INTERNATIONAL
HANDBOOK
OF
CURRICULUM
RESEARCH

STUDIES IN CURRICULUM THEORY

William F. Pinar, Series Editor

For more information about LEA titles, please contact
Lawrence Erlbaum Associates, Publishers, at www.erlbaum.com.

INTERNATIONAL HANDBOOK
OF
CURRICULUM
RESEARCH

Edited by

William F. Pinar
Louisiana State University

2003

LAWRENCE ERLBAUM ASSOCIATES, PUBLISHERS
Mahwah, New Jersey   London

Senior Acquisitions Editor   Naomi Silverman
Editorial Assistant: Erica Kica
Cover Design: Kathryn Houghtaling Lacey
Textbook Production Manager: Paul Smolenski
Composition: LEA Book Production
Text and Cover Printer: Hamilton Printing Company

Lawrence Erlbaum Associates, Inc., Publishers
10 Industrial Avenue
Mahwah, New Jersey 07430

Library of Congress Cataloging-in-Publication Data

International handbook of curriculum research / edited by William F. Pinar.

   p. cm. — (Studies in curriculum theory)
     Includes bibliographical references and index.
ISBN 0-8058-3222-X (casebound : alk. paper)
ISBN 0-8058-4535-6 (pbk. : alk. paper)
1. Curriculum planning—Research—Cross-cultural studies. 2. Education—
   Curricula—Research—Cross-cultural studies. 3. Curriculum change—
   Cross-cultural studies. 4. Comparative education.   I. Pinar, William F.
   II. Series.
LB2806.15 .I595   2003
375'.0007'2—dc21   2002026368
                                                             CIP

Printed in the United States of America
10 9 8 7 6 5 4 3 2 1

CONTENTS

PREFACE

This international handbook of curriculum research reports on scholarly developments *and* school curriculum development initiatives worldwide. Thirty-six essays on 29 nations—plus four essays of introduction—provide a panoramic and, for several nations (on which there are multiple essays), an in-depth view of the state of curriculum studies globally. There is, to my knowledge, no other such volume, at least not in English. As a library, personal, and pedagogical resource, I know it will be of use to scholars and students worldwide. This text may usefully serve as a supplemental textbook in general curriculum courses and as the main text in courses devoted exclusively to internationalization, globalization, and curriculum studies. For prospective and practicing teachers in the United States and elsewhere, it contextualizes national school reform efforts. The collection contributes, I trust, to the complicated conversation that is the internationalization of curriculum studies and the formation of a worldwide field.

As this collection testifies, curriculum studies is a field that straddles the divide between contemporary social science and the humanities. Research in the field is sometimes quantitative, often qualitative, sometimes arts-based, and sometimes informed by humanities fields such as philosophy, literary theory, and cultural studies. It is influenced as well by social science fields such as psychology, political and social theory, and, not only in the United States (see, e.g., Ulla Johansson's essay on Sweden, this volume), by interdisciplinary fields such as women's and gender studies and postcolonial studies. I settled on the term *research* in the title to emphasize, despite its paradigmatic differences, the field's relative unity in the scholarly project of scholarly *understanding*—a term that includes theoretical as well as practical interests and initiatives.

As the field moves toward formalization within and across national borders, disciplinary infrastructure is being put into place. By the use of that term I intend to draw our intention to the interconnected character of intellectualization and institutionalization. I am thinking not only of those institutions with which we are preoccupied—schools—and how they structure our research; I am thinking of those institutional structures now in place and those we must build to support the academic field of curriculum studies, including professional and scholarly associations and societies, scholarly journals, and conferences, all of which support the intellectual and archival labor necessary for a field of study to come into (self-conscious) being. This interconnected character of our intellectual and institutional work at this stage of the field's development persuaded me, in the introduction, to situate the collection in the current movement toward the internationalization of curriculum studies, institutionalized in the

International Association for the Advancement of Curriculum Studies. I trust it is clear that I do not regard the movement toward internationalization as confined to that Association's history and future, although at this stage it is most visible there.

NOTE ON LANGUAGE

English was not the first language of most who have contributed chapters to the handbook. As a consequence, there are language constructions that may seem peculiar to those for whom English is their first language. However, these are always decodable and, moreover, often offer novel and instructive conceptualizations. Although we—both at LSU and at Lawrence Erlbaum—have worked to make the English accessible, we have decided to leave some unusual, but informative, conceptualizations unedited.

ACKNOWLEDGMENTS

I wish to thank Naomi Silverman, senior editor at Lawrence Erlbaum, whose support for and commitment to this handbook project and to the larger project of internationalization have been and continue to be of inestimable importance. In addition to the handbook, Naomi persuaded LEA to co-sponsor (with Peter Lang Publishing and the LSU Curriculum Theory Project) the 2000 LSU Conference on the Internationalization of Curriculum Studies, at which the Committee of 100 (which became the International Association for the Advancement of Curriculum Studies) constituted itself. Moreover, Naomi supported the German *didaktik* book project mentioned in the introduction (and cited in the references). As well, Naomi has pledged her support for future projects in which curriculum studies around the world will be described in book form. I am grateful to you, Naomi.

I wish to acknowledge two LSU graduate assistants without whose labor this handbook would not have come to form. Seungbin Roh worked on the project in its early phases, and Nicholas Ng-A-Fook brought it to conclusion, reading the entire manuscript and making editorial suggestions. Thank you, Nicholas and Seugbin, very much. My thanks go as well to Professor Hongyu Wang for her editorial work on the essay on China. Finally, I wish to thank Professors Antonio Flavio Moreira and Janet L. Miller for suggesting the names of possible contributors.

—William F. Pinar
St. Bernard Parish Alumni Endowed Professor
Louisiana State University
Baton Rouge, Louisiana, U.S.A.

INTERNATIONAL
HANDBOOK
OF
CURRICULUM
RESEARCH

INTRODUCTION

William F. Pinar
Louisiana State University

This is, I believe, the first international handbook of curriculum studies. As such, it represents the first move in postulating an architecture of a worldwide field of curriculum studies. By worldwide, I do not mean uniform. As I have noted on another occasion, at this stage of formulation, curriculum studies tend to be embedded in their national and regional settings, often stipulated by national educational policies and/or in reaction to them (see Pinar, in press). This fact is evident in the chapters comprising this handbook. The point has a political dimension; it may work against the cultural and economic imperialism associated with the phenomenon known as *globalization*. In the preamble to the recently established (spring 2001) International Association for the Advancement, that point was prominent:

> The Association is established to support a worldwide—but not uniform—field of curriculum studies. At this historical moment and for the foreseeable future, curriculum inquiry occurs within national borders, often informed by governmental policies and priorities, responsive to national situations. Curriculum study is, therefore, nationally distinctive. The founders of the IAACS do not dream of a worldwide field of curriculum studies mirroring the standardization and uniformity the larger phenomenon of globalization threatens. Nor are we unaware of the dangers of narrow nationalisms. Our hope, in establishing this organization, is to provide support for scholarly conversations within and across national and regional borders about the content, context, and process of education, the organizational and intellectual center of which is the curriculum. (www.iaacs.org)

I regard this book as a companion event to the formation of International Association; both provide to the field much-needed infrastructure. Also important in this regard are Bjorg Gundem and Stefan Hopmann (Eds.), *Didaktik and/or Curriculum*, the proceedings of the 1995 Oslo conference, William E. Doll, Jr., William F. Pinar, Donna Trueit, and Hongyu Wang (Eds.), *The Internationalization of Curriculum Studies*, selected proceedings of the 2000 LSU Conference on the Internationalization of Curriculum Studies, a meeting that followed a 1999 LSU Conference which focused on the intersections and divergences between philosophy of education and curriculum studies worldwide. At the 2000 LSU conference, the organizational meeting was held—and the Committee of 100 formed—which led to the eventual establishment of the International Association for the Advancement of Curriculum Studies.

I chaired that organizational meeting, held on April 30, 2000, in Pleasant Hall on the LSU campus at which the Committee of 100 constituted itself. With the endorsement of those present, I called into "session"—I use quotation marks because our meetings were always over the Internet—a Provisional Executive Committee comprised of Ted Aoki (representing North America), Bjorg Gundem (representing Europe), Sid Pandey (representing Africa), Antonio Moreira (representing South America), and Qiquan Zhong (representing Asia). I served as secretary. During the final 4 months of 2000 and the first 4 of 2001, the committee met and formulated a constitution to propose to the Committee of 100. That proposed constitution was presented in March and ratified in April 2000; nominations were made and elections held during May–July, after which the Provisional Executive Committee disbanded and a new administration—to serve until 2004—moved into place to lead the International Association for the Advancement of Curriculum Studies (IAACS). Information concerning IAACS officers, members, and the constitution are accessible via the Association's Web site (www.iaacs.org).

At the LSU meeting in April 2000, informal agreement was reached regarding future meetings: The October 2003 meeting will be held in Shanghai, the 2006 meeting in Europe (perhaps Finland), the 2009 meeting in Africa (perhaps South Africa), the 2012 meeting in South America, and in 2015, the organization returns to North America. Proceedings from each meeting may be published, both in book form and in the IAACS scholarly journal. As well, I foresee handbooks, subsequent to this one, to be published perhaps every 10 years. These can become important markers of the field's advancement worldwide.

As the first such handbook, the present volume bears a heavy burden. Although I worked for as comprehensive a coverage as possible, I failed to secure chapters describing the history and present state of curriculum studies in a several important countries, perhaps most conspicuously Germany. I trust this particular failure on my part will be mediated by the appearance, just 2 years ago, of the Westbury–Hoptmann–Riquarts edited volume on German "didaktik," also published by Lawrence Erlbaum. Part of the difficulty I faced had to do with the lack of infrastructure, a difficulty future handbook editors—thanks to the existence of IAACS—should not face. Despite this limitation, there are significant, even ground-breaking, chapters from several contributors. All the chapters provide provocative glimpses into scholarly activity of those committed to the advancement of curriculum.

For four of those nations in which there are well-established and/or especially active fields, I solicited more than one chapter. (Regarding those countries with more than one contribution, I ordered the chapters according to the chronology of their content, not alphabetically according to authors' names.) This is *not* to say that those nations with one chapter (and those nations not represented at all) do not enjoy productive fields. Considerations of space forbade inviting multiple chapters from all nations with well-established and active fields. My motive was to provide more detailed commentaries from several nations—among them Argentina, Brazil, China, Japan, Mexico, and the United States—to allow readers something akin to a "photographic blow-up" of scholarship in certain areas, and to help readers gauge the broad level of generalization and conceptualization on which contributors were forced to operate. I believe readers will agree that sophisticated and sufficiently detailed portraits were achieved. My thanks to each of the contributors for their intellectual labor and commitment to the project.

FOUR ESSAYS OF INTRODUCTION

The handbook opens with four essays of introduction. These essays treat issues that traverse national boundaries. First, David Geoffrey Smith elaborates issues concerning the globalization of curriculum studies. Smith discusses the historical evolution of the term and, in so doing, explores several implications of globalization for the field of curriculum studies. He argues that there are three forms of globalization operating in the world today: Globalization One, Two, and Three. By "Globalization One," Smith refers to the *dominant form* associated with the revival of so-called radical liberalism, or neo-liberalism, dating back to the administrations of U.S. President Ronald Reagan and U.K. Prime Minister Margaret Thatcher in the 1980s. Globalization Two refers to the various reactions around the world to Globalization One, reactions spanning the spectrum from accommodation to resistance. Globalization Three refers to those conditions that may now be emerging to support a new global dialogue regarding sustainable human futures.

As becomes clear, *globalization* no longer refers only to such matters as trade between peoples and groups or even to various intercultural exchanges. Now globalization refers to those developments that may be functioning, in Smith's words, "to form a new kind of imaginal understanding within human consciousness itself. As a species, we may be imagining ourselves in new ways, especially with respect to issues of identity and citizenship." If so, we are imagining ourselves differently, according to nation and culture, as well as those forms of economic development that structure the various nations and cultures.

"Human self-understanding," Smith writes, "is now increasingly lived out in a tension between he local and the global, between my understanding of myself as a person of *this* place and my emerging yet profound awareness that this place participates in a reality heavily influenced by, and implicated in, larger pictures." Such a tension evokes, he suggests, not only a new sense of place, but also a new response to the world. It is a response one may feel before one can think, "given that so much about what seems to be going on is experienced preconceptually precisely because no one, no authority can tell me exactly what is happening." Consequently, globalization engenders "new kinds of identity crises," among them the erosion of national identities and the unprecedented losses of indigenous languages and cultures under the homogenizing pressures of global capital.

It is within these crises of identity that Smith finds vexing questions for curriculum studies, questions about epistemological authority, about how knowledge is produced, represented, and distributed, and questions too about the nature of curriculum work. Within the dominant mode of globalization theory, neo-liberal market theory, Herbert Spencer's classic question of the 19th century—What knowledge is of most worth—has been displaced by another: How much is knowledge worth? This question, Smith continues, begs another question: Is knowledge to be the ultimate arbiter of worth?

"The most important challenge for curriculum work in the new millennium," Smith suggests, "may be to develop the ability to deconstruct precisely *as* theory the unquestioned assumptions underwriting regnant forms of global economic procedure." Without such analyses, curriculum work, even when conducted explicitly in the name of justice and equity, will be in complicity with the politics of globalization. The key, Smith argues, is to find ways through complicity—through the complexity of globalization—to change the thinking that constructs it. This essay helps us do that and, in fact, furthers one strand of international conversation by asking: How do we understand curriculum in terms of politics, culture, economics, identity, and history? More particularly, how do the forms of globalization that Smith identifies inform the character of curriculum in the various nations, regions, and locales? Smith provides initial answers to these questions in his considerations of effects of Globalization One on curriculum reform developments in North America, Singapore, South Africa, Japan, the Caribbean region, and Mexico.

In the second essay introducing the collection, Noel Gough thinks globally about environmental education, focusing on the implications of such intellectual labor for the internationalization of curriculum studies. Despite its somewhat marginal status in the field of curriculum studies, environmental education is, Gough argues, a significant site for understanding curriculum internationally for at least two reasons. First, international organizations such as the United Nations and its agencies (e.g., UNESCO) have made substantial contributions to the development of environmental education over the past three decades. Second, the subject matter of environmental education is international and/or global in scope.

The global character of many environmental issues certainly implies that environmental educators should know how to *think globally*. But, Gough argues, after nearly 30 years in which the phrase *thinking globally* has circulated within discourses of environmental education, the concept remains "largely unexamined and undertheorized." Part of the problem, Gough suggests, has to do with environmental educators' uncritical acceptance of popular assumptions about the universal applicability of Western science. In so doing, he continues, environmental educators have tended to assume that Western scientific understandings of global environmental problems and issues provide and adequate basis for thinking globally. Environmental educators are not alone in making such assumptions, and Gough suggests that implications for other forms of curriculum work might follow from examining the limits to thinking globally in environmental education.

Gough recalls a number of studies in the history and sociology of scientific knowledge that demonstrate that Western science is a specific way of *thinking locally*, and that recognizing its local (rather than global) character enhances, not diminishes, its potential contribution to international knowledge generation and utilization. Gough suggests that understanding Western science as *one* among *many* local knowledge traditions might enhance its contribution to understanding and addressing the global environmental crisis. Additionally, understanding Western epistemologies as just *some* among *many* local knowledge systems that can be deployed in curriculum work might enhance their contributions to understanding curriculum internationally. From Gough's perspective, producing a "global knowledge economy" in/for an internationalized curriculum field can be understood as creating transnational "spaces"—among them, perhaps, the International Association for the Advancement of Curriculum Studies—in which local knowledge traditions can be "performed" together, rather than trying to create a global common market in which representations of local knowledge must be translated into (or exchanged for) the terms of a universal discourse. Gough's view provides sophisticated legitimation for a worldwide field of curriculum studies that is not uniform—that is, in fact, possibly antiglobalization in its intentions and effects.

Claudia Matus and Cameron McCarthy summarize "several critical developments now transforming social and cultural life outside and inside schools around the globe," which have "enormous implications for pedagogical practice and the educational preparation of school youth." These include: (a) *globalization*, which Matus and McCarthy define as "the intensification and rapidity of movement and migration of people, ideas, and economic and cultural capital across national boundaries"; (b) "the proliferation of new images, identities, and subjectivities now facilitated by the Internet," among them "TV, film, radio, newspapers, popular music, and aesthetic culture generally"; (c) stimulated by these is an "intensification of the work of the imagination of the broad masses of the people," which is to say, the appearance of "new interests, needs, desires, and fears gestated and amplified in the cultural landscape and aesthetic culture of the new media"; and (d) the generation of "new critical discourses and technologies of truth ... to address the challenges of this new historical period," among them cultural studies, postmodernism, multiculturalism, and postcolonialism. "Against the tide of these currents of change," Matus and McCarthy point out,

> educational thinkers, particularly in the United States, have tended to draw down a bright line of distinction between the established school curriculum and the teeming world of multiplicity and hybridity that now flourishes in the everyday lives of youth beyond the school. These educators still insist on a project of homogeneity, normalization, and the production of the socially functional citizen.

One consequence of this self-isolation from critical scholarship has been the under-theorization of concepts such as *culture* and *identity*—concepts Matus and McCarthy note, that are integral to curricular projects such as multiculturalism.

Matus and McCarthy problematize how the field has addressed the topics of cultural identity, cultural difference, and cultural community, concepts of striking educational significance during this period of rapid globalization. They read mainstream (i.e., technical or modernist) approaches to education and culture against the more critical possibilities of knowledge production and ethical affiliation that are explicit in postcolonial theory, postcolonial literature, art, and popular culture. Such issues of cultural identity and the organization of knowledge in schooling are pivotal, Matus and McCarthy argue, during this time of deepening cultural balkanization and curricular insulation in educational institutions—an insulation they argue is indeed precipitated by that proliferation of difference accompanying globalization.

In the final essay introducing the handbook, we return to matters of infrastructure for internationalization. Here we read of the genesis of the World Council for Curriculum and Instruction (WCCI), an ongoing organization. When I contemplated the idea of an international curriculum studies organization, I sought advice from Professor Norman Overly, the author of the WCCI essay. My request for the meeting was, in part, a matter of deference: Professor Overly had long been associated with that group, and I did not want the association I had in mind to be competitive with WCCI. Although he expressed no resistance to my idea, he was not enthusiastic about the prospects for an international curriculum conversation.

Professor Overly made two points. First, he warned that currency exchange problems make the matter of dues complicated. As a consequence, administrators—often with budgets for such professional opportunities—are able to join the association and attend international meetings. Dues would mean that junior faculty could not easily join and attend meetings. I kept this warning in mind as the Provisional Executive Committee and I worked (during fall 2000 and spring 2001) to formulate a constitution. We agreed to charge no dues to individuals; we did agree to ask affiliating organizations to make a donation. (Any funds that accrue, I hope, can begin to form a scholarship fund for travel to IAACS meetings, especially for graduate students and junior faculty, especially those working in nations and regions where currency exchange rates make international travel especially expensive.)

Norman Overly's second point concerns international politics. Rather than focusing on issues concerning curriculum studies. Overly reports, a number of WCCI members and conference participants, over the years, had used those opportunities not to discuss and debate curriculum matters, but instead to imagine themselves as representatives of their respective nations and carry on (often aggressive) attacks on curriculum scholars from other nations, whom they imagined, evidently, to be diplomatic representatives of those nations. The overall effects was to depress spontaneity, collegiality, and exchange over curriculum matters while reproducing global political disputes among those who enjoy few opportunities to resolve them. Overly discusses this point in his chapter (this volume).

This warning remains with me as well. In my opening night address to the 2000 LSU Conference on the Internationalization of Curriculum Studies, for instance, I discussed the problematics of my role in calling for an international conversation as an American. Of course, that acknowledgment of the problem hardly solved it, and the fact of international political tensions may well become the problem for IAACS that it has evidently been for WCCI. As IAACS' first president, I will work to persuade members to restrict criticism of other nations' policies to education and, specifically, *curricular* policies. It was for this reason that I declined many requests to make a statement as IAACS president regarding the terrorist attacks of September 11, 2001. I continue to believe that a focus on curricular issues makes it more likely that our debates and exchanges can stay focused on the *raison d'être* for being together—*our common cause*—the advancement of curriculum studies as indicated in the name of the association: the International Association for the Advancement of Curriculum Studies.

The WCCI came into existence on August 1, 1971. On that date, a sufficient number of ballots of the eligible voters was received in the offices of the (American) Association for Supervision and Curriculum Development (ASCD) to accept the initial constitution of the organization and to authorize the naming of officers (until the first election could be held). The prehistory of WCCI's founding moment dates many years earlier, however. It includes the activities of a dedicated group of internationalists—among them Alice Miel, Louise Berman, and Overly—who worked through the commissions and councils of ASCD for over 20 years to gain the attention and support of what Overly characterizes as "a generally unconcerned or even reluctant national membership for programming about international educational issues." My hope is that this handbook—and the IAACS—will honor and extend the important work done by Miel, Berman, Overly, and their colleagues at ASCD and WCCI.

ESSAYS ON CURRICULUM STUDIES IN 28 NATIONS

The main section of the handbook opens with Mariano Palamidessi and Daniel Feldman's study of curriculum studies in Argentina. Palamidessi and Feldman note that the definition if *curriculum theory* in Argentina has tended to focus on historical and social rather than epistemological elements: "The curriculum is a culture construction and its meanings depend on the way in which a political-educative tradition is built." They identify four periods in Argentine curriculum history, each with its own distinctive modes of production and dynamics of reception: (a) a period of centralized state regulation of schools and school knowledge (1880–1960), (b) a period of modernization characterized by a scientific emphasis in the university education courses and the emergence of experts and the appearance of curriculum theory (1960–1975), (c) the military dictatorship (1976–1983) characterized by political repression and a freezing of curricular debate, and (d) the return to democracy characterized by a proliferation of curriculum thinking (1984–2000).

During the 1990s, curriculum inquiry and research diversified in Argentina. Palamidessi and Feldman identify the following specializations and areas of initiative:

1. The planning, design, and organization of curriculum including attention to matters of content selection and emphasizing scientific and epistemological issues in the selection of school curriculum content. Scholarly production in this category formed much of the intellectual basis of the last decades' reform policies.

2. The governance and management of scholastic institutions. Scholarly works in this category have tended to analyze micropolicies and institutional cultures with an eye toward consensus building in both the education and public sectors. A number of scholars labor to explain the dynamics of institutional curricular processes in contexts of change, crisis, and uncertainty. Often these scholars propose conceptual tools for institutional planning. Such curriculum scholarship tends to be read by the ministries' technical staff as well as by school supervisors and directors.

3. The relationship among curricular policies, research, and school practices. Research in this category has focused on the development of curriculum in schools and the translation strategies that teachers and professors have employed, emphasizing rationales for curricular change.

4. The daily enactment of the school curriculum. In this category of research, scholars have focused on cultural issues, relying on the intellectual traditions of symbolic interactionism and neo-Marxism. Scholars working in this category of research have also drawn on ethnographic methodologies to analyze school experience as daily life, including issues of gender, identity, and teachers' work. Also in this category are studies of professionalization as well as studies of poverty and social marginalization.

5. The history of the curriculum and curriculum studies.

One problem the Argentine field faces, Palamidessi and Feldman suggest, is the absence of a sharp distinction between the intellectual field of education and the activities of official agencies—a problem America shares. Until the reconceptualization of U.S. curriculum studies during the 1970s, there was too complete an institutionalization of the field, with insufficient distance from the schools, state departments of education, and politicians' rhetoric.

After the military regime, there was an emphasis on political and sociological approaches, useful, Palamidessi and Feldman judge, for that moment of opening and democratization of the educative systems, but lacking a language of school improvement. Discourses on teaching and the school as institution remained in the context of the didactics—"a discipline with some difficulties to establish connections between what happens in classrooms, schools, and society." Argentine curriculum theory during the past 15 years has offered a site of intersection for both traditions.

A problem Silvia Feeney and Flavia Terigi identify in their chapter on curriculum studies in Argentina is the relatively few number of historical studies—a problem they help remedy themselves by writing a history of Argentine curriculum discourses for the period between 1983 and 1998. One major discourse Feeney and Terigi characterize as critical or sociopolitical, and this discourse has moved from a totalizing and utopian disposition to what North American readers recognize as identity politics, emphasizing ethnicity, gender, and cultural sphere generally. A second general discourse is also utopian—Feeney and Terigi characterize it as *the utopia of how* (in contrast to *the utopia of what* associated with the critical tradition)—but it focuses on "rationally directing the education of children, stimulated by new technologies, by scientific achievements in the field of cognitive psychology, and, often, by the prescriptions about what to teach and how in the curriculum."

Feeney and Terigi found that between 1983 and 1998, 29 books and 25 articles were published concerning curriculum. Many of these appeared after 1994. There is a "concentration of theoretical production on curriculum in the subject matters of design, development, and innovation of the curriculum," but, they judge, there remains "a weak structuring and a low relative autonomy of the field of curriculum studies in Argentina." There is evidence of imported traditions—Feeney and Terigi cite didactics as an example—and they conclude that the Argentine field suffers from a certain *satellization*. Although internationalization supports transnational communication, it would seem important for each nation (and/or region) to cultivate its own indigenous and conceptually independent strains of curriculum theorizing, inquiry, and research.

Perhaps there is a certain absence of infrastructure for the Argentine field because Argentina, Feeney and Terigi report, has few university departments of curriculum studies; the area is typically approached "within programs of education policy or didactics, the specialists of which are generally interested in research subjects that contribute little to the specific study of curriculum issues." There are few curriculum research projects underway as of this writing, and, they continue, there are no specialized journals that would support and encourage scholarly production in curriculum studies. For those interested in the curriculum field, opportunities have been primarily professional insofar as academic centers have, to date, provided little support. Perhaps the establishment of an Argentine Association for the Advancement of Curriculum Studies—with a scholarly journal—would contribute to the creation of the infrastructure necessary for the Argentine field to advance.

Bill Green begins his review of curriculum inquiry in Australia by noting that, as in Argentina and elsewhere, the field is relatively recent as a distinctive disciplinary formation. Only since the early 1980s has there been an official national organization (i.e., the Australian Curriculum Studies Association [ACSA], associated with the scholarly journal *Curriculum Perspectives*). Through its biennial conference and publication program, including its journal, ACSA provides a "certain measure of leadership with regard to formal curriculum inquiry." More recently, the Curriculum Corporation has provided "organizing oversight for the field, albeit from what tends to be an official, systemic, administrative orientation." What Green terms "the intellectual elaboration of curriculum thought and curriculum scholarship" has developed unsystematically, even sporadically, "overall ... instrumentalized, and largely technical in its orientation—subordinate[d] to policy."

Despite these conditions, there is, Green informs us, "an emerging presence in curriculum inquiry per se," and he names the scholarship of Noel Gough (see his chapter in this volume) as an example of "growing sophistication in the field." (Any serious student of the Australian scene would add Green's name as well.) In the remainder of the chapter, Green discusses the Australian scene, providing us with a "history of the present." Studies of the curriculum field in Australia are, Green tells us, still rare. There are as yet no major synoptic texts on the distinctive history and character of Australian curriculum and schooling, an understandable state of affairs given that the field, at least in its formal self-recognition, is still quite new. Green also points to "the archetypically *bureaucratic* character of Australian curriculum and schooling"—the fact that both have been dominated by an administrative logic—as another reason for the absence of interest in studies in Australian curriculum history.

As we saw in the case of Argentina, there is, Green notes, in Australian curriculum scholarship a heavy reliance on scholarship conducted outside the country. For the future, Green hopes to see "further investigations of the specificities and peculiarities of Australian curriculum work, both in its own right and in its historical, intertextual relation to the curriculum field more generally." He believes that the Australian field is "steadily gathering momentum" while still, as a field, somewhat "episodic and fragmented" and "under some threat, increasingly subsumed as it is within economic and cultural policy." A distinctively Australian curriculum will provide, Green concludes, "an epistemology of location, and due account of Australia' distinctive positioning and placement in a historically changing world order."

In their study of "The Decolonization of Curriculum in Botswana," Sid N. Pandey and Fazlur R. Moorad observe that, "despite the escalation in demands for more and better education, not much reflection or research has been done on the nature of the curriculum and how it relates to the whole process of change." Pandey and Moorad argue that the present educational system in Botswana remains rooted in its colonial past; there remains a hierarchical class structure resistant to that order of social transformation required to realize national education goals. Pandey and Moorad provide a history of colonial and postcolonial education, employing both critical pedagogy and African notions of oneness (*ubunto/botho*) to provide ethical and political grounding for a more emancipatory notion of education.

One example of such an ethical base for emancipatory education in Botswana is, Pandey and Moorad suggest, *Affirming Unity in Diversity in Education: Healing With Ubuntu*, by Maqhedeni Ivy Goduka. Born in the Xhosa tribe of South Africa, Goduka came of age under apartheid. For a time she lived and taught in the United States, Pandey and Moorad report, where she studied social reconstructionism, feminism, critical theories, deconstructionism, and other postmodernist theories. Goduka has been influenced by each of these traditions, as evident in her autobiographical narrative, a project for critical pedagogy she calls "healing with *ubuntu*." Pandey and Moorad argue that this notion is not only relevant for South Africa, but speaks also "to any setting where oppression has deprived people of their basic human rights." *Ubuntu/Yobuntu*, a concept borrowed from the Xhosa language, reflects values of respect and dignity for all humanity.

"To prepare ground for this pedagogy," Pandey and Moorad suggest, "the conception of curriculum must come out of its narrow confines to be reconceptualized." They conclude, "The narrowly conceived field of curriculum must give way to reconceptualizing curriculum theories and ideas to accommodate, appropriate, invite, and tolerate the old, new, outlandish, and so on to forge a new education including a vision of innovative curriculum, a project neglected until now, but must be undertaken in all immediacy to be decolonized." Decolonization will become an increasingly important subject, I suspect, in an internationalized field of curriculum studies.

In his study of the emergence and consolidation of curriculum studies in Brazil, Antonio Flavio Barbosa Moreira observes that, until the 1980s, an American influence was quite discernible in Brazilian curriculum studies. In the 1980s, American influence was rejected and European critical curriculum thought was imported to support the formulation of a more indigenous discourse—one more closely related to the unique educational problems faced by Brazil. Moreira chronicles the emergence of the Brazilian field during the 1920s and 1930s, continuing through to the 1970s, when courses on curriculum guaranteed their place in Brazilian universities and when specialized publications and research intensified. The new field of Brazilian curriculum studies, "although still in need of more autonomy," Moreira adds, has reached its maturity.

Moreira turns his attention to globalization—a phenomenon involving a "considerable movement of information and new knowledge." Such movement forces the realization that ideas do not exist in any pure state. In Moreira's view, "this movement [of information and new knowledge] suggests that there is a suspicion of ideas leaning toward a single culture in its pure state, uncontaminated by other manifestations, thus indicating a process of hybridization, in which the cultural elements of distinct origins and different hierarchies deterritorialize and reterritorialize." Moreira concludes with a call for studies that focus on curriculum practice in schools and universities—studies that show how hybrid curriculum discourses materialize when teachers and students work together in classrooms. He suggests that such studies may help us understand "the readings, interpretations, resistances, and adaptations that are made amid the discursive restrictions and the limits that curriculum theorizing and curriculum policies help to establish."

In their study of the curriculum field in Brazil during the 1990s, Alice Casimiro Lopes and Elizabeth Fernandes de Macedo note that the field of curriculum has been characterized by sociological rather than psychological approaches, focusing on curriculum as a forum for power relations. Studies emphasizing the field's administrative and scientific traditions have been deemphasized. By the end of the first half of the decade, the effort to understand postindustrial societies as producers of symbolic goods, more than material goods, altered this political emphasis: The Brazilian field began to incorporate postmodern and poststructural approaches—a major influence in the 1990s. There are historical studies as well. Because these various scholarly orientations have become interrelated, Lopes and Macedo suggest that the contemporary Brazilian field is characterized by hybridism or hybridity, a point Moreira makes as well.

New discourses are emerging, especially those valorizing culture, and in particular multicultural and cultural politics. As a consequence, Lopes and Macedo suggest, it becomes increasingly difficult to specify the boundaries of the Brazilian curriculum field. They write:

> This increasing imprecision, due to the undefined nature of the cultural capital to which it is associated, seems to us to be of some concern, because, at times, it disregards the specificity of education and curricular processes. With this, we do not wish to deny the importance of the flow of meanings established between different fields and subjects.... Within this perspective, as different flows of meaning come together, this may prove to be profitable for the curriculum field inasmuch as researchers manage to reevaluate discussions on the curriculum by trespassing on the traditional divisions established between areas of knowledge, thus taking better advantage of the elements available in their original field.

Silvia Elizabeth Miranda de Moraes focuses on a different aspect of Brazilian curriculum studies—namely, how this field is struggling to help rethink the key concept of *citizenship* in public education. She notes that the public school system in Brazil is undergoing profound curricular and administrative reform, animated by assessments that have prompted action by the Ministry of Education. As outlined in a document entitled "The National Curricular Parameters" (PCN), Brazilian curricular reform is structured around three main axes: (a) a new interdisciplinary vision of knowledge; (b) the inclusion of ethics, cultural pluralism, environment, health, and sexual orientation as transversal themes; and (c) to support the implementation of these reforms, each school is to develop its own pedagogical project.

Moraes situates current curriculum reform by situating it in a short history of the Brazilian curriculum. She then describes contemporary reform, concluding with an account of her own participation in it, relying on Habermas' theory of communicative action. Moraes acknowledges that "the school's sphere of action is limited, but our hope is that it will little by little shake up the whole system. Perhaps very soon we shall see the good results of this silent revolution." She concludes by quoting Habermas: "Against the horizon of an emerging global public sphere, such trends could signal the beginning of a new universalist world order.... This is naturally no more than a hope—indeed a hope born of desperation."

In her review of curriculum scholarship in Canada, Cynthia Chambers reports that many Canadian curriculum theorists have focused on the hidden curriculum, and specifically its function in reproducing social injustice. One domain of such scholarship concerns indigenous education. Such work challenges Western epistemology by articulating (in Western terms) an indigenous metaphysics. Other scholarship has focused on violence toward women—for instance, the massacre at the University of Montreal in 1989. That incident provoked scholarly narratives of resistance and redemption and teaching against the grain.

A second major domain of Canadian curriculum scholarship is phenomenological and hermeneutical in character. In reply to the question, "What might be the substantial interest that phenomenology holds for curriculum in Canada?," Chambers answers: "Perhaps phenomenology's focus on lived experience—the particulars of life lived in a specific place in relation to others—enabled scholars to at once be critical of the abstract discourses dominating curriculum and the violence they do the earth and children."

Although phenomenological inquiry aspires to make understanding possible, Chambers suggests, hermeneutic inquiry "identifies both the barriers to that understanding and the conditions that make it possible." Barriers to understanding can be located in both the discourse and the historicity of the educational situation or event, as well as in the life history and self-formation of the interlocutors and their collectivities.

The potential of the hermeneutic imagination to traverse national and cultural boundaries, enabling dialogical encounters among communities of difference,

> makes hermeneutics crucial for Canada, a country that is both colony (first politically of France and Great Britain, later economically of the United States) and colonizer (if indigenous people and later the French, within its own borders). Hermeneutics has made possible "cross-cultural mediation" in Canadian curriculum—for example, between dominant cultures and indigenous peoples. (Chambers, this volume)

The educational success of curricular conversations may depend, Chambers continues, on the self-reflexivity of the conversationalists, including their willingness to tell the (difficult) stories, to question the stories they tell, as well as to listen carefully to what others are saying. Chambers comments: "Autobiography and narrative inquiry offer creative ways to enter such conversations while carrying on the interpretive (i.e., the creative, linguistic, and political) work necessary for the conversations to continue." Autobiography, including feminist autobiographical theory and practice, is a major domain of contemporary curriculum research in Canada.

In recent years, the concept of *place* has emerged as a key concept in the effort to understand curriculum autobiographically and biographically. "Memory and history, both individual and collective, are," Chambers points out, "located in particular places, giving rise not only to concrete experiences, but local, personal, regional, and national identities. Curricular scholarship ignores the place of Canada in our peril." Chambers (1999) challenged curricular scholars and workers in Canada to write from a heightened sense of place, "to find and write in a curricular language of our own, to seek and create interpretive tools that are our own, and to use all of this to map a topography for Canadian curriculum theory, one that is begun at home but works on behalf of everyone."

There has also emerged in recent years considerable scholarly interest in arts-based curriculum inquiry, characterized by "reading poetry or literary texts instead of essays, dancing instead of sitting, performing stories instead of giving lectures, all in an effort to illustrate curriculum artistically" (Chambers, this volume). Contemporary curriculum theory and practice in Canada, including arts-based inquiry, has been profoundly influenced by postmodernism. Chambers characterizes postmodern culture as moving from past to present, unity to fragmentation, representation to a constant deferral of meaning, nationalism to global capitalism, and nature to text. Not a field submerged in the (postmodern) present, however, Canadian curriculum studies also investigates the past, especially the colonial past, as well as the future, specifically the dangers of globalization, the creation of a borderless global economy, and the dismantling of public institutions such as education (except to the extent it is training workers and consumers for the global economy). In contemporary Canadian curriculum scholarship, there is a call for intercivilizational dialogue—a call to which I hope this collection, as well as the IAACS, lends support.

Chinese cultural traditions are, Hua Zhang and Qiquan Zhong explain, nurtured and shaped by three main philosophies: Confucianism, Taoism, and Buddhism. Correspondingly, there are three main traditions of curriculum wisdom in China: Confucianism, Taoism, and Buddhism. Chinese curriculum thought is not recent; the Chinese term for curriculum, *ke-cheng*, first appeared in Confucian classics during the Tang Dynasty (618-907). During the 20th century, there have been four distinct periods, which Zhang and Zhong characterize as: (a) learning from the United States (1900–1949), (b) learning from the Soviet Union (1949–1978, during which the field of curriculum is replaced by the field of instruction), (c) the reemergence of curriculum field (1978–1989), and (d) the current movement toward independence for Chinese curriculum studies. Zhang and Zhong identify the following four features of Chinese curriculum research: (a) Curriculum research started early in China, but experienced an uneven developmental journey; (b) Chinese curriculum research is bound up with ideology; (c) Chinese curriculum theory depends on curriculum practice excessively; and (d) Chinese curriculum research has emphasized the study of curriculum history, connecting the exploration of curriculum development principles organically with the study of curriculum history.

In terms of prospects for the Chinese field, Zhang and Zhong make two points: (a) curriculum development will remain the dominant paradigm of Chinese curriculum research for the foreseeable future, and (b) the paradigm of *understanding curriculum* is the future direction of Chinese curriculum studies, meaning that the subservient position education occupied vis-à-vis ideology "has come to an end."

The field of curriculum studies has become a new and vigorous research specialization, attracting many researchers. Nearly every teachers' university and college has established a department of curriculum and instruction or center for curriculum research. This infrastructure provides "a solid basis for possible new theoretical explanations in an increasingly interdependent and changing global society." Zhang and Zhong conclude:

> To elaborate on what it means to know and be educated for the Chinese must be based on reflections of our own traditions and international conversation; nor can it be done without cultural, political, economical, global, and spiritual understanding of curriculum. Understanding curriculum at deeper levels must be accompanied by the difficult task of transcending the direct and concrete daily needs of curriculum practice, so that the critical and creative potential of theory can be released. The Chinese curriculum field will maintain its strong tradition of historical studies, attempt to inform curriculum research by traditional curriculum wisdom, participate and contribute to worldwide curriculum discourses, reflect on the reality of curriculum practice, and construct, finally, its own curriculum theory.

This phase of constructing a nation's own curriculum theory is identified by other scholars as well as a sign of the field's advancement or, to use Moreira's metaphor, *maturity*.

Writing from Estonia, Urve Laanemets suggests that in the present historical period education has acquired a new meaning and mission: the construction of human identities. The specification of identities from the local and regional toward the more global can work against, Laanemets argues, educational innovation. There remain "too many atheoretical and ahistorical curriculum documents used at the beginning of the 21st century." In the West as well as in postsocialist countries such as Estonia, Laanemets suggests that curriculum specialists maintain a balance between tradition and innovation. "It is particularly important to distinguish between the old and valuable and the old and outdated," she writes, for "if we fail to make this distinction, it may happen that some traditional human values may get lost and influence social stability within the country or even beyond." Yet such curricular questions cannot remain focused within national borders, she continues, because "no curriculum can exist in isolation and no national curriculum can ignore international developments." How to negotiate such complexity? Laanemets suggests the following questions:

> How diverse can diversity be? What can we accept and what is unacceptable considering our cultural and moral values and recognized traditions? What can we benefit from and what can we offer to the world? What has to be the common core of educational content and aspirations of the "knowledge society," if cohesion of societies and the world is desired? Can a global or European dimension really unite the nations, although language learning is really difficult to implement or that cultural diversity can be hard to accept? What are the strategically meaningful fields of knowledge and skills globally and regionally?

To illustrate how these questions might guide the curriculum scholar, Laanemets turns to language learning as "the central axis of global educational content." The task now, she writes, is "to develop flexible curricula, which would allow us to react and make changes in them according to the developments in technologies and culture." National curriculum decision making requires wide participation of all involved: students, teachers, parents, publishers, teacher trainers, employers, and so on. "All curriculum decisions are," Laanemets notes, "restricted by their adequacy for implementation.... Accordingly, different ideas, approaches, and structures can be used in different times.... It all depends on our powers of understanding the research and practical experience, those of conceptualization and reconceptualization of curricula and learning under diverse circumstances in the changing world."

In his study of "Postmodern Paradoxes: The Confinements of Rationality in Curriculum Studies," Finnish curriculum scholar Tero Autio makes the case that, although "the national imagery has been and arguably continues to be a major source of [curricular] ideas and practice, the infusion of the global horizon has nevertheless become more dominant even within national boundaries." This means that even nations' "restructuring" measures—"what overtly seems to be dissimilarity and national idiosyncrasy"—turns out to be strongly influenced by common, global trends. The same reform rhetoric that in one national context has been promoted by centralization measures (Autio uses the example of the United Kingdom) may in another be advocated by decentralization efforts. (Autio points to the United States; decentralization efforts are also underway in, for instance, Latin America [see Silva, 1993].) Underlying both national reform rhetorics, Autio argues, is the same process, if on two levels. Systemically, reform is driven by the *marketization* of the education, which includes the hegemony of Tylerian models of goals linked with standardized assessment tools. On the level of the school and teachers' work, restructuring employs business notions of *accountability, competitiveness,* and *performativity.*

Autio describes what he regards as unifying or globally shared themes as they are expressed on the level of national curricula, with particular attention to the influence of the Tyler Rationale: "the symbolic icon for the current curricular developments in the restructuring of education." Autio focuses on views that challenge a notion of curriculum understood as a proceduralism, concluding with an instructive discussion of Wolfgang Klafki's "critical-constructive Didaktik" and the American reconceptualization of curriculum studies.

Denise Egéa-Kuehne describes five domains of educational research in France: *science(s) de l'éducation, philosophie de l'éducation, pédagogie, didactique(s)*, and, most recently, *curriculum*. In her description and history of these sectors of scholarship, we see "how they intersect, blend, and complete, each vying to develop its own identity and define its own specially, while the same scholars may work in more than one of these domains." It has only been within the few years, Egéa-Kuehne tells us, that scholarly attention has been paid to the concept of curriculum. Such scholarship has tended to occur outside the field of education, in departments of sociology and history; curriculum as a separate field of study has not yet emerged in France, although several researchers have acknowledged it is "the subject of interesting approaches." Although there are semantic problems with the word *curriculum* in France—the terms *programmes d'études* or *plan d'études* are more frequently used, although with somewhat different meanings—at least one French scholar (Forquin) "deem(s) that the curriculum issue should be at the center of any thinking and any theory of education."

For Egéa-Kuehne, "the gaps and/or spaces of dissension and overlap among the fields of education studies (i.e., educational sciences, pedagogy, didactics, curriculum, philosophy of education) are sources of dynamic, rich reflection, and production of knowledge." Moreover, it is not possible or desirable to reconcile these diverse educational discourses. There is, in her view, "some danger in settling for an easy consensus, for facile 'transparency,' because, while claiming to speak in the name of intelligibility, good sense, common sense, or [supposedly] the democratic ethic, this discourse tends, by means of these things and as if naturally, to discredit anything that complicates this model." Clearly, the conditions are present in France for the evolution of a dynamic field of curriculum studies.

For his study of curriculum in Hong Kong, Edmond Hau-fai Law chooses the "classic framework proposed by Tyler." Law notes that, after 150 years of occupation, the British left Hong Kong (on July 1, 1997) with a system of education similar to the British system. Proposals for reforming the structure and contents of Hong Kong school curriculum started in October 1999. He reports that "Western practices in curriculum with an emphasis on experience-based and student-focused organization of learning have been a major theme in curriculum reforms in Hong Kong." This fact he understands has a consequence of Hong Kong's status as "a meeting place between East and West." Consequently, Law believes that "Hong Kong's experience in her search for a curriculum is a search for a compromise between Western ideas and Eastern practice in harmony."

In their portrait of "The Landscape of Curriculum Inquiry in the Republic of Ireland," Kevin Williams and Gerry McNamara note that the last decade has seen "vigorous and extensive" curriculum debate and inquiry. Participants have included curriculum specialists, philosophers, and sociologists, as well as those not directly involved in the academic study of education (e.g., representatives from industry and youth groups). Within the academic field, there exists, Williams and McNamara tell us, "an orthodoxy among curriculum theorists that is quite striking." First, most share the same critical view of current curriculum practice; second, Irish curriculum scholars tend to avoid issues that give rise to genuine disagreement.

To illustrate, Williams and McNamara observe that, although much has been written about low achievement, disadvantage, and the dominance of terminal written examinations, the voice of curriculum specialists has been largely absent from public controversies over state-sponsored programs of relationships and sexuality education. Williams and McNamara suggest that one might expect the theme of Irish identity to be the subject of curriculum debate, but the issue features little in the scholarly literature. The main concern of curriculum inquiry in Ireland today concerns that problem of low achievement. Williams and McNamara conclude:

> It seems safe therefore to argue that the current state of curriculum inquiry, in the broad context of school failure, alienation, and disaffection, is one of considerable alienation and disaffection. There is a feeling among curriculum thinkers and researchers that the process of curriculum reform has been heavily politicized in recent years. This process has enabled limited change, particularly the updating of subject syllabi, but has effectively restricted reform and even serious debate on the bigger questions of curriculum values, purposes, goals, and structures.

This problem of alienation and disaffection is hardly limited to Irish scholars, of course. It is a problem in U.S. curriculum studies and, I suspect, in all fields that have been distanced, in part by neo-conservative policies of marketization and in part by intellectual developments internal to those fields, from the schools. I return to this point in my concluding remarks.

M. Vicentini focuses her report of curriculum reform in Italy on debates concerning the university physics curriculum. Vicentini contextualizes her report within efforts to establish a European educational system that, while preserving national cultural identities, would support harmonization of existing systems across the continent. Italian curriculum reform has also been stimulated by the problems of underachieving and alienated students. Among the curricular issues that have surfaced include: (a) student workload, (b) the importance of English as a second language, (c) the organization of textbooks, (d) issues concerning the disciplines to be taught, and (e) the importance of computer literacy. Additionally, multicultural education is an important curricular issue, intensified by the recent arrival of many immigrants. Vicentini concludes that "the debate is actually quite heated and one has the feeling that it is driven more by the interests of the different sectors of the University staff than by a real interest in preparing better teachers for the schools of the future. Let us hope for the best."

Naama Sabar and Yehoshua Mathias detect a shift from a uniform to a multifaceted curriculum in Israel. This shift reflects sociocultural developments in Israeli society—developments that call on curriculum planners to create new interrelationships between compulsory elements and those elements that are open to variability and reflect the broad range of educational and cultural interests in contemporary Israel. These include: (a) ideological polarization, (b) the revolution of minorities and the failure of the *melting pot* metaphor of cultural assimilation, (c) cultural pluralism and postmodernism, and (d) Israel's entry into the postindustrial economy. Sabar and Mathias observe: "The polarization in ideology and values between sectors—for example, between the religious population and the nonreligious majority, and the strengthened status of national and cultural minorities—have demonstrated the shortcomings of the politics of a uniform and generally accepted curriculum."

In recent years, there has been support for decentralized curriculum development, a schema in which teachers play a prominent role. Sabar and Mathias characterize this "new approach to curricula" as "more holistic" and as taking "teaching into account." Under the influence of these ideas, the Ministry and various universities have worked with teachers to develop curricula; this development has, Sabar and Mathias report, increased teachers' curricular autonomy. "While autonomy engenders many hopes,"

Sabar and Mathias conclude, "it is also a cause for more than a few concerns." It is not clear, for instance, in what direction the Israeli school is headed: Will it work to achieve social solidarity and integration by providing equal opportunity for all? Will it perpetuate gaps and express mainly the division and disparity between cultures and social groups?" In Sabar and Mathias' view, these questions comprise the principal test of the Israeli school in the years ahead.

Miho Hashimoto explicates Japanese curriculum reform during the 1870s period of modernization. It was during this period, she argues, that modern curriculum in Japan developed its unique structure and practical meaning. Hashimoto suggests that the modernization of Japan's school curriculum amounted to "a process of coating Western notions on the traditional values of curriculum." This occurred because "it was very difficult for the Japanese to change their own intrinsic value of curriculum, which they had formed over a long term, despite their interest in Western notions of education."

Like late 19th-century Japan, Hashimoto suggests, many nations today face "one homogeneous and standardized development of curriculum around the world." Unless scholars appreciate the complexity of local cultures' encounters with globalizing curriculum discourses or, as Hashimoto puts it, "unless we scrutinize the internal process of the struggle for the modernization of curriculum in the individual countries, our understanding of curriculum worldwide will be simplistic." She concludes:

> I believe that curriculum studies must be based on in-depth understandings of the human nature. It is very important for one nation to establish a common base in order to understand the substantial meaning of other countries' civilization. Systematic transformation is possible in education, but it is very difficult to change the individual's values unless we understand the fundamental structure of human nature.

From the end of World War II to 1955, Tadahiko Abiko notes that curriculum development and inquiry in Japan were actively conducted by school teachers influenced by progressive notions imported from the United States. After 1955, state control was reasserted, and school curricula more closely followed national standards. State control was loosened in the 1980s, and in 1990, the Japanese Society for Curriculum Studies was founded and established on the principle that teachers, researchers, and education-related administrators should all work together for curriculum development. The Society has steadily attracted new members, and membership exceeded 700 in 2000, making it "one of the most pivotal academic societies related to pedagogy."

There are, Abiko reports, five major research groups in Japanese curriculum studies. The first group "critically analyzes political and social characteristics of curriculum"; the second focuses on curriculum development, emphasizing progressive, child-centered, open curricula, and integrated study to foster children's individuality and creativity; the third studies sociology of curriculum, focusing especially on analyses of hidden curriculum; the fourth criticizes public education from the perspective of Marxist educational philosophy; and the fifth, which includes school administrators, promotes school-based and teacher-led curriculum development. In addition to these five groups, there are two other groups: one composed mainly of the Japanese Teachers' Union, which develops its own curriculum proposals, and a second right-wing group.

In his study of "Japanese Educational Reform for the Twenty-First Century," Shigeru Asanuma analyzes "the basic structure and meanings in the curriculum reform in contemporary Japan." As in the United States, education in Japan has been used for political purposes. Politicians have invoked the image of a nation in crisis to mobilize public opinion to their political advantage. Although many publications report that strict discipline and intense pressures to perform on standardized examinations have enabled Japanese children to score well above average on various tests of school achievement, it is not well known that a flexible and progressive curriculum policy was initiated in April 2000.

In this reform—undertaken by the Central Council of Education—the most critical issue faced by contemporary Japanese children was judged to be the difficulty of living their everyday lives, underscored by the increase in the number of Japanese children committing suicide. The Council found that this fact derives from the "overloaded national curriculum content" based mostly on traditional subjects. The Central Council of Education proposed a reduction in the number of school hours and minimum essentials of curriculum content for all children. In effect, the Council supported less academic competition. There is, Asanuma reports, no solid evidence to demonstrate that these reductions have led, or will lead, to reduced school achievement, as reflected in Japanese school children's scores on International Educational Achievement tests.

How can one interpret contemporary curriculum reform in Japan? Asanuma tells us that contemporary reform cannot be understood in traditional Western curricular terms, such as discipline-centered curriculum versus child-centered curriculum. It must be situated in Japanese society, culture, and economy. Traditional curriculum, emphasizing the so-called *basics,* has done little to further children's psychological development—a judgment, Asanuma points out, even Japanese conservative political leaders have shared. Indeed, conservatives have pointed to the underdevelopment of ego identity as one important constituent element in the social dilemmas Japan faces today. The Japanese, Asanuma argues, "have never tried to change their own subjectivity because they think it is not a problem in their own ego but in others." Asanuma concludes, "For the Japanese, [contemporary] curriculum reform is a kind of cultural revolution, which sometimes accompanies pain and antagonism from the traditional groups, including socialist educators."

Angel Díaz Barriga's survey of curriculum research in Mexico begins with the acknowledgment that "the field of curriculum is an outstandingly practical domain." The distinction between *theory* and *practice* was expressed at the beginning of the 20th century by Durkheim, a distinction, in Barriga's view, that has led to "the conceptual impoverishment" of those disciplines that accepted it. In Mexico, curriculum studies has become a vast research field in which are studied "almost all the subjects that bear relation to the school system," including the school as institution as well as a wide range of pedagogical practices. For some, in fact, *curriculum* has become equivalent to the entire concept of education sciences; this fact makes necessary a rigorous demarcation of its scholarly borders.

In Mexico, the development of the field of curriculum is "tightly linked with higher education." Barriga understands this situation as a function of the high degree of curricular centralization in Mexico: "Study plans for the whole school system are made at a national level, a situation that causes a passive attitude in the teaching staff of the educative system." Consequently, the themes of Mexican curriculum research "bear a close relation to the educational problematics of the higher school system." Within the domain of Mexican educational research, Barriga continues, "curriculum research is gaining ground." Curriculum research can be classified into three orders of research: (a) exclusively conceptual studies, (b) conceptual studies with empirical referents, and (c) proposals to elaborate study plans.

Mexican curriculum design addresses: (a) education in professional competencies, (b) curricular flexibility, (c) application of constructivism in teaching, and (d) the incorporation of new information and curriculum evaluation technologies. Additionally, several themes "affect the entirety of the curriculum practices," among them: (a) education for peace and tolerance, (b) education toward the realization of human rights, (c) education and environment, (d) education and gender, and (e) education and citizenship. Barriga concludes:

> Curriculum research in Mexico is in a consolidation phase, and by that I am suggesting that there is a community of academicians who, from diverse traditions, have begun to conduct research in the field of curriculum. The conceptual and thematic diversity is huge, and I have intended merely to provide documentation of it. The greatest limitation curriculum research must defy is its reduced impact on basic education: As a matter of fact, the centralization of study plans constitutes an important obstacle that makes difficult the development of that kind of research.

The "Main Trends in Curriculum Research in Mexico," Frida Díaz Barriga reports, include: (a) a technologic-systemic trend, (b) a critical-reconceptualist trend, (c) a psychopedagogical trand, (d) a trend that deals with professional preparation and practice, and (e) an interpretive trend. Like her colleague, Barriga underscores that "it is difficult to fix the limits of what can be considered studies about curriculum with regard to the other areas of educational and psychological research." Research themes move across areas of specialization. The state of curriculum in Mexico is one of polysemy—a state of affairs reflected in the multiple meanings of the concept of *curriculum*. These include: (a) study plans and programs as products of formal curriculum structures; (b) learning and teaching processes; (c) the hidden curriculum and daily life in the classroom; (d) the preparation of professionals and the social function of teachers; (e) social and educative practice; (f) problems generated by the selection, organization, and distribution of curriculum contents; and (g) subjective interpretation of the subjects implied in curriculum. Such conceptual diversity has contributed, Barriga writes,

> not only to the term's polysemy, but it has also occasioned that curriculum research lost its outline with regard to other areas of education research, like the study of learning–teaching processes, specific didactics, sociological studies about professions, intersubjectivity, education interaction processes, and even multicultural and gender studies, to cite only a few.... In Mexico, we can find positions that are not only divergent, but also completely opposed regarding what is curriculum and how curriculum research must be performed.

There is in Mexico "a proliferation of courses about theory and methodology of curriculum ... dedicated to the formation [preparation] of teachers, educational planners, psychologists, pedagogues, and even functionaries and people with decision-making power in the educative institutions." There is, as well, "an important tension in the field of curriculum development between research and educative intervention." On the one hand, there is a major increase in scholarly production and the diversification of the field. However, in Barriga's judgment, "those developments have not been sufficiently applied to the domain of educative intervention in terms of the dissemination and consolidation of the real practice of new curriculum experiences and projects in accord with the settings and discoveries of the studies conducted about curriculum." In Mexico, as elsewhere, "[t]he practice of curriculum design is not always congruent with the theoretical or methodological approaches." As is the case in many countries, much curriculum work remains technocratic.

In their study of "Curriculum Theory in the Netherlands," Willem Wardekker, Monique Volman, and Jan Terwel point out that the Netherlands are wedged between political and philosophical spheres of influence—between the Continental (both German and French) and the Anglo-Saxon worlds, creating an in-between space for interpretations of education that are unique to the Netherlands. "Dutch thinkers," Wardekker, Volman, and Terwel write, "seem to have engaged mainly in connecting and 'trading' in ideas developed elsewhere. This commercial background may also be a reason that conflicts of interest tend to be solved by pragmatic compromise rather than by open conflict—a tendency that has also left its traces in the school system and educational theory."

This orientation toward commerce and industry, coupled with liberalism, translated into an empiricist and even positivist curriculum, Wardekker, Volman, and Terwel report, in which knowledge and abilities were prized more than personality development, the latter being regarded as a domain of the family and the church rather than the school. The position of the neo-humanist Gymnasium was accordingly devalued. Religious conflicts have also structured the Dutch school system and its curriculum. Protestants and Catholics each comprise about one third of the Dutch population, and each group has created its own organizations for nearly every aspect of public life, resulting in "a sort of voluntary religious apartheid system" that only began to break down during the second half of the 20th century, as secularization intensified. Each group claimed the right to decide the content of the school curriculum for its children; after a prolonged conflict, the issue was settled by creating the statutory right for any group to found its own schools, schools fully financed by the state as long as they conform to certain criteria of quality and number of pupils.

Curriculum theory in the Netherlands was, at first, empiricist (during the second half of the 19th century) followed (at the beginning of the 20th century) by a theological emphasis, what Wardekker, Volman, and Terwel term a *normative pedagogy*—that is, a "form of philosophy that concentrated on developing aims for education from a strictly normative (mostly Protestant Christian) perspective." Curriculum theory changed again about 1940 or so, partly due to the demands for objectivity—demands supported by a growing secularization of society. From 1940 to 1970, curriculum theory in the Netherlands was dominated by

a Dutch adaptation of the religiously more neutral, neo-humanist, and idealist German philosophy of the *Geisteswissenschaftliche Pedagogik,* a term chosen to denote that its methods were inspired on those by the humanities rather than by natural science. It was based in part on the philosophical ideas of Hegel, and thus shares some of its sources with the theories of John Dewey and Lev Vygotsky (although at the time, Dewey was viewed mainly negatively in the Netherlands, and Vygotsky was virtually unknown outside the Soviet Union).

Later, Langeveld's work was influential among some, especially Catholic, scholars. His child-centered emphasis resonated also with those who supported the progressive education movement. Langeveld's scholarship was obligatory for students of teacher education until the late 1980s.

Influential at that time was American empirical curriculum theory, committed to empirical research designed to improve educational practice. "The 'new' curriculum theory was just about everything *Bildung* theory was not," Wardekker, Volman, and Terwel write. "[I]t was empirical, down to earth, and transmission oriented, rather more sensitive to the 'needs of contemporary society,' and maybe, most important, closer to 'common sense' about education, which was still dominated by the empiricist view inherited from the 19th century; or maybe we should say that this empiricism had finally found an academic legitimation." At present, university-based researchers continue to focus on issues of effectivity and learning theory. If there is revival of continental European thinking, either in the form of *Bildungstheorie* or the newer and more promising approach of sociocultural theory, Wardekker, Volman, and Terwel suggest, "the pendulum might swing back from an emphasis on document construction to understanding the curriculum."

In Peter Roberts' review of "Contemporary Curriculum Research in New Zealand," we learn that as a field of academic inquiry, curriculum studies in New Zealand "never stands still." Important new theoretical currents have appeared each decade, as well as innovative reformulations of earlier traditions. During the last three decades of the 20th century, there were significant theoretical developments from Marxist, feminist, existentialist, hermeneutical, phenomenological, spiritual, biographical, and poststructuralist perspectives. Roberts writes:

> There is, as Paulo Freire might have said, a healthy level of scholarly "restlessness" in the field: Intellectual curiosity, a commitment to debate and rigorous investigation, and a determination not to remain too certain of one's certainties are qualities in abundant supply within the international curriculum studies community.

Curriculum inquiry in New Zealand is as well the study of curriculum policies and practices. As such, curriculum scholars critique policy documents, evaluate curriculum programs in schools and other institutions, appraise and construct new models for teaching different subjects and analyze structures and systems for curriculum implementation at local, regional, and national levels. Such labor often requires an examination of wider political changes. Calls for a return to the basics, for instance, might be understood as one dimension of a conservative restoration; demands for sex education or information technology curricula in schools might reflect, Roberts suggests, "changing ideas and social practices among younger people." "Massive changes" on the New Zealand educational system—rationalized by the ideology of neo-liberalism and its insistence on making education a "free market"—have demanded considerable attention by curriculum scholars in recent years.

Despite curriculum becoming a public issue New Zealand, drawing attention and comment from a wide range of interested groups individuals, including academics, teachers, students, administrators, politicians, parents, and business people, the number of academic books published by New Zealanders on curriculum theory and the nature of curriculum studies as a field of inquiry is relatively modest. The situation—relatively few book-length treatments of key theoretical issues—might be explained, Roberts suggests, in part by the institutional history of curriculum studies in New Zealand. Curriculum subjects have traditionally been compartmentalized according to school subjects; the concern has been more with the teaching of the subject than with curriculum studies as a field of inquiry. This is reflected in the absence of curriculum studies as a research category in the major professional organization for educational researchers in New Zealand, the New Zealand Association for Research in Education. Roberts concludes:

> I want to suggest, then, that although curriculum issues have attracted considerable comment in this country, a well-developed, multidisciplinary, interinstitutional program of curriculum studies is yet to emerge. This applies to both teaching and research. The lack of integrated, multilevel institutional course offerings in curriculum studies can be explained, in part, by time constraints and resource limits. These have been exacerbated by neo-liberal reform policies.

Norway, too, has recently undergone a period of thoroughgoing educational reform, report Bjorg B. Gundem, Berit Karseth, and Kirsten Sivesind. As is the case in many countries, curriculum studies in Norway since the 1960s and 1970s have tended to focus on the school subjects, in part due to political demands for a renewed emphasis on curricular content in terms of basic skills and a core curriculum. Research on curriculum history has tended to focus on the history of educational systems, institutions, and educational legislation on the other.

The sociology of education and, particularly, the sociology of knowledge have effected a shift from more traditional orders of curriculum research (i.e., from atheoretical attempts to chronicle the development of a school subject) to studies of the nature of education, including analyses of the antecedents of curriculum change. Gundem, Karseth, and Sivesind observe that Norwegian curriculum research has developed along lines similar to curriculum studies in other Nordic countries.

In addition to the impact of the new sociology of education on Norwegian curriculum studies, Gundem, Karseth, and Sivesind cite the work of French educational sociologists such as Pierre Bourdieu and Jean-Claude Passeron as a second and "overlapping influence." Relatedly, the concept and phenomenon of *curriculum codes*—underlying curriculum principles—has also become important. A third trend has been inspired, in part, by American revisionist historians, but more so by a specific British tradition that stresses the social construction of school subjects. This third trend is evident in Bjorg Gundem's studies on the development of English as a school subject, Britt Ulstrup Engelsen's studies of the development of the literature component in the teaching of Norwegian, and Berit Karseth's study of the development of new university subjects/courses of study at the University of Oslo. These studies elucidate a symbolic drift of school knowledge toward the academic tradition, and raise basic questions about social and philosophical explanation of the history of school subjects.

Gundem, Karseth, and Sivesind note that there seems to be a strong interest in examining the curriculum field from both empirical and theoretical points of view, employing a range of research methodologies. Additionally, there is a tendency to regard curriculum issues as embedded in complex philosophical, sociological, and cultural concerns. This complexity complicates efforts to classify specific curriculum studies. Therefore, a clear-cut description seems not possible or desirable. This may be reflected in the current interest in comparative studies. "For Norwegian curriculum studies," Gundem, Karseth, and Sivesind conclude:

> this challenge is complicated by a marked desire to find its own identity and, at the same time, see its role as subsumed within internationalization and the global society. A pertinent question to ask is whether Norwegian research on curriculum should in defining its tradition take as its starting point the imperatives of the national context and policies. As our overview shows, curriculum studies have, in a high degree, been open to international influences.

In his study of the Philippines, Malaysia, and Thailand, F. D. Rivera observes that one problem faced by those who speak "for the poor, the vulnerable, the dispossessed and the marginalized" is "their lack of any systematic grasp of the complexities of globalization." Rivera makes an intriguing proposal, one I hope IAACS can help actualize:

> A new architecture for producing and sharing knowledge about globalization could provide the foundations of a pedagogy that closes this gap and helps democratize the flow of knowledge about globalization. Such a pedagogy would create new forms of dialogue among academics, public intellectuals, activists, and policymakers in different societies, and its principles would require significant innovations. This vision of global collaborative teaching and learning about globalization may not resolve the great antinomies of power that characterize this world, but it might help even the playing field.

Many significant changes that have recently taken place in the curricula of many developing countries are attributable, Rivera suggests, to the internationalization of market economies and the globalization of the cultural economies. The phenomena of globalization and internationalization demand that these countries (130 developing countries account for at least 60% of the world's population), despite their unstable resource capital (human and otherwise), compete with the developed nation-states. Attempts made by individual countries to internationalize their curricula are often stimulated by the perception that they *must* develop globalized curricula. For instance, almost all countries deploy a stateless science, mathematics, and technology.

In Southeast Asia, various regional cooperations have led to the development of common curricular interests in the areas of literacy, science, and technology, as well as technical, vocational, environmental, and developmental education. As a consequence, curriculum theorizing in developing countries in Asia has been, by definition, an internationalized process. Despite the end of colonial rule, the need for a globally competitive school curriculum, stronger performances by students on cross-culturally based international examinations, and intensifying attention to global education, provide sufficient evidence, Rivera argues, curriculum has emerged as *international text*. What Rivera terms the "always-already internationalized component of curricula" is supported as well by developing countries' determination to build more stable and stronger local economies, requiring articulation with an international market economy. This economy is understood to depend on information and technological knowledge. As a consequence, there are vigorous curriculum restructuring efforts in developing countries designed to support technological transformation.

The internationalization of curriculum in developing Southeast Asian countries has had, Rivera judges, both productive and destructive effects on the formation of identities, nationalism, and the preservation of local heritage. Because the histories of the Philippines, Thailand, and Malaysia have historically been constructed by various colonial regimes, Rivera suggests, "they appear as always-already conditioned toward globalization. Consequently, curriculum theorizing in these cases is more or less a projection of the historical conditions that shaped them." Curriculum theorists in these developing countries are often asked by their governments to incorporate curricular responses to globalization and internationalization in ongoing school restructuring. Curriculum theorists thereby become elites, so-called "transnational cultural producers and consumers" who form "a global class with few real cultural allegiances to the nation-state, but who nevertheless need new ideologies of state and nation to control and shape the populations who live within their territories. As these populations are exposed, through media and travel, to the cultural regimes of other nation-states, such ideologies of nationalism increasingly take on a global flavor." Such complex and contradictory relations between nationalisms and globalization will take, no doubt, curricular forms.

After 1990, Nicholae Sacalis reports, "an influx of Americanism has flooded the Romanian language and culture." In fact, "we may talk about an American 'invasion.'" But to understand this situation, Sacalis advises, "we should go back a little bit in time." After World War II, as Soviet troops occupied the country, many felt certain that the Americans would be arriving soon. Many Romanians, Sacalis tells us, "were so deeply convinced that … they died, some in jail … hoping that one day, sooner or later, the Americans would show up to rescue Romania." It would be 45 years before Americans finally arrived in Romania.

After communism was established, educational reform became a priority; in 1948, "a radical reform of education took place." "As a matter of fact," Sacalis tells us, "it was not a true reform, but an imposition of Soviet education on the Romanian school." Especially impacted were humanistic studies at the university, where professors with doctorates taken abroad "were replaced, overnight, with illiterate party appointees." At all levels, the curriculum was fashioned after Soviet models; many textbooks were simply translation of Soviet textbooks. Science ruled the Soviet curriculum. Consequently, among the subjects eliminated were cybernetics, sociology, psychoanalysis, and, of course, all philosophy, except, of course, dialectical materialism. Romanian culture "was divided in two: the good and allowed culture and the bad and forbidden culture." When he obtained access to "forbidden culture," Sacalis recalls, "[w]hat a cultural shock I had suffered. [I] felt abused all those years when I had to learn all kinds of stupid things and that official trash that passed as scientific socialism or materialistic philosophy."

In his study of South Korea, Yonghwan Lee observes that before Japan annexed the Korean peninsula as its colony in 1910, Korea had maintained its own educational system and curricula for almost 5,000 years. Traditionally, Koreans have prized the humanities, regarding the technical and practical subjects as vulgar. This was, in part, a matter of class division: The nobility learned Confucian ethics and philosophy, whereas the practical subjects were reserved for the common people. During the colonial period, Korean education was characterized by "Japanization and mobocracy." *Japanization* was officially described as "educating subjects [to be] loyal to the Japanese Emperor" and *mobocracy* as "schools should educate aiming at making human workers according to the condition and standards of the people." In actuality, Lee asserts, the educational policy of colonial Japan was to differentiate and discriminate the Koreans from the Japanese.

Korean liberation from Japan in 1945 was, Lee tells us, more apparent than real. The Potsdam Declaration ruled that Korea would be under the trusteeship of the United States and Russia. Ignoring the will of the Korean people, the nation was divided in two according to the interests of these two countries who simply replaced Japan as the colonial power. The U.S. military appointed Captain E. L. Lockard as the administrator of education in South Korea. Lockard organized the Korean Committee on Education, composed of 10 boards. Although Korean language and history textbooks were promptly published by a few Independent Movement groups that had operated underground during the Japanese occupation, many classes depended on what could be written on blackboards as well as materials mimeographed by teachers. Curricular content did not change much from that of the Japanese period. "In other words," Lee writes, "despite getting their lost identity back (e.g., their own names, language, and history), they could not get rid of inertia because the Korean identity was not one they had won for themselves, but was one others had suddenly brought to them."

The postwar years were followed by a period of subject-centered curriculum (1948–1962), an experience-centered curriculum (1962–1973), and a discipline-centered curriculum (1973–1981), followed by a period of humanistic curriculum (1981–1995). In Korean curriculum studies, the new sociology of education (from England) and conflict theory (from the United States) were introduced. This had the effect of stimulating "some Korean curricularists reconsider the nature of curriculum itself, which had been only of an administrative significance." No American-style reconceptualization of the field has occurred, however.

In her study of curriculum research in Sweden, Ulla Johansson poses the following questions: (a) How have the research problems been defined, and what have the answers been? (b) Which interests and groups have the researchers served? She focuses on research published between 1990 and 2000. As is the case in nearly every country, Swedish curriculum research has been closely connected to school policy and school reform.

Beginning in the 1940s and continuing for approximately 30 years, Swedish curriculum researchers were engaged in efforts to provide politicians with knowledge to rationalize political decisions concerning the comprehensive school. At first, curriculum research was carried out within a scientific paradigm. Sharp distinctions were drawn between politicians who defined the goals of education and asked the questions on the one hand, and researchers who labored to provide answers on the other. Curriculum research was based on a linear input–output model of correlations. The curriculum researcher was a social engineer who produced knowledge for the schools. The teacher played the role of a technician who was expected to execute and follow the state's directives.

During the 1980s, it became clear that the goal to create a uniform and democratic school had not been realized. Research followed, which concluded "that standardized solutions could not be applied to a complex and refractory reality, and thus the rational large-scale philosophy of planning, characteristic of the Swedish welfare state, was cracked." Within Swedish curriculum studies, an attack on the scientific approach ensued, and a reconceptualization of the field followed, emphasizing political analyses.

More recently, Swedish curriculum research has been influenced by poststructuralism. Researchers emphasize the importance of language in the construction of curriculum, evidenced by the frequent use of the term *discourse* in many research reports. The intention of poststructuralist studies is to *deconstruct* the meanings of texts. Multiple interpretations of curriculum are possible and legitimate. Johansson notes that, in contemporary research, "the unstable meanings of curricular goals and content have been given the status of political truth."

In the past, feminist curriculum research has been subsumed within political analyses, but in recent years it has emerged as an important sector of Swedish curriculum research. Much feminist curriculum research finds schooling reproductive of women's subordination in society. The interplay between education and gender produces quite different trajectories for women and men in the labor market. Overall, Johansson reports, feminist curriculum studies show that the social construction of gender in schools is a multidimensional process; gender structures are both reproduced and challenged by education.

In his commentary on curriculum scholarship in Namibia and Zimbabwe, Jonathan D. Jansen reports that "the field of curriculum studies is underdeveloped in Southern Africa." He notes that, in these two countries, there are few curriculum scholars and, therefore, relatively little research, theory, and writing about the curriculum. The curriculum scholarship that is conducted tends to be dominated by visiting professors, international consultants, or masters and doctoral students from Europe and North America. Despite the relative absence of curriculum scholarship generally, and scholarship produced by indigenous writers, specifically, "what has been nevertheless makes a critical contribution to curriculum writing in education."

"The colonial histories of Zimbabwe and Namibia left an indelible legacy on the curriculum of these two nations," Jansen writes, "and this legacy is reflected in the curriculum scholarship of Southern Africa." This becomes evident in the first theme Jansen identified in curriculum scholarship in Zimbabwe and Namibia—namely, "writings about and against the colonial curriculum. These writings were in the main anticolonial descriptions, analyses, and judgments about the nature and effects of this foreign curriculum." The colonial curriculum was characterized as Eurocentric, dominated by European ideas and excluding African history, ideas, and movements.

The second theme Jansen identifies is evident in writings about curriculum innovations introduced after independence. In both Zimbabwe and Namibia, he reports, "ever major curriculum innovation became the subject of intense study by both national and international scholars eager to understand the possibilities and problems of changing the underlying ideological commitments of the inherited curriculum in forging a new social order." The third theme Jansen characterizes as "advocacy writings about what knowledge, ideas, and values the new education system should reflect after colonialism." The point of reference for these writings remains the system of colonial education and the Eurocentric curriculum it promoted. In Zimbabwe, Jansen notes, "these writings were deeply etched within the pre-independence socialist vision for education and curriculum." Jansen terms the fourth theme of curriculum scholarship in Zimbabwe "studies on the politics of curriculum—studies that analyze "the interface among politics, power, and privilege in the construction of curriculum in Southern Africa." In Namibia, for instance, writings on the politics of curriculum focused on the implementation of new language policies, identifying the ways in which political interests not only underpinned proposals for an English-only policy, but also explaining the limited success of such radical proposals in the schools and classrooms of the postcolonial Namibia. More recently, following a major restructuring of teacher education in Namibia, there has emerged scholarship on the politics of the teacher education curriculum.

The fifth theme of curriculum scholarship in Namibia and Zimbabwe concerns studies of school subjects; their nature, design, and organization; effects on learning and teaching; and attitudes among various classes of learners. In Southern Africa as elsewhere, "school subjects remain a powerful organizational reality in postcolonial institutions despite various initiatives for integration of subjects or interdisciplinary curricula." The sixth theme Jansen identifies concerns the administration of education and how patterns of administration influence curriculum planning in the two countries. A seventh theme has to do with examinations and assessment as part of the broader curriculum reform initiatives after colonialism. An eighth and final theme in the curriculum scholarship of Namibia and Zimbabwe concerns consultancy reports on curriculum reforms, typically those that received external funding from major international organizations such as the United States Agency for International Development (USAID), the World Bank, the Swedish International Development Agency (SIDA), and others, such as the various United Nations agencies (UNESCO, UNICEF, etc.). There are, Jansen writes, "critical silences in the curriculum writings from Namibia and Zimbabwe on matters of grave importance in the society around it (e.g., a dearth of writings on HIV/AIDS and education despite that this represents the single most important health crisis in Southern African schools and society)."

Writing from Taiwan, Jenq-Jye Hwang and Chia-Yu Chang characterize the study of curriculum as "the foundation of curriculum development and innovation" in which there is "a close connection" with the social context of a country. Although the study of curriculum "may lead to a social change and can promote human qualities," it is "also influenced by the sociopolitical situation." Social and educational changes since the late 1980s have had the effect of diversifying the study of curriculum in Taiwan. Among the diverse discourses Hwang and Chang identify are: (a) an analysis of political ideology in curriculum, (b) multicultural curriculum, (c) curriculum research on foreign language teaching, and (d) gender studies. Emerging social problems include environment protection, sex education, parents' education, human rights education, drug education, computer literacy, moral education, and career planning, all of which receive curricular attention.

As they contemplate the future of curriculum studies in Taiwan, Hwang and Chang call for: (a) the establishment of more research organizations at national, local, and school levels; (b) greater coordination of existing institutes, schools, and nongovernmental agencies; (c) the invitation of more experts to support international and interdisciplinary collaboration; and (d) the formation of systemic and integrated research programs emphasizing scholarly collaboration. "The task of curriculum study," Hwang and Chang conclude, "belongs not only to scholars in the library, but also teachers on the spot, and the aim of curriculum study is not only to establish theory, but also to improve practice."

F. Dilek Gözütok reports that studies of school program development activities have improved systematically in Turkey, especially since the 1950s. Contemporary studies of curriculum development were furthered by the National Educational Development Project (1990), a project supported by the World Bank. This project aimed to develop and improve school programs, in particular to improve the quality of school textbooks and other instructional materials and help teachers employ them more effectively. A new curriculum was prepared by the Department of National Educational Research and Development of Education in accordance with the National Educational Development Project in 1993. In this chapter, Gözütok details these and subsequent curriculum development activities in Turkey.

In their review of curriculum studies in the United Kingdom, David Hamilton and Gaby Weiner begin by stating the basic terms of their analysis—namely, that "courses of study entail notions of social order," which is to say: "To follow a curriculum is to be inducted into a social order. From this perspective, curriculum practice has the intention to foster social identities." In this sense, then, "the visible curriculum and the hidden curriculum are rendered as inseparable." Hamilton and Weiner focus on four areas of curriculum and practice: (a) the association of curriculum with social order, (b) the growth of curriculum federalism in the United Kingdom under the shadow of the fragile hegemony of the supernational state, (c) the advancement of new pedagogic identities (e.g., those nurtured by educational feminism) as a means of injecting social justice into curriculum practice, and (d) the centralist promulgation of a school effectiveness ideology/discourse as a technology of professional and pedagogic differentiation.

Hamilton and Weiner note that the concept of *curriculum* first appeared in the European educational lexicon during the 16th century. The much older term, *curriculum vitae* (*course of life*), was redefined to denote courses of schooling. The concept of curriculum was linked to the appearance of the concepts *class* and *didactics*, as well as the redefinitions of earlier conceptions of method and catechism. The evolution of these concepts was embedded in two historical developments: (a) educational thought became reflexive as the view emerged that human beings could redirect their own destiny, and (b) educational thought began to imagine that human powers of redirection could be applied not only reflexively, but also to other people. "The link among curriculum, class, method, catechism, and didactic," Hamilton and Weiner explain, "was that alongside the emergence of these notions, educational practice turned toward the conceptualization, organization, and accomplishment of instruction."

Contemporary educational rhetoric in the United Kingdom is marked, above all, by a market-oriented, neo-liberal discourse in education. In this discourse, formal education becomes a "service rendered to individuals," rather than an obligation of the state to its citizens. "All that remains common to the provision of education in the United Kingdom," Hamilton and Weiner tell us, "is that compulsory schooling is divided into two stages: primary and secondary. But even this division is not uniform: Whereas statutory schooling begins at 4 years in Northern Ireland, the equivalent figure for England, Wales, and Scotland is 5 years of age."

Because recent curriculum deliberation in the United Kingdom has been, in general, a response to "the centralist, neo-liberal, free-market policies of the 1980s and beyond," it had focused more on "human subjects than school subjects" in its "consideration of curricula as pathways through schooling, themselves also pathways through life." In this respect, curriculum practice and curriculum research in the United Kingdom attempt a "reconciliation of knowledge and pathways," between questions of "What should they know?" and "What should they become?" Hamilton and Weiner argue that the following developments have animated and will continue to animate curriculum research in the United Kingdom into the 21st century: (a) the impact on curricula and pedagogy of devolution, federalism, and globalism in the United Kingdom; (b) the breakthrough texts of Freire and Bernstein in linking curriculum and pedagogy to the social and educational order, and in offering the possibility of pedagogical plurality; and (c) two educational movements of late modernity—educational feminism and school effectiveness research—which have sought, in different ways, to challenge both the curriculum order and social order. "The extent to which the balance is tipped toward the human subject and away from subject knowledge in forthcoming curriculum considerations (or vice versa) will be important," Hamilton and Weiner suggest, "for the curriculum analysts and researchers of the future."

Because curriculum studies in the United States have been elaborated in a number of readily accessible texts, I have limited commentaries on the situation of curriculum scholarship in the United States to two chapters, the first historical, the second theoretical. In the first chapter, Craig Kridel and Vicky Newman provide a detailed report of research in American curriculum history. Animated by criticisms of the U.S. curriculum field of the 1960s and 1970s for its atheoretical and ahistorical concern for "basic principles" of curriculum, American curriculum historians have succeeded in making curriculum history an integral sector of scholarship in the contemporary field. With this accomplishment and recognition have come "divisions and conflict."

Although their view of curriculum history research is expansive, for the sake of this overview, Kridel and Newman focus on the work two overlapping groups of curriculum historians: (a) members of the Society for the Study of Curriculum History (a group founded in 1977 that meets prior to the Annual Conference of the American Educational Research Association [AERA]), and (b) those participants within Division B (i.e., Curriculum Studies) or AERA, Section 4, Curriculum History. From their study of conference presentations and scholarly publications, Kridel and Newman identify eight contexts for curriculum history research. These include: (a) curriculum history as social/educational history, (b) subject areas, (c) case studies, (d) synoptic introductions, (e) memoirs and oral histories, (f) archival documents, (g) biography, and (h) unsilencing voices. Kridel and Newman comment: "These contexts of curriculum history scholarship permeate and cut across one another as well as across recognized forms of curriculum discourse: political, racial, gender, phenomenological, auto/biographical, aesthetic, theological, institutional, and international texts."

Ultimately, Kridel and Newman see U.S. curriculum history scholarship as embracing two commonalities. First curriculum history is grounded in educational action. Many leaders in American curriculum history came to the area from a tradition of curriculum design and development immersed in educational practice (i.e., from the fields of curriculum, instruction, evaluation, and elementary and secondary education where involvement with the schools is assumed). A second common characteristic of U.S. curriculum history research pertains to "embraced understandings" toward both curriculum knowledge and interpretive perspectives.

Although Kridel and Newman do not endorse notions of "cultural and curricular literacy," they do accept that certain knowledge seems to permeate most, if not all, American curriculum history scholarship (e.g., the work of Herbert Kliebard, Thomas Kuhn, Joseph Schwab, John Dewey, Maxine Greene, and Ralph Tyler). "But new directions in curriculum history," Kridel and Newman add, should raise the question of *how* these embraced understandings are remembered and, perhaps more important, how traditional methods of analysis become means for consolidation and perpetuation of the oppositions among approaches in the field. Our review suggests that among curriculum workers, curriculum historians, and educational historians, rifts in purpose and scholarship have diluted the strength of the field of curriculum history. We wish to assert, however, that the nonlinear bricolage of practice and interdisciplinary approaches to scholarship, and not the narrow notion of historical research, provides great richness and possibilities.

Patrick Slattery rethinks the effort to understand curriculum as international text in light of research in hermeneutics, subjectivity, and aesthetics. Slattery argues that "the intersubjective nature of hermeneutics serves as a model for contemporary efforts to internationalize curriculum research." He believes that "a reconceptualized understanding of hermeneutics that foregrounds subjectivity and aesthetics" can support "the possibility of mutually collaborative projects for global justice and ethics." Foregrounding aesthetics as an integral dimension of the hermeneutic project supports, in Maxine Greene's phrase, "the release of imagination," but, Slattery argues, "agency and creativity" as well, all "essential elements for envisioning alternative possibilities to the international modern pathos of political hegemony; fundamentalist religious intolerance; economic caste systems; worker displacement; cultural annihilation; environmental degradation; and racial, gender, sexual, socioeconomic, and ethnic oppression." It is a "mutually interdependent understanding of hermeneutics, subjectivity, and aesthetics is a corrective not only to the current stalemate in the hermeneutic debates, but also has a language of possibility for international justice and cooperation in the postmodern era." Slattery's chapter illustrates well the hybridity of scholarly discourses now discernible in contemporary American curriculum studies.

NEXT STEPS

Several points become clarified in this first international handbook of curriculum research. As I suspected, the curriculum field is embedded in national and regional settings. Much curriculum work—research and curriculum development initiatives—functions in the service of school reform, stimulated and sometimes stipulated by governmental educational policy initiatives. As are elementary, middle, and secondary school teachers, the education professoriate is under intense pressure to improve the quality of educational experience, documented (too often from my point of view) in student scores on standardized examinations. Considerable curriculum scholarship worldwide is critical of the rhetoric of school reform; from this fact, we can conclude that the field is not merely a conceptual extension of the state's political and bureaucratic apparatus. There is a relative intellectual independence. This last point is heartening to those of us committed to an intellectually autonomous, vibrant scholarly field of curriculum studies worldwide. However, it cannot be taken for granted because politicians' manipulation of the political rhetoric of school reform represents an ongoing threat to the relative intellectual autonomy and freedom of curriculum scholars, not to mention of public school teachers.

It is also now clear that, to a considerable extent, the internationalization of curriculum studies has already occurred, except perhaps in the United States. Intellectual influences from the United States and the United Kingdom, especially in the area of critical curriculum thought (related to the new sociology of education), are evident in a number of non-North American fields. These influences do not seem to have been imported, in general, uncritically, but rather adopted somewhat self-consciously and for specific and local purposes (although this may not have always been the case with earlier waves of conceptual imports, especially, U.S. "empirical" research). Antonio Moreira (this volume) argues that the importation of "foreign material" involves "interactions and resistances, whose intensity and whose potential 'subversiveness' vary according to international and local circumstances." In the case of Canadian scholarship in phenomenology and hermeneutics (see Chambers, this volume), it is the United States that has been the importing nation (see Pinar et al., 1995, chap. 8). With the establishment of the IAACS and the publication of several international collections, including this handbook, the internationalization of the field will no doubt continue, perhaps at an accelerated rate. This reality asks scholars worldwide to become more knowledgeable, critical, self-conscious, and selective regarding the appropriation of scholarship from sources outside one's homeland.

What would constitute the advancement of the worldwide field of curriculum studies? Each of us is obligated to answer that question for ourselves as individuals and together as a field. To contribute to the conversation among us, permit me here to speculate, limited no doubt by my own national contextualization. That limitation acknowledged, and given the portrait of the worldwide field discernable in this handbook, I suggest the following might constitute next steps we might take to advance the field worldwide.

As Bill Green observed in his chapter on Australian curriculum studies, "understanding curriculum inquiry both as an international (global) phenomenon and as a local, situated practice is a complex undertaking and a constant challenge." I would emphasize that the project of understanding is both international *and* local, and that each of our national and regional fields might well be advised to support—through our teaching, scholarship, and scholarly journals, associations, and other forms of infrastructure—attention to both intellectual developments globally as well as locally. In the United States, for instance, for the first time an introduction textbook in American curriculum studies contained a chapter entitled "Understanding Curriculum as International Text." However, inadequate (and now outdated) our chapter 14 is in *Understanding Curriculum* (Pinar et al., 1995), it was, for the American field, a first step. This handbook is a second. I trust the establishment of an American affiliate to the IAACS—the American Association for the Advancement of Curriculum Studies (AAACS)—will provide additional needed infrastructure for the American field to undertake internationalization in earnest.

Attention to the local means not only attention to current, often politically instigated, waves of school reform. Indeed, to resist the danger of submergence in political rhetoric and overzealous governmental participation in the intellectual and psychosocial life of schools, curriculum studies as a field must labor to remain and/or become more intellectually independent. As Mariano Palamidessi and Daniel Feldman pointed out in their chapter on curriculum studies in Argentina, there can be an "absence of distinctions between state agencies and curriculum scholars in universities." To advance this field, I submit, vigorous debate and differences in point of view—not only among ourselves but from politicians—must be supported. Curriculum scholars must become intellectuals as well as technical specialists with bureaucratic expertise governments and their agencies employ (Said, 1996). A sophisticated field of curriculum studies would occupy, it seems to me, a broad spectrum of scholarship, from the theoretical to the institutional, from the global to the local.

We might think of our scholarly effort to understand curriculum as supporting the *horizontality* of the field, ranging from the global to the local. It is clear to me, from the studies published here, that for the field to "advance" or "mature" (to employ Antonio Moreira's formulation), the field must support *verticality* as well. That is to say, in each nation or region, as well as worldwide, the field needs historical studies and, I would add, future-oriented studies, the latter evident in Sabar and Mathias' reflection on the future of education in Israel, and Chambers' report on curriculum studies in Canada.

Historical studies enable us to understand and work through the specificities of our national cultures and the embeddedness of curriculum theory and practice within them, as underlined, for instance, the Zhang-Zhong chapter on Chinese curriculum studies, the Lee chapter on Korean curriculum studies and the Abiko, Asanuma, and Hashimoto chapters on Japanese curriculum studies. In this sense, historical studies enable us to resist any uncritical acceptance of globalization. Within our specific national and regional cultures, historical scholarship means that we are less vulnerable to political slogans (e.g., the *privatization* and *marketization* of public education), and to the discursive and material manipulations by specific regimes of reason and power. Although internationalization supports transnational communication, it would seem to me important for each nation (and/or region) to cultivate its own indigenous (including scholarship on historically indigenous peoples; see Chambers, this volume) and conceptually independent curriculum theorizing, inquiry, and research.

I emphasize this point because it is clear—I am thinking now of David Hamilton and Gaby Weiner's chapter on the United Kingdom, but nearly every chapter could serve as an example—that the field remains much focused on school improvement. We are less focused on the intellectual project of understanding. Although the two are, of course, intertwined and synergistic, in the near term, at least, *advancement* might mean, certainly in the U.S. context, a certain shift in the center of gravity of the field; from an exclusive and often bureaucratic preoccupation with instrumental interventions in the school as institution to the intellectual project of understanding. Although hardly abandoning bureaucratic protocols aimed at institutional improvement, some segment of the field, it seems to me, must be devoted to curriculum theory and history (i.e., scholarly efforts to *understand* curriculum, including curriculum development and evaluation).

In doing so, there are, as several chapters in this collection make clear, important ethical and political dimensions to the labor of curriculum development and scholarship. We cannot pretend, as mainstream social science once did, to be neutral. Especially in those nations in reconstruction after emancipation from colonial regimes, ethical and political dimensions are explicit, as indicated in Rivera's chapter on the Philippines, Malaysia, and Thailand, in Jansen's chapter on Zimbabwe and Namibia, and in the Pandey–Moorad chapter on Botswana. "The narrowly conceived field of curriculum," Pandey and Moorad tell us, "must give way to reconceptualizing curriculum theories and ideas to accommodate, appropriate, invite, and tolerate the old, the new, the outlandish, and so on, to forge a new education, including a vision of innovative curriculum, a project neglected until now but must be undertaken in all immediacy to be decolonized." Not only are those engaged in decolonization engaged ethically and politically. Wherever we are located "in the non-place of Empire" (Hardt & Negri, 2000, p. 208), we are all politically and ethically engaged, and in local and global ways that can usefully be articulated and elaborated in our research. For those of us facing and resisting the privatization and marketization of public education, we are forced to negotiate among complex and conflicting professional responsibilities, which are structured and animated by ethical obligations and political commitments.

The accelerating complexity of our work as curriculum scholars calls us to make scholarly efforts at self-conscious understanding of our work and the work of teachers and students in the schools, all of us situated culturally, historically, and, we are acutely clear, globally. I hope the chapters in this collection make a significant contribution to such scholarly self-understanding and understanding of the field and, thereby, contribute to the *advancement* of the field. May this collection give us pause to reflect on our respective national and regional fields, and to inspire us to renew our commitment to them as well as to the advancement of the field worldwide. In those nations and regions without infrastructure, may associations and societies of curriculum scholars be formed, scholarly journals established, and the project of understanding (collectively as well as individually) furthered. Let us, together, construct an intellectually sophisticated field of curriculum studies, one worthy of those school teachers and students who labor to understand themselves and the world they inhabit. May the complicated conversation that is the internationalization of curriculum studies continue.

REFERENCES

Chambers, C. M. (1999). The topography of Canadian curriculum theory. *Canadian Journal of Education, 24*(4), 1–14.

Gundem, B., & Hopmann, S. (Eds.). (1998). *Didaktik and/or curriculum: An international dialogue.* New York: Peter Lang.

Hardt, M., & Negri, A. (2000). *Empire.* Cambridge, MA: Harvard University Press.

Held, D., McGrew, A., Goldblatt, D., & Perraton, J. (1999). *Global transformations: Politics, economics, and culture.* Stanford, CA: Stanford University Press.

Pinar, W. F. (in press). The internationalization of curriculum studies. In D. Trueit, H. Wang, W. E. Doll, Jr., & W. F. Pinar (Eds.), *Internationalization of curriculum studies.* New York: Peter Lang.

Pinar, W. F., Reynolds, W. M., Slattery, P., & Taubman, P. (1995). *Understanding curriculum.* New York: Peter Lang.

Said, E. W. (1996). *Representations of the intellectual: The 1993 Reith lectures.* New York: Vintage.

Silva, E. (1993, November 3–5). *Trends and challenges in curriculum decentralization in Latin America.* Santiago, Chile: Regional Office for Education in Latin America and the Caribbean [OREALC], UNESCO.

Trueit, D., Wang, H., Doll, W., & Pinar, W. (Eds.). (in press). *The internationalization of curriculum studies.* New York: Peter Lang.

Westbury, I., Hopmann, S., & Riquarts, K. (Eds.). (2000). *Teaching as reflective practice: The German didaktik tradition.* Mahwah, NJ: Lawrence Erlbaum Associates.

PART I

Four Essays of Introduction

CHAPTER 1

Curriculum and Teaching Face Globalization

David Geoffrey Smith
University of Alberta

Globalization is a term now circulating frequently in both popular media as well as formal academic disciplines. It has many meanings, some of which are contestable, others simply descriptive. This chapter attempts to lay out the general parameters of the term as it has evolved historically and, in the process, explore some implications of globalization for the field of curriculum studies. Basically, my argument is that there are three forms of globalization operating in the world today: Globalization One, Two, and Three. Globalization One is the dominant form arising from what can broadly be called the revival of radical liberalism, or neoliberalism, dating back to the administrations of Ronald Reagan and Margaret Thatcher in the 1980s. Globalization Two represents the various ways that people around the world are responding to Globalization One through acts of accommodation or resistance. Globalization Three speaks to the conditions that may be emerging for a new kind of global dialogue regarding sustainable human futures. Especially in this last context, I restrict my remarks to the realm of curriculum and pedagogy.

The 1995 ninth edition of the *Oxford English Dictionary* contains no elaborated definition of *globalization,* noting it only as a noun drawn from the adjective *global,* meaning worldwide. This speaks of how the density of the term as now used is a relatively recent phenomenon, signifying the coalescence of a number of important developments within the political economy of world affairs. The late semantic arrival also speaks of how globalization does not refer simply to such things as trade between peoples and groups, or other kinds of intercultural exchange, because these have been part of human experience from the earliest of times. Instead, globalization has specific reference to fairly recent developments that may in turn be acting to form a new kind of imaginal understanding within human consciousness. As a species, we may be imagining ourselves in new ways, especially with respect to issues of identity and citizenship.

To say this, of course, displays in itself a certain intellectual conceit with its own history. After all, who has the right to speak for the world, for others? In terms of raw numbers, most people in the world have never heard of globalization and maybe never will.

Those who participate in its discussions do so out of privileged access to communications, travel, and information technologies, which are tied to various politics of representation, with legacies from the period of Euro-American colonialism extending from the 15th century to the present. Thus, although the technologies may be new, their production and use still reflect nonresolutions inherent within those legacy relationships. Eighty-five percent of all information about Africa, for example, lies in U.S. and European data banks (DeKerckhove, 1997). In a way, then, contemporary globalization is an old phenomenon in a new guise.

Globalization may especially refer to a particular kind of tension in the world, arising from what Arnove and Torres (1999) called "the glocal" (p. 14). Human self-understanding is now increasingly lived out in a tension between the local and the global, between my understanding of myself as a person of this place and my emerging yet profound awareness that this place participates in a reality heavily influenced by, and implicated in, larger pictures. This calls forth from me not just a new sense of place, but also a new kind of response to the world. It is a response I may feel uneasy about making given that so much about what seems to be going on is experienced preconceptually precisely because no one, no authority, can tell me exactly what is happening.

So it is that globalization is fraught with various new kinds of identity crises, ranging from eroding senses of national identity to unprecedented losses of indigenous languages and cultures under the homogenizing pressures of global capital. Within these crises of identity lie conundrums especially relevant for curriculum studies, difficult questions about epistemological authority, about how knowledge is produced, represented, and circulated, and perhaps especially about the auspices of curriculum work. Within the dominant mode of globalization theory, neo-liberal market theory, Herbert Spencer's classic question in the 19th century about what knowledge is of most worth has been replaced by another: How much is knowledge worth? In turn, another question is begged: Is knowledge to be the ultimate arbiter of worth?

A final introductory remark is needed on the importance of positionality as a marker within globalization debates. What Marshall McLuhan (cited in Benedetti & Dehart, 1996) once said of technology may also be true of globalization; whether it is good or bad in some philosophical sense may be beside the point. The real point is to carefully examine its effects within the life structure of human experience. Doing this, it can easily be seen that what is happening today in the name of globalization is benefiting certain rather small groups enormously, whereas for others the influence may be nothing short of catastrophic. In between are the many people simply trying to make a life together in new kinds of conditions. Within all of this is woven a form of economic theory that, in the words of political philosopher John McMurtry (1998), is embedded in "an acculturated metaphysic that has lost touch with the real world outside of its value program" (p. 136). The most important challenge for curriculum work in the new millennium may be to develop the ability to deconstruct precisely as theory the unquestioned assumptions underwriting regnant forms of global economic procedure. Without this, curriculum work, even in the name of justice and equity, will hit its head against a wall. The key is to find a way through the wall to change the thinking that constructs it. As economic historian Karl Polanyi (1944/1989) said earlier in this century, this is the age of *Homo Economicus*, economic man (sic). At least for those in power, everything has come to be defined in economic terms (Kuttner, 1996). Conflicts over globalization in the contemporary world may be driven by nothing less than the determination to put *Homo Economicus* in his place. All these and other issues are taken up later. First, however, attention is given to how globalization has arisen as a defining trope—not just for curriculum studies, but for everyone concerned about the future of the Blue Planet.

GLOBALIZATION ONE

To think about the future, it is best to work backward, tracing trajectories to the present moment, carefully working out the lineages that have brought current conditions into being.[1] Only then can thoughts of "what is to be done" be meaningful. Most immediately, the language of globalization began to emerge in the late 1980s with the collapse of the binary logic of the cold war, a political dualism that had defined the international balance of power since the end of World War II. If in the mouths of its espousers the language of globalization is today aggressively triumphalist in tone, this is because a moral and intellectual victory has been claimed, a certain right to speak and act in a way deemed vindicated by current events. This of course is short-sighted because the situation is not so simple. Especially dangerous is the historical amnesia suffered by those claiming "the road ahead" to be clear (Gates, 1996), that history has come to an "end" (Fukuyama, 1993), or that "there is no alternative" (Thatcher, 1995).

The cold war was a legacy of a particular struggle within the Euro-American empire dating from the Industrial Revolution of the 19th century. Contrary to popular opinion, constructed through Western media, the West did not win the cold war. Its conclusion was much more a compromise settlement to discontinue counterproductive policies that were draining the economies of both sides. The Eastern bloc had begun to suffer seriously from one form of implosion, the West from another. For the East, state control of a planned economy had produced high employment but limited innovation and stagnation of markets, with a consequent rise in social anomie ameliorated only by mythic patriotism and escalating militarization.

For the West, self-confidence was eroded by a number of converging factors: the failure to sustain public support for colonial venturing (Vietnam war); the determination of Middle Eastern states to assume greater control over their petroleum resources (OPEC oil crisis, 1971); the emerging economies of Asia (Japan, Korea, Taiwan, Malaysia, etc.) being able to produce goods for U.S. and European markets well below cost of those produced at home; the computer and technology revolutions that essentially gutted the middle class running paper-driven ships of state and Fordist manufacturing systems since World War II; and the emergence of *post* theory (poststructuralism, postcolonialism, etc.) that served to threaten both the autonomy and authority of the entire narrative underlying Western civilization.

The end of global binary logic made possible in the minds of some a vision of opening markets worldwide within a new borderless world guided not by states and nations per se, but by the newer institutions of global reach, such as the International Monetary Fund (IMF) and the World Bank (WB) along with the United Nations (UN) and the North Atlantic Treaty Organization (NATO). This vision, which was the foundation of both the Reagan and Thatcher administrations of the United States and United Kingdom, respectively, during the early 1980s became the lynchpin of the economic theory now known as *neo-liberalism*. Based on the ideas of Milton Friedman and Fredrick von Hayek, neo-liberalism redefined the rules of obligation between governments and peoples to privilege the free operation of a global market system over the state as the primary means for solving social problems. This policy turn provided the basis for an assault on public services especially in those countries falling under the orbit of Anglo-American influence (the United Kingdom and the United States, along with New Zealand, Canada, and Australia), with the application of business principles to most sectors of the public domain. Privatization of public services was emphasized, along with the cultivation of *enterprise culture* (Keat & Abercrombie, 1990).

---

[1] For a more detailed elaboration, see Smith (1999, 2000).

For education, the application of neo-liberalist principles has resulted in a host of actions designed to change both the nature and delivery of educational work. Some of the more important features can be noted as follows:[2]

1. vigorous attempts to delegitimize public education through documents such as *A Nation at Risk* and *The Holmes Report,* highlighting the failures of public schools rather than their successes;

2. treating education as a business with aggressive attempts to commercialize the school environment as well as make it responsible to outcomes or product-based measures;

3. emphasizing performance and achievement indicators as a way of cultivating competitiveness between schools and districts;

4. privileging privatization initiatives through strategies of school choice and voucher systems;

5. giving strict financial accounting procedures precedence over actual pedagogical need;

6. assaulting teacher unions to deregulate teacher labor to make it more competitive;

7. downloading educational management to local board authorities (site-based management) while retaining curricular and policy authority within state (hence now market) hands;

8. tying the financing of education to target projects, such as the technologization of instruction and the privileging of science and technology subjects in schools and universities to serve the needs of global industrial competitiveness;

9. adopting a human capital resource model for education, whereby curriculum and instruction work should be directed at producing workers for the new globalizing market system;

10. invoking the language of life-long learning to abate concerns about the end of career labor (expect to lose your job frequently, and reskill, as companies need to perpetually restructure to remain globally competitive);

11. aggressive generating of curriculum and educational policies by noneducation groups such as the Business Council on National Issues (Canada), the Business Roundtable (U.S.), the Trilateral Commission, the International Monetary Fund, and the World Bank (thereby accelerating efforts to harmonize curricula across nations and states to enhance the mobility of workers and bring more states into the globalizing web of the new economy);

12. separating debate and discussion of pedagogical issues, such as how children best learn and how teachers can best teach humanely from issues of educational management; and

13. pressuring governments around the world into accepting these actions as a condition for joining the new international trade cartels such as the World Trade Organization (WTO).

During the cold war, curriculum work was ideologically and rhetorically linked to the effort of producing citizens who would support one path over another. International aid programs in education were couched in the language of *development*; they were thinly veiled attempts to win ideological loyalty within a dichotomous structuration of global power. It may well be asked what shall be the organizing principle for curriculum work today? Many writers (Greene, Giroux, McLaren, Apple, etc.) speak to the need for more

---

[2]These are discussed more fully in Spring (1998); Ball (2000); Peters (1996); Barlow and Robertson (1994) and many other sources.

widespread vigilance in the protection of democratic principles, calling for increased participation of all the world's people in the decision-making processes that ultimately affect them. It is precisely on this point, however, that neo- liberalism, as the rallying call for global market liberalization (Globalization One), runs into difficulty.

Usually *market liberalization* is linked in a semantic pair with *democracy*, but in actual practice the two terms are contraindicative. For example, the installation of the various free trade agreements in the Americas since the late 1980s (The Free Trade Agreement [FTA]; The North American Free Trade Agreement [NAFTA]) made education linked to the language of tradeable goods and services. These agreements were both negotiated and implemented largely without public debate and certainly without due popular consent (McMurtry, 1998). Indeed, various writers have suggested that democracy is a problem for market liberalization because democratic process impedes the speed of decision making necessary for gaining and maintaining commercial advantage. Ian Angel (cited in Gwyn, 1996), professor of Information Systems at the London School of Economics, recently said that "(since) the disposable income of the majority is being reduced, the big question of the coming decades is how to find an acceptable means of scaling back democracy" (p. 16).

The Freidman/von Hayek argument that freedom of the market means freedom of persons is questionable on numerous grounds, not least of which is the way true freedom of thought is compromised when the results of thinking are judged by assumptions deemed to be beyond the scrutiny of thinking. Under such a condition, the end always justifies the means. Tight media control of information, subjugation of alternative knowledges, to say nothing of electoral fraud within constitutional democracies to produce desired results: All these are symptoms of the contemporary crisis of democracy under the reigning dispensation of neoliberalism.[3]

According to British writer, John Gray (1998), it is important to see the neo-liberalist version of globalization as essentially an Anglo-American vision that is attempting to haul the rest of the world into its rules of operation. Historically, it is linked to the history of the European Enlightenment ("The U.S. is the world's last great Enlightenment regime" p. 27), in which it was assumed that (a) because the operation of human reason is the same everywhere, (b) all reasonable people will abide by the version of reality that reason draws and maps for them. According to Immanuel Kant, the chief proponent of this view in the 18th century, any other response, such as that based on emotion, intuition, or deference to convention or other authority, is a sign of "self-incurred immaturity" (Schmidt, 1996).

Historically, it can be argued that the dream of the universality of a single logic (the Enlightenment ideal) is primarily a religious conception tied to monotheism and, in the European context, to Christianity and the vision of a unified Christendom that guided Europe from the days of Roman emperor Constantine in the 4th century C.E. (after his conversion to Christianity) to the breakdown of Christendom under scientific secularism in the 20th century. What we are left with today under Globalization One is a secular residue of the Christendom ideal, with economic theory providing a theological (Loy, 1998) justification for the new universal operation of The Market as God (Cox, 1999).

It is by this logic that a fundamental bifurcation is occurring within the global imaginary. Within the agenda of Globalization One, anything that does not fit the formula of its operations is described as an *externality* (McMurtry, 1998)—an anomaly that will

---

[3]The Internet has become the place of gathering for alternative research and interpretation of events in the public domain. By way of example, for evidence of the ways the U.S. Republican Party obtained the presidency for George W. Bush through tampering with the electoral rights of African American voters, see the website *www.GregoryPalast.com*.

eventually disappear through atrophy or irrelevance, but never to be addressed as bearing any pedagogical news, so to speak, something that could/should be engaged creatively. For example, one can think of neo-liberalism's appropriation of the postmodern emphasis on the ambiguity of language and the dynamic pluralism inherent in the human condition. Within the operation of neo-liberalism, ambiguity and pluralism get folded into another fetish of commodification, whereby the play of meaning becomes a rationale for the endless display of semiotic referentiality under the code of commercial innovation. A more creative response, pedagogically and globally speaking, might be to open the possibility of deconstructing economic theory to show not just how it subjugates alternative knowledges and ways of being, but also how its survival depends on the continuance of such subjugation.

The agenda of Globalization One has had a number of interlocking results that continue to reshape the landscape of both local communities as well as international human understanding. Control of the international economy is increasingly concentrated in fewer and fewer hands through the operation of giant multinational firms such as General Electric, IBM, Ford Motor Company, and Royal Dutch Shell. The largest 300 multinational corporations control 25% of all the world's productive assets, 70% of all international trade, and 99% of all direct foreign investment (see Clarke, 1997). The loyalty of these huge firms is less to the country of their national origin than to new virtual communities of international stockholders. The result is a diminishment of the tax bases that national governments are able to wrest from commercial ventures, which in turn affects the quality of social programs local communities can offer citizens.

The competitiveness of international enterprise also means that firms move frequently to take advantage of labor market conditions, regardless of the politics of local regions, so that in the name of market freedom and democracy, the corruption of local political regimes is often ignored.[4] Firms now enter into joint venture contracts with countries whose policies only 20 years ago would have been regarded as abhorrent. This has led critic William Greider (1997) to ask:

> What was the Cold War really all about? Was it about securing freedom for enslaved peoples, as every patriot believed, or was it about securing free markets for capitalism, as Marxist critics often argued? The goal of human rights that leading governments once described as universal has (now) been diluted by a new form of commercial relativism. (p. 37)

The technological innovation that has been pivotal in the development of globalization processes carries with it new kinds of moral consideration that especially arise when the impact of technology on struggling economies is revealed (Rifkin, 1996). For example, until recently, the islands of Madagascar, Reunion, and Comoros used vanilla production as their export ticket to the global economy. From the tropical climbing orchid, they produced 98% of the world's vanilla, selling it on global markets for U.S. $1200 per pound. By 1996, Escagenetics Co. of America was able to produce vanilla genetically for U.S. $25 per pound. The economies of three Indian Ocean islands have thus been completely undermined.

The most important influence of the new technologies of information has been the virtualization of international finance or the development of the new globalized "Casino Economy" (Clarke, 1997). Today, financial transactions of more than $3 trillion are conducted daily by banks, financial services institutions, and speculative market

---

[4]The support that the Canadian oil and exploration company, Talisman, indirectly gives to the government of the Sudan, and hence to its civil war with the local Muslim population, has been a topic of great controversy in Canadian media in recent years.

funds. The operation of the international economy is now profoundly disembodied. Entire countries like Brazil, Thailand, and Mexico have been bankrupted in a matter of days through the virtual flight of financial speculators. Although regulations are now in place to prevent the kinds of global collapse that seemed imminent in the mid-1990s, the vulnerability of the new international virtualized market system cannot be underestimated. Again, virtualization means neglect of the needs of concrete existence at the local level.

Other impacts of Globalization One that cannot be elaborated on here include: (a) the new feminization of labor through global electronics and garment industries, and women's politicization in developing countries (Sassen, 1998); (b) population migrations by political refugees, migrant workers, and postsecondary students who are changing the ethnic composition of Euro-American communities (e.g., in England, English is no longer the native tongue of the numerical majority; Pennycook, 1996); and (c) the emerging importance of global cities involving the transformation of traditional urban–rural linkages (Sassen, 1998).

Finally, brief but important mention needs to be made of the influence of the new information technologies as vehicles for the production and dissemination of knowledge under Globalization One. The Internet is a product of Euro-American technical development, and it is rapidly transforming traditional understandings of knowledge and pedagogy. Access to information (at least certain kinds of information) may be becoming more democratized at the same time as the Web is becoming a place of alternative kinds of community building and personal networking.[5] The long-range impact of these developments on curriculum and policy is difficult to assess at the present time. However, it is fair to say that, by and large, teachers are intimidated by the new technologies, and the costs of maintaining the technical infrastructure of Web-based instruction are proving prohibitive for local schools. If the 20th century was predicted by late 19th and early 20th century social planners to be "The Century of the School" (Tomkins, 1976), it may be safely predicted today that what survives of the school into the 21st century will be quite different from what currently prevails.

GLOBALIZATION TWO

If a radicalized interpretation of Market Logic is now providing the theoretical underpinning for social development of all kinds around the world, it is important to register that this interpretation is not univocally or unproblematically accepted.[6] Media control as a deliberate strategy of Globalization One (Schiller, 1989) has meant that citizens within the Anglo-American nexus have, to a large extent, been shielded from facing the true complexities, contradictions and contestations that are at work within the actual unfolding of globalization processes. This is partly because the orthodoxies of Globalization One rest on one important and troublesome assumption to which allusion has already been made, which is the belief that because history has been transcended by a new universal logic, history should be forgotten or rendered irrelevant to the true requirements of the contemporary situation. This is a problem that is endemic to the logic of power: Once power has been achieved, the process of getting there suffers amnesia. Slavery; subordination of women, gays, lesbians, and people of color; colonial history; genocide of aboriginal groups; environmental degradation—all these remain as mne-

---

[5]Outstanding sources of news include the Canadian Centre for Policy Alternatives (*www.po.icyalternatives.ca*) and the Black Radical Congress (www.blackradicalcongress.org).

[6]For an excellent survey of organizations and movements that are attempting to define civil life alternatively to the scripts of Globalization One, see Starr (2000).

monic ghosts within the imperial tale, either waiting in the wings for their own moment of truth or pushing hard against the grain of dominant interpretive frames.

In terms of economic theory alone, there are many different models at work in the world today, each connected to long traditions of civic obligation. Each plays into the emerging system of Globalization One, but on its own terms fighting to protect the rights of its citizens against the assumptions of radical monetarism. For example (see Broadbent, 2001), for most countries of the Organization for Economic Cooperation and Development, technical innovation and globalization forces have produced ever-widening gaps in income between social classes and regions. Anglo-American governments have allowed the disparities to deepen and become even more entrenched. Continental governments like Sweden, France, and Germany, in contrast, have taken steps to remain internationally competitive while maintaining strong social charters. In Canada today, child poverty levels stand at 25%; in Sweden, only 2.5% of children live in poverty. While the government of Ontario in Canada embarks on a program of dismantling its public education system in favor of privatization, the governments of Germany and the Netherlands have increased spending to enhance already fine public education systems.

Asian countries like Japan, China, and Korea have strong Confucian traditions that make loyalty to family and state virtually coterminous, in such a way that the state economy holds strongly to its social obligations (Gray, 1998). Full employment is more important than high GNP even if much employment is menial and could easily be replaced by technology, such as the operation of department store elevators.

In terms of curriculum policy, Singapore provides the example of preparing citizens who can work for the new multinational corporations that have set up in the country (Spring, 1998). Emphasis is on learning new international languages (English, German, etc.), but also on social attitudes of tolerance and harmony arising from Confucian values. As a reward for citizens, the government eliminated all individual taxes.

In the new South Africa, the path taken by the government for economic regeneration has meant forced compliance with educational and social policies dictated by the IMF and the WB, emphasizing an open door policy to educational institutions from overseas countries, especially England and the United States. The University of Lancashire, for example, now offers degree programs in different parts of the country. This creates new kinds of tensions for South Africans. As one teacher reported recently (Nwedamutswu, 2001), "We have only just won the war against the colonial oppression of apartheid. Now almost immediately our ability to produce and teach our own knowledge is being taken away from us again." This was not meant as a repudiation of globalization processes per se, but as a request that sensitivity be shown to the specific histories of people, and that concern for ownership of the means of knowledge production cannot be separated from those histories.

Japan, long admired in the West for an educational model based on a strict examination system producing high results on international math and science tests, has now acknowledged the human cost of such a system (Asanuma, 2000). Lack of creativity, severance of learning from learning to live, and the production of debilitating stress among students are all products of the old educational priorities. Today, a reform movement is afoot to make learning more relevant to learning to live: to live healthily, with respect for nature, and within a more harmonious rhythm balancing intellectual and social needs. A New Course of Studies has been developed, in which students learn how to grow their own vegetables, cook and sew, visit with the elderly and handicapped, and practice other basic life skills as part of a curriculum designed to foster a more well-rounded understanding of citizenship.

In Latin America and the Caribbean, under the Structural Adjustment policies (SAPs) of the IMF and WB (Globalization One), spending on education in the poorest

37 countries declined 25% between 1984 and 1994. Costa Rica, for example, once had the highest literacy rate in the Caribbean due largely to a public education drive between 1950 and 1980. In 1981, the government was given an IMF loan on condition that education expenditures be cut.

Mexico once had a public education system safeguarding equality of access for all students and staffed by teachers who had one of the strongest unions in the hemisphere. Most teachers were of peasant origin and were committed to land reform and other attempts to democratize Mexican life. In return for debt relief, Mexico was one of the first to inaugurate social reforms under the mandate and surveillance of the WB and IMF. Teacher salaries, already low, were cut by 50%. The public education system began to be dismantled, with industry-school partnerships put in place to transform education to serve the needs of industry (Barlow & Robertson, 1994).

Resistances are now growing against these kinds of Globalization One developments (Lemus, 1999). The Trinational Coalition (Canada, United States, and Mexico) in Defense of Public Education was formed to lobby governments to protect public education as a social right. The Coalition participated in the civil unrest surrounding the meetings of the World Trade Organization (WTO) in Seattle in 2000. Of particular concern was the potential under Globalization One practices for control of education to be taken over by foreign educational services companies, ostensibly to assist in the building up of the knowledge economy globalization processes are thought to require. What happens, then, to national identity when non-nationals take charge of education?

As John McMurtry (1998) suggested, the "knowledge based economy" might better be termed "the ignorance-based economy" because under it, "rationality" and "knowledge" become "absurd expressions" (p. 187). What genuine knowledge development requires quintessentially are conditions of impartiality and wider comprehension. A commercially based education system cannot provide these because the first canon of such a knowledge economy is that "what does not sell [directly or indirectly] corporate profits is refused communication" (p. 181). "As public education is increasingly stripped of its resources and bent to the demands of the global market, the only remaining institutional ground of human intelligence and reason is undercut" (p. 192).

The Pembina Institute of Canada has undertaken work to show that the standard measures of prosperity used by governments as yardsticks of civil progress—the Gross National Product (GNP) and Gross Domestic Product (GDP)—do not actually provide a realistic measure of the overall health of a population (see *www.pembina.piad.ab.ca*). For example, for both GNP and GDP, marriage breakdown is a positive contributor to the economy. Many sectors of society benefit economically from divorce (e.g., counseling services, legal professions, furniture companies, automobile companies, the real estate industry, etc.); all these stand to gain from the troubles of family breakdown. But what is the human cost of such troubles, even into the second and third generations, as capacities for trust and commitment are imperiled by experiences of betrayal and the breaking of faith between persons? The Pembina Institute developed what is called the *Genuine Progress Indicator* (GPI), which attempts to more realistically balance the social gains and losses from the different economic policies that governments put into effect.

Richard Sennett's (1998) excellent study of the effects of the new workplace under Globalization One ("Just in Time" production processes, the need for a highly mobile contract-based labor force instead of career-based labor, the need for constant reskilling as technology changes, etc.) illustrates that the most fundamental change in human experience currently underway may concern the experience of time. As Sennett expressed it: "The conditions of time in the new capitalism have created a conflict between character and experience, the experience of disjointed time threatening the ability of people to form their characters into sustained narratives" (p. 31). What is created is a new kind of character that is "both successful and confused"; monetarily successful perhaps, but highly confused over the question of what it means to live well with others. The idea of *lasting values* that can sustain a character over time remains nothing but an idea—something to discuss with vigor and passion, but also something completely disconnected from personal experience.

It is on this question of values that the enduring issues of globalization will be worked out. If *Homo Economicus* is just one *homo* among many, and one whose values are increasingly seen as problematic, what shall be the source and nature of alternative values? This is a matter of central preoccupation for writers in the field of globalization studies. Burbules and Torres (2000) have linked this to "the question of governability in the face of increasing diversity" (p. 22).

Responses to the issues surrounding governability and values vary. Huntington (1999) suggested that uncertainty inherent in the current situation may lead to a *clash of civilizations* as global power blocs fight for dominance in a time when no one bloc seems capable of maintaining control over the totality.

Another response is to retreat into the perceived security of past responses—what may be named as the response of *fundamentalism* (Marty & Appleby, 1994). Fundamentalism today takes many forms, from religious fundamentalism, to neo-tribalism, to a dogmatic entrenchment in the realm of pedagogy of such notions as *back to the basics* and *tough love*. Fundamentalism always thrives in times of cultural confusion, offering clear and simple answers to questions that are difficult and long range in implication.

In the next section, under Globalization Three, some suggestions are made regarding how the future may best be engaged during this time of permeable borders, increased worldwide mobility, and media and technology that are changing the shape and character of human self-understanding. The remarks are organized and sketched out specifically around issues of curriculum and pedagogy, and some personal examples are provided.

GLOBALIZATION THREE

In the 1980s, East Indian social theorist Ashis Nandy (1988) undertook a study of assumptions about childhood that can be perceived in various global contexts. He then developed a taxonomy for those assumptions—a heuristic that can be useful in exploring directions for curriculum and pedagogy in the age of globalization. According to Nandy, children and the young around the world are typically used and abused in four different ways:

1.   When they are used as projection targets for unresolved adult desires and conflicts (i.e., when parents, teachers, and significant adults use children to complete their own personal senses of lack);

2.   When *childhood* is used in a semantics of dystopia against the utopian logic of development. In such a case, terms like *childish, infantile,* and *immature* are used against an idealized and mythical binary of *adult* maturity as a way both to discipline the young as well as protect adulthood within a static and contained self-definition. This was/is a primary strategy of colonial domination, in which the colonized were/are infantilized within the power logic of the "adult" colonizer;

3.   When children and childhood are used as the battleground of cultures. A key example of this is when school curricula are written specifically to induct the young into a particular ideological viewpoint or historical perspective. For example, as part of its new neo-liberal agenda, the Grade 3 Social Studies curriculum for Alberta, Canada defines *community* as "a place where people trade in goods and services."

Current Palestinian textbooks do not depict Israel on maps of the Middle East as a way of teaching that the Middle East is an Arab-Muslim world (Steinitz, 2001). Until recently, Japanese textbooks legitimized Japanese imperial invasions of Asia during World War II as acts of liberation against Western domination; and

4. When, in technical/rational cultures like the West, the *idea of childhood* takes precedence over *the real child*. Here, a number of things can happen. For example, children become isolated as a sociological variable that can then be used by social engineers within a calculus of social and capital development. Within this set of assumptions, children have no interlocutionary power within the overall social framework. Also under this assumption, the specific flesh and blood needs of specific children can be ignored under generalized theories of childhood, perhaps the most insidious being the romanticization of the young, which leaves them abandoned to the cage of their own subjectivity.

As a political psychologist, Nandy suggested that, instead of using children as projection targets, as a model of dystopia against adult maturity, as ideological puppets, or as the object of scientific research and management, adults and children best live together in a condition of *mutuality*. It is in recognition of this condition of mutuality between adults and children that may lie the unique contribution of the field of pedagogy to discussions of globalization and curriculum.

Donald Tapscott (1998), an influential writer about the Digital Age, suggested that if schools are to survive at all, they should be places not of teaching and pedagogy in the usual senses, but gathering places for people wanting both information and a place where information can be shared and deliberated.

Teaching is becoming a less unidirectional process and much more collaborative and heuristic. I've heard many tales of students and teachers working together to implement technology in the classroom and more important new models of learning. All this gives evidence to the view that one of the most powerful forces to change the schools is the students themselves. (pp. ix–x)

Indeed, one of Tapscott's main arguments is that it is the Net Generation of young people who are leading the way in globalization's *techne*. From this viewpoint, globalization is a generational issue.

Here we see an inversion of the orthodox understanding of pedagogy as being always adult driven. Instead, there is a recognition of the young as partners in the journey toward a mutual maturity. This does not mean a relinquishment of responsibility of elders for the young, but a noting that one of the key responsibilities is to try to genuinely hear the young, to engage them conversationally about the affairs of life so that the world between them might be a truly shared one. This can be suggested in response to the findings of a recent documentary film team of the Public Broadcasting System (2001) for the program "Frontline." The film, *Lost Childhood*, documents the youth culture of a suburban Georgia community in the United States (see *http://www.pbs.org* for details) ironically just prior to a shooting incident at the school that received international attention. One of the most outstanding features of the culture was the apparent abandonment of the young by the adult community under a logic of self-interest. Each person, adult and youth, is given the right to follow his or her own interests, but the human consequences are astonishingly somber. There seems to be no basis for an ethic of mutual caring under a rubric of radical autonomy. No common meals: pick up your food and go to your own private bedroom to watch your own private TV. In this condition, both adults and children are lost to each other.

"Adultomorphism," as David Kennedy (1983) described it (endeavoring to turn children into replications of the adult self to serve the needs of that self) is a foundational strategy of conservative culture, whether that culture be religious, ethnic, economic, or pedagogical. The most notable characteristic of all educational reform prescriptions coming from Globalization One institutes and think tanks is indeed their adultomorphic nature: They show virtually no interest whatever in the impact of their formulations on the lives of children and youth. Nor do they show any interest in what possible contribution the young might make to any shared future, other than the future imagined within the neo-liberal agenda. It is on this point that further work is needed, the point of mediation between old and young with respect to how to proceed together, how to share a life. It is a point on which experienced teachers may have some important things to say. Here, two aspects are noted and then elaborated as examples.

First, in any condition of healthy living together, humanly speaking, there must be a sharing of the horizons of understanding among the people involved. Second, the subjects and practices of study must be taken not as inert and self-contained (e.g., commodifiable), but as always and inherently conversational, open-ended, and teleologically oriented to overcoming the alienation between human beings and between humans and the larger world (the sense of Self as different from Other and from World). In other words, successful study is oriented to peace, which is not to prescribe a suffocating absence of conflict, but to acknowledge that all learning involves resolving the resistances that demarcate the line between what is known and what is yet to be known. True learning means breaking the barriers and chains of ignorance and entering a new world in such a way that I and the Other become understood as One, as participating in a reality whose commonness transcends us both. In this case, Other can be understood as curriculum, as other person, as tradition, even as enemy. Learning to share a life together involves acknowledging and accepting that the work of this sharing, and the labor of coming to a mutual understanding of it, is never over, always ongoing, and sustainable only under the shadow of love. These points can be elaborated as follows.

Curriculum and Pedagogy as a Sharing of the Horizons of Understanding

As a teacher, I enter the pedagogical relationship through my own biography, which includes my formative experiences in the world, my training, and my aspirations for both myself and my students. So too does each of my students enter the pedagogical relationship in such a way. Unless there can be a sharing of these stories as a condition of our coming together, there can be no basis for our mutual advancement because it remains perpetually impossible to know who is talking; without such knowledge, what is present to be learned can only remain detached and alienated from those involved. Biographical stories do not need to be shared all at once, but their presentation within the ongoing work of the pedagogical journey is what makes the difference between a pedagogy of domination/subordination and one based on a relation of trust and mutual engagement. In the Advanced Curriculum Research course for doctoral students at the University of Alberta, for example, both students and professor participate in the Who Is the One Researching? (WITOR) project. Members work together to clarify the relations between their own biographies and the respective research projects that holds their interest.

The effect of such efforts is twofold. On the one hand, actually hearing the stories of others becomes a liminal reminder of the impossibility of corralling all of these stories into one conceptual or interpretive schema, except of course the schema of difference. On the other hand, it is precisely the schema of difference that brings people to an awareness of the need for deep tolerance and acceptance—the qualities without which there can be no community, no sense of common belonging. Sometimes the conundrum inspired by the irony is the site of provocation—a prelude for hermeneutic breakthrough. This was the case, for example, in another class discussing an article on gay and lesbian experience. Students from China reacted in horror to the possible sociocultural acceptance of gays and lesbians, relating stories from their own cultures of how such people are treated. Facing a lesbian student in the class, someone who had already gained their respect and trust before *coming out* induced a genuine sense of bewilderment and puzzlement, a new genuine openness to learning, and a reciprocal sharing of assumptions and understandings about sexuality generally.

The sharing of horizons can easily become stuck in a kind of self-aggrandizing narcissism if an effort is not vigilantly made to show how the dynamic at work in the pedagogical situation has reference in the broader world. That is, the sharing of horizons points to the way my horizon is never just *my* horizon, but one that opens out onto that of another and, as such, is in a condition of perpetual revision toward a more comprehensive understanding and appreciation of the broader world. In this instance is gained the appreciation for how no one story can tell the whole story, and that hermeneutic suspicion is best directed at pretensions to the same—pretensions to a univocal and monological theory of globalization, for example. The economistic determinism at the heart of the neo-liberal agenda of Globalization One must be exposed for the way it limits other ways of human expression and common living (e.g., through aesthetics, spirituality, and altruism).

The sharing of horizons within communities of difference helps break down the dichotomy between the private and public spheres, and may serve as a kind of prelude to a theory of justice that honors difference while holding every difference accountable to its influence in the broader public realm. It is one thing to hold private views and to honor the right to privacy for those views. Yet in the age of globalization, where persons and groups now rub shoulders in new and unforeseen ways, the time may soon be near when more open expression of personal convictions is necessitated by the requirement to understand more fully and more publicly the lived-out implications of privately held (including privately held by groups and communities) beliefs. In my graduate seminar on religious and moral education, for example, each person is encouraged to publicly articulate the convictions of their own faith community regarding other faith communities. This becomes a means of facing difference, lifting it out of the realm of abstraction and conceptualization, and embodying it in relations between persons. It is one thing for a Seventh Day Adventist student to state as an abstract principle of theology for his faith community that "the Pope is the Antichrist"; it is quite another to state it while facing directly a Roman Catholic friend and colleague in the class, surrounded by others now deeply invested in the outcome of such facing. These others are invested partly because the future of the class—its tone, its pedagogical receptiveness, its future possibilities as a place of secure freedom—depends on it. They are also invested because they recognize in such a confrontation an exemplification of their own relations of difference, so that the outcome of this specific case becomes prototypical for the resolution of their own personal challenges.

This kind of *outing* of difference also assists in helping students better understand the way their assumptions about others are historically constructed; as such, they must be reexamined and reinterrogated for their time boundedness. Of course, historicization as a strategy for opening dialogue contains its own theory of history, and it must be recognized that it does not work well within and among communities where history is taught as a rigid anamnesis—a memorization of how we got to this point as a way of legitimizing why at this point we should never change. Resolving that difficulty must be reserved for another day; here the pedagogical assumption is that history is open or better, that the future is always open, and that an orientation in the present to an open future is an absolutely necessary precondition not only for a world that is more fair and just, but also for one that may be inspired by hope.

One of the conditions, then, that the sharing of horizons brings into the classroom can be called the condition of *mnemonic reparation,* which has special relevance for curriculum in the age of globalization. Nigerian playwright, essayist, novelist, and poet, Wole Soyinka (2000), has called for an international movement to make possible a new kind of reparation in the world for past wrongs, past injustices. This new kind of reparation would not be monetary ("Reparation is not monetary recompense"), but a recovery and making public of the subjugated memories of oppressed peoples. For an example, Soyinka pointed to the UNESCO commitment to the preservation of the slave routes in West Africa, establishing a scientific committee to document, preserve, and open up the landmarks of the slave routes for posterity. In such a way, Africans around the world can better concretize their history to turn it into a living voice within the emerging global community. Also, such mnemonic acts reveal the interdependent nature of every identity.

Curriculum and Pedagogy as Being Oriented to Peace

The best way to understand this is through a kind of phenomenology of learning, which may be exemplified through attending closely to the learning act. Good examples can be found in the practice of learning to play a musical instrument. Contrary to conventional Western theories of musical practice, which are oriented by the desire for personal pleasure, performance, or even aesthetic achievement narrowly understood, the Confucian tradition of ancient China always taught music as a way of shaping character—helping students understand something important about relations in the world. In Confucianism and Chinese, *wen* denotes "the arts of peace" (Waley, 1992, p. 39), and they include music, dance, and literature.

How is learning to play a musical instrument an art of peace or an act of peacemaking? One does not need to be an expert to come to appreciate this; every diligent student has moments of realizing what is happening through good practice. To every student, beginner or experienced, come occasional moments of sensing deeply that what is at work in the playing can be ascribed to neither the instrument nor the practitioner nor the musical score alone. Instead, a mysterious unity has been achieved when all three seem to participate in a reality, a truth even, that transcends any of the individual aspects. It truly is a moment of peace, a moment of letting go—of ego, culture, worry, or otherness. It becomes an entry into quiet wonder—a sense that as a human being one participates in a most amazing and wonderful mystery. In piano playing, sometimes simply striking a single note and listening deeply and carefully to its reverberation into the broader world can produce a sense of participating in something that is large and beyond easy conceptual rationalization. In flute playing, there come moments when the breath seems to lose all resistance to the instrument, so that breathing into the instrument becomes the perfect extension of breathing naturally. It is an experience of amazing freedom, in which as a player one feels completely in communion with the instrument, and the air seems pure, clean, cool, and fresh.

Other examples are easy to find. Suddenly discovering the sheer beauty of a Wordsworth poem, the elegance of a quadratic equation, or the wonderful variegation of wood grain in a shop class: All of these experiences constitute a new kind of reconciliation with the world. The finding of the poem not to be brute and inert perhaps as expected, the equation not to be simply a mad random puzzle, and the wood to speak its own story:

This kind of finding is a form of self-finding, a finding of oneself in the things of the world, indeed a finding of the world to be a place where I can find myself to be truly at home. This is what is meant in saying that genuine learning is oriented to peace.

Such learning, however, has its own requirements, and it is precisely these that find little support in a view of education driven solely by commercial or economic interests. For one thing, such learning requires the nurturing of sustained attention. Staying with the subject or object of study until it begins to reveal itself to you so that you may engage it requires discipline (<L. *discere*, "learn"), which also means the ability to follow something to its true end—that is, to the end of its revelation. In this sense, true learning is a life's work. Margaret Atwood, Canada's leading novelist and writer, recalled once being at a cocktail party talking with a famous heart surgeon, who proclaimed, "When I retire I'm going to write a novel," to which Atwood replied, "When I retire I'm going to perform heart surgery!" Real learning can never be fickle or supercilious; it involves deep attunement to the Way of life.

Commercial culture is built on a phenomenology of distraction, and children who are raised in it lose the capacity for sustained attention. The principle of lifelong learning that undergirds the new economy depends on keeping people off-balance, ready to move at a moment's notice, ready to leave one job to take another, to reskill for this, then that. What is undercut is the capacity for a job to be not just a job, but a life—a place to grow, develop character, learn about living, share relations with others deeply, and complexly. "Having a job," without being able to "make a living," is a recipe for social disaster, the manifestations of which first present themselves in the lives of children and youth.

For the classroom to be a place of peace seeking and peace finding, privilege must be given to it being a place where people can find themselves through their inquiries and through their relations with one another. Above all, it must be a place of care, having its own requirements. There needs to be an adequate material base; the size of the group must not be allowed to intrude on the possibility of forming healthy relations; the teacher must be possessed of true hermeneutic skill, to show the essential openness of life, and its conversational character; there must be a balance of relations between speech and silence; the curriculum must address real human issues and problems, connected hermeneutically to the lives of the students; and the teleological purpose of learning must not be determined in advance of its creative engagement, or at least its given auspices must be held up for regular reexamination. Perhaps above all, pedagogical living in the classroom oriented to peace operates in the tension between completion and incompletion, between knowing and what is yet to be revealed. Such is the foundation of hope.

CONCLUSION

It is in the nature of such a broad discussion of globalization and curriculum that *conclusion* is a misnomer. Yet what may be said by way of drawing things to an informal summation? Perhaps the most relevant thing to say about globalization in the contemporary context is to note it as a topic of widespread discussion. Indeed, the fact that people everywhere are using the term as a new kind of backdrop to discussions about a multitude of different issues may signify a new kind of awareness about the underlying singular comprehensiveness of the human condition—a condition in which, to paraphrase a principle from the field of ecology, each one of us is connected irreducibly to every other one. This may be taken as a new foundation for ethical relation in a human world increasingly aware of itself as sharing a common home on the earth, and any efforts to regress into older more parochial visions must be noted with alarm.

REFERENCES

Arnove, R., & Torres, C. (1999). *Comparative education: The dialectic of the global and the local.* Lahman, MD: Rowman and Littlefield.

Asanuma, S. (2000, October 14). *The Japan educational reform for the twenty first century: The impact of New Course Studies toward post-modern era in Japan.* A paper presented at the Internationalization of Curriculum conference, East China Normal University, Shanghai, China.

Barlow, M., & Robertson, H.-J. (1994). *Class warfare: The assault on Canada's schools.* Toronto, Canada: Key Porter Books.

Benedetti, P., & Dehart, N. (Eds.). (1996). *On McLuhan: Forward through the rearview mirror.* Toronto, Canada: Prentice-Hall.

Broadbent, E. (2001, May 25). It is all about rights. Political direction: The future of the left. *The Globe and Mail,* p. A11.

Burbules, N., & Torres, C. (Eds.). (2000). *Globalization and education: Critical perspectives.* London: Routledge.

Clarke, T. (1997). *Silent coup: Confronting the big business takeover of Canada.* Ottawa, Canada: Canadian Centre for Policy Alternatives.

Cox, H. (1999, March). The market as God: Living in the new dispensation. *Atlantic Monthly,* 21–27.

DeKerckhove, D. (1997). *Connected intelligence: The arrival of web society.* Toronto, Canada: Somerville House.

Fukuyama, F. (1993). *The end of history and the last man.* New York: Avon.

Gates, W. (1996). *The road ahead.* Harmondsworth, England: Penguin.

Gray, J. (1998). *False dawn: The delusions of global capitalism.* London: Verso.

Greider, W. (1997). *One world, ready or not: The manic logic of global capitalism.* New York: Touchstone.

Gwyn, R. (1996, October 6). Voice of Angell provides hard truths. *The Toronto Star,* p. A17.

Huntington, S. (1998). *The clash of civilizations and the remaking of world order.* New York: Touchstone.

Keat, R., & Abercrombie, N. (1990). *Enterprise culture.* London: Routledge.

Kennedy, D. (1983). *Toward a phenomenology of childhood.* Unpublished PhD dissertation, University of Kentucky.

Kuttner, R. (1996). *Everything for sale: The virtues and limits of markets.* Chicago: University of Chicago Press.

Lemus, M. (1999, Fall). The millennium round and the social right to education. *Journal of Curriculum Theorizing,* pp. 97–103.

Loy, D. (1998). The religion of the market. In H. Coward & D. Maguire (Eds.), *Visions of a new earth: religious perspectives on population, consumption and ecology* (pp. 55–78). Albany: State University of New York Press.

Marty, M., & Appleby, S. (Eds.). (1994). *Fundamentalisms observed.* Chicago: University of Chicago Press.

McMurtry, J. (1998). *Unequal freedoms: The global market as an ethical system.* Toronto, Canada: Garamond.

Nandy, A. (1988). Reconstructing childhood. *In Tradition, tyranny and utopia.* Delhi: Oxford University Press.

Nwedamutswu, H. (2001, May 21). *Challenges in South African Education today.* A talk given to the Department of Secondary Education, University of Alberta.

Pennycook, A. (1996). *The cultural politics of English as an international language.* Toronto, Canada: Addison-Wesley.

Peters, M. (1996). *Poststructuralism, politics and education.* New York: Bergin & Garvey.

Polanyi, K. (1944/1989). *The great transformation: The political and economic origins of our time.* Boston: Beacon.

Public Broadcasting System. (2001). *Frontline: Lost childhood.* A documentary film.

Rifkin, J. (1996). The new technology and the end of jobs. In J. Mander & E. Goldsmith (Eds.), *The case against the global economy and for a return to the local* (pp. 108–121). San Francisco: Sierra Club Books.

Sassen, S. (1998). *Globalization and its discontents: Essays on the new mobility of people and money.* New York: The New Press.

Schiller, H. (1989). *Culture inc.: The corporate takeover of public expression.* New York: Oxford University Press.

Schmidt, J. (Ed.). (1996). *What is enlightenment? Eighteenth century answers and twentieth century questions.* Berkeley: University of California Press.

Sennett, R. (1998). *The corrosion of character: The personal consequences of work in the new capitalism.* New York: W.W. Norton.

Smith, D. (1999). Economic fundamentalism, globalization and the public remains of education. *Interchange, 30*(1), 93–117.

Smith, D. (2000). The specific challenges of globalization for teaching and vice versa. *The Alberta Journal of Educational Research, XLVI*(1), 7–26.

Soyinka, W. (2000). Memory, truth and healing. In I. Amadiume (Ed.), *Memory: The politics of truth, healing and social justice* (pp. 21–37). New York: Zed.

Spring, J. (1998). *Education and the rise of the global economy.* Mahwah, NJ: Lawrence Erlbaum Associates.

Starr, A. (2000). *Naming the enemy: Anti-corporate movements confront globalization.* London: Zed.

Steinitz, Y. (2001, June 2). It is an existential conflict about the very existence of the Jewish state. *Edmonton Journal,* p. H3.

Tapscott, D. (1998). *Growing up digital: The rise of the net generation.* Toronto, Canada: McGraw-Hill.

Thatcher, M. (1995). *The path to power.* New York: HarperCollins.

Tomkins, G. (1976). *A common countenance: Stability and change in Canadian curriculum.* Toronto, Canada: Addison-Wesley.

Waley, A. (1992). *Confucianism: The analects of Confucius.* New York: Book-of-the-Month Club.

CHAPTER 2

Thinking Globally in Environmental Education: Implications for Internationalizing Curriculum Inquiry

Noel Gough
Deakin University

In this chapter, I critically appraise attempts to think globally in environmental education and consider some implications of this critique for internationalizing curriculum inquiry. Despite its somewhat marginal status in the field of curriculum studies writ large, environmental education is a significant site for understanding curriculum internationally for at least two reasons. First, international organizations such as the United Nations (UN) and its agencies (e.g., UNESCO) have made substantial contributions to the development of environmental education during the past three decades. Second, many of the subject matters of environmental education are explicitly international and/or global in their scope.

As evidence of its marginal position in the curriculum field, I note that Pinar, Reynolds, Slattery, and Taubman (1995) did not mention environmental education as such in chapter 14, "Understanding Curriculum as International Text," of their synoptic text, *Understanding Curriculum: An Introduction to the Study of Historical and Contemporary Curriculum Discourses.* Despite this apparent silence, these authors alluded to both of the attributes that I suggest give environmental education considerable significance for understanding curriculum internationally. For example, Pinar et al. drew attention to the importance of the UN's entry into international curriculum discourse in the 1970s and 1980s; they illustrated this by reference to *A World Core Curriculum* published in 1982. However, the United Nations (through UNESCO–UNEP[1]) had in fact entered international curriculum discourse 8 years earlier by establishing the International Environmental Education Programme (IEEP) in 1974.[2] Pinar et al. described the world core curriculum as "an outgrowth of the global crises of the 1970s and the urgent concern for a school curriculum to address pressing international issues of the day" (p. 801), which de-

This chapter revises and expands the following paper: Gough, Noel (2002). Thinking/acting locally/globally: Western science and environmental education in a global knowledge economy. *International Journal of Science Education,* 24(11), 1217–1237. the author hereby acknowledges the prior publication of substantial portions of this chapter by Taylor & Francis Ltd.

scribes the IEEP equally well. Environmental issues are no less pressing (and no less international) today—a point that Pinar et al. clearly recognized and emphasized in the conclusion to their chapter where they reiterated a call "for education to accept full responsibility in addressing global survival issues" (p. 841). They supported the idea of a "curriculum for ecology" (p. 840), in which "ecological problems become educational problems" (p. 841) and suggested that in "the internationally-focused ecological proposals" of many educators (including Bowers, 1993a, 1993b; Gutek, 1993), "curriculum is elevated to a level of global strategic importance" (Pinar et al., 1995, p. 841).

In the light of these considerations, curriculum scholars might reasonably expect environmental education to exemplify a mode of curriculum inquiry that is already internationalized to a large degree. The transnational character of many environmental issues certainly raises expectations that environmental educators should possess some knowledge and experience of what it means to *think globally* in this specific area of curriculum. I argue here that after nearly 30 years in which the phrase *thinking globally* has circulated within discourses of environmental education, the concept remains largely unexamined and undertheorized. I offer evidence and argument for the proposition that many environmental educators have accepted uncritically popular assumptions about the universal applicability of Western science and have thus assumed that Western scientific understandings of global environmental problems and issues provide an adequate basis for thinking globally. Environmental educators are not alone in making such assumptions. Therefore, I suggest that implications for other forms of curriculum work might follow from examining the limits to thinking globally in environmental education. In particular, I explore the implications of a number of studies in the history and sociology of scientific knowledge that demonstrate that Western science is a specific way of *thinking locally,* and that recognizing its localness enhances rather than diminishes its potential contribution to international knowledge work. Thus, I suggest that seeing Western science as one among many local knowledge traditions might enhance its contribution to understanding and resolving global environmental problems. Similarly, seeing Western epistemologies as just some among many local knowledge systems that can be deployed in curriculum work might enhance their contribution to understanding curriculum internationally. From this perspective, producing a global knowledge economy in/for an internationalized curriculum field can be understood as creating transnational *spaces* in which local knowledge traditions can be performed together, rather than trying to create a global common market in which representations of local knowledge must be translated into (or exchanged for) the terms of a universal discourse.

THINKING GLOBALLY IN ENVIRONMENTAL EDUCATION: A SHORT HISTORY

Think globally. Act locally. These familiar exhortations have circulated within the slogan system of environmental education for nearly three decades. Usually they are invoked as a pair, but environmental educators have not necessarily translated them into practice in comparable or commensurate ways. School curricula often incorporate local action on environmental issues effectively (see e.g., Gough, 1992; Malcolm, 1988), but evidence of thinking globally is more elusive, equivocal, and problematic. We can readily observe learners performing a school energy audit, participating in a recycling project, propagating locally indigenous plants to revegetate a degraded site, and so on. But what constitutes compelling evidence of learners, teachers and curriculum writers thinking globally? In practical and performative terms, what do environmental educators *mean* when they say they are thinking globally and, perhaps more important, what *should* they mean?

According to Ruth and William Eblen (1994), Rene Dubos, a Nobel Laureate and molecular biologist, coined the phrase *think globally, act locally* in 1972, when he chaired the group of scientific experts advising the United Nations Conference on the Human Environment held that year in Stockholm. We might thus interpret the establishment of the aforementioned UNESCO–UNEP International Environmental Education Programme (IEEP) in 1974 as an early (post-Stockholm) manifestation of thinking globally in environmental education. This intergovernmental program has sponsored many projects that promote and support local and regional educational action in response to concerns about the quality of the global environment. However, the products of thinking globally in such projects are determined, at least in part, by the differential power relations that accompany intergovernmental cooperation (or the appearance thereof). For example, critics of the IEEP, including Gough (1999), argue that since its inception it has cultivated a neo-colonialist discourse in environmental education by systematically privileging Western (and especially U.S.) interests and perspectives.

By the mid-1980s, "think globally, act locally" was an axiom of environmental education, a self-evident truth that no longer needed an expert's authorization.[3] For example, in *Earthrights: Education as if the Planet Really Mattered,* Greig, Pike, and Selby (1987) treated "think globally, act locally" as a taken-for-granted principle apparently without seeing any need to cite its author(ity). Other texts published in the late 1980s that implicitly or explicitly valorize variations on this principle include Pike and Selby's (1987) *Global Teacher, Global Learner,* Fien's (1989) *Living in a Global Environment,* Hicks and Steiner's (1989) *Making Global Connections,* and the World Wide Fund for Nature's (WWF) Global Environmental Education Programme (see e.g., Huckle, 1988).[4] These texts equate "thinking globally" with knowing and caring about the global dimensions and significance of environmental problems and issues. For example, as part of the curriculum rationale for *What We Consume,* John Huckle (1988) wrote:

> Starting with products such as a tin of corned beef, a packet of potato crisps or a unit of electricity, teachers and pupils are encouraged to trace commodity chains and recognize their connections to such environmental issues as deforestation in Amazonia, the draining of wetlands in Britain and the debate over acid rain in Europe. (p. 2)

Although all of these texts infer that *thinking globally* means making connections between one's (local) experience and conditions elsewhere in the world, there are discernible differences of emphasis between them. For example, *What We Consume* emphasizes the material linkages of commodity chains, whereas many of the activities in *Living in a Global Environment* begin by encouraging readers to empathize with the lived experience of people enduring (and suffering) different circumstances from those enjoyed by most people in industrialized nations. *Living in a Global Environment* draws extensively on material first published by *New Internationalist* magazine, including first-hand accounts by people living in developing countries as well as reports by Western aid workers and journalists.

These approaches do not exhaust the possible and potential meanings of *thinking globally.* For example, I recall that when I first saw *Global Teacher, Global Learner* in a publisher's display, its title triggered a fleeting memory of a juvenile novel, *School in the Skies,* that I had read in the early 1950s. Other than the title, I remember only that the story recounted the fictitious adventures of some children and their teachers whose school for one term was an airplane that took them from country to country around the world. *School in the Skies* reminds me that, although "travel broadens the mind" is a cliché, it is also part of a constellation of meanings that informs our understanding of thinking globally. However, none of the texts to which I have referred suggests that shifting our geographical locations might enhance our capacity to think globally. More important, although all of these texts make some effort to encourage readers to shift their perceptual locations—to see the world from other standpoints—for the most part they do not question the privileged status of the Western knowledge systems within which their truth claims are produced. I confess that I espoused similar conceptions of thinking globally around this time (see Gough, 1992), and therefore I make this judgment with the benefit of considerable hindsight. Thus, I admit that it might be unreasonable to expect school textbooks published 10 or more years ago to generate such questions. Books such as Fien and Gerber's (1988) edited collection, *Teaching Geography for a Better World*, introduced teachers to feminist, antiracist, and multicultural perspectives on educational values and practices, but the underlying paradigms of knowledge production in Western natural and social sciences received scant attention. However, my main purpose here is not to disparage texts produced more than a decade ago, but rather to draw attention to the limited range of meanings of *thinking globally* that are sedimented in them.

To bring my discussion of thinking globally into the present, I focus on some of the implicit and explicit ways in which this concept is represented in *Environment, Education and Society in the Asia-Pacific: Local Traditions and Global Discourses* edited by David Yencken, John Fien, and Helen Sykes (2000a). This book brings together some of the significant findings of a large comparative study of attitudes to nature and ecological sustainability, particularly among young people, in 12 countries in the Asia-Pacific region.[5] Some of the key questions explored in this study concern the relative influence of, and relationships between, local traditions and practices and global environmental discourses. Indeed, Yencken (2000) began the book's first chapter by restating—and then inverting—Dubos's familiar maxim:

> To protect the planet, we have long been told to think globally and act locally. But we can readily see that there are as many reasons to think locally and act globally. If we do not think locally, we may ignore rich sources of environmental knowledge and devalue local understanding and experience of environmental problems. If we do not act globally, we will never solve the big issues of the global commons: atmospheric and ocean pollution and the impacts of environmental degradation across national boundaries. Sustainability has many local and global dimensions. (p. 4)

Yencken provided a thoughtful and culturally sensitive comparison of the various attitudes toward nature that can be found in both the Eastern and Western nations of the Asia-Pacific region. He focused not only on contemporary ecopolitical positions in the countries studied, but also reviewed the history of Western engagement with the environmental philosophies of Eastern cultures. Yencken's judgments on these philosophies are circumspect and descriptive, rather than evaluative (most of his critical comments concern other Western academics' appraisals of Eastern philosophies). However, the conclusions toward which he drew reveal his hopes for "the emergence of a global ideology of nature that transcends individual cultures" (Yencken, 2000, p. 23):

> The environmental problems now facing the world are global problems stemming from the process of industrialization and capitalist development that has been taking place in every country, albeit at different speeds and intensities. We therefore need contemporary concepts to help frame both the nature of the problems and their likely solution, together with simple, widely applicable models for analyzing and approaching environmental problems. These concepts (sustainability, ecology, biodiversity, natural capital, intergenerational equity, precautionary principle and the like) and working models and techniques (metabolism, ecological footprint, natural step, environmental space, industrial ecology, etc.) need to gain widespread international acceptance. They should be developed cooperatively by scientists, environmental thinkers, local communities and others working hand in hand, with contributions from all cultures. (Yencken, 2000, pp. 24–25)

Although Yencken clearly respects "contributions from all cultures," he neverthe-less privileges (albeit implicitly) Western science as the prime source of the "contempo-rary concepts … working models and techniques" that "need to gain widespread internuational acceptance." Many of the concepts, models, and techniques that Yencken listed as examples—ecology, biodiversity, metabolism—are already foreclosed by their production within Western scientific discourses, and thus I find it difficult to imagine how they could be "developed cooperatively by scientists, environmental thinkers, lo-cal communities and others." I find at least four assumptions underlying Yencken's po-sition somewhat troubling.

First, Yencken's use of the term *contemporary* is problematic, in part, because some of the concepts to which he refers already have long histories in some cultures. For exam-ple, the concept of *intergenerational equity* is emphasized in the oral traditions of a num-ber of Native-American peoples, although the extent to which various groups actually managed natural resources in ways that would achieve such equity is a matter of de-bate (see e.g., Nabhan, 1995). More important, Yencken used the term *contemporary* as if it were coterminous with *Western scientific*. That is, he usually contrasted *contemporary* with *traditional* and seemed to see only Eastern traditions as persisting in any signifi-cant way into the present.

For example, Yencken (2000) described the "great environmental awakening" that took place in the United States and elsewhere in the wake of Rachel Carson's (1962) *Silent Spring* and the "new consciousness of Spaceship Earth" (p. 13) that led citizens of West-ern industrialized nations to recognize that at least some of their environmentally dam-aging behaviors were rooted in the Judeo-Christian tradition. Yencken (2000) cited research suggesting that this tradition of environmental thought has now been super-seded by a form of contemporary environmentalism that constitutes a "single cultural consensus about the environment" (p. 24) in countries such as the United States, Austria, and Sweden. Although Yencken (2000) rejected attempts "to project Western priorities onto Eastern countries or Eastern traditions into Western cultures," he also asserted that "Western cultures undoubtedly have … much to learn from Asian traditional attitudes to nature in the same way that Eastern cultures have much to learn from Western environ-mentalism" (p. 25). Here only Western environmentalism is tacitly contemporary and only in Eastern cultures do traditional attitudes to nature persist into the present. For ex-ample Yencken did not assert that Western cultures have much to learn from contempo-rary Asian attitudes to nature or that Eastern cultures have much to learn from traditional Western (i.e., Judeo-Christian) environmentalism.

Second, I am puzzled by Yencken's assumption that models for analyzing and ap-proaching environmental problems should be simple and widely applicable. My point here is simple and need not be labored: Recent developments in many fields of science and technology have exposed the limits of simple, reductionist, context-free models for analyz-ing and predicting change in complex, dynamic systems, including those we think of as evolutionary and ecological (see e.g., Khalil & Boulding, 1996; Schneider & Kay, 1994).

A third difficulty with Yencken's formulation of contemporary concepts is the as-sumption that such concepts can meaningfully be shared across cultures in ways that might be helpful in framing global environmental problems and their possible solu-tions. For example, the term *ecology* does not command shared meaning even *within* the culture that has been most responsible for its development as a key knowledge cate-gory in environmental thinking. To which and to whose ecology is Yencken referring? Many current school environmental education programs continue to represent ecology in ways that resemble the systems ecology promulgated by Odum (1971) in the various editions of his textbook, *Fundamentals of Ecology*, between 1953 and 1971. For example, the new study design for Environmental Science, a subject offered to students in the se-nior secondary school years 11 and 12 as part of the Victorian Certificate of Education

(Victoria, 2000), presents an atomistic and reductionist view of large-scale ecosystem structure and function. In Unit 1: The Environment, the first area of study is titled "Ecological Components and Interaction," and its specification begins:

> The Earth's structure may be classified into four major categories: hydrosphere, lithosphere, atmosphere and biosphere. This area of study examines the processes occurring within the spheres of the Earth and the interactions that occur in and between the ecological components of each major category. (Victoria, 2000, p. 12)

The second area of study in Unit 1, "Environmental Change," focuses on the ecosystem as the unit for analysis. Neither the arbitrary categorical separation of the spheres or the emphasis on ecosystems is consistent with many contemporary approaches to environmental analysis. For example, Worster (1993) described in detail the ways in which ecologists over the past two decades and more have repudiated Odum's portrayal of orderly and predictable processes of ecological succession culminating in stable ecosystems, yet this is an explicit item of curriculum content in Victoria's Environmental Science course (Victoria, 2000, p. 13). Typical of such repudiations are the essays collected by Pickett and White (1985), which deliver the consistent message that the concept of the ecosystem has receded in usefulness and, to the extent that the word *ecosystem* remains in use, that it has lost its former implications of order and equilibrium. Similarly, Jamison (1993) described "the failure of systems ecology to contribute very much to the actual solution of environmental problems":

> By the late 1970s, systems ecology had lost much of its public appeal, although it continued to develop as a research program. Within ecology, however, new evolutionary approaches had become increasingly popular, so that systems ecology today is only one (and not even the most significant one at that) of a number of competing ecological paradigms. (p. 202)

Why should a school Environmental Science course in the year 2000 privilege an approach to ecology that many environmentalists regarded as a failure more than 20 years ago? If indeed there are "a number of competing ecological paradigms" within contemporary Western environmental science, how does Yencken see ecology functioning as a concept that might help to "frame both the nature of the problems and their likely solution" when it is at the same time a site of conceptual contestation?

These questions bring me to the fourth and most troubling assumption that I perceive in Yencken's position. Yencken (2000) clearly believes in the *possibility*—and perhaps even the *necessity*—of a unitary and universal understanding of nature that "transcends individual cultures" (p. 23), and he also appears to accept that Western science is the best approximation to such an understanding that humans have imagined to date. Yencken and his coeditors elaborate their position on Western science in a subsequent chapter of *Environment, Education and Society in the Asia-Pacific* (Yencken, Fien, & Sykes, 2000b), in which they are at pains both to recognize and respect feminist, postcolonialist, and multiculturalist critiques of modernist Western science. Nevertheless, they maintain the position that a culturally transcendent environmental science is possible—that what they name as *science* provides the key to both thinking and acting globally. For example, Yencken, Fien, and Sykes (2000b) asserted that: "It is generally accepted that most scientific research takes place within global theoretical assumptions …" (p. 30). This is a curious statement because many of the feminist, postcolonialist, and multiculturalist critiques that these authors claim to respect do *not* accept that the theoretical assumptions within which most scientific research takes place are global. Indeed, as I demonstrate, one extreme way to characterize many of these critiques is, to paraphrase Latour (1993), to assert that *we have never thought globally.*[6]

WESTERN SCIENCE:
THINKING LOCALLY, ACTING IMPERIALLY

Until relatively recently in human history, the social activities through which distinctive forms of knowledge are produced have, for the most part, been localized. The knowledges generated by these activities thus bear what Harding (1994) called the idiosyncratic "cultural fingerprints" (p. 304) of the times and places in which they were constructed. The knowledge signified by the English word *science* is no exception because it was uniquely coproduced with industrial capitalism in 17th-century northwestern Europe. The internationalization of what we now call *modern Western science*[7] was enabled by the colonization of other places in which the conditions of its formation (including its symbiotic relationship with industrialization) were reproduced.

The global reach of European imperialism gives Western science the *appearance* of universal truth and rationality, and many people (regardless of their location) assume that it is a form of knowledge that lacks the cultural fingerprints that seem much more conspicuous in knowledge systems that retain their ties to specific localities, such as the "Blackfoot physics" described by Peat (1995, 1997) and comparable knowledges of nature produced by other indigenous societies. This occlusion of the cultural determinants of Western science contributes to what Harding (1993) called an increasingly visible form of scientific illiteracy—namely, "the Eurocentrism or androcentrism of many scientists, policymakers, and other highly educated citizens that severely limits public understanding of science as a fully social process":

> In particular, there are few aspects of the "best" science educations that enable anyone to grasp how nature-as-an-object-of-knowledge is always cultural.... These elite science educations rarely expose students to systematic analyses of the social origins, traditions, meanings, practices, institutions, technologies, uses, and consequences of the natural sciences that ensure the fully historical character of the results of scientific research. (p. 1)

Over the last few decades, various processes of political, economic, and cultural globalization, such as the increasing volume of traffic in trade, travel, and telecommunications networks crisscrossing the world, have helped to make some multicultural perspectives on "nature-as-an-object-of-knowledge" more visible, including the indigenous knowledge systems popularized in terms such as *wisdom of the elders* (Knudtson & Suzuki, 1992) and *tribal wisdom* (Maybury-Lewis, 1991). The publication in English of studies in Islamic science (e.g., Sardar, 1989) and other postcolonial perspectives on the antecedents and effects of modern Western science (e.g., Third World Network, 1988; Petitjean, Jami, & Moulin, 1992; Sardar, 1988) has raised further questions about the interrelationships of science and culture. However, economic globalization simultaneously (and contradictorily) encourages both cultural homogenization *and* the commodification of cultural difference within a transnational common market of knowledge and information that remains dominated by Western science, technology, and capital.

Skepticism about the universality of Western science provokes a variety of responses. At one extreme are aggressive defenders of an imperialist position such as scientists Gross and Levitt (1994), who heap scorn and derision on any sociologists, feminists, postcolonialists, and poststructuralists who have the temerity to question the androcentric, Eurocentric, and capitalist determinants of scientific knowledge production.[8] I prefer to attend to the more subtle and insidious forms of imperialism manifested by educators whose ideological standpoints are much closer to my own. That is why I focus much of my critical attention here on the work of Yencken, Fien, and Sykes (2000a), whose respect for non-Western cultures is, I believe, sincere. Nevertheless, I argue that for all of their undeniably good intentions, these authors maintain a culturally imperialistic view of science through their use of rhetorical strategies that privilege Western scientists' representations of reality and that reproduce the conceit that Western science produces universal knowledge.

For example, one way in which Yencken et al. (2000b) privilege Western science is to stipulate its uniqueness—"we depend on science for the formal analysis of the physical world and the monitoring of environmental change" (p. 32)—and to insinuate that its unique object (the physical world) somehow renders it acultural: "*While* science is culturally shaped …, environmental science is *nevertheless* dealing with physical reality" (p. 32; italics added). Yencken, Fien, and Sykes (2000b) clearly intended the word *formal* to signify something special about Western science because they repeated and amplified this claim: "We rely on science for the formal analysis of environmental conditions and change. We have no more informed source to depend upon" (p. 33). Other environmental educators, such as Ashley (2000), questioned this dependence and asked whether science might not be "an unreliable friend to environmental education."[9]

Yencken, Fien, and Sykes (2000b) implied a universal *we*, but their assertions are culture-bound. Are they suggesting that non-Western knowledge traditions *ignore* "the formal analysis of the physical world" and do *not* "[monitor] environmental change"? Or are they merely saying that non-Western analyses of the physical world and environmental change are informal? What differences are they implying between what is formal and what is not? What rhetorical work are the words I have emphasized in the previous paragraph ("*While … nevertheless*") doing? What has "dealing with physical reality" got to do with the cultural shaping of knowledge traditions? In what sense is Western science an informed source? Informed by what (or by whom)?

I fear that Yencken, Fien, and Sykes (2000b) overstated the uniqueness of Western science. For example, Peat's (1997) discussion of Blackfoot knowledge traditions demonstrates that Western cultures have no monopoly on forms of knowledge production that have the qualities that these authors attribute to science. Peat described "the nature of Blackfoot reality" as "far wider than our own, yet firmly based within the natural world of vibrant, living things … a reality of rocks, trees, animals and energies" (p. 566):

> Once our European world saw nature in a similar way, a vision still present in poets like Blake, Wordsworth and Gerard Manley Hopkins who perceived the immanence and inscape of the world. Nevertheless our consciousness has narrowed to the extent that matter is separated from spirit and we seek our reality in an imagined elsewhere of abstractions, Platonic realms, mathematical elegance, and physical laws.

> The Blackfoot know of no such fragmentation. Not only do they speak with rocks and trees, they are also able to converse with that which remains invisible to us, a world of what could be variously called spirits, or powers, or simply energies. However, these forces are not the occupants of a mystical or abstract domain, they remain an essential aspect of the natural, material world. (pp. 566–567)

I am not suggesting that the Blackfoot view of reality is in any way superior (or inferior) to Western environmental science. Rather, I argue that the Blackfoot people analyze the physical world (and more) and monitor environmental change in ways that are no less formal than Western environmental science. They, like us, are interested in dealing with physical reality. They rely on their knowledge tradition "for the formal analysis of environmental conditions and change." They have no more informed source on which to depend.

Cultures other than those found in modern industrialized nations have developed ways of dealing with physical reality and monitoring environmental change that are formal in different ways from those privileged by Western science. They cannot be diminished by insinuating that they are not formal or not informed. For example, as

Turnbull (1991, 2000) pointed out, people from southeast Asia began systematically colonizing and transforming the islands of the southwest Pacific some 10,000 years before the "birth of [Eurocentric] civilization" is alleged to have occurred in the Mediterranean basin. The Micronesian navigators combined knowledge of sea currents, marine life, weather, winds, and star patterns to produce a sophisticated and complex body of natural knowledge that, when combined with their proficiency in constructing large sea-going canoes, enabled them to transport substantial numbers of people and materials over great distances in hazardous conditions. They were thus able to seek out new islands across vast expanses of open ocean and establish enduring cultures throughout the Pacific by rendering the islands habitable through the introduction of new plants and animals. Although the knowledge system constructed by these people did not involve the use of either writing or mathematics, it is patronizing and indefensible to suggest that it is any less concerned with physical reality than Western science or that it lacks a formal analysis of environmental conditions.

Indeed, some anthropologists are convinced that indigenous people decipher physical reality using homologous assumptions to Western scientists, including a disposition to use systematic empirical inquiry as a means of revealing the inherent orderliness of nature. For example, Berlin's (1990) field research suggests that the biological classification systems developed by many indigenous groups are *intellectualist*—that is, they are driven by curiosity about natural order and structure, rather than motivated only by a need to know which organisms are useful for practical purposes. Therefore, Berlin sees the difference between, say, Linnean taxonomy and an indigenous classification system as chiefly one of degree: Assisted by European imperialism, Linnaeus had access to a much larger sample of organisms than taxonomists who sampled relatively smaller locations and classified fewer organisms. Given the vast numbers of organisms populating the earth, however, no system of classification—including contemporary Western phylogenies—can claim universality. Reviewing a number of similar anthropological studies, Goonatilake (1998) concluded:

> The world, it appears, is thus littered with indigenous starting points for potential trajectories of knowledge—trajectories which, if they were developed, would have led to different explorations of physical reality. The existence of all this anthropological evidence does not solve the problem of Western ethnocentricity or of the distinctive rise of Western science, but it does help to further problematize them. (pp. 70–71)

If the knowledge produced by Western scientists was consumed only in cultural sites dominated by Western science, then their claim to its universality would be a relatively harmless conceit. However, attempts to generate global knowledge in areas such as health (necessitated, in part, by the global traffic in drugs and disease) and environment (e.g., global climate change) draw increasing attention to the cultural biases and limits of Western science. For example, Wynne (1994) reported that until the early 1990s the Intergovernmental Panel on Climate Change (IPCC) used models of climate change that equated global warming mainly with carbon emissions and largely ignored other factors such as cloud behavior, marine algal fixing of atmospheric carbon, and natural methane production. Western scientists and policymakers represented the IPCC models as a means for producing universally warranted conclusions, but to many non-Western observers these same models promoted the interests of developed nations by obscuring the exploitation, domination, and social inequities underlying global environmental degradation. If global warming is understood as a problem for *all* of the world's peoples, then we need to find ways in which *all* of the world's knowledge systems—Western, Blackfoot, Islam, whatever—can jointly produce appropriate understandings and responses. I do not presume to suggest (indeed, I cannot imagine) what a Blackfoot or Islamic contribution to such jointly produced knowledge might be, but I am willing to assert that different knowledge systems cannot coexist if the adherents of one local knowledge tradition insist that we *must* rely and depend on theirs.

The successive failures of the Kyoto Climate Change Summit in December 1997 and The Hague World Conference on Climate Change in November 2000 to reach effective transnational agreements on limiting greenhouse gas emissions demonstrate the difficulty of turning the rhetoric of *thinking globally* into tangible environmental action. Press reports from The Hague Conference indicate how deeply the putative global science of climate change is enmeshed in local contexts, even among Western nations. This is not just because the conclusions Western scientists draw about aspects of global warming—such as how forests and farm crops function as *carbon sinks*—are contradictory or controversial, but also because the same scientific facts produce different meanings for different people. Thus, for example, Mann (2000) reported that the definition of a *forest* was among at least 30 areas of disagreement between negotiators from the European Union and the United States and its allies in the so-called *umbrella* group, including Australia, Canada, Japan, New Zealand, and Russia. I suspect that the impulse to attempt such a definition results from the false hope that some useful scientific truth claims can be made about all forests in the world and their effects on atmospheric warming, regardless of their location. But each forest's local history and contingencies uniquely determine the quantities of atmospheric carbon it fixes and the solar heat it absorbs and radiates.

However, as a curriculum scholar, I am less concerned about the warrant for Western scientific knowledge of the relationship between global warming and atmospheric carbon fixing by vegetation than with the conflation of Western science and global science. Press reports and educational texts alike give the impression that the concept of a *carbon sink* is now a legitimate component of thinking globally (and scientifically) about climate change. For example, one of the required outcomes of Unit 3, "Ecological Issues: Energy and Biodiversity," in Victoria's Year 12 Environmental Science course (Victoria, 2000) is that students "should be able to describe the principles of energy and relate them to the contribution of a fossil and a non-fossil energy source to the enhanced greenhouse effect" (p. 22). To achieve this outcome, students are expected to demonstrate knowledge of, among other things, "scientific application in options for reducing the enhanced greenhouse effect, such as Greenhouse Challenge, National Greenhouse Strategy, Kyoto protocol, emission trading and vegetation sinks" (p. 23). Associating "emission trading and vegetation sinks" with scientific approaches to "reducing the enhanced greenhouse effect" affords them a global legitimacy they do not warrant. The scientific facts of carbon fixing by plants do not legitimate the metaphorical representation of forests as carbon sinks. The *sink* metaphor is a rhetorical device for recruiting scientific facts to assist the political efforts of industrialized nations to discount their greenhouse gas emissions.

By associating emission trading and carbon sinks with scientific application and international conferences on climate change, the authors of Victoria's Year 12 Environmental Science course insinuate that these terms have global currency—that they are part of the semiotic apparatus that supports thinking globally. Yet emission trading and carbon sinks are terms for thinking locally—terms that allow Western politicians and bureaucrats to represent mysterious[10] physical realities in the familiar language of economic rationalism. Examples such as these lead me to dispute Yencken, Fien, and Sykes's (2000b) claims, quoted previously, that "we depend on science for the formal analysis of the physical world and the monitoring of environmental change" and that "while science is culturally shaped …, environmental science is nevertheless dealing with physical reality" (p. 32). We cannot *depend* on Western science to the extent that Yencken, Fien, and Sykes suggest because environmental science deals not only with physical reality, but also with the culturally shaped representations of this reality. Pretending that these representations are acultural is an imperialist act—an act of attempted intellectual colonization.

HOW CAN WE THINK GLOBALLY?

My story so far is a cautionary tale. In Wagner's (1993) terms, I have tried to identify some of the *blind spots and blank spots* that configure the *collective ignorance* of environmental educators as we struggle to realize defensible ways of thinking globally. In Wagner's schema, what we "know enough to question but not answer" are blank spots; what we "don't know well enough to even ask about or care about" are blind spots— "areas in which existing theories, methods, and perceptions actually keep us from seeing phenomena as clearly as we might" (p. 16). Much of the research reported by Yencken et al. (2000a) and their coresearchers clearly responds to blank spots in our emerging understandings of the complexities that arise from the interreferencing of local traditions and global discourses of environmental education. My principal concern here is with the blind spots that may still remain in the vision of even the most culturally sensitive environmental educators. The detectable traces of Western scientific imperialism in the Yencken et al. (2000a) work underscore the difficulties we face when we attempt, as Lather put it, "to decolonize the space of academic discourse that is accessed by our privilege" (cited in Pinar & Reynolds, 1992, p. 254). How can we think globally *without* enacting some form of epistemological imperialism?

As Code (2000) observed, "addressing epistemological questions along a local-global spectrum raises timeworn questions about relativism versus absolutism" (p. 68). For example, Hess (1995) argued that understanding science and technology in a multicultural world demands that we think in terms of social constructivism and cultural relativism, but he explicitly eschewed the need to invoke epistemological, metaphysical, or moral relativism. However, Code (2000) argued that "responsible global thinking *requires* not just cultural relativism but a *mitigated epistemological relativism* conjoined with a 'healthy skepticism'" (p. 69; italics in original). She continued:

> I am working with a deflated conception of relativism remote from the "anything goes" refrain which anti-relativists inveigh against it. It is "mitigated" in its recognition that knowledge-construction is always constrained by the resistance of material and human-social realities to just any old fashioning or making. Yet, borrowing Peter Novick's words, it is relativist in acknowledging "the plurality of criteria of knowledge ... and deny[ing] the possibility of knowing absolute, objective, universal truth" (1988, p. 167). Its "healthy skepticism" in this context manifests itself in response to excessive and irresponsible global pretensions, whose excesses have to be communally debated and negotiated with due regard to local specificities and global implications. (p. 69)

Code's "mitigated epistemological relativism" bears a strong resemblance to what Hayles (1993) called "constrained constructivism" (although Code did not acknowledge this resemblance). Put briefly, Hayles argued that, "within the representations we construct, some are ruled out by constraints, others are not," and that "by ruling out some possibilities ... constraints enable scientific inquiry to tell us something about reality and not only about ourselves" (pp. 32–33). Hayles emphasized that constraints do not—indeed cannot—tell us what reality *is*, but rather that constraints enable us to distinguish between representations that are consistent with reality and those that are not. For example, Isaac Newton's representation of gravity as a mutual attraction between masses is different from Albert Einstein's representation of gravity as a consequence of the curvature of space. These are in turn different from a Native-American belief that objects fall because the spirit of Mother Earth calls out to kindred spirits in other bodies. Yet no representation of gravity that is constrained by the material and human–social realities to which Code referred could predict that when someone steps off a cliff she would remain suspended in midair. Different cultures interpret these constraints in different ways, but they operate multiculturally—and globally—to eliminate some constructions. Hayles (1993) noted that, for any given phenomenon, there will always be other representations, unknown or unimaginable, that are consistent with reality: "The representations we present for falsification are limited by what we can imagine, which is to say, by the prevailing modes of representation within our culture, history, and species"[11] (p. 33). Hayles (1993) concluded:

> Neither cut free from reality nor existing independent of human perception, the world as constrained constructivism sees it is the result of active and complex engagements between reality and human beings. Constrained constructivism invites—indeed cries out for—cultural readings of science, since the representations presented for disconfirmation have everything to do with prevailing cultural and disciplinary assumptions. (pp. 33–34)

As I argued in greater detail elsewhere (Gough, 1998), Hayles clearly articulated a philosophical position that should commend itself to science and environmental educators—a position that problematizes the nondiscursive reality of nature without collapsing into antirealist language games. Constrained constructivism is not anything goes, but neither does it disallow representations that fail to meet criteria that disguise their Eurocentric and androcentric biases behind claims for universality. However, as the example of systems ecology referred to earlier demonstrates, many science and environmental educators (including those who espouse constructivism) often seem to do the precise opposite of what Hayles suggested by requiring learners to *confirm* representations that conform to "cultural and disciplinary assumptions" that no longer prevail even in the West.

The literatures that I find most useful for thinking about thinking globally—and about the articulations between global (or transnational) and local knowledge production—are, broadly speaking, those that Harding (1998b) called Post-Kuhnian and postcolonial science and technology studies, and in particular the work of Turnbull (1994, 1997, 2000). Turnbull argued that all knowledge traditions are spatial in that they link people, sites, and skills. He recognized that knowledge systems (including Western science) are sets of local practices, which makes it possible to decenter them and develop a framework within which different knowledge traditions can equitably be compared rather than absorbed into an imperialist archive. From the postcolonialist and antiimperialist standpoints that Harding and Turnbull share, all knowledges are always situated and constituted initially within specific sets of local conditions and cultural values.

However, there are subtle and thought-provoking differences between their respective positions. Put crudely, Harding seems more interested in the universalizing tendencies that accompany the travel of knowledges beyond the localities in which they were initially produced, whereas Turnbull is more concerned with how trust is established between heterogeneous knowledges that arrive (or are produced) in the same space. For example, after reviewing the various implications of postcolonialist and feminist science and technology studies for research epistemologies and methodologies, Harding (1998b) argued that the distinction between universally valid knowledge and merely local opinion (e.g., superstitions, folk knowledges) is much less useful than older epistemologies supposed:

> If, as the post-Kuhnian, postcolonial and feminist accounts argue, all knowledge systems have integrity with the cultures that produce them and continue to find them useful, then nothing in principle is possible but local opinion—though some local opinions (e.g., the laws of gravity) definitely travel farther and retain usefulness lon-

ger than do others. (...) More productive is the project of seeking to understand the devices through which originally local knowledges (as all are) get to circulate and travel far from their origin, and how the most effective balances between these universalizing tendencies and the necessary localizing tendencies have been and can be nourished and maintained. (p. 46)

Elsewhere, Harding (1998a) again used travel metaphors to capture her sense of the ways in which "different modern scientific projects have maintained valuable tensions between the local and the global":

The most widely successful [knowledge systems], such as many parts of modern sciences, manage to travel effectively to become useful in other sets of local conditions—parts of nature, interests, discursive resources, ways of organizing the production of knowledge—that are different in significant respects from those that originally produced them. Without claiming a universality for them that we can now see is historically and conceptually misleading, how could we usefully think about valuable tensions between the local and this movability, or ability to travel, that has characterized parts of modern sciences in particular, but also parts of other knowledge systems (e.g., the concept zero and acupuncture)? (p. 182)

Turnbull detached a knowledge tradition's "ability to travel" from assumptions about its "universalizing tendencies," and instead looked for ways in which different knowledge systems can coexist. An important feature of Turnbull's (1997) strategy is to abandon an "overly representational view of knowledge" and to recognize that all knowledge is "both performative and representational" (p. 553). In other words, Turnbull is less interested in characterizing science's ability to travel by reference to the movement of representations and abstractions (such as "the laws of gravity" or "the concept zero" to which Harding referred and more concerned with the *activity* of knowledge production in particular social spaces. Thus, Turnbull argued that we can reconceive the social history of knowledge production "in a variety of intersecting and overlapping ways which move beyond simple contextualization" (that is, cultural relativism):

Science may be seen as a history of visualization or as a history of measurement and rational calculation. However, I would like to argue that a particularly perspicuous cross-cultural history of knowledge production is as a social history of space. That is as a history of the contingent processes of making assemblages and linkages, of creating spaces in which knowledge is possible. (p. 553)

Turnbull used diverse examples, including gothic cathedral building in medieval Europe, establishment of modern cartography, and rice farming in Indonesia, to show how particular knowledge spaces are constructed from differing social, moral, and technical components in a variety of cultural and historical contexts—from assemblages of people, skills, local knowledge, and equipment linked by various social strategies and technical devices. Turnbull (1997) suggested that from this spatialized perspective, concepts such as universality, objectivity, rationality, efficacy, and accumulation "cease to be unique and special characteristics of techno-scientific knowledge":

Rather these traits are effects of collective work of the knowledge producers in a given knowledge space. To move knowledge from the local site and moment of its production and application to other places and times, knowledge producers deploy a variety of social strategies and technical devices for creating the equivalences and connections between otherwise heterogeneous and isolated knowledges. The standardization and homogenization required for knowledge to be accumulated and rendered truth-like is achieved through social methods of organizing the production, transmission and utilization of knowledge. An essential component is the social organization of trust.[12] (p. 553)

Turnbull (1997) argued that a major analytic advantage of this spatialized perspective is that, because all knowledge systems have localness in common, many of the small but significant differences between them can be explained in terms of the different kinds of work—of *performance*—that are involved in constructing assemblages from the people, practices, theories, and instruments in a given space. Although some knowledge traditions move and assemble their products through art, ceremony, and ritual, the productivity of Western science has so far been accomplished by forming disciplinary societies, building instruments, standardizing techniques, and writing articles. Thus, Turnbull (1997) concluded that each form of knowledge production entails

> a process of knowledge assembly through making connections and negotiating equivalences between the heterogeneous components while simultaneously establishing a social order of trust and authority resulting in a knowledge space. It is on this basis that it is possible to compare and frame knowledge traditions. (p. 553)

Turnbull (2000) analyzed knowledge construction among different groups of people in different locations and times, including medieval masons, Polynesian navigators, cartographers, malariologists, and turbulence engineers. He demonstrated that, in each case, their achievements are better understood performatively—as diverse, messy, contingent, unplanned, and arational combinations of social and technical practices—rather than as the result of logical, orderly, rational planning or a dependence on internal epistemological features to which universal validity can be ascribed. As already noted, the purpose of Turnbull's emphasis on analyzing knowledge systems comparatively in terms of spatiality and performance is to find ways in which diverse knowledge traditions can coexist rather than one displacing others. The significance of his analysis for thinking globally is demonstrated by two examples of Western scientists attempting to displace the knowledge spaces constructed by Indonesian rice farmers with their own importations. Turnbull (1997) wrote:

> The Green Revolution and the introduction of high-yield rice turned Indonesia from being a net importer of rice unable to feed its own population to being one of the biggest rice exporters. This was achieved [in Java] at the price of using massive amounts of fertilizer and pesticides and in the abandonment of indigenous rice strains. That success, as we have become accustomed to expect, was short-lived. Insect pests started reaching plague proportions in the monocrop environment and increased applications of pesticide only made the problem worse. The solution was the banning of fertilizer and pesticide imports and the introduction of "integrated pest management." This is an ... approach to pest control which recognizes there will always be pests and the best way to manage them is to ensure that the populations of competing insects remain in balance. For this system to work, the local farmers had to become local experts, they had to monitor the insect populations on their own farms and to use locally appropriate rice strains.
>
> A similar reversal occurred in Bali where rice is grown under an irrigation system controlled by the temples. The Indonesian government thought this old fashioned and superstitious and introduced modern scientific methods of water control and distribution. The result was the same as in Java: initial success followed by a crash in production. So they brought in more Western experts, but this time they included a rather unusual anthropologist and a computer expert. Between them they were able to show on the computer screen how the old system of temple control worked and why it was the most efficient. This resulted in the knowledge and power being given back to the

local people while satisfying the central government's yen for high-tech solutions. (pp. 559–560)

These examples suggest to me that the globalization of knowledge production depends on creating spaces in which local knowledge traditions can be "reframed, decentered and the social organization of trust can be negotiated" (Turnbull, 1997, pp. 560–561). Tambiah (1990) and Soja (1996) named the space that Turnbull envisaged as a "third space," whereas Bhabha (1994) called it "an interstitial space" (p. 312)—a space created through "negotiation between spaces, where contrasting rationalities can work together but without the notion of a single transcendent reality" (Turnbull 2000, p. 228). The production of such a space is, in Turnbull's (1997) view, "crucially dependent" on "the re-inclusion of the performative side of knowledge":

> Knowledge, in so far as it is portrayed as essentially a form of representation, will tend towards universal homogenous information at the expense of local knowledge traditions. If knowledge is recognized as both representational and performative it will be possible to create a space in which knowledge traditions can be performed together. (pp. 560–561)

Turnbull invites us to be suspicious of importing and exporting representations that are disconnected from the performative work that was needed to generate them. For example, representing forests as carbon sinks arises in Western industrialized nations because their emissions of greenhouse gases are of sufficient magnitude to motivate and make meaningful the work of producing sinks to which excessive atmospheric carbon can be removed. The resistance of some developing nations to accepting carbon sinks as a way for Western nations to discount their greenhouse gas emissions is only to be expected because the *sink* metaphor has no cultural purchase in their localities. Jasanoff argued that global knowledge must be coproduced and that its legitimacy cannot be tied to any one culture's social and political traditions for conferring legitimacy on knowledge construction (see Turney, 1997).

If we think about coproducing knowledge in interstitial transnational spaces, it becomes clear that some of the most revered processes of Western knowledge production do not necessarily appear to be trustworthy. For example, many of the truth claims that constitute Western scientific knowledge of nature are produced under laboratory conditions.[13] However, as Code (2000) argued, developing "methodological strategies for ecologically-framed global thinking" requires a more naturalized epistemology than laboratory work assumes:

> I maintain that the laboratory is neither the only nor the best place for epistemologists to study "natural" human knowing in order to elaborate epistemologies that maintain clearer continuity with cognitive experiences—"natural knowings"—than orthodox *a priori*-normative epistemologies do. I advocate turning attention to how knowledge is made and circulated in situations with a greater claim to the elusive label "natural." My interests are in ways of gathering empirical evidence and in assumptions about the scope of evidence as it plays into regulative theories. My contention, briefly, is that evidence gathered from more mundane sites of knowledge production can afford better, if messier, starting points for naturalistic inquiry than much of laboratory evidence, for it translates more readily into settings where knowing matters in people's lives and the politics of knowledge are enacted. (p. 71)

For example, despite claims for the objectivity of experimental methods, the methodological principle of controlling variables produces knowledge that can be incomprehensible in locations where this principle is not taken for granted. Again, as Code

(2000) noted: "Descriptions, mappings, and judgments that separate evidence from extraneous 'noise' are always value-saturated, products of some one's or some group's location and choice; hence always contestable" (p. 71).

IMPLICATIONS FOR INTERNATIONALIZING CURRICULUM INQUIRY

In light of the prior considerations, I suggest that internationalizing curriculum inquiry might best be understood as a process of creating transnational spaces in which scholars from different localities collaborate in reframing and decentering their own knowledge traditions and negotiate trust in each other's contributions to their collective work. For those of us who work in Western knowledge traditions, a first step must be to represent and perform our distinctive approaches to curriculum inquiry in ways that authentically demonstrate their localness. This may include drawing attention to the characteristic ways in which Western genres of academic textual production invite readers to interpret local knowledge as universal discourse.

For example, in their chapter "Understanding Curriculum as International Text," Pinar et al. (1995) began a section dealing with research perspectives and paradigms by asserting that: "Studying curriculum internationally is conducted in seven different traditions of research" (p. 793). The traditions they listed include descriptive, analytical, interpretive, evaluative, predictive, organizational, and theoretical studies. They concluded by stating that, "The diversity of research orientation and of theme underlines the complexity of understanding curriculum internationally" (p. 794).

The authors' declarative and generalized mode of address occludes the local (and even parochial) character of their assertions. The authors are speaking principally for U.S. and Canadian scholars and almost exclusively for those who work in Eurocentric traditions. The research orientations and themes they listed are a diversity only within Western registers of difference in approaches to disciplined inquiry (e.g., they are limited to the exoteric interests that motivate most Western researchers rather than also including the more esoteric interests of many non-Western and indigenous scholars).[14] The seven traditions listed by Pinar et al. (1995) seem less diverse when they are compared with Smith's (1999) list of 25 indigenous research practices: claiming, testimonies, storytelling, celebrating survival, remembering, indigenizing, intervening, revitalizing, connecting, reading, writing, representing, gendering, envisioning, reframing, restoring, returning, democratizing, networking, naming, protecting, creating, negotiating, discovering, and sharing. Of course, these lists are not strictly comparable, although some of the items in Smith's list suggest silences in the list of Pinar et al. (1995). For example, where are the critical-emancipatory studies suggested by terms such as *celebrating survival, intervening, revitalizing, restoring, returning, democratizing,* and *protecting*? Are these subsumed under one or more terms in the Pinar et al. (1995) list? (The examples listed for each category do not suggest that this is the case.)

The more important question that arises from juxtaposing the Pinar et al. (1995) seven traditions of studying curriculum internationally with Smith's 25 indigenous research practices is to ask how the types of curriculum work that each set of practices represents might be performed together in the same transnational knowledge space. Here we must heed Turnbull's cautions about adopting an overly representational view of knowledge, with the attendant risks of homogenizing and universalizing different knowledge traditions. But performing both local knowledge traditions together seems more likely to provide opportunities for the mutual recognition of performative equivalences and develop the capacity for new transnational knowledge to be coproduced in the space. For example, Pinar et al. (1995) exemplified analytical studies "that seek to specify cause-and-effect relationships" by reference to "a study of the educational remnants of colonialism in the Pacific Islands" (p. 793). Smith (1999) illustrated the project of *connecting* by reference to "connecting people to their traditional lands through the restoration of specific rituals and practices" (p. 148).

Let us imagine that these two projects are quite literally being performed in the same space: A doctoral student from a U.S. university is pursuing the analytic project on the same Pacific island as another doctoral student from the International Research Institute for Maori and Indigenous Education at the University of Auckland (Aotearoa/New Zealand). Both researchers are interested in analyzing the educational remnants of colonialism, but the University of Auckland student is also a member of the island's indigenous community and wants her research to go beyond analysis to include a restorative dimension. If these researchers choose to work together, and if Turnbull's analysis of knowledge systems in terms of spatiality and performance is warranted, their most constructive achievements will arise from negotiated co-performances—from messy, contingent, unplanned combinations of their social and technical practices—as they struggle to find ways in which their different local knowledge traditions (Western and hybrid Western/indigenous, respectively) can coexist. I have had sufficient personal experience attempting to produce such transnational spaces (in southern Africa) to admit that *struggle* is much too weak a term for the effort that working in this way demands, but I also have experienced the ambiguous and humbling pleasures that have made the effort worthwhile (see e.g., Gough, 2000, 2001).

I have no conclusions to offer in this chapter, merely cautions. We may not be able to speak—or think—from outside our own Eurocentrism, but we can continue to ask questions about how our specifically Western ways of "acting locally" in curriculum inquiry might be performed with other local knowledge traditions in curriculum work. By coproducing curriculum inquiry in transnational spaces, we can, I believe, help to make both the limits *and strengths* of Western epistemologies and methodologies increasingly visible.

REFERENCES

Ashley, M. (2000). Science: An unreliable friend to environmental education? *Environmental Education Research, 6*(3), 269-280.

Berlin, B. (1990). The chicken and the egg-head revisited: Further evidence for the intellectualist bases of ethnobiological classification. In D. A. Posey & W. L. Overal (Eds.), *Ethnobiology: Implications and applications. Proceedings of the First International Congress of Ethnobiology* (Vol. 1, pp. 19–35). Belem, Brazil: Museo Emilio Goeldi.

Bhabha, H. K. (1994). *The location of culture.* New York: Routledge.

Bowers. C. A. (1993a). *Critical essays on education, modernity, and the recovery of the ecological imperative.* New York: Teachers College Press.

Bowers. C. A. (1993b). *Education, cultural myths, and the ecological crisis: Toward deep changes.* Albany: State University of New York Press.

Carson, R. (1962). *Silent spring.* New York: Houghton-Mifflin.

Code, L. (2000). How to think globally: Stretching the limits of imagination. In U. Narayan & S. Harding (Eds.), *Decentering the center: Philosophy for a multicultural, postcolonial, and feminist world* (pp. 67–79). Bloomington: Indiana University Press.

Eblen, R. A., & Eblen, W. R. (Eds.). (1994). *The encyclopedia of the environment.* Boston: Houghton-Mifflin.

Fien, J. (Ed.). (1989). *Living in a global environment: Classroom activities in development education.* Brisbane, Australia: Australian Geography Teachers Association.

Fien, J., & Gerber, R. (Eds.). (1988). *Teaching geography for a better world* (2nd ed.). London: Oliver & Boyd.

Goonatilake, S. (1998). *Toward a global science: Mining civilizational knowledge.* Bloomington: Indiana University Press.

Gough, A. (1997). *Education and the environment: Policy, trends and the problems of marginalisation.* Melbourne, Australia: Australian Council for Educational Research.

Gough, A. (1999). Recognising women in environmental education education pedagogy and research: Toward an ecofeminist poststructuralist perspective. *Environmental Education Research, 5*(2), 143–161.

Gough, N. (1992). *Blueprints for greening schools: Principles, policies and practices for environmental education in Australian secondary schools.* Melbourne, Australia: Gould League of Victoria.

Gough, N. (1998). All around the world: Science education, constructivism, and globalization. *Educational Policy, 12*(5), 507–524.

Gough, N. (2000). Interrogating silence: Environmental education research as postcolonialist textwork. *Australian Journal of Environmental Education, 15/16,* 115–122.

Gough, N. (2001). Learning from *Disgrace*: A troubling narrative for South African curriculum work. *Perspectives in Education, 19*(1), 109–128.

Greig, S., Pike, G., & Selby, D. (1987). *Earthrights: Education as if the planet really mattered.* London: World Wildlife Fund and Kogan Page.

Gross, P. R., & Levitt, N. (1994). *Higher superstition: The academic left and its quarrels with science.* Baltimore: The Johns Hopkins University Press.

Gutek, G. L. (1993). *American education in a global society: Internationalizing teacher education.* New York: Longman.

Harding, S. (1993). Introduction: Eurocentric scientific illiteracy—a challenge for the world community. In S. Harding (Ed.), *The "racial" economy of science: Toward a democratic future* (pp. 1–22). Bloomington: Indiana University Press.

Harding, S. (1994). Is science multicultural? Challenges, resources, opportunities, uncertainties. *Configurations: A Journal of Literature, Science, and Technology, 2*(2), 301–330.

Harding, S. (1998a). *Is science multicultural? Postcolonialisms, feminisms, and epistemologies.* Bloomington: Indiana University Press.

Harding, S. (1998b). Multiculturalism, postcolonialism, feminism: Do they require new research epistemologies? *Australian Educational Researcher, 25*(1), 37–51.

Hayles, N. K. (1993). Constrained constructivism: Locating scientific inquiry in the theater of representation. In G. Levine (Ed.), *Realism and representation: Essays on the problem of realism in relation to science, literature and culture* (pp. 27–43). Madison: University of Wisconsin Press.

Hess, D. J. (1995). *Science and technology in a multicultural world: The cultural politics of facts and artifacts.* New York: Columbia University Press.

Hicks, D., & Steiner, M. (Eds.). (1989). *Making global connections: A world studies workbook.* Edinburgh, Scotland: Oliver & Boyd.

Huckle, J. (1988). *What we consume: The teachers' handbook.* Richmond, Surrey, England: Richmond Publishing Company.

Jamison, A. (1993). National political cultures and the exchange of knowledge: The case of systems ecology. In E. Crawford, T. Shinn, & S. Sörlin (Eds.), *Denationalizing science: The contexts of international scientific practice* (pp. 187–208). Dordrecht, The Netherlands: Kluwer.

Khalil, E. L., & Boulding, K. E. (Eds.). (1996). *Evolution, order and complexity.* London: Routledge.

Knudtson, P., & Suzuki, D. (1992). *Wisdom of the elders.* Sydney, Australia: Allen & Unwin.

Latour, B. (1987). *Science in action: How to follow scientists and engineers through society* (C. Porter, Trans.). Milton Keynes: Open University Press.

Latour, B. (1993). *We have never been modern* (C. Porter, Trans.). Cambridge, MA: Harvard University Press.

Levitt, T. (1983). The globalization of markets. *Harvard Business Review, 83*(3), 92–102.

Malcolm, S. (1988). *Local action for a better environment.* Ringwood, Australia: Author.

Mann, S. (2000, November 22). Hill puts case on greenhouse gas. *The Age,* p. 15.

Maybury-Lewis, D. (1991). *Millennium: Tribal wisdom of the modern world.* London: Viking.

McLuhan, M., & Fiore, Q. (1967). *War and peace in the global village.* New York: Bantam Books.

Nabhan, G. P. (1995). Cultural parallax in viewing North American habitats. In M. E. Soulé & G. Lease (Eds.), *Reinventing nature? Responses to postmodern deconstruction* (pp. 87–101). Washington, DC: Island.

Odum, E. P. (1971). *Fundamentals of ecology* (3rd ed.). Philadelphia: W.B. Saunders.

Peat, F. D. (1995). *Blackfoot physics.* London: Fourth Estate.

Peat, F. D. (1997). Blackfoot physics and European minds. *Futures, 29*(6), 563–573.

Petitjean, P., Jami, C., & Moulin, A. M. (Eds.). (1992). *Science and empires: Historical studies about scientific development and European expansion.* Dordrecht, The Netherlands: Kluwer.

Pickett, S. T. A., & White, P. S. (Eds.). (1985). *The ecology of natural disturbance and patch dynamics.* Orlando, FL: Academic Press.

Pike, G., & Selby, D. (1987). *Global teacher, global learner.* London: Hodder & Stoughton.

Pinar, W. F., & Reynolds, W. M. (1992). Appendix: Genealogical notes: The history of phenomenology and post-structuralism in curriculum studies. In W. F. Pinar & W. M. Reynolds (Eds.), *Understanding curriculum as phenomenological and deconstructed text* (pp. 237–261). New York: Teachers College Press.

Pinar, W. F., Reynolds, W. M., Slattery, P., & Taubman, P. (1995). *Understanding curriculum: An introduction to the study of historical and contemporary curriculum discourses.* New York: Peter Lang.

Popper, K. (1965). *Conjectures and refutations: The growth of scientific knowledge* (2nd ed.). New York: Basic Books.

Sardar, Z. (Ed.). (1988). *The revenge of Athena: Science, exploitation and the third world.* London: Mansell.

Sardar, Z. (1989). *Explorations in Islamic science.* London: Mansell.

Schneider, E. D., & Kay, J. J. (1994). Complexity and thermodynamics. Towards a new ecology. *Futures, 26*(6), 626–647.

Shapin, S. (1994). *A social history of truth: Civility and science in 17th century England.* Chicago: University of Chicago Press.

Smith, L. T. (1999). *Decolonizing methodologies: Research and indigenous peoples.* London: Zed Books and Dunedin, Australia: University of Otago Press.

Soja, E. (1996). *Thirdspace: Journeys to Los Angeles and other real-and-imagined places.* Cambridge, MA: Blackwell.

Tambiah, S. J. (1990). *Magic, science, religion, and the scope of rationality.* Cambridge, England: Cambridge University Press.

Third World Network. (1988). *Modern science in crisis: A third world response.* Penang, Malaysia: Author.

Turnbull, D. (1991). *Mapping the world in the mind: An investigation of the unwritten knowledge of the Micronesian navigators.* Geelong, Australia: Deakin University.

Turnbull, D. (1994). Local knowledge and comparative scientific traditions. *Knowledge and Policy, 6*(3/4), 29–54.

Turnbull, D. (1997). Reframing science and other local knowledge traditions. *Futures, 29*(6), 551–562.

Turnbull, D. (2000). *Masons, tricksters and cartographers: Comparative studies in the sociology of scientific and indigenous knowledge.* Amsterdam: Harwood Academic Publishers.

Turney, J. (1997, August 13). Can science studies save the world? *The Australian,* p. 37.

Victoria, Board of Studies. (2000). *Environmental science: Study design.* Carlton, Australia: Author.

Wagner, J. (1993). Ignorance in educational research: Or, how can you *not* know that? *Educational Researcher, 22*(5), 15–23.

Worster, D. (1993). *The wealth of nature: Environmental history and the ecological imagination.* New York: Oxford University Press.

Wynne, B. (1994). Scientific knowledge and the global environment. In M. Redclift & T. Benton (Eds.), *Social theory and the global environment* (pp. 169–189). London: Routledge.

Yencken, D. (2000). Attitudes to nature in the East and West. In D. Yencken, J. Fien, & H. Sykes (Eds.), *Environment, education and society in the Asia-Pacific: Local traditions and global discourses* (pp. 4–27). London: Routledge.

Yencken, D., Fien, J., & Sykes, H. (Eds.). (2000a). *Environment, education and society in the Asia-Pacific: Local traditions and global discourses.* London: Routledge.

Yencken, D., Fien, J., & Sykes, H. (2000b). The research. In D. Yencken, J. Fien, & H. Sykes (Eds.), *Environment, education and society in the Asia-Pacific: Local traditions and global discourses* (pp. 28–50). London: Routledge.

ENDNOTES

1. UNEP: United Nations Environment Programme.

2. See Annette Gough (1997, pp. 17–20) for a succinct account of the early development of this still active program.

3. Note, however, that environmental educators were not alone in appropriating Dubos's aphorism. Theodore Levitt (1983) used a similar phrase—'Think global. Act local'—to encapsulate his view that 'the globalization of market is at hand' (p. 92) in an article for the Harvard Business Review. Of course, the imperative to think globally has a longer history. For example, in 1967 Marshall McLuhan noted that with the advent of an electronic information environment, 'all the territorial aims and objectives of business and politics [tend] to become illusory' (MdLuhan & Fiore, 1967, p. 5). 'Think global. Act local' is still a popular trope in both environmental and economic discourses. For example, I conducted an Internet search on 30 October 2000 that identified several hundred sites in which the phrase (or minor variants on it) was used. Within the top ten, two sites featured articles titled 'Think Global. Act Local': one was GLOBE (Global Legislators Organization for a Balanced Environment) International, the other was Invest in Britain Bureau.

4. For convenience, I have cited only one volume in the WWF Global Environmental Education Programme, namely, the teachers' handbook for the *What We Consume* curriculum module. In addition to Huckle's (1988) teachers' handbook, the module consisted of ten book-length units. *What We Consume* is one of four modules in the program.

5. The countries in which this comparative research was conducted are Australia, Brunei, Fiji, India, Indonesia, Japan, New Zealand, Papua New Guinea, the Philippines, Singapore, South China and Thailand.

6. This deliberately provocative formulation is inspired by the title of Latour's (1993) book, *We Have Never Been Modern*. Normally, I am reluctant to use terms like 'we'(which implies that I can speak for others) and 'never' (which suggests an absolutism that I cannot defend).

7. I realize that the term 'modern *Western* science' (as distinct from 'science' or 'modern science') reproduces a problematic 'West versus the rest' dualism and seems to overlook the historical influences of other cultures, such as Islam, India, and China, on its evolution. However, I also want to emphasize that I am referring to science and it was produced in Europe during a particular historical period and to those of its cultural characteristics that have endured to dominate Western (and many non-Western) understandings of science as a result of Euro-American imperialism.

8. Gross and Levitt (1994) give the impression that the academic left's 'quarrels with science' are chiefly the result of ignorance, scholarly incompetence, irrationality and/or ideological prejudice, an impression they underscore with a litany of personal abuse: for example, they refer to Sandra Harding's 'megalomaina' (p. 134), and Katherine Hayles's 'mathematical subliteracy' (p. 104) for whose work 'the work *crackpot* unkindly leaps to mind' (p. 103, emphasis in original).

9. Ashley here follows David Pepper (1996) who describes science as an unreliable friend to environmentalism.

10. I use the term 'mysterious' out of suspicion that very few of the people who take political positions on emission trading and on discounting emissions by counting carbon sinks—including many of the 5,000 delegates from the 180 nations or more represented at The Hague World Conference on Climate Change—have even a rudimentary understanding of the molecular biology and cellular physiology of atmospheric carbon fixing by plants.

11. Note that analyzing the consistency between reality and a representation is different from applying Karl Popper's (1965) doctrine of falsification, because Popper maintained that congruence is a conceptual possibility. However, as Hayles (1993) explains, the most we can say is that a representation is 'consistent with reality as it is experienced by someone with our sensory equipment and previous contextual experience. Congruence cannot be achieved because it implies perception without a perceiver' (p. 35).

12. Turnbull here echoes Steven Shapin (1994) who argues in his social history of science in 17th century England that the basis of knowledge is not empirical verification (as the orthodox view of 'scientific method' has it) but trust: 'Mundane reason is the space across which trust plays. It provides a set of presuppositions about self, others, and the world which embed trust and which permit both consensus and civil dissensus to occur' (p. 36). In a gesture towards Bruno Latour's (1987, 1993) 'actor network theory,' Turnbull (1997) also suggests that the linking of heterogeneous components of a knowledge system is achieved by both social strategies and 'technical devices which may include maps, templates, diagrams and drawings, but are typically techniques for spatial visualisation' (p. 553).

13. I write 'under laboratory conditions' rather than 'in laboratories' because Western scientists typically try to create (or assume) laboratory conditions when they are working elsewhere. Indeed, Latour (1983) notes that a large proportion of national budgets for scientific activity is contributed to the work of international agencies that maintain standard weights and measures so that, in effect, the world at large can be treated as a giant laboratory.

14. The terms 'parochial' and 'indigenous'—which I have used here in fairly close proximity— carry different connotations. From where I stand (which, most of the time, is in Australia), US curriculum scholars are easy targets for charges of parochialism. But why do we disparage the ignorance of US curriculum scholars as parochialism and celebrate the local knowledge of indigenous people who may be equally ignorant of the knowledges produced outside their localities? I suspect that the difference lies in tacit assumptions (by both authors and readers) about the 'exportability' of the knowledges produced. Indigenous knowledges tend to be closely tied to specific geophysical locations and bioregions and this local specificity usually is recognized by both the producers and 'readers' of the textual products of indigenous knowledge systems. In a very real sense, Pinal et al.'s (1995) *Understanding Curriculum* represents indigenous knowledge. Its contents can only be seen to be 'parochial' if either its authors or readers insinuate that the knowledge it represents is exportable or 'universal.' However, authors of synoptic textbooks for large English-speaking markets should not be naïve about their prospective readerships. If Pinar et al. had written 'In the localities with which we are familiar (including Canada, the USA, … etc.), studying curriculum internationally is conducted in seven different traditions of research,' they would be less likely to be suspected of parochialism and less likely to be interpreted as representing a universal 'truth'. I note that it is very easy to offer such advice in hindsight and emphasize that I have no quarrel with Pinar et al.'s assertions as representations of local curriculum knowledge.

CHAPTER 3

The Triumph of Multiplicity and the Carnival of Difference: Curriculum Dilemmas in the Age of Postcolonialism and Globalization

Claudia Matus and Cameron McCarthy
University of Illinois

Modern curriculum thinkers and practitioners have tended to look askance at several critical developments now transforming sociocultural life outside and inside schools around the globe. These developments have enormous implications for pedagogical practice and the educational preparation of school youth. Some of these developments can be summarized as follows.

First, there is that whole broad set of processes that has come to be known as *globalization* or the intensification and rapidity of movement and migration of people, ideas, and economic and cultural capital across national boundaries. Driven forward by the engines of modern capitalist reorganization and the expanded interests, needs, and desires of ordinary people everywhere, globalization is now sweeping all corners of the contemporary world. These processes are rapidly shrinking spatial relations among hitherto far-flung parts of the world and, as a consequence, deepening the imbrication of the local in the global and the global in the local as Giddens (1994) maintained.

Second, electronic mediation and computerization have set off new, powerful energies that have precipitated an explosion in the proliferation of new images, identities, and subjectivities now facilitated by the Internet, TV, film, radio, newspapers, popular music, and aesthetic culture generally.

Third, these latter developments have both stimulated and bolstered the intensification of the work of the imagination of the broad masses of the people. The expansion of representational technologies and capacities has meant that people now put together their sense of past, present, and the future, their very destinies and their sense of self, in collusion with new mediascapes. These new mentalities and self-imagings are propelled by an ever-expanding sense of possibility as well as terror and constraint as modern humanity cultivates new interests, needs, desires, and fears gestated and amplified in the cultural landscape and aesthetic culture of the new media.

73

Fourth, new critical discourses and technologies of truth have been generated, largely outside the field of education, to address the challenges of this new historical period. We are living in the age of the centrifugal proliferation of interpretation and genres. As a consequence, new critical discourses abound. In the academic realm, these discourses include programs of thought such as cultural studies, postmodernism, multiculturalism, and postcolonialism—the latter being the framework that informs and integrates the various disparate elements and threads of our argument in this chapter. Yet in the realm of the popular, these discourses of interpretation are formulated in the language of moral panic and its obverse the language of panaceas and instant fixes now deluging the modern subject. We are talking here about the panic/panacea discourses of psychic networks, extreme sports, stock options, investing, E-trading, retirement annuities, and the like that now dominate commercial advertising and the calculations of private citizenry as well as business. All of these developments represent the triumph of multiplicity and the carnival of difference now overtaking our daily lives. They incite, in the Foucauldian sense, new tasks and challenges for the practices of cultural reproduction generally and the practices of classroom pedagogy more specifically. Indeed, we are being compelled at every point to reconsider what pedagogy means in these circumstances.

Against the tide of these currents of change, however, educational thinkers, particularly in the United States, have tended to draw down a bright line of distinction between the established school curriculum and the teeming world of multiplicity and hybridity that now flourishes in the everyday lives of youth beyond the school. These educators still insist on a project of homogeneity, normalization, and the production of the socially functional citizen. This is true even of contemporary progressive approaches to curriculum reform, such as multiculturalism, that have sought to bring the problems of multiplicity and difference into a framework of institutional intelligibility and manageability. Thus, proponents of the modern curriculum have sought to emphasize a technicist discourse—a discourse of experts, professional competence, and boundary maintenance that has separated, for example, multiculturalism from more critical discourses such as Marxism, pragmatism, Frankfurt school critical theory, cultural studies, poststructuralism, and postcolonialism.

One consequence of this self-isolation from critical scholarship has been the fact that concepts such as *culture* and *identity*—concepts integral to curricular projects such as multiculturalism—are undertheorized and undigested within the curriculum field. As Rothstein (2000) noted in a recent *New York Times* article that looks at education and society in Japan, culture and identity are treated problematically in the educational arrangements of industrial societies. He maintained that the contemporary hierarchical arrangement of schooling in countries such as Japan and the United States works to produce differentiating processes, such as testing and streaming, that undermine and fragment student identities. These differentiating processes, in turn, help to generate a powerful ground of culturally significant distinctions between student and student, student and teacher, and so forth.

In what follows, we problematize the way in which the educational field has addressed the topics of cultural identity, cultural difference, and cultural community in these times of rapid globalizing change. We read such mainstream approaches to education and culture against the open possibilities of knowledge production and ethical affiliation that are foregrounded in postcolonial theory, postcolonial literature, art, and popular culture. We believe that addressing these critical issues of cultural identity and the organization of knowledge in schooling is pivotal in a time in which there are deepening patterns of cultural balkanization and disciplinary insulation in educational institutions—a product of the uncertainty precipitated by the proliferation of difference as a consequence of globalization.

As such, we confront the heart of Friedrich Nietzsche's (1967) diagnosis of the modern condition, which we think speaks adroitly to our contemporary educational and social dilemmas and to the antithesis of center-periphery relations more generally. In *On the Genealogy of Morals,* Nietzsche insisted that a new ethical framework had come into being in the industrial age that informed all patterns of human exchange in the bureaucratic arrangements of social institutions. He called this moral framework *ressentiment* (resentment), or the practice in which one defines one's identity through the negation of the other. This is a process governed by the strategic alienation of the other in forms of knowledge building, genres of representation, and the deployment of moral, emotional, and affective evaluation and investments. We see this in operation in the whole contemporary stance in educational institutions toward the topics of difference, multiplicity, and heterogeneity. School practices mediate the ability of individuals to manipulate their identity. Moreover, school processes work to dissociate youth from their identities and reassemble and deploy these within an economy of social control and regulation (Valenzuela, 1999).

As an example provided by Valenzuela (1999), the English as a Second Language programs implemented throughout the United States provide the fallacy of inclusion of Latino students within the mainstream, but the powerful institutional language they communicate is that Spanish is a second-class language. These conditions bring about that "Immigrant youth may acquire successful skills and knowledge, but at the cost of losing significant cultural resources, including a rich and positive sense of group identification" (Valenzuela, 1999, p. 162). Consequently, "Schools are an instrument of the maintenance of colonial relationships in that they constitute an arm of the state through which belief systems and cultural associations are taught" (Valenzuela, 1999, p. xviii).

We see all these dynamics at work especially now in the fratricidal wars going on at campuses across the country over the question of the canon versus multiculturalism and the traditional disciplines versus alternative forms of knowledge, such as cultural studies and postcolonial theory. We also see this antipathy to difference in popular culture and public policy in the United States—a country in which the professional middle-class dwellers of the suburbs have appropriated the radical space of difference onto themselves, occupying the space of social injury, social victim, and plaintiff. In so doing, this suburban professional class denies avenues of social complaint to its other: the inner-city poor. It projects its suburban worldview out into the social world as the barometer of public policy displacing issues of inequality and poverty and replacing these with demands for balanced budgets, tax cuts, and greater surveillance and incarceration of minority youth. All of this is accompanied by a deep-bodied nostalgic investment in Anglo-American cultural form and its European connections.

Of course, this framework of oppositions can be mapped a thousandfold onto third world–first world relations. Ironically, these developments are taking place at a time when, all over the world, the processes of migration, electronic mediation, and the work of the imagination of the great masses of the people have effected the diremption of culture from place (Appadurai, 1996). For example, the movement of peoples from Latin America, the Caribbean, Asia, Africa, and the Middle East to the United States has reworked American culture and its demographic character from within. In schools in Los Angeles, Texas, and New York, it is now usual to encounter classrooms in which the minority child is Anglo-American and in which English has been supplanted by Spanish, Armenian, Chinese, Korean, or Ebonics. This situation also can be seen more broadly beyond the United States in the third world, particularly in the linguistic and cultural patterns that follow migration from rural to urban settings in Latin America

and elsewhere. New cultural forms are produced at the point of encounter between indigenous groups and dominant society. This new cosmopolitanism places enormous
strains on formal institutions of society (Waxer, 1999).

These vastly transformed circumstances consequent on the movement and collision
of people impose new imperatives on curriculum and pedagogy in schooling. In our era,
however, we seem evermore to lack the qualities of empathy; the desire for collaboration,
cooperation, and negotiation; or the magnanimity of spirit to engage with the other as a
member of our community or even our species. How should we address the topics of culture and identity in the organization of school knowledge? These have proved to be difficult questions indeed. In the following section, we first assess the mainstream approach
of cultural monologists to culture and identity in curricular organization. We then explore the response of postcolonial theorists and artists. The chapter concludes with a call
for a new postcolonial direction toward theory and practice of curriculum organization
in this era dominated as it is by multiplicity and difference.

THE DOMINANT PARADIGM

The dominant approach to the contemporary challenges of multiplicity and difference
in schooling, and one increasingly associated with minority practitioners as well, is to
think of *culture* and *identity* within the crisis language of imaginary unity, of singular
origins, singular ancestry, bounded nationality, and so forth. *Culture* is thus defined as a
tightly bounded set of linguistic, aesthetic, and folkloric practices specific to a particular group. *Group identity* is seen as the true self within the collective association—as the
fulfillment of a linear connection to an unsullied past and ancestry. "These are our people." "We are different from all other groups." "These are our cultural forms and meaning of style."

Thus, in the United States, hegemonic Anglo school critics such as Arthur
Schlesinger, George Will, and William Bennett maintain that the U.S. school curriculum
should have a unitary and homogenizing focus around Western Eurocentric culture.
Will (1998) made the point in direct language:

> Our country is a branch of European civilization. ... "Eurocentricity" is right, in
> American curricula and consciousness, because it accords with the facts of history,
> and we-and Europe are fortunate for that. The political and the moral legacy of Eu-
> rope has made the most happy and admirable of nations. Saying that maybe indeli-
> cate, but it has the merit of being true and the truth should be the core of any
> curriculum. (cited in McCarthy, 1998, p. 109)

However, minority school critics such as Afrocentrist, Molefi Asante, argue for placing African culture at the heart of the curriculum, maintaining that the curriculum for
African Americans should be organized around "solid identities" with Africa (Asante,
1993). These discourses now dominate the Eurocentric/Afrocentric debate over curriculum reform. Both Eurocentric and Afrocentric discourses of cultural monologism rely
on the simulation of a pastoral sense of the past in which Europe and Africa are available to American racial combatants without the noise of their modern tensions, contradictions, and conflicts. The dreaded line of difference is drawn around glittering objects
of cultural heritage and secured with the knot of ideological closure. The modern
American school has become a playground of this war of simulation. Contending paradigms of knowledge are embattled as combatants release the leavers of atavism holding their faces in their hands as the latest volley of absolutism circles in the air. Nowhere
is this sense of cultural antagonism more strongly articulated than in debates over the
canon versus minority and third world knowledges and cultural form.

THE CANON VERSUS THE THIRD WORLD

The effect of these ethnocentric projects in the curriculum field has been to create an arbitrary divide between the traditions and cultural forms of the West or the first world and those of indigenous minorities of the United States and third world peoples. This is now foregrounded in the hot debates taking place in the United States about the merits of the Western canon versus multiculturalism and postcolonial third world cultural form. Curriculum organized around this monological interpretation of culture and identity is constituted around some of the following kinds of ideological assumptions.

First, curricular monologists conceptualize culture and identity as consisting of a clearly demarcated and bounded set of lived and commodified cultural forms and practices specific to particular groups. These practices are defined as forms of some kind of final property and are seen as constituting the totality of group capacity and definition.

Second, mainstream theorists motivated by the manipulation of this model of culture and identity propose that curriculum reform should take the form of content addition to the dominant Eurocentric core curriculum, adding selectively from the stock of knowledge and experiences associated with minority groups.

Third, monologists suggest that only the members of a given minority group are fully competent to understand the knowledge and experiences pertinent to that particular group. This often leads to a dangerous tendency to construct as *other*, as internal enemies, those who are not part of the monologist's preferred group or who do not share his or her real or imagined ancestry. The *other* in this context is then targeted for exclusion. The history, knowledge, and culture of such an other is consequently perceived as illegitimate and, often therefore, suppressed.

With the impact of this dominant monologizing framework, the school institution has become paralyzed. Its formal, symbolic, and emblematic forms and structures have been a battle ground of competing narrow-minded interests. The hierarchy, verticality, arbitrariness, lack of participation, and bureaucratic rituals that dominate schooling have also effectively compromised genuine democratic discourse over these symbols. Adding to this, the monologist curricular conception produces fragmented knowledge that displaces a sense of interdisciplinarity and association across established programs of thought and curricular organization.

THE POSTCOLONIAL RESPONSE

Postcolonial writers and critics such as Hommi Bhabha, Stuart Hall, Octavio Paz, and Gyatri Spivak have pointed to the limitations of these monological and homogenizing approaches to culture, identity, and curriculum. They argue, instead, that culture and identity are the products of human encounters, the inventories of cross-cultural appropriation and hybridity, not the elaboration of the ancestral essence of particular groups. Within this alternative framework, culture and identity are conceptualized as the moving inventories and registers of association across narrowly drawn boundaries of group distinction. In his important essay, "Cultural Identity and Diaspora," Hall (1990) maintained that within any given community there are several other hidden or alternative communities wrestling to come to the surface. Postcolonial writers such as Michael Ondaatje, Latin American writers such as Isabelle Allende, Julia Alvarez, and Gabriel Garcia Marques, African American novelist, Toni Morrison, or the Guyanese philosophical novelist, Wilson Harris, point to the unsuspected horizons and trestles of affiliation across human groups and cultures normally regarded as separable and distinct.

To illustrate this point about cultural hybridity, the Cuban historical novelist, Alejo Carpentier (1985), told the story of an intriguing encounter he had while visiting the remote forest community of Turiamo on the Caribbean coast of Venezuela. Here the villagers introduced Carpentier to the poet—an illiterate Afro-Latin griot who was regarded as the keeper of communal history, the people's poet. In this illiterate, itinerant peasant, Carpentier came face to face with the multiaccented, polyphonic presence of these anthropologically defined natives. At a late-night communal gathering, which Carpentier attended, this Afro-Latin griot, the poet, recited for his forest dwellers gathered by the sea extensive passages of eighth-century French epic verse in an indigenous Venezuelan language.

Carpentier (1985) told the story this way:

> Let me tell you an anecdote which illustrates the poetic tradition in Latin America. More than twenty years ago, when I was living in Venezuela, my wife and I went to stay in a small fishing village on the Caribbean cost called Turiamo. There were no hotels, no bars, and you get there by crossing kilometers and kilometers of virgin forest. All the inhabitants of the village were black, there were no schools and almost everyone was illiterate. We soon got to know the village people and they told us about the Poet, a person who enjoyed a great deal of prestige there. He hadn't been to the village for about two months and the people missed him. One day he reappeared, bringing news from other areas. He was a colossal African, illiterate and poorly dressed. I told him, I'd like to hear his poetry. "Yes," he replied, "Tonight, by the sea." And that night all the village people, children, old folk, everyone, gathered on the beach to wait for the Poet. He took off his hat with a ritual gesture and, looking out to sea, began in quite acceptable octosyllables to recite the wonderful story of Charlemagne in a version similar to that of the Song of Roland. That day I understood perhaps for the first time in our America, wrongly named Latin, where an illiterate black descendant of Yorubas could recreate the Song of Roland—in a language richer than Spanish, full of distinctive inflections, accents, expressions and syntax—where wonderful Nahuatl poetry existed long before Alfonso the Wise and San Isidoro's Etymologies, in our America, there were a culture and a theatrical disposition which gave poetry an importance long lost in many countries in Europe. (p. 160)

The St. Lucian playwright, Derek Walcott (1993), also called attention to this theme of hybridity in his 1992 Nobel lecture, "The Antilles: Fragments of Epic Memory." Walcott talked about taking some American friends to a peasant performance of the ancient Hindu epic of Ramayana in a forgotten corner of the Caroni Plain in Trinidad. The name of this tiny village is the happily agreeable, but Anglo-Saxon, "Felicity." The actors carrying out this ritual reenactment are the plain-as-day East Indian villagers spinning this immortal web of memory, of ancientness and modernity. Here Walcott is "surprised by sin" at the simple native world unfurling in its utter flamboyance:

> Felicity is a village in Trinidad on the edge of the Caroni Plain, the wide central plain that still grows sugar and to which indentured cane cutters were brought after emancipation, so the small population of Felicity is East Indian, and on the afternoon that I visited it with friends from America, all the faces along its road were Indian, which as I hope to show was a moving, beautiful thing, because this Saturday afternoon Ramleela, the epic dramatization of the Hindu epic of Ramayana, was going to be performed, and the costumed actors from the village were assembling on a field strung with different-colored flags, like a new gas station, and beautiful Indian Boys in red and black were aiming arrows haphazardly into the afternoon light. Low blue mountains on the horizon, bright grass, clouds that would gather colour before the light went. Felicity! What a gentle Anglo-Saxon name for an epical memory. (Walcott, 1993, p. 1)

The world on the Caroni plain integrates the ancient and modern, as Indian peasants, historically displaced to the Caribbean, create in their daily lives a rememory of their past before modern colonialism. In so doing, they add an extraordinary ritual and threnodic nuance to the folk culture of the Caribbean as a whole. In the art of living, these East Indian peasants triumph over the imposed history of marginalization and the middle-passage history of indentureship.

Carpentier and Walcott's vivid vignettes point us toward the complex flow of humanity across presumptive borders. What these authors highlight is the radical encounter of ancient and modern peoples and Western and indigenous third world cultures in the postcolonial setting, and the unanticipated trestles of affiliation that link up disparate populations. They highlight the difficulty, indeed the futility, of atavistic attempts to maintain group purity. By quoting and combining elements of Western and third world cultural forms, writers such as Walcott are engaged in a radical aesthetics of double coding.

One finds this strategy of double coding foregrounded in the work of postcolonial visual artists as well. A good example is the painting of Australian aboriginal artist, Gordon Bennett. In his art, Bennett, the son of an Aborigine mother and European father, documents his struggle with the profound personal and political issues historically surrounding identity formation in Australia.

Bennett came to art relatively late in life, graduating from art school in 1988, the year Australia celebrated the bicentennial of European settlement. His work registers the attendant tensions and concerns of this historical moment. We would like to foreground here, one of his pivotal paintings, "Outsider." This painting combines methods of Aboriginal pointillism and European perspectival painting to stunning effect. In "Outsider," Bennett ironically quotes and densely refigures Vincent Van Gogh's "Starry Night" and his "Vincent's Bedroom at Arles," intensifying and heightening the atmosphere of brusque, startling anxiety that works through Van Gogh's paintings. Bennett's double coding of European and native Aboriginal traditions exposes an unsettling environment of cultural hegemony. Most important, Bennett interposes a new scenario into the settings in Van Gogh's paintings: a decapitated native body stumbling toward a blood besmirched cradle on which lay two classical Greek heads. Against this backdrop of a reconfigured "Starry Night" and "Vincent's Bedroom at Arles," the essential ground of Aboriginal and hegemonic Anglo-Australian identities is now populated with trip wire questions located in this motif of hybridity and double vision. The work of hybridity unearths the symbolic violence of Australian history and the brutality of European "discovery" and subjugation of the native. At the same time, through this double coding, Bennett highlights the incompleteness of the modern Aboriginal search for identity. This is sharply underscored in Bennett's use of space. Avoiding the linear arrangement of space of the European colonial oil painting, in which the native is clinically separated from the colonizer, Bennett deliberately yokes the colonizer and colonized into the same space indeed the same body. Boundaries between the European and Aboriginal are collapsed, and antagonistic spaces of colonized and colonizer are folded into each other in a violent and eruptive manner (McLean & Bennett, 1996).

The work of the postcolonial imagination then points toward a larger inventory of associations in the conceptualization of culture and identity than one finds in the educational thought of the cultural monologists. Refusing monologism and ethnocentrism, postcolonial writers such as Said (1993) suggested that a complex and dynamically relational treatment of culture and identity should deeply inform curriculum organization in schooling as we enter the new millennium. Curriculum change to address the new challenges of culture and identity and predicated on the framework suggested by postcolonial theorists operates on the following assumptions.

First, postcolonial theorists maintain that the opposition between the Western canon and third world cultural form is illegitimate. They suggest that this opposition is not empirically based. Proponents of postcolonial theory insist instead that there is a vigorous critique of the West taking place in the literature, music, and paintings of third world artists.

Second, postcolonial school critics argue that curricular knowledge should be the interdisciplinary product of heterogeneous sources. They maintain that pedagogy in the classroom should be organized around the thesis of the constructed nature of all knowledge. Postcolonial theorists assert that the accumulation of the latter is not a linear or singular process, but one that is best facilitated by an open practice of knowledge production rooted in a plurality of methodologies and strategies of inquiry.

Third, postcolonial theorists suggest that the contemporary context of all school knowledge and experiences is profoundly shaped by globalization and the ever-expanding pattern of integration of local realities into more global dynamics. The world, they argue, is now more interdependent. Contemporary students and teachers must be prepared for this changing reality precipitated by the dynamics of globalization.

The lines that separate the philosophical and practical approaches of cultural monologists and postcolonial theorists to curriculum formulation about culture and identity are therefore firmly drawn. Monologists see the curriculum as the servant of the core cultural values, knowledges, and experiences of particular groups. They believe that the integrity of these groups is best preserved by curricular recognition of group distinctiveness and specificity. In contrast, postcolonial theorists argue for the interminable process of cultural integration and co-articulation of majority and minority cultures in the modern world. These theorists see contemporary reality as defined by globalization and the blurring of the boundaries of the cultural and economic distinctions that exist between the inhabitants of industrialized countries of the West and third world people. These social actors of the third world have long been consigned to marginalization in the curriculum formulations of U.S. educators. These developments provide extraordinary challenges, but also great opportunities for curriculum reform in the contemporary U.S. school context.

CONCLUSION

The great task confronting teachers and educators as we move into the 21st century is to address the radical reconfiguration and cultural rearticulation taking place in educational and social life. As underscored at the beginning of this chapter, a set of new developments have presented themselves to the modern educator in this new millennium. These developments are foregrounded and driven forward by the logics of globalization, the intensification of movement and migration of people, the heightened effects of electronic mediation, the proliferation of images, and the everyday work of the imagination of the great masses of the people affecting their sense of the past, present, and future.

All these developments have shifted the ground of commonly taken-for-granted stabilities of social constructs such as *culture, identity, race, nation, state,* and so forth. One response, indeed the dominant response to this proliferation of difference and multiplicity, is to suppress the implications for rethinking the ethical, political, and epistemological basis of education by imposing a program of homogeneity. To a large extent, such a hegemonic approach is deeply informed by the long history of intellectual and academic colonialism in U.S. educational institutions where Anglos define the history and other groups serve as the objects of such definitions. Within this framework, curriculum works to divest youth of their identities and impede prospects for a fully invested multiculturalism. This hegemonic approach constitutes a top–down project that attempts to hold the Eurocentric and establishment core of the curriculum in place, inoculating it by simply adding on selective, nonconflictual items from the culture and experiences of minority and subaltern groups.

But this monological approach to culture is also to be found in the curricular formulations of some minority school critics as well. Cultural monologists within subaltern groups argue for the simple inversion of the Eurocentric dominance of the curriculum. They maintain that the cultural knowledges and experiences of their specifically embattled minority group—be it African American, Chicana/o, Asian American, Native American—should be foregrounded, and in a manner that would effectively displace the Eurocentric core of the curriculum, replacing it with a specific minority program of affirmation of cultural heritage.

But these monological approaches to curriculum reform, hegemonic or minority, merely lead us down the path of a cultural illiteracy of the other—an illiteracy that we cannot afford in a world context of deepening globalization and interdependence. We cannot afford a continued blissful ignorance of groups that are different from ours: a practice that is still perpetuated in the dominant school curriculum. The ideal of community that monologists envision presumes a singular metasubject at the heart of the curriculum. This desire for the monological community relies on the same desire for monochromatic social wholeness and identification that underlies racism and ethnic chauvinism. This program of community building may help reproduce a sameness and a reassuring familiarity to curricular knowledge, but this occurs at the price of the suppression of the dynamism of the difference and alterity that excluded or marginalized knowledges and subjectivities bring to any educational setting.

By contrast, the postcolonial approach to curriculum change is based on the recognition of the plurality of subject positions operating at any given moment in the educational context. This approach seeks to integrate the logics of globalization into curriculum and educational frameworks by creatively interweaving the past, present, and future needs, interests, and desires of the full plurality of educational actors. It is recognized here that modern school subjects are better comprehended in their historical and contemporaneous heterogeneity than through structurally imposed categories or binary positions. Therefore, postcolonial theorists reject outright all imperializing forms of the self/other binary as they are expressed in contemporary schooling. Instead proponents strive for the creative fusion and vitalization of those mininarratives that every student and teacher brings to the curriculum and pedagogical context, reinforcing their particularities without allowing the dominant worldviews to fix their identities into structurally enforced categories.

As postcolonial theorists suggest, then, a fundamentally new direction is needed in the approach to culture and identity in education as we enter the new millennium. This approach must begin with an effort to reject the simplistic economy of the canon versus the third world opposition in education. It must involve a radical rethinking of the linkages of knowledge, culture, and association among all peoples. For instance, as dependency theorists such as Andre Gunder Frank, Samir Amin, and Benjamin Cardoso have pointed out, the links between first world development and third world underdevelopment must be throughly explored in the curriculum so that today's school youth might have a fuller understanding of the vital imbrication of industrialized countries like the United States in the underdevelopment of third world countries, and how these relations are transposed onto core–periphery relations within developed countries.

Thinking in postcolonial terms about the topic of difference and multiplicity in education means thinking relationally and contextually. It means bringing back into educational discourses all those tensions and contradictions that we tend to suppress as we process experience and history into curricular knowledge. It means abandoning the auratic status of concepts such as culture and identity for a recognition of the vital porosity that exists between and among human groups in the modern world. It means foregrounding the intellectual autonomy of students by incorporating open mindedness and inquiry that comes from letting traditions debate with each other under the rubric that we learn more about ourselves by learning about others. It means ultimately thinking across disciplinary boundaries and the insulation of knowledge—linking the syndical and the pedagogical in the way we do our work.

REFERENCES

Appadurai, A. (1996). *Modernity at large*. Minneapolis, MN: Minnesota Press.

Asante, M. (1993). *Malcolm X as cultural hero and other Afrocentric ideas*. Trenton, NJ: Africa World Press.

Carpentier, A. (1985). The Latin American novel. *New Left Review, 154*, 159–191.

Giddens, A. (1994). The consequences of modernity. In P. Williams & L. Chrisman (Eds.), *Colonial discourse and postcolonial theory* (pp. 181–189). New York: Columbia University Press.

Hall, S. (1990). Cultural identity and diaspora. In J. Rutherford (Ed.), *Identity: Community, culture, difference* (pp. 222–237). London: Lawrence & Wishart.

McCarthy, C. (1998). *Uses of culture: Education and the limits of ethnic affiliation*. New York: Routledge.

McLean, I., & Bennett, G. (1996). *The art of Gordon Bennett*. Roseville East, New South Wales, Australia: Craftsman House.

Nietzsche, F. (1967). *On the genealogy of morals*. (W. Kaufmann, Trans.). New York: Vintage.

Rothstein, R. (2000, October 11). When culture affects how we learn. *The New York Times*, p. 25.

Said, E. (1993). The politics of knowledge. In C. McCarthy & W. Crichlow (Eds.), *Race, identity and representation in education* (pp. 306–314). New York: Routledge.

Valenzuela, A. (1999). *Subtractive schooling. U.S.–Mexican youth and the politics of caring*. Albany: State University of New York Press.

Walcott, D. (1993). *The Antilles: Fragments of epic memory*. New York: Farrar, Strauss & Giroux.

Waxer, L. (1999). Consuming memories: The record-centered salsa scene in Cali. In C. McCarthy, G. Hudak, S. Miklaucic, & P. Saukko (Eds.), *Sound identities: Popular music and the cultural politics of education* (pp. 235–252). New York: Peter Lang.

Will, G. (1989, December 18). Eurocentricity and the school curriculum. *Baton Rouge Morning Advocate*, p. 3.

CHAPTER 4

A History of the World Council for Curriculum and Instruction (WCCI)

Norman V. Overly
Indiana University

The World Council for Curriculum and Instruction (WCCI) came into existence on August 1, 1971. On that date, sufficient ballots of the eligible voters were received in the offices of the Association for Supervision and Curriculum Development (ASCD) accepting the initial constitution of the organization and authorizing the naming of officers until the first election could be held. However, the history of its germination goes back many years before that date. It is rooted in the activities of a dedicated group of internationalists who worked through the commissions and councils of ASCD for over 20 years to gain the attention and support of a generally unconcerned, or even reluctant, national membership for programming about international educational issues.

AN AD HOC COMMITTEE

As was noted in the "Introduction" of a short history of WCCI (Berman, Miel, & Overly, 1982), "Organizations ordinarily come into being as a result of the creative thinking of a small group of persons who are sensitive to a problem" (p. 5). From the beginning of ASCD in the late 1940s, there was a small, but insistent, group of educators who were intent on keeping before the curriculum leaders and supervisors in American schools the global significance of the issues and problems they were addressing at the local community level. For 14 years, ASCD appointed a committee on international understanding. For reasons not immediately clear, the practice was discontinued in 1964 and 1965. However, Louise Berman, then Associate Secretary of ASCD, formed an ad hoc committee to develop recommendations for ways in which international understanding and related issues could be addressed by ASCD in the future.

While ASCD had grown with the involvement of persons from the progressive education movement, local leadership in some states was more traditional or conservative than the national leadership. Certainly the post-World War II years, the national struggle to come to grips with international relations, and the threat of international communism created a conservative atmosphere that caused some educators to draw back from controversial topics. The McCarthy era and the schism within American education over how to address relationships with communist nations and how to teach about nondemocratic forms of government led to some cautious moments among the ASCD leadership. To some extent, those active in the international arena were thought to be too liberal or leftist in their perspectives. ASCD's progressive outlook was permissive in encouraging expression of diverse ideas, but tended to marginalize groups with agendas outside the mainstream by providing minimal support. Many of the early Committee on International Understanding members were also members of the World Education Fellowship (WEF), which supported agendas of peace, nonviolence, and cooperation among persons of all nations irrespective of political leanings. The words *world* and *fellowship* used in the same title were enough to raise concerns about the patriotic convictions of such members in many quarters during this era in American history.

Alice Miel, professor at Teachers College, Columbia University, served as the chair of the ad hoc committee formed by Berman, her former doctoral student. Miel had attended an international conference in Denmark the year before her appointment. The format of the Denmark meeting, held "far from any large city" (Bermen et al., 1982, p. 5) at a folk high school, lent itself to the collegial atmosphere of formal lectures and data presentation, followed by discussion groups around the campus, participants eating meals together, and informal socializing until the wee hours of the morning. The collection of international conferees became a learning community of peers for the 10 days of the conference. Miel's position as chair of the ad hoc committee provided the platform from which she could explore a similar plan with and for ASCD.

As the ad hoc committee pursued its charge, the discussions soon focused on the limitations of the name, if not the perspective, of the earlier committee. International understanding suggested an academic perspective in keeping with traditional studies of comparative education that sought intellectual clarity about differing approaches to education and understanding of the national systems that supported them. In addition, international understanding often involved excursions into the political landscape in search of insights into the political and economic systems that undergirded national agendas. The primary interests and focus of the ASCD-based group was tied directly to elementary and secondary level practice of curriculum development and instruction rather than academic debate and research on differing international educational issues. The outcome of their early deliberations led the ad hoc committee to a recommendation that ASCD form a commission on international cooperation in education. Within ASCD, commissions were appointed for a limited period of time with regular review and the possibility of an extension depending on their productivity and success in meeting their charge. Usually a proportion of the membership on commissions was rotated off each year to ensure fresh ideas and the expectation of productivity. The proposal set forth the charge in this way:

(1) In addition to education for international understanding, the concerns of the commission would include caring about and helping others beyond national borders.

(2) Instead of aiming to develop a global perspective only in citizens of the U.S.A., the new commission would cooperate with other educators in the world in attempting to develop such a broad perspective in citizens of many nations.

(3) The charge would include working with educators from other nations to improve all facets of education world wide. (Berman et al., 1982, p. 5)

THE COMMISSION

The proposal was accepted by the ASCD Executive Committee in 1966 and the six members of the ad hoc committee (Arthur Adkins, Kenneth A. Bateman, George Dickson, Alice Miel (chair), Harry V. Scott, and Charles M. Shapp) were joined by Joseph Alessandro, Gertrude M. Lewis, and Willard Leeds. Louise Berman served as the ASCD coordinator of the work of the Commission until she took a position at the University of Maryland. At that time, (August 1967), Norman Overly replaced her in the ASCD office and took over the liaison coordination for commissions and councils of ASCD.[1]

Alice Miel set in motion an effort to replicate the Denmark experience that had made such an impression on her. Her plan won quick acceptance from the committee, and detailed planning on prospective sites, themes, program components, and identification of prospective participants soon dominated the considerations of the Commission. In the International Education Act of 1966, U.S. President Lyndon Johnson had projected 1970 to be International Education Year. He attended the International Conference on the World Crisis in Education in October 1967, which was a governmental model of the type of meeting Miel had in mind.[2] Using the prospect of 1970 as International Education Year defined the time for the Commission. At its September 1966 meeting, the newly formed Commission decided to hold an international conference at the Asilomar Conference Center at Pacific Grove, California, on March 5–14, 1970. All were intent on holding the meeting at a location some distance from any cities or major institution with their usual distractions, which tend to draw some participants away from a focus on the topics at hand to sightseeing, shopping, and cultural events. Because they were planning a working conference, the decision was made to limit the number of participants to 300 and to keep the U.S. participants to no more than half the total. The conference was to be conducted in English, with the requirement that all participants be able to function fully in that language. Although there was a desire to have as broad an international representation as possible, there was a recognition that multiple languages and translations would lead to a different type conference from what was envisioned and that the expenses of simultaneous translation would be prohibitive. Both language and expenses were to be issues to be worked on as WCCI emerged from its seminal conference.

Planning for Asilomar

The driving force for the conference was Alice Miel, and her ideas came to permeate every aspect of the program; she led the group through careful evaluation of endless sets of suggestions. Her ideas usually gained acceptance because they were presented with thoroughness and were supported by the depth of her experience in international and local education, the breadth of her knowledge, and the strength of her spirit, grounded in a tough gentleness.

---

[1]Others appointed to the commission over its 6-year life, besides Berman, were Ira B. Bryant, Delmo Della-Dora, Prudence Dyer, D. Edward Fleming, Leonard A. Herbst, Raymond Muessig, Vincent Rogers, Robert Smith, Robert W. Wagner, and Pearl N. Yamashita. Overly joined the Commission when he left ASCD in August 1970 for a position at Indiana University.

[2]The International Conference on the World Crisis in Education convened in Williamsburg, Virginia, on October 5, 1967. One hundred fifty educational leaders from 52 countries participated in the conference. *"Principal Addresses and Summary Report"* of the *International Conference* on the World Crisis in Education, Department of Health, Education and Welfare, undated.

The theme of the conference came from the Unesco motto, which begins: "Wars are made in the minds of men...." Although this perspective resonated with the position of the Commission, there was an additional, pragmatic reason for making this not so subtle connection to an organization that would provide worldwide legitimacy to the idea of a world meeting run by a group of Americans. By unanimous agreement, the Commission adopted the conference theme, "In the Minds of Men: Educating the Young People of the World." It echoed favorably among the members of the Commission, who belonged to the WEF and promised to reflect favorably on the fundamental assumptions that had motivated the ASCD group since its formation.

The Commission sought input from ASCD conference participants at their annual meetings in Dallas, Atlantic City, and Chicago from 1967 through 1969. Additional input came from a New York City conference sponsored jointly by the Commission and the U.S. Section of the World Education Fellowship (WEF) in March 1968 and an October 1969 meeting at Lake Mohonk, New York. Speakers such as E. R. Braithwaite, author of *To Sir with Love*, and Otto Klineberg, a social psychologist noted for his cross- cultural research, participated in the New York City conference, along with Zbigniew Brzezinski, later National Security Adviser to President Carter. The Mohonk conference provided an opportunity to investigate possible British and Canadian connections and ideas for incorporation in the planning for the Asilomar meetings. Wilfred Wees of Canada became a leading contributor to the planning and subsequent creation of WCCI.

The Initial Conference Program

In preparation for the conference, three booklets were prepared with financial assistance from the Longview Foundation. These publications[3] were designed to provide a common background for all the conference participants. Titles and authors were: *Cooperative International* Education by Willis Griffin and Ralph Spence, *The International Dimension of Education* by Leonard Kenworthy, and *Bases for World Understanding and Cooperation: Suggestions for Teaching the Young Child* by Joan Moyer. The Commission also planned what would become an award-winning issue of *Educational Leadership* on the theme, "International Cooperation in Education."[4]

The conference program had 10 plenary sessions. The topics of the plenary papers and the presenters were set forth in the conference report (Miel & Berman, 1970). Among them were:

1. "Men of Tomorrow: A Challenge for Education" by Alvin D. Loving, Sr., President-Elect of ASCD, U.S.A.;
2. "Is the School an Obsolete Institution?" by W. Senteza Kajubi, Makerere University, Uganda;
3. "Useful Functions for the Schools of the Future" by Torsten Husen, University of Stockholm, Sweden;
4. "Maintaining a Supportive Physical Environment for Man" by Pauline Gratz, Duke University, U.S.A.;
5. "Maintaining a Supportive Physical Environment for Man: How Schools Can Help" by Denis Lawton, University of London, U.K.;
6. "Maintaining a Supportive Social Environment for Man" by D. K. Wheeler, University of Western Australia;

---

[3]The three background papers were edited by Norman V. Overly and published by ASCD in 1970.
[4]*Educational Leadership*, 25(2), November 1969.

7. "Building a Socially Supportive Environment" by Edmund W. Gordon, Teachers College, Columbia University, U.S.A.;

8. "How to Accomplish School Reform" by K. G. Saiyidain, Asian Institute of Educational Planning and Administration, India;

9. "Toward a World Community of Educators: Unity with Diversity" by Alice Miel, Teachers College, Columbia University, U.S.A.;

10. "Aspirations for Education Around the Globe: A Visual Production" by Robert Wagner and Alexander Frazier, ASCD President, The Ohio State University, U.S.A.

Reaction papers were prepared and presented after the first nine plenaries (as noted before) by persons from Jordan, Colombia, Egypt, The United Kingdom, The Netherlands, South Africa, Japan, Peru, and Mexico. Preidentified discussion groups met to discuss the ideas generated by the papers and the reactors. In addition, a central focus of the meetings was the working parties which spent 13 hours exploring a preassigned special topic that was pursued in 60- or 90-minute periods over the 10 days of the conference. In all cases, the persons selected to present the reaction papers and provide leadership for the discussion groups and working parties were selected for their abilities to carry out their functions at a high level. In no small measure, the success of the conference was due to the careful planning and selection of these important contributors. Furthermore, persons from outside the United States were selected to preside over several of the plenary sessions.

Global Tensions Intervene

After 4 years of planning, the conference time came and went with widespread acclaim. Three hundred educational leaders from 53 nations joined together for 10 days of intense and close interaction on global professional issues. During the meetings, "one unpleasant and unexpected episode occurred" that was a foreshadowing of a continuing issue that WCCI has had to address in many ways and in many guises during its history. From the beginning, conferees had been identified and selected to attend on the basis of their potential contributions to the mix of the conference on the basis of their personal accomplishments, not as representatives of any government. Yet when the day approached when one of two South Africans participating in the conference was scheduled to serve as a reactor to a plenary speech,

> [b]lacks from Africa, supported by blacks from the U.S.A., threatened to leave the conference unless the reactor (a white South African) was cancelled. Following discussions with the protesters and the South Africans and after much soul searching, the Commission decided to prepare a carefully worded statement to answer questions that had been raised and to announce its decision in the matter. (Berman et al., 1982, p. 13)

Commission member and subsequent chair, Vincent Rogers, presented the Commission's hotly debated and carefully worded response to the concerns that had been raised. Among the points he made was a defense of the nature of the participants. He quoted from the letter of invitation that all participants had received. "We hope to have at least two educators from each country of the world plus 150 Americans. All participants will be outstanding professionals and will be expected to contribute to some aspect of the program." A working paper used by the Commission pointed out that no participants were to be restricted by any official or national point of view. Rogers continued by noting that nominations were solicited from professional organizations and their members, and in the cases where no representatives from a country were nominated, embassies and ministers of education were approached. Representation was not gained from all countries, including the USSR and most of Eastern Europe.

Pointing to the purpose of the conference, Rogers again quoted from the letter of invitation:

> Realizing that educators from various parts of the world share many concerns, we propose that the conference purpose shall be building a commitment to make schools and colleges around the world more effective instruments for full development of human resources, and achieving cooperation between persons and among nations.... We would expect each person who comes to present his own ideas in as straight-forward a manner as possible.

Such a noble intent failed to take into consideration the long history of social, religious, economic, and racial hegemony that was the experience of many of the participants. The specific conflict that arose provided no easy solution. Try as the Commission might, it was unable to come up with a win/win solution. Finally, the South African reactor was requested to withdraw from his formal presentation, but to remain as a participant. He was unwilling to accept the conditions and decided to leave the conference. However, the second South African participant did remain and was cordially involved in all aspects of the conference without prejudice.

The clear learning from this confrontation was the realization that international cooperation or understanding is a much more difficult ideal to realize than the intent to foster it. The history of conflicts among groups of persons around the world intrudes on efforts to cooperate in unexpected ways and at unexpected times. Generalizations and expectations about groups and individuals are equally unreliable. To a large extent, the intent of the organizers was affirmed. Conflicts and their solutions ultimately must be addressed individually "in the minds of men." In many ways, the history of WCCI is a story of efforts to address the issues arising from individual and group relationships. In turn, these efforts have had a major impact on the development of programs for publications and research and development undertaken by the organization.

Impact on ASCD

Following the 10-day Asilomar meeting, all of the conferees were bussed to San Francisco to attend the annual national ASCD conference. This provided an opportunity for the larger parent organization to have contact with the international conferees; in turn, the international participants experienced a major professional organization's annual meeting. The personal interactive nature of the conference was enhanced by the opportunity for all international participants to have a week of home stay and visits to local schools with a host ASCD family if they desired. Thus, the pattern of person-to-person professional interchange was set, and the contacts and ideas considered at Asilomar were extended to the wider ASCD membership. In addition, the ASCD Board of Directors requested a report on the *incident* with the South African participant.

During the Asilomar conference, heavy emphasis had been placed on small-group work and informal interchanges during refreshment breaks and at meals. As participants arrived at the dining room for meals, they were seated around tables holding 10 persons, thus mixing the discussion groups at each meal. It became a major time of sharing with new groupings at every meal. Also, although unplanned, an informal network developed for evening interactions that became a highlight of the conference for many.

By the time the group members arrived in San Francisco, they had bonded into a familiar group of friends who were regularly found leading social interchanges in the lobbies of all the major hotels. It is clear that the pattern of inviting participants to agree to be housed with persons from another culture during the conference in shared motel-style housing of two, three, or four persons per room had accelerated the bonding and making of friends. For many from the United States, it was the first time they had ever been in direct contact with persons from other cultures, not to say having to share sleeping and bathroom facilities with others. Although some private rooms were available, over 90% of the participants shared living space with at least one other person.

NEXT STEPS

When Asilomar was over, a question remained for many of the conferees: "Now what?" The question had been discussed prior to the conference, but no decision had been made. Within a few weeks of the conference, letters and telephone calls began coming into the ASCD offices asking what was to follow the conference. Many of the participants were unwilling to let the experience of close interaction and initial efforts at cross-cultural cooperation fade into the background as a once-in-a-lifetime experience. As a follow-up, the Newsletter of the World Conference of Educators was launched in June 1970 from funds not expended for conference planning. It was edited by Overly and sent to all Asilomarians in an effort to establish a regular format for communication among the conference participants.

The suggestion that an international organization be formed to incorporate the concepts explored at the Asilomar conference was made so frequently that an ad hoc committee of Asilomarians met in New York City in October 1970 to develop a proposal. Six members of the Commission—Berman, Dickson, Herbst, Miel, Overly, and Rogers—were joined by Sam Awudetsey of Ghana, John Bigala and Enoka Rukare of Uganda, and Richard Brown from the ASCD headquarters staff. Overly, now editing the newsletter from Indiana University, reported on the meeting. With the assistance of international students from New York area colleges and universities, Miel took responsibility for pulling the ideas together and drafted a constitution that incorporated ideas for organizational patterns, officers, financing, purpose, and objectives. A major outcome of the ad hoc committee's deliberations on the constitution was the decision to change the name of the future organization to the World Council for Curriculum and Instruction. Miel explained the significance of the name in a later article, "What's in a Name?," published in the February 1975 issue of the newsletter.

When the World Council for Curriculum and Instruction was named by the transnational framers of our constitution, the choice of each word was deliberate. *World* was selected, rather than *international*, partly to play down a division into nations and partly to cause us to aim higher than cooperation among only a few nations in one part of the globe. *Council* was chosen to signify a group of persons ready to give and take educational advice within the membership as well as outside.

It was decided that persons performing various functions in education would be more likely to feel included and needed if the new organization were named as a council for two key aspects of education. The first of these aspects was *curriculum,* a term then used to cover the intended, planned offerings of educational institutions. The second was *instruction,* used to cover the interactive process of teaching–experiencing–learning. The inclusion of "curriculum and instruction" in our name was intended to direct attention to this pair of central concerns and give us a unique function among world organizations.

The draft of the constitution was reworked on the basis of feedback supplied by Asilomarians who were able to meet at the annual conference of ASCD held in St. Louis, Missouri, in March 1971. As noted by Miel, the "constitution guaranteed international representation by providing for a board of directors composed of members elected by each of eleven regions into which the nations of the world had been grouped. A smaller executive committee was to consist of two elected officers, president and vice president, two appointed officers, secretary and treasurer, plus six members from different parts of the world elected as members at-large. Members of the executive committee were also to be part of the board of directors" (Berman et al., 1982, pp. 16–17).

A BRIDGE TO INDEPENDENCE

The ASCD Working Party on World Cooperation in Education, 1971–1972, served as the formal body that put the constitution into effect by naming interim officers once the Asilomarians had voted to form the organization by accepting the draft constitution. The officers represented an international mix, held a commitment to the principles on which WCCI had been founded, and were located within a reasonable geographic proximity to permit them to meet at least twice a year. It was also thought to be important to have a mix based on gender. The ASCD heritage brought with it a commitment to diversity insofar as possible in all official representation. Attendees at the Asilomar conference formed the pool from which the officers were selected.

Margarita Quijano (Mexico), who had become active in ASCD the prior 3 years, was selected as the interim president. Because the organizers were still hopeful that WCCI might expand beyond the limitation imposed by requiring English language proficiency, having a leader for whom English was a second language was viewed as a plus. Norman Overly was chosen as interim vice president because he had directed the Asilomar conference and had been the chief correspondent with each Asilomarian during the pre- and postconference communications, first through his position at the ASCD headquarters office and then through the newsletter.

Chandos Reid Rice from the Detroit region of Michigan was selected as secretary, and Hulman Sinaga from Malaysia was the choice for treasurer. Sinaga, an experienced educator, graduate student, and instructor at Wayne State University, represented another culture and different world region. Because two signatories were required for financial transactions, it became a pattern that the treasurer would always be in the United States because U.S. funds were used and that one other officer would be at hand to sign checks. In addition, the interim Executive Committee included Louise Berman (United States), Jean Burion (Belgium), Alexander Grey (Australia), Mary Jarma (Nigeria), Enoka Rukare (Uganda), and Wilfred Wees (Canada). Miel had taken a temporary position in Afghanistan at the time, but she continued her close work with the group as an advisor via correspondence.

The Interim Executive Committee began its deliberations with attention to the assumptions that formed the foundation of the organization and the purposes that were to inform its programming. The first issue of the newsletter in 1972 set forth the six assumptions on which WCCI had been established:

1. There are many and variable answers to problems for those who accept education as problem solving in an open universe.
2. Education throughout the world can be changed and improved through sharing of experiences and ideas.
3. Education starts with being in touch with reality.
4. A sense of world community is best fostered through person-to-person contacts.

5. Education is a process of becoming for individuals and groups as well as ideas.
6. All people have the potential to contribute significantly to the emergence of others.

Seven purposes were noted in the same article:

1. To examine the meaningfulness to the learner of existing educational assumptions, practices, and institutions.
2. To engage our members and others in a critical examination of controversial issues.
3. To propose and test approaches and evaluations of problems and needs.
4. To increase and broaden the body of professional knowledge.
5. To explore ways in which dissemination of theory and practice can be facilitated in all parts of the world.
6. To cooperate with other international and national organizations having compatible purposes.
7. To provide professional, ideological, and moral support to free people from prejudices and strengthen them to find ways and means to solve the problems they face.

A nominating committee was appointed at the first meeting of the Interim Executive Committee held in Detroit at the Rice home in November 1971. Lucille Jordan (North America) chaired the committee composed of one member each from Africa, Asia, Europe, and South America. Dues were set at $10 per year, with a $2 minimum being set in recognition of the differences in ability of persons from some cultures and countries to meet the regular fees. By May 1972, eighty persons had paid their dues. By the end of the first year, the membership had doubled.

Other action by the Interim Executive Committee included the decision to place the headquarters in Bloomington, Indiana, at the home of Overly, with whom the Asilomarians and new members were used to communicating. In addition, George Monroe was appointed as the editor for the newsletter, and he developed a logo with the motto, "Unity with Diversity," which continues to serve as a visual representation of the organization.

The first election was held during the first year, and the results were published in the October 1972 issue of the newsletter. Quijano and Overly were elected to 3-year terms as president and vice president, respectively. Burion and Grey were elected to 1-year terms on the Executive Committee, Berman and J.M. Obando (Colombia) were to serve 2-year terms, and Catherine Russell (U.K.) and Ziya Bursalioglu (Turkey) were the 3-year members. Representation on the Board of Directors was determined according to geographical (regional) areas with proportional membership by region. Those elected represented the Near East and South Asia, Mediterranean Africa, North America, Subsaharan Africa, Eastern Europe, and South America. Term lengths of 1 to 3 years were determined by lot. Those elected officially took office on October 1, 1972.

Prior to transferring responsibility to the elected officers, the Interim Executive Committee held a final meeting in New York in September 1972. Besides making specific administrative appointments, they held a wide-ranging discussion of principles and themes that would be a recurring concern and focus of future groups. They stressed that it was important to maximize the involvement of all members, focus on youth and education rather than professional roles, emphasize individual participation with diverse and pluralistic objectives, commit the organization to improving transnational communication, and, notably, consider holding a world conference on education in 1974.

A NEW REALITY UNDER WAY

Although most of the Executive Committee and several of the Board Members had been involved with the interim arrangements, the urgency of the problems of running an organization independent of the supporting parent became immediately apparent. Attention had to be given to membership development, financial stability, programming, and a secretariat to conduct the ongoing communications and coordination of the programs.

Conferences

Having been born from the experience of the Asilomar conference, it is not surprising that the central focus of the organization turned to opportunities to provide similar experiences for those who had not savored the stimulation of an Asilomar style conference. The distinctiveness of that meeting was the result of the residential nature of the setting, the extended period of time the participants spent together, and the working nature of a program that included meaningful interactions that led to future cooperation on development and research projects across national and cultural systems.

At the same time, the Asilomar conference demonstrated the difficulty of taking action on global problems or common educational concerns when persons are strangers to each other and often unfamiliar with the assumptions and context of each others' approaches. Yet the close, extended human interaction and the possibility of continuing and deepening friendships begun during a 10-day conference led members to treasure a similar experience for others. From the organizational perspective, a conference also provided an effective vehicle for familiarizing persons with the organization and for recruiting members. In addition, a conference provided a legitimate reason for gathering professionally to renew contacts and create new networks for cooperation.

The first conference was held at Keele University in England in September 1974. A conference has been held every 3 years since then. The Keele conference carefully mirrored the structure and plan of the Asilomar gathering. However, subsequent conferences were modified because of local customs, particular venue, time of year, climate of the site, and experience with the conferencing process. The Istanbul, Hiroshima, Cairo, and Bangkok locations made use of hotels in major cities as the venue. Tagaytay City, The Philippines, which used a military officers training center, and the Noordwijkerhout Conference Center, The Netherlands were the most like Asilomar in being removed from major cities and having self-contained housing. In Keele, England; Edmonton, Canada; and Amritsar, India, college campuses were used. In two cases, dormitories provided housing accommodations, but in India, hotels in the city provided sleeping accommodations. Although all the locations had adequate space for plenary sessions and small-group discussions, the impact of the site on the types of interchanges and the formality or informality of interactions between sessions was marked. Over the years, the length of the meetings has gradually decreased as costs have risen.

Another factor influencing the duration of the meetings has been the time of year of the meetings. Because vacation time from educational responsibilities varies greatly around the globe, and because seasonal rains and temperatures vary from region to region, the triennial conferences have been held from July to December, with the Philippine conference bridging the New Year holiday in 1980–1981.

Financing the triennial conferences depends on the ability of the sponsoring country and its institutions' ability to identify local resources and support that help them underwrite the expenses of the program and provide scholarship funds for persons from economically underdeveloped areas. The conferences regularly bring together about 300 persons from about 50 nations.

Finances

One of the priorities of the new organization was to establish its independence from ASCD. Although there was a desire to maintain a close cooperative relationship with many organizations, it was deemed critical to have a unique and independent identity. To achieve that goal, it was necessary to have a financial base. This was a noble goal, but one the organizers soon found was more difficult than they had imagined. A Finance Committee was formed to develop the necessary financial base for establishment of a headquarters with a secretariat to centralize communication and administration. The committee soon discovered that philanthropic organizations and government agencies were not interested in supporting the administration and structure of organizations no matter how worthy their purposes. In turn, they came to recognize that the best they could hope for was to develop projects for research and publications that philanthropists found worthy of support. Because cross-cultural and cross-national cooperation was a significant part of the purposes of the founders, attention turned to the development of proposals for short-term projects.

At the same time, the matter of membership dues was a complex issue that had to be addressed. In light of the wide diversity in ability to pay and in national policies for remitting funds, it became clear that any hope of having membership from all nations, or at least a wide spectrum of countries, would be dependent on finding a way to be as inclusive and flexible as possible in financial transactions. A number of plans were advanced and tried at different times in the early years. Members from more affluent regions were encouraged to sponsor persons from other countries, a two- or three-tiered dues system was tried, countries were encouraged to collect dues at the local or national levels and transmit them as a unit with individual names attached, and institutional memberships were encouraged with one person being permitted as the voting member or representative of the institution.

No matter the pattern of membership that was developed, it met with concern from a number of quarters. Members from countries with lower economic levels of support were concerned that they would feel like second-class members if they paid lower dues. Others objected to having their funds channeled through a national office in their country if membership was to be individual. Efforts to transfer non-U.S. funds met with difficulties in conversion rates and the reliability of differing banking systems. Sometimes checks from non-U.S. banks were found to have no legitimacy. Ultimately, with donated legal assistance from a noted Washington, DC law firm, WCCI received tax exempt status as a publicly supported organization from the U.S. Internal Revenue Service. This permitted U.S. donors to WCCI projects to gain U.S. tax deductions and attracted gifts from some philanthropically minded individuals.

Charter member Maxine Dunfee established a Membership Exchange Plan. Dunfee explained her plan in the February 1975 newsletter. Because there are countries abroad whose citizens are unable to send dollars outside their homeland, WCCI members in these lands are using the WCCI Exchange Plan. They send merchandise in lieu of dollars; their choices reflect the culture of their countries and are designed to give pleasure to the recipients. Ten lucky WCCI members who participated in the Exchange Plan by contributing membership fees in addition to their own have received the packages from abroad, each an interesting surprise.

A subsequent modification of this plan, the Conference Bazaar, again organized by Dunfee, became a regular part of the triennial conferences. Not only did it provide financial resources for support of scholarships for the conferees, but the bazaar became an important meeting place during the conference and occasion for discussion of cultural differences, economics of different areas, traditional crafts, and regional histories.

Costs associated with publications of the newsletter, conference proceedings, a journal, and occasional papers made the development of financial underwriting critical. The most significant publication costs always involved the journal and conference proceedings. Costs related to the former were meant to be covered by dues and subscriptions. Conference proceedings' expenses were usually built into the conference costs. A major expense that continued to increase was the cost of postage for publications and other communications. With the advent of the Internet and e-mail, postage expenses declined slightly, but costs of mailing publications remains high, and the international postal system is unreliable in many nations. Because the headquarters and publications were handled in the United States, the expenses in communicating with the membership in regions paying the lowest membership dues were the highest.

To combat this problem, efforts were made to handle preparation and mailing of publications from different regions. However, differing quality standards for paper and editing, along with the problematic nature of the postal systems for some countries, made those efforts difficult to maintain in most cases. In one case, nearly the entire mailing of an issue of the journal, *FORUM*, was lost in the mails or went down with a ship, never to be heard from again.

Headquarters and the Secretariat

The temporary headquarters in Bloomington served to get the organization started. The resources—primarily space and postage for international mailings—made available through the School of Education at Indiana University helped keep the organization afloat through the initial years. As was to be the pattern in every move of the headquarters, having a supportive dean at the head of the college or school of education was necessary for the organization's survival.

When Alice Miel returned to the United States from her assignment in Afghanistan, she accepted the position of Executive Secretary on an unpaid, volunteer basis. Space and support was gained from Teachers College, Columbia University in New York City for the new headquarters. With that transition, the treasurer's position also moved from Bloomington to New York, where it remained through the administration of Miel and then Betty Reardon, who was employed as a part-time Executive Secretary on Miel's retirement to Florida in the autumn of 1977. Under Reardon's leadership, the headquarters remained at Teachers College, and student volunteer help continued for office functions as it had during Miel's tenure. Helene Sherman was appointed as assistant to the executive secretary in recognition of her heavy volunteer contributions, and this allowed her to function as a legal agent of the organization. Reardon augmented her income by raising funds through projects on behalf of WCCI, which also served to expand the programming. However, by November 1979, the strain of her heavy workload and the uncertain nature of the financial support from WCCI made it necessary to change the secretariat once more.

Maxine Dunfee, Professor of Education at Indiana University, stepped into the breach in 1980 by agreeing to volunteer her services as the Executive Secretary. Again the administration of the School of Education at Indiana University (IU) provided space for the headquarters and support in the form of mailing privileges and office support. Dunfee established a consistent administrative style and leadership that stabilized the organization for many years. In 1993, several years after her retirement from IU, she turned the reigns over to Estela Matriano, Professor of Education at the University of Cincinnati. Matriano had been a long-time member of WCCI and had directed the third triennial conference in Tagaytay City in her native Philippines. The headquarters then moved to Cincinnati, Ohio, with the blessing and support of the Dean of the

College of Education. At that time, the title of the position was changed from Executive Secretary to Executive Director. This helped avoid some of the confusion engendered by having an executive secretary and a recording secretary with distinct, but sometimes similar responsibilities for communicating with the membership and officers.

As was the pattern throughout WCCI's history, the treasurer has been located in close proximity to the secretariat. For several years, the treasurer had been at Indiana University, then Teachers College, back to Indiana University, then the University of Cincinnati, for a time at the University of Nevada at Las Vegas, and then back to the University of Cincinnati.

Records of the organization have been maintained by the Recording Secretary. Merle Monroe initiated a policy and procedures handbook when she served in that position. With occasional updating by her and subsequently by Dunfee and Claudia Crump, another long-serving recording secretary, the administration established regular operating procedures with records of Executive Committee and Board meetings being maintained at the site of the secretariat.

Elected Leadership

As noted in the discussion of the headquarters and administrative leadership, the work has nearly always been voluntary. Likewise, the officers have served with minimal or no support. In those cases when officers have been from areas with a low economic base and when they lacked personal resources, the organization set aside funds to make it possible for the officers to attend official meetings. But local resources have routinely been used to support the president's local office. The secretariat has been supported by purchase of office supplies and equipment if the institution in which it is located has not been willing to supply it. But in all cases, space has been made available without charge.

Care has been taken in every election to nominate a wide cross-section of the membership for positions and to attempt to guarantee that no one region would dominate. The globally elected officers, president and vice president, have reflected these efforts. However, the lack of local or personal resources has made it difficult for some very able persons to stand for president.

PROGRAMS AND PROJECTS

Over the life of the organization, a number of projects have involved different groups of members. Frequently they have arisen from working or study groups at the triennial conferences. Members have pursued such topics as a cooperative, transcultural teacher preparation program; a world geography project; and a number of peace conferences and publications. The most recent Constitution of WCCI sets forth three relationships that projects may have with the organization:

The sponsorship project is an official activity of the World Council with formal involvement of the Board in formulating objectives and methods of operation and assisting in raising funding for pursuit of the project.

The affiliation project meets the needs of some WCCI members, helps fulfill our purposes, and may require involvement of members in association with another organization. Funding is not involved.

The endorsement project demonstrates a consistency of purpose with WCCI and may be carried out by an individual or other agency with the concurrence of a majority of the Board.

WCCI Presidents and Vice Presidents

Term	President	Vice President
1971–1972 (Interim)	Margarita Quijano, Mexico	Norman Overly, USA
1972–1975	Margarita Quijano, Mexico	Norman Overly, USA
1975–1978	Edward Edmonds, Canada	Anne Akpofure, Nigeria
1979–1981	Louise Berman, USA	Jaime Diaz, Colombia
1982–1984	Jaime Diaz, Colombia	Estela Matriano, USA
1985–1987	Estela Matriano, USA	Frithjof Oertel, Germany
1988–1990	Norman Overly, USA	Frithjof Oertel, Germany
1991–1993	Swee-Hin Toh, Malaysia (resigned as president-elect) Frithjof Oertel, Germany (Board-elected replacement)	Gulab Chaurasia, India
1994–1996	Gulab Chaurasia, India	Shigekazu Takemura, Japan
1997–1999	Shigekazu Takemura, Japan	Piyush Swami, USA
2000–2002	Piyush Swami, USA	Olu Odusina, Nigeria

In addition to programs that grow out of the global relationships, regional and local affiliates are encouraged to organize and develop local programs and projects. When they have been realized, it has been common for them to result in publications, conferences, and various types of professional meetings as well as in sponsorship of cross-cultural and nationally specific research and development projects. National or regional groups have been formed in North America, The Philippines, Japan, India, Chile, Nigeria, and the Mediterranean Africa and Arabic Speaking Middle East. Most have conducted conferences and produced publications that cut across national and cultural lines. It has been an especially important mode of operation because local education is seldom conducted in English only. The practice of involving WCCI members from the wider world organization in the particulars of local and regional programming has helped local educators improve their international understanding and access to global educational knowledge, strategies, and programs.

COMMUNICATIONS AND PUBLICATIONS

Approximately every 3 years a directory of membership is published under the title, "Persons as Resources." The directory is a major vehicle for maintaining communication among the members. It provides complete addresses, and other information when it is made available, such as telephone number, e-mail address, professional responsibilities, research interests, and areas of special interest. The advent of e-mail improved speed of communication, but it has not overcome the problem of heavy local professional responsibilities, which mitigate against the type of systematic, intense interaction on global professional issues envisioned by the founders.

A regular journal was inaugurated by the Board of Directors in June 1987 under the editorship of Virginia F. Cawagas of the Philippines. It continued publication from the

Philippines for 4 years until the editor began residency for her doctorate in Canada. In 1991, publication was transferred to Hunter College in New York City, with Nondita Mason and Helene Sherman as editors. After a brief hiatus, it was returned to the editorship of Cawagas in 1998 when she returned to the Philippines. The journal contains articles on significant issues in global education, viewpoints, reports of research, and occasional conference papers. Most of the conference proceedings have been published in bound volumes following the conferences. These publications have usually been the responsibility of the conference planning committee. In addition, working groups have developed special projects for publication under the auspices of WCCI.

Regional groups have published their own reports of proceedings of their conferences and established a variety of modes of communicating within their own regions. Region VI, Canada–USA Chapter of the World Council for Curriculum and Instruction began the WCCI Region VI FORUM in 1997 under the editorial direction of Penelope Flores and Larry Hufford. It continued to flourish and grow through Volume 4 in 2000. Other regions that have had occasional publications include the Philippine chapter, the Arabic speaking chapter in the Middle East and North Africa, the Chilean chapter, and the India chapter. Each holds regional conferences and serves as a major professional organization in their region.

PROBLEMS

The history of the organization has been marked by many problems that were anticipated in part but seldom in their specificity. To some extent, the major problem—cultural hegemony—is the natural outcome of some of the decisions that have been made to make the organization possible and to keep it viable. Fortunately, the participants have recognized that WCCI is a work in process—an effort by individuals to enhance the dialogue and understanding of persons around the world about each other, their cultures, their educational concerns, and their aspirations. Understanding is severely compromised at times because of the difficulties encountered in comprehending the nuances of language among the members when many are forced to function in a second or third language rather than their native tongue.

The financial control resulting from having to function with U.S. currency and the concomitant high cost of functioning on an American financial base makes it nearly impossible for significant numbers of persons from less affluent societies to participate. In addition, the diversity and range of educational issues frequently lead some members to feel marginalized or the issues seem irrelevant or trivial depending on the particular local needs. Perspectives on the nature of knowledge can be a stumbling block, and perspectives on social agendas, which so closely align with educational programs, reflect all the conflicts that continue to ravage the world's people. In some measure, the issues of Palestinian rights, apartheid, religious intolerance, and economic inequities that were present at Asilomar continue to arise as topics of debate and anguish. Yet the triumph is found in the continuing desire and willingness of persons of good will to maintain the dialogue and work on incremental steps toward greater cooperation and understanding.

REFERENCES

Berman, L. M., Miel, A., & Overly, N. (1982). *The World Council for Curriculum and Instruction: The story of its early years.* Bloomington: WCCI, Indiana University.

Miel, A., & Berman, L. (Eds.). (1970). *In the minds of men: Educating the young people of the world.* Washington, DC: Association for Supervision and Curriculum Development.

PART II

Thirty-Four Essays
on Curriculum Studies
in 28 Nations

CHAPTER 5

Curriculum Studies in Argentina: Documenting the Constitution of a Field

Silvina Feeney
University of Buenos Aires, Argentina

Flavia Terigi
University of Buenos Aires, Argentina

Today it is possible to clearly visualize the constitution of a field of curriculum studies at an international level. Many are works that, since the 1970s, disclose the main production centers of curriculum studies and the different theoretical approaches characterizing the field. Moreover, the creation of specialized journals and magazines and the organization of national and international congresses are evidence of the consolidation of this field.

We consider curriculum studies a *discipline or field*,[1] in which not only is an object (the curriculum understood as a text containing a generalized prescription for schools) produced, but discourse on such curriculum is produced as well: expression of problems, debates, and topics that make an impact on practice.

Although the curriculum subject has been present within the academic circles of Argentina for some time, we can assert that there are some distinctive signs of the constitution of a field that are still missing. For example, there are still no specialized publications on the subject. Under the label *curriculum studies*, there are often works of a disputable specialty. However, there are few universities in which there are departments specialized in the subject, often presented rather as a matter of didactics, which, in the local tradition, is focused on the topics related to the theory of education or educational procedures (or of educational policy with its focal point on normative analysis and macroeducational relations). The curriculum could be considered as an object be-

---

[1]The aspects that, according to Schwab (1964), define a theoretical discipline are: (a) Which are the limits of the discipline field? (b) Which are the ways in which evidence is provided and the veracity of certain statements or generalizations? What kind of methodology is legitimate within a certain field of research, which Schwab called *syntax*; and (c) the identification of basic concepts that guide the research and give rise to generalizations of different types—that is, the substantive structure of the discipline.

longing to both fields, but we should not overlook the fact that such a fate would imply the suppression or reduction of some of its central aspects, particularly its connections with a diverse and complex field of culture.

At the same time, the centrality that the curriculum design has gained as a tool for policies of reform of the educational system in our country has promoted multiple experiences of curriculum design, some works on curriculum assessment, and the formation of teams for research on processes for the implementation of curriculum changes.

In this work, our goal is to present the main issues regarding discourse on curriculum that we have surveyed for the period 1983–1998, and to attempt an assessment of the curriculum field in Argentina.

ON THE SURVEYED DOCUMENTATION

Within the proposed frame of concerns, we began the work of collecting the local materials with the objective of covering the majority of the production of discourses on curriculum for the period 1983–1998. In the last 40 years, we have witnessed a real explosion of the theoretical production in the international curriculum field, strongly innovative from the conceptual point of view. Throughout this century, Argentina has been able to receive and put itself on a par with every intellectual innovation, yet it has been late in incorporating those related to the curriculum, even relative to other Latin American countries such as Mexico and Brazil. If the years of military dictatorship were unfavorable for these incorporations, later we understood that, with the beginning of the democratic transition in 1983 and the consequent additional need for restructuring in the education field, a favorable atmosphere was created for the incorporation of a series of foreign productions that were extremely useful for the analysis of the problems of local curriculum practice.

In this work, attention shall be paid to theoretical discourses in those texts that may express ideas and knowledge specialized in the matter in question, generated within what Bernstein (1993) called *primary context.* According to Bernstein, the primary context of production is the place for the development and production of cultural texts, ideas, and specialized knowledge, which are selected for their transmission. In the secondary context, contents are reproduced and transmitted through institutions (schools, high schools, universities, institutes), levels, and specialists (teachers, professors), thus postulating a third type of context (called *recontextualization*) in which the organization of the texts used in the secondary context is based on the production of the primary context.

Although the curriculum field as a whole may be formed by the three types of contexts defined by Bernstein (1993), if we truly want the creation of a field of studies at a national level, it is essential to understand the role of the primary context of production, and that context is the main objective of this work. Regarding this subject, the universe includes the discourses on curriculum—in their primary context—produced by Argentine educationalists during the period 1983–1998, which are circulated in the following formats:

- Books (published in the country by publishers specialized in education).
- Magazines specialized in education (in this country, there are no magazines specializing in curriculum, as is the case in other countries). Many of these magazines belong to departments or institutes for the Research on Education Science from different national universities of this country.
- Other periodical spreading publications, with significant levels of reception at the different levels of the school system.

It was also absolutely essential for us to retrieve documents prior to the time period to be studied—that is, before 1983—and carry out interviews with some educationalists, with the objective of rebuilding pedagogic traditions that may have influenced the consolidation and present condition of the curriculum field in this country.

Before presenting the characteristics of the curriculum discourse in Argentina, we allow ourselves a brief digression on the role that, in our opinion, curriculum studies have played in the broadest field of education. In turn, this digression allows us to better understand how the discourse on curriculum has settled in Argentina.

THE GROWTH IN CURRICULUM STUDIES: TOWARD THE END OF EDUCATIONAL UTOPIAS?

It seems reasonable to assert that the growth in curriculum (focal point of the education reforms in Western countries since the 1980s) and curriculum studies expresses some kind of response to the criticism issued about the function and value of school. We agree with Dussel (1997) when she said that, "Recovering the cultural contents and the notion of transmission within the teaching activity seem to be relatively agreed ways to face the extended crisis of school systems" (p. 11).

In his work "The End of Educational Utopias," Narodowski (1999) performed an analysis of the transdiscursive paradigms of modern pedagogy and pointed out several features of postmodern pedagogy. This analysis is interesting when it comes to considering the field of curriculum studies in Argentina. The author held that the characteristic devices of modern pedagogy have undergone a sort of mutation in the so-called postmodern era.

One of the characteristic devices of modern pedagogy is that of educational utopias. The function that these utopias provide is to delimit great finalities that guide the order of practices and tend to legitimate different proposals. In modern pedagogy, it is possible to find two dimensions in the formulation of utopias: one related to social order and the other related to the education activity.

During the last years of the 20th century, we saw a growing vacancy of utopian postulations that provided totalizing responses. A review of current pedagogic literature shows that pedagogy has lowered its strongly disciplinary tone, which used to guide and properly establish what was right, fair, and true in the education of children and young people. It seems that the school culture crisis entails the possibility of a conciliation between the traditional ideological antagonists, those who are now adversaries, exponents of difference, tolerant, and respectful for the others. Old modern educationalists objected to be combined with the others because that would, presumably, diminish their critical capacity, whereas educationalists of the postmodern condition of culture opt for certain positionings as long as they can maintain their identity.

We could say that at the beginning of this century, there are two different theoretical paths. One recognizes its origin in the critical theories of education. On this path, the sociopolitical utopias of pedagogy—although they are no longer totalizing—have burst out in favor of the understanding of singular elements: class, ethnic group, gender, and cultural option. What the utopian scholars once wanted to discipline within a uniform frame must now be respected and preserved.

On the other path, the utopia of *what for* shuts itself away within the utopia of *how*. Along this line, some educationalists attempt to build an educational will capable of rationally directing the education of children, stimulated by new technologies, scientific achievements in the field of cognitive psychology, and often prescriptions about what to teach and how in the curriculum.

An event that clearly shows the tension between the paths to be followed is the case of the change in the title of the journal *Curriculum Studies* to *Pedagogy, Culture and Society.* In the words of Hamilton (1999), one of the important reasons for the change in the title is that the Anglo-American conceptions of curriculum have become both limited and limiting. Since *Curriculum Studies* was established in 1993, the theorizing on curriculum has become numb. It has lost contact with more profound topics that for centuries have inspired pedagogy and didactics. It has been reduced to issues on the content of education and its distribution within school classrooms. The idea that a curriculum might be a vision of the future and that, in turn, matters of the curriculum might be related to human education has become peripheral. The short-term question—What should they know?—came to replace the strategic curriculum question—what should they become?

The curious aspect of this is how different countries of Latin America have gradually taken a stand regarding curriculum studies. Regarding this subject, the cases of Brazil and Argentina, for our region, are really significant examples of different theoretical positions in curriculum studies.

One of the most important curriculum theorists in Brazil, da Silva (1999a, 1999b), suggested a curriculum conception based on a dynamic notion of culture understood in terms of creation, in terms of production within a context of negotiation, conflict, and power relations. In another one of his works, together with Moreira (Moreira & da Silva, 1999), the authors mentioned subjects and issues—old and emerging—in the field of curriculum in Brazil. Among them is the concept of *hidden curriculum* (not from the point of view of its frequent and easy use, which has led to a certain trivialization of the concept, but with the purpose of denaturalizing and historicizing the curriculum to propose alternatives that may transgress the existing curriculum order). They also expressed the need to review the disciplinary structure that seems to be one of the untouchable elements of the curriculum, especially for the purpose of understanding that this is one of the issues that have such a profound impact that they contribute to the indifference that the school curriculum shows to the ways in which popular culture (TV, music, video games, magazines) is presented to young people and adults. They also highlighted the role of new technologies—not only as regards the transmission of knowledge, but as regards the specific contents of knowledge as well.

Although these debates have taken the center stage within the field of curriculum studies today, they can only be slightly related to certain issues that are part of the curriculum discourse in Argentina. We can assert that the situation of the Argentine field is rather different from the subject matters characteristic of its international peers.

MAIN NOTES OF THE DISCOURSE ON CURRICULUM IN ARGENTINA

What are the central issues and debates in the field of curriculum studies in Argentina? What is the role of curriculum specialists? What are the features of the intellectuals and scholars who work in this field?

Between 1983 and 1998, 29 books on curriculum were published and 25 articles on this subject were written in academic magazines specialized in education. The progression year by year tells us that, for the studied period, the publication of books on curriculum has only recently begun to show a significant increase in volume since 1994, with a similar situation in the case of magazine articles.

If we analyze the list of authors of books and magazine articles, we would not find significant recurrences. There are only a few cases of authors who have published articles in magazines about something that, prior to or after its publication, became a book on that subject matter.

If we consider the subject matters, in our country there is a concentration of theoretical production on curriculum in the subject matters of design, development, and innovation of the curriculum.

Up to the present day, we have seen a significant separation of knowledge as regards the curriculum: The surveyed discourses account for a wide range of subjects with little development about the theoretical problems of the field. Two types of recurrent subjects appear: One involves prescriptions about the construction of curriculum design, and another involves the subject of curriculum innovation.

If we consider the field conceptualization by Bourdieu (1995)[2] regarding curriculum studies, the interchange among producers of curriculum discourse in Argentina becomes difficult because there are no game rules common to all of them: There is no single market where intellectual production may circulate. Moreover, the limits that separate them from other similar fields are not clear (e.g., from didactics, educational sociology, or educational policy).[3] We can also say there is no degree of accumulated capital—a specific capital the possession of which may act as a requirement for entering into the field.

All of this reveals a weak structuring and a low relative autonomy of the field of curriculum studies in Argentina, which have such an impact that the decision about what is researched and how, and the assessment of those productions, is imposed from the outside from other disciplinary fields with a greater tradition in our country, such as didactics for instance. This characteristic, which we call *satellization*[4] of the discourse regarding curriculum in Argentina, is the fundamental feature that allows us to identify the type of discourse productions by Argentine educationalists.

As mentioned earlier, the majority of the productions on curriculum, according to their subject matter, can be grouped in matters of design or curriculum innovation. This seems to be clearly in keeping with the issues mentioned by Narodowski regarding pedagogy in the postmodern era: concerns focused on how, with a real interest in finding ways to perfect practice, infallible methods and educationalists considered as specialists. This trend is partly justified by the big movement of Education Transformation, which has settled in our country since the year 1989, in which everything related to curriculum policies has played a central role.

---

[2]According to Bourdieu (1995), a field can be defined as a network or configuration of relations among positions. The field can be compared to a game. Thus, there are bets resulting from the competition between the players, an investment in the game, illusion: the players become trapped by the game. If there are no antagonisms, sometimes ferocious, between them, it is because they place a belief (doxa) in the game and the bets—an acknowledgment that is not called into question (the players, by participating in the game, accept that such a game is worth playing). In every field, there are valid and efficient cards—called *victories*—the relative value of which varies according to the fields and the successive states of a single field. In every field, there is also a capital that is the efficient factor of a given field and allows its holder to exercise a power—an influence—to exist in a determined field.

[3]It is appropriate to mention the impact of the disciplinary field of Education Sociology or to insist on that of Education Policy in the configuration of the field of curriculum studies in Argentina. However, it is the central objective of this analysis to refer to the relations that link the field of curriculum with that of didactics.

[4]Satellite (from the Latin *satelles*, member of an escort) is applied to the state or country that is theoretically independent, but in fact subject to the tutelage of another one more powerful, generally its neighbor. In the field of curriculum, powerful countries would be represented by didactics and education policy, whereas the curriculum would act as a satellite.

This may also be related to the satellization of curriculum studies, which have been included within disciplinary fields with a greater tradition in our country. Understood in terms of negotiation, conflict, and power, as mentioned by Tomaz Tadeu da Silva, the characteristics of the production on curriculum are governed by the theorizing practices[5] considered as valid by didactics. If we are within the paradigm of how, we can expect the production on curriculum to be focused fundamentally on matters of argumentative logic of a technical nature.

Certain conditions of the professional field explain the situation of curriculum theorizing in Argentina. As said earlier, our country has few university departments on this issue, and curriculum is usually approached within the programs of education policy or didactics, the specialists of which are generally interested in research subjects that contribute little to the specific study of curriculum issues. Moreover, there are even fewer research projects, and there are absolutely no specialized magazines that may encourage specific production. For those who are interested in the curriculum field, the best opportunity for development has been the professional activity, insofar as academic centers pay little attention to this matter.

Nevertheless, the processes of educational reform of the 1990s have triggered the work of curriculum elaboration. Thus, today, there are many professionals who have taken part, at least once or for a while, in the elaboration of a curriculum. As a result, curriculum issues have become part of the contemporary pedagogic agenda. Today we talk about curriculum and curriculum devices, whereas years ago we talked about planning, minimum contents, or study plan. Within the frame of the reform processes, the curriculum is outlined as a specific object that is becoming the focal point of relevant analyses. It is also presented as a set of contents in the training of future teachers and professors, which is in line with its importance for the understanding of contemporary education processes.

It is beyond the scope of this chapter to perform a detailed analysis of the consequences that this proliferation of curriculum design works has had in the production of a normative nature on the processes of curriculum elaboration. Our goal is to focus on specialists, not analyze the curriculum reform. Along this second line, it would be essential to resort to the analysis of the texts elaborated by the Federal Education Council and other technical entities in education of our country.

However, it is necessary to point out that the growing political importance of curriculum and its impact on the configuration of new professional entities do not have a recognizable correlative in curriculum production. In particular, in the case of Argentina, there has been little change in the situation that Feldman and Palamidessi (1994) defined once as a normative weakness of curriculum theorizing: The reform processes have not even produced recognized design procedures, parameters for the assessment of curriculum policies, or research programs aimed at producing knowledge on the curriculum processes in its different areas.

---

[5]In the words of Carr (1996),

... One of the ways in which we can begin to take an interest in the relation between theory and practice as a public process is to consider theory and practice in terms of social relations and social structures. We could begin by contemplating this social relations in terms of roles (...) it is not only about separating the places and times in which to theorize from the places and times of practice. (...) The analysis of theory and practice in terms of roles quickly becomes confusing when we think about the complexity of the relations between the theories and practices of the so-called theorists and the theories and practices of the so-called practicalists. We need to clarify exactly what practices (and whose) and what theories (and whose) are considered in each moment. ... (p. 33)

RECENT PRODUCTIONS

Education discourses and theories regarding education are placed within the frame of Social Sciences and are affected by the controversy that has developed around knowledge, science, the notion of reality, the methodology problem, scientific validity, and conceptual rigor, which, although we do not explain specially, we cannot refrain from mentioning.

The set of meanings that appears in Social Sciences and education as a part of them requires a conceptual approach that may bear in mind its complexity: Like any discourse on education, the discourse on curriculum refers to an object that implies a social action. Because of that, it articulates different functions related to practice, and it uses a type of code that characterizes it.

Understanding that messages overlap and have referents in different universes, and that despite that they still become a type of knowledge, means realizing that the visions generated from a center tend to deny the differences—that is, the others. In the case to which we refer, this allows us to understand why, in our country, the discourse on curriculum appears as a satellite of the didactic and political discourses.

However, it is our intention to point out the lack of continuity present in what we could consider the transdiscursive paradigm of curriculum studies in Argentina. Ruptures regarding certain subject matters are beyond the purely technical question (in line with the paradigm of how) and which do not refer to matters of ethnic groups, gender, or singularities.

Regarding this subject, there are many works that, since the 1990s, have begun to account for a growing concern about the generation of a space of production and research on curriculum studies in our country, although late compared with other countries in our region. These scholars point out the need to encourage the consolidation of a space to consider curriculum in Argentina, which, as we have attempted to show, cannot be replaced with other academic traditions.

All of these works have been frequently published in academic magazines or papers in congresses, rather than in a book format. Authors are mostly young and work on different subject matter and from perspectives that are different from one another. Some of them are more focused on theoretical issues concerning the normativity of the curriculum—issues related to teaching practices regarding curriculum. Others are definitely in favor of theoretical reflections and practical actions about what they call *curriculum in action.*

If a place can be defined as a place of identity, relational and historical, how can we relate this concept to the issue we are dealing with? By showing another interpretation of the search for a place for curriculum knowledge in Argentina, trying to understand what this knowledge is generated around, its genealogical construction referring to an instrument (curriculum design), and understanding didactics as a field for reflection, which is the constituent element in the constellation of curriculum knowledge in Argentina.

REFERENCES

Bernstein, B. (1993). *The structuring of pedagogic discourse.* Madrid, Spain: Morata.

Bourdieu, P. (1995). *Respuestas por una antropología reflexiva* (Responses for a reflective anthropology). (1st ed.). Mexico: Grijalbo.

Carr, W. (1996). *Una teoría crítica para la educación* (A critical theory for education). (1st ed.). Madrid, Spain: Morata.

da Silva, T. T. (1999a). *O curriculo como fetiche* (The curriculum as a fetish). (1st ed.). Belo Horizonte, Brazil: Autêntíca.

da Silva, T. T. (1999b. *Documentos de identidade. Uma introduaao ás teorias do currículo* (Identity documents. An introduction to the theories on curriculum). (1st ed.). Belo Horizonte, Brazil: Autêntíca.

Dussel, I. (1997). *Curriculum, humanismo y democracia en la enseñanza Media* (Curriculum, humanism and democracy in secondary education) (1863–1920). (1st ed.). Buenos Aires, Argentina: FLACSO/UBA.

Feldman, D., & Palamidessi, M. (1994). Viejos y nuevos planes: el curriculum como texto normative (Old and new plans: The curriculum as a normative text). In the Magazine *Propuesta Educativa* (Educational Proposal). FLACSO-Miño y Dávila, Buenos Aires Year VI, N_ 11, 69-73.

Hamilton, D. (1999). La paradoja pedagógica (The pedagogical paradox). *Revista Propuesta Educativa* (*Educational Proposal Magazine*), X, N_20, 6–13.

Moreira, A., & da Silva, T. T. (1999). *Curriculo, cultura e sociedade* (Curriculum, culture and society). (3rd ed.). San Pablo: Cortez.

Narodowski, M. (1999). El fin de las utopías educativas. Un adiós sin penas ni olvidos (The end of educational utopias. A goodbye without sorrows or obscurities). (http://argiropolis.com.ar)

Schwab, J. (1964). Structure of the disciplines: Meanings and significances. In *The structure of knowledge and curriculum*. Chicago: Rand McNally.

CHAPTER 6

The Development of Curriculum Thought in Argentina

Mariano Palamidessi
Latin American School for Social Sciences, Buenos Aires, Argentina

Daniel Feldman
University of Buenos Aires, Argentina

This chapter studies the emergence and development of curriculum thinking in Argentina. It intends to present a survey of the changing conditions that have marked curriculum theory's reception, production, and use. For this reason, rather than presenting in detail all the contents in this field of ideas, this chapter focuses on the analysis of forces that model and condition their orientations and operations in the context of Argentine education. On behalf of this effort, the chapter displays a periodization that takes into account the action of the state, the university's activity, and the role of experts within the educational field.

The definition of the field or theory of curriculum has been discussed for more than 30 years.[1] This definition does not seem to be an epistemological matter, but rather a problem related to the characterization of a series of social and historical practices. The curriculum is a cultural construction, and its meanings depend on the way in which a political-educative tradition is built. The different conceptions are a product of diverse ways of understanding the relations among schools, state, and society. Hence, a way to study curriculum—and the ideas on curriculum—is to study the course of a tradition characterized by certain governments, classifications, and control strategies. If this point of view is adopted to study the development of the curricular thinking in Argentina, it is necessary to analyze how policies on educative contents and the processes for scholarly transmission have changed, and what tools were used for the understanding and decision making on these matters. This is why this chapter describes the evolution of curriculum thinking in Argentina, taking into account the relationship between the action of the state's educative agencies and the intellectual field of education. According to the variations of these agencies' roles, the universities, and the specialized professionals in educa-

---

[1] From the classic works by Pinar (1978), Kliebard (1977), and Huebner (1976), to the more recent ones by Jackson (1992) and Pinar, Reynolds, Slattery, and Taubman (1995).

tion, in Argentina there are four periods with distinctive production, reception, and use of curriculum thought:

1. The hegemony of centralized state regulation on schools and school knowledge: National Education Council's *Planes de Estudio y Programas* (1880–1960).
2. The modernization of the pedagogical field characterized by a scientific shift of the university education courses, the emergence of experts, and of curriculum theory (1960–1975).
3. The military dictatorship (1976–1983) characterized by political repression and the freezing of the educative and curricular debate.
4. The return to democracy and the educative reforms, where a proliferation of curriculum thinking takes place (1984–2000).

THE HEGEMONY OF CENTRALIZED STATE REGULATION ON SCHOOLS AND SCHOOL KNOWLEDGE: THE NATIONAL EDUCATION COUNCIL'S *PLANES DE ESTUDIO Y PROGRAMAS* (1880–1960)

In the last two decades of the 19th century, the mass school system was organized in Argentina with a centralized model, in which the state's action was preeminent. In 1884, the Law N§ 1420 of Common Education was sanctioned. It established 6 years of primary schooling as common and obligatory, the laicism of education, and it sanctioned the curriculum for the common school. With this law, the state subordinated the Catholic Church and the different national and religious communities to state control of the contents and orientations of the educative system. This monopoly of the state would not be questioned until the end of the 1950s.

In the Argentine case, education was organized in relation to a central organism: the National Education Council or the Ministry of Education, which designed educative policies, established the norms, determined the contents and education methods, formed and assigned teachers, administered and supervised education, and controlled the alignment of text books. During its first 80 years, the Argentine educative system guaranteed its unity and coordination through a hierarchic and highly centralized structure. Despite the constitutional dispositions that consecrated political federalism, the actual government of the system was centralized.

School knowledge and objectives were defined by a political-administrative norm. Through the *Planes de Estudios*[2] of the Capital and National Territories, the National Education Council established the guideline used by the Provincial Councils to compose their plans. Until the 1960s, the Program Commissions of the National Council and Provincial Education Councils, in charge of the elaboration of the *Planes de Estudio y Programas*, were constituted almost exclusively by personnel that belonged to the educative system (professors, directors, or supervisors).

Within this institutional frame, there were few possibilities for the development of alternative definitions of school knowledge. This did not imply the lack of discussion concerning school knowledge or the objectives of education, but the centralization of the government and curriculum definition was barely questioned because, as Puiggrós (1990) pointed out, "... with exception of the anarchists, all the sectors accepted the

---

[2]*Planes de Estudios* is the official document that sanctions and organizes a course of studies, as well as prescribes the subjects and levels that correspond to a school grade along with its mission, objectives, and groups of contents. Generally, a *Plan de Estudios* presented a series of methodological directions for teachers. The *Programas* gave analytic details on the subject's contents.

State educative system as the unique or privileged scene for the struggle over curriculum" (p. 264).[3] Although throughout 80 years intense debates related to contents and methods took place, the instructional matrix defined in the 1880s continued regulating primary school curriculum until the beginning of the 1970s (Palamidessi & Feldman, 1999; Palamidessi, Dodero, Larripa, & Oelsner, 2000). During this period, the theoretical tradition that maintained the educative language and referred to education activities did not employ the idea of curriculum. From the conformation of its educative system, education in Argentina was organized according to the pedagogy and didactics tradition. The former is taken as a general education theory, and the latter like a theory of method or a specification of instruction processes. Much later, the theoretical references are expanded and other languages are integrated in the discussion on educative matters.

MODERNIZATION OF THE EDUCATIONAL FIELD AND THE EMERGENCE OF CURRICULUM THEORY (1960–1975)

In the educational field, the end of the 1950s and 1960s were characterized by a process of modernization and professionalization. National technical planning organisms were created, and the modernization of the state was promoted through the fortification of a new body of professionals (sociologists; economists; statistics professionals; experts in management, planning, and evaluation). In 1966, the military government (1966–1973) created the National Development Council, which made the first scientific diagnosis of Argentine education.[4] In the same year, the Ministry of Education created a Curriculum office.

At the same time, university studies on education acquired a scientific status and professionals' education began to differ from professors' education. In 1958, the Educational Sciences degree was initiated at the University of Buenos Aires, replacing the degree in pedagogical studies, which were clearly generalist and philosophical. During this period, the sprouting and expansion of these university careers consolidated a new professional, permanent, and specialized sector: the B.Sc. in Educational Sciences. This new professional group became part of the staff of the technical offices that supported the modernization of the state.

Curriculum theory began to appear in Argentina toward the second half of the 1960s through continental initiatives like the Alliance for Progress and the actions of organisms like the Organization of American States, UNESCO, and the International Evaluation Association. Along with Mexico, Argentina became a center of diffusion of this bibliography for Spain and Latin America. The preparation of human resources and the constitution of national centers for curriculum development was promoted through publications, seminaries, scholarships, and other activities.[5] Along with other specialized discourses, the appearance of curriculum reading material indicated the growing influence of the North American production in the Argentine pedagogical thinking. During this period, the first works on curriculum, coming mainly from the United States, were published in Argentina. Publishing houses like Troquel, El Ateneo,

---

[3]Although the author referred to the period of 1880–1916, the observation is valid for all the decades considered here.

[4]We are referring to the CONADE report (1967).

[5]In 1971, sponsored by UNESCO, an Argentine commission participated in the International Seminary on Curricular Development in Granna (Sweden), presided by B. Bloom and R. Tyler. The aim of this seminary was to promote the creation and strengthening of national curriculum planning units. Professor Alicia W. de Camilloni participated in this seminar and, on her return, coordinated the elaboration of the 1972 Curricular Outlines (Prof. Alicia Camillioni, personal interview, May 2000).

Kapelusz, Marymar, Paidós, or Losada, offered a great amount of translations of American authors like R. Tyler, H. Taba, R. Doll, J. Schwab, J. Michaelis, B. Bloom, and W. Ragan.[6] Other works came from Mexican and Spanish publications. New technologies were spread through the curriculum theory—evaluation theory, the formulation and taxonomies of operational objectives—and at the time were taken to represent the modernization of education.

The diffusion of curriculum theories took place in the middle of an intense process of renovation of the Argentine didactic-pedagogical thought. This process included the reformulations and questioning related to Jean Piaget's work, the modernization of the curriculum for science education, the proposal for the integration of curricular areas, the debates on global teaching methods, the introduction of modern mathematics and structural grammar, a nondifferentiated education by genders, and the questioning of nationalist and patriotic tradition. Curriculum discussion entered into a discursive field crossed by pedagogical and methodological discussions that acknowledged manifold theoretical references.

In the heart of this complex renovation process, it was due to the state's action that the concepts of *curriculum* and *curricular planning* spread throughout the pedagogical field. The Educative Reform carried on between 1968 and 1971[7] actively promoted the planning and operative formulation of didactic objectives that became the official technical-pedagogical discourse. Although the implementation of the reform failed, a new language was installed. Toward the beginning of the 1970s, the word *currículo* replaced the denomination *plan de estudios* in initial and primary level.

From that moment on, and in an increasing way, the national and provincial commissions in charge of the curricular design were controlled and led by university experts. This new professional group assumed spaces and functions formerly occupied by directors, professors, and supervisors. Despite its failure, the Educative Reform managed to modify teachers' training. The functions of secondary level schools for teacher education (*Escuelas Normales*) were transferred to higher education institutes for teacher training. This contributed to an increase in curricular bibliography. Works on curriculum had begun to spread in some professorate institutes in the mid-1960s, mainly through published works and personal translations of the most relevant works, like those of Tyler and Taba. In opposition to the normalist tradition that was hegemonic in the educational field, the university's scientist-positivist line and the prolongation of the teacher training career created a market for these new discourses.

In the university, there was little production on curriculum. Between 1966 and 1973, during the military government, the university lost its autonomous status. Many professors from Educational Sciences courses resigned from their positions. This situation ended a decade of university blossoming and modernization.

The first systematical works produced in Argentina on curriculum issues were, in the first place, textbooks for professorate students for primary level and, in some cases, for university students. The authors were generally graduates from the new higher education courses. Their intellectual production was oriented mainly to the demand of the editorial market. With their entrance in this field, new reading material occupied

---

[6]We are referring to the Spanish versions of the books by Saylor and Alexander (1966), Doll (1968), Ragan (1968), Bloom (1971), Tyler (1973), Schwab (1974), Taba (1974), and Michaelis, Grossman, and Scott (1974).

[7]The Educative Reform (1968–1971), impelled during General Onganía's military government, tried to reform the organization of the educative system, which was constituted by a 7-year primary school (ages 6–12), and a 5-year secondary school (ages 13–17). This reform created the intermediate school (ages 11–14). Due to the opposition of the greatest part of the public opinion and teachers and professors, the project was abandoned when the government fell.

the place formerly occupied by the general didactic manuals used in the Normal Schools. Among others, works like *Curriculum* by Sarubi (1971), *Curricular Planning* by Combetta (1971), *School Planning* by Galacho (1973), and *The Teacher's Task* by Avolio de Cols (1975) were published. They were the first Argentine texts on this matter. These authors systematized curriculum perspectives in a canonical presentation of Tyler's rationale. This initial curricular Argentine bibliography is structured around the following points:

- Curriculum is identified with a rational and scientific approach for decision making in educative matters. Opposed to the *plan de estudios* and the teaching programs, where the predominance of the study subjects is consecrated, curriculum supposes an integral and systemic methodology oriented to a planned production of educative experiences: "*Currículo* is synonymous of integral planning of the activities in school life" (Combetta, 1971, p. 46).
- New divisions of the pedagogical work are legitimized. According to this, the experts must consider the aspects related to the scientific grounds and the structural conception, whereas teachers must make operative the subordinated objectives (didactic, classroom objectives) of the curriculum.
- Curriculum theory is located in the traditional modern line. As the author of the prologue of Doll's (1968) book emphasizes:
    Perhaps the time has come for the real formulation of a curriculum that takes into account our present society's demands and the technological culture that identifies it. If Latin American countries, in their diverse degrees of development, have not obtained that culture still, there is no doubt they are on their way or about to obtain it, and consequently they must be prepared to live according to that model. Therefore, the transformation of curriculum is urgent. This is a responsibility of those who conduct education and this task will help those who must be prepared in all the levels of the educative system to orchestrate and put a start to the curriculum that our education demands. (p. 2)[8]

In these local versions, Tyler's scheme coincides with the existing bureaucracy of the government of the educational system. Modern planning does not modify the official levels in which curriculum is planned. Although they emphasize the school's innovating role, the state remains the central player in curricular change and decision making.[9]

Many of the professionals who used the curricular theory assumed the dominant systemic premises in the bibliography of the time. Nevertheless, curricular inquiry became highly contentious, and these disputes influenced Argentine curriculum inquiry. The Argentine reaction was diverse. The interpretation conducted by the Argentine pedagogical field in these years recognized two great lines. On the one hand, a technical version of the curriculum theory based on operational objectives, standard evaluation, and efficiency. On the other and opposing hand, a democratic perspective regarding what was taught and how it was taught in schools. This latter group, the progressives, promoted an integral planning as a possibility for strengthening teacher's autonomy. Bounded partly by these sectors, and accompanying the radical political movements that grew in the Argentine society, incipient university groups were

---

[8]The same considerations can be found in the works of Lafourcade (1970) and Martínez (1970).

[9]As Avolio de Cols (1975) affirmed, "It is essential for the curriculum to respond to a country's Educative Policy, which is at the same time part of a National Policy. Curriculum must serve a type of man and a type of society, it must defend the achievement of the established goals in each country's National Project. A curriculum that does not instrument an authentically national Educative Policy will fail and will be rejected" (p. 130).

formed, and they used broad theory references to criticize extant scholarship. A younger group of scholars in the University of Cordoba started off a scholarly production that articulated pedagogical thought with social class and cultural power primary; this production was based on a questioning of the technical paradigm.[10]

During these 15 years, the reception of the North American theory and the local thought on curriculum became associated with the different movements and modernizing projects of Argentine education. Curriculum matters came across a series of conflicts characterizing this field: the modernizing projects of the traditional educative system that the state—first civilian and soon military government—tried to impose, and the resistance that society and teachers expressed to this. In this context of increasing political conflicts, the appropriation and reading of curriculum theory were part of a wider movement that began to question pedagogical traditions at issue.

THE MILITARY DICTATORSHIP: REPRESSION AND THE POLITICAL-EDUCATIVE "FREEZE" (1976–1983)

In 1976, in a context of acute social and political antagonisms, the armed forces took control of the state and suspended constitutional guarantees. The so-called *National Reorganization Process* did not intend to modernize society with a government of technicians and planning experts as a main goal. This government attempted to refound the political, economic, and cultural behaviors of the Argentine society through a militarized authoritarian state and an open market.

During this period, the educational system was a privileged target for the military repression: the disappearance or expulsion of professors and students, the banning of certain books, and the imposition of rules that reinforced traditional ways of relationship and authority. The military government and the Catholic Church hierarchy agreed on the necessity of *cleaning* and *putting order to the educative system*: to eliminate the opposition in schools and universities, and reform the curricula to fight the spreading of *subversive* ideas. Many of its actions were guided by a sense of *war* against the subversion of *order*. Universities were closed and soon were administered by authorities designated by the military power.

In a public scene that was almost exclusively dominated by the unilateral decisions of the state power, a freezing of the educative debate took place, with a profound retrocession of pedagogical reflection. The expulsion (or exile) of professors deeply affected the faculties of Social Sciences and Humanities. The chairs were assigned to personnel who had bonds with the church or nonpolitical technicians. The intervention in universities and the military control of the educative system radically modified the production conditions of the recently born curricular theory and practice. Censorship and ideological control obstructed the arrival of authors or critical points of view on the subject.

During those years, the provinces modified their curricular norms to apply the Minimum Contents defined in 1977 by the military government. In fact, technicians' activ-

---

[10]This group, constituted between others by Eduardo Remedi, Alfredo Furlan, Gloria Edelstein, Susana Barco, and Azucena Rodríguez, developed a critical view on the educative processes, articulating the pedagogical reflection with sociological, anthropological, and historical perspectives. Without using the pedagogical language yet, this group thought about the methodological aspects of teaching, setting a difference with the technical rationality (Edelstein & Rodríguez, 1974). In this sense, they created lines of thought that anticipated postdictatorship curricular thinking. Many of these ideas and discussions circulated in meetings, debates, and events without being written, which was quite common in the university activity at the moment (Prof. Gloria Edelstein, personal interview, September 2000). Some years later, members of this group (Eduardo Remedi and Alredo Furlan) continued working on these lines of thought in exile, contributing to the development of curricular thinking in Mexico.

ity continued and was even expanded, but this happened without any debate or public discussion. In a context of strong censorship and political vigilance, the only curricular theory published followed a technical profile.

RETURN TO DEMOCRACY AND EDUCATIVE REFORMS: THE DIVERSIFICATION OF CURRICULAR THINKING (1983–2000)

In 1983, Argentina returned to constitutional order. The government of President Alfonsín (1983–1989) marked a period of cultural reactivation and reopening of possibilities for expression. In that context, the educative system was considered a central medium to modify the authoritarian culture. The democratization of education was carried out by expanding the matriculation, increasing participation in the school government (Student Centers, School Councils), and promoting a pedagogy focused on the student.

At the same time, the normalization of the universities and renovation of its professorate took place. This process was significant in the fields constituting Education, Humanities, and the Social Sciences, all of which had been especially affected by the military repression. This produced an updating of theoretical approaches and specialized bibliographies. The courses comprising programs in the Educational Sciences and the Institutes for teacher training modified and updated their curricula. For the first time, some universities created curriculum chairs.

During the second half of the 1980s, political debate understood modernization as the democratization of society's structures and institutions. In the educational field, the debate was centered on the school's reproductive or democratic function, including the possibilities of participation provided by school government and the updating of the curricular content. Toward the end of the 1980s, certain critical perspectives on curriculum had begun to spread through texts of a small group of Mexican and Spanish authors who translated and systematized the debates and thoughts of the Anglo-Saxon curriculum field.[11] Thanks to those works and translations, the Argentine academics got to know the discussion between the Tylerian tradition and the reconceptualization of curriculum studies. The British curriculum sociology and the neo-Marxist versions began to be considered in Argentine scholarship (see e.g., Bernstein, 1985; Apple, 1987; Giroux, 1990). These years allowed the academic community to update its knowledge of curriculum scholarship—a concept that was becoming more and more elusive and compelling.

The educative agenda changed during the 1990s. If the previous years were marked by democratization as the main issue, the 1990s were characterized, as in almost all of Latin America, by a process of general reform of the educative system. In a context of deepening market reforms and an opening up of the national economy, in 1992, an important administrative reform that transferred the whole national educative system (except for national universities) to the provincial states was completed. In 1993, the first organic and general law on education was sanctioned: the Federal Education Law. This law modified the structure and functions of the cycles and levels in the educative system. The Ministry of Education began a complex reform of school organization and design, and an updating of curriculum content on a big scale at national and provincial levels was undertaken. As a result of this process, the decentralization promoted by the reform was limited by new mechanisms of control on the composition of curriculum, evaluation, and teacher training.

The reform process stimulated the diffusion of curricular bibliography that had recently begun to circulate in universities toward the educative system. This occurred

---

[11] Among these works, we can mention Gimeno Sacristan (1984), Gimeno Sacristan and Gómez (1985), Glasman and Ibarrola (1987), and Furlan (1989).

through two mediums: (a) with the fluent circulation of personnel between the universities and the political-educative organisms from the national state and the provinces, and (b) with the generalization of processes of teacher professionalization. Consequently, notions of hidden, implicit, explicit, and prescript curriculum began to circulate among school teachers, professors, directors, and supervisors. Soon curricular language colonized the pedagogical language, working like a vehicle for the diffusion of slogans and educational mottos.

Unlike what happened during the 1960s and 1970s, this second moment of incoming curricular theory recognized manifold sites of scholarship, among them scholarly work from Spain, Brazil, Mexico, Great Britain, and Australia. The Argentine scholarly discussion of curriculum in these years recognized a noticeable influence from the educative reform debates in Spain. The point is that the controversy between an educational reform promoted by the National State—based on a neo-Tylerian outline and materialized in the work of Coll (1985)—and the critical position of a group in the education academy that vindicated the reform centered in the school, the professor's professional role, and the curriculum as a process.[12] In Argentina, both lines of thought coexisted with tension. The Reform vindicated the ideas of local problem resolution and the new role of the professor as a reflexive professional. But in Argentine conditions, due to the lack of resources, pedagogical traditions, and the usual ways of government, these projects turned into hybrids that tried to bring together a top–down rationality of curricular reform with the idea of change centered in the school.

In the 1990s, local productions of curriculum issues recommenced. In these productions, curricular problems and issues became diversified. At the present time, curriculum had different uses and was studied from different frames of interpretation (a detailed analysis of local bibliography produced in the last decade can be found in Feeney, 1999). For the needs of this work, it is enough to identify some aspects of this production based on the relevance they have acquired in the game of positions between the pedagogical field and the state. We outline the following sectors of scholarship and development:

1. *The planning, designing, and organization of curriculum.* These works intend to define conceptual and/or methodological models to orient the processes of curricular design (see Terigi, 1993; Braslavsky, 1996). Many of these works have come from technical documents produced in official organisms. A particularly influential line within this group has focused on content selection, emphasizing scientific and epistemological update of school content (see Frigerio, 1991). These works have been an important part of the intellectual basis of the last decade's reform policies.

2. *The government and management of scholastic institutions.* These works analyze the micropolicy and institutional cultures to generate processes of consensus building in the educational sector and in the community. In some cases, they try to explain the dynamics of curricular processes of an institution in contexts of change, crisis, and uncertainty. Usually these texts propose intervention models and tools of for institutional planning (see Frigerio, Poggi, & Tiramonti, 1992; Birgin, 1996; Poggi, 1998). With the bureaucratic demands that reform initiatives imply, this bibliography is read by the ministries' technical staff, school supervisors, and directors.

3. *The relationship among curricular policies, professors' action, and school practices.* Research on the development of curriculum in schools and the translation strategies that teachers and professors have toward official plans has been carried out in the

---

[12]Among others, Gimeno Sacristan, Pérez Gómez, and Contreras Domingo, whose production is influenced by English works (specially by the works of Lawrence Stenhouse and John Elliot).

university. Employing a nonrationalist vision, these works focus on curricular change. They develop a more complex perspective on the effects of the educational reforms in schools and try to produce local theory on the conditions and possibilities of educational change (see Palamidessi, 1993; Feldman, 1994; Feldman & Palamidessi, 1994; Gvirtz, 1997; Dussel, Tiramonti, & Birgin, 1998).

4. *The curriculum's daily accomplishment.* This issue has concerned investigators related to cultural approaches, symbolic interaction perspectives, and developments on neo-Marxist theory in education. These works, based on ethnographic methodologies, analyze school experience from a daily life perspective. Some of the topics taken are gender, identity, teachers' work, discourses of professionalization, and intensified scholarship regarding conditions of poverty and marginality (see Morgade, 1993; Duschatzsky, 1999).

5. *The history of the curriculum.* Recently, there have been approaches to aspects related to curriculum development in the Argentine educative system. These works analyze traditional aspects of the Normal Schools, the origins of secondary school, or the evolution of curriculum in elementary education. In some cases, these studies are connected with the analysis of the present articulations among state, school, and curriculum.[13]

It is possible to find works concerned about teacher training or university curriculum that disclose diverse intersections with the sectors mentioned earlier (see Suárez, 1994; Diker & Terigi, 1997; Davini, 1998; Edelstein & Litwin, 1993; Araujo, 1994).

Despite the increase and diversification of the production shown by these trends of scholarly work, by some indicators it is possible to affirm that curriculum as a field of study has not been formally established in Argentina. First, Argentine curricular production continues to be scarce and unsystematic.[14] Systematic research programs practically do not exist. Theoretical works are scarce, and a good part of these are written for the market of teacher education and training (see Gvirtz & Palamidessi, 1998; Terigi, 1999). Second, the identity and institutionalization in the processing of curricular matters is weak. It is improbable for the authors of each one of the issues identified here to recognize themselves as part of a common space. There are no publications, associations, or specific congresses that define agenda issues with certain regularity. It is also not possible to recognize a body of experts in design and curricular development with specific credentials and systematic written production. Finally, the academic incorporation of the curricular problematic is still recent. Although by the mid-1990s a market for postgraduate study had opened, much of it was oriented toward management, educative policies, or didactics.

In the preceding periods, curriculum was bonded to the state (which had a privileged role in the educational change), the modernization tasks, and the rational design methods. Curriculum was a language for experts. However, in this last decade, there was a diversification of the agents of curricular change. The meanings and uses of the term *curriculum* were also diversified and became part of educators' common sense. The theoretical-academic field related to curriculum theory has not managed to acquire a strength

---

[13]We must mention the academic work produced over the APPEAL project lead by Adriana Puiggrós. The work on curriculum history has been stimulated in the last years by the creation of the Argentine Society for Education History. Among many other works, we can quote those of Puiggrós (1990), Dussel (1993, 1997), and Caruso (1995).

[14]This lack of local works on curricular matters has been documented by Feeney (1999). The author concluded by pointing out that, "although there were curricular practices since the decade of 1960, there was little or no theoretical work in this field to accompany them (...)" (p. 6).

that is concomitant with the prestige and enormous diffusion that the idea of curriculum has acquired as well as with the use that educational policies have made of it.

THE PRESENT AND FUTURE
OF CURRICULAR THINKING IN ARGENTINA

Up to this point, we have focused on the different periods that mark the development of the curricular thought in Argentina. Based on this description, the possibilities and restrictions for their development as a field of studies are reviewed.

As a synthesis of what has been discussed, we can say that the period from 1880 to 1960 was characterized by a monopoly of the state over the control of decisions and educative management, and by the absence of a body of experts. A new period began in the decade of 1960. In this phase, projects to reform the structure of the educative system and modernize state management were activated. At the same time, the consolidation of a scientific direction in university studies and the preparation of specialized staff increased the participation of the academic field in educational matters. However, this process was frozen during the military dictatorship in the 1970s.

From 1984 on, with the return of constitutional institutions and the normalization of university life, a new incoming of curricular theory took place, with greater emphasis in its critical approaches. In this period, local production on curriculum was diversified. Approaches, topics, and concerns proliferated, and the curriculum discourse began to be used in the debate on issues previously discussed in terms of the conceptual language of pedagogy or didactics. In a context of structural system reforms in the 1990s, curricular discourse played an important part in legitimizing the state policies and the expert's role.

Unlike the first moment of diffusion of curricular thought, which was more worried about design and implementation problems, the production of the last 15 years paid more attention to aspects related to the processes of implementation, institutional dimensions, and the role of teachers in the development of curriculum. Yet the increasing acceptance of certain principles among educators and experts—like the idea of curricular development based on the school, the role of the professor as an investigator, and the institutional autonomy—were not seen in a sustained and increasing theoretical production.

In this last period, the development of curriculum thought increased remarkably. Nevertheless, there is still a noticeable disproportion between the popularization of curricular language and systematic theoretical production. Despite the early and quick development of its educative system and the solid tradition of its pedagogical thought, Argentina did not make important advances in the consolidation of research and theoretical production on problems related to the definition and distribution of school content and to the debate over the sense schooling has now. From our point of view, this can be partly explained by the converging of three characteristics.

The Permanence of a Centralizing Tradition

Many authors have pointed out the close relationship between the development of curriculum theory and the educative system's organizational guidelines (see Lundgren, 1992; Furlan, 1989). It is logical to think that the generation of this theory acquires different outlines in centralized or decentralized educative traditions. As described before, the centralizing tradition marked the origin and evolution of the Argentine educative system up to the present time. A discursive motto of the reforms initiated in the last decade consisted of praising the advantages of the system's decentralization and the autonomy of schools. Nevertheless, despite these declarations, the processes undertaken maintained the power of decision making, the technical capacity, and the resources and funding centralized in the National State (and in the provincial states in a smaller degree). In this scheme, schools and the professor bodies do not have effective curricular and programmatic autonomy. This was only possible in some institutions of the private school management subsystem, which counted on resources and instruments to adapt itself to the reform processes.

The Incomplete Professionalization of Academic Institutions

The modernization and differentiation of the university studies on education began toward the end of the 1950s. Nevertheless, the preparation of professionals is still determined by a generalist matrix: The academic organization did not change substantially, and the structure of long degree courses, with little development of postgraduate education, was maintained. In addition, Argentina suffered the impact of the military dictatorships (1966–1973 and 1976–1983) that did not allow the consolidation of lines of thought in the universities or the creation of continuity among the various groups with interests in curriculum matters.

Continuing fiscal restrictions have prevented the sustained provision of research funding. In the areas of Social Sciences and Humanities, the figure of the full-time professor is not too common, which has made research and reproduction of academic bodies quite difficult. The scholarships and subsidies systems are extremely scarce. The process of professionalization of the academic work, which began over 40 years ago, is still incomplete. When the basic characteristics of the Argentine university system are compared with those of other Latin American countries like Mexico and Brazil, it is possible to see that they have supported more fully the development of the fields constituting the social sciences, humanities, and education. These countries count on important postgrade systems, a full-time academic staff, and institutional continuity. In these countries, the curriculum thinking has reached a greater degree of development, specialization, and institutionalization.

National universities have not adequately supported important works related to schools or educative policies. Despite the influence of the 1918 University Reform that tried to strengthen the connections between universities and social activities, significant associations with the educative system, pedagogical reform movements, or groups of teachers and professors have not been formed.

Little Distinction Between the Intellectual Field of Education and the Activities of Official Agencies

The limitations of the academic activity in Argentina let us understand the conformation and dynamics of the intellectual field of education.[15] This field includes the academic activities that focus on education, some auto-financed research centers, and nongovernmental organisms. It also includes publications directed to a wider public, didactic proposals, books for teachers or text books, diffusion of innovations, consultancies, and teacher training. These professionals carry on educative activities without being involved in the direction or supervision of the elementary or secondary state educative institutions. Generally, they accomplish an important role as pedagogical opin-

---

[15]This sector brings together academic staff and professionals with university credentials that intend to "modify or change ideologies, theories or practices in the process of production of the educative discourse" (Díaz, 1997, p. 358).

ion producers. This specialized field has diverse connections and contact with the state management in Argentina. In fact, many of their members work in state offices with contracts as temporary personnel for technical tasks and, in some cases, like political functionaries. There is high staff mobility, and they are usually not part of the permanent bureaucracy.

In this process of permanent circulation among academic life, professional activity, and state functions, the official and nonofficial pedagogical positions disclose little difference. The members of political management and the members of the academy—even the opponents to the state education policies—frequently have similar references and theoretical positions. The state keeps a wide margin of imposition of the agenda and the rules because of its great capacity to convene personnel. The university academic who works on social and educative subjects has been quite dependent on the funding of the state agencies dedicated to the definition of educative policy and the educative system management.

What is the present role of curricular thought in Argentina? In the period of university reopening, the political and sociological approaches that thought on the authoritarian and excluding aspects installed by the military regimes had a great influence in education courses (see Tedesco, Braslavsky, & Carciofi, 1983). These works offered a useful platform of ideas for the moment of opening and democratization of the educative system, but they lacked a language to approach the problem of school improvement. Howver, the discourse on teaching and school as institution remained with the tradition of didactics—a discipline unable to establish connections between what happens in classrooms, schools, and society. In this context, the curricular theory of the past 15 years offered a zone of intersection for both traditions. The references on curriculum began to work like a kind of franc language for the different specialties and professional educational activities. Curricular language has adapted to the necessities of a professional community with little sense of institutional support and with ever-changing roles. It also legitimized the role of the experts in planning tasks in state offices.

Given global changes in its socioeconomic structure, Argentina has had to face the incorporation of market logics in education management and the accelerated weakening of the state's role as a promoter of a progressive distribution of knowledge and educative opportunities. The consequences of this restructuring of Argentine education should comprise important issues for research and theory development. At the moment, the debate appears as a discursive struggle between the old educating state tradition and the promises of the market. Yet a discussion in these terms will not answer the crucial question about how the new reforms have modified the school's functions and repositioned us as actors. This forces us to think in other terms, and it establishes the need for an intellectual production that recovers the task of articulating, under a pedagogical perspective, the changing connections among social structures, educative policies, and school practices.

Yet this prospect will not be occur if it only rests on an exhortation to theoretical willpower. The future depends on the multiplication of voices and the advances toward a greater autonomy of the different social agencies. Of course, perspectives are uncertain, but the point of such scholarly work is not to assert certainties, but to theorize the conditions for possible progress.

REFERENCES

Apple, M. (1987). *Educación y poder.* Madrid, Spain: Paidós-MEC.
Araujo, S. (1994). Curriculum universitario: Notas para su diseño, evaluación e innovación. *Revista Argentina de Educación, 12*(22), 81–94.

Avolio de Cols, S. (1975). *La tarea docente*. Buenos Aires, Argentina: Marymar.

Bahler, R. (1968). Prólogo. In R. Doll (Ed.), *El mejoramiento del curriculum* (pp. vii–viii). Buenos Aires, Argentina: El Ateneo.

Bernstein, B. (1985). Clase y pedagogías visibles e invisibles. In J. Gimeno Sacristán & A. Pérez Gómez, (Eds.), *La enseñanza: Su teoría y su práctica* (pp. 54–72). Madrid, Spain: Akal.

Birgin, A. (1996). Reflexiones sobre el Proyecto Educativo Institucional y el curriculum. In P. Caballero Prieto (Ed.), *Memorias foro proyectos educativos institucionales*. Bogotá, Colombia: Enfasis Currículo.

Bloom, B. (1971). *Taxonomía de los objetivos de la Educación*. Buenos Aires, Argentina: El Ateneo.

Braslavsky, C. (1996). Gestión curricular, transformaciones y reformas educativas latinoamericanas contemporáneas. Paper at the *I Congreso Internacional de Educación*, Universidad de Buenos Aires.

Caruso. M. (1995). Navidad en febrero: el curriculum liberal clásico y el socialismo argentino (1940–1946). *Revista del Instituto de Investigaciones en Ciencias de la Educación*, 4(6), 64–72.

Coll, C. (1985). *Psicología y Currículum*. Barcelona, Spain: Laia.

Combetta, O. (1971). *Planeamiento curricular*. Buenos Aires, Agentina: Losada.

Consejo Nacional de Desarrollo. (1967). *Educación y recursos humanos en la Argentina*. Buenos Aires, Argentina: Author.

Davini, C. (1998). El curriculum de la formación del magisterio. *Propuesta Educativa*, 9(19), 36–45

Díaz, M. (1997). El campo intelectual de la educación. In J. Larrosa (Ed.), *Escuela, poder y subjetivación* (pp. 333–361). Madrid, Spain: La Piqueta.

Diker, G., & Terigi, F. (1997). *Hoja de ruta. La formación de maestros y profesores*. Buenos Aires, Argentina: Paidós.

Doll, R. (1968). *El mejoramiento del curriculum*. Buenos Aires, Argentina: El Ateneo.

Duschatzky, S. (1999). *La escuela como frontera*. Buenos Aires, Argentina: Paidós.

Dussel, I. (1993). Escuela e historia en América Latina. Preguntas sobre la historia del curriculum. *Revista del Instituto de Investigaciones en Ciencias de la Educación*, 2(2), 62–70.

Dussel, I. (1997) *Curriculum, humanismo y democracia en la enseñanza media* (1863–1920). Buenos Aires, Argentina: EUDEBA.

Dussel, I., Tiramonti, G., & Birgin, A. (1998) Nuevas tecnologías de intervención en escuelas. Programas y proyectos. *Revista de Estudios del Currículum*, 1(2), 132–162.

Edelstein, G., & Litwin, E. (1993). Nuevos debates en las estrategias metodológicas del curriculum universitario. *Revista Argentina de Educación*, 11(19), 79–86.

Edelstein, G., & Rodríguez, A. (1974). El método: factor definitorio y unificador de la instrumentación didáctica. *Revista de Ciencias de la Educación*, 12.

Feeney, S. (1999). *El campo del curriculum en la Argentina. Notas sobre los discursos de pedagogos argentinos a propósito del curriculum (1983–1998)*. Paper at the Primer Congreso de Investigación Educativa, Universidad Nacional del Comahue, Cipoletti.

Feeney, S. (2000). *Documentando los intentos de construcción de un campo. Argentina (1983–1998)*. Paper at the LSU Conference on the Internationalization of Curriculum Studies Conference, Louisiana State University.

Feldman, D. (1994). *Curriculum, maestros y especialistas*. Buenos Aires, Argentina: El Quirquincho.

Feldman, D., & Palamidessi, M. (1994). Viejos y nuevos planes: el curriculum como texto normativo. *Propuesta Educativa*, 11.

Frigerio, G. (Comp.). (1991). *Curriculum presente, ciencia ausente*. Buenos Aires, Argentina: Miño y Dávila.

Frigerio G., Poggi, M., & Tiramonti, G. (1992). *Las instituciones educativas. Cara y Ceca*. Buenos Aires, Argentina: Troquel.

Furlan, A. (1989). Curriculum e investigación. In A. Furlan & M. Pasillas (Comps.), *Desarrollo de la investigación en el campo del curriculum* (pp. 66–79). México: UNAM.

Galacho. N. (1973). *Planeamiento escolar: fundamentos y técnicas para la elaboración de planes por el maestro*. Buenos Aires, Argentina: Kapelusz.

Gimeno Sacristán, J. (1984). *La pedagogía por objetivos: la obsesión por la eficiencia*. Madrid, Spain: Akal.

Gimeno Sacristán, J., & Pérez Gómez, A. (1985). *La ensenanza: su teoría y su práctica*. Madrid, Spain: Akal.

Giroux, H. (1990). *Los profesores como intelectuales*. Madrid, Spain: Paidós-MEC.

Glasman, R., & Ibarrola, M. (1987). *Planes de estudio. Propuestas Institucionales y realidad curricular*. México: Nueva Imagen.

Gvirtz, S. (1997). *Del curriculum precripto al curriculum enseñado. Una mirada a los cuadernos de clase*. Buenos Aires, Argentina: Aique.

Gvirtz, S., & Palamidessi, M. (1998). *El ABC de la tarea docente. Curriculum y enseñanza*. Buenos Aires, Argentina: Aique.

Huebner, D. (1976). The moribund curriculum field: Its wake and our work. *Curriculum Inquiry*, 6(2), 153–167.

Jackson, P. (1992) Conceptions of curriculum and curriculum specialist. In P. Jackson (Ed.), *Handbook of research on curriculum* (pp. 3–40). New York: Macmillan.

Kliebard, H. (1977). Curriculum theory: Give me a for instance. *Curriculum Inquiry, 6*(4), 257–269.

Lafourcade, P. (1970). Filosofía de la educación y diseño curricular. *Revista de Ciencias de la Educación, 3*, 46–56.

Lundgren, U. (1992). *Teoría del curriculum y escolarización.* Madrid, Spain: Morata.

Martinez, M. (1970). El programa de estudios. *Revista Latinoamericana de Educación, 82*, 344–360.

Michaelis, J., Grossman, R., & Scott, L. (1974). *Nuevos diseños para el currículo de la escuela elemental.* Buenos Aires, Argentina: Troquel.

Morgade, G. (1993). El género. Un prisma válido para analizar las relaciones escolares cotidianas. *Revista Argentina de Educación, 20.*

Palamidessi, M. (1993). Del curriculum a la planificación. La construcción del contenido enseñado. Unpublished research report, SECyT-UBA.

Palamidessi, M., Dodero, C., Larripa, S., & Oelsner, V. (2000). De los ramos de estudio a las áreas: Una primera lectura de las clasificaciones del curriculum para la escuela primaria común. Paper at the II Congreso Internacional de Educación: Debates y utopías, Universidad de Buenos Aires.

Palamidessi, M., & Feldman, D. (1999). Principios clasificatorios en los Planes de Estudio para la educación primaria argentina. Paper at the XI Jornadas de Historia de la Educación, Universidad Nacional de Quilmes.

Pinar, W. (1978). The reconceptualization of curriculum studies. *Journal of Curriculum Studies, 10*(3), 205–214.

Pinar, W., Reynolds, W., Slattery, P., & Taubman, P. (1995). *Understanding curriculum.* New York: Peter Lang.

Poggi, M. (1998). *Apuntes y aportes para la gestión curricular.* Buenos Aires, Argentina: Kapelusz.

Puiggrós, A. (1990). *Sujetos, disciplina y currículum en los orígenes del sistema educatvo Argentino.* Buenos Aires, Argentina: Galerna.

Ragan, W. (1968). *El curriculum en la escuela primaria.* Buenos Aires, Argentina: El Ateneo.

Sarubi, M. (1971). *Curriculum. Objetivos. Contenidos. Unidades.* Buenos Aires, Argentina: Stella.

Saylor, J., & Alexander, W. (1966). *Planeamiento del currículo en la escuela moderna.* Buenos Aires, Argentina: Troquel.

Schwab, J. (1974). *Un lenguaje práctico para la elaboración del currículo.* Buenos Aires, Argentina: El Ateneo.

Suárez, D. (1994). Formación docente, curriculum e identidad. *Revista Argentina de Educación, 12*(22), 29–56.

Taba, H. (1974). *Elaboración del currículo.* Buenos Aires, Argentina: Troquel.

Tedesco, J. C., Braslavsky, C., & Carciofi, R. (1983). *El proyecto educativo autoritario. Argentina 1976–1982.* Buenos Aires, Argentina: FLACSO-GEL.

Terigi, F. (1993). *Diseño, desarrollo y evaluación del currículum.* Buenos Aires, Argentina: PTFD-Ministerio de Educación.

Terigi, F. (1999). *Curriculum. Itinerarios para aprehender un territorio.* Buenos Aires, Argentina: Santillana.

Tyler, R. (1973). *Principios básicos del curriculum.* Buenos Aires, Argentina: Troquel.

CHAPTER 7

Curriculum Inquiry in Australia: Toward a Local Genealogy of the Curriculum Field

Bill Green
Charles Stuart University

Curriculum inquiry in Australia is relatively recent as a distinctive (sub)disciplinary formation. In the early 1980s, an official national organization was created to address Australian initiatives in both curriculum inquiry and curriculum work—the Australian Curriculum Studies Association (ACSA). A now well-established journal (*Curriculum Perspectives*) was also formed. Through its biennial conference and publication program, including its journal, ACSA seeks to provide a certain measure of leadership with regard to formal curriculum inquiry, although this is not its primary area of interest or responsibility. More recently, the Curriculum Corporation has provided organizing oversight for the field, albeit from what tends to be an official, systemic, administrative orientation. However, it is certainly not interested in nor charged with the pursuit of formal curriculum inquiry as such. Instead it focuses its endeavors on the practical provision of curriculum leadership and the development of curriculum materials, moreover within more or less received and traditional terms of reference.[1] Hence, the intellectual elaboration of curriculum thought and scholarship has emerged as a more or less unsystematic, sporadic matter, to some extent located in universities or related sites and with varying, arguably limited impact on policy. Perhaps more to the point, curriculum thinking overall has become instrumentalized and largely technical in its orientation: subordinate(d) to policy.

Nonetheless, there is an emerging presence in curriculum inquiry per se, in the work of curriculum scholars such as Noel Gough, and a growing sophistication in the field that warrants attention in this context. Exploring and explicating what is happening in this regard, with particular reference to the Australian scene at the beginning of the 21st

---

[1]Note, however, its conference theme for 2001—"New Curriculum for the Knowledge Age," featuring presentations from a variety of academics, politicians, and senior bureaucrats. Whether it is possible to step outside current-traditional frameworks and think (and speak) differently about curriculum and schooling remains to be sen. On the Curriculum Corporation, see Kemmis (1990) and Piper (1997) [Chapter6].

century, is the task I undertake in this chapter. Given the inevitable limitations on such an exercise, and hence the equally inevitable partiality of any such account, I seek to engage with this topic in two main sections. First, I review what I see as the current situation vis-à-vis curriculum inquiry in Australia, understood expressly as a brief *history of the present*. I then turn my attention more squarely to the early part of the 20th century, as in many ways an exemplary and particularly illuminating episode in the emergence and consolidation of the curriculum field in Australia. To begin with, I present a brief account of the theoretical and methodological resources and perspectives as a necessary context for the discussion that follows.

Basically, in describing this account as a local genealogy of the curriculum field, I want to bring together methodological insights and arguments from Foucault and Bourdieu. The latter is important with regard to grasping the specificity of the curriculum field, particularly as it becomes more professionalized and self-referential, even self-serving, *repetitive*, and reproductive of its own self-understandings (Ladwig, 1994). Foucault's influence is evident not only in my commitment to historical inquiry per se, and more specifically the notion of *history of the present* (Tyler & Johnson, 1991), but also in my sense of genealogical investigation as encompassing a nonteleological view of history and change. That is to say, I do not subscribe to the progressivist view of historical practice—that history moves toward what, in the present, is a necessarily more enlightened position. This is not to deny progress or improvement in either scholarship or praxis. Rather, it is to seek to narrate another story, as a *different* catalogue of possibilities and intelligibilities (Tamboukou, 1999).

Reflexive scholarly accounts of the curriculum field in Australia are still rare. There are as yet no major synoptic texts on the distinctive history and character of Australian curriculum and schooling, although there are certainly some that more than usefully gesture in that direction (e.g., Musgrave, 1979; see also Collins & Vickers, 2001). The relative scarcity of scholarship of this kind is perhaps understandable, given that the field, at least in its formal self-understanding, is still quite new. As Marsh (1987) observed some time ago now, "[t]he field of curriculum is very young in Australia, certainly no more than a decade" (p. 7). Yet there have been clear indications that the situation *is* changing. "Curriculum theory has a foothold in Australia at the present time," as Marsh (1987, p. 23) also noted, referring specifically to the late 20th century, and there are signs of growing maturity, sophistication, and innovation in the Australian scene. Among many such signs, one that is especially relevant here is a steadily growing recognition of and engagement with new theoretical discourses. Linked to this is the emerging significance of curriculum history, moreover increasingly and explicitly within a reconceptualist frame of reference (e.g., Cormack & Green, 2000). As Pinar and his colleagues (1995) wrote: "The study of curriculum history … has emerged in the 1980s as one of the most important sectors of contemporary curriculum scholarship" (p. 42). Their work suggests that a properly informed historical awareness is an appropriate sign of paradigmatic maturity:

> Scholars are acutely aware that curriculum work exists in time, in history, and this self-consciousness regarding the historicity of curriculum work, theoretical or institutional, has helped support the increasing interest in historical studies of curriculum. (Pinar et al., 1995, p. 42)

The paucity of readily available Australian curriculum history has been noted by various commentators, as has its effect. As Seddon (1989) observed: "The dearth of Australian curriculum history is to be regretted. It means that Australian curriculum workers do not know their own past; neither the curricular past, nor the history of their profession" (p. 1). Understanding educational change as a temporal process with its own rhythms and durational texture, she suggested, requires a historical imagination—one that takes full account of the complex relationships among past, present, *and* future. This is echoed by Marsh and Stafford (1988), in a chapter acknowledged to be one of the first substantive accounts of Australian curriculum history: "knowing and understanding the past assists us in placing all we do in perspective" (p. 195).

Similarly, Musgrave (1987) pointed to the fact that curriculum research and development as a distinctive field is not only relatively recent, dating back at most to the 1970s, but, until recently, largely unorganized and without a supporting archive. As he wrote: "Before the 1960s, almost all curricular development was undertaken at the state level by the Curriculum and Research (or similarly named) branches of state education departments." Although "[s]ome work was also done by state examination bodies and subjects associations," he continued, "[v]ery little was or is known about the activities of these bodies," mainly because "the reports, particularly the official ones, are brief" (Musgrave, 1987, p. 104). Moreover:

> What is even stranger is the paucity of work exploring the outcomes of the different curricula[r] and administrative arrangements in the various Australia states. Comparative education has been taught, and research has been undertaken on overseas systems, but it has not often been defined to include comparisons between the states. (Musgrave, 1987, p. 104)

Such observations remain pertinent today at the onset of the new century. Marsh (1987) pointed to a number of contributing factors (e.g., the lack of a large-scale, fully professionalized and institutionalized curriculum inquiry scene, such as characterizes the United States). Indeed, Australia's population density and attendant demographics might also be noted in this regard. Something else to take into account here is the archetypically bureaucratic character of Australian curriculum and schooling: the fact that it has long been dominated by an administrative logic. Among the effects of such a logic, in practice, has been a general policy amnesia and a lack of due regard for history, manifested as much as anything else in huge gaps and silences in the archive—in sharp contrast, for instance, with the North American scene. The net effect of all this is a profound loss of public-professional memory and increasing interest in the project of curriculum history.

Accordingly, a younger generation of curriculum scholars either based in Australia or with Australian connections, such as David Kirk, Terri Seddon, Bill Green, Bernadette Baker, and others, have sought to build on earlier historically oriented work by people such as Musgrave (1987) and Connell (1970) and also Marsh. Ranging across both general and applied curriculum areas and topics, their work draws eclectically on post-New Sociology of Education literatures and various postmodern critical-theoretical positions and perspectives. Influenced by Foucault and other poststructuralist thinkers, such work often seeks not only to contribute to the historical record, as a resource for praxis, but also to challenge and change the game of curriculum history or, at the very least, to problematize and supplement it. This work needs to be placed alongside and in specific relation to a range of innovative and exciting work also drawing on such influences, and ranging increasingly across feminism, postcolonialism, environmental activism, and cultural studies.

Although curriculum work in Australia remains by and large pragmatic and instrumental in its focus, classroom- and school-oriented, and policy-minded, there is increasingly acknowledgment and exploration of reconceptualist thinking and some indications of a willingness to countenance moving away from a more or less exclusively technical interest. This is partly driven by economic imperatives, but also by the social effects of significant technocultural change and a growing sense of the crisis in modernist mainstream schooling. Among other things, the new digital media has emerged as a rival didactic institution, actively and increasingly engaged in precisely those forms of identity work and capacity building that were once the major task and sacred responsibility of the school.

Work by Boomer (Boomer et al., 1992; see also Green, 1999a, 1999b) is particularly significant in this regard. Described by one commentator as "perhaps Australia's most creative curriculum expert" (Collins, 1995, p. 13), Boomer's explorations of the theory and practice of curriculum negotiation represent a distinctive contribution to the field, ranging as they do from classrooms to systems. Up to his untimely death in 1993, he was also heavily involved in national curriculum developments and debates in Australia. He chaired a major committee of the Australian Educational Council (AEC) charged with organizing and overseeing the introduction of national curriculum statements and profiles (Hughes, 1993). Otherwise he played an important leadership role in what has been undeniably a controversial initiative in Australian curriculum and schooling. What has not been recognized is that his work, originally grounded in English teaching, literacy studies, and language and learning, was emphatically of a reconceptualist stamp, increasingly engaging with new forms of theory and scholarship and in a sense always-already attuned to the so-called *linguistic turn*. As I have written elsewhere, he warrants being more widely acknowledged "not simply as an innovative curriculum thinker but as a leading curriculum theorist, albeit … 'in the practical state'" (Green, 1999b, p. 1–2). An unfinished project *par excellence,* his work nonetheless remains, to my mind, a crucial reference point in late 20th-century curriculum inquiry in Australia.

A further initiative bridging the 20th and 21st centuries in Australian education is the New Basics project—an ambitious attempt to review and redesign curriculum and schooling in and for Queensland. Specifically directed at and initiated by the public education system, the project brings together new principles and practices of curriculum making, organized around the conceptual and rhetorical categories of "new basics," "rich tasks," and "productive pedagogies." What distinguishes this work is its explicit futures orientation, based on "a philosophy of education committed to the preparation of students for new workplaces, technologies and cultures," and its equally explicit positioning in what can be called a critical-reconceptualist discourse in educational theory and practice. As well as drawing on Dewey, Vygotsky, and Freire in its formulation of the rich tasks, the project identifies the need for a major shift in curriculum-theoretical orientation—from "Tylerian approaches to curriculum" to what is described as "the Reconceptualist model developed by William Pinar and his colleagues." This is presented as proposing that "curriculum not be built on specific behavioral objectives, knowledge or process outcomes." Rather, the "reconceptualist model" is based on a phenomenological approach to curriculum and education. Reconceptualist and critical models argue that the multiple objective and outcome approach tend to fragment, molecularize, and disintegrate knowledge and practice, and to de-skill teachers […] (Luke et al., 2000, p. 25).

Moreover:

The Reconceptualist Model argues that curriculum can be built by envisioning the kinds of life world and human subjects that the education system wants to contribute to and build. In this way, a curriculum approach to curriculum is better suited to a futures orientation than the Tylerian approach, which by definition tends to reproduce existing categories, knowledges and skills rather than build new ones. (Luke et al., 2000, p. 26)

On the face of it, this may seems curiously dated, to specialist eyes at least—at best, what might be called *first-generation* reconceptualist thinking. However, it needs to be borne in mind here that this is referring emphatically to *systemic* reform on a scale and to a degree rarely attempted before. As such, it is an intriguing exercise (and experiment) in the integration of institutionalized school education policy and practice with curriculum-theoretical innovation.

Important, the project's principal architect is Allan Luke, at once a distinguished academic scholar in literacy and curriculum studies and (at the time) a senior educational-administrative leader in the Queensland Education Department. Much like Boomer, who was similarly a high-level educational bureaucrat in the latter stages of his life and career, Luke has worked from *within* the public education system to *change* it.[2] That is not at all insignificant, especially given the peculiarities and specificities of the Australian scene. It continues the tradition of major curriculum and schooling reform in Australia being initiated by educational bureaucrats rather than by academics per se, as Marsh and Stafford (1988) noted:

Changes to the curriculum have not occurred frequently and when they have occurred, they have come as edicts from directors-general. [...] it has been directors-general rather than theoreticians who have initiated curriculum change in Australia. (p. 231)

Hence, at this point, I turn to more general features of Australian education, expressly from a curriculum-historical perspective, and of the forms of scholarship and inquiry associated with it over the last century, in the formation and consolidation of a distinctive curriculum field.

A major and enduring feature of the curriculum field in Australia is its bureaucratic and administrative character. In this, it is quintessentially representative of what Pinar et al. (1995) called the "Curriculum as Institutionalized Text" tradition in curriculum inquiry and curriculum work—the dominant form, in fact, for much of this century. Part of what is at issue here is the relatively late professionalization of education in Australia. Thus, it is only since Federation in 1901, and hence the official formation of Australia as a separate nation, that a full-scale educational apparatus has been built, ranging from differentiated mass schooling at all levels and stages to systematic and formalized teacher education and training.[3] Enormous effort went into reconstructing, in particular, public education during the first several decades of the 20th century (Spaul, 1998; Turney, 1983). That this corresponds to the development of the curriculum field more generally—in North America, for instance (Schubert, 1984)—is only partly coincidental because there would seem to be scholarly consensus that this was a significant period of nation building across many countries.

In this regard, commentators point to the persistence of "centralized, efficiency-oriented curriculum decision making" (Marsh, 1986, p. 210) as a recurring feature of Australian education, distributed since the 19th century across seven states and ter-

---

[2]In this instance, at least, under secondment to Education Queensland. For a clear statement of an at least congruent position, however, see Luke (1995, 2000).

[3]Primary schooling was established in the mid-19th century, and consolidated in the early 20th century; comprehensive secondary schooling developed from the early 1900s, but was only consolidated half a century later.

ritories. Indeed, commonwealth–state relations and politics need to be accounted for here. Each state funds and runs its own educational bureaucracy and is responsible for public schooling provision within its own borders. Traditionally, there has been little real dialogue or exchange across these borders; consequently (among other things), much duplication of effort and expense has occurred (Boston, 1994). The emergence of a "national curriculum" debate in the late 1980s compelled some attention to what was happening nationally across the various jurisdictions. However, this remains a controversial, contested issue, partly, one suspects, because of the difficulty that bureaucracies have in imagining let alone initiating the dismantling of their own empires.

It is worth noting, too, that earlier commentators similarly noted the centralized, bureaucratic character of Australian education, especially those from overseas. In an account originally published in 1955, R. Freeman Butts of Teachers College, Columbia University, observed the following:

> Underlying [Australia's] centralized systems of state education are two basic assumptions: (1) a uniform policy for all schools in a state is a good thing, and (2) a uniform policy can be achieved only when the basic decisions are made by a relatively few people. (Butts, 1961, p. 12)

He went on to link this with similar kinds of standardization in both teaching methods and the educational programme—for example, "the dominance of the academic hierarchy of studies" (p. 44), "the efficient expression of knowledge" (p. 50), a general emphasis on "orderliness, discipline and developments of skills" (p. 47), and "a prevailing assumption that traditional methods are better than experimentation with newer methods" (p. 52). As he wrote, apropos secondary schools: "Almost everywhere I found the tyranny of the notebook, the tyranny of speed, and the tyranny of uniform standards" (Butts, 1961, p. 52). Although it would certainly be unwise to rely entirely on such an avowedly etic account, nonetheless this is suggestive, and all the more disturbing, when it is considered that, *despite* enormous advances since then and also great variety, Australian education may still exhibit similar features, notwithstanding references to post-1960s "breakouts" (Connell, 1993; Musgrave, 1988). Another way of putting this might be to point to an enduring grammar of curriculum and schooling in Australia—a persistent overarching *continuity* (e.g., Boomer, 1999a; Ely, 1978) despite more or less cosmetic shifts and changes. This is highlighted in more recent times with the challenge of postmodern media culture, digital networks, and new formations of popular identity and global entertainment, and the attendant prospect of curriculum being increasingly decoupled from schooling (Fitzclarence, Green, & Bigum, 1995; C. Luke, 1996).

In an important account of distinctive discourses, frames, or *mentalités* in different state (provincial) cultures, Collins and Vickers (2001) pointed to what they call an educational *archetype* in the Australian scene, manifested for them particularly in New South Wales as the largest and arguably most bureaucratic of the state systems. In short, this comprises and also sustains a competitive academic curriculum structure, formalized (high-stakes) testing and assessment regimes, and a stringent final tertiary-entrance examination, along with prescribed, centrally produced syllabi. As they wrote, apropos educational policy formation and associated forms of curriculum regulation, it behooves "those who attempt to influence curriculum decisions to acknowledge the fallacy of treating the archetypal system as somehow 'natural'" (Collins & Vickers, 2001, p. 20), and therefore at once normalizing and normative.

What they also noted, along with a range of other commentaries (e.g., Musgrave, 1987), is that different state systems in Australia rarely reference each other, seek to learn from each other, or rationalize their provision accordingly. Yet much is remarkably consistent and in common in the curriculum scene across Australia—understandably so, perhaps, given what I suggest is its paradigmatic investment in this normative understanding of the structure and function of curriculum and schooling. The governing idea is that of the mainstream modernist school, linked to which is "batch processing" and a transmission- and subject-oriented curriculum. This is a recognizable and enduring educational technology—a now long-established, almost viscerally familiar way of "doing education" (Pinar & Grumet, 1981, p. 31). Yet for all its monumentality and materiality, it is historically constructed and contingent *artificial*. The pedagogic problem here is a pervasive, unreconstructed *realism*. In Boomer's terms, we should "[c]onsider the curriculum as a kind of Hollywood western town teaching set." He argued that, "[I]f we don't take students, all students, behind our teaching set, then they are being terrorized, however benign our intentions are." Further:

> What we should be doing, I believe, is saying, "Come behind here and I'll show you how it works." By that I mean, letting students into one's seemingly magic curriculum tricks, or, to put it another way, leaving uncovered the footprints so often carefully dusted over. (Boomer, 1988a, p. 163)

As he later put it, in the context of counterposing two modes of teaching, the "naturalistic" and the "epic":

> The curriculum becomes almost like doing what comes naturally. Children are surprised, delighted, entertained, and engrossed. And thus they are manipulated—because the curriculum is not, in fact, natural but, rather, *constructed*, and the teacher, in seeming not to design, has palpable designs on the learners. (Boomer, 1999b, p. 91)

Yet this kind of meta-curriculum criticism is hardly recognized for what it is: an exercise in thinking and talking differently about curriculum and pedagogy. Instead, school is above all else *serious* and emphatically, insistently so; play is on the margins, literally. We are urged to work hard at school to move more or less willingly and well prepared into the wider world of work, thoroughly schooled and appropriately skilled.

As a distinctive form of curriculum inquiry, that is by and large a road not taken in Australian curriculum inquiry and scarcely even considered.[4] How could it be? As Marsh (1987) indicated, the problem is basically one of scale and opportunity: There are simply not enough avenues and forums in a country as small, population-wise, as Australia to sustain and encourage curriculum conversations of this kind. Other factors include a long tradition of social efficiency and a persistent, instrumentalized vocationalism in educational theory and practice. In addition, as various commentators have observed, Australian culture is characterized by a pervasive anti-intellectualism, or at least a suspicion of the intellectually trained, of abstraction and rhetoric, of *speech*—of *wanking with words*.[5] In such an environment, there is little opportunity for anything

---

[4]A notable exception here is the recent work of Noel Gough, which has moved from an earlier interest in and commitment to the "Deliberation" tradition (e.g., Reid, 1999) toward a more systematic engagement with Reconceptualist initiatives and positions (e.g., Gough, 1995, 1998).

[5]A typically irreverent Australianism that is a chapter title in Boomer and Spender (1976), an early foray into practical curriculum and language politics.

other than the pragmatic, purposeful, precise discourse of curriculum planning, design, and development. Hence: "It might be concluded that Australian curriculum books focus too much on classroom activities, and upon applying theoretical principles to classrooms, without undertaking the vital task of critiquing and perhaps discarding extant theories and formulating and shaping new theories" (Marsh, 1987, pp. 21–22). Indeed.

This has implications for the originality and vitality of curriculum thought in Australia. Much is made in the literature of its "derivateness" and its heavy reliance on overseas influences (Marsh & Stafford, 1988; Turney, 1983). Yet even that is colored by a seeming lack of assurance and tentativeness—perhaps all the more understandable when Australia's (post)colonial insecurities are taken into account. It may even be that when we have borrowed from elsewhere, we have done it badly. As Musgrave (1987) put it:

> In this matter of curricular decision-making and indeed throughout the field of curriculum, we do not now have the least idea whether we should or can, as so often has been done in the past, borrow overseas frameworks and theories. The Australian curricular cringe has been a special case of the more general cultural cringe. (p. 109)

Marsh sees this as symptomatic of a more serious lack of mature curriculum thinking and understanding—an *amateurism*. This points to the power and significance of politicians and senior educational bureaucrats—their official agency, especially compared to that of academics and curriculum specialists:

> The fact that these eclectic borrowings were often poorly implemented and short-lived in Australian education attest to these officials' inability to conceptualize curriculum implementation factors (Marsh, 1987, p. 10; see also Marsh & Stafford, 1988).

Yet I wonder how sustainable the charges are of derivativeness, lack of originality, second-handedness—or at least if it might not be productively read otherwise or differently? What would happen, I wonder, if more were made of notions of translation, traveling theory, *différance* in rereading and reassessing the historical record?

A related feature, to my mind, is the significance of geography. Australia's location in the southern hemisphere, and its vast spaces and distances, need to drawn explicitly into an account such as this. It is something often referred to, but hardly ever thematized. For instance:

> The vast areas of Australia led to the establishment of separate centralized education departments in each State which tried to stretch scarce resources to the limit to ensure that some semblance of equality of education occurred, and this meant a very meager, economical system for all. Centralized systems with extremely limited funds had the effect of restricting the school curriculum to a narrow range of subjects. The inspectorial system ensured that particular teaching methods were the only ones used and that these were based upon economic concerns rather than pedagogical ones. (Marsh & Stafford, 1988, p. 214)

What is to be noted here is that bureaucracy, centralization, and uniformity are presented as, above all else, a practical solution to the linked problems of scant resources and the so-called *tyranny of distance*. How *do* governments manage not simply populations, but territories as well? Hence, the fact that there has been a consistent efficiency orientation in Australian education, as Marsh (1986) and others observe, is partly due to the influence of overseas curriculum specialists and educational thinkers, notably from the United States (e.g., Bobbitt, Tyler, etc.), thus paralleling the story of curriculum contestation that Kliebard (1986) told of the North American scene. Could it also have to do with managing large distances and territories, of extending the project of public schooling into the vast geographic space of Australia—in the words of our first prime minister, "a nation for a continent and a continent for a nation?" I come back to this issue later.

The 1970s can be seen as the period of emergence of the formal curriculum field in Australia. Reviewing a number of initiatives and developments, including the importation and influence of new work in philosophy and sociology of education, Musgrave (1987) pointed among other things, to the Commonwealth Government's establishment of the Curriculum Development Centre in Canberra in 1975. At about the same time, a number of subject-area and cross-curricular initiatives emerged on the scene (Connell, 1993), representing new energies and synergies in curriculum inquiry and curriculum work. A Curriculum Interest Group resulted in the foundation of *Curriculum Perspectives* in 1980 and the Australian Curriculum Studies Association (ACSA). A series of Point and Counterpoint forums in 1984 provided one of the first occasions for the staging of curriculum inquiry as such. American contributions from William Pinar, William Schubert, George Willis, and Ed Short were supplemented and sometimes critiqued by Australian contributions from Garth Boomer, Noel Gough, David Tripp, Patrick Brady, and David Smith, "penn[ing] their own positions on curriculum theorizing" ("Editorial," 1984, p. 57). Something of the flavor of a distinctively Antipodean takeup of curriculum discourse can readily be discerned in these exchanges, although to some extent this is framed within an all-too-familiar theory-practice binary. The relative recency of the field is acknowledged:

> The word "curriculum" has only come into vogue in the past fifteen years, at least in Australia. Before that I suppose we talked about the principles and practice of teaching and learning, about students, subjects, courses, textbooks and tests, the *stuff* of education which we now call "curriculum." (Boomer, 1984, p. 58)

This echoes Marsh's (1987) historical observation that *curriculum* has tended to be subsumed within, or otherwise associated with, *teaching*. Although this is perhaps a legacy of Australia's practical and institutional orientation, it should be noted that, even in Britain, curriculum studies at least in the formal sense developed only from the mid-1960s (Lawn & Barton, 1981). Similarly, and perhaps not surprisingly, for much of the century, there was little interest in Australia, as in the UK, in the somewhat alien concept of *pedagogy* (Hamilton, 1999; Simon, 1985). So what was happening prior to this in Australia with regard to curriculum discourse, curriculum thinking, and curriculum inquiry? What were the precedents or the pioneers? What were the characteristic ways of talking about curriculum and schooling? What were the forms of rhetoric and rules of reasoning?

Musgrave (1987) pointed to changes in the definition of curriculum over the course of the 1960s and 1970s, and the emergence of a more comprehensive formulation in the early 1980s. Yet for decades previously, it would seem that curriculum had been understood in more or less classic, conventional terms, as referring essentially to prescriptions of educational knowledge, moreover with specific regard to the practicalities of schools and teaching. A 1954 paper published in *The Forum of Education* is illustrative and symptomatic. Written by Bill Connell, it is based on courses of study in curriculum and related matters at the University of Sydney. It begins thus:

> During the last 25 years curriculum study has become both more popular and more intensive. University schools of education, content formerly to treat the curriculum in the standard methods courses by a brief review on how to plan the syllabus, have launched into full-scale curriculum studies. Curriculum specialists have arisen, and

in many overseas universities, curriculum laboratories too. The literature in the field has multiplied, and several journals devoted exclusively to the discussion and reporting of research on curriculum problems have come into being. (Connell, 1954, p. 16)

It goes on to present a glossary of curriculum terms, describing the need for this as an effect of "the development of a technical language whose terms are not always clearly understood by those outside the charmed circle of curriculum specialists" (Connell, 1954, p. 16). That it is presented as a glossary is significant: A retrospective operation in effect, it is an attempt at once to fix categories and formalize meanings, synthesizing usage to date and drawing on the authority of what is presented as a growing field of scholarship. It is thus "science" and a measure of the emerging scientification of the field. Note, for instance, the previous reference to curriculum laboratories, later glossed as referring to "a building usually associated with a teacher-training institution or the headquarters of an educational authority, staffed by specialists in curriculum work, and equipped with offices, conference rooms, and materials of value in the study of curriculum problems" (Connell, 1954, p. 20). Part of what is at issue here is the struggle for recognition, respectability, and parity of professional esteem in the university—in this case, the University of Sydney—and hence also status and resources. However, due consideration must also be given here to the 20th-century emergence worldwide of education as a discipline (Bessant & Holbrook, 1995).

It is clear, too, what is at issue here is essentially the *written, preactive* curriculum (Goodson, 1988). Although *curriculum* and *syllabus* are seen as separate, distinguishable terms, at least in principle, the point is made nonetheless that "no good purpose is served by trying to maintain a distinction between these two terms" (Connell, 1954, p. 16).[6] A further category addressed is the notion of *course of study,* presented as "the details of subject-matter to be studied in a given time or for a particular purpose, a formal statement of a curriculum arranged to show the desired sequence of study" (Connell, 1954, p. 19). Usually "put together in advance for the coming year, term etc," it is evidently to be distinguished from *units* and *topics,* although certainly related all the same. "Most courses of study consist of a collection of topics concerned with some particular subject," whereas a unit "is to be distinguished from a topic by the greater sophistication of its approach" (Connell, 1954, p. 21). Already an implicit hierarchy has been established or at least a division of labor: teachers and classrooms, on the one hand, and educational authorities and curriculum specialists, on the other. Reference is also made here to curriculum councils and committees engaged in bringing together stakeholders and negotiating with the community, working toward "commonly agreed upon lines of general policy," and providing context and rationale for "curriculum construction" —"the process of building a curriculum" (Connell, 1954, p. 19). The impression is of a systematic, comprehensive, increasingly professionalized operation—an emergent grid of specification and a technology for generating curriculum statements.

It is useful at this point to look back three decades earlier. Published in 1932, *The Primary School Curriculum in Australia* was edited by Percival R. Cole, for many years vice principal of Sydney Teachers' College, a graduate of Teachers' College, Columbia, and perhaps Australia's foremost educational scholar in the first part of the century (Turney, 1983). The volume brought together a distinguished group of Australian educators, comprising both academics and senior administrators—figures such as Browne (1932) and Mackie (1919), as well as noted administrative intellectuals such as Peter

---

[6]In this regard, note Musgrave's (1987) refernce to Connell et al.'s 1962 definition of curriculum, within the context of tracing a growing sophistication in the field. The emphasis in 1962 is still clearly on more or less formal statements ("usually, though not necessarily, made explicit in a written document"). The Connell book was reprinted and revised a number of times; see Connell [ed] (1974) for the Third Edition.

Board, Frank Tate, and Cecil Andrews. It also represents something of a watershed moment in Australian educational history—a changing of the guard, so to speak, with a new breed and a younger generation stepping forward to take up the project of understanding *and explicating* education as a social-scientific practice.[7] It should also be noted here that this is one of several significant publications of the period, with a direct bearing on the formation of the curriculum field in Australia (Marsh, 1987; Marsh & Stafford, 1988). I want to treat this volume as a representative instance of curriculum discourse, expressly in the Foucaultian sense, keeping in mind, however, his cautions against reducing discourse to *text* or *language,* let alone *book* (Foucault, 1991).

The Table of Contents is suggestive, understood as a text in itself and immediately familiar:

CONTENTS—*THE PRIMARY SCHOOL CURRICULUM IN AUSTRALIA* (1932)

Introduction (P. R. Cole)

Chapter 1 *The Theory of the Curriculum* (A. Mackie)

Chapter 2 *The Relation of the Curriculum to Industrial and Social Needs* (H. T. Lovell)

Chapter 3 *The Influence of Other Institutions on the Curriculum of the Primary School* (Cecil Andrews)

Chapter 4 *Curriculum Making* (P. Board)

Chapter 5 *Organization and Administration* (F. Tate)

Chapter 6 *The Activities Which the Curriculum Entails* (R. G. Cameron)

Chapter 7 *Programmes of Study and Local Adaptation* (H. M. Lushey)

Chapter 8 *Questions of Time and Order* (H. T. Parker)

Chapter 9 *Revision of the Curriculum* (G. S. Browne)

Chapter 10 *Educational Measurement and the Curriculum* (K. S. Cunningham)

What is immediately noticeable here is that this remains familiar territory seven decades on. This is the language of current-traditional curriculum discourse: *theory* followed by *context* and *system,* to *practice* (or *methods*), followed by *testing and assessment.* A synoptic text, it is moreover orderly and regulative, rational and scientific, and organized entirely around schooling. In short, it neatly encapsulates the discursive field of the volume as a whole, although that is understandably more elaborated, more complex, and contradictory. This is not the place to undertake a comprehensive, fully rigorous discourse analysis, although that would be productive and extremely useful. Rather, I select various aspects that will illuminate my concern to display the complex rationality of such a monumental utterance. I begin with its frame: Cole's own Introduction to the volume.

The early decades of the century were marked by an intense interest in thinking education anew—a veritable fever of reform. Central to this was the rich discursive field of the so-called *New Education*—a somewhat uneasy amalgam of different traditions, perspectives, theories, and ideologies gathering force and momentum over the 19th century mainly in Europe (Selleck, 1968). Exported overseas, it became folded into the millennial and national(ist) fervors of the early promise of the new century, in Australia as elsewhere. As Turney (1983a) wrote: "In general the New Education represented a

---

[7]All of whom were men—again, a marker of both the field (then?) and the historical moment (Baker, 1996).

decided reaction beginning in the late nineteenth century against the prevailing narrow, mechanical, and subject-based instruction tightly controlled by prescription and inspection" (p. 1).

This legacy is clearly evident in Cole's Introduction. It opens with a swirl of metaphors and images of nature, with the curriculum "likened to seed" and "the teacher, like a wise agriculturalist, ... sowing with seed of different sorts to suit a variety of soils" (Cole, 1932a, p. ix). Immediately there are tensions and even contradictions evident—between uniformity and standardization, on the one hand, and the need to cater for and attend to individual differences, on the other. Hence: "The primary course should include nothing that does not conform to social standards, nothing that does not conform to natural tendencies. It must satisfy at once the requirements of society and the aspirations of the individual pupil" (Cole, 1932a, p. x). The child is presented as inheriting "the kingdom of civilization," "taking possession of [his] legacy"—within the responsible limits of the designated curriculum. The centralized character of Australian schooling is acknowledged: "In each of the Australian States, ... where the support and administration of public education are more highly centralized than in any other country in the world, there is only one primary curriculum to be followed by all." In a telling statement:

> The local adaptations which are and should be made within the primary curriculum adopted by an Australian State do not detract from, and fail to disguise, its essential unity. *The same subjects are taught in Sydney and at Tibooburra.* (Cole, 1932a, p. x–xi; italics added)

Claims are made as to the distinctively Australian perspective on, and experience of, curriculum and schooling, with Australian conditions described as "foremost in [the contributors'] minds." The outcome is presented as "a Report unprecedented in this country for the scope of its ideation and the originality of its outlook," notwithstanding account taken of reviews and survey overseas, "in the United States and elsewhere":

> The aim has not been to build a new curriculum, but to investigate the principles which govern curriculum-making on modern scientific lines. (Cole, 1932, p. xii)

In this regard, it is also notable that three of the contributors were clearly and formally designated as psychologists, whereas at least one other (Cunningham) was associated with the new sciences of measurement and assessment (Cleverley, 1983). In fact, it is impossible to disengage the volume as a whole from the disciplinization of education as a field of study, specifically in Australia. This is to refer to the Australian emergence of "educational science," again with all due reference and deference to elsewhere, notably the United States although also to some extent England (e.g., the Hadow report).

Three chapters in particular are of interest here: those by Mackie, Board, and Tate. What makes these especially relevant to consider in this context is that these three figures together represent what might be called the first wave of post-Federation educational thinking in Australia. Moreover, Mackie (originally from Scotland) was instrumental in developing a modern system of teacher education and training, and Board and Tate were both directors of education in New South Wales and Victoria, respectively, and indeed key architects of public education in Australia. Not only were all three heavily invested with the ethos of the New Education, but also identified in various and varying ways with a distinctive sense of mission with regard to nation-building and the formation of national identity. Certainly all three were significantly involved in the first phase of 20th-century public education in Australia, as a distinctive expression of the project of modernity.

Mackie's chapter has been described as "[his] major publication on the curriculum" (Spaull & Mandelson, 1983, p. 103), although his *The Groundwork of Teaching* (1919) must also be noted here (Marsh, 1987). Viewed in context, it seeks to bring together a social efficiency framework with a child-centered, Deweyian view of curriculum and schooling. What is especially significant in this regard is Mackie's sense of "public education ... as a necessary form of social service" (Mackie, 1932, p. 1), linked to his emphasis on "the whole life of the child" (Mackie, 1932, p. 4). This articulates with a notion of curriculum as dependent on and mediated through the figure of the Teacher as an exemplary moral personnage—an emulable subject. As the first principal of Sydney Teachers College, Mackie worked closely with Board, seeking to forge a distinctive new identity for teachers as active, informed professionals—a view that indeed is still characteristic of Australian curriculum inquiry more generally (Boomer et al., 1992; Grundy, 1987; Kemmis, 2000).

The links with Board's chapter on curriculum making are clear. This is especially with regard to his emphasis on the teacher's influence, although Board's concern here is with the larger picture of nation-building, personal culture, citizenship, and national character. Nonetheless, elsewhere Board and Mackie constantly sought to stress the importance of what they called *teaching character*—something they saw as necessarily forged in the *joint* work of the training college and the beginning years of teaching service (Fletcher, 1995). For Board, curriculum making was thoroughly implicated in nation building. Moreover, it needed to be seen as a *cultural* practice, and not simply as technical and instrumental: "Intellectual and moral refinement are certainly as necessary in nation-building as reading, writing and arithmetic. *The cultural is nationally utilitarian*" (Board, 1932, p. 81–82). Schools are charged with providing the child with "an equipment for life," which he saw as comprising "skill, knowledge and character" (Board, 1932, p. 75). Thus, shaping curriculum is linked to the social formation of subjectivity: the subject–citizen and the nation–state.

Curriculum and schooling are therefore always framed locally, systemically, and nationally. As Tate (1932) wrote: "Any discussion of the curriculum necessarily involves a consideration of the organization within which schools work" (p. 92). Moreover, "The internal organization of the school must be kept in mind by the framers of a curriculum" (Tate, 1932, p. 114). Hence, matters of administration and organization are crucial in curriculum inquiry, although arguably they must always serve the needs of particular pedagogic constituencies. At the same time, Tate's own positioned practice and administrative experience meant that he clearly saw the need to attend to larger contexts and the governmental challenges of linking uniformity of provision and equality of opportunity.

Accordingly, he was alert to the complexities and tensions evident in the heavily centralized, highly bureaucratized character of the Australian system, expressly seeing this in comparative terms as a recurring problem of "mass-production in popular education" (Tate, 1932, p. 92). What is especially noteworthy here is the solution offered for this complex of problems. On the one hand, he stressed the importance of institutionalizing regular reports from the *front* as a key aspect of the work of inspectors in their marshalling and monitoring of what is literally presented as "an army of teachers" (Tate, 1932, p. 107)—a proliferating network of writing and representation. "In an education system of any extent, in which administration is centralized, the reports of the inspectorial staff are of greatest importance" (Tate, 1932, p. 112). On the other hand, he was equally insistent on the *personal* qualities of those representing the department, and on the quality and character of both teachers and inspectors, and also other officials, at all levels. Hence, he pointed to the need for "vigorous and stimulating personalities in the higher command," and in fact all throughout the educational system, linking this to the need for "constant vigilance" (Tate, 1932, p. 106).

A number of issues can be isolated here. A certain kind of official pedagogic subject is being produced in these accounts of curriculum, the child, and the nation—a certain image of the Australian public school and of teaching and the teacher. It is significant, first of all, that it is located firmly at the center of things, both positionally and (as it were) geographically. Therefore, it is looking outward from this center, into and toward the expanses and margins of its own territories, and seeking to encompass within its gaze the full sociospatial field—New South Wales and Victoria, respectively, in the first instance and, more generally, Australia. Moreover, this is quintessentially a male, patriarchical gaze—the gaze of the Father. This applies equally for the classroom, the school, and the system as a whole. However, the task is one of managing not simply territories, but populations as well, and of mapping them onto each other. Consequently, a social analysis is needed that brings together notions and problematics of governmentality, gender, and geography. Indeed, in many ways, this can now be seen as a key distinguishing feature of Australian education viewed historically, especially when its vast, sparsely populated spaces and distances are taken into full account.

At this point, I draw more explicitly on the resources of communication studies, including both theory and history, to extend the account emerging here of curriculum inquiry in Australia. This means addressing the relations among communication, culture, community, and curriculum as concepts *and* practices. An important feature of the Australian experience has been the effect of geography and location on meaning making. As distinctively a "nation-continent" organized into seven states and territories, Australia has always been characterized by the need to negotiate the huge distances involved in social life and human interaction, and in agricultural and administrative practice—what one commentator has famously called the *tyranny of distance* (Blainey, 1966).

However, this has often been neglected or slighted in educational accounts and analyses. For example, Marsh seemed to gloss over this aspect in referring to the role and significance of senior administrators in the Australian curriculum scene, noting that, although they "have to grapple with many educational problems ... most are associated with stretching the funds to provide a uniform standard of education across vast geographical areas," and hence "[t]hey have to be efficient, practical leaders and to be able to delegate powers in systems which tend to be highly bureaucratic and structured" (Marsh, 1987, p. 9). Elsewhere, as already noted, he referred to "the vast areas of Australia ... separate centralized education departments ... stretch[ing] scarce resources to the limit," with noticeable constraining effects with regard to curriculum and pedagogy (Marsh & Stafford, 1988, p. 214). This links directly to Tate's observations on the perils and possibilities in centralization, on the role and significance of the inspectorate, and, in particular, on the oft-noted historical tendency toward educational conservatism in the Australian system (Tate, 1932).

In this regard, Livingston's (1997) work on communication history in relation to what he called the *federation story* is pertinent. Observing that "communication played the crucial role in Australia's federation that transportation played in the history of Canada's confederation," Livingston enabled a useful link to be made with work such as that of Carey (1989) and Innes (1991) in North America—in particular, the manner in which national identity and development are intricately associated with communicative practices and ideologies and with technological development and technocultural change. One incident he noted as particularly emblematic of this relationship is the technical and symbolic articulation between telegraphy as a "federalized communication system" and "the simultaneous raising of the national flag, the British Union Jack, at state schools throughout the nation" (Livingston, 1997, p. 184). As he wrote: "The children's flag-raising ceremony on 14 May 1901 ... reflected that ambivalent mixture of federalism, nationalism, colonialism and imperialism that characterized Australians in the first year of the

Commonwealth" (Livingstone, 1997, p. 185). This supports Osborne and Lewis' (1995) point that "[n]ation-building and communication were seen to be mutually reinforcing" in the early part of the 20th century, and moreover that "[a] more historically aware approach to communication in Australia ... may be a useful contribution to the process of making the people articulate" (Osborne & Lewis, 1995, p. 172). It is equally pertinent, I suggest, for reassessing curriculum inquiry in Australia.

Little has been done on the conceptual relationship between communication and curriculum—one notable exception being, of course, Barnes' (1976) classic work on classroom practice and collaborative learning. However, there would appear to be real value in examining so-called *popular education* as mass communication[8] and, hence, curriculum making, especially on a national scale, as meaning making and as communicative practice. For instance, Tate (1932) wrote of the need for "Directors of education, chief inspectors and inspectors" *not* regarding themselves as "a privileged few imposing their will on the teaching many, but rather ... the stimulating leaders of a loyal team" (p. 105). This is surely an emphasis on communication and rhetoric, rather than on the exercise of coercive or sovereign power.

He is elsewhere insistent on the personal qualities of teachers and administrators alike, and on leadership and pedagogy as stimulating, persuasive, and *engaging*. This connects readily with the constant emphasis that Mackie and Board (and others) put on the personal exchanges of the classroom, and also the significance of the teacher's influence, thus effectively linking curriculum, communication, charisma (personality), and the practice of community. It also enables a reassessment of the bureaucratic character of Australian education as one manifestation historically of what Beniger (1986) called *the control revolution,* and it highlights the relationship between communication and governmentality with all their attendant and complicit technologies.

Connections between the period in question here and more recent times and events become all the more clearer, too. Note, for instance, Boomer's aforementioned catalytic role in national curriculum debates, his declaration that "[t]he lasting lesson is the demonstration of the [teacher's] self as it handles its authority and those under its authority" (Boomer, 1988b, p. 31), and his vision of classrooms in which there are "quite amazing flows and ebbs of affect and primal resistance in teachers and taught from moment to moment" (Boomer, 1988c, p. 191). Clearly a complex view of communication is needed here—one that draws as much on Foucault and poststructuralist thinking more generally as it does on the received traditions of communication and cultural studies.

In this chapter, I have endeavored to present an avowedly partial view of curriculum inquiry in Australia. As well, I have sought to initiate and lay the foundations for what I hope are further investigations of the specificities and peculiarities of Australian curriculum work, both in its own right and in its historical, intertextual relation to the curriculum field more generally. Understanding curriculum inquiry both as an international (global) phenomenon and as a local, situated practice is a complex undertaking and a constant challenge. Australian work in this regard is steadily gathering momentum. Even so, it is as yet still episodic and fragmented, by and large, and indeed arguably under some threat, increasingly subsumed as it is within economic and cultural policy and still heavily mortgaged to and invested in a modernist project of schooling. Among other things, a widely acknowledged crisis in public education at

---

[8]Note in this regard, however, the proposition that central to "[t]he tradition of thinking about communication that emerged in Australia ... was the concept of communication as *public* communication, rather than simply as *mass* communication" (Osborne & Lewis, 1995, p. 8; italics added)—something that they link to "the 'public service' mission of State and Federal administration."

the onset of a new century may well prove a stimulus to creative and radical re-imaginings of what curriculum and schooling must now become, in a new age of digital culture, global networks, hybrid identities, and transnational imaginaries.

Opportunities to tell *different* stories, *supplementary* stories, are crucial. This means not only revisiting and rereading the available historical record, but seeking to add to the archive by encouraging and engaging in careful, informed, critical curriculum-historical inquiry. It means folding into a never-ending, dynamic, ever-revisable story rich with accounts of past, present, *and* future formulations of curriculum and schooling in Australia. That means, in turn, properly acknowledging that there are, and have long been, ongoing, active curriculum conversations that Australian curriculum workers have justifiably sought to refer to and participate in. Whether this has always been realized in original inquiry is not all that important. Rather, such charges must now be redescribed in the light not only of postmodern(ist) understandings of text, culture, and cognition, but also of new views of performativity and representation in curriculum inquiry (Gough, 2000).

A final issue is the likelihood, or perhaps even the desirability, of what Musgrave (1987) described as "a peculiarly Australian curriculum theory." Should such a thing emerge, there is little doubt there needs to be an epistemology of location and due account of Australia's distinctive positioning and placement in a historically changing world order. This involves taking into account Australia's geographical features and geopolitical trajectories. It also involves being sensitive and attuned to the particular realization in Australia of the conceptual and empirical relationship between communication and curriculum.

In summary, it is appropriate to observe that "[w]hat has been distinctive about the more general body of Australian ideas on communication … is the particular regional and local inflections given to those overseas debates, and how these have been shaped by Australia's history and geography" (Osborne & Lewis, 1995, p. 157). What are the possibilities and challenges here for curriculum inquiry in Australia? What might be the implications of such work for the international curriculum field as a larger discursive formation?

REFERENCES

Baker, B. (1996). The history of curriculum or curriculum history? What *is* the field and who gets to play on it? *Curriculum Studies, 4*(1), 105–117.

Barnes, D. (1976). *From communication to curriculum.* Harmondsworth, England: Penguin.

Beniger, J. R. (1986). *The control revolution: Technological and economic origins of the information society.* Cambridge, MA: Harvard University Press.

Bessant, B., & Holbrook, A. (1995). *Reflections on educational research in Australia: A history of the Australian association for research in education.* Coldstream, Australia: Australian Association for Research in Education.

Blainey, G. (1966). *The tyranny of distance: How distance shaped Australia's history.* Melbourne, Australia: Sun Books.

Board, P. (1932). Curriculum making. In P. R. Cole (Ed.), *The primary school curriculum in Australia* (pp. 74–91). Melbourne, Australia: Melbourne University Press.

Boomer, G. (1984). Space and Meta Space. *Curriculum Perspectives, 4*(2), 57–59.

Boomer, G. (1988a). Reading the whole curriculum. In B. Green (Ed.), *Metaphors and meanings: Essays on English teaching by Garth Boomer* (pp. 151–167). Adelaide, Australia: Australian Association for the Teaching of English.

Boomer, G. (1988b). Negotiation revisited. In B. Green (Ed.), *Metaphors and meanings: Essays on English teaching by Garth Boomer* (pp. 168–178). Adelaide, Australia: Australian Association for the Teaching of English.

Boomer, G. (1988c). Struggling in English. In B. Green (Ed.), *Metaphors and meanings: Essays on English teaching by Garth Boomer* (pp. 31–41). Adelaide, Australia: Australian Association for the Teaching of English.

Boomer, G. (1999a). Curriculum and Teaching in Australian School, 1960–1990: A Tale of Two Epistemologies. In B. Green (Ed.), *Designs on learning: Essays on curriculum and teaching by Garth Boomer* (pp. 127–146). Canberra, Australia: Australia Curriculum Studies Association.

Boomer, G. (1999b). Literacy: The epic challenge beyond progressivism. In B. Green (Ed.), *Designs on learning: Essays on curriculum and teaching by Garth Boomer* (pp. 83–98). Canberra, Australia: Australia Curriculum Studies Association,.

Boomer, G., Lester, N., Onore, C., & Cook, J. (1992). *Negotiating the curriculum: Educating for the 21st century.* London: Falmer.

Boomer, G., & Spender, D. (1976). *The spitting image: Reflections on language, education and social class.* Adelaide, Australia: Novak.

Boston, K. (1994). A Perspective on the So-Called 'National Curriculum." *Curriculum Perspectives, 14*(1), 43–45.

Browne, G. S. (1932). *The case for curriculum revision.* Melbourne, Australia: Australian Council for Educational Research.

Butts, R. F. (1961). *Assumptions underlying Australian education.* Melbourne, Australia: Australian Council for Educational Research. (Original publication 1955)

Carey, J. W. (1989). *Communication as culture: Essays on media and society.* Boston: Allen & Unwin.

Cleverley, J. F. (1983). Research director and educator—K. S. Cunningham. In C. Turney (Ed.), *Pioneers of Australian education* (Vol. 3, pp. 272–295). Sydney, Australia: Sydney University Press.

Cole, P. R. (1932a). Introduction. In P. R. Cole (Ed.), *The primary school curriculum in Australia* (pp. ix–xiii.) Melbourne, Australia: Melbourne University Press.

Cole, P. R. (Ed.). (1932b). *The primary school curriculum in Australia.* Melbourne, Australia: Melbourne University Press.

Collins, C. (1995). Introduction. In C. Collins (Ed.), *Curriculum stocktake: Evaluating school curriculum change* (pp. 3–19). Canberra, Australia: Australian College of Education.

Collins, C., & Vickers, M. (2001). *How state cultures have framed the post-compulsory curriculum.* Paper presented at the biennial conference of the Australian Curriculum Studies Association, Perth, Western Australia, September 29–October 2, 1999 [Revised 2001].

Connell, W. F. (1954). A Glossary of Curriculum Terms. *The Forum of Education, 14*(1), 16–22.

Connell, W. F. (1970). Myths and traditions in Australian education. *Australian Journal of Education, 14*(3), 253–264.

Connell, W. F. (1993). *Reshaping Australian education 1960–1985.* Hawthorn, Australia: Australian Council for Educational Research.

Connell, W. F., et al. (1962). *The foundations of education.* Sydney, Australia: Novak.

Cormack, P., & Green, B. (2000, April 23). *Re-reading the historical record: Curriculum history and the linguistic turn.* Paper presented at the annual meeting of the Society for the Study of Curriculum History, New Orleans, LA.

Editorial. (1984). Point and Counterpoint. *Curriculum Perspectives, 4*(2), 57.

Ely, J. (1978). *Reality and rhetoric: An alternative history of Australian education.* Chippendale, Australia: Alternative Publishing Cooperative in association with the NSW Teachers Federation.

Fitzclarence, L., Green, B., & Bigum, C. (1995). Stories in and out of class: Knowledge, identity and schooling. In R. Smith & P. Wexler (Eds.), *After postmodernism: Education, politics and identity* (pp. 131–154). London: Falmer.

Fletcher, B. (1995). Shaping the College, 1906–1920. In G. Boardman (Ed.), *Sydney Teachers College: A history 1906–1981* (pp. 28–57). Sydney, Australia: Hale & Iremonger.

Foucault, M. (1991). *The Foucault effect: Studies in governmentality.* London: Harvester Wheatsheaf.

Goodson, I. (1988). *The making of curriculum: Collected essays.* London: Falmer.

Gough, N. (1995). Manifesting cyborgs in curriculum inquiry. *Melbourne Studies in Education, 29*(1), 71–83.

Gough, N. (1998). Refractions and diffractions: Functions of fiction in curriculum inquiry. In W. F. Pinar (Ed.), *Curriculum: Towards new identities* (pp. 94–127). New York: Peter Lang.

Gough, N. (2000). Locating curriculum studies in the global village. *Journal of Curriculum Studies, 32*(1), 329–342.

Green, B. (Ed.). (1999a). *Designs on learning: Essays on curriculum and teaching by Garth Boomer.* Canberra, Australia: Australia Curriculum Studies Association.

Green, B. (1999b). Introduction: Garth Boomer—Curriculum worker for the nation. In B. Green (Ed.), *Designs on learning: Essays on curriculum and teaching by Garth Boomer* (pp. 1–12). Canberra, Australia: Australia Curriculum Studies Association.

Grundy, S. (1987). *Curriculum: Product or praxis?* London: Falmer.

Hamilton, D. (1999). The pedagogical paradox (or why no didactics in England?). *Pedagogy, Culture and Society, 7*(1), 135–152.

Hughes, P. (1993). Similar but different: The curriculum scene in Australia. *Educational Review, 45*(2), 143–154.

Innes, H. A. (1991). *The bias of communication.* Toronto: University of Toronto Press. (Originally published 1951)

Kemmis, S. (1990). *The curriculum corporation: Observations and implications.* Canberra, Australia: Australian Curriculum Studies Association, Occasional Paper No 1.

Kemmis, S. (2000, December 4–7). *Educational research and evaluation: Opening communicative space.* The 2000 Radford Lecture presented at the Annual Conference of the Australian Association for Research in Education, Sydney.

Kliebard, H. M. (1986). *The struggle for the American curriculum 1893–1958.* Boston: Routledge & Kegan Paul.

Ladwig, J. G. (1994). For whom this reform? Outlining educational policy as a social field. *British Journal of Sociology of Education, 15*(3), 3341–363.

Lawn, M., & Barton, L. (1981). Introduction. In M. Lawn & L. Barton (Eds.), *Rethinking curriculum studies: A radical approach* (pp. 11–19). London: Croom Helm.

Livingstone, K. T. (1997). *The wired nation continent: The communication revolution and federating Australia.* Melbourne, Australia: Oxford University Press.

Luke, A. (1995). Getting our hands dirty: Provisional politics in postmodern conditions. In R. Smith & P. Wexler (Eds.), *After postmodernism: Education, politics and identity* (pp. 83–97). London: Falmer.

Luke, A. (2000). Critical literacy in Australia: A matter of context and standpoint. *Journal of Adult and Adolescent Literacy, 43*(5), 448–461.

Luke, A., Matters, G., Herschell, P., Grace, N., Barrett, R., & Land, R. (2000). *New Basics Project: Technical paper.* Brisbane, Australia: Education Queensland. (http://education.qld.gov.au/corporate/newbasics/)

Luke, C. (1996). ekstasis@cyberia. *Discourse: Studies in the Cultural Politics of Education, 17*(2), 187–207.

Mackie, A. (1919). *The groundwork of teaching.* Sydney, Australia: Sydney Teachers College Press.

Mackie, A. (1932). The theory of the curriculum. In P. R. Cole (Ed.), *The primary school curriculum in Australia* (pp. 1–14). Melbourne, Australia: Melbourne University Press.

Marsh, C. J. (1986). Historical developments in curriculum. In C. Marsh (Ed.), *Curriculum: An analytical framework* (pp. 195–214). Sydney, Australia: Novak.

Marsh, C. (1987). Curriculum theorizing in Australia. *The Journal of Curriculum Theorizing, 7*(2), 7–29.

Marsh, C., & Stafford, K. (1988). Historical background to curriculum in Australia. In C. Marsh & K. Stafford (Eds.), *Curriculum: Practices and Issues* (pp. 197–232). Sydney, Australia: McGraw-Hill.

Musgrave, P. W. (1979). *Society and the curriculum in Australia.* Sydney, Australia: Allen & Unwin.

Musgrave, P. W. (1987). Curricular research and development. In J. P. Keeves (Ed.), *Australian education: Review of recent research* (pp. 90–114). Sydney, Australia: Allen & Unwin.

Musgrave, P. W. (1988). Curriculum history: Past, present and future. *History of Education Review, 17*(2), 1–14.

Osborne, G., & Lewis, G. (1995). *Communication traditions in 20th-century Australia.* Melbourne, Australia: Oxford University Press.

Piper, K. (1997). *Riders in the chariot: Curriculum reform and the national interest 1965–1995.* Camberwell, Melbourne, Australia: Australian Council for Educational Research.

Pinar, W., & Grumet, M. (1981). Theory and practice and the reconceptualisation of curriculum studies. In M. Lawn & L. Barton (Eds.), *Rethinking curriculum studies: A radical approach* (pp. 20–42). London: Croom Helm.

Pinar, W. F., Reynolds, W. M., Slattery, P., & Taubman, P. M. (1995). *Understanding curriculum: An introduction to the study of historical and contemporary curriculum discourses.* New York: Peter Lang.

Reid, W. A. (1999). *Curriculum as institution and practice: Essays in the deliberative tradition.* Mahwah, NJ: Lawrence Erlbaum Associates.

Schubert, W. F. (1984). *Curriculum books: The first eighty years.* Lanham, MD: University Press in America.

Seddon, T. (1989). Curriculum history: A map of key issues. *Curriculum Perspectives, 9*(4), 1–16.

Selleck, R. J. W. (1968). *The new education: The English background 1817–1914.* Melbourne, Australia: Sir Isaac Pitman & Sons.

Simon, B. (1985). Why no pedagogy in England? In B. Simon (Ed.), *Does education matter?* (pp. 77–105). London: Lawrence & Wishart.

Spaull, A. (1998). Public education in Australia: An historical essay. In A. Reid (Ed.), *Going public: Education policy and public education in Australia* (pp. 3–8). Canberra, Australia: Australian Curriculum Studies Association.

Spaull, A. D., & Mandelson, L. A. (1983). The college principals—J. Smyth and A. Mackie. In C. Turney (Ed.), *Pioneers of Australian education* (Vol. 3, pp. 81–166). Sydney, Australia: Sydney University Press.

Tamboukou, M. (1999). Writing genealogies: An exploration of Foucault's strategies for doing research. *Discourse: Studies in the Cultural Politics of Education, 20*(2), 201–217.

Tate, F. (1932). Organization and administration. In P. R. Cole (Ed.), *The primary school curriculum in Australia* (pp. 92–119). Melbourne, Australia: Melbourne University Press.

Turney, C. (1983a). Introduction. In C. Turney (Ed.), *Pioneers of Australian education* (Vol. 3, pp. 1–11). Sydney, Australia: Sydney University Press.

Turney, C. (1983b). Scholar and writer—P. R. Cole. In C. Turney (Ed.), *Pioneers of Australian education* (Vol. 3, pp. 296–330). Sydney, Australia: Sydney University Press.

Tyler, D., & Johnson, L. (1991). Helpful Histories? *History of Education Review, 20*(2), 1–8.

CHAPTER 8

The Decolonization of Curriculum in Botswana

Sid N. Pandey
Fazlur R. Moorad
University of Botswana

This chapter examines the nature of curriculum reforms in the light of educational expansion and curriculum innovation in Botswana. We argue that, despite the escalation in demand for more and better education, not much reflection or research has been done on the nature of the curriculum and how it relates to the whole process of change. We begin by providing a contextual background on Botswana's geographical, political, social, and economic situation and an overview of the development of education from the precolonial era to the present time. The present system of education is critiqued in the light of a review of research on the implementation of the new curriculum. Like most developing countries, Botswana has planned educational policies in phases and developed educational goals, a national philosophy, and a vision to create an ideal society to enable its people to realize their potentials and live in peace and prosperity. Unfortunately, a review of research on classrooms in Botswana indicates that the teaching patterns and the teachers' attitudes have not changed as required by an innovative curriculum. We argue that the nature and structure of the present educational system still rooted in the colonial history relate to the perpetuation of a hierarchical class structure and not to a radical change or social transformation required to realize the educational goals and national visions. Finally, critical pedagogy grounded in the radical theories is invoked as an alternative. The ethical value of humaneness and human oneness (*ubuntc/botho*) inherent in African cultural heritage and espoused by various African countries, including Botswana, is found worthy to provide an ethical dimension for critical pedagogy suitable for emancipatory education in Africa and other developing countries. To prepare ground for this pedagogy, the conception of curriculum must come out of its narrow confines to be reconceptualized.

DISTINGUISHING FEATURES OF BOTSWANA AS A NATION

Botswana, earlier known to anthropological researchers on Kalahari bushmen and tourists interested in wildlife of the Okavango Delta, has recently attracted world attention for its three distinguishing features: diamonds, democracy, and demography.

143

The discovery of diamonds in increasing proportions since its independence in 1966 from the yoke of British colonialism, which gave it a historical name, the Bechuanaland Protectorate, has made it resourceful and prosperous. A country of peace-loving people with a tradition of resolving their tribal and other kinds of differences in a specified meeting place (called *kgotla* in Setswana) has sustained three decades of successful modern democratic government. The National Development Plan–8 (NDP–8: 1997/98–2002/03; Government of Botswana, 1997b) emphasized: "The Botswana Constitution established a non-racial democracy which maintains freedom of speech, freedom of the press and freedom of association, and affords all citizens equal rights" (p. 1). The geophysical feature of this new nation is no less significant. In a landlocked area the size of France or Texas, only the eastern portion has some rain to encourage human settlement; the rest of the region is increasingly arid as one moves toward the west bordering Namibia. This aridity threatens the country with water scarcity and frequent cycles of drought. NDP–8 noted the main demographic features as such:

> It is small relative to the size of the country; it is growing rapidly as a result of high fertility and declining mortality rates; there is, consequently, a high proportion of children and young people; infant mortality is declining and life expectancy is increasing; and the pattern of settlement is changing rapidly. (p. 11)[1]

Surrounded by Zambia, Zimbabwe, South Africa, and Namibia, Botswana has approximately 1 million inhabitants. The money from the well-managed diamond industry, augmented by the income from the sale of beef processed in the largest slaughterhouse of the southern hemisphere, as well as funds derived from the production of other materials and products, provides for state spending on the improvements of people's lives.

Development and Change

Since its independence, phenomenal changes have taken place. Botswana was among the poorest countries of Africa in 1966, when 30% of its people between the ages of 20 and 40 worked as migrant laborers in South Africa. The country was dependent on foreign aid not only for its developmental efforts, but also for financing its recurrent expenditures. The implementations of policies in seven preceding National Development Plans have increased access to roads, water, health, and education. The capital city of Gaborone, a village of 4,000 people at the time of independence, now has a population of well over 100,000. The city has become a major center of government, commerce, and industry. It has attracted the global attention to host political, cultural, economic, and educational conferences and seminars on local, national, African, and international themes and topics. An international airport in Gaborone connects itself to the major cities of the world, and paved roads running across the country link the major urban centers and places of tourism. Comfortable hotels, well-stocked supermarkets, adequately equipped travel and transport agencies, and other facilities have spotted the whole country to meet the needs of a modern nation. The discovery of the internal resources and the political stability have encouraged outsiders to start local business and industry. The combined effects of these developmental changes have led to other related developments as well.

Before independence, there were over 200 primary schools and only 2 full-fledged secondary schools in the nation. Today the primary schools have multiplied over 3 times while the secondary schools have increased almost 50 times. School enrollment has improved over the years, with 90% of primary age children attending schools. The expansion of secondary education has been most notable. With the expansion and establishment of Community Junior Secondary Schools, most primary school graduates have access to secondary education (Government of Botswana, 1997b). Before outlining the major developments in education, it is relevant to trace the historic past of precolonial and colonial education to understand the context of the present educational curriculum we intend to discuss.

EDUCATIONAL DEVELOPMENT: PAST HISTORY, PRESENT EXPANSION, AND FUTURE PROJECTIONS

Precolonial and Colonial Education

It must be noted that a kind of education, in both formal and informal forms, existed in Botswana, like in all African countries, prior to the coming of missionary and Western education. Parsons (1983) documented the precolonial education in these words:

> Traditional education—as was Western education too—was part of the whole system of belief, or religion as well as a means of socializing children into the accepted norms of society. It therefore consisted of, in all cases, informal education in the home—largely a matter of parenting, and of relations between siblings, with special emphasis on the aged as repositories of wisdom. Formal education—i.e. schools—catered for the political and economic needs of the state power, particularly of the Tswana states which emerged and covered most of Botswana during the 19th century. Vocational training—besides general informal training in the household, agriculture, and hunting techniques—consisted of part-time individual apprenticeships in trades such as medicine, mining and smelting, and occasional demands by the state for drilling in techniques of mass hunting and warfare. (pp. 22–23)

Formal education, which must have been as old as the tribes, consisted of the initiation ceremonies called in Setswana *bojale* for girls and *bogwera* for boys. *Bojale* gave instruction in matters concerning motherhood, sex behavior toward men, housekeeping, agriculture, and other related activities. *Bogwera* for boys was conducted in bush camps under the supervision of skilled persons, including a local surgeon (*ngaka*) for circumcision and other activities related to adult male responsibilities, such as warfare preparation, livestock care, modelling, folk songs, precepts, dance drama, and other skills and attitudes relevant to the survival and functioning of the tribes.

These were intended to teach the boys how to behave in their adulthood, accept the adult roles of family and societal responsibilities, and respond to survival needs. Informal education took place in the family, neighborhood, and the environment. Education was an inseparable part of the totality of life. Needless to say, this type of education integrated into life or rather growing out of life enabled the people to survive for thousands of years until external interference seriously challenged and threatened its continuance.

Missionary and Colonial Education

In 1844, missionaries brought Western education to Botswana. David Livingstone was the pioneer in setting up schools in the southern part near Gaborone, and his wife, Mary, started an infant school with "60 to 80 pupils, though drought scattered the children to collect roots and locusts in 1848" (Parsons, 1983, p. 24). Various mission bodies, such as the London Missionary Society (LMS), the Dutch Reformed

Church, the Lutherans, the Roman Catholics, and the Anglicans, established primary schools starting from the mid-19th century. The curriculum consisted mainly of the 3Rs and the reading of scripture in Setswana. Little English was taught. In the late 1800s, the missionary education emphasis on "saving souls," rather than improving the economic or social life, led to some misunderstanding and conflict with the natives, who wanted to learn useful vocational skills. The lack of funds for education was another major barrier. Until 1904, the British Protectorate administration did not fund education at all. Thus, the poor education and lack of practical subjects led the natives to control and finance their education. The native groups, called *merafe,* started their own self-help (*ipelegeng*) schools. These were also called *ward* or *kgotla* schools. These did not charge tuition fees and were supported by the *merafe* or a special education tax levied for the purpose (Tlou & Campbell, 1984, pp. 136–141). Along with these, attempts were made to inculcate the value of Western culture, the notion of development, and the dignity of labor. The missionary influence is evident in the meaning of the Setswana word, *thuto,* which is commonly used today for *education* in the secular sense; it meant "Western civilization as well as Christian doctrine" up to 1880. Such doctrinal conceptions of education (*thuto*) also indicate the neglect of comprehensive education (Parsons, 1983, p. 25).

Colonial education also conflicted with the native way of life. For example, the young boys would be required for herding at the cattle posts and the girls would be needed for domestic work. A kind of social stratification brought in the notion of elitism and inequality. In the early days of formal education, only the children of the higher classes and royalty were encouraged to attend school. They did not want to raise the aspiration of the poor through education in general and make them acquainted with the idea of social equality inherent in Christian teachings. Although these patterns started changing in the 20th century, the quality of education during these periods remained poor because no money was available for teacher training, teaching materials, and other facilities. However, by 1880, every major village had a primary school. By 1900, there were about 20 primary schools, with approximately 1,000 pupils in the Protectorate. For this accomplishment, the credit goes to the missionaries who laid the foundations of Western education in Botswana (Tlou & Campbell, 1984). Credit should also go to those chiefs who spearheaded the community initiatives in establishing what were then known as *tribal schools.*

Postindependence Education

The main impetus for educational expansion and reform came a decade after independence from the Government of Botswana document, *Education for Kagisano: Report of the National Commission on Education* (NCE; Government of Botswana, 1977). The Commission, as appointed by the first president of Botswana who gave priority to education in nation building, consisted of a well-conceived team of six persons, among them African educationists, Botswana people's representative from the Parliament, and European and American academicians chaired by the Swedish scholar, Torsten Husén. The Commission's purpose was to clarify the goals of the educational system as perceived by the key parties within and outside government, review the current educational system, and present recommendations for the implementation of an effective program to overcome educational problems and achieve goals. The Report noted the fast transformation Botswana had undergone since its independence and made it clear at the outset that "a world entirely different from the present awaits today's children by the time they are in middle age." It stated:

So a relevant education for Botswana cannot be one which clings blindly to ancient tradition. It is rather one in which customs are adapted and culture is renewed, enabling the society to respond to new opportunities with confidence. (p. 9)

The Commission conducted survey research and a needs assessment all over the country to know the aspirations of the people of Botswana. It outlined major goals of education as expressed by those surveyed. It made attempts to clearly spell out philosophical as well as policy decision guidelines for improvement and reform measures for "the organization, content and style of education." Its intent was to make the curriculum relevant for the challenge of a fast changing world. It stressed:

The principal aim of education is individual development. The individual is of unique value and it is only through changes in the developed capacities and attitudes of individuals that society changes. The focus of education in the school and classroom should therefore be upon the learner; enabling them to acquire the knowledge, skills, attitudes and behavior that will give them a full, successful life and continued personal growth; and equipping them to participate effectively in a rapidly changing society. (Government of Botswana, 1977, p. 23)

The Commission, then, related the development and learning of the individual to the values of the society by adopting the already existing four national principles. The important Setswana word *kagisano* in the main title of the NCE Report means "social harmony," which provides the national goal of education in Botswana. Underlying this encompassing and broad national goal are the following four national principles to support the educational edifice:

Democracy

Development

Self-reliance

Unity

For the purpose of implementation, attempts were made to clarify the meaning of the four national principles. *Democracy* implies a voice for all the people in all important matters affecting their future. *Development* involves the management and use of the nation's physical and human resources to create a strong economy. *Self-reliance* means bringing the economy under the national and local control to enable the people to progress through self-help. *Unity* is the awareness of national identity, loyalty, and pride. "Combination of these four principles produce the national philosophy of *Kagisano*, meaning social harmony, and embracing the concepts of social justice, interdependence and mutual assistance" (p. 24).

We pointed out that education on its own cannot be relied on to change society. Other social forces, policies, and practices must work hand in hand to bring about social change. Education and training can help in the realization of *Kagisano* if the four national principles are represented and practiced in the organizational structure and translated into the curriculum of the school. In preparing the report, the Commission was apprised of the mistakes of other developing countries where educational curriculum has tended to become regurgitation of academic content, imitation-prone, lecture-oriented, dependence-generating, second-rate, and finally leading to the "diploma disease" syndrome. It was hoped that the late coming of independence in Botswana gave it an opportunity to learn from the mistakes of others. The Commission took care to emphasize the positive points and warn against possible pitfalls to eliminate the likelihood of repeating the history of other African countries.

DEVELOPMENT AND EXPANSION OF PRIMARY EDUCATION

The decade following independence focused on secondary and higher education, with scant attention paid to primary education. More secondary schools were started; through self-help efforts, called Botswana University Campus Appeal (BUCA), funds were collected to start a university in 1966. The idea of expanding primary education did not make sense because the educational planners were concerned about finding places for the further education of the primary school graduates.

The NCE report (Government of Botswana, 1977) gave importance to primary education development. In the interest of the nation's future economy and on the grounds of equity, it recommended for "immediate priority for quantitative and qualitative improvement in primary education" and "a reorientation of the curriculum to embody the national principles." To overhaul the whole educational system, the Commission made 156 recommendations with priorities and a time frame for their implementation. Primary education received 34 recommendations and focused on the improvement of the following specific areas: access to education, curriculum, medium of instruction, promotion and progression policy, examination, books and materials, building and furniture, and distribution of resources. This paved the way for the abolition of school fees in 1980 to make primary education universal. The minimum age was stipulated from 6 to 12. The structure of the school system from primary to higher education had to move from 7 + 3 + 2 + 4 to 6 + 3 + 3 + 4. One or two teachers' schools had to be established in outlying and remote areas to meet the needs of isolated areas. New school buildings with adequate classroom space and proper furnishing had to be created. Primary curriculum had to be practical without being narrowly vocational; the syllabus had to be revised to include a basic core of Setswana, English, and Mathematics. It was recommended that Setswana be given equal status to English and become the medium of instruction from Standard 1 to 4. English was recommended as the medium of instruction from Standard 5, although it remained a subject to be taught from Standard 1. The non-Setswana-speaking children had to be compensated in some ways during marking. The provision for the development of teaching materials for Setswana teaching and teacher training was emphasized. Facilities had to be provided to enable teachers to make their own teaching aids. For the training of primary teachers, recommendations were made to establish more training colleges and improve the existing ones. The Ministry of Education was asked to review and improve the service conditions and salary scale of teachers to entice them to work in remote and rural areas. It was also requested to explore ways of encouraging the writing and publication of books and local teaching material, as well as the creation of facilities for their proper storage and distribution.

ACTION BY THE GOVERNMENT

Following the NCE report (Government of Botswana, 1977), the Government of Botswana has been persistently active in implementing these recommendations. The National Development Plan–5 (NDP–5; Government of Botswana, 1979), following the Report of the Commission, showed its commitment in these words:

> [The] government attaches the highest priority within education to the primary education sector. First, in the interest of equality of opportunity and of developing the po-

tential of all children, the Government seeks to provide universal access to primary education. Secondly, since primary education lays the foundation for further education and training and for productive employment, the Government seeks to improve its quality and relevance. (p. 107)

Because many improvements and reform undertakings are complex and long-term processes, these are still underway. However, to address the immediate need to reform primary education, in 1979–1980, the Government of Botswana entered into an agreement with the USAID to start a Primary Education Improvement Project (PEIP). It consisted of two 5-year phases from July 1981 through November 1991. Ohio University was the institutional contractor for the project. The purpose of the PEIP–I (1981–1986) was to establish at the University of Botswana a permanent capacity for inservice training through the creation of a 4-year B.Ed degree program to upgrade senior primary school staff. Another objective was to strengthen the capacity of the Ministry of Education to organize and implement other effective inservice programs for primary teachers and supervisory staff. The second phase, the PEIP–II (1986–1991), was intended mainly to help the University build appropriate graduate training in primary education, expand and improve the inservice training in both B.Ed. and Diploma in Primary Education programs, establish and institutionalize the network for providing inservice education, and finally "coordinate and assist in the evaluation, revision, and implementation of PTTC curricula appropriate to the training needs of primary teachers" (Evans & Knox, 1991, pp. 40–41). This project deliberately left out curriculum reform, which was the domain of the Curriculum Development and Evaluation Unit. The evaluation of the PEIP summed up by Evans and Knox (1991) shows that the project was successful. They quoted from the last evaluation report:

Given such an enthusiastic beginning, the contractor (evaluator) must warn that a temptation to "declare victory" in primary education at this time would not only be premature because of the fact that the project is only a beginning of reform of primary education, but it might also result in damaging the improvements in teacher training and behaviour which is now evident. To paraphrase Sir Winston Churchill, this project is not at the "end of beginning," but at the "beginning of the beginning" in reform of primary education. (pp. 49–50)

DEVELOPMENTS IN SECONDARY EDUCATION

Although secondary education had been given more attention than primary, it still needed a lot of reform and expansion to meet the needs of the nation. The Commission first recommended changing the structure of education from 7 + 2 + 3 to 6 + 3 + 3 (i.e., from 7 years of primary, 2 years of junior secondary, and 3 years of senior secondary to 6 years of primary, followed by 3 years junior secondary, and 3 years of selective senior secondary). It was proposed that the first 9 years (6 + 3) be open to all children followed by 3 years of selective senior secondary. A quota had to be introduced to reserve places for each primary school to ensure that all qualified students could receive and accept the offer. Unaided schools became the recipients of government financial support. Measures had to be adopted to reduce the dropout rate of girls because of pregnancies. Junior Secondary curriculum included Tswana culture, English, mathematics, practical subjects, science, and social studies; Senior Secondary retained the same six subjects, as a core, plus two optional units for specialization. It was stressed that curriculum continuity had to be strengthened between junior secondary and senior secondary levels. In the new curriculum, Setswana as a medium of communication,

Tswana culture, and the indigenous content and approaches got the needed importance. Recommendations were made for the establishment of a testing center, a Botswana National Examination Council, and a Senior Secondary Board of Certificate of Education. The Cambridge Board Junior Certificate Examination was requested to test explanatory and reasoning powers of the pupils and Senior Secondary Examinations to include international as well as locally oriented papers, to be graded according to international standards, but the performance to be standard to Botswana needs.

Along with the secondary education, other types of education were also considered for improvements and expansion to meet different types of educational needs. It was noted earlier that during the colonial period, the curriculum offered was mainly academic, although the people wanted practical and occupational subjects and skill training. To achieve this, the Botswana Training College (BTC) was converted into the Botswana Institute of Accounting and Commerce (BIAC). The government was asked to develop facilities for continuing education and vocational studies to encourage and establish programs for part-time and evening classes to enable the employees of various sectors to upgrade their skills. Thus, along with the formal education, out-of-school and extramural education was also recommended. The inclusion of Botswana Brigades in the plans for the improvement of skill training and practical subjects became an important consideration.

It should be noted in passing that Botswana became internationally known in the 1970s for its Brigade Education Movement and for its education typified by a production approach. Patrick van Rensburg, who established several secondary schools in Botswana in the wake of its independence during the difficult times, pioneered the Brigade Movement in Botswana to instill a sense of self-help and self-employment among the young, and to find a remedy for the usual drawbacks of academic curriculum in developing countries. The Brigade Movement attracted the attention of international educators and researchers who visited Botswana and wrote reports about its education and training potentials. For various reasons, the Brigades started declining when the Commission was appointed. To rectify the situation, the Commission recommended that the government support the brigades and make provisions for the systematic improvement of training for the brigade school staff, including instructors and managers. The need for managerial training of the administrative staff appeared to be crucial not only among Brigade staff. The Commission made recommendations for upgrading and improving the training of headmasters, deputies, and education officers in collaboration with the Unified Teaching Service (UTS).

To increase the supply of teachers and prevent the turnover of the expatriate teachers, the Commission suggested certain incentives and improvements in the conditions of service. For the training of secondary teachers, besides improvement of courses and programs at the Teacher Training Colleges, a close cooperation between the Colleges and the University was recommended.

The government of Botswana responded to the recommendations for the improvement of secondary education quite positively. The NDP-5 (Government of Botswana, 1979) following the NCE report (Government of Botswana, 1977) shows the concern and budget allocations to meet the improvement needs of secondary education, particularly the improvement of teacher education and the implementation of a 9-year basic education up to junior secondary. To meet the challenge of the enormous expansion and the subsequent demands arising from the implementation of the 9 years of basic curriculum, the government once again signed another collaborative project with the USAID—the Junior Secondary Education Improvement Project (JSEIP). The JSEIP in Botswana, a part of a larger international project called Improving the Efficiency of Educational Systems (IEES), was under the contract of the Florida State University with the Institute for International Research and the State University of New York at Albany. Since 1986, the JSEIP initiated and pioneered a series of junior secondary curriculum, quantitative and qualitative research, specifically on the schools and the classrooms studies using questionnaire, observation techniques, and ethnographic approaches to make data available on instructional activities required to support improvement and innovation efforts. This was one of the most significant achievements; the studies were published later in a volume, *Curriculum in the Classroom* (Snyder & Ramatsui, 1990). The implications of these research studies are discussed later.

DEVELOPMENT OF HIGHER EDUCATION

The main seat of higher education, the University of Botswana, originated as the University College of Botswana, one campus of a university serving three protectorate countries in 1962 in Roma, Lesotho. Gradually the other two countries got out of this collaboration, and the University of Botswana (UB) was inaugurated in 1982. The two functions of the University are "to engage in improving the quality and in expanding the quantity of the human resources needed for the development, and to act as the repository of the collective knowledge and experience of the nation and the world" (University of Botswana, 2000, p. 5). The staff is committed to teaching, service, and research. The programs offered by the University and its affiliated institutions lead to degrees, diplomas, and certificates. Through research, consultancies, and information services undertaken by the staff, the University creates new knowledge and renders service to the nation. It also renders service by moderating and scrutinizing the curriculum and evaluation of six affiliated Colleges of Education that prepare primary and junior secondary teachers.

Several health training institutions belonging to the Ministry of Health are the affiliates of UB. The Faculty of Education office and staff renders a variety of service to the whole system of education and the Ministry of Education. At present, there are six faculties in operation. The university started with a few hundred students at the time of independence in 1966. In 1990–1991, the enrollment exceeded 3,500. In 2001, it reached almost 12,000.

To meet the aspiration of the people, the campus is expected to teach around 15,000 students in the future. It offers primarily bachelor's and master's level courses. Gradually the affiliated institutions have taken over the function of preparing most of the diploma programs. The Faculty of Education started first with the M.Ed. program with three students in 1984. Today it has 60 students. In 2001, three doctoral candidates also were admitted in Educational Administration and in the Guidance and Counseling section of Educational Foundations. Through the expansion of the Center of Continuing Education and its Distance Education Unit, plans are being implemented to bring education at a tertiary level to the doors of those who need higher education in remote and difficult-to-reach areas. This will be accomplished mainly through the development of modular courses and distance education methods used by the Open University systems, and through the use of educational technology and electronic media presently available to the modern world. There are plans to expand education in Botswana at all levels. The time is now ripe for a second university as the demands for more education and new programs continue to grow.

DEVELOPMENTS IN THE 1990s

Among many developments, two significant reports with serious implications for education in the 1990s and beyond need to be mentioned. In the 1990s, some educators felt that the NCE (Government of Botswana, 1977) needed a review in terms of the various changes affecting Botswana in fast changing times. In 1992, the president appointed a new commission on education to review and reexamine the educational system and its relevance in view of the fast changes that had taken place. It advised on the organization and diversification of secondary school curricula, particularly on postschool vocational and technical training systems for junior secondary and senior secondary graduates. In 1996, the president appointed a task force to provide a set of long-term goals for what kind of society and nation people envisioned Botswana ideally to be in the next 20 years by 2016.

The new commission on education submitted its report with the Revised National Policy on Education (RNPE) in 1994. It identified several important issues dealing with access and equity; training needs for the national economy; improving the quality of the educational system; improvement of teaching profession; and effective management of the educational system, including cost-effectiveness and sharing the cost of education. The commission noted problems despite the implementations of the NCE (Government of Botswana, 1977) recommendations in these areas and suggested remedies. It noted a low level of access and lack of equity. "According to the 1991 Census, about 17% of primary school age children (7–13 year age group) were not enrolled in formal education contrary to earlier projections of only 10%" (p. 2). It highlighted similar imbalances in human and material resource allocation, rural and urban school disparities, significant gender gaps in academic performance in science and mathematics, and so on. The RNPE (Government of Botswana, 1994) revisions and recommendations refined and updated the whole educational process to enable Botswana to catch up with world developments.

The new commission recommended the reintroduction of the 10-year basic core curriculum $(7 + 3 + 2)$, instead of the 9-year basic core curriculum $(6 + 3 + 2)$, for all students for the award of Junior Certificate at the end of junior secondary education. The new curriculum aimed to prepare the young for the changing times, the world of work, the use of electronic-age technology, with emphasis on the children's participation and interaction in learning, critical thinking, and problem solving. It included Setswana and English from Standard 1, science and technology, computer skills, practical subjects like business, everyday commerce, and environmental education. It also aimed to develop understanding of society, appreciation of culture, a sense of citizenship, and other necessary skills and attitudes to make the young ready for the world of work. It demanded immediate localization of the Senior Secondary syllabus and examination to be fully achieved by 2003. It stressed the recognition of continuous assessment in the evaluation process, improvement of career guidance and guidance and counseling services, incorporation of environmental education in all subjects, provision for vocational and technical education, and a National Book Policy to promote local books, publishing industry professionalism, and culture of reading in Botswana. It recommended the establishment of a National Council on Education to guide the government, a Pre-Primary Unit to oversee and guide the activities to support primary education, and the changing of the name of the National Setswana Language Council to Botswana Languages Council with revised terms of references. The committee recommended the establishment of a Tertiary Education Council to formalize and coordinate the activities and policies of various tertiary education institutions and relevant sectors in the economy to ensure the maintenance of the standards of courses and their evaluation, and to advise the government on all matters concerning human resources.

The second significant report was submitted by a nine-person Presidential Task Group, later expanded to 31 persons representing various sections, in a booklet entitled, *Long Term Vision for Botswana: Prosperity for All* in 1997. The document presents a long-term vision for the year 2016, the 50th year of Botswana's independence. It is now popularly called *Vision 2016*. The document has been distributed to the public and to government and private organizations for incorporation in their programs, plans, and policies. Vision 2016 asks: "Why Does Botswana Need a Vision?"

> Botswana finds itself in a period of history when social attitudes and values around the world are changing at an unprecedented rate. The people of Botswana must adapt to the challenge of global society while retaining the positive aspects of their cultural values that distinguish them from other nations. After thirty years of independence we must take stock of our past aspirations, and the extent to which we have realized them. At the same time, we must formulate our aspirations and dreams for the future. What kind of society would we like Botswana to be by the year 2016, when we will be celebrating our fiftieth anniversary of independence? Some of the changes we need to make will only take effect after a number of years. This includes improvements in education and public health. We must therefore have a long term view of the right directions to take. For us to be active in the rapidly changing global economy and social order, we must take advantage of the opportunities that change will present. The targets we set for ourselves will come with many challenges, some of which we cannot anticipate today. We must prepare for continuous innovation, resilience, commitment and fortitude. We will have to dedicate ourselves to shaping the destiny of our country. Nobody will do it for us. These changes will entail effort and hardship, but the reward will be prosperity for all Botswana. (Government of Botswana, 1997a, p. 69)

Vision 2016 is widely publicized. An impressive logo appears in public places, including the posters by the roadside, to make people aware of its importance. Various organizations and institutions in Botswana have been asked to send their responses to the Interim Council on how they think they can contribute to making the Vision a reality. *Long Term Vision for Botswana* (Government of Botswana, 1997a) adds a fifth national principle, *Botho,* to the already existing four principles stated earlier (Democracy, Development, Self-Reliance, Unity). Thus, Botswana now has five national principles intended to enrich its philosophical goals and guide its policies, plans, and activities. The Setswana word, *Botho,* is the equivalent of *compassion.* Yet the real meaning and importance of *Botho* in the national life and future plans of Botswana are given in these terms:

> The fifth principle for Botswana will be *Botho*. This refers to one of the tenets of African culture—the concept of a person who has a well-rounded character, who is well-mannered, courteous and disciplined, and realizes his or her full potential both as an individual and as a part of the community to which he or she belongs. *Botho* defines a process for earning respect by first giving it, and to gain empowerment by empowering others. It encourages people to applaud rather than resent those who succeed. It disapproves of antisocial, disgraceful, inhuman and criminal behavior, and encourages social justice for all. *Botho* as a concept must stretch to its utmost limits the largeness of the spirit of all Batswana.[2] It must permeate every aspect of our lives, like the air we breathe, so that no Motswana will rest easy knowing that another is in need. The five principles are derived from Botswanas's cultural heritage, and are designed to promote social harmony, or *kagisano*. They set the broader context for the objectives of national development, which are: Sustained Development; Rapid Economic Growth; Economic Independence; Social Justice. (p. 2)

After adding a new ethical dimension to the national goal and philosophy, the document states seven principal visions as "a national manifesto for the people of Botswana":

By the year 2016, Botswana will be
an educated, informed nation
a prosperous, productive and innovative nation
a compassionate and caring nation
a safe and secure nation
an open, democratic and accountable nation
a moral and tolerant nation
a united and proud nation. (pp. 70–72)

The Vision 2016 features prominently in the short "Foreword" by President Masire to the National Development Plan-8, 1997/98-2002/03 (NDP–8). *Sustainable Economic Diversification* is the keyword, the burden of NDP–8. Chapter 15, "Education and Training," gives strong support to the RNPE (Government of Botswana, 1994) recommendations: "During NDP–8 the education sector will contribute to producing such a workforce through continued implementation of the recommendations of the Revised National Policy on Education (RNPE) of 1994" (Government of Botswana, 1997b, p. 337). Although it notes the implementation of some of the recommendations, such as the access to Universal Primary Education, the establishment of National Council of Education, and so on by NDP–7 (1991/92–1996/97; Government of Botswana, 1991), it promises to implement other recommendations as prioritized and to spur the progress of those already implemented. Thus, there is full governmental support for what the RNPE (Government of Botswana, 1994) has recommended. In the foregoing pages, an attempt has been made to provide the context and detailed information to acquaint the reader with Botswana's educational setup and its plans and policies for years to come. The next section provides an examination and critique of the achievements and the promises of the educational establishment in the light of research studies, scholarly reviews, and realities of national life.

RESEARCH FINDINGS ON THE IMPLEMENTATION
OF THE NEW CURRICULUM

Various research studies on the implementation of the new curriculum indicate that three decades of sincere human efforts and ample financial resources expended to expand and improve education in Botswana to meet the needs and aspirations of the people have not yielded results to be enthusiastic about. The new curriculum for the 9-year basic education up to junior secondary for all was implemented in the mid-1980s. The teaching and the teachers of this curriculum became the focus of research, particularly under the guidance of the Junior Secondary Education Improvement Project (JSEIP). The findings of selected research studies reveal how the new curriculum is taught in Botswana classrooms. The new curriculum guides for teachers and others distributed to the schools make it clear that the learners have to be active and expressive by being involved in the teaching–learning process; the teaching has to be child-centered and based on the learner's everyday life experiences, and what used to be *academic* is expected to be *practical*. Prophet and Rowell (1990) used ethnographic research procedures involving direct classroom observations and interviews to collect data from five junior secondary schools. This study indicates little change in the delivery of the new curriculum. Authoritarian teachers talking to passive pupils involved in drills and stock responses to close-ended questions dominate the classrooms in Botswana:

The classroom interactions documented in this study show the curriculum-in-action, and as such, present a predominantly instrumental view of the term "practical." An emphasis or the acquisition of limited skills associated with the specific responses required to achieve success on the terminal examination prevails. The dominant mode of interaction is that of transmission of information from teachers to students accompanied by repetitions and drills. Knowledge is a commodity to be poured into empty vessels and the more the better. What is missing from these interactions is any recognition of the beliefs and values which students bring with them to the classroom or even acknowledgment that students have already constructed schemes for interpreting the world. (pp. 27–28)

Rowell and Prophet (1990), in their detailed analysis of ethnographic data collected on the multiple facets of practical curriculum in action, came to similar conclusions about the classroom interaction. The teachers and pupils involved in the practical remain confined to merely technical aspects. The interpretive and critically reflective aspects of the practical, in terms of the real-world knowledge brought into the classroom by the pupils, are neglected. Thus, "this school knowledge becomes trapped by its context and separated from the outside world, becomes criticized as academic" (p. 24). Fuller and Snyder (1990) undertook a broader study of junior and primary school teachers involving observation of quantifiable teacher behaviors across the entire country to balance the small study by Prophet and Rowell (1990) cited earlier. They concluded: "Our findings confirm Prophet and Rowell's earlier work: teachers tend to stand before the class talking at pupils, encouraging few questions, little manipulation of ideas, and even infrequent application of textbooks and basic instructional materials" (p. 68).

The ecology of Botswana primary and junior secondary classrooms has been studied quantitatively by Fuller and Snyder (1990, 1991) and Chapman and Snyder (1992). Fuller and Snyder (1990) used 406 classrooms in 57 primary schools and 603 classrooms in 32 junior secondary schools for their study. They concluded that the school and its environment prove to be more ambiguous and less nurturing as the pupils move from primary to secondary in terms of unclear classroom objectives, more complex teaching methods, and more difficult content leading to student confusion and lack of interest. Fuller and Snyder (1991) investigated the teacher's use of instructional materials and time and the classroom social interaction in 127 primary and 157 junior secondary schools. They concluded that textbooks as materials are less frequently used than expected (although textbooks in English and mathematics are used more). The use of textbooks makes teaching less teacher-centered.

Chapman and Snyder (1992) investigated teachers classified as untrained, diploma holders, and postgraduate diploma (PGDE) holders. The largest difference reported was between the untrained and the PGDE holders, and the next largest difference was between the untrained and the diploma holders. The PGDE holders showed the skills of logical presentation of content and the use of teaching aids. However, the untrained group asked more open-ended questions and devoted more time in lesson preparation than the PGDE holders. The untrained teachers also appeared to be more oriented to student development. The researchers concluded that the formal training of the PGDE holders make them more content-oriented and teacher-centered and prone to neglect lesson preparation and student development. These negative characteristics of the PGDE holders, as compared with the untrained teachers, have implications for the design of preservice programs offered to the students.

Five years later, Prophet (1995) observed and ethnographically interviewed 2 junior secondary schools selected from among the 11 chosen by the Curriculum Development Unit for the trial of English curriculum materials. He summarized the findings:

From the extensive observations in these schools it can be said that there has been little or no visible change in the nature of the classrooms from that observed in the earlier studies by Prophet and Rowell (1990) and Fuller and Snyder (1990; 1991). This appears to be true not only for English lessons, but across the curriculum where it was expected that the positive effects of the new curriculum, would lead to more student-centered classrooms. The teaching-learning situation in the classrooms of these two schools can be easily summarized as follows:

> There is a continuing emphasis on teacher-centered whole-class teaching. There is a continuing student involvement in listening and silent desk work with a minimum of verbal participation. There is little or no time spent by the teacher working with individual students or small groups of students. Teachers are generally continuing to ignore incorrect student responses and are not offering remedial help. (p. 135)

This type of teaching and learning can be witnessed in the senior secondary classes in state schools as well. Tabulawa (1997) employed qualitative methods to study the teaching of state-prescribed geography curriculum at Cambridge level in two senior secondary schools of different status situated in different locations (a government rural school, School A; a private urban school, School B). This study found significant differences in the teaching styles contrasting the two schools: "in the case of School A, a stress on the transmission-reception mode of teaching and learning, and in the case of School B, a stress on the dialogue-participation pedagogical style" (p. 223). The difference in the quality of teaching and learning discovered in the two schools was explained in terms of their organizational structures, the teachers' notion of curriculum knowledge, and the sociocultural context.

All the studies on the 9-year basic curriculum implemented in junior secondary schools concur that the functional curriculum is opposed to the intent of the official curriculum launched by the Ministry of Education. The teachers' interpretation of the content and their involvement in the process as perceived by them negate what the new curriculum intends the pupils to experience in the classrooms. One scholar, Marope (1997), in her review of these studies, made critical observations of the researchers' positions with respect to their findings on the ground that "there is a need to establish a database on the state of teaching quality and to institute a program of research through which improvement can be monitored" (p. 33). Still this does not invalidate the basic findings that what the new curriculum aims at and what actually happens in Botswana classrooms are in conflict. Why? The next section attempts to answer this relevant question.

A CRITICAL ANALYSIS
OF THE BOTSWANA EDUCATIONAL SYSTEM

The context of Botswana surveyed in the light of its sociocultural transformation, and its colonial and postcolonial educational history, makes it evident that Botswana has always relied on education in its various developmental phases to meet the challenge of life and sustain progress. Even during the colonial period, when no financial assistance was available for education, it harnessed local community resources to support relevant curriculum in its self-help schools. In the decade following independence, education got its priority in the successive plans to supply the skilled manpower required for the country's economy. In the 1980s and later, when the financial resources became available in more abundance, education got the support required to expand and meet the national needs. According to the current estimate, the share of spending in educational developments in the national budgets has been increasing: "A significant increase in the share of the total expenditure is recorded for Education, from 16.8% in 1991/92 to 25.1% - 1996/97 due to increased expenditure arising from the implementation of Parallel Progression and the Revised National Policy on Education during the last years of the Plan period" (Government of Botswana, 1997b, p. 107).

Lack of funds has always been blamed for the poor and inadequate educational facilities in Africa, which in turn is considered the main cause of the continent's backwardness. In this respect, it must be noted that Botswana has been an extremely fortunate country to be among the few self-supporting and solvent nations of Africa. Of all the developing countries, it is able to fully finance its educational plans and still have foreign reserves for future use. According to a recent study by German Africa experts, despite the bleak future for most African countries, Botswana is among eight "potential reform countries" of Africa based on the criteria of GDP growth rates, per capita income, investment levels and productivity, UNDP index of human development, income distribution, and existence of stable institutions (Kappel, 2001, p. 23). Only a fortunate confluence of factors has brought about this happy situation.

Education in Botswana enjoyed the best possible consultancy from internationally reputed educational advisers and agencies, and its will and resources to implement their proposals, plans, and recommendations aimed to create the right kind of curriculum to realize the laudable national goals and people's aspirations. If this kind of educational effort fails or falls short, then questions must be raised about the fundamental nature of things guiding the educational endeavors. The lessons learned and insights gained through these critical questionings may help guide the policy decisions for the expansion of education and development of curriculum in Botswana and other African countries.

Why does the Botswana educational system not relate to curriculum innovations designed to achieve the national goals and aspirations? The answer lies in the examination of the deep structure of education and schooling inherited from the colonial past. The educational system received from the colonial past was not intended to help the colonies develop and achieve the ideals and objectives leading to national development and progress. The educational systems imported by the missionaries and colonial masters served their own respective purposes efficiently. Studies on colonial education indicate that the main purpose of the school was to produce intermediaries and literate clerks to assist the masters in ruling the natives.

The studies of Carnoy (1974) and Altbach and Kelly (1978) spearheaded the leftist-radical interpretation of postindependence educational developments embedded in the colonial history and the hierarchy of class structure. This interpretation still remains valid despite the attempts of some scholars, such as Ball (1983), who argue against the Marxist and class-based interpretation of the colonial education history. It is argued that it is the natives who demanded European education, curriculum, and medium of instruction for their benefit. This is apparently true as recorded in the available documents of the ex-colonies, including Botswana, but the hidden design and deeper motives must be investigated. The native elites, who made vigorous demands for the newly imported and cleverly imposed education, lacked insights into the far-reaching consequences of this education. Unfeeling toward the oppressed masses and concerned with their own immediate gains, they were no better than opium eaters. Once institutionalized, the educational system created a demand for itself.

What has it produced? In Fasheh's (1990) description of hegemonic education, it produced

> intellectuals who have lost their power base in their own culture and society, and who have been provided in a foreign culture and ideology, but without the power base in the hegemonic society-they tend to sharply overvalue symbolic power and tokens such as titles, degrees, access to prestigious institutions, and awards associated with the dominant culture. (p. 25)

In fact, Thomas Macaulay, who came to India in 1835 to lay the foundation of the earliest colonial education system, knew thoroughly well that it was intended to produce "a class of persons Indian in blood and colour, but English in tastes, in opinion, in morals and in intellect" (Zastoupil & Moir, 1999, p. 171). This is exactly what happened to the native intellectuals in every colony. The colonial educational system created almost a religious fervor for the colonial master's language and culture and reduced the indigenous knowledge, skills, and attitudes to the level of superstition. Scientific knowledge and methods, along with rationalism taught in foreign languages, enhanced the prestige of new education to the level that anything conceivably modern and progressive had to be Western. This almost uprooted indigenous approaches to knowing and living, at least for the newly educated flocking to the urban centers. Tangible rewards in the form of new jobs under the empire benefited those who had the advantage of the new education and the language of their colonial masters.

Obviously, the ruling royalties and landlords who maintained their power over the masses, while remaining loyal to the colonial masters, benefited most from this education. They also played the role of petty bourgeoisie in light of their gains. The common mass of people at the socioeconomic bottom remained the most exploited. In Botswana, commoners started working as migrant laborers in the mines of South Africa after the British Protectorate was established. After the colony became independent, despite all the noble intentions and grand goals and visions in the white papers, the old educational system has continued root and branch. The postcolonial phase has been aptly labeled *neo-colonial.*

After the independence, the demand for education intensified. To meet the manpower needs of a new nation dependent on expatriates, it was necessary to develop education at all levels, first starting with the existing secondary and tertiary education to absorb the primary school graduates. When the need for a comprehensive educational plan and policy was felt, the National Commission of Education (Government of Botswana, 1977) was appointed. This Commission accomplished admirably what it was supposed to do. It gave a coherent philosophy, policy guidelines, plans, and strategies for the expansion, adaptation, modification, and reformation of the educational system inherited from the colonial masters. The idealists among the national leaders and educated elite who wanted to raise the nation had to rely on hired consultants and skilled manpower from outside, mostly from Britain and other ex-colonies. It is questionable that this kind of staff and officers hired would do anything other than just operate the given machinery of the educational system. Also there prevailed a lack of confidence in the locally available resource persons capable of doing the task. The colonial rule, as stated earlier, had destroyed the roots of self-reliance and sown the seeds of dependency. Hence, the idea of surface change inherent in the expansion and reform of the inherited educational system was easier and more acceptable than bringing about a total radical change based on a curriculum newly conceptualized and worthy of being called innovation. This generally happened in all ex-colonies. Postindependence education in Botswana tended to repeat the histories of India, Kenya, Nigeria, Ghana, and a host of other colonies. Because we are speaking of Botswana, one grand example of how indigenous innovation was slighted is illustrative.

The Brigade Movement was hailed all over the world as holding great potential to provide a relevant curriculum for "education with production" in a developing country. It was designed to instill self-reliance and create self-employment opportunities required to ward off "the diploma disease" syndrome common in the developing countries (Dore, 1980). Under the leadership of an African educator naturalized in Botswana, Patrick van Rensburg, this movement with indigenous efforts aimed to regenerate the nation's youth to solve major socioeconomic problems. Two curriculum experts in Botswana, Noel and Ramatsui (1994), using Miller and Seller's (1985) categorization, assessed it as the "most notable effort to implement a transformation position in Botswana" (p. 110). Yet it started losing the support of the educated elite who favored "academic" and white-collar jobs and relegated the Brigade schooling to a substandard, second-rate vocational stream.

After the initial success of the 1960s and 1970s, it never got back to its original prestige despite the recommendations in its favor by the NCE (Government of Botswana, 1977) and the RNPE (Government of Botswana, 1994). The attitude to the national language, Setswana, compared with English shows the spell of colonial education. In their critical review of research on Setswana teaching, Chebanne and Molosiwa (1997) pointed out that "there is absolutely nothing written about the teaching of Setswana … but what is striking is that if at all there are publications or research on language teaching matters it is almost always on English curriculum and achievement" (p. 187). Chebanne and Molosiwa and other researchers have placed the blame on attitude of the government and its policy concerning Setswana for this neglect since independence.

The importance of English in the curriculum undermines the interest and research needs of the national language, Setswana, and contributes to the total neglect of other native languages. English as the medium of instruction increased its importance beyond the early conceptualization. The National Commission on Education (Government of Botswana, 1977) recommended the use of English from Standard Five. Following the recommendations of the National Commission on Education (Government of Botswana, 1993) as amended by the revised policy, English was used from Standard Two. It was recommended to be used from Standard One in 2000. Primary children face considerable problems communicating when they have to do code switching from Setswana or other native languages to English in the classroom. In his study relating the understanding of science teaching to language and culture in Botswana, Prophet (1990) pointed out that "no research appears to have been carried out concerning the extent to which fundamental world views of Setswana culture reinforce or contradict the views being put forward in schooling" (p. 114). He concluded on a pessimistic note:

> The classroom here in Botswana may not be drastically improved by curriculum reform which simply alters the surface features of that which is on offer to the pupils. Whilst the minority of bright pupils appear to get by, the majority struggle and fall by the wayside. The problem is more fundamental and is related to the issue of culture and language. The knowledge acquired by the pupils through the curriculum is dependent on both their experience and the language they use to describe that experience. This needs to be accepted, the effect of this on educational outputs researched, and if necessary, change introduced. (p. 116)

Arthur (1996) alluded to "the early start fallacy" practiced in the teaching of English in Botswana and to the neglect of the mother tongue. He pointed to a deeper reason for the supremacy of English:

> Although the elite social group in Botswana is mainly composed of Setswana speakers, English is assimilated into their social and cultural life, and they tend to send their children to English-medium schools. They have a vested interest therefore in sustaining the symbolic value of English which can be viewed as linguistic capital. The interest of this national elite coincides with that of dominant world powers in promoting the global hegemony of English. (p. 51)

This state of affairs has continued despite the recommendations favoring the use of home languages by some native research scholars (Nyati-Ramahobo, 1989, 1991). According to Arthur (1996), the "needs of learners, whether in pragmatic terms of understanding lesson content or in terms of their emotional well-being as young children, are clearly not central to the aims and models of English language pedagogy operating in Botswana" (p. 53).

Beyond the focus on language, some scholars have used sociological insights to interpret the role of education in social reproduction and inequality. Chilisa (1987, n/d) examined inequalities of educational access related to socioeconomic status differences among children in the village of Mochudi in Botswana. She found a proportional representation of children in primary schools, but the disparities of representation emerge as children climb up the educational ladder. Using Gramsci's concept of hegemony, Maruatona (1996) showed how in Botswana the ruling class, the elite achieved through education, language and other forms of ideological state apparatus, the consent of the general population. He critically examined the thinking behind the two Education Commissions (1977 and 1993), which shaped the national educational plans and policies, the state education apparatus such as the Curriculum Development Unit, and the relationships between the teachers and pupils and the teachers and the curriculum development. He argued that the precolonial social structure was reinforced by the colonial system to increase the dependency of the people on authority by collaborating with the ruling elite. These developments further aggravated by the endemic poverty and illiteracy of the people did not allow them to actively participate in the political and other decision-making processes. Thus, the democratic process becomes a show once the election fever is over. "In Botswana, the political and the economic elite are the same groups and are answerable to their former 'colonial masters' who still control the economy" (p. 53).

The involvement of people in Education Commissions as respondents serves to allow them "to rubber stamp the decisions of the elite." The Ministry of Education is a centralized machinery with departmental officers bound in hierarchical relationships. The Curriculum Development Unit operates under the assumption: that education is a neutral process and curriculum development is a rational-technical process through which a body of expert knowledge worthy for all is offered. This eliminates teachers' and students' participation in the curriculum development process. With English given top priority as a medium of instruction and Setswana, all other languages are ignored. The English medium school children are prepared to compete for the best available jobs from which the poor are eliminated. Maruatona (1996) concluded:

> The thesis being articulated is that the education system in Botswana serves to widen the gap between the rich and the poor through reproducing class inequalities by preserving the culture of the dominant groups and institutionalizing it as a common culture. (p. 63)

This brings to the relevant points of teacher education and curriculum development ideas prevalent in African countries including Botswana. First, the demand for education has been escalating since independence in every country without much reflection and research on the nature of the curriculum and how it relates to people's attitudinal change to work habits and life patterns conducive to the required progress, development, and change. Learning is inseparably attached to formal schooling so that new and innovative ideas such as freeschooling, deschooling, reconceptualizing curriculum, and other alternatives appear to be senseless. The promise of universal access to free education, if possible up to the highest level, has universal appeal. It also provides advance solutions for many problems likely to be created by the opposition. The models most dominant in curriculum development departments and courses offered for teachers have been technical-rational ones. Most educational research means empirical data gathering, mostly surveys, or replications of British and American studies, although ethnographic studies have been undertaken. For some time and more so now, a great faith in technology has been evident. Technology and its adjuncts carry the prestige of being modern, efficient, and scientific, although it is costly. Thus, the mainstream curriculum experts and researchers, the lecturers and teachers, and all involved at all levels of education are convinced that these alone work. This is probably an indication of a conservatism getting stronger, to break the spine of radical-leftist educational ideas and alternative theories, in view of the rise of commercialism, consumerism, and the market economy following globalization. This seems a parallel to the resurgence of neoconservatism in the Western world, which is discussed later in this chapter.

AN ALTERNATIVE TO THE MAINSTREAM REFORMS

Botswana is among the few African nations that has brought together its democratic process of government and the resources for developing its educational system. Education based on formal schooling inherited from the colonial masters has been subjected to extensive expansion, various curriculum reforms, and general innovation during the last three decades. At present, more than a quarter of the total national budget is allocated for education alone. Despite the resources expended and all the possible attempts in terms of improvements in teacher training, teacher–pupil ratio, provisions for curriculum guides, and other necessary paraphernalia, the implementation efforts have been largely unimpressive. Contrary to the Curriculum Development Unit's expectations, the students are taught as in traditional classrooms, dominated by teacher talk and their authoritarian approaches, compounded by the communication difficulties created by the pupils learning through English as the medium of instruction. What should be done? What are the possible alternatives? What other directions are available?

Suggestions from educational scholars and researchers locally and elsewhere abound. The local educational institutions and associations, the governmental and other organizations hold frequent conferences and seminars where papers are presented, educational problems are discussed, and remedies are prescribed. The ideas and proposals from the mainstream scholarship and research are largely oriented to making piecemeal and persistent reform endeavors in terms of improving teacher education programs, course offerings, job market-oriented education, teaching practice, teaching methods, evaluation procedures, curriculum materials, use of technology, administrative measures, research undertakings, parents and community relations, budgetary provisions, and other measures likely to overcome and solve the problems gradually. However, radical-leftist theorists of education, particularly the reproduction theorists, hold that the educational system, including schooling, is not a neutral machinery in need of repair and improvements to solve the ills of the society. In fact, the educational system is doing effectively and efficiently what it has been designed to do. Its aim has been misconstrued as libertarian and emancipatory while in reality it works toward perpetuating the existing social stratification in favor of the ruling class and elite.

LEFTIST-RADICAL CRITIQUES AND THEORIES AND CRITICAL PEDAGOGY

The leftist-radical critiques of education and schooling provide insightful and powerful analyses, demonstrating how education reproduces various forms of socioeconomic inequalities that result in exploitation and oppression of one class by another. In the educational discourses of the last three decades, reproduction theories have influenced educational scholars to develop what has been loosely called *resistance theory*. Basically, these theories point out that schools are structurally designed to achieve their main objectives of efficiently reproducing the dominant social order; schools are not neutral agencies because they serve the purpose of transmitting the ideology and knowledge of the dominant social class. This is necessary to persuade the majority and gain their support or consent to maintain the status quo and reproduce the existing class structure. The major impact of the reproduction theorists' critique of education and their contribution to curriculum has been felt since the 1970s. According to Giroux (1983), Paulo Freire's early works, particularly his *Pedagogy of the Oppressed* (1970), was a precursor of the cultural reproduction theories of Pierre Bourdieu (Bourdieu & Passeron, 1977). The hegemonic-state reproduction model based on Gramsci (1971) is reflected in Apple (1979), Sarup (1984), and Dale (1986) to explain how intellectual and moral influence as well as coercion are used to win approval of the majority and eliminate their opposition. The insights of the reproduction theorists generated resistance theory to provide a new, optimistic perspective concerning the potentials of education. Education is conceptualized as having considerable autonomy, capable of offering serious resistance or opposition to the dominant and oppressive socioeconomic forces.

Radical-leftist theories, including the resistance theory, have empowered education and encouraged libertarian educators. Nevertheless, these theories have their weaknesses. Based on the analysis of various scholars, including Giroux, Apple, and others, Stanley (1992) identified several problems. Resistance theories have overemphasized class as an explanatory variable and neglected the analysis of race and gender as modes of domination. Feminists like Ellsworth (1989) have been extremely concerned about the neglect of feminist aspects of dialogue in critical pedagogy. The views of Apple have been adduced to show that the radical discourse is "too abstract to have significant impact" and "much of the critical scholarship in education has been elitist, because it is written for a narrow academic audience—an escape into theory disconnected from the concerns of real world teachers and students."

In the meantime, neoconservatism revival has gained strength. The conservative conception of curriculum favors a technical approach in which *science* is "defined in terms of its utility for economic productivity and technological development" (Stanley, 1992, p. 105). The same situation can be discovered in many developing countries particularly when the multinationals are looking for cheap skilled labor. In Botswana, some progressive native scholars have argued that the technical rational model approaches to curriculum development have led to the failure of curriculum reform. Maruatona (1996, 1998) and Tabulawa (1997, 1998) support radical and paradigmatic change in the conceptualization of curriculum problems and their solutions in Botswana. The findings of both include an indictment of the technical-rational model of curriculum development pursued in Botswana.

In third world countries, the reliance on science and technology has remained undiminished because these are held mainly responsible for the developments and economic superiority of the Western world to be emulated. Therefore, models and methods interpreted in terms of science and technology are likely to get priority over those originating from alternative sources. New and borrowed terms abound, sometimes meaninglessly, in the papers and articles on teacher education: teaching problem solving, developing critical thinking, striving for computer awareness and literacy, interactive learning, virtual class, teaching for occupational skills and vocational education, and so on. These are used more as fad words or slogans or panaceas for all the social ills. The conservative revival has become forceful in Africa after the radicals were muted following the failure of the Marxist regime in Soviet Russia and the internal communal wars, which brought miseries and suffering in several African countries under the influence of Marxist politics.

Why has neoconservatism been so popular? Stanley (1992) thought that its rhetoric, based on common-sense perceptions applied to the real problems of most working- and middle-class people, was appealing. However, the liberal and radical discourse has failed to provide an adequate response to the neoconservative challenge. Giroux (1988) found that the liberal faith in science and reason and the dominance of empiricism and scientism in education and other social sciences divert the liberal discourse away from everyday life. As indicated earlier, Apple found the critical approaches to the study of schooling too abstract and elitist to cater for the concerns of concretely existing teachers and students. Besides these, the most important is "the failure of radical educators to construct an adequate moral theory" (Stanley, 1992, p. 111; see also Pinar et al., 1995, chap. 5).

A CONCEPTION OF MORALITY/ETHICS FOR CRITICAL PEDAGOGY

In his various writings, Giroux has struggled intellectually to forge a conception of ethics to support radical pedagogy. He also noted that it requires a language of protest grounded in a vision of a preferred community fighting for democratic rights. Apple (1986a, 1986b) agreed with Giroux that critical pedagogy requires both a "language of critique" and "language of possibility." To move away from a society based on privatization and greed and for the reconstruction of a society based on the principle of common good, it is an educator's prominent task to convince people that the current and emerging economic and political institutions reproduce current inequalities and inequities (Stanley, 1992). Giroux (1992) indicated the main issues involved in the creation of ethics for critical pedagogy:

> Ethics must be seen a central concern of critical pedagogy. Ethics, in this case, is not a matter of individual choice or relativism but a social discourse that refuses to accept needless human suffering and exploitation. Ethics becomes a practice that broadly connotes one's personal and social sense of responsibility to the Other. (p. 74)

He went on to say:

> The issue of human rights, ecology apartheid, militarism, and other forms of domination against both humans and the planet affect all of us directly and indirectly. This is not merely a political issue; it is also a deeply ethical issue that situates the meaning of the relationship between the self and the other, the margin and the center, and the colonizer and colonized in broader context of solidarity and struggle. Educators need to develop pedagogical practices that not only heightens the possibilities for a critical consciousness but also for transformative action. (p. 79)

For critical pedagogy to be on sound and solid footing, it requires ethical imperatives that have been critically missing. The required ethics, as pointed by Giroux in the prior two quoted passages, must be grounded in social discourse and in the relationship between the self and the other for the educators to raise critical consciousness and get involved in transformative action.

The history of education shows that critical pedagogy in some form was always there to preserve the essentially progressive nature of education. During the course of time, it has steadily strengthened its hold among those concerned with emancipatory education. Stanley (1992) related the current radical education and critical pedagogy to social reconstructionism in American education between the two World Wars. A coterie of

some profound American thinkers and educators were associated with social reconstructionism as a stream in the larger movement of Progressive education. Its aim was to
bring about a planned social transformation that could avoid the extremes of the right
and the left: the prevalent Social Darwinianism and the laissez-faire capitalism on the
right and the radical model for social change under the influence of Marxism and Lenin-
ism on the left. Stanley shows that the current critical pedagogy comprising a variety of
theorists and educators represents the reemergence of social reconstructionism with
some differences. Stanley's arguments are not only valid and cogent; they are attested by
the evident similarities of aims and interests pursued by the two educational movements
that emerged in two different milieux. Although both social reconstructionism and critical pedagogy have a common vision of creating a democratic society through direct involvement and empowerment of teachers and educators, the former relied on the
Enlightment tradition, whereas the latter appropriated the insights of postmodernism
and poststructuralism to question the Enlightment legacy. The changed milieu should
also be noted to understand critical pedagogy as a radical movement.

Critical pedagogy wants to address the long-standing need for emancipating the colonized and the oppressed and to bring about equity and social equality through education
in a time when the world is caught between the commercial greed-creating consumerism
and multinational cartels in the global economy on the one hand, and the helpless, disorganized, and directionless masses on the other hand. The middle-class elite capable of
providing the leadership are engaged in the service of commercialism. A similar role
played by the elite supporting the ruling class led to the expansion of the colonial empires globally in the last two centuries. The history of education is evoked here to show
that the critical pedagogy is neither an upstart nor abrupt as an educational movement. It
is in the service of a long-standing ethical cause—the education of the oppressed and the
deprived all over the world. It is needed for the development of the potentials of each
member of the society and the self-realization of each individual by democratic means.
Everything else is less important than this project if humanity wants to preserve its humaneness and call itself civilized. What can be more important than this?

In response to this need, Henry Giroux, who holds a prominent position among the
supporters of critical pedagogy, points to the problems in providing an ethics for critical pedagogy. Stanley (1992) admirably summarized the views from Giroux's *Schooling
and the Struggle for Public Life: Critical Pedagogy in the Modern Age.* The left has failed to
focus on theoretical dimensions of morality. The right posits an essentialist view of morality to endorse transmission of traditional values and forms of knowledge. The liberal theorists support a "naive view of the value of reason and scientific progress." The
liberals promote an abstract view of morality depending on procedural justice and a
conception of the individual abstracted from history and community, which is likely to
lead to "a morality designed for a society of strangers." Deconstructionist approaches,
arising from postmodernism, poststructuralism, and neopragmatism, have led to a collective assault on foundationalism, which has further decentered the unified subject essential for conservative, liberal, and radical theorists while resulting in a "one sided
methodological infatuation with deconstructing not simply particular truths, but the
very notion of truth itself." This has encouraged the current flight from ethics and politics. Giroux wants critical theorists to appropriate progressive aspects of postmodernist movement and resist the tendency of flight from politics and ethics. "Those who
hold that critical educators have no right to impose their positions on students misrep-
resent critical pedagogy and argue from a flawed theoretical position that contributes
to the flight from ethics and politics while reinforcing status quo." This view of Giroux
is "consistent with Freire that teachers have an obligation to make their positions clear
to students but not to impose a given position on them" (Stanley, 1992, pp. 164–167).

In search of an ethics for his reconceptualized reconstructionist approach to critical pedagogy, Stanley (1992) traced the concept of *phronesis* in Aristotle's politics. *Phronesis* means "practical competence required for praxis, understood as inherently social and interpretive mode of activity characteristic of human beings" (p. 214). It represents a fundamental human interest embracing all dimensions of human thought, action, linguistic and interpretive competence, and ethical capacity. Practical competence exists as intrinsic to human beings, and critical human judgment has survived historically under adverse circumstances (p. 215). Stanley pointed out that a critical pedagogy supported by an ethics of practical competence would involve value analysis in three ways: critically examine whether a society is functioning according to its professed aims, provide a utopian speculation of how the good or human betterment should be defined, and consider the values and conditions to conceptualize preferred communities and societies. Evidently, a critical pedagogy based on practical competence would involve value analysis, judgment, and social reconstruction. "The realization of basic human interests requires the practical competence denied by racism, sexism, class discrimination, and so forth" (p. 216).

AN AFRICAN PERSPECTIVE ON ETHICAL DIMENSIONS FOR CRITICAL PEDAGOGY

The question that remains to be addressed is: What kind of pedagogy can be relevant to solve the educational problems and implement curriculum change for social transformation required to bring about equity and social justice? Reconceptualized reconstructionist critical pedagogy as currently conceived through the incorporation of the ideas of social reconstructionism, the new sociology, critical theories, neo-Marxism, feminism, neopragmatism, postmodernism, and poststructuralism appears foremost in its fight against existing social oppression, inequities, and inequalities. Because these social problems are more intensely prevalent in Africa and other developing countries, critical pedagogy can be relied on for antihegemonic and emancipatory education to bring about social transformation. The second question then is: What kind of ethics can these nations provide for critical pedagogy? What follows is an attempt in that search.

In her recent work, *Affirming Unity in Diversity in Education: Healing with Ubuntu,* Goduka (1999) provided an ethical base for critical pedagogy—an educational project designed to transform the conflict-torn South African multicultural society. Born in the Xhosa tribe of South Africa, Goduka grew up experiencing the oppression of apartheid. Subsequently, she lived and taught in the United States and developed Western intellectual awareness of social reconstructionism, feminism, critical theories, and deconstructionist postmodernist theories. She assimilated and utilized all these perspectives in her autobiographical narrative, a project for critical pedagogy she called *healing with ubuntu.* This educational project by a thoroughgoing African is relevant for South Africa, but it also applies equally well to any setting where oppression has deprived people of their basic human rights. *Ubuntu/Yobuntu,* a concept borrowed from the Xhosa language "reflects the oneness of humanity, a collectivity, a community and set of spiritual values that seek respect and dignity for all humanity" (p. 9). A few sentences from her "Prologue" disclose the nature of her project:

> My job as an educator is to take *ubuntu bene*—your humaneness, *nobuntu bam*—my humaneness, *nobuntu be-Afrika iyonke*—and the humaneness of the continent of Africa and use it to undergird the curriculum and pedagogy in order for the present and the future generations to inherit the legacy *yobuntu* and pass it on. (p. 17)

When I was thinking about writing *Healing with Ubuntu,* and after the process of writing began, I invoked and summoned the ancestors with me to guide me, protect me, and allow their spirits to engage with my spirit to give me the wisdom, respect, humility and sensitivity to tell my story, and to tell my truth, yet not to become oblivious to other stories and other truths. (p. 17)

The project I am proposing in *Healing with Ubuntu* does not originate with me. It is grounded in the spiritual values embedded in the world view embraced by indigenous people from different continents. (p. 18)

Thus the goal of both my narrative and the text is to provide educators with the philosophy and theoretical framework that will help them move beyond the role of a technician to that of a thinker, a creator, a writer, a healer and a visionary. (p. 19)

The author built "a theoretical and philosophical foundation and a solid scaffolding for an inclusive yet diverse" curriculum affirming unity in diversity. She took an African concept *ubuntu* (oneness of humanity, commonality, and unity amid diversity) and related it to the Greek word *agape* (altruistic/unselfish love), to the Lakota Native-American worldview of reverence for all life in the saying *mitakuye oyasin* ("we are related"), and finally to the ideas of Freire and Giroux to ground a critical pedagogy curriculum for social transformation and antihegemonic education. By losing the bond of oneness, the commonality, and the communitarian spirit, we have become each other's oppressors. The new curriculum bound by the universal principle of unity in diversity must be grounded in "the biological relatedness," "the common spiritual capacity," and "the common destiny" of all human beings (p. 45). "The maxim upon which transformation rests is reflected in the Xhosa proverb (*umntu ngumntu ngabantu*—I am we; I am because we are; we are because I am; I am in you—you are in me; therefore, we are one life)." This spirit of human unity is embraced by "the indigenes of Africa, Asia, Australia, North and South America, and Africans in Diaspora.... It stands in opposition to the western European individualistic axiom I think; therefore I am" (p. 191).

Inspired by Giroux's view of teachers as transformative intellectuals and encouraged by the postmodern and poststructural deconstructionists, a teacher in this critical and liberatory curriculum for social reconstruction and transformation understands and challenges the canon of accepted ideologies, assumptions, and foundations to create learning conditions and restore human dignity lost during colonial oppression. Students must be involved and encouraged "to think critically and to develop the skills to formulate, document and justify their conclusions and generalizations" (p. 191). Pedagogy is not neutral, apolitical, and value-free. This raises questions with respect to who defines and organizes school knowledge, who has access to it, and whose culture is included and excluded in the curriculum. It speaks of optimism and visionary leadership required for teachers to be "transformative intellectuals, cultural awakeners, spiritual and bone healers for all forms of oppression—*Izangoma*, in order to heal first, before engaging learners in this process" (p. 187).

CONCLUSION

The foregoing reflections have been critical about the developments and the state of curriculum innovation in Botswana, which has been one of the few African countries to enjoy the socioeconomic and political conditions, financial resources, and social will to execute its educational plans. It has been critical of the prevalent mainstream educational policies and conceptions of curriculum development that pay little attention to what one can learn from the history of education and the nature of schooling grounded in the class structure. The lesson learned from the success and failures of Botswana can be extended to understand, inform, and develop relevant curriculum in other African countries and elsewhere in the world. Jansen (1989) pointed out that one of the reasons for the emergence of critical models of curriculum in postcolonial Africa is the perception of the irrelevance of Western models of curriculum development in an African setting, especially after the rapid and unplanned expansion of an existing educational infrastructure undertaken initially created serious political dilemmas. Ironically enough, this occurred in Botswana, although the educational expansion and curriculum innovation were seriously and professionally planned by the experts. The consideration of critical pedagogy as relevant to the process of decolonization of the educational setup in Africa including Botswana, inevitably led to this question: What can Africa contribute to critical pedagogy in search of an ethical dimension for its application in African classrooms?

African countries invoking the spirit of Africa have always shown optimism and bold visions for social reconstruction in their attempts to replace, rather than heal, their colonized and oppressed status. Most of these visions are attempts to realize the best that was felt in African cultures. These visions also show their readiness to appropriate the advantages of developments in science, technology, the political democracy, and other ideas that come from the West. Less is known about the real powers, potentials, and regenerative capacities of the best in indigenous cultural traditions of Africa, grounded in the oral tradition that sustained social life for millions of years. This relative lack of knowledge is a function of the absence of infrastructure for allowing the natives to speak and give expression to their feelings. Certainly such infrastructure is not as fully and readily available as dancing, making music, and being sportive—all highly evolved social forms of expression in Africa.

The conceptions hidden in the terms *African socialism, African humanism, Africanism, ujamaa, kagisano, botho, siumuniye, umuntu* and so on are more meaningfully complex than the English expressions indicate. They indicate the lived experiences that cannot be fully expressed in literal forms or discourse. These are informed by the oral traditions that are silently articulate. But they all want to create an ideal, humane, and peaceful habitat—a society where individuals develop to contribute to the development and prosperity of others in the community. Estrangement and dissociation from the community are inconceivable to a healthy African mind. The idea of sharing, so commonplace to an African, is an invasion of the personal privilege and privacy to the individualistic and competitive mind. Therefore, it is not surprising that Goduka (1999) found a social concept, *ubuntu*, in her Xhosa worldview. It is not different from the Setswana term *botho*, accepted in Botswana as the fifth national principle to add an ethical dimension to the philosophy of life.

The two terms, coming from adjacent languages, are synonymous. Both mean "humaneness, human oneness," which is of universal ethical significance and applicable to critical pedagogy in Africa or elsewhere. This just shows the dynamism of the African traditions. It was this inherent potential of African cultures and traditions that gave Nelson Mandela the power to forgive his oppressors, liberate South Africa, and ground it constitutionally in a modern, multicultural democratic republic. We also tend to forget that it was Africa, under the oppressive rule, that created Mahatma Gandhi's powerful political weapon of passive resistance based on truth and nonviolence. To say all this is not to be accused of romanticizing; it is envisioning and forging a future for human beings and their healthy survival in togetherness. It is the ability to feel the sameness with others that brings a sense of communion, oneness, compassion, *ubuntu/botho*, and so on that can be extended to all and discovered in all cultures and climes that exist inherently by virtue of our belonging to the human species. A critical pedagogy to raise this consciousness of individuals must be grounded here. This is the ethics of emancipatory education required to decolonize the new nations coming out of the throes of oppression.

To create a condition for this critical pedagogy, we need to clear the ground. The narrowly conceived field of curriculum must give way to reconceptualizing curriculum theories and ideas to accommodate, appropriate, invite, and tolerate the old, the new, the outlandish, and so on to forge a new education, including a vision of innovative curriculum—a project neglected until now, but one that must be undertaken in all immediacy to be decolonized.

REFERENCES

Altbach, P. G., & Kelly, G. P. (1978). *Education and colonialism.* New York: Longman.

Apple, M. W. (1979). *Ideology and curriculum.* London: Routledge & Kegan Paul.

Apple, M. W. (1986a). National reports and the construction of inequality. *British Journal of Sociology of Education, 7*(2), 171–90.

Apple, M. W. (1986b). *Teachers and texts: A political economy of class and gender relations in education.* New York: Routledge & Kegan Paul.

Arthur, J. (1996). Language pedagogy in Botswana: Paradigms and ideologies. *Mosenodi* (Journal of Botswana Educational Research Association), *4*(1), 47–57.

Ball, S. J. (1983). Imperialism, social control and the colonial curriculum in Africa. *Journal of Curriculum Studies, 15*(3), 237–263.

Bourdieu, P., & Passeron, J. C. (1977). *Reproduction in education, society and culture.* Beverley Hills, CA: Sage.

Carnoy, M. (1974). *Education as cultural imperialism.* New York: David McKay.

Chapman, D. W., & Snyder, C. W. (1992). Teacher training and teachers' classroom behavior. In H. J. Walberg & D. W. Chapman (Eds.), *Advances in educational productivity* (Vol. 2, pp. 195–209). Greenwich, CT: Jai Press.

Chebbane, A. M., & Molosiwa, A. (1997). Research on the teaching of Setswana. In P. T. M. Marope & D. W. Chapman (Eds.), *A handbook of research on education: Teaching and teacher education in Botswana* (Vol. 1, pp. 187–204). Gaborone, Botswana: Lenstwe La Lesedi.

Chilisa, B. (1987). *Who gets ahead in education: A cross- sectional survey of primary, secondary and university students from Mochudi.* Unpublished master's thesis, University of Botswana, Gaborone, Botswana.

Chilisa, B. (n/d). *Education and social class representation in Botswana: A case for Mochudi* (mimeo).

Dale, M. (1986). Stalking a conceptual chameleon: Ideology in Marxist studies of education. *Educational Theory, 36*(3), 241–257.

Dore, R. (1980). *The diploma disease: Education, qualification and development.* London: Allen & Unwin.

Ellsworth, E. (1989). Why doesn't this feel empowering? Working through the repressive myths of critical pedagogy. *Harvard Educational Review, 59*(3), 297–324.

Evans, M. W., & Knox, D. M. (1991). The primary education improvement project. In M. W. Evans & J. H. Yoder (Eds.), *Patterns of reform in primary education: The case of Botswana* (pp. 38–58). Gaborone, Botswana: Macmillan Botswana.

Fasheh, M. (1990). Community education: To return and transform what has been made invisible. *Harvard Educational Review, 60*(3), 19–35.

Freire, P. (1970). *Pedagogy of the oppressed.* New York: Seabury.

Fuller, B., & Snyder, C. W. (1990). Colorful variation in teaching practices? In C. W. Snyder & P. T. Ramatsui (Eds.), *Curriculum in the classroom* (pp. 57–71). Gaborone, Botswana: Macmillan Botswana.

Fuller, B., & Snyder, C. W. (1991). Vocal teachers, silent pupils? Life in Botswna classrooms. *Comparative Education Review, 35*(2), 274–94.

Giroux, H. A. (1983). *Theories of reproduction and resistance in education.* South Hadley, MA: Bergin & Garvey.

Giroux, H. A. (1988). *Schooling and the struggle for public life: Critical pedagogy in the modern age.* Minneapolis: University of Minnesota Press.

Giroux, H. A. (1992). *Border crossing: Cultural workers and the politics of education.* New York: Routledge, Chapman & Hall.

Goduka, M. I. (1999). *Affirming unity in diversity in education: Healing with ubuntu.* Kenwyn, South Africa: Juta & Co. Ltd.

Government of Botswana. (1977). *Education for kagisano: Report of the National Commission on Education.* Gaborone, Botswana: Government Printers.

Government of Botswana. (1979). *National Development Plan 5: 1979–85.* Gaborone, Botswana: Government Printers.

Government of Botswana. (1991). *National Development Plan 7: 1991/92–1996/97.* Gaborone, Botswana: Government Printers.

Government of Botswana. (1993). *Report of the National Commission on Education.* Gaborone, Botswana: Government Printers.

Government of Botswana. (1994). *Revised national policy on education.* Gaborone, Botswana: Government Printers.

Government of Botswana. (1997a). *Long term vision for Botswana: Prosperity for all.* Gaborone, Botswana: Government Printers.

Government of Botswana. (1997b). *National Development Plan 8: 1997/98–2002/03.* Gaborone, Botswana: Government Printers.

Gramsci, A. (1971). *Selections from the prison notebook.* New York: International Publishers.

Jansen, J. (1989). Curriculum reconstruction in post-colonial Africa: A review of the literature. *International Journal of Educational Development, 9*(3), 219–31.

Kappel, R. (2001, March/April). The end of the great illusion: Most African countries face uncertain future. *Development and Cooperation, 2,* pp. 23–24.

Marope, P. T. M. (1997). Government inputs and research findings on teaching quality in Botswana's basic education system: A stereo in discord? In P. T. M. Marope & D. W. Chapman (Eds.), *A handbook of research on education: Teachers and teacher education in Botswana* (pp. 3-38). Gaborone, Botswana: Lentswe La Lesedi (Pty) Ltd.

Maruatona, T. (1996). Hegemony and the curriculum process: A critique of curriculum development and implementation in Botswana. In R. Charakupa, J. Odharo, & M. Rathedi (Eds.), *Botswana's challenge for quality education into 21st century.* The proceedings of the 2nd National Conference on Teacher Education, May 2–5, 1995 (pp. 49–64). Gaborone, Botswana: Ministry of Education.

Maruatona, T. (1998). Facilitating dialogue: The quest for effective learning across the curriculum in Botswana. In C. D. Yandila, P. Moanakwena, F. R. O'Mara, A. K. Kakanda, & J. Mensah (Eds.), *Improving education quality for effective learning: The teacher's dilemma.* Papers presented at the 3rd biennial conference on teacher education, August 26–29 (pp. 87–95). Gaborone, Botswana: Ministry of Education.

Miller, J. P., & Seller, W. (1985). *Curriculum, perspectives and practice.* New York: Longman.

Noel, K. L., & Ramatsui, P. T. (1994) Linkages between research, curriculum development and policy: Lessons from the 80s, suggestions for the 90s. In S. Burchfield (Ed.), *Research for educational policy and planning in Botswana* (pp. 99–144). Gaborone, Botswana: Macmillan Botswana.

Nyati-Ramahobo, L. M. (1989). *The national language and education for democracy in Botswana.* Paper presented at the Symposium on Educational Research in the SADCC Region, University of Botswana, Gaborone.

Nyati-Ramahobo, L. M. (1991). *Language planning and education policy in Botswana.* Unpublished doctoral dissertation, Microfilm International, Ann Arbor, Michigan.

Parsons, Q. (1983). Education and development in pre-colonial and colonial Botswana to 1965. In M. Crowder (Ed.), *Education for development in Botswana* (pp. 21–45). Gaborone, Botswana: Macmillan.

Pinar, W. F., Reynolds, W., Slattery, P., & Taubman, P. (1995). *Understanding curriculum.* New York: Peter Lang.

Prophet, R. B. (1990). Experience, language, knowledge, and curriculum. In C. W. Snyder & P. T. Ramatsui (Eds.), *Curriculum in the classroom: Contest of change in Botswana's junior secondary school instructional programme* (pp. 109–119). Gaborone, Botswana: Macmillan Botswana.

Prophet, R. B. (1995). Views from Botswana junior secondary classrooms: Case study of curriculum intervention. *International Journal of Educational Development, 15*(2), 127–140.

Prophet, R. B., & Rowell, P. (1990). The curriculum observed. In C. W. Snyder & P. T. Ramatsui (Eds.), *Curriculum in the classroom* (pp. 1–56). Gaborone, Botswana: Macmillan Botswana.

Rowell, P. M., & Prophet, R. B. (1990). Curriculum-in-action: The "practical" dimension in Botswana classrooms. *International Journal of Educational Development, 10*(1), 17–26.

Sarup, M. (1984). *Marxism/structuralism/education.* London: Falmer.

Snyder, C. W., & Ramatsui, P. T. (Eds.). (1990). *Curriculum in the classroom: Context of change in Botswana's junior secondary school instructional programme.* Gaborone, Botswana: Macmillan Botswana.

Stanley, W. M. (1992). *Curriculum for utopia: Social reconstructionism and critical pedagogy in the postmodern era.* Albany, NY: State University of New York Press.

Tabulawa, R. (1997). Patterns in geography teaching in Botswana: A comparative study. In P. T. M. Marope & D. W. Chapman (Eds.), *A handbook of research on education: Teacher and teacher education in Botswana* (Vol. 1, pp. 205–231). Gaborone, Botswana: Lentswe La Lesedi.

Tabulawa, R. (1998). Teachers' perspectives on classroom practice in Botswana: Implications for pedagogical change. *Qualitative Studies in Education, 2*(2), 249–68.

Tlou, T., & Campbell, A. (1984). *History of Botswana.* Gaborone, Botswana: Macmillan.

University of Botswana. (2000). 2000/2001 Calendar. Gaborone, Botswana: Author.

Zastoupil, L., & Moir, M. (Eds.). (1999). *The great Indian education debate: Documents relating to the Orientalist–Anglicist controversy, 1781–1843.* Surrey, England: Curzon Press.

ENDNOTES

1. It is important to note that in the last five years the incidence of HIV/AIDS has curtailed life expectancy significantly in Botswana. See further information on the impact of HIV/AIDS in Botswana: Government of Botswana and United Nations Development Programme (2000). *Botswana human development report 2000: Towards an AIDS-free generation.* Gaborone, Botswana: United Nations Development Programme.

2. Botswana is the country, Batswana denotes the citizens of Botswana.

CHAPTER 9

The Curriculum Field in Brazil: Emergence and Consolidation

Antonio Flavio Barbosa Moreira
Federal University of Rio de Janeiro

The North American influence on the curriculum field in Brazil is emphasized in a number of studies (Cardoso, Santana, Barros, & Moreira, 1984; Ferreira, Domingues, Alves, & Carletti, 1985; Saul, 1988; Silva, 1988). The discipline curriculum studies, offered and taught in our teacher education courses, is indeed seen, in its early stages, as a copy of the technical approach to curriculum and instruction forged in the United States (Domingues, 1985). In synthesis, it is thought that curriculum theories and practices developed here illustrate a case of educational transfer, understood by Ragatt (1983) as a movement of ideas, institutional models, and practices from one country to another.

Up to the end of the 1970s, the American influence was really marked, although not yet exclusive, both in the emergence and consolidation of our curriculum discourse. During this period, the resistance against foreign material was not strong due to the political, economic, cultural, and educational contexts of the country and the power relations in the international scenario. There is a dominant endeavor to adapt American and European theories and proposals so that they can be more easily applied in the Brazilian context. In the 1980s, significant changes occurred in both national and international contexts. On the one hand, there was a swing between a strong movement of rejection of foreign experiences, especially American, and, on the other, a movement that both draws on European social theory and American and English critical curriculum thought, and invests in the preparation of a more indigenous discourse more closely related to the educational problems faced by Brazil.

The purpose of this study is to examine the first of these periods. The intention is to focus on the emergence of the field during the 1920s and the 1930s, continuing up to the 1970s, when courses on curriculum guarantee their place in our universities and when specialized publications and research intensify. The new field, although still in need of more autonomy, reaches its maturity.

The metaphor of *copy* is not adequate enough to explain the paths followed by the Brazilian field. Being overly simplistic, it is rejected in a study (Moreira, 1988) in which I argue that the reception of foreign material involves interactions and resistances, whose intensity and potential subversiveness vary according to international and local circumstances. Therefore, all efforts to copy are bound to fail. On rejecting the idea of copy, the category of *educational transfer* is opted for. It is analyzed and reconceptualized with reference to the paths taken by the curriculum field in Brazil. It is argued that traditional accounts of educational transfer—the cultural imperialism approach (of which Martin Carnoy is one of the main authors) and the neocolonialism approach (to which are associated names such as Philip Altbach and Gail Kelly)—based on dependency theories also simplify the question. This underemphasizes, in the analyses, the interactions among cultural, social, political, and economic contexts of central (or so-called *first world*) and third world countries, as well as the importance of resistance, adaptations, arrangements, rejections, and substitutions that take place during the process. In the forementioned study (Moreira, 1988), the nonmonolithic character of the American discourse that influences us is stressed, and it is showed that our first theorizing, in fact, constitutes a combination of different ideas, trends, and interests more than a submission to either this or that American current of thought.

A more recent study (Moreira & Macedo, 1999) points out that the complex and contradictory character of the global contemporary society is still not sufficiently studied and understood. In this society, the ideas of imperialism and colonialism, keys to the analysis of the educational transfer phenomenon in the 1970s and 1980s, have acquired new meanings and dynamism. Based on the studies of globalization developed by Ianni (1993, 1995, 1997), tensions, contradictions, and convergence involved in the considerable movement of information and new knowledge that promote global culture in the world are highlighted. This movement suggests there is a suspicion of ideas leaning toward a single culture in its pure state, uncontaminated by other manifestations, thus indicating a process of hybridization, in which the cultural elements of distinct origins and different hierarchies deterritorialize and reterritorialize.

The term *hybridization* has been applied to a variety of contemporary cultural phenomena. However, according to Dussel, Tiramonti, and Birgin (1998), hybrid discourses in education have been present since the public school emergency. The term *curriculum* can be analyzed as being hybrid if we conceive it as the result of a selection of a part of the most available culture and its transformation, so that it can be taught, in a given moment, in a specific institution to a specific group of students. Curriculum discourses can also be studied as hybrid as they correspond to transitory configurations that result from different traditions and pedagogic movements. To understand these discourses, it is necessary to analyze them not only as results of dispute among conceptual currents, but also as manifestations of unresolved conflicts. Thus, the hybridization category can be considered especially useful for a study that focuses on the process in which distinct trends, models, and curriculum theories, both new and previously existent, are mobilized and articulated in a determined place, thereby creating, within possible limits, new meanings.

It is therefore argued that the category of hybridization furnishes a more exact view of the shaping of the Brazilian curriculum field. Its employment in this text is based on the theories put forward by Latin American authors (Dussel, Tiramonti, & Birgin, 1998; Garcia Ganclini, 1990; Sarlo, 1999) who, on analyzing new social space mappings of our postmodern contemporary peripheries, stress the specific hybrid profile of the Latin American cultural panorama—a heterogeneous continent where multiple development logics coexist and where one deals with contradictory and hybrid movements within which the traditional and the modern, the national and the foreign, the cult and the popular, the internal and the external participate with results that are not always predictable nor always democratic.

Based on the assumption that the phenomenon of hybridization is affected by historic conditions and cultural particularities in which it develops, the study puts forward the ones that reveal themselves to be more influent in regard to the paths taken in the curriculum field in Brazil. It is argued that three kinds of conditions contribute toward the establishment of the intellectual state into which the field is shaped: international conditions, social conditions, and institutional conditions (Moreira, 1990; Sousa Santos, 1995).

International conditions embraced the beginning of American influence in the 1920s, agreements signed between our country and the United States, the intense American influence on the reform of the Brazilian educational system as from the military coup in 1964, direct assistance afforded by American specialists in the taking of decisions in the country, and the wide range of theories and books emanating from the United States. The main intention is to understand how such factors expressed themselves in the emergence and initial evolution of the curriculum field in Brazil.

Social conditions refer to the wider context in which communities of teachers and specialists in curriculum work. Such conditions affect the way the field is formed, altered, and transmitted in the universities. Consequently, the principal characteristics and events of Brazilian social space have to be highlighted and related to the educational scenario.

The institutional conditions correspond to the infrastructures within which studies, research, congresses, seminars, courses, and publications concerning curriculum are developed. In these spaces, priorities are established, resources are provided, trends and parameters to be followed are defined, and ideas and theories are reterritorialized.

The purpose of this study is to understand how the three conditions are articulated in the configuration of the hybrid discourses that compose the Brazilian curriculum tradition in its early stages. First, there is a focus on the emergence of the field in the 1920s and 1930s, under the influence of American progressivism. Second, the concern is with the approach to curriculum issues developed in the National Institute of Educational Studies and Research (INEP), one of the first infrastructures of the field. The third focal point is the curriculum discourse formulated in the Program of American Brazilian Assistance to Elementary Education (PABAEE), another important infrastructure of the field. Thereafter, the study examines the moment of maturity of the field, in the 1970s, when curriculum studies was actually introduced into Brazilian university. Principal publications of the moment are analyzed, seeking to identify the main themes approached, influences and theoretical trends, as well as underlying interests. Attention is called to how such elements are articulated in the formation of hybrid discourses. Finally, some conclusions are outlined.

THE EMERGENCE OF THE FIELD: THE 1920s AND 1930s

The beginnings of Brazilian curriculum thought can be placed in the 1920s and 1930s, when significant economic, social, political, cultural, and ideological transformations occurred in the country. After World War I, an incipient industrial sector was organized, caused mainly by changes in relations Brazil had with industrialized countries, rather than as a result of the war. Literacy was seen as necessary for more specialized workers who, at the same time, gradually started to make demands for educational expansion. In addition, a program of literacy for the masses, prevented from voting, meant a significant increase in the number of voters and a change in political power up to that point in the hands of rural oligarchies. Furthermore, literacy was seen as a cure for the incredible poverty of the country, associated with the industrialization and urbanization process that had started very slowly (Moreira, 1988).

Brazilian pedagogic literature reflected the increasing influence of the United States in Latin America and matched the ideas proposed by North American thinkers, associated with the pragmatism and theories formulated by a number of European authors. Our specialists insisted on the need to face the more pressing problems of national education, proposing that education be renewed on the basis of the contributions of psychology and sociology. The new education models then spread throughout the country.

Imbued with these ideas, leaders of the educational renewal movement—the so-called *New School Pioneers*—sought to overcome the limitations of the Jesuit heritage and the encyclopedic tradition, a derivative of French influence on our education, striving to make an almost inexistent educational system consistent with the new context. As far as they were concerned, the new education is "a categorical, intentional, systematic reaction against the old artificial and verbalist educational service structure, mounted for an outdated conception" (Romanelli, 1980, p. 146). Traditional and modern elements combine in the hybrid perspective that characterizes the pedagogic discourse of the time and informs the efforts to reform some of the educational systems in the country, such as those of Bahia, Minas Gerais, and the Federal District.

At the time of these reforms, a systematic proposal as to how curriculum issues were to be approached was not known throughout Brazil. However, there were curriculum traditions founded on a hybrid philosophical basis that matched the principles of Herbart positivism, Pestalozzi, and the Jesuit tradition. These trends were characterized by: (a) emphasis on literary and academic subjects, (b) encyclopedism, and (c) division between intellectual and manual work (Figueiredo, 1981). Both in relation to the reforms that they lead, as well as in respect to the numerous works published, the Pioneers advocated a break with the elitist character of our traditions and our school, stressing the social nature of schooling and suggesting a renewal of curriculum work, teaching methodology, assessment, and, even more, a democratization of the classroom and the teacher–student relationship. Thus, the concern with social reconstruction become allied to the importance given to the technical aspects involved in the planning of instructional environments.

The Pioneers, including Anísio Teixeira, Lourenço Filho, Paschoal Lemme, and Fernando de Azevedo, did not form a homogeneous group: their trends varied from conservative liberal postures to more radical leftist positions. In this regard, seeds of both the critical approaches of the 1960s, which employed some of the elements and principles of the New School methodology in proposals for mass literacy, and the technical approach of the 1970s can be identified in the Pioneers' discourses.

In regard to curriculum matters specifically, although texts and reforms in this period did not reach the point of proposing detailed curriculum planning procedures, reflections were found in respect to primary school curricula, as well as guidelines for their development. Consequently, it can be argued that the emergence of Brazilian curriculum thought is located in the hybrid discourse that articulates the progressive ideas of Dewey and Kilpatrick; the renewal ideas of European authors such as Claparède, Decroly, and Montesorri; as well as the liberal ideas dominant in Brazil. All of them are gathered around the interests of the Pioneers so as to reduce the alarming degree of illiteracy and construct educational systems aimed at modernizing the country and meeting the needs created by the developing industrialization process.

Teixeira (1968), one of the most renowned Pioneers, presented his points of view on curriculum issues in some of his texts. He defended the child-centered curriculum, seen as the "origin and center of all school activity" (p. 53). His respect for the infant personality is derived from the belief that man develops naturally in the direction of a perfect social adjustment. The philosophy of curriculum work must be, then, one of "unlimited confidence in the infant spirit and religious respect held by the personality of the child" (p. 55).

Like Dewey, Teixeira conceived education as growth, growth as life, and, as a result, education as life. Again like Dewey, Teixeira defined *curriculum* as the set of activities within which children are engaged during schooling. Therefore, curriculum is viewed as part of the educative process that lasts throughout life.

The curriculum must center on activities, projects, and problems, and, above all else, be "derived from natural human activities" (Teixeira, 1968, p. 63). However, care must be taken to select only positive experiences: "the central criterion has to be to transform the school into a place where the child grows in intelligence, worldview and command over life" (p. 67).

Based on these conceptions, Teixeira (1968) presented his suggestions for curriculum construction. According to him, it is always possible to define the principal objectives to be reached and plan activities and strategies beforehand. Apart from this, minimum programs must be prepared in advance. "The teacher or the director of a school will organize, within general limits, a special program for each class, according to the progress of the work" (p. 65). A certain degree of regulation, characteristic of pragmatism, appears to permeate the proposal.

New curricula, programs, experiments, and methods are seen as indispensable to face the Brazilian educational crisis in the first half of the century. According to Teixeira (1969), our educational crisis is one aspect of the Brazilian crisis arising from institutional readaptation. In his view, the European models transferred to our environment were disfigured, thereby making our educational establishments real devices for the perpetuation of social injustices, instead of schools concerned with the problems of the time and with a more just social order. To adapt schools to the new conditions, added Teixeira, demands the rejection of uniform and rigid curriculum proposals, imposed programs, and weak and poor textbooks, in addition to new contents, methods, and techniques.

His suggestion was "an educational system created for the entire country, where an intelligent balance between liberty of teaching and central controls can give place to a more generalized expansion possible of schooling" (Teixeira, 1969, p. 53). To achieve this, it is necessary to fix a certain minimum of external conditions, such as the duration of courses and the number of daily class hours, a license or authority to teach, and a system of state exams during primary and secondary school, followed finally by the university entrance exam. On the basis of a fundamental, common, and public system of education, a practical and active school can be erected: "plasticity and flexibility of the school will permit the adjustment to student conditions and offer such student more appropriate conditions for his perfection, without mentioning only growth" (p. 58). Intentions of control, flexibility, and emancipation are integrated in a proposal that repudiates European traditional standards and aims to construct a new school—one that is more democratic, for all social classes, based on American models. The American progressivism themes are reterritorialized in the contradictory scenario in which capitalism is consolidated, in the midst of flagrant inequalities, misery, illiteracy, and precarious industrialization.

THE INSTITUTIONAL SPACE OF THE NATIONAL INSTITUTE OF EDUCATIONAL STUDIES AND RESEARCH (INEP)

The social and political conflicts in Brazil during the 1920s, together with the economic crisis of 1929, prepared the ground for the 1930 Revolution, supported by a heterogeneous coalition. As a consequence, Getúlio Vargas ruled Brazil for 15 years. A new economic model was adopted, involving a continuous tension between an independent nationalism and traditional national and international influences. The process sought to repeat, in different historic conditions, the form of industrialization that the developed countries had undergone. The industrialization process received government support, which employs a nationalist ideology to justify the control of the economic sphere.

Between 1930 and 1937, Vargas tried to construct a democracy on a popular basis, making concessions to both the middle class as well as the working class. In 1937, as a result of innumerous problems and protest marches in the country, Vargas started an authoritarian period under the name of the New State.

During the liberal period, the prestige enjoyed by the Pioneers continued and was extended to the institutional bases of the Minister of Education and Health and the National Council of Education, created in 1930 and 1931, respectively. The Pioneers also participated in important educational events in the country, such as the Francisco Campos Reform (which proposed rigid curricula for Brazilian schools), the creation of the University of São Paulo (USP), and the creation of the University of the Federal District (UDF). Catholic educators and the New School Pioneers struggled for influence on the 1934 Constitution, which included suggestions of both groups seeking a balance between the two positions.

The National Institute of Educational Studies and Research (INEP), created in 1938 to operate as a center for the study of educational issues related to the work being done by the Minister of Education and Health, constituted a great part of the institutional space for the study of curriculum as from the 1940s. Its objectives were as follows: (a) organization of pedagogic documents; (b) promotion of surveys and educational research; (c) interchange between national and international educational institutions: (d) development of investigations related to educational psychology and vocational guidance; (e) assistance to regional educational authorities; (f) diffusion of pedagogic knowledge; (g) cooperation with the Public Service Administrative Department (DASP) in the selection and training of public servants; and (h) coordination of pedagogic studies, projects, and plans developed by the Ministry of Education and Health (Costa, 1984; CBPE/INEP, 1956; Martins, 1975).

The strength of New School ideals diminished during the New State. The emphasis moved to vocational education, and a more conservative attitude returned to dominate the scenario. The Capanema Reform that took place in the 1940s reorganized the educational system, proposed rigid encyclopedic curricula for the whole country, and emphasized the importance of educational specialists (i.e., school supervisors, administrators, counselors, and inspectors).

Even with the loss of prestige, the Pioneers still exercised a marked influence on INEP and within *The Brazilian Journal of Pedagogic Studies* (RBEP), published under the sponsorship of this Institute from 1944. This journal became an important vehicle for the discussion of educational problems and the spreading of emerging curricular thought. In the first number of the journal, for example, Lourenço Filho signed an article entitled "Minimum Program," emphasizing the importance of the elaboration of curricula and programs, which should include the objectives to be achieved and strategies to be adopted. He defended the establishment of minimum programs, provided that, besides the concern with administrative aspects, the programs consider social needs and individual abilities. It is this curriculum development model, permeated by both regulation and emancipation aims, that was adopted by the Pioneers.

In 1953, the INEP promoted a "Campaign of Inquiries and Surveys of Elementary and Secondary Education." One of the results of the campaign was *An Introduction to Primary School Study,* under the authorship of Moreira (1955), the first Brazilian textbook on curriculum in which the dominant curriculum discourse of the INEP was expressed.

Moreira presented the state of the art of the curriculum field and proposed that incompatibilities between diverging ideologies be overcome. He offered a historic study of elementary school curricula and an analysis of curriculum reforms followed to the letter by Fernando Azevedo, Lorenço Filho, Anisio Teixeira, and other educators committed to the new education. In these reforms, there is a movement in the direction of curricula that have children at the center and the social environment as a motive.

Sharing the same view, Moreira maintained that the organization of curricula and programs must be local and appropriate to each school so that its integration—in terms of the surrounding social environment—is eased. Thus, there was a need to hear school teachers, students, and parents. The programming of activities, however, must obey techniques not available to all because they demand specialized knowledge. The need for guidance from a specialized organ that coordinates local suggestions and aids in the articulation and execution of these suggestions through appropriate planning was then justified. Elements of flexibility and control were present in the discourse, as well as a certain tension between the knowledge of the specialist and the knowledge held by other sectors of the school community.

According to Moreira, curriculum making should include the concern both with children's psychobiological possibilities and social problems and activities, and adopt the view of school subjects as instruments for action rather than as ends in themselves. The ideas proposed by Bobbit and Dewey, forerunners of curriculum theorizing in the United States, were combined in Moreira's discourse. The result was a proposal for curriculum development based on scientific studies of children's interests and capacities, and on problems of social, political, and economic life.

The author insisted on an examination of American and English curriculum theories, which was useful, in his opinion, to guide both the selection and organization of school knowledge. He restated his adhesion to a school and curriculum that contributed to the modernization of the country, to its integration with Western civilization of the 20th century, and to eliminate the existence of areas containing misery and pauper populations. Thus, he suggested that objectives be selected from diverse philosophies (Aristotelianism, Thomism, realism, modern idealism, pragmatism), which means integrating religious, progressive, and conservative ideas. Reflecting different influences and interests, Moreira's thought was supported by progressive and technicist ideas, originating from the United States and arriving recently in Brazil, as well as the European tradition spread among us, thereby constituting a hybrid mosaic of ends, principles, and techniques.

THE INSTITUTIONAL SPACE OF THE PROGRAM OF AMERICAN BRAZILIAN ASSISTANCE TO ELEMENTARY EDUCATION (PABAEE)

In 1956, Juscelino Kubitschek was elected president, promising 50 years of development in the 5 years of his mandate. During his administration, Brazilian and foreign businessmen, the middle class, workers, and leftists were invited to meet to further the aims of industrialization and modernization of the country. A developmental-nationalist discourse guided and justified the measures taken. Despite this, the government allowed and encouraged the entry of vast amounts of foreign capital. A number of multinational companies took advantage of the opportunity and opened factories and branches in the country.

The American influence increased considerably. A Program of American Brazilian Assistance to Elementary Education (PABAEE) was created as a consequence of one of the many agreements signed between Brazil and the United States during the 1950s (to be precise, in 1956) aimed at: (a) training elementary school supervisors and normal school teachers and teacher recycling courses; (b) producing, adapting, and distributing instructional material to be used in teacher training; and (c) selecting competent teachers to send them to the United States for training in elementary school education.

Within the departments created in the Program, that of curriculum and supervision was responsible for the organization of courses on curriculum, as well as for technical assistance, regarding curriculum issues, to educational authorities in a number of Brazilian states. The programs of curriculum subjects, organized by the Department, clearly emphasized how to plan and develop curricula—that is, "how to do it." In addition, curriculum and supervision were associated, which suggests the intention to instrumentalize the supervisor so as to help the teacher carry out the teaching program in a good and efficient manner—or, in other words, to improve the control of the curriculum process. From this perspective, the concern with methods, techniques, resources, and skills was not surprising.

The PABEAEE's approach to curriculum was presented in the book written by Marina Couto, *How to Elaborate a Curriculum,* published in 1966. As far as the author, Teixeira, and Moreira were concerned, the school must educate for life.

> The essential function of a school is to develop the child's thought and to discipline his behavior. It has the responsibility of integrating the student with its physical and social environment, to help the child to assimilate our cultural heritage. And it does this mainly through the content of school subjects. This is how the child is educated to face life. (Couto, 1966, p. 7)

A reasonable similarity was noticed in relation to progressivism, which was confirmed in the definition of *curriculum* adopted: "the totality of child experience at school, directed for the purposes of education. It is the entire life program for each and every student" (Couto, 1966, p. 1). The similarity was also confirmed in the concern for a good teaching plan to ensure that school work was characterized by being gradual, intentional, and integrated.

Couto defended a curriculum centered on areas of study, instead of a subject-centered curriculum. In this regard, she suggested programs for each of the areas, consecrating the traditional sequence of "objectives, contents, activities and evaluation." The use of behavioral objectives was clearly recommended: objectives must be formulated in such a manner as involve, at the same time, the sphere of the subject and aspects of change of behavior desired for the child. A significant concern with curriculum organization, planning, objectives, and evaluation gave the discourse, in which the presence of behaviorist psychological principles was noticed, a clear technical tone.

The book did not clearly explain the social and political ends that informed the process of curriculum development recommended. However, in the appendix, some indications were found. The underlying vision of human nature is based on Pope John XXIII's *Pacem in Terris.* A person was seen as being gifted with intelligence, sensitivity, and free will, and as the holder of the following rights: the right to a dignified standard of living; rights relative to moral and cultural values; rights to economic activities; the right to meet and associate; rights to migration: the right to pray to God; and the right to choose his or her own state of life. Equality, liberty, democracy, and private property—the main themes in liberal discourse—seemed to be the foundation of the analysis made by the author.

Couto (1996) stated the expectation that the student will contribute "in a certain way towards the improvement of his or her family's and community's standard of living" (p. 23). She also expressed the belief in a democratic way of life, as well as her intention to lead the student to "respect honest differences of opinions" (p. 12) and to "evaluate scientific progress by the contributions that it brings to the common good" (p. 13).

The American influence is noticeable in the bibliography. Authors such as Edward Krug, Florence Stratemeyer, and William Ragan, illustrious representatives of the concern for curriculum development, are very present. American technicism and pragmatism are reterritorialized in Couto's discourse and combined with traditional catholic elements, previously dominant among us. In the new configuration, instrumental rationality prevails, which can be observed in the strong emphasis on the techniques of curriculum planning.

Besides offering important institutional space for the development of the field, INEP and PABAEE are also responsible for the training of the first specialists in curriculum in Brazil, whose importance and necessity were highlighted in specialized literature during the 1950s and 1960s (Abreu, 1955; Bastos, 1959; Couto, 1966; Moreira, 1955, 1956). The new specialization aimed at favoring the control of curriculum elaboration, implementation, and regulation of teacher and student behavior. The increasing complexity of the Brazilian educational system, partially organized to meet industrial needs, required the presence of experts to help a nontrained staff teach efficiently those children so far absent from classrooms.

THE CONSOLIDATION OF THE FIELD

At the beginning of the 1960s, the contradictions between the nationalist discourse, which insisted on greater independence from the United States, and the modernization discourse, which moved toward a model of interdependent development, were clear. The contradictions between the two made it evident that the socialist model was seen, by part of the population, as a possible way out. J. Quadros and J. Goulart, who ruled the country from 1961 to April 1964, were not successful in their efforts to solve the problem. Quadros resigned in August 1961, and Goulart was deposed by the military in 1964.

Before the coup, institutional spaces increased with the introduction of curriculum studies into Brazilian universities. The Law of Guidelines and Bases of National Education (Law 4024/1961) favored the appearance of the subject. Expressing a vague concern with primary school education curricula, the Law, for the first time in Brazil, conceded a certain margin of flexibility in secondary schools, permitting them to define a part of their curricula. Of the total number of subjects to be studied, a few would be optional and chosen freely by the schools. Debates on and studies of curriculum spread more quickly throughout the country, including our university. In 1962, the university base of the field—the Pedagogy Course—was created, and curriculum studies became one of its elective disciplines.

Also before the coup, articles on curriculum reflected both the influence of progressive democratic ideals and the discourses of efficiency and nationalism. The articles emphasized that Brazilian schools cannot continue copying foreign models and be restricted to serving privileged groups. There was a strong urge to overcome underdevelopment and cultural dependency. Education was seen as an instrument necessary for industrial growth and a space for critical discussion of the paths to be followed. The main themes of the nationalist discourse were present, many times combined with the ideas of the American specialist Ralph Tyler and with the contradictory proposal of adopting models of curriculum organization elaborated in first world countries (Abreu, 1965).

The ambiguity that characterized the early 1960s context appears to have affected curriculum discourse. The oscillation between the support of an autonomous process of industrialization and development and the support of the establishment of strong links with the international market can be associated with the oscillation between a more autonomous curriculum approach and the search for foreign models. Furthermore, the simultaneous concern with efficiency and planning, with individual needs and experiences, and with social problems and issues can be related to the emergence of the efficiency and modernization discourse in a context permeated by nationalist and even radical proposals.

At this time, the beginnings of influence exerted by Paulo Freire in curriculum thought could be noticed. He was concerned with a form of education that allowed the oppressed to become more conscious of their situation, enabling them to critically reflect on their destiny, responsibilities, and role in overcoming the backwardness of the country, misery, and social injustices. Thus, new curricula became necessary because the traditional, abstract, theoretical, and alienated curriculum could never develop students' critical awareness.

Although Freire appraised, as progressive authors do, dialogue, active learning, and meaningful experience, his primordial concern was to radically transform the social reality in which the student was inserted. Despite this, Freire was accused, in the first stages of his work, of turning more toward the industrialization and modernization of the country than toward deeper structural changes (Paiva, 1980). Insofar as curriculum thought was concerned, however, his theory represented the emergence of a critical approach to curriculum and teaching matters in Brazil.

With the military coup in 1964, the entire political, economic, ideological, and educational panorama in the country underwent substantial transformation. Various agreements were signed with the United States aiming at the modernization and rationalization of the country. In 1969, based on the Brazilian university reform followed to the letter by the military, the study of the subject Curriculum Studies became compulsory, in Pedagogy Course, by future school supervisors. Thus it occupied effective space in our Faculties of Education. In the 1970s, the first MA courses in Curriculum began to appear in the country (Federal University of Parana, Catholic University of São Paulo, and University of Brasília) (Xavier, 1982), and curriculum studies became a discipline offered and taught in many graduate courses. Therefore, in Franklin's (1974) terms, the Brazilian curriculum field reached its maturity in the early 1970s.

The discourse on curriculum assumed a dominant instrumental tone, integrating the efficiency discourse adopted by the military, with a dilution of emphasis on the needs of the student, defended by progressives, as well as on the emancipatory intentions of emerging critical orientation and seeking, at the same time, to be in harmony with the doctrine of national security that started to guide governmental decisions. Consequently, there was a merger of the national security discourse and technological rationality aimed at adequately training and regulating the human capital supposedly necessary for the development of the country.

The military received the support of the American government, which was prodigious in both technical assistance and financial aid. Some of the technicians linked to USAID even occupied highlighted positions in various federal administrative areas. Because education was seen as an important resource for growth, various educational assistance programs were planned and implemented in our country.

The turn to American curriculum theories and models, in this scenario, was not surprising. However, the most influential authors in Brazil at that moment, such as Ralph Tyler, Hilda Taba, William B. Ragan, and Robert Fleming, joined together distinct approaches and interests (Moreira, 1988). Besides this, their proposal interacted with the dominant progressive epistemological nucleus of curriculum traditions previously developed in the country. In this regard, it is worth considering curriculum thought of this period as mainly corresponding to a hybridization of progressive and technical (or technicist) theories.

Various articles on curriculum issues, published in the 1970s, evidenced concern with curriculum planning, vocational education, curriculum legislation, industrial needs, and efficiency (Nascimento, 1974–1975; Peregrino, 1972; Pires, 1971). The presence of technicist authors in the bibliographies was well accentuated, although in some studies—as a way to counterbalance the dryness of technicism—a more humanistic perspective, derived from phenomenology, existentialism, progressivism, and Rogerian nondirectivity, was observed (Bordas, 1976; Martins, 1980; Mota & Santos, 1976). Hence, the influences observed in articles on curriculum, in the decade in question, suggest a more hybrid discourse than a strict adhesion to technicism.

The textbooks published in this period, written by Sperb (1966) and Traldi (1997a, 1997b, 1997c), focused on themes related to curriculum planning and development. The bibliographies and quotations of the texts illustrated the influence exerted by John Dewey and Hilda Taba, that of Havighurst and the Pioneers of the New School (in the case of Sperb), and that of Bloom, Bruner, Fleming, Piaget, Ragan, and Tyler (in the case of Traldi).

Insofar as curriculum organization was concerned, Sperb rejected the subject-centered curriculum and suggested the construction of curriculum centered on social problems. According to her, "it is very improbable that this curriculum organization (isolated subjects) serve the purpose of an education aimed at democracy" (1996, p. 63). Traldi (1997a) proposed curricula centered on areas of knowledge and emphasized the process of knowledge acquisition instead of knowledge in itself. The author stressed that curriculum knowledge must be seen not as a set of information, but as a system of learning. She said that the key to the selection of meaningful and educative experiences is that which

> leads an individual to mental opening, to the search for what is essential and meaningful in things, facts and people: to love and give value to the human being and to divine creation; to commune with peers, tolerate, respect and know how to accept; to persist and take decisions; to participate with authenticity and in a positive, creative, firm, constructive, honest, dignified and responsible manner with oneself and the common good ... therefore, that which leads to more human ends. (Traldi, 1997a, pp. 46–47; original in italics)

Sperb accentuated that curriculum organization appealed to the reunited forces of the educational specialist and the administrator. Drawing on Taba, she considered the scope, sequence, continuity, and integration of learning as the central problems of curriculum organization. As far as she was concerned, if the intention is to provide the student with solid knowledge within the different areas of teaching, curriculum organization must express this intention. If the idea is the integral development of the student, curriculum organization must include a series of aspects in which the subject matter functions as means and not as an end.

It can therefore be seen, in Traldi's and Sperb's books, besides an emphasis on curriculum planning and the creation of a system of decision making, the purpose of developing in the student a capacity to solve problems, creativity, scientific spirit and cooperation, as well as establishing a democratic atmosphere in school. All these principles reflect the influence of progressive authors and the adhesion to a liberal proposal of education—thus the concern with a more humane society and individual development of each child. The two theoretical frameworks reflect the American influence, derived from the studies that the authors carried out in the United States, but also indicate the interaction of American models with curriculum tendencies previously influential in our country and the effort to adapt them to our context. It further reflects the choice of more traditional authors such as Tyler, Taba, Ragan, Alexander, Saylor, and so on, instead of names more clearly associated with educational technology and systemic.

Why the preference for more traditional authors? It can be argued that, in the first half of the 1970s, when the curriculum field actually consolidated among us, there was a great affinity among these traditional authors and curriculum approaches previously dominant in Brazil, which consisted, fundamentally, of the way the Pioneers interpreted American progressive ideas. More than just an abrupt technicist invasion in a vacuum, the curriculum field seemed to consolidate itself in Brazil by means of the reterritorialization of ideas capable of simultaneously anchoring in our cultural context and serving the purposes of modernization, efficiency, and regulation—sought, in different forms, by our governors since the 1920s.

CONCLUSION

The paths followed by the curriculum field, after its consolidation in the Brazilian educational scenario, are beyond the scope of this chapter. Thus, these comments only make brief mention of the conformations that follow those discussed.

In the second half of the 1970s, technicism became hegemonic in the discourse on curriculum in Brazil. Attention veered to behavioral objectives and taxonomies of educational objectives, as well as individualized strategies of teaching and programmed instruction. However, the focus on the instrumental aspects of curriculum process was challenged at the end of the decade as a result of far-reaching changes in social and international conditions. In the early 1980s, amid a serious economic crisis and high inflation rates, the process of democratization gathered speed in the country and hastened the exit of the military from power. In 1985, José Sarney became the first civilian president after 21 years of military dictatorship. Political opposition gathered strength and intensified social movements. During the 1980s, as a whole, critical pedagogic literature strengthened and educational reforms were implemented in some states and municipalities, in which the materialization of new ideas was sought. Curriculum analyses assumed a different perspective, reflecting other influences and interests. The field widened and reached distinct autonomy. The critical discourse remained hegemonic up to the beginning of the 1990s, when new conditions, influences, themes, and approaches took form in research and publications and reshaped the field.

In this chapter, an endeavor was made, considering the period between the 1920s and 1930s and the beginning of the 1970s, to analyze how the curriculum field has been organized as a consequence of a hybridization process, within which different interests, traditions, and theories came together—originating approaches that are more or less creative and autonomous. It can be supposed that the category of hybridization would also ease the analysis of the paths followed by the field in the 1990s, during which period distinct international, social, and institutional conditions certainly contributed to new meanings and configurations.

In synthesis, what is being sustained is that the term *hybridization* appears to satisfactorily substitute the expression educational transference, in as much as it allows for the better grasping of the dynamic movement of ideas, theories, and models from different countries, as well as avoiding analyses that, although recognizing the occurrence of interactions and resistances, place the importance of the cultural sphere in the process of forming a field of studies on a secondary level. Considering that cultural activity relates to a much wider area of reality than the abstractions of socioeconomic experience (Williams, 1985), it can be stated that the dynamics of hybridization found in a field can support, redirect, or even neutralize the steps suggested by macrostructural factors.

Given the complexity of the question, new studies are suggested in an endeavor to confirm the contribution of the category toward the construction of other histories, both in the curriculum field as well as other fields of pedagogic knowledge.

Finally, it is suggested that future studies focus on curriculum practice that develops in schools and universities, seeking to verify how hybrid discourses on curriculum actually materialize when teachers and students work together. It is argued that such studies may furnish a better understanding of the readings, interpretations, resistances, and adaptations that are made amid the discursive restrictions and limits that curriculum theorizing and curriculum policies help to establish.

REFERENCES

Abreu, J. (1955). A educação secundária no Brasil. *Revista Brasileira de Estudos Pedagógicos, 23*(58), 26–104.

Abreu, J. (1965). Fatores sociais atuantes no currículo da escola secundária brasileira. *Revista Brasileira de Estudos Pedagógicos, 44*(99), 53–71.

Bastos, C. (1959). A flexibilidade dos currículos da escola secundária americana. *Revista Brasileira de Estudos Pedagógicos, 32*(75), 186–189.

Bordas, M. C. (1976). Integração curricular e humanização do ensino: Uma dupla dimensão de busca. *Educação and Realidade, 1*, 23–31.

Cardoso, E. A., Santana, M. C., Barros, A. M., & Moreira, F. A. (1984). Os livros tradicionais de currículo. *Cadernos CEDES, 13*, 7–25.

CBPE/INEP. (1956). Os estudos e as pesquisas educacionais no Ministério da Educação e Cultura. *Educação e Ciências Sociais, 1*(1, 2), 5–60.

Costa, L. C. B. F. (1984). INEP: Novos rumos e perspectivas. *Revista Brasileira de Estudos Pedagógicos, 65*(150), 241–254.

Couto, M. (1966). *Como elaborar um currículo.* Rio de Janeiro, Brazil: Ao Livro Técnico.

Domingues, J. L. O. (1985). *Cotidiano da escola de primeiro grau: O sonho e a realidade* (Ph.D. thesis). São Paulo, Brazil: Catholic University.

Dussel, I., Tiramonti, G., & Birgin, A. (1998). Hacia una cartografía de la reforma curricular: Reflexiones a partir de la descentralización educativa argentina. *Revista de Estudios del Currículum, 1*(2), 132–161.

Ferreira, I., Domingues, J. L., Alves, N., & Carletti, V. (1985). *Elementary school curriculum.* Research project, INEP, mimeo.

Figueiredo, M. C. M. (1981). Curriculum issues in Brazil: Traditions, policies and problems. *Compare, 11*(1), 89–98.

Franklin, B. (1974). *The curriculum field and the problem of social control, 1918–1938: A study in critical theory* (Ph.D. thesis). Madison: Wisconsin University.

García Canclini, N. (1990). *Culturas híbridas: Estrategias para entrar y salir de la modernidad.* México: Grijalbo.

Ianni, O. (1993). *A sociedade global.* Rio de Janeiro, Brazil: Civilização Brasileira.

Ianni, O. (1995). *Teorias da globalização.* Rio de Janeiro, Brazil: Civilização Brasileira.

Ianni, O. (1997). *A era do globalismo.* Rio de Janeiro, Brazil: Civilização Brasileira.

Lourenço Filho, M. B. (1944). Programa mínimo. *Revista Brasileira de Estudos Pedagógicos, 1*(1), 393–402.

Martins, E. R. (1975). INEP: *Linhas para uma administração por objetivos* (MA dissertation). Rio de Janeiro, Brazil: Federal University of Rio de Janeiro, 1975.

Martins, J. (1980). Modelo de planejamento curricular. In W. Garcia (Org.), *Educação brasileira contemporânea: Organização e funcionamento.* São Paulo, Brazil: McGraw-Hill do Brasil.

Moreira, A. F. B. (1988). *Towards a reconceptualisation of educational transfer: The case of Curriculum Studies in Brazil.* (PhD thesis). London: University of London Institute of Education.

Moreira, A. F. B. (1990). *Currículos e programas no Brasil.* Campinas, Brazil: Papirus.

Moreira, A. F. B., & Macedo, E. F. (1999). Faz sentido ainda o conceito de transferência educacional? In A. F. B. Moreira (Org.), *Currículo: Políticas e práticas.* Campinas, Brazil: Papirus.

Moreira, J. R. (1955). *Introdução ao estudo do currículo da escola primária.* Rio de Janeiro, Brazil: MEC/INEP.

Moreira, J. R. (1956). Os problemas do ensino elementar no Brasil. *Revista Brasileira de Estudos Pedagógicos, 26*(64), 44–59.

Mota, C. C. S., & Santos, D. G. (1976). Currículo pré-escolar: Uma tentativa de abordagem. *Revista Brasileira de Estudos Pedagógicos, 61*(140), 44–59.

Nascimento, M. A. O. (1974–1975). Algumas considerações sobre o currículo da nova escola de 1° grau. *Didactica, 11–12*, 131–141.

Paiva, V. (1980). *Paulo Freire e o nacionalismo- desenvolvimentismo.* Rio de Janeiro, Brazil: Civilização Brasileira.

Pires, N. (1971). Objetivos da educação fundamental. *Revista Brasileira de Estudos Pedagógicos, 56*(123), 10–24.

Peregrino, M. G. (1972). O currículo e a implantação da Reforma. *Revista Brasileira de Estudos Pedagógicos, 57*(125), 59–69.

Ragatt, P. (1983). One person's periphery. *Compare, 13*(1), 1–5.

Romanelli, O. O. (1980). *História da Educação no Brasil: 1930–1973.* Petrópolis, Brazil: Vozes.

Sarlo, B. (1999). *Escenas de la vida posmoderna: Intelectuales, arte y videocultura em la Argentina.* Buenos Aires, Argentina: Ariel.

Saul, A. M. (1988). *Avaliação emancipatória: Desafio à teoria e à prática de avaliação e reformulação de currículo.* São Paulo, Brazil: Cortez/Autores Associados.

Silva, T. R. N. (1988). *Conteúdo curricular e organização da educação básica: A experiência paulista* (Ph.D. thesis). São Paulo, Brazil: Catholic University.

Sousa Santos, B. (1995). *A crítica da razão indolente: Contra o desperdício da experiência.* São Paulo, Brazil: Cortez.

Sperb, D. (1966). *Problemas gerais de currículo.* Porto Alegre, Brazil: Globo.

Teixeira, A. (1968). *Pequena introdução à filosofia da educação: A escola progressiva ou a transformação da escola.* São Paulo, Brazil: Companhia Editora Nacional.

Teixeira, A. (1969). Escolas de educação. *Revista Brasileira de Estudos Pedagógicos, 51*(114), 239–259.

Traldi, L. L. (1977a). *Currículo: Conceituação e implicações.* São Paulo, Brazil: Atlas.

Traldi, L. L. (1977b). *Currículo: Metodologia de avaliação.* São Paulo, Brazil: Atlas.

Traldi, L. L. (1977c). *Currículo: Teoria e prática.* São Paulo, Brazil: Atlas.

Williams, R. (1985). *Marxism and literature.* Oxford, England: Oxford University Press.

Xavier, R. C. M. (1982). *O currículo como campo de estudos: Contribuições das teses e dissertações de currículo na década 70–80* (MA dissertation). Curitiba, Brazil: Federal University of Paraná.

CHAPTER 10

The Curriculum Field in Brazil in the 1990s

Alice Casimiro Lopes
Federal University of Rio de Janeiro

Elizabeth Fernandes de Macedo
State University of Rio de Janeiro

The emergence of the Brazilian curriculum field in the 1990s was marked by an intense American influence that resulted from an instrumental process of transference fostered by concrete associations between Brazil and the United States. The major point of this transference was to assimilate the technical perspectives that would enable curriculum development. It was only in the early 1980s that the field acquired greater complexity as it gained references in critical theories. Two national groups, pertaining to the critical-historical pedagogy and the pedagogy of the oppressed, strove for hegemony both in the educational discourse as well as their capacity for political intervention. By the end of the 1980s, the field's references assumed the multiplicity of perspectives that was to become a major trait of the 1990s field. This multiplicity included not only the appropriation of authors from the curriculum field, but also of thinkers from the fields of sociology and philosophy. This multiplicity and complexity is why the task of defining the curriculum field in Brazil today is such a difficult task.

An analysis of the research carried out in Brazil, as well as the literature published in recent years, shows that the term *curriculum* encompasses a variety of studies. The database of research groups from one of Brazil's main funding agencies (CNPq) contains 117 entries for the term *curriculum*—from research on curricula to literacy teaching, knowledge, and culture, as well as specific curricular innovations, new technologies, and interdisciplinarity. Among those studies that actually focus on the subject of curriculum, there are works referenced in discussions involving the practice and theory of the field, as well as studies based on constructivist theories or those regarding teaching propositions aimed at specific subjects.

In view of this reality and to study this field in Brazil in the 1990s, it is important to define what is to be understood by the curriculum field. For the sake of defining the term, we have adopted Bourdieu's concept of field. Bourdieu (1983, 1992) defined a *field* as a locus where actors engage in battles around the specific interests that characterize the area in question. Thus, the functioning of a scientific field not only produces

185

but also presumes a specific form of interest in a scientific activity, whether it is a discipline or sector of the discipline. A competition is thus established among these actors concerning the legitimacy of knowledge as well as whose authority it is to define such legitimacy. This does not mean to say that the social actors are the producers of the field: They act within the scope of a field that has been socially predetermined. All they do is execute the actions this field is able to actually accomplish (Ortiz; cited in Bourdieu, 1983). Thus, power relations are constituted in the field according to the different social quanta of the actors performing therein. These social quanta constitute the social capital of these actors: the sum of present or potential resources related to the individual's bondage to a group whose agents share common features and are united by permanent and useful ties (Bourdieu, 1998).

Not only does the social capital depend on the network of relationships that each actor is able to mobilize, but also on the bulk of his cultural capital. According to Bourdieu (1998), cultural capital comes into existence once it is incorporated as durable dispositions of the individual, scientific habits, and systems of schemes generated by perception, valuation, and action, all of which, produced by a pedagogical analysis, enable a choice of those objects to undergo research, problem solving, and evaluation of solutions. Cultural capital also exists in objective terms represented by a variety of cultural goods such as books, periodicals, works, instruments, and institutions. Cultural capital also exists on an institutionalized level, involving teaching institutions as a whole as well as others more dedicated to the production and evaluation of research. Such institutions are in charge of ensuring not only the production and circulation of scientific goods, but also the reproduction and circulation of the producers, reproducers, and consumers, mainly by granting diplomas. In other words, they objectify the cultural capital that legitimizes and guarantees this capital.

Therefore, practices aimed at preserving scientific authority and legitimate knowledge are developed by those who possess the highest sociocultural capital in a specific field as a result of the capacity to impose their conceptions and thus dominate the field; the heterodox practices of contention are developed by those who seek to question the holders of authority in the field—in other words, the dominated. On reaching this concept, it is possible to define the existence of different fields (sciences, arts, sports) according to the object around which each field stages its battles for legitimacy and authority—in other words, depending on the sociocultural capital required in each field.

Based on Bourdieu's perspective, we can understand that the curriculum field constitutes an intellectual field: a forum where different social actors possessing specific sociocultural capitals in the area legitimize certain conceptions regarding the theory of curriculum. These same actors contend for the power to define who is to constitute authority in the area. This is a field endowed with the power to exert influence on official curricular propositions and on pedagogical practices in schools as a result of the different processes of recontextualization of its discourse, although it is not constituted by these propositions and practices. The intellectual curriculum field produces theories of curriculum that are legitimized as such by the competitive struggles taking place within it. The production of the curriculum field thus constitutes part of its objectified cultural capital.

Hence, we believe that, to analyze the production of this field, it is necessary to objectify the knowledge produced by those subjects who are invested with legitimacy to speak about curricula. This legitimacy is conferred by their presence in institutionalized venues, such as research and teaching institutions, where they act as teachers, researchers, and counselors; funding agencies, in which they are advisors who define which kinds of studies are to be financed; and the forums of researchers, the most distinguished among which is the Work Group (WG) on Curriculum of the National Association of Post-Graduation and Research in Education (ANPEd). Participation in these groups has become a key factor in guaranteeing legitimacy and authority when dealing with curriculum.

Thus, we analyze the social production of the field, bearing in mind that the field is not to be defined by the use it makes of certain theoretical-methodological contributions. On the contrary, the power relations that dominate this field are responsible for the prevalence of certain contributions according to their specific interests and purposes. Our analysis takes into consideration the production of knowledge made by institutionalized research groups that have maintained a steady output throughout the decade. Therefore, instead of working with scattered productions of different subjects, we try to assemble it in larger trends, emphasizing the work developed by the leaderships of these groups. The sources for the present work encompass texts that have been published as books or specialized magazines, alongside other works presented by the WG on curricula at the annual meetings held by the ANPEd. As well, there are various research reports and projects carried out by researchers working on the lines of thought selected for their role in constituting the field.

At first, we present a general outlook on the production of curricula in Brazil in the 1990s, providing evidence of how this field has acquired its hybrid features. Subsequently, we analyze in further detail the production of three of the most consolidated and representative groups in the field in that decade to understand their process of constitution and consolidation. Finally, we indicate the trends of the production currently underway.

THE SOCIAL PRODUCTION IN THE CURRICULUM FIELD IN THE 1990s

The 1990s subjected the world to countless sociopolitical changes. In the previous decade, a 15-year military dictatorship had come to an end in Brazil. It featured economic dependence on the United States, along with a radical policy of nationalization as a result of national security ideology. The election of Fernando Collor in the early 1990s introduced the country to the discourse of globalization. The urgency for Brazil to be aligned with the modern worldwide economy became clear. Trade barriers for imported goods fell, market reserves collapsed, and the concern for control over government expenditure was reinforced, thus providing grounds for the establishment of a neo-liberal ideology in Brazil. This framework was not typical of Brazil alone because it was to be seen throughout Latin America, where, according to Anderson (1995), the growth of neo-liberalism proved its force as an ideology for salvation on a worldwide scale. Relations between Latin America and the hegemonic bloc, especially the United States, acquired a new profile. From the role as possible international allies against the threat of communism and as a large-scale consumer market, Brazil assumed the role of a satellite nation in a state of dissimulated dependence amid the powers at play in a globalized world.

The educational scene in Brazil in the 1990s, especially the curriculum field, deeply reflected an option toward alignment with neo-liberal policies. The insertion of the country in a globalized economy now required a new set of schooling standards, the cost of which the state saw fit to reduce partnerships with the productive sector. In its effort to streamline public expenditure on social sectors, including education, the government has been proposing exams and curricula on a national basis to funnel investments and guaranteeing control over academic work so as to forge a mentality more in accordance with the objectives of these policies. This experience with official curricula on a national basis has created a movement of criticism against government policies in the curriculum field and, in some cases, proposals of alternative curricula. Although we understand that the curriculum field is not made up of curricular practices or policies, we believe it is important to point out that many of the propositions did materialize the discussions being carried out in the field, whereas others subsidized the construction of consistent theoretical contributions. Although these studies did not characterize the 1990s, they were beyond any doubt one of the focuses of the period, especially in the latter half of the decade.

These social and political shifts are reflected in the references that enable us to grasp the meaning of curricular phenomena. In the 1980s, the direct influence of American technical thought would gradually lose force as it no longer held the official status of programs supported by international agreements. However, a tendency toward the incorporation of critical discourses on curricula arose both at the NSE matrix and at the American Marxist-oriented matrix. The influence did not occur by means of official processes of transference. It was subsidized by works carried out by Brazilian researchers in search of references in critical thought. This less directed process of integration between Brazilian curricular thought and foreign productions supplied grounds for the appearance of other influences, both from French literature and European Marxist theoreticians.

In the early 1990s, the field of curriculum experienced these multiple influences. Studies involving curricula adopted a deeper sociological approach, as opposed to the hitherto dominant psychological thought. Most works sought an understanding of curricula as a forum for power relations. Studies that discussed the field's administrative and scientific aspects were definitely left behind. Only but a few references to this kind of study still remained in the beginning of the decade, especially in the production of periodicals. Texts presented at scientific forums had definitely dismissed such an approach. Curricular propositions gave way to a more comprehensive literature of an eminently political nature on curriculum. In the first half of the decade, the vast majority of studies fell under the category of *political texts,* as defined by Pinar et al. (1995). The notion wherein curricula could only be within a political, economic, or social context was visibly hegemonic. Excepting Paulo Freire, most references were made to foreign authors, such as Giroux, Apple, and Young in the curriculum field, or Marx, Gramsci, Bourdieu, Lefèbvre, Habermas, and Bachelard in the fields of sociology and philosophy.

During this period, discussions involving curricula and knowledge were highlighted. Specialized magazines in the area, and especially the WG on curriculum, laid special emphasis on matters dealing with the relationship among scientific knowledge, school knowledge, popular knowledge, and common sense. Other matters were explored, such as those regarding the selection of contents that constitute curricula, the relationships between communicative action, the processes of criticizing knowledge, the processes of emancipation, and the need to overcome dichotomies between contents, methods, and specific school relations, all in tune with a broader understanding of curricula as social construction of knowledge. Side by side with topic themes related to knowledge, we can witness the development of works involving the aspect of multireferentiality (Burnham, 1993), indicating the complexity of the curriculum field and how it requires a multiple network of references for its interpretation.

By the end of the first half of the decade, the effort to understand postindustrial societies as producers of symbolic goods, more than material goods, started to alter the emphases that prevailed until then. Curricular thought began to incorporate postmodern and poststructural approaches, which now shared common grounds in modern discussions. Curricular theoretization thus incorporated the thoughts of Foucault, Derrida, Deleuze, Guattari, and Morin. These approaches represented a major influence in the 1990s. Nevertheless, they should not be seen as the sole orientation of the field. The typical multiplicity of contemporaneity gradually appears in opposition to theoretizations of a globalizing nature. Such multiplicity does not simply imply different theoretical and methodological orientations, but rather tendencies and orientations that interrelate so as to produce cultural hybrids. Thus, hybridism seemed to be the field's most prominent feature in Brazil in the latter half of the 1990s.

We see the processes of hybridization, resorting to García Canclini (1998), as diffuse cultural phenomena in a complex and fragmented world. Such phenomena are more keenly felt nowadays as a result of the acceleration of the processes of communication, the ever-growing territorial displacement of social groups and the speed in which different discourses are included, which leads to a loss of their original features as a consequence of these hybrid processes. Therefore, not only do we sustain that curricular practices constitute hybrids as a result of the different processes of selection and recontextualization, as stated by Dussel, Tiramonti, and Birgin (1998), but also that in the closing years of this century, the curriculum field is undergoing a process of acquiring hybrid characteristics of its own. García Canclini (1998) offered further explanation on the processes of hybridization by resorting to three fundamental mechanisms: the breaking down and blending of collections organized by the cultural systems, the deterritorialization of the symbolic processes, and the expansion of impure genres. We believe such mechanisms are able to explain hybridism in the curriculum field in the 1990s.

The processes of breaking down and blending collections organized by cultural systems are summarized by García Canclini (1998) as the process of *discollecting*. Modern collections served as a tool for the organization of symbolic goods in separate groups of different hierarchies. Therefore, the very fact of knowing a certain organization somehow guaranteed the power to establish differences vis-à-vis those who could not identify the organization of that collection. In opposition, what we see in current cultural systems is the multiplication of the processes of discollecting and the rupture of the organizations. This is better expressed as the frontiers between the erudite and the popular grow dimmer. With regard to the curriculum field, certain basic principles of field organization—the fundamental theoretical conceptions, the matters to be considered—used to guarantee some measure of identity. As a result, the mastery of these principles of organization of collections involving curricular ideas would in its turn assure the mastery of the field. Nowadays, we have been experiencing a process of discollecting to the extent that previous principles of organization are discarded regardless of their having been replaced by a new set of principles: There are no more collections of principles, but rather an alternation of contributions from different collections.

In association with the process of discollecting, there is the deterritorialization of the symbolic processes. Once again, according to García Canclini (1998), what is a stake is a loss of the natural relation among cultural, geographical, and social territories. Deterritorialization in its turn leads to processes of reterritorialization—in other words, relative and partial territorial relocations of old and new symbolic productions. We can no longer interpret cultural systems according to binary models of modernity: colonized and colonizers, cosmopolitans and nationalists. Such models prove to be insufficient in a globalized society with deterritorialized cultural processes. This process occurs quite clearly in the curriculum field, where mainly North American contributions of the past decade are maintained, although accompanied by major contributions coming from European, Australian, South African, and Latin American authors. This process of interchange reterritorializes the theoretical propositions of different authors in such a way that the original identification vis-à-vis a specific national territory is lost along the way.

Finally, García Canclini (1998) discussed the cultural process of expansion of the impure genres. In other words, genres in which the intersection between the visual and the literary, the erudite and the popular, craftsmanship and industrial output of massive circulation becomes evermore clear. In the curriculum field, the identification of impure genres may be achieved through a variety of theoretical associations, including between modern and postmodern theoretizations.

Along with the phenomena of discollection, deterritorialization, and the forming of impure genres, hybridism makes it impossible for the curriculum field to be characterized in terms of specific themes or theoretical and methodological approaches of its own. In previous decades, dominant groups constituted the field because they legitimized the priority of specific theoretical and methodological orientations. In the 1990s, however, the power relations in the field of curriculum privilege a variety of orientations. This is not to say that we sustain the inexistence of dominant groups, but rather that we deem it to be convenient for these dominant groups to maintain hybridism in the theoretical and methodological incorporations.

In the following section, we analyze the social production of the field of curriculum in the 1990s. We base ourselves on the constitution and consolidation of dominant groups in the field as we try to understand how such groups construct a field most characterized by its hybridism.

HYBRIDISM: THE PRIMARY CHARACTERISTIC OF THE CURRICULUM FIELD

Once the curriculum field has been outlined as an intellectual field created by the positions, relations, and practices arising from a context of discourse production in a specific area (Bernstein, 1996), we analyze the curricula production in Brazil based on the three major groups of this period: (a) the poststructuralist perspective, (b) the curriculum network, and (c) the history of curriculum and constitution of school knowledge.

The Poststructuralist Perspective

The poststructuralist perspective became prominent in the curriculum field in Brazil mainly as a result of the production in this area provided by the group of Curricula from the Federal University of Rio Grande do Sul (UFRGS). Headed by Tomaz Tadeu da Silva and formed by his graduate students and collaborators, the group has maintained a steady production since the first half of the 1990s, and its presence has been noteworthy in educational congresses throughout the country. Silva's expressive coordination of editorial works, as well as his edition and translation of foreign authors pertaining to a poststructuralist perspective, has stood as a major contribution toward the articulation of the group, by means of what Bourdieu referred to as the constitution of an institutionalized and objectified social capital. On analyzing the work in question, it is possible to identify the theoretical and methodological bases that served as guidelines for the group. Silva constituted a trajectory of publications from the beginning of the decade, which basically still incorporated historical-critical theoretical perspectives and later on, although with some restrictions, poststructuralist theoretical perspectives. Toward the end of the decade, his adhesion to these perspectives became even stronger. Michel Foucault, in this sense, constitutes his most significant theoretical basis. Works based on cultural studies, especially by Stuart Hall, feminist studies, and, to a lesser scale, theoretical contributions made by Derrida, Deleuze, and Guattari are also significantly incorporated. Although this theoretical base includes French authors, the incorporation in Brazilian curriculum studies was made by means of English-language authors, including at times references to English translations of French authors.

In one of his early works in the 1990s (Silva, 1992), Tomaz Tadeu started out from a synthesis of the field of Sociology of Education. His main object is an analysis of the connections among the processes of selection, organization, and distribution of school curricula and the dynamics involved in the production and reproduction of capitalist societies. Thus, the grounds for his analysis are based on the critical theoretization of such authors as Bourdieu, Althusser, Marx, Thompson, and Raymond Williams. With respect to the curriculum field, dialogues are established mainly with such authors as Apple, Jean Anyon, Bernstein, Paul Willis, and Michael Young. The work repudiates postmodernism as an ideology associated with the downfall of East European regimes and the triumph of new right-wing ideologies, whereas it reaffirms the standpoints of critical perspectives in the process of exposing social injustice and inequality.

Based on the judgment that his former views had been rather hasty and naive, Silva (1993) later endeavored to establish a dialogue between critical and postmodern theoretizations. He sketched out the continuities and ruptures between such theoretizations, as he identified the limitations, difficulties, and impasses between these theoretical perspectives. The concern in integrating analysis and political action, centered mainly on curricular alternatives, is identified as one of the continuities between critical and postmodern perspectives. According to Silva, inasmuch as poststructuralist perspectives dismiss metanarratives, universal knowledge, and staunch cultural distinctions, they provide grounds for a curriculum centered on students' culture much in the same way as critical theoretization does. Therefore, according to the author, the repudiation of what is seen as knowledge and school knowledge is where the continuity between these perspectives lies.

A clear sign of the rupture regarding the interpretation of knowledge, however, is the fact that poststructuralist thought centralizes matters concerning interests and power, not limiting itself to economic matters, but actually providing a broader scope of debate so as to encompass gender, ethnicity, and sexuality, as well as criticism on notions such as reason, progress, and science. In this sense, another clear rupture is the absence of a view toward the future in poststructuralist thought: Education, curriculum, and/or pedagogy are not feasible if they are escorted by a liberating, just, and egalitarian view of man and society. This possibility would constitute a metanarrative, which is denied by postmodernism because of its oppressive nature vis-à-vis the complexity and variety of the world.

Another discontinuity pointed out by the author refers to the concept of *ideology*. He understands that critical theoretization, mainly in its neo-Marxist orientation, is based on the concept of ideology as a false view of the social world in opposition to true discourse. Therefore, true discourse would constitute the discourse that best represents reality. Hence, such a conception of critical theoretization would be questioned in its foundations because, according to poststructuralism, language constitutes reality and meanings are never fixed but always constructed within certain practices. In this sense, there are no such things as false or true discourses, but several discourses constituting regimes of truth, according to Foucault. Therefore, according to Althusser's perspective of separating science from ideology, there would no longer be a place in science capable of disclosing ideology. However, as Silva analyzed, all narratives are partial and depend on the position of their spokesperson. Thus, a privileged position for the emission of a discourse would not exist.

In contrast, Silva performed an approximation between the postmodern perspective of the conception of reality and the conception of social construction present in the early works of Michael Young and the NSE. According to Young (1978), the true criterion for the validation of knowledge can be found in ethics and politics, more explicitly in their capacity to contribute toward the achievement of man's liberation. Silva pointed out that within this perspective one referent still exists—knowledge shared on an intersubjective basis—whereas postmodern perspectives have no referents. The

question involving the validity of knowledge, always present in the critical theoretizations of curricula, is no longer an issue in poststructuralist discussions. According
to the same author, NSE's form of relativism was faint, whereas that of poststructuralist
theories was powerful. This position strengthens his argumentation in the sense that
not all poststructuralist theses are as innovative as they may seem at first. According to
Silva, it is not a privilege of postmodern thought to be critical of metanarratives. As an
example, he showed how Michael Young and Michael Apple expressed some mistrust
of unicausal and total explanations as they questioned the premises of Marxism of a
more orthodox nature.

Another central issue is the understanding of the subject. In most modern critical literature, Silva understands that it is possible to find the premise for subjects with a unitary, homogeneous, and centered conscience—one that is able to break free from a state
of alienation and submitted to domination so as to reach a lucid, critical, and, therefore,
free and autonomous state. The questioning of this notion of subject by means of the
fragmented, decentralized, and contradictory aspects of subjectivity thus represents
one of the major traits of poststructuralism. Consequently, processes associated with
the notion of emancipation and awareness are also questioned. This conception of
poststructuralism and the consequent criticism made on educators seen as illuminated
beings capable of indicating the path toward awareness is one of the principles of
poststructuralism, soon to be incorporated by Silva and worked on throughout his
work. The author believes what is most important is to incorporate the concept of difference: Based on any possible universal validation criterion, no discourse possesses a
privileged epistemological point of view. There are different nonequivalent discourses
inasmuch as they are involved in asymmetrical power relations. Such asymmetry is a
matter Silva considered of the utmost importance to be questioned during a process of
valorization of differences.

In short, on reviewing his previous position, Silva argued that poststructuralist
theoretizations should be judged according to the fundamental principles of the Critical Theory of Education and its political project. As a criterion for the analysis of
postmodern thought, he proposed asking to what extent such theoretizations constitute a regression or conservative movement, and to what extent they provide grounds
for a better understanding of matters involving domination and power. Finally, he
pointed out how poststructuralism risks keeping us bound to micronarratives, neglecting to question the structures of inequality. His concern with such matters closer to critical theoretization can also be seen in other works of the same period (Gentili & Silva,
1996; Moreira & Silva, 1994; Silva, 1995a), wherein he maintained throughout his analysis the centrality of understanding curricula as a political text (Pinar et al., 1995).

A more thorough study of Michel Foucault's works (Moreira & Silva, 1995; Silva, 1994,
1995b) and, later, of Derrida, Deleuze, Guattari, and Lacan (Silva, 1999, 2000a, 2000b) fulfilled the process of incorporation of postmodern thought in Silva's work. In the curriculum field, the theoretical influences of Popkewitz, Walkerdine, and Gore became more
prominent. His work is most distinguished by the stronger link it establishes between
knowledge and power, for the processes of linguistic turnarounds, the links between curricula and social regulation, curricula, identity, and difference, and social epistemology.
As already mentioned, the matter of equating the consequences arising from the decentralization of the subject vis-à-vis educational projects is also still quite acute.

The link Foucault established between knowledge and power serves as Silva's premise to develop his questioning of the notion of theoretical criticism, which postulates that
knowledge constitutes sources for liberation, enlightenment, and autonomy. This results
from the fact that there is no such thing as a nonpower situation, but a permanent state of
struggle against positions and power relations. A change occurs in the conception of

power: According to Foucault, sources of power do not exist. What exists in fact are decentralized micropowers whose actions are not only coercive, but also productive. The author decisively incorporates the consequences of the so-called linguistic *turnaround* to question the philosophy of conscience. If the world is constructed prior to the subject in language and by means of language, there is no way we can consider speaking of an autonomous subject and conscience. Once a decentralized subject is accepted, it is necessary to accept coexistence with the instability and transitoriness of multiple discourses and those multiple realities constituted by these discourses. This perspective is further enhanced as it incorporates Derrida's thought, whereas subjectivity is dissolved into textuality, the presumed subject being sheer exteriority (Silva, 2000b).

These conclusions can only be developed by assessing the consequences of such interpretations in the educational field, especially the curriculum field—fields in which the principles of autonomy of the subject and sovereignty of reason and knowledge are of the utmost importance in their own constitution. Silva insisted that the consequence of these interpretations is not nihilism, cynicism, or desperation. Above all, the diffuse nature of regulating and controlling mechanisms needs to be emphasized: For instance, even critical pedagogies are involved in processes of regulation and power. Based on Derrida' questioning of essentialism, his concern lies on the deconstruction of such binaries as theory/practice, subject/object, and nature/culture.

Resulting from his conception of language as a transparent and neutral means of representing reality (Silva, 1994), Silva argued that the rationalist tradition of social and educational thought tends to conceptualize knowledge and epistemology as logical processes related to mental schemes of reasoning, unlike in his previous work, where he focused on critiques of meta-narratives and epistemological objectivism, pointing that neither was credible within poststructuralist thought. Silva came to understand that the categories used to define and divide the world are systems that make us ponder, see, and interpret objects the way we do. Such systems are social epistemologies (Popkewitz, 1994). Thus, the position that was previously closer to NSE's faint form of relativism appears to be redirected toward relativism of a more powerful nature.

Silva's "farewell to metanarratives" remains within the perspective that it may even be possible to live more comfortably in their absence, preventing discourses made by restricted groups from being oppressively presented as the only possible discourses and direction available for the educational and curricular fields. To Silva, this means conceiving that the theory of curriculum constitutes one of the nexus between knowledge and power: It is a governing technology. The curriculum field is a person's particular domain of knowledge. It involves government strategies and, therefore, seeks the production of particular subjects.

The production of these subjects can be better understood through the links among curricula, representation, and identity. According to Silva, representation is a process of production of social meanings by means of different discourses that operate through the establishment of differences: It is through the production of systems of differences and oppositions that social groups are made different and constitute their multiple identities. Therefore, curricula are forms of representation. They are both the result of relations between social identities and power, as well as their determiner. This is also how curricula are constituted as a system of control and moral regulation.

Although at times in an apparent contradiction with poststructuralist thought, Silva was still concerned with determining the political effect of these interpretations. He never neglected to consider how the present neo-liberal and neo-conservative project involves a global redefinition of the political, social, and personal spheres with complex and efficient mechanisms of representation and meaning. According to Silva, new discourses, among them contemporary educational discourses, are inserted into this social epistemology, thus enabling it to constitute a linguistic reality and limit the possibilities of conceiving the present world out of its neo-liberal and neo-conservative contexts. The author maintained that one of the fundamental conclusions of critical theory was the linking of curricula to processes of production of value and surplus value. Hence, his concern was not to abandon critical theoretization, but to associate it along with other concepts and metaphors capable of providing further possibilities for interpretation. Silva (1999) developed works containing metaphors such as curricula as a fetish, as representation, and as practices of meaning. In his recent works, he assembled texts that analyze constructivism as the main form of narrative in its regulation of subjectivities (Silva, 1998). He also presented other texts that, on considering the subject as sheer exteriority, interpret the consequences of the existence of monsters, cyborgs, and clones vis-à-vis the contemporary cultural theory and conceptions of subjectivity (Silva, 2000b). He never ceased to approach such recurring discussions as the issue of identity and of difference based on cultural studies (Silva, 2000c).

Tomaz Tadeu Silva's remarkable curriculum scholarship constitutes a major guideline for the group of poststructuralist curriculum researchers. In one of the group's most important works (Veiga-Neto, 1995), scholarly curriculum productions focus directly on an analysis of the following matters: those related to Foucault's standing in postmodern/poststructuralist theoretization; diversified discursive productions (environmental education, constructivism); processes of educational reform and change; and a better understanding of the potential of post-structuralist perspectives in expanding curriculum analysis, especially in criticizing neo-liberal perspectives in education.

Curricula and Knowledge Networks

Discussions involving knowledge networks highlighted the studies on curricula in the latter half of the 1990s, although they date back to the 1980s. This line of work was developed basically by researchers from Rio de Janeiro, coordinated by Nilda Alves at the University of the State of Rio de Janeiro (UERJ), and Regina Leite Garcia at the Fluminense Federal University (UFF), the latter working more closely with the areas of literacy and cultural studies (Garcia, 1995, 1997, 1999). Such studies are the centers of this perspective, although at the end of that decade studies based on this approach were not limited to the same groups, coordinated by the same researchers. The theoretical production of this group has increased in recent years, both in national and international congresses as well as editorially, especially after the publication of a book collection with 17 volumes, entitled *The Meaning of School*. Although not specifically related to the topic of curricula, this collection did create the necessary conditions for the circulation of discussions on knowledge network and on school activities on an everyday life basis.

Although most of the production on curriculum in Brazil is based on discussions originated in English-speaking countries, most studies focusing on curricula network find their references in French bibliography, mainly among such authors as Certeau, Lefèbvre, Morin, Guattari, and Deleuze. In recent years, Portuguese author Boaventura de Souza Santos has become an important reference for these studies. Another noteworthy aspect regarding the main theoretical bases of these studies is the little amount of dialogue established with authors belonging to the area of education, and, more specifically, to the area of curricula such as it is presented in local and foreign literature.

The elaborations involving curricula networks are based on Alves' studies in the curricular area, which focus mainly on the everyday life category (Alves, 1998c) and discussions regarding teacher training (Alves, 1998c). The origin of the concept of *network* such as it is used in the curriculum field in Brazil, dates back to 1985, when discussions involving changes in teacher training courses were being carried out. At the time, Alves (1998a) identified four different spheres in teacher training: academic training, government action, pedagogical practice, and political practice. Such spheres were considered intertwined so as to create a net of relationships in which practice occupied a central position. *Practice* was proposed as the setting where articulations between the sphere of theory and the other two more political spheres were to take place. The focus on the practice of the people who experience curricula on an everyday life basis, as well as the notion according to which training is processed by means of an articulation between different spheres, much in the same way as a web, are to be the central concepts of the theoretization involving the notion of curriculum networks.

During the process of elaboration of the Law of Directives and Bases of National Education 2 years after this first text, Alves (1998a) again approached the discussion involving teacher training, now including the idea of a common national basis that had been in the process of elaboration since 1983. In 1990, this was finally established in the same document that created the National Association for Teacher Training (ANFOPE), of which he was to become president. In defense of a common national basis for teacher training appears the concern with overcoming the subject-related approach within the context of schools. For this purpose, mention is made to curricular *axes*. These would serve as collective venues for discussion and action, pervading each subject in the curriculum and enabling collective propositions. Such axes were seen as producers of fields of action that would allow knowledge to be fully recovered. The analysis of the proposed axes for teacher training—the school–society relationship, the construction of knowledge, public schools, school and classroom everyday life activities, and the discourse of experienced cultures—brings again to light the centrality of social practice and the existence of many intertwined training forums. Notions regarding curricula with a common national basis and curricular axes capable of articulating training experiences brought forth a curricular proposition from the Fluminense Federal University in 1992. This proposition became the object of most texts discussed during meetings held with professionals who dealt with curricula during the first half of the decade. These texts were the first to incorporate the concept of *knowledge network* for the purpose of discussing curricula.

During the 1992 ANPEd meeting, Alves and Garcia (1997) presented their project for the UFF course on Pedagogy in the city of Angra dos Reis. They backed the notion wherein knowledge should be considered in practical, social, and historical terms, and that "man's way of seeing/acting (…) is determined on the one hand by class condition (objective dimension), and on the other by nationality, culture, generation, sex and religion (subjective dimension)" (p. 76). Resorting at this point to Lefèbvre, basically, they denied the ordination, linearity, and hierarchizing of knowledge, whereas they backed the notion of referential networks in social practice. Because theirs was a work based on the concept of complexity and an understanding that the contents dealt with in the duration of the course should fully incorporate culture, the curriculum assimilated the same propositions made by the teacher training movements back in the 1980s. The curricular net was constituted by the curricular axes of the common national basis, the principles of the movement that constructed this basis, the methodological processes, and the subjects that composed the curriculum. The curricular experience would thus develop in a spiral of growing intensity, in a process that alternated individual processes and collective moments, and in an atmosphere of tension between things collective and individual composed by disciplines and multiple activities (Alves & Garcia, 1992).

The degree to which the notion of *knowledge network* is developed is much greater than in its initial formulations. As the bases for the teacher training course at Angra dos Reis were developed theoretically, the authors constructed and sustained the central argumentation wherein different kinds of knowledge are woven in networks and therefore correspond to different everyday life contexts. Nevertheless, the notion of curricular unfolding as an open-ended spiral does not yet allow the proper integration between this notion and the structuring of the curriculum. The metaphor, previously used by Bruner, remained a repository for the modern ideals of growing complexity— of pathways toward perfection. Thus, by the early 1990s, this conception of knowledge network as a tool at the service of weaving curricular alternatives began to undergo greater theoretical elaboration. It is argued that the conception of curricula is formally a repository of the modern concept of knowledge, despite the countless appropriations of this object by social subjects. So long as our modern world lives in a state of crisis, new perspectives for curricular topic themes need to be created.

As they resorted to this central argument, studies on curriculum and knowledge network gradually distanced themselves from the specific discussions involving curricula and moved closer to a focus on the modern world crisis as a topic theme. This is expressed in three different spheres: labor, scientific production, and, mainly, the questioning of reason as a privileged form of understanding the world. Criticism on modernity appears through references made not only to Harvey (1993), Jameson (1994), Touraine (1995), and Santos (1995), but mainly to Morin (1995, 1996). As contemporary relations tend to become more fluid, horizontal, creative, and collective, the centrality of traditional knowledge, which would be the basis of modern curricula, starts to give way to other kinds of knowledge related to everyday life actions. Therefore, the centrality of reason, with its own privileged forum of expression—the sciences—begins to undergo its share of questioning. It is not only a matter of redefining what kind of knowledge is to be valued, but also the form according to which the weaving of social knowledge is done. Based mainly on Deleuze and Guattari (1995) and Lefèbvre (1983), the disciplinarization of knowledge, expressed in the metaphor of the *tree of knowledge,* is questioned and replaced by the understanding that knowledge is woven rhizomatically. Besides the visible depletion of the traditional sciences, with the creation of the inter- or transdisciplinary areas, the *rhizome* metaphor would enable questioning the frontiers established by modernity between scientific knowledge and knowledge woven within the everyday life spheres of society.

Discussions involving the kind of knowledge woven within the everyday life spheres of society are basic characteristics of works dealing with the notions of curricula and knowledge network. The incorporation of the notions of knowledge networks and the weaving of knowledge in networks becomes fundamental in view of the multiplicity and complexity of the relations in which we are permanently involved and in which we create knowledge, as we weave it together with that of other fellow human beings. Thus, weaving a theoretical understanding of curricula involves taking into consideration the everyday life venues where these curricula take place, valuing the making of curricula as a production of meaning.

The notion of weaving a *knowledge network* furthers the initial discussions on training in an effort to give it greater theoretical consistency. The works of De Certeau (1994, 1997), Lefèbvre (1983), and Santos (1995, 2000) constitute, for this purpose, the main references of the studies. The notion of knowledge network introduces a new basic referential—social practice—where practiced knowledge is woven with multiple contacts. Thus, an inversion of the modern polarization between theory and practice is proposed.

Practice is now seen as the venue where theory is woven. Once it reconceptualizes practice as the everyday life venue where knowledge is created, this proposition eliminates the frontiers between science and common sense, between valid knowledge and everyday life knowledge. To maintain this polarization, modern thought regarding school and curriculum creates a set of social processes that define what is official—the time/space instances of power. On the contrary, everyday life knowledge is woven by tactics that propose using what already exists, following the path to some extent of improvization (Alves, 1998b). This type of knowledge refuses the pretension of globalization: It is punctual and diffused throughout the networks in which it is practiced. Thus, the network metaphor purports to subvert the role of inferiority assigned to the kind of knowledge produced by common sense, as opposed to the role that is conferred by modernity to scientific knowledge. This relationship between the context of power and the everyday life context has been focused in depth in research projects developed by the group since 1996 (Alves, 1996; Alves & Oliveira, 1998; Oliveira, 1998). These projects focus on the everyday life construction of knowledge in curricula elaborated by pedagogical staffs in the secretariats of education of different municipalities.

As these research projects considered the everyday life contexts as the proper venues for the weaving of knowledge within curricula, Alves and Oliveira introduced Santos' (1995, 2000) discussions concerning the multiple contexts that constitute subjects as networks of subjectivity: family context, production context, context of citizenship, and context of worldliness. Each one of these contexts corresponds to a social practice, each with its own mode of rationality and forms of power. In each one of these contexts, people weave their knowledge based on the multiple networks to which they belong. This involves producing radical displacements within the limits of a single place, which is our place, displacements concerned with what is being done in times/spaces formerly considered common and even ignored, but which are of great importance because they are where we actually live our lives.

THE HISTORY OF CURRICULA AND THE CONSTITUTION OF SCHOOL KNOWLEDGE

Studies on school knowledge and curricula at the end of the 1980s constituted one of the main nuclei around which theoretical discussions on curricula were developed in Brazil. Early studies carried traits typical of the English-based New Sociology of Education as well as works produced by M. Apple and H. Giroux. Along with the circulation and study of political theories on curricula in foreign literature, an effort was beginning in the sense of understanding the development of the curricular field in Brazil through historical studies. These studies were to become one of the central themes developed by the Nucleus for Studies on Curricula (NEC) of the Federal University of Rio de Janeiro (UFRJ) coordinated by Antonio Flavio Moreira.

The works on the curriculum history produced by this group followed two major guidelines: the study of Brazilian curricular thought and the study of school subjects. Studies on Brazilian curricular thought have been developed by the NEC to understand the movements that constituted the curriculum field and the influence of foreign theoretization on its constitution. In an initial study carried out between 1984 and 1988, Moreira (1990) proposed a study on curricula from its appearance until the end of the 1980s focusing on foreign influences present in curricular theories and practices. On analyzing the limitations of the approaches traditionally used for the study of educational transference, Moreira proposed an alternative focus taking into consideration international, societal, and procedural conditions. As it delved into the interactions, mediations, and resistance witnessed in the process of development of this production, the purpose of its referential frame of analysis was to avoid oversimplified interpretations that reduced Brazilian scholarly production on curricula to a mere copy of the technicism being elaborated in the United States. Regarding the curriculum field, the study referred to critical productions on curricula—namely, by M. Apple, H. Giroux, and M. Young—and to the history of curricula, with contributions made by M. B. Franklin, I. Goodson, and S. Ball.

Along the same lines, between 1994 and 1996, the group coordinated by Moreira concentrated on rethinking the concept of *transference* by studying the development of the field in the 1990s, focusing on curricular thought as well as the teaching of curricula in Rio de Janeiro universities. At this point, discussions involving educational transference were broadened so as to encompass such categories as globalization, cultural hybridization, and cosmopolitanism (Moreira & Macedo, 1999). Besides references made to B. Franklin, I. Goodson, and S. Ball, studies by Hannertz and Garcia Canclini were added with a view toward a fuller understanding of cultural phenomena in contemporary societies. Working basically with the concept of hybridism and introducing the concern involving discussions on identity (Moreira & Macedo, 2000), in a recent study the group tried to analyze how the issue of multiculturalism has penetrated Brazilian production on curricula.

Within this theoretical framework, Moreira's studies on the constitution of the curriculum field in Brazil have enabled an analysis not only of the theoretical productions of the field and the policies on curricula introduced in the country, but also the existing curricula, the role of the professor and the intellectual in the constitution of the field, and their experienced practices. Moreira (1998) thereby analyzed the impasses and contributions of critical curricular theories in postmodern times, thus sustaining the existence of a reconfiguration in the curriculum field that jeopardizes the conception of curricula as political texts. The jeopardy in question is well expressed by the incorporation of a variety of theoretizations often capable of generating obscurely worded theoretical inconsistencies and of being at a distance from matters of a more practical nature. As he developed his argumentation, Moreira believed it is possible to maintain the process of integration of postmodernist insights into the theoretical body of critical theoretization. He also pointed out the need to elect pedagogical practice as the central focus of the analysis. Nevertheless, as he analyzed current curricular policies, Moreira endeavored to understand how they hybridize different social and curricular discourses. He also proposed an interpretation of the theoretizations on curricula that influence such policies, thereby underlining their association with traditional perspectives of curricula, their psychologizing bent and their focus on the tension between flexibility and control (Moreira, 1995, 1996).

As for the roles of teacher and researcher, Moreira defended them as critical and intellectual cosmopolitans able to appropriate themselves of different productions to construct alternative solutions and propositions for current models. This latest concern in Moreira's works glides between the curriculum field, per se, and the field of teacher training (Ludke & Moreira, 1996; Moreira & Silva, 1995). Particularly in these works, Moreira questioned the prescriptive focuses of the first decades of the curricula field, never neglecting to develop propositions aimed at teacher training, having in mind the valorization of the relations between theory and practice and the interrelation of scientific and political dimensions involved in training.

The group's second line of work is directed toward the history of school subjects. By establishing a dialogue with the production of T. Popkewitz, I. Goodson, and S. Ball, and referenced mainly in the work of the Goodson and Fall, these works have studied the development and consolidation of school subjects or knowledge areas, focusing on how they developed in specific institutions. Therefore, these studies have tried to focus on the intersection between school subjects, per se, and the study of educational institutions. Besides these two research projects, which approached the study of education by focusing on the creation and consolidation of the postgraduation course in education at UFRJ (Macedo, 1997; Moreira, 1994) and the subject of science at the Application

Schools of the city of Rio de Janeiro (Moreira, Lopes, & Macedo, 2000), this line of work has generated further studies dealing with other areas/disciplines documented in mastership dissertations and doctorate theses produced at the Nucleus by UFRJ and UERJ students.

Works by this group involving the history of disciplines are integrated by tentative hypotheses constructed by I. Goodson (1983) aiming at the systematization of studies in the area of history of school subjects. They follow a perspective in educational studies that valorizes a conceptual and historical enlargement of history, wherein ethnohistory and the effort to understand the everyday life of institutions gain special emphasis. Hence, studies involving the history of school subjects have been carried out in association with works that privilege schools as institutions with a relative level of autonomy—a totality wherein sociocultural aspects are mediated by the pedagogical. Therefore, because curricula are materialized in certain institutions presenting particular specificities, the works carried out by the group in the scope of history of school subjects have referenced specific institutions. As a result, the particularities of each case are evidenced in the global logic of the course each discipline has followed.

Based on these studies, Goodson's hypothesis is seen in its proper perspective and expanded. The hypothesis proposes that, during the process of consolidation of a school subject and its corresponding referential academic discipline, groups dealing with the academic disciplines tend to distance themselves from the utilitarian and pedagogical traditions within which they originally worked in favor of academic traditions that guarantee this consolidation. It is impossible to define a linear path from utilitarian and pedagogical traditions toward academic traditions. Both in the context of universities and schools, moments of crisis were to be witnessed in the process leading toward the academic. Within the context of universities (Macedo, 1997), a stress on objectives of a more utilitarian nature was noticed as a result of determiners either internal or external to the institution due to gaps between what was hegemonic in the institution and the broader scenario of the educational field. Within the context of schools (Moreira, Lopes, & Macedo, 2000), it was possible to notice that the teachers' concern in motivating their students by exploring the relations between their subject and the students' experiences, together with the specific institutional characteristics of teacher training laboratory schools, are both often capable of valorizing traditions of a more pedagogical and utilitarian nature, although a broader project oriented toward academic objectives does still exist.

However, specifically institutional factors may be added to the hypotheses in question. Among these factors, the following are worth mentioning: (a) the major role performed by discipline leaderships in a specific institution (such leaderships guide teachers according to their own conceptions, tending to represent models of curricular stability); (b) the significant influence of the institution's degree of autonomy vis-à-vis the official mechanisms of control over curricula; and (3) the substantial influence exerted by the professional training of the teaching staff. Academic traditions tend to be reinforced as the level of training reaches higher degrees of specialization in university courses.

Investigations on school subjects are also intertwined with analyses involving the constitution of school knowledge. This process of school-knowledge constitution was developed based on the understanding of school knowledge as a particular sphere of knowledge, which is defined vis-à-vis other social knowledges, particularly scientific and everyday life knowledge. Based on an interpretation according to which culture is constituted by a plurality of reasons and curricula is a cultural selection, Lopes (1999) developed an analysis of the relationships among school knowledge, scientific knowledge, and everyday life knowledge, sustaining the need to articulate Bachelard's historic epistemology with sociology of curriculum. The purpose of this articulation is to face the NSE's faint relativism. It understands that the hierarchies between scientific and everyday life knowledge must be questioned because they are to be seen as different types of knowledge, with different contexts for their application, and they must establish a dialogue between themselves and question each other. Therefore, we may conclude that school knowledge is constituted by processes of didactic transposition and disciplinarization that transform scientific knowledge and other social practices of reference according to the social objectives of schooling. In an effort to fulfill specific educational objectives, school subjects reorganize scientific knowledge in new subdivisions that do not necessarily correspond to the divisions of academic knowledge. Along the process, they undergo the influence of different factors other than those originating from universities and research centers—factors intrinsic to school institutions as well as issues of political and economic nature.

As long as discipline organization is seen as the dominant form of curricular organization in the history of curricular action, the focus on processes of disciplinarization leads to a better understanding on how an organization according to disciplines is capable of endowing school knowledge with cognitive configurations of its own. Delving deeper into this matter, one of the present research projects of the nucleus (Lopes, 2000) involves an investigation of how current discourses sustaining an integrated organization of school knowledge in secondary schools have been incorporating specialized literature produced in the curricula field by means of processes of recontextualization and hybridization. In this sense, the focus turns especially toward discourses on curricular integration (interdisciplinarity, transdisciplinarity, and transversality) and official curricular propositions aimed at the organization of an integrated curriculum.

TENDENCIES

Throughout the present text, we have sustained that hybridism is the major trait of the curriculum field in the 1990s in Brazil. Thus, we have tried to understand how it is possible to cope with the diversity of theoretical tendencies that define the field: (a) a field better characterized by its organic diversity than by its uniformity, (b) one in which different discourses are reterritorialized, and (c) a field inhabited by subjects who are cultural hybrids (Ladwig, 1998). In short, a field of contention in which influences, interdependencies, and rejections mingle.

The process of hybridization occurs as a result of the breakdown and blending of collections organized by different cultural systems—the deterritorialization of a variety of discourse productions that constitute and expand impure genres. Some discollections and recollections that characterize the field of curriculum in Brazil as impure, hybrid, and contentious can be pointed out.

One of the main traits of current Brazilian curricular thought is the blending of postmodern discourses with the focus on politics characterized by critical theorization. Thus, the teleological perspective of a future of changes, based on the philosophy of the subject, the philosophy of conscience, and the valorization of knowledge as a producer of autonomous and critical subjects, becomes associated with the decentralization of the subject, the discursive constitution of reality, and the constitutive linkage of knowledge and power. This kind of blending, more clearly seen in theoretizations involving poststurcturalist theories, may also be found in most of the other productions in the area.

Another trait related to postmodern changes is expressed by the reterritorialization of discourses produced beyond the limits of the educational field. Seeking an interpretation for schools in a postmodern context, references to sociology and philosophy are hybridized together with traditional references from the curriculum field. This new articulation has redefined the Brazilian curriculum field, producing new and advantageous questions and bringing forth new problems that have to be solved. However, as it expands its references, we believe this new hybrid framework has altered the field in such a way that it even manages to assimilate other areas, such as cultural studies or philosophy, within itself. In short, discourses that have penetrated discussions involving curricula have contributed toward the constitution of new identities for the field, making the constitution of a theory on curricula more diffuse and allowing some themes to glide from one field to another.

Therefore, we believe the curriculum field is undergoing some kind of redefinition—one that involves not only the reterritorialization of referential productions on curricula, but also the construction of new concerns. For that matter, we believe the main tendency of the field is to valorize certain discussions involving culture inasmuch as discussions on multiculturalism or social studies have been gaining intensity under a variety of theoretical references. A process of cultural change is underway—one that associates education and curricula with broader cultural processes, thus contributing toward a certain degree of imprecision in defining the boundaries of the intellectual curriculum field.

This increasing imprecision of the boundaries of the field, due to the undefined nature of the cultural capital to which it is associated, seems to be of some concern, because, at times, it disregards the specificity of education and of curricular processes. With this, we do not wish to deny the importance of the flow of meanings established between different fields and subjects. However, we do believe that being open to these meanings requires, according to Hannertz (1994), the ability to brave these new fields and manipulate their particular system of meanings. Thus, the relationship with other fields needs to be negotiated by means of interactions between domination and subordination, when the researcher dealing with curricula takes hold of that which is useful from other fields, yet upholds the notion of creative confrontation as a guideline for such appropriation. Within this perspective, as different flows of meaning come together, this may prove to be profitable for the curriculum field, inasmuch as researchers manage to reevaluate discussions on the curriculum by trespassing on the traditional divisions established between areas of knowledge, thus taking better advantage of the elements available in their original field.

REFERENCES

Alves, N. (1996). *Construção de conhecimento sobre currículo por equipes pedagógicas de secretarias municipais de educação* (Projeto de Pesquisa). Rio de Janeiro, Brazil: Faculdade de Educação, UERJ.

Alves, N. (1998a). *Trajetórias em redes na formação de professores*. Rio de Janeiro, Brazil: DP&A.

Alves, N. (1998b). *Redes de saberes: Questoes práticas e epistemológicas* (Projeto de Pesquisa). Rio de Janeiro, Brazil: Faculdade de Educação, UERJ.

Alves, N. (1998c). *O espaço escolar e suas marcas: O espaço como dimensão material do currículo*. Rio de Janeiro, Brazil: DP&A.

Alves, N., & Garcia, R. L. (1992). A construção do conhecimento e o currículo dos cursos de formação de professores na vivência de um processo. In N. Alves (Org.), *Formação de professores: pensar e fazer*. São Paulo, Brazil: Cortez.

Alves, N., & García, R. L. (1997). Uma infinidade de mundos passíveis: Fragmentos de um discurso em construção. XX Reunião Anual da ANPEd. Caxambu, Brazil.

Alves, N., & Oliveira, I. (1998). *Construção de conhecimento sobre currículo por equipes pedagógicas de secretarias municipais de educação* (Relatório de Pesquisa). Rio de Janeiro, Brazil: Faculdade de Educação, UERJ.

Anderson, P. (1995). Balanço do neoliberalismo. In E. Sader & P. Gentili (Org.), *Pós-liberalismo: As políticas sociais e o estado democrático*. São Paulo, Brazil: Paz e Terra.

Bernstein, B. (1996). *A estruturação do discurso pedagógico—classe, códigos e controle*. Petrópolis, Brazil: Vozes.

Bourdieu, P. (1983). *Sociologia. Introdução e organização de Renato Ortiz*. São Paulo, Brazil: Ática.

Bourdieu, P. (1992). *A economia das trocas simbólicas. Introdução, organização e seleção de Sérgio Miceli*. São Paulo, Brazil: Perspectiva.

Bourdieu, P. (1998). *Escritos da Educação. Introdução e organização de Maria Alice Nogueira e Afrânio Catani*. Petrópolis, Brazil: Vozes.

Burnham, T. F. (1993). Complexidade, multirreferencialidade, subjetividade: três referências polêmicas para a compreensão do currículo escolar. *Em Aberto, 12*(58), 3- 13.

De Certeau, M. (1994). *A invenção do cotidiano-artes de fazer*. Petrópolis, Brazil: Vozes.

De Certeau, M. (1997). *A invenção do cotidiano-morar, cozinhar*. Petrópolis, Brazil: Vozes.

Deleuze, G., & Guatarri, F. (1995). Mil platôs. *Rio de Janeiro, 34.*

Dussel, I., Tiramonti, G., & Birgin, A. (1998). Hacia una nueva cartografía de la reforma curricular. Reflexiones a partir de la descentralización educativa argentina. *Revista de Estudios del Curriculum, 1*(2), 132-162.

García Canclini, N. (1998). *Culturas híbridas—estratégias para entrar e sair da modernidade*. São Paulo, Brazil: Edusp.

Garcia, R. L. (1995). *Cartas londrinas*. Rio de Janeiro, Brazil: Relume Dumará.

Garcia, R. L. (1997). *Uma nova orientação para uma nova escola*. São Paulo, Brazil: Loyola.

Garcia, R. L. (1999). *Alfabetização dos alunos de classes populares*. São Paulo, Brazil: Cortez

Gentili, P., & Silva, T. T. (Orgs.). (1996). *Escola S/A*. Brasília, Brazil: CNTE.

Goodson, I. F. (1983). *School subjects and curriculum change: Case studies in curriculum history*. London: Croom Helm.

Hannertz, U. (1994). Cosmopolitas e locais na cultura global. In M. Featherstone (Org.), *Cultura global: Nacionalismo, globalização e modernidade*. Petrópolis, Brazil: Vozes.

Harvey, D. (1993). *Condição pós-moderna*. São Paulo, Brazil: Loyola.

Jameson, F. (1994). *Espaço e imagem-teorias do pós- moderno e outros ensaios*. Rio de Janeiro, Brazil: Ed. da UFRJ.

Ladwig, J. G. (1998). *World curriculum and the postcolonial subject*. Trabalho apresentado no X Congresso de Educação Comparada, Cidade do Cabo, mimeo.

Lefèbvre, H. (1983). *Lógica formal, lógica dialética*. Rio de Janeiro, Brazil: Paz e Terra.

Lopes, A. R. C. (1999). *Conhecimento escolar: Ciência e cotidiano*. Rio de Janeiro, Brazil: EdUERJ.

Lopes, A. R. C. (2000). *A organização do conhecimento escolar no "novo ensino médio" (Projeto de Pesquisa)*. *Rio de Janeiro, Brazil: Faculdade de Educação, UFRJ.*

Ludke, M., & Moreira, A. F. B. (1996). *Socialização profissional de professores* (Relatório de Pesquisa). Rio de Janeiro, Brazil: PUC-Rio, UFRJ.

Macedo, E. F. (1997). *História do currículo da Pós-graduação em Educação da UFRJ (1972–1994)* (Tese de Doutorado). Campinas, Brazil: Faculdade de Educação, UNICAMP.

Moreira, A. F. (1990). *Currículos e programas no Brasil*. Campinas, Brazil: Papirus.

Moreira, A. F. B. (1994). *O currículo da Pós- graduação em Educação da UFRJ: Os dez primeiros anos* (Relatório de Pesquisa). Rio de Janeiro, Brazil: Faculdade de Educação, UFRJ.

Moreira, A. F. B. (1995). Neoliberalismo, currículo nacional e avaliação. In L. H. Silva & J. C. Azevedo (Orgs.), *Reestruturação curricular: Teoria e prática no cotidiano da escola*. Petrópolis, Brazil: Vozes.

Moreira, A. F. B. (1996). Os parâmetros curriculares nacionais em questão. *Educação e Realidade, 21*(1), 9-23.

Moreira, A. F. B. (1998). A crise da teoria curricular crítica. In M. V. Costa (Org.), *O currículo nos limiares do contemporâneo*. Rio de Janeiro, Brazil: DP&A.

Moreira, A. F. B., Lopes, A. R. C., & Macedo, E. F. (2000). *Currículo de ciências: um estudo sócio- histórico* (Relatório de Pesquisa). Rio de Janeiro, Brazil: Faculdade de Educação, UFRJ, UERJ.

Moreira, A. F. B., & Macedo, E. F. (1999). Faz sentido ainda o conceito de transferência educacional? In A. F. B. Moreira (Org.), *Currículo: Políticas e práticas*. Campinas, Brazil: Papirus.

Moreira, A. F. B., & Macedo, E. F. (2000). *Multiculturalismo e o campo do currículo* (Projeto de Pesquisa). Rio de Janeiro, Brazil: Faculdade de Educação, UFRJ, UERJ.

Moreira, A. F. B., & Silva, T. T. (Orgs.). (1994). *Currículo, cultura e sociedade*. São Paulo, Brazil: Cortez.

Moreira, A. F. B., & Silva, T. T. (Orgs.). (1995). *Territórios contestados—o currículo e os novos mapas políticos e culturais*. Petrópolis, Brazil: Vozes.

Morin, E. (1995). *Introdução ao pensamento complexo*. Lisboa, Portugal: Instituto Piaget.

Morin, E. (1996). *Ciência com consciência*. Rio de Janeiro, Brazil: Bertrand Brasil.

Oliveira, I. (1998). *Redes de saberes e poderes no desenvolvimento e na implantação de políticas curriculares locais* (Projeto de Pesquisa). Rio de Janeiro, Brazil: Faculdade de Educação, UERJ.

Pinar, W. F., Reynolds, W., Slattery, P., & Taubman, P. (1995). *Understanding curriculum.* New York: Peter Lang.

Popkewitz, T. (1994). Historia do currìculo, regulação social e poder. In T. T. Silva (Org.), *O sujeito da educação: estudos foucaultianos.* Petrópolis, Brazil: Vozes.

Santos, B. S. (1995). *Pela mão de Alice.* São Paulo, Brazil: Cortez.

Santos, B. S. (2000). *A crítica da razão indolente.* São Paulo, Brazil: Cortez.

Silva, T. T. (1992). *O que produz e o que reproduz na educação.* Porto Alegre, Brazil: Artes Médicas.

Silva, T. T. (Org.). (1993). *Teoria educacional crítica em tempos pós-modernos.* Porto Alegre, Brazil: Artes Médicas.

Silva, T. T. (Org.). (1994). *O sujeito da educação: estudos foucaultianos.* Petrópolis, Brazil: Vozes.

Silva, T. T. (Org.). (1995a). *Neoliberalismo, qualidade total e educação.* Petrópolis, Brazil: Vozes.

Silva, T. T. (Org.). (1995b). *Alienígenas na sala de aula - uma introdução aos estudos culturais em educação.* Petrópolis, Brazil: Vozes.

Silva, T. T. (Org.). (1998). *Liberdades reguladas—a pedagogia construtivista e outras formas de governo do eu.* Petrópolis, Brazil: Vozes.

Silva, T. T. (1999). *O currículo como fetiche: a poética e a política do texto curricular.* Belo Horizonte, Brazil: Autêntica.

Silva, T. T. (2000a). *Teoria cultural e educação—um vocabulário crítico.* Belo Horizonte: Autêntica.

Silva, T. T. (Org.). (2000b). *Pedagogia dos monstros.* Belo Horizonte, Brazil: Autêntica.

Silva, T. T. (2000c). *Identidade e diferença.* Petrópolis, Brazil: Vozes.

Touraine, A. (1995). *Crítica da modernidade.* Petrópolis, Brazil: Vozes.

Veiga-Neto, A. (Org.). (1995). *Crítica pós-estruturalista e educação.* Porto Alegre, Brazil: Sulina.

Young, M. (1978). Taking sides against the probable: Problems of relativity and commitment in teaching and the sociology of knowledge. In C. Jenks (Ed.), *Rationality, education and social organization of knowledge.* London: Routledge & Kegan Paul.

CHAPTER 11

In Search of a Vision: How Brazil Is Struggling to Envision Citizenship for Its Public Schools

Silvia Elizabeth Moraes
Conselho Nacional de Desenvolvimento Científico e Tecnológico
Centro Universitário Central Paulista (UNICEP-São Carlos)

The public school system in Brazil is going through profound curricular and administrative reforms. The evidence that we are far behind other countries in students' achievement has made our leaders finally understand that, to be part of the globalized world in partnership conditions with developed countries, we must provide good basic education for all. Therefore, universalizing education and building high standards in Brazilian public schools has become the most important goal of the Ministry of Education (MEC).

Presented in a document entitled the *National Curricular Parameters* (PCN), this curricular reform is basically structured around three main axes: a new interdisciplinary vision of knowledge; the inclusion of ethics, cultural pluralism, environment, health, and sexual orientation as transversal themes;[1] and, to implement these changes, a democratic and autonomous administration of which a fundamental element is the development of a pedagogical project by each school.

The PCN was officially introduced to the educational community in 1996. At that time, I was engaged in research that consisted of an analysis of the curriculum of the public high schools in São Carlos, SP, and I had arrived at the same conclusions that motivated the reform: Our curriculum was based on a positivistic, fragmented, and alienated conception of science; quantity was given a more privileged place than quality; and pedagogical work resumed itself in the traditional, obsolete view of quiet, silent, passive classes with students working individually, facing one another's nape, and memorizing concepts that had no connection with their lives or even their remotest interests.

I saw in that reform a possibility of improving this dramatic situation and I decided to work for it. I presented a research project to the Brazilian research funding agency *Conselho Nacional de Desenvolvimento Científico e Tecnológico,* which consisted of devel-

---

[1]Cross-curricular themes in the United States and England; *objetivos fundamentales transversales* in Chile, *temas transversales* in Spain and Argentina.

oping interdisciplinary/transversal projects with public school teachers and student teachers of the Federal University of São Carlos (UFSCar). This experience (1997–1998) resulted in many interesting and exciting encounters and a book written in partnership with Dr. Angela B. Kleiman (Kleiman & Moraes, 1999).[2]

However, collective work—the basis of interdisciplinarity and transversality—has revealed itself more difficult than expected. The majority of our public school teachers had their formation in the same fragmented, alienated, individualized curriculum they are now supposed to abandon. Although the schools have included in their schedules collective planning hours, many of these opportunities are being spent in individual/disciplinary work. It was then that I thought of Habermas' theory of communicative action (TCA). In his work, Habermas developed a concept of communicative rationality no longer based on subjectivism and individualism: He talked about getting together and using our rationality to reach a consensus, giving voice to all participants in acts of communication, and rehabilitating the public sphere. It is indeed a theory of democracy.

Following the same steps, I presented a research project to CNOCT, who, once again, gave me full support: a postdoctoral action research that I am now developing, the objective of which is to situate the discussion of an autonomous and democratic school administration within TCA. The research participants are curriculum coordinators, directors, vice directors, teachers, and students of 12 schools of the São Carlos district, in São Paulo, Brazil. The first phase of the research consisted of 10 meetings of 3 hours each, in which the concepts of public sphere and public opinion, communicative action as opposed to strategic action, communicative rationality as opposed to cognitive-instrumental rationality, ideal speech situation, life world, and normative universalism (Habermas, 1984, 1989, 1995) were presented and discussed (March–June 2000). The second phase took place in September and was completed by November 2000. This involved visits to the participating schools, where I analyzed, together with the research participants, the situations where the concepts of communicative action could be applied. In the third stage of our research (January, February, and March), we evaluated and disseminated the results.

In this chapter, I present a brief account of the Brazilian public school reform. The chapter is divided into: (a) a short history of the Brazilian curriculum; (b) the PCN and its main concepts of interdisciplinarity and transversality; (c) the transversal themes of ethics, cultural pluralism, environment, health, sexual orientation, work and consumption, and local themes; (d) the concept of pedagogical project; (e) the vision of democracy and citizenship as an ideal to be attained by the Brazilian public schools; and (f) the theory of communicative action as a theoretical framework for our vision building.

HISTORICAL INEQUALITY

The history of our curriculum started in colonial times with the Jesuits who imported European medieval forms of thinking and dominant ideas. Uniform and neutral, concentrated on giving basic general culture, without any concern for qualifying for work, the Jesuit curriculum was completely alienated from colonial life. It was characterized by an attachment to forms of dogmatic thought for the reaffirmation of the authority of the Church, and for the practice of intellectual exercises with the purpose of strengthening memory and reasoning (Romanelli, 1978). The elitist character of the curriculum only began to be seriously questioned after World War I, when industry lacked literate workers. Moreover, the illiterate could not vote, and the emergent industrial bourgeoi-

---

[2]Dr. Angela B. Kleiman is a professor at the Instituto de Estudos da Linguagem (IEL) of the State University of Campinas, SP (UNICAMP).

sie saw in the literacy of the masses an instrument to change political power and defeat the rural oligarchies.

The idea of a curriculum at the service of a democratic society only appeared with Anísio Teixeira and the advocates of the New School. For the first time, school subjects were considered instruments for the attainment of certain goals, with the objective of qualifying individuals to live in society. Teixeira looked for the model of the ideal school in the American philosopher John Dewey. As a pupil of Dewey at Columbia University (1927), he was attracted to Dewey's democratic ideas and translated several of his books. Besides being the main propagator of Dewey's ideas in Brazil, Teixeira left several writings, conferences, and articles impregnated with those notions, then revolutionary, of a curriculum centered in the child—of a public, free, and universal school, of learning through experience, of a conception of a school as a citizenship, and democratic laboratory.

Teixeira defined *curriculum* as the group of activities in which children are engaged in their school life. Curriculum was part of an educational process that lasted for a lifetime; it should be centered in activities, projects, and problems directly taken from natural human experience. The students should be organized according to their interests, and the teacher should not be the sole and exclusive transmitter of knowledge, rather becoming an activator and advisor of learning of which the initiative would be the students'. The teacher, in this curriculum conception, became the facilitator of learning.

This form of individualized teaching raised school costs. Learning in such a stimulating atmosphere, which demanded an immense variety of didactic material, class libraries, learning centers, science, and language laboratories, restricted access to these schools to the power elite (Mills, 1981). Moreover, they conserved the mold of slavery times (i.e., a dichotomy between intellectual and manual work, racism and an excessively humanistic tendency). The public school, in turn, did not even have a chance to experience this new schoolism, and its teaching methodology remained traditional, based on a one-way teaching whereby students sat for hours passively copying empty and decontextualized concepts so that, later on, they would be submitted to evaluations that only tested their memorization ability. In the recent past of antidemocratic governments, our educational reforms only created policies and requirements that increased governmental control over and compounded the bureaucracy under which public schools had to survive. The private institutions took care of educating the elite while the rest of the population was left with a mediocre educational system.

Today, the idea of leaving the masses uneducated has been globally eroded by the evidence that modern products need qualified markets (illiterate and unemployed people do not buy computers), and that exporting raw materials will never make us rich. Our technological and educational delay is huge. It seems as if we are waking up after a long sleep.

INTERDISCIPLINARITY AND TRANSVERSALITY IN THE PCN

The present curricular reform has started with the implementation of the National Curricular Parameters (PCN)—a document elaborated by the Ministry of Education that is meant to function as a frame of reference to stimulate reflection and guarantee coherence in the development of education policies. The intention is that this would be achieved by socializing discussions, research and recommendations, subsidizing programs of improvement of teaching quality, and guiding the daily work of Brazilian teachers, mainly of those that are more isolated from current pedagogical information.

The elaboration of PCN included the study of different national and international curricular proposals, research, statistical data, publications, and classroom experiences disseminated in conferences, seminars, and publications. In 1995–1996, an initial proposal of PCN was presented in a preliminary version to be discussed among educators of public and private universities, state educational authorities, and institutions of different areas of knowledge. About 400 opinions on the initial proposal were put forward and served as reference for its reelaboration.

The PCN presents, as its basic proposal, the adoption of interdisciplinarity and transversality, which are based on the critique of a conception that takes reality as a group of stable data, subject to an exempt and distant act of knowing. For conceptualization, we can say that they differ from one another in the sense that interdisciplinarity refers to an epistemological approach to knowledge, questioning the segmentation among its different fields produced by a compartmentalized vision (disciplinary) of knowledge.

Transversality refers to a pedagogic approach that helps students acquire a wide and comprehensive vision of reality as well as their insertion and participation in this reality. Transversality and interdisciplinarity are inseparable concepts. Interdisciplinarity questions fragmentation and linearity, and transversality confronts alienation and individualism in the acquisition of knowledge. Both can only be put into practice through collective work.

The PCN emphasizes the role of the school in the process of construction of democracy, which necessarily concerns knowledge, understanding, and practice of rights and responsibilities in relation to personal, collective, and environmental life. The proposed themes express concepts and values that are fundamental and correspond to important and urgent issues for Brazilian society today. The PCN brings to the curriculum the problems focused on by the transversal themes, its general objectives, contents, and evaluation criteria. With transversality, the themes become integral parts of the areas and not external and/or attached to them, defining a perspective for educational work that starts from them.

In practice, these two concepts—interdisciplinarity and transversality—are interdependent and imply a radical change in teaching practice. Transversality is a new way of looking at the disciplinary contents. It is considering the subject matters of the curriculum in their different levels and ramifications, associating disciplines with real life, modernizing and contextualizing their content through discussions, examples, empiric observation, reading of newspapers, magazines, and watching TV. Both demand constant planning, evaluation, and replanning that can only be put into effect through wide interaction among the teachers of the different disciplines with a view to a common objective: an integrated curriculum. Collective work is therefore the sine qua non condition for the development of such a curriculum.

According to the transversal vision of the curriculum, the knowledge transmitted through conventional areas such as Portuguese, mathematics, sciences, history, and geography—without losing sight of their fundamental importance—is not enough to attain the goal of educating for citizenship. The transversal themes are situated beyond what has been traditionally taken as the field of concern of the conventional curricular areas and should therefore receive a transversal approach.

A recent study on curricular tendencies in some countries (Moraes, 2000) has indicated that there is a general concern with the inclusion of the transversal themes. Spain, England, the United States, Chile, Ghana, Sierra Leone, Liberia, Nigeria, Gambia, and Australia, among others, have proposed, throughout these last two decades, several initiatives of inserting in the curriculum of the fundamental school the transversal themes of ethics, human rights, respect for the environment, citizenship, and multiculturalism. MEC suggests that ethics, cultural pluralism, health, environment, sexual orientation, work and consumption, and local themes be approached transversally.

THE TRANSVERSAL THEMES

Ethics

Ethics concerns rules of social conviviality. Ethical reflection includes all the other themes because it encourages discussion on the freedom of choice, the legitimacy of practices and values consecrated by tradition and habit, and relationships among individuals, groups, and groups in institutions. The school work to be accomplished around *ethics* should be organized to help students be capable of:

- understanding the concept of *justice* and sensitizing them for the need for the construction of a just society;
- adopting respectful attitudes toward differences among people;
- adopting attitudes of solidarity, cooperation, and repudiation of injustice and discrimination;
- understanding school life as participation in the public space, using and applying the knowledge acquired in the construction of a society based on democracy and solidarity;
- valuing and using dialogue as a form of illuminating conflicts and taking collective decisions;
- building a positive image of oneself, self-respect expressed by trust in one's capacity to choose and accomplish one's life project, and for the legitimation of moral norms that guarantee everyone the same accomplishment;
- assuming positions according to one's own judgement, considering different points of view and aspects of each situation.

The transversal theme of ethics is organized in four blocks of contents: mutual respect, justice, dialogue, and solidarity.

A survey of public school teachers in São Paulo I conducted during 1998–1999 registered these teachers' total acceptance of the inclusion of ethics in the curriculum. They see it as an attempt to rediscover the sense and direction of the school. For them, ethics today presents itself as a social need. If we think of ethics as rules of social conviviality, they say, we will see that these rules need to be revised urgently: violence, corruption, disrespect toward the weakest and poorest, excessive valorization of money as the greatest goal to be reached by everybody. The discussion of ethical values is a question of survival.

The school sees an increase of violence among the students who confront one another in gangs as they come out of classes and sometimes even inside the classrooms. Scenes such as shootings and confrontations have become commonplace. According to the magazine *VEJA,* in the state of Sao Paulo in 1999, at least 10 students were murdered inside or in front of schools. A student told me that just looking at one another can cause a fight. Another manifestation of violence is vandalism against school materials. The influence of TV is notorious. Violence seems to increase the day after a violent film is shown in the local cinemas. The feelings of impotence and despair dominate most members of public schools, therefore, in the teachers' and students' vision, we need to speak of ethics at every possible opportunity.

Cultural Pluralism

According to the PCN, *cultural pluralism* concerns the knowledge and valorization of ethnic and cultural characteristics of the different social groups that inhabit the national territory, the socioeconomic inequalities, and the critical discriminatory relationships that permeate Brazilian society. It offers the student the possibility to get to know Brazil as a complex, multifaceted, and sometimes paradoxical country. To consider diversity is not to deny the existence of common characteristics, nor the possibility of constituting a nation or even the existence of a universal dimension of the human being. Cultural plurality means looking at diversity as a fundamental step in the construction of a national identity. Working with human diversity implies an amplification of horizons for the teacher and student—an opening for the conscience that the reality in which we live is part of a complex, fascinating, and challenging world in which the underlying universal element and defining factor of intersocial and interpersonal relationships should be ethics.

It is important to distinguish cultural diversity from social inequality. Different cultures are produced by social groups throughout their respective histories in their fight for subsistence, the organization of their social and political life, their relationship with the environment and with other groups, and the production of knowledge. The difference among cultures is the product of the singularity of those processes in each social group. Social inequality is a difference of another nature: It is produced from socioeconomic and political dominance and exploitation. In practice, Brazil is not a society governed by rights, but by privileges. The privileges generate discrimination and prejudice of all types. In other words, dominance, exploitation, and exclusion interact; discrimination is a result and an instrument of this complex of relationships.

However, despite discrimination, injustice, and prejudice, which contradict the principles of dignity, mutual respect, and justice, paradoxically Brazil has been producing experiences of conviviality and re-elaboration of original cultures. Embedded in the contradictions of an economic and social system historically constituted in an unjust way, Brazil has the following contribution to make: the possibility of a multiple singularity, multifaceted, complex conscious of its conflicts constantly open for transformation of itself. Therefore, what is longed for when working with cultural pluralism is not division of society in closed cultural groups, but conviviality.

There has been historical difficulty dealing with the theme of racial/ethnic prejudice and discrimination. The country has avoided the theme due to its image of a homogeneous country without differences—a racial democracy. However, at school, we have manifestations of racism and social and ethnic discrimination, sometimes unconscious or involuntary, on the part of teachers, students, and administrators. To contribute to the process of overcoming discrimination and building a fair, free, and fraternal society, the educational project has to deal with the ethical dimension—of how one develops attitudes and values directed toward the formation of new behavior and new bonds in relation to those that have been victims of injustice. Changing mentalities, overcoming prejudice, and fighting against discriminatory attitudes are goals for the school.

Another important point to be covered in the discussion of *cultural pluralism* is what Apple (1979) called *selective tradition*: the choice of certain meanings and practices that are neglected and excluded in favor of other meanings and practices in a dominant culture. The representations of history and culture of a society change with time because they reflect contemporary values and special interests. These representations are a continuous selection and reselection of the significant ancestors. The schools not only function as agents of this selective tradition, but they also reproduce people—with appropriate meanings and values—who do not see any other possibility than that of the dominant culture. Our significant past, at least the one taught in the schools before, was mainly European. We are now looking at our Indian, African, and European origins as well as the many immigrant groups that have formed and are forming the Brazilian people. It is a crusade in favor of self-esteem and self-respect, of discovery of knowledge and cultures that have almost been forgotten or eliminated.

This movement toward the valorization of local cultures has been well registered by contemporary authors like Harvey (1994), Featherstone (1994), Dussel (n.d.), Garaudy (1975, 1983), and Levinas (1988), among others. As Featherstone (2000) said, there is nothing intrinsically better in Beethoven, Shakespeare, or an erudite culture than in popular culture. All cultures are basically synchretic; cultural unity is a deceiving illusion that masks a multiplicity of voices and cultural forms in existence. The distinction between erudite and popular culture cannot be sustained because hierarchical distinctions of taste have been arbitrarily constructed. Curriculum knowledge contributes to the shaping of identity, capacity, attitude, and action, both individually and collectively, and questions of multicultural curriculum knowledge are important because how we understand ourselves, others, the nation, and the world is shaped by that knowledge (Cornbleth, 1995).

Environment

In the PCN, *environment* deals with the search for collective and personal ways to establish economic, social, and cultural relations to promote the quality of life for everyone in the present and the future. The environmental perspective consists of looking at the interrelation and interdependence of the various elements in the constitution and maintenance of life on this planet. In terms of education, this perspective fosters the need for commitment to the principles of dignity, participation and co-responsibility, solidarity and equity among humans, and the need to extend respect and commitment to life of all living beings.

For the incorporation of environmental issues and the valorization of life in educational practice, several initiatives have been taken by government and nongovernmental organizations. In 1968, UNESCO performed a comparative study in 79 countries on the work accomplished by the schools in relation to the environment. In that analysis, propositions were formulated that later would be accepted internationally, such as Environmental Education should not be considered a discipline—for environment we consider not just the physical, but also the interrelated social, cultural, economic, and political aspects.

In 1972, at the Conference of the United Nations for Human Environment in the Stockholm, a Plan of World Action and the Declaration on the Human Atmosphere (orientation for the governments) were elaborated. At that Conference, the importance of educational action in the environmental subjects was determined for the first time— a fact that generated the first International Program of Environmental Education consolidated in 1975 by the Conference of Belgrade.

In 1977, the Intergovernmental Conference of Environmental Education of Tbilisi defined the objectives of Environmental Education as a dimension given to the content and practice of education guided by the resolution of concrete problems of the environment through interdisciplinary approaches. In 1987, at the International Conference on Education and Environmental Formation in Moscow, summoned by UNESCO, there was consensus on the need for introducing Environmental Education in the world's educational systems.

One of the main conclusions and international proposals assumed by the participant countries of RIO-92, the International Environment Conference held in Rio de Janeiro in 1992, was the recommendation of investing in a change of mentality, making human groups aware of the need to adopt a new point of view and new attitudes toward the environment. More than 170 countries signed agreements in which they recognized the central role that education has to play in the construction of an ecologically fair and well-balanced world that demands individual and collective responsibility in local, national, and international contexts. Agenda 21 gathered proposals of action for the countries and the people in general, as well as strategies for those actions to be carried out. In complementation to that agenda, Latin American and Caribbean countries presented *Our Agenda* with the priorities of our countries. All those recommendations, decisions, and agreements document the importance now attributed by world leaders to Environmental Education.

Besides being one of the largest countries in the world, Brazil possesses countless natural resources of fundamental importance for the whole planet. The problem is the way in which natural and cultural resources are being negotiated, nationally and internationally. Hunger, poverty, social injustice, violence, and a low quality of living for many Brazilians are factors that strongly related to the development model and its socioenvironmental implications. In this context, alongside protection laws, the importance of educating future citizens is unmistakable.

More than teaching information and concepts, the school must work with attitudes, the formation of values, teaching and learning abilities and procedures, among them gestures of solidarity, habits of personal hygiene, and participation in small negotiations. An important procedure for action in the environmental area is the capacity to participate in collective and democratic decision-making processes even in the simplest circumstances. Working with that ability implies a reflection of the teacher regarding how a negotiation among several participants, with different points of view and interests, can be carried out.

The basic principles adopted by the PCN are:

1. respect and take care of the community you live in as an ethical principle that reflects our obligation towards other people and other life forms, now and in the future;
2. improve the quality of human life;
3. conserve the vitality of the earth's diversity;
4. minimize the exhaustion of nonrenewable resources such as minerals, petroleum, gas, mineral, and coal;
5. stay in the limits of support capacity of the earth;
6. modify attitudes and personal practices;
7. allow communities to take care of their own atmosphere;
8. generate a national structure for development integration and conservation; and
9. constitute a global alliance.

Working with the theme *environment* should encourage the students to:

- know and understand, in an integrated and systemic way, the basic notions related to the environment;
- adopt attitudes in the school, community, and at home to lead to constructive, just, and ecologically sustainable interactions;
- observe and analyze facts and situations of the environmental point of view, in a critical way, recognizing the need and opportunities for reacting and proposing to guarantee a healthy environment and good quality of life;
- notice in several natural phenomena cause and effect relationships that condition life in space (geographical) and time (historical), using that perception to position oneself critically before environmental conditions;

- understand the need and master some conservation procedures and handling of natural resources with which one interacts, applying them in one's daily life;
- perceive, appreciate, and value natural and sociocultural diversity, adopting respectful attitudes toward different aspects and forms of natural, ethnic, and cultural patrimony; and
- identify oneself as an integral part of nature, observing personal processes as fundamental elements for a creative, responsible, and respectful attitude toward the environment.

Health

The PCN understands *Education for Health* as promotion and protection of health and a strategy for the conquest of citizenship rights. Its inclusion in the curriculum responds to a strong social need that requires the development of a sanitary conscience of our population and our rulers so that the right to healthy conditions is considered a priority. Alone, the school will not make the students healthy. However, it can and should make them aware that they have a right to a healthy life.

The concept of *Healthy City* originated in Canada in the 1980s, is a good parameter for guiding projects in several parts of the world. A Healthy City should have: (a) a strong, fraternal community constituted on the bases of social justice, in which there is a high degree of participation of the population in the decisions of public power; (b) a clean and safe environment favorable to life quality and health; satisfaction of the citizens' basic needs, including food, housing, work, and access to good health, education, and social attendance services; (c) an active cultural life; and (d) a strong, diversified, and innovative economy.

Speaking of *health* implies taking into consideration the quality of the air that one breathes; the production, conditions, and use of nuclear or war equipment; wild consumerism and poverty; social degradation or malnutrition; personal lifestyles; and forms of insertion of different groups of the population in the work world.

At the end of their school life, the students should be capable of:

- understanding that health is everybody's right, valuing the actions that seek its promotion and protection;
- understanding health in its physical, mental, and social aspects as an essential dimension of human development;
- understanding that health is linked to the physical, economic, and partner–cultural environment, identifying personal and collective risk factors;
- knowing and using intervention forms on unfavorable factors, acting with responsibility in relation to one's personal health and collective health;
- knowing forms of access and use of the community resources that favor the promotion, protection, and recovery of health; and
- assuming responsibility for one's own health, adopting self-care habits, respecting the possibilities and limits of his own body, and identifying and taking precautions against risk factors.

Sexual Orientation

Sexual orientation in the school should be understood as a process of pedagogic intervention that has as its objective the transmission of information and problematization of subjects related to sexuality, including attitudes, beliefs, taboos, and values associated with it. Such intervention happens in a collective context, differing from individual work, of psychotherapeutic character and focusing on the sociological, psychological, and physiologic dimensions of sexuality. It also differs from the education accomplished by the family because it facilitates the discussion of different points of view associated to sexuality without the imposition of certain values on others.

The work of *sexual orientation* seeks to propagate to youths the possibility of exercising their sexuality in a responsible and pleasant way. The three fundamental axes for guiding the teachers are: the human body, relationships of gender, and the prevention of sexually transmissible diseases and AIDS (STD/AIDS). The vision of the body as the matrix of sexuality aims to impart to students the knowledge to respect and heed their own bodies. The discussion on gender foments a questioning of roles rigidly established for men and women in society, the valorization of each, and the flexibility of those roles. As for prevention, since the 1980s, the demand for discussion about sexuality in the schools increased due to the educators' concern with the growth of unwanted pregnancy among adolescents and the risk of contamination by HIV among youths. The transversal theme of sexual orientation works so as to offer scientific and up-to-date information on the various forms of prevention. It should also combat discrimination that HIV carriers suffer.

The contents were organized into three blocks: human body, relationships of gender, and prevention of STD/AIDS. At the end of their school life, the students should have acquired the following capacities:

- respect for the diversity of values, beliefs, and existing sexual behaviors once human dignity is guaranteed;
- understanding the search for pleasure as a healthy dimension of human sexuality;
- knowledge of their bodies value and take care of their health as a necessary condition for having sexual pleasure;
- recognition, as social and cultural determinants, of the characteristics attributed to the male and female;
- identification and expression of their feelings and desires while respecting the feelings and desires of others;
- protection of themselves from coercive sexual relationships or exploiters;
- recognition of mutual consent as a necessary condition for having pleasure in a relationship of two people;
- solidarity in relation to those who are HIV positive and to act in the sense of making proposals for the implementation of public policies to prevent and treat STD/AIDS
- knowledge and adoption of protected sex practices to avoid their own infection and that of others, taking precautions against STD/AIDS;
- development of a critical conscience and to take responsible decisions regarding their sexuality; and
- seeking orientation for the adoption of contraceptive methods.

Work and Consumption

The dilemmas and uncertainties of the world of work, practices and consuming habits, as well as consumerism concern everyone. Directly or indirectly, in an explicit or implicit way, the school works with values, conceptions, and attitudes in relation to work and consumption. This theme aims to question these values and practices, such as the acquisition, or not, of objects and of *brands* with high symbolic value.

The theme *work and consumption* proposes to analyze the relationship between production and consumption—considered as moments associated with social life because, through them, citizenship dilemmas are expressed every day. These relationships are obscured by the belief that we are all equally free to work and choose the type of work we want, as well as to consume. Under this conception, access to work, consumer goods, and services and their differentiated distribution among social classes is diluted. This theme is presented in an integrated way so that students know more about forms and organization of work and consumption, and understand the relationships, dependencies, interactions, their problems, the rights of citizens, contradictions, and values.

Local Themes

Under the denomination of *local themes,* the PCN intends to contemplate the themes of specific interest of a certain reality to be defined in the context of the state, city, and/or school. Once the social urgency of a local problem is recognized, it can receive the same treatment given to the other transversal themes. As an example, let us examine the problem of traffic. Although that is a matter that reaches a significant portion of the population, it gains significance mainly in great urban centers—the right to good transportation, associated with life and environmental standards, or disrespect toward the rules of road safety for drivers and pedestrians (road accidents in Brazil cause an extremely large number of deaths). Seen this way, the theme of *traffic* causes people to reflect on the characteristics of life manners and social relationships.

THE PEDAGOGICAL PROJECT

To strengthen the school as a unit of the educational system, to provide it with autonomy, it is essential to give it the responsibility of elaborating a pedagogical project. When doing this, the school discusses and makes explicit collective values, defines priorities and desired results, and incorporates self-evaluation of its work.

It is known that each school has its own identity. That identity is constituted by a plot of circumstances that crosses different factors. Each school has its own culture permeated by values, expectations, habits, traditions, and conditions historically built starting from individual and collective contributions. Each school is inserted in a reality with economic and sociocultural characteristics. That is why reform has as its fundamental element the school's pedagogical project: Teachers, parents, administrators, and students are supposed to meet and discuss the identity of the school (Who are we?), the utopia of the pedagogic action (Where do we want to get to?), and the dimension of the pedagogic practice (How do we get there?). Therefore, the construction of the pedagogic project is the result of collective work and, at the same time, organizes and articulates collective work. It should:

- be an effort of collective construction involving all members of the school's community;
- articulate theory and practice;
- favor the accomplishment of individual projects within the collective project;
- build a culture of dialogue among teaching staff, administrators, and parents; and
- be flexible enough to favor its own renewal.

The school staff should meet systematically to reflect about the accumulated experiences and renew their practices (action–reflection–action). A pedagogical project with this objective can be directed by three main guidelines:

1.   Take up a position in relation to social issues and interpret the educational task as an intervention in the present moment. This guideline necessarily implies much more than just the assimilation or reception of information, especially because the amount of information available today to the common citizen is such that its use becomes impossible if he or she does not manage to integrate it in significant nets that he or she should learn how to organize;

2.   Do not treat values as ideal concepts, which implies that the educator should direct his or her methodological options in such a way as to incorporate the value in the subject as an objective in daily activities. Thus, when we talk about respect toward one another, we must respect our students and colleagues and not just preach about respect and go on with our authoritarian and contemptuous classroom practices.

3.   Include that perspective in the teaching of the contents of the areas of school knowledge.

For Doll (1997), intentional cooperative behavior leads us to more elevated levels of organization. The community, with its sense of cooperation and critical judgment, can be essential for significant learning; individualism must be reevaluated. The postmodern paradigm is asking us to make this evaluation in many different fields such as architecture, biology, chemistry, mathematics, and theology.

A VISION OF CITIZENSHIP AND DEMOCRACY

For Staessens and Vandenberghe (1994), vision is the result of daily activities and experiences that shape the way teachers perceive their tasks and their school. It is a shared reality with a comprehensive and dynamic nature that implies reflection and understanding of an organization's future. "It does not mean the sum of individual goals but the degree of consensus among organizational members about the value of daily activities and decisions in relation to some goals and the future development of an organization" (p. 188). It can be defined as a goal consensus resulting from interactions among staff members reflected through daily activities, which, in turn, are shaped by an existing vision. In Manasse (1986), vision is the development, transmission, and implementation of an image of a desirable future. It gives life to an organization because it consists of the force that molds meaning for the people of an organization. Peterson (1986) defined *vision* as the beliefs concerning what the ideal state of the organization is or what should be achieved. For O'Sullivan (2000), cosmology, the well-being of the earth and the well-being of the human within the earth community, must be the central concern of education for the future: "The fundamental educational task of our times is to make the choice of a sustainable planetary habitat of interdependent life forms over and against the pathos of the global competitive marketplace" (p. 2).

In this crisis of social orientation, Küng (1999) preached a receptive dialogue with political and economic science in the shape of a realistic vision or an integrated vision that tries to fix boundaries of a more peaceful, more just, and more humane world. The central place should not be occupied by a regulating principle such as the state, market, or church, nor should we be under a narrow economist or partisan ideology because this would only multiply our problems. What we must have is a viable sketch of the future that takes into consideration historical experience, which comes from the present social reality and, at the same time, overcomes this reality and envisages a better world order. This would be an integrated vision that is argumentatively developed and ethically oriented, which distinguishes itself by:

- a diachronic and synchronic thought in great historical contexts,
- a critique without prejudice of the real existing conditions,
- constructive and rationally realizable alternatives, and
- concrete impulses that can be discussed so as to be put into practice.

Such vision can stimulate the experts and be responsible for different areas to develop and elaborate long-term strategies.

An educational vision for our public schools is the construction of citizenship and democracy for those placed at the bottom of the social pyramid; our goal is equality of educational opportunities for all. Although in a democratic society political equality can be ensured by institutions, effective equality demands full and indiscriminate access by citizens to the totality of public goods. Among these goods, in a special position, stands access to the knowledge that is socially important.

THE THEORY OF COMMUNICATIVE ACTION AND VISION BUILDING

Developing such a vision for education in a large, diverse, and unfair country such as Brazil is an enormous task. In the same way that economics lacks a guiding theory that should subsidize us in the regulation of world capitalism (Habermas, 1995; Moraes, 1995), our education needs a theory that would serve as a base, a foundation. Assuming that a vision is developed collectively through action–reflection–action—one that is socially constructed; the result of communication among the members of an organization and created through common experiences, shared comprehension, shared decision making, shared evaluation—a theory of communicative action seems to be an excellent theoretical framework in our vision building.

This movement toward a dialogical form of reason is based on the verification that, in our current societies, there is a plurality of opinions, of visions of good and evil, sometimes extremely conflicting, that limit the horizons of communication. Public systems, in general, are being menaced by the market economy and corruption. According to Habermas (1980), disturbances in systemic integration only threaten the continuous existence of the system when the consensual foundations of the normative structures become too damaged. The crisis then assumes the form of disintegration of the social institutions. To rehabilitate the public sphere, we need a democratic disposition of dialoguing and a reaching of consensus. Habermas defined *public sphere* as a realm of social life in which something approaching public opinion can be formed. He took the historical-philosophical project of modernity and attributed to public opinion the task of legitimating the political domain by means of a critical process of communication, sustained by the principles of a rationally motivated consensus. The question that we are all asking right now is whether contemporary democracies allow the possibility of structuring a public argumentative praxis that links the validity of the action norms to a rational justification originated from citizens' free discussion.

Communicative action, mediated by language and derived from communicative rationality, is action that seeks understanding, a consensus among the several social actors. It is opposed to strategic action, which results from cognitive-instrumental rationality and seeks domination. Rationality, for Habermas, is the way by which speakers and actors acquire and use knowledge. Reaching understanding is a process of arriving at an agreement among subjects on a rational basis; it cannot be imposed by any of the parts, be it instrumentally intervening directly in the situation or strategically influencing the opponents' decisions. The ideal speech situation (Habermas, 1984) is attained when all speakers have an equal chance to select and employ speech acts and when they can assume interchangeable dialogue roles. The speech acts are based on an underlying consensus formed in the reciprocal recognition of at least three validity claims:

1. that the statement made is true (or that the existential presuppositions of the propositional content mentioned are in fact satisfied);
2. that the speech act is right with respect to the existing normative context (or that the normative context that it is supposed to satisfy is itself legitimate); and
3. that the manifest intention of the speaker is meant as it is expressed. (Habermas, 1984, p. 99)

Social consensus derives from communicative action (i.e., an orientation that responds to the cognitive interest for a reciprocal understanding and to the practical interest for the maintenance of an intersubjectivity that is permanently under threat). The objective of a critical theory of democracy, normatively based, consists of explaining how complex societies admit the existence of a public opinion based on the guarantee of general conditions of communication that ensure a discursive formation of the will.

It is not enough, said Habermas (1995), to reiterate the importance of human rights and the need to ensure peace and democracy. We must improve political institutions so they are able to confront this technical universalization and impose the application of a normative universalism. The expansion of markets and administrative structures leads to the colonization of the life world—a cultural stock of knowledge from which the participants in interaction draw their interpretations. This intersubjectively shared life world forms the background for communicative action.

CONCLUSION

In a democracy, the exercise of citizenship presupposes political participation of everybody in the definition of directions assumed by the nation. The forms of political participation are expressed not only in the choice of political and ruling representatives, but also in the participation in social movements and even in one's involvement with themes and issues of the life of the nation. The reform put forward by Brazil is an enormous, ambitious project. It requires the effort of the whole nation. Although there has been disagreement around certain details of the reform, there is consensus about the need of a crusade in favor of basic education.

Sometimes in a school in the middle of a huge sugar plantation or cattle farm, the teachers, whose students are the children of *bóia-frias*[3] living in houses with no electricity or even piped water, ask me: What sort of citizenship should I talk about with my students? How can I tell them of their rights to participate in the destinies of the country if their struggle for survival takes over all their strength? I usually reply: It is like the work of the ants, slow but steady.

The school's sphere of action is limited, but our hope is that it will shake up the whole system little by little. Perhaps soon we shall see the good results of this silent revolution. As Habermas said, "against the horizon of an emerging global public sphere, such trends could signal the beginning of a new universalist world-order. [...] this is naturally no more than a hope—indeed a hope born of desperation" (cited in Outhwaite, 1996, p. 218).

---

[3]*Bóia-fria* means "cold lunch." The workers take their lunch to the fields and eat it cold at noon.

ACKNOWLEDGMENT

My thanks to Chloe Furnival for her help in revising the English.

REFERENCES

Apple, M. (1979). *Ideologia e currículo.* São Paulo, Brazil: Brasiliense.

Brasil, Ministério da Educação. (MEC). Parâmetros curriculares nacionais.

Cornbleth, C. (1995). Controlling curriculum knowledge: Multicultural politics and policymaking. *Journal of Curriculum Studies, 27*(2), 165–183.

Doll, W. (1997). *Currículo: Uma perspectiva pós- moderna.* Porto Alegre, Brazil: Artes Médicas.

Dussel, E. (n.d.). *Filosofia da Libertação* (Filosofia na América Latina). São Paulo, Brazil: Loyola.

Featherstone, M. (Coord). (1994). *Cultora global: Nacionalismo, globalização e modernidade.* Petrópolis: Ed. Vozes..

Featherstone, M. (2000). Da universidade à pós-universidade? Explorando as possibilidades de novas formas de comunicação. In S. E. M. Moraes & J. C. Santos Filho (Orgs.), *Escola e universidade na pós-modernidade.* Campinas, Brazil: Fapesp/Mercado de Letras.

Garaudy, R. (1975). *Palavra de homem.* São Paulo, Brazil: Difel.

Garaudy, R. (1983). *O ocidente é um acidente* (Por um diálogo das civilizações). Rio de Janeiro, Brazil: Forense-Universitária.

Habermas, J. (1980). *A crise de legitimação no capitalismo tardio. Tradução de vamireh chacon.* Rio de Janeiro, Brazil: Edições Tempo Brasileiro.

Habermas, J. (1984). *The theory of communicative—reason and the rationalization of society action* (Vol. 1) [T. McCarthy, Trans.]. Boston: Beacon.

Habermas, J. (1989). *The theory of communicative—lifeworld and system: A critique of functionalist reason* (Vol. 2) [T. McCarthy, Trans.]. Boston: Beacon.

Habermas, J. (1995). Interview given to Barbara Freitag and Sérgio Paulo Rouanet. *Jornal Folha de São Paulo,* Caderno MAIS!

Harvey, D. (1994). *Condição pós-moderna, trad. Adail Ubirajara Sobral e Maria Stela Gonçalves.* São Paulo, Brazil: Edições Loyola.

Kleiman, A., & Moraes, S. E. (1999). *Leitura e Interdisciplinaridade—tecendo redes nos projetos da escola.* Campinas, Brazil: Mercado de Letras.

Küng, H. (1999). *Uma ética global para a política e a economia mundiais.* Petrópolis, Brazil: Vozes.

Levinas, E. (1988). *Totalité et infini: Essai sur l'exteriorité.* Dordrecht, The Netherlands: Kluwer Academic.

Manasse, A. L. (1986). Vision and leadership: Paying attention to intention. *Peabody Journal of Education, 63*(1), 150–173.

Mills, C. W. (1981). *A elite do poder.* Rio de Janeiro, Brazil: Zahar Editores.

Moraes, S. E. M. (1995). *O currículo do diálogo* (Ph.D. thesis). Universidade Estadual de Campinas, SP (UNICAMP).

Moraes, S. E. M. (2000). Currículo, transversalidade e pós-modernidade. In S. E. M. Moraes & J. C. Santos Filho (Orgs.), *Escola e universidade na pós-modernidade.* Campinas, Brazil: Fapesp/Mercado de Letras.

O'Sullivan, E. (1999). Transformative learning: Educational vision for the 21st century. Toronto, Canada: University of Toronto Press.

O'Sullivan, E. (2000, April 27–30). *The project and vision of transformative learning: A vision statement.* Paper presented at the Internationalization of Curriculum Studies Conference, Louisiana State University, Baton Rouge.

Outhwaite, W. (1996). *The Habermas reader.* Cambridge, MA: Polity Press.

Peterson, K. (1986) Vision and problem finding in principals' work: Values and cognition in administration. *Peabody Journal of Education, 63*(1), 87–106.

Romanelli, O. (1978). *História da educação no Brasil* (9th ed.). Petrópolis, Brazil: Vozes.

Staessens, K., & Vandenberghe, R. (1994). Vision as a core component in school culture. *Journal of Curriculum Studies, 26*(2), 187–200.

CHAPTER 12

"As Canadian as Possible Under the Circumstances": A View of Contemporary Curriculum Discourses in Canada

Cynthia M. Chambers
University of Lethbridge

This chapter is offered with a profound sense of obligation first to those to whom I am writing—students and researchers, both Canadian and international, requiring an introduction to curriculum in Canada—and second to those about whom I am writing. My obligation has been to limit the injustice I do (to the extent that is possible) to their work, ideas, texts—by way of omission, limited understanding, and the infinite fragility of language in the creative work of interpretation and translation. Therefore, to the reader, I suggest that you use this chapter as a map to follow, rather than a novel (which might give you full access to a complete and possibly fictional world), a guide as you seek out the real texts reviewed here, and in journeying through them, perhaps locate those authors who were omitted here. Having just been, it is a trip I highly recommend. To those scholars overlooked, I plead the (concrete) limitations of word length and time, and within those parameters a conscious choice to focus on those areas of curriculum to which Canada has made (in my estimation) the most significant contribution to curriculum studies internationally.

Also I plead regionalism, which is as important a part of the Canadian imaginary as is nationalism and internationalism (Cameron, 1997). I am a uni-lingual Anglophone northerner who lives in the South (but only the far western and southern edge of the South)—and this means my relations with scholars residing in Central Canada and the Maritimes are limited, and with Francophone scholars, nonexistent. A vast territory with many regions, innumerable groups (with different traditions), and relentless (and competing) stories in a seemingly infinite number of languages—these are the challenges that face curriculum and curriculum scholarship in Canada today.

To those authors reviewed, I say "thank you" for the opportunity to engage critically (but I hope not crabbily) and creatively with your texts, and forgive any impoverished (or mis-) interpretations. In this writing, I have been at times "lost in translation" (Hoffman,

1989), awestruck by the Canadian voice(s) in international curriculum scholarship. If this introduction sounds apologetic, it is; knowing how to say you are sorry is an important aspect of being Canadian (Ferguson & Ferguson, 2001); if it is self-deprecating, then it is "as Canadian as might be expected under the circumstances" (Cameron, 1997, p. 8).

MAPPING CANADA

While the second largest country in the world, Canada has only 31 million people (one tenth the population of the United States), 40% of whom live in six major cities, the remaining 60% spread out along a narrow strip just north of the 49th parallel (Government of Canada, 2001) or scattered around the various geographical margins. Prior to colonization, there were over 600 indigenous language groups (often called First Nations in Canada). Although the number of indigenous peoples and languages wiped out through epidemics and war (what some indigenous scholars like Chrisjohn [1997] call *genocide*) are unimaginable, today there are approximately 1 million aboriginal people in Canada (Government of Canada, 1998). With the highest birthrates in Canada, soon provinces like Manitoba and Saskatchewan will be predominantly aboriginal, whereas Nunavut, Canada's newest territory, already is. However, from the time of first European contact until recently, immigration has been the main source of population growth in Canada.

During the colonial era, immigrants first came from France, later from the primarily English-speaking countries of Scotland, Ireland, and England, creating a linguistic and political complexity that lives on today. Asian immigration shifted the racial and linguistic homogeneity of the West Coast created by early British colonization (and inhabitation of the periphery by indigenous peoples) in a way similar to that of how African-American refugees changed the face of Eastern and Atlantic Canada. Prior to World War I—and after the indigenous peoples of the prairies were forced to sign treaties and move to reserves opening up their land for "settlement" (McLeod, 1998)— Eastern and Germanic Europeans as well as the British carved homesteads and ranches on the prairies. In the 1960s and 1970s, people immigrated to Canada from all over the world: Those coming from the former French colonies, such as Haiti, settled in Québec, those from former English colonies elsewhere in the country. War and the rise and fall of communism in Eastern and Central Europe and Southeast Asia brought new waves of immigrants, many of whom spoke neither French nor English and certainly none of the indigenous languages.

Although Canada has been officially bilingual (i.e., French and English) since the mid-1960s (Cameron, 1997), this has not translated into practical bilingualism except in specific geographic regions or for those educated in specific circumstances, such as French language immersion programs in Anglophone Canada or where the infamous Bill 101 prevents (most) Québec families from educating their children in English. Today, the ethnic, racial, linguistic, and cultural complexity of Canada and its classrooms goes well beyond the "two solitudes" (MacLennan, 1945) of French and English Canada. For example, of the three remaining viable indigenous languages in Canada (out of the approximate original 600), Cree has only 77,000 speakers, whereas 10 times as many Canadians speak Mandarin or Cantonese (Government of Canada, 1996).

Canada is the place where—almost 40 years ago—communication theorist Marshall McLuhan (1964; McLuhan & Fiore, 1967; McLuhan & Powers, 1989) foretold the electronic interdependence that would make the world a global village. In the 21st century, particularly following the events of September 11, 2001, McLuhan's prophecy seems fully manifested. In many ways, Canada is the global village. Over 5 million residents were not born in Canada. Over 40% of the people who live in Toronto (Canada's largest city, with over 4 million residents) do not speak either official language as their mother tongue (Government of Canada, 1996), and 40% of children who enter Grade 1 in Vancouver (a population of 2 million) do not speak English as their first language. Spread over 3 million square miles of land, Canadians are different in ways unimaginable not long ago. Perhaps because of the extent of these differences spread over such vast distance, Canada is the most wired country in the world, embracing wired and wireless technology in all its most recent manifestations.

In the face of pluralism of this magnitude, Canada is still a federal parliamentary democracy in which responsibility for education, including curriculum, remains with the 10 provinces and three territories. Thus, education is not a federal matter (except in specific areas like education in the military or of indigenous peoples), is never an issue in federal elections, and is rarely a topic of public debate outside particular provinces, except in moments of crisis, such as a teachers' strike or when Canadian students rank poorly on international standardized tests. As such, unlike in the United States, there have been no national campaigns for educational reforms. Each province and territory must find ways to educate its students—as different as they are from north to south, city to town, east side to west—probably the most ethnically, racially, linguistically, and religiously diverse of any school population in the world. Governments mandate curriculum developers to create documents that guide life in such classrooms, but life on whose behalf ask curriculum scholars (Aoki, 1999). It is teachers and students who experience these rich organic differences—who live with "the whole world in one classroom" (Hasebe-Ludt, 1999, 2003).

Canadian curriculum theorists, working at universities, located in specific provinces (with their own curriculum) are challenged to interpret what is curriculum at this time and in this place? What is it significance? What would be the fitting response of curriculum in this time and place?

CANADIAN CURRICULUM AS POLITICAL TEXT

Curriculum is inherently political regardless of national context. Curriculum in Canada, as institutional texts and practices, reinforces normative definitions of gender and (hetero)sexuality (de Castell & Bryson, 1997; Forman, O'Brien, Haddad, Hallman, & Masters, 1990; Lewis, 1990; Sumara & Davis, 1999) as well as racial categories, stereotypes, and distinctions (Battiste & Barnum, 1995; Battiste, 2000b; Henry, 1992); and perpetuates racial/class distinctions in the society at large (Bannerji, 1993, 1995; Porter, 1965). Thus, Canadian curriculum has a great deal in common with curriculum internationally.

Many Canadian curriculum theorists, like their counterparts in other countries, have focused their intellectual efforts on strident critiques of the hidden curriculum and its role in perpetuating various forms of social injustice, both universal and those particular to Canadian society. The extent of those injustices—such as child poverty, homelessness, gutting of the social safety net, questionable immigration policies and practices—are ironic given that *peacemaker* and *multicultural* are Canada's international trademarks (McFarlane, 1995; Smith, 1991, 1998).

One site of Canadian curriculum that is particularly contentious and under-represented in (mainstream or contemporary) scholarship is Indigenous education. The primary goal of the Jesuits was evangelizing the Native people, and through the *Ratio Studiorum* their souls and bodies were to be converted from tribal religions, holistic medicine, and council fire to a (European) God and rituals and sacraments of His Holy Roman Church. For the next 200 years, Christian morals formed the basis of either the Catholic schools in Québec or the public systems (with Protestant curriculum) in Ontario, the crucifix dominating the walls of one, the portrait of King or Queen the other (Tomkins, 1979). Until the 1960s and 1970s, European-based churches, on behalf of the federal government, provided education to indigenous people in Canada, continuing the mix of catechism, vocational education, and basic literacy. Although attempts to subdue and evangelize Indigenous people were largely unsuccessful, Fanon (1963) cautioned the West about underestimating the psychological damage of colonization (of which church and education were key instruments).

Fifty years after Algerians fought for their independence from France, Canada faces the intergenerational effects of the "plan of studies" in all its derivations, particularly for aboriginal people (see Chrisjohn & Young, 1997; Haig-Brown, 1988). As survivors of the *Indian* residential schools sue the federal government and the churches, and institutions such as the Anglican Church of Canada face bankruptcy in the wake of court rulings favoring the litigants, there appears to be psychological damage enough for all.

"Telling tales of difficulty and danger," particularly those written by women scholars, while still marginal have gained some prominence in Canadian curriculum scholarship in the past decade. Suzanne de Castell was guest editor of a special issue of the *Canadian Journal of Education* (1993), "Against the Grain: Narratives of Resistance." She entitled her introduction "6 December 1989/1993, Je me souviens" in memory of the women murdered at Université de Montréal. This incident, and narratives of resistance told in this issue of the journal, highlight that, despite the predominance of "narratives of redemption" in educational theory and discourse, teaching against the grain in Canadian universities—and writing about it—is perilous work, especially for educators who "do not, as a matter of identity politics, may not, speak from positions of dominance" (p. 187).

Dealing with difficult topics, especially ones in which the (teacher and student) self is implicated, is difficult and dangerous work. In the essays, each educator speaks of matters difficult not only for the writer, but for education: Roxanna Ng narrates being charged with using her teaching as a platform for feminism; Linda Eyre describes what happens when she challenges the compulsive heterosexuality of health curriculum with prospective teachers in the Maritimes; and Mary Bryson and Suzanne de Castell (1993) speak out about the impossibility of naming oneself "queer" in school systems or universities, and the even greater difficulty of "queerying pedagogy" (p. 299), concluding from a graduate course they taught, "Lesbian Subjects Matter: Feminism/s from the Margin," that the distance from "queer theory to queer pedagogy" is great (p. 298). Bryson and de Castell reject the notion of a "dialogue across difference" as a solution to the difficulties they describe. Rather, their prescription lies in the power of narratives of resistance—that for those who still believe in queer pedagogy to come out and "tell it like it is, or, at least, how it might be ..." (p. 301).

Some curriculum scholarship has focused on the possibilities of pedagogy for transforming social relations. Over a decade ago, Lewis (1990) offered a feminist critique of patriarchy as well as a specific framework—pedagogical and strategic—of feminist teaching, the kind necessary to subvert the gendered text of teacher preparation and meet student resistance to the realities of violence against women in Canada. This article was published shortly after the massacre of December 6, 1989.

Recognizing these differences has implications for how we proceed in research as well as pedagogy. Te Hennepe (1997) describes what "respectful research" looks like in a university context for First Nations people and then when it is published. The topic of research always has something to say about how one shall proceed (Smith, 1999). For other Canadian scholars, the task is to decenter Western epistemology by articulating in (Western terms) an Indigenous metaphysics (O'Meara & West, 1996)—a kind of ethnometaphysics (McPherson & Rabb, 1993) that is articulated from the inside out.

Douglas Cardinal, one of Canada's most famous and innovate architects who also happens to have a sweat lodge, describes the phenomenology of the vision quest. Haig-Brown (1988, 1995), a long-time scholar and activist in aboriginal education, recently edited a volume (1997) that documents how such practices change the phenomenology of schooling for urban aboriginal students and hopefully transform political realities. Joe Duquette High School, in Saskatoon, Saskatchewan, the place of Haig-Brown's study, has been a site for others trying to figure the interconnections between Western and Indigenous epistemologies and how differences can be bridged especially in schools (Regnier, 1995).

The particular historical and geographical context(s) of Canada have given rise to unique political traditions and complex social realities. Each of the many groups who comprise that complexity is made up of people who live in the world not only as identities, but also as sentient beings. People experience the world in time, in and through their bodies. With language and through conversation and story, they struggle to give meaning to their lives and those experiences. Situated within phenomenological and hermeneutic discourses, Canada has a significant tradition of understanding curriculum as practical wisdom.

PRACTICAL WISDOM: INTERPRETING CANADIAN CURRICULUM THROUGH PHENOMENOLOGY AND HERMENEUTICS

Phenomenology was a major element in the "reconceptualization of curriculum studies" of the 1970s (Pinar, Reynolds, Slattery, & Taubman, 1995, p. 419). In the United States, Dwayne Huebner introduced phenomenology to curriculum studies (Pinar & Reynolds, 1992a) as a form of critique of the instrumental language of curriculum, dominated by the Tyler rationale, a move taken up by Maxine Greene and William Pinar. In Canada, most of the phenomenological research in curriculum has occurred at the University of Alberta. Originally under the leadership of Ted Aoki, Max van Manen, and Kenneth Jacknicke and later Terrence Carson, phenomenology became institutionalized in the Department of Secondary Education at the University of Alberta.

The Faculty of Education at the University of Alberta has the largest doctoral program in Canada, and thus the list of Ph.D. dissertations that were phenomenological in character is both lengthy and broad in scope (see Pinar et al., 1995, for a partial listing). Ted Aoki, David Smith (1983, 1988), and David Jardine (1987, 1988) engaged in significant phenomenal scholarship in the 1980s, but by the early 1990s, their scholarship had shifted directions, leaving Max van Manen as Canada's major phenomenologist.

van Manen's phenomenology focuses primarily on adult relations with the child rather than curriculum per se. Introduced to phenomenological pedagogy in his Netherlands homeland through the scholarship of Langeveld, van Manen kept phenomenology central to curriculum scholarship in Canada (van Manen, 1982, 1984, 1989) through mainstream journals such as *Curriculum Inquiry,* as well as a periodical *Phenomenology + Pedagogy,* which he founded and edited, but has since ceased to publish. Where conventional educational research, particularly in psychology, tends to label and categorize the child, van Manen saw phenomenology as a way to understand the child's experience and the adult's—parent and teacher—experience of the child, so that sensitivity and tact, rather than efficiency, remain the touchstones of pedagogy. He addressed teachers and parents directly in *The Tone of Teaching* (1986) through reflective anecdotes, and other curriculum scholars in *The Tact of Teaching: The Meaning of Pedagogical Thoughtfulness* (1991), where he identifies the characteristics of pedagogical thoughtfulness.

van Manen's (1990) other significant contribution to curriculum scholarship in Canada has been his efforts to articulate phenomenology as a method for conducting human science research that retains its sensitivity to pedagogy. As a member of the International Institute for Qualitative Methodology, he maintains *Phenomenology On-*

line (van Manen, 2002a), a Web site dedicated to mapping out the interrelated aspects of phenomenological inquiry, as well as identifying scholars, resources, and Web sites and maintaining a public forum on phenomenology. van Manen (2000) continues his interest the pedagogy of care, especially its moral character—never losing sight of the lived experience—as expressed in the anecdote, the key for phenomenological inquiry (van Manen, 2002b). Once articulated, these vignettes, and the researcher's interpretation of them, bring to life knowledge as it resides in action, in the body, in the world, and in relations (van Manen, 1999).

Stephen J. Smith, a graduate of the University of Alberta now teaching at Simon Fraser University, has adhered closely to phenomenological topics and writing. Also following Langeveld, where the world of the child is at least partially a secret one, Smith (1998) opens up how the child is vulnerable to harm while the risks encountered remain pedagogical. Rather than telling parents and teachers how this is so, Smith illuminates the value of risk taking through phenomenological writing that invites the reader to (re-)experience childhood and that draws attention to adult/parental responsibility to prepare children for the precarious world beyond the playground.

Aoki (1990) first made the distinction between the curriculum as lived and the curriculum as planned. Perhaps not the first, but in a succinct and heartfelt way that (teacher) audiences heard and responded to, Aoki invited educators to attend to the actual experiences they had with students in classrooms interpreting the curriculum (typically planned by others). Aoki saw this curriculum actualization as more significant than dominant notions of implementation. This move to the lived curriculum was at once phenomenological, in the attention paid to lived experiences, but it was also hermeneutic in that it sought the practical wisdom both gained, and already at work, in the situation.

Margaret Hunsberger at the University of Calgary (1985, 1988, 1989, 1992) took phenomenological inquiry directly to classrooms and became one of Canada's most prominent phenomenologists. She asks, what is the experience of reading? What is it like to be a reader? Her interest is the interpretive study of reading—oral reading, rereading—as a lived experience that is both embodied and individual, as well as, inherently social. Her research showed how understanding of text is achieved through a relationship between reader and text, and when rereading, between the reader and his or herself, as well as other readers.

Situated in a similar phenomenological hermeneutic tradition, Sumara (1994) seeks "the middle way" in curriculum—one that accounts for the lived experiences of teachers without losing sight of theory that might make such experiences intelligible and, in the tradition of action research, open to critique and change through genuine collaboration (Carson & Sumara, 1997; Sumara & Luce-Kapler, 1993). Borrowing from Buddhism, Sumara formulates the curriculum teachers actually enact, the one that co-emerges as a "path laid down by walking," one that is "particular and contingent rather than predictable and controlled" (p. 129).

Sumara (1996) has taken seriously the co-emergence not only of curriculum, but of understanding of text, teaching, self, and other made possible through public and collaborative renderings of experiences with literary texts. In his study of English teachers meeting to explore individual and collective responses to literary texts, Sumara (1996) articulates a new reader-response theory that makes visible a complex network of shared literary relations—a kind of "literary anthropology" (Wolfgang Iser, 1993; cited in Sumara, 1996) where what the reader has to say about the "literary text is far less interesting than what the literary text announces about the reader" (Pinar et al., 1995, p. 438). In collaboration with Brent Davis and Rebecca Luce-Kapler, Sumara continues his interest in curriculum—teaching and learning and text—as forms of knowledge that are a part of, and emerge out of, a complex system of interdependencies, larger ecologies of relationships (Davis, Sumara, & Luce-Kapler, 2000).

Phenomenology is not only a method or new empirical language for research. Rather, in the 1970s, it enabled a strident critique of the dominant discourses in curriculum: the traditions of consciousness where the mind becomes the location of all thought and meaning, and the critical discourses of (neo)Marxism, which were to emancipate both curriculum and society (Smith, 1991), ready or not, wanted or not. "The phenomenological interest is in how to stand with things in a way that the things can be seen for what they really are without the overlay of political agenda, dense theorizing or moralistic intent" (Smith, 1999, p. 143).

Jardine (1987, 2000) found in phenomenology—particularly through its attention to the local and concrete practices, embedded in actual lives and places, and to the temporal, contingent, and occasioned—a critique of Piaget and Descartes and their discourses of consciousness that continue to dominate early childhood education, particularly the constructions of the child (Pinar et al., 1995; Smith, 2000a). In the next decade, Jardine continued to unravel the dangers, for both ecology and pedagogy, of abstracting (and coercing) the "stubborn particulars" of person and place into explicit, rational schemata.

What might be the substantial interest that phenomenology holds for curriculum in Canada? Perhaps phenomenology's focus on lived experience—the particulars of life lived in a specific place in relation to others—enabled scholars to at once be critical of the abstract discourses dominating curriculum and the violence they do the earth and children, and to see, hear, and feel the "stubborn particulars of grace" (to quote Jardine quoting the now-deceased Canadian poet Bronwen Wallace) of everyday life wherever it is lived. Perhaps too it was phenomenology's interest in the ordinary because, as Charles Taylor observed, "More than most people, Canadians are prejudiced in favor of the ordinary; it is a function of our history, our climate and our geography" (Taylor, 1977/1997, p. 289).

Phenomenology also poeticizes the world and its ordinary particulars—reading a book, falling on the playground, finding a lump in the breast—and Canadians love poetry and their poets because poetry shows us what we cannot see and love, and yet always did, about each other and the world. Phenomenological inquiry endeavors to make understanding possible, whereas hermeneutic inquiry identifies both the barriers to that understanding and the conditions that make it possible.

Although phenomenology seeks the universal through the particular, hermeneutics requires continuous movement from part to whole and back again. Hermeneutics attends to the linguisticality of understanding—how it is given and understood through discourse (both words and action; speaking/writing and listening/reading)—as well as its historicity—how any understanding is made possible by attending to the historical context and how that context may have shaped language, events, institutions, practices, habits, and understanding. For hermeneutics, barriers to understanding can be found both in the discourse and historicity of the situation or event, and the personal history of the interlocutors as well as the collective history of the groups to which they belong. Thus, hermeneutics is particularly well suited to curriculum when the goal is understanding, and where the barriers to understanding are many (see Jardine, 1992; Smith, 1991, for excellent introductions to hermeneutics and curriculum from a Canadian perspective).

The power of the hermeneutic imagination is its "capacity to reach across national and cultural boundaries to enable dialogue between people and traditions superficially at odds," says Smith (1999), "to problematize the hegemony of dominant culture in order to engage it transformatively" (p. 35). This makes hermeneutics crucial for Canada—a country that is both colony (first politically of France and Great Britain, later economically of the United States) and colonizer (of Indigenous people, and later the French, within its own borders). Hermeneutics has made possible "cross-cultural mediation" in Canadian curriculum—for example, between dominant cultures and Indigenous peoples (Smith, 1998).

There are three additional ways in which hermeneutics has had a significant impact on curriculum studies in Canada. First of all, hermeneutics refuses foreclosure on the answer to any question; instead it requires scholars and practitioners to remain open to questions and possible answers, each answer being only a temporary resting place on the journey of deeper understanding. This is crucial in a country where many of the thorniest issues are not easily or pragmatically solvable (e.g., when Anglo Canada asks, "What does Québec want and can (should) that be guaranteed constitutionally?"). The "Québec question" is probably one without full resolution regardless of referenda on sovereignty or changes to the Constitution or education of the masses. Canadians—Francophone, Anglophone, or otherwise—must live with each other, in a state of tension, a result in part of the impossibility of foreclosure.

Second, hermeneutics invites those who encounter it to return to the original difficulty (Fowler, 1997, in press; Jardine, 1992) and to stay with that difficulty, working it for all of its pedagogical and transformative possibilities. This has been particularly powerful for practitioners turning to curriculum studies for solutions, where they begin to see that, although there may not be formulaic or expedient solutions to their problems, the solution may be in understanding the difficulty rather than trying to find a way to make it go away.

Third, the notion/word *hermeneutics* is derived from Hermes, the Greek god charged with translating the words of the gods and goddesses to the mortals, making intelligible that which was not. The necessity of translation is particularly crucial in Canada with all of its diversity/difference. Hermes was also a trickster; as such, he has a special place in Canada, where the trickster manifests itself in various forms depending on the people and region—for example, Raven (West Coast and Dene), Napi (Blackfoot, Blood, and Peigan), Wisahkecahk (Cree), Coyote (Central Kootenai), and Nanaboosh (Nanishnawbe or Ojibway). "The role of chaos also appears in mythology throughout the world in stories of the trickster, the sacred fool whose antics reminds us of the essential role of disorder in the creation of order" (Cajete, 2000, p. 17).

The trickster reminds humans of their fallibility and potential; something of which curriculum scholars and practitioners alike need constant reminding—we may not have it right (in fact, given our fallibility—our selfishness, greed and ego—we probably do not), but we may get closer to what is truth or right conduct as long as we do not take ourselves too seriously. The trickster always reminds us of the essential role of chaos in the universe and of the dangers of trying to secure order through personal achievement or satisfaction at the expense of the collective good. This, too, is an important lesson for curriculum, particularly in these times where capitalism requires individual achievement be the hallmark for success, and this business ethos has infused all aspects of Canadian life, including curriculum and schools.

Hermeneutics demands Canadian curriculum pay attention to the particularities of this place. However, hermeneutics does not offer Canadians a curricular isolationism. Rather, in hermeneutics, any understanding—of who we are as Canadians, of where Canada is as a place, or even who we are as individuals inhabiting this place at this time—is always arrived at in relation to others: other countries, peoples, places, traditions, and languages. In this way, hermeneutics is like the traditional teachings of Indigenous peoples (McLeod, 1998; Ross, 1996). Lived relationally, the difference that is Canada, rather than a problem to be solved, is what makes understanding, dialogue, and transformation possible in the first place (Hasebe-Ludt, in press).

In a similar vein, Carson (1984), in conversation with curricular workers, interpreted the deeper meanings of implementation for curriculum and beyond. This work produced an immensely helpful article (1986) about hermeneutic conversation as a mode of research. Carson (1990; Carson & Sumara, 1997; Carson & Sheridan-Carson, 1999) extended his understanding and practice of researching collaboratively and interpretively as he moved into action research, again turning the instrumentalist notions of action research upside down as he sought more interpretive and creative ways to act and research. Together with Sumara (1997), Carson was able to reconfigure action research as a *living practice.*

Aoki's (1999) journey through postmodern and postcolonial discourses (not a dissimilar intellectual odyssey to David Smith's) turned him against what he sees as the dangerous and romantic desire for the "tantalizingly holistic"—a fusion of self and other into an intersubjective "we"—embedded deeply within hermeneutics. However, Smith (1991) remains committed to the original hermeneutic impulse for understanding, through dialogue and cultural mediation, made difficult by difference but made possible by "the deep commonality of all people" (p. 190). Yet both agree with many curriculum scholars writing in Canada today (Chambers, 1999; Davis, 1994; Davis et al., 2000; Hasebe-Ludt, 1999; Pratt, 1994) that those working/writing/teaching (in) curriculum must continue to seek ways and opportunities to speak and listen to another, to find new ways of speaking with one another and in/with (the many) societies that comprise Canada. It may be that survival—whether local, national, or planetary—depends on our interpretations and whether we have these conversations (Smith, 1987).

The success of the conversations—beyond simply having them—may lie with the self-reflexivity of the conversationalists (Kelly, 1997) and with their willingness to tell the (difficult) stories that have to be told (de Castell & Bryson, 1997; Fowler, 1997), to call into question the stories they have always told (Aoki, 1999; Jardine, 1994), and to listen to what others are saying (Davis, 1994; Jardine, 2000; Smith, 1999, 2000a) and the "deep excavations of [our] own received [intellectual] traditions" (Smith, 2000a, p. xii). Autobiography and narrative inquiry offer creative ways to enter such conversations while carrying on the interpretive (i.e., the creative, linguistic and political) work necessary for the conversations to continue.

TAKING CURRICULUM PERSONALLY (AS WELL AS POLITICALLY)

As part of their reconceptualization of curriculum studies in the 1970s, Pinar and Grumet (1976) introduced the idea that curriculum is an autobiographical text. They proposed *currere,* meaning the running of the course, as an autobiographical theory. Pinar et al. (1995) described *currere* as a focus

> on the educational experience of the individual, as reported by the individual ... *currere* seeks to describe what the individual subject him or herself makes of these [experiences].... *Currere* ... communicates the individual's lived experience as it is socially located, politically positioned, and discursively formed, while working to succumb to none of these structurings. (pp. 414–417)

Believing the curriculum field had forgotten the existing individual, Pinar and Grumet (1976) outlined a method for *currere* that involved four steps: regression, progression, analysis, and synthesis while continuing to articulate autobiography as a theory for curriculum.

In Canada, Graham (1989, 1991)—a published poet and former teacher of high school English, now chair of the Department of Curriculum and Instruction at the University of Victoria—extended this work of mapping out the theoretical underpinnings of autobiography. Graham paid particular attention to the contribution of Dewey to any understanding of the significance of experience for the self and how it is both lived and understood socially and educationally. At the same time, he noted the "poststructural turn need not entail a turn away from auto/biography but can instead lead us toward 'a view of auto/biography as an intertextual and intersubjective project'" (Graham, 1991, p. 147; cited in Kelly, 1997, p. 49). Most Canadians working in autobiographical theory and practice are located somewhere along the continuum that Graham articulated between modernist and postmodernist discourses.

Starting at the modernist end of the continuum, Connelly and Clandinin (1988, 1990; Clandinin & Connelly, 2000), undoubtedly Canada's best-known curriculum scholars of narrative inquiry, claim Dewey as their intellectual ancestor. "Since it is experience, not narrative, that is the driving impulse" (2000, p. 188), and key to education they continue to elaborate a method for narrative inquiry that focuses on the experience of the individual and follows where that experience leads. Their earlier work (1988) was more interested in making transparent and explicit the enacted curriculum of teachers in classrooms. Their method offered teachers a way to document narratives of their own experiences as research data on their own practice. Connelly and Clandinin (1990) argue for an "empirical narrative inquiry" that is based in such data as field notes, journal records, interviews, storytelling, letter writing, and autobiographical and biographical writing. Concerned with methodological issues, they explicate a process for negotiating entry, collecting data, and structuring narratives as well as criteria for writing good narratives. Clandinin and Connelly (2000) maintain a practical focus—recounting what narrative inquirers do—rather than attempting to define the field. In so doing, they discovered that relationship is "at the heart of thinking narratively ... key to what it is that narrative inquirers do" (p. 190).

In the 1980s and early 1990s, Richard Butt—from the University of Lethbridge—and his collaborators (1987; Butt & Raymond, 1992) made "voluminous and important" (Pinar et al., 1995, p. 554) contributions to understanding the autobiographical character of curriculum and educational research. As clear as Connelly and Clandinin distinguish their method from autobiography (see Pinar et al., 1995), Butt and Raymond (1987) are clear that teaching, thinking, and praxis can best be understood autobiographically. However, like Connelly and Clandinin, Butt focuses on the individual while locating collaboration between teacher and research as imperative to "autobiographical praxis" (see Pinar et al., 1995, pp. 554–557).

This method conveys how teachers' knowledge is held and formed, as well as how it can be studied and understood. In his method, Butt asks four questions: "What is the nature of my working reality? How do I think and act in that context and why? How through my work life and personal history, did I come to be that way? How do I wish to be in my professional future?" (Butt, Townsend, & Raymond, 1990, p. 257; cited in Pinar et al., 1995, p. 556). Once the data are generated in response to these questions, he invites understanding through collaborative and collective interpretation—a process that makes transformation through autobiographical praxis possible. Butt's method enables teachers to articulate their professional knowledge, but such understandings occur as part of the whole story of their lives, rather than as disembodied fragments.

Antoinette A. Oberg is located at the University of Victoria where she created and, for many years, coordinated a highly successful graduate program in Curriculum Studies. The heavily subscribed summer school attached to this program regularly attracts international curriculum scholars such as William Doll, William Pinar, Noel and Annette Gough, and Thomas Barone, as well as Canadian scholars such Max van Manen, David Jardine, David Smith, Ted Aoki, Jacques Daignault, and Magda Lewis. Similar to Butt's, Oberg's (1987) earlier work mapped out teacher knowledge as a basis for professional development, retaining a distinction between research and teaching.

Then Oberg began documenting the ways in which she used journals in her graduate teaching, and her interest in collaborating with her students on common topics of inquiry—often their pedagogic relationship—only increased (Chambers, Oberg, Moore, & Dodd, 1994; Oberg, 1990; Oberg & Artz, 1992; Oberg & McElroy, 1994; Oberg & Underwood, 1992b).

Oberg continues her inquiry into the pedagogic relationship; what has shifted is her interest in the effect of that relationship on the inquiry produced (primarily as writing) in the context of that relationship, both by her students and herself. Recently, her own writing has become more explicitly autobiographical (cf. Chambers, Oberg, Fowler, Hasebe-Ludt, Leggo, & Norman, 2000) as she articulates narratively what really matters to her: her relationship with her father, her location within the academy, and the relations of power at work in her subject position as a radicalized and, at one time, marginalized professor.

Feminist autobiography theory and practice intentionally blurs the line—real, imaginary, or symbolic—between the public and private realms and the public and private selves, making the writing, topics, and mode of writing difficult. By the early 1990s, several Canadian women scholars were writing autobiographically about difficult matters. In 1988, Anne-Louise Brookes submitted an "autobiographical/theoretical/fictional analysis" of her experience of her childhood sexual abuse for her doctoral dissertation, the text of which was published in 1992 as *Feminist Pedagogy: An Autobiographical Approach.* In the tradition of feminist autobiography, Brookes credits the safe place and supportive community of scholars for making possible her writing of such difficult matters in such a (at that time) nontraditional format (an intertext where narrative is woven with quotations, letters to her committee members, and a series of extended essays). Brookes explains that she fictionalized characters in the narratives because her work was not intended to hurt anyone; "Rather, I wrote to reclaim my life" (p. 4).

Leah Fowler (1997, in press) also writes autobiographically about difficulty, her own as well as those common to teachers. Employing Caputo's radical hermeneutics and Britzman's (1992) notion of the "difficulty in knowing thyself," Fowler explicates how narratives of the "original difficulty of teaching" constitute a curriculum and a way to transform stories into research. In her method, the writer/researcher recursively moves the text (and herself) through "seven gates to narrative knowing"—beginning with naive storytelling (where many teacher narratives end), to the psychological constructions and psychotherapeutic ethics at work in their stories (where many writer/researchers are arrested), through narrative craft and hermeneutic interpretation of the texts (which many writer/researchers do not learn), to a curriculum of pedagogy and a (re-)articulation of the teaching self through a poetics of aesthetics, beauty, truth, and justice. Fowler's work addresses concerns of those critical of the naiveté of, and lack of narrative craft in, much educational autobiography and narrative. Fowler provides evocative but clear direction for educators wanting to transform their stories of difficulty into narratives that teach.

Norman (2001) addresses two questions central to autobiographical theory and practice in education: How is autobiography research? How does women's writing contribute to this research? Utilizing the leitmotif of the mirror, Norman both explores and performs autobiography in the thematic contexts of writing, mothering, and teaching. The intertextuality—where poetry (her own), personal essays and stories, journal entries, and theoretical-poetic ruminations are strategically juxtaposed—and self-reflexivity of the text (text as mirror) announce it as both feminist and postmodern. Writing from the hyphenated space of Jew–mother–teacher–poet, Norman's is consummately Canadian autobiography. However, her readings of Hannah Arendt and Doris Lessing move her readers and herself beyond national or personal hyphenated spaces to ones we hold in common. Autobiography can help us, Norman claims, to answer Arendt's call to *amor mundis*—to love the world.

Like A. Oberg, Aoki's approach to narrative has been intensely pedagogical and highly influential. Through his teaching, he invited teachers to narrate the "call of teaching," their lived experience of classrooms and thus revealing their practical wisdom through story (Aoki & Shamsher, 1991, 1993). Yet Aoki (2000) recently posed the question: Are there limits to narrative and autobiography? Recognizing that "auto/biographical writing has become both a prevalent and privileged form of educational practice," Kelly (1997) takes up a similar question in the context of poststructural pedagogy. She claims that the allure of autobiography for such a project is paradoxical because, although the notion invokes romanticized images of the "authentic and rational self" (a cornerstone of modernist education theory and practice), authenticity and subjectivity are highly contested within poststructuralist theory. Less interested in autobiography theory or research, Kelly's fascination lies with the "underbelly of autobiography"—autobiography as pedagogy (where submission of autobiographical writing leaves students vulnerable to exoticization and abuses of power by the teacher) and pedagogue as autobiographer (where the teachers operate in drag, masking their dark side). She asks: What do students need to know? What is it I need to know about myself? How do I carry those desires into my relationships with students through my pedagogies?

Kelly works with autobiographical fragments that "refuse their assumed status as evidence and, instead, resume the status of provocateur, that which provokes (further) questions" (p. 60). A poststructural autobiography, then, is one that decenters subjectivity while illuminating the desires that constitute it. Unsettling notions of what constitutes "the personal, self, memory, history, and truth, do, however, create the grounds for a more critical and reflective autobiographical practice," one that does not "diminish the intimacy of auto/biography" but "enhances the sociality of the self" (p. 66). The narratives of resistance, the intertextual constructions of complex identities, and the analysis of stories of difficulty cited in this section illustrate the emancipatory possibilities of autobiography that Kelly calls for.

Autobiography and narrative may limit curriculum if they continue with the naive and incorrect assumption that lived experience is individual, rather than that which arises out of the "deep sediment and texture of our collective life" (Smith, 1991, p. 191). As Jardine (1994) says, "ownership of 'my story' is a peculiar notion if considered ecologically" (p. 9). He (1997b) admits to finding many "teacher stories frankly boring" while also admitting that his own hyperpublication record originates from relentless self-narrativizing. Either way, conversation is shut down. In fact, Hans-Georg Gadamer uses the phrase "the conversation that we are" to indicate the fragile, infinite ways that we make something of ourselves over the course of our lives and in conversation with the (shared and contested) world(s) we inhabit (Jardine, 1997b, p. 391).

We cannot understand ourselves if we do not understand our relations with everything. The Cree, Blackfoot, and Ojibway (as well as others) say, "All my relations." This invocation of the ancestors and all living beings—to close ceremonies or end ceremonial talk—is a profound declaration of the extent and necessity of one's relations and the inherent (inter)dependency of the Universe, including story, memory, place, and life (King, 1990; Ross, 1996). "All my relations" is a rather short speech that says a lot. Maybe that is what Jardine meant when he asked us to consider "whether there is the possibility that [I/we] might, for one blessed moment, shut up— ... [and] quell what Buddhists call the 'monkey mind'" (p. 393). Putting down the pen and walking out into the world can sometimes do that. Curricular theorists in Canada have a particular interest in place—with its own curriculum from which we have much to learn, if we can listen.

THE TOPOGRAPHY OF CURRICULUM

"The concept of 'place' has emerged as crucial to understanding curriculum autobiographically and biographically" (Pinar et al., 1995, p. 532). Like the literature, which (some) autobiography emulates, curricular life writing (Kadar, 1993) has characters situated in actual places experiencing human life through (recalled) events. Memory and history, both individual and collective, are located in particular places, giving rise not only to concrete experiences, but local, personal, regional, and national identities. Curricular scholarship ignores the place of Canada at our peril. Chambers (1999) challenges curricular scholars and workers in Canada to write from this place—to find and write in a curricular language of our own, to seek and create interpretive tools that are our own, and to use all of this to map a topography for Canadian curriculum theory, one that is begun at home but works on behalf of everyone.

Some Canadian curriculum writers are quite specific about the locations in which they are writing. Aoki (1983) writes about living and teaching in Lethbridge, Alberta, as does David Smith. For some, like David Jardine (2000), it is the relationship with the place that is topical, not autobiographically, but (eco)pedagogically. Ecopedogogy is about "reawakening the sense of intimate connection between ecological awareness and pedagogy" (p. 87). As he walks on the land, meets a bear, watches a bird, Jardine reads the world and rereads himself, schools, classrooms, literacy, mathematics, early childhood education, Western philosophy, and its critics. But the world is not just a text, a book to be read. The world is already there and does not depend on human interpretation for survival (Ross, 1996). Rather, relations with places are like relations among all living things—kindred, connected, familial, and interdependent.

The living ecopedagogical relationship echoing through Jardine's essays are reminiscent of a Dene (Indigenous) elder, Eddie Cook, who said, "The land was the best teacher I ever had" (Chambers, 1989). Jardine (1994) reminds us that we find ourselves *in the world* as part of the world's story; a story that is infinitely interpretable and relentless. But stories and world are not metaphors. All places have names and stories, and wisdom sits in (those) places, the Apache say (Basso, 1996). The truth of those places and their stories can shoot through you like an arrow (Basso, 1996). For Jardine and Eddie Cook, as we walk and live on the land, we are shot through with the immense responsibility for "our children's children," to protect the earth, the young, and the traditions that make it possible for life to go on (Chambers, 1989; Ross, 1996).

Jardine has always been preoccupied with the power of the particular, both as a pedagogy and a critique of violence done to children by the abstractions and universals of curriculum language, policy, and practice. Through his supervision of hundreds of student teachers in Calgary schools and a large ongoing research project, Jardine and his colleagues in the school district and the university are conducting interpretive investigations of specific classrooms and the projects, events, writing, and conversations that go on in these places. Again this work focuses on the particularities of the place, and what happens there, as a way of constituting the disciplines (of the curriculum) as

> open, generous, living field of relations ... [and how] the work of education is to draw children into the real, complex, interrelated, often ambiguous, often contested work of a discipline, and not to fragment it into static, established structures, but in the living conversations that constitute their being passed on in ways that are healthy, whole and sustainable. (LaGrange, Clifford, Jardine, & Friesen, 2001, p. 189)

It is this spiritual connection between place and pedagogy, between health and holism that John Miller, from the Ontario Institute for Studies in Education, explores.

Miller offers holism as a theory and practice for teaching and teachers (1993) and for curriculum (1996), as well as a critique of the discipline-based curriculum that results in a fragmentation of knowledge and pedagogy. In his latest book, Miller (2001) shifts from teachers and the curriculum to the soul: what does it need and want; how ought it be educated? He explains why a curriculum of the inner life is a necessity for teachers and how it would work practically with students. He proposes a curriculum that "nurtures the inner life of the student and connects it to the outer life and the environment" (p. 12), and he explicitly explores the interrelations between soul and Earth. Rather than new-age mysticism, Miller reminds his audience that for ancient societies, such as the Greeks and the Indigenous peoples, and in the teachings of Christ and the Buddha, restoring our original relationship to the universe is the true purpose and responsibility of education.

In other curriculum work, place is not a location from where one can critique, but a site always open to critique. Barnes and Duncan (1992) problematize the naive realism of writing—not in curriculum, but in geography, reminding readers that texts, discourses, and metaphors construct our notions of place and landscape at least in the Western (literate) world. "Earth (geo) writing (graphy)," then, is not simply "telling it like it is," but rather "telling it like we are" (p. 3). In other words, writing about worlds reveals as much about those writing as it does about the worlds represented. This is something that Hasebe-Ludt (in press) discovered as she and the students of her cosmopolitan eastside Vancouver classroom (re)wrote and (re)read across difference into community. Thus, in poststructural discourses, classrooms too are places and landscapes, worlds to be read and written.

Other curriculum writers (Hurren, 2000) use postmodern and postcolonial discourses to deconstruct commonsense notions of space and place, landscape and land—ones that are constructed through the disciplines like geography and school subjects like social studies. The autobiographical fragments, poetry, and physical montages of words and images that perform curriculum and remap geography as a discipline and a practice neither originate in nor arrive at any romantic notion of Earth or landscape or what we might learn from it. Instead, Hurren's curiosity lies in the "relationship between our words and our worlds"—and in this space, she believes, resides the poetic possibility of curriculum, one of "writing the world in active, creative ways" (p. 79). She shares much with David Jardine and his colleagues in this project.

Hasebe-Ludt and Hurren (2003) edited a collection of essays from 20 established and emerging curricular scholars for whom place is a prominent notion in their work and Canada is their geographical location. Following on their own doctoral work and the scholarship of Ted Aoki, the essays they have collected call into question fixed notions of place, language, and pedagogy. The places of pedagogy explored in these works are as varied as films, haiku, performances, school literature, mathematics curriculum, the academy, stories, songs, the prairies, and metonymic moments. The texts illustrate postmodern themes of hybridity, strangeness, and ambiguity through the textual practices of intertextuality, montage, and performance. The aesthetic texture of this volume signals a wider movement toward text and research as performance, curriculum as poetry: a move visible in the work of those seeking to decenter (Western) epistemology to make room for poststructural theory and artistic practice as modes of curriculum inquiry in Canada. It is to these curriculum scholars that we turn next.

ARTS-BASED CURRICULUM INQUIRY

In the past decade in particular, there has been a proliferation of conferences, or sections of conference programs, dedicated to arts-based curriculum inquiry. Canadians have been particularly noticeable at these, reading poetry or literary texts instead of essays, dancing instead of sitting, performing stories instead of giving lectures, all in an effort to illustrate curriculum artistically.

Willis and Schubert's (1991) edited collection, entitled *Reflections from the Heart of Educational Inquiry: Understanding Curriculum and Teaching Through the Arts,* documented initial forays into arts-based inquiry. A disproportionately large number of Canadian scholars contributed to this volume. van Manen explored how he came to be interested in pedagogy, interweaving his recollections with actual text from an old childhood storybook that he found on a return visit to the Netherlands. Through personal essay, Stinson, a dance teacher and poet from Edmonton now completing her PhD, with Smith explored the relationship between dance and curriculum. Butt (see autobiography section) documented episodes of his life from working-class lad in Britain to teacher in Canada, each constructed as a dramatic scene, the climax of which was the transformation of the writer, which is, Butt claims, the power of autobiography in curriculum. As well in this collection, Aoki designed a text (that is being read) attuned to the ear through musical rhetoric and poetry that was critical of the eye as a predominant metaphor in curriculum.

More recently, Canadians—particularly in such places as the Centre for Curriculum Studies at the University of British Columbia and the Department of Secondary Education at the University of Alberta—have published dissertations that are both curriculum-focused and unquestionably arts-based. Luce-Kapler (1997), teacher/poet/novelist, published a thoughtful and beautifully crafted dissertation that weaves poetry and philosophical discourse, inquiry, and interpretation. Two years later at the University of British Columbia, Dunlop (1999), also a published poet and teacher and currently a professor at York University, crafted her doctoral inquiry as novel, the first to be published as an educational doctoral dissertation in Canada. In the same year, Fels (1999), also at the University of British Columbia, explored relationships and possibilities among curriculum, performance, and inquiry in her dissertation. A year later, Norman (2000), also studying at the University of British Columbia, completed her dissertation, which won an award and was published by Peter Lang the following year. Internationally renowned feminist curriculum scholar Miller (2000) points to these three dissertations as the cutting edge of scholarship in autobiography. For Miller, that all three are Canadians was irrelevant (that they are women was). However, it is relevant to this overview. Canadian women—who also happen to be poets and novelists, performers, and teachers, many of whom whose identities are hyphenated—are creating this scholarship.

It is not only women. In addition to his two books of poetry, Leggo (1999), mentor of Dunlop and Norman, explores the cartography of curriculum through gender, language, autobiographical poetry, and essayist rumination. In his doctoral dissertation, Rasberry (2001), also one of Leggo's students, maps out the intimate relationship between writing and pedagogy, between poet and teacher, between becoming a poet and becoming a teacher, in a way that is indelibly an arts-based inquiry. With its playfulness, irony, genre/crossing, juxtaposition of image and text, performativity, and gaze on the arts, arts-based inquiry in Canada arises out of a postmodern sensibility with one eye on poststructuralist discourses, and another on arts and culture both within and beyond the curriculum, schools, and places (cf. Neilsen, Cole, & Knowles, 2001). We turn now to face postmodernism, more directly, in light of Canadian curriculum scholarship.

CANADA AS A MULTI(POST) SOCIETY

As elsewhere in the world, curriculum theory in Canada has been profoundly influenced by postmodernism. Although postmodern culture may be characterized as moving from image to print, past to present, unity to fragmentation, representation to a constant deferral of meaning, nationalism to global capitalism, nature to text (Pinar et al., 1995), postmodern theory is a rejection of the tenets of modernism, key to which is the assumption that "concepts, formulations and ideas refer eventually to something fixable, enclosable and nameable once and for all as reality" (Smith, 1999, p. 121). As Smith says, this assumption gives rise to the binaries—such as the theory/practice split—that plague modern pedagogy, as well as the objectification of others "into formalized manipulable categories," a move that perpetuates master narratives and severs the connection between self and other (p. 121).

To call the space and moment in which we live as well as the sensibility we bring to this time and place postmodern has gained currency in the general social lexicon, in the arts and popular culture, as well as in educational discourse. Poststructuralist theory has less currency and is typically subsumed under postmodernism (see Pinar et al., 1995). Poststructural theorists such as Foucault, Deleuze, Lacan, Derrida, and Serres argue that, although structuralism proposed that meaning is derived from structures and systems of difference that underlie language (rather than the experience/world the language represents), it ignored that those structures and systems are dependent on language (see Pinar et al., 1995; Smith, 1999 for overviews). Moreover, structuralism did not take into account the sociopolitical construction of these systems—that is, that discourse or knowledge constructs reality rather than represents it, shifting the question from "what does this mean?" to "who has the power to shape reality?" (Pinar et al., 1995, p. 463).

Jacques Daignault, professor of philosophy of education and curriculum at L'Université du Québec, has been a major contributor to postmodern curriculum discourse and poststructural critique of curriculum in North America at large (Pinar et al., 1995). His command of these discourses is demonstrated in both the content and form of his writing, where he is playful, courageous, and honest, documenting the movement of thinking. Whereas Anglophone curriculum theorists awaited English translations of the French poststructuralists, Daignault has never had to wait.

Daignault's (1992b) writing illustrates, in his own words, "traces at work from different places" that cross "the Atlantic from France to Québec" (p. 202). Daignault's (1985) project is a curriculum of aesthetics; a third way (Daignault & Gauthier, 1982) that refuses both theory (as descriptive or objective discourse) and practice (as normative discourse), instead choosing writing and teaching as poetic practices that maintain the paradox of pedagogical complexity (1992a). Continuing with the project of keeping curriculum (theory, writing, and teaching) as an open working site (Daignault & Gauthier, 1982), he becomes interested in creating an aesthetics that problematizes the subject "instead of excluding it or placing it in the centre, an aesthetics that does not exclude emotion without reducing everything to it either. The aesthetics proposed by Deleuze goes beyond sentimentality and signification toward sensuality and sense" (Daignault, 1992b, p. 209).

For Daignault, a continual problem in curriculum is the gap between what students are and what one thinks they should be. When a teacher/curriculum ignores this gap, it is nihilism; when any means is used to close it, it is terrorism; either way students are encouraged to be stupid (Daignault, 1985). Daignault's (1992b) work returns to this third way; a way of writing, a way of teaching that neither hunts nor kills (referring to Serres), but rather, following Nietzsche, translates "life into joyful wisdom, thinking maybe" (p. 202). Daignault work—his reading (of texts), his (re)writing, his speaking/teaching, his writing—is a form of translation.

Daignault (2001; Daignault & Fountain, 2000) continues to seek the passage to the third way, most recently, in information technology in educational contexts. Information technology has been a key element in colonization and more recently globalization. Hot commodity computer companies like Microsoft highjacked the distribution of computer software from the computer "geeks" and hackers who created it for their own pleasure and the public domain. Once software became a marketable commodity, its copyright had to be protected for shareholders and profitability. Thus, the source codes no longer open were locked, hidden in such a way that prevented users from re-programming, altering, or improving software. Thus, information technologies became inextricably connected to the "new corporate colonialism" (Smith, 1999), where multinational computer companies hold countries, schools, and curriculum hostage with software developed and controlled by them. Open Source, for which Daignault and Fountain (2000) are activists, is committed to free redistribution of software and the inclusion of source codes (or free and easy access to it) so that programmers can modify software. LINUX, an Open Source operating system, allows countries—for example, in Africa—access to computers and the Internet that is (a) affordable, and (b) modifiable to the needs of local situations. Again, Daignault seeks the passage to the third way: to destabilize technology as necessary evil (terrorism that closes the gap at any cost) or technology as immoral practice (nihilism—do not really care what the effects are on students), but to keep technology as an open working site, multiple in its definitions, practices, and ways.

Daignault's work is "as Canadian as possible under the circumstances." He writes (and reads) in both French and English. He has always sought the third way—the one that refuses foreclosure on problems because they are difficult. He writes with profound respect for students and teachers, with candor about education, and with irreverence and even apology for curriculum theory and the harm it can do to teachers (Daignault, 1992b).

Aoki, a Japanese-Canadian, has made the journey through almost all the contemporary curriculum discourses in Canada. This odyssey began in the "curricular landscapes of practicing teachers and their students" (Aoki, 1993, p. 255), a landscape that claims him as a long-time teacher and school administrator and infuses his writing, no matter how seemingly theoretical, with a practicality that always returns himself and the reader to the pedagogic situation. This is a site inhabited by teachers and their students_ and his own experiences of being a student and being and becoming teacher at a time when, and in a place where, his difference was a lived experience of racism rather than a theoretical construct (Aoki, 1983).

Leaving the school for the university gave Aoki new opportunities and languages to critique curriculum documents, and the political contexts that gave rise to them and constrained the teachers and students who had to live with them. He published his ground-breaking, *Toward Curriculum Inquiry in a New Key* (1979) during this period. Eventually, Aoki (cf. 1986) moved from ideology critique to the situational, interpretive practicality of phenomenology and hermeneutics. This move allowed Aoki (1993) to "dwell near, if not in the midst of" (p. 255) curricular landscapes, listening thoughtfully to teachers and students; to articulate the "tensionality that emerges, in part, from in-dwelling in the difference between two curricula: the curriculum-as-plan and the lived curriculum" (p. 257). Aoki kept moving—from Emmanuel Levinas, Gilles Deleuze, Jean-François Lytoard to Jacques Lacan—finding language to speak of difference so that it does not slide into romanticized notions of diversity. His most recent writing, informed primarily by postcolonial theory, offers an even more radicalized working out of difference and the implications for Self and Other and curriculum (Aoki, 1993, 1999).

Aoki's journey was/is not as simplistic or unidirectional as such a summary might imply. Nor did a reader have to wait until the 1990s to trace the Canadian/postmodern themes in his work. In 1983, his article "Experiencing Ethnicity as a Japanese Canadian," Aoki was already articulating the deep sensitivity of those Canadians located on the margin(s) of race, language, history, and place. Reflecting on a preteen (pre-World War II) visit to Japan, he writes, "A British Columbian born Japanese Canadian in Japan? In Japan I felt that as a Japanese Canadian, I was both Japanese and non-Japanese. I felt I was both insider and outsider, 'in' and yet not fully in, 'out' and yet not fully out" (p. 323).

The interest in the hyphen, as well as in the conjunction "and" for which the hyphen stands, has a long history in Canada. The defeat of the French at the famous Battle of the Plains of Abraham in 1759, and the subsequent British decision, in the Québec Act of 1774, to grant New France continued rights of religion, language, and legal system made being bicultural, bilingual, and bilegal fundamental to the nation's identity, the beginning of the conviction that "there is more than one way to be Canadian" (Cameron, 1997, p. 13). Although the principle of difference within sameness was established with Canada's early history, how this principle occluded certain differences (Jewish, aboriginal, Asian, queer, etc.) is also Canadian history (and identity), documented and articulated in arts, culture, and literature as well as in autobiographical curriculum texts such as Aoki's. The short quote earlier resonates not only with the wider spread Canadian preoccupation with difference, but also with the turn in Canadian literature and humanities toward the postmodern—a direction that Aoki sees curriculum scholars (but not curriculum planners and supervisors) in Canada following.

In this early article on difference and multiplicity, both Aoki's use of *and* as well as his placement of presence and absence side by side foreshadows the next two decades of his scholarship, and his coaxing of Canadian curriculum studies from the modern to the postmodern and later to the postcolonial (foreshadowed in this article by his use of "(not)belonging" and "homecoming" and "unwanted strangers in our own homeland") and poststructural (again foreshadowed by his use of "totalizing," "mono-vision," "a homogenized reality" in favor of a personal and human "becoming"). Perhaps most interesting in this article is Aoki's metaphor of seeing both the Japanese *satura* and the Canadian rose, rather than one or the other, employing a double vision that keeps both in view.

Ten years later, Aoki (1993) still sees with double vision. Now he sees both the traditional curricular landscape that privileges the discourse of curriculum developers and planners, the curriculum as plan, and the phenomenological and hermeneutic landscapes of classrooms, the lived curriculum. The metanarratives of traditional curriculum discourse delegitimize the discourses of the lived curriculum, where life is embodied in the stories told and the language spoken. Rather than substituting one for the other, Aoki (1993) proposes that the traditional curriculum discourses be decentered to make room for the practical wisdom of teachers—the thoughtful everyday stories of those who dwell within the landscapes of classrooms legitimating their meanings and wisdom.

Deborah Britzman, professor of education and women's studies at York University in Toronto, writes from a different position of hyphenation—a gay American woman living and teaching in Canada. One of Canada's most prolific and provocative curriculum theorists, her earliest work analyzed the formation of teacher identities (1991, 1996), as well as sexual identities (1996/1999). More recently, her interests have shifted to the psychoanalytic study of teaching and learning (1998). Britzman (1991) was always interested in critical discourses and practices, and she continues to cite Adorno and Arendt, linking her critique to ethics, claiming curriculum and education as ethical practices. Drawing on Stuart Hall and Homi Bhabha, both of whom were interested in identity as displacement, Britzman (1996) works brilliantly to identify the overlapping territories of language, politics, and psyche as they map out teacher identity, sexual identity and what that means for gendered/sexualized curriculum and pedagogy.

The first ethical obligation of research, pedagogy, and curriculum is "to know thyself" (Britzman, 2000). Poststructural theory suggests that to "know thyself" is to understand that oneself, and one's understanding of oneself, are constructions, neither fixed nor complete, both given to us and created by us through discourse. Thus, the complex process of negotiating one's identity, say as a beginning teacher, should never simply be assuming an already given identity, say of teacher. With her current reading of psychoanalytic theory (1998), to know thyself does not mean to know just what you would like to know, but also to come to know, and face to face, that which is difficult to know and what we tend to project onto the other.

Seeking such knowledge requires educators to examine how they are implicated in what they research, how they live and teach, and with whom. Thus, in Britzman's view, those writing and working in curriculum cannot simply write narratives, do research, or teach; they must question their own narratives, research questions, and teaching practices. If identities are constructed rather than given or assumed, which is the great hope that poststructural discourses offers curriculum, then identities can change, and those who are negotiating them can also be changed. In education and curriculum, this shifts knowing thyself from the realm of individual psychological insight, according to Britzman (1992), to social action and possibly social change.

It was Britzman's (1997) experience of coming to Canada to teach that invited her to refuse explication as pedagogy. Faced with her Canadian students, who spoke the same language but shared few of the same cultural referents, Britzman decided these students did not have a lack (which could be filled through explication), but were of equal intelligence (which could be loved and cared for through authentic conversation). At this point, "What do you think?" became her pedagogical question. For Britzman (1996), curriculum and pedagogy should incite critique not shut it down, should proliferate the ways people identify with one another (across difference) not minimize the psychological and social effects of difference.

Curriculum—as a point of departure rather than a destination—and conversation—about texts that have the power to affect coupled with the invitation of questions—are her exploratory pedagogy. Britzman is a harsh critic of curriculum in Canada, particularly its seeming irrelevance to the important matters facing the world today, and its exclusion from the "ethical obligation that the existence of children entails for every human society" to make or remake the world. Britzman (2000) asks how teacher education—with its demand for compliance, fear of controversy, and unclaimed experiences all conducted in the name of professionalism—can come to notice that the world matters. This she asked only 1 year prior to the terrible events of September 11, 2001.

What is the appeal of postmodernism and poststructuralism to Canadian curriculum theorists? Canada is almost the postcard (post) society: It is postmodern, postcolonial, and almost postnational. The Canadian postmodern is visible in the visual arts and architecture—from the National Gallery in Ottawa to the Museum of Civilization in Hull Quebec to the public library in Vancouver. While postmodernism is frequently critiqued for its apolitical character, the fragmented and regional politics of Canada—where the national government has become a parody of its former modern self under Pierre Elliot Trudeau—is perhaps postmodernism gone bad. Canadian fiction is consummately postmodern, preoccupied with difference and what Linda Hutcheon calls "ex-centricity," employing parody and irony as the major forms of critique and artistic practice, allowing writers and artists to "speak to their culture, from within, but without being totally co-opted by that culture" (Hutcheon, 1997/1988, p. 68).

Canadians have a keen sense of marginality, earlier to Britain's colonial power, and now to U.S. economic power. When any particular place becomes located as center or mainstream, Canadians immediately look for another margin. This may account, in part, for the Canadian penchant for self-deprecating satire (Cameron, 1997). It is the many Canadian eccentrics—those living outside the mainstream (White, Anglo-French, heterosexual)—"whose split identities—as Japanese- or Italo-Canadians, for instance—have made them feel closer to the postmodern concerns for difference and multiplicity rather than sameness and single identity" (Hutcheon, 1997, p. 67). Hutcheon's analysis sheds light on the intersections of postmodernism in Canadian curriculum theory.

Like Hutcheon, Smith believes that postmodernism heralds an era of hope for education and Western societies such as Canada. As modernism and its grip on education die, postmodernism makes possible a "motility of meaning … [that] works in favor of a deep relationalism," a character that is "relational, ecological, modest, conversational and somewhat mysterious." Postmodernism makes possible pedagogy that "begins with a sense of the deep interconnectedness between adult and child," (p. 123), and curriculum, quoting Derrida, that is "the as-yet-unnameable-which-is-constantly-proclaiming-itself" (p. 124), giving us all, but children in particular, hope that we may creatively participate in the task of interpreting the world and creating a future.

GLOBAL CHALLENGES TO CURRICULUM IN CANADA

George S. Tomkins (1979) claims that curriculum in Canada has been international since the Jesuits brought the Ratio Studiorum to New France in the 1630s. Their "plan of studies" was arguably the most systematic and highly centralized curriculum ever devised, and became the basis for secondary education in Québec for the next 300 years. Tomkins (1986) unravelled these origins as part of a modernist project to objectively describe the "origin and growth" of curriculum in Canada from its early colonial, "preindustrial" period through to the 20th century with its "rapid industrial and technological change" and resulting shifts in notions of the child and into the post-1945 periods with its affluence and "breakdown of the long established consensus based on Judeo-Christian and Anglo-conformist imperatives" and the "new social consensus based on a new ethic of respect for cultural diversity and the persistence of nationalizing imperatives" (pp. 5–7). Each of these eras brought demands for curriculum change that were countered by a deeply entrenched desire for cultural and political stability (Tomkins, 1981b). Although curriculum originating primarily in France and Britain—each with different histories but similar purposes and effects—can hardly be considered international, it is implicated in the global challenges facing curriculum studies in Canada today.

More recent Canadian scholarship is considerably more critical but equally hopeful. John Willinsky (1993, 1995, 1998), professor of language and literacy at the University of British Columbia and Fellow of the Royal Society (one of the most prestigious academic honors bestowed in Canada), claims education and curriculum as explicit tools of colonialism, essential elements in European imperialism, through which Western notions of race, language, and nation were constructed, exported, and continue to be reproduced in classrooms throughout the world.

Willinsky's scholarship traces how language and literature, as well as history, geography, and science, became the building blocks of the colonial mindset, but he proposes that what was constructed can be deconstructed. Given that in Canadian classrooms today, students from the colonies and beyond gather, Willinsky believes that students have the intellectual right to learn, and curriculum has the responsibility to make explicit the relationship between nation and language (Willinsky, 1995), imperialism and the academic disciplines and school subjects (Willinsky, 1998), and the part education has played in making it so. His proposal is to "supplement our education with a consideration of imperialism's influence on the teaching of history, geography, science, language, and literature in the hope that it will change the way this legacy works on us" (Willinsky, 1998, p. 247). Such a postcolonial curriculum would make it possible for students to feel at home in Canada as well as a sense of responsibility and belonging to a world that through such curriculum change can become "more openly and equitably interdependent" (Willinsky, 1995, p. 142).

David G. Smith (1999, 2000b) argues that for public life generally, and liberal democratic institutions such as schools and universities specifically, the "new corporate colonialism" is a far more urgent matter than the vestiges of the old colonialism in the academy and public school curriculum, or the imaginaries of those who work in those domains or are required to suffer them. Smith draws the parallel between religious fundamentalism and "economic fundamentalism," illustrating how the initiatives of globalization—to create a new borderless global economy and to dismantle public institutions such as education except where they can train workers and provide markets and consumers for the global economy—are religious and theological in their intent and purpose. As Director of An International Forum on Education and Society, Smith's project is to "rethink the nature and character of education in the context of the new configuring of global order" (p. 109; see *http://www.ualberta.ca/~smithdg/*).

Smith documents the origins of this global economy—the rise of U.S. global domination after World War II, the resulting Bretton Woods Agreement of 1944, and institutions such as the International Monetary Fund and World Bank, and subsequent international trade agreements like the North American Free Trade Agreement (NAFTA) and the European Union—which ensure the fluid movement of capital, goods, and services. He maps out the effects of globalization—exploitation of poor countries and the poor in rich countries; education under siege, its legitimacy eroded; traditional liberal democratic aims to create citizens given way to training for competitiveness and consumption; and loss of control over national and local economies eroding traditional state protections and services for citizens. Smith's project is to draw attention to the critical impact of globalization on education and to make transparent the strategies North American corporations use to remake or take over public education, particularly in Canada. International trade agreements like NAFTA give corporations rights equal to those of citizens and national corporations and in Canada this enables U.S. takeovers of curriculum, textbooks, and testing. NAFTA also secures agreements for harmonization of reforms in curriculum and teacher education— among the United States, Canada, and Mexico—ostensibly to meet the needs of the global economy (Barlow & Robertson, 1994).

For Smith, the greatest challenge educators face is how to respond in the face of the media-disseminated belief that these change are inevitable. For Smith doing nothing and being silent is not responsible. The public must be educated and economic theory demystified; and who better to do this than teachers and professors of education. Smith's (2000b) most recent writing calls us all "to think creatively about how a new global economy might be managed to honor and safeguard the human necessities of place and security" (p. 111), and to commit ourselves to "intercivilizational dialogue." Here we see Smith's origins as a teacher; although his critique is economic, his hope and commitment are fundamentally pedagogical and hermeneutic, that transformation is made possible through dialogue.

However, is colonialism a post that Canada is beyond? Is Canada and its curriculum postcolonial? As noted earlier, the entire history of Canada is about colonization: both of being colonized by foreign imperial powers, and of internalized colonialism as Anglophones suppress the French in Québec, and the Cree and Inuit fight Québec for recognition of their Indigenous rights. Canada is a hyphenated nation—where everyone wears and uses the hyphen, and as Canadian playwright John Gray says, "we created a hyphenated national vocabulary, a verbal railway ... that allows Canadians to go forward, backward, or to writhe somewhere in between" (cited in Grace, 1995, p. 131).

This railroad of hyphenated vocabulary ties individuals to the social world in which they live, and which they produce collectively. Indigenous Canadian writers such as Tomson Highway, Marilyn Dumont, and Eden Robinson, as well as those novelists and poets born elsewhere who have made Canada their home—for example, Kristjana Gunnars, Michael Ondaatje, Rohinton Mistry, and Dionne Brand—are writing a new language, a new way of telling stories of Canada and what it means to be Canadian. These languages are not idiolects nor are they dialects unintelligible to those outside the particular community of the author. Rather these new Créole or Michif languages write and tell, "epic narratives that recuperate and interpellate the silenced voices, suppressed realities, and hitherto unimagined communities into the always incomplete discourse of Canadian nationalism" (Grace, 1995, p. 131; see also Chambers, 1999). If the arts and culture in Canada can take up the challenge of finding new ways to speak to, and with, one another—in and across difference—can Canadian curriculum, and those who produce and teach it, do the same? As in arts and culture, curriculum writers in Canada are interested in difference in its various manifestations—as multiculturalism, diversity, globalization, nationalism, and citizenship.

Ted Aoki's is probably the most recognizable hyphenated voice on the Canadian curriculum airwaves. In his most recent work, he rereads his own narratives of attending public school in English ("school for whites" in translation from Japanese) as well as Japanese language school; and growing up in "Japanese" town on the periphery of the small mining community of Cumberland, British Columbia. (The peripheral situation of the Japanese language and town in relation to the central position of the English language and towns are exemplary of the Canadian experience of, and preoccupation with, margin and center.) This "doubled schooling"—with its double-language standard—led to Aoki becoming a "mixed-up hybrid kid."

After a long career in Alberta, he returned to a British Columbia (from which he was expelled during the Japanese internment of World War II) operating under a new language code, one in which Japanese and other Asian languages are legitimate (even preferred, as part of the new economic preoccupation with the Pacific Rim) curriculum subjects, an irony that does not escape Aoki. Now the language he could not speak without getting the strap, the culture and race to which he belonged that was grounds for exile and incarceration, is part of the diversity of a "multicultural" Canada.

Reading Homi Bhabha and other postcolonial critics and theorists, Aoki rejects the "metaphorical language of diversity" that has become the "bedrock of multi-cultural, multi-national education" (Bhabha, 1990) in countries like Canada. This unity in community arises from a liberal pluralism that "paradoxically permits diversity but masks difference" (p. 32) and the norm of the dominant culture, which says "these or other cultures are fine, but we must be able to locate them within our own grid" (Bhabha, cited in Aoki, 1999, p. 32).

Aoki (1999) calls for the location of new places to speak that are "inhabited often by the colonized, the minorities, the migrants in a diasporic community whose productive voices are now beginning to come forth" (p. 33). Aoki begins the project with himself, questioning the "narrative imaginary within which I've been inventing my stories of personal experiences of my schooling days, and as well upon my own life experiences as a Canadian with the label of an Asian minority" (p. 37). Canadian philosophers like Charles Taylor (1991, 1992), and postcolonial scholars such as Homi Bhabha (1990) and Trinh Min-ha help Aoki to "transform the sting of the strap" he received for speaking Japanese during recess at the English school, to write from a space where the "otherness of others is not buried," and he can begin to speak a "vitally new language" (p. 36). He invites all curriculum workers and teachers to do the same.

On what grounds will the intercivilizational dialogue that David G. Smith calls for take place? What is the new language that Aoki is learning to speak and wishes others to find for themselves? Indigenous scholars find the discourses of postcolonialism powerful tools in their effort to critique Indigenous education and to map out a curriculum and a pedagogy in response to real and devastating consequences of colonialism. For Indigenous people, the experience of postcolonialism is not language play or a theoretical strategy for getting equal representation in literature or critiques of it; rather, colonialism (without the post) resides in bones, personal and collective memory, dreams, family stories, myths, dances, and poems (McLeod, 1998). However, "aboriginal people need a new story ... the old one is one of destruction, while the emerging one is that of the ongoing vitality of Aboriginal people, from whose experience we can learn" (Battiste, 2000a, pp. viii–ix).

Marie Battiste's (2000b) most recent edited volume of essays offers a métissage (Chambers, Hasebe-Ludt, & Donald, 2002) of writing from Indigenous (in one sense of the term or another) scholars, all of whom are not Canadian. The U.S.–Canadian border is not a border that makes a difference—either colonially or postcolonially—where alliances are at once older and deeper—both in wounds and time—than any ones founded on "national" (in the sense of nation state) identities. Robert Yazzie's essay entitled "Indigenous Peoples and Postcolonial Colonialism" perhaps best captures the sense of irony with which new Indigenous scholars approach Western theories and theorizing about Indian as Other, be they postcolonial subject or otherwise. This appropriation of a discourse to one's own ends is a trickster move, and, unfortunately many Canadian curriculum scholars will never see it—mostly because they are not watching borders or peripheries (unless it happens to be their own).

Terrance Carson and Ingrid Johnson (2000) confront the very difficult task of making these issues topical in teacher education; "teaching for diversity" becomes one more thing that already anxiety-ridden student teachers have to master. When difference becomes a topic, especially in lived stories of racism, and particularly of racism against Indigenous peoples, the anxieties of the (mostly) white Canadian student teachers are heightened. "Young white males, in the midst of negotiating the contradictory discourses of teaching in the formation of their own identities, are unlikely to be receptive to charges of their own complicity in racism and the maintenance of white privilege." In response to their question of what the pedagogical task of the teacher is in this situation, Carson and Johnson call for a pedagogy of compassion, one that is not a panacea but a "starting place for productive conversations."

Charles Taylor, professor of philosophy at McGill University in Montréal, is mapping out the *Malaise of Modernity,* the title of his 1991 book based on the Massey Lecture series broadcast on CBC radio (and published outside of Canada as *The Ethics of Authenticity*), and the politics of recognition and how those are mapped onto multiculturalism. An unfair oversimplification of the work of the world's most eminent scholar of modernity might be that the concern for (finding and being true to) the self, the preoccupation with the individual (and his or her uniqueness) rather than equality, and the desire for public recognition (of the individual)—all of which have become confused with authenticity—have littered our public lives with meaninglessness, catharsis, and political apathy, leaving lives and our significant relationships, particularly with those we love, devoid of meaning. It has also rendered us apathetic toward loss of freedom and the social (ecological, economical, and political) crisis brought about by the predominance of instrumental reason.

Of particular interest is how this notion of the unique self maps onto identity, so that the curriculum (and society) are required to support the individual in two contradictory ways: one based on his or her abstract humanity and the other based on his or her uniqueness as an individual. What is our way out of this acute self-consciousness and the dangerous precipice to which it has brought us? Taylor argues that we are individuals only in so far as we are social, and that being authentic or faithful to ourselves is "being faithful to something which was produced in collaboration with a lot of other people" (Rorty, cited in McNeill, 1997).

Taylor, another hyphenated Canadian—an Anglophone Catholic living in Québec—believes our way out of this fatal malaise is to recognize that human life is dialogical (Taylor 1991, 1992), and that we can only discover and recover (authenticity and) our identity in dialogue with "significant others." This is the challenge for curriculum studies in Canada, for curriculum planners, supervisors, and practicing educators. Taylor proposes that is it through dialogue with significant others that both come to understand who we are, where is here, and how we can live authentically and responsibly together in this place. Those who work in curriculum in Canada are charged with no less a responsibility.

PAST THE LAST POST: HAVE WE GONE POSTNATIONAL?

It seems that Canada and its curriculum studies have moved into the postmodern and the (post)colonial, albeit not always gracefully. Have we gone postnational? Can we afford to go postnational? Is postnational the same as international? How can such a "group of groups" possibly experience nationalism, asks Elspeth Cameron (1997). At three specific points in our history, Canadians experienced nationalism. First at Confederation in 1867; second during World War I, particularly following the Canadian success at Vimy Ridge (when the paintings of the Group of Seven flourished); and finally during the first Centennial celebration in 1967 when Expo 67 in Montreal and the strong federalist Prime Minister Pierre Elliot Trudeau inspired a generation to be Canadian (Cameron, 1997). As the Vietnam War raged on and OPEC control over Middle Eastern oil supplies created American demand for Canadian petroleum, cultural critics wondered how "national" Canada's foreign and defense policy was. Canadians wondered if they had too little of American-type patriotism, what the two great wars in Europe had previously made suspect.

As cultural and political sovereignty became the topic of the literary and political elite, similar questions found their way into curriculum scholarship and practice. Milburn and Hebert (1973) pondered the relationship between national consciousness and the curriculum, and the responsibility of school curriculum to create and maintain a Canadian identity. Following this fervent period, Canadian Studies became a university and school subject and Canadian textbooks (or adaptations) were published. Eventually nationalism and Canadian identity moved off the curriculum screen until 1988, when NAFTA was signed. With NAFTA, Canada lost the right to protect its cultural "industries," including publishing, through federal government subsidies. Textbooks became an international commodity, schools a marketplace, and the question of cultural autonomy, national identity, and Canadian content in textbooks returned as a serious curriculum matter (Altbach, 1991; Chambers, 1999; Smith, 1999).

Yet, George Tomkins (1979, 1981a) makes the case that the curriculum was always an overt instrument for nation building in Canada, particularly for making Canadians out of the waves of immigrants in the 19th and early 20th centuries. It was the postmodernist, poststructuralist, and postcolonial discourses that made Canadian curriculum theorists hypercritical of "actual" curriculum and teaching practices, the public policies and institutional practices that give rise to them (Blades, 1997; Couture, 2000; Richardson, 1999; Smith, 1998), and the explicit and implicit intent to construct Canadian identity and patriotism. Multiple identities or postcolonial contexts notwith-standing, Canadian curriculum still standardizes a "curriculum of national identity" (Richardson, 2001).

The "post" theories counter that national identity as a narrative of "belonging"—and nation-building as a project—are constructed through very particular state appa-ratuses—like the media (Canadian Broadcasting Corporation), the military, the police (Royal Canadian Mounted Police), and the schools (Chambers, 2000; Penrose, 1997), vi-sual symbols such as the railway, the Canadian flag and its maple leaf (Cameron, 1997); and stories such as the one about the "two founding nations"—English and French—transformed into a "vertical mosaic" (Porter, 1965) by official bilingualism and official multiculturalism (McFarlane, 1995; Rukszto, 1997). This essay suggests that such a nar-rative has a few gaps, or perhaps gaping holes.

The place called Canada is part of the narrative of belonging as well. "Much in the Canadian identity is tied to the land itself" (Cameron, 1997, p. 9). Why is that? Canada's eminent historian of the fur trade era, Harold Innis, claims that Canada emerged, not in spite of geography, but because of it (cited in Cameron, 1997, p. 9). Canadians, perhaps because of the sheer size of the land mass, are preoccupied with space and place, land and landscape. The roots of this obsession are neither symbolic nor imaginary, but real; the winters long and harsh, varied topography, massive topographical diversity that made travel difficult (and still does in regions, especially in the North, in Labrador, Nunavut, and the Northwest Territories, where great distances and unpredictable weather make travel more dangerous than one might assume it would be).

Historically, Canada's economy has been primarily resource-based—fur, lumber, mining, petroleum, fishing, and agriculture. Survival, individual and collective, de-manded that people remain attuned to the weather and the land, powerful forces that could neither be alienated nor succumbed to. As southern Canada became more popu-lated, and technology for surviving the elements more advanced, surviving the long, cold winters or fly-infested summers shifted from the real to the imaginary, from the south to the north, from real life to literature and art. The motif of Canada as concerned with survival is a strong one in Canadian literature, and this thematic is tightly woven with the immense role that the North and its landscape play in the Canadian imagina-tion and sense of identity (Atwood, 1972, 1995; Chambers, 1999).

Thus the Canadian identity is a fractured, multiple one, constructed by state appara-tus, language, place, and metanarratives; lives are lived in one place with imaginaries shaped elsewhere—the North, or Toronto, the shopping mall (that great Canadian con-tribution to urban landscapes) or MuchMusic (the Canadian equivalent of MTV). As it becomes apparent that a single national identity no longer seems practical nor perhaps all that desirable, Canadian curriculum workers are left to wonder not only what it means to be Canadian but what Canadian means for curriculum—particularly in these postmodern times and in this postcolonial space—when narrating Canada has become so problematic (Ruskzto, 1997). Does it mean that we give up any narration about na-tion? Do we omit all mention of nation from our narration? Have we gone past the last post? Some would argue we have; that the imaginary geographics we inhabit are part of a global field rather than a Canadian home-ground (see Frank Davey cited in Grace, 1995), and this review of curriculum in Canada would support this.

Sherrill Grace, in her essay "Canada Post," a play on the name of the federal postal service in Canada, is very reluctant to give up on a citizenship that mediates the indi-vidual's relations with the multinational or global community. If the flip side of postnationalism is globalization, then the choice—between a "collapse back into trib-alism, racialized nationalisms, ethnic cleansing, political fragmentation and violence on the one hand, and our seduction by the blandishments of global corporatism on the other" (Grace, 1995, p. 133)—isn't a real choice. As uncomfortable as Canadians are with nationalism (Hlynka, 2001), as problematic as the concept might be theoretically or politically, at this point in time a national identity may be a "pivotal mediating context through which I negotiate my individual, local and global selves" (p. 133) even as those selves, and that national identity are multiple and shifting. Richardson (1997) ironically suggests that nationalism has become the "new love that dare not say its name," and argues that if Canadians are to create a shared public space that is tolerant of difference and inviting to youth, curriculum must address identity and nationalism directly in a way that is invested with, rather than divested of, emotion and passion.

In this sense, national identity may be a third way, a middle passage through globalization and the new corporate colonialism, ironically our best defense against globalization and its "superimperialism" of information technology that masquerades as neutral (Hlynka, 2001), but is as imperialistic—and alienating—as the old forms we remember from the past—"fighting for territory, world markets and discursive control" (Grace, 1995, p. 134). Grace predicts this particular imperialist war could mean the death of Canadian education, particularly for universities, as degrees become virtual, and curricula are sold electronically to Canadians from the United States. The community that might forestall such an apocalyptic vision does not have to be of the "either/or, two founding nations, one land, one flag" variety; rather we need to imagine a national community that "embraces a plurality of national identities co-existing, co-operating, sharing and articulating differences" (p. 135). Hopefully this can be done with the humor, humility, and goodwill on which (most) Canadians pride themselves.

This is difficult work, and yet, the need has never been greater.

AS MUCH OF AN ENDING AS IS POSSIBLE
UNDER THE CIRCUMSTANCES

That "Head Office is somewhere else," as Northrop Frye quipped, is not only an economic and cultural fact, but also a characteristic of much Canadian curriculum scholarship—both historical and contemporary. Curriculum scholars are like the many immigrants to Canada, inhabited by traditions received from a (intellectual Father/Mother) homeland elsewhere. Rather than ignoring or rejecting these inherited discourses, for any immigrant, this (new) place requires that the traditions and the languages they speak be made anew, infinitely re-created in and with a land and people that seem to refuse easy definition.

This is the "middle or third way" that many Canadian curriculum scholars seem to be calling for. Through their work they are braiding languages and traditions, stories and fragments, desires and repulsions, arguments and conversations, tradition and change, hyphens and slashes, mind and body, earth and spirit, texts and images, local and global, pasts and posts, into a métissage, one that is perhaps as Canadian as possible under the circumstances. It is our way, and it is what we have to offer any international conversation that is curriculum.

REFERENCES

Altbach, P. G. (1991). Textbooks: The international dimension. In M. Apple & L. Christian-Smith (Eds.), *The politics of the textbook* (pp. 242–258). New York: Routledge.

Aoki, T. T. (1979). *Toward curriculum inquiry in a new key.* Edmonton, Canada: University of Alberta, Department of Secondary Education.

Aoki, T. T. (1983). Experiencing ethnicity as a Japanese Canadian teacher: Reflections on a personal curriculum. *Curriculum Inquiry, 13*(3), 321–335.

Aoki, T. T. (1986). Interests, knowledge and evaluation: Alternative approaches to curriculum evaluation. *JCT, 6*(4), 27–44.

Aoki, T. T. (1990). Inspiriting the curriculum. *The ATA Magazine,* 37–42.

Aoki, T. T. (1993, Spring). Legitimating lived curriculum: Towards a curricular landscape of multiplicity. *Journal of Curriculum and Supervision, 8*(3), 255–268.

Aoki, T. T. (1999). In the midst of doubled imaginaries: The Pacific community as diversity and difference. *Interchange, 30*(1), 27–38.

Aoki, T. T. (2000, July). *Opening address.* The Symposium on Writing Teachers' Lives, The University of Lethbridge, Alberta, Canada.

Aoki, T. T., & Shamsher, M. (Eds.). (1991). *Voices of teaching, Vol. 2: Program for quality teaching.* Vancouver, Canada: British Columbia Teachers' Federation.

Aoki, T. T., & Shamsher, M. (Eds.). (1993). *The call of teaching.* Vancouver, Canada: British Columbia Teachers' Federation.

Atwood, M. (1972). *Survival: A thematic guide to Canadian literature.* Concord, Canada: House of Anansi Press.

Atwood, M. (1995). *Strange things: The malevolent north in Canadian literature.* Toronto, Canada: Clarendon.

Bannerji, H. (Ed.). (1993). *Returning the gaze: Essays on racism, feminism and politics.* Toronto, Canada: Sister Vision Press.

Bannerji, H. (1995). *Thinking through: Essays on feminism, Marxism and anti-racism.* Toronto, Canada: Women's Press.

Barlow M., & Robertson, H.-J. (1994). *Class warfare: The assault on Canada's schools.* Toronto, Canada: Key Porter Books.

Barnes, T. J., & Duncan, J. S. (1992). Introduction: Writing worlds. In T. J. Barnes & J. S. Duncan (Eds.), *Writing worlds: Discourse, text, and metaphor in the representation of landscape* (pp. 1–17). New York: Routledge.

Basso, K. H. (1996). *Wisdom sits in places: Landscape and language among the Western Apache.* Albuquerque: University of New Mexico.

Battiste M. (2000a). Foreword. In M. B. Castellano, L. Davis, & L. Lahache (Eds.), *Aboriginal education: Fulfilling the promise* (pp. vii–ix). Vancouver, Canada: University of British Columbia Press.

Battiste M. (Ed.). (2000b). *Reclaiming indigenous voice and vision.* Vancouver, Canada: University of British Columbia Press.

Battiste M., & Barman, J. (Ed.). (1995). *First Nations education in Canada: The circle unfolds.* Vancouver, Canada: University of British Columbia Press.

Bhabha H. (1990). *Nation and narration.* New York: Routledge.

Blades, D. (1997). *Procedures of power and curriculum change: Foucault and the quest for possibilities in science education.* New York: Peter Lang.

Britzman, D. P. (1991). *Practice makes practice: A critical study of learning to teach.* Albany: State University of New York Press.

Britzman, D. P. (1992). The terrible problem of knowing thyself: Toward a poststructural account of teacher identity. *JCT, 9*(3), 23–46.

Britzman, D. P. (1996/1999). On becoming a "little sex researcher:" Some comments on a polymorphously perverse curriculum. In W. F. Pinar (Ed.), *Contemporary curriculum discourses: Twenty years of JCT* (pp. 379–397). New York: Peter Lang.

Britzman, D. P. (1997). On refusing explication: Towards a non-narrative narrativity. *Resources for Feminist Research, 25*(3–4), 34–37.

Britzman, D. P. (1998). *Lost subjects, contested subjects: Toward a psychoanalytic inquiry of learning.* Albany State University of New York Press.

Britzman, D. P. (2000). Teacher education in the confusion of our times. *Journal of Teacher Education, 51*(3), 200–205.

Brookes, A.-L. (1992). *Feminist pedagogy: An autobiographical approach.* Halifax, Canada: Fernwood.

Bryson, M., & de Castell, S. (1993). Queer pedagogy?/!: Praxis makes im/perfect. *Canadian Journal of Education, 18,* 285–305.

Butt, R., & Raymond, D. (1987). Arguments for using qualitative approaches in understanding teacher thinking: The case for biography. *JCT, 7*(1), 63–69.

Butt, R., & Raymond, D. (1992). Studying the nature and development of teachers' knowledge using collaborative autobiography. *International Journal of Educational Research, 13*(4), 402–449.

Butt, R., Townsend, D., & Raymond, D. (1990). Bringing reform to life: Teachers' stories and professional development. *Cambridge Journal of Education, 20*(3), 255–268.

Cajete, G. (2000). *Native science: Natural laws of interdependence.* Sante Fe, NM: Clear Light.

Cameron, E. (Ed.). (1997). *Canadian culture: An introductory reader.* Toronto, Canada: Canadian Scholar's Press.

Carson, T. (1984). *A hermeneutic investigation of the meaning of curriculum implementation for consultants and teachers.* Unpublished doctoral dissertation, University of Alberta, Edmonton, Canada.

Carson, T. (1986). Closing the gap between research and practice: Conversation as a mode of doing research. *Phenomenology + Pedagogy, 4*(2), 73–85.

Carson, T. (1990). What kind of knowing is critical action research? *Theory into Practice, 29*(3), 167–173.

Carson, T., & Johnson, I. (2000). The difficulty with difference in teacher education: Toward a pedagogy of compassion. *The Alberta Journal of Educational Research, XLVI*(1), 75–83. Retrieved February 14, 2002 from the World Wide Web: http://www.ualberta.ca/~tcarson/

Carson, T., & Sheridan-Carson, R. (1999, Winter). Action research: Building a strong culture of professional development. *Alberta Teachers Association Magazine,* 11–12.

Carson, T., & Sumara, D. (Eds.). (1997). *Action research as a living practice.* New York: Peter Lang.

Castellano, M. B., Davis, L., & Lahache, L. (Eds.). (2000). *Aboriginal education: Fulfilling the promise.* Vancouver, Canada: University of British Columbia Press.

Chambers, C. M. (1989). *For our children's children: An educator's interpretation of Dene testimony to the Mackenzie Valley Pipeline Inquiry.* Unpublished doctoral dissertation, University of Victoria, Victoria, Canada.

Chambers, C. (1994). Looking for a home: A work in progress. *Frontiers: A Journal of Woman Studies, 15*(2), 23–50.

Chambers, C. (1997). On taking my (own) medicine: Memory work in writing and pedagogy. *Journal of Curriculum Theorizing, 14*(4), 14–21.

Chambers, C. M. (1999). The topography of Canadian curriculum theory. *Canadian Journal of Education, 24*(4), 1–14.

Chambers, C. M. (2000, May). *Globalization and the north.* Presentation to Canadian Society for the Study of Education, Edmonton, Canada.

Chambers, C. M., Hasebe-Ludt, E., & Donald, D. (2002). Creating a curriculum of métissage. *Educational Insights.* Retrieved August 9, 2001 from the the World Wide Web: http://www.csci.educ.ubc.ca/publication/insights/index.html

Chambers, C., Oberg, A., Fowler, L, Hasebe-Ludt, E., Leggo, C., & Norman, R. (2000, April). *What does writing autobiographically do to us?* Performance conducted at the annual meeting of the American Educational Research Association, New Orleans, LA.

Chambers, C., Oberg, A., Moore, M., & Dodd, A. (1994). Seeking authenticity: Women reflect on their lives as daughters, mothers and teachers. *Journal of Curriculum Theorizing, 10*(4), 73–108.

Chapman, M. L., & Anderson, J. (Eds.). (1995). *Thinking globally about language education.* Vancouver, Canada: Centre for Study of Curriculum and Instruction, University of British Columbia.

Chrisjohn, R. D., & Young, S. L. (1997). *The circle game: Shadows and substance in the Indian residential school experience in Canada.* Penticton, Canada: Theytus Books.

Clandinin, D. J., & Connelly, F. M. (2000). *Narrative inquiry: Experience and story in qualitative research.* San Francisco: Jossey-Bass.

Clifford, P., & Friesen, S. (1993, Fall). A curious plan: Managing on the twelfth. *Harvard Educational Review, 63*(3), 339–358.

Connelly, F. M., & Clandinin, D. J. (1988). *Teachers as curriculum planners: Narratives of experience.* New York: Teachers College Press.

Connelly, F. M., & Clandinin, D. J. (1990). Stories of experience and narrative inquiry. *Educational Researcher, 19*(4), 2–14.

Couture, J.-C. (2000). *The gift of failure: Teacher commitment in the postmodern classroom.* Unpublished doctoral dissertation, University of Alberta, Edmonton, Canada.

Daignault, J. (1985). *Pour une esthétique de la pédagogie.* Victoriaville, Canada: Editions NHP.

Daignault, J. (1992a). The language of research and the language of practice: Neither one for the other: Pedagogy. In T. R. Carson & D. J. Sumara (Eds.), *Exploring collaborative action research: Proceedings of the ninth invitational conference of the Canadian Association for Curriculum Studies* (pp. 121–143). Edmonton, Canada: Canadian Association for Curriculum Studies.

Daignault, J. (1992b). Traces at work from different places. In W. F. Pinar & W. M. Reynolds (Eds.), *Understanding curriculum as phenomenological and deconstructed texts* (pp. 195–214). New York: Teachers College Press.

Daignault, J. (2001, May). *Internationalization of curriculum studies.* Presentation to the annual meeting of the Canadian Society for the Study of Education, Université du Québec, Laval, Canada.

Daignault, J., & Fountain, R. (2000, April). *Linux, a philosophy and operating system for education.* Paper presented at the 1st Internationalization of Curriculum Studies Conference, Louisiana State University, Baton Rouge, LA.

Daigrault, J., & Gauthier, C. (1982). The indecent curriculum machine: Who's afraid of Sisyphe? *JCT, 4*(1), 177–196.

Davis, B. (1994). Mathematics teaching: Moving from telling to listening. *Journal of Curriculum and Supervision, 9*(3), 267–283.

Davis, B., Sumara, D., & Luce-Kapler, R. (2000). *Engaging minds: Learning and teaching in a complex world.* Mahwah, NJ: Lawrence Erlbaum Associates.

de Castell, S. (1993). 6 December 1989/1993, Je me souviens. Introduction to S. Castell (Ed.), Against the grain: Narratives of resistance [Special Issue]. *Canadian Journal of Education, 18*(3), 185–188.

de Castell, S., & Bryson, M. (Eds.). (1997). *Radical In<ter>ventions: Identity, politics, and difference/s in educational praxis.* Albany: State University of New York Press.

Dunlop, R. (1999). *Boundary Bay: A novel as educational research.* Unpublished doctoral dissertation, University of British Columbia, Vancouver, Canada.

Fanon, F. (1963). *The wretched of the earth* (C. Ferrington, Trans.). New York: Grove.

Fels, L. (1999). *In the wind clothes dance on a line: Performative inquiry, a (re)search methodology, possibilities and absences within a space-moment of Imagining a universe.* Unpublished doctoral dissertation, University of British Columbia, Vancouver, Canada.

Ferguson, W., & Ferguson, I. (2001). *How to be a Canadian (even if you already are one).* Vancouver, Canada: Douglas & McIntyre.

Forman, F., O'Brien, M., Haddad, J., Hallman, D., & Masters, P. (Eds.). (1990). *Feminism and education: A Canadian perspective.* Toronto, Canada: Ontario Institute for Studies in Education.

Fowler, L. C. (1997). *Re/Constituting the teaching self: Narrative explorations of difficulty in teaching.* Unpublished doctoral dissertation, University of Victoria, Victoria, Canada.

Fowler, L. C. (in press). *A curriculum of difficulty: Stories and narrative analysis in education research.* Mahwah, NJ: Lawrence Erlbaum Associates.

Grace, S. E. (1995). Canada Post: -Modern? -Colonial? -National? *Transactions of the Royal Society of Canada,* Series 6, Volume 6, 127–137.

Graham, R. (1989). Autobiography and education. *The Journal of Educational Thought, 23*(2), 92–105.

Graham, R. (1991). *Reading and writing the self: Autobiography in education and the curriculum.* New York: Teachers College Press.

Government of Canada, Statistics Canada. (1996). *Aboriginal population by mother tongue, 1996 Census.* Retrieved February 13, 2002 from the World Wide Web: http://www.statcan.ca/english/Pgdb/People/Population/demo36b.htm

Government of Canada, Statistics Canada. (1998). 1996 Census: Aboriginal data. Retrieved February 13, 2002 from the World Wide Web: http://www.statcan.ca/Daily/English/980113/d980113.htm

Government of Canada, Statistics Canada. (2001). *Population by sex and age.* Retrieved February 14, 2002 from the World Wide Web: http://www.statcan.ca/english/Pgdb/People/Population/demo10a.htm

Haig-Brown, C. (1988). *Resistance and renewal: Surviving the Indian residential school.* Vancouver, Canada: Tillicum Library.

Haig-Brown, C. (1995). *Taking control: Power and contradiction in First Nations adult education.* Vancouver, Canada: University of British Columbia Press.

Haig-Brown, C. (Ed.). (1997). *Making the spirit dance within: Joe Duquette High School and an Aboriginal community.* Toronto, Canada: James Lorimer.

Hasebe-Ludt, E. (1999). The whole world in one classroom: Teaching across traditions in a cosmopolitan environment. *Interchange, 30*(1), 39–55.

Hasebe-Ludt, E. (in press). *In all the universe: Placing texts of culture and community in only one school.* New York: Peter Lang.

Hasebe-Ludt, E., & Hurren, W. (Eds.). (2003). *Curriculum intertext: Place/language/pedagogy* (with an afterword by W. Pinar). New York: Peter Lang.

Henry, A. (1992). African Canadian women teachers' activism: Recreating communities of caring and resistance. *Journal of Negro Education, 61,* 392–404.

Hlynka, D. (2001, May). *The national discourses of instructional technology.* Paper presented at the meeting of the Canadian Society for the Study of Education, Laval, Canada.

Hoffman, E. (1989). *Lost in translation: A life in a new language.* New York: Penguin.

Hunsberger, M. (1985). The experience of re-reading. *Phenomenology + Pedagogy, 3*(3), 161–166.

Hunsberger, M. (1988). Teaching reading methods. *The Journal of Educational Thought, 22*(2A), 209–218.

Hunsberger, M. (1989). Students and textbooks: What is to be the matter? *Phenomenology + Pedagogy, 7,* 115–126.

Hunsberger, M. (1992). The time of texts. In W. Pinar & W. Reynolds (Eds.), *Understanding curriculum as phenomenological and deconstructed text* (pp. 64–91). New York: Teachers College Press.

Hurren, W. (2000). *Line dancing: An atlas of geography curriculum and poetic possibilities*. New York: Peter Lang.

Hutcheon, L. (1988/1997). The Canadian postmodern (an excerpt from The Canadian postmodern: A study of contemporary English-Canadian fiction). In E. Cameron (Ed.), *Canadian culture: An introductory reader* (pp. 65–71). Toronto, Canada: Canadian Scholars' Press.

Jardine, D. W. (1987). Reflection and self-understanding in Piagetian theory: A phenomenological critique. *Journal of Educational Thought, 21*(1), 10–19.

Jardine, D. W. (1988). Piaget's clay and Descartes wax. *Educational Theory, 38*(3), 287–298.

Jardine, D. W. (1992). Reflections on education, hermeneutics, and ambiguity: Hermeneutics as a restoring of life to its original difficulty. In W. Pinar & W. Reynolds (Eds.), *Understanding curriculum as phenomenological and deconstructed text* (pp. 116–127). New York: Teachers College Press.

Jardine, D. W. (1994). *Speaking with a boneless tongue*. Bragg Creek, Canada: Mákyó Press.

Jardine, D. W. (1995). On the integrity of things: Ecopedagogical reflections on the integrated curriculum. In G. Vars (Ed.), *Current conceptions of core curriculum: Alternative designs for integrative programs* (pp. 33–38). Kent, OH: National Association for Core Curriculum.

Jardine, D. W. (1997a). "To dwell with a boundless heart:" On the integrated curriculum and the recovery of the Earth. In D. Flinders & S. Thorton (Eds.), *The curriculum studies reader* (pp. 213–223). New York: Routledge.

Jardine, D. W. (1997b). A silence that is not being silenced (A critical review of *The Stories we are: An essay in self-creation*). *Interchange, 28*(4), 389–393.

Jardine, D. W. (1998). *To dwell with a boundless heart: Essays in curriculum theory, hermeneutics, and the ecological imagination*. New York: Peter Lang.

Jardine, D. W. (2000). *"Under the tough old stars:" Ecopedagogical essays*. Brandon, VT: Solomon Press/The Foundation for Educational Renewal.

Jardine, D. W., LaGrange, A., & Everest, B. (1998). "In these shoes is the silent call of the earth": Meditations on curricular integration, conceptual violence, and the ecologies of community and place. *Canadian Journal of Education, 23*(2), 121–130.

Kadar, M. (Ed.). (1993). *Reading life writing*. Toronto, Canada: Oxford University Press.

Kelly, U. (1997). *Schooling desire: Literacy, cultural politics and pedagogy*. New York: Routledge.

King, T. (Ed.). (1990). *All my relations: An anthology of contemporary Canadian Native fiction*. Toronto, Canada: McLelland & Stewart.

LaGrange, A., Clifford, P. A., Jardine, D. W., & Friesen, S. (2001). "Back to basics:" Rethinking what is basic to education through an interpretive study of teachers and students in elementary classrooms. *Alberta Journal of Educational Research, 47*(2), 187–190.

Leggo, C. (1999). Twenty-six ways of listening to light. *Journal of Educational Thought, 33*(2), 113–133.

Lewis, M. (1990). Interrupting patriarchy: Politics, resistance, and transformation in the feminist classroom. *Harvard Educational Review, 60*(4), 467–488.

Luce-Kapler, R. (1997). *As if women writing*. Unpublished doctoral dissertation, University of Alberta, Edmonton, Canada.

MacLennan, H. (1945). *Two solitudes*. Toronto, Canada: Collins.

McFarlane, S. (1995). The haunt of race: Canada's Multiculturalism Act, the politics of incorporation, and writing thru race. *Fuse, 18*(3), 18–24.

McLeod, N. (1998, Fall). "Coming home through stories." *International Journal of Canadian Studies Révue Internationale d'Études Canadiennes, 18*, 51–66.

McLuhan, M. (1964). *Understanding media: The extension of man*. New York: McGraw-Hill.

McLuhan, M., & Fiore, Q. (1967). *The medium is the message* (coordinated by J. Bell). New York: Bantam.

McLuhan, M., & Powers, B. (1989). *The global village: Transformations and world life and media in the 21st century*. New York: Oxford University Press.

McNeill, R. (1997, April 4). *Soft relativism and the malaise of modernity* (Malispina College-University Web site). Visited February 8, 2002.

McPherson, D. H., & Rabb, J. D. (1993). *Indian from the inside: A study in ethno-metaphysics* (Occasional Paper No. 14). Lakehead, Canada: Lakehead University, Centre for Northern Studies.

Milburn, G., & Herbert, J. (Eds.). (1973). *National consciousness and the curriculum: The Canadian case*. Toronto, Canada: Ontario Institute for Studies in Education.

Miller, J. L. (2000, April). *Defiant curriculum acts: Feminist auto/biography*. Paper presented at the 1st Internationalization of Curriculum Conference, Louisiana State University, Baton Rouge, LA.

Miller, J. P. (1993). *The holistic teacher*. Toronto, Canada: OISE Press.

Miller, J. P. (1996). *The holistic curriculum*. Toronto, Canada: OISE Press.

Miller, J. P. (2001). *Education and the soul: Toward a spiritual curriculum*. Albany: State University of New York.

Neilsen, L., Cole, A. L., & Knowles, J. G. (Eds.). (2001). *The art of writing inquiry.* Halifax, Canada: Backalong Books.

Norman, R. (2001). *House of mirrors: Performing autobiograph(icall)y in language/education.* New York: Peter Lang.

Oberg, A. A. (1987). Using construct theory as a basis for research into teacher professional development. *Journal of Curriculum Studies, 19*(1), 55–65.

Oberg, A. A. (1990). Methods and meaning in action research: The action research journal. *Theory Into Practice, 29*(3), 214–221.

Oberg, A. A., & Artz, S. (1992). Teaching for reflection: Being reflective. In T. Russell & H. Munby (Eds.), *Teachers and teaching: From classroom to reflection* (pp. 138–155). London: Palmer.

Oberg, A. A., & Underwood, S. (1992). Facilitating teacher development. In A. Hargreaves (Ed.), *Understanding teacher development* (pp. 162–177). New York: Teachers College Press.

Oberg, A. A., & McElroy, L. (1994). "If a body meets a body ...." *Curriculum Inquiry, 24*(2), 229–246.

O'Meara, S., & West, D. A. (Eds.). (1996). *From our eyes: Learning from indigenous peoples.* Toronto, Canada: Garamond.

Penrose, J. (1997). Construction, de(con)struction and reconstruction: The impact of globalization and fragmentation on the Canadian nation state. *International Journal of Canadian Studies/Révue Internationale d'Études Canadiennes, 16*, 15–49.

Pinar, W. F., & Grumet, M. (1976). *Toward a poor curriculum.* Dubuque, IA: Kendall/Hunt.

Pinar, W. F., & Reynolds, W. M. (1992a). Appendix, section one: Genealogical notes on the history of phenomenology in curriculum studies. In W. F. Pinar & W. M. Reynolds (Eds.), *Understanding curriculum as phenomenological and deconstructed text* (pp. 237–244). New York: Teachers College Press.

Pinar, W. F., & Reynolds, W. M. (Eds.). (1992b). *Understanding curriculum as phenomenological and deconstructed text.* New York: Teachers College Press.

Pinar, W. F., Reynolds, W. M., Slattery, P., & Taubman, P. M. (1995). *Understanding curriculum: An introduction to the study of historical and contemporary curriculum discourses.* New York: Peter Lang.

Porter, J. (1965). *Vertical mosaic: An analysis of social class and power in Canada.* Toronto, Canada: University of Toronto Press.

Pratt, D. (1994). Curriculum and human well-being. In D. Pratt (Ed.), *Curriculum planning: A handbook for professionals* (pp. 1–34). Toronto, Canada: Harcourt Brace.

Rasberry, G. (2001). *Writing research/Researching writing: Through a poet's I.* New York: Peter Lang.

Regnier, R. (1995). Bridging Western and First Nations thought: Balanced education in Whitehead's philosophy of the organism and the sacred circle. *Interchange, 26*(4), 383–415.

Richardson, G. (1997). The love that dare not speak its name: Nationalism and identity in the Alberta social studies curriculum. *Canadian Social Studies, 31*(3), 138–141.

Richardson, G. (1999). *The death of the good Canadian: Teachers, national identities, and the social studies curriculum.* Unpublished doctoral dissertation, University of Alberta, Edmonton, Canada.

Richardson, G. (2001). *A modernist curriculum for postmodern times: The Western Canadian Protocol for Social Studies and the (re)creation of national identity.* Paper presented at the annual meeting of the Canadian Society for the Study of Education, Laval, Canada.

Ross, R. (1996). *Returning to the teachings: Exploring aboriginal justice.* Toronto, Canada: Penguin.

Ruskzto, K. (1997). National encounters: Narrating Canada and the plurality of difference. *International Journal of Canadian Studies/Révue Internationale d'Études Canadiennes, 16*, 149–162.

Smith, D. G. (1983). *The meaning of children in the lives of adults: A hermeneutic study.* Unpublished doctoral dissertation, University of Alberta, Edmonton, Canada.

Smith, D. G. (1987). Children and the gods of war. *Elements, 19*(1), 2–4.

Smith, D. G. (1988). Experimental eidetics as a way of entering curriculum language from the ground up. In W. Pinar (Ed.), *Contemporary curriculum discourses* (pp. 417–436). Scottsdale, AZ: Gorsuch Scarisbrick.

Smith, D. G. (1991). Hermeneutic inquiry: The hermeneutic imagination and the pedagogic text. In E. C. Short (Ed.), *Forms of curriculum inquiry* (pp. 187–209). Albany: State University of New York Press.

Smith, D. G. (1998). *Pedagon: Interdisciplinary essays in the human sciences, pedagogy and culture.* New York: Peter Lang.

Smith, D. G. (1999). Economic fundamentalism, globalization, and the public remains of education. *Interchange: A Quarterly Review of Education, 30*(1), 93–117.

Smith, D. G. (2000a). Preface. In D. W. Jardine (Ed.), *Under the tough old stars: Ecopedagogical essays* (pp. xi–xv). Brandon, VT: Solomon Press Book/The Foundation for Educational Renewal.

Smith, D. G. (2000b). The specific challenges of globalization for teaching and vice versa. *Alberta Journal of Educational Research, 46*(1), 7–26.

Smith, S. J. (1998). *Risk and our pedagogical relation to children: On the playground and beyond.* Albany: State University of New York.

Sumara, D. J. (1994). A path laid down by walking: Curriculum development in high school English programs. In M. C. Courtland & T. J. Gambell (Eds.), *Curriculum planning in the language arts, K–12: An holistic perspective* (pp. 123–150). Toronto: Captus.

Sumara, D. J. (1996). *Private readings in public: Schooling the literary imagination.* New York. Peter Lang.

Sumara, D. J., & Davis, B. (1999). Interrupting heteronormativity: Toward a queer curriculum theory. *Curriculum Inquiry, 29*(2), 191–208.

Sumara, D. J., & Luce-Kapler, R. (1993). Action research as a writerly text: Locating co-laboring in collaboration. *Journal of Educational Action Research, 1*, 387–396.

Taylor, C. (1991). *The malaise of modernity.* Concord, Canada: House of Anansi Press.

Taylor, C. (1992). *Multiculturalism and "the politics of recognition."* Cambridge, England: Princeton University Press.

Te Hennepe, S. (1997). Respectful research: That is what my people say, You learn it from the story. In S. de Castell & M. Bryson (Eds.), *Radical In<ter>ventions: Identity, politics, and difference/s in educational praxis* (pp. 153–181). Albany: State University of New York Press.

Tomkins, G. S. (1979). Towards a history of curriculum development in Canada. In *Canadian Society for the Study of Education, 6th yearbook* (pp. 1–13). Vancouver, Canada: Canadian Society for the Study of Education.

Tomkins, G. S. (1981a). Foreign influences on curriculum and curriculum policy making in Canada: Some impressions in historical and contemporary perspective. *Curriculum Inquiry, 11*(2), 157–166.

Tomkins, G. S. (1981b). Stability and change in the Canadian curriculum. In J. D. Wilson (Ed.), *Canadian education in the 1980s* (pp. 135–157). Calgary, Canada: Detselig Enterprises.

Tomkins, G. S. (1986). *A common countenance: Stability and change in the Canadian curriculum.* Scarborough, Canada: Prentice-Hall.

van Manen, M. (1982). Phenomenological pedagogy. *Curriculum Inquiry, 12*(3), 283–299.

van Manen, M. (1984). Practicing phenomenological writing. *Phenomenology + Pedagogy, 2*(1), 36–69.

van Manen, M. (1986). *The tone of teaching.* Richmond Hill, Canada: Scholastic.

van Manen, M. (1989). By the light of the anecdote. *Phenomenology + Pedagogy, 7*, 232–256.

van Manen, M. (1990). *Researching lived experience: Human science for an action sensitive pedagogy.* London, Canada: Althouse Press.

van Manen, M. (1991). *The tact of teaching: The meaning of pedagogical thoughtfulness.* London, Canada: Althouse Press.

van Manen, M. (1999). The practice of practice. In M. Lange, J. Olson, J. Hansen, & W. Blunder (Eds.), *Changing schools/changing practices: Perspectives on educational reform and teacher professionalism.* Luvain, Belgium: Garant.

van Manen, M. (2000). Moral language and pedagogical experience. *Journal of Curriculum Studies, 32*(2). Retrieved February 14, 2002, from the World Wide Web: http://www.ualberta.ca/~iiqm/

van Manen, M. (2002a). Phenomenology online. Retrieved February 14, 2002, from the World Wide Web: http://www.ualberta.ca/~iiqm/

van Manen, M. (Ed.). (2002b). *Writing in the dark: Phenomenological studies in interpretive inquiry.* London, Canada: Althouse Press.

Willinsky, J. (1993). After 1492–1992: A post-colonial supplement for the Canadian curriculum. *Our Schools/Our Selves: A Magazine for Canadian Education Activists, 4*(3), 101–124.

Willinsky, J. (1995). Language, nation, world. In M. L. Chapman & J. Anderson (Eds.), *Thinking globally about language education* (pp. 135–148). Vancouver, Canada: Centre for Study of Curriculum and Instruction, University of British Columbia.

Willinsky, J. (1998). *Learning to divide the world: Education at empire's end.* Minneapolis: University of Minnesota Press.

Willinsky, J. (1999). *New technologies of knowing: A proposal for human science research.* Boston: Beacon Press.

Willis, G., & Schubert, W. (Eds.). (1991). *Reflections from the heart of educational inquiry: Understanding curriculum and teaching through the arts.* Albany: State University of New York.

CHAPTER 13

Curriculum Studies in China: Retrospect and Prospect

Hua Zhang
Qiquan Zhong
East China Normal University

The issue of curriculum occupies a central position in an educational system. The most basic and broad project in educational reform in contemporary China is curriculum reform, which calls for serious curriculum research. The process of curriculum research is a process of seeking curriculum wisdom embodied in the true, the good, and the beautiful and of understanding curriculum history, reality, and process. To be in quest of curriculum wisdom and curriculum theory is our vocation as Chinese curriculum scholars. Therefore, this chapter intends to make a historical reflection of ancient curriculum wisdom, depict a comprehensive picture of the development of curriculum studies in the 20th century, and look ahead to the prospect of curriculum theory in contemporary China.

THREE KINDS OF CURRICULUM WISDOM IN CHINA

Curriculum wisdom is an in-the-world being, so it has local character. In this era of globalization, it is particularly important to understand locality of curriculum wisdom (Smith, 1997, 2000). The idea of place is important in the seeking of curriculum wisdom. Curriculum wisdom is also a historical being. The history of curriculum discourse dwells in the reality of curriculum. The concept of historicity also becomes important.

Chinese cultural traditions are nurtured and shaped by three main philosophies: Confucianism, Taoism, and Buddhism. Correspondingly, there are three main traditions of curriculum wisdom in China: Confucianism, Taoism, and Buddhism. When we explore these three kinds of curriculum wisdom, we are not limited to what ancient philosophers have said about education. We intend to understand what curriculum meanings and curriculum questions can be derived from the discourses of ancient philosophers. In other words, we base our study on hermeneutics, not on positivism.

Confucian Curriculum Wisdom

The Chinese term for curriculum is *ke-cheng*. The term curriculum (*ke-cheng*) first appeared in Confucian classics in the Tang Dynasty.[1] There are two syllables in the word *ke-cheng*. Before the Tang Dynasty, these two syllables *ke* and *cheng* appeared independently. According to the most authoritative book of Chinese etymology, *Xu Shen's Exploring Etymology of Chinese Words* (in the Eastern Han Dynasty), *ke* means "function" and *cheng* means "many persons gathering in one room and sharing." Both the original meaning of *ke* and the original meaning of *cheng* are different from today's meaning of curriculum.

The first man who created the word *ke-cheng* (curriculum) was named Kong Yingda. He is one of the most famous Confucian philosophers in the Tang Dynasty. His representative book is called *Understanding the Five Confucian Classics*. The main content of this book is to explain some of the most important Confucian classics: *Book of Songs, Book of Changes, Book of History, Book of Rites,* and *Spring and Autumn Annals.* In this book, when he explained one sentence from the *Book of Songs*[2] he created the word *ke-cheng* (curriculum). In *Book of Songs,* it says:

Magnificent indeed is the temple,
Which has been constructed by the moral person.

Kong Yingda explained this sentence as what follows:

It is the moral person
Who plans, supervises, and upholds the curriculum (*ke-cheng*).
That is legitimate.

In ancient China, *temple* did not only mean a kind of architecture, but also symbolized "great cause," "great contribution." So curriculum (*ke-cheng*) originally pointed to temple, signifying "great cause," "great contribution." In the Tang Dynasty, curriculum was not limited to school curriculum; it included all the great undertakings in the society (H. Zhang, 2000c, p. 66).

Zhu Xi, one of the greatest Confucian philosophers in the Song Dynasty,[3] frequently used the word *ke-cheng* (curriculum). In *Complete Works of Zhu Xi On Learning*, he said, "You should provide plenty of time for students, and make good use of the time to teach curriculum." He also said, "You should develop curriculum not in many books, but put a lot of work on what's chosen for learning." Zhu Xi's conception of curriculum is limited to school curriculum. Certainly, school curriculum is a "great cause" (H. Zhang, 2000c, p. 66).

How can we understand the temple metaphor in the Confucian conception of curriculum? What is the meaning of "great cause"? To solve these questions, we must turn to Confucian metaphysics. What is the intrinsic feature of Confucian metaphysics? Confucian metaphysics is moral metaphysics. In other words, Confucian metaphysics is based on morals. If we have to use one word to summarize the basic principle of Confu-

---

[1]The Tang Dynasty ranged from 648 to 907.

[2]*Book of Song* is a general collection of the most ancient Chinese poetic works. This book consists of 305 pieces. All the poetic works included in the book were produced over 500 years ranging from early years of the Western Zhou Dynasty (the 11th century BC) to the middle part of the Spring and Autumn Period (the 7th century BC).

[3]The Song Dynasty ranged from 960 to 1279.

cian metaphysics, we can say: Cosmic order is moral order. Because Confucianism holds moral metaphysics, Confucian philosophy can be said as a philosophy of the subject. However, this subject integrates and internalizes the heaven (*tian*). So it is the Eastern subject, Chinese subject, not the Western subject. The most important theme of Eastern culture is the unity between the subject and the heaven. That is the most crucial difference between Eastern culture and Western culture (Mu, 1997).

The nature of the subject is "benevolence" (*ren*). Benevolence is the core idea of Confucius and the core idea of the most important Confucian classic, *The Analects.* According to *Xu Shen's Exploring Etymology of Chinese Words,* the original meaning of *benevolence (ren)* is intimacy. This intimacy is not limited to family relatives; it is extended to the society. Confucius said, "Benevolence is to love all men." Benevolence is not limited to human society, either. It is extended to all beings. Xunzi said, "Benevolence should be extended to loving all things." Through benevolence and caring, the world goes into a new state of the "unity between heaven and man."

How does Confucianism think about being (ontology)? Being is the "unity between heaven and man." The first chapter of *The Doctrine of the Mean* wrote:

> What is endowed by heaven is called the nature; to follow that nature is called the way; to cultivate the way is called education.

> One cannot depart from his way for a moment, what can be departed is not the way. A moral man is always discreet and vigilant when he is beyond others' sight, apprehensive and cautious when beyond others' hearing. One should never misbehave even when he is in privacy, nor should he reveal evil intentions even in trivial matters. So a moral man remains circumspect especially when he is alone.

Confucians paid great attention to "remaining circumspect especially when one is alone " That means the process of going into the unity between heaven and man is a process of conscious moral practice.

How does Confucianism think about the question of becoming (cosmology)? *The Doctrine of the Mean* wrote:

> The way of the universe can be completely described in a single sentence: as it is constant to taking honesty as the only proper course, its way of bringing up all things is extremely subtle because it creates one thing as the only thing, and it creates things unpredictably.

What an insightful description of the way of creation! The world is an organism, not a clock Every thing is the only thing. All things are co-emergent. This is the cosmology of Confucianism.

What curriculum horizons does Confucianism open up for us? First, Confucian curriculum philosophy is based on moral metaphysics. The unity between heaven and man is the basic platform of values to understand curriculum. The ideal of unity between heaven and man is the highest level that curriculum should attain. To cultivate moral persons is the direct purpose of curriculum. Is this ideal mysterious or unreachable? No, it is not. According to Confucianism, the state of unity between heaven and man is permeated throughout ordinary life. Confucius said, "Is benevolence indeed so far away? If we really wanted benevolence, we should find that it was at our very side" (Shu Er, *The Analects*). When we cultivate our benevolent behaviors from now on and from ourselves, we are starting the journey to this ideal state.

Second, curriculum is a sociopolitical text. Confucianism emphasizes the idea of the mean or harmony (*zhong-he*), so it has founded a sociology of mean–harmony. Confucius said, "How transcendent is the moral power of the mean! That it is but rarely found among the common people is a fact long admitted" (Yong Ye, *The Analects*). *The Doctrine of the Mean* expanded Confucius' thought:

> Feelings like joy, anger, sorrow and happiness are in the state of the mean when they are kept in heart; they are in the state of harmony when expressed in conformity with moral standards. The mean is the fundament of everything under heaven, and harmony the universal law. With the mean-harmony, the heaven and the earth move orderly, and everything thereon grows and flourishes.

So Confucian sociology of curriculum is based on the sociology of mean–harmony. This curriculum focuses on balance, harmony, interaction, and communication. This is quite different from various conflicting sociologies of curriculum in the Western world (Pinar et al., 1995).

Finally, according to Confucianism, curriculum is a moral event, so curriculum research is a values-laden process. Every aspect of curriculum process and curriculum research is soaked by values and moral elements. So the efforts to find universal and value-free laws and models of curriculum development are naive and impossible considering what this ancient wisdom can teach us.

Generally speaking, Confucian curriculum wisdom is a curriculum discourse based on moral metaphysics. To build a harmonious society and eventually reach the state of unity between heaven and man is the basic and ultimate aims of curriculum research and curriculum process. Is not this the meaning of the *great cause* and what the temple metaphor implies?

Confucian curriculum wisdom is one of the main growing interests in Chinese contemporary curriculum theories. A few Chinese curriculum scholars have begun to explore the contemporary meaning of Confucian curriculum wisdom (e.g., H. Wang, 1999; H. Zhang, 1996, 2000a).

TAOIST CURRICULUM WISDOM

To understand the essence of Taoist curriculum wisdom, we need to first understand Taoist metaphysics. What is the intrinsic feature of Taoist metaphysics? In one word, Taoist metaphysics is the metaphysics of Nature. *The Book of Laozi* (chap. 25) wrote:

> Man follows the way of Earth,
> Earth follows the way of Heaven,
> Heaven follows the way of Tao,
> Tao follows the way of Nature.

If man does not go against the way of Earth, he will be safe. If Earth does not go against the way of Heaven, it will be complete. If heaven does not go against the way of Tao, it will be in order. To follow the way of Nature is the intrinsic character of Tao. So, in Taoist view, Nature is the *noumenon* of the cosmos. What is the meaning of Nature? Nature is a transcendent spiritual state of freedom, independence, and autonomy. Tao is not only the core feature of Nature, but it also is the realization of Nature. The first chapter of *The Book of Laozi* wrote:

> The Tao that can be spoken of is not the eternal Tao;
> The name that can be named is not the eternal name.

The nameless (*wu- ming*) is the origin of Heaven and Earth;
The named (*you- ming*) is the root of all things.

Therefore, the subtleties of Tao are always apprehended through their forms:

The limits of things are always seen through their form.
These two (*wu* and *you*) have the same source but different names.
Both of them can be called profoundness (*xuan*),
The most profound, the door of all mysteries.

This chapter revealed the meaning and character of Tao. As the realization of Nature, Tao (the Way) is dynamic and moving. It is the origin and mother ground of all things. Tao has double character: *wu* (no-thing) and *you* (being). When all the artificial things are excluded, a pure, vacant, and quiet spiritual state manifests itself. This state is called *wu* (no-thing). *Wu* is the basis for the changes of all things. *Wu*, as an infinite and universal state, has an orientational tendency to point to a certain being. So *wu* generates *you* (being). *You* is the concrete content of *wu*. Laozi said, "All things under Heaven come into being from *you*, and *you* comes into being from *wu*" (chap. 40). *Wu* is one, *you* is many. There is a dialectical thinking in Taoism. *Wu* is the *wu* of *you*. *You* is the *you* of *wu*. The dialectical unity of *wu* and *you* is called *xuan* (profoundness). *Xuan* (profoundness) is the realization of Tao. The profoundness is the door of all mysteries.

So according to Taoism, Nature is the unity of Tao, Heaven, Earth, and Man. Taoism also worships the state of unity between heaven and man.

How does Taoism think about becoming? In the Taoist view, the nature of every thing is good. The nature of every thing should be kept well and actualized. So Taoism advocates the principle of actualization. For Taoism, it is not so much to say creating a thing as to say returning a thing itself. Laozi said (*The Book of Laozi*, chap. 16):

Try the utmost to make the heart vacant,
Be sure to hold fast to quietude.
All things are growing and developing,
And I see thereby their cycles.
Though all things flourish with a myriad of variations,
Each one will eventually return to its root.
This return to its root means "tranquility,"
It is called "returning to its destiny."
"To return to its destiny" is called "the eternal,"
To know "the eternal" is called "enlightenment."
Not to know "the eternal" and to act blindly (will necessarily) result in disaster.

Returning to the root of a thing and returning to its destiny is the process of actualization for a thing. This is the essence of growth and development.

How can we interact with things? The main points are *wu-wei* (doing nothing), *jing-guan* (tranquil observation), and *xuan-lan* (profound insight). *Wu-wei* means not to act blindly, but to realize Nature, to attain the state of Nature. *Wu-wei* is not inaction, but to act with Taoist wisdom. Laozi said, "Tao invariably does nothing, and yet there is nothing left undone" (*The Book of Laozi*, chap. 37). "Doing nothing and nothing left undone" concentratedly embodied Taoist practical wisdom. *Jing-guan* (tranquil observation) and *xuan-lan* (profound insight) are the methods of understanding things. To understand things is to be integrated with things. To attain this ideal state, we should "make the heart vacant," "hold fast to quietude," "keep the unity of the soul and body," and "achieve gentleness like an infant," as Laozi wrote (*The Book of Laozi*, chap. 10):

Can you keep the unity of the soul and the body without separating them?

Can you concentrate the vital energy, keep the breath and achieve gentleness like an infant without any desires?

Can you cleanse and purify your profound insight without any flecks?

Because both Confucianism and Taoism worship the state of unity between heaven and man, what are their differences? First, Confucian unity between heaven and man is the inevitable outcome of moral metaphysics. Confucianism bases the unity between heaven and man on morals. It focuses on harmony of human relations. Taoist unity between heaven and man is the necessity of metaphysics of Nature. Taoism bases the unity between heaven and man on nature. It focuses on the state of Nature. Second, Confucianism emphasizes positive benevolent action as the way to realize the unity between heaven and man. In contrast, Taoism proposes that the state of *wu-wei* is the essential way to achieve the unity between heaven and man. The state of unity between heaven and man is not an artificial product, but an internal quest and inevitable outcome of Nature and Tao.

What curriculum horizons does Taoism create for us? First, if we understand curriculum as a Taoist text, we should borrow Taoist metaphysics of Nature to reflect on today's curriculum field. Do not more and more miscellaneous school materials go against Nature? Are not richer and richer curriculum discourses artificial? According to Taoist curriculum theory, all the school materials and curriculum discourses need to be thoroughly deconstructed.

Second, what Taoist curriculum wisdom provides for us is the teleological meaning of the nature in curriculum development and curriculum theory. The educated man, according to Taoist curriculum wisdom, is authentic man (natural man). From John Dewey (1897, 1899, 1902) to Ralph Tyler (1949) to today, the paradigm of curriculum development based on anthropocentrism has been built. This paradigm establishes the nature as the object conquered, dominated, and utilized by human beings. The anthropocentric character of curriculum development is one of the main reasons leading to curriculum alienation. Taoist curriculum wisdom based on the teleology of the nature can open up a new vision for curriculum development and curriculum theory.

Finally, can we introduce the methods of *jing-guan* (tranquil observation) and *xuan-lan* (profound insight) to the methodology of curriculum research to transcend the positivist character and technical orientation in present curriculum research? We think Taoist methodology and the Western qualitative methodology (e.g., phenomenological methodology) both point out new directions for curriculum research.

BUDDHIST CURRICULUM WISDOM

In all the traditions of Chinese wisdom, Buddhism is the most complicated and abstruse one. If Western philosophy has been struggling with the wisdom of being, self-identity, Buddhist philosophy, on the contrary, has been struggling with the wisdom of nonbeing. That is the intrinsic feature of Buddhist philosophy (Mu, 1997, 1998). So the general principle of Buddhist philosophy is causal occasioning (*yuan-qi*) and nature emptiness (*xing-kong*). *Causal occasioning* means that all beings come into existence dependent on conditions. *Nature emptiness* means that all beings do not have eternal nature and they keep changing. All beings are causal occasioning because of nature emptiness. The nature of all beings is empty (*kong*) because of causal occasioning. In the Buddhist view, all things that Western philosophy has been pursuing (essence, being, self-identity, personality, independence, freedom, God, etc.) and the pursuit itself are attachments that are necessary to be emptied. When the Sixth Patriarch Huineng died, he told his disciples, "You should behave as if I were alive: sit decorously together, neither rush about nor refrain from movement, think neither of life nor of annihilation, neither of coming nor going, neither of right nor wrong, neither of abiding nor departing. Just be still. That is the supreme Way" (*Platform Sutra*). So when all the attachments and blind will are thoroughly emptied, the supreme Way will manifest itself.

What does Buddhism think about becoming? Because all beings are causal happening as such, all beings immediately emerge and immediately disappear. That means all beings change and transform forever. The time when a thing emerges is the time when the thing disappears. The body, thinking, feeling, and behavior of human being are not eternal. So the world is always changeable, like floating clouds and flowing water. What can we do in this changeable world? The only choice is to know our own mind, discover our nature, and attain the moment of enlightenment in seeing Buddha. Huineng said (*Platform Sutra*):

> Without enlightenment, a Buddha is just like any other man; but in a moment of enlightenment, any man can become a Buddha. This means that the Way of Buddha is in one's own mind. So why do we not discover our own nature of suchness in the instant of revelation in our minds?

The nature of suchness means to treat the world as such. Embrace the world and let it go. *The nature of suchness* means the pure and tranquil mind, the nonego self. In the moment of enlightenment, you see Buddha, all things in the world come from the same source, and they return to the One.

What curriculum horizons can Buddhism expand? First, Buddhist curriculum wisdom can help us purify today's curriculum field. There are so many external wills controlling the curriculum field, among them political interests, economic interests, cultural hegemony, and so on. On the one hand, "everything for children's interests!" is called on. On the other hand, children's rights are sold by imposing adult's own benefits and wills. In the process of curriculum reform, more often than not, adult's obsession with national interests, technological advancements, and scientific superiority is projected onto our young children, forcing them to carry an unbearably heavy *schoolbag*. What would it be like if both attachments to the selves of human beings and attachments to the selves of things were emptied in the curriculum field?

Second, in the view of Buddhist curriculum wisdom, the educated man is the enlightened man. The enlightened man is not a knowledge cabinet, but a man of spirituality. Wonder, awe, reverence, imagination, transcendence, quietude, empathy, and caring are essential elements of spirituality. Can we find them in our curriculum? Our curriculum is so disenchanted. Both curriculum theory and curriculum practice need to be reenchanted if we do not want to produce one-dimensional persons and dull souls.

Finally, Buddhist pedagogy is quite instructive and enlightening. It is a real pedagogy of wisdom. For example, "to teach through the mind not through the written word," "Zen meditation," "to know your own mind and to discover your own nature," and "to work things out for yourself" all touch the core of pedagogical wisdom and make today's technology-oriented instructional methods look simple, dull, and poor.

In the Western curriculum field, there are some wonderful studies on Buddhism. For instance, Smith's (1996, 1999) exploration on the question of identity in the conduct of pedagogical action and Hwu's (1998) study on the comparison of Zen/Taoism and poststructuralism (1998) are fascinating. We believe Smith's study is a milestone in the East/West dialogue of curriculum field.

RELATIONSHIPS AMONG THE THREE KINDS
OF CURRICULUM WISDOM

A spiritual state of unity between heaven and man is the common theme of Confucian, Taoist, and Buddhist curriculum wisdom. What is the educated man? Confucianism understands the educated man as a moral man. Taoism understands the educated man as a natural man. Buddhism understands the educated man as an enlightened man. In other words, Confucianism, Taoism, and Buddhism realized their ideal of spiritual state of unity between heaven and man from the angle of society, nature, and self, respectively. But confirming relatedness and co-origination as the essence of the world is the common intrinsic character of the three theories of wisdom.

If we want to utilize and learn from Chinese ancient curriculum wisdom to inform contemporary curriculum theory and practice, it is necessary to transform our traditions and ask questions relevant to our own times:

> How can we get rid of the ancient instrumental rationality (the logic of control) and other out-of-date aspects from Confucian, Taoist, and Buddhist curriculum wisdom and imbue traditions with present curriculum spirit?
>
> How can we create possibilities of dialogue between Chinese curriculum wisdom and Western curriculum theories and form a dynamic relationship between the two?
>
> How can we create possibilities of dialogue among Confucian, Taoist, and Buddhist curriculum wisdom to provide fertile soil for its further growth into Chinese contemporary curriculum philosophy and curriculum sociology?
>
> How can we create possibilities of dialogue between the ancient curriculum wisdom and today's curriculum practice to provide insights to transform curriculum practice?

FOUR STAGES OF CONTEMPORARY CHINESE
CURRICULUM STUDIES

During the 20th century, with the tortuous journey of social changes and educational development in China, Chinese curriculum studies experienced the following stages: learning from the United States, learning from the Soviet Union, reemergence of curriculum field, and seeking for the independence of Chinese curriculum studies.

Stage I: Learning from America, Making Curriculum Field
Relatively Independent (1900–1949)

During the first half of the 20th century, the main social and historical mission of Chinese people was to "save the nation from extinction." A group of persons with breadth of vision looked on education as a main way to do this. This function of education was embodied in the national spirit reconstruction. The core of spiritual reconstruction was "democracy" and "science." The concrete strategies of reconstruction consisted of two aspects: one, plunging into rural areas and organizing educational activities in accordance with the semicolonial, semifeudal Chinese social reality; the other, drawing fully on the experience of Western educational ideas and institutions of which the United States was a representative and transplanting American educational culture into China.

In the early 20th century in America, with the rapid growth of educator training programs during the "progressive period," and the increasingly rise of curriculum-making literature, "curriculum studies" gradually developed into a professional research field of education sciences. The famous American curricularist Franklin Bobbitt's book, *The Curriculum,* published in 1918, was generally considered the symbol of independence of the curriculum field. Nearly at the same time, Chinese scholars undertook curriculum research effectively to meet the need of curriculum reform in China. Such studies included the following four aspects.

Translating American Curriculum Literature into Chinese.   To lay a primary foundation for curriculum research in China, scholars studying in America pioneered to translate famous works of American curriculum theory. During this period, there were several well-known works translated into Chinese: Bobbitt's *The Curriculum* was translated by Zhang Shizhu and published by Commercial Press in 1928. It was part of the series of translation works called *Modern Famous Works of Education,* and it was widely circulated after its publication. Another Bobbitt book, *How to Make a Curriculum,* first published in America in 1924, was translated by Xiong Zirong and published by Commercial Press in 1943. F. G. Bonster's book, *The Elementary School Curriculum,* was translated by Zheng Zonghai and Shen Zishan and published by Commercial Press in 1925. It was probably the first American works on curriculum theory published in China. These translation works widened the horizon of Chinese education and Chinese curriculum research.

Research on the General Principles of Curriculum Development.   The earliest Chinese curriculum scholars not only fully attempted to learn from curriculum studies in America, but they also paid attention to explore the general principles of curriculum development under the context of Chinese curriculum reform at the very beginning. As early as in 1923, Chinese scholar Cheng Xiangfan's book, *The General Principles of Elementary School Curriculum,* published by Commercial Press, although named *Elementary School Curriculum,* in fact contributed greatly to the study on the general principles of curriculum development (Cheng, 1923). It was published only 5 years after Bobbitt's (1918) *The Curriculum.* Thereafter K. Wang's (1928) book, *The Principles and Methods of Curriculum Making,* systematically explored the general principles, rules, and methods of curriculum making. Z. Zhu (1931) compiled and wrote the book *Elementary School Curriculum Study,* which systematically elaborated on conceptions, principles, and strategies of curriculum making. On the basis of this book, Zhu published another book with the same title in the same press in 1933, then compiled and wrote another book with the same title in 1948, therefore contributing much to the field of curriculum studies in China. Z. Xiong's (1934) work, *The Principles of Curriculum Making,* systematically expounded the function of curriculum, the research fields of modern curriculum, the principles of modern curriculum making, and school curriculum-making strategies at different levels. It was one of the most systematic works on curriculum studies compiled and written by Chinese curriculum scholars in the first half of 20th century (Z. Xiong, 1934).

Further Research on Specific Fields of Curriculum Studies.   Early curriculum research in China not only dealt with the general principles of curriculum development, but connected the study of general curriculum development principles organically with the study of particular principles of specific fields. During this period, Chinese curriculum scholars studied in depth the questions of elementary school curriculum development in connection with practice, and published a great number of research achievements. The study of elementary school teaching materials grasped some curriculum scholars' attention (Sun, 1932; Z. Wu, 1934; W. Wu & Wu, 1933; Y. Yu, 1934; Zhu, 1932). Some studies further specifically explored the curriculum development questions of low-grades in elementary schools, such as Li's (1934) book, *Low-Grades Comprehensive Curriculum Theory In Elementary School.*

Research on Curriculum History.   Chinese curriculum research emphasized the study of curriculum history and connected the exploration of curriculum development principles organically with the study of curriculum history from the beginning. As early as 1929, Xu's work, *The Evolvement and Reform History of Chinese School Curriculum,* systematically explored the Chinese curriculum history and tried to understand the long and well-established Chinese curriculum traditions. Sheng (1934) compiled and wrote the work *The Evolvement and Reform of Elementary School Curriculum,* which explored the evolving history of elementary school curricula. Chen (1944), the famous curriculum specialist, published his work, *The Evolvement History of Modern Chinese Elementary School Curriculum.* These works laid a foundation for Chinese curriculum history studies.

The early studies of Chinese curriculum theory not only emphasized theoretical construction, but also responded to the practical needs. It not only respected Chinese traditions, but also made use of American curriculum theoretical achievements. It not only explored the general principles of curriculum development, but also specifically studied the particular rules of specific curriculum fields. As a response to the need of educational reform, curriculum research was fully developed to expand educational theory. Curriculum research in China accomplished substantial achievements and became a conspicuous, relatively independent research field during this period. It might not be exaggerated to say that curriculum research in China was leading the world during the first half of the 20th century, at least not too much behind the advanced level in the world. Unfortunately, this tradition did not continue, and curriculum research in China almost became extinct in the second half of the 20th century.

Stage II: Imitating the Soviet Union, the Curriculum Field Is Replaced by the Field of Instruction (1949–1978)

A new period of constructing socialism started after the People's Republic of China was founded. At the early time of founding the state, China modeled itself after the former Soviet Union and built up a highly centralized socialist system. Although the great divergence in ideology occurred later between China and the former Soviet Union, a highly centralized socialist system remained intact in China. Socialistically planned economy is the mode of production in this social system, which had lasted for almost 30 years in China. Under this system, education was regarded simply as social superstructure, so it had no independence and could function only as the mouthpiece of economics, the loudspeaker of politics, and the defender of culture. In a planned economy system, central authorities determined curriculum—the core of education—and curriculum implementers could not deal with curriculum development issues directly. Curriculum administration was also centralized. The central authorities managed curriculum by bureaucracy through unified teaching plan, and syllabus, textbook, and the principals and teachers in elementary and secondary schools had no power to make curriculum decisions.

During this period, education and curriculum research also followed the Soviet Union model. The basic theoretical framework of the mainstream pedagogy in Soviet Union was composed of four sections: foundation, instruction, moral education, and management. In this framework, curriculum was treated as teaching content within instructional section. Because curriculum was made by central government, it was unnecessary for others to explore its value orientations and principles of design. What was needed was to rationally interpret the curriculum documents, such as teaching plans, syllabus, textbooks, and so on. Thus, curriculum studies turned into a state of vacuum. Curriculum as teaching content was separated from instruction: Curriculum was aims and orientations, whereas instruction was processes and means.

This period from 1949 to 1978 was an important time for curriculum studies to blossom in the Western world. In the year when the People's Republic of China was founded, one of the most famous American curricularists, Ralph Tyler, praised as "the father of modern curriculum theory," published *The Basic Principles of Curriculum and Instruction*. The book was called "the Bible" of curriculum development and marked that curriculum development had reached a new stage. But the achievement of curriculum studies in Western countries had been excluded from coming into China for almost 30 years because of the prejudice in ideology and the policy of cutting off our country from the Western world. The tradition of Chinese curriculum research in the first half of the 20th century was discarded too. The Chinese curriculum research declined and fell greatly behind the Western world.

Stage III: The Resurgence of the Chinese Curriculum Field (1978–1989)

After the Third Conference of the 11th National Congress of the Chinese Communist Party, China began the new period of all-round societal recovery and development of which economical construction is the core, reform and opening to the outside world is the theme. This provided new opportunities and challenges for education. In 1985, the Central Committee of the Communist Party of China declared *Decision About Educational System Reform*. It attempted to remedy the malpractice of the educational system (such as too many regulations and restrictions, inflexible management under permanent control), empower grass-roots educational organizations, and initiate a new system in which principals took responsibility for schools. In 1986, China promulgated Compulsory Education Law. To implement the decree, in 1988, *An Instructional Plan for Full Time Students at Primary Schools and Junior Middle Schools in Compulsory Education* was drawn. In 1986, a significant event happened in the history of Chinese curriculum development. The first authoritative organization for the examination of subject matters was established: National Committee for the Examination of Subject Matters in Elementary and Secondary Schools. The committee enacted the curriculum policy of one guideline, and many textbooks with examination and subject matter development separated. Because localities had the power to make their own decisions to develop curriculum materials, the high tide of curriculum and instructional reform surged in China, starting during the late 1980s.

When curriculum implementers have the power to make their own decisions in curriculum development and curriculum construction, the importance of curriculum theory became obvious. At this stage, the curriculum field started to recover in China, which was mainly manifested as follows.

First, specialized academic curriculum periodicals and academic organizations were established. In 1981, the first organization whose main mission was to do research on curriculum theory and guide the practice of curriculum development—the Study Workshop of Curriculum and Subject Matters at the People's Educational Publishing House—was founded. At the same time, this study workshop established the first academic curriculum journal *Curriculums, Subject Matters, and Instructional Methods*. The journal studied not only the general foundations of curriculum and instruction, but also the specific principles of subject curriculum and instruction. It became an important theory frontline in curriculum studies. In 1983, Chinese Ministry of Education gave the approval for the founding of the Institute of Curriculum and Subject Matter, which was under control of Chinese Ministry of Education and People's Educational

Publishing House. As a result, the original Study Workshop of Curriculum and Subject Matter was upgraded to the Institute of Curriculum and Subject Matter. The study of curriculum and subject matter was strengthened not only in quantity, but also in quality. In addition to specialized curriculum academic organizations, there were specialized scholars engaged in curriculum studies in many educational departments and institutes of educational sciences at universities. The Specialized Committee for Instructional Theory in Chinese Educational Academy undertook the function of curriculum research too. Columns of curriculum theory were set up in many academic educational periodicals to publish research papers.

Second, a number of foreign curriculum works were introduced to China. In 1985, People's Educational Publishing House started to publish the first set of *Curriculum Research Series.* Some curriculum works from England, Japan, America, and the Soviet Union were translated into Chinese. For example, *Theory and Practice of Curriculum Studies* (Lawton et al., 1978) and *Curriculum Theory: Meaning, Development and Use* (Beauchamp, 1961) were among them. These works made their contributions to the recovery of Chinese curriculum field.

Third, some important academic achievements on curriculum were accomplished. During the resurgent period of curriculum studies, many academic works, which have had important influence on Chinese curriculum research, were published (Ban, 1988; Chen, 1981, 1985; Dai, 1981; Shi, 1984; Wang, 1985; Xiong, 1985; Zhong, 1989b). These works analyzed the subject and scope of curriculum research, explored the direction for the development of curriculum theory, discussed the basic questions of curriculum development and reform, and did critical research of current conditions of curriculum studies. They initiated the efforts to establish curriculum theory as one of the independent fields in education sciences, and they laid a preliminary foundation for the further development of Chinese curriculum field.

These shifts in Chinese educational policy provided a basic guarantee for the resurgence of curriculum research. Curriculum reform's call for theoretical considerations was the basic motivation. Under this context, the development of curriculum theory was mainly to respond to the urgent needs of curriculum practice, and the nature of curriculum theory was not taken into account systematically. Although scholars appealed for the independence of curriculum theory from instruction, the professional activities and academic research were not enough to achieve it. At large, the research achievements on curriculum theory were mainly gained in the framework of instructional theory at this stage.

Stage IV: The Reindependence of Curriculum Field and Its Initial Prosperity (1989–2001)

Chinese reform has expanded since 1989. Chinese society has gradually turned its attention to building the socialist market economy. In this context, unprecedented vigor emerged out of education reform. Curriculum reform at elementary and secondary schools has been catching on like fire in Shanghai, Zhejiang Province, and several other regions. All these are the macrocontext under which curriculum theory develops now in China.

It was under certain historical conditions that curriculum theory was substituted by or subject to instructional theory. After more than 10 years development of curriculum reform and accumulation of curriculum research in the late 1970s and throughout the 1980s, the time for curriculum theory to become independent from instructional theory was at hand.

1989 was an important year in the history of Chinese curriculum theory. In March 1989, People's Educational Publishing House published a book *Curriculum Theory*, which was the first systematic work on curriculum theory after the foundation of new China. The book was written by Chen (1989). He had studied curriculum theory extensively with depth for several decades, learning from curriculum theory in the former Soviet Union and the Western countries while maintaining close ties with Chinese curriculum practice. He expounded systemically the intent, subject, and method of curriculum studies, including:

- Histories of school curriculum in China and Western countries.
- Different schools of curriculum theory.
- Factors that influence school curriculum development.
- Position and role of school curriculum in cultivating student as a whole person.
- Relationship among educational aims and natures, roles, types, development, implementation, and assessment of curriculum.
- Directions of curriculum development.

After only 1 month (April 1989), Shanghai Educational Publishing House published Zhong's book *Modern Curriculum Theory* (1989a), which has been the most complete, systematic, and detailed book dealing with the fundamental questions about curriculum theory so far; it can even be called an encyclopedia on curriculum research. In this book, in a style of narrating rather than assessing, Zhong made a clear presentation of the fundamental achievements of curriculum theory and curriculum practice, and of their latest trends in Western countries, dating back to Greco-Roman traditions and extending into the late 1980s. He narrated the history of curriculum theory and the basic schools of curriculum thought. Especially, he explored the fundamentals of curriculum development and new forms of modern curriculum. He also did cross-cultural and comparative studies on curriculum systems and policies.

Both books, Chen Xia's *Curriculum Theory* and Zhong Qiquan's *Modern Curriculum Theory*, share the same name of curriculum theory, but have different styles. The former explored the principles of curriculum development in terms of the particular features of Chinese educational practice, whereas the latter investigated the principles of curriculum development without the boundaries between countries. The former has the features of theoretical thinking and reasoning, whereas the latter was inclined to illustrate the principles based on substantial evidences. The former was published in Beijing, whereas the latter was published in Shanghai. Both books replenished each other and constructed the cornerstone of the development of Chinese curriculum theory. It can be said that these two books, published separately in March and April 1989, symbolized the independence of Chinese curriculum theory from instruction and, in fact, became parallel to instructional theory.

Since then, Chinese curriculum theory sprang up like mushrooms. Many academic achievements have been made. First, there is research on general principles of curriculum development, whose representatives include Liao (1991), Jin (1995), Shi (1996), Zhong and Li (2000), and Zhang (2000b, 2000c). These researches constructed a platform for the conversation between curriculum theory and practice.

Second, research on specific fields of curriculum theory has been conducted. Representative works include Zhong (1993), Zhang (2000a), Cui (2000), Jin (1996), and Huang (1996). These works deepened the study of Chinese curriculum field.

Third, research on Chinese curriculum history was done. The representative academic achievements include two books: Lu's (1994) *The Modern History of Chinese Curriculum* and C. Xiong's (1996) *Research on the School Subject Matter in Ancient China*. These achievements laid a primary basis for future studies.

Fourth, there was research on subject curriculum. The representative academic achievements include Zhang (1996), Zheng and Yu (1996), and He and Bi (1996). The study of subject curriculum in China is still at its beginning stage, but has a brilliant future.

Fifth, representative curriculum works in the world have been introduced to China and international curriculum conversation has been launched between China and other countries. Institute of Curriculum and Instruction at East China Normal University is the national center for curriculum research. It is a window of communication between China and many other countries in the curriculum field. It has translated and introduced many contemporary curriculum works in the world (e.g., Doll, 1993; Smith, 2000; van Manen, 1991, 1997; Pinar et al., 1995, 1998; Noddings, 1992). All these have been or are being published in China and have promoted Chinese scholars' enthusiasm regarding curriculum theory. Meanwhile, Chinese curriculum scholars are participating in international conversation concerning curriculum discourses and trying to make their own curriculum theories international (Zhang et al., 2000).

Sixth, curriculum theories have been constructed in Chinese style. Zhong, as one of the founders of Chinese curriculum field, has been establishing a curriculum theory for quality education (Zhong, 1994, 1995, 1997, 1999, 2000, 2001). His theory makes individual development as the core of curriculum and individualized curriculum as an important and necessary part of reforming curriculum structure. Zhang based his curriculum inquiry on Chinese ancient curriculum wisdom and contemporary Western curriculum discourses. He constructed a theory of lived experience curriculum (Zhang, 1997, 1998, 1999, 2000a). Wang did a study on the dialogue among great Chinese Confucians such as Confucius, Zhu Xi, and the great French philosopher Michel Foucault in an attempt to build a theory toward a curriculum for creative transformation of selfhood (H. Wang, 1999). These curriculum theories contributed to a possible transition of Chinese curriculum field toward the paradigm of "understanding curriculum" (Pinar et al., 1995).

Those works mentioned earlier are unprecedented not only in scope, but also in depth in the history of Chinese curriculum theory. Under the contexts of long-term curriculum reform and rigorous pursuit of continuous curriculum research, Chinese Educational Society approved to found the National Committee of Curriculum Theory in March 1997. This is the first national and professional academic organization for curriculum research. It provided the organizational support to make curriculum field go further toward specialization and independence.

FEATURES OF CHINESE CURRICULUM RESEARCH

Looking back on the 100-year development of Chinese curriculum theory, we can reflect on some basic features:

1. *Curriculum research started early in China, but experienced an uneven developmental journey.* At the beginning, Chinese curriculum research followed the example of America where the discipline of curriculum theory was born. At that time, Chinese curriculum research kept close ties with the advanced studies in the world. However, when China followed the model of the former Soviet Union, the research tradition stopped instantly. Thus, Chinese curriculum research fell far behind the Western world. At the end of the 20th century, the lost tradition of Chinese curriculum theory was recovered, which made curriculum field independent from instruction theory. Chinese curriculum research experienced an uneven road, but will have a bright future.

2. *Chinese curriculum research is bound up with ideology.* One of the reasons that the development of Chinese curriculum theory was uneven is that curriculum studies were greatly tied with the mainstream ideology during certain historical periods. In the 1950s and 1960s, curriculum studies were transmuted almost completely into policy annotation and could not be called a *study* at all. Of course curriculum theory cannot develop in a vacuum. It is not surprising that it is influenced by certain ideologies. However, it should keep its own relative independence. Regarding the relationship between the two, curriculum theory is not only influenced by ideology, but it also can mutually influence the development of ideology. Interaction rather than one-way control provides a good basis to form a dynamic relationship between curriculum theory and ideology.

3. *Chinese curriculum theory depends on curriculum practice excessively.* To get a bird's-eye view of the 20th century, we can find that curriculum research in China did not flourish until curriculum reform had an urgent demand for theory. Thus, to a certain degree, curriculum theory followed the needs of curriculum practice. The discipline of curriculum theory has strong practicality. Undoubtedly, there exists an inherent relationship between curriculum theory and practice. However, without the critical ability of reflecting on practice, curriculum theory cannot be called a *theory*. Without a strong theoretical orientation, Chinese curriculum theory cannot participate in reform and practice in a more creative and critical way. Therefore, Chinese curriculum theory needs to be independent of curriculum practice rather than dependent on it in a simple way.

4. *The Chinese curriculum field emphasizes the study of curriculum history.* The whole process of developing Chinese curriculum theory is accompanied by the study of curriculum history. Some great works on curriculum history came out during the 20th century. During the long history of Chinese civilization, curriculum discourses arising in different historical phases interacted with each other and formed vigorous curriculum traditions in terms of curriculum wisdom, which influences today's curriculum theory in both implicit and explicit ways. Curriculum traditions are the root of today's curriculum discourses. Therefore, the study of curriculum history is indispensable in the construction of curriculum theory and the development of curriculum practice. Chinese curriculum researchers understood this point at the beginning and paid close attention to the study of curriculum history, which may make its own contribution to the worldwide field of curriculum theory.

PROSPECTS FOR THE CHINESE CURRICULUM FIELD

After a long journey of exploring Chinese curriculum concepts, curriculum wisdom, and curriculum studies, we can think about where Chinese curriculum studies might go in the future.

First, the study of curriculum development as the dominant paradigm of Chinese curriculum research will last for a long time. China is now carrying on an unprecedented curriculum reform. How to develop curriculum effectively is an urgent call for Chinese scholars. Chinese curriculum field has lost touch with the technology of curriculum development, which needs to be rethought and reutilized. Chinese curriculum reform is confronted with many questions: How to develop curriculum standards? How to develop subject matters? How to define curriculum objectives? How to select curriculum contents? How to organize curriculum contents? How to evaluate curriculum? How to adjust curriculum policy to adapt the need of new curriculum? Hence, the study of curriculum development will dominate the Chinese curriculum field or, at least, co-exist with the efforts of theoretical (such as cultural, social, political, aesthetic, spiritual) explorations of curriculum in the near future.

Second, the paradigm of *understanding curriculum* is the future direction of Chinese curriculum studies. In China, the traditional study of education and instruction that served mainstream ideology has come to an end. In its place, the field of curriculum studies has become a new and vigorous research area. This area has gathered many researchers, and nearly every teachers' university or college has established a department of curriculum and instruction or center for curriculum research. All these expansions and transitions provide a solid basis for possible new theoretical explorations in an increasingly interdependent and changing global society. To elaborate on what it means to know and be educated for the Chinese must be based on reflections of our own traditions and international conversation, nor can it be done without cultural, political, global, and spiritual understanding of curriculum. Understanding curriculum at deeper levels must be accompanied by the difficult task of transcending the direct and concrete daily needs of curriculum practice, so that the critical and creative potential of theory can be released. The Chinese curriculum field will maintain its strong tradition of historical studies, attempt to inform curriculum research by traditional curriculum wisdom, participate and contribute to worldwide curriculum discourses, reflect on the reality of curriculum practice, and, finally, construct its own curriculum theory.

REFERENCES

Ban, H. (1988). Hidden curriculum and the forming of personal morality. *Educational Research, 9*(4), 10–14.

Beauchamp, G. (1961). *Curriculum theory: Meaning, development and use.* Wilmette, IL: The Kagg Press.

Bobbitt, F. (1918). *The curriculum.* New York: Houghton-Mifflin.

Bobbitt, F. (1924). *How to make a curriculum.* Boston: Houghton- Mifflin.

Chen, X. (1944). *The evolvement history of modern Chinese elementary school curriculum.* China: Commercial Press.

Chen, X. (1981). An introduction to curriculum studies. *Curriculum, Subject Matters, and Teaching Methods, 1*(2), 44–50; 1(3), 7–12.

Chen, X. (1985). The dialectics of curriculum reform. *Curriculum, Subject Matters, and Teaching Methods, 5*(5), 12–18.

Chen, X. (1989). *Curriculum theory.* Beijing, China: People's Educational Publishing House.

Cheng, X. (1923). *The general principles of elementary school curriculum.* China: Commercial Press.

Cui, Y. (2000). *School-based curriculum development: Theory into practice.* Beijing, China: Educational Science Press.

Dai, B. (1981). On the importance of research on school curriculum. *Curriculum, Subject Matters, and Teaching Methods, 1*(1), 3–7.

Dewey, J. (1897). My pedagogic creed. *The School Journal, 54*(3), 77–80.

Dewey, J. (1899). *The school and society.* Chicago: University of Chicago Press.

Dewey, J. (1902). *The child and curriculum.* Chicago: University of Chicago Press.

Doll, Jr., W. E. (1993). *A post-modern perspective on curriculum.* New York: Teachers College Press.

He, S., & Bi, H. (1996). *Research on curriculum of chemistry.* Guangxi, China: Guangxi Educational Publishing House.

Huang, F. (1996). *Introduction to ladder-like curriculum.* Guizhou, China: Guizhou Educational Publishing House.

Hwu, W.-S. (1998). Curriculum, transcendence, and Zen/Taoism: Critical ontology of the self. In W. F. Pinar (Ed.), *Curriculum: Toward new identities* (pp. 21–40). New York: Garland.

Jin, Y. (1995). *Modern curriculum theory.* China: Southwest Normal University Press.

Jin, Y. (1996). *Research on hidden curriculum.* Jiangxi, China: Jiangxi Educational Publishing House.

Lawton, D., Gordon, P., & Ing, M. (1978). *Theory and practice of curriculum studies.* London: Routledge.

Li, L. (1934). Low-grades comprehensive curriculum theory. In *Elementary school.* Beijing, China: Press of China.

Liao, Z. (1991). *Curriculum theory.* China: Central China Normal University Press.

Lu, D. (1994). *The modern history of Chinese curriculum*. Beijing, China: People's Educational Publishing House.

Mu, Z. (1997). *Nineteen lectures on Chinese philosophy*. Shanghai, China: Shanghai Classics Press.

Mu, Z. (1998). *Series lectures on the theory of four causes*. Shanghai, China: Shanghai Classics Press.

Noddings, N. (1992). *The challenge to care in schools: An alternative approach to education*. New York: Teachers College Press.

Pinar, W. F., Reynolds, W. M., Slattery, P., & Taubman, P. M. (1995). *Understanding curriculum*. New York: Peter Lang.

Pinar, W. F. (Ed.). (1998). *Curriculum: Toward new identities*. New York: Garland.

Sheng, L. (1934). *The evolvement and reform of elementary school curriculum*. China: Press of China.

Shi, G. (1984). The scope and guiding principles of curriculum research. *Research Information of Shanxi Education Sciences, 1*(2), 31–37.

Shi, L. (1996). *Curriculum theory: Foundations, principles and problems of curriculum*. Beijing, China: Educational Science Press.

Smith, D. (1996). Identity, self and other in the conduct of pedagogical action: An West/East inquiry. *JCT: Journal of Curriculum Theorizing, 12*(3), 6–12.

Smith, D. (1997). The geography of theory and the pedagogy of place. *JCT: Journal of Curriculum Theorizing, 13*(3), 2–4.

Smith, D. (1999). *Pedagon: Interdisciplinary essays in the human sciences, pedagogy and culture*. New York: Peter Lang.

Smith, D. (2000). *Globalization and postmodern pedagogy*. Beijing, China: Educational Science Press.

Sun, Y. (1932). *Study of elementary school teaching materials*. Beijing, China: Peking Culture Society.

Tyler, R. W. (1949). *Basic principles of curriculum and instruction*. Chicago: University of Chicago Press.

van Manen, M. (1991). *The tact of teaching: The meaning of pedagogical thoughtfulness*. Albany: State University of New York Press.

van Manen, M. (1997). *Researching lived experience: Human science for an action sensitive pedagogy*. Ontario: The Alt House Press.

Wang, H. (1999). Toward a curriculum for creative transformation of selfhood: An East/West inquiry. *JCT: Journal of Curriculum Theorizing, 15*(2), 143–155.

Wang, K. (1928). *The principles and methods of curriculum making*. China: Commercial Press.

Wang, W. (1985). *An inquiry on the scope of curriculum research*. Sichuan, China: Sichuan Educational Publishing House.

Wu, Y. Y., & Wu, Z. (1933). *Study of elementary school teaching materials*. China: Commercial Press.

Wu, Z. (1934). *Study of elementary school teaching materials*. Shanghai, China: Enlightening Press of Shanghai.

Xiong, C. (1985). Research on curriculum and subject matters in ancient China. *Curriculum, Subject Matters, and Teaching Methods, 5*(3), 39–42.

Xiong, C. (1996). *Research on the school subject matters in ancient China*. Beijing, China: People's Educational Publishing House.

Xiong, Z. (1934). *The principles of curriculum making*. China: Commercial Press.

Xu, Z. (1929). *The evolvement and reform history of Chinese school curriculum*. Shanghai, China: Shanghai Pacific Bookstore.

Yu, Y. (1934). *Study of elementary school teaching materials*. Nanjing, China: Zhongshan Press of Nanjing.

Yu, Z. (1935). *Study of new elementary school teaching materials*. Shanghai, China: Children Press of Shanghai.

Zhang, H. (1996). On transcendence of Chinese traditional moral education from a comparative view between Eastern and Western cultural traditions. *Journal of Educational Theory and Practice, 16*(2). 53–58

Zhang, H. (1997). An inquiry on the curriculum theory of existential phenomenology. *Journal of Foreign Education Studies, 26*(5), 9–14.

Zhang, H. (1998). An inquiry on critical curriculum theory. *Journal of Foreign Education Studies, 27*(2), 18–23; 27(3), 76–80.

Zhang, H. (1999). A theory of lived experience curriculum. *Journal of Educational Theory and Practice, 19*(10), 26–31; 19(11), 30–33; 19(12), 38–44.

Zhang, H. (2000a). *Research on experience curriculum*. Shanghai, China: Shanghai Educational Publishing House.

Zhang, H. (2000b). *Research on curriculum and instruction*. Shanghai, China: Shanghai Educational Publishing House.

Zhang, H. (2000c). On the integration of curriculum and instruction. *Educational Research, 21*(2).

Zhang, H., Shi, W., & Ma, Q. (2000). *Research on the schools of curriculum theories*. Shandong, China: Shandong Educational Publishing House.

Zhang, Y. (1996). *Research on the curriculum of mathematics*. Guangxi, China: Guangxi Educational Publishing House.

Zheng, J., & Yu, G. (1996). *Research on curriculum of physics*. Guangxi, China: Guangxi Educational Publishing House.

Zhong, Q. (1989a). *Modern curriculum theory*. Shanghai, China: Shanghai Educational Publishing House.

Zhong, Q. (1989b). Several questions on modern curriculum development. *Educational Research, 10*(5), 53–58.

Zhong, Q. (1993). *A perspective on the curriculum reform in foreign countries*. Shanxi, China: Shanxi Educational Publishing House.

Zhong, Q. (1994). Elective system and individual development. *Research on Comparative Education, 14*(3), 19–23.

Zhong, Q. (1995). On the pedagogical model of curriculum design for qualities education. *Educational Research, 16*(2), 30–36.

Zhong, Q. (1997). Individual differences and quality education. *Journal of Education Theory and Practice, 17*(4), 8–12.

Zhong, Q. (1999). Quality education and the reform of curriculum and instruction. *Educational Research, 20*(5), 46–49.

Zhong, Q. (2000). School knowledge and curriculum standards. *Educational Research, 21*(11), 50–54.

Zhong, Q. (2001). Dialogue and texts: Transmission of teaching standards. *Educational Research, 22*(3), 33–39.

Zhong, Q., & Li, Y. (Eds.). (2000). *The basis of curriculum design*. Shandong, China: Shandong Educational Publishing House.

Zhu, Y. (1932). *Study of elementary school teaching materials*. Shanghai, China: World Press of Shanghai.

Zhu, Z. (1931). *Elementary school curriculum study*. China: Commercial Press.

Zhu, Z. (1933). *Elementary school curriculum study*. China: Commercial Press.

Zhu, Z. (1948). *Elementary school curriculum study*. China: Commercial Press.

CHAPTER 14

In Search of a Quality Curriculum in Hong Kong

Edmond Hau-fai Law
Hong Kong Institute of Education

It is a formidable task to contemplate writing a chapter on Hong Kong curriculum research, albeit the task of putting writing the essay into practice. The field of curriculum, as it has been understood and investigated for a decade or so since its appearance in public discourse, has been characterized by its multifaceted nature. Curriculum carries equally valuable meanings to frontline teachers, school heads, curriculum developers, teacher educators, and researchers regardless of their interests and focus, but their uses capture quite different things and functions to different people in the educational community. No stakeholder alone is able to claim its domination in its interpretation, although its interpretation could hardly be refuted due to its power of encompassing almost innumerable activities that are provided and implemented in the school education for the upbringing of children. A definition of the field of curriculum would put its liveliness to a dead end, and for fear of this I would choose to leave it wide open to the readers. Curriculum may mean a series of planned course of study for children in schools or it may mean the total experience of a group of children in schooling. For classroom teachers, it may easily and comfortably mean a teaching subject to them (Marsh, 1997).

This state of confusion in definitions of *curriculum* and its practices seems to have a cultural perspective to it. In Chinese language, curriculum definitions can be translated differently using different characters: *ke mu* (subject curriculum), *xue xiao jing yan* (school curriculum experience), and *jiao xue nei rong* (curriculum content). The most commonly used characters are *ke cheng* (curriculum); their literal translation is "study course or process," which is close to the dictionary definition of *curriculum* (i.e., a course of study). With the nature of the curriculum definitions in mind, for this chapter I choose a classic framework proposed by Tyler with minor adaptations. My choice is a convenient one, not a purely academic one. Yet the chosen frame gives readers some conceptual clarity in understanding a selected collection of research studies organized around Tyler's (1949) four fundamental curriculum questions:

1. What educational purposes should the school seek to attain?

2. What educational experiences can be provided that are likely to attain these purposes?
3. How can these educational experiences be effectively organized?
4. How can we determine whether these purposes are being attained?

The first question asks for a statement of aims and objectives (goals), which is necessarily derived from the culture and values of the social community. The second issue is the choice of curriculum contents and activities that are thought to be valuable in achieving the aims and objectives. The third issue is a pedagogical one that demands curriculum decisions on the sequence and structure of learning experiences. The last question is about the forms of collecting evidence of learning—forms that may serve a selection or formative purpose.

Another consideration about selecting research studies to be reported is that interests of investigating curriculum issues are multidirectional. There are studies focusing on the individual subject curriculum, such as the most common core subjects of the school curriculum in Hong Kong, English and Chinese languages, mathematics, and science that have featured prominently in the only academic journal on curriculum matters, *Curriculum Forum,* from 1991 to 1999, leaving general and nonsubject-based curriculum issues to only around 29 papers in contrast with the 113 subject-based curriculum papers. These 29 papers cover issues such as contemporary curriculum reforms in Hong Kong, curriculum policy guidelines, mastery learning, integration, core curriculum, curriculum implementation, curriculum changes, and other teacher education topics. I deliberately focus on major research projects and studies related to major curriculum reforms in Hong Kong because these projects have been conducted with clear policy implications and thereby asserted influences on the direction of the contemporary curriculum reforms. For international readers of curriculum, I have purposefully inserted sections that outline some salient features of the Hong Kong educational system with which the curriculum decisions have been operating.

FEATURES OF THE EDUCATION SYSTEM IN HONG KONG

The British left Hong Kong with a system of education similar to its own in terms of structure after over 150 years of occupation before she returned Hong Kong's sovereignty to China on July 1, 1997. Children start nursery school or kindergarten at age 2 or 3 and proceed to primary schools at age 6. They enter secondary schools at age 11 and complete 5 years of secondary education at age 16. Two-year sixth form prepare one third of school leavers for university entrance examinations; 18% of this age group is able to cover 14,500 first-year degree places in eight higher institutions funded by public money through University Grants Committee.

I focus on two issues that have influenced curriculum thinking and practice in Hong Kong. First, compared with international practice in terms of resource funding, Hong Kong has been spending only less than 3% of her GDP on education, whereas developed countries are spending an average of 5.1% of their GNP on education. The distribution of resources seems negatively biased toward basic education. The unit cost of a primary pupil is 6% of the expenditure for each university student. It is fair to say that Hong Kong education is underfunded in general terms with a bias strongly against the provisions of basic education. The implications of this policy are twofold. Bisessionalism in primary education, which was a temporary measure to accommodate a large amount of immigrant children from China in 1954, became a common phenomenon, and attempts to convert these half-day schools have received some resistance from teachers. Class size is around 40, and chairs are in rows. Primary schools hardly have decent sport grounds, gymnasiums, or special rooms for arts and crafts.

The second issue relates to the management of the schools in the public sector. Only 10% of the schools are under direct control of the government, with similar terms of service being offered to the teachers and heads as civil servants in government departments. Over 80% of primary schools and 70% of secondary schools have been managed by 60 religious bodies and other charitable organizations (Ho, 1996). Private sectors amount to only 10%, with a substantial proportion of these schools, such as Singapore and Canadian International Schools, organized by international bodies Their curriculums follow their national requirements. One implication of the diversity of the school backgrounds is the impact on the curriculum contents for the students who are required to read bibles and observe religious practices while others may not have these spiritual experiences. The third observation is about the school curriculum. Organization of learning activities for primary and secondary education is largely subject based, with an emphasis toward studies of Chinese and English languages and mathematics, which may dominate two thirds of the total study hours on the timetable. Curriculum differentiation and choice of studies for students are rare among school practices. Whereas 5% of secondary school students study a curriculum with bias toward technical or vocational subjects, the rest of the students study a common core curriculum up to secondary three. For the fourth and fifth years, students may choose among three curriculum streams—science, arts, or business. Preparatory years for university entrance focus on only three to five subjects, and the curriculum experience tends to narrow itself down to a few subjects before the universities. The fourth issue concerns culture.

There is some good reason to believe that British practice of student-centered education has not taken root in the Hong Kong educational community, although the local educational rhetoric is still dominated by language common to student-centered approaches to learning and teaching (Biggs, Wong, & Stimpson, 1994; Wong, 1997). The promotion of focusing our curriculum on student needs and interests started in 1974, with additional resource support for schools that proclaim the practice and adoption of the activity approach (AA). These AA schools enjoy smaller class sizes and appropriate resources. Toward the end of last year, government statistics have shown that 50% of primary schools have opted for AA practice. However, research studies have indicated the choice of AA is manipulated by the pragmatic intentions of the schools, rather than the beliefs in the educational underpinnings of AA on student learning. The methods of teaching are still didactic and expository even in these AA schools: "AA is found to have, to some extent, degenerated into a form of teaching very similar to the traditional one" (The Board of Education, 1997, p. 45).

Discipline prevails and is valued as part of moral training of students. Success is attributed to hard work, rather than students' ability. Efforts compensate stupidity, as the Chinese say. Competition for educational excellence dominates and is still thought essential for personal social mobility as it is the case with the ancient Chinese. Educators and people with good education enjoy a higher social status and are believed appropriate for government positions. Merchants and traders enjoy far less social respect than the well educated. Book knowledge is preferred, rather than the relevance of life experience to students. Regardless of social class and educational backgrounds, most parents share these values and expectations of school education. The Chinese traditional goals of education aim at achievement in five developmental areas: moral, intellectual, physical, social, and aesthetic. These various aspects of development seem to find home in the statement of the overall educational goals in the recent educational reform documents issued by the government:

> To enable every person to attain all-round development in the domains of ethics, intellect, physique, social skills and aesthetics according to his/her own attributes so that he/she is capable of life-long learning, critical and exploratory thinking, innovating and adapting to change; filled with self-confidence and a team spirit; willing to put forward continuing effort for the prosperity, progress, freedom and democracy of their society, and contribute to the future well-being of the nation and the world at large. (Education Commission, 2000, p. 30)

It seems that these East Asian ideas and conceptions of learning, school education, knowledge, and values all go in harmony with the Western practices in Hong Kong (Cheng, 1997; Gardner, 1989).

IN SEARCH OF A QUALITY CURRICULUM
FOR THE 21ST CENTURY

The desire and need to search for a modern curriculum began with the achievement of universal 9-year basic education in 1978, when the elitist and selective curriculum practice was facing the challenges of a mixed ability school population. Homogeneous classrooms in primary schools became diversified with students' needs and interests. To many educators, the traditional curriculum practices seemed unbearable. With able students in secondary schools, the use of English language as the medium of instruction had no obvious problems, but for mixed ability classes, the language issue became acute and affected the quality of learning and teaching in many schools. The 1982 Lewellyn Report, authored by a group of invited international educators, has been well respected. Its observations of the classroom practices have often been quoted to argue a case for curriculum reforms in line with the Western practices.

> The lessons we observed tended to be teacher-centred, with little use of aids beyond chalk and blackboard. In 'non-exam' years, the atmosphere seemed fairly relaxed, but in the examination preparatory forms all was deadly earnest and students were seen taking notes, laboriously completing model answers and learning texts by rote. (Lewellyn Report, 1982, p. 50)

> Since the students are desperate to obtain their qualifications, and as teachers are judged professionally in terms of their students' results, the whole business is understandable. Discovery methods, team teaching and individualized instruction have little appeal to parents, students and teachers in a situation where the ends require more didactic means. Obtaining a credential to ensure a job offer and if possible, upward social mobility (rather than providing an interesting and intellectually broadening curriculum) is the almost universally agreed objective. Teacher-dominated instruction of passive student audiences seems, with rare exception ..., to be the accepted way. (Lewellyn Report, 1982, p. 51)

Some scholars used the "3 Ts" to characterize the curriculum practice that has been shaped and dominated by teachers, textbooks, and tests (Adamson & Morris, 1998).

These observations led to a series of responses to improve the curriculum practice in Hong Kong. From the Education Commission Report No. 1 in 1984 to Report No. 6 in 1996, the first focus was on improving the school environment, such as encouraging the adoption of activity approach to curriculum practice and the speeding up of establishing whole-day schools. The second focus was on upgrading teacher qualifications by introducing graduate posts into the primary schools, as well as the establishment of the Hong Kong Institute of Education, which aimed to provide degree programs for student teachers in 1994. The third focus was on curriculum development, which used to be under the auspices of the Education Department. It was proposed and accepted that a Curriculum Development Institute was set up in 1992 with the employment of frontline professionals on contract terms. It is expected that these contract professionals are able to provide expertise in various curriculum development areas.

Four curriculum areas were identified in the Education Commission Report No. 4 in 1990 and recommended further studies by the CDI. These four areas include the feasibility studies of introducing modular curriculum, mastery learning, program of learning for less able and gifted children, and the integrated studies in formal curriculum. These were the first attempts by the government to investigate the possibility of reforming the structure and organization of the current curriculum practice in schools. The move toward encouraging more school-based initiatives in curriculum development was identified in the Lewellyn Report in 1982 (Cheng, 1999). Early in 1988, a scheme of school-based curriculum projects was introduced and schools were encouraged to design and adapt curriculum materials on the basis of the formal curriculum structure laid down by the Curriculum Development Council—the central agency with specific responsibility in curriculum policies across the country. Substantial direct resources to encourage school-based improvement initiatives were evidenced in January 1998 after the setting up the $5 billion Quality Education Fund (QEF) to finance projects for the promotion of quality school education in Hong Kong. Since its establishment, $1,547 million have already been allocated to 2,744 school-based initiatives.

The need for reforms in the direction of a more student-centered approach to learning, and a curriculum designed for diverse needs and ability of the students, were proposed in 1989. This time the scale of restructuring the curriculum practice was massive and the resources invested were unprecedented.

The Target Oriented Curriculum (TOC) is a fundamental curriculum reform that attempts to address the curriculum issues raised in the Lewellyn Report—namely, the excessively academic orientation of the school curriculum contents, the teacher-dominated pedagogy, and an assessment system based on the selective function. The TOC framework brings changes in three dimensions of the school curriculum: (a) identification of learning outcomes in a hierarchical structure within each subject, (b) assessment on the basis of student achievement of learning targets at each of the three key stages, and (c) student-centered and task-based learning with diffusion of five cross curricular principles of learning such as communicating, enquiring, conceptualizing, reasoning, and problem solving. Curriculum strategies include emphasis on integrated studies, spiral curriculum, increase in capability of learning independently, and equal values of achievement of learning targets as well as learning processes. Curriculum contents include four aspects—namely, knowledge structure, intellectual skills, study and communication skills, and attitudes. The following is a diagrammatic representation of the curriculum change embodied in the TOC proposal (Adamson & Morris, 1998).

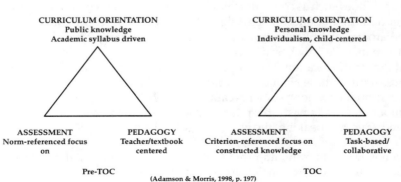

(Adamson & Morris, 1998, p. 197)

The history of implementing the TOC reform met with resistance and hostility in the early 1990s. Teachers found it alien and complicated to understand the educational jargons used in the documents. The practice of TOC was even more time-consuming, and conditions in schools are far from conducive to change of this magnitude. Interpretations of the TOC are diverse from subject to subject. Its mission went to a dead end when new curriculum reforms were prepared in 1999, and a proposal was published for consultation in 2000 without clear statements from the government on the changing policies. One speculation suggests that the possibility of the changing personnel at the top leadership positions in the decision-making mechanism in Hong Kong after the return of sovereignty in 1997 justifies the need for new initiatives in key strategic development areas in Hong Kong.

New proposals for reforming the structure and contents of the Hong Kong education and its school curriculum started in October 1999. The strategy to reform education and the school curriculum was taken holistically. The review started with redefining the aims of education for the 21st century and moved to the structure and organization of the education system. The issues with each level of education and its curriculum were studied within the contexts of achieving the aims of education and the vision of the Hong Kong society.

Justifications for reforms could be broadly understood in three perspectives—economical, social, and political. Manpower needs change due to the changing infrastructure of the Hong Kong economy from a basically manufacturing and export-oriented model toward a model heavily relying on finance, trade, and tourism. It is argued that the service economy requires manpower of qualities such as independent and higher order thinking skills, communication skills, and critical thinking skills. People in contemporary Hong Kong should have an international outlook and a diverse cultural perspective. The knowledge-based economy requires a life-long learning attitude and the ability of every citizen to be equipped with information technology knowledge and skills. Socially, Hong Kong is an open society with a fair amount of freedom and autonomy, although democracy is perceived to be lacking behind the Western standards and practice. To maintain an open society within a global community, civic and moral values, with a balance between the communal good and individuality, should become the core elements in our school curriculum.

Politically, Hong Kong enjoys the privilege of "one country, two systems," but the need for more understanding of the national system and its development becomes urgent for establishing national identity and affiliation with the mainstream Chinese culture of the next generation. Focuses of the reform relate strongly to the curriculum problems discussed earlier. Examination formats and admission systems should be reformed with an emphasis on formative purposes providing feedback on teaching and learning effectiveness, rather than on summative purposes (Education Commission, 2000). The school curriculum should be student centered, with due emphasis on building up students' life-long and generic capabilities such as communication, creativity, numeracy, problem solving, collaboration, and information technology skills. Contents of the school curriculum should be organized around eight key learning areas—namely, the languages of Chinese and English; Mathematics; Personal, Social and Humanities (PSH); Natural Science; Technology; Arts; and Physical Education. The purpose of building learning activities and educational experiences around these eight areas is to allow flexibility for integration. Moral training and values formation among students capture another focus of reform in the school curriculum. Values such as honesty, hospitality, and perseverance with open mindedness are highlighted. Overall speaking, the aim of the school curriculum is:

> The school curriculum should provide all students with essential life-long learning experiences for whole person development in the domains of ethics, intellect, physi-

cal development, social skills and aesthetics, according to individual potentials, so that all students could become active, responsible, and contributing members of society, the nation and the world.

The school curriculum should help students to learn how to learn through cultivating positive values, attitudes, and a commitment to life-long learning; develop generic skills to acquire and construct knowledge, which are essential for whole-person development to cope with challenges of the 21st century.

A quality curriculum for the 21st century should therefore set the directions for teaching/learning through a coherent and flexible framework which could be adaptable to changes and different needs of students and schools. (Curriculum Development Council, 2000, p. 17)

CURRICULUM RESEARCH

A select sample of curriculum research studies has been organized around the essential components of a curriculum proposed by Tyler (1949) with minor changes to his original conception. This approach presents to international audiences a convenient conceptualization of the research studies conducted in Hong Kong.

Aims of Education Redefined

Until 1992, Hong Kong had only sketchy explications in various Education Reports on her aims of the school education:

[E]ducation should strive to develop individuals who are curious, imaginative and creative, who will have an appreciation of their cultural heritage, and an awareness of the moral social aesthetic values of our present day society and of the role they can play in its improvement. Inherent therefore in our overall aim of education is the efficient development of intellectual, vocational and inter-personal skills relevant to the individual as he takes his place in Hong Kong. (Hong Kong Government 1973 Green Paper on Secondary School Education)

A systematic approach to provide a statement of the overall and specific aims of education emerged in 1993 when the Education Commission published *School Education in Hong Kong: A Statement of Aims*. The fundamental aim of the Hong Kong education is:

The school education service is to develop the potential of every individual child, so that our students become independent-minded and socially aware adults, equipped with the knowledge, skills and attitudes which will enable them to lead a full life and play a positive role in the social and economic development of the community. (Education and Manpower Branch, 1993, p. 8)

The expected learning outcomes include:

1. Learning skills: literacy and numeracy, thinking and reasoning, acquiring knowledge;
2. Practical and technical skills: develop abilities and attitudes useful in their further study and adult life;
3. Social, political, and civic awareness;
4. Personal and ethical qualities;
5. Physical development; and
6. Aesthetic and cultural development: developing creativity and aesthetic awareness as well as respect of the achievements of other cultures.

To a certain extent, the statement of aims addressed the issue raised in the Lewellyn Report—that education in Hong Kong is predominantly a highly utilitarian means to economic and vocational ends. It is also observed that the emphasis in schooling has been, by necessity, on academic success at some cost to personal development and sense of personal fulfillment to the majority of students.

The aims and objectives of the Hong Kong education system have not attracted researchers' interests. One research study is reported here, together with the commissioned research on the achievement of aims by the Board of Education, which is an advisory body to the Education Department. The first research conducted in 1992 and its purpose was to investigate the attitudes of primary teachers toward the aims of education. Six hundred teachers were randomly selected from the 17,800 members of a professional association in Hong Kong. Its total membership constituted 90% of the total number of primary teachers in Hong Kong. Questionnaires were sent to these teachers and 317 (52.8%) were returned. Distribution of teachers across gender and ranking in schools was in accordance with the general patterns of the primary population. The first issue asked them to rate between the social and personal functions of education, and preference was indicated. It was found that, although 53.1% indicated their preference to the personal aim of education, the difference was not statistically significant: 213 teachers rated between the medium numbers 3 and 2, indicating a more balanced view toward the function of education. The second issue was with the rating of importance on the six dimensions of curriculum aims—namely, moral, intellectual, social, emotional/personal, aesthetic, and physical developments: 79.2% voted on moral aim, whereas only 14% thought intellectual development was the most important curriculum aim.

The ratings on the importance of intellectual development for primary pupils were even lower than aesthetic and physical development. It would be revealing to contrast this perception of curriculum aims with the distribution of time and resources on studies of subject curriculum, which have a stronger academic flavor than arts and physical education. The academic subjects received the largest amount of curriculum time in the primary and secondary school timetables. The finding of the study was contrasted with another similar study in England in 1975, with moral education being in fourth place and social education and emotional/personal development being in the first and second places, respectively. The investigation included ratings of 67 statements deriving from the six dimensions, such as aesthetic and moral developments (e.g., "expressing feeling through different artistic forms" and "diligence, perseverance and responsibility"). The findings confirm earlier ratings on the six dimensions that, for the first eight statements with the highest ratings, the first two, the fourth, the sixth, and the seventh belong to the moral aspect of the curriculum aims. Development of personal ethical values is considered the most important for the aim of the school curriculum, whereas aesthetic and physical education received the least attention. These data reflect the unbalanced allocation of curriculum time to arts and physical education (Poon et al., 1997).

The second study was commissioned by the Board of Education and was reported in the Report on Review of 9-year Compulsory Education published in 1997. The research solicited through questionnaires opinions from 7,609 pupils, 723 teachers, and principals of 60 local primary schools and 47 secondary schools. They also interviewed 295 pupils, teachers, and principals in schools and 22 administrators of school-sponsoring bodies and decision makers in the central government. The findings focused on the extent that the current provision of education is able to achieve the stated aims of education published by the government in 1993. For example, on Aim 12, which is about the needs for social, political, and civic awareness, the Board found that documents and guidelines on civic education have been developed and distributed among schools that can choose to implement the guidelines by conducting civic education either as a separate subject or through an integrated approach in the formal and informal curricula.

The Report recommends that the teaching of civic education should be strengthened and learning activities should be organized to promote a better understanding of the "one country, two systems," the roles and responsibilities of citizens, and the Chinese culture and history. Another example of using the aim in evaluating the effectiveness of the school curriculum is Aim 10, which is about developing students' learning skills. It was found that most primary schools have no school library, and for schools with libraries there is no librarian or clerical support. Only secondary schools are provided with computer rooms. It is recommended that additional resources be invested in these areas, and training of teachers with skills in information technology should form part of the teacher education programs.

Teaching and Learning

The persistence in advocating Western practices in curriculum with an emphasis on experience-based and student-focused organization of learning has been a major theme in curriculum reforms in Hong Kong. One-sided beliefs in constructivist approaches being more powerful and necessarily the models of reforms lead to the emergence of one curriculum reform after another. Careful study of official TOC and Learning to Learning documents easily gives evidence of the use of common educational terminology in contemporary education theories and practices. It seems to the officials and policymakers that the practice is taken as deficient and something new should replace the traditional practices.

Australian scholar, John Biggs, who worked in the Faculty of Education Hong Kong University since 1987, conducted numerous research studies on the learning styles of Chinese students and attempted to seek answers to the charge that Chinese students are used to rote learning and memory training and that their creativity suffers. However, he saw it as a paradox that, although teachers in Confucius Heritage Culture (CHC) classrooms are adopting expository methods with large class sizes of 40, learning is largely examination oriented, atmosphere is intense toward examination periods, and most classrooms are underresourced, the academic achievements of these CHC students outperform their Western counterparts in science and mathematics. To Western wisdom, good learning conditions include adoption of various methods of learning, emphasizing student activity, cooperative, and group work. Small classes and warm classroom climate are necessary for effective learning. Learning must be meaningful. It seems all these contrast well with the conditions described as CHC classrooms. He closely examined the conception of learning to the CHC students and their ways of dealing with learning tasks. He found that CHC students operate within a culturally different milieu of learning, which encourages highly adaptive modes of learning. CHC students do not rote learn materials, but repeat learning in meaningful ways for the insurance of good results in a highly competitive environment. This repetition encourages possibility of transformation and internalization of positive dispositions to learning without much motivation, as is the case in the West. Teacher and student relations may be hierarchical, but are typically marked by warmth and a sense of responsibility on both sides. Gardner (1989) observed that the sequence of learning arts in China is contrary to the Chinese way of learning arts. The Chinese students start with the acquisition of skills and are allowed to explore, whereas the American children start with the exploration and acquisition of skills. As mentioned in previous sections, the attributions for success and failure by CHC students are different from the Western traditions. Efforts play a strong motivational force for most students to achieve and continue learning (Watkins & Biggs, 1996).

I chose to discuss Biggs' work because it contradicts much of our current thinking about the curriculum problems in Hong Kong. Boggs' work deserves serious consideration by educators and curriculum decision makers. His work may also explain, partially, the persistence of the traditional conceptions of teaching and learning among school teachers and parents, and the failure of the introduction of the activity approach in Hong Kong schools. His works and the research studies challenge the conventional wisdom in Hong Kong about what the real issues are with our school curriculum. Does the deficiency model of thinking about our school curriculum work? Hong Kong's experience seems to have a deeper meaning to the current curriculum theory internationally, in that the role of culture should deserve further attention in theorizing curriculum practice.

Reflections on Major Curriculum Reforms

Reforms in improving the school curriculum in Hong Kong have been moved from a piecemeal to a holistic approach in the last 20 years (Cheng, 1999). Reforms such as TOC aim to transform the traditional curriculum practice to a model of practice close to student-centered philosophy and constructivism. Two research studies on TOC are reported here because of their magnitude and scale. The first one was conducted by Professor Paul Morris and his team at Hong Kong University, and the second was investigated by John Clark and his team at the Hong Kong Institute of Education. Morris and his team started with questions at policy level, school level, and classroom level. At policy level, they wanted to find out what the main features of the innovation were, who was involved in making decisions, why TOC was introduced, and what strategies were used. At school level, the research questions included how schools responded to the quest for change, what processes schools used to support and implement the innovation, and what the problems emerged in these processes. At classroom level, the issues included how teachers implemented TOC, how pupils perceived the change, and what problems emerged in these processes. Research methods covered documentary analysis, interviews, questionnaires, and case study schools. At policy level, the TOC initiative is probably the most ambitious attempt to radically change the current practice in the school curriculum. Innovations were introduced and implemented in three core components of curriculum—aims, pedagogy, and assessment style.

Findings pointed to the need for the localization of innovative ideas imported from overseas countries with participation of frontline teachers at the planning, reviewing, developing, and implementing stages. The shifting and revising of the original proposal was seen defective and thus damaging its credibility among teachers. Experience emerging from the implementation should become an integral part of the reform package. Innovations at the three core components of curriculum increased its complexity of change, and fidelity to its original conception becomes extremely different among teachers and schools that carry with them a diverse sociocultural milieu. Coordination between various curriculum initiatives, such as activity approach and mastery learning promoted by the government, becomes confusing to the teachers and schools in terms of their priority of change. Commitment to additional resources in support of the implementation came only when resistance became strong. This indicated the lack of a strategy policy on the part of the government to implement innovations of this magnitude. Messages from government officials about TOC differed, and sometimes reports of no confidence were heard in the news. Concern about the commitment to TOC was raised after 1997, and the lack of clarity in long-term commitments further deteriorated the confidence of the schools.

At the organizational level, the implementation of TOC in schools created opportunities for teachers' professional development. Collaboration and team work was enhanced, and the spirit and morale of the staff improved. However, schools had different orientations toward adopting TOC. Some desired to obtain advantage, whereas others wanted to enhance prestige among schools. Decisions to join TOC were rarely taken by teachers; where teachers were involved in decision-making process, the impact was greater. TOC brought changes to the curriculum practice of some schools, which allowed common periods among TOC teachers to develop materials and planned for integrated studies. The climate in some schools was not conducive to change.

At the classroom level, it was found that most teachers had difficulty interpreting the key concepts of TOC, and thus TOC was adapted to assimilate the current practice of the teachers, rather than changing the practices to accommodate TOC. The latter is significantly essential for implementing innovations. In classroom pedagogy, group work and individual work were rare, and whole-class teaching still dominated. Pupil–pupil interaction was still not prevalent in TOC classrooms. Attempts to introduce problem-solving and inquiring activities were evidenced, but observations of these classrooms could not distinguish the difference between these two. Teachers showed a limited understanding of the nature and purpose of formative and criterion-referenced assessment. The traditional assessment patterns were retained in most lessons. Textbooks were not perceived to be consistent with TOC and were rejected by some teachers for use in classrooms.

One theme from the study emerges. It relates to the influence of the contextual constraints in disseminating innovations in a system culturally different from the place where the reform originates. The role of culture becomes a focus of study again. The conception of TOC started with an assumption that the curriculum practice is problematic and thus innovations are necessary. As it was written in the offical documents, the problem with the education lies in their perception that the qualities of our graduates do not meet the standards and needs of Hong Kong's market economy.

The second major study was conducted by John Clark, who was one of the major proponents of the TOC innovation. The focus of this study was to find out the necessary professional competencies that were needed for successful implementation of TOC. Interviews with teachers of TOC subjects, panel chairpersons, TOC coordinators, and school heads were conducted, together with questionnaires being sent to 141 schools; 125 (89%) responded. Case studies involved six schools. It was found that the competencies of the teachers required for successful implementation of TOC include:

1. Developing learning activities in line with the TOC requirements;
2. Selecting and adapting materials in textbooks;
3. Managing group work without having discipline problems;
4. Responding to individual differences; and
5. Improving teaching with formative feedback from assessment.

For teachers and administrator who assume leadership responsibility in implementing TOC, the following is required:

1. Understanding the rationale and the basic concepts of TOC;
2. Understanding the processes of introducing school based curriculum development; and
3. Planning and developing appropriate strategies for school based development of TOC.

Judging from the previous findings listed, one might wonder whether these competencies are simply the general skills and capabilities of classroom teachers. Another observation is that the TOC innovation may be too ambitious in its attempts to bring drastic changes to a system of practice that is seen to be in harmony with the expectations of the teachers and parents. One might wonder whether a deep structural issue lies at the heart of this contradictory perception of the curriculum problems in Hong Kong education.

CONCLUSION

Hong Kong is a meeting place between East and West. Her history, cultural background, and commitment to a global perspective in all walks of life make her more cosmopolitan than many other great cities in the world. Her history of searching for a quality education and curriculum comparable to the aspirations and practice of the developed countries is sufficient evidence of her commitment. The efforts of moving away from traditional conceptions of knowledge, learning, and schooling have been met with resistance and suspicions. Western models of teaching and learning do not find a home in the mainstream schools in Hong Kong. There is some evidence that the resistance has been a function of Chinese cultural values and conceptions of knowledge and education. Empirical research on cultural studies has indicated learning activities in CHC classrooms, although traditional in forms, have deeper and long-term cognitive meanings to most of their students. Learning to these students is not rote and based on memory at low cognitive levels, but rather deep and meaningful—with life-long effects on their dispositions to learning and moral development. Deficiency models of thinking do not agree with these observations, which have asserted less influence on the conception of curriculum problems in Hong Kong schools. Advocates of the deficiency models find passivity, docility, and boredom the essential components in the traditional curriculum practice. They urge reforms.

To a great extent, most curriculum reforms are modeled on Western conceptions of learning, knowledge, and society. Official documents are couched in language fashionable among educators and university researchers in education. From their perspective, resistance to change is a combination of various factors and inadequacies in planning, coordination, and dissemination strategies. The problem is a function of technology. Hardly can one find challenges to the student-centered beliefs and practice in education and curriculum. Progressivism has its appeal for many kind-hearted teachers and teacher educators, especially in its romantic and humanistic approaches to fundamental curriculum issues. The dilemma is far from being resolved, and Hong Kong's experience in its search for a curriculum is a search for a harmonious compromise between Western ideas and Eastern practice.

REFERENCES

Adamson, B., & Morris, P. (1998). Primary schooling in Hong Kong. In J. Moyles & L. Hargreaves (Eds.), *The primary curriculum: Learning from international perspectives* (pp. 181–204). London: Routledge.

Cheng, K. M. (1997). The education system. In G. A. Postiglione & W. O. Lee (Eds.), *Schooling in Hong Kong* (pp. 25–42). Hong Kong: Hong Kong University Press.

Cheng, Y. C. (1999). The pursuit of school effectiveness and educational quality in Hong Kong. *Journal of School Effectiveness and School Improvement, 10*(1), 10–30.

Clark, J., Lo, Y. C., Hui, M. F., Kam, C. K., Carless, D., & Wong, P. M. (1999). *An investigation into the development and implementation of the TOC initiative with special reference to professional competencies, professional development and resources.* Hong Kong Education Department.

Curriculum Development Council. (2000). *Learning to learn: The way forward in curriculum development.* Hong Kong Special Administration Region of The People's Republic of China.

Education and Manpower Branch. (1993). *School education in Hong Kong: a statement of aims.* Hong Kong Government.

Education Commission. (1984). *Education commission: Report.* Hong Kong: The Commission.

Education Commission. (1990). *The curriculum and behavioural problems in schools.* Hong Kong: Government Printer.

Education Commission. (1996). *Quality school education: Consultation document.* Hong Kong: Government Printer.

Education Commission. (2000). *Learning for life/learning through life.* Hong Kong Special Administration Region of The People's Republic of China.

Gardner, H. (1989). *To open minds.* New York: Basic Books.

Ho, K. K. (1996). The past, present and future of the religious schools in Hong Kong. *Compare, 26*(1), 51–59.

Lewellyn, J. (1982). *A perspective on education in Hong Kong.* Hong Kong: Government Printer.

Marsh, C. (1997). *Perspectives: Key concepts for understanding curriculum.* London: Falmer.

Poon, T. C., Wong, H. W., Tang, S. F., Yu, L. S., & Yip, S. H. (1997). The expectations of the Hong Kong primary school teachers on the aims of the primary curriculum. In H. W. Wong (Ed.), *Compulsory university school education: System and curriculum* (pp. 139–164). Hong Kong: Chinese University of Hong Kong.

The Board of Education (1997). *Report on Review of 9 year Compulsory Education.* Hong Kong Government.

Tyler, R. W. (1949). *Basic principles of curriculum and instruction.* Chicago: University of Chicago Press.

Watkins, D., & Biggs, J. (Eds). (1996). *The Chinese learner: Cultural psychological and contextual influences.* Hong Kong: Comparative Education Research Centre, Hong Kong University.

Wong, E. M. O., & Stimpson, P. (1994). Teaching styles of Hong Kong's environmental educators in secondary schools. *Journal of Research in Education, 52,* 1–12.

Wong, M. (1997). Concepts of learning and teaching in Hong Kong: An insider's perspective. *Journal of Education and Society, 15*(2), 13–23.

CHAPTER 15

Learning for the Future in Estonia: Content Revisited and Reconceptualized

Urve Laanemets
Education Policy Centre at the Jaan Tonisson Institute, Estonia

Problems of curriculum design and specification have obtained a particular meaning all over the world. Experience of both—the Western as well as that of Eastern block countries after the collapse of the socialist empire—have offered new insights into educational development and possible innovation. Aspirations for political and social cohesion on the global level demands unavoidable common values and approaches. Development of new curricula for different educational levels and types of school requires common understanding of possible structures for the specification of the content of education and the organization of learning processes.

Design of curricular documents remains culture specific and time bound historically. However, some common principles and models could be considered usable under different sociocultural circumstances. Hopefully these could help establish a more balanced approach toward a constantly changing educational situation, especially regarding personal expectations of individuals as well as more explicitly expressed social demands for education in official documents. In this contribution, an attempt has been made to introduce some models of curriculum planning that could be considered capable of implementation and not only in periods of great social change.

INTRODUCTION

Although education has been considered a powerful social factor historically, today we have come to understand its boundaries and limitations as well. Education is not omnipotent in the contemporary world, but despite the change of its role, it has acquired a new meaning on the level of greater social abstraction: It is primarily supposed to help people build their identities. Identity building for the 21st century, however, means a wide choice and wise interpretation of different options to find out which are acceptable and which are not. Due to new and multiple means of communication, many individuals have multiple identities, which build hierarchies and influence social action according to subject positionings in this system. Education has to help people make decisions about how to construct these hierarchies and also envisage the results of their functioning (Pinar, 1998).

Still, we have to bear in mind that perception and interpretation of particular educational values is always limited by its temporary constraints, which restrict the arguments by the scope of available knowledge and skills at that particular moment of time. When thinking about theoretical findings and experience regarding general education and action research so far as a basis for development of content of studies and organization of learning processes, we often tend to forget that studies of that type are closely related to their time and specific conditions, particularly to sociocultural conditions. Accordingly, first, when offering data and conclusions about action research, those data should be introduced by a precisely description of the conditions of the study. Second, longitudinal analyses in similar conditions merit greater attention.

The content and organization of education remains highly debatable globally as well as locally. In particular, there are continuing debates over what is considered worth learning or what should or could students learn about various subjects, themes or facts. The proponents of absolutely free personality development try to avoid any impositions made by teachers on students. Usually we come across discussions about the two: democratic and authoritarian approaches for selection not only of the content of learning, but also that of activities. Again, a third approach tends to be forgotten—one that balances the two extremes: one based on understanding and competence, which can offer versions for meeting the changing educational demands under most diverse circumstances.

The constant change of the contemporary world has its influence on education as well, and the key word *flexibility* has caused intense debates over what could be considered meaningful in education at large. Attempts have been made to specify dimensions of education, such as global and regional education (Darinski, 1996), European dimensions (White Paper, 1995), and others relevant on a smaller scale of applicability. We should acquire an improved ability to read and learn from theories, practices, and proposals and gain a surer understanding of the cultural and philosophical roots of issues in curriculum design, which in turn could create educational options for managing the change on the level of an individual, group, or nation. However, the concept of change has become somewhat overexploited, and considerably less has been written about using the resources of different times for creating meaningful and wise sequences of desired educational developments.

Systems of compulsory general education are supposed to guarantee some kind of educational minimum, which would enable students to meet the needs of society not only regarding the demands of the labor market, but also capabilities of all people to manage their lives and become involved in life-long learning. Observing educational developments in compulsory schooling in different countries, we cannot fail to notice the general tendency toward the lengthening of studies. It also means that society at large has recognized equal access to education as a social benefit every country has to provide their people with if development and social stability are the agreed and acknowledged common goals. Time spent on learning usually specifies the content that can be made available, but it also has its particular meaning of inclusion. In some places, the time of compulsory schooling has reached (or is going to do so) 10 years or 18 years of age (e.g., Norway, Russia). Recent school reforms in several countries have had the meaning of a cultural reform, which, for example, "help to provide good conditions for children and adolescents as they grow up with a wealth of impulses in varied learning environment and where creative activities and forms of expression will become an important part of everyday life of the school, in collaboration with local cultural institutions" (Reform, 1997, Norwegian Ministry of Education, Research and Church Affairs, p. 1).

According to the UNESCO report, all societies have to overcome the controversies of our time in their own way. The following have been listed: controversies between the local and global, universal and individual, traditional and contemporary, long- and short-term aspirations and decision making, competition and equal opportunities, information flood and capability to process it, and, finally, between the mental and material ideals and values (Delors, 1996, pp. 16–17).

Educational and curriculum reforms in particular have to help overcome some of these controversies and reflect change of values in a society and consensus about new goals considering the more distant future. Aspirations to establish national curricula in the countries where they traditionally have not been used show a tendency to come to a common understanding in educational matters. The new social agreement about changing values means innovation within the country, but it may also have a broader effect that influences educational change globally, considering, for instance, the influence of new information technologies developed in different parts of the world.

We also have to admit the growth of regional, national, and ethnic differences, whereas new space levels have become evident, and we have to study processes of globalization in education similar to those carried out in sociology of economics. Mutual influence of globalization and local developments offers new opportunities for specification of different identities and belonging to new associations. Progress in education can be similarly expected as it is in economy—by the development of new resources, those being new skills and means of communication (Raagma, 1999).

The specification of identities on different levels, starting from local and regional to more global, allows the development of stability in educational innovation and the avoidance of educational pollution (i.e., innovation for the sake of innovation, an expression of the so-called *zero tolerance* toward whatever is extant). Developments of that kind are the reason there are still too many atheoretical and ahistorical curriculum documents in place and under development at the beginning of the 21st century.

IS IT POSSIBLE TO DEVELOP AN ADEQUATE CURRICULUM AND HOW DO WE DO IT?

There are various approaches, rationalized theoretically, as well as field-tested cases, all to guide curriculum planning and design, that may lay stress on different aspects and stretch over different periods of time considering their implementation. Practical processes of planning and text compilation usually start with paradigm specification, which is followed by compilation of a curriculum text or texts based on it and meant for practical implementation on different educational levels. The following discussion is dedicated to two phenomena: specification of a paradigm and selection of the content for general education.

Education has to meet the demands of society, but these are rarely clearly specified. As aptly marked by Johnson in 1967, socioeconomic power groups and politicians are usually interested in some kind of improvement, whereas understanding and more specific fields of new interests remain vague (Johnson, 1967). A paradigm shift can be manifested if there really develops a new mind set expressing an essential change in comprehension of needed educational content and activities in society. If this new way of understanding is well provided with arguments and implementable prognosis for action, reforms are designed and implemented.

Paradigm shifts have covered all approaches. The approach through content as a structure for curriculum has been the most traditional and most widely used by practitioners. This particular approach has proved to be unavoidable if the national educational system is meant to offer equal access to studies or is designed as a unified system.

Approach through objectives is also a well-spread version of curriculum design, but unfortunately there is no commonly accepted definition of objectives or goals, and they are all based on some kind of ideology, expressing recognized values within a society. Ideologies may develop in different directions. Some postsocialist countries have even manifested deideologization of education, which seems to be partly true considering the rejection and loss of many universal ideas of education.

Democratization and humanization of curricula, often related to humanitarization (more time and space allotted to languages and social sciences), have been dedicated to the substitution of the so-called *red ideology* with a democratic one. However, in many cases, the concept has become obscure, and the new slogan of democracy in education may also mean voluntarism in many fields of educational actions. Ideology of some kind, even if not manifested, always remains. The most fashionable approach in the discussion of curriculum design of the last 30 years is the one through process. The supporters of this approach usually reject means–end rationality and, according to Eisner (1979), "purpose need not precede action, purposes may grow out of action" (p. 100). It has led to different forms of modeling that, most often in the form of different projects, have produced curricula complex in their structure and difficult for teachers to put into practice because the expectations of the learners as well as those of employees may be greatly changed, if not shattered. This approach through process has become popular in postsocialist countries mainly because of American educational influence as well as new and unlimited opportunities for experimentation. Active methods offering more participation, learning by doing, and so on created a kind of new approach to learning process in general and was undoubtedly innovational by its varied project work. In a way, it also offered an opportunity to diminish the traditional content of subjects and avoid hard and unpopular work of learning concepts and facts highly typical of the former Soviet education. The main aim (the development of critical thinking skills in a meaningful study process), which has been the aim of the constructivist approach of many scholars (see Gagne et al., 1992; Kearns & Doyle, 1991; Piaget, 1975), has been substituted by a simplified child-centered approach. Not in the sense of Nunan (1991) and others who have understood the concept as an aspiration to make study material feasible and meaningful for the learner (child). However, development of systematic knowledge and critical thinking has been somewhat neglected as the content for those activities has been selected according to their suitability for a particular study technique.

The fourth approach is based on assessment. Measure-driven assessment of instruction (MDI) has been the basis of curriculum development in America for a long time. The use of achievement tests directs the instructional process, and the high performance level requires a content relevant to these objectives. The higher the stake, the greater the impact on the content and instruction. The system of national examinations has been established in many European countries as well, but characteristics of educational standards for passing tend to be limited, and it is extremely difficult to keep complex and complicated testing systems updated. Assessment-led curriculum also tends to be limited because many educational outcomes, especially acquisition of moral and ethical values, creativity, and artistic skills, are and probably remain immeasurable. Assessment-led curricula usually leave out broader cultural values as well as the so-called *nonutilitarian knowledge,* which is indispensable for development of different types of intelligence and human mind. Nobody has managed to give a satisfactory answer to the question of what knowledge, skills, and so on should be tested to specify the grade of social and academic maturity of a person, who could be considered capable of managing one's own life, under the circumstances of the ever-growing mobility of labor force and changing times.

All four approaches have positive and negative characteristics. In aspirations to seek a balance among educational objectives, content of education, processes of learning, and desired social and individual outcomes, all of them have to be managed. Because there are countries providing their people with good educational opportunities and achieving generally high academic results with which those societies are generally satisfied, I think it is possible to create adequate curricula. However, it requires wise planning and effective implementation. It has to start with a paradigm specification, which undoubtedly is no easy task. It has to create a philosophical approach that could serve as basis for general understanding of education and learning in a particular society positioned in the diverse educational world at large.

THE IDEA MODEL FOR PARADIGM SPECIFICATION: AN ATTEMPT TO CREATE A SOCIAL MIND SET FOR THE DEVELOPMENT OF CURRICULA

This model attempts to offer a structure for understanding educational processes within a society considering basic relations among the global, regional, local, and individual. The model has been named after the initial letters of its components: ideology, design of curriculum structures and content, evaluation of educational developments, and results and adjustments to regional and local needs (IDEA).

I–Ideologies

Curriculum ideologies have been defined by E. Eisner as beliefs about what schools should teach, for what ends, and for what reasons. Ideologies are belief systems that provide the value premises from which decisions about practical educational matters are made (Eisner, 1992).

Despite the six curriculum ideologies identified by Eisner—namely, religious orthodoxy, rational humanism, progressivism, critical theory, reconceptualism, and cognitive pluralism—there are practically few, if any, clear-cut classical ideologies used as a basis for curriculum development. However, all contemporary ideologies, official or hidden, that are used for selection of education content and the organization of school studies tend to use various elements of all the aforementioned in their own particular configurations.

The term *ideology,* derived from the word *idea,* has to specify the basic assumptions of what deserves to be included into the concept of educated person on agreed levels of academic and social competencies by which we hope the new generation is able to adjust itself to future circumstances, even if the preparation we provide for those circumstances can only necesssarily be partly correct.

When designing any models for curriculum development and implementation, the previous stage of educational organization of the system has to be considered as well as the traditions of pedagogical culture in the society. From the point of view of educational change in the Western and postsocialist countries, the problems of establishing a balance between the traditional and innovational deserves special attention. It is particularly important to distinguish between the old and valuable and the old and outdated. If we fail to make this distinction, some traditional human values may get lost and influence social stability within the country or even beyond. When again the lost values become desirable, their restoration means new efforts and spending resources (time finances, and human resources), which could be used in a more meaningful way. When deciding about the ideologies, we have to bear in mind that no curriculum can exist in isolation, and no national curriculum can ignore international developments

(Pinar et al., 1996), and even *big* countries have to look beyond their borders. Although there is a lot of ethnocentricity in educational decision making, there are more curricularists who have understood that we all can gain in competence if we can track the new and interesting ideas in the right time regardless of where or who they may come from.

To specify an ideology relevant to a particular educational situation, some basic questions should be asked:

How diverse can diversity be?

What can we accept and what is unacceptable considering our cultural and moral values and recognized traditions?

What can we benefit from and what can we offer to the world?

What has to be the common core of educational content and aspirations of the knowledge society if cohesion of societies and the world is desired?

Can a global or European dimension really unite the nations, although language learning is really difficult to implement or that cultural diversity can be hard to accept?

What are the strategically meaningful fields of knowledge and skills globally and regionally?

What kind of content could create balance between different social and cultural values?

What is the desired educational quality, considering both, the process and the content of learning?

What quality of education could be considered adequate and sufficiently flexible, capable to meet the challenge of changing labor market and tendencies toward "the end of the work" (Rifkin, 1995)?

What kind of new activities could be designed as meaningful for people in information societies?

The specification of an ideology, which could serve as the basis for development of educational strategy documents, remains an object of political debate and negotiations. A special subdiscipline—curriculum policy—has been developed, which Elmore and Sykes have called anything but a well-organized distinctive field of inquiry (Elmore & Sykes, 1992; McLaughlin, 1987). Quite often rational analyses can influence ideological change. However, the more data there are, the more there is opportunity for interpretation and deeper understanding. The more complex our world becomes by different social and political structures, the more we need specified and specialized ideologies for clarification of the meaning for particular fields of human activities, including education and learning in general (Walsh, 1993).

D–Design of Curriculum Structures and Content

The shortest definition of *curricula* was given by Hilda Taba, who, in 1962 called them "plans for learning." She suggested several ways of organizing particular activities, which could lead the students to expected results considering their capabilities to comprehend the world around them—to see possible causes behind social developments and to become able to participate in everyday life as responsible citizens (Taba, 1962). What kind of plans for learning should we work for today? Different structural models have been developed. We can distinguish broadly between the *Lehrplans* (study plans), which have been generally more prescriptive, and curricula, which can be considered more open for interpretation as they are built as frameworks. Developments in the German-speaking world have also led to *Rahmenprogramme* and didactic models, such as

Berlin and Hamburg model, open models, and plans for different school levels (Peterssen, 1992/1998), which have allowed to plan the content as well as processes of learning. A third approach could be followed in the Soviet curriculum theory (Krajewski & Lerner, 1983), proceeding in contemporary Russia today, where the main attention has been dedicated to development of classical encyclopedic approach and integrated organization of academic content.

Today, at the beginning of the 21st century, educationists try to compile the most acceptable plans for learning for the young people who we expect not only to adjust themselves to new circumstances, but also to make our world a better place in which to live. It requires a dialogue among all concerned about education at large as well as on an individual level. Several international organizations have tried to offer their guidelines for education.

In 1995, the European Commission issued a White Paper on education and training with the message, "Teaching and learning—Towards the Learning Society." This document manifests three major trends or "factors of upheaval in societies": internationalization of trade, the dawning of information society, and the relentless march of science and technology with all their different impacts. The mentioned commission has offered two possible solutions that education and training can provide in eliminating the pernicious effects of the mentioned factors—namely, reintroducing the merits of a broad base of knowledge and building up employability. Among the guidelines, there are five suggested educational objectives developed primarily for the needs of the business world and labor market.

1 Encourage the acquisition of new knowledge (i.e., raise the general level of knowledge);
2 Bring school and business sectors closer together by developing apprenticeship in Europe in all its forms;
3 Combat exclusion: Offer a second chance through school by complementary system;
4 Encourage proficiency in three community languages because language proficiency has become essential for getting a job and having mobility in the labor force in general; and
5 Treat material investment and investment in training on an equal basis, making education and training a priority. (White Paper, 1995)

The previously mentioned objectives clearly indicate an aspiration toward the cultivation of a world outlook by students—one that would provide them with more sophisticated (world-class) skills for informed decision making. One of the basic truths recognized by researchers and practitioners is that the globalization of education has led, in particular, to investigations for a common core of general education.

The development of a core curriculum, offered as a necessary aspect of democracy, could be characterized as something "establishing publicly known and acknowledged agreements about the substance of universal schooling" (OECD/CERI, 1994), which could create a basis for common values and better mutual understanding. First of all, it means specification of particular fields of human knowledge and skills we cannot do without for meaningful international communication in all spheres of social life. These fields have to be represented as structural elements in curricula, probably in different forms of traditional school subjects, integrated subject cycles, or other. It is difficult to specify them due to different sociocultural values. However, we should first think about what we need for the development of a culture of intercultural communication. Hasanow (1998) established theoretical and methodological principles for development of this particular type of culture with relevant personal social skills, which deserves particular attention for designing the content of civics and other social sciences as school subjects.

Accordingly, some priority fields of knowledge can be specified, which would enable us to develop the previously mentioned intercultural communication skills. This probably has been the reason for the special attention given to learning regional and community languages, history, and civics in all societies in the East as well the West. This field of educational content is of particular importance for small countries considering the number of people speaking a particular ethnic language and the unavoidable need to learn some world language for international communication. They are destined to be multilingual, as Allardt (1979) has well argued.

Let us study the case of language learning as an element of the common core curriculum. Language cycles in NCs usually contain courses for learning the native languages and one to two foreign languages according to their instrumental position in a particular geopolitical region. Functional demand for various language skills is best specified by a longitudinal research. In Estonia, such studies have been carried out in 1984 (Laanemets), 1988 (Laanemets), 1994 (Laanemets & Rebane) 1995, (Laanemets & Hutt), and 2002, with the aim to specify the dynamics of social demand for competence in different languages and in particular language skills. These are of special importance in Europe and particularly for small states that are destined to be multilingual. Social demand for language competencies is a changing phenomenon in all societies, especially in those undergoing great political and social transformations. Despite short time or politically colored preferences, practical needs reestablish their position and required language competencies, and skills become balanced to reality as the situation becomes more stabilized. The use of different languages is clearly influenced by economic, political, and cultural contacts of a particular country in particular times. Studies of that kind also help gain some information about hidden curricula, which might influence implementation of manifested curricula in different directions. Hidden curriculum in Estonia and several other postsocialist countries has clearly supported the learning of English, whereas learning of Russian has been in disguise since the 1990s. Political developments toward European Union (EU) membership have created a wish to have some competence of French. Even the United States is facing the problem of organizing education and learning in regionally important languages despite English is a world language.

Civic education as one of the cornerstones for building democratic societies has required a particular meaning from the point of view of a common and shared core curriculum. Civic education should be required at every level of the school curriculum and should be a central goal of education. Moreover, civic education should be interdisciplinary and of high quality and sufficient quantity; emphasis in the civic education should be on how to think rather than what to think. It should include historical as well as contemporary topics. As well, civic education should reflect community realities and a balance between conflicting social values and political viewpoints and enable participation in the community life. Civic education methodology should be primarily interactive (Valdmaa, 1996).

Another field that has recently gained importance, especially considering globalization of economy and business in particular, is usually represented in curricula as economic geography of the world, but it is closely related to culturally specific developments in particular regions. Attempts made in Germany in this field deserve special attention (e.g., Dichtl, 2000) because they also contribute to an understanding of cultural diversity and its influence on socioeconomic developments in the world. This modernized school subject is of great educational meaning and potential, which can develop a broader comprehension of the world as a social, cultural, ecological, and economic system that has to be kept in balance for our survival.

Representation of traditional math and science subjects also deserves revisiting due to nationally established core curricula with their four compulsory subjects—one's mother tongue, math, science, and social studies—have left all other disciplines available. Even if young people tend to choose in favor of the so-called *easier* subjects, these decisions seem to be short sighted individually as well as nationally because several countries are facing the lack of adequately educated student candidates for learning medical and technical disciplines on the university level. European and Russian experience in content design for general education in particular has shown the role and meaning of wisely modernized academic disciplines. Another approach for the concept of the core curriculum was elaborated, by which the most essential body of knowledge and skills was specified for all traditional sciences, which covered about 60% to 70% of the time for studies and was compulsory to all learners. The rest of the time (30%–40%) could be used optionally for learning new subjects; learning math, sciences, languages, or arts on a more advanced level; and preparing them directly for entrance to university. The so-called *encyclopedic approach,* with the content consisting of many school subjects, represents available knowledge and skills in the respective field of human experience. Each subject, be it languages or math, offers a new mental structure for the comprehension of the world around us, specifically thinking skills. As we see, even the concept of the core curriculum needs to be agreed on.

We may conclude that core curriculum can be the central axis of global educational content. Its perspective is to make academic and practical sense to all young people by clarifying the common and shared core of knowledge and moral values, prepare their minds for constant adaptation, as well as help them understand the meaning and inevitability of life-long learning in their own lives. The common core of the content can be specified by particular fields of knowledge, subject cycles, or some other form. However, the content of learning as well as its organization must be periodically revised and redetermined considering that intellectual flexibility is the main object of education. The core curriculum constructs the shared identity of every single person being one of the humankind, as a human being in our controversial world. The organization of learning environment and processes, however, including methods of instruction, learning strategies, and other, remains culture specific and open for different interpretation for educational practice.

E–Evaluation of Educational Developments and Results

In general, societies are primarily interested in academic achievement. Politically powerful groups express their satisfaction or criticism, sometimes considering comparative data that indicate how competitive graduates are in terms of university admissions or the labor market. Such judgments are often considered to be the most reliable indicators of quality of a particular curriculum or education at large. Although not all educational results are measurable, evaluation is crucial. For a generalizing paradigm, we have to focus on two basic points: the quality of the curriculum and the stability of the established paradigm.

There are several systems for curriculum evaluation, starting with Tyler (1949), according to whom the process of evaluation is essentially the process of determining to what extent the educational objectives are actually being realized by the program of curriculum and instruction. Today we have to analyze curricula in a broader perspective that differentiates between assessment and evaluation in various forms of implementation (see Lawton, 1994; Madaus & Kellaghan, 1992) with all their psychological impacts under highly diverse circumstances. Measure-driven assessment instruction (MDI) approach has led to the development of systems of national examinations in many countries, which, despite their aspirations for objective feedback, have remained controversial. No testing system has succeeded in uniting acquired knowledge and skills with individual ethical and moral development, regarding the new values and identities a person may or may not have acquired by learning via formal or informal education again, it leads to the need for deeper comprehension and understanding of educational processes at large and value-added evaluation in particular, which allows to consider the impact of the implemented curricula in their sociopolitical context. Quite often, new curricula and education at large are supposed to change students' attitudes (e.g., their motivation for life-long learning, attitudes toward positive thinking, cultural tolerance, caring, and sharing—all needed for social stability). Even if we cannot collect concrete data (no matter how sophisticated the research) to document these changes, we can trace the desired effect by emergence of new social phenomena or institutions. The best example of that kind is the establishment of various NGOs for educational or charity purposes.

Another field of evaluation, which deserves greater attention, is the evaluation of quality of the learning environment in a broader sense of the concept, which in turn specifies the implementation of the curriculum. Learning environment could be evaluated by three basic criteria:

- physical environment, which is aimed at functionality, describing the premises designed for learning according to the principles of school architecture, curriculum-specified conditions (a stadium, lab, library, etc.), and health requirements;
- study aids, which are aimed to meet the curriculum requirements, describing how the content, specified in curriculum documents, has been made available and how it has been methodologically organized for learning with the help of various traditional textbooks, handbooks, and so on, but also using it; and
- human environment and school culture, aimed at professionalism, describing qualification of the teaching staff, opportunities for cooperation, individualized curricula, and achievement (Laanemets, 2002).

If feedback by different forms of evaluation, either by qualitative ranking or quantitative marks or coefficients, have provided data proving the achievement of the manifested aims, we may speak about suitability of the specified paradigm for a society. This in its turn gives ground for stability of this paradigm for a strategically designed period of implementation of the curriculum (e.g., a national curriculum).

A–Adjustments to Regional and Local Needs

This part of the paradigm is related to two phenomena: (a) specification of these sections of curricula reflecting the regionally and locally meaningful educational content, and (b) if monitoring at large and more specific evaluation has given unfavorable results. Implementation of the commonly accepted and shared global core curriculum cannot be put into practice in the same way due to diverse educational cultures, and nationally specific parts of the curriculum have to meet the demands for particular knowledge and skills required in their geopolitical region. This can be decided on using well-documented research for curriculum implementation in different parts of the world.

A MODEL FOR THE DEVELOPMENT OF NATIONAL CURRICULA FOR GENERAL COMPREHENSIVE SCHOOLS

National or state curricula have been compiled in countries where compulsory schooling has been legitimized and access to general education has been accepted as a principle for organizing education. According to Mader (1979), all theory for developing national curricula as documents of educational content and learning for all the population of the country should be dedicated to fostering development of the culture, society in the organization of a state, and an individual person. It means that, in addition to globally accepted values and contents, there has to be a special field of developing one's individual characteristics and identities.

The more information people encounter by different communication channels, the more there are and will be opportunities to discover the acceptable and meaningful in rather numerous fields of human culture. These in turn may develop different feelings of belonging to some particular values or fields of knowledge as education can make them comprehensible and acceptable. Because the competitive world of today is participating in some kind of hard brain race (Kearns & Doyle, 1991), the problem of the 21st century is not that of what to include into the content of learning, but just the opposite: what to exclude? Due to unmanageable amount of information, it has become more and more complicated to decide what could we do without. The acceptance of values means identity building, as we have discussed before. In addition to traditional family and ethnic identities, new identities of belonging to rather different and often international social groups and organizations can influence all of them. The more identities the person may find likely to take, the quicker he or she has to establish a personal priority list of belonging, so some identities become accepted and some rejected. When people and societies at large are unable to identify themselves, identity crises can develop, expressed by intolerance and even conflict, which can endanger social stability on any level of social organizations.

If culture, society, and individual are considered as a meaningful existing whole and understanding of that is expected to be conveyed and developed by public schooling, the following principles could be considered for compilation of the basis or general part of the curriculum, which in turn gives guidelines and enables to establish particular structures for designing study fields, school subjects, modules, or other elements of the system: preservation of globally accepted code of ethics for human behavior; preservation of ethnic cultures and their enrichment by globally and regionally relevant values; aspirations toward social cohesion on local, regional, and global levels; stability of society and development of democratic participation; and development of an informed, competent, and responsible citizenry.

DEVELOPMENT OF CROSS-CURRICULAR CONTENTS WITH DEVELOPMENT OF PERSONAL COMPETENCIES IN VARIOUS FIELDS FOR BUILDING DIFFERENT IDENTITIES

Accordingly, for organizing learning, development of particular curriculum area, or cross-curricular contents and activities can be identified for consistent treatment that can result in required content consisting of particular subject cycles in the curriculum. These cycles may be related to each other with different types and levels of integration. If learning with comprehension is understood as the basis for saving knowledge and skills in the long-term memory for future operational use, curricula have to be designed and compiled in a way that enables this. It might be called a thinking culture-specific approach to curriculum development able to meet demands of a particular society in the best rational and emotional way, considering the content required for everyday human activities as well as the establishment of a basis for future developments.

To make a smart selection for designing a curriculum as an integrated and meaningful whole, several basic principles derived from instructional psychology should be considered:

- Curricula should motivate students for active learning by developing external or internal motivation (Buck, 1985; Deci, 1975; Good & Brophy, 1997), which can explain the value of particular knowledge, skills, attitudes, and so on;
- All learning has to be planned considering its dynamics, content, and process (Taba, 1932);
- Educational change will be productive if provided with three things: a source of innovations in teaching and learning strategies, an efficient way to communicate these innovations, and an incentive system that rewards productive innovations and quickly eliminates bad ideas (Kelly, 1991);
- Curricula can be compiled as a system, where all new information for learning can be related to the previous knowledge of students acquired by formal or informal learning. Frameworks to fit in the new information have to be established before the new material is learned (Ausubel, 1960);
- More specific learning material for traditional school subjects or study fields can be rationally selected by meaningful vertical and horizontal integration of the content (Pring, 1976; Talyzina, 1975);
- All learning has to provide students with operational knowledge and skills, implementable in practical physical or mental activities;
- Education for identity development will always remain an individual and moral enterprise in which education has a crucial role for establishing the hierarchies of different identities;
- Possibility of transfer of basic concepts, facts, and skills offered by different subjects, study fields, modules, and so on has to be planned and sequenced logically;
- Balance between study time and content of studies can be achieved by specification of the developmental level of students and "hidden curriculum" of the sociocultural environment supporting or hindering learning.
- Content of studies has to allow implementation of different learning strategies, techniques, and relaxation activities considering the age and capability of learners. Small children in primary grades are more successful at acquiring enactic knowledge of how to do something as a procedure, whereas teenagers and adult learners become capable of metacognition (Bruner, 1990). Accordingly, skills of cooperation and other learning techniques constitute a particular field of processual knowledge, which has a particularly important role in the content of learning.
- Specified school subjects or study fields have to contribute to development of basic human competencies—namely, communicative and arithmetical competence, competence of critical and creative thinking, and technical-technological and social competencies—because they usually develop during people's lifetime, leading to an integrated competence of individual autonomy allowing one to manage one's life. Content of studies should follow roughly the same sequence in their organization, reaching particular levels of autonomy by the end of a specified educational (primary or secondary) level.

The goal of participation in the life of learning society presumes skills of decision making and talking about one's learning activities during different periods of life. Accordingly problems of learner autonomy have cropped up in numerous educational discussions in recent years. The most essential components of learner autonomy are considered to be the following:

- skills for selecting an educational level, school type, and more precise content of learning;
- skills for organizing one's learning process; and
- skills for evaluating personal academic achievement and educational and career opportunities for the future.

Considering the aforementioned, a model for development of subject syllabi and their implementation on a school level has been developed with the main emphasis on key concepts; development of structured, integrated, and operational knowledge; and specification of educational standard as minimal expected achievement and meaningful evaluation. Theoretical foundations for these models have been derived from the works of Taba (1962), Ausubel (1960, 1965, 1969), Pring (1976), Mader (1979), Orlov (1997), Daniljuk (1997), Goodson (1998), Klippert (1994), Peterssen (1982/1998), and Razumowski (1997). These models also allow a more rational use of the available time for studies, and they enable teachers to develop their own plans of action regarding the implementation of the NC. Although these models have only been designed and field tested in general comprehensive schools so far, similar models could be developed for other types of schools and courses of learning.

We have called this model of comprehensive learning for curriculum design a COPE model considering its basic constituting elements, and namely:

C–Content areas or school subjects based on development of six human competencies, helping people adjust themselves to contemporary culture and socio-political structures.

O–Operational knowledge and skills offered by specified school subjects or study fields empowering people for the learning society.

P–Practical process skills for learning culture-relevant ways of organizing learning activities and experiences.

E–External evaluation and self-evaluation against established educational standards as educational minimum.

According to this model, a more specific structure for selection of the subject content can be used. The following structure is an attempt to organize subject syllabi or study field programs into a holistic curriculum if compiled by a common or similar structure.

1. Nomination of the subject.
2. Main objectives of the subject (specification of the objectives this particular subject can support considering the agreed general goals of education; explanation for why this subject must be included in the NC).
3. Allotted time for studies (hours, modules, credits, etc.) for the whole subject course and in different grades.
4. Contingency of learners (considering their age and level of development).
5. Previous courses and experience constituting the starting level of learners for the course.
6. The content of the subject course with expected minimal attainment targets (standards or educational minimum) with specification of integrated knowledge and skills (operational level) by grade and school levels.

7. Evaluation (forms and implementation by grades and school levels).
8. Recommended basic study aids for implementation of the NC.

In case the subject syllabi in the NC could offer the aforementioned information, it could easily be put into practice on the school level. At schools all the teachers have to agree on teaching a particular course or subject following a common content and general approach. Schools are the places of practical implementation of the NC, where both the success or failure may occur in the process. The real outcome of curriculum implementation depends on how educationists and society at large understand and interpret the document, what the role of hidden curriculum is, what the circumstances are of a particular school, and what is actually learned and acquired by the students.

CONCLUSION

Nowadays there is an acknowledged need to develop flexible curricula that would allow us to react and make changes in them according to the developments in technologies and culture in the broad sense of the word. Decision making about national curricula requires wide participation of all involved (students, teachers, parents, publishers, teacher trainers, employers, etc.) as it burdens the people compiling the document with high ethical responsibility. Educational change by curriculum reforms should find solutions and alleviate tensions between the balance and coherence as well as choice and diversity, which is of special meaning for small societies (Estonia among the many). Social perspectives of educational change have to be considered in a much broader fields and context of interaction in society than the changes in the system (Eurydice Survey, 1999). Educational change in a small country offers opportunities for a considerably faster and shorter implementation. However, if managed the wrong way, it may cause devastating effects on the whole system.

All decisions about curricula or any other educational activities are restricted by their adequacy for implementation or, plainly spoken, their lifespan. Accordingly, different ideas, approaches, and structures can be used in different times and interpretations. It all depends on our powers of understanding the research and practical experience, those of conceptualization and reconceptualization of curricula, and learning under diverse circumstances in the changing world.

REFERENCES

Allardt, E. (1979). *Implications of the ethnic revival in modern industrialized society.* Helsinki, Finland: Societas Scientarum Fennica.

Ausubel, D. (1960). The use of advance organizers in the learning and retention of meaningful verbal material. *Journal of Educational Psychology, 51,* 267–272.

Ausubel, D. (1965). An evaluation of the conceptual schemes approach to science curriculum development. *Journal of Research in Science Teaching, 3,* 255–264.

Ausubel, D. (1969). *School learning: An introduction to educational psychology.* New York: Holt, Rinehart & Winston.

Bruner, J. (1990). *Acts of meaning.* Cambridge, MA: Harvard University Press.

Buck, R. (1985). *Human motivation and emotion* (2nd ed.). New York: Wiley.

Daniljuk, A. J. (1997). A school subject as an integrated system (in Russian). *Pedagogika, 4,* 24–28.

Darinski, A. V. (1996). A regional component of the content of education (in Russian). *Pedagogika, 1,* 18–20.

Deci, E. (1975). *Intrinsic motivation.* New York: Plenum.

Delors, J. (1996). *Learning: The treasure within* (in Estonian). Paris: UNESCO.

Dichtl, H. (2000). *Vorbereitung auf das Abitur Geographie.* Stuttgart, Germany: Manz Verlag.

Eisner, E. W. (1979). *The educational imagination: On the design and evaluation of school programs.* New York: Macmillan.

Eisner, E. W. (1992). Curriculum ideologies. In P. W. Jackson (Ed.), *Handbook of research on curriculum* (pp. 302–326). New York: Macmillan.

Elmore, R., & Sykes, G. (1992). Curriculum policy. In P. W. Jackson (Ed.), *Handbook of research on curriculum* (pp. 185–214). New York: Macmillan.

Eurydice Survey 1. (1999). *Forward planning in education in the member states of the European Union.* Luxembourg.

Gagne, R. M., Briggs, J. L., & Wager, W. W. (1992). *Principles of instructional design* (4th ed.). San Diego, CA: Harcourt Brace Jovanovich.

Good, T. L., & Brophy, J. E. (1997). *Looking in classrooms* (7th ed.). New York: Longman.

Goodson, I. F. (1998). *Subject knowledge.* London: Falmer.

Hasanow, Z. (1998). *Education towards intercultural communication culture.* Mahatshkala.

Johnson, M. (1967). Definitions and models in curriculum theory. *Educational Theory, 17*(2), 127–140.

Kearns D. T., & Doyle, D. P. (1991). *Winning the brain race.* San Francisco: ICS Press.

Kelly, H. (1991). Technology and transformation of American education. *Curriculum Perspectives,* pp. 357–374.

Klippert, H. (1994). *Methoden-training.* Ubungsbausteine den Unterricht. Weinheim und Basel Verlag.

Krajewsky, V. V., & Lerner, I. Y. (1983). *Curriculum theory in the USSR.* Paris.

Lawton, D. (1994). The National Curriculum and Assessment. *Forum, 36*(1), 7–8.

Laanemets, U. (1988). Functional load of languages in Estonia. *Nukogude Kool* (Soviet school), *1.*

Laanemets, U. (2002). *Education in Russian medium schools by 2007: Quality and management problems.* Jan Tonisson Institute.

Laanemets, U., & Hutt, V. (1995). *Research Report No. 2: Bilingualism and multilingualism of Russian-speaking population in Estonia.* Estonian Science Foundation, Project 13A.

Laanemets, U., & Rebane, J. (1994). *Languages in the context of culture of Russian-speaking students in Estonia.* Tallinn, Estonia: Avita.

Madaus, G., & Kellaghan, T. (1992). Curriculum evaluation and assessment. In P. W. Jackson (Ed.), *Handbook of research on curriculum* (pp. 119–154). New York: Macmillan.

Mader, O. (1979). *Fragen der Lehrplantheorie. Beitrage zur Pedagogik.* Berlin, Germany: Volk und Vissen Volkseigener Verlag.

McLaughlin, M. W. (1987). Learning from experience: Lessons from policy implementation. *Educational and Policy Analysis, 9,* 171–173.

National Curricula of the Republic of Estonia 1923, 1928, 1930, 1938.

Nunan D. (1991). *The learner-centered curriculum.* Cambridge, England: Cambridge University Press.

OECD/CERI. (1994).

Orlov, V. I. (1997). Content of the information for studies (in Russian). *Pedagogika, 1,* 53–55.

Peterssen, W. H. (1992/1998). *Handbuch Unterrichts planung.* Munich, Germany: Oldenburgverlag.

Piaget, J. (1975). *The child's conception of the world.* New York: Littlefield.

Pinar, W. (Ed.). (1998). *Curriculum: Toward new identities.* New York: Garland.

Pinar, W., Reynolds, W., Slattery P., & Taubman, P. (1996). *Understanding curriculum.* New York: Peter Lang.

Pring, E. (1976). *Knowledge and schooling.* London: Open Books.

Raagmaa, G. (1999). *Global change in economic environment and regional developments* (http://www.e.2010.ee/teemad/raagmaa 1htm # 1).

Razumovski, V. G. (1997). *Teaching and scientific cognition* (in Russian). *Pedagogika, 1,* 7–13.

Reform 1997, Norwegian Ministry of Education, Research and Church Affairs: 1).

Rifkin, J. (1995). *The end of the work: The decline of the global labor force and the dawn of the post-market era.* Hew York: Putnam Book.

Taba, H (1932). *The dynamics of education.* London: Kegan Paul.

Taba, H (1962). *Curriculum development: Theory and practice.* New York: Harcourt, Brace & World.

Talyzina, N. F. (1975). *Upravlenie protsessom usvojenija znanij* (Management of the processes of knowledge acquisition). Moscow: Moscow State University Press.

Tyler, R. (1949). *Basic principles of curriculum and instruction.* Chicago: University of Chicago Press.

Valdmaa, S. (1996). *About civics and curriculum development.* Jaan Tonisson Institute.

Walsh, P. (1993). *Education and meaning. Philosophy in practice.* Cassell.

White Paper on Education and Training. (1995). *Teaching and learning—towards the learning society.* Luxembourg: Office for Official Publications of the European Communities.

CHAPTER 16

Postmodern Paradoxes in Finland: The Confinements of Rationality in Curriculum Studies

Tero Autio
University of Tampere, Finland

The last two decades or so have witnessed quite dramatic changes in the arena of education. These changes have covered the whole world of education: theoretical advancements, breakthroughs in the field of curriculum studies, and, at the same time, strongly mandated changes in educational governance and financing often in sharp contrast with practical implications of those theoretical contributions. These incommensurate shifts and transitions in education and schooling reflect wider cultural, social, political, and economic transitions throughout the world. The traditional national and local imagery is increasingly absorbing a global horizon in the entire range of human action: from economy and politics to individual and intimate formations of self. These processes are difficult to capture within the uniform categories of change: The reasons and motivations, as well as their outcomes and effects, are at best complex and intertwined.

In education and schooling, where the national imagery has been and arguably continues to be a major source of ideas and practice, the infusion of the global horizon has nevertheless become more dominant even within national boundaries. Although the restructuring measures seem to organize around national interests and principles, they might actually involve more unifying and converging elements than before. Thus, what overtly seems to be dissimilarity and national idiosyncrasy proves to be strongly influenced by common trends. The same reform rhetoric, which in one national context has been promoted by centralization measures, may in another be advocated by decentralization efforts. The examples of restructuring in the United Kingdom and the United States may illuminate this principle in action. The implementation of the National Curriculum in England and Wales by the 1988 Education Act has left little or no room for teachers' professional autonomy and deliberation (see Kelly, 1999), whereas in the United States policy texts would seem to be a tendency to reverse the traditional image of the teacher as an obstacle to change and efficiency and to see teachers now as the subjects of restructuring not as the objects of it: "In the USA the teachers are the reformers, in the UK they are 'the reformed'" (Maguire & Ball; cited in Klette et al., 2000, p. 328). Yet what seems different turned out to be so only rhetorically: In educational restructuring, seemingly different policies in different national settings share same underlying principles and "implementation mechanisms."

Ingrid Carlgren (cited in Klette et al., 2000) divided the shared underlying principles under different restructuring processes into two levels: on a system level the *marketization* of the educational sector, which includes new forms of governance (steering by goals/objectives and results); and on the level of school and teachers' work, the restructuring mechanisms used include the insertion of *accountability, competitiveness,* and *performativity.* Reiterating Stephen Ball's claim that "the combination of market and performative reforms bites deep into the practice of teaching and into the teacher's soul," Carlgren recorded the replacement of the profession's value orientation from professional-ethical regimes to entrepreneurial-competitive ones. The combined effect of competition and performativity turns educational processes more into a matter of economic efficacy and competition than a matter of building societies, which means that education is becoming increasingly commodified.

This situation is in a multilayered way confused. At a time when curriculum studies has been claimed since the 1970s, and, at least in the United States, to have "emerged as a vibrant field, replete with excitement, creative energy, and a body of theoretically informed scholarship" (Kincheloe, 1997, p. xiii), the enacted curriculum has experienced an educational degeneration. When the complexities of the curriculum are being understood better than ever before, the actual curriculum has been taught in conditions of late modernity as "an incontestable fixity" and with "procedural fidelity." Focusing specifically on the teachers' new situation, Goodson (1998) spoke about

> one of the *paradoxes of postmodernism*: that at precisely the time teachers are being "brought back in," their work is being vigorously restructured. Teachers' voices and stories are being pursued as *bona fide* reflective research data at a time of quite dramatic restructuring. In fact, at precisely the time the teacher's voice is being pursued and promoted, the teacher's work is being technized and narrowed.... As teachers' work intensifies, as more and more centralized edicts and demands impinge on the teacher's world, the space for reflection and research is progressively squeezed. (pp. 18–19)

In the first part of this chapter, an attempt is made to question these unifying or globally shared themes manifested on the level of national curricula with broader maps of the developments in social theory and the philosophy of science. Notably, the influence of the Tyler rationale as the symbolic icon for the current curricular developments in the restructuring of education is of interest. Although based on instrumental rationality and the continuation of empiricist tradition, the rationale succinctly captured the spirit of Western rationalism with its emphasis on procedural and pragmatic effectiveness. Within this order of value, the design of curriculum would mean the psychologization of its dimensions feasible both to the bureaucratic and then to the commodified, neo-liberal uses of curriculum. The second part briefly focuses on curriculum views that both challenge the notion of curriculum in terms of proceduralism and consequently seek to identify alternative ways to conceive it. The first of these views would represent one version of the German hermeneutically inspired version of curriculum and pedagogic studies (*geisteswissenschaftliche Pädagogik*)—Wolfgang Klafki's "critical- constructive Didaktik." The other view, the Reconceptualization Movement, which initially began as an American domestic dispute by criticizing Tyler's notion of curriculum, has only been recognized more internationally after the publication of the monumental theoretical mapping of the movement, *Understanding Curriculum* (Pinar et al., 1995).

The Reconceptualization is not treated here as an internal dispute within the curriculum field, but is linked to paradigm change in the philosophy of science in the change of the self-understanding of science in general. Both those curricular views draw on hermeneutics (or in any case postempiricism) as their respective methodological attitude. Yet common features exist as well as interesting distinctions between them that might be informative while seeking the complex identities of curriculum in the globalizing world of education.

BASIC PRINCIPLES OF CURRICULUM AND INSTRUCTION

Tyler's (1949) *Basic Principles of Curriculum and Instruction* has been treated as "a Bible of the curriculum" (Jackson, 1992) or "the fundamental icon of the American curriculum field" (Westbury, 1998, p. 49). His four-step synthesis of curriculum planning, known as the *Tyler rationale*, became the commonsense of the field:

> The first is the development of objectives—a crucial first step since all other aspects of curriculum planning depend on the precise articulation of achievable ends. The second step involves the creation of learning experiences that will lead to the attainment of those objectives, with the third step involving the ordering of those activities in an effective way. In the final step the curriculum designer/teacher evaluates how successfully students have accomplished the objectives identified in step 1. (Tyler, 1949, p. 1; Beyer & Liston, 1996, p. 25)

The obvious commonsensicality of those maxims might have been one reason for the success of the Tyler rationale in educational settings not only in American curriculum work, but increasingly with the advent of postindustrial society all over the world—if not literally at least symbolically. The rationale might be claimed to be more than one suggestion for an effective curriculum as Tyler saw it. In a succinct form, it is a consummation of American curriculum thought; even more, it might be argued to include the main characteristics of Western rationality at large. Although Tyler (1949) was concerned about the narrow purposes of social efficiency, he could not prevent the destiny of the Basic Principles from becoming a manifesto for the ideological efforts of effectiveness ("education should help people to carry on their activities more effectively": p. 20), neutrality, and objectivity in curriculum work. It promoted the search for a utilitarian curriculum that would respond to societal and economic needs and prepare future citizens to meet these needs.

Of course, all this has its roots. Westbury (cited in Gundem & Hopmann, 1998) stressed the continuity of the American school system and curriculum work, starting from the first half of the 19th century, when New York City experienced a tenfold population increase between 1800 and 1850. Rapid urbanization hastened the need to create a school system that first

> drew heavily for the inspiration for its institutional development both on the notion of a school based on universal, general rules about how human affairs might be ordered and on the imaginings, and the practices, of the industrial and organizational revolution of the 19th century. (Gundem & Hopmann, 1998, p. 51)

The result was a school system that

> applied collective decisions to a large mass of people; it promulgated detailed procedures and then attempted ensure quality by eliminating deviation from these procedures. The system's governors employed supervision, inspection, punishments, and rewards to encourage uniform performance, and they made explicit the relationships

between levels in the authoritative hierarchy for teachers and the curriculum hierarchy for students. (Kaestle; cited in Westbury, 1998, p. 51)

The second critical feature of the New York system was that

> it was a system developed within an institutional context which offered common di-
> rection from a single authoritative center. This center directed and provided the orga-
> nization within bureaucratically organized, monopolistic provision of "public"
> education. Almost all the forms of modern American school system can be seen encap-
> sulated in the early 19th century school system ... (Westbury, 1998, p. 51)

These administrative arrangements were completed by novel curricular tasks associated not with elite preparatory schools, but with the organization of mass terminal
secondary education. The needed curriculum changes required a new kind of ideological and public legitimation, which the new class of university curricular intellectuals
like Tyler undertook.

> In this new mutation curriculum work became an activity which supported, rational-
> ized, directed and sought to legitimate the changes being undertaken in the schools,
> and a source of authority vis-à-vis publics for the emerging professional, administra-
> tive "leadership" of such social change. It was "movement" which sought sanction for
> its prescriptions in new versions of "science" (i.e., Tyler's "psychology"), the system-
> atic ("scientific") analysis of social "needs," and images of a "modern" school; and
> while it identified itself with the curriculum, and with the school programs and teacher
> practices that would support the new schools, its target of concern was still the "sys-
> tem." (Westbury, 1998, p. 52)

Westbury's critical conclusion is that the history of the (American) curriculum field
summarized in the Tyler rationale would reflect and only extend 19th-century procedures of systemic curriculum making.

> Thus, from the origins of curriculum work in the urban school bureaucracies of the
> 19th century, through the period of reform of the 1920s and 1930s which created the
> modern comprehensive high school, through the curriculum reforms of the Sputnik
> era to the concerns of of today with nation-wide "systemic reform" and the national
> curriculum, the focus has been on public needs and on the adjustment of the system to
> the perceived public "needs" of each time. (Westbury, 1998, p. 52)

One of the astonishing paradoxes of this picture Westbury is painting would be, at
least from a non-American point of view, how restrained a role seems to have been reserved for the teacher in the promised land of individual freedom:

> Within the perspective of curriculum, teachers are always, ..., the invisible *agents* of
> the system, to be remotely controlled by that system for public ends, *not* independent
> actors with their own visible role to play in the schools. They are seen as "animated"
> and directed *by* the system and not as sources of animation *for* the system.... The cur-
> riculum and its transmission, teaching, is ideally "teacher-proof." Thus both tradi-
> tional curriculum theory and "practical" curriculum work have seen the abstracted
> teacher as a (if not the) major brake on the necessary innovation, change, and reform
> that the schools always require, a "problem" which must be addressed by highly elab-
> orated theories and technologies of *curriculum implementation*. Teachers are seen as the
> conservative source of the "failure" of much innovation. It is the task of teacher educa-

tion to prepare teachers as effective vehicles for delivering the curriculum and and its goals to students by equipping them with most effective methods for delivering that content. *It was and is not their task to reflect on that content.* (Westbury, 1998, pp. 52–53)

Despite Westbury's focus on the American curriculum field, his speculation might be illustrative in many other Western countries, too. The advent of neo-liberal discourses and political practices since the end of 1970s made those trends described by Westbury more perceptible in other Western countries, too, which Kelly, for the part of the United Kingdom (especially England and Wales) has featured as following principles: (a) a simplistic concept of "standards," (b) instrumentalism, (c) commercialism, and (d) an increased emphasis on management (Kelly, 1999). The practical outcome of this kind of educational policy has proved to be rather similar to that of the United States.

Teachers are, or should be, merely operators, passive agents, technicians rather than professionals, whose task it is to carry out the policies made for them elsewhere and by others, to instruct children in those things their political masters wish to have them instructed in. ... Whether, in reality, teachers can be thus operated by remote control is another question, but it is certainly a premise and an assumption of current policy that they can and should be. (Kelly, 1999, pp. 192–193)

The question remains whether educational and curriculum policies and practices are becoming more similar than ever in different parts of the world. Might these developments shortly mean globalization in educational terms? At the center of these efforts are the principles Tyler hesitantly proposed as just one—his—alternative to curriculum design, but his suggestion might have been transformed in the hands of educational stakeholders throughout the world as *the* universal model and ideology of curriculum work. In any case, in the United States at least, the ideas of Tyler and his predecessors (Bobbitt, Charters, Snedden, and Finney) have been claimed to be "... very much alive and well in contemporary society":

... the attempts of the new right to reconfigure the school and and college curriculum are tied to yet another attempt to make the curriculum reflect the needs not of industrial or corporate capitalism but of what has been called postindustrial society. *Such an attempt in many ways reinstantiates the curriculum movement at the turn of the twentieth century.* (Beyer & Liston, 1996, p. 27; italics added)

THE RATIONALE AND OCCIDENTAL RATIONALISM

An attempt might be made to render more intelligible the critical account of the Tyler rationale as a symbol of Western curriculum thought when viewed from within the development of the *Occidental rationalism*. In his classical but fragmentary studies of Western or Occidental rationalism Max Weber (1864–1920) explained the peculiarly rationalized nature of "our European-American social and economic life," which is manifest specifically in the establishment of the capitalist economy and the modern state.

Weber's treatment of the development of rationalization might be pertinent from a curriculum theory point of view because he had a two-way focus on the processes of rationalization. On the one hand, Weber was interested in the processes of the motivational anchoring of an individual to societal institutions; on the other hand, he tried to articulate how posttraditional moral or psychological remakings of self would emerge as institutional embodiments. In other words, for Weber, rational action functioned like a glue between single individuals and societal institutions. In a similar fashion, the differently stressed mediations between self and society might be argued to form the kernel of educational agendas through the history of education. To understand the historical and theoretical roots of the Tyler rationale, it might be informative to take a look at it through the lenses provided by Weber's (1978) exposition of types of social action in *Economy and Society*:

Social action, like all action may be oriented in four ways. It may be:

(1) *instrumentally rational (zweckrational),* that is, determined by expectations as to behavior of objects in the environment and of other human beings; these expectations are used as "conditions" or "means" for the attainment of the actor's own rationally pursued and calculated ends;

(2) *value-rational (wertrational),* that is, determined by a conscious belief in the value for its own sake of some ethical, aesthetic, religious, or other form of behavior, independently of its prospects of success;

(3) *affectual* (especially emotional), that is, determined by the actor's specific affects and feeling states;

(4) *traditional,* that is, determined ingrained habituation. (pp. 24–26)

Instrumental rationality stood for Weber as an ideal type of Western rationalism—as a yardstick against which three other orientations could be ordered and against which they could be assessed. Instrumental rationality is closely related to knowledge. However, there would be a specific emphasis on knowledge that is nicely manifested in Tyler's opening words in the *Basic Principles*: "Instead of answering the questions, an explanation is given of procedures by which these questions can be answered" (p. 2). This is just what Habermas (1984) said about rationality in his preliminary specification linked to Weber:

When we use the expression "rational" we suppose that there is a close relation between rationality and knowledge ..., for rationality has less to do with the possession of knowledge than with how speaking and acting subjects *acquire and use knowledge.* (p. 8)

The methical and pragmatic stress would be characteristic for instrumental rationality, where knowledge is assessed by its feasibility to instrumental mastery of reality. Habermas (1984) introduced "the concept of *cognitive-instrumental* rationality that has, through empiricism, deeply marked the self-understanding of the modern era" (p. 10). This mode of rationality, with its modernist scientific outlook, leans on two basic premises that are peculiarly present in the Tyler rationale, too. The first is the notion of *truth* conceived in empirical terms; the other is the notion of *effectiveness*:

As *truth* is related to the existence of states of affairs in the world, *effectiveness* is related to interventions in the world with whose help states of affairs can be brought into existence. (Habermas, 1984, pp. 8–9)

This abstract philosophical expression is concretely present in the rationale: Empirical truths and pragmatic effectiveness stripped of all metaphysical or moral considerations would form a kind of circular reasoning in curriculum planning, where educational goals are constantly revised in the light of scientific findings and needs of society, which, in turn, are to be tested against their effective applicability indicated as students' preferred behavior changes.

Method, Effectiveness, and Moral Concern

Although Tyler (1949) dedicated almost half the space available (62 pages) to the treatment of educational purposes and their determination, his approach contained no genuine ethical or value-rational search for a source of setting ends. His straightforward and pragmatic focus on contemporary life is akin to Locke's and other early empiricists' interest in the experience and rational organization of the human mind and society. While preferring contemporary life to ethics or metaphysics, Tyler actually affirmed everyday life as a source of morality, like Descartes and Locke at the dawn of modernity. This emphasis on everyday practice might prove to be anything but unproblematic: It instantly brings the question of social and political power and control to the forefront, and this issue is addressed in the next brief excursion into the moral and ideologial features of the rationale.

Yet the overt lack of moral concern and the stress on instrumental rationality is not to be interpreted one-sidedly as theoretical naiveté or moral indifference. Tyler (1949) continued—perhaps not yet consciously—that long tradition of the proponents of instrumental rationality that see morality embedded within scientific method or methodism in life conduct in general. Already for Descartes, the skills of "rightly conducting reason " like methodical life conduct in the Protestant-Calvinist devotion to paid work, meant a conscious effort for moral improvement. The whole cultural context that gave birth to instrumental rationality was imbued with moral concern.

This initial morality immersed in the methodical thinking of the founders of modern philosophy and science might have created a first appeal to instrumentalism lasting to this day while trying to solve social, political, and educational problems by science. Taylor (1991) illuminated the moral of instrumentalism, which "has by no means been powered by an overdeveloped *libido dominandi* and thus has served exclusively the ends of greater control or technological mastery" (p. 105). According to Taylor, the domination of nature is not the whole story; there are two other important moral contexts from which the stress on instrumental reason has arisen.

The first of these is the Cartesian theoretical initiative of disengaged reason: "we are pure mind, distinct from body, and our normal way of seeing ourselves is a regrettable confusion" (p. 102). Here the Calvinist image of the self as imperfect and being in constant need of betterment would fit to the Cartesian view. The idea of human as disengaged reason in turn "is grounded in a moral ideal, that of a self-responsible, self-controlling reasoning" (p. 103). From a historical point of view, one of the secrets of the great success of this thought might be that initially the idea of instrumental rationality was not restricted to the controlling function of reason, but it was "an ideal of freedom, of autonomous, self-generating thought" (p. 104). This bond between bodily self-control and cognitive-mental freedom would render a powerful modern image of self and personality on which the Enlightenmental ideas of progress in general and modern education in particular could be anchored:

> Instrumental reason has grown, along with a disengaged model of human subject which has a great hold on our imagination. It offers an ideal picture of human thinking that has disengaged from its messy embedding in our bodily constitution, our dialcgical situation, our emotions, and our traditional life forms in order to pure, self-verifying rationality. This is one of the most prestigious forms of reason in our culture, exemplified by mathematical thinking, or other types of formal calculation. Arguments, considerations, counsels that can claim to be based on this kind of calculation have great persuasive power in our society, even when this kind of reasoning is not really suited to the subject matter.... (Taylor, 1991, pp. 102–103)

The moral core in this methodical freedom is tied to a need to give an explanation to the problem that has been common to all world religions: "the question of justifying the unequal distribution of life's goods" (Habermas, 1984, p. 201). The need to reduce inequality and individual suffering no longer fell from heaven, but resulted from "learning processes that set in as the ideas of justice established in tribal societies clashed with the new reality of class societies" (p. 201). In these novel social situations, the common good as an ethical ideal presupposed an idea of a free and rational agent whose destiny was no more bound by the habits of tradition. In that model of thought, the disengagement of the human subject, an ideal of self-determining freedom, and instrumental rationality would create the minimal conditions for common good in the constitution of modern society.

In Taylor's second suggestion for the initial moral strain of instrumental rationality, the moral ideal of free, yet self-responsible and self-controlling reasoning is related to the notion of new science, whose main task would be to reduce human suffering. The desire for the common good would mean the stress on pragmatic truth criteria by "the affirmation of ordinary life" because

> the life of production and reproduction, of work and family, is what is important for us, for … it has made us give unprecedented importance to the production of the conditions of life in ever-greater abundance and the relief of suffering on an ever-wider scale. Already in the early seventeenth century, Francis Bacon criticized the traditional Aristotelian sciences for having contributed nothing to "relieve the condition of mankind." He proposed in their stead a model of science whose criterion of truth would be instrumental efficacy. *You have discovered something when you can intervene to change things.* Modern science is in essential continuity in this respect with Bacon. But what is important in Bacon is that he reminds us that *the thrust behind this new science was not only epistemological but also moral.* (Taylor, 1991, p. 104; italics added)

Seen from this historical perspective, the Tyler rationale seems anything but a morally indifferent or isolated piece of work, as it might appear separated from its theoretical forerunners: Bacon, Descartes, Locke, and the Calvinist forms of the Reformation. Pragmatism as its epistemology and criterion of truth, psychology as a major means to methodize the pursuit for pragmatic educational goals (the needs of society), would form the operational core of the Tyler rationale. However, more important perhaps is the way of moral justification in the rationale. Actually, education in its proper sense is a moral and political enterprise. Within the Cartesian and Calvinist legacies, there is a tendency to subsume the moral and political under the rules of procedure or method, often ideologically clothed in scientific objectivity and political neutrality. The Tyler rationale faithfully follows this scheme in its tacit moral justification. There is no factual need for the analysis of moral or political aspects of educational goals because those requirements would be automatically satisfied by the "rightly conducting" scientific methods, which means that the best available morality is embedded within the instrumental use of rationality.

PSYCHOLOGY OF LEARNING: LOGIC WITHOUT CONTEXT

The central status of psychology in the Tyler rationale is interestingly related to that general scheme of thought. It should be found as a way to mediate the initial moral concern at the level of personality. Here there is a striking similarity with Calvinist and Cartesian attempts to design a program for the promotion of cultural and societal ideals of rationalization on the level of personality. This would mean the fostering of a decentered (i.e., scientific) understanding of the world and a psychological objectification of interpersonal relationships. The overall but tacitly assumed aim of those efforts would be the common good and human welfare. Thus, there is no real incentive to exercise genuine moral or political deliberation in the choice and justification of educational ends as such. The real problem is about a proper procedure: how to make these ends psychologically accessible and feasible to instructional arrangements.

The rational and calculative aspects of knowledge that Tyler wanted to include in his notion of psychology might arguably be interpreted as a 20th-century version of Calvinist and Cartesian notions of self. The reduction of the complexities of economic, social, and political life into psychological orders would reinstantiate the initial Calvinist requirements for the remaking of the self.

Psychology does not function merely as a means in the pursuit of selected ends, but also has an active role with philosophy while screening out educational objectives from the three main sources of curriculum: contemporary life, learners, and subject matter specialists. However, the role of philosophy remains a minor one among those two screens within the structure of the rationale. Philosophy at its best seems to function as a preparation for the psychologization of curriculum planning. First of all, the Tylerian definition of *education* essentially restricts the scope of philosophy to behavioral aspects of human action: "education is a process of changing the behavior patterns of people" including "thinking and feeling as well as overt action." Thus, in practice, an auxiliary role has been reserved for philosophy as "the first screen" for selecting and eliminating educational objectives. "In essence," wrote Tyler, "the statement of philosophy attempts to define the nature of a good life and a good society" (p. 34), but the way Tyler used philosophy is a negative one: "selecting and eliminating," not using it, for instance, as a theoretical tool for an analysis of power relations in society or what the preconditions of good life might be in modern society.

Such a definition of *philosophy* might raise a further fundamental problem that is related to the problem of a good life and a good society: the Lockean-like reduction of values and morality to the behavioral sphere of experience. This stand is reflected later in positivism according to which ethical questions and values are not scientific and thus not real problems because they cannot unequivocally be reduced to experiences based on sense perception or sense data. The inherent problems of Tyler's positivistically and instrumentalistically inspired curriculum theory might assume their most serious expressions in his "screens thinking." He never made it quite clear what those values inherent in his philosophical screen were. Yet the main function of the philosophical screen is to guide the choice making among an infinite number of objectives that can be drawn from the three sources. But

> since the philosophical screen (and the psychological screen for that matter) are essentially arbitrary statements of beliefs, they can just as easily screen out what is worthy and commendable as what is trivial and senseless. Because we have no guidance as to what a good 'philosophy' is as opposed to a bad one, we also have no guidance as to what objectives to choose. We are enjoined only to make the objectives consistent with the two screens. Needless to say, if there were no necessity to choose objectives in the first place, there would be no need of a mechanism for sorting them out ... it may even be possible to to engage in an educational activity for good reasons that have nothing to do with objectives in the Rationale's sense of the term, and, I dare say, many excellent teachers have done so for centuries. (Kliebard, 1995, p. 82)

Kliebard's critique shows how that kind of "very rough and commonsensical" use of philosophy in determining educational objectives functions only as curricular lip service to philosophy:

Stating philosophies in this sense is only one of many extant rituals of schooling. These rituals continue to exist not because they are actually instrumental in resolving curriculum issues or in guiding the choice of objectives but as a kind of secular analogue to prayer. What the Rationale asks us to do is to invoke divine philosophy (rather than a deity) in order to bless the objectives of the curriculum that are born out of the process. They are good objectives not by virtue of their demonstrable merit but because they have the philosophy's benediction. A typical school's philosophy expressing such bromides as 'meeting the needs of children' excludes nothing because it says virtually nothing and therefore will not serve to guide the process of curriculum making even in the unlikely event that it is taken seriously. Don't get me wrong. Philosophy is important, but its significance lies in the way it can illuminate the problems we face and not as an inventory of sanctimonious platitudes. (p. 85)

The real and ideological core of the *Basic Principles* is not in philosophy but in the psychology of learning: how motivational and psychological anchoring of people to the institutions of modern society could be educationally established. Maybe, contrary to what Kliebard claimed, the psychological screen is not arbitrary. It seems to be in the service of societal rationalization. The tacit ideological interest of the psychological screen is to connect personality to system by "the rationalization of the personality system" (Habermas, 1984, p. 166). By the personality system Habermas denoted, "the behavioral dispositions or value orientations that are typical of the methodical conduct of life" (p. 166). Historically, the rationalization process within the personality system has been manifested in the transposition of the initially Protestant ethic into professional-ascetic orientations "above all in economic and administrative spheres of life" (p. 166). The structuration process of modern society as the embodiment of moral-practical structures of consciousness has been heavily dependent on the rationalization of the personality system, where in turn the role of education has been, and continuously is, vital.

The methodical conduct of life is now justified and promoted by scientific-psychological arguments, not by religious or philosophical ones. The thrust of the rationale is to psychologize educational theory and practice. Complexities of social, economic, and political life create the psychological individual. To strip education from its socially situated character is legitimated by the ideological maneuver where the systemic interests are contained within the personality system.

By the psychologization of education, the rationale may wish to transcend race, gender, class, and religious divisions and create a universal paradigm of curriculum design. But just that kind of procedural universalism suggested by empirical generalizations might have caused the inherent problems of the rationale. Universalism has been bought at the price of content despite Tyler's explicit insistence on the inclusion of the content aspect with the behavioral one in a valid choice of educational objectives.

One of the most instructive single expressions of that universalistic bias based solely on formal procedures is Tyler's account of critical thinking as an educational objective. Critical thinking could be appreciated as one of the most important goals of education, and the treatment of this topic in the Tylerian framework is illustrative of the inherent problems of the rationale. Critical thinking, wrote Tyler (1949), "implies some kind of mental operation involving the relating of facts and ideas in contrast to mere apprehension or memorization of them" (p. 60). Referring to the formative experiences of secondary school teachers during the 8-Year-Study, Tyler defined *critical thinking* to include three sorts of mental behavior:

The first involved *inductive thinking*; that is, the interpretation of data, the drawing of generalizations from a collection of specific facts or items of data. The second involved *deductive thinking*; the ability to begin with certain general principles already taught and to apply them to concrete cases which, although new to students, are appropriate illustrations of the operation of the principles. The third aspect of thinking identified by these teachers was *the logical aspect* by which they meant the ability of the student to make material purporting to be a logical argument and analyze this argument so as to identify the critical definitions, the basic assumptions, the chains of syllogisms involved in it and detect any logical fallacies or any inadequacies in the logical development of it. (p. 60; italics added)

It is characteristic that the procedural recommendation of the rationale seems to extend the behavioral aspect of an educational objective to the extreme that it engulfs the content aspect of critical thinking. There is no material hint—a content aspect of an educational objective—what critical thinking might be. This model of critical thought might be partly valid in the context of laboratory experimentation, but it is definitely insufficient in dealing with social issues. However, Tyler took the case of critical thinking as a model for transforming any vaguely stated term into a valid educational objective:

By defining critical thinking in this way the teachers gave meaning to a term which previously has been vague to them, and thus provided a base for understanding what curriculum implications there might be whenever such a term was set up as the behavioral aspect of an educational objective. (p. 60)

The content-free methodism might unveil the ideological nature of such a notion of psychology. From the Weberian–Habermasian standpoint, behaviorist psychology forms an essential part of modern rationalism. In the reductive creation of the psychological individual, the Tyler rationale nevertheless mirrors and shares the spirit of larger institutional contexts like (a) rationality of market, (b) formal legal system, (c) rational administration, and (d) methodical professional ethic. The rationale, along with its psychologized curriculum suggestions, maintains the ideal of rational actor as an indispensable part of modern Western nation-state institutions. Educational psychology assumes its tacit responsibility to connect people to nation-state not by force, but by methodical and rational self-control, where self-interest comes to be subordinated to the requirements of society. To be a good citizen and a good worker in a modern society means a constant remaking of the self inclined toward more and more deliberate, rational, and predictable behavior, where the outer control is increasingly removed and replaced by a psychological, inward, and subtler one.

FROM RATIONALIZATION TO COMMODIFICATION

Rationalization, differentiation, and commodification are the main constituents of modernization. These three processes are closely related: "modern social systems have a high or complex level of differentiation and are equally characterized by progressive commodification and rationalization" (Crook et al., 1992, p. 16). The concept of *differentiation* specifies a dimension of modernization that is more "power neutral" than the other two. But,

as Marx and Weber respectively make clear, commodification and rationalization are closely connected to the forms and distribution of power in society. The level of their development is an index of the extent to which commodity producers and "rule producers" are able to extent their control over material and cultural objects and over other human beings. (Crook et al., 1992, p. 10)

The symbolic tools Tyler well meaningly offered for the school bureaucracy and rule producers in his rationale have experienced rather vulgarized, but comprehensible transformations in the most recent, commodified developments in curriculum work. The result in many countries has been that the school institution has become something of a hybrid of traditional bureaucratic organization and a business enterprise. Yet this development is no great surprise because both models of organization are manifestations of the same type of modern thinking and practice: instrumental rationality. Kelly described this shift as the imposition of the commercial and industrial metaphors on the education system of England and Wales, but probably they are known everywhere (Blenkin et al.; cited in Kelly, 1999, p. 42):

> throughout the official literature on the National Curriculum, we are offered a commercial/industrial imagery which encourages us to see schools as factories. Teachers are invited to view their task as one of "delivering" a "product," they are subjected to "quality-control mechanisms"; they are encouraged to focus their efforts on "increased productivity," usually at a more "economic costing" (i.e. on the cheap); inspectors and advisers have in many places acquired new titles as "quality control" specialists. Soon education will be run, like the Rev. Awdry's railway system by a "Fat Controller"—if this is not happened already. (p. 42)

One might conclude that "all was quiet in the western front" if we compare this description with Westbury's account of the development of teacher-proof curriculum from the beginning of the 19th century. The metaphors that reflect a new, commodified phase in societal rationalization are mirrored again and consequently at the level of personality. The subtle manipulation of language readily led to self-censorship—"the most difficult of all kinds of censorship"—where teachers as the agents of the system cannot comprehend their vocation in any other terms than those in accord with commercial/business metaphor: competition, productivity, instrumentalism, quality, and value for money:

> the loss of other values and attitudes perhaps more appropriate to education in a democratic society (caring, human development, intrinsic value) has been almost completely absorbed by the teaching profession, and has come to dominate not only the education debate but also educational policies and practices. (Kelly, 1999, p. 43)

In this context, educational psychology seems to continue the tradition of proceduralism and systemic concerns with all their alienating effects in constantly new guises (situated cognition, constructivism, etc.). Any thoroughgoing redefinition of its task would come to be supplanted by or situated in the systemic interests of society and schooling:

> I argue for *refinement* rather than *redefinition*. Our foundations as an applied science are sound, in my opinion. The challenge ahead is to bring together the scattershot elements of our accomplishments to date. A cornerstone for coherence can be found in the object of our investigation: the institution of schooling. In an effort to satisfy diverse clientele, American schools have virtually "disintegrated" during the past 50 years. By focusing our efforts - theoretical, methodological, and empirical,—on the integration of schooling, we can both assist education and re-establish a sense of disciplinary integrity. (Calfee, 1992, p. 163)

Alternative Options for Curriculum Work

The current curriculum field contains responses and contributions that have attempted to transcend the obvious *ad hoc* character of educational psychology with its nonproblematic institutionalism and revitalize the deintellectualized and mandated field of teacher practice and teacher education. This part of the field has realized that "all curriculum development is teacher development" (Stenhouse; cited in Kelly, 1999, p. 11)—how a teacher is able to grasp the nature of the profession not only in terms of what and how, but also theoretically and comprehensively in terms of why. In that respect, two important instances could be briefly raised—one from the United States, the other from Germany as a programmatic summary for the field—each of which has attempted to name the world of education, curriculum, and teachership differently. Despite the long historical and cultural roots of the traditions, there are in each of them some common reminders of the indispensable and enduring moral and social complexities of curriculum as the centerpiece of education. The subsequent, partly historical treatment supported by a short excursion into the recent philosophy of science would ultimately aim to illustrate of the chosen order of values in those theory suggestions—and as contrasted to curriculum models guided by more instrumental orientations.

The theoretical avantgarde in curriculum studies—in North America especially—gained its power of influence since the 1970s and was organized as the Reconceptualization Movement. One of its culmination points was the publication of *Understanding Curriculum* by William F. Pinar et al. in 1995. Inspired by the growing dissatisfaction within the American domestic curriculum work, which was based on the Tyler's rationale, the Reconceptualization, as it is exposed in the *Understanding Curriculum*, has gradually begun to remind curriculum people outside the United States of the serious restraints to understanding curriculum merely in its institutional terms. The institution of schooling forms just one aspect in the Reconceptualist effort to conceive curriculum differently. To remove it from its conventional status as an administrative-bureaucratic document, curriculum came to be understood in the Reconceptualist sense as a form of praxis and a project of understanding. To introduce theory into the study of curriculum decisively expanded the often taken-for-granted realm of curriculum in two ways: substantive and methodological. The institution of schooling was viewed as indispensable, although only as one possible way to conceive the curriculum. The other points of view, which are denoted in chapter headings of the *UC*, would be: history, politics, race, gender, phenomenology, postmodernism, autobiography, aesthetics, theology, and international and global concerns. On a methodological (and worldview) level, the Reconceptualization meant a paradigm shift from an ideal of causal *explanation* to hermeneutic *understanding*—from an image of human sciences as seeking cause–effect relationships as in the natural sciences to viewing human studies as a linguistic (textual, discursive) interpretation of human action and its institutional embodiments.

Hermeneutic Critiques

This feature of the Reconceptualization is linked to an alternative posture in the philosophy of science, which has roots reaching back to the latter part of the 19th century to the Neo-Kantian dispute, the so-called *Methodenstreit*, between Explanation (*Erklären*) and Understanding (*Verstehen*). Hermeneutics as a viable approach in human and cultural studies was established as a result of this debate. The recognition of some basic issues in that debate might be useful in the reappraisal of the American curriculum debate during the recent two decades, and it would also demonstrate the usefulness of both debates for the current internationalization of curriculum studies.

Among the pioneers of hermeneutics, there was a certain distrust of science and its methods when modeled according to the study of inanimate nature. Without losing confidence in the possibilities of science as such, their critique and concern was aimed at the validity of the study of human history, culture, and society when the applied methods were uncritically adopted from natural sciences or rationalist-empiricist philosophy.

This posture was expressed in the words of the chief architect of hermeneutics, Wilhelm Dilthey (1833–1911), when he targeted his criticism of rationalism and cognitivism to both British empiricists and Continental rationalists. His fragmentary project, *Einleitung in die Geisteswissenschaften,* aimed at theory of human studies (*Geisteswissenschaften*) as opposed to arid reason and abstract speculation of philosophy and mechanistic causality of natural sciences. These reductionist endeavors in philosophy and science have also led to inactive and static images of human subject and action:

> There is no real blood flowing in the veins of the knowing subject fabricated by Locke, Hume, and Kant, but only the diluted juice of reason as mere mental activity. (Dilthey, 1988, p. 73)

Dilthey's goal was to outline a theory of concrete human subject that was to challenge the theories devised by "earlier epistemology, both empirical and Kantian, [which] explains experience and knowledge on the basis of a framework which is purely ideational" (p. 73). He strove for a holistic appreciation of human powers, which are embodied in the outcomes of historical processes as well as the principles of psychology, which form the object of human studies. The kind of comprehensive conception of human life and reality fostered by Dilthey as an irreducible and complex object of hermeneutic studies cannot live with the demands of methodological monism and proceduralism promoted by both rationalism and empiricism.

Hermeneutics drew ideas from *Lebensphilosophie,* a romanticist opponent of the Enlightenment, which sought to promote a more comprehensive and complex view of human life and agency than that dictated by methodical reason like in Cartesian thought. In hermeneutics, the picture of human reality is a social picture—individuality is to be conceived not in terms of self-sufficiency, but rather as a formative process between I and World. The content of this basic relation is not to be reduced to cognitive-solipsistic assertions, but needs a recognition of human being as a willing-feeling-perceiving totality. Thought is preceded by this fundamental or primordial subjective experience of reality, which Dilthey called *Erlebnis* (from *Leben,* life) or *lived experience*: It is "a reality of consciousness that is ultimate and prior to reflection, 'behind which' one cannot go" (Betanzos; cited in Dilthey, 1988, p. 13). "It is not thought or reason that is at the core of life, on the contrary 'the core of what we call life is instinct, feeling, passions, and volitions'" (p. 13). Lived experience is contrasted with the notion of *Erfahrung,* which would mean an objectifying or evaluative attitude toward lived experience—a kind of secondhand experience, which Dilthey saw in use in associationist psychology. "It is not the immediate, inner, and preconscious 'lived experience' of life" (p. 13).

These hermeneutic insights regarding the study of human and social reality are symbolically reiterated in the struggle of identity of (American) curriculum. The Reconceptualist critique claimed the barrenness of psychologism and cognitivism in Tylerism and bureaucratized pseudopractice related to it (see Pinar, 1999, pp. xvii–xviii).

Theory as procedural recommendation like the rationale is challenged in hermeneutic tradition, where theory means an effort to understand a particular practice in terms of a larger conceptual network. According to the 19th-century German hermeneuticians, social world is an internally contested one in which dissensus is pervasive and, consequently, educational and curriculum theory should start from this baseline, not from uncritical pursuit of methodological ideals of natural science. Friedrich Schleiermacher, one of main figures in early hermeneutics, with his follower, Wilhelm Dilthey, and a lesser-known contemporary of Johann Friedrich Herbart, noted in his pedagogy lectures of 1826 that the task of educational theory would have to provide the actors in the field of education with an awareness of a dialectical nature of educational activity where the enlightened deliberation (*Besonnenheit*) is able to make appropriate but provisional and context-bound choices among often contradictory aims and interests of education, which necessarily escape predetermined rigid procedures (see Schleiermacher 1983/1826, p. 55).

Schleiermacher's teaching for curriculum theorizing would be that the world of education is historically layered by misunderstandings, controversies, and contradictions; societal-political circumstances are basically antagonistic, where under the thin and provisional veil of consensus there are few a priori shared ethical or political standards for the orientation of good life education to be concerned about.

This insight that every practice is already infused by different kinds of worldviews, scientific, or commonsense theories was argued for by Martin Heidegger, with whom hermeneutics took a radical turn. Our relationship with everything, in his view, is hermeneutic. The basic feature of human existence is understanding (*Verstehen*). Understanding forms the basis of all our relationships with surrounding world as with ourselves. Heidegger (1986) named the cultivation of understanding interpreting (*Auslegung*; p. 148). What is a most important implication of Heidegger's notion is that our existence is always intentional: to experience, perceive, and understand something will denote to do it *as* something. This *as-structure* of experience would mean that our understanding is never free from presupposition: We are not dealing with brute data, with things *in the raw* while apprehending something presented to us.

The Postempiricist Turn

This necessarily constant business of interpreting as a basic modus of human existence has subsequently informed not only the *Verstehen* tradition, but also the postempiricist philosophy of natural science. In the latter, the emphasis has been moved toward what might be depicted as a hermeneutic turn or critique in the overall understanding of natural sciences—and what emphasis would arguably be useful for the appreciation of the relation between theory and practice in social and educational studies. In a traditional empiricist view of natural science,

> it is assumed that the sole basis of scientific knowledge is the *given* in experience, that descriptions of this given are available in a theory-independent and stable language, whether of sense data or of common sense observation, that theories make no ontological claims about the real world except in so far as they are reducible to observables, and that causality is reducible to mere external correlations of observables. (Hesse, 1980, p. 172)

The theory ladenness of the descriptive language of observables has become increasingly apparent through the works of Wittgenstein, Quine, Kuhn, Feyerabend, and others. The interpretative element makes the concepts of *meaning* and *value* intrinsic to natural science, too. At this point, the *Verstehen* tradition and postempiricist accounts of natural science intersect. On this occasion, Habermas drew on the tradition initiated by Schleiermacher and Dilthey, both of whom set a prime concern of science and study on enlightened and informed practice. Habermas' starting point, which he explicitly described in *Knowledge and Human Interests* (1972), consists of three major interests with their respective validity claims and around which the human endeavor called *science* has been organized: (a) technical interest, which aims at mastery of nature, constitutes knowledge as successful prediction, and dictates the methodology of the empirical sciences; (b) practical interest, where knowledge is constituted in free communication between persons as interpretation of meanings and that dictates the methodology of hermeneutic sciences like history and cultural studies insofar as they aim at understanding; and (c) emancipatory interest, which is the third mode of knowledge that Habermas claimed to be essential in liberating from constraints of all kinds, of natural necessity as well as of social domination. Habermas motivated his project by the critique of scientism, which is parallel to that of postempirical philosophers of science in Anglo-American context. For Habermas, scientism means two things:

> First, the view that empirical knowledge is co-extensive with knowledge, and is adequate for knowledge of persons and societies as well as things. Second, scientism implies the view that empirical knowledge is sufficient for its own explanation. His arguments against the first thesis follow lines made familiar by Winch and others, namely that knowledge of persons and societies involves interpretations of meaning implicit in human language and social institutions. Moreover Habermas adds the thesis that the *interest* of hermeneutic science lies in such interpretive understanding with the aim of interpersonal communication, and not (or not exclusively) in the empirical interest of prediction and successful test. (Hesse, 1980, p. 211)

With a critique of the supposed ultimate rational grounds undergirding natural science, Habermas' aim was to show by a hermeneutic analysis of the *theoretical* aspects of natural science its dependency on human practical interests and value judgments—that no autonomous superstructure for science detached from life can be figured out just as early hermeneuticians asserted. Hesse (1980) suggested that, "it is not alternative internal rationalities that are required in the aftermath of empiricism, but rather a wider perspective on scientific theory in its social and ideological content" (p. xx).

That novel picture of natural science inspired by postempiricist and hermeneutic influences, which might be instrumental when we are taking a critical view of curriculum studies, might be captured as in Hesse's (1980) summary:

> 1. Theories are logically constrained by facts, but are underdetermined by them: that is, while, to be acceptable, theories should be more or less plausibly coherent with facts, they can be neither conclusively refuted nor uniquely derived from statements of fact alone, and hence no theory in a given domain is uniquely acceptable.
>
> 2. Theories are subject to revolutionary change, and this involves even the language presupposed in "statements of fact," which are irreducibly theory-laden: i.e., they presuppose concepts whose meaning is at least partly given by the context of theory.
>
> 3. There are further determining criteria for theories which attain the status of rational postulates or conventions or heuristic devices at different historical periods—these include general metaphysical and material assumptions, for example, about substance and causality, atoms or mechanisms, and formal judgments of simplicity, probability, analogy, etc.
>
> 4. In the history of natural science, these further criteria have sometimes included what are appropriately called value judgments, but these have tended to be filtered out as theories developed.
>
> 5. The "filtering-out" mechanism has been powered by universal adoption of one overriding value for natural science, namely the criterion of increasingly successful prediction and control of the environment.... I shall call this the *pragmatic criterion*. (pp. 187–188)

According to Hesse (1980), "value judgments related to natural science may be broadly of two kinds. They may be evaluations of the *uses* to which scientific results are put, such as the value of cancer research or the disvalue of nuclear bomb." Yet value judgments "may enter more intimately into theory-construction itself as *assertions* that it is desirable that the universe be of such and such a kind *and* that it is or is not broadly as it is desired to be."

After all, what is of crucial importance here is the issue of scientific truth. It has been believed since the 17th century that natural science was a progressive, cumulative, and convergent approach to truth. Truth was understood as a correspondence between a system of objective knowledge and the real world. Yet this realist interpretation of scientific theory as something that would progressively reveal the hidden essences of nature has become untenable:

> It soon became apparent that in the subsequent history of science (…) that there is no such cumulative approach to description of a real world of essences by scientific theory. The conceptual foundations and premises of theories undergo continuous and sometimes revolutionary change. And this occurs not merely *before* the so-called scientific revolution in method of the seventeenth century, but subsequently, when the method of science remained comparatively stable. The succession of theories of the atom, and hence of the fundamental nature of matter, for example, exhibits no convergence, but oscillates between continuity and discontinuity, field conceptions and particle conceptions, and even speculatively among different topologies of space. (Hesse, 1980, p. 174)

Just this instability of theory in natural science and the consequent impossibility of maintaining a view of science as constituted essentially by accumulating knowledge of fundamental, but hidden nature of things has resulted in a pragmatic interpretation of scientific truth. This view would prefer accumulating knowledge of phenomena and observables that

> issues in technical application, the cumulative character of which cannot be in doubt. Thus the claim of science to yield objective knowledge comes to be identified with the cumulative possibilities of instrumental control rather than with theoretical discovery, and this in fact is the conclusion drawn by Habermas and most other hermeneutic philosophers when they come to compare the forms of objectivity of the natural and human sciences. (Hesse, 1980 pp. 174–175)

Hesse's points are of special interest while seeking the identity of social sciences in general and curriculum studies in particular. It may be argued that the main task of theory in those studies since Comte has been viewed in the accomplishment of the interest: "To see in order to predict and control." Yet the difficulty here is that there is no unequivocal pragmatic criterion or the notion of *truth* in the sense of prediction and technical control comparable to that of natural science.

> There is no *a priori* guarantee, …, that the pragmatic criterion will be as successful in the social sciences, in other words there is no guarantee that these sciences will, can, or even should attain comprehensive and progressive theories like those of physics or biology. This fact, together with the admittedly character of adoption of the pragmatic criterion in the first place, suggests that the social sciences may properly adopt goals other than that of successful prediction and control of their domain. (Hesse, 1980, p. xxi)

The long-standing debate between social and natural science has not yet resulted in a deeper gulf between them, but rather in the acknowledgment that we know today that the separating of *Verstehen* from *Erklären* was a misleading way to characterize both social and natural science. Summarizing complicated matters briefly, advances in the philosophy of the natural sciences have made it plain that understanding or interpretation are just elemental to these sciences as they are to the humanities. On the other hand, while generalizations in the social sciences are logically discrepant from those of natural science, there is no reason to doubt that they involve causal attributions. (Giddens, 1987, p. 18)

In the same vein, Hesse (1980), in a critical discussion with the Habermasian interests, developed a continuum of the sciences and concluded her scrutiny by distinguishing two kinds of objectivity within both natural and human science:

1. Technical interest in external instrumental control, whose objectivity is ensured by the method of self-corrective learning. This interests applies to the more predictive aspects of the human sciences as well as to natural science proper.

2. Communicative interest, which includes the interpretive understanding of the human sciences, and also the social function of theoretical science, not as pure ontology, but as a mediation of man's views of himself in relation to nature. (p. xxi)

One thing seems evident about the nature of theory briefly discussed here. Because, as Hesse (1980) pointed out, the adoption of the pragmatic criterion implies a value judgment, it is possible to adopt other value goals for social science and so decide against a straightforward pragmatic criterion as an overriding goal for social science. The most prominent achievements of sociology and social theory might be interpreted as manifestations of being able to decide differently: Weber's desire to rescue human ideals from dominance by substructures, whether economic or bureaucratic; Durkheim's sense of the need for social cohesion and stability in face of man's inordinate and irrational desires; the note of protest inseparably bound into Marx's scientific concept of exploitation of man's labor power. All of these instances of social phenomena, like the French Revolution, the Great Depression of 1929, or the collapse of the Soviet Union, rather than requiring explanation in the sense of natural sciences, can be made more intelligible "as redescription (interpretation, understanding) in terms which make them cohere with the chosen order of values" (Hesse, 1980, p. 199).

Thus, in social research, the intentional (i.e., value-laden) aspect of it also justifies the *theoretical* motivation of research by personal interests and intentions. Alvin Gouldner's description of the sociologist's task after empiricism captures this point:

Commonly, the social theorist is trying to reduce the tension between a social event or process that he takes to be real and some value which this has violated. Much of theory-work is initiated by a dissonance between an imputed reality and certain values, or by the indeterminate value of an imputed reality. Theory-making, then, is often an effort to cope with threat; it is an effort to cope with a threat to something in which the theorist himself is deeply and personally implicated and which he holds dear. (cited in Hesse, 1980, p. 199)

This voice of personal concern and implication is clearly echoed in the intellectual breakthrough in North American curriculum studies—in the Reconceptualization Movement. In the introduction to his edited *Contemporary Curriculum Discourses*, Pinar (1999) situated the whole layer of the recent changes in the philosophy of science in the paradigm shift in curriculum studies:

The thoughtful practice of everyday educational life requires us to understand practice theoretically. So understood, curriculum becomes intensely historical, political,
racial, gendered, phenomenological, postmodern, autobiographical, aesthetic, theological, and international. When we say that curriculum is a site on which the generations struggle to define themselves and the world, we are engaged in a theoretically
enriched practice. When we say that curriculum is an extraordinarily complicated
conversation, we are underscoring human agency and the volitional character of human action. When curriculum specialists understood their work only in institutional
terms, they had in fact retreated from politically engaged and phenomenologically
lived senses of practice. When curriculum was understood only institutionally, the
classroom became a mausoleum, not a civic forum. We rejected a bureaucratization of
the everyday, what was in fact pseudopractice. We embraced *praxis*. Over the past
twenty years the American "curriculum" field has attempted "to take back" curriculum from the bureaucrats, to make the curriculum field itself a conversation, and in so
doing, revitalize practice theoretically. (pp. xvii–xviii)

Conversation, understanding, interpretation, and dialogue as defining modes of research activities might seem uninformative, odd, and indefensible. As Hesse put it:

The model of dialogue as a form of objectivity is unfamiliar and somewhat shocking to
those accustomed to empiricist presuppositions, but it is one of the few alternatives to
the model of natural science in dealing with the human sciences. (p. 180)

HERBARTIANISM, DIDAKTIK,
AND THE RECONCEPTUALIZATION

Through its commitment to a dialogical model of science and hermeneutics, where
substance (content) and value are preferred to procedures, the Reconceptualist Movement shares many interests and topics with the tradition of hermeneutically inspired
theory of education (*geisteswissenschaftliche Pädagogik*), whose theoretical principles
were to be realized in *bildungstheoretische Didaktik*. Although education is always
deeply rooted in national institutions, histories, and future projections, there may be
strikingly similar, even intertwined trends in the course of events. The rise of the
Reconceptualization Movement in the aftermath of Tylerism might, without being
guilty of excessive anacronism, be argued to share common structural and content features with some forms of *geisteswissenschaftliche Pädagogik* as the critical reappraisal of
Herbartianism.

Both critics might have experienced theory-making (in Alvin Gouldner's words) "in
an effort to cope with threat." The threat was to educational values and principles,
which used to be considered worthwhile for a single individual as well as to humankind at large. Education and teaching were to be enshrined in institution-bound, mechanistic, and dull routines. Tyler's suggestion for basic outline of curriculum and
instruction, through a four-foci procedure (goals, learning experiences, organization,
and evaluation), came to be considered the universal, content-free, and teacher-proof
paradigm of curriculum development and implementation. Herbart's theory of
erziehende Unterricht (educating instruction) "combined classical rhetorical education
with modern psychology" and "argued for an active interplay of all components, the
content, the teacher, and the learner," but "Herbartians like Ziller reduced the content
to a fixed array of school subject matter to be poured over passive learners. The rules
dictated that, for instance, that every lesson should follow the same formal pattern, that
is, the five formal steps of *preparation, presentation, association, generalization,* and *applica-*

tion." The less good image of something being didactic can be traced back to the rigorous procedure of practice the Herbartians seemed to promote (Hopmann & Riquarts, 2000, pp. 5–6).

Yet there are some intriguing features behind these developments that might illuminate some of the historical roots of the Reconceptualization Movement. In a mediated fashion, Herbart might too have played a pivotal role. During the last decade of the 19th century in the United States, a small but dedicated group of his proponents, like Charles de Garmo and Charles and Frank McMurry, effectively spread the ideas of Herbart among American educators. But also in the American interpretation, the holistic ideas of Herbart were supplanted not this time by formal steps, but by "the superficial features of the psychology of apperception masses and sequential instruction [which] were annexed to the new conceptions of positivistic science" (Bowen, 1981, p. 367). The drive to seek scientific grounding for education led to the adoption of Herbart's educational psychology while discarding other elements in his theory. For that purpose, Herbart's psychology, especially his theory of apperception masses, fit well. Herbart's zest for universalizable laws of mind made his theory eligible to positivism but also suitable for the purposes of mass education. Therefore, it was understandable why in the United States, "Prussian Herbartianism became relevant to the mass training of teachers in the late nineteenth century" (Bowen, 1981, p. 370). What Hesse (1980) called the *pragmatic criterion* of natural science advised the adoption of the Herbartian psychology of apperception. The pragmatic criterion—"the criterion of increasingly successful prediction of and control of the environment" (Hesse, 1980, p. 188)—had displayed its power in natural science and emerging technology with industrial, mass-scale applications. Now stripped of its unnecessary metaphysics and epistemology, the Herbartian theory of apperception masses seemed to guide the way to the science of psychology—how to deal with human objects in the spirit of pragmatic criterion. The natural scientific "prediction and control of the environment" came to be turned to an interest of psychological prediction and control of the human mind in educational environment. Bowen (1981) commented on Charles McMurry:

> All the time, the teacher, using the Herbartian psychology of apperception, must be guiding the perception and leading to the formation of "correct" results, working by the processes of logical induction to assist the otherwise confused mind of the child to "the formulation of the general truths, the concepts, principles, and laws which constitute the science of any branch of knowledge"; to organize the contents of knowledge in 'well-arranged textbooks' and ensure that they are "stored in the mind in well arranged form." The apperception of mass of each child, McMurry wrote, is different because backgrounds vary; the task is, by means of a curriculum of many-sided interest, by sequentially organized lessons, to develop common apperception masses. The essence of the position was to produce an identity of outlook among the mass of the population; the image of the industrial system demanding uniformity and interchangeability is dominant. The morality and character being sought was a conformity of wills and predictability of behaviour; there was no intention of accepting individuality or personal autonomy. (p. 371)

Thus, what seemed to have been changed in the transition from Herbartian psychology to scientific psychology of learning in the United States would have been that apperception was replaced in the spirit of positivism by behavior as the center of curriculum. Yet the basic order of values from Herbartianism onward has arguably remained the same even though in a more subtle scientific guise. The ideological preference for standardization of thinking and behavior creates the quintessence of this order as the predetermination of a good citizen and competent worker. This consequence is partly due to the thought of Herbart, not merely Herbartianism. Herbart's own intention was to develop a universal model of mechanics of mind (*eine Mechanik des Geistes*) and remain in history as the Newton of Psychology (*als Newton der Psychologie in die Geschichte einzugehen*; Benner; cited in Herbart, 1986, p. 43). Herbart's belief in the feasibility of establishing *eine Mechanik des Geistes* (viz. mechanical lawlike relations as the contituents of human consciousness) might have led the Herbartians to discard the metaphysical and ethical elements of his original theory. This reduction of Herbart's ethics to a normative theory of *Gesinnungsethik* (Benner; cited in Herbert, 1986), with conformity of wills and concomitant predictability of behavior, might have been consequential to a discursive production of educational and psychological goal of self-sufficient and self-controlling individual in terms of suggested normativity. Individuality and personal autonomy are to be conceived not in their genuine idiosyncrasies, but in universal (viz collectivistic) terms.

The intertwining of Herbartianist normativity and educational psychology is not confined to the United States. For instance, in Finland, the German influence on educational theory and practice was dominant until World War II, and the Herbartian–Zillerian formal patterns of teaching had formed the base of teacher education programs, and they still have some appeal. But after the war, official educational relations with Germany weakened, English replaced German as the first foreign language in schools, and authoritative sources and partners of education and curriculum were sought in the Unites States. Yet the *Didaktik* (in Finnish, *didaktiikka*) as the cover name of some core courses in teacher education programs still persists, but without references to *Didaktik* in terms of its theoretical sense, rather in terms of learning designated by educational psychology. The proceduralism of Herbartianism seemed to have been updated and reproduced by the context- and institution-free proceduralism of educational psychology.

In general, this transition from Herbartianism to the psychology of learning might claim an increase in the hold of control than any real change in thought patterns. In the Herbartianist dual focus on a "conformity of wills" and "predictability of behavior," the former has been displaced by the more manageable "predictability of behavior." From the contemporary point of view, the question remains whether, for instance, psychological constructivism will denote a "return inside the head," where the ideology of a conformity of wills still lingers.

In German-speaking countries, the criticism against Herbartianism grew in an unmediated fashion as an emergence of reform pedagogy and a proliferation of varying versions of *geisteswissenschaftliche Pädagogik*. The response in the United States has taken place in a prolonged fashion because the Herbartianist order of values was tacitly implied and sustained in the interests of those in charge of the industrialization of society and the enculturation of immigration masses. Accordingly, those values were also supported in the preunderstandings of rapidly expanding and academically prestigious educational psychology. "Thus Herbart became one of the fathers of the American spelling of pedagogy as educational psychology" (Hopmann & Riquarts, 2000, p. 7). The reduction of pedagogy as well as curriculum studies to educational psychology in terms of natural scientific pragmatic criterion and instrumental rationality is succinctly manifest in the Tyler's (1949) rationale.

This kind of intellectual background, articulated here in all its complexity, might have been one among the many initial incentives to challenge curricular orders of educational psychology by an attempt to "reconceptualize" the field of American education and curriculum studies by introducing theory in its postempiricist or hermeneutic sense to the field.

IDEOLOGICAL CAUSES BETWEEN *BILDUNGSTHEORETICAL DIDAKTIK* AND THE RECONCEPTUALIZATION

The subsequent brief inquiry would interrogate some of the assumptions and practices of *German Didaktik*—the American Reconceptualization. In the large *Didaktik* tradition, I prefer the so-called "critical-constructive *Didaktik*" by the presentation of some main ideas of its creator, Wolfgang Klafki. In the closing remark of his essay, Klafki (1998) hinted interestingly, but somewhat mysteriously, at the possibility that "the reconceptualists' position is similar to critical-constructive Didaktik in significant areas" (p. 327).

What might those significant areas be? Besides the different historical and national backgrounds of each view, the further question would be whether there may be found a shared space for dialogue for the partners dedicated, respectively, to modernist and postmodernist approaches. Here it is possible to deal with only one significant topic—the role of ideology in curriculum studies—from both perspectives to extend the Hessean discussion about the value-ladenness of study and research in respective cases.

Klafki's critical-constructive *Didaktik* has its origin in the German Movement, which developed during 1770 to 1830 through the contributions of philosophical, pedagogical, and literary avantgardists (e.g., Lessing, Kant, Goethe, Schiller, Pestalozzi, Herbart, Schleiermacher, Fichte, and Hegel) to a German-speaking version of the Enlightenment. It had a decisive influence on the rise of hermeneutics in the latter half of the 19th century through the holistic and relational image of the human being advocated by the movement (see Klafki, 1998). The central concern of the movement reflected the old Greek microcosmos–macrocosmos model of thought as an ideal representation between I and World. This ideal could be best approached by the process of *Bildung*. This concept also has a theological connotation that refers to the human being as a reflection of God, where the process of *Bildung* would enhance the fulfillment of this likeness. Klafki's notion of *Bildung* designed for his critical-constructive *Didaktik* is, however, determined by more secular and pedagogical concerns that consist of three main aspects or "abilities which Bildung is to promote" (Klafki, 1998):

> Self-determination: Each and every member of society is to be enabled to make independent, responsible decisions about her or his individual relationships and interpretations of an interpersonal, vocational, ethical, or religious nature.
>
> Co-determination: Each and every member of society has the right but also the responsibility to contribute together with others to the cultural, economic, social, and political development of the community.
>
> Solidarity: As I understand the term, it means that the individual right to self-determination and opportunities for co-determination can only be represented and justified if it associated not only with the recognition of equal rights but also with active help for those whose opportunities for self-determination and co-determination are limited or non-existent due to social conditions, lack of priviledge, political restrictions or oppression. (pp. 313–314)

Those three principles of Bildung form a basic order of values for critical-constructive *Didaktik* in the settings of education. In his notions of science, educational theory, and *Didaktik*, Klafki's attitude is that of a modernist in a way initially present in the German Enlightenment and that has been embodied in the long tradition of German critical theorists (from Adorno and Horkheimer to Habermas). The constant and critical search for the mode of rationality best suited to contemporary challenges of each time been featured by their work without ever losing its unshakeable faith in reason as such. Klafki belonged to that tradition in his treatment of key issues of our own times (*epochale Schlüsselprobleme*) and in his efforts regarding how the rational potential latent in every human being could be educationally articulated and transformed into practice. It is characteristic of the notion of the reason those German scholars stressed that they focus on the social preconditions and consequences of science and, subsequently, as in Habermas in his theory of communicative action, on egalitarian social practice. This feature of reason pursuing egalitarian practice, rather than instrumental effectiveness (*Vernunft / Verstand*), imparts to the German Enlightenment its characteristic flavor. With this notion of reason, the Germans have never felt a burning urge for postmodern discourses that have resulted—as they might see it from their intellectual background—from the critical response to the comprehensive and absurd dominance of instrumental rationality.

Solidarity as a precondition of egalitarian practice is in turn based on the moral conviction intrinsic to the very meaning of *Bildung* "as general Bildung *for all*, as the right of every person, without qualitative or quantitative gradations in status determined by social origins or future positions in society" (Klafki, 2000, p. 103) or, as in Humboldt, "that each and every person, even the poorest, should receive a complete education" (p. 89). "This basic demand," Klafki noted, "implicitly contains a fundamental criticism of society and a perspective that points far into future" (p. 89). This order of values would determine the adoption of critical theory as a core of critical-constructive *Didaktik. Didaktik*, in a Klafkian sense, is to be conceived in a historical-hermeneutic perspective, yet oriented to the future.

> All problems of Didaktik are set within the wider context of educational history and, beyond that, the context of social history, often with an international perspective. This applies regardless of whether those concerned—curriculum developers, teachers, students—are aware of the fact or not. But at the same time, the didactical meanings mediated sociohistorically, which are contained in, for example, curricula, instructional concepts, school books, instructional planning, etc., refer to presumed or desired future. The didactical meanings, the intentions, the purposes for teaching and learning also contain certain ideas concerning the meaning of human life, the relationship between the individual and society, the significance of childhood and adolescence in the process of life, in other words philosophical and, not least, ethical preconditions. (Klafki, 1998, p. 320)

Bildung in its original sense may not have much purchase in the conditions of postmodernism or late modernity with its perverted neo-liberal discourses of commodification. The moral concern that formed the essence of *Bildung* as well as of other notions of education has been drastically commodified. The former Prime Minister of Great Britain, Margaret Thatcher, while advocating the unholy alliance between neo-conservatism and neo-liberalism, declared one particular economic system—capitalism—as an embodiment of the Biblical ethic. Consequently, many personality features we have advocated as worthwhile in terms of *Bildung* and education have been badly depreciated by the political subordination to the sheer interests of commodification and economy:

> Capitalism encourages important virtues, like discipline, industriousness, prudence, reliability, fidelity, conscientiousness, and a tendency to save in order to invest in the future It is not material goods but *all the great virtues exhibited by individuals working together that constitute what we call the market place.* (Thatcher; cited in Spring, 1998, p. 128)

The preconditions for *Bildung* have experienced a radical shift from edifying cultural potential to a real option for market determination of self and education. Terhart

(1998) depicted the difficult transition from educational modernism to educational postmodernism by the tripartite line of development from *Bildung* to Learning to Experience in (West) Germany from the 1960s to 1990. The confidence in reflective, non-instrumental reason invested in the *Bildungstheories* and the optimism regarding the science-oriented curriculum movement in the 1970s, parallel to that of curriculum development in the United States, has been turned into

> scepticism when it was quite clear that reality is always much more complex than even the most complex model, when the political consensus concerning "reform" faded away—and when money became scarce because it moves to other themes and places. So today a nostalgic, some say, a cynical attitude can be observed (...): letting things go, little hope in intervention, systems/cultures do regulate themselves—let's observe this! No planning and reforming of curricula—just learn and live together with your students and strive for conversation and collaborative experience. *Obviously this is an attitude of an asthetically interested indifference typical of post-modern thinking.* (Terhart, 1998, pp. 120–121; italics added)

The cynicism expressed by Terhart about the state of curriculum studies is not restricted to the old continent. In his article on American curriculum development, Davis (1998) described the struggle between the theoretic and the practical in the formation of actual curriculum. By the theoretic, he meant to such early American pioneers of curriculum studies as Bobbitt, Charters, and Tyler. Davis' point is that actual curriculum development has seldom if ever followed the recipes of curriculum theories designed to be followed, but curricular decisions have been and are to result from more complex processes rooted in local administrative, educational, ideological, religious, and political deliberations and struggles.

Davis' enthusiasm over the practical is almost overwhelming, and the question remains whether he saw any sense in the entire undertaking of curriculum theorizing. Sympathetic to Tyler's expertise on local and practical curriculum development, Davis denied the value of the Tyler rationale such as it is written for actual curriculum work: "... little substantial evidence supports its asserted influence on local school curriculum development. Likely, the Tyler Rationale's general usefulness has been exaggerated beyond any reasonable estimate" (Davis, 1998, p. 94). Theory no doubt will acquire ironic tones if the final worth of theorizing would be that "... Tyler's modest course outline has served well the careers of a number of prominent advocates and critics and has been the intellectual foil for an entire school of curriculum reconceptualists" (p. 94). Yet Davis' reluctance to see theory at work in local curriculum development paradoxically and unintentionally claims for that kind of theory what the advocates of *geisteswissenschaftliche Pädagogik* have underscored as the "dignity of practice" theory should try to illuminate—or what the Reconceptualists have been sought to attain in their respective projects as to *understanding* curriculum.

The shift from *Bildung* to experience as a constitutive core of education in Terhart's account, and the theoretical despair that accompanied this move, was remarkably similar to the respective American comments of the state of the curriculum field in general:

> Enthusiasm and optimism, ..., are far from what one finds. Indeed, were one to choose a single word to capture both the state of affairs reported on as well as the recurrent mood of those doing the reporting, it would have to be the adjective "confused." (Jackson, 1992, p. 3)

These feelings shared transatlantically would remove the issue from the internal debate concerning the scholarly status of curriculum studies to a broader context of cultural and ideological transitions, which those feelings would signal. At this time, the system of values of those who advocate the legacy of the Enlightenment in terms of instrumentality (empiricism or pragmatism) or universal morality (*Bildungstheory*) have been felt to be under threat. Moreover, what is experienced as threatening would be the entire mentality of modernity, which has been embodied in modern society and modern education.

> The kind of society that, retrospectively, came to called modern, emerged out of the discovery that human order is vulnerable, contingent and devoid of reliable foundations. That discovery was shocking. The response to the shock was a dream and an effort to make order solid, obligatory and reliably founded. This response problematized contingency as an enemy and order as a task. It devalued and demonized the "raw" human condition. It prompted an incessant drive to eliminate the haphazard and annihilate the spontaneous. As a matter of fact, it was the sought-after order that in advance construed everything for which it had no room or time as contingent and hence lacking foundation. The dream of order and the practice of ordering constitute the world—their object—as chaos. And, of course, as a challenge—as compulsive reason to act. (Bauman, 1992, p. xi)

The practice of ordering has been a characteristic of curriculum work in the (Baumanian) sense of *legislation*, rather than *interpretation* of curriculum. Bauman's account of the relationship of modern rulers and philosophers could be read as a metaphorical story of the relationship between modern education administration and modern curriculum specialists:

> Modern rulers and modern philosophers were first and foremost *legislators*; they found chaos, and set out to tame it and replace it with order. The orders they wished to introduce were by definition *artificial* (emphasis added), and as such had to rest on designs appealing to the laws that claimed the sole endorsement of reason, and by the same token delegitimized all opposition to themselves. Designing ambitions of modern rulers and modern philosophers were meant for each other and, for better or worse, were doomed to stay together, whether in love or in war. As all marriages between similar rather than complementary spouses, this one was destined to sample delights of passionate mutual desire alongside the torments of of all-stops-pulled rivalry. (Bauman, 1995, p. 24)

From this wider symbolic and historical perspective, as well as from current political practices, the openly ideological nature of education as an epitome of modern mentality has been revealed. This point would have methodological consequences with implications beyond the developments of empiricism of educational psychology as well as the horizon of hermeneutics dealt with in this chapter. Curriculum theories *of* or *for* practices (in its empiricist or hermeneutic-*bildung*-theoretical terms) are to be seen both as authoritative accounts of reality where "ideology can only be understood, not escaped" (Lather, 1999, p. 250) as might have been evidenced here in the case of the Tyler rationale. Poststructuralism, on which the Reconceptualists have broadly drawn (see Pinar et al., 1995), is a cultural and methodological response to the crisis experienced not only within curriculum studies, but also across other fields where the crisis of representation with all its validity and truth claims has become evident.

The most supportable Klafkian interest to enhance the possibilities of egalitarian practice has to start from the recognition of the complexity of our current key problems (*epochale Schlüsselprobleme*), but where "the sole endorsement of reason" might hardly dispense with novel autobiographical, cultural, and methodological sensitivities in unveiling the "relationship between the conscious and unconscious dynamics embedded in social relations and cultural forms."

> The material ground of poststructuralism is the information age of complex and ever-unfolding knowledge in a world marked by gross maldistribution of power and resources. The postmodern world is one of multiple causes and effects interacting in complex and nonlinear ways, all of which are rooted in a limitless array of historical and cultural specificities. The intent of poststructuralism is to open the future to a new form of knowledge, to come up with ways of knowing appropriate for a new world, *forced by the weight of the present horror to go beyond present constructions.* (Lather, 1999, p. 253; italics added)

From a poststructural or postmodern perspective, ideology is viewed as a constitutive component of reality:

> There is no meaning-making outside ideology. There is no false consciousness, for such a concept assumes a true consciousness accessible via "correct" theory and practice. As we attempt to make sense in a world of contradictory information, radical contingency, and indeterminacies, ideology becomes a strategy of containment for beings who, …, cannot "Stop Making Sense." (Lather, 1999, p. 253)

"In some ways we are only beginning to understand, perhaps the postmodern turn is about more freely admitting politics, desires, belief into our discourse as we attempt to solve the contradictions of theory and practice" (Lather, 1999, p. 254). But the lust to also receive postmodernism in some scholarly corners of curriculum studies as "aesthetically interested indifference" has neglected the possibility of understanding that, by admitting the fragmented, ideologically constituted reality, postmodern curriculum studies is actually and seriously striving for a new balance between the Klafkian *bildungstheoretical* "self-determination," "co- determination," and "solidarity" in a different world. In this sense, the Reconceptualization Movement could be appreciated as an updated, postmodern theory of *Bildung* when old truths are increasingly losing their theoretical and practical appeal.

> Since "education" sounds a bit too flat, and *Bildung* a bit too foreign, I shall use "edification" to stand for this project of finding new, better, more interesting, more fruitful ways of speaking. The attempt to edify (ourselves or others) may consist in the hermeneutic activity of making connections between our own culture and some exotic culture or historic period, or between our own discipline and another discipline which seems to pursue incommensurable aims in an incommensurable vocabulary. But it may instead consist in the "poetic" activity of thinking up such new aims, new words, or new disciplines, followed by, so to speak, the inverse of hermeneutics: the attempt to reinterpret our familiar surroundings in the unfamiliar terms of our new inventions. In either case, the activity is (despite the etymological relation between the two words) edifying without being constructive—at least if "constructive" means the sort of cooperation in the accomplishment of research programs which takes place in normal discourse. For edifying discourse is *supposed* to be abnormal, to take us out of our old selves by the power of strangeness, to aid us in becoming new beings. (Rorty, 1980, p. 360)

REFERENCES

Bauman, Z. (1992). *Intimations of postmodernity*. London and New York: Routledge.

Bauman, Z. (1995). *Modernity and ambivilance*. Oxford, England: Polity.

Beyer, L., & Liston, D. (1996). *Curriculum in conflict: social visions, educational agendas, & progressive schoo' reform*. New York: Teachers College Press.

Bowen, . (1981). *A history of Western education* (Vol. 3). London: Methuen.

Calfee, R. (1992). Refining educational psychology. The case of missing links. *Educational Psychologist, 27*(2), 163-175.

Calgren, I. (2000). The implicit teacher. In K. Klette, I. Carlgren, J. Rasmussen, H. Simola, & M. Sundkvist (Eds.), *Restructuring Nordic teachers* (pp. 325-362). Oslo, Norway: University of Oslo, Institute for Educational Research.

Crook, S., Pakulski, J., & Waters, M. (1992). *Postmodernization: Change in advanced society*. London: Sage.

Davis, O. L., Jr. (1998). The theoretic meets the practical: The practical wins. In B. Gundem & S. Hopmann (Eds.), *Didaktik and/or curriculum* (pp. 87-106). New York: Peter Lang.

Dilthey, W. (1988). *Introduction to the human sciences: An attempt to lay a foundation for the study of society and history* (R. J. Betanzos, Trans.). London: Harvester Wheatsheaf.

Giddens, A. (1987). *Social theory and modern sociology*. Cambridge, MA: Polity Press.

Goodson, I. (1998). Storying the self: Life politics and the study of the teacher's life and work. In W,. F. Pinar (Ed.), *Curriculum: Toward new identities* (pp. 3-20). New York: Garland.

Gundem, B., & Hopmann, S. (Eds.). (1998). *Didaktik and/or curriculum: An international dialogue*. New York: Peter Lang.

Habermas, J. (1972). *Knowledge and human interests*. Cambridge, MA: Polity.

Habermas, J. (1984). *The theory of communicative action: Volume 1. Reason and the rationalization of society*. Boston: Beacon.

Heidegger, M. (1986). *Sein und Zeit*. Tübingen, Germany: Max Niemeyer Verlag. (Original publication 1927)

Herbart J. F. (1986). *Systematische Pädagogik. Eingeleitet, ausgewählt und interpretiert von Dietrich Benner*. Stuttgart, Germany: Klett-Cotta.

Hesse, M. (1980). *Revolutions and reconstructions in the philosophy of science*. Brighton, England: The Harvester Press.

Hopmann, S., & Riquarts, K. (2000). Starting a dialogue: A Beginning conversation between didatik and the curriculum traditions. In I. Westbury et al. (Eds.), *Teaching as a reflective practice* (pp. 3-11). Mahwah, NJ: Lawrence Erlbaum Associates.

Jackson, P. (1992). Conceptions of curriculum and curriculum specialists. In P. W. Jackson (Eds.), *Handbook of research on curriculum: A project of the American Educational Research Association* (pp. 3-40). New York: Macmillan.

Kelly, A. V. (1999). *The curriculum. Theory and practice* (4th ed.). London: Paul Chapman.

Kincheloe, J. (1997). Introduction. In I. F. Goodson (Ed.), *The changing curriculum. Studies in social construction* (pp. ix-xi). New York: Peter Lang.

Klafki, W. (1998). Characteristics of critical-constructive Didaktik. In B. Gundem & S. Hopmann (Ed.). *Didaktik and/or curriculum studies* (pp. 307-330). New York: Peter Lang.

Klafki, W. (2000). The significance of classicaltheories of Bildung for a contemporary concept of Allgemeinbildung. In I. Westbury et al. (Eds.), *Teaching as a reflective practice* (pp. 85-107). Mahwah, NJ: Lawrence Erlbaum Associates.

Klette, K., Carlgren, I., Rasmussen, J., Simola, H., & Sundkvist, M. (Eds.). (2000). *Restructuring Nordic teachers: An analysis of policy texts from Finland, Denmark, Sweden and Norway. Report No. 10*. Oslo, Norway: University of Oslo, Institute for Educational Research.

Kliebard, H. (1995). The Tyler rationale revisited. *Journal of Curriculum Studies, 27*(1), 81-88.

Lather, P. (1999). Ideology and methodological attitude. In W. F. Pinar (Ed.), *Contemporary curriculum discourses* (pp. 241-246). New York: Peter Lang.

Pinar, W. F. (Ed.). (1999). *Contemporary curriculum discourses: Twenty years of JCT*. New York: Peter Lang.

Pinar, W., Reynolds, W., Slattery, P., & Taubman, P. (1995). *Understanding curriculum*. New York: Peter Lang.

Rorty, R. (1980). *Philosophy and the mirror of nature*. Oxford, England: Basil Blackwell.

Schleiermacher, F. (1983). *Pädagogische Schriften: I. Die Vorlesungen aus dem Jahre 1826*. Frankfurt am Main, Germany: Klett-Cotta.

Spring, J. (1998). *Education and the rise of the global economy.* London: Lawrence Erlbaum Associates.

Taylor, C. (1991). *The ethics of authenticity.* Cambridge, MA: Harvard University Press.

Terhart, E. (1998). Changing concepts of curriculum: From "Bildung" to "learning" to "experience." Developments in (West) Germany from the 1960s to 1990. In B. Gundem & S. Hopmann (Eds.), *Didaktik and/or curriculum* (pp. 107-125). New York: Peter Lang.

Tyler, R. (1949). *Basic principles of curriculum and instruction.* Chicago: University of Chicago Press.

Weber, M. (1978). *Economy and society.* Berkeley: University of California Press.

Westbury, I. (1998). Didaktik and curriculum studies. In B. Gundem & S. Hopmann (Eds.), *Didaktik and/or curriculum* (pp. 47- 78). New York: Peter Lang.

CHAPTER 17

Understanding Curriculum in France: A Multifaceted Approach to Thinking Education

Denise Egéa-Kuehne
Louisiana State University

A number of factors make understanding education in France and its approach to thinking education a serious challenge, especially for someone not familiar with the French system of education or the politics of its institutions. One must keep in mind that the French educational system has traditionally been highly centralized,[1] and that France has striven to remain "an encyclopaedic heartland" (McLean, 1990).[2] Another major difficulty is a lack of consensus on a terminology which would be common to all education specialists. Consequently, there exists a certain "anarchy" (Avanzini, 1997, p. 17), sometimes resulting from sheer carelessness, sometimes nurtured by a misplaced concern with originality, popularity and/or publicity. This is nothing new as even a cursory look at the history of education in France reveals. Yet in a 1997 publication,[3] Avanzini stressed how the resulting polysemy and erratic if not contradictory use of basic notions continue to fuel the never-ending debates on what he called "false problems" (p. 17).

Based on a close exploration of the field of education in France, its publications, and its institutions, I introduce five domains where a reflection on education is currently carried out under different labels and on different levels. They include: *science(s) de l'éducation, philosophie de l'éducation, pédagogie, didactique(s),* and, more recently, *curriculum.*[4] A de-

---

[1] In France, school programs and teaching and learning activities are determined by the Ministry of Education and published in the *Journal Officiel,* as any and all other forms of French public law. The National Education is the group of services responsible for the organization, direction, and management of all aspects of public education in France and for the control of private education (for further details, see e.g., Gauthier, 1994; Prost, 1968).

[2] All quotes from original French texts are translated by D. Egéa-Kuehne. Original British spellings are respected in quotes from original English texts.

[3] Although Avanzini's (1997) text focused on pedagogy, his remarks on a need for consensus on terminology are relevant to the entire field of French education.

[4] In the French context, the term *curriculum* refers to its recent meaning in British educational literature, that is, "the educational itinerary proposed to learners" (Perrenoud, 1993, p. 61).

scription of these fields and a look at their history reveal how they intersect, blend, and compete, each vying to develop its own identity and define its own specificity while some scholars work in more than one of these domains under more than one title.

It is obvious that this project cannot be exhaustive, and it is only one approach to understanding the complex phenomenon and genealogy of educational thinking in France. Furthermore, not all the works or authors who have contributed and are currently contributing to its development can be acknowledged here, and I apologize to those who may not be mentioned in this chapter. Finally, few of these publications are available in English. However, for those who can read French, the present text is no substitute for reading the numerous authors cited. My hope is that it prompts a desire to further explore the work done in France.

EDUCATIONAL SCIENCE(S): THE NEW DISCIPLINE

According to Gautherin (1995), it is the "founders of the *École de la République*" who, in the last part of the 19th century, "totally invented educational science [singular]" (p. 45). Its genealogy highlights its complex roots and partially explains its difficulties in finding an identity, defining its specificity and goals, and obtaining institutional recognition.

Ambiguous Beginnings

In 1812, Marc-Antoine Jullien de Paris[5] had already introduced a new expression, *"science* [singular] *de l'éducation,"* in *L'Esprit de la méthode d'éducation de Pestalozzi.* Four years later, in his *Esquisse d'un ouvrage d'éducation comparée,* he expanded on this new concept. His hope was that "education should become a more or less positive science" (cited in Gautherin, 1991, p. 40). *More or less* associated with *positive science* is already an interesting oxymoron—a harbinger of future ambiguities and of the difficulties this new discipline would encounter to find its own path. However, when reviewing the history of scientific approaches to education, it is an English author, Alexander Bain, who is most often cited (*Education as a Science,* 1872). His work was brought to France through Compayré's translation, *La Science de l'éducation,* in 1879. However—and this will have echoes in later developments—rather than try to establish a specific and autonomous educational science, both Bain and Compayré were more interested in applying a psychological approach to "the art of teaching," with Compayré mostly concerned with the history of educational doctrines.

1883–1914: Marion and Durkheim

After 1803, educational science was introduced in humanities departments by way of complementary courses (*cours complémentaires*), rather than through specifically designated tenured positions. Then in 1883, under the initiative of Jules Ferry and René Goblet—Ministers of Public Instruction—and their Directors of Instruction (including Buisson), the first course of educational science was institutionalized at La Sorbonne. It included a *cours magistral* and a *conférence pratique.* Prior to this, only two other courses had been offered in the *Faculté des Lettres*: a course in philosophy of education by Gabriel Compayré in Toulouse in 1874, and a course in pedagogy by Alfred Espinas in Bordeaux in 1882. Gautherin (1995) identified 14 educational science *or* pedagogy courses created

---

[5]Marc-Antoine Jullien de Paris was a jaded revolutionary and one-time collaborator of Pestalozzi at the Yvedon School in Switzerland, a member of the Society of Education, and author of numerous publications. For further details, see Gautherin (1991, 1995, 2001).

between 1882 and 1914 (Table 17.1).[6] She also indicated that of the nearly 38 professors responsible for those courses at various times, most of them were originally *professors of philosophy*—half of them graduates from the *École Normale Supérieure*.[7] Gautherin (2001) stressed that they were not in the least ready to teach instructional practices, much less to turn education into a science. The universities of Bordeaux, Lyon, and Paris (La Sorbonne) were to offer these courses without interruption until 1914. Four years after the onset of the first *cours complémentaire*, the first tenured position in educational science per se was created at La Sorbonne, in 1887, and Henri Marion became the first professor of educational science in France. Previously, he was a professor of philosophy[8] and had taught psychology applied to education.[9] Hence, from its onset, educational science was closely linked with philosophy, pedagogy, and psychology.

TABLE 17.1
Courses in Educational Science Opened 1882–1914

University	Date Created	Course Title	Taught by	Specialty	Created by
Bordeaux	1882	Pedagogy	Espinas	Sociologist	City Council
Paris	1883	Educational Science	Marion	Philosopher	French Ministry of Education
Lyon	1884	Educational Science	Thamin	Philosopher	French Ministry of Education
Montpellier	1884	Educational Science	Dauriac	Philosopher	French Ministry of Education
Nancy	1884	Educational Science	Egger	Philosophe	French Ministry of Education
Toulouse	1887	Educational Science	Dumesnil		French Ministry of Education
Lille	1887				City Council
Douai	1887				City Council
Grenoble	1888				
Dijon	1889				
Besançon	1903				
Alger	1906				
Rennes	1907				
Caen	1910				

Note The data summarized in this table was gathered from Gautherin's (1995) text.

---

[6]For a detailed analysis of the "first birth" of educational science, see Gautherin's (1995) introductory text to the CORESE report (*Commission de réflexion sur les Sciences de l'éducation*, under the direction of Charlot, 1995), and her doctoral dissertation (1991).

[7]One of the most prominent and prestigious higher education institutions in France, called *Grandes Écoles* (not part of the university system). Georges (2000) described the ENS as "the tip of the pyramid [of the *Grandes Écoles*]" (p. 48). The ENS has traditionally been dedicated to forming teachers of philosophy.

[8]At the prestigious *Lycée Henri IV*. In France, philosophy is taught the last year of high school, called *année de philo*.

[9]At the *École Normale Supérieure* (Fontenay).

In fact, in his inaugural address at La Sorbonne on December 6, 1883, *Leçon d'Ouverture du cours sur la Science de l'Éducation,* Marion stressed the importance of the philosophy of education. He wanted to extend the legitimacy of "the doctrine of education" (p. 492) taught in the *écoles normales* (for elementary school teachers) to higher education, especially to the formation of secondary school teachers. The point was to rely no longer on what he called "instinctive reason," but to develop "the bases of a rational culture" (p. 493). Trying to redefine *pedagogy,* Marion (1888) fell back on the notion of pedagogy as "the science and the art of education" commonly accepted by the specialists of his era. He also attempted to narrow it further: "Pedagogy is the science of education, that is to say the methodical study, the rational research of the goals we must propose by raising the children, and the means most appropriate to this end" (cited in Buisson, 1911, p. 2238).

Although Marion saw the necessity of being attentive to theoretical reasons, he considered educational science a practical science, which nevertheless could not be assimilated to either mathematical science (logical sequences of notions) or physical science (laws). He perceived it as being closer to moral and political sciences because of its relative uncertainty due to the nature of its object—the free individual (*l'être libre*). He believed that, to be able to elaborate such a science—or at least a body of doctrines coherent enough to provide support for concrete action—one must tap a variety of sources including "personal experiences …; the history of doctrines, methods, and school institutions; [and] the 'positive' data from physiology and psychology" (Plaisance & Vergnaud, 1999, p. 8).

Psychology seems to be the discipline on which Marion relied in his analysis of education as the most appropriate instrument to gain knowledge of the faculties (intelligence, sensitivity, will), which education is, by definition, supposed to ensure of a harmonic development. These synonymies and parallels among pedagogy, philosophy of education, and educational science are not so surprising if we recall that, for the philosophers trying to establish *une science de l'éducation,* philosophy and science were one and the same thing. Following Auguste Comte's positivist thought, the founders of French educational science considered that, "The attempt to reduce the art of education to scientific rules, deducted from the laws of psychology, today is as legitimate in many respects as that of scientifically founding medicine upon the exact knowledge of the [human] organism and its functions" (Marion, 1883, p. 493). So in his attempt to define a science of education, Marion moved from *philosophy* to *pedagogy* to *psychology* without attaching clear boundaries to those terms.

If, for Marion, "pedagogy [was] the science of education," it was not the case for Durkheim, for whom it was a "practical theory." Durkheim's first appointment in 1887 was at the University of Bordeaux, in the department of humanities, to teach one of those complementary courses called Social Science and Pedagogy.[10] In 1902, he was assigned to La Sorbonne, where he distinguished himself from his predecessors (Henri Marion and Ferdinand Buisson) by bringing a sociological approach to education. Durkheim made a distinction between *education* and *pedagogy.* He realized that education could be given several definitions. In its largest meaning, he believed that it referred to the abundance and variety of influences to which any human being may be exposed. He preferred to give *education* a narrower meaning as "the action exerted by adult generations upon those who are not yet mature enough for social life" (cited in Buisson, 1911, p. 1255). Durkheim distinguished between the definitions based on values (normative) and those based on facts (positive). The former, following Kant and Stuart Mill, conceived education as ideal and perfect, whereas the latter defined *educa-*

---

[10]Course title and guidelines set by the French Ministry of Education.

tion by its practices and institutions: "Sets of practices, behaviors, customs which constitute perfectly defined facts and have the same reality as other social facts" (cited in Buisson, 1911, p. 1255). In this context, education was a system characteristic of a specific society at a specific time.

For Durkheim, pedagogy was not an art either. According to him, the objective of pedagogical theories was not "to describe nor to explain what is or has been, but to determine what must be," and to "edict precepts of behavior" (Plaisance & Vergnaud, 1999, p. 9). This, according to Plaisance and Vergnaud (1999), situates pedagogy halfway between art and science, where reflection is oriented toward acting rather than explaining. Hence, Durkheim's famous formula, "practical theory," which "does not study systems of action scientifically, but which reflects upon them in order to provide the educator with ideas to guide him/her in his/her activity" (cited in Plaisance & Vergnaud, 1999, p. 9). Under Durkheim's influence, the Sorbonne teaching position originally designated as Educational Science took the title of Sociology and Educational Science. After his death in 1917, the department committee changed this title again to Social Economy, and Bouglé, a follower of Durkheim, found himself in charge of a position which no longer made any reference to education.

Wartime: A Hiatus

Those newly established university departments and courses would not survive World War I. Their specificity gradually disappeared as they were either renamed (e.g., La Sorbonne) or terminated altogether. It may have been a sign of the devalued status of pedagogy, which only worsened, especially during the late 19th and early 20th centuries, within humanities (i.e., philosophy) departments where a humanist tradition prevailed. Two other new human sciences—psychology and sociology—also experienced some opposition from the proponents of the humanist tradition, but pedagogy seemed to be "the most vulnerable" (Plaisance & Vergnaud, 1999, p. 9). Plaisance and Vergnaud (1999) believed that it may have been due to the fact that pedagogy was associated with the education of elementary school teachers. Gautherin (1995) saw an indication of this negative status in the limited number of doctoral theses in education.[11] Educators who taught educational science and pedagogy preferred to rely on philosophy or another academically established discipline to gain professional recognition in academia.[12]

Although pedagogy tried to maintain some specificity, the confusion between *pedagogy* and *educational science* continued. Plaisance and Vergnaud (1999) recognized that "the university programs of instruction inaugurated in 1883 [were] not maintained as such" (p. 12). They included other types of courses and programs. For example, the Institute of Pedagogy was opened in 1920 in the humanities department at La Sorbonne, a Practical School of Psychology and Pedagogy was created in 1945 in Lyon under the direction of Bourjade, and courses taught by human sciences specialists were developed in some *écoles normales* (e.g., Versailles and La Seine schools; Avanzini, 1987). In France no document reveals the use of the plural form *sciences de l'éducation* between the two World Wars, but in Switzerland the Jean-Jacques Rousseau Institute was opened in 1912 under the name of *École des sciences* [plural] *de l'éducation*.

---

[11]Between 1885 and 1914, Gautherin (1995) identified only 9 humanities doctoral theses on topics related to education, none of those by any of the scholars who taught educational science.

[12]For example, when Durkheim was appointed to his position at La Sorbonne, it was on the strength of his reputation as a sociologist; in this case, pedagogy was seen as a "province of sociology" during one of the faculty meetings in the humanities department in 1902 (Gautherin, 1995).

After World War II: Institutionalization of a New Field

The first efforts in France to develop a discipline identified as *educational science* had not included the creation of specific degrees. It was with a concern for institutional recognition in mind that, in 1962, several projects were elaborated under the direction of Jean Château (Bordeaux), Maurice Debesse (Paris), and Gaston Mialaret (Caen). In Bordeaux, a project of university curriculum in pedagogy was formulated by Château, who proposed the creation of an undergraduate degree in pedagogy (*licence de pédagogie*) in the humanities department. It included four certificates: history of educational doctrines and institutions, psychology of the child and the adolescent, psychophysiological and clinical pedagogy, and philosophy of education and pedagogy (Hermine & Vigarello, 2000). Although his first intention was to create this proposed undergraduate cursus and degree in educational sciences (plural) (*licence de sciences de l'éducation*), Château chose to keep the term *pedagogy* (*licence de pédagogie*) in his proposed project, deeming this title "shorter, therefore more elegant" (cited in Marmoz, 1988, p. 13). As a consequence, the reference to or inclusion of a diversity of sciences was omitted, and the titles of the previously mentioned certificates reveal that this program included "'only' history, philosophy, and psychology" (Hermine & Vigarello, 2000, p. 3).

In 1962, Château did not believe that the new fields of sociology of education and economy of education had a research program established enough to be included in the curriculum of an undergraduate degree in pedagogy. Also indicative is the student population this program was trying to reach: "It will be an undergraduate teaching degree (*licence d'enseignement*), at least for the *École Normale* professors who are currently responsible for this discipline, and for this discipline only" (Château, 1962, p. 208). In other terms, this curriculum and its degree concerned only future elementary teachers.[13] In the end, this project appears deeply rooted in past disciplinary and institutional traditions. Only the degree would have represented a novelty. Yet faced with a strong resistance from the Sorbonne's philosophy and psychology departments, Château's project had to be abandoned (Hermine, 1978).

A few months later, in Paris, Debesse proposed a new version of this project, suggesting to better "balance psychology and the other educational sciences" (Marmoz, 1988, p. 43). However, his intention did not materialize, as is apparent in the names designating the certificates included in the curriculum and the degree: philosophy, history, psychology, and methodology. But the public they addressed was more specifically defined: the "administration will be urged to require the *licence de pédagogie* or to recommend it for certain professions, for example regarding the functions of Inspector of instruction, the direction of special education institutions, and so on" (Marmoz, 1988, p. 43). Like Château's, this project did not actualize either, but it still helped establish new certificates for the philosophy and psychology undergraduate degrees (*certificat de licence de philosophie* and *certificat de licence de psychologie*).

In 1966, a different context was created by the "Fouchet reform"[14] following an increase in student population and discipline diversity. Mialaret (2000) recalled that on December 7, 1966, he received an urgent call for a meeting at the Ministry of Education. This meeting brought together university scholars (Debesse, Fraisse, and Mialaret) and administrators (Corraz, Rachou, and Poignant). The purpose was to plan the creation

---

[13]This is understandable when one realizes that, at that time in France, secondary teacher education and its degrees were not determined by the universities, but by the central administration called *Inspection Générale*, part of the Ministry of Education.

[14]Fouchet was then Minister of Education.

of a program in pedagogy to begin after the second year of university (*2e cycle*). Mialaret (2000) reported how he, Debesse, and Château had previously met many a time to discuss such a project. Soetzel and Fraisse, from psychology, would also join them on occasion. Furthermore, at that time, many pedagogy courses and curricula were already organized. For example, La Sorbonne offered an Advanced Certificate of Pedagogy (*certificat d'études supérieures de pédagogie*), and its program was not attached to any undergraduate teaching degree per se. Since 1956–1957, the university of Caen, with Mialaret, had accepted the creation of a university degree in psychopedagogy (*diplôme universitaire de psycho- pédagogie*), and its program was regularly offered. Meanwhile, in Bordeaux, Château organized courses with "a pedagogical orientation" (Mialaret, 2000, p. 16). In Lyon, following in Chabot's steps, Bourjade taught a course on child psychology, which had much in common with pedagogy.

The elements of a beginning were there, but the administration balked at its formalization for several reasons. Pedagogy was not considered a noble subject (i.e., not a higher education subject), and, in Mialaret's (2000) words, "[t]o see pedagogy invading the universities was for some people, at that time, inconceivable" (p. 16). Furthermore, outside the universities, the *écoles normales* directors, who had been teaching pedagogy, did not see kindly this job being taken away from them, and neither did the general inspectors. For many of them, pedagogy was the domain reserved to the *écoles normales*. Aside from experience and personal reflection, no one saw the necessity of engaging in research, much less scientific research.

New projects were elaborated, and a title had to be agreed on, but under the label of *psychopedagogy* to give the notion of pedagogy an added element of apparent scientific legitimacy. For example, the program committee of the psychology section at La Sorbonne submitted a request for an undergraduate degree in psychopedagogy (*licence de psycho-pédagogie*). Concurrently, the creation of a graduate degree (*maîtrise*) was discussed and provided the opportunity to insist on the "necessity of a basis for French pedagogical research, currently very poorly directed" (May, 1966; cited in Hermine & Vigarello, 2000, p. 6). This new project met with stronger support from the Ministry of Education, which consulted with Debesse, Mialaret, Oléron and Fraisse. Debesse was charged with writing a summary of the debates. Published in October 1966 under the title *Projet de création d'une licence et d'une maîtrise de sciences de l'éducation,* this summary soon became *the* document of reference. For the first time, the term *educational sciences* (plural) was introduced in an official document and explained in great detail: "The title 'Educational Sciences' eventually appeared to be preferable to that of 'Psycho-pedagogy' which was more limiting, and whose content might duplicate that of the undergraduate degree in psychology (*licence de psychologie*)" (cited in Hermine & Vigarello, 2000, p. 6). This document also introduced disciplines which had not been mentioned so far, including educational sociology, educational law, and comparative education. Hermine and Vigarello (2000) declared: "[t]his 1966 project is indeed the precursor of the current curriculum" (p. 6).

A mandate from the Ministry of Education dated February 11, 1967, finalized the creation of two specific programs: one leading to an undergraduate degree (*licence de sciences de l'éducation*) offered to students with 2 years of previous university experience, and the other to a graduate degree (*maîtrise de sciences de l'éducation*). For these degrees, the reference was no longer pedagogy or psychopedagogy, but *educational sciences.* It marked a definite break from the content of general pedagogy and its public. Applied linguistics, social and political economy, and demography were added to the fields mentioned in the 1966 project. These changes indicated a concern with affirming not only the necessity for a plural scientific approach to education, but also the need for broadening the notion of pedagogy toward a public of adults and beyond problems of educational practices. Hermine and Vigarello (2000) wrote: "In the space of a few years, the texts are no longer comparable. A cultural maturation occurred which has totally disrupted them" (p. 6). In fall 1997, the application of this mandate led to the opening of programs in educational sciences at the universities of Bordeaux (where Wittwer joined Château), Caen (Mialaret), and Paris-Sorbonne (Debesse).

One example of the new goals set by these educational sciences departments is found in the text of the project out of the university of Paris-Sorbonne drafted in August 1968 by several educators, including Cambon, Contou, Delchet, Filloux, Léon, Snyders, and Vial. Title I of this document states that:

> this department will have to respond to:
> - the demands of a formation to interdisciplinary educational research;
> - the necessity of thorough pedagogical teacher education at all levels;
> - the needs expressed in diverse contexts where problems of group leadership, communication, and relation arise within educational settings; and
> - the demands of comparative education. (Title I, Paris-Sorbonne, 1968, cited in Hermine & Vigarello, 2000, p. 7)

The importance of this document is obvious in as much as it reveals to what extent the field had progressively asserted itself since the early 1960s, and it states the directions along which educational sciences were to be opened and promoted. It underscores the vastness of a field which proposed to address teacher education (elementary and secondary) and adult education in and out of the context of educational institutions. It also outlines a number of approaches and themes which, although linked to social sciences, were beginning to gain autonomy. Hermine and Vigarello (2000) recognized that "[a]t least in its aims, the discipline 'educational sciences' had clearly asserted itself. Now, it had to live" (p. 7).

The establishment and growth of the educational sciences field are revealed by the creation of new departments and an increase in the number of students, educators, and researchers. After Bordeaux, Caen, and Paris-Sorbonne, the three original programs created in 1967, eight more opened in 1970 and another five in 1980. Keeping in mind that degrees specifically in educational sciences were delivered only after at least 4 years of studies at the university (*licence* or *maîtrise*), student population growth in educational sciences is summarized in Table 17.2, and teacher-researcher population growth in Table 17.3. In 1971, the *Association des Enseignants et Chercheurs en Sciences de l'Éducation* (AECSE) was founded.[15] It organizes a conference on the actuality of educational research every other year.[16]

The texts of 1967 attempting to construct the field of educational sciences indicated that a number of sciences were expected to be applied to education as their object. Psychology (e.g., Compayré and Marion) and sociology (e.g., Durkheim) were associated from the beginning. Other disciplines were added later, including history, economy, linguistics, and, later still, anthropology. However, although the first educators in-

---

[15]In January 2002, two co-presidents were elected: Michèle Guigue and Patrick Rayou. The AECSE is the French educational research association and sends representatives to the European Educational Research Association (EERA) executive committee. Its 450 members are mostly educators and scholars in education. *http://www.inrp.fr/aecse*. Last accessed May 19, 2002.

[16]The last AECSE conference was held jointly with ECER (European Conference on Educational Research) and EERA in Lille in September 2001. The year with no conference, AECSE holds a symposium more specifically focused on educational and social issues, such as adult training (Strasburg, 1998), or practices in higher education (Toulouse, 2000).

TABLE 17.2

Student Population Growth in Educational Sciences 1990–1999

	Number of University Students	Undergraduate Licence	Graduate Maîtrise	Advanced Studies DEA***	Doctoral Theses	Habilitation to Direct Research
1990–1991	11,500*	71%	24%	5%		
	12,000**	72%	24%	4%		
1993–1994	14,000*	2,600 degrees delivered	400 degrees delivered	200 degrees delivered	80 degrees delivered	
1998–1999	15,283*	NA****	NA	NA	718 students	8 students
Increase 1990–1999	33%					

Sources:

* Plaisance and Vergnaud (1999, pp. 13–14)
** Charlot (1995, p. 73)
*** Diplôme d'Études Approfondies (DEA)
**** Not Available

TABLE 17.3

Educator-Researcher Population Growth in Educational Sciences 1978–1999

	Total Number of Educators in Educational Sciences	Professeurs (P) (Habilitated to Direct Research)	Maîtres de Conférence (MC) (Generally Not Habilitated to Direct Research)	Paris	Provinces
1978*	82	29	53	NA****	NA
1988*	172	48	124	26P and 77MC	22P and 47MC
1990–1991**	254	82	172	60%	40%
1991–1992***	265	89	176	59%	41%
1992–1993***	315	96	219	62%	38%
1998–1999**	415	116	299	66%	34%
Increase 1990–1999	63%	41%	74%		

Sources:

* Hermine and Vigarello (2000, p. 7)
** Plaisance and Vergnaud (1999, p. 16)
*** Charlot (1995, pp. 247–248)
**** Not Available

volved with the teaching of educational sciences were teachers of philosophy for the most part, philosophy as a subject was essentially absent from the various projects proposed to construct the field. Nevertheless, it was specifically mentioned in one of the certificates in Château's 1962 project for an educational sciences undergraduate degree ("philosophy of education and pedagogy"). Hermine and Vigarello (2000) indicated that, especially after the mid-1970s, "philosophy as such becomes relatively absent … from education and from research in educational sciences" (p. 10)—a trait shared with all other human sciences.

PHILOSOPHY OF EDUCATION: THE FOUNDATION

Yet like Fabre (1999), many scholars believe that a philosophical reflection is "more than ever necessary" in education (p. 277). However, Barthelmé (1999) asked whether there is such a thing as philosophy of education: "Does philosophy of education exist?" (p. 11). According to what he presented to be the thesis of his book, Barthelmé (1999) argued that "philosophy of education remains to be constructed" (p. 7). Indeed, philosophy of education was named as such relatively recently. According to Charbonnel (1988), the first book with the general title *Philosophy of Education* was by Édouard Roehrich and published in 1910 (cited in Charbonnel, 1988, p. 109). In France, the expression was coined in the latter part of the 19th century in the context of the efforts on the part of several philosophers to elaborate a new discipline—educational science (singular then). Their names were Buisson, Compayré, Gréard, Marion, Pécaud, and Thamin. In his inaugural address, Marion (1883) declared: "Today, for the first time, philosophy of education is admitted to take its due place in public education" (p. 481).

Olivier Reboul[17] appears to some as a philosopher who believed that "the existence of one [philosophy] was sufficient to legitimize the other [philosophy of education]" (Barthelmé, 1999, p. 10); to others (e.g., Bouveresse, 1993; Houssaye, 1999), he was a leading figure of philosophy of education in France.[18] In any case, his work and influence cannot be ignored.[19] In his introduction to *La Philosophie de l'éducation* (1989a), Reboul stressed that philosophy in general—and philosophy of education in particular—is "not a body of knowledge, but a questioning of all we know or believe that we know on education" (p. 3), characterized by the following points:

- It is a "total" questioning in as much as no object can escape it. The specificity of philosophy consists in the way it poses problems or proceeds in its reflection. (p. 3)
- It is a "radical" questioning. Distinguished from reflection in general, philosophical reflection reaches deeper, all the way to the foundations, or to the end, to the first or the last questions, where, in Aristotle's words, "one must eventually stop." "[Philosophy] does not attempt to build a school program, but asks what is worth

---

[17]Reboul created a program of philosophy of education in Montreal (1969–1975) and at the university of Strasburg (after 1975) where he also participated in the creation of the *Unité de Formation et de Recherche (UFR)* in educational sciences and became director of the educational sciences doctoral program.

[18]Other philosophers, while presenting themselves as proponents of philosophy of education, have some problem with the concept of *a* philosophy *of* education, arguing that "education is not an *object* dissociated from philosophy" (Morandi, 2000, p. 11). Houssaye (1999) also "refuse[d] to reduce a priori the relation between philosophy and education" (p. 14). He posited the four following "aspects": "there is philosophy outside education; there is education outside philosophy; there is philosophy within education; there is education within philosophy" (p. 14).

[19]See Bouveresse (1993).

teaching, and why. It does not look for the most reliable and efficient means, but asks what the ends of education are." (p. 3–4)

• It is "vital" in as much as it is not prompted by a "purely speculative interest." For example, when asking, "What is time?" it concerns time of course, but also our human existence with and through time, "our anguish and our joy, our life and our death." Its quest is not merely knowledge, but also a knowing how to be, a kind of being through knowledge. (p. 4)

Fabre (1999) added a fourth characteristic:

• It is a questioning conducted according to reason. It recognizes reason as its only norm. Fabre (1999) pointed out how, even when philosophy acknowledges intuition (e.g., Bergson), or faith (e.g., Reboul), this reckoning always comes following a process of reasoning, of "reasonable adhesion." (p. 272)

Reboul (1989a) stressed that *philosophy* defined as such is not the panacea of experts. He added: "[t]he moment an educator reflects on the meaning of his enterprise, the moment he asks why, or better still, what for he does what he does, he philosophizes [original gender[20]]" (p. 5). What the experts bring is a method or, rather, said Reboul, a number of methods created by the philosopher or borrowed and/or adapted from the scholars who preceded him or her, this very choice, according to him, being philosophical. He described the five methods he used: those which rely on traditional doctrines whereby all great philosophers have questioned education and discussed its problems (Plato, Aristotle, the Stoicists, St. Augustin, St. Thomas d'Aquin, Erasmus, Hobbes, Locke, Hune, Helvetius, Rousseau, Kant, Fichte, Hegel, Nietzsche, etc.); reflection on sciences; logical analysis; argument "a contrario"; and dialectics. Fabre (1999) believed that only the first type of approaches, those based on the history of philosophy, "come under a specific professional knowledge" (p. 272).

For Fabre (1999), philosophy's three cardinal functions of epistemology, elucidation, and axiology should guide this reflection. The epistemological function concerns the knowledge issued from educational sciences, the identification of the specific characteristics of this field, and the evaluation of its validity and pertinence to the elevation of humanity. The function of elucidation explores the systems, mechanisms, and procedures of education to bring to light what is at stake in them, as well as their implications and meaning. The axiological function addresses values in education, particularly moral values, analyzing the goals to be promoted and the principles to be disseminated. However, the advent of educational sciences brought into question the status and functions of a philosophy of education. Avanzini (1987) wondered whether philosophy of education and educational sciences are competitive or complementary, while Fabre (1999) believed that "[t]he very fact of assigning a space [to philosophy in education] (above? Next to it? In the margins?) must be questioned" (p. 277). He wondered how to define the conditions in which philosophy would exert its heuristic power to support the questioning and

---

[20]The masculine grammatical gender, *homme, il*, is most frequently used in the French texts. Charlot (1995) explained this continued use, indicating that, "By 'man' we understand 'human being,' which includes, of course, women" (p. 21). He added that, "[b]y becoming 'man' [through education], one always becomes also a specified human being—by his/her sex, social or familial belonging, era, singular history, and so on" (p. 21).

explaining of the theories and practices of a field he also designated as "the field of pedagogy and didactics" (p. 277).[21]

Fabre (1999) recalled that, at the end of the 19th century, with Compayré, Marion, and Durkheim, educational sciences began amid a complex set of tensions between scientific and philosophical objectives. We saw that while advocating his general project to develop an *educational science* (singular then), Durkheim was in fact more interested in sociological research. Avanzini (1994) noted that the ambiguity of Durkheim's project was first denounced by the philosophers charged with teaching this new educational science (e.g., Chabot, Thamin). However, as philosophical reflection seemed to be increasingly pressured out of these new projects focused on a more scientific approach, the philosophers did not appear free of responsibility in minimizing the role of philosophy in education. In fact, Fabre (1999) believed that the lack of distinction among terms and notions and the laxity in terminology started with Compayré and Marion, who "indifferently—according to the old custom—spoke of 'Philosophy of education' and 'Science of education' to characterize any organized knowledge whatever its modes of legitimization" (p. 278). For example, the "Compayré moment"—described by Charbonnel (1988)—combined Victor Cousin's spiritualist philosophy, Anglo-Saxon empirical psychology, and Auguste Comte's positivism to investigate human nature. As a glaring example of what he called *this eclecticism,* Fabre (1999) also cited the famous *Dictionnaire de pédagogie et d'instruction publique,* which Dubois (1994) analyzed. Dubois exposed the weaknesses contained in this dictionary, which advocated

> either to keep to principles so general that the most diverse practices could be inferred, or to venture to practical prescriptions which then owe less to initially posited principles than to "extra-pedagogical concerns whose assumed philosophical soundness seems sufficient to authorize the ignorance of the didactics which support them." (cited in Fabre, 1999, p. 278)

This brand of what Fabre called *confusionism* is a serious problem, and he saw it as undermining any attempt at a meaningful reflection on education, be it in the past or today.

In 1984, Duborgel warned against another risk he saw in a reductionistic use of philosophy by education. Going back to the three functions of philosophy (elucidation, epistemology, and axiology) may help one understand his point. Swept along with the enthusiasm following the development of sciences and the technologies they produce, with the belief that humanity finally held the key to a thorough understanding and control of the world, one could trust that unlimited progress and knowledge were now also available to education. However, as in other disciplines and areas of scholarship, especially after 1945, it was soon evident that truth remained elusive, and progress was an ever-moving horizon, a continuing search, reminding us that perhaps the most meaningful knowledge is not so much gained in the answer as in its quest. Scholars who even now talk about their hope for a *true, rigorous, exact* science able to *demonstrate* and offer *certitudes* forget that numbers are generated by humans, statistics are but probabilities interpreted and manipulated by humans, and even computers give back only as good as we humans put in. Science cannot bring any guarantees, and the necessity of developing an epistemological and ethical reflection which would keep up with the scientific and technological advances is one major issue in education as well as in science today.[22] Moreover, several authors have pointed to the weaknesses of some

---

[21]It is somewhat reassuring that Fabre devoted the next two paragraphs to discussing the *eclecticism* and *confusionism* among the terms used by his predecessors and therefore among the notions they convey in both fields of philosophy and education (pp. 277–278), thus indicating an awareness of the problem specifically discussed by Avanzini (1997). As previously pointed out, this problem of vocabulary and semantics in the French field of education is one major issue.

methodological approaches[23] which carry their own risks as they might lull us into the smugness we may derive from a so-called *scientific education.* In addition, Fabre (1999) also noted the danger of "assimilating philosophy to a catalogue of doctrines or of conceptions of the world" (p. 279).

Furthermore, French scholars generally seem to look to traditional philosophy either for an explanation of current issues in education or an application to educational situations toward a resolution of their problems. Fabre (1999) saw some limits in the way the epistemological function of philosophy may be used to examine problems, methods, and results at work in educational sciences. Although he agreed that some "anchoring in educational positive knowledge" appears "absolutely necessary," he warned against "reducing epistemology to its positivist variant" (p. 279). He recalled Auguste Comte, who did not limit philosophy to thinking sciences, but rather to establishing connections among the various scientific fields, and between sciences and all fields of knowledge, in the hope of giving sciences the *proper* direction. However, in contemporary education, those Duborgel (1984) called "neopositivist officer[s] of coordination" are faced with the unmanageable complexity of "pluri-, multi-, inter-disciplinarity" or are immersed in a "super-discipline" (p. 24) which claims to be able to manage all the relations, orders of dependence, and interferences among the basic disciplines. Yet Duborgel (1984) wondered what an epistemology severed from all theories of knowledge would be worth.[24]

It seems more difficult to divert, misdirect, or misuse the axiological function of philosophy since "[t]o philosophize is first to question, to ask questions which address the meaning and the values attached to the individual and collective transformation of humanity, the meaning of its future, the responsibility for the future" (after Jonas, 1993; cited in Morandi, 2000, p. 6). In education, it means to question the values and ends of education; it also means to go back to the foundations of its theories and practices and the very conditions of their possibility (Fabre, 1999). Although Durkheim held that the ends of education were determined by society and uncovered by sociology, some philosophers of education maintain that philosophy cannot renounce its mission to seek the meaning of education—to ask "Why?" as well as "What for?" to develop a critique of its directions, orientations, institutions, and so on, guided by ideal values.

For example, Fabre (1999) discussed the necessity of a philosophical reflection on and about education, but specifically *of education.* Using a double-bind type of argument, he showed how "any attempt to do away with [philosophy of education]—be it in the name of the prestige of science or the urgency of practice—assumes what it is precisely supposed to be denying" (p. 270). Hadji (1994) argued that this philosophical questioning bears on legitimacy, and its criteria on values and the value of our values, in search of a fulcrum conceived as objective principle (Plato), reason (Kant), origin (Nieztsche), or originary (Husserl, Heidegger). Fabre (1999) insisted that education must remain opened to questioning, beyond issues of technicity or scientificity. Like Socrates's irony, Plato's wondering, and Aristotle's metaphysics, this questioning bears on a knowledge and know-how which may otherwise grow too smug in their confidence that they hold *the* truth. According to Fabre (1999), philosophy of education does not question the inadequacy of sciences or the imperfection of practices, but the self-satisfaction or certainty of either sciences or

---

[22]For further discussion on this topic, see Serres (especially 1994, 1995, and 1999) and Egéa-Kuehne (1998, 2001a, 2001b).

[23]They include: "temptation of the dictionary or the authors catalogue; hunting for precursors; systematic 'comparatism' which gives priority to the elements external to a work (sources, influences, and so on); reconstructivism or temptation to think by proxy, sheltered by someone else's work; and finally, typologism or art to fit all the works into a limited number of small drawers" (after Rosenvalon; cited in Fabre, 1999, p. 279; see also Charbonnel, 1988; Dubois, 1996).

[24]See also Serres (1994, 1995, 1999) and Egéa-Kuehne (1998, 2001a).

practices when they believe they have found *the* solution or *the* answer. Such questions include: What do we mean when we say we intend to form someone? (Fabre, 1994); What do we claim we do when we evaluate? (Hadji, 1989); To educate, what for? (Hocquard, 1996); On what do we pretend to found our authority as educators? (Houssaye, 1996); What is worth teaching? (Reboul, 1989b); and so on.

Earlier we noted how philosophers were at the origin of educational science (singular then) in the early 1880s. While attempting to work pedagogy through applied psychology to create a science of education, they did so within philosophy. Thus, in 1880, through a series of shifts in terms, if not in the depth of the concepts, educational science (singular still) appeared as the "apex of Philosophy of Education" (Charbonnel, 1988, pp. 101–102). However, Gautherin's (1995) analysis revealed that this educational science never did assert itself as a science. It remained speculative and estranged from empirical research. Although professors of educational science essentially produced general theories seemingly of little use to educators, they managed to "justify an educational policy, reinforce belief in the powers of education, and strengthen the social connection" (Gautherin, 1995, p. 53). Based on such blurring of definitions, responsibilities, domains, and so on, it is professors of philosophy who became professors of psychopedagogy in 1947, teaching general pedagogy, philosophy of education, child psychology, and social anthropology to future teachers. Again, in 1969, two years after the creation of the first departments of educational sciences, philosophers were asked to teach general pedagogy and the history of the doctrines of education. According to Houssaye (1997), this is how philosophy of education became "the specialist of generalities" (p. 86) and continues to justify the role of philosophers in the programs of initial teacher education.

As a consequence, unlike other traditional philosophical disciplines (e.g., epistemology, esthetics), philosophy of education has had some identity problems related to its place and the place of philosophers of education in French universities, made worse by institutional constraints. This is evident in the lack of philosophy of education tenured positions within departments of philosophy, or even in departments of educational sciences, and in its restriction to teacher education. Fabre (1999) and Hocquard (1996) also regretted the absence of a reflection on education on the part of established French philosophers. I would differ on that point since such contemporary philosophers as Deleuze, Derrida, Foucault, Lyotard, Ricoeur, and Serres, for example, have indeed seriously addressed problems of education. However, they are seldom or not at all mentioned in even the most current reflection on education, except by a few authors such as Morandi (2000), albeit briefly.[25] Especially in France, these authors are not read often enough if at all by educators, or not read for what their reflection can bring to education.[26] Therefore, in France, philosophy of education has not been very visible and has appeared to be treated as "a minor occupation" (Fabre, 1999, p. 272).

---

[25]One finds Arendt, Deleuze, Lyotard, and Ricoeur cited occasionally. See Egéa-Kuehne's publications on Derrida, Serres, and Levinas, for example.

[26]The position of the author is that, when reading the works of these philosophers, one should not be looking for guidelines, rules, or prescriptions to apply to education to fix its problems. The point is not to reduce "the profound arguments which form in [their] work … to trivial statements used to talk about implications for schooling." In fact, "[a]ny attempt to summarize complex concepts, to recall them more or less exactly, more or less precisely in order to try and draw some specific 'implications' to be applied to education would not carry much meaning, and would amount to a misreading" of these authors. For "[i]t is not a matter of relating [their] thought to issues of pedagogy or didactics either." Rather, reading them "in the context of education calls for an engagement of [their] forms of reasoning and analyzing with educational issues. It needs an attentive and respectful reading 'through work which actually requires time, discipline and patience, work that requires several readings, new types of reading, too, in a variety of different fields' (Derrida, 1995, p. 401)" (Egéa-Kuehne & Biesta, 2001, p. 4).

Yet more recently, philosophy of education has found itself in the limelight. In 1998, branches of the Paris *Institut National de Recherche Pédagogique* (INRP) were opened in Lyon and Rouen. These institutes were placed under the direction of one of the French leading scholars in education, Philippe Meirieu, a specialist in educational sciences who identifies himself as a pedagogue and likes to call himself "a tinkerer in education."[27] A few months later, a new department was opened at the Institute in Paris. The department of *Philosophie de l'éducation et pédagogie* (distinct from the department of *Sciences de l'éducation*), under the direction of François Jacquet-Francillon, is "still in the process of being created" (Institut National de Recherche Pédagogique, 1999, p. 14)—still caught between the "objective limits of its embryonic state" and the necessity of projecting in the future "something which will be per force more ambitious" (Institut National de Recherche Pédagogique, 1998, p. 14). The main incentive behind its creation was "an increasingly acute sense of severe gaps and shortcomings in discourses on and about schools and education" (Institut National de Recherche Pédagogique, 1998, p. 14). The need was keenly felt for something more solid than "ill informed interventions by some intellectuals essentially concerned with their media image," as was the need for a more problematized, more reflexive approach to education, "going beyond summaries of empirical research" (Institut National de Recherche Pédagogique, 1998, p. 14). The main objective of the Department of Philosophy of Education and Pedagogy is "to promote an interdisciplinary questioning of the theories, concepts and problems of education" (Institut National de Recherche Pédagogique, 2000, p. 14). This department identified three priorities as main directions for research: philosophy of education, controversial issues in the school, and memory and history. Teams of professors are collaborating on various projects, particularly on "Controversial Issues in Education" under the leadership of Sophie Ernst. The Philosophy of Education section, under the direction of François Jacquet-Francillon, declared three goals for 2000–2001:

- to know the state of the art and the results of philosophy of education scholarship abroad (notably the US);
- to gather and publish (with an appropriate critical apparatus) series of texts dedicated to education in the historical corpus of philosophy and pedagogy;
- to examine philosophical questions related to the evolution of the teaching professions and the missions of education (ethical and deontological reflection). (Institut National de Recherche Pédagogique, 2000, p. 14)

When, after the demise of Claude Allègre, Minister of Education, Meirieu resigned from his position as director of the INRP in May 2000, a fierce debate had already been raging for several months through the daily *Le Monde*, the monthly magazine *Le Monde de l'éducation*,[28] as well as in a number of books.[29] It exposed the antagonism between the "owners of knowledge" (i.e., university professors and researchers, working essentially in philosophy and the humanities) and the "pedagogues" (i.e., researchers in sciences of education, historians, sociologists, teachers) (Guibert, 2000, p. 15). These publications are an indication that nowadays "education becomes an object which

---

[27]Philippe Meirieu, specialist in educational sciences and labeled "the pedagogue most read by educators" (Etévé & Gambart, 1992), identifies himself as a pedagogue rather than as a philosopher of education. His work in theory of education and the tight connection he always maintained with the schools seemed to hold a powerful potential for the leadership of the INRP.

[28]For example, *Le Monde*, September 8, 1999; April 8, May 12, May 19, and June 22, 2000. *Le Monde de l'éducation*, May 2000, July–August 2000, and October 2000.

[29]For example, Finkielkraut (2000a), Kambouchner (2000), and Meirieu (1998).

philosophical reflection … meets as it were by accident, because one must condescend to thinking the educational crisis [when it is discussed in the news] and to responding to journalists" (Fabre, 1999, p. 272). Unfortunately, this kind of exchange is often in the style more of pamphlets than of scholarly debates. Several observers and commentators (e.g., Guibert, 2000) explained how, in fact, this debate harks back to old intellectual positions and recalled Brunetière's words in 1895. Professor of philosophy at the *École Normale Supérieure,* he declared: "One does not need to teach pedagogy to these young men [students], they have discovered it themselves and by themselves. Let's first have teachers who think of nothing but to teach and let's not care about [*moquons-nous*[30]] pedagogy" (p. 8).

PEDAGOGY: THE PERENNIAL

Indeed, pedagogy has always been the underdog in the field of education. In the introduction to a special issue of what Houssaye (1997) called the "Mecca of French journals in educational research and in sciences of education" (p. 96)—that is the *Revue Française de Pédagogie,* Forquin (1997) wrote:

> In the face of the accumulation of "positive knowledge" produced in the name of "research in education," and also in the face of some powerful systematizations of philosophy but without a directly practical purpose, pedagogy as thinking, as a mode and posture of thinking, seems to have recently come to being devalued. (p. 5)

Yet as Forquin (1997) indicated further: "any and all pedagogical thinking remains tightly linked to teaching situations and practices" (p. 6).

Pedagogy has a long history of being caught and torn between practical theory (Durkheim) and empirical practice (Avanzini), and it is characterized in French by a highly inconsistent use of the term.[31] From the beginning, an opposition has existed between "the content of education and its form, the matter to be taught and the manner to teach it" (Reboul, 1989a, p. 52). At times, the debate currently raging has taken a vicious turn.[32] In fact, this antagonism has existed ever since the Ancient times, when the pedagogue was a slave taking the children to the preceptor in charge of instructing them. However, the word *pedagogy* entered the field of education much later. The Robert dictionary sets its appearance in the French language around 1485 (cited in Mialaret, 1984, p. 3). Littré found it in Calvin's (1536) *Christian Institution,* and the *Académie Française* accepted it in its dictionary in 1762 (cited in Mialaret, 1984, p. 3). Not until the 19th century did its usage become more frequent (Mialaret, 1984). In 1690, Furetière gave this definition of *pedagogue* in his dictionary (whereas *pedagogy* did not figure as an entry): "a master to whom is given the care to instruct and govern a pupil, to teach him grammar, and to watch over his actions [original gender]."

Throughout the centuries, the meaning of this word has fluctuated, and its connotations have taken different directions—from the most positive (e.g., *German pedagogues* designates the greatest thinkers of the 19th century) to the most negative (e.g., "a pedantic, authoritarian, narrow-minded master" in the Robert dictionary, 16th century).

---

[30]It also means "to make fun of," "to ridicule." Although in this context the intent of the message is most likely to drop pedagogy out of the program, the term *moquons-nous* nevertheless leaves a pejorative connotation.

[31]See Avanzini (1997) and Beillerot (1997).

[32]See, for example, Blanchard (2000), Dupuis (2000), Finkielkraut (2000a, 2000b), Guibert (2000), Le Bars (2000), Meirieu (1998, 2000a, 2000b), and Prost (2000).

Reboul (1989a) suggested that "the word 'pedagogy' has at least two meanings" (p. 51). On the one hand, it refers to being a pedagogue, "to possessing the art of teaching and educating, the know-how which is essentially learned through practice" (p. 51). On the other hand, it refers to "the theory of that art, a 'practical theory,' as Durkheim put it, since it concerns itself with applying human sciences to the art of education" (p. 51). In his analysis of Reboul's definition, Avanzini (1997) set pedagogy as synonymous with the common usage of *didactic procedures* and of Marion's (1888) *educational science*. Reboul's second meaning also echoes the definition of *pedagogy* given by the *Revue Française de Pédagogie* (RFP) in the Editorial of its first issue (1967). The editorial board of the *Revue Française de Pédagogie* (Institut National de Pédagogie, 1967) had set its goal as "familiarizing educators, but also a broader but wiser audience, to the most important problems posed by the evolution of Education, in its principles, its methods, and, as the case may be, its structures" (p. 7).

But Avanzini (1997) found Reboul's characterization of pedagogy "insufficient" (p. 18). He stressed that its referring only to the child was adequate up to the 20th century, but is no longer appropriate today because it does not cover contemporary adult education, continuing education, and so on. De Lansheere (1986) is one of the rare scholars to note that "the word pedagogy etymologically limits the field of investigation to the child, particularly in a school context, whereas nowadays, education is a lifelong endeavor" (p. 13), and he saw there a justification to shift the terminology from *experimental pedagogy* to *research* (i.e., *scientific research*). Durkheim (1966) added a reflexive dimension to pedagogy, writing that it "consists not in an action, but in a theory ... it consists in a certain manner of reflecting on educational issues" (p. 67). However, making a distinction between doctrines (i.e., intellectual constructions) and pedagogy, Durkheim denounced these intellectual constructions, which rather than focusing on the knowledge of "the genesis or the functioning of educational systems" remain merely speculative, only aimed at "enacting rules of behavior" (p. 67).

In 1967, when the new projects were named, the term *pedagogy* was replaced with *educational sciences* to designate programs and degrees. Mialaret (1993) recalled various stages: "before this creation [of educational sciences departments in 1967] one commonly talked about 'pedagogy'" (p. 162). He added:

> If my memory serves me right, it is Maurice Debesse who tossed the idea of an undergraduate degree in educational sciences (*licence en sciences de l'éducation*) and had it adopted. But we were not all totally agreed on what, outside the traditional pedagogy (history and philosophy of educative thought and pedagogical theories, sociology of education, Compayré, Durkheim, Hubert, and so on), we were going to put there. One must recall what the opinion was in that domain, and at that time: for some, on a theoretical level, to speak of pedagogy was to cover only the history and philosophy of thought and of pedagogical theories; whereas for others, it was to fall into an initiation to a narrow professional practice, practically amounting to recipes on "how to teach well?" (Mialaret, 1993, pp. 164–165)

Concerning these shifts in the meanings of *pedagogy*, Beillerot (1997) conducted an analysis of several texts which mark the development of educational sciences from 1967 to the present time (Debesse & Mialaret, 1969; Ferry, 1983; Filloux, 1971; Isambert-Jamati, 1983; Mosconi, 1982). It revealed that, through the years, several viewpoints confronted one another. However, they all eventually shared a common goal (i.e., the formation of teachers). Houssaye (1997) offered a synopsis of this shift in the vocabulary following the movements of the concept which "took some time to stabilize itself," using successively, or sometimes alternatively if not simultaneously, the following terms:

- *scientific pedagogy* (Binet, Boughet, Bovet, Claparède, Fabre);
- *experimental pedagogy* (Binet, Claparède, Dottrens, Simon);
- *pedagogical science* (Claparède);
- *educational science* (Bain, Buyse, Compayré, Marion, Lapie, de la Vaissière); and
- *educational sciences* (Malche, Mialaret, and everyone else). (Houssaye, 1997, p. 87)

Discussing the nature of pedagogy in France, Avanzini (1997) identified two components. The first one is normative and elaborates doctrines. It attempts to explain the meaning of the practice at hand and to determine its ends and ideals. Because the educational act is fundamentally one of being, the normative approach proceeds from three main sources: philosophy, politics, and theology. The second one is descriptive, covering a range from empirical to scientific and constructs theories. It studies the phenomenon of education as such, that is as cultural phenomenon in essence, analyzing how, why, what for, and so on, it functions as it does. Through this study is gained knowledge about the institutions and people involved. Furthermore, to do that, different venues are needed, including sociology, psychology, and history. Over the years, the normative and descriptive approaches received a varying amount of support. For example, up until Rousseau, the normative approach seemed to be in favor. However, at the end of the 19th century and beginning of the 20th century, its popularity started to wane when, under the pressure of the positivist movement, there grew a demand for better understanding of educational apparatuses and their functioning through a deliberate shift toward a "rigorously scientific methodology" (Avanzini, 1997, p. 20). The development of educational science(s) which followed brought about a devaluation of pedagogy, although it is not incompatible with so-called *objective methods*.[33] In fact, the normative and scientific approaches are not incompatible as long as the researcher knows and makes clear where he or she stands. This is reflected in these words in Laeng's (1974) dictionary: "pedagogy as philosophy was born out of the necessity to give a valid critical foundation to the educational action, going from man to man and consequently implying the essential problems of nature and the destiny of humanity [original gender]" (p. 208). Laeng added:

> Pedagogy as a science, especially in contemporary times, has shown the necessity of positive research, experimentally founded on facts; it has taken the form of an interdisciplinary study of several ancillary sciences (psychology, sociology, anthropological-cultural sciences) and of a compared assessment of plans, systems, methods and techniques. (pp. 208–209)

This debate on the nature of pedagogy and its relation to educational sciences is not singular to France. In other countries (e.g., Germany), a similar debate is also taking place (Geulen, 1995). According to Avanzini (1997), this is one more indication that pedagogy is alive and well and is "neither obsolete nor superfluous" (p. 21). For Mialaret (1991) pedagogy is "a reflection on the ends of education and an objective analysis of its conditions of existence and functioning; it is directly related to the educational action which constitutes its area of reflection and analysis, yet without ever getting confused with it" (p. 7). Avanzini (1997) maintained that, among other writers, Soëtard is the scholar whose work has "most efficiently and most justly achieved a rehabilitation of this concept [pedagogy]" (p. 21). Soëtard (1985) argued that to do pedagogy is "to formalize the combination of 'the scientific perspective' which assesses the means, and 'the practical perspective'" (p. 248) which determines everyday behavior.

---

[33]See Binet and *scientific pedagogy* or Buyse and *experimental pedagogy.*

For some scholars, it is not a problem to situate pedagogy in relation to educational sciences, sometimes also called *pedagogical sciences* (Debesse & Mialaret, 1969). For example, it is clear for Mialaret (1993), one of the *fathers* of educational sciences, that educational sciences "do not have the normative aspect which pedagogy itself may have, since they claim to adopt a scientific approach in the study of this educative action" (p. 172). Moreover, Mialaret (1993) situated pedagogy as a "subset of educational sciences" (p. 172), certainly not a classification with which everyone will agree. However, it enabled him to see the benefits of using both angles to get a better understanding of education. Avanzini (1997) reported him as perceiving educational sciences as objectively concerning themselves with the entire range of educational phenomena, whereas pedagogy focuses specifically on the child, from both an objective and a normative standpoint. He did not see how, once this relation is thus perceived in its simple clarity, it should not cease to be a source of fierce controversy, unless the fun is in the controversy for controversy's sake.

Looking at the media and professional publications (journals and books) made available in the past few years, one can see that the debate did not rest. It just shifted grounds. Besides pedagogy, caught between sciences of education and philosophy of education, another approach to educational issues is trying to assert its identity and define its specificity as distinct from all three preceding domains.

DIACTICS:[34] A CONFLUENCE OF OPPORTUNITIES

Emergence of a "New" Field

Develay (1997) believed that the emergence of the didactics ushered in positivist knowledge as they hoped to resolve the problem of cognition. The term *didactics* came into common use relatively recently, especially in connection with specific disciplines, and tends to project a more modern image than does pedagogy, which is perceived as more traditional. Yet Coménius had already defined it as "the art of teaching" (p. 29), in a work published in Czechoslovakia in 1649. Houssaye (1997) recalled that Coménius's *La grande didactique* is considered "the first attempt at a synthesis to constitute pedagogy as an autonomous science" (p. 88). Note that even then the terminology was not free of semantic ambiguity.[35] This same definition of *didactics* as "the art of teaching" (Houssaye, 1997, p. 88) found its way into dictionaries after 1955—but had not pedagogy already been defined in those terms? (e.g., Marion; cited in Plaisance & Vergnaud, 1999, p. 8).

Develay (1997) preferred to situate the emergence of the current brand of didactics (singular, *la didactique*) in the 1970s as a reaction against educational sciences. In this perspective, aiming to be pragmatic, didactics viewed educational sciences as too disconnected from practical issues. Develay (1997) offered "two viewpoints to analyze the conditions of emergence of didactics … institutional, and speculative" (p. 60). He described how, beginning in the early 1970s and in reaction to approaches to educational issues in terms of relations as promoted by the departments of educational sciences, a new movement placed the emphasis on questions of students' appropriation of the contents. This movement was emerging from the structures associated with the fragmentation of the disciplines and manifested itself mainly in two institutions: the Insti-

---

[34]In French texts, we find *la didactique* (singular) to designate a field and *les didactiques* (plural) as a reference to the distinct didactics specific to each discipline (e.g., didactics of sciences, didactics of history, didactics of mathematics, etc.).

[35]More on the mutations of the term *didactique* in Develay (1997).

tutes of Research on the Teaching of Mathematics (*Instituts de Recherche sur l'Enseignement des Mathématiques* [IREMs]) and the National Institute of Pedagogical Research (INRP). Develay (1997) recalled that in the IREMs, scholars were rather dubious about the knowledge issued from social and human sciences. They were not satisfied with psychosociological or psychoanalytical explanations. Formed essentially in their discipline of origin, with little contact with human and social sciences and a concern with a democratization of knowledge, at times these scholars would construct didactical concepts without ensuring that they had not already been established in the field of educational sciences (e.g., theory of situations, didactic contract). Vergnaud (1990) defined *didactics* as

> the study of the teaching and learning processes pertaining to a particular domain of knowledge: for example a discipline, a trade, or a profession. It rests on pedagogy, psychology, [epistemology] and of course the discipline studied. But it cannot be reduced to that. (p. 55)

Although relying on psychology, pedagogy, and epistemology, didactics as a field is still striving to develop its own concepts and theoretical frameworks.

The emergence of this brand of didactics had an impact on two levels: on institutions and programs in the *écoles normales,* and on professional development and career advancement of university professors and teacher educators. At the *écoles normales,* teacher education used to begin before the last 2 years of high school. When the *Instituts Universitaires de Formation de Maîtres* (IUFM) replaced the *écoles normales,* students entered these new teacher education programs at the university level, and their formation entailed a project of action research in coordination with the IREMs or the INRP. Hence it was no longer sufficient to teach some academic content. Instead, future teachers also had to focus on the conditions of appropriation of these contents by pupils (didactic transposition). Teacher educators were seeking a new professional identity for which "didactics [would] constitute the hard core" (Develay, 1997, p. 60). Current didactics were constructed at "the interface between practical questions of classroom management and more theoretical concerns corresponding to a demand for an explanation of the modes of learning and teaching" (Develay, 1997, p. 60). The development of didactics coincides with a growing interest in issues of teacher education and learners' formation.

Current didactics also had an impact on professional development and career advancement. To university professors, the field of didactics offered a venue for promotion within the university; for teacher educators in training centers, it constituted a point of access to the university. This movement corresponds to the introduction of new approaches to education into educational sciences departments when teaching became a subject of content knowledge, and positions were opened in didactics of the various disciplines (i.e., didactics of mathematics, of sciences, didactics of foreign languages, etc.). Develay (1997) saw a "not-yet-assumed filial relationship" between the "mother" pedagogy and the "daughter" didactics (p. 60).

In the 1970s, when didactics emerged out of the movement toward a more active involvement of children in early learning activities in elementary schools, two main currents of ideas developed. Authoritative references to established scholars were sought, and two names seemed to be prominent: Bachelard and Piaget. Bachelard's work helped explain two things: the potential which children's representations offered in some didactics, especially in sciences; and how access to rationality can be founded on non-rational dimensions which structure any thinking. Hence, the notions of *epistemological obstacle* and *school epistemology* entered the field of didactics even before those terms were actually coined (Bachelard, 1938, 1940, 1949). For psychological references, didacticians turned to Piaget (Piaget & Ibhelder, 1966; Piaget, 1974a, 1974b). His work on experience and exchange and his notion of *conflit socio-cognitif* helped develop an understanding of knowledge as derived from the activity of the child and from exchange. Yet Develay (1997) pointed to a paradox of some consequence in the didacticians' use of Piaget in as much as it enabled them to leave out the ethical aspect of educational reflection. He wrote: Piaget's "viewpoint on the development of intelligence—open to communication, expression, conflict, and to the debate of ideas—enabl[es] a striking shortcut bypassing ethical reflection which many didacticians frequently feign to forget in their conceptualization of the processes of teaching rather than of education" (p. 61). Thus, in didactics, a major aspect of reflection on education was left out while this venue enabled didacticians to introduce a positivist approach to their field of study.

The second current of ideas emerged at the intersection of social and cognitive psychologies, and it took two directions. In some didactics (e.g., sciences), the notion of *representation* or conception played a central role and was perceived both as an obstacle and a fulcrum for the child's learning. Social psychology supported this line of thinking. In other didactics (e.g., mathematics), the notion of *representation* was less important than the notions of *didactic situation, didactic transposition, didactic contract*, and the learning processes of diverse concepts.[36] Cognitive psychology was developing and provided the references for this domain of reflection. Richard (1990) and Vergnaud (1983, 1990) are credited with contributing to the development of theoretical bases for a type of didactics suitable for the more formalized disciplines.

Still in mathematics, Develay (1997) acknowledged the work of several scholars whose influence extended to all the disciplines precisely around the previously mentioned notions of *theory of situations, didactic contract*, and *didactic transposition*. In the theory of situations (including didactic engineering), Brousseau (1998) distinguished diverse types of teaching/learning situations according to what is at stake: action and success; formulation of a message or an element of knowledge; and validation of a judgment or an argument. For Brousseau (1984, 1990), didactic contract focused on the relationship between the teacher and the individual being taught and on the responsibility of each toward the other, and more specifically concerned the content. However, in this context, more frequent references are made to Filloux's (1974) position contract, based on psychoanalysis, and the institution of knowledge in the pedagogical relation. In the notion of didactic contract, it is assumed that the specificity of the content, rather than the pedagogical method at work, determines the particular nature of the respective expectations of the teacher and the individual being taught. As a consequence, the problem of teaching is placed at the core of the didactic reflection, which posits that the specificity of a content is determined by the specificity of a learning. "Often referred to, this hypothesis is rarely illustrated," wrote Develay (1997), "as if the didactic reflection could not manage to satisfy its intentions, leaving it to pedagogical reflection" (p. 62). As to the notion of didactic transposition, it was borrowed by Chevallard (1985) from a sociologist, Verret (1975), to explain the processes necessary to go from academic knowledge to a knowledge which can be taught in the classroom. Thus, originally borrowed from sociology, the concept of didactic transposition now appeared to be characteristic of didactics. This is one example, noted Develay (1997), of the didactics' generous propensity to borrow concepts from other fields and of the necessity to be vigilant for any alteration in the transit. It is also an example of the need for concepts the field of didactics may have in its search for a legitimacy and an identity. Astolfi (Astolfi, Darot, & Ginsburger-Vogel, 1997) was less tolerant, suggesting that "undoubtedly, didactics have led to some interesting

---

[36]See, for example, Vergnaud's (1983) work on subtraction.

contemporary developments, but it should acknowledge [that it is] stepping into a tradition and it should recognize its precursors" (p. 68).

Contemporary Issues in Didactics

Within each discipline, discipline-specific didactics developed their own concepts (e.g., the didactics of mathematics is not the same as the didactics of history). Yet one can identify a common trend: In all cases, focus is on learning and teaching contexts within the respective disciplines. Hence, one talks about didacticians in mathematics, in history, and so on. Dissention, divergence, misunderstanding, and/or differences appear when addressing the functions of didactics, their objects, and the trends in research.

Develay (1997) identified three different "attitudes" corresponding to different "functions" which seemed to emerge in didactics (p. 63). At the university level, didactics play a role of elucidation, explanation, and clarification. University didacticians deal with learning/teaching situations removed from "the concrete environment of specific children in a particular school institution at a given time" (p. 63). Their goal is to make sense out of the situation at hand, not to offer suggestions for action beyond this decontextualized setting. Theirs is a *didactics of elucidation.* A *didactics of injunction* refers to the inspector didactician whose role is to prescribe, recommend, and indicate "what must be done and what must not be done" (p. 63). In this case, didactics are understood according to norms not always explicit, which may refer to a domain other than didactics. For a *didactics of suggestion,* the instructor is expected to use the discourse of the researcher to clarify the new practices he or she is promoting. This may take into account and offer a critical analysis of already existing practices. Develay (1997) pointed out that these three functions are not always clearly distinguishable because overlapping and intersecting are frequent. They do not refer to any institutionalized status either as the labels of *university scholar, inspector,* or *instructor* might lead to believe. Each, in turn, can elucidate, prescribe, or suggest.

There is a divergence between two schools of didacticians as to the objects of their reflection. Some believe that, to create situations of learning, there is no need to investigate content epistemology. Only theories generally from the field of psychology are relevant. This type of didactics is akin to psychopedagogy, and it is illustrated by Aebli (1951) and the psychological didactics based on Piaget's theories. Opponents of this approach believe that it is not possible to suggest learning situations without considering the epistemology of the content to be taught/learned. For example, before one can teach history or biology, one must determine which history or which biology is at stake. The epistemology of knowledge uncovers the discrepancies, relations, and reconstructions in acquired university knowledge. It identifies what was borrowed from social practices, for example, to make academic knowledge gel into a body of contents which can be taught, working through axiological reflection, psychological assumptions, and biases from fads and lobbies. This kind of didactics, using didactic transposition, didactic reconstruction, notions of paradigms, and/or disciplinary matrixes, no longer relies on psychology only. Develay (1997) underscored that these two positions are but the two extremes of a continuum.

Develay (1997) further noted that the borders of didactics are still not clear. The distinctive character of didactics, especially as compared with pedagogy, is most apparent when placed in actual situations of learning, in schools, with real children. Didacticians consider that the specificity of the contents is determinant to explain success or failure, whereas pedagogues focus on the relations in the classroom among students and between students and teachers. Pedagogues also pay attention to relations of power, love, hate, and indifference, which can be identified at the conscious and subconscious levels. At the same time, pedagogues are attentive to the values constructed or exchanged through these relations, and communications ethics are a main concern. The controversy played out between these two positions brought to caricature-like extremes—with pedagogues focusing on relation and didacticians on content—is at the heart of one of the most virulent debates currently taking place (Guibert, 2000).

Specificity of Didactics

Didactics are said to offer a new approach to thinking education precisely through their relations to contents and through their identifying themselves as discipline specific: "the particularity of the contents to be taught determines the modes of learning and the modalities of teaching," wrote Develay (1997, p. 64). Not everyone agrees. For example, Houssaye (1997) declared that "[i]nstitutionally speaking, in fact, didacticians seem to begin talking about questions which were traditionally allotted to what was recognized as pedagogy" (p. 88). Four viewpoints attempted to clarify the question of didactics relation to knowledge (Beillerot, Blanchard-Laville, Bouillet, & Mosconi, 1989; Charlot, 1997; Develay, 1976, 1997).

- Psychoanalysis can help us understand the relation to knowledge of one specific student … through the role played by desire in learning, and therefore by the fantasmagoric dimensions any knowledge holds for one particular learner (Santos, 1999);
- Sociology can clarify the relation of a student to knowledge through the identity ties he/she lives with his/her peers, and especially with his/her family. Didactics must understand what relation to knowledge as relation to culture a child lives in school, within a specific discipline (Bertrand, 1999);
- The epistemology of school learning constitutes a reflection on contents taught in school in order to explain their foundations, methods, and conclusions. It makes addressing the issue of the relation to knowledge possible. An epistemology of school learning must specify the nature of the relation to the truth which is to be built within a given discipline (Develay, 1995);
- The anthropological dimension of the relation to knowledge, as basic foundation to didactics … would prompt the examination of what questions are posed today by a specific discipline in respect to its initial goals, and what vision of humanity is thus revealed. … When these fundamental questions are overlooked, we teach only some elements of knowledge, but not the culture of this knowledge. … However, didacticians would need to accept to consider that the nature of knowledge constitutes the core variable of its conditions of appropriation by the learners. (Develay, 1997, pp. 64–65)

In 1997, Develay believed that scholars in the domain of didactics still needed to resolve some serious problems. They claimed not merely to be designing methods to teach some given content with a maximum of efficiency, but also aimed to understand the relation of the student to knowledge and to establish ethical precepts issued from that comprehension. Develay (1997) emphasized that, to achieve that, they still had a lot of research to do, especially on questions of anthropology, epistemology, logic, and ethics.

CURRICULUM: THE NEW KID ON THE BLOCK

In the past few years, in addition to the approaches offered by educational studies in France under the terms of *educational sciences, philosophy of education, pedagogy,* and, more recently, *didactics*, a reflection has developed around the concept of *curriculum*. However, in France, this work takes place mostly outside education. Forquin (1995) stressed that although "such an approach does exist … [it is] in a more scattered way than in the form of a unified and structured field of study" (p. 200). In fact, he indicated that curriculum issues have been addressed mostly indirectly and essentially by sociologists or historians. In any case, although curriculum is not a field of study clearly identified in France, several researchers have been claiming it as "the subject of interesting approaches" to understanding education (Forquin, 1995, p. 199).

The French Context

In a 1995 article in *The Curriculum Journal,* Forquin presented a review of the work done in France in previous years, "illustrating how sociological research in curriculum [was] breaking new ground in reconceptualizing recurring themes such as the structural conditions of equal opportunity and the ideological presuppositions of the now ubiquitous 'hidden curriculum'" (Moon, 1995, p. 159). Forquin (1995) also discussed how the concept of *didactic transposition* contributed to understanding issues of content knowledge, curriculum, teaching, and learning. He was careful to indicate the semantic problems around the word *curriculum* in a French context, where the terms *programme d'études* or *plan d'études* are more frequently used, though with different meanings. Perrenoud (1993) also stressed the difference in meanings of the word *curriculum* in French and in English. He wrote:

> In Anglo-Saxon countries, one speaks of curriculum to designate the educational itinerary proposed to learners, whereas in French one will more readily say plan of study, program or cursus, depending on whether the accent is placed on the progression in the acquisition of knowledge, the subsequent contents, or the structuring of the school career. (p. 61)

In the United States, curriculum studies is a well-developed field with rich "curriculum theory"[37] scholarship (Egéa-Kuehne, 1999a, 1999b; Pinar, 1988; Pinar, Reynolds, Slattery, & Taubman, 1995). Following the (British) English common use of the word *curriculum*, Forquin (1995) posited that "the concept of curriculum … implies taking into consideration the whole course of studies and not just one aspect or one stage considered separately" (p. 200). In this context, he considered that it raises two major questions:

- the issue of educational coherence between the various forms of content, the various subjects taught, and the different learning experiences included in a course of study (p. 200); and

- the issue of educational progression … in relation to explicit ends or objectives … over a given period of time. (p. 200)

In the study of curriculum, Forquin (1995) also suggested to include "what students are actually taught," which may be different from the prescribed formal syllabus; "the underlying content of teaching or of school environment," acquired albeit unwittingly

---

[37]"Curriculum theory is that field of scholarly inquiry which labors to understand curriculum across the subject matter/academic disciplines. While subject matter specialization (such as the teaching of English or science or mathematics) tends to focus on teaching strategies and curricular issues within single teaching fields, curriculum theory aspires to understand the overall educational significance of the curriculum, focusing especially upon interdisciplinary themes, as well as the relation among curriculum, the individual, and society" (Pinar, 1999).

within a school context in form of "skills, abilities, habits and attitudes ... through experience, persuasion, familiarity or pervasive conviction"; and "the cognitive and cultural dimension of education" (p. 200). Based on these aspects of educational thinking, Forquin "deem[ed] that the curriculum issue should be at the center of any thinking and any theory of education" (p. 200).

The question of curriculum coherence and relevancy, raised by Durkheim (1938) earlier in the century, is, according to Forquin (1995), "one of the main strands of present thinking about curriculum in France" (p. 202). A report presented to the French Ministry of Education in 1989 by Bourdieu and Gros supports this point. It indicated that it has been a constant problem through the years—one which continues to feed current debates if not conflicts between the proponents of "an encyclopaedic ideal aiming at rationality, universality, and fairness and [the proponents of] the new requirements for flexibility, individuality and usefulness" (Forquin, 1995, p. 202). In the British model of curriculum studies, which seems to have some influence on francophone scholars, content knowledge has been the main concern of British curriculum sociologists. However, in 1995, Forquin had indicated that "in France and French-speaking countries, the issue of curriculum has appeared only recently and is usually tackled only indirectly in works of educational sociologists" (p. 203). Plaisance and Vergnaud (1999) also found that French-speaking sociologists of education seldom addressed issues of content knowledge per se.

Curriculum and Sociological Research

Sociological research has contributed more specifically to the scholarship on social structures and equal opportunity. Cherkaoui (1976, 1978) recalled the influence of Durkheim's work, one of the pioneers who brought a sociological approach to the first attempts at establishing educational science. Yet Durkheim seems to have a larger readership abroad than he does in France. So does Bourdieu, whose works and his colleagues', according to Forquin (1995), contributed "many analyses shedding light on teaching and assessment practices, academic language and school culture (Bourdieu, 1989; Bourdieu & Passeron, 1964, 1970; Bourdieu, Passeron, & De Saint-Martin, 1965)" (p. 203). Thus, in France, Durkheim's and Bourdieu's works did not have the following they did in the Anglophone community, and recent scholarship in French sociology offers few studies directly concerned with curriculum. However, Forquin (1995) brought attention to research conducted by Tanguy in the 1980s. Her work (1983a, 1983b) contributed to revealing "the contrast in France between general subjects and technical and vocational ones" (Forquin, 1995, p. 204). Her study (1991) on vocational education revealed that modifications in the profession of vocational teachers contributed to changes in the curriculum, now more oriented toward technical content knowledge. Her research parallels some work carried out by British curriculum sociologists on skills and knowledge selection, distribution and hierarchy, otherwise discussed by Forquin (1983, 1984, 1989).

Another important line of investigation into curriculum came from French-speaking Switzerland. In 1984, Perrenoud suggested a distinction between the intention to instruct, as laid out in programs, study plans and formal curricula, and the actual experiences of the learners, the actual curriculum. In a more recent analysis (1993), he revisited his constructs of *formal* and *actual* curricula, but added a third concept, the *hidden curriculum*, well known in the Anglophone literature. According to Perrenoud (1993), it is this notion of hidden curriculum which "gives the concept its status in human sciences" (p. 61). Using Merton's notion of *latent functions* in social systems and Boudon's (1977) concept of *pervert effects*, Perrenoud (1993) pointed out that the hidden curriculum is a sociological construct which helps account for the "involuntary effects of human actions and institutions" (p. 61). Thus, Perrenoud stressed that schools teach something different from, or in addition to, what they announce, and proposed to explore the consequences of this discrepancy. In France, Isambert-Jamati followed up on Perrenoud's line of inquiry with some empirical research. On her own (1984) as well as with Grospiron (Isambert-Jamati & Grospiron, 1984), she had already explored the relationship between, on the one hand, the French high school exit examination (*bacca-lauréat*) results of students from diverse backgrounds and, on the other hand, their teachers' pedagogical ideologies and methods. In a more recent study, Isambert-Jamati (1990) studied differences in the objectives and contents of detailed early learning activities in relation to pupils' socioeconomic backgrounds and that of the teachers. Other scholars carried out similar types of investigations on formal and actual curricula, but at different levels: for example, Dannepond (1979) and Plaisance (1986) in nursery school, and Demailly (1985) in middle school.

The relationship between students and the curriculum has also been an object of research. In these studies, Charlot, Bautier, and Rochex (1993) and Charlot (1999) used a survey approach on students' self-perceptions. They revealed that "this type of relationship is indissolubly a social relationship expressing conditions of existence and expectations regarding the future, and a singular and subjective relation" (cited in Plaisance & Vergnaud, 1999, p. 100). Linked to the concept of *curriculum*, some current concerns are specifically analyzed, such as the notion of proficiency (Ropé & Tanguy, 1994), and evaluation (Thélot, 1993). Growing scholarship on assessment addresses the question of educational progression. For example, Mitterand (1992) expressed concern about a growing emphasis on accountability and what he called *an obsession with objectives*. In addition, Forquin (1993) pointed to the role played by public opinion when it responds to the polemic raised by media and "books dealing with such themes as 'lower level' learning or the presumed culturally damaging effects of policies of 'democratization' and innovation" (Forquin, 1995, p. 202). In the context of increased demands for accountability and efficiency, more research directly focused on curriculum issues is needed. Ropé and Tanguy (1994) showed that these factors all contribute to putting pressure for a greater focus on behavioral objectives and measurable outcomes, thereby calling for a restructuring of curricula.

Curriculum and Didactics

Forquin (1995) saw the emergence of didactics and some work done in this field as "a major breakthrough in French thinking about curriculum" (p. 205). We saw earlier that the borders of didactics were still in the process of being defined. However, relying on Martinand's (1994) work, Forquin (1995) stressed a "strong tendency to define didactics by referring specifically to the transmission of knowledge content" (p. 205). This definition is useful, as is the concept of *didactic transposition* mentioned earlier (Chevallard, 1985), to understand some major issues in curriculum—in particular the gap between *original knowledge* (learned/acquired by the future teacher in university courses) and its didactic substitute, the *school knowledge* (what the teacher is able to teach in his or her classroom). Forquin (1995) provided a good discussion about the constraints on "the morphological and stylistic features of the discourse" in textbooks and/or in the classroom and at the "epistemological level," as they may "[affect] the very nature of knowledge" (p. 205). Knowledge then goes through what Chevallard (1985) called a process of "didactic dressing [*apprêt didactique*]" (p. 59). In France, Forquin (1995) saw "a whole trend of research" trying to identify "the route taken by knowledge" going "from laboratory to classroom" as in Grosbois, Ricco, and Sirota

(1992) or the specific elements of "school epistemology" as in Astolfi and Develay (1989) and Develay (1992) (Forquin, 1995, p. 205).

Nevertheless, based on some work on the history of education, Forquin (1995) explained that "the deep logic of school culture is not only a 'transpositive' one, but also a 'creative' or 'constructive' one" (p. 205). He cited Chervel's (1977) research on "school grammar" over 200 years as a fine example of an ad hoc theory elaborated under the pressures of political unification through language and of school attendance made mandatory. Chervel (1988) further showed that the same phenomenon occurred in other parts of the curriculum at other times (e.g., Latin culture and Christian values in the *Ancien Régime*[38]). Another interest of these historical studies is that they are not limited to the school setting. For example, Chervel (1988) explored how the Greek and Latin civilizations taught in secondary schools influenced the whole European elite culture through linguistic and cultural patterns.

If, according to Forquin (1995), the work published in sociology, the history of education and didactics informs studies in curriculum, do these scholars see themselves as curriculum theorists? Besides Forquin, Perrenoud (1993), who teaches in the Department of Psychology and Educational Sciences at the University of Geneva, seems to be one of the scholars who acknowledges working directly on curriculum from a theoretical viewpoint, although he does not see it as a "scientific concept" (p. 61). Yet Perrenoud (1993) recognized that curriculum has gained a "status in human sciences," especially through the notion of "hidden curriculum" (p. 61). Forquin (1995) declared that "[n]ew prospects are now open for a sociological research more directly centered on curriculum issues and more cogently linked to other research fields such as the history of education, cognitive psychology or didactics" (p. 205). But are these sociologists or other scholars from other fields or areas of educational studies who write on and about curriculum ready to identify themselves as curriculum theorists? Do they need to redefine themselves and their scholarship? If in France there is indeed a reflection on curriculum, it is still, in Forquin's (1995) words, "very scattered," and 5 years later it is still a long way from being anywhere close to organizing itself into a "unified and structured field of study" (p. 200).

CONCLUDING REMARKS:
CURRENT DEBATES AND CONTEMPORARY ISSUES

Throughout the years, neither the ambiguity among terms and the concepts they carry nor the antagonism among their respective proponents have abated (e.g., Avanzini, 1997; Barthelmé, 1999; Beillerot, 1997; Finkielkraut, 2000a; Froment, Caillot, & Roger, 2000; Houssaye, 1997; Kambouchner, 2000; Meirieu, 1998; and media[39]). In 1976, Mialaret wrote: "one must recognize that a great disorder rules the terminology and that interferences and confusions among teaching, education, pedagogy, and so on are numerous and complex" (1984, p. 3). In 1997, Houssaye concluded a discussion on the overlapping of terms and concepts with these words: "Undoubtedly, it is really very difficult to find one's way" (p. 89).

In this web of meanings, we saw that educational sciences, philosophy of education, pedagogy, didactics, and curriculum all contribute to thinking and understanding education, and pedagogy appears as a common link. Yet all other educational areas have repeatedly tried to deny it, reject it, and/or devalue it while trying to appropriate it. In 1967, had not Ferry declared "Death to pedagogy" (cited in Houssaye, 1997, p. 84)?

---

[38]See, for example, Ariès (1960).

[39]Especially *Le Monde* and *Le Monde de l'éducation*.

Houssaye (1997) developed a fine argument to show how "pedagogy has always navigated between rejection and appropriation.... By denial of its specificity. Yet pedagogy never dies" (p. 84). Might it be because the "pedagogical thought" (whatever other label it may be given) represents a form of

> elaborated or reflective thinking, which—even when rooted in the concrete experience of teaching and finalized by a concern for evaluation and improvement of the efficiency of its practices—finds itself nourished by elements of scholarly culture (science, history, philosophy, law, and even literature) which it integrates into discursive configurations to which it can give the names of "theories" or "doctrines" (Forquin, 1997, p. 6)?

In the same text, "Argument," opening a special issue of the *Revue Française de Pédagogie*[40] whose theme is precisely "the question of the 'theoretical status' of pedagogy," Forquin (1997) also declared: "It is easier to perceive pedagogy as a form of action or a type of competence than as a mode of thinking" (p. 5), which has been one of the limits at once imposed or projected on it and held against it. Meirieu (1995) wrote: "it is indeed the pedagogical discourse and the work it proposes or incites which create a specific space for research in education.... In this sense, pedagogy and educational sciences are not exclusive of each other, but they are not inclusive either" (p. 241).

Nevertheless, the field of educational sciences seems, in turn, to present itself as containing all other areas of educational studies, where pedagogy, philosophy of education, didactics, and now curriculum would be subsets. Mialaret (1984) defined educational sciences as being "constituted by the totality of the disciplines which study the conditions of existence, functioning, and evolution of the situations and acts of education" (p. 32). "'Untangling the factors at play' requires many different scientific disciplines," of which Plaisance and Vergnaud (1999) gave a long list. Making an inventory of the contributing sciences may lead to too fragmented a vision of the education field. This may be why Mialaret (1984) also analyzed what appeared to him to constitute the unity of educational sciences: "It is in respect to their object that educational sciences find the principle which gathers them into a family whose borders are rather well defined compared to other domains of scientific research" (p. 86). Because the complexity of the phenomenon to be analyzed (i.e., education) cannot be reduced to a simple and unidimensional explanation, some scholars believe that an internal pluridisciplinarity would be the key to this unity (Plaisance & Vergnaud, 1999, p. 22). This approach does not satisfy all researchers. In opposition to positivist analyses, which require a fragmentation of the objects they study, a multireferential approach has been suggested which would try to restitute "the 'molar,' holistic character of the reality under study" by choosing a systemic, comprehensive, and hermeneutic approach (Ardoino & Vigarello, 1986, p. 185). Ardoino and Vigarello (1986) stressed that actual educational situations, practices, and acts "did not easily let themselves be transformed by theoretical perspectives which postulate homogeneity and linear continuity, at the cost of a reduction" (p. 185). According to them, a multireferential approach could account for the complexity of these practices, situations, and acts in a way similar to social ones for inherent to them are rich and abundant meanings "which resist being reduced by a mono-disciplinary scientific explanation" (Plaisance & Vergnaud, 1999, p. 22). In 1990, Morin discussed the continuum from "interdisciplinarity which can be a simple co-existence, poly- or pluridisciplinarity which im-

---

[40]Houssaye (1997) commented on the symbolism of this professional journal—"the Mecca of French journals in education and educational sciences" (p. 96)—first published in 1967, the same year as when educational sciences were institutionalized and the first three universities opened their programs in educational sciences.

plies an association of disciplines around a common project, and, the most ambitious, transdisciplinarity, which demands shifts of cognitive schemes across disciplines" (cited in Plaisance & Vergnaud, 1999, pp. 27–28).

In any case, despite the enduring vocabulary and semantic "ambiguities, uncertainties, epistemological metissage" (Charlot, 1995, p. 26), most French scholars agree that any reflection on education rooted in and enriched by research from the sciences would remain insufficient if not misleading if it did not engage in a specific analysis of the ends and values of education. In 1989, Reboul had already declared that "[t]he solution cannot be purely scientific" (1989a, p. 9). In his investigation on the specificity of research in education, Legrand (1997) recalled the two classic main categories in educational research: studies which lead to a better knowledge of the existing educational system, on the one hand, and those which lead to innovations in the domains of behavior, content knowledge, and educational structures, on the other hand. In both cases, Legrand (1997) distinguished between research which endeavors to understand and which he deemed most "important if not fundamental" (p. 39) as opposed to research which tries to explain. Besides discussing current issues in research methodology, he also pointed to the main areas being explored. Houssaye (1999) with Soëtard also identified several themes which appear as the most "pertinent in regard to current tendencies and debates" among contemporary major questions on and in education (p. 15), as have Plaisance and Vergnaud (1999).

The same factors which make understanding education in France a challenge—highly centralized system, traditional encyclopedic approach to knowledge, lack of consensus on terminology—explain why it is also closely linked to French political life and vulnerable to political upheavals, and why its debates and controversies play themselves on the public forum through popular media, before unfolding in books. In an article published in the daily *Le Monde*, educational historian Antoine Prost (2000) summarized the latest developments in the debates around some current issues in education, particularly virulent following the demise of Claude Allègre, Minister of Education, in May 2000. Referring to several articles published in *Le Monde*,[41] Prost recognized that a debate should take place, but underscored and regretted "the tone and methods employed by these polemics, which cause surprise, distress, and sometimes indignation" (p. 17). Otherwise called the *missions war* ("*La guerre des missions*," October 2000), and apparently triggered by the new reforms initiated by Allègre,[42] in fact these debates reopened some very old intellectual oppositions (Guibert, 2000) between contents and pedagogy, philosophers and pedagogues, republicans[43] and pedagogues, those who are anti- and those who are propedagogy. This quarrel between philosophers and pedagogues is epitomized by, and reaches its paroxysm in, the exchanges between Finkielkraut (2000a, 2000b) and Meirieu (1998, 2000a). Prost (2000) strongly emphasized that such a debate would be better served by a work of research and analysis characteristic of academic scholarship, rather than by "diatribes" and a "rhetoric, empty of meaning" (p. 17).

---

[41]March 4, 2000 (panel of over 100 teachers, researchers, and writers, including Finkielkraut), April 8, 2000 (Bourdieu & Christophe), and May 19, 2000 (Finkielkraut).

[42]The Allègre project was based on three closely linked elements: new school programs refocused on the basics (i.e., speaking, reading, writing, and arithmetic); new school rhythms better adapted to those of the children, thus restructuring the daily schedules in order to give everyone "a true equality of chances," and a new definition of the teaching profession whereby the teachers' responsibilities become those of an "orchestra conductor" with a team of teacher assistants and outside participating guests.

[43]In this context, the term *republican*, which emerged in the 1960s (Touraine, 2000), designates those who oppose the proposed reforms. It refers to the Republican School as defined and structured by Jules Ferry in the 19th century (free, secular, and mandatory school).

Beillerot (1997) acknowledged that "the expressions educational sciences and pedagogy"—and one may add philosophy of education, didactics, and curriculum—are not interchangeable as one would believe when reading certain texts, they are not "univocal, because they cover different realities, and have different uses" (p. 76). However, whether the names of educational specialists, departments, or degrees are changed within the institutions, the questions remain fundamentally the same (Houssaye, 1997). But when considering the same problems (e.g., the educability of the student [child or adult], knowledge contents, teacher/student relations, classroom heterogeneity, evaluation and accountability, technology, exclusion, racism, violence, etc.), each different perspective throws a different light on the given problem, and each brings a different element to a better knowledge and assessment of the issue, each substantially enriching the others. Each lights up a new facet of the possible approaches to thinking education.

These various perspectives are not subtractive, and there is no reason why they should be in competition unless one is looking for personal media attention or institutional promotion, which are undeniably, and unfortunately, among some of the most influential factors, but which hardly do anything toward a better understanding of education and a better resolution of its problems. Meirieu (1998), responding to Finkielkraut, asked him to recognize that "[t]here is no reason ... for the philosopher, the pedagogue, and the educational sciences specialist not to get along ... as long as one of them does not claim absolute hegemony" (p. 79).

In fact, the gaps and/or spaces of dissention and overlap among the fields of educational studies (i.e., educational sciences, philosophy of education, pedagogy, didactics, and curriculum) are a source of dynamic, rich reflection and production of knowledge as they constitute at one and the same time "the link, the very impossibility of reducing one to the other, and the dialectical movement which envelop them in an indissoluble way" (Houssaye, 1997, p. 91). It is not possible to reconcile these diverse approaches to education and educational issues, and it is not even desirable. Because there is some danger in settling for an easy consensus, for facile "transparency," since, while "claiming to speak in the name of intelligibility, good sense, common sense, or [supposedly] the democratic ethic, this discourse tends, by means of these very things, and as if naturally, to discredit anything which complicates this model" (Derrida, 1992, p. 55).[44] As soon as we settle for a common space, we turn all possibilities into a program or an "ontotheological or teleo-eschatological scheme" (Derrida, 1992, p. 126). A common consensus among educational sciences, philosophy of education, pedagogy, didactics, and curriculum is not necessarily to be hoped for, but a respect for, and recognition of, serious scholarship is.

When reading French scholarship, one major aspect of education emerges in any area of educational studies. For example, Charlot (1995) recalled that "education is an ensemble of practices and processes via which humanity occurs within man [original gender]" (p. 21), reminding us of Aristotle's quest for this same "principle of humanity," "what is proper to man." In fact, this notion can be found in almost every French author. It sets the end of education as a striving for a perfection which would help set the individual "in harmony with the world as well as with his/her liberty, it would help him/her accomplish his/her nature, construct a collective progress, invent ..." (Morandi, 2000, p. 6). It is also the tradition of the Republican School, which has presented education first as a movement whereby a child becomes an adult. "But the adventure does not stop" there, added Charlot (1995), for "the appropriation of what is human can never be total ... it can never be considered either ... as achieved and complete" (p. 22). Reboul (1989a) went

---

[44]See also Egéa-Kuehne (1995, 1997).

even further, insisting that education is successful only if it is "unfinished" (p. 121). This concept of the very essence of education as a never completed task has been expressed over the years by several authors. Morandi (2000) added that education "is something ... which is imagined" (p. 26). He saw education not as "a finished work but as a work marking a beginning, which one 'imagines' as one goes on" (p. 26). For Charlot (1995), it means that "to study education is to deal with virtuality," since "no education is possible without assuming that the person [child or adult] can be educated" (p. 25). In that sense, and also because in the end there is no guarantee that the individual can be educated or will accept to be educated, education is a promise. As such, the future holds a promise. Meirieu (1998) believed that "[t]he pedagogue is at the heart of the construction of *demos*, looking for the necessary conditions so that each and every one may have access to speech, and that each and everyone may hear one another [*s'entendre*, also get along], if not listen to one another" (p. 129).[45] At the core of the concept of education, there is a promise—that of an ideal of education.

Here, Derrida's notion of *to-come*[46] is helpful to better understand the profound meaning of education and its promise, and the hope Meirieu (1998) wrote about. For Derrida (2001) the notion of *to-come* entails "some openness to the future, and ... openness to the other" (p. 180). That is why when you speak of something-to-come (e.g., education), you refer to something experienced as always possible. In this case, it does not mean that education will realize itself only in a future time, nor does it refer to a "regulatory idea in the Kantian sense, nor a utopia" (Derrida, 1994, p. 64). Extending Derrida's concept of *to-come* to education, education can be understood "as the concept of a promise" (p. 64) which can manifest itself only where there is disruption and upheaval, when there exists a gap between the present state of education, in this case, and the possibility of an ideal of education. Thus, the apparent failure of education would be "a priori and by definition" characteristic of *all* education. In fact, it is in this very gap that education would be shaped, and Derrida's following words can aptly apply to education:

> ... between an infinite promise (always untenable because it at least calls for an infinite respect of the infinite singularity and the infinite alterity of the other as much as for the calculable, subjectable equalities among these anonymous singularities) and the specific, necessary, but necessarily ill fitting forms which must measure themselves against that promise. (Derrida, 1994, p. 65)

It is in this gap that heterogeneity must be preserved, "as the only chance of an affirmed, or rather re-affirmed future" (Derrida, 1992, p. 68). Without this gap, without this disjunction, education may simply believe, in all good conscience, that it has succeeded, that "its duty is accomplished," and therefore education may "miss its chance for the future, for the promise or the call ... (in other words, for its very possibility)" (Derrida, 1994, p. 56). Meirieu (1998) saw there a "duty toward the future," "a principle of responsibility" all educators must assume (p. 44). But, wrote Derrida (1992), "there is no responsibility that is not the experience and experiment of the impossible" (p. 45).

Derrida (1992) defined *responsibility* as "a certain experience and experiment of the possibility of the impossible: the testing of the aporia from which one may invent the only possible invention, the impossible invention" (p. 41). Derrida described and discussed extensively in several of his texts how ambiguities and dilemmas are inherent to the concept of responsibility, and are, in fact, *the very condition* of its possibility. For "at a

---

[45]See Derrida (1992): "[L]isten how I speak in my language, me, and you can speak to me in your language; we must hear each other, we must get along [*nous devons nous entendre*]" (p. 61).

[46]Especially as developed around the theme of democracy-to- come—a concept clearly linked to education.

certain point, the promise and the decision, that is to say the responsibility, owe their possibility to the test of undecidability which will always remain their condition" (Derrida, 1994, p. 126). He stressed repeatedly that if there is an easy decision to make, there is in fact no decision to be made, no possibility of decision, therefore no responsibility to be taken, only a set of rules to follow, a program to implement. He linked this concept—this condition of responsibility as being dependent on the simultaneous necessity of a condition of impossibility—to a notion of *messianism,* to the experience of the promise. It is by opening a space for the affirmation of this promise, of the "messianic and emancipatory promise," of the impossible event as a promise, that it preserves its capital of possibilities, of dynamic ideal of education in-the-making, to-come.

In closing, I reiterate that this chapter has hardly scratched the surface of the work done in France and contains wide gaps impossible to cover within the constraints of this text. I apologize to any scholar whose work may have been omitted or not given the weight it deserves. When looking at the broadness of the field covered in France and the richness of the scholarship, it certainly gives hope that, if only these scholars would bring up their quarrels to the level of challenging scholarly debates, huge steps could be taken toward actually building the future of education—of education-to-come. With Meirieu (1989), we might be able to say: "The situation is neither better nor worse than yesterday. It is radically different and the true courage is to accept this difference as an invitation to invent new hope" (p. 40)—an invitation to the "impossible invention" (Derrida, 1992, p. 41), to responsibility.

REFERENCES

Aebli, H. (1951). *Didactique psychologique: Application à la didactique de la psychologie de Jean Piaget.* Paris: Delachaux et Niestlé S. A.

Ardoino, J., & Vigarello, G. (1986). Identité des sciences de l'éducation. In M. Guillaume (Ed.), *L'état des sciences sociales en France* (pp. 185–188). Paris: La Découverte.

Ariès, P. (1960). *L'enfant et la vie familiale sous l'Ancien Régime.* Paris: Plon.

Astolfi, J.-P., & Develay, M. (1989). *La didactique des sciences.* Paris: Presses Universitaires de France.

Astolfi, J.-P., Darot, E., & Ginsburger-Vogel, Y. (1997). *Pratiques de formation en didactique des sciences.* Paris and Bruxelles: De Boeck Université.

Avanzini, G. (1987). *Introduction aux sciences de l'éducation.* Toulouse: Privat.

Avanzini, G. (1994). Les trois fonctions de la philosophie de l'éducation. In H. Hannoun & A.-M. Drouin-Hans (Eds.), *Pour une philosophie de l'éducation.* Dijon: CNDP-CRDP de Bourgogne.

Avanzini, G. (1997). Les déboires de la notion de pédagogie. In J.C. Forquin (Ed.), *Penser la pédagogie* (special issue), *Revue Française de Pédagogie, 120,* 17–24.

Bachelard, G. (1938). *La formation de l'esprit scientifique.* Paris: Vrin.

Bachelard, G. (1940). *La philosophie du non.* Paris: Vrin.

Bachelard, G. (1949). *Le rationalisme appliqué.* Paris: Presses Universitaires de France.

Bain, A. (1872). La science de l'éducation (G. Compayré, Trans., 1879). In G. Compayré, *Histoire critique des doctrines de l'éducation en France depuis le 16e siècle.* 2 volumes. Paris: Hachette.

Barthelmé, B. (1999). *Une philosophie de l'éducation pour l'école d'aujourd'hui.* Paris and Montreal: L'Harmattan.

Beillerot, J. (1997). Sciences de l'éducation et pédagogie: un étrange manège. In J.C. Forquin (Ed.), *Penser la pédagogie* (special issue), *Revue Française de Pédagogie, 120,* 75–82.

Beillerot, J., Blanchard-Laville, C., Bouillet, A., & Mosconi, N. (1989). *Savoir et rapport au savoir.* Paris: Éditions Universitaires.

Bertrand, Y. (1999). Expérience et éducation. In J. Houssaye (Ed.), *Éducation et philosophie: Approches contemporaines* (pp. 49–62). Paris: Editions Sociales Françaises.

Blanchard, S. (2000, September 27). Philippe Meirieu, le prof au coeur gros. Horizons-Portraits. *Le Monde,* p. 16.

Boudon, R. (1977). *Effets pervers et ordre social.* Paris: Presses Universitaires de France.

Bourdieu, P. (1989). *La Noblesse d'État: Grandes écoles et esprit de corps.* Paris: Les Éditions de Minuit.

Bourdieu, P., & Christophe, C. (2000, April 8). Un ministre ne fait pas le printemps. Point de vue. *Le Monde de l'Éducation,* p. 1.

Bourdieu, P., & Gros, F. (1989). *Principes pour une réflexion sur les contenus d'enseignement* (Committee for Content Teaching). Paris: Ministère de l'éducation nationale.

Bourdieu, P., & Passeron, J.-C. (1964). *Les Héritiers: Les étudiants et la culture.* Paris: Les Éditions de Minuit.

Bourdieu, P., & Passeron, J.-C. (1970). *La Reproduction: Éléments pour une théorie du système d'enseignement.* Paris: Les Éditions de Minuit.

Bourdieu, P., Passeron, J.-C., & De Saint-Martin, M. (1965). *Rapport pédagogique et communication.* Paris and La Haye: Mouton.

Bouveresse, R. (Ed.). (1993). *Education et philosophie: Écrits en l'honneur de Olivier Reboul.* Paris: Presses Universitaires de France.

Brousseau, G. (1984). Le rôle central du contrat didactique dans l'analyse et la construction des situations d'enseignement et d'apprentissage des mathématiques, 3e école de didactique des mathématiques. Olivet.

Brousseau, G. (1990). Le contrat didactique: le milieu. In *Recherche en Didactique des Mathématiques, 9*(3), 308–336.

Brousseau, G. (1998). *Théorie des situations didactiques: Didactiques des mathématiques 1970–1990.* Grenoble: La Pensée Sauvage.

Brunetière, F. (1895). *Education et Instruction.* Paris: Firmin Didot.

Buisson, F. (Ed.). (1911). *Dictionnaire de pédagogie et d'instruction primaire* (1st ed. 1882–1887). Paris: Hachette.

Charbonnel, N. (1988). *Critique de la raison éducative.* Berne: Peter Lang.

Charlot, B. (Ed.). (1995). *Les sciences de l'éducation: un enjeu, un défi. (Rapport CORESE).* Paris: Editions Sociales Françaises.

Charlot, B. (1997). *Du rapport au savoir: éléments pour une théorie.* Paris: Anthropos.

Charlot, B. (1999). *Le rapport au savoir en milieu populaire: une recherche dans les lycées professionels de banlieue.* Paris: Anthropos.

Charlot, B., Bautier, É., & Rochex J.-Y. (1993). *École et savoir dans les banlieues et ailleurs.* Paris: A. Colin.

Château, J. (1962). Letter from Jean Château to Maurice Debesse dated February 9. In S. Hermine (1973), *Les sciences de l'éducation: public, objectifs, méthodes et moyens. Essai d'analyse historique et prospecive* (p. 208). Doctoral dissertation (thèse de IIIe cycle), University of Paris V.

Cherkaoui, M. (1976). Socialisation et conflit: les systèmes éducatifs et leur histore selon Durkheim. *Revue Française de Sociologie, 17*(2), 197–212.

Cherkaoui, M. (1978). Système social et savoir scolaire. Les enjeux politiques de la distribution des connaissances selon Durkheim. *Revue Française de Science Politique, 2,* 313–349.

Chervel, A. (1977). *Et il fallut apprendre à écrire à tous les petits Français: Histoire de la grammaire scolaire.* Paris: Payot.

Chervel, A. (1988). L'histoire des disciplines scolaires: Réflexion sur un domaine de recherche. *Histoire de l'Éducation, 38,* 59–119.

Chevallard, Y. (1985). *La transposition didactique: du savoir savant au savoir enseigné* (1st ed.). Grenoble: La Pensée Sauvage.

Comérius, J. A. (1649). *La grande didactique ou L'art universel de tout enseigner à tous.* (M.-F. Bosquet-Frigout, D. Saget, & B. Jolibert, Trans., 1992). Paris: Klincksieck.

Compayré, G. (1879). *Histoire critique des doctrines de l'éducation en France depuis le 16e siècle.* 2 volumes. Paris: Hachette.

Dannepond, G. (1979). Pratique pédagogique et classes sociales. Étude comparée de trois écoles maternelles. *Actes de la Recherche en Sciences Sociales, 30,* 31–45.

Debesse, M., & Mialaret, G. (1969). *Traité des sciences pédagogiques* (1st ed. 6 volumes). Paris: Presses Universitaires de France.

De Landsheere, G. (1986). *La Recherche en éducation dans le monde.* Paris: Presses Universitaires de France.

Demailly, L. (1985). Contribution à une sociologie des pratiques pédagogiques. *Revue Française de Sociologie, 26*(1), 96–119.

Derrida, J. (1992). *The Other Heading: Reflections on Today's Europe* (P.-A. Brault & M. B. Nass, Trans.). Bloomington and Indianapolis: Indiana University Press.

Derrida, J. (1994). *Specters of Marx: The State of the Debt, the Work of Mourning, and the New International* (P. Kamuf, Trans.). New York and London: Routledge.

Derrida, J. (1995). *Honoris Causa*: "This is *also* extremely funny." In E. Weber (Ed.), *Points …: Interviews, 1974–1994.* (pp. 399–421) (P. Kamuf, Trans.). Stanford: Stanford University Press.

Derrida, J. (2001). "Talking liberties." In G.J.J. Biesta & D. Egéa-Kuehne (Eds.), *Derrida & Education.* (pp 176–185). London: Routledge.

Develay, M. (1976). *Donner du sens à l'école.* Paris: Editions Sociales Françaises.

Develay, M. (1992). *De l'apprentissage à l'enseignement.* Paris: Editions Sociales Françaises.

Develay, M. (Ed.). (1995). *Savoirs scolaires et didactiques des disciplines*. Paris: Editions Sociales Françaises.

Develay, M. (1997). Origines, malentendus et spécificités de la didactique. In J.C. Forquin (Ed.). *Penser la pédagogie* (special issue), *Revue Française de Pédagogie, 120*, 59–66.

Dubois, P. (1994). Les philosophes, dans le Dictionnaire de pédagogie et d'instruction primaire de Ferdinand Buisson. In H. Hannoun & A.-M. Drouin-Hans (Eds.), *Pour une philosophie de l'éducation*. Dijon: CNDP-CRDP de Bourgogne.

Dubois, P. (1996). L'historiographie composite du Dictionnaire de Pédagogie de Ferdinand Buisson. *Penser l'éducation, 1*.

Duborgel, B. (1984). Phénomènes éducatifs et questionnement philosophique. In *Éducation et recherche, 3*.

Dupuis, M. (Ed.). (2000, July–August). Un siècle d'éducation. Dossier spécial. *Le Monde de l'éducation*. pp. 19–76.

Durkheim, E. (1911). Éducation. In F. Buisson, *Nouveau dictionnaire de pédagogie*. Paris: Hachette.

Durkheim, E. (1938). *L'Évolution pédagogique en France*. Paris: Editions Sociales Françaises.

Durkheim, E. (1966). *Éducation et sociologie*. Paris: Presses Universitaires de France.

Egéa-Kuehne, D. (1995). Deconstruction Revisited and Derrida's Call for Academic Responsibility. *Educational Theory, 45*(3), 293–309.

Egéa-Kuehne, D. (1997). Neutrality in Education and Derrida's Call for "Double Duty." In F. Margonis (Ed.), *Philosophy of Education 1996* (pp. 154–163). Urbana, IL: Philosophy of Education Society. Also published online: *http://www.ed.uiuc.edu/pes/96_docs/egea-kuehne.html*. (last accessed May 19, 2002).

Egéa-Kuehne, D. (1998). Michel Serres's Connections Through the Multiplicity of Time: A Metaphor for Curriculum. *JCT: An Interdisciplinary Journal of Curriculum Studies, 14*(3), 8–13.

Egéa-Kuehne, D. (1999a). Analyse d'un livre: Understanding Curriculum (Pinar 1995). *Revue Française de Pédagogie, 127*, 183–187.

Egéa-Kuehne, D. (1999b). Les reconceptualistes: histoire d'un phénomène américain. *Revue Française de Pédagogie, 128*, 89–96.

Egéa-Kuehne, D. (2001a). Levinas: Teaching "Conscience" and the Other. In L. Stone (Ed.), *Philosophy of Education 2000* (pp. 213–216). Urbana, IL: Philosophy of Education Society.

Egéa-Kuehne, D. (2001b). Derrida's ethics of affirmation: The challenge of educational rights and responsibility. In G.J.J. Biesta & D. Egéa-Kuehne (Eds.), *Derrida & Education* (pp. 186–216). London: Routledge.

Egéa-Kuehne, D., & Biesta, G. J. J. (2001) Opening. In G.J.J. Biesta & D. Egéa-Kuehne (Eds.), *Derrida & Education* (pp. 1–24). London: Routledge.

Etévé, C., & Gambart, C. (1992) *Que lisent les enseignants?: lectures et diffusion des connaissances en éducation*. Paris: Institut National de Recherche Pédagogique.

Fabre, M. (1994). *Penser la formation*. Paris: Presses Universitaires de France.

Fabre, M. (1999). Conclusion. Qu'est-ce que la philosophie de l'éducation? In J. Houssaye (Ed.), *Éducation et philosophie* (pp. 269–298). Paris: Editions Sociales Françaises.

Ferry, G. (1983). *Le trajet de la formation: les enseignants entre la théorie et la pratique*. Paris: Dunod, Bordas.

Filloux, J. (1974). *Du contrat pédagogique: ou comment faire les mathématiques à une jeune fille qui aime l'ail*. Paris: Dunod.

Filloux, J.-C. (1971). Le processus enseigner-apprendre et la recherche en sciences de l'éducation. *Orientations, 37*, 5–23.

Finkielkraut, A. (2000a). *Une voix qui vient de l'autre rive*. Paris: Gallimard.

Finkielkraut, A. (2000b, May 19). Point de vue: La révolution culturelle à l'école. Point de vue. Horizons-Débats. *Le Monde*, p. 1.

Forquin, J.-C. (1983). La "nouvelle sociologie de l'éducation" en Grande-Bretagne: Orientations, apports théoriques, évolution. *Revue Française de Pédagogie, 63*, 61–79.

Forquin, J.-C. (1984). La sociologie du curriculum en Grande-Bretagne: Une nouvelle approche des enjeux sociaux de la scolarisation. *Revue Française de Sociologie, 25*(2), 211–232.

Forquin, J.-C. (1989). *École et culture: le point de vue des sociologues britanniques*. Bruxelles: De Boeck Université.

Forquin, J.-C. (1993). Savoirs et pédagogie: Faux dilemmes et vraies questions. *Recherche et formation, 13*, 9–24.

Forquin, J.-C. (1995). The curriculum and current educational thinking in France, *The Curriculum Journal, 6*(2), 199–209.

Forquin, J.-C. (1997). Argument. In J.C. Forquin (Ed.), *Penser la pédagogie* (special issue), *Revue Française de Pédagogie, 120*, 5–6.

Froment, M., Caillot, M., & Roger, M. (2000). *30 ans de Sciences de l'Éducation à Paris V*. Paris: Presses Universiatires de France.

Furetière, A. (1978). *Le Dictionnaire Universel* (1st ed. 1690, Hollande). Paris: S.N.L.-Le Robert.

Gauthein, J. (1991) *La formation d'une discipline universitaire: La science de l'Éducation, 1880-1914 (essai d'his-oire sociale).* Doctoral dissertation (thèse de IIIe cycle), University of Paris V.

Gauthein, J. (1995). La science de l'éducation, discipline singulière. In B. Charlot (Ed.), *Les sciences de l'éducation: un enjeu, un défi* (pp. 45–54). Paris: Editions Sociales Françaises.

Gauthein, J. (2001) *Une discipline pour la république.* Berne: Peter Lang.

Gauthier, R.F. (1994) Les programmes d'enseignement dans l'institution scolaire française: problématique juridique et pédagogie générale. In C. Demonque (Ed.), *Qu'est-ce qu'un programme d'enseignement?* Paris: CNDP-Hachette.

Georges, J. (2000, July–August). Dans les grandes écoles, l'élite forme toujours l'élite. *Le Monde de l'éducation,* pp. 48–49.

Geulen, D. (1995). Les sciences de l'éducation en Allemagne. *Cahiers Binet-Simon, 645*(4), 87–102.

Grosbos, M., Ricco, G., & Sirota, R. (1992). *Du laboratoire à la classe, le parcours du savoir: Étude de la transposition didactique du concept de respiration.* Paris: ADAPT.

Guibert N. (2000, June 13). École: regarder la réalité en face. Horizons - Analyses. *Le Monde,* p. 15.

Hadji, C. (1989). *L'évaluation, règles du jeu.* Paris: Editions Sociales Françaises.

Hadji, C. (1994). La philosophie de l'éducation, un luxe inutile. In H. Hannoun, & A. M. Drouin-Hans (Eds.). *Pour une philosophie de l'éducation.* Dijon: CNDP-CRDP de Bourgogne.

Hermine, S. (1978). *Les sciences de l'éducation: public, objectifs, méthodes et moyens. Essai d'analyse historique et prospective.* Doctoral dissertation (thèse de IIIe cycle), University of Paris V.

Hermine, S., & Vigarello, G. (2000). In M. Froment, M. Caillot, & M. Roger (Eds.), *30 ans de Sciences de l'Éducation à Paris V* (pp. 3–13). Paris: Presses Universitaires de France.

Hocquard, A. (1996). *Éduquer, à quoi bon?* Paris: Presses Universitaires de France.

Houssaye, J. (1996). *Autorité ou éducation?* Paris: Editions Sociales Françaises.

Houssaye, J. (1997). Spécificité et dénégation de la pédagogie. In J.C. Forquin (Ed.), *Penser la pédagogie* (special issue), *Revue Française de Pédagogie, 120,* 83–97.

Houssaye, J. (Ed.). (1999). *Éducation et philosophie: Approches contemporaines.* Paris: Editions Sociales Françaises.

Institut National de Recherche Pédagogique. (1998). *Guide des recherches et des chercheurs 1998-1999.* Paris: INRP.

Institut National de Recherche Pédagogique. (1999). *Guide des recherches et des chercheurs 1999-2000.* Paris: INRP.

Institut National de Recherche Pédagogique. (2000). *Guide des recherches et des chercheurs 2000-2001.* Paris: INRP.

Institut Pédagogique National (Collective Co-Authors). (1967). Editorial. *La Revue Française de Pédagogie.* Paris: Institut Pédagogique National.

Isambert-Jamati, V. (1983). Fonctionnement du système éducatif. In R. Carraz (Ed.), *Recherche en éducation et socialisation de l'enfant. Rapport de mission au ministre de l'Industrie et de la Recherche.* Paris: La Documentation française.

Isambert-Jamati, V. (1984). *Culture, technique et critique sociale à l'école élémentaire.* Paris: Presses Universitaires de France.

Isambert-Jamati, V. (1990). *Les savoirs scolaires. Enjeux sociaux des contenus d'enseignement et de leurs formes.* Paris: Editions Universitaires.

Isambert-Jamati, V., & Grospiron, M.F. (1984). Types de pédagogie du français et différenciations sociales des résultats. L'exemple du "travail autonome" au deuxième cycle long. *Études de Linguistique Appliquée, 54,* 69–97.

Jonas, H. (1993). *Pour une critique du futur.* Paris: Le Seuil.

Kambouchner, D. (2000). *Une école contre l'autre.* Paris: Presses Universitaires de France.

Laeng, M. (1974). *Vocabulaire de pédagogie moderne.* Paris: Le Centurion.

La guerre des missions. (2000, October). Dossier: le débat qui divise l'école. *Le Monde de l'éducation,* pp. 23–43. *http://www.lemonde.fr/mde/anciens/octo2000.html* (last accessed May 19, 2002).

Le Bars, S. (2000, May 27). M. Meirieu, directeur de l'INRP, a remis sa démission à M. Lang: Il s'estime "désavoué" par son ministre. Société. *Le Monde,* p. 12.

Legrand, L. (1997). Qu'est-ce que la recherche pédagogique? *Revue Française de Pédagogie, 120,* 39–47.

Marior, H. (1883) Leçon d'ouverture du cours sur la Science de l'Éducation, *Revue Pédagogique, 3*(12).

Marior, H. (1888). Pédagogie. In F. Buisson (Ed.) (1911), *Dictionnaire de pédagogie.* Paris: Hachette.

Marmoz, L. (1988). *Les Sciences de l'éducation en France, histoire et réalités.* Issy-les-Moulineaux: Éditions EAP.

Martinand, J.-L. (1994). Didactique. In P. Champy & C. Étévé (Eds.) *Dictionnaire encyclopédique de l'éducation et de la formation.* Paris: Nathan.

McLean, M. (1990). *Britain and a single market Europe: Prospects for a Common School Curriculum*. London: Kogan Page.

Meirieu, P. (1989). *Enseigner, scénario pour un métier nouveau*. Paris: Editions Sociales Françaises.

Meirieu, P. (1995). *La pédagogie entre le dire et le faire*. Paris: Presses Universitaires de France.

Meirieu, P. (1998). *Lettres à quelques amis politiques sur la République et l'état de son école*. Paris: Plon.

Meirieu, P. (2000a, May 12). Une odieuse chasse au pédagogue. Horizons - Débats. *Le Monde*, p. 16.

Meirieu, P. (2000b, September 5). Enseigner: le devoir de transmettre et les moyens d'apprendre. Horizons - Conférences. *Le Monde*, p. 20.

Mialaret, G. (1984). *Les sciences de l'éducation*. Paris: Presses Universitaires de France.

Mialaret, G. (1991). *Pédagogie générale*. Paris: Presses Universitaires de France.

Mialaret, G. (1993). *L'éducateur, le pédagogue, le chercheur*. Paris: Presses Universitaires de France.

Mialaret, G. (2000). La création des sciences de l'éducation. In M. Froment, M. Caillot, & M. Roger (Eds.), *30 ans de Sciences de l'Éducation à Paris V* (pp. 15–21). Paris: Presses Universitaires de France.

Mitterand, H. (1992). Les obsédés de l'objectif: L'enseignement du français en question. *Le Débat, 71*, 164–172.

Moon, B. (1995). Editorial. *The Curriculum Journal, 6*(2), 159–160.

Morandi, F. (2000). *Philosophie de l'éducation*. Paris: Nathan.

Mosconi, N. (1982). Les sciences de l'éducation du point de vue de leur objet, de leur unité, et de leurs rapports à la pratique. *Les sciences de l'éducation pour l'ère nouvelle, 4*, 77–90.

Panel - Multiple Authors. (2000, March 4). C'est la littérature qu'on assome rue de Grenelle. Débat sur l'enseignement des lettres. Pannel – Horizon Débat. *Le Monde*, p. 18.

Perrenoud, P. (1984). *La Fabrication de l'excellence scolaire: Du curriculum aux pratiques d'évaluation: vers une analyse de la réussite, de l'échec et des inégalités comme réalités construites par le système scolaire*. Genève: Librairie Droz.

Perrenoud, P. (1993). Curriculum: le formel, le réel, le caché. In J. Houssaye (Ed.), *La pédagogie: une encyclopédie pour aujourd'hui* (pp. 61–76). Paris: Editions Sociales Françaises. Available online: *http://www.unige.ch/fapse/SSE/teachers/perrenoud/php_main/php_199 3/1993_21.html*. (last accessed May 19, 2002).

Piaget, J. (1974a). *La Prise de conscience*. Paris: Presses Universitaires de France.

Piaget, J. (1974b). *Réussir et comprendre*. Paris: Presses Universitaires de France.

Piaget, J., & Ibhelder, B. (1966). *La Psychologie de l'enfant*. Paris: Presses Universitaires de France.

Pinar, W. F. (Ed.). (1988). *Contemporary Curriculum Discourses*. Scottsdale, Arizona: Gorsuck Scarisbrick, Publishers.

Pinar, W. F. (1999). Curriculum Theory Project Intenational Conference Flyer. Baton Rouge: Louisiana State University Curriculum Theory Project Document.

Pinar, W. F., Reynolds, W., Slattery, P., & Taubman, P. (1995). *Understanding Curriculum: An Introduction to the Study of Historical and Contemporary Curriculum Discourses*. New York: Peter Lang.

Plaisance, É. (1986). *L'enfant, la maternelle, la société*. Paris: Presses Universitaires de France.

Plaisance, É., & Vergnaud, G. (1999). *Les sciences de l'éducation*. Paris: Éditions La Découverte.

Prost, A. (1968). *Histoire de l'enseignement en France, 1800-1967*. Paris: A. Colin.

Prost, A. (2000, June 22). La trahison des clercs: encore. Horizon - Débats. *Le Monde*, p. 17.

Reboul, O. (1983).

Reboul, O. (1989a). *La philosophie de l'éducation*. Paris: Presses Universitaires de France.

Reboul, O. (1989b). *Les valeurs de l'éducation*. Paris: Presses Universitaires de France.

Richard, J. F. (1990). *Les activités mentales*. Paris: Armand Collin.

Ropé, F., & Tanguy, L. (Eds.). (1994) *Savoirs et compétences: De l'usage de ces notions dans l'école et l'entreprise*. Paris: L'Harmattan.

Santos, L. F. dos (1999). Désir et éducation. In J. Houssaye (Ed.), *Éducation et philosophie: Approches contemporaines* (pp. 17–48). Paris: Editions Sociales Françaises.

Serres, M. (1994). *Atlas*. Paris: Julliard.

Serres, M. (1995). *Conversations on Science, Culture, and Time* (R. Lapidus, Trans.). Ann Arbor: University of Michigan Press.

Serres, M. (1999). *La Légende des Anges*. Paris: Flammarion.

Soëtard, M. (1985, October–November). De la science aux sciences de l'éducation: France, où est ta pédagogie? *Rassegna di pedagogia, 4*.

Tanguy, L. (1983a). Savoirs et rapports sociaux dans l'enseignement secondaire en France. *Revue Française de Sociologie, 24*(2), 227–254.

Tanguy, L. (1983b). Les savoirs enseignés aux futurs ouvriers. *Sociologie du Travail, 3*, 336–354.

Tanguy, L. (1991). *L'enseignement professionnel en France: des ouvriers aux techniciens*. Paris: Presses Universitaires de France.

Thélot, C. (1993). *L'évaluation du système éducatif: coûts, fonctionnement, résultats*. Paris: Nathan.

Touraine, A. (2000, July–August). L'école est active, elle crée ou diminue l'inégalité. Interview by M. Dupuis. In M. Dupuis (Ed.) Un siècle d'éducation. Dossier spécial. *Le Monde de l'éducation*, pp. 50–53.

Vergnaud, G. (1983). Quelques problèmes de la didactique à propos d'un exemple: les structures additives. Premier atelier international de recherche en didactique de la physique à Lalonde-Lès-Maures. (pp. 391–402). Paris: CNRS.

Vergnaud, G. (1990). La théorie des champs conceptuels. *Recherches en Didactique des Mathématiques, 10*(2.3), 133–170.

Vergnaud, G. (1999).

Verret, M. (1975). *Le Temps des études*. Paris: Honoré Champion.

CHAPTER 18

The Landscape of Curriculum Inquiry in the Republic of Ireland

Kevin Williams
Gerry McNamara
Dublin City University, Ireland

Over the last decade, curriculum inquiry in Ireland has been vigorous and extensive. Contributions have come from curriculum specialists, philosophers and sociologists as well as from those not directly involved in the academic study of education (e.g., from representatives of industry and youth groups). Although academic inquiry has been critical of current curriculum provision and practice, there exists an orthodoxy among curriculum theorists that is quite striking. First, most share the same critical view of the system. Second, they tend to avoid issues that give rise to genuine disagreement. For example, much has been written about low achievement, disadvantage, and the dominance of terminal written examinations, but the voice of curriculum specialists has been largely absent from the public controversy about the state-sponsored program of Relationships and Sexuality Education. Likewise, readers might expect the theme of Irish identity to be the subject of curriculum debate, but the issue features little in the literature.

The major themes of curriculum inquiry in Ireland are of universal interest to curriculum scholars, and it is difficult to identify anything specifically Irish about them. The main concern of inquiry is with low achievement, particularly among young people, who, for socioeconomic or other reasons, do not flourish at academic learning. The first part of the chapter gives an account of inquiry into low achievement and school failure, the theoretical principles underpinning the curricular response to these problems, and an appraisal by theorists of the value of these responses. The second part of the chapter examines two main approaches to curriculum inquiry. On the one hand, there are the reformers who argue that *via* different educational structures new school programs can meet the needs of all young people. On the other hand, there are those who, although not dismissive of the work of the former, suggest that only more radical approaches can result in real change. According to the advocates of the first strand of the radical approach, reform of society must precede reform of the curriculum. Proponents of the second strand of radical thinking argue for a reconceptualization of the nature of intelligence. A third, philosophical strand consists of the desire to uncouple school learning from selection for third-level education and employment and to concentrate on the internal goods of curricular pursuits. The arguments of the advocates of reform of educational structures and those who argue in support of the various strands of the radical approach overlap and are not mutually exclusive, but they do reflect different emphases. The chapter concludes with some comments on a neglected strand of inquiry—namely, the relationship between the curriculum and Irish identity.

CURRICULUM INQUIRY: CONTEXT AND DEFINITION OF PRINCIPLES

Alienation and disaffection, school failure, and early dropout have been major themes in Irish curriculum inquiry for the past 25 years, effectively since curriculum has been an area of study and debate. This is partly because, as Hyland (2000a) remarked, "the problem of early school leaving has proved to be more intractable than originally envisaged" (p. 5). It is also because, uniquely in the Irish context, significant funding—mostly of European Union origin—has been available for research in this field. A further reason for interest in these issues is that, although school failure in its most dramatic form of early dropout is highly visible, most educationalists are well aware that alienation and disaffection blight the school experience of many other young people who never reach the ultimate stage of dropping out of the system. The situation in Ireland is similar to that in Britain. There, according to British scholar, John Elliott (2000), alienation and disaffection among many of those remaining in school constitute the biggest single problem facing the education system. He dubbed such students *rhinos ... on the roll but here in name only.* He suggested that, despite some 30 years of research, there is no sign of improvement. He argued that most of the current government's policies, stressing goals, targets, appraisals, and so on are motivated primarily by the need to tackle this issue.

DISADVANTAGE, LOW ACHIEVEMENT, AND SCHOOL FAILURE

Despite three decades of dramatic increase in public investment in education and an equally dramatic increase in the numbers benefiting from education, the problem of school failure and dropout remains significant. Educational opportunities have been revolutionized so that now close to 80% of the age cohort completes a full cycle of secondary education compared with 25% 30 years ago. Of those who complete secondary schooling, roughly 85% continues on to some form of further or higher education, and the numbers enrolled in third level education have risen more than tenfold in 30 years. Although employment levels have dropped, worries remain that economic growth may be halted by labor shortages (Fitzgerald, 1998).

Yet the problem of early school leaving and underachievement among those who stay in school remains. Despite a series of initiatives in the past 25 years to combat this problem, over 20% of young people continue to leave school with either no or inadequate qualifications. Because school failure is linked to poverty and disadvantage, this figure is much higher in certain districts than in others (McNamara & Quinlan, 2000). The issue of educational disadvantage and school failure is a recurrent theme in national policy documents. It was considered in the Report of the Pupil Transfer Committee (Government of Ireland, 1981), in the Irish Government's White Paper on Education (Government of Ireland, 1980), in the Government's Green Paper on Education (Government of Ireland, 1992a), in the National Development Plan (Government of Ireland, 1992b), in the Report of the National Education Convention (Coolahan, 1994), in the Government's White Paper on Education (Government of Ireland, 1995a), in the Operational Programme for Local, Urban, and Rural Development (Government of Ireland, 1995b), and in the Government's Green Paper on Adult Education (Government of Ireland, 1998).

In addition to these reports, the Department of Education and Science has produced a range of papers dealing with aspects of educational disadvantage in Ireland. Agencies such as the Conference of Religious of Ireland (1988), the Irish National Teachers' Organization (1997), the Economic and Social Research Institute (Smyth, 1998), the Organization for Economic Co-operation and Development (1995), and the National Economic and Social Forum (1997), among others, have also published their concerns on educational disadvantage and school failure.

THE CURRICULAR RESPONSE
AND ITS UNDERPINNING PRINCIPLES

In tandem with the previous reports, extensive curriculum reform designed to address issues of school failure and low achievement has been undertaken in the past two decades. During the 1980s, the European Union funded an extensive series of pilot projects designated the First and Second Action Programmes on the Transition of Young People from School to Adult and Working Life. Many of these projects were primarily concerned with the development of programs designed to interest and remotivate underachieving young people throughout their school careers. The literature generated by the two Action Programmes is extensive (there were some 60 pilot projects in all, 6 of them in Ireland). From this literature, what might be called *transition education principles* relevant to the development of potentially successful alternative programmes emerged. These principles were enunciated by curriculum theorists and can be summarized as follows:

1. Philosophy and methodology are of greater importance than content in curriculum development and reform;
2. Curriculum to be designed around pupil needs in terms of coping successfully with the demands of adult and working life and to stress relevant knowledge and practical learning;
3. Input from the pupil into the development of the curriculum by means of a process of negotiation;
4. Active learning methodology involving modular units, block timetabling, integrated studies, project work, pupil-directed learning, small-group and individual work, and team teaching;
5. Extensive use of the out-of-school environment as a learning resource through such methods as work experience, community tutors, community service, work shadowing, and residential courses;
6. Broad course content involving vocationally relevant studies, but also social and personal education and the arts;
7. Personal and educational guidance for each pupil;
8. An appropriate social context involving cooperation and more democratic relationships with staff, smaller teaching teams, and group tutors, with time to develop closer links with individual students;
9. An appropriate physical context including purpose-prepared base areas within the school for project work and use of outside facilities for course elements;
10. Involvement of parents and the broader community in the program through home–school links and school–community liaison;
11. Emphasis on gender equality through specific courses and nontraditional vocational training and work experience for girls;
12. Closer cooperation and link/shared courses between schools and other bodies such as training agencies and industry;

13. Ongoing assessment of a wide range of pupil knowledge, skills, and personal qualities through school-based profiling systems and records of achievement;
14. Modular programs involving widely recognized certification leading to further education/training and employment (McNamara, 1992).

	Traditional Design	Transition Design
Emphasis on	Cognitive skills	Skills related to future work environment and noncognitive skills
Organized around	An educational model common to the whole age group in which ranking according to scholastic achievement is the major objective	A wide diversity of courses tailored to a variety of needs of specific groups of young people
Learning Experiences	Based on established disciplines and subjects of knowledge	Subject matter is integrated and focuses on practical areas
Student/Teacher Relationships	Tend to be formal and hierarchical	More informal and democratic
Teaching Methods	Transmission of knowledge from teacher to student	Student-centered, activity-based, and experiential learning methods used
Focus	Learning mainly confined to school and the classroom	Extensive use of out-of-school environment as a place of learning
Cooperation and partnership	Involvement of the community is limited and dominated by the educational partners	Developing methods of real cooperation and partnership locally or regionally, in which other schools, other institutions, community groups, parents, and employers play an equal role in facilitating the transition of young people to adult life

The distinction between this approach to curriculum design and that underlying the traditional Leaving Certificate is illustrated in the above schema developed by Jim Gleeson (Gleeson, 1990; see also Leonard, 1990).

These principles have influenced, to a greater or lesser degree, curriculum reform since the mid-1980s. Alternative programs designed for early school leavers, such as Youth-reach, or for the less academically inclined within the school system, such as the Junior Certificate Schools Programme and the Leaving Certificate Applied Programme, are largely based on these ideas. Even within mainstream education, the revision of the junior cycle owes a lot, at least in theory, to elements of transition education principles (e.g., in relation to areas such as teaching and learning methods and modes of assessment).

However, despite extensive analysis and considerable expenditure on a range of interventions, there is little sign of significant improvement. The results of the 1994 Leaving Certificate Examination, reviewed by the National Council for Curriculum and Assessment (1995), show that between 1992 and 1994 an annual average of 8,000 young people left school at around 15 years of age, having completed the Junior Certificate only. An annual average of 4,000 young people left second-level school between 1992 and 1994 with no qualifications whatsoever. In 1995, the White Paper on Education (Government of Ireland, 1995a) set a target of 90% of the year 2000 cohort staying on to take the Leaving Certificate (the senior cycle of Irish secondary education). However, as Ann Louise Gilligan, Co-ordinator of the Educational Disadvantage Centre, acknowledges, it has become widely accepted that the Leaving Certificate has probably reached a plateau of around 81% (see Byrne, 2002). One reason for this is the economic growth of recent years that has encouraged children from poorer families to leave school early to take up low-paid jobs.

In March 1999, a report for the Junior Certificate Review Group analyzed the statistics for early school leavers (National Council for Curriculum and Assessment, 1999a). According to the report, around 60% of early school leavers are male, and 85% of these come from working class or small farming backgrounds. Over half of early school leavers come from families where fathers are unemployed. The Review Group found deterioration in the job prospects of those leaving school after the Junior Certificate. The Review Group also found that the students leaving school before Junior Certificate have the lowest chances of getting jobs due to employers' demands for credentials seeping down through the recruitment process for all levels of work, further marginalizing the early school leaving group.

THEORISTS APPRAISE THE CURRICULAR RESPONSE

What has been the response of theorists to the initiatives designed to enhance the educational experience of low achievers? In his recently completed study of curriculum policy in Ireland, Gleeson (2000) provided a number of interviews with leading Irish curriculum researchers and thinkers designed to ascertain the current state of curriculum inquiry in the field of low achievement in this country. It makes for depressing reading. For example, Teresa McCormack believes that the curriculum inquiry of recent decades has largely been a failure: "we don't have a coherent, integrated curriculum policy and change involves tinkering around the edges of a framework that is seen as by and large OK. You just add a bit to make it more holistic and add on bits for also rans" (Gleeson, 2000, p. 5).

Tony Crooks, who worked with the innovative City of Dublin Curriculum Development Unit, which (with the Shannon Curriculum Development Centre) was one of two independent curriculum units active in the 1970s and 1980s, takes an equally pessimistic view: "too much educational reform comes from within a circle; classroom doors are closed. Everything operates to perpetuate something that doesn't change, from the exam system to the timetable" (Gleeson, 2000, p. 5). He is even critical of his own work in the Curriculum Development Unit: "now that I am outside of it, I see more starkly how (the system) is self-perpetuating and to a degree how the CDU was helping it to self-perpetuate by innovating within the system" (Gleeson, 2000, p. 5).

Equally pessimistic is Anton Trant, former director of the same curriculum unit:

the emerging models of the teacher [are] very functional, there is rhetoric about the freedom of the teacher, the variety in approaches. I don't think anything much will happen unless all of these things become reality. Today's situation is much more frightening than it was in the seventies. (Gleeson, 2002, p. 6)

Jim Callan, Director of the Innovative Schools for Active Learning Project, asserts that the dominant focus in mainstream development has been an updating of curriculum content in order to get into the curriculum subject knowledge relevant to changing demands in the labor force and to addressing economic and technological needs. New curricula have been modified through the power of existing systems both within and without the school to shape it into their own likenesses. (Gleeson, 2000, p. 6)

Perhaps of even greater concern is the notion that, through mainstreaming, these voices subversive of curriculum orthodoxy have been largely silenced. The burden of Gleeson's argument is that, although researchers in the curriculum development units and universities have largely been voices in the wilderness, even this role has been eliminated by involving them in research and support work for centrally developed initiatives. This view is shared by Diarmuid Ó Donnabháin, Director of the Shannon Curriculum Development Centre, the *éminence grise* of Irish curriculum inquiry, who describes the current situation as follows: "the big danger here is that we are not challenging anybody anymore and that worries me. I have absolutely no power, no authority. There is no innovation as such, I just implement the policy as it is given to me from above" (Gleeson, 2000, p. 6).

Therefore, it seems safe to argue that the current state of curriculum inquiry, in the broad context of school failure, alienation, and disaffection, is one of considerable alienation and disaffection. There is a feeling among curriculum thinkers and researchers that the process of curriculum reform has been heavily politicized in recent years. This process has enabled limited change, particularly the updating of subject syllabi, but has effectively restricted reform and even serious debate on the bigger questions of curriculum values, purposes, goals, and structures. O'Sullivan and Mulcahy state a view that is still dominant among curriculum specialists in Ireland—namely, that:

the liberal functionalism which developed during the expansionary period under discussion, persists as the only salient paradigm for linking school and society. Educational expansion was expected to at once advance equal opportunity and provide for the skill needs of the economy. Fundamental questions about this remained not merely unanswered but unposed despite the raising of many critical issues about Irish social structure by social researchers and religious and church groups in recent years. (O'Sullivan & Mulcahy, 1989, p. 261)

Outside of the mainstream, in the realm of area partnerships in deprived areas, and in the context of special programs for seriously alienated groups of young people such as Youthstart (Canavan, 2000; McNamara & Campbell, 1999), innovative thinking and experimentation continue. In the mainstream, however, there is a feeling that the era of curriculum change is over for the present—that schools and teachers need to be allowed to recover from change fatigue.

CAN THEORISTS TAKE US FARTHER?

The relative failure of research and interventions to impact on the core problem of school failure has resulted in renewed intense curriculum debate. As stated in the introduction, two approaches can be identified within recent work: reformist and radical. Reformist theorists essentially argue that curriculum reform cannot be said to have failed because it has not been fully tried. Among these (Boland & McNamara, 1994; Callan, 1994, 1997; Gleeson, 1996, 2000; McNamara, 1991), it is suggested that key elements of curricular and structural reform identified as central to making schools more responsive to the needs of the less academically inclined have never been followed through with any real vigor. For example, Callan (1997) pointed out that, despite rhetoric to the contrary, little evidence of any fundamental shift in teaching and learning strategies toward more experiential, activity-based learning is to be found in practice. Gleeson (1996) argued that "the rhetoric of educational reform is one thing; the reality is often a pale shadow" (p. 64). He pointed out that the essentially centralized process of curriculum decision making has remained fundamentally unaltered, giving little room to teachers to respond imaginatively to particular needs.

Boland and McNamara (1994) were concerned with structural issues, which, they argued, limit and perhaps even negatively affect a great deal of the reform to date. For example, McNamara (1991) pointed out that school design, timetables, and teacher and principal training remain completely incompatible with key curricular imperatives, such as project-based learning, integrated studies, use of the out-of-school environment for teaching and learning, and so on. For most young people, the curriculum remains subject-based, school-centered, and rigidly timetabled. Boland and McNamara (1994) also pointed out that the supposedly reformed programs for potential early school leavers remain cyclical rather than truly modular. This provides little motivation to continue in education and no transferable credit to enable young people who leave school to continue education elsewhere or reenter it at later stage. These shortcomings combined have produced what Gleeson (1996) referred to "as innovation without change" (p. 65) and therefore not surprisingly have been disappointing in terms of effectiveness. However, these curriculum theorists remain largely of the view that more extensive and successful reform within existing programs and structures is possible and still offers the best way forward.

Reforming Society

The perceived failure of reform has foregrounded the work of those who hold more radical views. The first group places school failure in the broader context of inequality and suggests, in effect, that school as currently organized is an unlikely or even an unhelpful forum to address this issue. In this category, Lynch (1988, 1989, 1992, 1999, 2000) and Lynch and Drudy (1993) argued that widespread educational provision and other liberal public policies have failed to promote radical social change in society in the postwar era. Lynch (2000) suggested that research indicates that on questions such as "social-class related inequality, gender inequality and poverty, liberal social policies are not effective in eliminating major social problems either nationally or internationally" (p. 56). In Lynch's view, education as currently structured has embedded within it the business of cultural production and reproduction; as such, it is clearly inimical to the interests of those whose culture does not coincide with the dominant culture in society. Moreover, as Gleeson (2000) pointed out, control of curriculum and other aspects of schooling is highly centralized in the Irish system. Therefore, the planning and implementation of reform remain in the hands of experts who generally operate without systematic dialogue or collaboration with those who must use the service provided regardless of whether it meets their needs.

Clearly at one level, the type of critique offered by sociologists and curriculum theorists such as Lynch and Drudy implies dramatic upheavals in the socioeconomic order, which are unlikely in the present centrist political climate. At another level, however, this type of critique has become influential in promoting community education. This has developed in the form of collaborative area partnerships in deprived areas designed to bring about a greater degree of community stakeholder involvement in decision making in education and in other fields. The type of coalitions and partnerships suggested by Lynch (2000) as being central to equality and emancipation may have begun to emerge. Whether this process becomes a truly emancipatory partnership or simply another form of the colonization of the deprived by middle-class experts, as feared by Lynch, remains to be seen.

Reconceptualizing Intelligence

A second strand in radical theory challenges what are perceived as unhelpful concepts of what counts as intelligence, and mechanistic, reductionist, and instrumental approaches to curriculum and assessment. One strand of this inquiry that has gained considerable recent influence in Ireland is in the area of multiple intelligences (Hanafin, 1997; Hyland, 2000b). This approach could be considered alongside those that suggest that reform of curriculum may be the panacea for school failure and dropout. However, the extent of the conceptual challenge offered to the dominant culture of education probably positions the multiple intelligences movement far beyond more modest curriculum reform proposals.

It is not proposed to say a great deal here about the underpinning theory because it is based on the widely known work of Howard Gardner. The Multiple Intelligence and Assessment Project at University College, Cork, which has been the driving force in this field in Ireland, was closely linked to Project Zero at Harvard Graduate School of Education. The outcomes of the multiple intelligences project in Ireland, which concluded in 1999, have offered a radical blueprint for reform, which suggests that:

> A significant minority of young people do not experience success in the system; teaching, learning and assessment approaches need to be broadened to take account of the differences between learners; and the schooling experience overall is too heavily influenced by terminal written examinations. (Hyland, 2000b, p. 47)

The work of the multiple intelligences project has been particularly radical and innovative (Hanafin, 1997) in the field of assessment—an area that has become central to the concern of many curriculum theorists writing about the Irish education system (Hyland, 1998; Kellaghan, Madaus, & Raczek, 1996; National Council for Curriculum and Assessment, 1999b; Williams, 1992, 1998a). It is widely held that "rigidity in assessment approaches has done more to stultify curriculum improvement than perhaps any other factor" (National Council for Curriculum and Assessment, 1999b, p. 59) and reform of assessment has moved to the top of the curriculum agenda.

Realizing the Internal Goods of Curricular Pursuits

There is yet another strand of inquiry that has radical implications for how we design and deliver the school curriculum. This further strand consists in the desire to uncouple school learning from selection for third-level education and employment and to concentrate on the internal goods of curricular pursuits through promoting personal engagement in learning.

This strand of inquiry emerges conspicuously in the work of philosophers of education writing on the school curriculum (Dunne, 1995; Gaden, 1979, 1983, 1990; Hogan, 1995). This philosophical work reflects a general concern within the entire educational community regarding the connection between assessment and selection for third-level education and employment. The use of educational performance to determine suitability for particular kinds of employment and further education (what is called the *credential effect* or *exchange value of education*) is considered to compromise the character of learning for its own sake and to subvert personal commitment to learning. A cautionary note is struck in the work of Williams (1995a) against indicting everything currently being taught and learned in school as morally and educationally deficient. In a society where demand for jobs and third-level places exceeds supply, educational achievement is almost inevitably going to be invested with an exchange value. A tension is almost unavoidably present in a system that uses academic success for instrumental purposes—to determine suitability for further education or employment. Although it would be foolish to deny that some students only study for reasons of crude personal ambition, rather than out of love for their subjects, it is hardly inevitable. The educational value of all learning conducted in the context of examinations does not have to be compromised by the intrusion of external motivation. Human behavior can spring from multiple motives, and there is no reason that students studying for examinations should not also derive pleasure and satisfaction from their studies.

The Role of Specialization

In the context of a single chapter, it is not possible to deal with the work of three scholars in a way that would do them justice. Therefore, we propose to concentrate on the work of Gaden because it is the most detailed in respect of curriculum design and has not received the recognition that its imaginative character merits. Gaden accepted that society will have certain legitimate expectations of publicly sponsored schools. Young people must develop the enabling skills of literacy, numeracy, and, perhaps, computer skills, as well as a corpus of knowledge and understanding of the world useful, if not indeed necessary, to function in contemporary society. Schools must also seek to cultivate and promote the personal qualities and virtues necessary for civic participation. Having said this, Gaden looked at the quality of the engagement of young people in what they are required to learn.

In making his case for specialization at second level, Gaden (1983) claimed that "we have for many years contrived the means to support highly complex curricula which have no clear rationale, and through which it is likely that the majority of pupils learn very little" (p. 53). He argued that a "curriculum which attempts to incorporate every kind of knowledge and human concern in a complex program of formal instruction" (p. 55) cannot equip a pupil with the self-confidence which s/he will need to be "ambitious and adventurous" (p. 56) in later learning situations. The school should instead concentrate on teaching young people to engage in activities that contribute to their human flourishing by endeavoring to identify and teach those activities (academic, sporting, craft, artistic) in which are likely to enjoy success and find fulfillment. In other words (see Williams, 1998b), the school must become more assertive in recovering its classical mission to be an arena of *scholé* or *ludus*—that is, an arena for the pursuit of leisure.

Although immense social approval is bestowed on competence in intellectual skills of a linguistic/mathematical character, which are linked to access to status-bearing occupations, Gaden argued that success at *any* activity that enjoys an acknowledged status within the student's community promotes confidence. *Self-confidence*, defined by Gaden (1983) as "confidence in one's own worth or significance" (p. 48), is essential to human flourishing. Although self-confidence can be diminished by certain experiences of failure (e.g., in relationships, a career, etc.), it can be boosted by the experience of success in almost any pursuit. Most important, in the school situation, self-confidence can be promoted through the organized learning of something seen by the learner to have value and significance and which the learner can expect to succeed in mastering through sustained effort. It is unlikely that we can do much about society's hierarchy of values, but as educators we need to present to young people an opportunity to engage in activities that can enhance their confidence.

Sustained effort on the part of the learner is part of her or his gradual assumption of responsibility, which, like self-confidence, can be promoted through organized learning. Children become responsible through engaging in learnable activities, not just at the level of procedural competence and correctness, but by grasping the central purposes and values (i.e., the spirit of the activities in question). This spirit depends on the internal coherence of the body of skill and knowledge to be learned. As well as self-confidence and responsibility, another crucial notion here is that of identification—what young people require is activity with which they can identify in a positive way. The absence of any activity of this nature is often to be found among disaffected young people and, indeed, among those who find themselves at a loose end following retirement. What schools should seek to promote is "a degree of identification or a relationship of some personal significance between the learner and his or her chosen pursuits" (Gaden, 1990, p. 36) or "competence in and personal identification with at least something which can contribute to the sustenance and enjoyment of one's own life and that of others" (Gaden, 1983, p. 52).

Gaden proposed that from second year onward, one third of the pupils' time in second level schooling should be given to specialized pursuits, which, he suggested, might be taken two at a time for a least 2 years each. This would allow the pupils to acquire the essential skills and bodies of factual knowledge relevant to each activity and a grasp of its traditions, its spirit, and its social and economic significance. It would also allow the learning to be the subject of sustained effort on the part of the learner and of a serious commitment by teachers and school authorities to the development of the learner's competence. Teachers would be enabled to engage in what Hogan (1995) referred to as a genuine "courtship" of their youthful sensibilities and energies. Reasonably, Gaden argued that it would not be possible to provide the time and commitment to get young pupils to seriously engage in more than two pursuits at a time.

Gaden's specialized pursuit has clear parallels with Dunne's (1995) account of an educational practice as "a coherent and invariably quite complex set of activities and tasks that has evolved cooperatively and cumulatively over time" and which is "alive in the community who are its insiders" (p. 72). Central to this notion of a practice are "standards of excellence, themselves subject to development and redefinition, which demand responsibleness from those who are, or are trying to become, practitioners" (p. 72). Acquiring competence at a practice involves a submission that imposes a discipline; but it is also, of course, "this discipline which enables or empowers people" (p. 72). Through "real engagement with, and in, a practice a person's powers are released, directed and enlarged" (pp. 72–73). Dunne argues that it is through such engagement that a person comes to find her or himself (p. 76). This is the way, he suggested, to a "real, and deeply grounded 'self-esteem'" (p. 76).

NEGLECTED INQUIRY:
CURRICULUM, CULTURE, AND IDENTITY

As readers have no doubt learned, curriculum inquiry in Ireland has been energetic and creative. Nevertheless, one area that has not attracted sustained attention is that of Irish identity. As noted in the introduction, the absence of this theme from the literature is surprising and disappointing. This is not to claim that the theme is entirely neglected. James Bennett has published a fine series of articles on the conceptions of Irish identity informing the different subjects of the primary curriculum (see e.g., Bennett, 1994, 1995; see also Alvey, 1992). But it is an area that remains conspicuously undertheorized.

For example, the issue of the relationship between religion and the secular curriculum received extended treatment only from Williams (1998c) and Alvey (1992). This is an area about which theorists could have been expected to comment. In Ireland, parents have the constitutional right to withdraw their children from religious education in the formative sense, but it was hard to see how such withdrawal could be complete or absolute in practice because the rules of the Department of Education required the maintenance of a religious ethos in all primary schools. An essential element of this ethos was a mandatory relationship between religion and other subjects through the integrated curriculum. A similar integrative role was attributed to religion in the regulations that govern the operation of vocational schools at second level. The assumption underlying this aspect of curriculum policy is that being religious is part of being Irish. The initiative on the issue was actually taken by the State, and the revised document on the primary school curriculum (Department of Education and Science, 1999) changes the State's policy in the area. The document affirms the significance for most Irish people of a religious perspective on life, but it does not commit the State to a direct endorsement of the Christian view of human destiny. Therefore, it is no longer State policy to insist that the curriculum endorse a single worldview. This aspect of curriculum policy was changed with minimal input from curriculum theorists.

The concern with issues of nationality and identity that has exercised philosophers of education and curriculum theorists internationally (see e.g., White, 1996) and is addressed in the works of Williams (1995b, 1999a, 1999b), features little in the writings of other theorists in this part of the island. An area of the curriculum where issues of identity are very much to the fore concerns the place of Irish in schools. Must one speak Irish to be truly Irish? Is it realistic to expect the learning of Irish in school to lead to a revival of the language? Critical debate on the relationship between knowledge of the Irish language and Irish identity and on the project of reviving Irish through the classroom is rare (see Williams, 1989). What discussion there is concerns only the effectiveness of different teaching methods (see De Bhál, 1994). Anecdotal evidence suggests that significant numbers of young people seem to have opted out in spirit from Irish class, but this has not led to a critical inquiry into the status of compulsory Irish in the school curriculum.

There seems to be only one area where cultural matters are addressed. This is in the almost universally shared view that the European dimension to political and cultural life is to be welcomed and vigorously promoted. Only in the work of Williams (1996a, 1996b, 2000) has the widespread, uncritical endorsement of the policy of using the school curriculum to promote the ideology of a united Europe been challenged. As with the concern about low achievement and disadvantage, this is an issue on which consensus is nearly total. It is hard to avoid the conclusion that scholars fight shy of contentious topics that give rise to genuine disagreement. The notion of *critique* is tied almost exclusively to standard denunciations of the socio-economic and educational system.

The issue of identity, like that of sexuality, is fraught with potential disagreement and so tends to be avoided. In the light of political developments designed to end the conflict in Northern Ireland and to engender respect and harmony between the principal traditions on the island, the paucity of research literature on the interrelationship among culture, curriculum, and identity is a source of regret. The growing immigrant population also requires response from curriculum theorists about these matters. It is time to go beyond clichés about multiculturalism and engage in serious and sustained critical inquiry regarding the relationship among religion, politics, culture, and the curriculum. The excellent work done in other areas of curriculum inquiry needs to be reflected in inquiry into the place of the school curriculum in reflecting culture and shaping identity.

REFERENCES

Alvey, D. (1992). *Irish education: The Case for secular reform*. Dublin, Ireland: Church and State Books.

Bennett, J. (1994). History textbooks in primary schools in the Republic of Ireland, 1971–1973, *Oideas, 42* (Official Journal of the Department of Education and Science, Ireland), 25–38.

Bennett, J. (1995). Changing values in primary education, *Studies: An Irish Quarterly Review, 84,* 71–79.

Boland, J., & McNamara, G. (1994). The reform of senior cycle educational provision in the Republic of Ireland: A proposal for radical change. *Irish Educational Studies, 13,* 190–196.

Byrne, A. (2002). St. Patrick's is targeting disadvantage in education. *The Irish Times, Education and Living Supplement,* 2 April 2001, p. 4.

Callan, J. (1994). *Schools for active learning—Final Report*. Maynooth, Ireland: St Patrick's College.

Callan, J. (1997). Action learning in the classroom: A challenge to existing educational values and practices. In Hyland, A. (Ed.), *Issues in education* (pp. 21–29). Dublin, Ireland: Dublin Association of Secondary Teachers in Ireland.

Canavan, J. (2000). *The Mol an Óige Project—The view from the schools: An evaluation of the project*. Galway, Ireland: Department of Political Science and Sociology, NUIG.

Conference of Religious of Ireland. (1998). *Inequality in schooling in Ireland*. Dublin, Ireland: CORI Education Commission.

Coolahan, J. (Ed.). (1994). *Report of the National Education Convention*. Dublin, Ireland: The Stationery Office.

De Bhál, P. (1994). The Irish language and education: A review of recent research. *Studies in Education, 10,* 37–46.

Department of Education and Science. (1999). *Primary school curriculum*. Dublin, Ireland: The Stationery Office.

Dunne, J. (1995). What's the good of education. In P. Hogan (Ed.), *Partnership and the benefits of learning: A symposium on philisophical issues in educational policy* (pp. 60–81). Maynooth, Ireland: Educational Studies Association of Ireland.

Elliott, J. (2000, June). *Action research and global trends in curriculum reform*. Paper delivered to the 2nd Educational Studies Association of Ireland Theme Conference on Action Research, Dublin City University, Dublin, Ireland.

Fitzgerald, J. (1998). Education and the Celtic Tiger. In B. Farrell (Ed.), *Issues in education* (pp. 33–44). Dublin, Ireland: Association of Secondary Teachers in Ireland.

Gaden, G. (1979). Depth of knowledge as an educational aim. In *Proceedings of the Educational Studies Association of Ireland 1979* (pp. 224–233). Galway, Ireland: University of Galway Press.

Gaden, G. (1983). The case for specialization. *Irish Educational Studies, 3,* 47–60.

Gaden, G. (1990). Rehabilitating responsibility. *Journal of Philosophy of Education, 24,* 27–38.

Gleeson, J. (1990). Spiral II: The Shannon Initiatives. In G. McNamara, K. Williams, & D. Herron (Eds.), *Achievement and aspiration: Curricular initiatives in Irish post-primary education in the 1980s* (pp. 71–91). Dublin, Ireland: Drumcondra Teachers Centre.

Gleeson, J. (1996). Senior cycle curriculum policy. In P. Hogan (Ed.), *Issues in education* (pp. 57–69). Dublin, Ireland: Dublin Association of Secondary Teachers.

Gleeson, J. (2000, June). *The cultural and political context of Irish post-primary curriculum reform*. Paper delivered to the 2nd Educational Studies Association of Ireland Theme Conference on Action Research, Dublin City University, Dublin, Ireland.

Government of Ireland. (1980). *White paper on education*. Dublin, Ireland: The Stationery Office.

Government of Ireland. (1981). *Report of the pupil transfer committee*. Dublin, Ireland: The Stationery Office.

Government of Ireland. (1992a). *Education for a changing world: Green paper on education*. Dublin, Ireland: The Stationery Office.

Government of Ireland. (1992b). *National development plan*. Dublin, Ireland: The Stationery Office.

Government of Ireland. (1995a). *Charting our education future: White paper on education*. Dublin, Ireland: The Stationery Office.

Government of Ireland. (1995b). *Operational programme for local, urban and rural development*. Dublin, Ireland: The Stationery Office.

Government of Ireland. (1998). *Adult education in an era of lifelong learning*. Dublin, Ireland: The Stationery Office.

Hanafin, J. (ed.) (1997). *Towards new understandings: Assessment and the theory of multiple intelligences*. Cork, Ireland: Multiple Intelligences Curriculum and Assessment Research Project, UCC.

Hogan, P. (1995). *The custody and courtship of experience: Western philosophy in philosophical perspective*. Dublin, Ireland: The Columba Press.

Hyland, Á. (ed.) (1998). *Innovations in assessment in Irish education.* Cork, Ireland: Multiple Intelligences Curriculum and Assessment Research Project, UCC.

Hyland, Á. (2000a). *Teacher education in the south—Systems; current developments; issues and emerging themes.* Paper delivered to the Conference for Teacher Education Professionals in Ireland—North and South, Belfast, Ireland.

Hyland, Á. (Ed.) (2000b). *Multiple intelligences curriculum and assessment research project, final report.* Cork, Ireland: Multiple Intelligences Curriculum and Assessment Research Project, UCC.

Irish National Teachers Organization. (1997). *Teaching and learning: Issues in assessment.* Dublin, Ireland Author.

Kellaghan, T., Madaus, G. F., & Raczek, A. (1996). *The uses of external examinations to improve student motivation.* Washington, DC: American Education Research Association.

Leonard, D. (1990). The vocational preparation and training programme. In G. McNamara, K. Williams, & D. Herron (Eds.), *Achievement and aspiration: Curricular initiatives in Irish post- primary education* (pp. 33–46). Dublin, Ireland: Drumcondra Teachers Centre.

Lynch, E. (1988). Developing abilities: What are we doing in second-level education at present. *Compass, 17,* 47–60

Lynch, K. (1989). *The hidden curriculum: Reproduction in education a reappraisal.* Lewes, England: Falmer.

Lynch, K. (1992). Intelligence, ability and education: Challenging traditional views. *Oideas, 38,* 134–148.

Lynch, E. (1999). *Equality in education.* Dublin, Ireland: Gill & Macmillan.

Lynch, K. (2000). Equality studies, the academy and the role of research in emancipatory change. In J. McNiff, G. McNamara, & D. Leonard (Eds.), *Action research in Ireland* (pp. 26–55). Dublin, Ireland: Educational Studies Association of Ireland.

Lynch, K., & Drudy, S. (1993). *Schools and society in Ireland.* Dublin, Ireland: Gill & Macmillan.

McNamara, G. (1991). Curriculum innovation and teaching skills. *Oideas, 37,* 16–28.

McNamara, G. (1992). The senior cycle and the less academically inclined student. *Studies in Education, 8,* 15–27.

McNamara, G., & Campbell, H. (1999). *Learning to learn: An evaluation of a youthstart initiative.* Dublin, Ireland: Youthstart Support Unit.

McNamara, G., & Quinlan, C. (2000). *Early school leaving in Blanchardstown: Causes and cures.* Dublin, Ireland: Blanchardstown Area Partnership.

National Council for Curriculum and Assessment. (1995). *The 1994 leaving certificate examination: A review of results.* Dublin, Ireland: The Stationery Office.

National Council for Curriculum and Assessment. (1999a). *The junior cycle review: Progress report, issues and options for development.* Dublin, Ireland: The Stationery Office.

National Council for Curriculum and Assessment. (1999b). *Curriculum and assessment: Policy towards the new century.* Dublin, Ireland: The Stationery Office.

National Economic and Social Forum. (1997). *Early school leavers and youth employment forum report, No. 11.* Dublin, Ireland: Author.

O'Sullivan, D., & Mulcahy, D., (Eds.). (1989). *Irish educational policy, plans and substance.* Dublin, Ireland: Institute of Public Administration.

Organization for Economic Co-operation and Development. (1995). *Economic surveys, Ireland.* Paris, Author.

Smyth, E (1998). *Pupil performance, absenteeism and school drop- out.* Dublin, Ireland: Economic and Social Research Institute.

White, J. (1996). Education and nationality. *Journal of Philosophy of Education, 30,* 327–343.

Williams K. (1989). Reason and rhetoric in curriculum polity: An appraisal of the case for the inclusion of Irish in the school curriculum. *Studies: An Irish Quarterly Review, 78,* 191–203.

Williams K. (1992). *Assessment: A discussion paper.* Dublin, Ireland: Association of Secondary Teachers, Ireland.

Williams K. (1995a). Philosophy and curriculum policy. In P. Hogan (Ed.), *Partnership and the benefits of learning: A symposium on philosophical issues in educational policy* (pp. 83–106). Maynooth, Ireland: Education Studies Association of Ireland.

Williams, K. (1995b). Review article: National sentiment in civic education. *Journal of Philosophy of Education, 29,* 433–440.

Williams, K. (1996a). Education for European citizenship: A philosophical critique. *Studies in Philosophy and Education, 15,* 209–219.

Williams, K., (1996b). Promoting the "New Europe" education or proselytism? *Studies: An Irish Quarterly Review, 85,* 49–55.

Williams, K. (1997). On learning for its own sake. *Prospero: A Journal of New Thinking in Philosophy for Education, 3,* 10–13.

Williams, K. (1998a). Assessment and the challenge of scepticism. In D. Carr (Ed.), *Education, knowledge and truth: Beyond the post modern impasse* (pp. 221–236). London: Routledge.

Williams, K. (1998b). Review Article: The labor we delight in. *Journal of Philosophy of Education, 32,* 292–303.

Williams, K. (1998c). The religious dimension of the secular curriculum: The Irish experience. *Panorama: International Journal of Comparative Religious Education and Values, 10,* 95–105.

Williams, K. (1999a). Faith and the nation: Education and religious identity in the Republic of Ireland. *British Journal of Educational Studies, 47,* 317–331.

Williams, K. (1999b). Patriotism and respect for diversity, Presidential address to the Annual Conference of the Educational Studies Association of Ireland, 1998. *Irish Educational Studies, 18,* 1–13.

Williams, K. (2000). Realism, rationalism and the European project. In F. Crawley, P. Smeyers, & P. Standish (Eds.), *Remembering Europe: Nations and culture in European higher education* (pp. 47–65). New York: Oxford, Berghahn.

CHAPTER 19

Curriculum Planning at the Threshold of the Third Millennium: The Israeli Case

Naama Sabar
Yehoshua Mathias
Tel Aviv University, Israel

A review of the changes in curriculum planning in Israel from the establishment of the state to the present day shows a shift from a uniform curriculum to a multifaceted one. This development largely reflects sociocultural processes that have occurred in Israeli society and their influence on the educational system (Harrison, 1994; Sabar & Silberstein, 1998). In light of these social processes, curriculum planning in the third millennium will create new interrelationships between the compulsory elements dictated by the central authorities and those elements that are open to variability and reflect the range of educational and cultural interests in Israel. A historical survey of the development of curriculum planning in Israel since its establishment reveals this trend.

Another issue this chapter deals with relates to future changes in the knowledge the curricula represents and in the legitimate sources of this knowledge. Research on curricula indicates that the knowledge included in them depends on specific sociocultural contexts (Apple, 1990; Bordieu, 1979; Goodson, 1997). This distinction raises a series of questions about the social distribution of knowledge in curricula, the ownership of that knowledge, and the relationship between its distribution and economic and class stratification. Historical changes in the knowledge included in curricula, as well as in its conception and distribution, often denote changes in the balance of power between sociocultural groups—changes that are the outcome of struggles conducted within various arenas. However, in modern societies with complex educational and cultural systems, curricula are not merely reproductions of what is taking place in other sectors, but are influenced by autonomous educational factors too (Ringer, 1979). Hence, an analysis of changes in curricula must also seriously relate to the autonomy of the educational field and curriculum development as a professional realm in its own right.

FIRST-GENERATION CURRICULA: 1954–1967

Like other modern national movements, Zionism also strove to create a new, secular high (written) culture based largely on a readaptation of material from ancient and religious Jewish culture (Shavit, 1999). The Zionist movement assigned this role to the Hebrew elementary schools designed for the general population (Elboim & Dror, 1990). Nonetheless, since the 1920s, various political and ideological movements made their special imprint on the Hebrew educational system and its curricula (Reshef & Dror, 1999).

Each stream had its own curricula with special emphases dictated by the ideology of the roof movement. They were developed by its central pedagogical leadership and included a rationale and list of topics according to age groups. Their contents were arranged according to disciplines and included chapters in Jewish and Hebrew studies, science, mathematics, local geography, history, and English, with a stress on the acquisition of items of knowledge. Although the curricula of the various streams were quite similar, their existence aroused a great deal of criticism. The critics of the stream system argued that it perpetrated political distinctions and deferred the cohesiveness that a modern national society required (Reshef, 1987).

A marked change occurred only after the state's establishment when a large, culturally heterogeneous immigration doubled the population of the country within 4 years. The 1953 State Education Law canceled the separate streams and the affiliation between political movements and the schools. It laid down the aims of education in Israel and invested the state with absolute authority over the elementary school and its curricula, thus completely nationalizing elementary education.

The demand for a uniform curriculum was an important part of the ideology underlying state education. This curriculum was intended to be "a stabilizing factor in the multiplicity of cultures and ethnic groups" (Ziv, 1955, p. 11). Its major goal was to create a homogeneous, common cultural basis for the entire population—a prerequisite for a modern, industrialized society (Gellner, 1983).

THE STATE CURRICULUM AND ITS CULTURAL ORIENTATION

The state curriculum, like its predecessors, was based on a breakdown by subjects of study. It was prescientific, formal, and patriarchal, both in the way it was planned and its ideological educational approach. It was composed in a temporary manner because it was a result of the work of ad hoc committees, which almost never included teachers nor intellectuals, set up for the purpose and then dissolved after completing it. The planning was not based on any theories of curriculum planning, nor were any formal strategies of evaluation employed in the committees' work (Ben Peretz & Seidman, 1986; Dror & Lieberman, 1997). According to the State Education Law, the state is the sole source of legitimacy of the curricula.

The choice of goals as well as the formulation of achievements expected of the pupils attested to the strong nationalist orientation of the curriculum. A typical example is the goal set for teaching the Bible: "to instill in the pupils a love of the country in which their forefathers lived, in which the Jewish people took shape, in which our prophets prophesized and our poets wrote, the land in which the Book of Books was created and for which Jewish heroes have sacrificed their lives" (Ministry of Education and Culture, 1954, pp. 15, 64). The aim of the Bible curriculum, like that for literature and history, was to create a broad cultural common denominator for both the state religious and the state nonreligious elementary schools. The Ministry of Education also refused to commit itself to the secular nature of the state school, which educated "not for religion but not against religion" (Ministry of Education and Culture, 1959).

Nonetheless, the state curricula were not as uniform as their authors described them, if for no other reason, because the State Education Law that canceled the streams recognized that the religious had the right to pedagogical autonomy. Consequently, there are differences between the state elementary school curricula and those for the state religious schools, particularly in regard to the scope and content of Jewish and Oral Law studies. These subjects were naturally assigned a high priority in the religious schools. In the history curriculum, the chapter on prehistoric man was deleted because it did not fit in with the periodization of the Bible; it was replaced by "talks about the history of the First Temple period based on the Bible" (Ministry of Education and Culture, 1954, p. 31).

In this context, it is interesting to note how the leaders of the Ministry of Education coped with the cultural heritage of the immigrants from Islamic countries, who made up about half of the new immigration. Ben Zion Dinur, Minister of Education in the early 1950s, recognized the social value of integrating the heritage of the various ethnic groups into the curricula, so that "every Yemenite and Moroccan child can stand tall" (Dinur, 1953, p. 14). In his view, this combination was part of the Zionist movement's project to create an all-encompassing national culture reflecting the heritage of all ethnic groups that are part of the Jewish people (Dinur & Beer, 1936). However, he laid down a prerequisite for implementing this integration—the possibility of finding in the culture and history of the Oriental Jews patterns, content and artistic works compatible with the cultural models and historical concepts that had become an integral part of the culture of modern European Jewry (Dinur, 1953). Only those artistic works and cultural elements that met this test merited, in his view, inclusion in the curricula. This stipulation underscored that the state curricula represented the European Hebrew culture of the long-standing inhabitants of the country, who dominated Israeli society.

Officially, the state acknowledged the need to adapt curricula to the special needs of the Arab population. Although the language of instruction in schools in the Arab villages was Arabic, at that early stage, the state refused to recognize the right of Israeli Arabs to nurture a special national culture. As a result, Arab pupils learned more Bible than Koran, more Jewish and Zionist history than Arab history, and more Hebrew poetry than Arabic poetry. Modern Arab history was not taught at all, neither in the Hebrew schools nor in the Arab schools (Haj, 1995; Maari, 1975; Mathias, in press).

DIFFICULTIES IN IMPLEMENTATION AND VOICES OF RESISTANCE TO THE STATE CURRICULUM

The Ministry of Education realized that it was essential to enlist the teachers' support to introduce the new curricula into the schools. However, it did not place much trust in the teachers or their commitment to the national goals that the heads of the state and the shapers of state education wished to attain (Ben Gurion, 1954). The new situation created by the mass immigration and the concomitant rise in the number of students fueled this lack of trust; many of the teachers hired at the time lacked didactic training or had no suitable national education (Avidor, 1957). The situation was particularly bad in the immigrant towns and villages, where most of the teachers were new immigrants, not totally fluent in Hebrew, and hence not integrated into the Hebrew culture of the prestate community.

The center's lack of faith in the teachers was expressed in various ways in the policy underlying the uniform curriculum. According to the State Education Law, the Ministry of Education was supposed to write only the basic curriculum, covering up to 75% of the total number of study hours in the elementary school. The parents and teachers were entitled to suggest additional curricula covering the remaining 25%. In practice, because the basic curricula were so dense, they became both the minimum and maximum curricula, and only the more affluent populations succeeded in implementing them (Adar, 1956). Teachers were critical of the density of the state curriculum and the Teachers Federation even demanded that it be rescinded (Hed Hachinukh, 1956).

Isolated, but vociferous voices were harshly critical of the curricula's pedagogical and nationalist orientation. Zvi Adar of the Hebrew University claimed that uniform curriculum for the whole country will do away with the teacher's and the pupil's personality, will cause them to feel they are acting mechanically, and "will adversely affect the teachers' conscience and their relationship with their pupils, since they are obliged to teach them according to a uniform set curriculum regardless of whether or not it suits their abilities and needs" (Adar, 1956, pp. 43–44). He deplored as well the nationalist ethnocentric, narrow-minded spirit of the state curriculum.

Nevertheless, everyone, including critics of the curriculum, agreed that under the existing historical conditions a uniform curriculum was essential; the debate focused on its character and scope. Whereas critics were in favor of a minimal uniform curriculum beyond which each school could develop additional, special contents, the state officials wanted to control it in its integrality to maintain the national spirit. The greatest difficulties were encountered in those schools in which a large proportion of the pupils were immigrants from Islamic countries. The seriousness of this problem was fully revealed after 1955 when the Ministry of Education began administering national uniform tests to all eighth-grade graduates. These tests, known as the *seker* (survey), revealed a large gap between the achievements of children of immigrants from Islamic countries, on the one hand, and those from the veteran population and European immigrants, on the other (Lewy, 1994). These gaps seriously questioned whether the declared aim of the state curriculum (i.e., to create a common cultural basis for the entire Israeli population) was being attained.

Over the years, the assumption that one nation should have one curriculum was challenged. Dissatisfaction with the uniform curriculum and the poor achievements of elementary school pupils paved the way for an overall reform of the structure of the educational system.

ROOTS OF THE REFORM IN THE EDUCATIONAL SYSTEM: 1964–1968

The idea of reforming the structure of the Israeli educational system was born in the mid-1960s, largely under the influence of the academic trend that developed in the United States following the launch of the Sputnik (Kliebard, 1992). The Six Day War gave added momentum to the Israeli trend towards reform, the general lines of which had already been laid down (Shmida et al., 1971).

After the war, a new concept of the roles of the educational system took shape. In the 1950s, in the wake of the mass immigration, the role of elementary education, like that of the army, was to serve as a melting pot—to imbue the immigrants with the national culture so they would identify with the Jewish people and the state. The Six Day War, in which most of the soldiers were new immigrants, proved that the schools had succeeded in this task beyond all expectations. From then on, the goals were expanded, and the major role of education was to further Israel's economic and technological advancement. To achieve this goal, the knowledge defined by the curricula had to be updated and adapted to the requirements of a modern, highly technological economy (Yadlin, 1971). This demand was further validated in the aftermath of the Six Day War, which ended with a great military victory, but also led to a dramatic escalation in the intensity of the Israeli–Arab conflict. Defense expenditures grew considerably and could only be met through economic modernization. Following the war, Israel emerged from the economic recession that had prevailed previously, and the new prosperity led to the development of patterns typical of a consumer society.

Another aim of the reform was to reduce the gaps in achievement between stronger and weaker pupils. These gaps, which corresponded to disparities between Sephardic and Ashkenazi pupils, had created a segregative stratified structure—a potentially explosive social situation (Lissak, 1999). It gradually became clear that these two aims were not necessarily compatible (Dror & Lieberman, 1997; Lewy, 1979). The reform was first introduced in the 1960s and continued throughout the 1970s and 1980s. The most comprehensive of all educational reforms in Israel, it was a three-part program. The first part was organizational, which included the reduction of elementary school education from 8 to 6 years, and the creation of a 6-year secondary school based on two stages: 3 + 3. At the same time, compulsory education was extended to cover ninth grade. This meant that secondary education had become a part of compulsory education in Israel, which amounted to a major step up for the majority of the population. The second part included the academization of teachers in the middle school—a move that led to an increase in the number of applicants to institutions of higher education. The third part dealt with the development of a new generation of curricula, also known as the generation of scientific curricula.

THE GENERATION OF SCIENTIFIC CURRICULA: 1966–1978

The transition to scientific curricula was marked by the establishment of the National Curriculum Center in the Ministry of Education. The initial staff that founded the center received their training in curricula planning in American universities. Under their influence, an ongoing relationship between the academia and the Ministry of Education was established and was one of the striking innovations of this new generation of curricula. The Minister of Education took pride in the fact that "our greatest achievement is our success in enlisting so many university scholars to work on the preparation of new curricula" (Aranne, 1969, p. 2936).

The heads of the Ministry of Education believed that the development of new curricula was "one of the most effective investments in the educational system, implemented on the basis of a systematic and precise approach, in cooperation with the finest scientific and pedagogical minds, and under the teachers' guidance. The curriculum is meaningful not because it was written by a person of renown, but mainly because it has successfully been tested in the classroom" (Yadlin, 1971, p. 20).

The curricula were planned in two tracks (Sabar & Silberstein, 1998). In the general track, as in the first generation, syllabi were developed for the various disciplines. They included aims and principles, a suggestion for the content of study, basic terms, key ideas, and their allocation among the various classes. But unlike the previous generation, they systematically related to modes of learning. In the second, empirical track, learning materials were developed. One form this took was books written as an example for other writers. Another form was kits that reflected the new approach of the curriculum developer, who regards it as his or her duty to suggest learning activities that may make it possible to achieve the aims the curriculum has set for itself. These kits ostensibly contained everything the teacher needed to do his or her work in the classroom, including teacher guides that describe activities in detail as well as equipment required for experiments. The range of teaching and learning materials expanded significantly. The pupils were no longer perceived as a homogeneous group, as in the past. To cope with this variance, special curricula were prepared for heterogeneous classes (Sabar & Silberstein, 1998). The development process was based on a multistage planning model according to Tyler's (1949) approach. This model emphasized several components: a clear definition of aims, preferably in behavioral-operational terms; development of learning materials consistent with these aims; training teachers to teach the curriculum; and evaluation of the classroom implementation. The entire process was perceived as an ongoing task of development, evaluation, and revision. The contents were disciplinary.

Instead of items of information, the structure of discipline served as a key concept in the development process. This concept is based on the ideas of Bruner and Schwab (Bruner, 1965), and served as a basis for organizing and categorizing the contents of the various subjects. The contents are designed to represent the basic ideas of each discipline and the methods of research that characterize it.

Some latent functions of the structure-of-discipline approach also had the effect of deskilling teachers, thus undercutting their enhanced professional status. It legitimized the development of curricula by universities and national institutes of curriculum planning, thus relegating teachers to the status of consumers (Eden, 1986; Silberstein, 1984). This was based on the assumption that disciplinary knowledge, which was given clear priority in these curricula, could be found mainly among the experts in academic institutions (Seixas, 1999). Teacher's guidebooks and special courses accompanied the development and operation of the new curricula and by this means, the developers attempted to persuade the teachers to use them while remaining faithful to their aims. This effort proved that, unlike the first-generation curricula, the scientific curricula related to teachers as intelligent consumers giving them the possibility to select and choose among various components (Apple, 1982).

EDUCATIONAL INNOVATIONS AND PUBLIC CONSENSUS

The structure-of-discipline approach and the close cooperation with the academic community produced innovative and, at times, daring curricula in terms of that period. Their developers justified them via a combined ideology that spoke, on the one hand, in favor of developing the individual's abilities and intellectual capacity, and on the other, in favor of strengthening his or her loyalty to the society and its national objectives. Nonetheless, a large proportion of the innovations did not infiltrate into the field at the time. It is important to take note of these because efforts to apply them are continuing to the present day. Beginning from the middle school, the scientific curricula attempted to nurture scientific thinking at the expense of memorization and absorbing information (Adar & Fox, 1977; Sabar, 1988). They stressed the empirical, critical nature of the process of knowledge acquisition and the temporary nature of scientific truth. They attempted to make the biological experiment or the historical source a part of routine learning in the classroom. Consequently, these curricula imparted a pluralistic image of science. Scientific truth was depicted as the outcome of an ongoing process conducted according to rules that would guarantee the rationality of the achieved results (Scheffler, 1964). In this process, the student tests his assumptions according to scientific facts and rules and arrives at his own conclusions. This meant that the emphasis had to be shifted from the knowledge of details to the development of skills, including the development of the individual's judgment and his or her mastery of the rules of scientific thought.

Under the influence of this systematic approach, curricula were then developed to grapple with topics that had been repressed in the Israeli educational system, like the Arab–Israeli conflict, political and social conflicts in the pre-state Jewish community, social gaps, and interethnic conflicts in Israel. In the new curricula studies, the aesthetic judgment of literary works was no longer submitted to national and ideological criteria (Yaoz & Iram, 1987).

A particularly interesting illustration, in this context, is the curriculum dealing with the Israeli–Arab conflict, which aroused a stormy public debate (Mathias, in press). It paved the way for a change in the negative stereotype generally associated with the Arab enemy (Bartal, 1999). The incentive for addressing the topic arose after the Six Day War, when military commanders complained, at a meeting with the management of the Ministry of Education, that their soldiers knew nothing about Arab countries and the Arab population in the areas conquered in the war (Ministry of Education and Culture, 1968). Although the basic assumption underlying the curriculum was at the core of Israeli consensus, its form and texture evoked a strong public reaction. Faithful to the demand made by the historical discipline—namely, to understand from within each side in the conflict—the curriculum, for the first time, presented authentic voices of the enemy, his or her reasoning, and his or her narrative version of the conflict. This included the voices of the Palestinians, their demand for recognition of their national identity, their national struggle against Zionism, and the refugee problem. These positions were presented in the name of their adherents, without any comments by the authors of the curriculum, and this at a time when the Israeli political establishment and Prime Minister Golda Meir were denying the very existence of a Palestinian national identity (Mathias, in press). The curriculum also encouraged students to critically examine all these positions, including that of Israel. In this sense, the curriculum preceded politics in two decades.

The new curriculum on Zionist history also presented a more critical picture of the past than the one previously accepted. It related to conflicts and power struggles between ideological movements and political parties in prestate Israel, and it also left it up to the students to assess which of them was right. The history curriculum for the upper classes in secondary schools abandoned the approach of all-encompassing narratives and instead offered specialization on specific topics (patch history). The civics curriculum enabled the students to learn about the contemporary Israeli reality, its negative as well as its positive aspects. For the first time, the Israeli student was able to learn about the life of the Arab minority in Israel, their cultural and national aspirations, and special problems. The same holds true for the interethnic and class conflicts that divided Israeli society and the disadvantaged status of Oriental Jews. One of the principles adhered to by the writers of the new curricula was not to deviate from the consensus in Israel society in relation to ideology and values (Eden, 1976). In post-1967 Israel, consensus was a key issue in politics that had to be taken into account (Pedatzur, 1996). Therefore, although the writers of the curricula introduced the latest research findings into them, they tried to maintain a balance and avoid contradicting widely accepted views. Nonetheless, their pluralistic and academic approach was enough to arouse opposition. The argument was that as long as Israel was fighting for its existence, an approach of this kind was liable to arouse doubts in the minds of the students about the rightness of Zionism. Principals, educators, teachers, experts on education, and supervisors in the Ministry of Education also felt that the trend of academization was undermining the main function of humanistic subjects in the school, which, in their view, was to shape the students' identity (Shremer, 1979; Zameret, 1980).

The vociferous opposition to the scientific curricula confronted the Ministry of Education with an awkward dilemma. The Minister of Education and many of the top officials in his ministry and the Curriculum Center believed that national education according to the academic approach was more suitable than indoctrination because it provides answers to all the existential questions that preoccupy the young generation in a time of violent and unresolved conflict. Nevertheless, the Minister of Education hastened to reassure the Knesset that he was committed "to achieve a coalition with all Israeli children but also to form a coalition with all sectors of Israeli society, and in the political sphere, with both the ruling parties and the opposition parties." He also stressed that "I am not in favor of neutrality when it comes to the basic values of our national consensus" (Yadlin, 1974, p. 2836).

This reaction clearly illustrates the limitations that prevented the Ministry from carrying out a comprehensive reform in a society fraught with social, cultural and ideological conflicts. Moreover, national education was not imparted only through the formal curricula. In fact, most of it, as previously, was still imparted through a system based on ceremonies, festivals, memorial days, social activities, and texts that complemented formal education (Ben Amos & Beit El, 1999; Dror, forthcoming). The structure-of-discipline approach was also not compatible with the aim of reducing the gaps between weak students and high achievers. The new curricula and their accompanying material were far more sophisticated than the previous ones. Teachers and principals believed they were particularly suitable for the better students, but would not be appropriate for weak students (Lewy, 1979; Wolf, 1992).

From other standpoints as well, the reform was disappointing. Studies on the implementation of the new curricula forced their advocates to view them in a more realistic light. Although some of the most important innovations were rejected by teachers and students, many innovations were adopted. For example, the new biology curriculum was successful in making the experiment and the class discussion a part of teaching already in the middle school (Sabar, 1988). The same is true of the use of historical sources (Adar & Fox, 1977). The new curricula also led to a revolution in the form of textbooks, which reflected the epistemological and didactic changes of the scientific curricula. The new books were much more attractive—their pages were richer in various types of texts, in visual material, charts, maps, and a range of activities and assignments for the student. In addition, they were written in a more factual style, free of high-flown language.

However, in general, it still turned out that the new curricula were not successful in instilling students with high scientific and independent critical thinking, neither in history nor in the sciences (Adar & Fox, 1977; Sabar, 1988).

Nevertheless, studies proved that the new curricula could not be evaluated solely on the basis of the teachers' fidelity to the developers' intentions, and that other unplanned advantages that teachers gain when teaching the curricula had to be taken into account as well (Sabar, 1988). Gradually all those involved began to realize that the quality of operation is a key factor in achieving the curriculum's aims, and that the school must participate in defining these aims so that the curriculum will meet its needs (Sabar, 1988). Along with this realization, mixed approaches were developed involving the Center and the periphery, and these laid the groundwork for the transition to the third generation of curricula in Israel (Eden, 1986).

THE THIRD GENERATION OF CURRICULA

From the 1980s, the Curriculum Center in the Ministry of Education gradually lost its monopoly and the way for a new generation of curricula was paved. An eclectic approach to planning, new concepts about knowledge and the form of its representation, the decentralization of sites of development, and changes in the identity of the developers—these were the characteristics of the new curricula. Along with these innovations, there is also a large measure of continuity of key curricula that still represents the scientific approach.

The reasons for these changes and the erosion of the Ministry's monopoly lie in a series of processes that are changing the face of Israeli society and its culture, including its educational system. The following sections describe four such processes and their influence on changing the educational policy. An expansion will be placed on the third-generation curricula, with a concluding forecast about the issues to be grappled with in the future.

Processes Changing the Face of Israeli Society and Its Culture

Ideological Polarization.   Since the 1970s, Israeli society has been marked by a process of political and ideological polarization. Whereas the secular public is largely turning *left* and adopting liberal, democratic, and hedonist values, the religious public is largely turning right toward nationalistic, collectivistic values and toward religious conservatism with a focus on the settlement of the Land of Israel (Harrison, 1994).

The Revolution of Minorities and the Failure of the Melting Pot.   Present-day Israel continues to be an immigrant society because of the continuous flow of immigrants from CIS, thus the society has a multiplicity of cultures and a large Palestinian Arab minority, along with national minorities and, taken together, constitute close to half of the population. Each of these groups maintains a more or less separate cultural system, with a separate marriage market, population concentrations, and singular lifestyles (Kimmerling, 1998). The ethnic revival has also had an impact on the Oriental Jews of Israel. Members of the middle class and intellectuals who were well integrated in the political and cultural establishment take part in this revival along with Orientals from the periphery that belong to an ultra-orthodox Oriental party. It is no wonder then that even the staunchest advocates of the melting pot now admit that it has failed (Lissak, 1999). The significance of these moods is that the population holding to the values of the secular Zionism that molded the state's institutions has shrunk. Nonetheless, these values and the Hebrew culture that expresses them continue to dominate the government, army, economy, and culture. However, under the influence of the minorities' growing strength, the state has abandoned the melting pot ideology and has adopted an approach of cultural pluralism (Mautner & Sagi, 1998; Yonah, 1999).

Cultural Pluralism and Postmodernism.   The ideas of cultural pluralism are now feeding a lively debate in Israel. In this framework, criticism is being voiced against Zionism for suppressing non-European cultures: that of the Arab minority, Oriental Jews, and the ultra-orthodox. Liberal Zionists assume today that, as a liberal democracy, the state of Israel should protect the right of each individual to his or her own particular culture whatever that implies for the national character of the state (Margalit & Halbertal, 1998).

On the face of it, cultural pluralism denies the validity of any attempt to grade cultures according to external criterion or the existence of universal and objective criteria for such grading. This view creates a meeting point between multiculturalism and postmodernism (Hassan, 1993). In present-day Israel, as in the West, postmodern ideas are resounding in culture and art as well as in the academic community. Postmodernism questions the positivistic legitimation of science as a rationalist, unbiased activity striving for the truth (Lyotard, 1979). Rationalism and the scientific method are, in the views of postmodernist critics, a sort of social or linguistic game dependent on specific (Western) historical, social, and cultural contexts, and, as such, are arbitrary. This criticism challenges the traditional division into disciplines that developed in university research. With the collapse of science's metanarrative, the distinction between *soft* and *hard* knowledge, between popular and scientific knowledge, as well as popular and high art is no longer justified (Gurewitz, 1997).

Postmodern art argues in favor of the pleasurable and entertaining surface and also blurs the distinction between the commercial and the artistic. There are some who define the project of enlightenment and science in terms of oppression, control, or cultural dispossession in the service of the particularistic interests of the West, of the patriarchal order, or, alternatively, of capitalism or all of these (Best-Keller, 1991; Hassan, 1993).

This criticism also has clear implications for education and curricula. Although only few persons in Israel systematically advance postmodern ideas, their influence is definitely felt in the pedagogical and curricular discourse (Aviram, 1999; Gur-Zeev, 1996). They challenge the legitimacy of the traditional curriculum based on a division into disciplines and subjects differentiated according to a hierarchic grading of their knowledge, as well as challenging the views that the school and curriculum are imparting values and canonical cultural texts to the coming generation.

Israel's Entry into the Postindustrial Economy.   Alongside the forces operating to break "the Western scientific and cultural hegemony," there are other forces in Israel stemming from economic and technological needs. As the Israeli economy joined processes of globalization, the stature of technological and managerial knowledge was enhanced. The spread of computerized communication raises the importance of new ways of learning and of displaying and storing knowledge.

Changes in Curriculum Planning in the Third Generation: Autonomy and Variability

These processes have an impact on the present agenda of curricula and affect the forecasted opportunities for the future. In the following section, we relate to what exists at present while projecting ahead to future curricula for the first generation of the coming millennium.

The polarization in ideology and values between sectors (e.g., between the religious population and the nonreligious majority) and the strengthened status of national and cultural minorities have demonstrated the shortcomings of the politics of a uniform and generally accepted curriculum.

The Ministry of Education is attempting to adapt to the new reality and to the expanding cultural disparities. From the 1980s, this adaptation has placed on the Ministry's agenda the politics of educational autonomy, on the one hand, and cultural pluralism, on the other (Director General's Circular, 1983, 1984, 1985). Probably what is defined as the *politics of difference* will dictate the Ministry's policy in the next generation.

The idea of autonomy embraces various models—from increased cooperation between the center and the periphery to turning the periphery into the center and creating a polyarchic system. The need for autonomous curriculum planning in each school was one of the lessons learned from the Ministry's unfulfilled expectations of the reform in curricula it had introduced in the 1970s. One of the conclusions drawn from the studies on the implementation of these curricula was that their success depends first and foremost on the professional empowerment of teachers. However, that can be done only by expanding their curricular authority (Sabar, 1998).

A new theory of curriculum planning further validated the demand to move the emphasis in the development of new curricula by the teachers. According to this theory, the teacher's pedagogical content knowledge is the best guarantee of the curriculum's success (Schwab, 1983; Shulman, 1987). This personal knowledge is made up of a combination of propositional knowledge, of "know what" in the particular disciplines, and practical didactic "know-how" (Ben Peretz, 1991). As a result of this approach, the structure of discipline idea, which assigned the leading role in development to academic institutions, was no longer in favor. The new approach to curricula is also more holistic and, as part of its definition, takes teaching into account Hence, it becomes obvious that the demand to avoid any discrepancy between intentions and performance is not only unrealistic, but also undesirable. However, the mutual adaptation approach (Fullan & Pomfret, 1977) speaks in terms of a curriculum that is broken down according to the views and needs of all those involved in its development. Under the influence of these ideas, the Ministry and universities went out to the field and tried to develop curricula through cooperation with teachers and schools, thus paving the way for expansion of the teachers' curricular autonomy (Sabar, 1987; Sabar & Silberstein, 1998).

Various Aspects of Autonomy

The scope of curricular autonomy can be measured according to a variety of models and criteria: One balanced model tests autonomy on the basis of the degree of school participation in curriculum planning, even if it is not planned from beginning to end by the local staff. In this approach, autonomy is tested according to the contribution added by the school and its teaching staff to the curricula planned by the Center (Emmanuel, 1994; Reshef, 1990). This contribution can be manifested in curricula planned by the local staff or curricula created through cooperation between the local staff and outside parties connected to the Center and the academia.

Another, more radical model stems from the concept of *personal autonomy* and attempts to apply it to school curriculum planning. In this case, the test of autonomy is whether the curriculum is authentic—namely, whether its goals and contents grow out of teacher and pupil needs, whether it provides freedom of choice for teachers, and whether teachers' choices are rational (i.e., whether they choose the most appropriate means to achieve their goals; Kopelman, 1997).

According to the latter model, most curricula in today's educational system are only partially autonomous: Even if they meet the second and third criteria, only infrequently do they meet the first. This is not surprising, considering the fact that even when teachers in Israel develop materials, these are usually connected to national curricula planned by central organizations or with the assistance of the Education Ministry or university institutes. Over the last two decades in Israel, there have been plentiful examples of the success of autonomy according to the balanced model (Sabar & Silberstein, 1998). The success of this model derives, among other things, from the fact that the Ministry of Education initiated and adopted it. It also encourages schools to act accordingly (Green & Danilov, 1994; Inbar, 1990; Sabar, 1990).

In this system, teachers' curricular autonomy is expressed in several ways: the right to choose between alternatives proposed by the state curriculum; the possibility of planning their own curriculum linked to topics and goals set by the state; and the teachers' right to develop their own topics and materials on condition that these constitute an additional concentric element in the compulsory national curriculum. The Ministry also offers to help teachers and teaching staffs in schools (Ben Eliyahu, 1989). This policy, despite its limitations, indicates how far the Education Ministry has come from being a system whose major function was to impose authority to a system responsive to the needs of its schools. The next obvious step is for the Ministry of Education to transfer cultural and material resources directly to the schools to enable its teaching staff to plan special curricula and expand their authority to plan and assess authentic curricula. For this to be implemented, teachers must assess their own professional knowledge, identify their professional needs, and develop personal and school credos. This cannot take place without an egalitarian dialogue between school staffs and outside consultants from central, professional organizations.

CURRICULAR AUTONOMY AND VARIABILITY

Up to the third-generation curricula, the differences between school curricula were determined primarily on the basis of the schools' affiliation with an ideological-educational sector and the educational level (e.g., religious, elementary; Harrison, 1994). In most subjects, curriculum differences existed among orthodox schools, Arab state schools, state schools, and state religious schools, and among the curricula of elementary schools, middle schools, and high schools. Today, too, educational level and sector continue to be the major factors in determining the differences between curricula and between levels of autonomy. However, in the last generation, some schools, particularly on the elementary level, have developed enrichment curricula in the sciences, the arts, environmental studies, and others. Most of these schools operate in upper middle-class communities and towns (Dror & Leiberman, 1997).

At the same time, schools emerged that differed from others—not in terms of the formal level of curricula, but rather in terms of teacher and pupil perception: child-oriented, egalitarian, participatory schools in contrast to elitist, competitive ones, open schools as opposed to regular ones. This variability is also found in great part in the state sector at the elementary school level. In contrast, there is little variability of this type in the state religious sector, whereas in the Arab sector there is none at all within the state educational framework (Harrison, 1994). Nonetheless, approximately half of the Arab urban population sends its children to private Catholic schools, where they study in most traditional ways and according to separate curricula (Ichilov & Mazawi, 1997).

In summary, the higher the level of education, the more limited teacher and school autonomy are; curricular variability decreases, and the Ministry retains a larger degree of authority, both organizational and moral because of the threat of the matriculations. Most probably, the struggle for a change in the structure of matriculation examinations and greater flexibility will also gradually bring about a change in the degree and nature of variability in high school education, and school autonomy will expand at that level, too. However, the fact that today variability is enjoyed primarily by upper class populations is a cause for concern and calls for a reexamination of its ramifications. This fact does not undermine the fact that excellent schools exist in the periphery like in Beit Shean, Shderot, and so on.

MULTICULTURALISM, POSTMODERNISM, AND VARIABILITY IN THE THIRD-GENERATION CURRICULA

Despite their latent dangers, postmodernist and multicultural values have a beneficial effect on the democratization of the educational system, as well as on the curriculum planning process. Under the influence of democratization, the social composition of curriculum developers expands and becomes more varied. Today, more teachers are involved in curricular planning than in the past, as are more private and public institutions that are not subject to the authority of the Ministry. In addition, the new curricula give greater expression than in the past to contents and values of minority cultures and heritages. Not that this does not lead to vigorous public conflicts and debates. The question that once again arises is how to present a more balanced picture of Israel that will take into account the criticism of Zionism that exists today without relinquishing its national modern and democratic ideals.

In the struggle for recognition, the proponents of cultural pluralism demand that full and direct expression be given to minority cultures from the internal point of view of their members (Taylor, 1994). This is not a completely new idea because, in the past, scientific curricula recognized the need to introduce such a perspective. They did so, however, in connection with the values and ideas of the dominant culture, which has enjoyed many privileges. In the 1970, representatives of Oriental Jews demanded that they be integrated into the historical narrative of Zionism. This demand resulted in the expansion of research on Oriental Jews, the establishment of institutions for the study of Oriental Jewry and the nurturing of their heritage, as well as the founding of suitable periodicals. At the same time, changes also occurred in the history curricula in the schools. These changes took place under the rubric of the dominant Zionist ideology, and they underscored the similarity between the history of Oriental and European Jewry (Ettinger, 1981). In contrast, the cultural pluralism ethnic approach, which emphasizes the special features of Oriental Jewry under the colonial regime, has not yet gained full recognition, neither in the schools nor in historiography (Ben Amos, 1995; Mathias, 2002; Shetreet, 1997).

Moreover, on the level of formal and perceived curricula, there are substantial differences between state and state religious schools; in state schools, the culture and history of Oriental Jewry is usually a marginal topic, whereas in state religious schools, where students from Oriental Jewry are the majority, these topics are compulsory subjects (Ministry of Education and Culture, 1979; National Supervisor's Circular, 1998).

Another example is the struggle of the Arab population in Israel for recognition of their national Palestinian identity. Since the 1970s, Education Ministry policy has been revised with regard to the Palestinian identity of the Arab minority in Israel, gradually shifting from disregard to limited recognition (Haj, 1995). The proposed history curriculum for high schools published some years ago indicates how far curricula in the Arab sector have come in the last generation. According to this curriculum, Arab schools teach parallel histories that offer both the Palestinian narrative and the Zionist narrative of the people and the country. These narratives are presented from the internal point of view of Jews and Palestinians alike (Ministry of Education and Culture, 1997).

The Intifada in the late 1980s also forced the schools to confront the moral dilemma of the Israeli occupation of the territories. The political debate that rocked the country found its way into the schools, and the Ministry of Education had difficulty in providing answers to the incisive questions with which teachers and principals were coping. In any case, it was clear that the issue of Palestinian identity and a discussion of ongoing Israeli rule of the Palestinian population in the territories could no longer be avoided (Mathias, 2003). In addition, the history curricula in the Jewish state sector require more critical inspection today than in the past of the Zionist version of the conflict between the two peoples. New textbooks recently published portray the Jewish–Palestinian conflict as a struggle between two national movements, each of which has a legitimate right to exist (Bartal, 1999; Podeh, 1997). The refugee problem now appears as an inseparable part of the story of the war between Arabs and Jews and of the Israeli victory in the 1948 War of Independence. With these changes, the Ministry of Education takes leave of the apologist approach vis-á-vis the refugee problem.

Simultaneously, a new consensus is being formed with regard to the recognition of the Arab minority's civil rights in Israel as one of the decisive tests of the country's democratic character. This recognition is manifest mainly in civics studies, where educational efforts in Israel are concentrated on nurturing universal, democratic values (Director General's Circular, 1985; Ichilov, 1993). A long series of curricula were developed for nurturing democratic ideals and strengthening understanding between Jews and Arabs. Most of these curricula were developed by nongovernmental public institutions, though with Education Ministry funding (Hochman, 1986).

Since the 1990s, civics curricula have adopted cultural pluralistic language. According to the new civics curriculum published in 1994, Israeli Arabs are entitled to "nurture their cultural, religious and national heritage and enjoy as well their civic rights as Israeli citizens" (On Being a Citizen, 1996, p. 33). The structure and contents of the new civics curriculum reflects "the politics of difference" (Walzer, 1996). It has compulsory topics that form its core and is shared by all sectors. These topics deal with democratic government and its values; it also has elective topics adapted to the interests of every one of the sectors in the Israeli educational system. Inherent in this structure is a proposal for the creation of a shared civic identity based on universal values, and at the same time, a recognition of the right of all ethnic and national groups in Israel to their own special cultures (On Being a Citizen, 1996).

THE NEW GENERATION'S INFORMATION POLICY IN THE FACE OF THE CHALLENGE OF THE INFORMATION EXPLOSION AND POSTMODERNISM

The information explosion and specialization, on the one hand, and the influence of postmodernist ideas, on the other, are enhancing the search for new organizational forms and ways to present information in schools, attempting to decrease the gap between what is taught and the enormous growth of knowledge. This problem is particularly severe in light of accepted educational ideology that seeks to enable every pupil to specialize in whatever interests him or her. One solution proposed by the Ministry of Education in the mid-1990s was the concentration of studies according to clusters, each of which represents a language or form of knowledge. This proposal related to five clusters: languages (including mathematics), the humanities and the social sciences, Jewish studies, the sciences, and the arts (Director General's Circular, 1996). The cluster method intended to respond to the need to deal with the growth of information and, simultaneously, make possible personal choice and specialization for pupils (Gordon, 1995; Levin & Nevo, 1996).

In the meantime, this proposal has been removed from the agenda because it was not supported by teachers, whose training is subject-based, nor by the academic community. Additionally, matriculation examinations, which are a condition for acceptance into the university, continue to dictate a structure-of-discipline approach particularly in the high schools.

Postmodernist ideas also have an impact on new curricula, mainly in the humanities and social sciences. Supposedly inferior genres like mystery fiction are being recognized today in literature curricula (Ministry of Education and Culture, 1992). This is also true for the viewing of popular film dramas, which has today replaced the reading of literature. In history, dramatic films based on historical events have become a major source for learning about the past (Angvick & Borries, 1997). Teachers, however, find it difficult to reconcile themselves to the ongoing use of these forms, which they were trained to believe to be inferior. They are also aware that movies have succeeded in arousing interest and pleasure where teaching sources and others have failed. The use of movies is also consistent with the emphasis placed nowadays on personal pleasure as an element of and legitimate goal of the learning process, particularly in the state schools (Harrison, 1994).

The constructivist, individualistic, and social approach to learning has shaken the positivist, objective paradigm of the essence of knowledge and how it is created. The brain is not a camera that photographs what is outside of it. An individual's knowledge, as well as the reality in which he or she lives, is imbued with interpretive elements that result from social construction and interrelationships (Terwell, 1999). There is no justification, therefore, for the assumption that knowledge and the conditions leading to it are always identical. At the same time, there is a growing recognition that formal thinking is nothing more than one type of intelligence among many, and the schools must relate in a just manner to all of them (Gardner, 1993).

The Postindustrial Economy and Information Policy in the Third Generation

In the face of the changes surveyed previously, however, economic needs have given rise to opposing trends. The economy today gives greater preference to scientific, technological knowledge and to knowledge related to the management of complex, supranational organizations, including those that deal with the creation, storage, and distribution of knowledge. The stratification of knowledge in schools, primarily in state schools, reflects the needs of a knowledge economy. Even in elementary education, mainly in state schools, a subject is evaluated according to market needs. That is why mathematics and English are considered more important than other subjects by teachers and pupils alike, as well as by parents (Harrison, 1994). The situation is similar in high schools, too, where pupils from higher socioeconomic classes choose to specialize in math, sciences, and English, whereas those of lower socioeconomic classes focus on the humanities (Ayalon & Yogev, 1995).

CONCLUSION AND FORECAST FOR THE FUTURE

Although autonomy engenders much hope, it is also a cause for more than a few concerns. The question is, in what direction is the Israeli school heading? Will it be an institution of solidarity and social integration that provides equal opportunity for all, including the weaker members of society, or will it perpetuate gaps and express mainly the division and disparity between cultures and social groups? In the past, the school aspired to integration imposed from above. Today, Israeli society is sufficiently varied and strong, so that such imposition will not succeed. In addition, the character of the state's educational policy has changed over the years; instead of defining needs, it responds to needs from below. The next step required by the process is this: On the one hand, the Ministry must provide the schools with the tools and the moral, organizational, cultural, and financial resources it needs to be autonomous; on the other, it must act for social integration and the closing of social gaps. In our view, this will continue to be the principal test of the Israeli school in the future.

In the future, we may also see more autonomy—not only in the elementary schools, but also in the secondary schools and, primarily, in the high schools. Therefore, it will be necessary to shift to at least internal assessment of matriculation examinations, with some regional or multiinstitutional control by universities or colleges. Without such a change, it will be impossible to develop authentic curricula in schools. This is a difficult struggle with more than a few risks because the question is how to ensure that internal examinations are recognized as having the same value as external ones. The key lies in cooperation between schools and institutions of higher education, on the one hand, and between the latter and the Ministry of Education, on the other.

The dilemma of autonomy versus integration calls for a curricular discussion of the core, how it is to be created, and whose knowledge is to be represented in it. Is it sufficient that it should comprise Hebrew, English, and math, which are required for integration into the postindustrial economy? Is it important to include in it knowledge of civic and moral abilities as well (Salomon & Almog, 1994)?

Liberals who espouse the pluralist approach believe that the desired situation is one in which the core is comprised of three concentric elements (Tamir, 1998): one element of the knowledge of values and abilities common to all, a second element of each group's cultural origin, and a third in which members of every culture become acquainted with the cultures of the other groups. It is desirable that every school at every educational level be required to give representation to all three concentric elements. Exposing the learner to all three concentric elements will ensure greater freedom of choice for every individual in each of the different cultures.

However, this is precisely the situation that members of nonliberal groups, such as ultra-orthodox and ethnic minorities, wish to avoid at almost any price. Thus, the desire to build a common core of three concentric elements is not suited to present Israeli reality. The cultural gaps in Israel are large; therefore, in the near future, there may be no choice but to reconcile ourselves to a situation in which the shared concentric element is minimal. This means that we must ensure that pupils are instilled with the abilities that will enable them to participate in the Israeli economy, thereby avoiding the creation of large social gaps. With regard to the development of a concentric element of civics education common to all pupils, at this stage, minority groups, such as the ultra-orthodox, who reject the liberal, democratic moral and political order, will only accept it as the best of a bad choice (Tamir, 1998).

It may be, in the present conflict-ridden reality, that none of the other groups is ready for a serious curriculum comprised of three concentric elements either. However, an effort should at least be made with regard to them on the condition that the Center makes an effort to shift from being a coercive system to a supportive one. In the framework of this change, the Center should change its attitude to the schools, expand their pedagogical authority, and initiate and support a dialogue among the various schools.

Despite what appears to be a reality of division, it should be underscored that the Ministry continues to maintain its dominant status. Even as groups develop their own special heritages, they do so with its consent and under its supervision. Moreover, the Ministry maintains a pendulum policy. At the same time that it encourages variability and autonomy, it attempts to preserve homogeneity through national, comprehensive examinations for all. If we want the educational system to answer most of the educational needs of the population, and also ensure full social and national integration, it is important for diverse arrangements to exist side by side: autonomy along with centralization, a certain degree of homogeneity along with variability, and an expansion of the social basis of that variability. This is also true for the knowledge policy of curricula, the types of knowledge they represent, and teaching methods.

During the first generations, the state school was an institution of solidarity based on particularistic Jewish nationalist values and the Hebrew culture. Today, there are those who claim that it should be expanded and nurtured on the basis of democratic and liberal civic values. Nonetheless, liberalism and the market economy weaken the school's status as an institution of social solidarity. Therefore, the question is, will the school cease to be an institution of solidarity, or will it succeed in creating a new, broader solidarity than that of the past, based on national identity and general civic values?

REFERENCES

Adar, L., & Fox, S. (1977). *Analysis of a history curriculum and its implementation in schools* (Heb.). Jerusalem: The Hebrew University.

Adar, Z. (1956). Critique of the state curriculum (Heb.). *Megamot, 7,* 41–76, 254–264.

Angvick, M., & Borries, V. B. (1997). *Youth and history.* Hamburg, Germany: Korber Stiftung.

Apple W. M. (1982). Curricular form and the logic of technical control—Building the possessive individual. In W. M. Apple (Ed.), *Cultural and economic reproduction in education: Essays on class, ideology and the state* (pp. 247–274). London: Routledge & Kegan Paul.

Apple, W. M. (1990). *Ideology and curriculum.* New York: Routledge.

Aranne, Z. (1969). *Knesset record* (Heb.) vol. 55, 2936.

Avidor M. (1957). *Education in Israel—Jerusalem, Youth and Hechalutz department.* 89–99.

Aviram, R. (1999). *Navigating in a storm: Education in postmodern democracy* (Heb.). Tel-Aviv: Masada.

Ayalon, H., & Yogev, A. (1995). The status of humanistic studies in secondary education in Israel (Heb.). In D. Chen et al. (Eds.), *Education on the verge of the 21st century* (pp. 221–248). Tel-Aviv, Israel Ramot.

Bartal, D. (1999). The Arab–Israeli conflict as uncontrolled, and its reflection in Israeli textbooks. (Heb.) *Megamot, 39*(4), 445–491.

Ben Amos, A., & Beit El, I. (1999). Ceremonies, education and history: Holocaust Day and Memorial Day in Israeli schools (Heb.). In E. Etkes & R. Feldhay (Eds.), *Education and history: Cultural and political contexts* (pp. 457–479). Jerusalem: Zalman Shazar Center.

Ben Amos, A. (1995). Is pluralism impossible? Jews from Europe and Jews from Oriental communities in the history curriculum (Heb.). In D. Chen et al. (Eds.), *Education on the verge of the 21st century* (pp. 267–276). Tel-Aviv, Israel: Tel-Aviv University.

Ben Eliyahu, S. (1989). The second decade of the National Curriculum Center (Heb.). *Halakhah leimeiaseh betikhnun halimudim, 6,* 9–16.

Ben Gurion, D. (1953). *The government's objectives* (Heb.). Jerusalem: The Government Yearbook.

Ben Gurion, D. (1954). The goals of state education (Heb.). *HaiHinuch, 27*(1), 3–8.

Ben Peretz, M. (1991). The structure of discipline as a guiding concept in curriculum planning (Heb.). In M. Silberstein (Ed.), *The structure of discipline and a uniform approach in curriculum planning* (pp. 10–21). Jerusalem: Ministry of Education.

Ben Peretz, M., & Seidman, M. (1986). Three generations in curriculum development in Israel (Heb.). *Yiunim Behinuch, 43/44,* 317–327.

Best, S., & Keller, D. (1991). *Postmodern theory: Critical interrogations.* New York: Guilford.

Bruner, J. (1965). *The education process* (Heb.). Tel-Aviv, Israel: Yachdav.

Dinur, E. Z. (1953). Education for citizenship as a principle and a subject (Heb.). In *Education of the Israeli citizen* (pp. 14–16). Jerusalem: Federation of Secondary Schools.

Dinur, E. Z., & Beer, Y. (1936). Our purpose (Heb.). *Zion, 1,* 1–5.

Director General's Circular. (Heb.). Ministry of Education, Jerusalem: May 1983 - 43/5; September 1983 - 43/9; 1984 - 44/6, 2–4; 44/9.

Director General's Special Circular. (Heb.) Ministry of Education, Jerusalem: V - May 1985; XX - June 1996

Dror, Y. (forthcoming). *The educational system as an agent of Jewish patriotism in the State of Israel: From pioneering Zionism to balanced Israeliness in its relationship to Jewry and other nations* (Heb.) Tel-Aviv, Israel: Tel-Aviv University.

Dror, Y., & Lieberman, Y. (1997). The curriculum in practice: The State of Israel (Heb.). *Halakhah leimeiaseh betikhnun halimudim, 12.*

Eden, S. (1971). The new curricula: Principles and processes (Heb.). In S. Eden (Ed.), *On the new curricula* (pp. 21–69). Tel-Aviv, Israel: Maalot.

Eden, S. (1976). *Aims of education in Israel* (Heb.). Tel-Aviv, Israel: Maalot.

Eden, S. (1980). The new curricula, experiences and lessons learned (Heb.). *Halakhah leimaiaseh betikhnun halimudim, 3,* 8–21.

Eden, S. (1986). The center and the periphery in curriculum planning (Heb.). In S. Eden, R. Aviad, & S. Mozes (Eds.), *Interaction between the center and the periphery in curriculum planning* (pp. 1–25). Jerusalem: Ministry of Education and Culture, Curriculum Division.

Elboim-Dror, R. (1990). *Hebrew education in the Land of Israel, 1914–1920* (Heb.). Jerusalem: Mosad Bialik.

Emmanuel, D., Silberstein, M., & Sabar, N. (1994). How to improve curriculum planning in the school (Heb.). In R. Shapira, R. Green, & Y. Danilov (Eds.), *School autonomy, its application and the lessons learned* (pp. 80–113). Jerusalem: Ministry of Education and Culture.

Ettinger, S. (1981). General introduction. In S. Ettinger (Ed.), *History of the Jews in Islamic countries Part I* (pp. 7–11). Jerusalem: Shazar Center.

Fullan, A., & Pomfret, A. (1977). Research on curriculum and instruction implementation. *Review of Educational Research, 47*(2), 335–397.

Gardner H. (1993). *Multiple intelligences.* New York: Basic Books.

Gellner, E. (1983). *Nations and nationalism.* Oxford, England: Oxford University Press.

Goodsor, F. I. (1997). *The changing curriculum: Studies in social construction.* New York: Peter Lang.

Gordon, D. (1995). *All together and each one on his own, a proposal for discussion* (Heb.). Jerusalem: Ministry of Education.

Green, R., & Danilov, Y. (1994). Autonomy in education, from experiment to application (Heb.). In R. Shapira, R. Green, & Y. Danilov (Eds.), *School autonomy, its application and the lessons learned* (pp. 15–33). Jerusalem: Ministry of Education.

Gur-Zeev, I. (Ed.). (1996). *Education in the era of the postmodern discourse* (Heb.). Jerusalem: Magnes.

Gurewitz, D. (1997). *Postmodernism, culture and literature at the end of the 20th century* (Heb.). Tel-Aviv, Israel: Dvir.

Haj, M. (1995). *Education, empowerment and control: The case of the Arabs in Israel.* Albany: State University of New York Press.

Harrison, J. (1994). *Unity and diversity of culture and curriculum in the Israeli education system.* Jerusalem: Institute for the Study of Educational Systems.

Hassan, I. T. (1993). Toward a concept of postmodernism. In T. Docherty (Ed.), *Postmodernism: A reader* (pp. 146–156). New York: Columbia University Press.

Hed Hachinukh (1956, 28 September). The state curriculum from the end of its first year (editorial), 32–33, 4.

Hochman, R. (1986). *Education for Arab–Jewish co-existence: A manual* (Heb.). Jerusalem: Van Leer.

Ichilov, O. (1993). *Civics education in a formative society, Palestine-the Land of Israel-the State of Israel* (Heb.). Tel- Aviv, Israel: Sifriat HaPoalim.

Ichilov, O., & Mazawi, A.. (1997). Choice and its social implications in the Arab community (Heb.). *Megamot, 38*(3), 421–432.

Inbar, D. (1990). Is autonomy possible in a centralized education system? (Heb.). In I. Friedman (Ed.), *Autonomy in education* (pp. 50–75). Jerusalem: Szold Institute.

Kimmerling, B. (1998). The new Israelis: A multiplicity of cultures without multiculturalism (Heb.). *Alpaim, 16,* 226–308.

Kliebard, H. (1992). *Forging the American curriculum: Essays in curriculum history and theory.* London: Routledge.

Kopelman, H. (1997). *Teachers' autonomy in implementing the Ministry of Education curriculum developed in the nineties* (Heb.). Unpublished master's thesis, Ben-Gurion University.

Levin, T., & Nevo, B. (1996). *The future elementary school as a reality of life: Towards a new concept of curriculum as a dynamic learning space; a working paper* (Heb.). Jerusalem: Ministry of Education and Culture.

Lewy, A. (1979). *New curricula in the Israeli educational system, their distribution and value* (Heb.). Jerusalem: Ministry of Education and Culture.

Lewy, A. (1994). *Eighteen years of an eighth-grade survey test: Its history and influence, and the factors that led to its cancellation* (Heb.). Generation to generation VII, Collections on the study and documentation of the history of Jewish education in Israel and in the Diaspora, Tel-Aviv, Israel.

Lissak, M. (1999). *The mass immigration of the fifties and the failure of the melting pot* (Heb.). Jerusalem: Mossad Bialik.

Lyotard, F. (1979). *La condition postmoderne.* Paris: Minuit.

Maarii, S. K. (1975). *Comparative review of curricula in schools in the Arab sector* (Heb.). Jerusalem: Ministry of Education and Culture.

Margalit, A., & Halbertal, M. (1998). Liberalism and the right to culture (Heb.). In M. Mautner, A. Sagi, & R. Shamir (Eds.), *Multiculturalism in a democratic Jewish state* (pp. 93–105). Tel-Aviv, Israel.

Mathias, Y. (in press). The thorny way to recognition: Palestinians and Arabs in the Israeli curriculum. In F. Pingel (Ed.), *Contested past, disputed present: Curricula and teaching in Israel and Palestine,* vol. 110/2. Braunschweig, Germany.

Mathias, Y. (2002a). Nationalizing education: The emergence of state history curriculum. (Heb.). In A. Ben Amos (Ed.), *History, identity and memory: Images of the past in Israeli education* (pp. 15–46). Tel-Aviv, Israel: Tel-Aviv University.

Mathias Y. (2002b). The crisis of the national paradigm: History in Israeli curriculum during the 1990s. *International Textbook Research, 24*(4), 427–443.

Mautner, M., & Sagi, A. (1998). Reflections on multiculturalism in Israel (Heb.). In M. Mautner, A. Sagi, & R. Shamir (Eds.), *Multiculturalism in a democratic Jewish state* (pp. 67–76). Tel-Aviv, Israel: Tel-Aviv University.

Ministry of Education and Culture. (1954). *Curriculum for the state and state religious elementary school* (Heb.). Jerusalem.

Ministry of Education and Culture. (1959). *Deepening Jewish consciousness.* (Heb.). Jerusalem.

Ministry of Education and Culture. (1979). *History curriculum for the state religious secondary school* (Heb.). Jerusalem.

Ministry of Education and Culture. (1992). *Literature curriculum for the middle school* (Heb.). Jerusalem.

Ministry of Education and Culture. (1997). *History curriculum for the Arab state secondary schools* (Heb.). Jerusalem.

National Supervisor's Circular. (1998). *History for the upper level of the state secondary school.* Jerusalem: Ministry of Education and Culture.

On being a citizen. (1996). *Civics education for all in Israel.* Jerusalem: Ministry of Education and Culture.

Passeron, J., & Bourdieu, P. (1979). *Reproduction in education, society and culture.* Beverly Hills, CA: Sage.

Pedatzur, R. (1996). *The triumph of confusion: The policy of Eshkol's government in the territories after the Six-Day War* (Heb.). Tel-Aviv, Israel: Zmora Bitan.

Podeh, E. (1997). *Kudos for the cover-up and disapproval of confusion: The Arab–Israeli conflict reflected in history and civics textbooks in Hebrew (1953–1995)* (Heb.). Jerusalem: The Harry Truman Peace Center, the Hebrew University.

Reshef, S. (1987). Ben Gurion and state education (Heb.). *Katedra, 43,* 91–114.

Reshef, S. (1990). School autonomy: A new era in state education (Heb.). In I. Friedman (Ed.), *Autonomy in education* (pp. 13–31). Jerusalem: Szold Institute.

Reshef, S., & Dror, Y. (1999). *Hebrew education in the national home 1919–1948* (Heb.). Jerusalem: Mossad Bialik.

Ringer, F. (1979). *Education and society in modern Europe.* Bloomington: Indiana University Press.

Sabar, N. (1987). School-based curriculum: The pendulum swings. In N. Sabar, J. Reddick, & W. Reid (Eds), *Partnership and autonomy in SBCD* (pp. 1–4). Sheffield, England: University of Sheffield.

Sabar, N. (1988). *The metamorphosis of a curriculum* (Heb.). Tel- Aviv, Israel: Yachdav.

Sabar, N. (1990). School curriculum planning: Meaning of the concept, opportunities and dangers of its applications (Heb.). In I. Friedman (Ed.), *Autonomy in education* (pp. 133–144). Jerusalem: Szold Institute.

Sabar, N. (1998). Curriculum development at school level. In T. Husen & N. Postlewaite (Eds.), *The international encyclopedia of education* (pp. 1267–1272). Oxford, England: Pergamon.

Sabar, N., & Silberstein, M. (1998). From uniformity to variability: The development of curricula in Israel (Heb.). In E. Peled (Ed.), *The fiftieth anniversary of the Israeli educational system* (Vol. 1, pp. 193–204). Jerusalem: Ministry of Education.

Salomon, G., & Almog, S. (1994). The desirable image of the school graduate (Heb.) In Y. Danilov (Ed.) *Educational policy: Position papers 1994* (pp. 343–368). Jerusalem: Ministry of Education and Culture.

Scheffler, I. (1964). Philosophical models of teaching. *Harvard Educational Review, 32,* 131–143.

Schwab, J. J. (1983). The practical4: Something for curriculum professors to do. *Curriculum Inquiry, 13*(3) 239–265.

Seixas, F. (1999). Beyond content and pedagogy: In search of a way to talk about history education. *Journal of Curriculum Studies, 31*(3), 317–337.

Shavit, Y. (1999). The status of culture in the process of creating a national state in Eretz-Israel, basic positions and concepts (Heb.). In Z. Shavit (Ed.), *Building a Hebrew culture in Eretz-Israel* (pp. 9–30). Jerusalem: Israeli Academy of Sciences.

Shetreet, S. (1997). The Ashkenazi Zionist eradicator (Heb.). *Maznayim, 71,* 55–58.

Shmida, M., & Bar-Lev, M. (Eds). (1971). *Educational reform in Israel and the nations and its implementation through the comprehensive school: A collection of sources* (Heb.). Ramut Gan, Israel: Bar-Ilan University.

Shremer, O. (1979). Towards education to cope with history: A curricular discussion (Heb.). *Hachinukh, 42,* 64–72.

Shulman, S. L. (1987). Knowledge and teaching: Foundations of a new reform. *Harvard Educational Review, 57*(1), 1–22.

Silberstein, M. (1984). The role of the teacher in curriculum planning in Israel (Heb.). *Iyunim Bechinukh,* 131–151.

Tamir, Y. (1998). Two concepts of multiculturalism (Heb.). In M. Mautner, A. Sagi, & R. Shamir (Eds.), *Multiculturalism in a democratic Jewish state* (pp. 79–92). Tel-Aviv, Israel: Tel- Aviv University.

Taylor, C (1994). The politics of recognition. In A. Gutmann (Ed.), *Multiculturalism: Examining the politics of recognition* (pp. 25–73). Princeton, NJ: Princeton University Press.

Terwell, . (1999). Constructivism and its implication for curriculum theory and practice. *Journal of Curriculum Studies, 31*(2), 195–199.

Tyler, R. W. (1949). *Basic principles of curriculum and instruction.* Chicago: The University of Chicago Press.

Walzer, M. (1996). The politics of difference (Heb.). In M. Lissak & B. Kney-Paz (Eds.), *Israel on the verge of the year 2000* (pp. 28–38). Jerusalem: Magnes.

Wolf, Y. (1992). *The place of evaluation in preparing a new history curriculum* (Heb.), Jerusalem: Ministry of Education, 88.

Yadlin, A. (1971). The shift in curriculum planning (Heb.). In S. Eden (Ed.), *On the new curricula* (pp. 9–20). Tel-Aviv, Israel: Knesset Publication.

Yadlin, A. (1974). *Knesset Record, 71,* 2836–2837.

Yaoz, H., & Iram, Y. (1987). Changes in the literature curriculum—a comparative study (Heb.). *Iyunim Bechinukh, 46/47,* 157–170.

Yonah, Y. (1999). The third arrangement (Heb.). *Panim,* 5, 3–7.

Zameret, Z. (1980). A special-purpose historical approach (Heb.). *Petachim,* 47–48.

Ziv, M. (1955). *With the curriculum* (Heb.). *Proposed curriculum for the secondary school.* Jerusalem: Ministry of Education and Culture.

CHAPTER 20

Curriculum Reform in Italy in a European Perspective

M. Vicentini
Università La Spienza, Italy

One may define a *curriculum of study* as everything (content knowledge, skills, abilities, methodologies) planned to bring students from an initial state of competence (again in terms of content knowledge, skills, abilities, methodologies) to a final state. Therefore, many different components contribute to innovations in a curriculum: subject-related components for the definition of contents of a discipline or some interdisciplinary theme; method-related components for the definition of skills and abilities that characterize the disciplinary field; experimental skills for any experimental discipline; as well as social communication components and general skills. Moreover, any curriculum must take into account the organization of course of study (duration and disciplines to be included) and the definition of the teaching methodologies for efficient communication to students.

In brief, curriculum development may concern: (a) the introduction of new contents, (b) a reorganization of contents, (c) changes in teaching methodology, and (d) the architecture of the course of study. A schematic summary of the curriculum components in an experimental science (Black et al., 1997; Tobias, 1997) is shown in Table 20.1.

The context of a curriculum reform may range from a single school in a single region of a single state (at an experimental level) to a state new curriculum definition to a cooperation among different states.

Over the last 40 years, Italy has witnessed changes in the Lower Secondary School Curriculum and in the Primary School Curriculum dictated by national political decision (following research and experimental trials in the school), and the development of a curriculum for teacher training. We are now involved in studying changes in University Studies in a European perspective and in rethinking the architecture of preuniversity schooling.

In fact, political changes have been taking place in Europe since World War II: Europe, a set of states with different histories, cultures, and languages, is aiming at becoming a union. Reaching this aim does not seem to pose particular difficulties monetarily (we have a common currency, the Euro, in 2001) or in adopting of a common work language (English), but when culture (and therefore the school systems) is considered, debates arise. In fact, each State of the European Union is proud of its culture. Although

TABLE 20.1
Curriculum Components

Subject-Related Components	Method-Related Components	Social Communication Components
Knowing facts, laws, terms, definitions Understanding phenomena, arguments, explanations Recognizing relations, patterns, structures Judging hypotheses, arguments, statements	Looking up references, taking notes Organizing and planning work Visualizing tables, graphs Structuring, ordering material Writing reports and protocols	Listening Using arguments Questioning Discussing Cooperating, integrating Presenting
Experimental Skills	*Skills Component*	*General Skills*
Planning an experiment Handling of apparata Taking measurements Collecting data Analysing and interpreting data		Reading nonscientific reports (including newspapers) Researching library sources and archives Simulating multidimensional systems Oral communication, presentation skills Written communications of arguments and summary of arguments (not just findings) Analysis of argument: Not just what is the right answer? But why do we (or they) disagree? Communicating with and understanding nonspecialists Team work, budgets and budget making, management

willing to recognize some drawbacks in its educational system, it is also prone to see more drawbacks in the systems of the other states.

In this chapter I present some aspects of the debate at the European level concerning the university system and the correlated debate at the Italian national level.

In particular, due to my specific expertise, I exemplify the debates from the point of view of physics while glancing at other disciplinary fields. I then illustrate the factors of resistance to change of the university staff members. I conclude with some consideration about curriculum reforms at other school levels: the preuniversity school system and teacher training courses.

THE EUROPEAN DEBATE OVER THE "HARMONIZATION" OF UNIVERSITY COURSES OF STUDY

Many countries in Europe may reasonably claim that they have the oldest universities in the world and also some prestigious ones for the preparation of the elite class. In the second half of the century, however, with increased welfare and democracy, all countries have seen an increase in the population of university students, and yet this increase has not generally been followed by changes in the organization of studies and teaching methodology.

The principal aim of the university remained the preparation of the elite class (i.e., in mathematics and the experimental sciences, the preparation of researchers in pure math or sciences). Of course, the increasing number of students also implied an increased number of good or very good students (competitive at an international level on research grounds), but the university staff failed to observe problems with the average student. Each country, then, did not program changes in the traditional organization of the studies.

Problems became apparent both internally in each country (i.e., high number of dropouts, longer actual duration than legal specified) and externally in comparison with countries. In fact, when the European community started to organize exchange programs (Erasmus and Socrates) of study, it became imperative to compare the different organizations.

Many countries then started to reflect on their organization, often, however, in the belief that more changes were needed in other countries. An example is the document by the French Minister Attali (1999) and the discussions in Italy presented in a later section. An example of the difference among the countries is the physics course with varying duration (4 or 5 years), in some countries with an intermediate degree, in some countries with entrance examinations (Ferdinande & Petit, 1998). In physics and other natural sciences, due to the existence of a strong research community, there were minor differences in content organization (however, more math courses were required in France and Italy in contrast to the United Kingdom), which paid attention to the knowledge needed for research. The differences among the human sciences, due to the importance for these of the cultural components specific to each country, were larger.

While debates were taking place in each country with regards to specific disciplinary fields, the European Community, after some evaluation of the Erasmus exchange programs and the organization of European meetings on specific disciplines or fields (Physics 1995 Gand Belgium, Teacher training Osnabruck Germany 1995), opened the way to some thematic Networks for an accurate comparison across Europe (EUPEN for Physics).

While university staff members were involved in thinking about ways to improve university education at a national level and in a European comparison in Thematic Networks, political steps were taken to establish a European educational system that, while preserving national cultural identities, could favor the development of a European system in the spirit of an harmonization of the existing systems. Two meetings (Sorbonne 1998, Bologna 1999) were then organized, with the participation of the Ministries of Education and University, to define the architecture of such a system of tertiary education (Haug, 1999; Modica, 1999).

The two declarations prepared in the meetings were the subject of analysis and debate in each single state of the union. The main points of the declarations were as follows:

> We are heading for a period of major change in education and working conditions, to a diversification of courses of professional careers, with education and training throughout life becoming a clear obligation. We owe our students, and our society at large a higher education system in which they are given the best opportunities to seek and find their own area of excellence.

> An open European area for higher learning carries a wealth of positive perspectives, of course respecting our diversities, but requires on the other hand continuous efforts

to remove barriers and to develop a framework for teaching and learning, which would enhance mobility and an ever closer co-operation.

The international recognition and attractive potential of our systems are directly related to their external and internal readabilities. A system, in which two main cycles, undergraduate and graduate, should be recognized for international comparison and equivalence, seems to emerge." (Sorbonne Declaration, 1998, Ministers of France, Germany, Italy, the United Kingdom)

While affirming our support to the general principles laid down in the Sorbonne Declaration, we engage in co-ordinating our policies to reach in the short term, and in any case within the first decade of the new millennium, the following objectives, which we consider to be of primary relevance in order to establish the European area of higher education and to promote the European system of higher education world-wide:

> Adoption of a system of easily readable and comparable degrees, ... Adoption of a system essentially based on two main cycles, undergraduate and postgraduate. Access to the second cycle shall require successful completion of first cycle studies, lasting a minimum of three years. The degree awarded after the first cycle shall also be relevant to the European labor market as an appropriate level of qualification. The second cycle should lead to the master and/or doctorate degree as in many European countries.

Establishment of a system of credits system as a proper means of promoting the most widespread student mobility. ... (Bologna Declaration, 1999, Ministers of Education of 29 European Countries)

It is worth noting that, as the declarations were formulated in the different languages of Europe, some semantic problems appeared. An interesting one concerns the meaning of *harmonization*. In all Latin countries, the semantic root of the word *harmony* suggested the analogy of an orchestra of musical instruments: Each instrument plays a theme of its own in an integrated supertheme. Therefore, in these countries, there was no fear of losing cultural identity while trying to harmonize with other cultures. In some Anglo-Saxon countries, however, *harmonization* was interpreted more rigidly and resistances appeared.

Because the European declarations limit themselves to giving guidelines for the decision of the single states, more debates were taking place at the national levels than at the union level. An example of European confrontation for one disciplinary field is available for physics in the inquiry of the European Network (Ferdinande & Petit, 1998, 1999). The inquiry was conducted by providing to the participating members of the Network a questionnaire on the state of the organization of the course of study concerning content knowledge, teaching methodologies, and innovations. I do not report the detailed results here, but focus only the answers to the questions related to educational innovation.

The inquiry showed that in many countries the study of a global reorganization of the university physics curriculum was underway. The answers of some European countries to the question of "why innovation is needed" are reported in Table 20.2. In some cases, the motivations are connected to local characteristics of political and social changes (Poland, Latvia). Other needed innovations are generally attributed to common problems in Europe: The first is the acknowledgment that the initial preparation of students entering university seems to have declined in recent years, the second is the decline in the number of students who choose physics, and the third is the duration of the total course of study, which is, for the average student, longer than the legal duration.

TABLE 20.2

Some Reasons for Innovation

Country	Reason
Belgium	"The major need is to improve learning-effort, to stimulate "life long learning—and to present physics as a science in which knowledge is experienced and constructed and that social interaction plays a significant part in the process."
Germany	"To have separate courses for experimental and theoretical physics seems an unnecessary waste of effort." For the "teachers: we need a wide but not necessarily very detailed knowledge."
Greece	"The students are not interested to participate in the course the way it is done. More and more we realize that, if we teach at a higher level what they have already heard at school (Mechanics, Electricity, Oscillations) they are not interested, they don't assimilate the different aspects, and finally they keep in their mind their previous knowledge only."
Latvia	"These innovations are introduced to adjust education obtained at the department of Physics to the needs of Latvia and its science, reborn industry and small businesses on one hand and to make Physics department more attractive for secondary school graduates on the other hand."
Netherlands	"The physics education at this moment is focused too much on the vocational aims of a physics researchers, but many students choose another professions. So the actual education may be too narrow (more skills needed) and too selective. The incoming students (from VWO (= high school)) have changed (and will change even more): they have been taught less (formal) physics and mathematics and a more active and independent way of learning is emphasized. So the university has to adapt itself to these changes."
Poland	"Currently in Poland the Ministry of National Education is working on elaboration of a complex education system reform. It is connected with: i) great transformation of our political, governmental system and administrative structure, ii) challenges resulted from integration of Poland with EU), iii) a new model of Polish education on the turn of ages. Educational system should be adjusted to the changes of economical needs and job market. As a result it is anticipated to get an increasing number of graduates from universities in general, namely also physicists. In educational system and program particular attention will be paid on a suitable balance among transmission of knowledge, formation of competences (know-how, skills) and development of student personality."
Portugal	"One may support and construct a web site developed at the European level, with input and interactivity from different countries and with a compilation of the several initiatives and innovations sprung at each country. It will serve as a reservoir of teaching products (programs, problems, simulation codes, lab experiments, exams), as well as a site where questions from students all over Europe can concentrate to be answered by professionals from several universities. These questions and respective replies will form a data basis which will enlarge the horizon scope of students in each country as well as constitute a rich and helpful material for teachers all over Europe, validated scientifically."

Although the overall contents for the preparation of a researcher in physics were not really questioned, some issues were raised about the need for the training of particular types of physics trained professionals. In particular, the issues raised for the beginning introductory courses were:

- the need to establish a stricter relationship between theory and lab courses;
- the study of simplified versions of existing courses with particular attention to conceptual and phenomenological aspects;
- the organization of laboratory courses;
- the relation between basic math and physics courses;
- the importance of a reflection on epistemological aspects;
- the opportunity to adopt a modular basis for the development of the courses; and
- the need to change examination procedures.

The inquiry also showed that many different changes in the teaching methodology were underway, such as:

- use of educational research results (Italy, Belgium in particular),
- computer-aided instruction both for problem solving and laboratory work,
- use of multimedia,
- problem solving,
- group work,
- projects,
- peer instruction,
- interactive teaching in general,
- evaluation procedures,
- development of communication skills, and
- development of software by the students.

A flavor of the debate among university physicists on changes in introductory courses may be drawn from the following comments, which may be extended to other scientific fields that have witnessed great development during the 20th century:

"To update and adapt curricula and courses to the new advances of knowledge is important. But also important is to give the students a solid background in fundamental principles of Physics, which is essential to develop their intuition for interpreting and solving problems.

The question of updating to the new developments is not more important than the question of preventing the university and the courses from being behind the society. It is vital for the universities to be open to quality from any origin. That may mean to adapt and to bring to learning and teaching the most recent resources of communication and information used everyday, and at an increasingly larger scale, by the society in general."

"[I]ntroductory courses are in many cases used to provide a broad perspective on a subject and not to give the deepest insight in every sub-area of the subject. To be up to date with the development of knowledge seems as a wish that every student should learn the deepest secrets within every sub-field and that cannot be provided in an introductory course."

"It depends on the content and structure of the courses following the introductory ones. Semiconductors, superconductivity, magnetic materials should be briefly treated."

Other comments focus more on the epistemological aspects:

"We tackle this question from the perspective of what science is. Following Harrè every scientific activity is characterized by two part activities. One is some form of observation/perception, either direct through the senses, more often indirect through instruments. The other part is thought-activity. It surrounds, penetrates, precedes the observation, directs attention, chooses observations. It distinguishes between different parts of observations, gives names, makes conceptual analyses of them, quantifies and relates them, logically or mathematically. A dynamic combination of those two activities produces theories and models, which on the one hand represent our human understanding and seeing of the world, on the other hand allow us to manipulate the world to control and use it. Here technology arises.

Concerning new technology, what should be taken up ? Evidently, choices have to be made, since not everything can be incorporated. We propose that technology which profoundly affects our everyday lives, at the service of overall human well-being deserves attention (so not only based on economic grounds or simply because they are used, like gadgets). Concerning our understanding of the world, options are much clearer. Facts which challenge our present-day understanding (which results from a long historic process) should be taken up. In particular those phenomena are at the heart of science as a dynamic activity, and students should be engaged in them (since Popper, falsification much more than confirmation is a driving force in science)."

The results of the inquiry were summarized in the following issues for a European debate

a. *Definition of the final states of knowledge.* It seems difficult to shift the preparation of master's degrees from the training of scientists to the training of "science-trained professionals." However, many examples of bachelor courses open to different professions are available. Does this trend fulfill the aim of preparing "science-trained high-level professionals"?

b. *Changes in the global organization.* We have seen that in many countries the organization of physics courses is structured in two cycles (bachelor, master's/PhD). At the political level, the same organization has now been agreed on by the ministers of various countries. However, harmonizing the architecture is a first step toward a European homogeneous system of university education. To complete the scheme, it is necessary to reach an agreement on the basic contents of the two cycles. A particular point may concern the quality of the thesis work. Some countries consider this part of the curriculum crucial for a good level of preparation for any profession. There are, however, trends to strongly limit or cancel the thesis work to reduce the time needed to obtain a degree.

c. *Changes in the content organization.* Some examples of changes have been reported. A comparison of the different proposals is useful. Particular attention should be focused on introductory courses in terms of "quantity and quality" of the contents for a solid background preparation for different professions.

d. *Changes in teaching methodology.* The results of educational research point out some necessary changes in the teaching methodology. However, it appears difficult to apply these changes at the university level. This may be due to the communication gap between the physics and education departments. However, examples of radical changes in those departments involved in teachers' training are available. The issue of how to obtain good quality preparation in disciplinary knowledge and expertise in educational aspects should be discussed. In particular, a problem worthy of attention is that of the educational expertise of university teachers, whose training is generally based only on disciplinary knowledge and whose careers are based mainly on research results with little attention to the quality of teaching.

THE ITALIAN DEBATE

The Context

Italy has 75 universities throughout the national territory, the majority (55) of which are state universities. The courses of study range from 2- to 3-year courses (diploma) to 4-, 5-, and 6-year courses (*laurea*). The *laurea* courses are followed by doctoral studies and specialization schools for particular professions (e.g., Schools of Medicine).

Until 1989, the university system was strongly state-centralized. Generally, there is no entrance examination: Anyone with a secondary school diploma may decide to follow any university course.

As seen in Table 20.3 (which gives the data on students' flow in 1997–1998), there is a large number of dropouts at all levels. The average ratio of students to professors is 37 to 1.

Figure 20.1 shows that in all knowledge sectors the duration of studies is longer than the legal duration (in physics, the students take about 3 years more than the legal 4 years duration).

The figure also shows that about 60% of the students coming from secondary school enter university courses, and that only 40% of those students leave the university with a degree. Changes are therefore needed to (a) guide students in the choice of university courses, (b) allow students to finish their studies within the legal duration, and (c) reduce the number of dropout students.

The Process of Change

The first change had its start in 1989 with the shift from a centralized system to an autonomous local system (the so-called *autonomy of the Universities*) in a statewide coordination. A schematic sequence of the process of change is shown in Fig. 20.2.

First came the definition of the rules concerning the statutes of the universities, which was soon followed by the rules concerning financial support. Some years later, the problem of didactical autonomy was initiated by stimulating universities to organize activities for guiding secondary school students in their choice of university courses. Different kinds of activities were thus begun, ranging from the simple dissemination of information to the organization of meetings between secondary school students and university teachers to the organization of didactic activities for specific courses of study. As an ex-

TABLE 20.3
Student Flow in the Italian Universities, 1997–1998

Degree	Incoming	Enrolled	Outcoming
Diploma 2/3 years	35,000	77,000	9,000
Laurea 4 years	198,000	1,164,000	84,000
Laurea 5 years	69,000	458,000	32,000
Laurea 6 years	8,000	72,000	7,000
	310,000	1,771,000	132,000

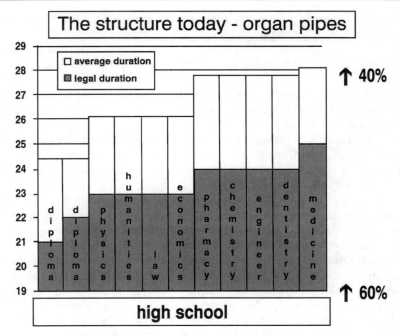

FIG. 20.1. Duration of courses of study.

1989	First document on the autonomy of the university system
1993	Document on financial autonomy
1997	Didactic autonomy: actions for guiding secondary school students in their choices of university courses
1997	The Martinotti document
May 1998	The Sorbonne Declaration
1998 June. Sept.	The so-called first and second nota di indirizzo (documents for analysis and debate in the universities)
1998/1999	Drafts of Decreto Quadro and Decreti d'Area
1998	Document on the autonomy in the recruitment of university professors
1999 June	The Bologna Declaration
1999 Sept.	Decreto Quadro approved by the Parliament
2000 July	Decreti d'area approved
Sept. 2001	Reform due to start in all universities

FIG. 20.2. The sequence of the process of change in Italy.

ample, in my university, we have two general meetings with the students (one in spring and one in September) to illustrate the characteristics of each course of study of the Faculty of Sciences. Then in the second half of September, the new physics students are offered a self-evaluation questionnaire and a series of activities aimed at discussing the answers to the questionnaire and issues like "the language of physics," "the methodology of experimental sciences," "mathematics and physics."

In October 1997, a first document (the so-called *Documento Martinotti,* named after the coordinator of the group) was produced by a study group of the Ministry of University and Research composed of university professors of different disciplinary fields.

The document suggested the following as general principles for didactic organization:

- a clear definition of an *educational contract* between the students and the university,
- the need for some kind of competition among universities with a plurality of offerings and flexibility in the curriculum,
- the adoption of the credit system analogous to the ECTS for the mobility of students,
- the importance of stimulating bottom–up innovations, and
- the need for introducing forms of evaluation of educational offerings.

Following these principles, the document gave indications for the main direction of intervention: (a) changes in the structure, (b) coordination/differentiation throughout the territory, (c) connection with other European systems, (d) guiding secondary school students, and (e) studying the form of evaluation of the changes.

The document thus started discussions at all levels of the university, which showed on the one side the real interest in imagining reasonable changes in the university structure and, on the other, the existence of strong resistance to any kind of changes.

The discussions following the Martinotti document and the Sorbonne declaration of May 1998 led to the constitution of new groups of study and the development of a definite proposal of change (*Nota di indirizzo,* June 1, 1998; *Nota di indirizzo,* October 2, 1998), which has been formalized into a general scheme (*Decreto Quadro,* May 1999). In the meantime, study groups on the different knowledge areas (science, humanities, engineering) have been examining the specific organization of each area. The *Decreto Quadro* was the object of detailed discussions at various levels: The University National Committee (CUN), The Conference of University Rectors, and The Conferences of Faculty Deans.

The final overall structure, approved by law in September 1999, is shown in Fig. 20.3.

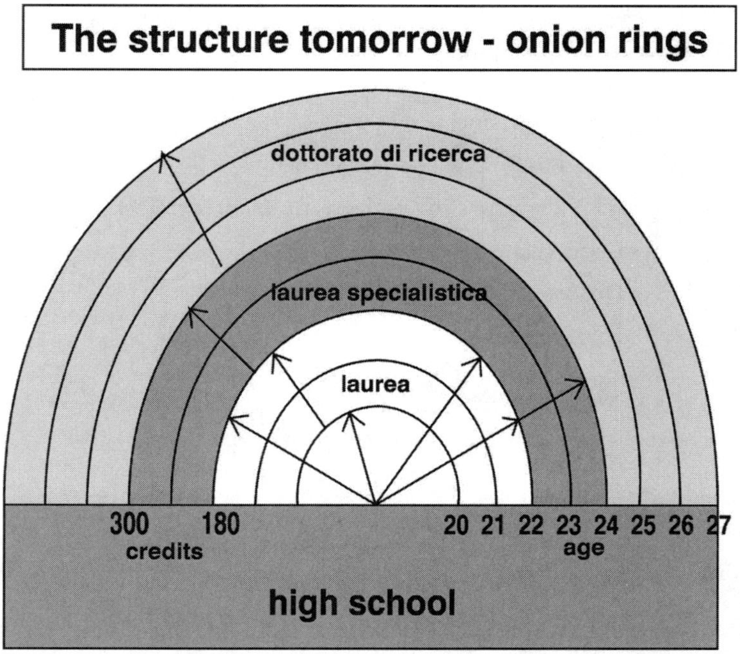

FIG. 20.3.   The new structure of the university system.

A second *Decreto,* defining the number of knowledge areas and specific objectives and overall structure of each area, after a similar procedure of discussion including the level of the councils of specific study courses and the conferences of study courses, was approved in July 2000. The reform was due to take effect in all universities in 2001.

We recall the main features of the new structure:

1. All Universities and most of the knowledge sectors must offer students the possibility of taking different degree levels (laurea, 180 credits; laurea specialistica, 180+120 credits; dottorato di ricerca, 180+120+180 credits). State rules fix 66% of the credits referring them to large disciplinary areas. University rules fix the total number of credits referring them to narrow disciplinary sectors. Faculty rules fix the details and credits of each learning activity.

2. The knowledge sectors are subdivided into areas (i.e., the scientific-technological area) with common rules over the territory, and each area comprises different classes of degrees with some central rules (i.e., the class of "Physics and Physical Technology"). The definition and denomination of each degree is left to the autonomy of each university.

State rules also establish the kind of activities to be organized by each university. For each class of first degree, it is thus compulsory to organize the curriculum reserving at least:

- 10% of the credits to basic knowledge,
- 10% of the credits to specific knowledges items,
- 10% of the credits to integrating and context knowledges items,
- 5% of the credits to activities freely chosen by the students,
- 5% of the credits to the final examination and a foreign language, and
- 5% to crossover skills.

An Example: Physics

The proposed class of "Physics and Physical Technology" for the first-level degree is aimed at giving the students:

- basic knowledge in classical and modern physics,
- familiarity with scientific methodologies of inquiry,
- experimental abilities,
- competence in using mathematical and computational tools,
- the ability to act professionally in particular sectors of application,
- competence in communicating in one European language other than Italian, and
- ability to cooperate in work groups.

The structure of the curriculum must follow the state rules to include:

- Basic knowledge (mathematics, information, computation), at least 18 credits;
- Specific knowledge (physics), at least 54 credits;
- Additional knowledge (chemistry), at least 18 credits;
- Optional knowledge, at least 9 credits;

- Dissertation, 10 credits; and
- Professional knowledge, 9 credits.

The remaining credits are left to the definition of each university and course of study. However, for physics, national coordination is activated through the Conference of the Chairs of the Physics Courses and the auspices of the Italian Physical Society.

The Conference has been studying the framework of a general curriculum with common basis for the mobility of the students and teachers while allowing some flexibility.

Questions that have become object of debate are:

What is basic knowledge in classical and modern physics?
What mathematical and computational tools are needed?
What changes in didactic methodology should be stimulated?
How can we induce such changes?
Should we work on the development of new didactical material (textbooks, audiovisual aids, computer software) at a national level or in a European cooperative effort?
How can we establish links with the work world?
Should we think of specific professionally oriented curricula (like environmental physics, health physics, physics and astronomy, biophysics)?

As I write, curriculum proposals are being developed across the country with partially different solutions to the issues.

RESISTANCE TO CHANGE AMONG UNIVERSITY STAFF

Why should we change? Our graduates are competitive internationally for their research competence and abilities. Of course this claim is valid for top-level students, but it does not take into account that, in the second half of the 20th century, the university changed from an elite course of study to a mass university.

We have thus seen a heavy increase in the number of students even in scientific courses. An example may be given of the physics course at the University of Roma "La Sapienza," where in 1950, just 30 students were enrolled, whereas in 1980, the number had gone up to about 400. Of course, the increase in the number of students forced an increase in the number of staff members and, thus, in a way, the change from an elite to a mass university was effective on both sides: the students and staff. In particular, the staff, chosen more for their research merits than for their didactic abilities, did not care much for the average students, but continued to focus their attention on the top-level students whose number, while constant in percentage, was increasing in absolute number and was therefore more than sufficient to maintain the high-quality standard for research. At the same time, at least for the scientific disciplinary fields, the century saw a large increase in the quantity of knowledge needed to enter the research field. Thus, the courses became more dense in content, and more difficult for the average students.

Why change? It is surprising that, even in the scientific fields where logical abilities are a necessary tool for research and the capacity for looking at a problem in a systemic way is usually developed, the university professors seem to fail to apply logical abilities and systemic capacity to the educational problem of dropouts students and the length of time studying.

Of course, belief systems play a role: Students fail because they lack the inborn capacity for the discipline or because they are not willing to work hard.

Often the problem is shifted to other study levels: The university is a good educational system, but the quality of secondary school has deteriorated and students arriving at the university lack the basic knowledge and abilities needed.

Why change? Often *change* is interpreted only for its negative aspect—that is, in terms of the decrease in the quality of study. But, of course, if something is perfect—by definition—any change alters the perfection.

In reality, what I now list as apparent logical objections are but emotional reactions to the prospect of having to afford a process that requires time, energy, and creativity. Thus, the main resistance factor may be identified in the fear of having less time, energy, and creativity for research. Research, not education, is their main reason for working in a university.

The belief that *teaching is an art* brings with it a disregard for any kind of research in educational matters. Therefore, a positive change guided by improvements in teaching practice, informed by results of educational research, is, by and large, not considered possible.

CORRELATED CURRICULUM REFORMS

Preuniversity School Reform

Up to now, the preuniversity school in Italy has been divided into three cycles: primary (6–11 years), lower secondary (11–14 years), secondary (14–18 years). Primary and lower secondary form the compulsory years, and maternal (3–5 years) schools are also available. Secondary school is subdivided into many different streams, from the *liceum* to technical and artistic.

Therefore, there are two principal differences with other European systems: the length of compulsory school (14 years as opposed to 16 years) and the age of university access (19 years as opposed to 18 years).

A reform has designed the architecture of a basic compulsory cycle (5–14 years) followed by two compulsory years, in which students are offered options that should guide them in their choice of the concluding years of study or in work activities. Two noncompulsory, final years are then offered for entrance to the university. In these years, options should be available for the students as a guide for their choice of university course of study.

Programs are as yet undefined in details, but some debate has taken place with the work of a commission discussing the general aims. The debate has concerned: (a) student work load, (b) the importance of English as a second language, (c) textbooks organization, (d) general ideas about the disciplines to be taught, and (e) the importance of computer literacy.

The future carries the problem of multicultural education: Italy has gone from a country of emigration to a country of immigration. Children from many third world countries are now entering Italian schools, bringing with them their languages, cultures, and religions. Religion has always been a topic for debate concerning the relation of Christian Protestant and Jewish minorities to the Catholic majority. (It must be remembered that Catholic religion teaching was compulsory by an agreement—*Concordato*—with the Vatican State. Now the new agreement does not pose the question of compulsory Catholic teaching, but the tradition, for the Italian state, of offering Catholic optional courses continues with less care for other religions.) Now the religious landscape has been enlarged to include Muslims and Buddhists with reasonably large communities. The gender problem has not been particularly relevant in the past at the educational level. We may then hope that the new organization does not raise the issue as it has in some Anglo-Saxon countries.

Teacher Training

In Italy until few years ago, the training of primary school teachers was done in a particular stream of higher secondary schools (*scuola magistrale*), whereas no training at all was considered for secondary school teachers, who entered the school system through a national examination (*concorso*) after having followed disciplinary university courses.

A law established in 1990 states that primary school teachers should be prepared by a 4-year university course and that secondary school teachers should be prepared by a 2-year special course (*Scuola di Specializzazione*) after graduation in the specific disciplinary fields (4–5 years of university). The law was enforced in 1997 for the primary teachers and in 1999 for secondary teachers.

The curricula for the two training courses was defined in detail by working groups composed by university teachers from the different disciplinary fields concerned with the issue. The working groups were organized on a single university basis and coordinated at the national level.

The university participation in the working groups was formed by two main components: the educationalists (pedagogy and psychology experts) and the disciplinarians (experts in educational research of some disciplinary fields). In particular in Italy, a community of educational researchers is active in the fields of mathematics and natural sciences. The community is centered on the disciplinary departments, and cooperation with educational departments is usually confined to personal relations. At both levels of the training courses, a main issue for debate has been the weight of pedagogical matters as compared with disciplinary educational matters. Of course, one of the reasons for the debate was recognized in the search for new teaching opportunities for both kinds of experts. Therefore, the working groups had to define the respective areas of intervention in addition to the specific contents of didactic activities.

The final curricula sees a wider space for educational matters with respect to the disciplinary ones for primary school than for secondary school training. In both courses, practical activities in the school take up a large portion of the didactic activities. They should be organized through the cooperation of both kinds of university experts. School teachers seconded at the university for full or part time are then in charge of conducting activities with student teachers.

Although the university course for primary school teachers is a course pertaining to the faculties of education, the *Scuola* for secondary school teachers is a collaboration among different faculties of different universities. The problems of cooperation between the two kinds of experts are, as a consequence, more visible in the *Scuola*. Therefore, I will illustrate in more detail the school organization. The main features are as follows:

- The school is open to graduates of the various disciplinary fields on the basis of a fixed number decided by the Ministry of Education. Students must then pass an examination for acceptance.
- The schools are organized on a regional basis with the cooperation of the universities active in each region (i.e., in Lazio 7, universities are involved).
- The curriculum is divided into four different knowledge areas: Area 1 concerns the psychopedagogical/socioanthropological disciplines, Area 2 concerns the specific disciplinary fields (math, physics, Italian, foreign languages, etc.), Area 3 concerns the application of knowledges in analyzing and programming didactic activities, and Area 4 concerns training in practical activities in the school (*Tirocinio*-Apprenticeship). The teachers of Areas 1, 2, and 3 are university professors, and the activities of Area 4 are coordinated by secondary school teachers seconded from the school for a partial time (half of the contract hours).
- Each area is structured in specific modules (corresponding to a specific number of credits).

The number of examinations must be fewer than six each year. The restriction is imposed on one side to stimulate the use of evaluation procedures during the didactic activity (in *itinere*) and, on the other, to foster coordination among the modules of each area and among the areas. For the activities in the disciplinary fields, it is assumed that basic knowledge has been acquired in the specific university courses and that the activities of the *Scuola* should focus, besides the educational aspects, on the history and epistemology of the disciplines. The *Scuola* is now at the end of the first year of activation. The problems that emerged from this first year may be summarized as follows:

- the quality of the disciplinary knowledge acquired in the university course, which is not focused on the teaching profession and which is somewhat incoherent;
- the lack of pedagogical knowledge of university teachers;
- difficulties in cooperation among the university teachers, in particular if they belong to different knowledge areas;
- difficulties in the interaction among the university and the secondary school teachers.

With the University reform new problems arise that are actually the object of hot debate:

- Should primary school teachers be prepared by a 3-year *laurea* course or a 5-year *laurea specialistica?* The issue is not easy to solve because the definition of the teachers for the basic school cycle also change with the preuniversity reform. Some options are under discussion:

  a.   a 3-year *laurea* course for the teachers of the initial years of school, followed by 2 years of disciplinary training for the final years;

  b.   a 3-year *laurea* course in the Faculty of Education, followed by a year of practical application in Schools; a 3-year *laurea* course explicitly designed on interdisciplinary themes (mathematics and science, humanities, foreign languages), followed by a *Scuola* for didactic training.

- Secondary school teachers. For this level, the impact of the reform of preuniversity school is less relevant. Particularly relevant, however, is the university reform. The shortening of disciplinary preparation in the 3-year *laurea* course is seen by some disciplinary experts as dangerous for its specific content-based training. Therefore, they suggest that the educational training in the *Scuola* should follow a 5-year *laurea specialistica* course. However, this solution implies a total duration of 7 years for teacher training. Such a duration, larger than any other professional training (limited to the 5 years of the *laurea specialistica*), does not seem feasible. There comes the suggestion of restricting the *Scuola* to a 1-year course, possibly introducing some educational matters in the *laurea specialistica*.

Other experts claim that the duration of training should be concluded in 5 years. Therefore, the access to the *Scuola* (to be continued according to the present scheme) should follow the 3 years of *laurea* in the disciplinary fields. Eventually the school, in the definition of the necessary disciplinary background, may require specific additional credits for entrance. Those credits should not require more than 1 additional year. Of course, the thinking on the disciplinary knowledge needed for teaching could have a positive impact on the content organization of the 3-year *laurea* courses. As already stated, the debate is actually quite heated, and one has the feeling that it is driven more by the interests of the different sectors of the university staff than by a real interest in preparing better teachers for the schools of the future. Let us hope for the best.

REFERENCES

Attali, J. (1999). Pour un modéle europeen d'enseignement supérieur. In H. Ferdinande & A. Petit (Eds.), *Inquiries into European higher education in physics* (Vol. 2, pp. 251–253). Gent, Belgium: University of Gent.

Black, P., Holcomb, D. F., Jodl, H. J., Jossem, L., Lopez, R., Mataz, F., Rigden, J. S., Smit, J., Stith, J., & Yun Ying. (1997). A call for changes in the undergraduate physics education. In E. F. Redish & J. S. Rigden (Eds.), *The changing role of physics departments in modern universities* (pp. 1–6). New York: American Institute of Physics.

Bologna Declaration. (1999). In H. Ferdinande (Ed.), *Inquiries into European higher education in physics* (Vol. 3, pp. 261–272). Gent, Belgium: University of Gent.

Ferdinande, H., & Petit, A. (Eds.). (1998). *Inquiries into European higher education in physics* (Vol. 1). Gent, Belgium: University of Gent.

Ferdinande, H., & Petit, A. (Eds.). (1999). *Inquiries into European higher education in physics* (Vol. 2). Gent, Belgium: University of Gent.

Ferdinande, H. (Ed.). (1999). *Inquiries into European higher education in physics* (Vol. 3). Gent, Belgium: University of Gent.

Haug G. (1999). *Trends and issues in learning structures in higher Education in Europe. The Bologna Forum.* http://www.unige.ch/ere/activities/Bologna%20Forum/texts

Modica, L. (1999). *Introductory address to the Bologna Forum.* http://www.unige.ch/ere/activities/Bologna%20Forum/texts

Sorbonne Declaration. (1998). In H. Ferdinande & A. Petit (Eds.), *Inquiries into European higher education in physics* (Vol. 2, pp. 237–248). Gent, Belgium: University of Gent.

Tobias, S. (1997). The science trained professionals: A new breed for the new century. In E. F. Redish & J. S. Rigden (Eds.), *The changing role of physics departments in modern universities* (pp. 49–60). New York: American Institute of Physics.

Post Scriptum April 2002

It is worth mentioning the developments in the reforms that have followed the description available in the year 2000.

- University reform: In all Italian universities and in the different fields, the reform is being applied starting in the Academic Year 2001–2002 with the first year of the new 3-year degree.
- Teaching training: The "Scuola di Specializzazione" had its first graduates in the year 2001 with reasonable success. Now we are planning the fourth year of activation.
- Secondary school: With the political changes in the year 2001, the reform planned by the previous Ministry has been abandoned and a new one is being proposed. Hot debates on the issue are going on at the moment.

CHAPTER 21

Japan's Struggle for the Formation of Modern Elementary School Curriculum: Westernization and Hiding Cultural Dualism in the Late 19th Century

Miho Hashimoto
Tokyo Gakugei University, Japan

This chapter is an attempt to analyze and interpret the dualistic phases of curriculum reforms in the 1870s, a key period in Japan's modernization. Japan's modern curriculum uniquely developed in terms of both the form and practical meaning of knowledge. Through my analysis, it is clearly disclosed that the modernization of Japan's school curriculum is a process of coating Western notions on the traditional values of curriculum. This process is likely to accompany the alteration of the practical meanings of Western curriculum through the symbolization of new school subject matters such as oral teaching. It was difficult for the Japanese to change their own intrinsic value of curriculum, which they had formed over the long term, despite their interest in Western notions of education.

In particular, Japan experienced the drastic change of curriculum in the middle of the 19th century when the Japanese encountered Western civilization. Economists and sociologists are likely to assume the universal structure concerning the modern school curriculum. Many scholars have assumed that primary schools of almost all countries have a curriculum comprised of modern school subject matters such as mathematics and sciences. However, we could find the alteration of the meaning of curriculum if we examine the history of the implementation and practices of modern curriculum. Japan's formation of the modern school curriculum is not the way as many have assumed There have always been political battles in forming the modern curriculum despite the appearance of Japanese homogeneity. Political conflicts regarding curriculum have been obscured in the history of Japan. Thus, the dualism of curriculum values have been penetrated into the school culture that teachers and educational administrators have developed. The modern curriculum may have been appeared standardized, but this is the case only on the surface. It is necessary for curriculum researchers to understand the political struggles and the internal contradictions under the surface to comprehend the substantial meanings of curricular modernization in Japan.

Most critics of contemporary curriculum discourses have addressed the fallacy of modern curriculum in terms of its fundamental feature of rationalism and bureaucracy. Most criticisms are concerned with the bureaucratic and inflexible structure of modern Japan's curriculum influenced by Western countries. It is often argued that the leading status of Western civilization is so solid around the world that developing countries have to follow the model of Western school curriculum, composed of traditional subject matters such as math, science, language, social studies, and others.

The modern school system developed the standardized style of curriculum within the rigid structure of subject matter. Yet those critics have not recognized or have ignored the fact that there existed the traditional Japanese curriculum, which had been implicitly formed at the in-depth level of the school culture. Because of the explicit structure of the modern curriculum, the critics have overlooked that traditional Japanese curriculum thoughts permeated the foundation of Japan's modern school curriculum. Modern Japanese schools integrated the traditional values in the curriculum, which is not able to be interpreted in terms of the Western notion of curriculum. To understand the traditional Japanese curriculum thoughts, it is necessary to identify and illuminate the function and characteristics of the Japanese transformation of the Western notion of curriculum, which has not been made explicit in the contemporary curriculum discourses.

For example, Dore (1976) found the curriculum development in Japan is still at an immature developmental stage in terms of its predominant concern with the selection of the student at the entrance of the upper schooling. The selection has always been a keen issue for Japanese children, rather than what they actually learn in schools, because it is related to the social stratification in Japan. In this type of curriculum model, the curriculum standard is the same for each individual; merely the degrees of the individuals' achievements are different. In this model, a learner has to be motivated merely for the aspiration of the advancement of the social status, not for the curriculum content. If this assumption is true, the knowledge and skills in the curriculum content simply would function as the tools for selecting the people, and there would be no value in the process of learning knowledge and skills.

Meyer (Meyer, Kames, & Benavot, 1992) also addressed the simplistic model of curriculum in his world system theory. He assumed the educational system and the school knowledge convert into the standardized structure from a global perspective. In this model, the children have to study universally ordered standardized knowledge in this one world. There are no pluralistic differences in the knowledge that the mass of children have to learn around the world. He stated, "As a consequence, the general outlines of mass education and its curriculum often show surprising degrees of homogeneity around the world" (Meyer et al., 1992, p. 2).

Meyer et al. (1992) observed the homogeneity of the curriculum around the world. He asserted the homogeneity as a result of functional analysis of mainly focusing on the primary schools around the world. He said that his findings and functional analysis unexpectedly could turn out to be a kind of ideology because "the labels, at least, of mass curricula are closely tied to great and standardized worldwide visions of social and educational progress, they tend to be patterned in quite consistent ways around the world" (p. 2).

We are likely to believe that the curricula of various countries are directed toward a worldwide standard. In this kind of functional analytical model, we can see the universal meaning and role of curriculum as far as the structure and goals of curriculum are concerned. We find the curriculum is the certain system of knowledge and skills that all human beings have to learn. However, no matter how widely the standardized system expands around world, the explicitly prescribed curriculum cannot avoid generating struggles among various interest groups within a country.

I try to point out that the alteration and transformation were inevitable for the Japanese educational modernization when the Japanese educational leaders began to accept the information of American school curriculum. Many curriculum concepts were introduced in Japan in the middle of the 19th century. Yet the substance of these concepts has never been implemented into Japanese schools without distortion of its original meaning. I analyzed the biography and other related historical materials of Shuji Isawa.

Shuji Isawa was a Japanese educational leader who studied at Bridgewater Normal School in Massachusetts from 1875 to 1877. Before he studied in the United States, he devoted himself to the struggle of formulating the modern school curriculum by interpreting the information of curriculum in the Western world. Then he encountered the overwhelming tide of educational information in the United States.

JAPAN'S CURRICULUM: A MODEL OF DIVERSION

In this study, I analyzed the work of Shuji Isawa, a pioneer of modern curriculum making in the midwest region of Japan in the early Meiji era. In 1874, Isawa was appointed a principal of the normal school in Aichi prefecture, which was one of the major normal schools in Japan and was leading curriculum reform in Japan. He introduced the new curriculum in his primary school, which was based on American educational thoughts. In his pedagogical practices, he understood the importance of children's psychological developmental stages in curriculum making, which is constituted of the integrated spheres of human development. Before he was appointed to study in the United States in 1875, he was reading the following books:

> Matilda H. Kriege. *The Child, Its Nature and Relations.*
> David Perkins Page. *Theory and Practice of Teaching.*
> Charles Northend. *The Teacher's Assistant.*
> J. and B. Ronge. *A Practical Guide to the English Kindergarten.*

These books explicate Froebel's pedagogy—pedagogy based on child psychology. The theory of children's developmental stages was an epoch-making innovation because the educational significance of children's interests was not a major concern for teachers' training in this era. The influence of Froebel's realism was so radical at that time that he functioned as a missionary of educational reforms in Japan. What he introduced into the schools includes such concrete items as a world globe for geography. He also argued that musical gymnastic exercise was important for generating motivation and balanced activities for children. Froebel advocated art education, songs, musical gymnastic exercise, physical education, and object lessons.

It is plausible that Isawa was the first pioneer of child-centered curriculum in the modern history of education in Japan (Hashimoto, 1998). Psychology was a frontier discipline for the Japanese. They had not thought that child development could be a subject of scientific research. In the traditional framework, the curriculum content had not been sequentially ordered in terms of the child's developmental age (Hashimoto, 1998).

It should be noted that new curriculum activities in Isawa's school were quite uniquely developed, different from both traditional Japanese schooling and Western-style schooling in other prefectures. He emphasized the arts and musical gymnastic exercise for balancing the body and soul. Moral education and physical education were valued equally as cognitive fields. That corresponds to the idea of Pestalozian education. *The True Method of Teaching,* his prominent book summarizing three pedagogical human resources, including Kriege, Page, and Northend, demonstrates the essences of curriculum making. The book consists in the mosaic integration of American curriculum thoughts. The first, the order of the subject matters, is cited from Page's book, Kriege's object lesson is introduced, and the order of the unit and content of each subject matter came from Northend.

The steering committee was organized in the parliament of the second large school region, which was one of the seven largest school regions in Japan at that time. The steering committee members were from the former Samurai class. They kept the Samurai education culture because they were raised in this culture. They were the delegates of the individual prefectures and the individual school areas. In the parliament, they intensively discussed the standards of the selection and legitimacy of the subject matters for elementary schools for 5 days in June 1876. This steering committee played the most important role in determining the direction of the standards of curriculum in each school region in Japan. The meeting of the second region proceeded under the strong initiative of Shuji Isawa's epoch-making idea. It should not be taken for granted that Japanese curriculum was standardized in those days. On the contrary, it can be observed that the curriculum was decentralized in the respective prefectures (Hashimoto, 1998).

The first school region, the central area including Tokyo, explored the quite different direction in curriculum making. Their preference was to edit the prescribed manual and handbook for the spec of instruction. For instance, in 1873, the principal of Tokyo Normal School, Nobuzumi Morokuzu's manual for teaching actions, a book of Tokyo Normal school, *Shogaku Kyoushi Hikkei,* was distributed as a kind of course of study. It describes no principle or reasoning for the action, but the specifications of instruction for teachers. That fact demonstrates that Japanese educational culture has been inherited for many generations and was a part of the general Japanese cultural disposition (Hashimoto, 1998).

The members of the committee were the representatives of the individual subject matters as well as the individual school areas. The discussion at the Council of the Educational Code of Elementary School (Shogaku Kyosoku) pertained to the future direction of education in Japan. We can interpret that the council was the field of Japan's educational culture encountering Western educational culture. In particular, "Oral Teaching," "Songs," "Musical gymnastic exercise," and "Drawing" were the center of discussion.

Oral Teaching

The *object lesson* was introduced to the younger children, and oral teaching was considered an important principle for curriculum development and teaching method. The order of geographical content was organized in the spiral expansion from the immediate surrounding area to the distant regions in the world. The learning content was also organized in order from the easy to the difficult. Such a curriculum organization was based on the epoch-making principles in curriculum making. The learner is situated in the center of organizing the order of curriculum content. The grading is composed not of the linear model, but of the developmentally transitional stages. This shows the rational understanding of the Western curriculum because those principles stem from the original books of pedagogy. Page's idea in organizing the cognitive sphere influenced Isawa's conceptualization of the order in the curriculum content (Hashimoto, 1998).

The mosaic constitution of the American pedagogy drove on the expansion of the curriculum content beyond the cognitive sphere into the affective and physical spheres, including drawing, songs, musical gymnastic exercise, book keeping, gymnastics, and object lessons. Among those subject matters, oral teaching played the central role as a means to integrate various areas of study, which involved object lessons, moral education, hygiene, geography, history, physics, chemistry, economics, and politics. Oral teaching did not integrate the content of knowledge, but prescribed the planning of lesson units because teachers did not use the textbook in the oral teaching, but it merely determined the features of teaching method. This method has more creative and flexible traits than catechism. It likely aimed at designing a child-centered curriculum.

There were controversies among the teachers of the normal schools concerning the oral teaching. Teachers in favor of Isawa's conceptualization of curriculum emphasized the priority of children's understanding of the meanings or the reasons of the things of nature and society, rather than the forms of learning. Therefore, they had a pedagogical thought oriented toward the heuristic process. On the other hand, the teachers in Tokyo Normal school opposed the teachers of the Aichi Normal School directed by Isawa. Tokyo teachers were more inclined to depend on the tacit means of teaching such as textbooks and rote learning. The basic structure of this controversy of the teaching method has been inherited by contemporary educators. Tokyo teachers inherited the traditional educational culture of Samurai class. They tend to lean toward the method of rote learning and textbook reading. This tendency implies that, for the traditional educational culture of Samurai class, the form of curriculum is more important than the practical values in their curriculum. The form of knowledge had priority in their learning. Knowledge did not have to be used for their vocational lives. The basic assumption is that forging the children's ethical attitude into a certain disposition is the most valuable principle in their learning (Hashimoto, 1998).

School Songs and Gymnastic Exercise

The second controversy of the Normal School in Aichi concerned musical gymnastic exercise and school songs. Those two subject matters were the fields avoided by the most traditional educators. Those who were raised in Samurai culture were likely to criticize musical gymnastic exercise and free physical movement. Isawa's proposal of musical gymnastic exercise was rejected because the traditional teachers had images of strict discipline regarding physical movements. They assumed that the physical exercise with song was inconsistent with the terms of their Samurai code. But the subject matter of singing songs was accepted by the traditional teachers because it was already prescribed in the School Act of 1872 (Hashimoto, 1998).

Drawing

The controversy over drawing illustrates the typical attitude of Samurai culture. The Japanese had developed their own unique esoteric aesthetic culture in fine arts. The traditional artists could not tolerate the school popularization of the intricacies they had developed over a couple of centuries. They feared that the introduction of the Western school curriculum could lead to the degrading of the arts and their dignity. It should be noted that the Samurai class developed their own educational culture, which is independent of the secular values of education. The curriculum is the means of keeping their own identity and distinction from other social classes. Even the humanistic value of educational culture including arts was intrinsically unrelated to their everyday lives. Thus, the form of the traditional curriculum was the source of identity and nobleness, which they had to rely on as a tool for making distinction (Hashimoto, 1998).

The traditional Japanese educators ignored the developmental stages of children. They did not understand that children would not have freedom to draw and express their own feelings intensively and extensively. For the Samurai class, play and joyfulness were considered anathema to education. Curriculum was not about life, but for making those distinctions necessary for the perpetuation of the Samurai class. What was important for the Samurai was not the practical value of knowledge, but the symbolic value of the form of knowledge. Their interest in education was predominantly directed toward the style of forming their own social class dignity. They were concerned with the form of knowledge, but not with the intrinsic values of knowledge itself (Hashimoto, 1998).

PERMEATING DUALISM: GENERATING HIDDEN CURRICULUM IN MODERN JAPAN'S SCHOOL CURRICULUM

As noted earlier, the transformation of Japan's modern school curriculum should not be oversimplified or characterized in terms of modern Western notions of curriculum, which has formed the order of instruction and curriculum content in the form of subject matters. Several researchers of Japan's educational history have been occupied with the stereotyped interpretation about the modernization of Japan's school curriculum, which emphasizes the one-way direction of information flow. Japan's modernization of curriculum had not been attained only by importing the ideas and systems of the Western higher education curriculum. It could be true if we focused on the history of the higher education curriculum in Japan. The structure of higher education curriculum had been organized in terms of the sequential order of content, from the basic to the advanced, culminating in knowledge specialization and expertise.

However, a number of tacit grassroots movements altered the meanings of Westernization at the elementary school curriculum level. The basic characterization of the elementary school curriculum cannot be simplified as a matter of the sequence of subject matters. It was related to the area of the children's activities. The proceedings in the educational parliament discussed the possibility of the expansion of the concept of children's study. Yet the implementation of that idea had to wait for Isawa's returning home from the United States. Physical education and music were founded as standardized subject matters in Japan's schools after he came back home.

It should be noted how radical Isawa's curriculum planning was. In the era of Samurai culture, body is an entity in the individual's self-regulation. Silence and static physical movement are their common aesthetic virtues. The inwardness of the individual's own voices has never been turned outward. They were concerned with impression rather than expression. Isawa challenged those who still believed in traditional values. Those who believed the values of the Samurai culture were opposed to curriculum innovation, especially given its Western style. Traditional curriculum believers neglected the element of body movement in music, the element of play in physical education, and the integration of play with work.

Although the curriculum thought of Isawa demonstrates fundamental traits of Western modern curriculum thought, his notion of Western modern curriculum was used to enforce modernization. His notion of curriculum was not understood by the educators at an in-depth level, but was superficially used for implementing the educational policy of the central government on the surface. Thus, the central government's struggle for the Westernization of school curriculum had to confront the Japanese traditional curriculum thought, which was rooted in the Samurai spirit (Hashimoto, 2000). The Samurai spirit has been interwoven with the various values in the modern curriculum. The values of self-control and well-disciplined characters of the independent individual have been developed in this integration. The most prominent trait of the Samurai spirit is the individual's inner autonomy. The virtue of the self-discipline contributed to the growth of industrial production in the early capitalism of Japan in terms of its character, similar to the Protestant ethics.

The Japanese conflict between the traditional values and the modernization of school curriculum had driven on the formation of the hidden curriculum of Japan's modern school (i.e., the formation of the dual curricula). This dual system is subtly related to the cast system in the feudal period. The schools for the Samurai class did not prefer materialistic culture, but rather Confucian ethics, which had contributed to formation of the traditional humanistic values. However, the masses, including merchants, technicians such as carpenter, and farmers, preferred the practical knowledge and skills for their own efficacy for their future lives. The children of those social classes went to *Terakoya*, a kind of community school. They were naive and practical enough to accept those innovative curricula, but it took a long time for the influence of Samurai's spiritual values to disappear from the school curriculum. Actually, they have not yet completely disappeared, but have been hidden as a hidden curriculum in Japan's school culture. Thus, Japan's modern school curriculum has been developed through hiding the conflict between underlying traditional curriculum notions and an explicit Westernized curriculum structure.

SAMURAI'S EDUCATIONAL CULTURE RECONSIDERED

Let us examine the Samurai culture and its influence on the modernization of the school curriculum in Japan. Before the Meiji era, it had been taken for granted that Samurai should not complain of physical difficulties and pains. The practical values in the secular world were neglected in their lives. Nobleness was one of the major causes of the collapse of the caste system because of their inability to manage the economic system of the whole society. The Samurai were economically defeated by the ordinary social caste, but they struggled to maintain their legitimacy in the school curriculum. That was a last site where they could insist on their own cultural identity. They stubbornly opposed the introduction of the concept of *play* into the school. They could not believe that children's own interests and egos would have their own intrinsic values separated from the traditional arts and humanistic academic classics. They did not believe in the values of commercial and technical skills for industry. The sources of their identity were narrow, but were passed on in the educational culture as school curriculum.

Terakoya teachers, on the one hand, understood the idea of developmental stages. On the other hand, the Samurai curriculum functioned as a means for becoming something even if it was to be modernized. But Samurai culture sustained the meaning of school curriculum as an important part of the growth of human beings and maintaining the social caste system. In that social structure, this was the only form of curriculum considered valuable for education. Its practical value was likely to be neglected.

For the Samurai class, the curriculum was the sum of tasks the individuals could accomplish in their life-long terms. They assumed that the important function of education is in the socialization for morality, but not in the transmission of the practical skills and knowledge for the social life. The developmental stages are not important for the socialization because the individuals could be socialized whenever they decided to start studying. Even the apprenticeship for the masses was built on the idea of life-long education. The individual has a chance whenever they can start to learn. The curriculum for the laymen is built on the needs for life. Therefore, the social life is the center of curriculum making in the traditional educational culture. In the traditional educational culture, play, music, drawing, and dancing were not considered a part of learning. Work was strictly separated from play. For the Samurai class, curriculum was a symbol for their social class identity. For the laymen class, curriculum was the sum of knowledge and skills useful for the social life and the means for meaningful practical life.

The dualism of the meanings of *curriculum* has been maintained for many decades in the modernization of curriculum in Japan. Besides, this major contradiction has not been made explicit even after World War II. As it were, it functioned as a foundation of Japan's hidden curriculum for over a century. It was the foundation, as Vallance (1973–1974) pointed out in her analysis of American's experience of "hiding the hidden curriculum," of the nationalization of modern curriculum.

DUALISM: A GLOBAL PERSPECTIVE

I argue that the experience of Japanese educational modernization in the mid-19th century was highly suggestive of our understanding of contemporary trends in the globalization of education. In this era of the third world countries, prevailing views of the modernization of education tend to be too simplistic and sometimes dangerous, given that these views tend to posit one homogeneous and standardized development of curriculum around the world. Japan's experience of educational modernization in the late-19th century suggests that we carefully scrutinize the internal struggles provoked when curricula are modernized in the various countries.

Japan's experience of educational modernization is likely to be cited by developing countries as one of the successful cases of modernization. The nation state was born after the long internal fight among the local state governments in Japan. Traditional culture and provincialism were not completely discarded after the battle for rising modern Japan. Traditional cultural heritage was hidden in the course of Westernization. Westernization was proclaimed by some to be the only means of educational modernization in Japan. Therefore, a number of educational leaders studied in the United States to establish the curriculum model for Japan's schools.

I believe that curriculum studies ought to be based on in-depth understandings of human nature. It is important for one nation to establish a common base to understand the substantial meaning of other countries' civilizations. Systematic transformation is possible in education, but it is difficult to change individuals' values unless we understand the fundamental structure of human nature. Because Isawa understood humanistic values in the Western curriculum, he had to face the critical problem of cultural dualism in the Japanese modern curriculum. This cultural dualism is inevitable for the government's effort of implementing Japan's curricular modernization. I assume that we can find the phenomenon of cultural dualism of curriculum in many contemporary countries struggling for educational modernization (Shibusawa, 1994).

REFERENCES

Dore, R. P. (1976). *The diploma disease: Education, qualification and development*. London: Allen & Unwin.

Hashimoto, M. (1998). *The study of the modernization of the Japanese education through actively processing the information of American education in the early Meiji era*. Tokyo: Kazama-shobo.

Hashimoto, M. (2000). Shuji Isawa, a pioneer of Western curriculum thoughts, and the struggle for implementing his curriculum thoughts: The formation of the modern elementary school curriculum in Japan. *The Japanese Journal of Curriculum Studies, 9*, 42–44.

Meyer, J. W., Kamens, D. H., & Benavot, A. (1992). *School knowledge for the masses*. Washington, DC: Falmer.

Shibusawa, T. (1994). Octavio Paz: The present seeker. *Journal of Intercultural and Transdisciplinary Studies, 30*, 42.

Vallance, E. (1973–1974). Hiding the hidden curriculum: An interpretation of the language of justification in nineteenth-century educational reform. *Curriculum Theory Network, 4*(1), 5–21.

CHAPTER 22

Present State
of Curriculum Studies in Japan

Tadahiko Abiko
Waseda University, Japan

From the end of World War II to 1955, curriculum studies in Japan were actively conducted by school teachers, with a focus on the areas of curriculum formation and development. Influenced by the philosophies and theories of progressive education in America, an organization for educational activism called the *Koa-Karikyuramu Renmei* (Association of Core Curriculum) was established in 1948 by researchers and teachers to convert the prewar curriculum based on subject matter to a new one centered on children, and an original, truly Japanese theory of core curriculum was developed and put into practice as well.

After the Course of Study was developed by the government in 1958, however, the state control based thereon became stricter, and the content of the curriculum became strongly restricted by the Course of Study (i.e., the national standard). As a consequence, the impetus on the part of teachers at school for self-governing and subjective curriculum formation was immediately weakened. As teachers then shifted the subject of their research and activism to those related to instruction, their efforts in the Analysis of Instruction or Research on Instruction came into bloom after 1960, and this trend continued up to the 1980s. As a matter of course, research on curriculum development of some study subjects was also conducted during these years, producing the *Suido-hoshiki* (Doing sums on paper-oriented mathematics education) in arithmetic and mathematics and the *Kasetsu-Jikken* (hypothesis–experiment instructions) in science during the 1960s, followed by the *Kyokuchi-hoshiki* (polar method) in science at the beginning of the 1970s. These methods are all examples of the active development of truly Japanese study material formation, which is still ongoing now in response to the new global trend of the modernization of education content. However, research that directly deals with the whole curriculum, including nonacademic matters, has been quite sterile.

ESTABLISHMENT OF THE JAPANESE SOCIETY
FOR CURRICULUM STUDIES IN 1990

The aforementioned situation changed with the loosening of state control in the content of the Course of Study in 1983 and the establishment of the Japanese Society for Curricu-

425

lum Studies in 1990. With the revision of the Course of Study in 1983, it was decided that free hours used at each school's discretion be set up, which the school (or teachers therein) could spend at liberty. It has become a major issue for teachers to form a curriculum for these free hours. In accordance with this change of surroundings in which schools and teachers were situated, and with the increase of research results that questioned the content of education as well as the increase of requests from society at large, the Japanese Society for Curriculum Studies was founded in December 1990 on the basis of the judgment that teachers, researchers, and education-related administrators should be further committed to curriculum development. The foundation was proposed by Professors Shigemitsu Kinoshita (Osaka Kyoiku University) and Tadahiko Abiko (formerly of the University of Nagoya), whose main appeal was as follows.

Until recently, there has been no academic society in Japan that deals with the entire curriculum, except for the Japan Curriculum Research and Development Association, although such a society normally exists in other Western countries. Hence, the National Association for the Study of Educational Methods has accepted curriculum researchers as well. Still, one cannot deny curriculum research in Japan is behind compared with other countries, both in terms of quality and quantity. However, discussions concerning school curricula have become active for the last several years, and large-scale changes and reforms, including consolidation of study subjects and implementation of new subjects, are anticipated, with the introduction of the 5-day school system just around the corner.

However, interest in the state of curricula has started to grow larger among researchers and academics in various fields, who all base their approach in asking themselves again how the structure of knowledge in their respective specialized field should be. This is the case with education-related researchers such as those in the field of educational methods, subject-matter pedagogists, comparative pedagogists, and educational psychologists, as well as cultural scientists such as philosophers and anthropologists; social scientists such as sociologists, economists, jurists, and historians; and natural scientists such as mathematicians, medical scientists, and biologists.

In addition, educational practitioners have also come up with new approaches, results, and questions from a variety of different angles, and related discussions have become increasingly active, including discussions on viewpoints from theories of school education, problems of hidden curricula, research on the curricula during the postwar educational reform, environmental education and sex education, relevance of information and internationalization with education, issues concerning the study subject of home economics, and elective subjects. The proposed foundation of this society is in response to these movements. Its purpose is to create a venue for mutually presenting these issues on a national scale and discussing them in a synthetic and interdisciplinary manner.

Taking into consideration the possibility of research exchanges with overseas societies, we are of the opinion that an academic society would be more appropriate than a mere study group. This would make it easier for each researcher to independently present his or her ideas to the curriculum administration in Japan as well. Based on these assumptions, we have made it a basic principle to make this society completely open to researchers, practitioners, administrators, and the general public regardless of position. The fact that nearly half the members are practitioners is another major feature of this society. We would like to develop this society into a new brand of academic society, where everyone's wisdom is put together and research and discussions abound.

As society at large is going through a tremendous change now, an image of a new educationalist and researcher is required toward the 21st century. We would like to welcome many membership applications for our society so that it could develop into a research network, a research venue, and a base camp for practice for the education-related circle. Not only curriculum researchers, but also course development researchers, subject-matter pedagogists, educational sociologists and educational psychologists, educational business administration researchers, and education administrators supported this call, and 30-odd founders gathered. As already mentioned, because developing the ability of school teachers was thought to be particularly important as one of the roles of the society, teachers and education practitioners were widely solicited as well, resulting in the attendance of 150-odd members at the inaugural meeting. The society has steadily attracted new members ever since, and the membership finally exceeded 700 in 2000—10 years after its foundation—making it one of the most pivotal academic societies related to pedagogy. Various research groups have joined the society during these years; some researchers steadily conduct historical research on an individual level, and others have formed a group to carry out nationwide movements.

Because the society does not merely function as a venue for presenting research results, but also serves as a space for information and idea exchanges among various groups, it has been quite well received by its members and academics for the past 10 years. This was possible because the society has secured support from various fields due to the sincere attitude toward research and significant research results of its first representative director, Professor Yoshimatsu Shibata (Professor Emeritus at University of Tokyo). The second executive director, Professor Tadahiko Abiko, who took the position in October 1999, was the very person who proposed the foundation of the society in cooperation with Professor Shigemitsu Kinoshita. The roles required of him as new representative director are to promote the creation of research results that could work as guidelines for school curriculum reform in Japan, and to promote communication and idea exchanges with overseas researchers and academic societies to expand and develop curriculum studies in Japan in the years to come.[1]

FIVE MAJOR RESEARCH GROUPS AND TWO ADDITIONAL GROUPS IN THE CURRICULUM STUDIES SPHERE IN JAPAN

As a next step, let me overview the present state of curriculum studies in Japan, placing a special focus on researchers who join the Japanese Society for Curriculum Studies. Among other things, I summarize the situation of curriculum studies in Japan in the past 10 years or so from my own perspective. Although curriculum researchers in Japan are strongly influenced by the research trends in America and England, they also have unique perspectives. The same situation is probably shared by researchers in any field in any country.

First, Japanese researchers can be roughly divided into five major groups. Because a division of this kind differs depending on who does it, the one presented here is only based on my own benchmarks. My benchmarks focus on the difference in research objectives rather than research styles. The five groups are as follows:

1. A group that critically analyzes political and social characteristics of curriculum.

---

[1]The activities of the Japanese Society for Curriculum Studies include the organization of annual conferences, publication of three or four newsletters every year and joint research by volunteer members. The society annually publishes the *Japanese Journal of Curriculum Studies* (since its first issue in 1992, nine issues have been published) to publicize research results. Various types of academic papers appear in this publication, including historical research, sociological research, theoretical research, investigative research, development research, as well as practical research conducted by practitioners.

2. A group focusing on curriculum development that emphasizes progressive and child-centered open curricula and integrated study to foster children's individuality and creativity.
3. A group that studies sociology of curriculum by focusing on analyses of hidden curriculum.
4. A group that has consistently criticized public education from the perspective of Marxist educational philosophy.
5. A group that aims to promote curriculum development on the part of schools and teachers (school administration researchers also belong to this group).

In addition to these five groups, there are several other groups that should be mentioned. One is composed mainly of the Japan Teachers' Union, which attempts to develop its own curriculum. Major characteristics of this group are, among other things, its criticism of Monbu-Kagaku-sho, the Ministry of Education, Culture, Sports, Science, and Technology (formerly the Ministry of Education) and the continuous efforts cooperatively made by education practitioners, consisting mainly of teachers and researchers who support them to draw up a counterplan against the Ministry's Course of Studies. Their movement has a history of nearly 50 years. However, there have been fewer conflicts between the group and education administrators for the last 10 years or so, compared with the past, and now they mutually exchange ideas and information concerning curriculum development in a fairly active manner.

Another group is characterized by a wide range of figures with right-wing political influence, including researchers who are concerned with curricula of history education. This group advocates the justifiability of the history of Japan from nationalistic perspectives and lobbies the administrators, journalists, and politicians to develop history education intended to form a consciousness of Japanese people in that direction. Although the group's political clout has little impact on the academic sphere, it has quite a large influence on the political world. Accordingly, it is something that cannot be ignored and one should be careful about. Among the leading pedagogists in this group is Professor Nobukatsu Fujioka (University of Tokyo).

FIVE STREAMS OF SCHOLARSHIP
IN CURRICULUM STUDIES IN JAPAN

I proceed to summarize the opinions and activities of each of the five major groups to clarify the total picture of curriculum studies in Japan and their respective characteristics.

A Group That Critically Analyzes Curricula

First and foremost, researchers and practitioners belonging to this group are largely influenced by the opinions of Michael Apple, who is one of the central figures in curriculum studies in America, from which the analytical perspectives of the group stem. This suggests that the group cannot accept the basic characteristics of current curricula in public schools in terms of education philosophy, and its activities are rather focused on sharply criticizing them.

In particular, this group finds the actualities of *curriculum politics,* as Apple put it, in the curricula in Japanese public schools and tries to reveal, by focusing on discrimination, how the current curricula are structured on behalf of the ruling class, rather than of children, by the hands of various political, economic, and social powers of politicians and industries. In modern Japan, issues of inequality in sex, social classes, haves versus have-nots, cultures (capital), and so on are taken up as research topics.

For example, the content of the Industrial Arts/Homemaking subject used to differ between male and female students at junior high school 10 years ago. Now male and female students study exactly the same content. The background of this change was the movement initiated by female activists who demanded equal rights for both sexes as well as equal opportunities, who received support from this group.

Another characteristic of this group is its ardent efforts toward integrated study. The basis of these efforts is the voluntary movement towards the realization of interdisciplinary study, which was proposed by the Japan Teachers' Union in 1976. The movement has been led by some eager believers in the idea of interdisciplinary study. In fact, interdisciplinary study was quite similar to integrated and lateral study that appeared in the first recommendation of the Central Education Council in 1997 while its emphasis was based on a different, newer perspective. Therefore, the group connected the Japan Teachers' Union's idea of interdisciplinary study with this council recommendation and started a large-scale endeavor to reform the existing school education, which is study-subject-centered and devoid of consideration toward children in compliance with the subject-based learning method currently applied, to children-initiated study based on themes beyond study subjects. Although this movement follows the examples of *theme learning* in America and *topic learning* in England, it also recommends various other endeavors be developed at each school level.

One of the leaders of this group is Professor Akio Nagao (Osaka Kyoiku University). He also belongs to the theorist group supporting the Japan Teachers' Union and constantly criticizes, while giving partial praise to as well, the fundamentals of the current administration in education and science. He asserts that responsibility in school education should fundamentally rest with teachers, and the Ministry of Education, Culture, Sports, Science, and Technology should confer teachers necessary authorities accordingly. By coauthoring books such as *Curriculum Politics* (1994) with Apple and Whitty, Professor Nagao clarified the political and social characteristics of curriculum and also pointed out potential problems in curriculum. As a whole, this group agrees on the voluntary curriculum development by the Japan Teachers' Union and confronts the education-related administration in cooperation with the Union for the purpose of increasing its capability.[2]

Group That Criticizes Central Education Administration From Perspectives Emphasizing Children's Independence, Individuality, and Creativity

Viewing progressive education and children- or learner-centered education in America as its models, and based on ideas of Dewey et al., this group criticizes group-oriented, uniform education in Japan and also sharply criticizes the public education administration of the Ministry of Education (currently the Ministry of Education, Culture, Sports, Science, and Technology), which has been promoting it. From these standpoints, the group supports the idea of open education, which is actually losing its momentum in America. Furthermore, the group criticizes subject-divided education from the perspective of the child-centered philosophy and strongly advocates an inte-

---

[2]The following is a list of major books written in Japanese by researchers belonging to this group:

Nagao, A., Apple, M., Whitty, G. (1994). *Curriculum Politics.*

Nagao, A. (1996). *Gakko-Bunka Hihan no Karikyuramu-Kaikaku* (Curriculum reform via criticism against school culture).

Apple, M. (1992). *Kyoiku to Kenryoku* (Education and power). (S. Asanuma, Trans.).

Apple, M. (1986). *Gakko-Genso to Karikyuramu* (Ideology and curriculum). (M. Kadokura, Trans.).

grated curriculum by actively working hand in hand with practitioners to spread integrated study to each school.

What differentiates the idea of integrated study advocated by this group with that by the first group is that this group places curiosity and interest of children at the center, not themes or topics such as environment or peace. This child-centered idea, together with that of open education, has been increasingly spread at the elementary school education level in Japan, and integrated study is considered to be the symbol of this idea.

Within this group, Professors Yukitsugu Kato (Sophia University) and Shigeru Asanuma (Tokyo Gakugei University) have grouped together and are actively working on the movement of spreading education practices of these kinds to schools nationwide. Influenced by the postmodern ideological trend, which is a trend for new curriculum research in America, this group is also carrying out practical and research activities in parallel with that trend. Pinar and Giroux also have a relatively large impact on their activities.

In the meantime, another movement has been initiated by Professor Manabu Sato (University of Tokyo). It is concerned with criticism of curriculum. Professor Sato calls for a child-centered curriculum and the improvement on the part of teachers to increase their abilities. Sato is also engaged in critiquing activities against related issues in various fields, including the deregulation policy and liberalization measures and the introduction of competition and market principles into school education, all of which are promoted by the Ministry of Education (currently the Ministry of Education, Culture, Sports, Science, and Technology). From his standpoint, this opts for the establishment of professionalism in school teaching.

Professor Sato does not emphasize the virtue of integrated study as much as he did before and instead criticizes the education administration by stating that subject-based learning should also be emphasized so that the level of academic achievement does not decrease. However, he is still sensitive to the trend in America and is recently working on teacher research more actively than before due to his realization that the American education sphere is shifting from curriculum studies to teacher research. At the same time, he always targets schools in Japan as his research subject and is thereby widening the depth of his curriculum studies and teacher research in a practical manner.

Today, Professor Sato (and Professor Hidenori Fujita, an educational sociologist at the University of Tokyo) is drawing attention as a leading figure who squarely opposes the educational reform implemented by the Ministry of Education, Culture, Sports, Science, and Technology of Japan. His discussion is placed not so much on the curriculum, but on his belief that the education administration makes light of the publicness that public education should inherently encompass because it asserts that the further expansion, via liberalization, of the discretion by parents and guardians in choosing a school would deprive children of the equal opportunities in education, and economic as well as class gaps between the rich and the poor would be further broadened. Professor Sato argues that it is against the principles of publicness of public education and equal opportunities for the administration to not allow freedom in school selection while it agrees that parents and guardians have the right of education. Although the standpoints of the two professors are inherently quite different, they cooperatively oppose the current education administration because, after all, their opinions coincide in terms of their social aspect.[3]

---

[3]The following is a list of major books written by researchers belonging to this group:

Asanuma, S., Nakano, K., Yamamoto, T., Okazaki, M., Nagao, A., & Sato, M. (1995). *Posuto-Modan to Karikyuramu* (Post-modernism and curriculum).

Sato, M. (1996). *Karikyuramu no Hihyo* (Criticism of curriculum).

Sato, M. (1997). *Kyoikuhoho-gaku* (Educational methodology).

Sato, M. (1997). *Kyoshi to Iu Aporia* (An aporia called a teacher).

Kato, Y. (1997). *Sogo-Gakushu no Jissen* (Practice of Integrated Study).

Group That Gives Criticism From the Standpoint of Sociology of Curriculum

Supporters of this group are found among educational sociologists as well as curriculum researchers. Strongly influenced by sociology of curriculum in England and America, the group carries out various research activities particularly based on research results of sociologists such as Jackson, Bernstein, and Goodson. The leader of this group is Professor Toji Tanaka (University of Tsukuba). What is unique about Professor Tanaka is his method of observing actual results of curricula in connection with a teacher's awareness on study subject matters (i.e., the teacher's viewpoint on subject matters and traits of the teacher's identity based thereon).

Although curriculum studies by this group naturally cover various fields, including issues of hidden curriculum, languages used in curriculum, and historical and social background to be introduced as study subjects, the group is recently inquiring into the foundation and principles of curriculum from historical and social perspectives. Discovering *currents of the times* as a result of the research in this direction, which might also be called *historical and social limits of curriculum*, the group attaches importance to the ever-changing aspects of curriculum that depend on social, political, and economic requirements of each era. The group positively accepts the idea of integrated study, which is introduced eventually, as something that serves as a response to the requirements of times and emphasizes the shift of practices and opinions toward that direction.

However, the most prominent feature of this group rests with its research methodology. Researchers in this group do not directly address the education administration in a criticizing manner, but rather conduct experimental and ethnographic research to clarify social causes lying behind the education administration as exemplified by the research by Professor Kokichi Shimizu (University of Tokyo). In this fashion, the group is working on the clarification of actualities of hidden curriculum and the clarification and analyses of the actual state of "curriculum that promotes reproduction of social strata via cultural capital" and "various causes existing in and outside of school that determine results of curriculum."

The group is characterized in particular by the concentration of its interest in the result stage in curriculum observation, which is the final one among the three stages (i.e., planning, practice, and result). In fact, it is obvious that a success level of a curriculum should be determined by actual effects and results because it would be useless to discuss the curriculum in the planning stage when it has not been put into practice yet. In addition, although one is observing a curriculum in the form of ongoing classes, one could not conclude the curriculum in the practice stage to be an absolute success without observing how much quality and quantity of capacities children would obtain as a result even if one could improve the curriculum in the practice stage through formative evaluation. In this sense, it is probably correct to conclude that the actual growth of children can only be grasped in the result stage of curriculum.

Nevertheless, when asked "So what?," research results by this group would not casually give a straight answer. It naturally makes a certain judgment on the value of curriculum, but it rarely touches on what kind of situation should be best realized because its utmost focus rests with the mere clarification of facts.[4]

---

[4]The following is a list of major books written by researchers belonging to this group:

Tanaka, T. (1996). *Karikyuramu no Shakaigakuteki-Kenkyu* (Sociological research on curriculum).
Shibano, S. et al. (Eds). (1992). *Kyoiku Shakaigaku* (Educational sociology).
Shimizu, K. (Ed.). (1998). *Kyoiku no Esunogurafi* (Ethnography of education).

Group That Gives Criticism From the Marxist Standpoint

Having been in the mainstream in the education-related academic sphere in Japan after World War II, this group still remains in the center of the sphere, although its impact has recently declined. This group's position in opposing the Ministry of Education, Culture, Sports, Science, and Technology from the left wing is theoretically clear. Although the group partially supports the recent trend of deregulation on the part of the administration concerning curriculum, it consistently opposes the introduction of liberalization measures, competition, and market principles to education. This is basically due to the philosophy of the group, from its socialistic and communistic perspective, of considering education as a social service, because these measures are not given a certain level of guarantee by the state.

With regards to curriculum studies, the group opposes each and every measure proposed by the government—the Liberal Democratic Party and the Ministry of Education, Culture, Sports, Science, and Technology—and makes special efforts in preparing counterproposals against them. More specifically, Professor Toshio Umehara (Wako University) is a leading figure in this movement, and those who share the same uniquely Japanese Marxist philosophy gather around him, forming a group. This group is characterized by its basic beliefs in, among other things, group-focused rather than individual-focused education, maintenance of publicness to ensure equal opportunities in education given by public authorities, and vigilance and criticism of ideology-driven nationalism in education. Policies that stem from these kinds of perspectives include the emphasis on mandatory subject matters and criticism of the expansion of elective courses, the guarantee of a certain level of academic achievement, and the emphasis on achievement level evaluation for that purpose. Professor Koji Tanaka (Kyoto University) is quite active in research on such evaluations.

The utmost *Japaneseness* in the Marxist educational philosophy lies in its *egalitarianism*. Although special education for the gifted is agreed on as well as encouraged in Marxist education in other countries, it has been consistently viewed negatively in Japan since World War II. Consequently, the basic image of Marxist education in Japan lies in its policy of fostering capacities equally and uniform education pursued in terms of ideology. The undercurrent of such thought is the assertion that the state should assume responsibility for guaranteeing its people a common, minimal education level—in other words, that gaps in sex, academic achievement, social classes, and economy (income) should not be generated.

Although this group criticizes those curricula that bring about socioeconomic gaps, it allows those that emphasize independence of children or teachers. Child-centered features are acknowledged as democratic, and a curriculum independently developed by teachers is also considered good due to its democratic nature. Therefore, the group regards the deregulation measure per se by the Ministry of Education, Culture, Sports, Science, and Technology as something that should be welcomed, but criticizes that teachers and children on the accepting side are still ill-prepared at this time. However, it does not say when they will be prepared. In short, the group squarely criticizes every attempt from above to reform by relegating it as something that is done for the convenience and benefit of the authoritative ruling class.

As a result of the collapse of the former Soviet Union, the attitude and views of Marxist pedagogists toward America have recently changed, and the trend of considering, if partially, American democracy to be favorable is on the increase. Accordingly, more people in the group value democratic characteristics in the American education administration. In such a trend, the group has been gradually accepting some ideas of curriculum studies, including integrated study, and developing them on its own, however limited it may be.[5]

Group That Promotes School-Based Curriculum Development

This is a joint and cooperative group consisting of teachers and researchers. They cooperatively conduct research to determine what kinds of measures are required to develop a curriculum best fit to each school. Thus, this group has a strong intention to have teachers acquire curriculum development ability as well as to further improve it for the utmost purpose of promoting school-based curriculum development. One of the leaders of this group is Professor Tadahiko Abiko (Waseda University).

Previously, it was hard for individual school teachers to foster an ability to develop and compose a curriculum because of the central curriculum administration by the Ministry of Education. Curricula were developed by educational administrators and veteran teachers (practitioners) who were close to them, and that was done with little involvement of researchers. Therefore, the teachers' awareness was directed to teaching and instruction skills rather than the curriculum, and curriculum studies in Japan were merely counted as one category of research on instruction methods and skills. This is one of the major reasons that there was no academic society specializing in curriculum in Japan until 10 years ago, and the only society that was founded a long time ago was the National Association for the Study of Educational Methods.

Accordingly, this group is currently encouraging and soliciting teachers to actively engage themselves in curriculum-related issues so they can improve their skills in curriculum development, composition methods, procedures, viewpoints, and so on through their own experience. Among other things, the fact that the deregulation carried out by the educational administration has begun to require teachers to acquire these skills is increasingly directing teachers' awareness toward curriculum. In particular, the major issue that teachers are currently facing is how to define the relationship between curriculum of each study subject matter and newly introduced periods of integrated study.

Professor Abiko also addresses that theories on curriculum development have been too broad (i.e., the problem-solving curriculum and discovery-method curriculum), and curriculum formation in response to more detailed objectives has been neglected. Accordingly, he proposes that hybrid model curriculum development should be conducted, which is a combination of more refined curricula established for each different objective.

At the same time, with regards to the relationship between children's developmental stages and school curriculum, he insists that a curriculum that could work effectively on each developmental stage of children cannot be formed without clarifying the entire structure of curriculum throughout the entire schooling from infancy to adolescence. He proposes a curriculum so structured by collecting results from brain science and developmental psychology or empirical facts on the part of teachers and children.

Due to this group's research content, researchers from various backgrounds participate in it, including educational psychologists, brain scientists, subject-matter pedagogists, and school administration researchers, making it possible for them to ex-

---

[5]The following is a list of major books written by researchers belonging to this group:

Umehara, T. (1999). *Gakushushido-yoryo wo Koeru Gakko-zukuri* (School formation beyond courses of study).

Group Didactica et al. (Ed.). (2000). *Manabi no Tame no Karikyuramu-ron* (Curriculum methodology for learning).

change opinions and information in an open and interdisciplinary manner. Although the group is weak on analyses from social perspectives, it learns about them from the research results of other groups and tries hard to help teachers develop a better fitting, even if only slightly, curriculum.[6]

---

[6]The following is a list of major books by researchers belonging to this group:

Abiko, T. (Ed.). (1985). *Karikyuramu Kenkyu Nyumon* (Introduction to curriculum studies).

Abiko, T. (Ed.). (1999). *Shinpan: Karikyuramu Kenkyu Nyumon* (New edition: Introduction to curriculum studies).

Abiko, T. (Ed.). (1998). *Gakko Chi no Tenkan* (School knowledge and change: How to undertake curriculum development).

Abiko, T. (Ed.). (1997). *Chugakko Karrikyuramu no Dokujisei to Kosei-genri* (Uniqueness and construction principles of junior high school curriculum).

CHAPTER 23

Japanese Educational Reform for the 21st Century: The Impact of the New Course of Study Toward the Postmodern Era in Japan

Shigeru Asanuma
Tokyo Gakugei University, Japan

This chapter is an analysis of the basic structure and meanings of the curriculum reform in contemporary Japan. Japanese education was broadly publicized among American educational researchers in the 1980s. As LeTendre (1999) pointed out, it is well known that Japan coincidentally became interested in a political agenda of American educational policies. As the Sputnik shock typically demonstrated, the topic of education has been used for rationalizing politics and budget allocation. A nation at crisis is always eroded as a chance to expand public concern. In the 1980s and 1990s, a number of publications and broadcast news concerning Japan's education was distributed to the public as a case of those politicized interest in the United States.

A number of publications have reported that the strict discipline and consequent pressure for entrance examinations have brought Japanese children up to the point of highly above the average scores of school achievement around the world. However, the fact is not well known that a flexible and progressive curriculum policy has been administered in Japan since April 2000. Among the global issues of curriculum in Japan, only part of the descriptions on the history of wars and racial discrimination in social studies textbooks is likely to be argued as a target of political agenda in the discourse of international politics. As a consequence, the textbook issue is likely to be reduced to the social studies textbooks in Japan as well as other countries. The Japanese popular condemnation is typically represented in avoiding the historical duty of teaching its bloody modern history, such as the Nanking massacre and *comfort* women from Korea.

In the United States, Japan's education has been of interest for longer than a century as a public discourse. On the one hand, Japan's education has been used for reflecting and changing American educational policies since 1872 (Hashimoto, chap. 21, this volume). On the other hand, Japan has used American education to formulate Japan's educational policies and public discourses. Japan's education is used as a tool for changing American educational policy without the scrutiny of the real educational practices. But the attitude of American educators changed in the 1990s after Japan's economic *miracle* ended in the late 1980s. A number of American educators began to observe Japan's schools without the economic interest. As a result, American researchers' stereotyped views of Japan's education gradually corrected due an increasing number of publications reporting on education in Japan. In particular, the development of American researchers' ethnographic studies of Japan's teachers' classroom teaching contributed to the changing traditional view of Japan's education. As LeTendre (1999) pointed out, the mutual examinations of videotaped classes helped to correct their stereotyped views of education in Japan. For instance, "American teachers interviewed often spoke of the strict discipline of Japanese schools" (p. 43), and *cleaning schools* is an example of how American teachers' image of Japanese education is created. The American teachers' image of Japanese education changed by scrutinizing the videotapes; they saw that cleaning schools actually created an enjoyable environment and a cooperative atmosphere for Japanese children.

Studies like LeTendre's have contributed to the correction of stereotyped images of Japan's education prevalent in the United States. However, there is always a critical problem in those behavioral comparative studies of schools. For in-depth curriculum studies, it is indispensable for a researcher to grasp and illuminate the internal state of the individual learner: what she or he thinks and how he or she interprets the world. Those studies do not elucidate the children's curriculum experiences because the language difference always hinders the in-depth mutual understanding of the quality of children's curriculum experiences. This is the reason that a number of comparative studies between the United States and Japan are likely to be limited to visible facts such as the children's test scores or social behavior such as fashion. Therefore, LeTendre (1999) rightly pointed out: "Because many of the social changes experienced by Japan are common to nations making the transition to a 'post industrial' economy, this area of research offers significant potential for researchers and educators interested in the impact of social change on cultural values and education" (p. 4). It is necessary to add more to this statement. Japan is confronted not only with a postindustrial economy, but also with the postmodern world in curriculum. A simplistic economic explanation does not clarify the direction the new generation is heading in the 21st century.

THE NEW COURSE OF STUDIES IN JAPAN

The Ministry of Education announced the New Course of Studies (NCS) for elementary and secondary schools in Japan in 1999. NCS emphasized the phrase *ikiru chikara* (living power; passion for life) as the most important educational goal for Japan's future. Those involved in the educational reform in 1990s, the Central Council of Education, argued about the goal of education for many years. This council consists of experts appointed by the Ministry of Education. It is in charge of steering Japan's most important educational policies. This council addressed the main pillars of educational reform for the first decade of the 21st century as following three key words.

Ikiru Chikara (Living Power; Passion for Life)

The Central Council of Education assumed that the most critical issue of contemporary Japanese children was their inability of living in their everyday lives. The council members assumed that demographic and economic changes have influenced children's basic abilities in sustaining their fundamental lives. The most shocking fact they have to consider is the increase of the number of children committing to suicide. The number of children committing suicide increased in the 1980s for many reasons (e.g., bullying a boy in a middle school). In that case, three classmates forced him to steal money from home and elsewhere. The victimized student was bullied in various ways, such as being submerged in a river whenever he failed to steal. In another instance, three junior high school girl students jumped out of the top of a tall building because they lost the sense of the meaningful life by abusing drugs. They hated schools and lost the motivation to survive in this world.

Those incidents are not sufficient conditions for justifying the new national education policies. Nevertheless, those cases were symbolically used for rationalizing the goals of educational reform. As a matter of fact, the older generation had a hunch that their children's world has been transformed into the stage of their own experienced world. They found that the symptoms of their children's behavior deviated from the decency in the former years in their children's age in Japan. The older generation used common sense to understand their children's behavioral changes not in terms of the concept of the generation gap, but from the drastic changes of intrinsic values of children's lives. Children losing the realistic senses surrounding their circumstances damaged the natural development of the individual's sanity as biological and social existence. The inspiration generated from those natural senses became the foundation of forming the national goals of curriculum in modern Japan. There is no country in this world that advocates basic abilities such as living power as a national goal of education except Japan. How do we interpret this kind of educational goal? It is a biological terminology. But it is now becoming a goal of national policy.

Yutori (Relaxation or Slowing Down)

The council found that the lack of children's living power was generated by the overloaded national curriculum content that is mostly based on traditional subject matters. Hence, the council proposed trimming the number of school hours and minimum essentials of curriculum content for all children. *Yutori* means relaxation—reducing the overloaded curriculum and competition in education.

A number of people assumed that the total number of school hours would be less than those in the United States on the completion of this reform. The most prominent point in this reform is the prescription of practicing the project method type learning at all grade school levels for 2 or 3 school hours a week on the basis of school initiative. At the middle school level, a school has the freedom to let the students choose certain subjects for 2 or 3 school hours a week. Theoretically, ninth-grade children would gain the freedom to decide what they want to learn for one third of school hours, including about 1000 hours of project type learning for a year. As a result, Japanese schools have legally attained the highest point of flexibility in making curriculum on the school basis.

The Ministry of Education set up the minimum standard instead of the maximum. It seems to the public that Japanese national curriculum has been reduced and downsized. Recently, a number of mass media started a campaign against the educational reform by the Ministry of Education. It was alleged that reducing the number of school hours for the traditional subject matters would lead to the lowering of Japanese children's school achievements. This conservative campaign stirred the antagonism among the Japanese masses against educational reform. The conservatives suddenly amplified their voice in 1999. They started listing a number of false facts (e.g., indicating the decrease of children's home study hours; college students who cannot calculate multiplication or division of numbers; college students who do not know the basic historical facts). The controversy over the new national curriculum was hyperbolic rather than factual. There was no solid evidence demonstrating that the reduction of curriculum standard courses leads to the lowering of students' school achievements. Even International Educational Achievement test scores do not show it lowering students' school achievements despite that conservatives have pointed out the decrease of the international ranking of Japanese students' mathematics scores. Almost all evidence the conservatives submitted is irrelevant for rationalizing their own argument. From the controversy over educational reform, it is possible to observe the character of Japanese national hysteria, which is based on pseudoconsciousness and general rumors.

Japan's contemporary curriculum reform is so drastic that it is plausible that many school teachers cannot follow its radical changes. However, this reform has been made as a result of the national consensus on education over the last decade. A number of educational practitioners found that the discourse of curriculum would be based not on a rational procedure, but on the politics where various interests groups struggle for hegemony and ideology.

Kokoro no Kyoiku (Education for Mind, Psychological Treatment)

The key word *Kokoro no Kyoiku* was added at the last stage of the council in 1998. A number of victims were sacrificed before the formation of this pillar. One of the crucial incidents was that of a middle school teacher killed by a student who was carrying a knife because of his stressful and psychologically disordered condition. This murder case shocked all over Japan. The controversy about the students carrying knives became the sensational topic in education in 1998. The council found that the school circumstance—in particular, the traditional curriculum—has damaged the children's normal psychological development. The council started emphasizing the need to introduce school counselors or psychological clinics in schools. As a result, the Ministry of Education accelerated the process of administering NCS. Those three major pillars were the main resources drawing on the curriculum reforms in the 1990s. Those pillars were basically a continuum of the educational reform of the 1980s. The unique individual development (*Koseika*) and globalization (*Kokusaika*) were the fundamental drives for educational reform in 1980s. The most noticeable implication of the educational reform was their attempt to deconstruct the traditional concept of curriculum and instruction, which merely emphasized the ability of rote learning and factual knowledge.

CURRICULUM REFORM FOR DEMOCRATIC CITIZENSHIP

How can we interpret Japan's curriculum reform as it has been stated? It should be noted that we cannot correctly understand this reform in terms of the traditional frameworks such as discipline-centered curriculum versus child-centered curriculum. We have to take into account the fundamental changes in the economic, social, and cultural environments in Japan.

Japan entered the postindustrial era in the 1980s. Even conservative political leaders had predicted the coming economic crisis in the future. The neo-conservatives started fighting not only with the socialists, but also with the old conservatives who used to benefit from the socialist pseudoegalitarian bureaucracy. The farmers and working class, such as the National Railroad Corporation, were typical cases who used to enjoy monopolistic benefits from the Japanese socialist type economic system. The destruction of the socialist type egalitarian economic system became imperative for the conservative government for sustaining their economy, which was supported by the corporate industries. The curriculum reform has been accompanied with the deconstruction of traditional corporate economic system because Japan has had to face various crisis in the postindustrial society, which has not been accomplished before.

It is obvious that postindustrialism is not equal to the postmodernism. However, the cultural milieu surrounding schools has changed since the 1980s. Most Japanese were not aware that they were living in an era of cultural transition toward postmodernism. Educational reform was the most important task for the government in the 1990s. The government began to formulate new educational policies slowly at first. Their first target was the traditional curriculum, emphasizing *the basics*. Even conservative political leaders started asserting the lack of the individual ego development in Japanese citizenship education. The conservatives assumed that the lack of the development of ego identity hindered the development of the individual's ability to make judgments when faced with dilemmas or social conflicts. They even started reflecting on their own attitude that they cannot live without the authority to consult.

The problem of the individual's excessive dependency has been publicized and disclosed by a number of psychiatrists and psychoanalysts in Japan. Phrases such as *amae* (sweat dependency) or *moratorium* (holding the decision of the ego identity) are popular among the Japanese, although they have not tried to change their own subjectivity because they think it is not a problem in their own ego, but in others. Western philosophers like Hegel and Weber have pointed out the problems of the lack of the individual ego identity in the Confucian ethics. They assume that Confucian ethics permeate into the individuals' mentality and psychologically motivate them to obey the community leaders, and therefore volunteer for slave labor. Thus, they alleged there is no democratic process based on the individual ego identity in Confucian ethics.

For the Japanese, curriculum reform represents a kind of cultural revolution, which sometimes accompanies pain and antagonism from the traditional groups, including socialist educators. Teachers cannot communicate the importance of human rights or social justice when their efforts are focused on entrance examinations. Students do not have to hold the memory of the factual knowledge after they attain their own private goal of education, which simply means gaining university diplomas. They would never believe that there are significant values in university curricula because they assume that the values of knowledge are not in the knowledge, but in schools' entrance exams. Even if they passed the examinations, which are composed of heavily loaded factual knowledge for good citizenship, there is no guarantee for them to become good citizens. For many Japanese, knowledge is separated from their practical lives. This dichotomy between theory and practice has always existed in the history of Japanese school curriculum. Education for a good citizenship typically represents this dichotomy in Japanese curriculum. The critical problem in the field of curriculum study in Japan is that there are not many educators who take this dichotomy seriously.

THE THEORY AND PRACTICE FOR A GOOD CITIZENSHIP BEYOND THE KNOWLEDGE-BASED CURRICULUM

To solve the problem of the dichotomy between theory and practice, the Ministry of Education began to formulate and introduce a new sphere of curriculum called *Sougouteki Gakushu no Jikan* (Time for Comprehensive Learning). Japanese schools started the new subject matter, called *Seikatsuka* (The Study of Life), for first and second grades at elementary schools in the mid-1990s, it is a subject integrating science and social studies. The Ministry of Education introduced the new curriculum, which is similar to *Seikatsuka,* into all other school in Grades 3 to 12. The *Sougouteki Gakushu* aims to implement the project method type learning as demonstrated in the United States in the era of progressive education movement since the 1890s. The council assumes that *Ikiru Chikara* will be attained through the process of problem solving in this type of learning.

It is also expected to provide educational programs for a good citizenship through community-based curriculum. NCS encourages teachers and children to use community resources, including human environments surrounding schools.

NCS prescribes that *Sougouteki Gakushu no Jikan* should include activities for international understanding, environmental learning, information, welfare and health, and others. These learning units used to be taught in social studies, sciences, and home economics. However, the Ministry of Education found it necessary to clearly promulgate the school hours for those areas of study besides the hours of traditional subject matters because they assumed it is difficult to include those areas of study in the area of traditional subject matters. Among many subject matters, social studies still has important status for educating citizenship. However, many social studies teachers have failed to prepare children for citizenship.

Because many educators are frustrated with the failure of traditional subject matters, *Sougouteki Gakushu no Jikan* (the project method type learning) was introduced to attain the new goals of education. It is time for students to create their own activity through their own projects for a good citizenship. Instead of memorizing factual knowledge, they are required to explore topics on the basis of their own judgment. Children are encouraged to establish authority by developing their own autonomous activities, which means they are responsible for their own planning and activities. Children's interests and needs are respected because the motivation to explore the topic is the most important factor for successful learning. For successful learning, it is important for children to listen to their internal voices in their individual minds. Beyond the surface of the factual textbook knowledge, educators and children are required to think critically about the ethics they can practice in their everyday lives. Many outstanding practices and cases developing these activities were reported before Japanese schools officially started the integrated curriculum. It is important to know how the educators have developed their own theories and practices.

CONCLUSION: PROSPECTS FOR THE PIONEERING PRACTICES OF THE INTEGRATED CURRICULUM

Many of the practices of curriculum integration have been attempted at all levels of school. For instance, Ogawa Elementary School (Aichi-Ken) has organized the program of exchanging friendships with the elder people, the handicapped, Korean-Japanese, the people from other countries, the staff of international organizations, and the people in the community. Most practices have shown good performances in terms of students' scholastic achievement and passion, and self-discipline in their everyday lives. However, we need clear-cut analytical frameworks to interpret those practices because it is not well defined to interpret the direction and future society oriented by those educational reforms. Thus, I assume that age definition is necessary to identify the epoch of those curriculum integration (Asanuma, 1998). Here I find the transition of Japan's school curriculum from modernism to postmodernism. The first pillar of modern Japanese curriculum consists of self-discipline, punctuality, regularity, autonomy, structural consistency, standardized forms, individuality, and utilitarian value orientation. These characterizations are based on the bureaucracy and economic structure of the environments surrounding school. The school is a microcosmos of the virtual reality of modern society.

Ogawa Elementary School is a well-known open school in Japan. There is a large amount of freedom in time management for school life. The children have freedom to run their own meetings in the morning, freedom to plan their own lessons, freedom to control their own time, and freedom to have so-called *open time*. Freedom to make one's own decisions requires self-responsibility. The freedom of time management means that the children are obliged to obey their own time rules once they decide. The freedom to determine what they explore means they have to have responsibility to pursue their own goals once they have alleged to attain. Therefore, the freedom of decision making means the responsibility for their own judgment. The freedom leads to the self-discipline of the children. The punishment from the internal voice is more realistic for the individual than the punishment from the others. Thus, the self-regulation comes from the internal voice. Nobody can reach the individual self except through subjectivity. The individual is likely to believe that somebody would call you for the discipline, but this voice actually arises in the individual ego. This internalized voice voluntarily springs from the monad of the ego identity.

The automatic body movement is clearly observed when we see physical education and school assemblies in Japan's schools. Even in school baseball games, students are expected to run and take regulated forms in their team formation. As physical education demonstrates, the power comes from the bottom to the top rather than the top to the bottom. As Foucault described, the modernism of education is based not on power relations of the human body, but on the psychological structuring of human relationships. The internalization of the voice made it possible to volunteer to regulate one's own self. External physical punishment is not necessary for the society to control individuals. Individuals are motivated to punish themselves psychologically. This punishment is likely to accompany action to shape the body physically.

It is possible to see the modernism in the contemporary curriculum reform movement in Japan. Japan's modernization of curriculum implies the liberation of the individual from the outer control of human body and soul. If the freedom of the individual's spirit is the ultimate goal of modernism, then the aim of curriculum reform movement has to be directed toward the consistent spontaneity of self-control.

The modernization of Japan's school curriculum demonstrates a optimistic faith in the future. The future is the *promised land* for those who have developed a work ethic in their self-disciplined day-to-day labor. They can enjoy their lives as long as they work hard for the production. As long as they follow standardized procedures, they are satisfied with their realization of utilitarian values.

Japan's curriculum reform movement has a postmodernism value in its practice. The traits of the postmodernism are typically characterized by reciprocity, mutuality, dialogue, flexibility, situation dependency, virtual reality, style, marginality, chaos, and exchanging value orientation. Most curriculum reforms are defined in terms of these traits. Most practices include the reciprocal action in its teaching method and program.

For instance, the touching program in various schools means that the children have contact with the elder, the city people, and foreigners. The children have curiosity and interest in people who are different and unfamiliar. The difference inspires the creative motivation. The discrepancy between the day-to-day life and the ideal produces the inspiration for the future. Deviation from the taken-for-granted world provides the opportunity to question and wonder at the world. Children are encouraged to experiment with the real world.

Modernism and postmodernism have to be mixed in their curriculum practices. It is conceivable that Japan's curriculum practices for integration are in the midst of the transition from modern curriculum to postmodern. There is no distinctive boundary in this transition. It is chaotic, but creative. It is not a type of activity of establishing order, but of deconstructing the traditional structures of the curriculum at first.

REFERENCES

Asanuma, S. (Ed.). (1998). *Making cross-curriculum/integrated curriculum for living power.* Nagoya, Japan: Reimei Shobo.

Foucault, M. (1988). *Politics, philosophy, culture: Interviews and other writings 1977–1984.* [Edited by L. Kritzman]. New York: Routledge.

LeTendre, G. K. (1999). The problem of Japan: Qualitative studies and international educational comparisons. *Educational Researcher, 28*(2), 38–45.

CHAPTER 24

Curriculum Research:
Evolution and Outlook in Mexico

Ángel Díaz Barriga
National Autonomous University of Mexico

Like other disciplinary groups of educational sciences that have to do with the school system, the field of curriculum is an outstandingly practical domain. Scholarly reflection about education becomes concrete in action, and this is the reason that historically many parts of educational sciences have been considered as completely lacking in theoretical dimension, which is not acceptable at all.

It is also generally accepted that educational disciplines can be classified into theoretical and practical—a separation that does not necessarily reflect what happens, neither in the conceptual constitution of the research field nor in practice, and this distinction is observable in the entire history of education. This separation was first expressed at the beginning of this century by Durkheim (1979),[1] who came to consider the professor as a practitioner, entirely different from the person who has conceptual responsibility to build the educational knowledge.[2] All this contributed, in my view, to the conceptual impoverishment of those disciplines.

What we call the *field of curriculum* is fully concerned with this problem. The first tension comes from the absence of an appropriated articulation between theory and practice. On the one hand, there was a trend that only worried about the technical dimension of the formulation of plans and programs and its development in the classrooms; the other tradition, as a reaction to a reductionist technicality, began to build up an exclusively conceptual discourse in many instances rather remote from practice.

---

[1] *"Se puede ser un perfecto educador y ser, sin embargo, completamente incapaz para las especulaciones de la pedagogía. … El pedagogo puede carecer de toda habilidad práctica; no habríamos confiado una clase a Rousseau, ni a Montaigne"* ("Someone may be a perfect educator and nevertheless be completely unable to reach the high spheres of pedagogical speculation. … The pedagogue can be completely lacking in practical ability: we would never have entrusted a class to Rousseau nor Montaigne," my translation).

[2] The German tradition of pedagogy granted an important place to theory in the teacher's job. That is what Herbart demanded in 1806: *"He exigido del educador ciencia y reflexión. No me importa que la ciencia sea para los demás como unos lentes, para mí es como unos ojos y los mejores sin duda que tienen los hombres para mirar sus asuntos. … La pedagogía es la ciencia que necesita el educador para sí mismo"* ("I require from the educator science and reflection. I don't care about the fact that science is considered by the others like glasses, for me it is like eyes, and certainly the best eyes that people have to look at their business. … Pedagogy is the science the educator needs for himself," my translation).

We consider curriculum as a practical domain articulated by theory whose object is to delineate the school subjects, from the global conception of skills and knowledges that are required at every level of the educational system, to the working processes generated in the classrooms, to the evaluation systems in their relation with the complete scholastic process. The clarification of the different objects of what we call *curriculum* has led to a debate. In this perspective, two problems arise whose solution is important for a better comprehension of the curriculum research in Mexico. In the first place, it is necessary to start with a conceptualization about what we understand as curriculum research; in the second place, we need to proceed to a conceptual demarcation of the domain of curriculum.

CONCEPTUALIZATIONS OF CURRICULUM RESEARCH

One of the deepest reflections about what we must understand as curriculum research can be found in the *Estado de Conocimiento* (State of Affairs), wherein curriculum specialists are recognized as specialists (Díaz Barriga et al., 1995). In this document, curriculum specialists are contextualized in the conception that Durkheim[3] formulated about the educational sciences, from which can be derived three levels of the educational research:

1. the basic or conceptual research whose object is to make conceptual constructions;
2. applied research with a double purpose: It uses the characteristic methods of this research model to analyze the results of diverse educative programs, and these results can be studied from different disciplines (sociology, psychology, etc.) and multiple conceptual points of view (functionalism, genetic psychology, etc.), as well as its own methodologies for the study of the different subjects that have to do with the field of curriculum; and
3. we also considered as relevant the acknowledgment of a third level, which consists of the systematized reflection about curriculum experiences.

This reflection makes possible an articulation between practical cases and their conceptual grounds. Curriculum research has, if we see it from this perspective, an ample field for further development: The methodologies to which the curriculum researcher can resort depend on the stress he puts on anyone in the educational sciences.

Surely this classification of research options in the field of curriculum occasions some complications. There is a huge contrast between research with empirical referent (case 2) and the other two investigation models. In the case of the so-called *conceptual studies* (case 1), it is not easy to pass judgment on the contribution that a study—generally expressed with the form of an essay—offers to the domain of curriculum. In the same way, the conceptualization of a curricular experience (case 3), whose advantage is that it shows the ranges and limits of a particular experience, confronts the difficulty of realizing a theoretical-practical articulation, which makes possible a documentary reconstruction that formulates the conceptual basis of this articulation with its results and that—thanks to this formulation—can be the origin for further developments of the field. I have come to recognize that this conceptualization of the curriculum research has been convenient and fecund to analyses of research conducted in the field of curriculum in Mexico.

---

[3]As I mentioned earlier, for Durkheim, the research that leads to the formulation of laws is built by the educational science, whereas the pedagogy is a practical theory whose purpose is to give an orientation to the educational action; the action of the educator is determined only by practice.

THE SUBJECTS OF STUDY
SUBJACENT TO THE FIELD OF CURRICULUM

The range of methodological possibilities for the research that we have shown increases significantly when we recognize the great diversity of the subjects of study that are subjacent in the delimitation of what can be considered as curriculum. From its beginning, curriculum studies has confronted difficulties specifying the limits of the research field. In the first texts, it is possible to notice the conformation of two traditions: The first is linked to the analysis of the contents and the learning experiences generated in individuals, like we can see in the study of Dewey (1902), *The Child and the Curriculum*. The other is a formal perspective about the organization of the contents integrated to the study plans, like in the study of Bobbit (1918), *The Curriculum.*[4] This perspective becomes dominant in the development of the field, particularly because of its practical utility for the organization of the educative systems and in the school establishments; it clearly answers the question, How can I organize a study plan?

In the development of this field of research, other subjects arose—in some cases, like a specialization derived from the construction of study plans; in others, like a specific development of the field. In the first case, we find topics like the elaboration of the grounds of a study plan (in many cases, best known as analysis of necessities), the selection and organization of the contents of a study plan,[5] the curriculum evaluation, and, especially in Mexico, professional formation. In the second case, the most relevant is undoubtedly the concept of *hidden curriculum,* which has become the axis of interesting outlooks. As a result, Dewey's vision of paying attention to the educational experiences that the school system promotes gave, in the Mexican case, the conception of curriculum as a process. This led Furlán (1996) to formulate the concepts of *curriculum pensado* (thought-out curriculum) to refer to the proposal of the educative institution and *curriculum vivido* (lived curriculum or curriculum based on personal experiences) to refer to the educational experiences that happen in a classroom.

The field of curriculum has become a vast research field in which almost all the subjects that bear relation to the school system are studied, including the educative institution and pedagogical practices. Some scholars even consider *curriculum* as a concept comparable with the concept of educational sciences, and this makes necessary a rigorous demarcation of its conceptual borders. We recognize, from a historical perspective, that it was initially conceived to tell of the elaboration of programs and plans and the entirety of educational experiences based on these programs that can be realized in the classroom. However, it is also true that both subjects have become more complex because of the natural evolution of the research field as well as the apparition of new themes, which once were subdisciplines and then came to establish themselves as typical developments of the research field (like the case of the hidden curriculum concept and the curriculum in development or in process). Like specific applications of mutations made in other disciplines (like the case of the relationship between institutional theory and the educative institution; the administrative disciplines; and particularly the focus on total quality and themes of management and operation of a study plan),

---

[4]We cannot forget that, for Cremin, the works of Bobbitt, which include another *How to Make the Curriculum* (1924) together with Charter's (1923) book *Curriculum Construction,* represent "*el esfuerzo para desarrollar una ciencia de elaboración del plan de estudios de las escuelas públicas*" ("The effort to develop a science to elaborate the study program in public school establishments," my translation).

[5]A meta-reading of Tyler's book makes it possible to assert that, beyond what the author calls *sources* for a curriculum (a theme that Taba translates as "analysis of necessities"), what he really proposes is a working system that can be subdivided in determination of the grounds and methodological formulations to design them. Compare Díaz Barriga (1996).

the tension that there is between the didactical tradition (so important in the Latin countries) and instruction theories (linked with the experimental psychology and different kinds of constructivist psychology) is noteworthy.

In this situation, the domain of curriculum research had to tackle a multiplicity of themes that bear relation to the school institution, and these can be examined from the most diverse methodologies (e.g., a study about professional performance may combine elements of profession sociology with aspects of educative economy, or a research about thought construction may be based on diverse methodologies of cognitive sciences). The field of curriculum covers plenty of studies about education.

CURRICULUM RESEARCH IN MEXICO

The development of the field of curriculum in Mexico is tightly linked with higher education. To understand this situation, it is necessary to keep in mind that the study plans of the Mexican educative system are characterized by their centralization except at the level of public universities[6] and in the private system of higher education. Study plans for the whole school system are made at the national level—a situation that causes a passive attitude in the teaching staff of the educative system. Each public university or private institution of higher education states a curricular proposal for the different specializations that it offers. In this way, the themes that can be identified in the curriculum research bear a close relation to the educational problematics of the higher school system.

We can assert that, in the domain of Mexican educational research, the curriculum research is gaining ground. As a matter of fact, it is now possible to identify several formed groups that reflect different traditions. The results of their work have a national and sometimes even international circulation.

For a best comprehension, we assemble the themes that comprise the subjects of study into three categories: (a) exclusively conceptual studies, (b) conceptual studies with empirical referents, and (c) proposals to elaborate study plans. Each of these categories includes distinct modalities and thematic emphases.

Exclusively Conceptual Studies

Under this category, we find three kinds of studies. First, there are studies whose purpose is to realize a conceptual construction of the field. There are three basic supports for such work: psychology, sociology, and philosophy, especially in their relation with epistemology and cognition theory. Surely history is a discipline present in such approximations as well. Two questions orient those approximations: What do we understand as field of curriculum? Is there a specific theory for this knowledge? If the answer to the latter is positive, we question, How can the conceptual ground of the diverse curricular proposals be built?

In the facts, we can find a conceptual obstacle to delimit the studies of what we consider the curriculum discipline; the classroom and the educative institution are directly connected with it, and also the explicit educative project, which becomes concrete through the study plans and programs and the real educational practices. Many of these are neither foreseen nor conscious. Because of the notable quantity of topics and/or subjects that it includes, the field of curriculum is multidisciplinary. It is a field in which the knowledge of several diverse disciplines converge—where the principal

---

[6]Part of the public higher education system are also the institutes for technological education and the teacher training colleges or normal schools. In those cases, the study program is made in a centralized way by the Federation.

dangers are to exclude the traditionally educational disciplines[7] and assign to curriculum discipline the place that belonged once to educational theory. However, in regard to the simplifications that psychology—and specifically experimental psychology—went through during the development of curriculum, sociology has become a privileged approximation to analyze the social relations in the educational system.

Finally, an important group of studies realized in Mexico has to do with curriculum history. Those studies present two directions: (a) an analysis of the origin and evolution of curriculum problem in Mexican Federation, whose aim is to make evident which are the most important themes it has to tackle with; and (b) a study about the incorporation, evolution, and Mexicanization of the curriculum debate in Mexico,[8] as well as the evolution of the institutions that offer different study plans (like the modular system) or some professions in particular (medicine, nursery, psychology, education, etc.). In all those cases, the problem of practice has been casted into relative oblivion.

Conceptual Studies With an Empirical Referent

In this category, we find five subjects of research in the field of curriculum. This kind of research is the one that fits best into what we traditionally used to understand as research particularly because it relies explicitly on empirical referents.

Studies About Professions.   With contributions from the professions of sociology, educational economy, and history, it has been possible to carry out a group of research studies about the performances of students who graduated at the university, as well as the evaluation of those students and their employers about the intellectual formation they received, and about the following of graduated students to appraise the processes of incorporation into the labor world. Some educational economists have realized studies about the increasing trend of the demand of professionals for the labor market. In the same way, there are studies about the formation of specific professionals, sometimes by comparing the study plans that diverse institutions offer for the same professional (architect, physician, psychologist, pedagogue). To understand this situation, it is necessary to keep in mind that, in the Mexican higher educational system, it is not obligatory to specify a minimum of contents in the study plans of similar professions, unlike the Spanish norms, which stipulate that *"un núcleo mínimo de contenidos deba estar presente en los planes de estudios conducente a una misma titulación"* ("there must be a minimum of contents in study plans that lead to the same degree," my translation; Murillo, 1997, p. 128). In the same way, in Mexico, no institutional accreditation practice exists that can assume the position of an external guarantee for the different professional formation projects. Thus, the curriculum research in relation with the professional formation has filled an important function: It offers

---

[7]This seems to be a usual problem for all the people who undertake that kind of research study. Likewise, when Hameyer (1993) made a balance of curricular research in Germany, he affirmed: "*La investigación curricular se mueve en parte en el terreno de la didáctica clásica y la teoría educativa, aunque con diferente metodología. ... Los críticos advierten también que los investigadores curriculares no debían dejar en el olvido os conceptos básicos de la teoría educativa y la didáctica*" ("Curricular research moves part in the sphere of classical didactic and part in the educational theory, although it uses different methodologies. ... The critics also notice that the curricular researchers could not forget the basic concepts of educational theory and didactic," my translation).

[8]It is possible to identify several concepts that have been forged in the Mexican experience and that have had a fundamental impact in Latin America (e.g., the modular study program by transformation subjects, the analysis of professional practice by considering it as decadent, domineering, and emergent, or a framework for curriculum design).

valuable information about the performances of graduated students and the characteristics of the diverse formation projects.

Studies About Content.   The studies about selection and organization of contents in the study plans are one of the research lines in the field of curriculum. Those are based on four axes: The structure of contents in each discipline; the construction of knowledge and its impact on the organization of the contents in a study plan; the cultural imposition and socialization of values through the selection of contents; and those that recently have been considered as emergent themes in the treatment of contents, especially environmental perspectives, human rights, and gender subjects.

In the realization of those research studies, the starting points are conceptual approximations, such as theory of knowledge, cognitive psychology, didactic field, and aspects of educational sociology. The subject of study consists of the analysis of the formal contents that can be found in the programs of a study plan. In each research, a conceptual approximation is privileged, and this aspect defines the content of the whole study. It is important to notice that this research line has a particular relevance, although the methodologies developed in it still present serious challenges that make its generalization difficult. The studies about the manners in which subjects such as human rights, gender, and environment can be approached in the contents of a study plan seem to be more consistent because their comparative elements are relatively more structurated.

Studies About the Curriculum as a Process.   These studies constitute what we generically call *real curriculum,* meaning the entirety of actions that are performed in the classroom in relation to the teaching. This model is useful because it reveals the ways teachers work as well as the activities students realize in their comprehension process of a discipline. This type of investigation must be clearly distinguished from the research studies about the hidden curriculum because they tackle the intentional teaching process, starting from the dynamics that a real school situation impresses on the interaction between teachers and students. Certainly this curricular perspective is the one that links with didactics (it practically fuses with didactics). However, it is surprising that this discipline tends to be neglected in the research studies that are performed.

We can affirm that curriculum research as a process is performed on the basis of the incorporation of the proceedings of anthropology, ethnography, and ethnology, although, as it has been sensibly said (Inclán, 1992), this incorporation is made by eliminating the cultural context that is constitutive in the anthropological sciences. This has led to a methodology that starts with an exhaustive record of observations in the classroom—many of them realized without conceptual referents—and then moves to perform an interpretation of them. Specialists in the field of curriculum in Mexico have dedicated themselves to these investigations, as they make possible a cognitive apprehension of the real functioning of the school system through what teachers and students actually can do.

Studies About Hidden Curriculum.   The conceptualization about hidden curriculum has been an especially successful theme of research. What we consider as hidden curriculum is a whole set of beliefs and values that are transmitted in a nonintentional and, thus many times, unconscious way in the educational relation, particularly through the pedagogical actions that are performed in the classroom work. The purpose of several research studies is to "know this whole of beliefs and values" that are transmitted in the school relation. An analysis of the research studies that are realized from this point of view shows in the community of researchers a significant confusion: Many times the research studies that are performed have to do with the curriculum process and do not tackle the analysis of the values and beliefs that are transmitted through curriculum practice. Therefore, in our 1993 study (Díaz Barriga), we concluded that the methodologies for hidden curriculum research find themselves beyond the ethnographical methodology.

Studies About Curriculum Evaluation. The educational evaluation takes part in the modernization politics of higher education that are evident globally. Among the actions of educational evaluation, we can identify the curriculum evaluation. In the Mexican case, this evaluation is based on two fundamental paradigms: A perspective of results whose purpose is to give information—generally to people with decision-making power—about the efficiency of curriculum. This is done in an internal (degree of fulfillment of the educational aims, teaching and learning work, fulfillment of the teaching contents) as well as an external perspective, meaning the performance of students in higher education or in the labor world once they have finished a study plan.

A second perspective in curriculum evaluation assembles studies whose purpose is to allow us to understand the functioning of a study plan. These research studies assume that it is the researcher's responsibility to determine his or her subject of study as well as the theories he or she uses to realize his or her investigation. These studies try to supply complete and complex information not only about the functioning of the study plan, its grounds, and internal structure, but also about the evaluation that teachers, students, administrators, and actors of labor world (employers and graduated students) present of the formation that each particular plan proposes.

THE DESIGN OF STUDY PLANS

The third type of studies in the field of curriculum we accept as results of curriculum research studies are the proposals worked out to formulate study plans. Those studies are performed in an eminently practical perspective because their main aim is to set themselves up as designers of the strategies that people who are responsible of a curriculum formation or restructuring may follow.

We must confess that it is rather difficult to discern the real value these studies present in the research field because of their practical emphasis. This difficulty created a trend in the field of curriculum in which that kind of study is devalued: Many scholars assert that every proposal of curriculum intervention corresponds to an exclusively technical logic, and they even refer to the classification Pinar (1975) proposed at the end of the 1970s, in which he stated that those studies had to do with a technical rationality.

However, posterior analyses also considered that the proposals for the elaboration of study plans were senseless because of the difficulty to apply this formal study plan on school practice (Furlán, 1996). Therefore, curriculum planning was censured because it was considered a formal activity many times performed without conceptual grounds, and whose only purpose was to attain the formal approbation of a study plan. The authors also considered that this formal plan was totally unknown, inept, or inadequately employed in the classrooms. The results of those negative opinions were not only that curriculum planning completely lacked in sense, but also that no educational planning was possible. Instead of recognizing the limits of the planning task or its sense, this trend invalidated any form of planning.

Both trends discouraged the realization of studies to orient the elaboration of study plans, although the educative institutions are kept under pressure to elaborate or re-elaborate their study plans. Several universities reelaborated the entirety of their study plans for the formation of professionals, which meant in some institutions that more than 80 study plans were reelaborated, many times over short time periods.[9] In 1993, in a study about the evolution of curriculum research in Mexico, we came to the conclusion that, as a result of this disregard of the studies about the elaboration of study plans, the norms used by universities to elaborate their plans had not changed since the 1970s, and therefore our institutions reflected a significant conceptual and technical lag with regard to the debate that took place in the research field.

The fundamental problem with analyzing the studies whose reference is the elaboration of study plans is double: First, it is necessary to confirm whether they are a practical proposal that precisely helps the teachers devise study plans and programs, in many cases by fostering a reflection about their experiences, expectations as teachers, and institutional insertions. An interesting proposal for the elaboration of plans and programs is not only an orientation for the realization of that teaching work, but it is also an important aspect of the professionalization process of the teachers by encouraging reflection processes and a study about the contents and forms of teaching.

A second element that must be taken in account consists of the analysis of both the conceptual support of the proposal and its practical viability. This creates specific problems because it is particularly difficult to analyze the conceptual grounds subjacent to a proposal. The great obstacles are, on the one hand, the permanency of a technical vision that eliminates *de facto* any conceptual perspective, and, on the other hand that, because of the presence of too many conceptual elaborations, when they experience difficulties to become concrete in a conceptual proposal, techniques tend to be considered again as independent of the conceptual development. The ideal we have maintained for many years (Díaz Barriga, 1997)—to achieve a theoretical-technical articulation— has not been attained yet. The appropriate value of those studies is difficult when it is possible to notice that some curricular proposals, which have undeniable merits, build up with many difficulties their conceptual reflection to achieve their translation in the technical domain.

In the case of higher education, we can assert that there are three distinct trends about the elaboration of proposals for the realization of study plans and programs.

The first case concerns those elaborations that aim to constitute themselves as an alternative for curriculum elaboration. The most significant experience in this perspective is the modular design by transformation subjects (e.g., professional activities).[10] This experience, established at the Universidad Autónoma Metropolitana (Metropolitan Autonomous University), Xochimilco campus, boiled down the almost 50 subjects that must be attended in the professional formation process to 12 curriculum stages, basically organized around professional problems that must be studied in 4 years. The whole curriculum structure rests on the analysis of *professional practice*, and this concept, which refers to the consideration of professional activity as a social practice, is built on the Marxist concept of practice, particularly from the Althusserian perspective, to show the links between theory and action in the professional performances.

Each curriculum stage—called modular—is organized around a specific problem of the professional activity (e.g., transformation subject), and for its study different disciplinary approximations are performed according to what every discipline can offer for the comprehension of the study problem. For instance, anatomy, physiology, biochemistry, zootechnics, and management for a problem of raising mammals; or mathemat-

---

[9]For example, the Universidad Autónoma de Baja California (Baja California Autonomous University) elaborated during its expansion years 82 study programs, and from 1990 to 1997 it reelaborated 84 of its study programs. In 1995, the Benemérita Universidad Autónoma de Puebla (Puebla Autonomous University) restructured 30 study programs.

[10]There is a long bibliography on the subject; we refer to Díaz Barriga, Martínez, Reygadas, & Villaseñor (1989).

ics, physics, structural calculus, service distribution, and sociology for an architectural design problem.

The purpose was to integrate the three substantive functions of university in the modular work; the axes of school work are teaching, research, and service to community. The concept of *teaching* refers to a learning process in an approximation that is closer to what can be conceived as learning like problem resolution and from a perspective centered on the student's activity. The concept of research demanded a distinction between research with didactical purposes and research for production of knowledge. This distinction made it possible to show that the research performed by students is only with didactical purposes, and this kind of research has become a basic activity of the learning assignments. The point was also to take over the study of those research studies from a problem in professional activity, seeking in the election of the problem a social content so the academic space could bring some aid for the resolution of the problems experienced by the most needy sectors of society. Thus, we assert that this academic model adopted a work methodology similar to the teaching by problem resolution.

This experience, which began to work in 1976, had an important impact on diverse study plans at a national level, particularly in the master's degrees in the sector of farming and animal husbandry. In its development, it had to build up a curricular conceptualization that made possible the elaboration of concepts and design methodologies that had to be different from the ones traditionally applied. For example, the stage of diagnostic of necessities was substituted by another stage called *framework for curriculum design*, whose central element consisted of the study, elaborated on the basis of profession sociology and professional practice. Although concepts like outline of the graduated students and objectives (in relation with the behavior) were preserved, the notion of transformation subject was incorporated: To bring out the election of a professional problem from the real world, this curriculum theory calls it a reality problem, from which they can organize the learning contents that orient the teaching, research, and service activities of each module.

The practice of this curriculum theory has been difficult because it implies working with small learning groups. This is a problematic aspect in a country that has experienced an unprecedented expansion in its higher education system, which has grown 65 times in the last 50 years and has a significant lag in coverage because only 17% of the 18-year-olds can enter the university (and this is the reason that Mexico shows one of the lowest coverage rates of the continent).[11]

Otherwise, the modular system becomes exigent toward the education staff, who has to modify the working patterns formerly acquired. The staff's main task consists of creating optimal conditions so the students can begin to grasp knowledge and to deal with a subject from the diverse disciplines of the professional problem (transformation subject) that integrates each module. Therefore, the teacher needs to have a thorough knowledge of different disciplines and be able to integrate the learnings that proceed from them. Furthermore, the teacher must pay attention to the fact that such integration is done with a simplification of the discipline contents. This situation required different teachers, usually full time, to take charge of one module. The modular functioning significantly raised

---

[11]According to information from the Secretaría de Educación Publica (Secretariat of Public Education), in 1950, 29,892 students were registered in the higher education system in Mexico (the global population counted 25,791,017 inhabitants), and so the coverage rate was less than 2% of the 18-year-old people. In 1999, in contrast, 1,837,884 students matriculated at the university, whereas there are 93,716,332 Mexicans in the country. The number of inhabitants quadrupled since 1950, whereas the higher education system increased 65 times in the same period. However, in 1999, only 17% of the people who are of age are matriculating at the university, whereas the rates of enrollment in other Latin American countries is much higher (e.g., Bolivia, 27%; Argentina, 35%).

the costs when the fiscal crisis compelled the government to reduce the financing of higher education and the institutions were not able to continue to attend to the expansion demanded of the system.

Finally, it was not easy to translate an experience that came from the domain of health sciences, and especially from the group of experiences that the Pan American Health Organization (PHO) had impelled in the 1960s in several faculties of medicine in Latin America. The experience they had in the health sector could not be extrapolated to 15 different professions: some professions from social sciences (sociology, economy, communication sciences, psychology), design sciences (architecture, industrial design), and basic sciences, particularly biology and the licenciate degree in pharmaceutics (*Químico-farmacéutico-biólogo* [QFB]). Furthermore, not all the disciplines can be taught from a global point of view, such as mathematics and basic sciences.

Diverse evaluations and studies have been conducted regarding the functioning of the modular system, proving that on many occasions it has produced unquestionably valuable educational practices from the perspective of professional formation, the resolution of several specific problems of professional practice and the development of a research and/or service activity in a particular community. However, those evaluations also noticed educational practices that left important blanks in the formation process of the students.

In 1984, I (Díaz Barriga, 1996) published a book in which I showed it was possible to identify the articulation points that could be established in the curriculum design work between the Tyler and Taba perspective and the developments of the modular curriculum system.

At the end of the 1980s, in several institutions of the health sector, they began to encourage postgraduate programs with a mix of curriculum integration. Some of the stages of the study plan are modular or integral, and in the other ones the knowledge is split up into disciplines. This alternative is worth more experimentation because it offers great possibilities to overcome several deficits found in the modular system.

In the second place, we find the elements that in the 1990s became the axes of curriculum debate. In a context of the equilibration of the higher school system, according to the internationalization of the debate as a result of the globalization politics, those subjects bring some help in the modernization process of education in the domain of curriculum work.

We distinguish two kinds of themes: Some of them have a direct effect on the design processes or the actions realized in relation with them; the others express a whole set of problems and ideals of the educational system and can be considered as transversal subjects of the curriculum work.

GENERAL THEMES

In the case of subjects that have a direct effect on the curriculum design process, we identify the following themes: Education in professional competencies, curricular flexibility, application of constructivism in teaching, and incorporation of new information and curriculum evaluation technologies. The four cases are perspectives that aim to have a bearing on the curriculum design and the development processes.

Unlike what happened in the modular system, where a complete alternative proposal was built for the curriculum design and development work, in the 1990s, the contributions seemed to point to the construction of an element that allows partial modifications in the context of the educative modernization, directly connected with the internationalization of education and the reduction of the governmental financing for higher education.

The two first themes proceed from the labor world. The development of disciplines close to management and production has raised a discussion about the professional competencies and the flexible formation. Although it is necessary to recognize the specificity of each theme, we can assert that both themes are directly linked with the thesis that promotes a flexible formation. This proposal finds support in several grounds, and the most important are the following: The labor world is in a permanent changing process that is caused by the profound transformations of technology as well as by the radical changes in the labor situation of workers;[12] the human capital theory has been accompanied by two formulations that go with the flexibility proposal. The first one concerns the necessity of training the worker in the abilities he or she requires for his or her incorporation into the job; the second one affirms that it is only necessary to train him or her in those abilities. Finally, flexibility can be justified by an important and consistent critical examination of the stiffness that appears in the study plans in the Mexican higher education system—a stiffness that impedes a student from attending similar courses in other faculties or colleges of his or her institution or attending similar courses in other national or foreign institutions. It is even difficult for a Mexican student to get a recognition of the partial studies he or she realized in a university when, for one or another reason, he or she has to change residences.

In regard to its specificity, it is important to notice that there is no univocal interpretation about what can be understood as competencies, nor about its integration into the field of curriculum. In the European case, the study of competencies is closely related to: (a) the necessity to take steps to make easier the professional mobility in the European Union; (b) the adaptation of the professional formation systems to the apparition of a new labor organization and new contracting strategies in the firms, which means to obtain a greater flexibility in the educational system; and (c) the fulfillment of some formation and efficiency norms.

The ever higher unemployment rates, in connection with the exigencies of better qualification in the work demand (a trend that can be observed clearly in the advanced industrial economies), are one of the subjacent elements in the conceptualization of the competencies as an instrument that helps to articulate *"la formación teórica con los conocimientos prácticos para facilitar la adquisición de destrezas adaptables a las profesiones establecidas."*[13]

However, the theme of competencies has been used with more success in the domain of technical formation, and, in a peculiar combination with work analysis, it has been possible to promote training processes for work.

The concept of *flexibility* has different effects on the structure and organization of a study plan. When we say *flexible curriculum* (Díaz Barriga, 1999), we understand: (a) the establishment of optional areas of prespecialization at the end of a study plan; (b) the organization of a plan by formation areas that allow the student to attend freely the courses of every line; (c) the adaptation of the last parts of curriculum to the changes that are generated in the labor world; (d) the establishment of formation options that make richer the trunk formation that a professional must master; (e) the acceptation of courses offered by other educative institutions, national or foreign; and (f) the academic recognition of professional experience through adequate certification mechanisms.

---

[12]The types of flexible work are: Contracts handled by temporal work agencies or firms that work with subcontracts; personnel hired for specific projects or temporally; part-time workers; freelance workers, including people who work at home (Carnoy, Castells, & Benner, 1997).

[13]("The theoretical formation with the know-how to make easier the acquisition of skills that are adaptable to established professions," my translation; Marsden, 1990).

The impact of constructivism on teaching is one of the themes that is part of the research agenda as well as the teacher formation practices. This impact is important to promote the studies about particular teaching of diverse disciplines: Natural sciences (biology, physics, chemistry), social sciences (history, sociology), mathematics, and linguistics. This is one of the domains of curriculum research that not only worries about the problems of higher education, but has also fomented relevant studies about basic education.

Likewise, the new technologies have created another domain to modify curriculum practice. Their development possibilities are tightly linked with the economical reality, which means that it is in the domain of higher education where teaching with the Internet and still isolated distance education experiences are in way of generalization. Among those distance education experiences, the most important are the programs of Postgraduate of Education[14] and several teachers' preparation courses.

Evaluation has become one of the central subjects in the educational debate at the end of this century. To this effect, there are also actions that seek to develop the curriculum evaluation as a task that makes sense both for the study plan and the curriculum practice, and also for an institutionality that is reflected in the system of program credit and the professional certification of graduated students. The challenge consists in the development of curriculum evaluation models that attend to the curriculum process and respond to those two institutional exigencies; if this cannot be done, the risk is that those mechanisms will take the place of evaluation in the sphere of curriculum.

TRANSVERSAL CURRICULUM THEMES

Different spaces need different themes that affect the entirety of the curriculum practices, and that also need to find unification in the treatment of the contents of all the subjects that shape a study plan. Its importance takes root in the formation of the values that are required by the professional or the student in general. Those themes are education for peace and tolerance; education toward the realization of human rights, education, and environment; education and gender; and education and citizenship.

Certainly because of their relevance, they are part of the educational reflection that will be present in the next decade; those themes are also subjects of reflection for international organizations, particularly the UNESCO.

Its importance consists in the necessity to incorporate a perspective that allows a clearly human formation, although it has been difficult to specify the place they must occupy in a study plan. So the development of environmental education resulted in the study plan of two secondary subjects: ecology and environment. This had a negative effect on the possibilities of this theme to be incorporated in the treatment of many contents of other disciplines like geography, sociology, history, and so on.

This showed that the articulations between such themes and the field of curriculum were realized too formally. Only recently has it been possible to see that a transversal perspective could resolve that problem because it does not deal with the incorporation of a content or subject into the study plan, but with the adoption of a focusing that goes through the treatment of contents by diverse disciplines that integrate the plan.

---

[14]The Instituto Tecnológico de Estudios Superiores Monterrey (Higher Studies Technological Institute of Monterrey [ITESM]) has developed an experience during the last 10 years in a national distance postgraduate program. The Secretaría de Educación Pública (Secretariat of Public Education) has established a satellite program for all the units of the Universidad Pedagógica (Pedagogical University), and the Instituto Latinoamericano de Comunicación Educativa (Latin-American Institute for Educational Communication [ILCE]) also has a postgraduate program in education.

The writings about such themes, although it is still in a conformation stage, are more important than the practices that are possible in the treatment of contents. The challenge finds itself in this dimension, and resolving the tranversality allows one to discern other possibilities for the curriculum practice.

TOWARD A CONCLUSION

Curriculum research in Mexico is in a consolidation phase, which means a community of academicians from diverse traditions have begun to conduct research in the field of curriculum. The conceptual and thematic diversity is huge, and I have intended merely to provide documentation of it.

The greatest limitation curriculum research must defy is its reduced impact on basic education. As a matter of fact, the centralization of study plans constitutes an important obstacle that makes difficult the development of that kind of research. The studies about this level practically are condensed to the problem of the teaching diverse disciplines (mathematics, language, natural and social sciences) by using different foci of the cognitive theories, or ethnographically oriented studies to recount what happens in the classroom. Other perspectives of the curriculum discipline have had no impact.

The opposite happens in the higher education. Due to the vertiginous expansion of this system, it grew from approximately 30 institutions in the 1950s to more than 1,200 today. The opportunity to formulate study plans in each institution has made possible the development of a field of intervention, reflection, and research. The community of researchers that produces studies about the field of curriculum is concentrated at this level.

Until now, two states of affairs about curriculum research have been realized—the first one in 1981 and the second in 1993. They recount the incorporation and evolution of this discipline in the country. Actually, a third state of affairs is being realized to offer a document that allows a balance of the development of research, so this can orient its evolution.

REFERENCES

Berruecos, L. (Coord.). (1997). *La construcción permanente del sistema modular*. México: UAM-Xochimilco.

Bobbit, F. (1918). *How to make the curriculum*. New York: Hougton- Mifflin.

Carnoy, M., Castells, M., & Benner, C. (1997). Mercados laborales y formas de empleo en la era de la flexibilidad. Estudio monográfico en Silicon Valley. *Revista Internacional del Trabajo, 116*.

Dewey, J. (1902). *The child and the curriculum*. Chicago: University of Chicago Press.

Díaz Barriga, A. (1996). *Ensayos sobre la problemática curricular* (rev. ed.). México: Trillas.

Díaz Barriga, A. (1997). *Didáctica y curriculum. Convergencias en los programas de estudio*. México: Paidós, Colección Educador.

Díaz Barriga, A. (1999). *La flexibilización profesional y su impacto en los planes de estudio*. Paper presented at the 5th Congreso Nacional de Investigación Educativa, Consejo Mexicano de Investigación Educativa, Aguascalientes.

Díaz Barriga, A., Martínez, D., Reygadas, R., Villaseñor, G. (1989). *Práctica docente y diseño curricular (un estudio exploratorio en la UAM-Xochimilco)*. México: Universidad Autónoma Metropolitana-Xochimilco/CESU-UNAM.

Díaz Barriga, A., Barrón, C., Guzmán, J. C., Díaz Barriga Arceo, F., Torres, R. M., Spitzer, T., & Ysunza, M. (1995). La investigación en el campo del currículo 1982–1995. In A. Díaz Barriga (Coord.), *Procesos curriculares, institucionales y organizacionales* (pp. 19–172). México: Consejo Mexicano de Investigación Educativa.

Díaz Barriga Arceo, F. (1993). *Diseño curricular: II. Ejercicios de un método específico para el diseño curricular*. México: PROMESUP/OEA/ILCE.

Durkheim, E. (1979). *Educación y sociología*. Bogotá, Colombia: Linotipo.

Furlná, A. (1996). *Curriculum e institución*. Morelia, México: Cuadernos del Instituto Michoacano de Ciencias de la Educación.

Hameyer, U. (1993). Situación actual de la investigación curricular: Balance de una década. *Paidea, 18*.

Inclán, C. (1992). *Diagnóstico y perspectivas de la investigación educativa etnográfica en México. 1975–1988*. México: UNAM, Cuadernos del CESU.

Marsden, D. (1990). Cambio industrial, competencias y mercado del trabajo. *Revista Europea*.

Murillo, J., Arrimandas, I., & Calzón, J. (Coords.). (1997). *Sistemas educativos nacionales*. Madrid, Espãna: Ministerio de Educación y Cultura/Organización de Estados Iberoamericanos para la educación, la ciencia y la cultura (OEI).

Pinar, W. (Ed.). (1975). *Curriculum theorizing: The reconceptualists*. Berkeley, CA: McCutchan.

CHAPTER 25

Main Trends of Curriculum Research in México

Frida Díaz Barriga[1]
National University of México

This chapter offers a brief analysis of the main trends in the research about curriculum that have been conducted in México during the last decade. In my opinion, those trends are the following: (a) a technologic-systemic trend, (b) a critical-reconceptualist trend, (c) a psychopedagogical trend, (d) a trend that deals with professional formation and practice, and (e) an interpretative trend. These categories represent the most relevant and fertile sectors of the national production in theorization and intervention in the field of research. Although one cannot talk in strict sense about paradigms or programs of curriculum research in the way those concepts are interpreted by authors like Thomas S. Kuhn or Lee Shulman (see Hernández, 1998), nevertheless we can clearly recognize trends or research lines about diverse themes that are linked to curriculum, in which it is possible to distinguish, on the one hand, an explicit conception of what we understand as curriculum as well as study subjects and specific theoretical assumptions, and on the other, those inherent methodologies employed to conduct these studies or the educative interventions that derive from those approaches. In our case, the mentioned trends are delimited in regard to their importance and presence in the domain of research, theoretical reflection, intervention, and teaching in the Mexican teaching institutions. They are defined on the basis of the subjacent notion of curriculum and the domain of specific problems to which they pay attention. It is also possible to identify in those trends the predominance of any discipline or particular theoretical focusing (e.g., behaviorism, constructivism, critical theory, new educational sociology, etc.).

The purpose of this chapter is not only to be an exhaustive inventory of the production generated in the country, nor a state of affairs that would exceed its own limits. Basically it aims to discuss the *polysemy* and diversity of conceptions that coexist in regard to what can be understood as studies about curriculum and to bring out the contributions of several Mexican authors whose authority has been widely recognized. Regarding the research trends that are described in this chapter, to situate them in a wider context, I connect them with some of the possible focusings and contemporary interna-

---

[1]PhD of Pedagogy, regular professor at the Faculty of Psychology, UNAM. e-mail: fdba@servidor.unam.mx

tional authors who have tackled with studies about curriculum. It is important to point out that this chapter owes a lot to the state of affairs about curriculum research performed by A. Díaz Barriga et al. (1995), in which the authors analyzed the production of curriculum research generated in México between 1982 and 1992, as well as to a former research study I conducted (F. Díaz Barriga, 1993).

CURRICULUM RESEARCH: THE TERM'S POLYSEMY AND THE TRENDS OF RESEARCH

It is difficult to fix the limits of what can be considered as studies about curriculum with regard to the other areas of educational and psychological research. This problem is tightly linked to the polysemy and characteristical dispersion of the concept of curriculum, and this originates the diversity of focuses for its study and generates a superposition with other research themes.

In the field of curriculum in our country, it is impossible to find a unique focusing that could include all and each of the subjects of study, problems, or situations that pertain to the field. Depending on the way curriculum is conceived, the idea of curriculum research and its method are determined, and so are fixed, at the level of intervention, the conceptual and technical character of its design and evaluation. In their analysis of the research generated between 1982 and 1992, Díaz Barriga et al. (1995) discern the following meanings for the word *curriculum*:

(a) study plans and programs as products and formal curriculum structures;

(b) learning and teaching processes;

(c) hidden curriculum and daily life in the classroom;

(d) formation of professionals and social function of the teachers;

(e) social and educative practice;

(f) problems generated by the selection, organization and distribution of curriculum contents;

(g) subjective interpretation of the subjects implicated in curriculum. (p. 31)

This conceptual diversity has contributed not only to the term's polysemy, but it has also occasioned that the curriculum research lost its outline with regard to the other areas of educational research, like the study of the learning–teaching processes, the specific didactics, the sociological studies about professions, the intersubjectivity, the educational interaction processes, and even the multicultural and gender studies, to quote only a few.

We also consider that the knowledge generated in the field of research is not the cumulative result of specific research projects, but a complex work of conceptual construction performed by a community of people who realize research regarding the theme, perspectives, working styles, shared interests, and takings of positions necessarily imply compromises and exclusions. In México, we can find postures that are not only divergent, but also completely opposed to what is curriculum and how curriculum research must be performed. For several authors who consider curriculum as the entirety of courses or subjects in a study plan, curriculum research should seek to evaluate the fulfillment of the aims that were established in the normative papers, whereas other authors think curriculum should be studied as "a whole about education."

It is necessary to admit that the curriculum research methods performed in México are intimately linked to a rank of social problems and demands inherent to the country and to the Latin American region. In particular, we believe that the main engagements assumed by the curriculum researchers have to do with problems such as the massification of teaching; the obsoleteness and stiffness of the study plans and teaching models; the inequality of teaching quality and offer; the educational institutions' incapacity to give a positive answer to the demands of the labor world; and the serious deficiencies in the formation of primary and secondary school students or the ignorance of the educational practices that occur in the Mexican classrooms.

A CHARACTERIZATION OF THE MAIN TRENDS OF CURRICULUM RESEARCH IN MÉXICO

The Technologic-Systemic Vision

The studies about curriculum that we can situate in this trend are based on the so-called *classical* or *traditional* authors (those epithets seem unsuitable, above all the second one) of the field of curriculum theory and of the so-called systematization of teaching, which have been successful in our country since the 1970s. Those authors and their most widespread works in Spanish are Ralph Tyler (*Principios básicos del currículo*), Hilda Taba (*La elaboración del currículo*), Mauritz Johnson (*Curriculum y educación*), Robert Mager (*Confección de objetivos*), and Benjamin Bloom (with his widely known taxonomy of cognitive objectives). Their interests lie in the resolution of the four basic questions raised by Tyler: Which are the educational objectives? Which educational experiences allow to achieve them? How can we organize efficiently those experiences? How can we evaluate the attainment of those objectives? The authors who join this focusing are inscribed in a technological rationality because they are interested in the formal structures and programmatic components. As a matter of fact, their mission is to make more efficient the educational processes through the application of scientific techniques frequently extrapolated from the world of industry.

In México, Glazman and Ibarrola's (1976) and Arnaz's (1981) proposals to design study plans by objectives were the most representative of this trend. Their outlines concurred with those educative techniques derived from the behaviorist paradigm, and this provoked the appearance of teaching systemization models (Gago, 1978), the elaboration of descriptive charters (Gago, 1982), techniques for the analysis of curriculum contents (Huerta, 1981), and programed teaching (Comisión de Nuevos Métodos de Enseñanza, 1976).

Afterward, in the proposal developed by Arrendondo (1981) for the development of curriculum, the influence of the systemical focusing shows up with a perfect definition (vid. Stufflebeam, 1971), and this focus oriented the processes of educational planning and curriculum design according to the context-input-process-product diagram during the 1980s. The Asociación Nacional de Universidades e Instituciones de Educación Superior (National Association of Universities and Higher Education Institutions [ANUIES]) and the extinct Comisión de Nuevos Métodos de Enseñanza (Comission for New Teaching Methods [CNME]) are two instances that assemble the authors who follow this trend and that foster resolutely the dissemination of its proposals by means of publications and formation courses for teachers and educative planners.

Despite the wide diffusion of this trend and notwithstanding until now the Mexican institutions that keep working on the design of their educational projects according to the logic of methodological proposals like the ones we have just quoted, the criticisms to this posture arose almost from the beginning. A. Díaz Barriga (1984) synthetizes them like this: they are too reduced, rigid, and acontextualized approach to the curriculum problems; the realization of pretended diagnoses that concealed the real problem of social exercise of professions; the fragmentation and trivialization of learning by behavioral objectives (we even could talk about "objectives"); the superficial treatment and the atomization of content; the lack of a historical and social treatment; the emphasis on administrative control and the technical treatment that does not pay attention to the academic processes.

THE CRITICAL-RECONCEPTUALIST MOVEMENT

In the context of the social movements of the 1960s and 1970s, important criticisms to the social system and education arose in several countries; they had an important repercussion in México and made possible the appearance of a new generation of authors who were considered the "critics" of curriculum. Actually, in this trend, we can identify diverse currents of thinking like the English new sociology of education headed by Michael Young; the North American reconceptualization movement represented by Basil Bernstein, William Pinar, Henry Giroux, Michael Apple, and Peter McLaren; the neo-Marxist analysis and the reproduction and resistence theory of the French Althusser, Bourdieu, Passeron, Baudelot, and Establet; these and, in the Latin American context, Paulo Freire's pedagogy of liberation and his censure of the "banking education" are going to be the main influences of this new trend. In De Alba's (1991) opinion, more than a unidirectional influence of the Anglo-Saxon authors on the Mexican thought, what we can observe is the arising of two parallel movements that coincided in their theoretical referents and in the search for emancipating educative experiences.

From this point of view, the academic institutions became highly questionable, and the main discussion was that the real function of school is to perpetuate the social inequalities and injustices and to validate the hegemonic ways of knowledge and culture of the domineering ranks of society. But in the case of the Mexican authors, other domains of criticism arose with regard to the cultural and ideological hegemony of the imperialist countries on Latin America and the phenomenon of scientific and technological dependence.

Leaving out the behavior psychology focusing and the technical conception of curriculum—actually rebelling openly against both of them and taking as reference different social theories (mainly Marxism, hermeneutics, or the Frankfurt school)—we can observe in México during two decades the generation of critical essays and alternative curriculum proposals. In those critiques, diverse theoretical approximations and research focuses are manifested. However, in Silva's (1999) opinion, the critical theories of curriculum share what he calls "impulsos emancipadores y liberadores" ("emancipating and liberating impetuses," my translation; p. 13).

We cannot perform here an exhaustive inventory of works (those interested should take a look at the state of affairs Díaz Barriga et al. published in 1995), but we attempt to mention the most representative authors. In the first place, at the conceptual level, we must recognize the relevance, especially at the moment of their publication, of the articles of authors such as Angel Díaz Barriga, Alfredo Furlán, Eduardo Remedi, Margarita Pansza, María de Ibarrola, Alicia de Alba, Roberto Follari, and Porfirio Morán, all of whom are university-based researchers.

In the second place, it is important to mention several curriculum models and methodological proposals that arise from a critical discussion about the social and political function of education, in which the authors openly reject technical rationality. The most illustrative example of those models is the curriculum project at the Universidad Autónoma Metropolitana-Xochimilco, which encourages an innovative epistemological and pedagogical vision by means of the creation of a modular system. In our opinion, this is the most important and original contribution to the curriculum theory from a perspective that is centered on historical and sociopolitical dimensions. Particularly interesting is the notion of module (contrary to the organization by subjects), which is based on the analysis of a rank of relevant social problems for a profession, what we call *transformation objects [subjects]*. Against the then imperative vision, the modular model presented a situational and contextualized curriculum design centered on the problem of the social exercise of professions and not on discipline, which sought to link theory to practice and that openly claimed a social engagement. This proposal functioned as a pattern to other curriculum projects in the main Mexican institution of secondary and higher education, and also provoked important debates in the field of university curriculum development.

However, according to Furlán (1996:59), it is possible to notice a serious breakdown between the projected level and level of actual realizations in innovative curriculum experiences as well as in the traditional experiences, and this creates a new field of reflection and research. This field consists of the analysis of thought-out curriculum in opposition with lived curriculum (or curriculum based on personal experiences); this means the study of *"las relaciones entre la racionalidad de la planificación y las dinámicas que los sujetos actores establecían en sus prácticas"* ("the relations between planning rationality and the dynamics acting subjects establish in their practices," my translation). The works of J. Eggleston (*Sociología del desarrollo curricular*), P. Jackson (*La vida en las aulas*), and L. Stenhouse (*Investigación y desarrollo del curriculum*) are important antecedents of various local studies about the social construction of curriculum, the problem of power, and the dynamics of social relationships in the classroom. Another important characteristic of this trend is the change in the methodological focusing of the studies about curriculum: Quantitative studies decrease or are left aside to make space for ethnographical and naturalistic[2] studies about the educational reality. It is easy to understand that from then on it has been difficult to fix the limits with other areas of educational research.

At this point, it is important to mention that the use and appropriation in our country of the concept of *hidden curriculum* (*curriculum oculto* or *escondido*, as several authors call it) is not univocal either. For some authors, it represents the transmission mechanisms of the domineering ideology in the classroom; for others, it consists of the study of the school reality or daily life in the classroom. We also find this notion to refer to the domain of interpersonal relations between teachers and students, to the psychological affective processes, or to any kind of incidental learnings not foreseen in the formal curriculum.

We also must emphasize that the research which approaches the curriculum as the study of reality in the classrooms find themselves in a domain whose focuses are the educational processes and practices, not products nor formal structures. Hence, when they go into the classroom, they are evermore interested in the daily school experiences, and this inevitably leads to the investigation of the protagonists of the educational act's behaviors, creeds, values, feelings, and so on. Part of those works can be situated within this critical trend because they consider curriculum as a space for social reproduction, and they analyze it from a basically sociological perspective, but several authors perform their studies by appealing to other theoretical referents. However, Díaz Barriga et al. (1995) and Silva (1999) agree that, at the beginning of the 1990s, it was possible to observe a new line of curriculum research, which, although relatively close to the critical vision and centered on the study of curriculum processes, tackled with

---

[2]It is important to clarify that not all the ethnographical, naturalist, or ethnological studies are studies about curriculum, nor are those studies necessarily centered on a critical or sociological perspective. Although it is sometimes difficult to fix the limits between studies, we find in México an acknowledged corpus of educational research with ethnographical or naturalist studies made of descriptive, anthropological, psycholinguistic, or psychological studies that could not easily be classified as curriculum research.

the curriculum problems from an interpretative point of view; that is why we discuss this trend here.

Ruíz (1992: 40) thinks that the national authors' most important works refer to theoretical analyses about the dual character of curriculum—"real and formal"—and that the main challenge is *otorgar significancia teórica a las acciones pedagógicas que se realizan en el salón de clases* ("to give a theoretical significance to the pedagogical actions that are performed in the classroom," my translation).

Paradoxically, despite their interest in the analysis of what happens in the classrooms, an important problem of this research is that the educators who are not knowledgeable in curriculum theory cannot easily understand them. To derive from this curriculum theory any practical application to school curriculum development is a complex operation. De Alba (1991) asserts that a large part of the teachers, students, and educative authorities lack in the basic formation elements to understand this critical trend's complex discourse about curriculum, and therefore at the end of the 1980s this trend, became a myth for the people who were uninformed about the subject. According to the author, this situation generated a communication gap between the producers of discourse and the actors of the problem. In our opinion, this situation explains, at least partially, that the practice of curriculum design in the educational institutions keeps supporting on the previously-mentioned technological focusings or that we can perceive the production of what A. Díaz Barriga et al. (1995) call *hybrid curriculum projects,* whose grounds are in the critical discourse, but that make operational the design of plans and programs by means of the focus on technological rationality. In short, the principal censure used to receive the authors of this trend is that in the past decennia we can notice the expansion of the critical discourse, but not the crystallization of the practical alternatives formulated from the inside of this trend.

CURRICULUM STUDIES ON THE FORMATION AND SOCIAL PRACTICE OF PROFESSIONALS

In our opinion, it is important to situate in the field of curriculum research a rank of works focused on the formation and social practice of professionals. Although there is not really a theoretical or methodological orientation that unifies them, they can be assembled according to the subject of research (what happens with the formation and/or social practice of professionals in México?) and to their interest in the educative intervention (which models can be proposed for the development and evaluation of curriculum in higher education?).

The original interest of most of those studies, at least in the 1970s and the 1980s, was not centered on the theorization about curriculum questions, but rather resided openly in the analysis of curriculum projects in vogue with regard to the formation at the university and to the performances of graduated students in the labor world. Generally we find plenty of descriptive studies with a demographical and statistic character, which were performed by means of surveys without a clear relation to one or another curriculum theory, although they were occasionally linked to the systemic focusing to evaluate the university curriculum by following its graduated students. In other cases, the central reference of the works is the analysis of the discipline(s) that are subjacent to the study plan. We find that is mainly in the research performed by professionals of the educational field where there were explicit assumptions about the curriculum theories.

Despite those limiting factors, these kinds of studies are valuable because they allow an approach to the reality of social practice of professions in México and they make it possible to demarcate of the real profile of the graduated students at the university or the higher education institutions. They also led to a discussion about the encyclopedic study plans that focus on the discipline structures and that are organized by subjects with little or no curriculum flexibility. Finally, they oriented the reflection inside of the professional associations about the formation that higher education institutions were giving and the chasm that existed between this formation and the needs of ruling social elites and the working classes.

Nevertheless, the development of university curriculum in the last 20 years has progressively ceased responding to the ideal of "the satisfaction of social needs," which characterized the formation of professionals in the public universities during the 1970s and part of the 1980s. Barrón (1997) considers that the formation of Mexican professionals at the end of the 20th century responds to the governmental project of industrial reconversion, which seeks to adapt the national productive apparatus to the technological innovations and to the globalization trend. So, in an uncertain international context *sujeto al vértigo del cambio* ("subject to the accelerated rhythm of evolution," my translation), the tendency resides in the modernization of university curricula to adjust them to the necessities of the firms—not only at the national level, but rather transnationally. This fertilizes the ground for the entrance of curriculum models based on the delimitation of international professional standards (the EBC or education based on the competence norms), the certification and evaluation of professional quality, or the homogenization if study plans of other countries, particularly Canada and the United States. The curriculum discourse of those models gives the priority to the concepts of efficiency, quality, and excellence o a highly competitive human capital.

However, in México, the development of curriculum as a university domain of research and intervention is a field where we frequently see the participation of educative psychologists and pedagogues as curriculum experts, but in the last two decades the participation of other professionals has increased, above all proceeding from the social, human, and health disciplines (nurses, physicians, social workers, odontologists, economists, teachers, etc.). This occurs partly because they stop considering that curriculum development is an exclusive assignment for experts. Hence, a participative focusing can be promoted where teachers, students, educational authorities, experts in the discipline, and even promoters and members of the community ideally are allowed to participate.

In many instances, such works are part of efforts made by an educative institution to change the curriculum, so they are linked to periodical seminars or academical administrative working groups, or they are the result of the exigencies of the normative framework or legislation imposed by the institution to approve curriculum projects. The results of those efforts are diverse with regard to the quality and profoundness of their attainments as well as in the conception of what we understand as studies about curriculum and professional formation. But we also have noticed that many of those studies, which are generated in the course of the curriculum evolution processes in schools and faculties, do not get around to being published because they constitute documents destined for the restricted circulation inside the commissions designated for this purpose. However, the staff that is responsible for those studies does not always have a suitable formation about questions related to curriculum processes and development and still less about theoretical focuses (Jiménez, 2000).

As an example for those research studies that illustrate this interest in the study of formation and social practice or the confection of innovating educative proposals in higher education from different perspectives, we can mention the works of Díaz Barriga and Saad (1997), Ducoing and Rodríguez (1990), Esquivel (1991), González (1985) Ruíz (1997), and Urbina (1989).

In connection with those studies, alternative proposals were generated for the design of curriculum and of study plans at a higher level (high school, university, and technological institutions), which aimed to transcend the technical vision of curriculum. The nuclear interest of those proposals was to offer theoretical and methodological resources for curriculum design and evaluation, and for the study of professions and the following of graduated students. Among those proposals, we can mention A. Díaz Barriga's (1984, 1997), from a critical point of view; F. Díaz Barriga's (1993), which allies contributions of the systemic focus with instructional cognitive psychology; or De Ibarrola's (1992) proposals, which are based on the notion of curriculum structure and were applied in technological education and in high school. We also find alternative proposals for curriculum evaluation from integrating social (Galán & Marín, 1988; Marín, 1993) or qualitative (Ruíz, 1998) perspectives.

Parallel with the course of time in this decade, we can observe in the case of several researchers that the study of formation and professional practice begins to get a firmer theoretical consistence and that it defines itself as a field of sociological studies about professions (see A. Díaz Barriga & Pacheco, 1990, 1997; Marín, 1993). Another perspective that is incorporating in this trend is Schön's (1992) study about the formation of reflective professionals (see Díaz Barriga & Saad, 1997).

THE PSYCHOPEDAGOGICAL APPROACH TO CURRICULUM

This trend arises and consolidates around the concern to implement new forms of knowledge and teaching organization that would make it possible to overcome the learning difficulties experimented by students, especially at the primary and secondary school levels. This curriculum research trend is related not only to learning and developmental psychology, but also to the ideas defended by the pedagogues of the new European school and the so-called North American progressive education.

According to Posner (1998), new forms of curriculum organization emerge when educational psychologists make important criticisms to the study plans that only reflect the structure of discipline and that are organized deductively (e.g., the subject curriculum), but ignore the psychological structure of knowledge and the complex human learning processes. Díaz Barriga (in the same volume) asserts that this is one of the two most important traditions of studies about curriculum, whose origin can be found at the beginning of this century in Dewey's book called *The Child and the Curriculum,* first published in 1902. From its beginning, this trend is connected with the analysis of contents and the learning experiences; the premise is that curriculum must reflect the way in which people learn. It is important to observe that in this perspective the point is to link the curriculum development to the instruction theory and design.

Although in México there was an important influence of behaviorist psychology in the conformation of school curriculum (e.g., Robert Gagné and his proposal to organize knowledge by means of a "task analysis" and a progressive ordering of atomized abilities that go from simple to complex), the major developments of those trends can be found in the contributions of cognitive psychology and the psychogenetical focusing. Since the 1970s, but especially in the 1980s, we can observe the proliferation of research and the development of important projects about curriculum—several public and national—cognitively orientated and inspired by Jean Piaget and his followers, however the influence of Jerome Bruner or David Ausubel is undeniable. In the 1990s, we observe an amplification of the postulates of constructivism under the influence of important Anglo-Saxon and Spanish authors. Among the latter, we can highlight the work of César Coll (1987, 1990) and the group of authors whose mission was to process the Spanish curriculum reform in primary and secondary education. This influence is perceptible not only in México, but also in different Latin American countries such as Chile, Brazil, and Argentina.

Yet we believe that in our country the main achievements of the psychopedagogical focus on curriculum with a cognitive orientation can be found in the development of far-reaching curriculum projects, some of them at a national level. The most acknowledged attainments can be observed in preschool, special, and primary education (the Initial Education curriculum (*Currículo de Educación Inicial*: 1979–1991); the Preschool Education Program (*Programa de Educación Preescolar*: 1981–1992); CONAFE-DIE's Community Education Program (*Programa de Educación Comunitaria*: since 1980; the Cognitive Orientation Curriculum (*Currículo de Orientación Cognitiva* of SEP-UNAM: since 1982); the Program of Integrated Groups for Special Education (*Programa de Grupos Integrados de Educación Especial*: operative until the mid-1990s), to mention only a few. Subsequently, we can notice the dissemination of this trend at the level of secondary and higher education levels, with a special emphasis on natural sciences and mathematics. However, we must say that, because of its purpose and study subject, this kind of research generally should be situated in the field of specific didactics or in research in the teaching–learning processes, not in studies about curriculum.

The planning and setting in operation of those curriculum projects was accompanied by diverse efforts of educational research in connection with curriculum as well as with cognitive development and learning processes, and they attained variable quality, diffusion, and results. For Díaz Barriga, Hernández, García, and Muriá (1998), there are two main obstacles that such educational proposals have had to confront. First, the quarrel between the organized culture of the Mexican educative institutions—and their own management processes and the philosophy and operative demands of an approach such as the constructivist. In the second place, the deficiencies in the formation of teachers. According to these authors, the eternal absents of curriculum intervention experiences in the domain of national public education are the possibility to create really flexible and situational curricula and to rely on the managership and real disposition of the teaching staff for the creation and setting in operation of those curricula, the transformation of the classrooms into enriching stages, and to abandon a traditionally centralized, transmissive, and authoritarian education.

INTERPRETATIVE STUDIES

Those studies about curriculum that constitute a typical research line of the 1990s, focus on the analysis of the subjective meanings of the pedagogical and curricular experiences. Their main interest is to analyze the subjective and intersubjective meanings reported by the protagonists of the educational actions, and therefore they aim to get to the bottom of the interpretation performed by the subjects of curriculum. In some cases, they are works that can be classified in the critical current of naturalist research in the classrooms. As a matter of fact, several authors who are considered part of the critical pedagogy actually are realizing research about intersubjectivity and curriculum themes. In the case of the interpretative trend, the curriculum is examined with as corpus the "texts" and discourses generated by the subjects. Therefore, it is interesting to see how the identity construction process occurs. In this point, those studies differ from the authors of the critical trend, who emphasize the role of the economic structures and institutions.

Silva (1999) considers that this new trend reflects poststructuralist and postcritical conceptions of curriculum. According to this author, this trend includes relevant multicultural research (which emphasizes the role of minorities or vulnerable social groups in curriculum)—research whose purpose is to study the gender relations or feminist pedagogy as well as research that deciphers curriculum as an ethnical and racial narrative.

In our opinion, more than a trend unified by its theoretical referent, what we find here is a diversity of perspectives that coincide in the previously-mentioned aspects. So we can notice in those works, which investigate the meanings that subjects build up about curriculum diverse foci, a range that goes from phenomenological and Freudian influences to hermeneutical visions, passing through research that studies the subjects' implicit representations and theorizations. The most convenient methodological resources are profound interviews or clinical cross-examinations, lives, and biographical narratives or discourse analyses. Several works that illustrate this trend are Remedi's (1992) studies about management in the school institution, Pliego's (2000) about the identity of educational researchers, or the research performed by Moreno (1999) about the subjective vision presented by high school teachers with regard to the curriculum and relations inside the classroom. It is important to bring out that, in those works, the researchers' main interest is not the curriculum, but the analysis of the subjects through the curriculum. We find here again crossovers with other domains of educational research that pose the prior dilemma: Are those studies strictly or exclusively about curriculum? Does this notion include the entirety of the meanings and identities that are built up by the subjects? It is evident that this trend withdraws from any pragmatical interest, at least with regard to the elaboration of curriculum politics and projects, or even to the transformation of the educational practices in the classroom.

CONCLUSION

The curriculum research produced in México during the 1970s was oriented principally to the design of study plans and programs. It showed the predominance of its own approach to the so-called *technological rationality* based on behaviorist psychology. Since then, scholars have appeared who have expressed important criticisms and alternative proposals to this approach from contrary positions, particularly from critical theory and cognitive psychology. But we must wait to the 1980s to notice a substantial increase in this area of research because in this period, a diversity of conceptual and methodological foci concerning curriculum questions showed up. It was also in the 1980s that studies about curriculum got institutionalized (i.e., many educative institutions at primary, secondary, and higher levels created departments or working groups focused on the study of curriculum and the design and evaluation of study plans and programs). Likewise, we saw a proliferation of courses about theory and methodology of curriculum (e.g., subjects, training seminars, diplomats, postgraduate studies) dedicated to the formation of teachers, educational planners, psychologists, pedagogues, and even functionaries and people with decision-making power in the educative institutions.

In regard to the scientific production, in the previously-mentioned state of affairs (see A. Díaz Barriga et al., 1995), we notice that between 1982 and 1991, 45 specialized publications appeared about curriculum questions (books, anthologies, booklets) and 9% (180) of the articles published in national reviews specializing in education and psychology treated the theme of curriculum in essays, research reports, or presentation of proposals and experiences. The theme and approaches of those publications coincides generally with the trends we identified in this chapter. The pending business is now to analyze the production at the end of the 1990s to know whether the scientific production kept growing and which were the prevailing themes and approaches.

We also find an important tension in the field of curriculum development between research and educative intervention. In the former, and because research as knowledge-building work lies in the hands of curriculum theoreticians and specialists, we find a major increase and diversification in the field and a considerable opening to innovating and internationally valid psychological, anthropological, social approaches.

However, those developments have not been sufficiently applied to the domain of educative intervention in terms of the dissemination and consolidation of the real practice of new curriculum experiences and projects in accord with the settings and discoveries of the studies performed about curriculum. Several authors agree that the link between curriculum and design of study plans is the most represented basic reference in México, but the practice of curriculum design is not always congruent with the theoretical or methodological approaches.

After my participation in the state of affairs about the field, and above all on the base of my professional experience in diverse educative private an public institutions, I consider that the generation of curriculum projects still follows the technocratic line and that it keeps centering on the elaboration of formal documents and on the stage of planning. This means that it does not achieve the articulation with the work in the classrooms nor with the formation of teachers. In this sense, excepting meritorious experiences, it has not been possible to give a satisfactory answer to basic problems such as the change in rhetorical and authoritarian educational practices, the organization and construction of contents according to the characteristics of the students, or the connection between social exercise of professions and the most urgent social demands.

Nevertheless, it is important to recognize that it is impossible to find in México the favorable institutional, economical, and salary conditions to allow the exclusive dedication to the chore of educational research. In the concrete case of curriculum research, we can see that the debate and scientific production are mainly centralized in five public higher education institutions,[3] all of which are located in the metropolitan area. This means that all of them are situated in México City or bordering towns. The conditions that have made possible this consolidation as a community of educational researchers have to do with the presence of recognized researchers with an important trajectory and leadership who devote themselves to form new researchers; obtain financing or subventions for their projects; have important editorial connections; take part in conventions, seminars, and formal curriculum experiences where the curriculum is studied; have exchange links with other national or international communities; and rely on the adequate infrastructure. In the case of other institutions that achieve to realize research about curriculum, such as the universities outside the capital and the normal schools, a survey performed in 1992 (see Díaz Barriga et al., 1995) shows that the research work is secondary to the teaching job, that the maximum dedication time of the academic staff to research is about 10 hours a week, and they do not rely on adequate infrastructure. It is important to notice that in those cases the largest part of the research works they report is centered on the establishment or evaluation of curriculum projects or on the analysis of their graduated students' performance in the labor world.

Finally, the curriculum research trends presented here do not aim to be a rigid classification of the national production in this field of study. On the contrary, they represent

---

[3]Those institutions are the Centro de Investigaciones y Servicios Educativos (Center for Educational Research and Services [CISE]), which disappeared in the mid-1990s; the Centro de Estudios sobre la Universidad (Center of Studies About the University [CESU]); the Faculty of Psychology; the *Escuela National de Estudios Profesionales Iztacala* (National School for Professional Studies [ENEP-I]), all of them part of the *Universidad Autónoma Nacional de México* (National Autonomous University of México [UNAM]). The other institution is the *Departamento de Investigaciones Educativas* (Department of Educational Research [DIE]) of the *Instituto Politécnico Nacional* (National Polytechnical Institute [IPN]). Since the 1980s, but much more present in the 1990s, we find interesting developments at the *Universidad Pedagógica Nacional* (National Pedagogical University [UPN]), several departments of the *Secretaría de Educación Publica* (Department of Public Education [SEP]), in the Normal Schools, and in several public universities in the provinces and several private institutions. Taking into account the impulse received by the latter, we think that in an average time they will increase their presence in the field of educational and curriculum research.

only one among many possible perspectives to arrange this production to identify consequent working lines. In any case, we can observe that all those trends coexist, that they are more or less in vogue, and that they receive important influences from the international debate about the theme. Nevertheless, we also opine that the national curriculum research has its own physiognomy and that it reflects the characteristics and problems of the Mexican education, although it has not achieved the proper repercussion in the transformation of the educational practices and the curriculum development processes.

REFERENCES

Arnaz, J. A. (1981). *La planeación curricular.* México: Trillas.

Arredondo, V. (1981). Fundamentación de la Comisión Temática sobre el desarrollo curricular. *Documento Base del Primer Congreso Nacional de Investigación Educativa* (Vol. 1). México.

Barrón, C. (1997) Perspectivas de la formación de profesionales para el siglo XXI. In A. de Alba (Coord.), *El currículum universitario de cara al nuevo milenio* (2nd ed.). México: UNAM.

Coll, C. (1987). *Psicología y currículum.* Barcelona, Spain: Laia.

Coll, C. (1990). Un marco psicológico para el currículum escolar. In *Aprendizaje escolar y construcción del conocimiento.* Barcelona, Spain: Paidós.

Comisión de Nuevos Métodos de Enseñanza. (1976). *Enseñanza programada.* México: CNME/UNAM.

De Alba, A. (1991). Algunas reflexiones sobre el desarrollo del discurso crítico del currículum en México. In A. De Alba, A. Díaz Barriga, & E. González (Comps.). *El campo del currículum. Antología.* México: CESU/UNAM.

De Ibarrola, M. (1992). Primera aproximación a la revisión del plan de estudios del bachillerato CCH. *Gaceta del CCH, 6,* 2-8.

Díaz Barriga, A. (1984). *Ensayos sobre la problemática curricular.* México: Trillas.

Díaz Barriga, A. (1997). *Didáctica y currículum.* México: Paidós.

Díaz Barriga, A., Barrón, C., Carlos, J., Díaz Barriga, F., Torres, R., Spitzer, T., & Ysunza, M. (1995). La investigación en el campo del currículo. In A. Díaz Barriga (Coord.), *Procesos curriculares, institucionales y organizacionales.* México: Consejo Mexicano de Investigación Educativa.

Díaz Barriga, A., & Pacheco, T. (Comps.). (1990). *Cinco aproximaciones al estudio de las profesiones.* Coll. Cuadernos del CESU, 21, México: CESU/UNAM.

Díaz Barriga, A., & Pacheco, T. (1997). *La profesión, su condición social e institucional.* México: CESU/UNAM.

Díaz Barriga, F. (1993). Aproximaciones metodológicas al diseño curricular. *Tecnología y Comunicación Educativas, 8*(21), 19–39.

Díaz Barriga, F., Hernández, G., García, B., & Muriá, I. (1998). Una aproximación al análisis de la influencia de la obra piagetiana en la educación. In *Piaget en la educación: Debate en torno a sus aportaciones.* México: Paidós.

Díaz Barriga, F., & Saad, E. (1997). La formación en la práctica del profesional universitario: Un modelo integral de docencia-servicio-investigación en el ámbito de la psicología educativa. In A. Díaz Barriga (Coord.). *Currículum, evaluación y planeación educativas.* México: COMIE/CESU/ENEPI.

Ducoing, P., & Rodríguez, A. (Comps.). (1990). *La formación del profesional para la educación.* México: UNAM/ANUIES/UNESCO.

Esquivel, E. (1991). Los egresados de los posgrados de educación. *El caso de la Universidad Iberoamericana.* Col. Cuadernos del CESU, 22, México: CESU/UNAM.

Furlán, A. (1996). *Currículum e institución.* México: Instituto Michoacano de Ciencias de la Educación.

Galán, I., & Marín, D. (1988). Investigación para evaluar el currículo universitario. In *Antología para la actualización de profesores de enseñanza media superior.* México: UNAM/Porrúa.

Gago, A. (1978). *Modelos de sistematización del proceso de enseñanza-aprendizaje.* México: Trillas.

Gago, A. (1982). *Elaboración de cartas descriptivas.* México: Trillas.

Glazman, R., & de Ibarrola, M. (1976). *Diseño de planes de estudios.* México: CISE/UNAM.

González, O. (1985). Procedimientos alternativos en la preparación del ingeniero. *Universidades, 101,* 104–121.

Hernández, G. (1998). *Paradigmas en psicología de la educación.* México: Paidós.

Huerta, J. (1981). *Organización lógica de las experiencias de aprendizaje.* México: Trillas.

Jiménez, E. (2000). *La participación de los académicos en el diseño curricular de planes y programas de estudio de la UNAM*. Master's thesis of Educational Psychology, Faculty of Psychology, UNAM, México.

Marín, D. E. (1993). *La formación profesional y el currículo universitario*. México: Diana.

Moreno, A. (1999). *Las relaciones en el aula: una mirada desde la subjetividad a un encargo constructivista*. Master's thesis of Social Psychology, Universidad Autónoma Metropolitana, México.

Pliego, A. (2000). *La identidad de los investigadores sobre la educación. El caso de los psicólogos*. Master's thesis of Clinic Psychology, Faculty of Psychology, UNAM, México.

Posner, G. (1998). *Análisis de currículo*. Bogotá, Colombia: McGraw-Hill.

Remedi, E. (1992). *Desórdenes, sentidos y signos de la gestión: Voces de los sujetos*. Santiago, Chile: UNESCO.

Ruíz, E. (1992). La investigación curricular en México. *Perfiles Educativos, 57–58*, 38–43.

Ruíz, E. (1997). Nuevos requerimentos de formación de ingenieros frente a los nuevos esquemas de la producción industrial y la función empresarial. In A. Díaz Barriga (Coord.), *Currículum, evaluación y planeación educativas*. México: COMIE/CESU/ENEPI.

Ruíz, E. (1998). *Propuesta de un modelo de evaluación curricular para el nivel superior. Una orientación cualitativa*. Coll. Cuadernos del CESU, 35, México: CESU/UNAM.

Schön, D. (1992). *La formación de profesionales reflexivos*. Barcelona, Spain: Paidós.

Silva, T. (1999). *Documentos de identidade*. Belo Horizonte, Brazil: Autentica Editora.

Stufflebeam, D. I. (1971). *Educational evaluation: Decision making*. Itasca, IL: Peacock.

Urbina, J (Comp.). (1989). *El psicólogo: Formación, ejercicio profesional y prospectiva*. México: UNAM.

CHAPTER 26

What Education Scholars Write About Curriculum in Namibia and Zimbabwe

Jonathan D. Jansen
University of Pretoria, South Africa

The field of curriculum studies is underdeveloped in southern Africa. There are few curriculum scholars and, therefore, relatively little research, theory, and writing about the curriculum. The curriculum scholarship that does exist tends to be dominated by visiting professors, international consultants, or masters' and doctoral students from mainly Europe and North America, giving a particular slant to the writings that emerge from this region of the world. Despite the dearth of curriculum scholarship generally, and especially scholarship produced by indigenous writers, what has been written nevertheless makes a critical contribution to curriculum writing in education. The purpose of this short record of curriculum scholarship in Namibia and Zimbabwe is to both describe the emergent curriculum scholarship from these two countries and assess its significance for curriculum thought elsewhere in the world.

THE BROADER POLITICAL CONTEXT SHAPING CURRICULUM THOUGHT IN SOUTHERN AFRICA

The political, economic, and educational systems of Southern African countries are inextricably linked to the patterns of European colonization in the region and the dominant role of apartheid South Africa.

The colonial histories of Zimbabwe and Namibia left an indelible legacy on the curriculum of these two nations, and this legacy is reflected in the curriculum scholarship of Southern Africa. In extracting themes in the curriculum writings from this region, I have relied on three sources: my own research on curriculum in Namibia and Zimbabwe after independence in both countries (Jansen, 1991, 1995), a survey of the curriculum literature on the two countries since independence, and writings that appear in the two most prominent educational research journals of the two countries (i.e., the *Zimbabwe Journal of Educational Research* and *Reform Forum: Journal for Educational Reform in Namibia*). As elsewhere in Africa, there is no journal specifically dedicated to curriculum like the *Journal of Curriculum Studies* (UK) or *Curriculum Perspectives* (Australia).

471

Hence the title of this contribution: what education scholars write about curriculum in Namibia and Zimbabwe.

EMERGING THEMES IN CURRICULUM WRITINGS FROM ZIMBABWE AND NAMIBIA

The first theme to emerge from curriculum scholarship in Zimbabwe and Namibia involves writings about and against the colonial curriculum. These writings were in the main anticolonial descriptions, analyses, and judgments about the nature and effects of this foreign curriculum. It was described as racist because it was founded on an ideology that extolled the belief in inherent differences between the races, and because it portrayed Whites as heroes and Blacks as savages. The colonial curriculum was described as Eurocentric because it was dominated by a history of European ideas and events to the exclusion of African history, ideas, and movements. It was denounced as divisive and demeaning because it justified social, economic, and political segregation among the races in favor of White minority rule. It was dismissed as exploitative and unjust because it portrayed the capitalist system as the only viable economic system for African development, thereby denying the history of communal socialism of precolonial times. This strong anticolonial theme dominated the curriculum writings of Namibian and Zimbabwean writers, whether in exile or in the universities and social movements of those countries for much of the 20th century (see Amukugo, 1993; Chung & Ngara, 1985; Jansen, 1990; Salia-Bao, 1989, 1991).

The second theme of curriculum scholarship in Zimbabwe and Namibia concerns those curriculum innovations introduced after independence. In both countries, every major curriculum innovation became the subject of intense study by both national and international scholars eager to understand the possibilities and problems of changing the underlying ideological commitments of the inherited curriculum in forging a new social order (Mungazi, 1985; Zeichner & Dahlstrom, 1999; see also Hungwe, 1992). In Zimbabwe, for example, extensive studies were conducted during the early 1980s on an innovation called *education with production* (Jansen, 1990; Lewis, 1988). This educational program, first pioneered in Botswana, intended to create new conditions for teaching and learning, which reconciled education and work in the context of a broad socialist education. The problem identified was the capitalist disjunction between formal education (what happened in schools) and the world of work (what happened in society). This distance between education and work contributed to a class structure that valued mental labor more than manual labor, and the credentialing associated with schooling more than the transformation of especially rural communities. In Namibia, for example, the national requirement that English would be the language of instruction was widely interpreted as a swift move by the new government to displace Afrikaans (a South African variant of the original settler Dutch) as the linguistic and ideological vehicle through which Namibian children used to learn. Several studies tracked the implementation of the new language policy in Namibian schools—a position that received criticism from both sympathetic writers (on the grounds of denying the primacy of indigenous languages) as well as colonialists who saw the new policy as impractical given the long history of Afrikaans in the schools (Harlech-Jones, 1998; Mutumba, 1999). Other major studies of innovation in Namibia concerned the new curriculum for teacher development, Bachelor of Teacher Education Diploma (BETD) for teacher training (Dahlstrom, 2000; Zeichner & Dahlstrom, 1999) and the implementation of learner-centered education in the school curriculum (Narimab, 1999; Swarts, 1998).

The third theme of curriculum scholarship in Zimbabwe and Namibia could be described as advocacy writings about what knowledge, ideas, and values the new education system should reflect after colonialism. The point of reference for these writings clearly was the system of colonial education and the curriculum vision that it espoused. In Zimbabwe, these writings were deeply etched within the preindependence socialist vision for education and curriculum (Amukugo, 1993; Chung & Ngara, 1985; Nekhwevha, 1999). These writers were concerned with the termination of the racist and Eurocentric biases of the colonial curriculum, and they were preoccupied with the capitalist and exploitative nature of colonial education. Such writings typically called for greater educational opportunities for the children of those colonized, greater equality and improved quality in the educational system, breaking down distinctions between education and training, the removal of racism and sexism from the curriculum, and solidarity with socialist or antiracial models of education elsewhere. Although perhaps not strictly scholarship, such writings had an important political influence in these emerging democracies and in rallying sentiment against the colonial curriculum as the basis for imagining a postcolonial curriculum. Such writings were typically contained in conference proceedings and unpublished papers rather than in peer-reviewed journals.

The fourth theme of curriculum scholarship in Zimbabwe and Namibia could be called *studies on the politics of curriculum*. This rare but critical component of curriculum writings in southern Africa offers analyses of the interface among politics, power, and privilege in the construction of curriculum in Southern Africa. Such writings provided critical assessments of curriculum initiatives of the state, often pointing to the contradictions between radical visions for curriculum change and the conservative forces that maintain curriculum continuity with colonial knowledge and values (Harber, 1985, 1997; Jansen, 1990, 1991, 1995). In Zimbabwe, the most persistent writings under this theme concerned those radical proposals for creating a socialist curriculum called *The Political Economy of Zimbabwe* (Jansen, 1991). This radical curriculum was introduced by the new government and then rapidly withdrawn from schools as a consequence of unprecedented resistance from the general public, the Church, and other influential groups in Zimbabwean society. A similar radical initiative that gained the attention of curriculum scholars in Zimbabwe was Education with Production—a program seeking to instill socialist values and skills in the postcolonial experiences of youth through greater vocationalization of the curriculum (Lewis, 1988; see also Gustafsson, 1988, Nherera, 1998; Jansen, 1993). In both cases, the tensions between change and continuity constituted the focus of these critical studies. In Namibia, writings or the politics of curriculum were focused on the implementation of new language policies, showing the ways in which political interests not only underpinned the original proposals for an English-only policy, but also explained the limited success of such radical proposals in the schools and classrooms of the new Namibia. More recently, there has emerged a more coherent body of writing on the politics of the teacher education curriculum following a major restructuring of teacher education in Namibia (see Zeichner, Dahlstrom, & Swarts, 1999).

The fifth theme of curriculum scholarship in the two countries concerns studies of school subjects, their nature, design, organization, effects on learning and teaching, and attitudes among various classes of learners (Alausa, 1999; Kafupi, 1999; Liswani, 1999; Mandebvu, 1991; Marira, 1991; Mtetwa, 1990; Nyagura & Riddell, 1991; Swarts, 1998; Wilmut, 1996). In Southern Africa, school subjects remain a powerful organizational reality in postcolonial institutions despite various initiatives for integration of subjects or interdisciplinary curricula. Such studies are often conducted by specialists within the subject (e.g., science education students or language scholars). Studies of school subjects are often fragmented and proceed with the insular discourses of the discipline. These studies also tend to be conservative, focusing on technical limitations or deficiencies in teaching, learning, curriculum, and assessment within the context of a particular school subject or discipline (Nziramasanga, 1989). It is rare that cross-curricular themes are researched (see Amukushu, 1999) or critical studies of school subjects are pursued in Namibian or Zimbabwean curriculum writings; the closest writings in this regard concern content analyses of the racial and colonial content of school textbooks and syllabuses (outlines of subject material to be taught) that define a school subject in southern Africa (Jansen, 1990; Salia-Bao, 1989).

The sixth theme in curriculum writings in Namibia and South Africa concerns the administration of education and how patterns of administration influenced curriculum planning in the two countries. These writings are typically historical-descriptive in nature and span both the colonial and postcolonial periods. This literature places emphasis on both the formal and informal organization of administration and curriculum and tends to constitute detailed documentary studies of education over time. In Zimbabwe, the classical study *Teaching Rhodesians,* by Atkinson (1978), is typical of the formal, organizational studies of schooling under colonialism (see also Welle-Strand, 1996). In Namibia, Cohen's (1994) study on the administration of education is a similar documentary account from the colonial period to the present (see also Katzao, 1999). However, studies by Harber (1985, 1997) in both Namibia and Zimbabwe have concentrated on the informal organization of schools, curriculum, and pedagogy during the liberation wars against colonialism. Studies of curriculum organization are, however, quite rare; and where matters of curriculum are dealt with, they are often contained within broader studies of educational administration.

A seventh theme in curriculum writings concerns those examinations and assessments as part of the broader curriculum reform initiatives after colonialism (Jansen, 1995). Examinations formed the focus of much controversy and conflict in curriculum reforms and the end of colonial rule for three broad reasons. First, examinations served a powerful selection role under colonialism, giving White and small Black elite access to further and higher education, employment opportunities, class status and social position, and a wealth of other privileges. Second, examinations were strongly influenced by external forces widely seen as part of the ongoing colonial control over African education. In Namibia, the South African government controlled the end of school examination, called *Matriculation Examinations.* In Zimbabwe, the Cambridge Examination Syndicate controlled the important exit examinations at O and A levels. But here an interesting divergence occurred. To shake off the shackles of South African control, Namibia brought in the International Cambridge Syndicate, whereas Zimbabwe has always, at least in public and political rhetoric on curriculum, tried to unshackle itself from the admittedly Eurocentric and expensive Cambridge Examination Syndicate. Not surprisingly, in both countries, curriculum writers have debated and analyzed the instruments and effects of assessment and examination after colonial rule (Association for the Development of Education in Africa, 2001; Legesse & Otaala, 1998).

An eighth and final theme in curriculum writings of Namibia and Zimbabwe concerns consultancy reports on curriculum reforms, and typically those that received external donor funding from major international organizations like the United States Agency for International Development (USAID), the World Bank, the Swedish International Development Agency (SIDA), and others like the various United Nations agencies (UNESCO, UNICEF, etc). Typically, these consultancy reports are either stocktaking exercises or sector assessments concerned with education reforms broadly or the evaluation of specific curriculum projects (Association for the Development of Education in Africa, 1999; Atkinson, Agere, & Mambo, 1993; Chikombah et al., 1999). Sometimes these reports are generated from within national government agencies using national consultants or academics, although such local scholars in such contexts often work alongside international consultants or academics (Creative Associates International, 1990). In Namibia, such a national agency is the National Institute for Educational Development (NIED), where a strong contingent of academics from Florida State University in the United States worked with local scholars to conduct monitoring and implementation studies on curriculum-related policies after independence in 1990 (e.g., see Fair, 1994). In Zimbabwe, the Curriculum Development Unit (CDU) had a similar function, although individual Zimbabweans were more often hired as consultants from the local university to work independently on international consultancy teams dealing with sector studies or curriculum evaluation of new projects and policy receiving external aid support (Maravanyika, 1990). Consultant reports driven by donor agencies have become influential in curriculum decision making in Namibia and Zimbabwe, and they often appear in international journals as curriculum scholarship from Southern Africa. In addition, such reports hold considerable significance for decisions on donor aid to such countries and, as critical scholars often point out, can strengthen the dependency of education in developing countries on the power and influence of external agencies. The postcolonial imprints of external agencies have left an indelible mark on curriculum innovation and scholarship in Southern Africa (as elsewhere), and one of the principal instruments in this process is international donor aid (see Samoff, 1992).

COMPARING CURRICULUM SCHOLARSHIP IN NAMIBIA AND ZIMBABWE

There is a clear pattern of education scholarship on curriculum in both countries. Anticolonial writings on curriculum mark the period before political independence in both states; these writings were largely critical reports on colonial education and its manifestation in the school curriculum. In the period prior to and following independence, advocacy writings emerged more prominently, with an emphasis on "what should be" in the new curriculum. Also at about the point of independence, international agencies normally commenced sector studies that typically estimated the state of readiness in the new nation for large-scale education reforms, with sections on the status of the curriculum (examinations, assessment, content, teaching styles, etc). After independence and in the wake of the announcement of major initiatives by the new state, case studies on innovation began to appear in the literature. Down the road from independence, innovation studies were replaced by milestone studies, in which progress was reviewed and monitored, often again in the form of earlier sector studies driven by international agencies with participation by local academics or consultants.

Despite these broad trends, the curriculum writings by individual scholars in Zimbabwe tend to be dispersed and cover a range of disparate topics from sex education in the curriculum, to second-language teaching, to special education, to code switching in mathematics, to the relative performance of boys and girls in science classrooms (see the *Zimbabwe Journal of Educational Research*). Namibian writings, in contrast, tend to be more focused on the topic of curriculum reform and are less dispersed in focus than in the case of Zimbabwe (see the *Reform Forum: Journal for Education Reform*). This could be explained as follows. Zimbabwe has a relatively strong and independent university (with new ones created recently) that is only weakly coupled to the Ministry of Education in terms of its research and publications agenda. Namibia, in contrast, has a small university with a weak Faculty of Education, so that the bulk of the research on education is produced in and through the Namibian Institute for Educational Development (NIED), which is part of the Ministry of Education and produces its research journal from within the institute.

In both Namibia and Zimbabwe, the content of education writings on curriculum tend to be similar. The scholarly writings tend to follow, almost mechanistically, the research agendas of international agencies (see Samoff, 1996). The most obvious example is the sudden fixation with education quality that has tied down the resources and staffing of government behind the quality agenda. The Southern African Consortium for Monitoring Educational Quality (SACMEQ), funded and managed by UNESCO using its in-house consultant expertise, is the main player in framing Namibia and Zimbabwe's education and curriculum writings at the time of writing (see Machingaidze et al., 1998; Voigts, 1998). The curriculum writings tend to be based on simple research designs such as thin case study reports (qualitative) or basic statistical summaries (quantitative). The writings locate their conceptual roots in Europe and North America, with little cross-referencing of the research (small though it may be) from other parts of the third world, from Africa, or even from the Southern African region. The bulk of the education and curriculum writings are atheoretical as well as apolitical. There are fairly standard and mainstream studies on school effectiveness, student questioning, learner attitudes, perceptions of school subjects, and so on. There are critical silences in the curriculum writings from Namibia and Zimbabwe on matters of grave importance in the society around it (e.g., a dearth of writings on HIV/AIDS and education despite that this represents the single most important health crisis in Southern African schools and society).

CONCLUSION

As stated earlier, there is no established curriculum scholarship in Namibia and Zimbabwe. Curriculum writing is often submerged under general education writings. Curriculum writing in this region of the world is often dominated by professors, students, or consultants from other parts of the world. Curriculum writing had a strong political focus under and against colonialism, but lost this quality at independence in favor of more staid technical and administrative accounts of curriculum change and innovation. Curriculum scholarship does not exist, and there does not appear to be a critical mass of curriculum specialists or writers (the same is true in other states of the region such as Botswana and South Africa) that have defined the field of inquiry in southern Africa. Curriculum writing is often reflexive on a colonial legacy (like the Eurocentric curriculum), new international controls (like the Cambridge Examination Syndicate in Namibia), or external ideologies (like socialism during early independence in Zimbabwe). The reasons for this dearth of indigenous curriculum scholarship are many and include the fact that there are few universities in the region (until recently, one each in Namibia and Zimbabwe), education research is weak in these institutions, curriculum writing has been mainly focused on school subjects with a teacher education and practical bias, and the fragmented group of curriculum writers is transient, leaving after a short while to their home universities in Europe and North America. As is the case in the economic domain, curriculum scholarship in southern Africa has been underdeveloped and remains dependent on what happens in the West. As in the political domain, curriculum developments in Southern Africa, however small and limited, provide significant insights for curriculum scholarship in the rest of the world in three ways. One, it demonstrates the powerful legacies of colonialism and, some would argue, neo-colonial dependency in the themes emergent in Namibian and Zimbabwean writings. Two, it demonstrates how curriculum change and innovations unfold under conditions (economic, political, social) of transition that are poorly understood in the international curriculum literature. Third, it points to obvious areas for further research and development, including a sustained and critical curriculum scholarship that focuses on new conditions (such as globalization) that threaten to reinforce the marginalization of Southern African curriculum scholars and writings in this part of the world.

REFERENCES

Alausa, Y. A. (1999, September). Teacher's feedback through the learners: A case of my biology class. *Reform Forum, 10*.

Amukugo, E. M. (1993). *Education and politics in Namibia: Past trends and future prospects*. Windhoek, Namibia: New Namibia Books.

Amukusu, A. K. (1999). Developing cross-curricular themes from storytelling in grade one. In K. Zeichner & L. Dahlstrom (Eds.), *Democratic teacher education reform in Africa: The case of Namibia* (pp. 198–206). Boulder, CO: Westview.

Association for the Development of Education in Africa. (2001). *What works and what's new in African education: Africa speaks*. London: Author.

Association for the Development of Education in Africa. (1999). *Curriculum reform and development in Namibia reflecting equity, access and quality*. London: Author.

Atkinson, N. D. (1978). *Teaching Rhodesians*. London: Longman.

Atkinson, N. D., Agere, T., & Mambo, M. N. (1993). *A sector analysis of education in Zimbabwe*. Harare, Zimbabwe: UNICEF.

Chikombah, C. E. M., Chivore, B. R. S., Maravanyika, O. E., Nyagura, L. M., & Sibanda, I. M., (1999). *Review of education sector analysis in Zimbabwe 1990–1996*. Paris: Working Group on Education Sector Analysis.

Chung, F., & Ngara, E. (1985). *Socialism, education and development: A challenge to Zimbabwe*. Harare, Zimbabwe: Zimbabwe Publishing House.

Cohen, C. (1994). *Administering colonial education in Namibia: The colonial period to the present*. Windhoek, Namibia: Namibia Scientific Society.

Creative Associates International. (1990). *Final evaluation: Basic education and skills training sector assistance program, Zimbabwe*. Washington, DC: Author.

Dahlstrom, L. (Ed.). (2000). *Perspectives on teacher education and transformation in Namibia*. Windhoek, Namibia: Gamsberg Macmillan Publishers.

Ellis, J. (1984). *Education, repression and liberation: Namibia*. London: Catholic Institute for International Relations and the World University Service.

Fair, K. (1994, September 22). *Passing and failing learners: Policies and practices in Ondangwa and Rundu in grades 1 to 3*. Ministry of Education and Culture and UNICEF, with support from UNICEF and the MEC/Florida State University Project, Volume II.

Gustafsson, I. (1988). Work as education—perspectives on the role of work in current educational reform in Zimbabwe. In J. Lauglo & K. Lillis (Eds.), *Vocationalizing education—an international perspective*. Oxford, England: Pergamon.

Harber, C. (1985). Weapon of war: Political education in Zimbabwe. *Journal of Curriculum Studies, 17*(2), 163–174.

Harber, C. (1997). *Education, democracy and political development in Africa*. Brighton, England: Sussex Academic Press.

Harlech-Jones, B. (1998). Viva English! Or is it time to review language policy in education? *Reform Forum, 6*.

Hungwe, K. N. (1992). Issues in computer-oriented innovations in Zimbabwean education. In S. G. Lewis & J. Samoff (Eds.), *Micro-computers in African development: Critical perspectives*. Boulder, CO: Westview.

Jansen, J. (1990). *State, curriculum and socialism in Zimbabwe, 1980–1990*. Unpublished doctoral dissertation, Stanford University, Stanford, CA.

Jansen, J. (1991). The state and curriculum in the transition to socialism: The Zimbabwean experience. *Comparative Education Review, 35*(1), 76–91.

Jansen, J. (1993). Curriculum reform in Zimbabwe: Reflections for the South African transition. In N. Taylor (Ed.), *Inventing knowledge—contests in curriculum construction*. Cape Town, South Africa: Maskew Miller Longman.

Jansen, J. (1995). Understanding social transition through the lens of curriculum policy: Namibia/South Africa. *Journal of Curriculum Studies, 27*(3), 245–261.

Kafupi, P. (1999, September). Some male learners in grade 10 geography. *Reform Forum, 10*.

Katzao, J. (1999). *Lessons to learn. A historical, sociological and economic interpretation of education provision in Namibia*. Windhoek, Namibia: Out of Africa Publishers.

Kristensen, J. O. (1999). Reform and/or change? The Nambian broad curriculum revisited. *Reform Forum, 10*, 1–7.

Legesse, K., & Otaala, B. (1998, February 25–27). *Performance at (H)IGCSE in Namibia, 1995–1997*. Implications for Teaching and Learning, A Report of a Workshop held at Rossing Education Centre, Faculty of Education, University of Namibia, Namibia.

Lewis, M. (1988). *The theory and practice of theory and practice. The continuing debate over linking school and work and a case study from Zimbabwe.* MA Monograph, Stanford University School of Education.

Liswani, V. (1999). Improving the participation of girls in my grade nine agricultural lessons. In K. Zeichner & L. Dahlstrom (Eds.), *Democratic teacher education reform in Africa: The case of Namibia* (pp. 94–99). Boulder, CO: Westview.

Machingaidze, T., Pfukani, P., & Shumba, S. (1998). *The quality of primary education: Some policy suggestions based on a survey of schools.* Paris: Zimbabwe, Ministry of Education and Culture; UNESCO International Institute for Educational Planning (IIEP), SACMEQ Policy Research: Report No. 3. Published by the IIEP, UNESCO Paris.

Maravanyika, O. E. (1990). *Implementing educational policies in Zimbabwe.* Washington, DC: The World Bank (World Bank Discussion Papers 91, Africa Technical Department Series).

Ministry of Education. (1989). *The political economy syllabus, Zimbabwe junior certificate.* Harare, Zimbabwe: Author.

Ministry of Education and Culture. (1993). *Towards education for all.* Windhoek, Namibia: Gamsberg Macmillan.

Mungazi, D. (1985). Educational innovations in Zimbabwe: Possibilities and problems. *Journal of Negro Education, 54*(2), 196–212.

Mutumba, J. (1999, April). Language policy in Namibia. *Reform Forum, 9.*

Nagel, T. (1992). *Quality: Between tradition and modernity. Patterns of communication and cognition in teacher education in Zimbabwe.* Dr. Polit. Avhandling, Pedagogisk Forskningsinstitutt, Universitetet I Oslo, Host.

Narimab, G. (1999). Developing learner understanding through learner-centered activities. In K. Zeichner & L. Dahlstrom (Eds.), *Democratic teacher education reform in Africa: The case of Namibia* (pp. 82–87). Boulder, CO: Westview.

Nekhwevha, F. (1999). No matter how long the night, the day is sure to come: Culture and educational transformation in post-colonial Namibia and post-Apartheid South Africa. In C. Soudien, P. Kallaway, & M. Breier (eds), *Education, equity and transformation* (pp. 491–506). The Netherlands: Kluwer.

Nherera, C. M. (1998). Post-independence reform policies and vocationalization of the secondary school education in Zimbabwe. In L. Buchert (Ed.), *Education reform in the south in the 1980s* (pp. 89–112). Paris: UNESCO.

Nziramasanga, C. T. (1989). Social studies curriculum development in Zimbabwe. *International Journal of Social Education, 4*(2), 44–52.

Salia-Bao, K. (1989). *Curriculum development and African culture.* London: Edward Arnold.

Salia-Bao, K. (1991). *The Namibian education system under the colonialists.* Randburg, South Africa: Hodder & Stoughton Educational.

Samoff, J. (1992). The intellectual/financial complex of foreign aid. *Review of African Political Economy, 53*, 60–87.

Samoff, J. (1996). The structural adjustment of education research: Reflections. In L. Buchert & K. King (Eds.), *Consultancy and research in international education: The new dynamics* (pp. 65–83). Bonn, Germany: German Foundation for International Development.

Swarts, P. (1998, June). *Evaluation and monitoring exercise of the mathematics curriculum.* Research Report, Namibian Institute for Educational Development, Okahandja, Namibia.

Voigts, F. (1998). *The quality of education: Some policy suggestions based on a survey of schools, Namibia.* UNESCO International Institute for Educational Planning (IIEP), SACMEQ Policy Research: Report No. 2. Published by the IIEP, UNESCO Paris.

Welle-Strand, A. (1996). *Policy, evaluation and leadership: The context of educational change in Zimbabwe.* Stockholm: Stockholm University, Institute of International Education.

Wilmut, J. (1996). *Evaluating syllabus within the Namibian schools curriculum from grade 1–12.* Okahandja, Namibia: National Institute for Education Development.

Zeichner, K., & Dahlstrom, L. (Eds). (1999). *Democratic teacher education reform in Africa: The case of Namibia.* Boulder, CO: Westview.

Zeichner, K., Dahlstrom, L., & Swarts, P. (1999). Reconstructive education and the road to social justice: The case of postcolonial teacher education in Namibia. *International Journal of Leadership in Education, 2*(3), 149–164.

Zvobgo, R. J. (1986). *Transforming education: The Zimbabwean experience.* Harare, Zimbabwe: The College Press.

CHAPTER 27

Curriculum Theory in the Netherlands

Willem Wardekker
Monique Volman
Jan Terwel
Vrije Universiteit Amsterdam, the Netherlands

Although the Netherlands are wedged between the spheres of influence, both in a political and philosophical sense, of the Continental (both German and French) and Anglo-Saxon worlds, a space for some specific developments in and interpretations of education that are unique to the Netherlands has existed most of the time. The history and present state of its school system, the curriculum, and curriculum theory and research are all closely connected to the waxing and waning of these spheres as they came to dominance, but they cannot be understood if we do not take into account some specific characteristics of the Dutch mind set and the solutions and structures to which it gave rise.

As in most European countries, the school system in the Netherlands developed to meet the needs of a shifting social order. This could be described as a process of *massification* of education: More and more people gained admission to formal education until compulsory enrollment for all was reached as late as 1920. It may be interesting to note right away that the dependence of the country on foreign trade has led to an important amount of curriculum time being devoted to foreign languages, while nationalist tendencies, both in the curriculum and in the general way of thinking, are rather less marked than in most other countries. It is unclear whether the fact that the Netherlands cannot boast of many great names in philosophy or the humanities (Nauta, 2000) should be seen as a consequence or cause of this situation. Dutch thinkers seem to have engaged mainly in connecting and trading in ideas developed elsewhere. This commercial background may also be a reason that conflicts of interest tend to be solved by pragmatic compromise rather than by open conflict—a tendency that has also left its traces in the school system and in educational theory. Such conflicts have existed between social classes or strata, but also, more markedly than in other countries, between religious groups. A description in terms of massification of education tends to hide such conflicts of interest and their solutions.

As to social conflict, each time a new social group emancipated itself and demanded admission to the structure, a new school type in secondary education was added instead of changing the curriculum of the existing schools. Ostensibly, the purpose of this was to cater to the specific needs of such groups. Thus, for instance, in the second half of the 19th century, the Higher Citizen's School (HBS) was formed next to the gymnasium, addressing itself to the children of the higher middle class and providing a curriculum inspired mainly by the needs of commerce. Yet the idea of creating special schools for special needs may also be viewed as an ideology that hides the purpose of maintaining the class structure of society against the dangers that this emancipation process presented. The net result has been a rather rigid structure with many types of schools in secondary education, the boundaries between which are difficult to pass for pupils. Although Dutch society is much less class oriented than, for example, the British, it is still true that enrollment in these school types is class related. Until recently, the most important feature of this system was a strict separation in secondary education between schools for general education and schools for industry-oriented vocational training. This separation grew historically from the development of different education systems, and is thus class related, but was (and still is) legitimized by an ideology of separate student abilities: Some students are better with their heads, others with their hands.

These 19th-century developments have also left their mark on the curriculum. According to Lenders (1988, 1992), the orientation toward commerce and industry, coupled with a dominant liberalism, translated itself into an empiricist and even positivist curriculum, in which knowledge and abilities were valued more than personality development, the latter being seen as an area belonging to the family and the church rather than the school. This empiricist curriculum became the factual norm both in primary and secondary education. The position of the neo-humanist gymnasium, for instance, became quickly marginalized once the more empiricist HBS curriculum (and others like it) was established.

The history of the Dutch school system and its curriculum is at least as much one of religious conflicts and the emancipation of religious groups as it is one of class conflicts and emancipation. This element had important consequences in the second half of the 19th and throughout the 20th century.

Protestants and Catholics each comprise about one third of the Dutch population, and each group traditionally has created its own organizations for just about every aspect of public life: The struggle for emancipation and power of each group resulted in a sort of voluntary religious apartheid system (Sturm et al., 1998) that has only begun to break down with the growing secularization in the second half of the 20th century. Of course, each group claimed the right to decide the content of the curriculum of its children; after a prolonged conflict, the issue was settled by creating the statutory right for any group to found its own schools, which are fully state financed as long as they conform to certain criteria of quality and number of pupils. Most of these schools (now about 60% of all schools) are of an either Catholic or Protestant signature; the state provides schools only in those cases where this system does not suffice, and these public schools form the third pillar in this system of what is commonly called *pillarization*—recruiting their students from social democrats and conservatives alike. (One of the unforeseen consequences of this system has been that it is now being used to found state-financed Islamic or Hindu schools.)

The consequences of this model have been different from what one might expect. Apart from obvious differences in religious education as a subject, the impact on the actual curriculum is limited. The dominance of an empiricist tradition has largely prevented thinking in other terms than those of the transmission of objective knowledge. Neither group has succeeded in creating a curriculum that is inherently Catholic or Protestant in nature. In fact, the curricula (both formal and informal) in all three denominational streams are largely the same; the more so as schools that have a religious background admit pupils, and often teachers as well, who do not have the same background and the importance attached to religion as a dominating aspect of life is diminishing anyway. This is now leading to a situation where parents, irrespective of their religious background, choose the *best* school for their children—a practice that tends to emphasize class and ethnic differences. From the point of view of curriculum theory, the most important consequence of the so-called *freedom of education* is that the state cannot prescribe detailed curricula or textbooks because this is quickly interpreted as state interference in private matters. Schools are largely autonomous in their choice of source books, marketed by independent commercial publishers (originally catering each to their own pillar) or even created by the teachers. There is a state institute for curriculum development (SLO), but its influence is limited to creating example curricula with no binding power. Although in recent years SLO has gained influence by coordinating and directing the processes of deliberation concerning the national curriculum within and between the various interest groups, the educational publishing houses have not lost their position of power.

Because of the relative autonomy of schools, the margin for curriculum changes imposed by the state is relatively small. However, based on the fact that schools in all three pillars are fully financed by the state, the right to assess the quality of education is claimed by the state, and it exercises this right by imposing central examinations in secondary education and an inspection system at all levels. Some major changes in the curriculum have been imposed by changing the content of the examinations. In addition, the national curricula and goals are evaluated by the National institute for educational testing (CITO). Both CITO and SLO are instrumental in an educational policy toward accountability. Still the space for curriculum change initiated in the schools is much greater than in countries with a more centralized curriculum; given the uncoordinated nature of such efforts, coupled with the rather conservative policies of publishers, this may have resulted in a rather slow rate of change.

The relative autonomy of schools and the relative ease of founding state-financed schools, even if they are not religious in character, have also created the possibility for the success of several strands of the Progressive Education movement in the Netherlands. In the beginning of the 20th century, these began as isolated initiatives, sometimes inspired by internationally recognized practical efforts like those of Montessori (who lived in the Netherlands for some time), Petersen, Freinet, Steiner, and Helen Parkhurst, and sometimes founded by more nationally known educators like Boeke and Ligthart. Such initiatives were often dependent on one person's special charisma, but the freedom of education made it relatively easy to continue these efforts. Even now, the number of Montessori, Jenaplan, and Waldorf schools is still growing, and *progressive* ideas have had a distinct impact on the pedagogy of *normal* schools. The actual influence on the pupils' curriculum of these movements is much greater than that of the religious affiliation of schools.

At the moment, it would seem that the position of the state relative to that of the schools is shifting. This shift may be partly caused by the growing disinterest in a religion-based school system and partly by the rising costs of education that have resulted in drastic budget reductions (to the point where the Netherlands is now spending a smaller portion of its national income on education than most other Western countries) accompanied by the requirement to the schools that they present themselves in an open market and be accountable for their results. Finally, it is partly due to the problems created by the relatively large influx of non-Dutch-speaking pupils, which is seen as a threat to quality. On the one hand, schools are nominally being given even more (financial) freedom to realize a distinct mission; on the other hand, the state is exerting more control than ever by taking measures to ensure the quality of education. These take the form of imposing regulations that have a direct impact on the aims and content of the curriculum. One example of this tendency is the formulation of mandatory curriculum aims for primary and lower secondary education; although at the moment these are little more than a collection of rather loosely formulated and incoherent descriptions of subject areas to be covered, it is a clear break with the tradition of nonintervention in the curriculum. Another example is the recent compulsory introduction of a pedagogy based on principles of self-regulated learning in the second phase of secondary education. Here, too, the basic principles are rather loosely formulated, and schools can implement these in diverse forms of actual curriculum. At the same time, such an intervention would probably have met with insurmountable resistance 20 years ago.

THE STRUGGLE FOR A COMMON CURRICULUM IN SECONDARY EDUCATION

The history of Dutch education in the second half of the 20th century was marked by a struggle to get rid of the more problematic aspects of the school system as it had developed in the past because the state had limited power over the curriculum. The aim was to abolish the institutionalized form of curriculum tracking and create a more meritocratic form of education. Most of these attempts concentrated on changing the structure of the system, diffusing or eliminating the boundaries between school types. None of these attempts has fully succeeded partly because of the resistance of conservative political forces and partly because of the inherent resilience of the system, which in the Netherlands may be greater than in some other countries because of the limited power of the state over the curriculum. The latest example is the creation of a common curriculum in the first 2 or 3 years of secondary education, which we go into in some detail herein.

Both developments in society and notions of social justice and equality of opportunity in education were important motives for curriculum innovation in the first stage of secondary education. In the Netherlands, Leon van Gelder, professor of education at Groningen University from 1964 to 1981, was one of the proponents of a radical innovation of the first stage of secondary schooling in the Netherlands. In the 1960s and 1970s, he proposed a new curriculum for all 12- to 16-year-olds. The resulting concept of a comprehensive school (middle school) was inspired by similar innovations in Sweden, England, and Germany. Some of the European scholars who inspired this innovation were Bernstein and Klafki. In the 1970s, when the social democrats became a coalition partner in the Dutch government, plans were launched and experiments were initiated to design and implement the middle school. One of the main issues was to overcome the traditional division between general education and vocational education, and the accompanying system of curriculum tracking between and within schools.

The curricular innovations in the middle school experiments were supported by the National Institute for Curriculum Development (SLO). However, the main burden of the development of new curriculum materials was on the teachers. This included integrating subjects into broader curriculum domains; connecting teaching and learning to real-life situations; integrating the cognitive, affective, and psychomotor dimensions of learning; and having students of different abilities work together in heterogeneous classes and small groups.

As soon as a new conservative minister of education was in charge, the experiments gradually lost their political legitimation and support and were finally abandoned. It took more than 15 years before a political consensus could be found for a new secondary curriculum. At the start of the school year (1993–1994), a major innovation was introduced for the first stage of Dutch secondary education. All students were to participate in a national core curriculum called *basisvorming* (basic education). The new curriculum contained common objectives for 15 subjects to be covered in 3 years, with some differentiation in time for high- and low-achieving students in the various streams, but without any changes to the existing structure with its heavy emphasis on external differentiation.

In the core curriculum, new subjects, aims, and classroom procedures were formulated. Some of the elements of the new curriculum were also part of the middle school curriculum, like learning in real-life situations and integrating the cognitive, affective, and psychomotor dimensions. More or less new is the accentuation of skills and cognitive strategies, and a new role of the teacher in guiding students in the process of reinvention instead of whole-class teaching from a transmission perspective. The development of learning strategies and self-regulated learning is a central goal seen as a longitudinal process to be fostered both in the junior and senior levels of secondary education. The new curriculum marks a change in outlook from the middle school ideas: There, a way of thinking inspired by progressive educators was plainly visible; here, the perceived demands of a market economy led to a greater emphasis on qualification, whereas the progressive element is visible only in some of the arguments for self-regulated learning.

It is noteworthy that this was a curriculum innovation without any corresponding institutional reform, as intended by the earlier comprehensive (middle) school movement. Recently, Roelofs and Terwel (1999) concluded that the development and implementation of this innovative curriculum are still far behind the expectations of educators and policymakers. First, the formally stated aim of postponing early selection of students has not been reached. As a consequence of the weak compromise (changing the content, but maintaining the traditional school structure), students are already selected into different school types or tracks at the beginning or during their first year in secondary education. Although the same 15 subject areas form the curriculum for every school type, virtually the only common factor in the curriculum in use at the present time are the names of these subjects. The contents differ greatly between school types, both in scope and degree of difficulty. Second, 5 years after the introduction of the national curriculum, the learning results are lower than before the introduction of the new curriculum (Van der Werf, Lubbers, & Kuyper, 1999). Third, differences (inequalities) in learning results and opportunities between categories of students relating to gender, SES, and ethnicity have not changed after 5 years of curriculum innovation. Last, the intended new teaching methods were only observed in a small minority of schools and classrooms. One of the striking results was the discrepancy between students' and teachers' perceptions of the learning environment. Whereas teachers indicated that they regularly or often practiced new innovative teaching methods, the students indicated that teachers did so infrequently. Although school and class climates were evaluated in more positive terms, the rather disappointing overall conclusion must be that, in terms of curriculum levels, the intentions, aims, and characteristics of the new curriculum are more idealistic than experienced and far from being attained (Roelofs & Terwel, 1999; Van den Bergh, Peters-Sips, & Zwarts, 1999; Van der Werf, Lubbers, & Kuyper, 1999). However, in its evaluation of the implementation of the common curriculum, the inspectorate concluded that the learning results, relative to the stated goals, are satisfactory. Two thirds of the attainment targets the results are at or above the minimum level, although results differ between subjects (*Inspectie van het Onderwijs*, 1999).

The peculiarities of the Dutch system (of which the foregoing was only one example) have to be kept in mind when, in the next sections, we describe the history and present situation of curriculum theory, research, and development in the Netherlands.

THE FIRST WAVE OF CURRICULUM THEORY: EMPIRICISM AND THEOLOGY

In the 19th century, curriculum theory in the Netherlands was not established in the universities. Rather, those concerned with the curriculum were school inspectors, school leaders, and teachers (Lenders, 1992). It was they who wrote instruction books for teacher training, materials for (mostly primary) education, and articles in education journals. As noted in the first section, their dominant outlook, especially in the second half of the 19th century, was empirist, if not empiricist. This led them to value direct experience and inquiry, which was a marked improvement on the book knowledge-oriented curriculum dominant until then. According to Lenders, they had a lot of direct influence on the actual curriculum. At the end of the 19th century, their position culminated in adopting the psychological and didactical ideas of the neo-Herbartians based on association psychology. This resulted in a quite formal and uniform outlook on the curriculum, in which the three stages of learning need to be exactly passed through, and direct experience was replaced by carefully restructured and re-presented curriculum contents. It was this formal and methodical type of teaching/learning process that, around 1900, became dominant at the same time that it was criticized by the proponents of progressive education. However, as noted before, the influence of the latter was initially limited to isolated schools, and the majority of schools continued in the old way.

In the beginning of the 20th century, thinking about education obtained a stronghold in the universities. This was not a direct continuation of the work of school inspectors and leaders noted earlier; rather, their work was largely disregarded. Instead, it took the form of normative pedagogy—a form of philosophy that concentrated on developing aims for education from a strictly normative (mostly Protestant Christian) perspective. Its proponents—like Gunning, Waterink, Casimir, Perquin, and Hoogveld, who had a background in theology or philosophy—saw schools above all as a specialized extension of family education, where character education in obedience to God's laws was the ultimate goal. Thus, their actual work was in creating an apology for the religion-based divisions in the school system, not primarily making a contribution to greater effectiveness or more relevant content of the curriculum, as was the tendency in Northern American curriculum thinking in the same period. Consequently, their influence on the curriculum was limited, and, in this period, the actual curriculum in the schools was still mainly inspired by neo-Herbartian psychology.

THE HEYDAY OF IDEALISM

The focus of curriculum theory changed in 1940 or so partly because of the pressure for objectivity exerted on the newly founded academic discipline, helped later by a growing secularization in society. Thus, from 1940 to 1970, curriculum theory in the universities was dominated by a Dutch adaptation of the religiously more neutral, neo-humanist, and idealist German philosophy of the *Geisteswissenschaftliche Pädagogik*—a term chosen to denote that its methods were inspired by those of the humanities rather than by natural science. It was based in part on the philosophical ideas of Hegel, and thus shares some of its sources with the theories of Dewey and of Vygotsky (although at the time Dewey was viewed negatively in the Netherlands, and Vygotsky was virtually unknown outside the Soviet Union). Its main category is the concept of *Bildung,* which is most aptly described as a transformation (as opposed to transmission) model of learning (Jackson, 1986). Learning, to this theory, is not a purely cognitive process. Rather, by being submerged (via the curriculum contents) in the wealth of culture (seen by Hegel as the manifestation of the unfolding Geist of humanity), the pupil's whole personality is transformed and civilized. Curriculum subjects were supposed to have a particular motivating and civilizing power (*Bildungsgehalt*); a great deal of the efforts of this paradigm's curriculum theory (Didaktik, originally as opposed to Methodik, the theory of handling classroom situations, although Klafki later abolished this distinction; confusingly, what Klafki called *Methodik* is often called *didaktiek* in Dutch) was directed at finding the best possible ways of identifying, selecting, and re-presenting elements of the academic disciplines (with an emphasis on the humanities) that have a strong *Bildungsgehalt* (cf. Westbury, Hopmann, & Riquarts, 2000).

Langeveld's work resonated with some of the other education professors, especially in the Catholic pillar (Perquin), who went from a normative view to a more humanist and ecumenical view, in which responsibility, conscience, and inner resilience were seen as more important goals of education than willingness to observe traditional values or acquiring knowledge and skills. This may have created a breeding ground for the later popularity of self-regulated learning, to which we return shortly.

The direct practical impact of this work on education, however, was rather small due partly to its high level of abstraction, partly to the strong influence that the transmission-oriented theories of the neo-Herbartians still had. Thinking in terms of transformation did not fit well into the ways of thinking about education that had become common sense.

In the same period, the more practice-oriented work of the progressive education movement (known here under its German-oriented name of *Reformpedagogiek*) did have a lot of impact. No wonder, then, that the most important educational theorist of the time, Langeveld, tried to integrate the child-centered approach of these educators with the more content-centered approach of the *Bildung* theory. This approach led him to conceive of the school as the child's way (curriculum) through educational experiences, as expressed in the title of one of his works originally written in German: "*Die Schule als Weg des Kindes*" (*The School as the Way of the Child*, 1960).

Langeveld's work became well known because it was obligatory material in teacher education until well into the 1980s. However, it failed to change the curriculum; its impact was largely limited to creating an awareness of the need to pay attention to the personality development of children. Quite contrary to Langeveld's intentions, however, in common educational thinking this has been translated into the idea of a dual task of the school: Both an instructional and a developmental (pedagogical) task needs to be fulfilled, with possible conflicts between the two normally solved in favor of the instructional task. One reason for this unintended interpretation was the influence of the empirically oriented new curriculum theory, discussed later, in which questions of norms and personality are viewed as bordering on the unscientific; another may be that Langeveld had little to offer in terms of the selection of curriculum content or the management of teaching–learning situations. For him, as for a number of his contemporaries like Stellwag and for later defenders of this position like Lea Dasberg, the supposedly universal qualities of culture as represented in the material of curriculum subjects remain the source of transformation to be effected in the pupils. For instance, Dasberg (1996) related a number of curriculum subjects directly to five essences of being human (collective memory, morality, language, critical power, and creativity), so that these subjects should never be removed from the curriculum, whereas other subjects, related more to the current needs of society, are seen as less important and more subject to change. To many, such a position seems to lead to a singularly detached curriculum that has difficulties meeting the concrete needs of contemporary society.

A remedy for this was proposed in 1969 by Jacob Bijl, a student and colleague of Langeveld. He suggested to found the curriculum in an analysis of life tasks, such as being a member of a religious community, family, society, and profession. This was a clear break with the idea of a curriculum based on academic subjects. Superficially, his proposal may look like that of the American educationist Bobbitt (1918), but where Bobbitt's intention was to analyze the exact cognitive qualities necessary to fulfil exact tasks, Bijl was thinking in terms of the personality transformations necessary to be a member of such communities.

THE TURN TOWARD AN EMPIRICAL AND CONSTRUCTIVE VIEW

Although elements of his concept were adopted in some social studies curriculum projects, Bijl's proposal had little impact. For by this time, the tide had turned. After World War II, the power of education to produce civilized personalities became questionable. In Germany, where educationists had to find a way of living with their own past, critical pedagogy was developed in the 1960s and 1970s as a variant of *Bildung* theory, which is more aware of its societal position (Miedema & Wardekker, 1999). In the Netherlands, however, the impact of this theory was limited. Rather, a beginning cultural hegemony of the United States had already led to the discovery and adoption of American curriculum theory, which was based on an approach adapted from the natural sciences. To some extent, it had a precursor in the person of Philip A. Kohnstamm, a natural scientist by training, but also a theologian, banker, politician, and educationist, who had considerable influence in the 1930s. Although in his theoretical outlook he was a representative of the first wave of theology-inspired philosophers, due to his training as a scientist he had a strong interest in promoting the use of empirical research to improve educational practice.

The new curriculum theory was just about everything *Bildung* theory was not: It was empirical, down to earth, transmission oriented, more sensitive to the needs of contemporary society, and maybe most important, closer to common sense about education, which was still dominated by the empiricist view inherited from the 19th century, or maybe we should say that this empiricism had finally found an academic legitimation. Moreover, it concentrated on the curriculum as a planning document and its construction, not on education as a whole. In one important respect, however, it resembled the old theory: Its idea of curriculum structure was also predominantly based on academic subjects. However, even here there are two important differences. Formerly, the subjects were seen as capable of inducing personality formation by means of their *Bildungsgehalt*. Now the subjects were valued because of the specific knowledge and skills they contain, which must be transmitted to the pupils. Also, whereas in the old paradigm the emphasis was on the legitimization of curriculum content, this was now seen as an area for politics rather than human science, and researchers concentrated on teaching and learning theories—on the *how* rather than on the *what*.

This changing outlook on the proper subject of academic curriculum theory is demonstrated by the CURVO project, carried out by Langeveld's successors in Utrecht university (De Kok-Damave, 1980). The aim of this project was to devise an empirically founded procedure for the development of curriculum documents. Inspired by American curriculum theorists like Tyler, Schwab, and Walker, the CURVO group held the view that curricula cannot be prescribed (as to concepts, aims, content, and criteria) by scientists. In their view curriculum development was a matter of deliberation and choice in a group in which teachers, curriculum specialists, experts in learning and instruction, and evaluation experts work together. This line of curriculum thinking, development, and research is still vivid in the Netherlands and became interwoven with computer-supported approaches for designing educational programs. It is typical not only of scientific caution in making value-laden decisions, but also of the penchant for compromise in a situation where no official body has final authority over the curriculum.

For a while, attempts were made (e.g., by Langeveld's pupil Van Gelder) to integrate the old and new points of view, but these attempts were doomed to fail, on the one hand, because of the totally different views of the task, scope, and methods of scientific work related to education, and, on the other hand, because of the sheer number of researchers working within the new empirical paradigm. Whereas the old paradigm had been the nearly exclusive domain of educationists, the new one was introduced by, and attracted mainly, research-oriented psychologists (like De Groot and Meuwese) concentrating on learning theory, and sociologists (e.g., Van Heek, Vervoort, Jungbluth) whose main topic was inequality of access and results. De Groot, basing himself on earlier work of test psychologist Luning Prak, intended to create a science in which testing and assessment, rather than the subjective judgments of teachers, would provide objective grounds for social justice. In the universities, this led to the establishment of a new interdisciplinary field of educational studies, in which the position of those educationists who tried to maintain a more philosophical and anthropological point of view quickly became marginalized, and the emphasis was on the instrumental side of education.

It was mainly from this position that in the 1970s, under a social democrat government intent on eradicating class differences in education, a number of large curriculum projects were launched. The common goal of these projects was to create a curriculum that would raise the achievements of children from low socioeconomic status (SES) to the level of other children. Most of these projects did show some effects in the expected direction. However, the retention of the results of learning over a long time was disappointing. In the most prestigious one, based on rather strict prescriptions for teachers, no long-term effects could be found (Slavenburg, 1989). Such large-scale projects came to be considered too big a risk, both financially and in terms of their results, and thus were discontinued—a development that also tied in with a diminishing political will to regulate such things from above and the ascendance of the idea that schools should be made accountable for their results.

The mainstream of research and theory in the Netherlands since that time has followed international developments, and at this moment it is not very different from that in the United States, with an emphasis on cognitivist-constructivist models of learning and teaching. Curriculum theory and research in the mainstream may be said to be internationalized. In an important product of this work, the *Handboek Curriculum* by Nijhof et al. (1993), curriculum theory is explicitly said to be based on the American example. This form of internationalization is also evidenced by the fact that universities now require educational researchers to publish in international (English language) journals rather than in Dutch ones, to the detriment of their relevance to the teaching profession. Another sign of this internationalization may be found in the recent political decision, mentioned earlier, to base the pedagogical structure of the last years of secondary education on the model of self-regulated learning, which by itself is certainly not a Dutch invention.

An interesting aspect of this last development is that, in the concept of self-regulated learning, although it may be seen to result from the development of the cognitive tradition in psychology, a theme returns that was central in the first period: that of the development of personality. It is certainly no accident that the theme of personality or personal identity is now rather popular in educational theories. The condition of late modernity implies that individuals need to make many more life choices than before, and making and entertaining such commitments has become a major life task. This points to the necessity and problems of personality formation. However, although in the *Bildung* paradigm this was seen as primarily a moral development made possible by the civilizing influence of culture (as represented by the subject matter), in the cognitivist paradigm it reduces to the more technical version of self-monitoring of motivation and emotions in the service of the ongoing acquisition of knowledge and skills (cf. Prawat, 1998). The moral side of personality development has here become a separate issue—an issue that is being much discussed at the moment following an initiative of the Minister of Education to pay more attention to the task of the schools in moral development.

A further point of interest is that here we indeed seem to have a situation in which theoretical developments in educational psychology that depart significantly from the traditional views on teaching and learning have been implemented. However, given the leeway schools have in the actual implementation, and the lack of proper preparation of teachers for their new tasks, it remains to be seen how much of these theories will actually be realized. Also, it is an open question why self-regulated learning was introduced; it may well be that the most alluring factor (for bureaucrats) was the promise of higher effectivity at equal or lower costs. Generalizing somewhat, this leads us to a remark on the position of educational researchers.

The freedom of education we spoke about earlier has consequences for the position of curriculum theorists, researchers, and developers. In most cases, they do not feel they are working either for or against the state. Rather, they are working in the space opened up by the principle of relative noninterference, helping to create better conditions for the schools to fulfill their mission. (It should be noted here, however, that teacher education takes place in separate institutions, mostly outside the universities; researchers do not have a teacher education task.) This was especially true in the 1970s, when the state was (ostensibly) engaging in a proactive policy for creating equal educational opportunities for all. Much of educational research in the Netherlands is state funded, but that does not imply that it has to be in line with current government policies even though it is frequently perceived to be so by practitioners. However, the mainstream models of educational theory and research, with their emphasis on exactness and predictability, on outcomes rather than on processes, lend themselves more easily to bureaucratic use and control than other models of teaching and learning. Hence, it can be said that, because this model became dominant, researchers work if not for or against specific political or departmental policies then often in the service of the educational bureaucracy. This may be one more form the Dutch tendency toward compromise takes.

We end this section by noting that a reconceptualization of curriculum thinking, as advocated in the United States by Pinar, has not found many adherents in the Netherlands probably because it is perceived in a way as too reminiscent of the outmoded paradigm of *Bildungstheorie*. However, there are areas of overlap with the social constructivist paradigm, a way of thinking that does have proponents, as becomes clear in the next sections.

CURRICULUM AND CONTENT: THE CASE OF MATHEMATICS

To do justice to the whole picture of curriculum theory and practice in the Netherlands, the role of subject matter and subject matter specialists needs to be mentioned (Freudenthal, 1991; Gravemeijer, 1994; Van der Sanden, Terwel, & Vosniadou, 2000). In various university departments (mathematics, languages, history, etc.) in the Netherlands, subject matter specialists play an important role in theorizing and developing curricula. These groups often have direct working relationships with teachers, teacher educators, and curriculum developers. As a consequence, their curriculum work is conten: oriented and practical. There is often some tension between these groups and the general curriculum theorists in the departments of education. However, some groups maintain strong relationships with both the practice of teaching and the theory of curriculum, learning, and instruction. Curriculum thinking and development in mathematics in the Netherlands is a successful example.

In the recent history of curriculum concepts in mathematics, as in most other disciplinary subjects, three long waves may generally be discerned as answers to the traditional approach: the structure of the curriculum approach, mathematics in real-life contexts, and a constructivist approach in mathematics education. In the 1960s, Dutch teachers of mathematics were aware of the failures of traditional mathematics education, with its emphasis on the transmission of knowledge and the process of explanation by the teacher, as well as its accent on basics: algebraic equations, calculations, and drills (cf. De Miranda, 1966). At that time, a new curriculum movement, called *New Math*, swept across Western countries. This movement may be considered an example of the structure of the discipline approach. In the context of the New Math movement, however, the structure of the discipline approach never became popular in the Netherlands.

Instead, the traditional approach of the 1950s gradually changed into a curriculum wave that can be characterized as *mathematics in real-life contexts,* which was at that time popularized under the banner *mathematics for all and everyone,* of which Hans Freudenthal was the principal proponent in the Netherlands. Freudenthal defended his concepts of *mathematics as a human activity, mathematics in real-life contexts,* and *realistic mathematics education* against advocates of the structure of the discipline approach and was strongly opposed to the New Math movement, with its introduction of sets, relations, and logic—a position similar to that of Wagenschein in Germany. For Freudenthal, New Math was "mathematics as a system," divorced from its context. He highly valued the process of mathematization, rather than the results of the process. He and his coworkers consequently embraced the idea of mathematics in real-life contexts (Terwel, 1990; Terwel, Herfs, Mertens, & Perrenet, 1994). These ideas were later brought together under the new acronym RME (Realistic Mathematics Education).

More and more, RME has become related to constructivism. Consequently, in the 1980s a new wave in the innovation of the Dutch mathematics curriculum emerged: mathematics education from a constructivist perspective. This is a remarkable development because Freudenthal was strongly opposed to constructivism (and any other form of educational ism) and considered it an empty philosophy and poor developmental psychology (Freudenthal, 1991). The main problem for him was the lack of clarity or the lack of consensus on what constructivism is. He reacted to this lack of clarity by introducing his own terms: *(re-)construction, (re-)creation,* and *(re-)invention.* However, Freudenthal was inspired by traditional European conceptions of education and learning as expressed by Decroly, Wagenschein, Langeveld, Selz, Kohnstamm, Vygotsky, and Piaget.

Phenomenology, cognitivism, and progressive education were important sources for Freudenthal's conception of the mathematics curriculum. The same holds true for his concept of *guided reinvention.* Although he rarely referred to these sources explicitly, Freudenthal may be considered, in a sense, a constructivist *avant la lettre.* This connection with European curriculum traditions is the main reason that it was comparatively easy for Freudenthal's coworkers and, more in general, Dutch mathematics educators to relate to the constructivist movement. Gravemeijer (1994), one of the current leading researchers in the Freudenthal Institute, expressed the relation between realistic mathematics education and constructivism as follows: "The central principle of constructivism is that each person constructs his or her own knowledge, and that direct transfer of knowledge is not possible. This idea of independent construction of knowledge supports the central realistic principle" (p. 195; see also Gravemeijer & Terwel, 2000). Sometimes there is opposition to the basic idea that students should proceed from the real world to the mathematical world from inside mathematics and the mathematics education communities.

The main criticism of the RME approach is that it is often impossible to proceed from everyday life situations to mathematics. Reinvention, in this view, is a waste of time (Keune, 1998; Verstappen, 1994). The group around Gravemeijer, however, has gone more and more in the direction of social constructivism, in which every theory about the world is considered one of many possible theories that equally well describe a certain state of the world. The choice among such theories is considered to be a social choice made for reasons of efficiency in actions or, in some instances, for reasons of power. This way of thinking, for which in mathematics education Cobb and his colleagues (Cobb & Bowers, 1999) may be considered the leaders, implies that students should be made aware that there are multiple solutions for a given problem, that they are able to think of some solution themselves, and only then be shown why and in what cases the canonical solution of mathematics might be the best one. There is a clear connection here to the sociocultural approach to curriculum, which is considered in the next section.

At the level of the formal curriculum, innovation in mathematics education may be said to have been successful. There are new examination programs and curriculums for the full range of the general streams in secondary education in the Netherlands. The principles of RME have to some extent been integrated into all published mathematics methods. With regard to the operational curriculum, mathematics education is at a transitional stage. Many of those involved have noticed a lack of systematic evaluation and support for the way teachers have translated innovation into concrete actions. It is still unknown how lessons are being modeled according to the new ideas. Therefore, it remains partly an open question whether Stoller's (1978) description and prediction will come true when he said that Wagenschein and Freudenthal are laughed at because of their idealism and because they do not fit in with any bureaucratic model and forgotten when it comes to real classroom practices.   •

THE RECEPTION OF VYGOTSKY'S LEGACY

As may have become clear from the mathematics example in the last paragraph, the field of curriculum studies in the Netherlands is currently not a unity. Next to the neo-humanist and empirical-scientific strands of theory, a third form has developed—more humanist in its principles than the new empiricist paradigm, but more oriented toward research and the development of educational practice than the old *Geisteswissenschaftliche* way of thinking, deriving its basic ideas from Vygotsky and (lately) Dewey. In a sense, the work of the previously-mentioned Kohnstamm may have also provided some leads for this movement. For although he was in favor of empirical research, he opposed various elements of the empirical educational psychology of his day, especially the idea that intelligence was one capacity of which the magnitude was fixed genetically. Taking the German *Denkpsychologie* as a point of departure, he showed that IQ could be boosted by adequate education. This led him to promote forms of education in which understanding, not memorizing, was central. Understanding could be reached by giving students the opportunity to relate curriculum content to a context of practices in daily life. This principle was expressed in a rather influential method for reading in which understanding of the text was central. Training what would now be called problem-solving strategies in reading was essential to his method. But for Kohnstamm, understanding was not the ultimate aim: He saw all education as ultimately contributing to the personal development of all students, as opposed to the mere intellectualism, which he discerned in the stance of other educationalists of his time.

Elements of Kohnstamm's thinking are visible in the work of several later educationists; they prepared the ground for an arrival of Vygotskian theory that was rather earlier than in most other countries outside the Soviet Union. Vygotsky's work was made known in the 1960s through the efforts of Van Parreren (who studied with Kohnstamm) and Carpay, who translated and adapted parts of his work and especially that of his follower Galperin for use in teacher education. Their initial emphasis was on the conditions for transfer (cf. Van Oers, 2000). This work was widely used in the education of primary school teachers and thus formed the beginning of a number of developments One of these can be discerned in primary education, where developmental teaching (also known, if related to the first stage of primary education, as basic development) along Vygotskian lines is now a well-known approach that about 200 schools for primary education use, at least for the earlier years, and that is being constantly developed by the school consultancy center APS. An emphasis in this work is on bridging the gap between playing and learning (cf. Van Oers, 1999). A second development is taking place in educational sciences, where theory development and research have realized a connection to the international community of sociocultural research in education and where now also the similarities between this theory and the ideas of Dewey are being explored. However, the number of adherents to this paradigm remains small, and cognitive constructivism remains the dominant paradigm into which some of Vygotsky's ideas become integrated.

Whereas Van Parreren's interpretation stayed close to the cognitivist paradigm, with a strong emphasis on problem-solving strategies, recent developments have gone in the direction of a social-constructivist theory in which many of the themes of *Bildung* theory are revived but also transformed. This is maybe to be expected given the common roots of both paradigms in late 19th-century European philosophy. Thus, the contribution of education in personality development (cf. Wardekker, 1998) is a research theme as well as the differences and similarities between the home and the school as contexts for learning, and the importance of engaging the pupils' motivation. An important difference, however, is that motivation is no longer sought in a mysterious force, *Bildungsgehalt*, that is in the subject matter. Instead, motivation is related to the pupils being able to connect subject matter to their own participation in societal practices (cf. Van Oers, 2000). In this connection, it is interesting to note that Bijl's idea of an analysis of life tasks as the foundation for the curriculum was echoed recently in a proposal to connect the curriculum to life areas instead of academic subjects (Meijers & Wijers, 1997). Also, elements of this way of thinking can be found in recent work in the mathematics curriculum by the Freudenthal Institute, as noted before. This paradigm, among other things, gives an impetus to re-opening the discussion on curriculum content and its function, like the reconceptualization did for the curriculum field in the United States.

INTERNATIONALIZATION OF THE CURRICULUM?

We have noted that curriculum theory and research in the Netherlands have always been internationally oriented, although the international research communities it was connected to have differed according to the paradigm that was selected. An interesting question, which we cannot go into here, would be why it is that, in the last century, French thought on curriculum issues has had virtually no impact in the Netherlands, although some important documents were translated.

In a sense, the same international orientation can be found in the curriculum, at least in its explicit part. Foreign languages have always been seen as important, for instance. Still, present conditions require a more intrinsic form of questioning the national identity that is also undoubtedly part of the curriculum background.

These conditions, part of the changes occurring in late modernity, can be summarized as constituting processes of simultaneous globalization (resulting in forms of greater unity) and localization (resulting in diversity and plurality). These processes most visibly express themselves in, on the one hand, the tendency toward a unified Europe and the freer movement of persons across it, on the other hand, in the confrontation of cultures and values resulting from this tendency and from the influx of immigrants. Another such process is the secularization of society, which in the Netherlands, with a social organization based on religious differences, has especially far-reaching consequences.

At the moment, those aspects of these processes that are seen as threatening to the social order receive the most attention. A fear of degeneration of values has inspired the government to ask schools to give more attention to their task in moral education (Wardekker, 2001). The coming of children from other cultural communities is seen as a problem rather than an opportunity. Discussion concentrates on the problem that most of them do not know the Dutch language, which is then countered by the demand that schools become more effective in teaching them. The number of those who see the educational value of plurality of views and values is still small, and multiculturality in this sense is not much of an issue in educational thinking. The concept of a *European identity*, although promoted by the European organizations, does not seem to be a significant part of the curriculum yet either.

This situation has a broader background. Questions of internationality and multiculturality, along with all other questions of curriculum content, are viewed by the dominant empiricist paradigm as belonging in the realm of politics, not of academic inquiry. Academic educationists concentrate on issues of effectivity and learning theory mostly. However, there is no national debate (or anything like it) on the contents of curriculum either. This seems one area in which a revival of continental European thinking, either in the form of *Bildungstheorie* or the newer and more promising approach of sociocultural theory, could be beneficial. If that happens, the pendulum might swing back from an emphasis on document construction to understanding the curriculum as a contribution to the pupils' life course while not abandoning, of course, the attention to teaching practice and the problem of inequality in education, which we thank to the empirical paradigm.

ACKNOWLEDGMENT

The authors wish to thank Ed Wendrich, Arjan Dieleman, and Siebren Miedema for their helpful comments.

REFERENCES

Bijl, J. (1969). *Over leerplanonderzoek* [About curriculum research]. Groningen, The Netherlands: Wolters Noordhoff.

Bobbitt, F. (1918). The curriculum. Cambridge, MA: Riverside Press.

Cobb, P., & Bowers, J. (1999). Cognitive and situated learning perspectives in theory and practice. *Educational Researcher, 28*(2), 4–15.

Dasberg, L. (1996). *Menswording tussen mode, management en moraal* [Educating for humanity between fashion, management and morality]. Amersfoort, The Netherlands: CPS.

De Kok-Damave, M. (Ed.). (1980). *De Curvo-strategie: Handboek voor leergangontwikkeling* [The Curvo strategy, handbook for curiculum development]. Den Haag, The Netherlands: Staatsuitgeverij.

De Miranda, J. (1966). Vragen naar de identiteit van de didactiek [Questions regarding the identity of didactics]. *Vernieuwing van Opvoeding en Onderwijs, 25,* 122–137, 162–173.

Freudenthal, H. (1991). *Revisiting mathematics education: China lectures.* Dordrecht, The Netherlands: Kluwer.

Gravemeijer, K., & Terwel, J. (2000). Hans Freudenthal, a mathematician on didactics and curriculum theory. *Journal of Curriculum Studies, 32*(6), 777–796.

Gravemeijer, K. P. E. (1994). *Developing Realistic Mathematics Education.* Doctoral dissertation. Utrecht, The Netherlands: Utrecht University, CdBèta Press.

Inspectie van het Onderwijs. (1999). *Werk aan de basis. Evaluatie van de basisvorming na vijf jaar.* Algemeen rapport [Work at the basis. Evaluation of the common curriculum after five years. General report]. Den Haag, The Netherlands: SDU.

Jackson, P. (1986). *The practice of teaching.* New York: Teachers College Press.

Keune, F. (1998). *Naar de knoppen* [Inaugural lecture]. Nijmegen, The Netherlands: Catholic University.

Langeveld, M. J. (1960). *Die schule als weg des kindes. Versuch einer anthropologie der schule.* Braunschweig, Germany: Westermann.

Lenders, J. (1988). *De burger en de volksschool. Culturele en mentale achtergronden van een onderwijshervorming.* Nijmegen, The Netherlands: SUN.

Lenders, J. (1992). Liberalisme en positivisme: de ontwikkeling van een uniform schoolmodel in Nederland 1850–1900 [Liberalism and positivism, the development of a uniform teaching method in the Netherlands 1850–1900]. *Comenius, 12,* 265–284.

Meijers, F., & Wijers, G. (1997). *Een zaak van betekenis. Loopbaandienstverlening in een nieuw perspectief* [A meaningful matter: career guidance in a new perspective]. Leeuwarden, The Netherlands: LDC.

Miedema, S., & Wardekker, W. (1999). Emergent identity versus consistent identity: Possibilities for a postmodern repoliticization of critical pedagogy. In T. S. Popkewitz & L. Fendler (Eds.), *Critical theories in education. Changing terrains of knowledge and politics* (pp. 67–83). New York: Routledge.

Nauta, L. W. (2000). *Onbehagen in de filosofie* [The embarrassment of philosophy]. Amsterdam: Van Gennep.

Nijhof, W. J., Franssen, H. A. M., Hoeben, W. T. J. G., & Wolbert, R. G. M. (Eds.). (1993). *Handboek curriculum. Modellen, theorieën, technologieën* [Handbook curriculum: Models, theories, technologies]. Amsterdam: Swets & Zeitlinger.

Prawat, R. S. (1998). Current self-regulation views of learning and motivation viewed through a Deweyan lens: The problems with dualism. *American Educational Research Journal, 35,* 199–224.

Roelofs, E., & Terwel, J. (1999). Constructivism and authentic pedagogy: State of the art and recent developments in the Dutch national curriculum in secondary education. *Journal of Curriculum Studies, 31*(2), 201–227.

Slavenburg, J. H. (Ed.). (1989). *Het project onderwijs en sociaal milieu: een eindbalans* [The education and social class project: A final balance]. Rotterdam, The Netherlands: Rotterdamse School Adviesdienst.

Stoller, D. (1978). Anspruch und Wirklichkeit der Reform des Mathematikunterrichts. *Neue Sammlung, 6,* 540–560.

Sturm, J., Groenendijk, L., Kruithof, B., & Rens, J. (1998). Educational pluralism—a historical study of so-called "pillarization" in the Netherlands, including a comparison with some developments in South African education. *Comparative Education, 34*(3), 281–297.

Terwel, J. (1990). Real maths in cooperative groups. In N. Davidson (Ed.), *Cooperative learning in mathematics* (pp. 228–264). Menlo Park, CA: Addison-Wesley.

Terwel, J., Herfs, P. G. P., Mertens, E. H. M., & Perrenet, J. C. (1994). Cooperative learning and adaptive instruction in a mathematics curriculum. *Journal of Curriculum Studies, 26*(2), 217–233.

Van den Bergh, H., Peters-Sips, M., & Zwarts, M. (1999). Deelstudies in het kader van de evaluatie van de basisvorming [Studies for the evaluation of the common curriculum]. *Pedagogische Studiën, 76* (4), 224–236.

Van der Sanden, J. M. M., Terwel, J., & Vosniadou, S. (2000). New learning in science and technology. In P. R. J. Simons, J. L. van der Linden, & T. M. Duffy (Eds.), *New learning: Three ways to learn in a new balance* (pp. 119–140). Dordrecht, The Netherlands: Kluwer Academic.

Van der Werf, G., Lubbers, M., & Kuyper, H. (1999). Onderwijsopbrengsten en onderwijskansen voor en na de invoering van de basisvorming [Educational outcomes before and after the introduction of the common curriculum]. *Pedagogische Studiën, 76*(4), 273–287.

Van Oers, B. (1999). Education for the improvement of cultural participation. In G. Brougère & S. Rayna (Eds.), *Culture, childhood, and preschool education* (pp. 317–338). Paris: UNESCO.

Van Oers, B. (2000, July 16–20). *Continuous recontextualization and the generalization of knowledge and skills.* Paper presented at the third Conference for Sociocultural Research, Campinas, Brazil.

Verstappen, P. (1994). Het dogma: Van de leefwereld naar de wiskundewereld [The dogma: From the daily life world to the world of mathematics]. *Tijdschrift voor Didactiek der Bètawetenschappen, 12*(2), 104–129.

Wardekker, W. (1998). Scientific concepts and reflection. *Mind, Culture, and Activity, 5,* 143–153.

Wardekker, W. (2001). Schools and moral education: Conformism or autonomy? *Journal of Philosophy of Education, 35*(1), 101–114.

Westbury, I., Hopmann, S., & Riquarts, K. (Eds.). (2000). *Teaching as a reflective practice. The German Didaktik tradition.* Mahwah, NJ: Lawrence Erlbaum Associates.

CHAPTER 28

Contemporary Curriculum Research in New Zealand

Peter Roberts
University of Auckland, New Zealand

In curriculum studies, as in many other domains of human activity, one of the few constants is change. As a field of academic inquiry, curriculum studies never stands still. Important new theoretical currents emerge each decade, and in any given year fresh insights within established traditions can be identified. In the last three decades of the 20th century, there were significant developments in the study of curricula from Marxist, feminist, existentialist, hermeneutical, phenomenological, spiritual, biographical, and poststructuralist perspectives (Pinar et al., 1995). Curriculum studies lends itself, perhaps more readily than any other body of work within the broader field of education, to a multiplicity of theoretical approaches. Curriculum scholars have responded, often in highly original ways, to new scholarly trends in other disciplines. Thus, to take just one example, the postmodern turn in social theory has found creative expression in the diverse and sometimes conflicting voices of curriculum theorists such as William Doll, Henry Giroux, Peter McLaren, Joe Kincheloe, Shirley Steinberg, Patti Lather, and Bill Green, among others. Of course, these scholars have not merely applied the ideas of others; they have also played an important role in making the postmodern turn what it is. Indeed, a thorough examination of postmodern curriculum scholarship is likely to yield rich results for those seeking to understand what a postmodern perspective might have to offer beyond the curriculum domain. The same might be said of other theoretical approaches in curriculum studies: Many researchers in this area have been innovative and forward looking in responding to, and promoting, change. There is, as Paulo Freire might have said, a healthy level of scholarly restlessness in the field: Intellectual curiosity, a commitment to debate and rigorous investigation, and a determination not to remain too certain of one's certainties are qualities in abundant supply within the international curriculum studies community.

There is another sense in which the theme of change is important. Curriculum inquiry is, in part, the study of curriculum policies and practices. As such, it involves the critique of policy documents, evaluation of curriculum programs in schools and other institutions, appraisal and construction of new models for teaching different subjects, and analysis of structures and systems for curriculum implementation at local, regional, and national levels. Work of this kind often necessitates an examination of wider political changes. Calls for a return to the basics, then, might be understood as one dimension of a conservative restoration, just as demands for sex education or information technology programs in schools might reflect changing ideas and social practices among younger people. Politicians frequently remind us that we live in an ever-changing world. This may have become a cliché, but it is, for curriculum theorists, a statement of considerable significance. In attempting to respond to a variety of national and international pressures, governments in many Western countries have instituted seemingly endless reviews and reforms within the educational sector, often with a direct or indirect bearing on the curriculum. In such a climate, there has been no shortage of material for scholarly interrogation. In fact, this process of continuous policy change has become an object for critical analysis by curriculum theorists. Given a constantly shifting set of economic and social circumstances, those working in the field of curriculum studies have had to periodically and self-consciously reinvent themselves. While not neglecting traditional questions pertaining to aims, development, and organization, curriculum theorists have increasingly turned to matters of policy and politics—recognizing, if nothing else, the paramount importance of contextualizing their work. Curriculum researchers have expended considerable intellectual energy contemplating their own role as theorists and/or practitioners. The question of whether scholars should be concerned with merely analyzing curriculum changes or actively involved in making (or resisting) them has been a central concern.

New Zealand provides an interesting case study when examined in the light of these preliminary comments. A small country with fewer than 4 million inhabitants, New Zealand has nonetheless produced some first-class research on issues in curriculum policy. New Zealand has also been the object of intense scrutiny from other nations for its dramatic economic and social experiment (Kelsey, 1995). From 1984 to 1999, New Zealanders were subject to a series of sweeping neo-liberal policy reforms. In this chapter, I argue that this restructuring process has played a dominant role in shaping the development of an agenda for curriculum research in New Zealand, particularly over the past decade. The theme of change has become highly significant for scholars interested in curriculum issues in this period. Structural modifications, implemented on a scale and at a pace hitherto unseen in this country, have impacted on almost all areas of New Zealand life, including education. A number of important new curriculum documents have been released by the Ministry of Education, and major changes in the administration of schooling have come into being. There has been a reorganization of the entire qualifications system, and tertiary education has been given a more thorough shakeup (Butterworth & Tarling, 1994) than ever before in its New Zealand history. These massive changes—all underpinned (sometimes in rather different ways and to different degrees) by the ideology of neo-liberalism and a relentless drive to marketize education—have exerted considerable influence over curriculum discourses in recent years. Some commentators have supported the general direction of the reforms; many others have been strongly critical of them. No one concerned with curriculum issues, however, has been able to avoid them.

This chapter does not attempt to provide either a history of curriculum theorizing in New Zealand or a comprehensive review of the literature. It would be difficult to do justice to either of these tasks in the space available. Instead, I limit my focus to some of the key features of contemporary research by New Zealanders on curriculum issues and consider prospects for further investigation. Concentrating on work completed over the past decade, I try to show how debates over curriculum reform have been related to wider economic, social, and educational changes. I comment on the current status of curriculum studies as a field of academic inquiry in New Zealand, and I identify two areas for further development: one devoted to curriculum issues in higher education, the other based on an expansion of curriculum research in the literacy studies domain.

NEO-LIBERALISM, EDUCATIONAL REFORM, AND CURRICULUM RESEARCH

If the development of the contemporary curriculum field in New Zealand is to be understood, attention must be paid to the social changes that have both profoundly affected the lives of educational researchers and provided a focus for their thinking, theorizing, and teaching. The dominant theme for many critical researchers in recent years has been the marketization of education and the curriculum. This section sketches some of the key features of the marketization process in New Zealand and considers its influence on curriculum scholarship.

The tentacles of the market have spread to almost every sector of society in countries such as New Zealand, Australia, Canada, Britain, and the United States. The New Zealand neo-liberal experiment, sometimes referred to as the New Right revolution, has been particularly dramatic. The broad features of the economic and social reform process in this country are well known internationally, and indeed have sometimes been lauded by politicians as an example for other countries to follow. Over a period of 15 years, successive Labor (1984–1990) and National (1990–1999) governments pursued an aggressive agenda of corporatization, marketization, and privatization. Their policies were given strong support by influential members of the big business community in New Zealand, and key government agencies such as the Treasury and the State Services Commission played pivotal roles in making the New Right vision a reality. In promoting the new order, the political, bureaucratic, and corporate figures behind these changes have appealed to a neo-liberal view of human beings as self-interested, perpetually choosing individuals. Older communitarian ideals, once the hallmark of New Zealand's political system, have been ridiculed or dismissed, and competition among individuals, state-owned enterprises, and public institutions has been encouraged. Policies of user pays have been implemented in health, education, and other sectors. Education has been reconfigured in this process and now exists as just one more commodity: something to be bought, sold, traded, franchised, and consumed. The model of the market has become the basis for the whole organization of contemporary social life. The ideal, for those on the New Right, is one in which different individuals strive for advantage over others in an environment of largely unfettered competition, with minimal state interference and a heavy emphasis on the bottom line in all policy and decision-making processes.

Most of the key reforms in the core public sector were initiated by Labor, including the selling off of state assets, removal of tariffs and subsidies, and adoption of corporate management practices for public institutions. Heavy bureaucratic structures were, in theory, to be trimmed and reorganized into smaller semiautonomous administrative units. Efficiency was seen as utterly compatible with equity, and was to be secured by staffing cutbacks, new systems of performance measurement, a move to fixed-term rather than permanent positions, and the contracting out of state services. When the National government came to power in 1990, the reform process was intensified, with health, education, and social welfare becoming the prime targets. Benefits for the sick and unemployed were slashed, private rental rates were imposed for state housing tenants, and hospitals became Crown Health Enterprises. Government departments remodeled themselves along corporate lines, placing greater emphasis on image creation, marketing, and profitability. Chief executives in these organizations earned enormous salaries, whereas workers suffered a considerable erosion in wages and conditions under the new Employment Contracts Act. There was a strong push, from the Prime Minister's office downward, for policy innovations conducive to enterprise, entrepreneurialism, and international competitiveness.

The key changes at the school level, signaled by the publication of *Tomorrow's Schools* in the late 1980s (Department of Education, 1988), were based on a model of decentralization in which control over educational decisions was ostensibly shifted from a central bureaucracy with a supporting regional network of Education Boards to the school communities. Each school was to have a Board of Trustees through which parents and other members of the local community would work collaboratively with teachers in decisions over staffing, charters, property management, and indirectly, some matters of curriculum and pedagogy. The reforms were intended to serve as a model of participatory democracy and community empowerment, but in practice have arguably contributed to higher stress levels and greater workloads for teachers and parents. There has been a devolution of responsibilities to teachers and Boards, but the resources necessary to meet these responsibilities have not been forthcoming, and considerable control has remained at the center. The ideology behind the reforms has, with the passage of time, become clearer. It was argued that, in the past, schools and the curriculum had suffered from "provider capture," and that a shift in decision-making power was necessary to avoid serving the narrow interests of one group (teachers). This allowed the elimination of one layer of bureaucracy (the Education Boards) and the creation of Boards of Trustees to be sold as an exercise in democratic reform while reducing costs and diminishing the role of the teacher as a professional (cf. Peters, 1995). The new system was thus promoted as both equitable and efficient. Later moves by the national administration to convert schools to bulk funding regimes pushed the market model even further. The final step in this process—the introduction of a voucher (individual entitlement) system—was mooted, but never implemented.

In the tertiary education sector, students have been portrayed as private beneficiaries from their investment in education and are now expected to cover a greater share of their tuition costs. The notion of education serving wider public goals has been systematically undermined. Neo-liberal reformists have supported full competition within and between institutions. A Board of Directors style of governance, with clear lines of authority and minimal representation on university councils by faculty members, has been favored over the collegial and democratic models of the past. New accountability mechanisms, couched in the language of "performance indicators," have been instituted. Universities, like schools, have had to do more with less over the past decade. Government funding per effective full-time student fell, in real terms, sharply in this period. Teaching loads have increased, and administrative work has escalated. Tertiary education leaders now talk of positioning their institutions in the market and devote considerable sums of money to TV and newspaper advertising. Contestability in research funding has been encouraged, and universities have frequently been told that the work they do should be more directly relevant to the demands of employers and the global economy.

The 1990s also witnessed major changes in curriculum policy. With a more explicit marketization agenda now in place, there was increasing pressure to ignore or downplay the progressive tendencies in earlier policy documents, such as the *Curriculum Review* (Department of Education, 1987). The National government shifted its focus to the development of a stronger enterprise culture in the New Zealand education system. Then Prime Minister, Jim Bolger, spoke of successful business people as heroic figures and urged young people to become more entrepreneurial and competitive. An Education for Enterprise Conference was held in 1992 to confirm the new direction. Meanwhile, the *National Curriculum of New Zealand: A Discussion Document* was released by the Ministry of Education in 1991. After submissions and revisions, this became *The New Zealand Curriculum Framework* (Ministry of Education, 1993). Couched in the language of both competitiveness and inclusiveness, the Foreword to the Framework states:

> Today, New Zealand faces many significant challenges. If we wish to progress as a nation, and to enjoy a healthy prosperity in today's and tomorrow's competitive world

economy, our education system must adapt to meet these challenges. We need a learning environment which enables all our students to attain high standards and develop appropriate personal qualities. As we move towards the twenty-first century, with all the rapid technological change which is taking place, we need a work-force which is increasingly highly skilled and adaptable, and which has an international and multicultural perspective. (O'Rourke, 1993, p. 1)

The *Framework* identifies seven *essential learning areas*: language and languages, mathematics, science, technology, social studies, the arts, and health and physical well-being. These are coupled with eight *essential skills*: communication skills, numeracy skills, information skills, problem-solving skills, self-management and competitive skills, social and cooperative skills, physical skills, and work and study skills. Consideration is also given to the place of *attitudes and values* in the school curriculum. It is claimed that the school curriculum will "reinforce the commonly held values of individual and collective responsibility which underpin New Zealand's democratic society." These values include: "honesty, reliability, respect for others, respect for the law, tolerance (rangimarie), fairness, caring or compassion (aroha), non-sexism, and non-racism" (Ministry of Education, 1993, p. 21). The document provides ' sets of achievement objectives describing what students are supposed to know and be able to do, arranged according to a progressive series of eight levels covering the 13 years of learning from Year 1 (New Entrants) to Year 13 (Form 7), and associated assessment programmes" (Philips, 2000, p. 145). The Framework was designed to establish "the principles which give direction to all teaching and learning" in New Zealand schools (O'Rourke, 1993, p. 1), and it has served as the foundation document for curriculum reform in other subject areas. Of these, three are particularly noteworthy. The English curriculum (Ministry of Education, 1994a), built on a recognition of three forms of language (oral, written, and visual), was seen by many teachers as an enlightened and innovative document, but criticized by others as an example of political correctness and a lowering of academic standards. The social studies curriculum attracted critical comment from groups on both the Right and Left, and had to be redrafted twice before the final version—a compromise between conflicting extremes—was produced (see Ministry of Education, 1994b, 1996, 1997). Finally, the curriculum document for a new subject introduced in the early 1990s by former Minister of Education Lockwood Smith—Technology (Ministry of Education, 1995)—has also been debated at length.

Much of the work conducted by academics on curriculum matters in the 1990s addressed the *Framework* (or its precursor, *The National Curriculum of New Zealand*) and the other subject-based documents that followed from it. Many authors have found it impossible to disentangle curriculum issues from broader debates over neo-liberal reforms in the economy, social policy, and education. In the last decade, books have been published on historical dimensions of the school curriculum (McCulloch, 1992b), teachers and curriculum decision making (McGee, 1997), the national curriculum in school classrooms (Barr & Gordon, 1995), the technology curriculum (Burns, 1997), and the social studies curriculum (Benson & Openshaw, 1998; Openshaw, 1992). In the same period, curriculum themes have also featured in a number of other New Zealand volumes on schools and society (Adams et al., 2000; Jones et al., 1990), the politics of education (Codd, Harker, & Nash, 1990), educational policy studies (Middleton, Codd, & Jones, 1990; Olssen & Morris Matthews, 1997), women and education (Middleton & Jones, 1992), learning and teaching (Coxon et al., 1994; McGee & Fraser, 1994), the history of education (Openshaw, 1992; Openshaw, Lee, & Lee, 1993; McKenzie, Lee, & Lee, 1993), and science education (Matthews, 1995).

Curriculum questions have been regularly addressed in the major New Zealand scholarly journals in the field of education: the *New Zealand Journal of Educational Studies,* the *New Zealand Annual Review of Education, Access: Critical Perspectives on Cultural and Policy Studies in Education, SET: Research Information for Teachers,* and *Delta: Policy and Practice in Education.* In addition to these refereed periodicals, several publications with wider readerships (e.g., the *New Zealand Education Review,* a newspaper-style weekly, covering contemporary issues in education across a range of formal and informal sectors; *New Zealand Principal,* a key vehicle for the circulation of ideas among school principals; and the *Education Development Newsletter,* a nonreferred journal consulted by many school teachers), have all included frequent commentaries on curriculum issues. To these might be added several periodicals on specific curriculum areas: *English in Aotearoa,* the *New Zealand Journal of Social Studies, Reading Forum New Zealand,* and *New Zealand Physical Educator,* among others. Finally, mention should be made of the *Education Digest,* published by the Education Forum, in which articles on curriculum issues have sometimes appeared. The curriculum has featured as a primary focus for a number of graduate student theses (examples from the University of Auckland in the 1990s include Allen, 1993; Bradley, 1998; Hannif, 1996; Mansfield, 1995; Wang, 1995), conferences and seminars (see, e.g., Capper, 1991), special issues of academic journals (O'Neill, 1996b), and funded research projects (among many other studies, compare Hall, Robertson, & Casey, 1995; Katterns, 1992; Peddie, 1994; Ramsay et al., 1990; Robertson, 1991). Philips (2000) claimed that most New Zealand schools have adopted the new curriculum "without serious reservations, partly because they are obliged to implement it." However, schools have raised concerns about "increased workload and monitoring by ERO [the Education Review Office]" (p. 145).

A number of positive features have been identified in the academic literature. The benefits of greater participation by parents, teachers, principals, and students in curriculum decision making have been noted by some commentators. Collaborative models of curriculum development have been found to work well where there has been effective leadership from principals, sufficient time for reflection, a strong emphasis on staff development programs, and inclusive rather than top–down implementation strategies (Ramsay et al., 1992). Others have argued that the new responsibilities teachers exercise in making decisions about courses and units can be advantageous, provided curriculum planning is conducted in a systematic and professional manner. A systematic framework can assist in setting parameters for learning without inhibiting the flair and individuality of the teacher. Understanding the complexities of the social settings within which curriculum decisions are made, ensuring thorough teacher preparation, and reducing outside restraints are important in allowing teachers to make the most of their professional autonomy (McGee, 1997).

Criticisms of the curriculum changes have taken a number of different forms. Some scholars have focused on shortcomings in the curriculum documents, whereas others have addressed problems relating to the wider reform process. O'Neill (1996a) drew a contrast between the input-driven curriculum changes in the past, characterized by extensive development systems, thorough trialing, and the genuine involvement of teachers, with the Treasury-driven, neo-liberal reforms instituted in the late 1980s and early 1990s. According to O'Neill, teachers have been supportive of the notion that ongoing curriculum development is necessary, but there has been "a high level of professional disquiet about curriculum content, resourcing issues and implementation strategies and procedures" (p. 6).

Several theorists have problematized the emphasis on skills and information at the expense of knowledge and understanding in the *New Zealand Curriculum Framework* and other documents. Marshall (1997) argued that the curriculum proposals of the early 1990s exhibit a lack of concern with the nature of knowledge and pedagogy. Documents such as the *Framework* ignore central questions about "what counts as knowledge, how it is defined and controlled, and whose knowledge is selected for inclusion" (p. 313). Marshall maintained that the *Framework* stresses a particular kind of "knowing how" (the acquisition of skills) over the teaching of content knowledge ("knowing what") A similar argument has been applied to curriculum initiatives employing the new information technologies, where the danger of replacing ideals such as breadth and depth in knowledge and understanding with goals such as skill in browsing have been highlighted (Roberts, 1997b). The former places a premium on knowing why and how X has come to be what it is (and in what context, and with what consequences), whereas the latter focuses on simply finding X (i.e., knowing that X is there). The same emphasis on skills can be found in other policy documents issued by the New Zealand government in the 1990s, particularly those on qualifications reform. Indeed, there was a deliberate attempt to "skill New Zealand" in this period (Education and Training Support Agency, 1993). What passes as knowledge in many of these documents could often be renamed as skills or information without any serious loss in meaning (Roberts, 1997d). Indeed, knowledge and information have often been conflated or confused (Marshall, 1995, 1996, 1997; Peters, 1995; Peters & Roberts, 1999; Roberts, 2000).

Critics have also alluded to problems with the links among content, aims, and outcomes across different subject areas and have questioned the sequencing of knowledge and skills in the *Framework.* Elley (1996), for example, argued that the division of curriculum areas into a multilevel structure cannot be supported on academic grounds (from either curriculum theory or learning theory), and suggested that New Zealand's outcome-based achievement model is unworkable.

The emphasis on economic and entrepreneurial aspirations has also attracted critical comment. Lee and Hill (1996) maintained that the reforms have been premised on a problematic view of national economic advancement, an impoverished concept of education, and a misplaced faith in predictions about the future needs of New Zealanders. Peters (1992) pointed out that the notion of enterprise promoted by politicians and officials has been unnecessarily narrow. Enterprise has been tied almost exclusively to competitive business practices and, as such, has wrongly excluded other forms of human activity (including those in the curriculum sphere) involving initiative, risk-taking, good management, team work, and the creative employment of diverse talents and skills.

Taking this a step further, Peters and Marshall (1996) identified a form of busnocratic rationality in the new curriculum discourses. One element of the position they critique is the idea that quality in the curriculum should be determined by educational consumers (particularly industry groups) rather than providers. Underpinning this idea, and arguably the entire curriculum reform process, is a problematic construct of human beings as autonomous choosers (Marshall, 1995). The individualistic assumptions on which this ontology turns have been analyzed in some detail (see e.g., Codd, 1993; Olssen, 1997). Appeals to student choice invariably ignore both the structural limits many students face in exercising choices and the ways in which choices come to be formed (Roberts, 1997e). Policy statements from the last 10 years are also littered with references to the importance of meeting the needs of consumer groups (students, employers, and parents, among others). Again, the notion of needs is typically superficial and misleading. In most cases, the needs to which curriculum documents and other policy statements refer might better be termed wants or preferences (Roberts & Peters, 1999).

A powerful political lobby group, the New Zealand Business Roundtable (NZBR), has been active in offering evaluative comments (via speeches, submissions to government commissioned reports, and occasional articles in academic publications) on many curriculum developments over recent years. In some cases, NZBR views have been conveyed indirectly, principally through a closely affiliated organization, the Education Forum (1994, 1995, 1996). Michael Irwin, a policy analyst with the Roundtable, has produced a number of careful critiques (Irwin, 1996, 1997, 1999), drawing attention to ambiguous, inconsistent, and contradictory claims in the *Framework* and other curriculum documents. Irwin (1999) argued that the reforms have been underpinned by a postmodernist view of the curriculum, a constructivist view of learning, needs-based and student-centered views of pedagogy, and a relativist view of values. He found fault with all of these approaches. Others connected with the NZBR have been more polemical in their criticisms. Roger Kerr, the Roundtable's executive director, suggested that there had been a politically correct dumbing down of curricula, supported by strong anti-Western and antibusiness sentiments. He portrayed the English curriculum as "vague and soporific" and the second draft of the Social Studies curriculum as "vintage edubabble" (Kerr, 1997). Myers (1993, 1996a, 1996b), a former chairman of the NZBR, laid similar charges of political correctness in the curriculum and, like Kerr, called for a firmer commitment to excellence and closer alliances between schools and businesses. Others (Roberts, 1998a; Snook, 1996, 1997), however, have argued that people such as Kerr and Myers, although heavily critical of those who seek to politicize the curriculum, fail to acknowledge their own non-neutrality as commentators on educational matters. They have highlighted the narrowness of the Roundtable's vision for education, identified the corporate interests served by their submissions, and commented on the moves made by some NZBR members to suppress criticism and dissent.

Although the curriculum reforms of the 1990s have been vigorously debated, it would be inaccurate to suggest that a clean line between Left and Right political camps can be drawn. There are important tensions not only between, but within, different positions in the debates. Indeed, there are some highly significant tensions in the curriculum documents. Over the years, NZBR and Education Forum commentaries have tended to combine economic liberalism with academic (and sometimes moral) conservatism. Thus, members of the NZBR have supported key elements of the neo-liberal restructuring program—less state interference, businesslike systems of governance and accountability, greater choice for educational consumers, bulk funding in schools, further privatization in the tertiary sector, and so on—while arguing vehemently against other aspects of the reform process. The changes in curriculum policy have, for the most part, been found seriously wanting by NZBR critics. The NZBR has also been critical of the shift to a standards-based system of assessment and a National Qualifications Framework.

Although many teachers and academics were concerned that politicians and government officials had been too heavily influenced by the business community and the language of managerialism, NZBR members claimed that the educational reforms had not gone nearly far enough. In their view, the curriculum documents still suffered from an unhealthy level of provider capture; what was needed was more competition, further privatization, and stronger connections with the world of work. On a number of points, however, NZBR commentators and opponents of neo-liberalism have found some agreement. Irwin's (1999) critique of the "Framework's assumption that all learning relevant to schooling can be packaged in a form determined independently of curricular content" (p. 157) is compatible with the criticisms advanced by Marshall (1997) and others. Reservations expressed in some *Education Forum* reports about the replacement of knowledge with skills have been shared by Snook (1997). Common ground can also be found in analyses of the qualifications reforms, particularly with regard to the breaking down of distinctions between academic and vocational modes of learning, development of outcomes statements, and implementation of a unit standards approach in universities (cf. Irwin, 1999; Roberts, 1997a). Snook (1997) and Irwin (1999) were both critical of relativism in the curriculum.

In some respects, the *New Zealand Curriculum Framework* attempts to do too much and, in the process, risks displeasing almost everybody. The *Framework* stipulates that the New Zealand curriculum will promote both competitiveness and cooperation, ignoring the fundamental tension between these two notions. References are made in the *Framework* and other curriculum documents to gender inclusiveness, yet there is little consideration of what this might mean in theoretical terms or how it might work in practice (cf. Gilbert, 1999). The *Framework* ostensibly "acknowledges the value of the Treaty of Waitangi" (O'Rourke, 1993, p. 1), yet fails to consider some of the radical implications of this goal. There is now an extensive literature on Maori curriculum initiatives at early childhood, school, and tertiary levels (see e.g., Jones et al., 1990; G. H. Smith, 1997; L. T. Smith, 1992; Stewart-Harawira, 1997). This body of work shows that appeals to the Treaty and biculturalism can become nothing more than empty rhetoric if they are not accompanied by wider educational and social changes. Addressing the crisis in Maori education requires structural transformation, not merely the addition of some language and culture classes. Issues of language and culture have been inadequately address in the curriculum reform process. Language has been conceived largely in instrumental terms and regarded as less important than new curriculum areas such as technology (Peddie, 1995). In the absence of adequate state support and mindful of the assimilationist and domesticating tendencies in previous curricular reforms, Maori have taken the initiative and developed total immersion systems of education via Te Kohanga Reo and the Kura Kaupapa Maori schools. When compared with this sort of critical activism, the changes suggested in the *Framework* seem like mere window dressing. The *New Zealand Curriculum Framework,* it might be said, promises much, but ultimately cannot deliver. It suffers from conceptual ambiguities, a lack of theoretical justification, and serious internal contradictions. Despite these faults (and others), it has served as a useful prompt for curriculum debate in New Zealand and has, indirectly and unintentionally, assisted in bringing some of the educational and political differences and similarities between various groups into sharper focus.

POSSIBILITIES FOR FURTHER RESEARCH

In New Zealand, as in many other nations in the Western world, curriculum issues have attracted comment from a diverse collection of interested groups and individuals, including academics, teachers, students, administrators, politicians, parents, and business people. Ideas on the curriculum have been presented in books, journal articles, conference papers, reports, newspapers, submissions, and professional newsletters. Given this broad literature, it might be stated with some confidence that curriculum themes have figured prominently in New Zealand educational thought. Yet, somewhat surprisingly, the number of academic books published by New Zealanders on curriculum theory and the nature of curriculum studies as a field of inquiry is relatively modest. In the 1990s, only McCulloch's (1992b) *The School Curriculum in New Zealand: History, Theory, Policy and Practice* (especially McCulloch, 1992a), Barr and Gordon's (1995) *The Curriculum in the Classroom* (especially McGee, 1995; Faire, 1995) and, particularly, McGee's (1997) *Teachers and Curriculum Decision-Making* addressed these questions in any detail. Another New Zealander, Michael Peters, has recently coauthored a book on postmodernism and curriculum theorizing with several scholars living in Mexico (Alba et al., 2000). Two edited collections published in earlier years, *Curriculum Issues in New Zealand* (Ramsay, 1980) and *Adventures in Curriculum* (Minogue, 1983), have also contributed to the New Zealand literature in this area. McGee's book, although not without its problems (see Peddie, 2000), stands out as the only text of the past decade to deal at length with questions about the nature of the curriculum field, models of curriculum development, curriculum intentions, perspectives on curriculum content, ideas on curriculum leadership, theories of curriculum change and planning, and curriculum decision-making processes.

The dearth of book-length theoretical material of this kind might be explained, in part, by the institutional history of curriculum studies in New Zealand. Curriculum subjects have traditionally had a strong presence in New Zealand teacher education programs. These are courses designed to prepare teachers for work in mathematics, English, or social studies classrooms. Their concern has been more with the teaching of the subject than with curriculum studies as a field of inquiry. Amalgamations between teachers colleges and universities in the 1990s have not altered the balance of curriculum offerings in any substantial way. Courses examining the curriculum from sociological, historical, philosophical, feminist, and other perspectives have been sprinkled across Education departments in New Zealand universities over the years, but they have seldom formed part of a comprehensive curriculum studies program. To some extent, this is a reflection of New Zealand's small size. The idea of having four or five specialists in curriculum theory in a Department or School of Education—a not uncommon occurrence in North American research universities—is unheard of in the New Zealand context. Yet it is also an indication of the way the field has been conceived. Curriculum studies has, in both New Zealand's institutions and its community of educational researchers, been deprived of the relatively independent theoretical status accorded other domains of inquiry, such as the history of education, educational philosophy, and the sociology of education. Scholars from each of these disciplinary areas (and others) have contributed to the development of the New Zealand literature on curriculum processes and practices, but curriculum studies has never emerged as a well-developed, self-contained body of work in this country. The field, perhaps more so today than in the past, is very much a hybrid one, a picture of which can only be developed by pulling together and examining the ideas of a wide range of theorists and practitioners.

The major professional organization for educational researchers in New Zealand, the New Zealand Association for Research in Education, lists 34 categories of research interests in its 1999 Membership Directory. These range from the traditional domains of disciplinary inquiry in education (e.g., educational psychology, history of education) to multidisciplinary, specialist, and applied areas such as teaching/teacher education, assessment, parent education, staff development, and computers in education. Each level in the formal education system (early childhood education, primary education, secondary education, and tertiary education) is well represented. Curriculum studies is a striking omission from the list of categories. This is not to say, of course, that curriculum issues are of little importance to any or many of the several hundred individual members in the association; the wealth of material on curriculum matters published in book, journal, and report form by past and present members of the organization suggests otherwise. What the omission does show is that curriculum studies has yet to gain the sort of cohesive support enjoyed by some other multidisciplinary fields of inquiry in the New Zealand community of educational researchers. Although it might be argued that many would tick a curriculum studies box if one were available in the form sent to members each year, the fact that such a category does not appear is significant. Given that other areas with smaller international literatures have been added to the list of research interests over the years, it seems likely that, had a sufficient number of individuals seen curriculum studies (or curriculum theory) as a key domain of their academic activity, this heading would now appear on the list.

I want to suggest, then, that although curriculum issues have attracted considerable comment in this country, a well-developed, multidisciplinary, interinstitutional program of curriculum studies is yet to emerge. This applies to both teaching and research. The lack of integrated, multilevel institutional course offerings in curriculum studies can be explained, in part, by time constraints and resourcing limits. These have been exacerbated by neo-liberal reform policies. The norm for preservice teacher education degrees in New Zealand is now 3 years. The move from 4-year to 3-year degrees was a response to market pressures. Questions of curriculum theory, where they are addressed at all in such programs, feature more prominently in educational studies courses than the curriculum papers. But the scattered nature of education in curriculum studies in New Zealand also reflects the underdevelopment of a well-defined, cohesive research base from which teachers in this area might draw. Of the many areas worthy of further investigation, I discuss two with strong potential for interinstitutional, multidisciplinary inquiry. First, I argue for more research on the higher education curriculum; second, I consider the possible expansion of literacy studies as a field of curriculum inquiry.

THE HIGHER EDUCATION CURRICULUM

In the late 1980s and first half of the 1990s, debates over political correctness, great books, and the university curriculum generated an enormous amount of popular and academic attention in the United States (see e.g., Aufderheide, 1992; Berman, 1992; Berube & Nelson, 1995; Gitlin, 1995; Gless & Smith, 1992; Graff, 1992). Prompted by the publication and unprecedented success of Allan Bloom's (1988) *The Closing of the American Mind,* North American commentators of varying political persuasions devoted considerable intellectual energy to questions about the nature and purpose of higher education. Some scholars (e.g., D'Souza, 1991; Kimball, 1991) argued that universities had become hotbeds of radicalism, subject to left-wing political dogma, cultural relativism, and a watering down of the curriculum standards. They claimed that, in an effort to make the university curriculum more reflective of America's diverse cultures, values and experiences, academics had abandoned many traditional classic works of literature, philosophy, and history in favor of more books by women, ethnic minorities, and third world writers. Others (e.g., Aby, 1993; Bartlett, 1992; Gates, 1992; Messer-Davidow, 1993) observed that education could never be neutral and that critics on the Right were simply waging a well-funded war to ensure their political position prevailed. In seeking an explanation for the deterioration of higher education in the United States, some focused on the neglect of teaching, problems of specialization, and a lack of attention to moral values (P. Smith, 1990; Wilshire, 1990) while others (e.g. Sykes, 1988) concentrated on greed and other character deficiencies in academic communities. The U.S. *culture wars,* as Graff (1992) called them, were concerned not just with issues of text selection—with questions about reading and books—but with the question of what university students should know. In the midst of these debates, the curriculum became a vital site for the struggle of worldviews. At stake were competing conceptions of education, learning, and democratic citizenship.

As noted elsewhere (Roberts, 1993, 1997c), New Zealand educationists have been inexplicably quiet in responding to these debates. Among the exceptions, the work of Michael Peters on cultural politics in the university (Peters, 1997) and disciplinarity (Peters, 1999) stands out. Controversies over political correctness surfaced periodically during the 1990s, but these seldom became the subject of rigorous academic inquiry. Instead, the debates were played out via sound-byte sized TV items and, occasionally, magazine articles (e.g., Stratford, 1990). To some extent, the lack of interest may reflect differences between U.S. and New Zealand universities. Contemporary New Zealand universities do not offer core courses on "Western Civilization," "Great Books," or "Cultures, Ideas and Values" for incoming students across multiple departments. It could be argued, then, that battles between traditionalists and revisionists are of little relevance to educators in this country. Yet questions about what, how, and why students should read are surely important for all teachers in humanities and social sciences programs. The idea of requiring, say, all Bachelor of Arts students to complete one or more courses devoted to questions of culture (broadly conceived) is seldom considered in the academic literature on education and the curriculum in New Zealand. In fact, higher education has been largely ignored in curriculum debates. Multiple dimensions of the New Zealand school curriculum have been discussed in books and articles over the past 10 years, but rather less has been said about what to teach, to whom, how, and with what possible consequences in universities. Some attention has been paid to questions about the nature and purpose of university life in the critical educational policy studies literature (see e.g., Peters & Roberts, 1999), but there is scope for a great deal more work in this area. Considerable energy is expended in university discussions over degree requirements, prerequisites, co-requisites, cross-crediting, and other regulatory matters, but deeper questions about knowledge, culture, intellectual inquiry, and the aims of higher education often never make it to the debating table.

In a market-driven system of education, where what counts is what sells, fundamental changes in university curricula are inevitable. At the broadest and most drastic level, institutions can be closed down for failing to offer a sufficient number of consumer-friendly courses. New Zealand's major universities do not appear to be in any danger of closure at present, but in some cases entire programs of study have been dropped. Most of the curriculum changes, however, are at a more subtle level. With universities under relentless pressure to do more with less—and in particular to generate more effective full-time students (EFTSs), increase external research funding, and reduce institutional inefficiencies—traditional academic justifications for programs and courses struggle to gain a foothold. Talk about curriculum aims and objectives now has a quaint ring to it: It seems somehow old fashioned, unrealistic, and too imprecise. Thus, instead of asking, "What do we expect a graduate with a major in Education to know?", the temptation is to say, "What are the numbers?" The logic becomes self-sustaining. Students are told (or decide for themselves) that some domains of study are not "marketable" or "useful" and move toward courses in other areas with supposedly greater "relevance." As the numbers in some areas decline, faculty members with expertise in these domains are either shifted sideways to take on teaching responsibilities in other areas, "let go" or encouraged to take early retirement, or not replaced when they go elsewhere. With fewer faculty appointments, research in these domains of inquiry diminishes, adding to the impression that such areas are not worth studying. Over time, what used to be regarded as essential in an Education degree begins to appear unnecessary, and eventually courses disappear altogether. Debates over these issues have, for the most part, stayed within institutional walls.

There is potentially fertile territory here, however, for research on the politics of curriculum reform. Attentive to developments in curriculum theory and the politics of education elsewhere, New Zealand scholars have perhaps missed an opportunity to add to the international literature by reflecting on their own institutional experiences. This, in part, involves facing up to the ways in which we, as researchers, have been shaped by neo-liberalism and the logic of performativity in contemporary universities. Indeed, if Lyotard (1984) was correct in his analysis of the changing status of knowledge in postmodern societies, human beings may not be necessary at all in teaching the curriculum of the future. When *knowledge* has been reduced to *information*, machines might conceivably overcome the need for any face-to-face instruction. We do not have to agree with Lyotard's "death of the professor" thesis to appreciate his point that the liberal university faces a crisis of legitimacy—one with far-reaching consequences for teaching and research. These institutional changes have significance not just at personal and professional levels, but also for curriculum studies as a field of academic inquiry.

LITERACY STUDIES AND CURRICULUM INQUIRY

The development of research on reading and literacy in Australia and New Zealand is instructive in considering these issues and others relating to disciplinary disputes, funding, and the politics of inquiry. New Zealand enjoys an enviable international reputation for its contribution to the psychological literature on reading. The advantages and disadvantages of whole-language and phonics approaches have been discussed at length, and Reading Recovery programs continue to generate debate in academic journals and the popular press. Most of New Zealand's universities can claim to have (or to have had in the recent past) at least one expert on reading among their faculty members. The University of Auckland is fortunate to have several internationally recognized scholars in this area. Across the country, a plethora of university courses devoted to the reading process, reading behavior, and reading problems can be found. Those who teach these courses have been successful in gaining external research grants, and university library shelves are well stocked with books, journals, and reports on the psychological study of reading. Yet the growth of literacy studies as a multidisciplinary field of academic inquiry has been stunted in New Zealand, particularly when compared with developments in Australia. New Zealand universities have made little effort to actively recruit scholars with expertise in sociological, anthropological, historical, or philosophical approaches to the study of literacy for academic appointments. Papers drawing extensively on the wider literacy studies literature have appeared from time to time (e.g., Lankshear, 1994; Roberts, 1995; Soler, 1998), but there has not been a sufficient critical mass of scholars with interests in this area to build and sustain a major research program.

These institutional imbalances both reinforce and perpetuate the dominance of psychological views of reading over other accounts. Most psychological studies assume a fixed, transcultural, ahistorical notion of reading. Reading, it is frequently believed, is the same everywhere regardless of the social circumstances under which it takes place. Psychologists seeking to gauge reading ability invariably assume a fixed notion of reading, both sociogeographically (from one school, region, nation, etc. to another) and historically (from one measurement date to the next). Behaviorist constructs of reading rely on quantitative measures of reading performance via standardized tests for their theoretical coherence. The entire logic of testing in this manner rests on an individualized, internalized, decontextualized conception of reading. For psychologists, reading is construed as a natural phenomenon, discernable and knowable through the empirical methods of the natural sciences (Baker & Luke, 1991, p. xii). As such, it is assumed that, provided sufficiently rigorous standards of scientific inquiry are observed, the elements of the reading process should be able to be isolated and observed or recorded irrespective of the time and space within which reading takes place. Reading is, in this sense, timeless and transcends the particulars of given social contexts. The objective for the investigator is to discover the essence of reading and map out in ever greater detail (through successive studies) its constituent components.

This view of reading is consistent with what Street (1984, 1993) called the *autonomous mode* of literacy. Street (1993) argued that, although this model has encountered a series of challenges in recent years, it nonetheless remains dominant in a number of educational spheres. In the arena of assessment, for example, it is (still) often assumed that texts can be understood independently from contexts. Supporters of the new literacy studies, however, have argued that conceptions and practices of reading and writing are socially embedded, contested, and ideological in character. Street observed that if scholars attempt to define and explain reading by focusing on psycholinguistic processes, the decoding of signs and interactions with texts, they are likely to turn to experimental methods and investigate individual action. The approach fostered by the new literacy studies, by contrast, requires research that can handle social "context" (p. 81).

A similar line of critique has been advanced by Luke (1991), who pointed out that, although reading psychologists have quarreled for years over the merits of skills-based as opposed to whole-language approaches in the teaching of reading, criticism remains confined within relatively narrow parameters. For advocates of either method, "reading is constituted as an observable, singular psychological phenomenon, and the adjudication of matters of pedagogy is seen to depend on psychometrically derived student performances and on psychologically theorized models of reading development" (p. 3).

Despite a shift in some quarters from behaviorist to cognitive approaches in explaining the reading process, the view of reading as a unitary, individual, neutral process remains intact in the psychological literature. Luke (1991) challenged these assumptions and highlighted the role of multinational publishers, governments, and educational experts in determining reading and teaching practices. He argued that reading psychologists have failed to recognize or critically address their own politicality. His analysis suggests that enclosure of discussion within overly narrow boundaries may not only result in a restricted view of a concept or subject, but may also mask the political interests served by particular theories and practices. For Street (1993), likewise, the battle over the meaning of literacy is not merely a semantic game; it is an arena for struggle between groups competing for "power and resources" (p. 82).

If Street, Luke, and others (e.g., McHoul, 1991) are correct in their assessment of the boundaries within which psychologists operate, it is not difficult to see how those with alternative conceptions might have to work hard to gain recognition and support in academic and popular discourses. Psychologists begin from premises that resonate strongly with popular conceptions of reading (as an internal, individual, unitary process) and in this sense have a head start over less conventional ideas. Commonsense presuppositions are fortified and bolstered, although in considerably more complex ways, by most courses on reading in institutions such as universities. In many cases, these are the only courses on reading available. Such courses, however, might appear to provide room for vigorous debate over reading issues because there is much dispute over the precise nature of the reading process among psychologists. Students interested in reading take these courses, pass on the knowledge they gain from them in classrooms, and reproduce the same fundamental assumptions with which their teachers began. The media frequently turn to universities in seeking expert opinions on complex academic subjects, and because most academics who deal with reading in universities tend to be psychologists, the domain for comment tends to be restricted to areas within the parameters of the psychological paradigm. When developing and implementing reading programs in schools, government agencies sometimes seek outside assistance from professionals in the field. Again, if there is a recognized authority on reading on a committee, the person is more likely to hold views compatible with the dominant perspective on reading than contrary ideas. The conceptual terrain of reading thus remains narrowly circumscribed—in both public and professional domains—despite healthy debate and obvious points of contention within the dominant paradigm.

Baker and Luke (1991) charted the political ramifications of psychological views assuming the mantle of legitimacy over other theoretical approaches to reading. They claimed that this dominance "complicitly services the politics of established research institutions and the interests of corporations successfully involved in the business of defining and deploying school literacies" (p. xix). They argued that this inhibits the development of other worthwhile lines of research, development, and classroom practice. Yet although it is not difficult to support the claim that research (in reading, literacy, or any other subject area) is always a political process, this does not mean that research is nothing but politics. Nicholson (1997) observed that, "[i]f certain findings support the teaching of phonics (sounding-out of words), the researchers are likely to be criticized as pawns of the religious or conservative Right." However, "whole language researchers are sometimes criticized as Communists and Left Wing" (p. 106). As Nicholson pointed out, these simplistic and misleading characterizations undermine the research enterprise and can be detrimental to the educational goals investigators seek to serve.

As is the case with other curriculum areas, research on reading and literacy does not fall into neat ideological camps. Nicholson (1997) expressed surprise, given "the scale of reading failure that exists, and the urgency of helping those in most need," that so little policy research has been conducted on "what works best for whom" in New Zealand (p. 107). There is a timely and welcome challenge here for researchers with "different solutions, and different perspectives" (p. 107) to become involved in investigating reading problems. There has, as Thrupp (1997) noted, already been some good New Zealand work published in this area by sociologists of education. For example, Nash (1993) conducted empirical research on the relationship between social class and reading achievement. There is, however, plenty of space for scholars from other disciplinary backgrounds to contribute to these debates. Luke (1991) and others remind us that what comes to be construed as worthy of debate is an important question. It is not simply a matter of adding more voices to existing debates; we also need to consider how questions about reading and literacy come to be conceived, framed, and addressed.

A research project conducted in Australia in the late 1990s (Roberts, 1998b) suggests that if the boundaries for inquiry are to be widened, national and institutional politics, curriculum reform, and money will all play significant roles. Like New Zealand, Australia has an impressive number of experts in the psychology of reading. In addition, however, Australian scholars have made a substantial contribution to the international literature in the broader field of literacy studies. This has been reflected in Australian tertiary education institutions, with the emergence of research concentrations, centers, and even entire academic departments devoted to the study of language, literacy, and education. The appointment of prominent literacy theorists to senior positions in Australian universities provides part of the explanation for this growth.

The leadership exercised by these scholars has been important in fostering a strong research culture in literacy studies. Multidisciplinary conferences have been organized, interinstitutional research projects have been developed, and graduate study in the literacy area has been encouraged. Of course, care must be taken not to read too much into the names given to institutional entities. A switch from *reading* to *literacy* in the name of a center or department can sometimes be a semantic shift only, with little change in conceptual categories, theoretical orientation, or research procedures. In most cases, however, there has been a genuine broadening of curriculum offerings and research activities in the reading, writing, and literacy domain.

This has been prompted, in part, by the status of literacy as a topic for public concern, popular debate, and governmental recognition in Australia. In the early 1990s, literacy became a major policy issue in Australia, and relatively large sums of government money became available for research projects in this area. To some extent, the growth of literacy studies reflected the increase in available funds. There were strong incentives for academics to become literacy experts, given the support their research could receive. Research projects that previously might never have materialized could, with appropriate initiative and attention to detail in the preparation of applications and proposals, be launched and sometimes sustained for considerable periods of time. The flow-on effects of better funding and greater recognition could be felt at multiple levels within universities and other organizations. More researchers and research assistants with expertise in the literacy domain could be appointed, some of the costs associated with the production of scholarly materials could be covered, visiting specialists from elsewhere in the world could be hosted and employed as consultants, and administrative support could be found.

In New Zealand, by contrast, many dimensions of literacy have been neglected or ignored. There has been a reluctance to acknowledge that adult literacy is an issue worth addressing (Sutton & Benseman, 1996). Most government-funded initiatives focus on the school sector (for one recent example, see Literacy Taskforce, 1999) and demonstrate only a minimal awareness of the wider literacy studies research literature. As the work of Green (1993) and others shows, this literature has much to offer curriculum theory. Among the many questions that might be addressed by curriculum researchers are these: What role do curriculum processes play in constructing concepts of "reading," "writing," and "literacy"? What forms of literacy should we be promoting through curriculum activities? What are the benefits of literacy? In what ways might literacy be harmful? What should we expect students to read and why? To what extent, and in what ways, might the selection of texts for reading classes be regarded as a political process? What can we learn from curriculum initiatives of the past in creating, restructuring, and rethinking contemporary literacy programs? To what extent, and in what ways, are reading and writing practices influenced by the hidden curriculum? What are some of the social consequences of different forms of literate practice? How might the new information technologies alter conceptions and practices of reading and writing? What values and ideals underpin curriculum reforms in the areas of reading and writing? How might the teacher's beliefs and commitments affect the content and processes of a literacy program? How might the different cultures, languages, and worldviews of participants be incorporated into reading programs? What is the relationship among context, content, and pedagogy in literacy learning? How should reading and writing be assessed? How might success and failure be gauged? How should decisions about curriculum content and processes in reading classes be made? What special curriculum requirements, if any, do adults have when they take up reading and writing? What is the optimal relationship between skills and knowledge in a reading and/or writing curriculum? What impact might inequities along class, gender, ethnicity, and other lines have on learning in the reading and writing classroom? To what extent is illiteracy a structural phenomenon? What limits and obstacles must teachers and other curriculum decision makers face when attempting to address illiteracy and reading problems?

If these questions, or others of a similar kind, are to form the basis for a well-developed research program, a number of developments are necessary. Those with interests in the study of literacy from philosophical, historical, sociological, and other perspectives need to demonstrate initiative and leadership in getting new projects off the ground and in seeking the support of colleagues in New Zealand and elsewhere. All participants in curriculum debates over reading and writing need to exhibit an open-minded willingness to consider literacy issues from other points of view. The curriculum in teacher education programs has to be changed, and there have to be stronger incentives for graduates to contemplate advanced study in the literacy area. Additional funds and resources have to be put aside by government agencies to stimulate and support literacy research. Equally important, researchers have to be active and committed in applying for grants, lobbying politicians and officials, and promoting their ideas in a range of popular and academic forums. These are ideal developments; as such, they need to be tempered with a sober assessment of the messy realities of contemporary institutional life. There are limits to what can be achieved in the current neo-liberal environment. Nonetheless, the potential benefits of a well-developed program in this area have been clearly demonstrated in Australia and other countries. Given those benefits, there is, despite obstacles and challenges, considerable merit in continuing to strive for the establishment of literacy studies as a coherent, well-supported, rigorous, and robust area of curriculum inquiry in New Zealand.

CONCLUDING COMMENTS

The 1990s were tumultuous times for educationists in New Zealand. In this period, curriculum issues were discussed and debated as part of a wider process of contestation over the nature and direction of neo-liberal reform. Arguably, the project of analyzing neo-liberal developments in the curriculum sphere is not yet complete, and further productive critical work remains to be done. There is much more that might be said, for example, about some of the underlying assumptions and curriculum implications of new discourses on information technologies and the knowledge society (see Marshall, 1999; Peters & Roberts, 1998, 1999). It must be acknowledged, however, that the need for a vigorous response to one form of change (the politics of neo-liberalism) can, in an environment where time and resources are strictly limited, sometimes make it more difficult for theorists to respond to and create other changes. Hence, although there are good reasons for encouraging curriculum scholars to continue engaging neo-liberal policies, it is also important that other lines of theoretical inquiry be developed. This chapter has identified some of the possibilities for future investigation, but these are hardly exhaustive. Reviving some of the concerns of earlier decades—including questions about the meaning of curriculum, curriculum aims and purposes, and the nature of curriculum processes—could be important in building and sustaining a rigorous, comprehensive program of teaching and research in curriculum studies in New Zealand. The key perhaps is not to fall into a form of abstract theorizing where the practical, policy, political, and pedagogical issues of the day are ignored, but rather to show how concern with fundamental curriculum questions can, by providing a new set of conceptual lenses through which to view those issues, deepen and extend an already rich and complex conversation.

REFERENCES

Aby, S. (1993). The political correctness debate: An essay review. *Discourse, 13*(2), 46–54.
Adams, P., Clark, J., Codd, J., O'Neill, A.-M., Openshaw, R., & Waitere-Ang, H. (2000). *Education and society in Aotearoa New Zealand.* Palmerston North: Dunmore.
Alba, A. de, Gonzalez-Gaudiano, E., Lankshear, C., & Peters, M. (2000). *Curriculum in the postmodern condition.* New York: Peter Lang.
Allen, G. L. (1993). *School-based curriculum review and development.* Unpublished master's thesis, University of Auckland, Auckland, New Zealand.
Aufderheide, P. (Ed.). (1992). *Beyond p.c.: Toward a politics of understanding.* St. Paul, MN: Graywolf.
Baker, C., & Luke, A. (1991). Toward a critical sociology of reading pedagogy: An introduction. In C. D. Baker & A. Luke (Eds.), *Towards a critical sociology of reading pedagogy* (pp. xi–xxi). Philadelphia: John Benjamins.
Barr, H., & Gordon, P. (Eds.). (1995). *The curriculum in the classroom.* Palmerston North, New Zealand: Dunmore.

Bartlett, K. T. (1992). Surplus visibility. In P. Aufderheide (Ed.) *Beyond p.c.: Towards a politics of under-standing.* St Paul, MN: Graywolf.

Benson, P., & Openshaw, R. (Eds.). (1998). *New horizons for New Zealand social studies.* Palmerston North, New Zealand: ERDC.

Berman, P. (Ed.). (1992). *Debating p.c.: The controversy over political correctness on college campuses.* New York: Dell.

Berube, M., & Nelson, C. (Eds.). (1995). *Higher education under fire: Politics, economics, and the crisis of the humanities.* New York: Routledge.

Bloom, A. (1988). *The closing of the American mind.* Harmondsworth, England: Penguin.

Bradley, L. (1998). *The origins and development of the history of art curriculum in New Zealand secondary schools.* Unpublished master's thesis, University of Auckland, Auckland, New Zealand.

Burns, J. (Ed.). (1997). *Technology in the New Zealand curriculum: Perspectives on practice.* Palmerston North, New Zealand: Dunmore.

Butterworth, R., & Tarling, N. (1994). *A shakeup anyway: Government and the universities in New Zealand in a decade of reform.* Auckland, New Zealand: Auckland University Press.

Capper, P. (Ed.). (1991, May 12–14). *Proceedings of the Post Primary Teachers' Association curriculum con-ference.* Christchurch, New Zealand: Post Primary Teachers' Association.

Codd, J. (1993). Neo-liberal education policy and the ideology of choice. *Educational Philosophy and Theory, 24*(2), 31–48.

Codd, J., Harker, R., & Nash, R. (Eds.). (1990). *Political issues in New Zealand education* (2nd ed.). Palmerston North, New Zealand: Dunmore.

Coxon, E., Jenkins, K., Marshall, J., & Massey, L. (Eds.). (1994). *The politics of learning and teaching in Aotearoa/New Zealand.* Palmerston North, New Zealand: Dunmore.

Department of Education. (1987). *The curriculum review.* Wellington, New Zealand: Author.

Department of Education. (1988). *Tomorrow's schools.* Wellington, New Zealand: Government Printer.

D'Souza, D. (1991). *Illiberal education: The politics of race and sex on campus.* New York: The Free Press.

Education and Training Support Agency. (1993). *Skill New Zealand: Lifelong education and training.* Wellington, New Zealand: New Zealand Qualifications Authority.

Education Forum. (1994). *English in the New Zealand curriculum: A submission on the draft.* Auckland, New Zealand: Author.

Education Forum. (1995). *Social studies in the New Zealand curriculum: A submission on the draft.* Auckland, New Zealand: Author.

Education Forum. (1996). *Social studies in the New Zealand curriculum: A submission on the revised draft.* Auckland, New Zealand: Author.

Elley, W. B. (1996). Curriculum reform: Forwards or backwards? *Delta: Policy and Practice in Educa-tion, 48*(1), 11–18.

Faire, M. (1995). Thematic approaches to teaching. In H. Barr & P. Gordon (Eds.), *The curriculum in the classroom* (pp. 225–240). Palmerston North, New Zealand: Dunmore.

Gates, H. L. (1992). Whose canon is it, anyway? In P. Berman (Ed.), *Debating p.c.: The controversy over political correctness on college campuses* (pp. 190–200). New York: Dell.

Gilbert, J. (1999). Gender equity statements in the New Zealand national curriculum documents: Their genealogy and likely effects. *New Zealand Annual Review of Education, 8*, 97–117.

Gitlin, T. (1995). *The twilight of common dreams: Why America is wracked by culture wars.* New York: Met-ropolitan Books.

Gless, D. J., & Smith, B. H. (Eds.). (1992). *The politics of liberal education.* Durham, CA: Duke University Press.

Graff, G. (1992). *Beyond the culture wars: How teaching the conflicts can revitalize American education.* New York: Norton.

Green, B. (Ed.). (1993). *The insistence of the letter: Literacy studies and curriculum theorizing.* London: Falmer.

Hall, A., Robertson, J. M., & Casey, G. (1995). *A resounding ACCO: The continuing effects of a curriculum project one year later.* Hamilton, New Zealand: Educational Leadership Centre, School of Educa-tion, University of Waikato.

Hannif, N. G. B. (1996). *Implementation of the 1993 New Zealand science curriculum: Some primary school teachers' perceptions.* Unpublished master's thesis, University of Auckland, Auckland, New Zea-land.

Irwin, M. (1996, October 18). *Curricular confusion: The case for revisiting the New Zealand Curriculum Framework.* Address at the seminar on "Implementing the Curriculum," Principals' Centre, Uni-versity of Auckland, Auckland, New Zealand.

Irwin, M. (1997, August 7). *Follies and fashions in New Zealand education.* Address at the Waikato Forum on Education, University of Waikato, Hamilton, New Zealand.

Irwin, M. (1999). A decade of curricular reform. *New Zealand Journal of Educational Studies, 34*(1), 156–166.

Jones, A., McCulloch, G., Marshall, J., Smith, G., & Smith, L. (1990). *Myths and realities: Schooling in New Zealand.* Palmerston North, New Zealand: Dunmore.

Katterns, B. (1992). *Curriculum and pedagogy* (Report no. 13 in the Monitoring Today's Schools Research Project). Prepared for the New Zealand Ministry of Education as part of a research contract between the Ministry and the University of Waikato.

Kelsey, J. (1995). *The New Zealand experiment: A world model for structural adjustment?* Auckland, New Zealand: Auckland University Press/Bridget Williams Books.

Kerr, R. (1997, September 17). *Upgrading New Zealand's human resources.* Address at a gathering of the New Zealand Institute of Personnel Management (Auckland branch), Auckland, New Zealand. (*http://www.nzbr.org.nz*)

Kimball, R. (1991). *Tenured radicals.* New York: Harper Perennial.

Lankshear, C. (1994). Literacy and empowerment: Discourse, power, critique. *New Zealand Journal of Educational Studies, 29*(1), 59–72.

Lee, G., & Hill, D. (1996). Curriculum reform in New Zealand: Outlining the new or restating the familiar? *Delta: Policy and Practice in Education, 48*(1), 19–32.

Literacy Taskforce. (1999, March). *Report prepared for the New Zealand Minister of Education.* Wellington, New Zealand: Ministry of Education.

Luke, A. (1991). The political economy of reading instruction. In C. D. Baker & A. Luke (Eds.), *Towards a critical sociology of reading pedagogy* (pp. 3–25). Philadelphia: John Benjamin's Publishing Company.

Lyotard, J.-F. (1984). *The postmodern condition: A report on knowledge* (G. Bennington & B. Massumi, trans.). Minneapolis: University of Minnesota Press.

Mansfield, J. (1995). *The death of the "dance of the cave weta": The marginalisation of the arts within state education.* Unpublished master's thesis, University of Auckland, Auckland, New Zealand.

Marshall, J. (1995). Skills, information and quality for the autonomous chooser. In M. Olssen & K. Morris Matthews (Eds.), *Education, democracy and reform* (pp. 44–59). Auckland, New Zealand: NZARE/RUME.

Marshall, J. (1996). The autonomous chooser and "reforms" in education. *Studies in Philosophy and Education, 15,* 89–96.

Marshall, J. (1997). The new vocationalism. In M. Olssen & K. Morris Matthews (Eds.), *Education policy in New Zealand: The 1990s and beyond* (pp. 304–326). Palmerston North, New Zealand: Dunmore.

Marshall, J. (1999). Technology in the New Zealand curriculum. *New Zealand Journal of Educational Studies, 34*(1), 167–175.

Matthews, M. (1995). *Challenging New Zealand science education.* Palmerston North, New Zealand: Dunmore.

McCulloch, G. (1992a). Introduction. In G. McCulloch (Ed.), *The school curriculum in New Zealand: History, theory, policy and practice* (pp. 9–25). Palmerston North, New Zealand: Dunmore.

McCulloch, G. (Ed.). (1992b). *The school curriculum in New Zealand: History, theory, policy and practice.* Palmerston North, New Zealand: Dunmore.

McGee, C. (1995). The primary school curriculum. In H. Barr & P. Gordon (Eds.), *The curriculum in the classroom* (pp. 17–37). Palmerston North, New Zealand: Dunmore.

McGee, C. (1997). *Teachers and curriculum decision-making.* Palmerston North, New Zealand: Dunmore.

McGee, C., & Fraser, D. (1994). *The professional practice of teaching.* Palmerston North, New Zealand: Dunmore.

McHoul, A. (1991). Readings. In C. D. Baker & A. Luke (Eds.), *Towards a critical sociology of reading pedagogy* (pp. 191–210). Philadelphia: John Benjamin's Publishing Company.

McKenzie, D., Lee, H., & Lee, G. (1993). *Scholars or dollars? Selected historical case studies of opportunity costs in New Zealand education.* Palmerston North, New Zealand: Dunmore.

Messer-Davidow, E. (1993). Manufacturing the attack on liberalized higher education. *Social Text, 36,* 40–80.

Middleton, S., Codd, J., & Jones, A. (Eds.). (1990). *New Zealand educational policy today.* Wellington, New Zealand: Allen & Unwin.

Middleton, S., & Jones, A. (Eds.), (1992). *Women and education in Aotearoa 2.* Wellington, New Zealand: Bridget Williams Books.

Ministry of Education. (1991). *The national curriculum of New Zealand: A discussion document.* Wellington, New Zealand: Learning Media.

Ministry of Education. (1993). *The New Zealand curriculum framework.* Wellington, New Zealand: Learning Media.

Ministry of Education. (1994a). *English in the New Zealand curriculum.* Wellington, New Zealand: Learning Media.

Ministry of Education. (1994b). *Social studies in the New Zealand Curriculum* (draft). Wellington, New Zealand: Learning Media.

Ministry of Education. (1995). *Technology in the New Zealand curriculum.* Wellington, New Zealand: Learning Media.

Ministry of Education. (1996). *Social studies in the New Zealand curriculum* (Revised Draft). Wellington, New Zealand: Learning Media.

Ministry of Education. (1997). *Social studies in the New Zealand curriculum.* Wellington, New Zealand: Learning Media.

Minogue, W. J. D. (Ed.). (1983). *Adventures in curriculum.* Sydney, Australia: Allen & Unwin.

Myers, D. (1993, March 13). *Schooling for the 21st century.* Address at the "Successful Schools–Successful Business" conference, Auckland, New Zealand.

Myers, D. (1996a, May 18). *Education: The way the world should be.* Address at the Independent Schools Council annual conference, Auckland, New Zealand.

Myers, D. (1996b, February 27). *Why not simply the best?* Address at a gathering of the Canterbury Manufacturers Association, Christchurch, New Zealand.

Nash, R. (1993). *Succeeding generations.* Auckland, New Zealand: Oxford University Press.

Nicholson, T. (1997). Social class and reading achievement: Sociology meets psychology. *New Zealand Journal of Educational Studies, 32*(1), 105–108.

Olssen, M. (1997). Reframing educational policy: Choice, Rawlsianism, communitarianism. In M. Olssen & K. Morris Matthews (Eds.), *Education policy in New Zealand: The 1990s and beyond* (pp. 391–428). Palmerston North, New Zealand: Dunmore.

Olssen, M., & Morris Matthews, K. (Eds.). (1995). *Education, democracy and reform.* Auckland, New Zealand: Research Unit for Maori Education/New Zealand Association for Research in Education.

Olssen, M., & Morris Matthews, K. (Eds.). (1997). *Education policy in New Zealand: The 1990s and beyond.* Palmerston North, New Zealand: Dunmore.

O'Neill, A.-M. (1996a). Curriculum development in Aotearoa New Zealand: An editorial introduction. *Delta: Policy and Practice in Education, 48*(1), 3–10.

O'Neill, A.-M. (Ed.). (1996b). Special Issue on "Curriculum reform: The political context." *Delta: Policy and Practice in Education, 48*(1).

Openshaw, R. (Ed.). (1992). *New Zealand social studies: Past, present and future.* Palmerston North, New Zealand: Dunmore.

Openshaw, R. (1995). *Unresolved struggle: Consensus and conflict in state post-primary education.* Palmerston North, New Zealand: Dunmore.

Openshaw, R., Lee, G., & Lee, H. (1993). *Challenging the myths: Rethinking New Zealand's educational history.* Palmerston North, New Zealand: Dunmore.

Openshaw, R., & McKenzie, D. (1987). *Reinterpreting the educational past: Essays in the history of New Zealand education.* Wellington, New Zealand: New Zealand Council for Educational Research.

O'Rourke, M. (1993). Foreword. In Ministry of Education, *The New Zealand curriculum framework* (pp. 1–2). Wellington, New Zealand: Learning Media.

Peddie, R. (1994). *What shall they learn? Junior secondary school curriculum in New Zealand.* Final report of a longitudinal study of short option courses in the third and fourth forms of New Zealand secondary schools, 1990–1993. Wellington, New Zealand: Ministry of Education.

Peddie, R. (1995). Culture and economic change: The New Zealand school curriculum. In D. S. G. Carter & M. H. O'Neill (Eds.), *Case studies in educational change: An international perspective* (pp. 140–156). London: Falmer.

Peddie, R. (2000). Review of Teachers and curriculum decision-making by Clive McGee (Palmerston North, New Zealand: Dunmore, 1997). *New Zealand Journal of Educational Studies, 35*(1), 91–93.

Peters, M. (1992). Starship education: Enterprise culture in New Zealand. *Access: Critical Perspectives on Education Policy, 11*(1), 1–12.

Peters, M. (1995). Educational reform and the politics of the curriculum in New Zealand. In D. S. G. Carter & M. H. O'Neill (Eds.), *International Perspectives on Educational Reform and Policy Implementation* (pp. 52–70). London: Falmer.

Peters, M. (Ed.). (1997). *Cultural politics and the university in Aotearoa/New Zealand.* Palmerston North, New Zealand: Dunmore.

Peters, M. (Ed.). (1999). *After the disciplines? The emergence of cultural studies.* Westport, CT: Bergin & Garvey.

Peters, M., & Marshall, J. (1996). The politics of curriculum: Busnocratic rationality and enterprise culture. *Delta: Policy and Practice in Education, 48*(1), 33–46.

Peters, M., & Roberts, P. (Eds.). (1998). *Virtual technologies and tertiary education.* Palmerston North, New Zealand: Dunmore.

Peters, M., & Roberts, P. (1999). *University futures and the politics of reform in New Zealand.* Palmerston North, New Zealand: Dunmore.

Philips, D. (2000). Curriculum and assessment policy in New Zealand: Ten years of reforms. *Educational Review, 52*(2), 143–153.

Pinar, W. F., Reynolds, W. M., Slattery, P., & Taubman, P. M. (1995). *Understanding curriculum: An introduction to the study of historical and contemporary curriculum discourses.* New York: Peter Lang.

Ramsay, P. (Ed.). (1980). *Curriculum issues in New Zealand.* Wellington, New Zealand: New Zealand Educational Institute.

Ramsay, P. D. K., et al. (1990). "There's no going back": Collaborative decision making in education: Final report, September 1990. Hamilton, New Zealand: Curriculum Review Research in Schools Project.

Ramsay, P., Harold, B., Hawk, K., Marriot, R., & Poskitt, J. (1992). Sharing curriculum decisions with parents: An overview of findings of Project C.R.R.I.S.P. *New Zealand Journal of Educational Studies, 27*(2), 167–182.

Roberts, P. (1993). Philosophy, education and literacy: Some comments on Bloom. *New Zealand Journal of Educational Studies, 28*(2), 165–180.

Roberts, P. (1995). Literacy studies: A review of the literature, with signposts for future research. *New Zealand Journal of Educational Studies, 30*(2), 189–214.

Roberts, P. (1997a). A critique of the NZQA policy reforms. In M. Olssen & K. Morris Matthews (Eds.), *Education policy in New Zealand: The 1990s and beyond* (pp. 162–189). Palmerston North, New Zealand: Dunmore.

Roberts, P. (1997b, July). *Literacies in cyberspace. SET: Research Information for Teachers* (Special issue on language and literacy).

Roberts, P. (1997c). Political correctness, great books and the university curriculum. In M. Peters (Ed.), *Cultural politics and the university in Aotearoa/New Zealand* (pp. 103–134). Palmerston North, New Zealand: Dunmore.

Roberts, P. (1997d). Qualifications policies and the marketisation of education: A critical reading of the green paper. *Access: Critical Perspectives on Cultural and Policy Studies in Education, 16*(2), 31–47.

Roberts, P. (1997e, October 11). *Scholarly life in virtual universities.* Keynote address at the conference on "Virtual Technologies in Tertiary Education: A Vision for New Zealand?," sponsored by the Association of University Staff of New Zealand, Auckland, New Zealand.

Roberts, P. (1998a). The politics of curriculum reform in New Zealand. *Curriculum Studies, 6*(1), 29–46.

Roberts, P. (1998b). *Multidisciplinarity in the academy: The case of literacy studies.* Project funded by University of Auckland Research Committee.

Roberts, P. (2000). Knowledge, information and literacy. *International Review of Education, 46*(2), 1–21.

Roberts, P., & Peters, M. (1999). A critique of the tertiary education white paper. *New Zealand Annual Review of Education, 8,* 1–22.

Robertson, J. M. (1991). *ACCO—Achieving charter curriculum objectives: A teacher development programme using a school development strategy.* Hamilton, New Zealand: Educational Leadership Centre, School of Education, University of Waikato.

Smith, G. H. (1997). *The development of Kaupapa Maori: Theory and practice.* Doctoral thesis, University of Auckland, Auckland, New Zealand.

Smith, L. T. (1992). Kura kaupapa Maori and the implications for curriculum. In G. McCulloch (Ed.) *The school curriculum in New Zealand: History, theory, policy and practice* (pp. 219–231). Palmerston North, New Zealand: Dunmore.

Smith, P. (1990). *Killing the spirit.* New York: Viking.

Snook, I. (1996). The Education Forum and the Curriculum Framework. *Delta: Policy and Practice in Education, 48*(1), 47–56.

Snook, I. (1997). Democracy, education and the new right. In M. Olssen & K. Morris Matthews (Eds.), *Education policy in New Zealand: The 1990s and beyond* (pp. 358–371). Palmerston North, New Zealand: Dunmore.

Soler, J. (1998). The politics of learning to read: 1940s debates over literacy instruction in the New Zealand primary school. *New Zealand Journal of Educational Studies, 33*(2), 155–166.

Stewart-Harawira, M. (1997). The impact of the state-welfare relationship on whanau: Implications for education. In M. Olssen & K. Morris Matthews (Eds.), *Education policy in New Zealand: The 1990s and beyond* (pp. 327–345). Palmerston North, New Zealand: Dunmore.

Stratford, S. (1990, December). Talking about my generation. *Metro*, pp. 82–94.

Street, B. (1984). *Literacy in theory and practice.* Cambridge, England: Cambridge University Press.

Street, B. (1993). The new literacy. *Journal of Research on Reading, 18*(2).

Sutton, A., & Benseman, J. (1996). Adult literacy and basic education policy in New Zealand: One step forward and two back. *New Zealand Journal of Educational Studies, 31*(2), 131–141.

Sykes, C. J. (1988). *Profscam: Professors and the demise of higher education.* Washington, DC: Regnery Gateway.

Thrupp, M. (1997). Taking a broader view: A response to "Struggletown meets Middletown." *New Zealand Journal of Educational Studies, 32*(1), 97–104.

Wilshire, B. (1990). *The moral collapse of the university.* Albany: State University of New York Press.

CHAPTER 29

Curriculum Theory and Research in Norway: Traditions, Trends, and Challenges

Bjrøg B. Gundem
Berit Karseth
Kirsten Sivesind
University of Oslo

As a general introductory note, we would like to point out that, like many other countries, Norway has recently been experiencing a period of thoroughgoing educational reform. From 1993 to 1995, new laws were introduced affecting every stage of education from kindergarten to college. In 1994, students in upper secondary education and vocational training were given new curricula. In the same year, the regional college system was reorganized, and in 1996, a new law for universities and regional colleges came into effect. In 1997, reforms were implemented for elementary and junior high schools. The new curricula for these levels of education emphasize comprehensive principles: All students are to have the chance to be educated in their local area and to experience the fellowship of being members of a class and student body. They are to encounter a common core of educational content, which will gradually broaden as they progress through the system (Royal Ministry of Education, 1994, 1999).

This chapter outlines the development of curriculum theory and research in Norway, using historical description and critical macrosociological analysis to lay out a social-constructivist perspective, focusing on a variety of levels of discourse. We mention various types of inquiry that we have found relevant for the empirical and theoretical conceptualization of curricular questions. We hope that our presentation gives an up-to-date portrayal of Norwegian research efforts that is of interest to curriculum researchers, both nationally and internationally. Further, an attempt is made to grasp the dimensions, conflicts, and dilemmas embedded in the perspectives, which can be brought to bear on current challenges to curriculum theory and research. The first part of the chapter outlines traditions, whereas the second part focuses on trends and challenges.

TRADITIONS OF CURRICULUM RESEARCH

In Norway, as in the rest of Scandinavia, curriculum studies have, from the 1960s and 1970s, preferred to focus on the subjects that make up the curriculum (Gundem, 1996a). This growing interest arises from a number of different causes. The societal importance of frequent efforts to reform the curriculum through plans for reconstruction has highlighted the centrality of school subjects. Moreover, a renewed emphasis on content in terms of defining basic skills or a core curriculum naturally focuses on school subjects. The introduction of school subject didactics in teacher education courses and as part of academic degree courses during the 1980s has also contributed to this trend (Gundem, 1992).

In our overview, we distinguish and discuss a variety of research approaches to explain how such a diversity of approach has arisen—a diversity that still exists, although development over time through different phases or stages can be discerned, because different research traditions can live side by side. The first of these traditions is dominated by historical, descriptive curriculum research following a well-established historical approach. The second one is curriculum research as curriculum development following, to some extent, a scientific approach. The third one is curriculum research according to macrosociology using a critical perspective related to structuralism. Finally, the fourth one is curriculum research based on curriculum theory and curriculum history theory following a poststructuralist perspective. As we give our overview, these different perspectives, to some extent, mingle and intersect.

HISTORICAL DESCRIPTIVE CURRICULUM RESEARCH

Historical research studies on the curriculum in Norway can be related, on the one hand, to the history of educational movements and ideas and, on the other hand, to the history of educational systems and institutions, and of educational legislation. The specific research interest may be the place and role of school subjects, together with their teaching/learning content, as well as teaching/learning materials, teaching methods, or even teacher education. Sometimes these studies are seen in relation to both the history of educational movements and ideas and the development of the overall school system. It is also the case that these kinds of studies have been dedicated to a historical descriptive research methodology—avoiding, as it were, theoretical constructs or theoretical overtones—and have often combined historical descriptive research with quantitative research methodology (Stensaasen, 1958).

Historical studies of the educational system provide important data and knowledge about curriculum reforms in Norway. The aim of these studies is to describe historical events rather than develop theory (Dokka, 1988; Harbo, 1969; Telhaug & Aasen, 1999). The history of educational and philosophical ideas related to the content of school subjects is another approach. A classic and influential study of the history of ideas in the Scandinavian context is Andersson's (1979) work on the aims of history teaching in Finland, 1843 to 1917. He placed the history of school subjects in a wide societal, educational, and philosophical/ideological context, anticipating the kind of school subject research that was later to be developed (Goodson, 1983). In a similar way, Steinfeld's (1986) study of the rise and development of mother tongue teaching in Norwegian schooling from the 16th into the 20th century merges viewpoints from history, philosophy, linguistics, economics, and educational science.

Similarly, more recent studies should also be mentioned, such as those of Lorentzen (1986, 1990), which showed how ideas about patriotism have influenced the content of history books in Norway, and of Gjone (1985) on the introduction of New Math in basic schooling. The history of school subjects has also been examined from the point of view of a more philological and linguistic research interest. A Norwegian study of this kind that should be mentioned uses a historical perspective to examine the debate about the role of instruction in grammar as it is linked to mother tongue teaching in Norwegian schools. Hertzberg (1995) disclosed the historical roots of the grammar teaching controversy and related the debate about its function, role, and value to predominant trends in linguistics and learning theory in different epochs.

CURRICULUM RESEARCH ON CURRICULUM DEVELOPMENT

Not much of the available research can be classified as research on general didactics, which apparently does not lend itself easily to programs of research, although there has been a certain amount of theorizing around didactical models and conceptions (Gundem, 1980). However, some research projects that encompass a variety of approaches to form and content, and also to research methodology, may, in the context of this chapter, be categorized as general didactical research. A characteristic they all share is a focus on curriculum development.

One of these is the Environmental Education Project - Miljæreprosjektet, 1969–1976 (Bjørndal & Lieberg, 1972; Bjørndal, 1980). The intention was to integrate subject matter from a variety of school subjects to develop a course of study in ecology for basic schooling. The aim was to give students insight into the natural environment, foster an attitude of caring for environmental values, and develop teaching materials and qualify teachers in the use of them. A team of qualified scientists was in charge of the project, including university educators and teachers in basic schooling, who together were able to cover the necessary subject matter and pedagogy. The team decided on the content, developed approximately 80 teaching-learning units, and prepared a manual.

This project has traits that imply use of science-oriented curriculum theory (Bjørndal, 1969). The didactical ambitions were obvious (Bjørndal & Lieberg, 1975, 1978). Where curriculum development theory is concerned, the project's pedagogy may be placed somewhere between discipline centered and student centered. The development of the teaching materials had its roots in teaching theories aimed at problem solving. There were elements of aims-means thinking, but without a stringent rationale to connect objectives to end results. A model for didactical analysis, reflection, and planning was elaborated—the model for didactical relational deliberation, which has in many ways influenced curriculum research and development in Norway (Gundem, 1995).

This model has inspired and given rise to concepts and thinking different from those stemming from more traditional approaches within curriculum theorizing and research. First of all, it represents a critique of the technocratic rationale for planning and teaching. Second, it focuses on commonplaces of practice, which are regarded as being of equal importance with theoretical conceptions. Consequently, it emphasizes the necessity of making relationships among these varied elements. The model has been used in a scientific way to analyze the ways in which teachers plan their courses, but is also promoted for its ability to contribute to the development of teacher thinking and to the advancement of their planning skills (Handal & Lauvås, 1983; Hiim & Hippe, 1989; Lillemyr & Søbstad, 1993).

Eventually, the model gained acceptance as part of the planning and curriculum development process on all levels of the educational system, and especially in situations where the pedagogical-practical aspects are the main objects of attention (Bjørnsrud, 1995). As a starting point, the conceptual framework offered by Goodlad et al. (1979) is used to distinguish and explain the relationship between different levels of decision making. Its substantive components are parallel to the didactical categories. This framework is found useful for systematically analyzing the connections between sociopolitical decisions, on the one hand, and substantive conceptualizations, on the other, which are constructed in different fields of curriculum practice as, for example, development, textbook production, implementation, and evaluation (Monsen, 1998; Solstad, 1994).

CURRICULUM RESEARCH RELATED TO MACROSOCIOLOGICAL THEORY AND REPRODUCTION THEORY

The influence of the sociology of education and knowledge has brought about a shift from more traditional types of curriculum research—that is, from atheoretical attempts to chronicle the development of a school subject to a different way of looking at the nature of education and, consequently, a new approach for analyzing the antecedents of curriculum change. Of course, Norwegian curriculum research has developed along lines that can be observed in other Nordic countries, as well as in other parts of Europe. Englund (1990) argued that research in Nordic curriculum history forms part of an international universe, historically related to the new sociology of education and critical curriculum theory, and that this tradition may be seen, in certain ways, as a critical correction to the optimistic, rational-scientific conception of curriculum and to studies of curriculum history based on it (Englund, 1990).

Three stages or trends of influence may be discerned: The first is linked to the new sociology of education, where the focus of influence exerted seems to be the nature of school knowledge as related to the social class of students (Young, 1971). A second and overlapping influence comes from French educational sociologists such as Bourdieu and Passeron (1970). Instrumental in bringing about this influence was especially Staf Callewaert, a Belgian Marxist and *d'éfroqué* who came to live in Sweden and Denmark and is now holding the chair in education at the University of Copenhagen. Through this influence, a move toward reproduction theory became noticeable, focusing on the function of school subjects and school knowledge in terms of sociocultural reproduction (Berner, Callewaert, & Silberbrandt, 1977).

The concept and phenomenon of *curriculum codes,* underlying curriculum principles, specifically coined and developed by Ulf P. Lundgren and his associates within the Research Group for Curriculum and Reproduction at the Stockholm Institute of Education, has also become important (Lundgren, 1972, 1979). It is seen as inherent in the development of school subjects and is consequently acknowledged in many studies related to the social history of school subjects. It may be looked on as a special Scandinavian contribution inspired by the new sociology of education, as well as by reproduction theorists. In 1983, some of these studies were collected in a volume edited by Basil Bernstein and Ulf P. Lundgren entitled *Power, Control and Education.*

One may or may not agree with Englund in emphasizing the influence of the new sociology of education on the rapid expansion of research on curriculum history in the Nordic countries in the 1980s. One may also disagree on the role and influence attributed to Lundgren as the main mediator of curriculum history research of a sociology of knowledge type (Englund, 1990). There is, however, no doubt that Lundgren's research in curriculum theory, and especially his research on curriculum codes, has had a major impact on most Swedish, Norwegian, and Finnish research in curriculum history. Code research is concerned with identifying and examining fundamental principles underlying the history of the school curriculum. Behind every syllabus there are certain fundamental principles—a certain curriculum code (Lundgren, 1979). To some extent, we may already talk about a sociological turn in educational theorizing in the 1970s (Dale,

1972; Hoëm, 1978; Monsen, 1978). At that time, the concept of *social pedagogy* became important, and discourse on pedagogy in the complexity of mass education, modern media, gender, and youth cultures was an obvious frame of reference (Jarning, 1998).

A third trend can be recognized, inspired to some degree by American revisionist historians (Franklin, 1986; Kliebard, 1986), but more especially by a specific United Kingdom tradition originating in, but gradually becoming a critique of the new sociology of education/the sociology of knowledge. This new tradition, which particularly stresses the social constructs of school subjects, is linked to the work of Ivor Goodson, who can be seen as an initiator of this tradition and as a person who has contributed toward an understanding of the need for continuity in historical descriptions of curricular events, and of the description of the development of school subjects (Goodson, 1983, 1988). The central role of the school subject as the written curriculum, and the interrelated impact of content and form embedded in most school subjects, must, according to this tradition, be focused through historical research to grasp the realities and complexities of the context within which school subjects exist today.

A beginning, but growing influence from the United Kingdom may be discerned in studies by Gundem (1989) on the development of English as a school subject, as well as in the studies by Engelsen (1988) on the development of the literature component in the teaching of Norwegian. Another example of a Scandinavian study drawing on the theoretical framework developed by Goodson is the work of Karseth (1994) on the development of new university subjects/courses of study at the University of Oslo. Following Goodson, these studies, to a certain extent, elucidate a symbolic drift of school knowledge toward the academic tradition. They also raise central and basic questions about societal, sociological, and philosophical explanations of the evolution of school subjects.

CURRICULUM RESEARCH BASED ON CURRICULUM THEORY AND THEORY OF CURRICULUM HISTORY

Following the curriculum history research done in the United Kingdom, the Swedish reproduction and curriculum code research, and the research done on school subjects at the German Institute for Science Education (IPN), we may talk about the generation of a fund of theory directly related to curriculum history as a scientific and academic discipline. To give an example, Haft and Hopmann (1990a) summarized determining factors to be taken into consideration when trying to historically understand the introduction of new school subjects:

(1) The scientific, cultural, and perhaps economic limits and merits of a school subject.

(2) The definition and transformation of those features into curricular concepts by experts, teachers, associations, and interest groups.

(3) The pattern and stability of the overall framework, as well as of the different interests inside and outside schools that are associated with their particular operational characteristics.

(4) The reactions and interventions of parents, teachers, and students, on the one hand, and of the society's or the economy's various purchasers of knowledge on the other.

(5) The political, administrative, and educational resources available for the new subject's implementation. (p. 3)

Nevertheless, we have to take into account the influence of curriculum theory. The fact that the history of the curriculum as a field of research and studies is also an artifact of the rapid expansion of the field of curriculum studies and curriculum development must be taken into account when highlighting curriculum research efforts, especially over the last decade. The theory of curriculum history and curriculum theory are intertwined to a high degree in Scandinavian research on school subjects and curriculum. This was already visible in the studies by Gundem and Engelsen, which have been cited, where, for example, the theoretical frameworks of Goodlad et al. (1979) or Schwab (1978, 1983) are used as analytical tools. In addition, Reid's (1991, 1994, 1999) contribution, focusing on curriculum as institution and practice, has been a significant source of ideas for approaching curriculum research. Reid's elaboration of Schwab's conception of curriculum, and his further development of the deliberative tradition of curriculum theorizing, should also be mentioned. When, as is the case today, studies try to relate specific questions of curriculum reform to a wider societal, cultural, and educational frame of reference, curriculum theory, and especially curriculum theory linked to the social and political sciences, assumes particular importance. Therefore, the mingling of sociological and curriculum theory is a marked characteristic of recent Scandinavian studies on curriculum history and development.

An example of this trend was the research project "Curriculum and School Subjects" (1989–1992). This was an umbrella project embracing many different studies (Gundem & Karseth, 1993). The overall aim was to illuminate the phenomena of curriculum and school subjects in their broadest sense to acquire insight into the shaping of the content of schooling and education as a whole. This project became important for network building, recruitment, and international cooperation. An international conference found place within the setting of the research project in 1990: Curriculum Work and Curriculum Content; Theory and Practice; Contemporary and Historical Perspective (Gundem, Engelsen, & Karseth, 1991). At this conference, researchers from the United States and Germany met and decided on the international dialogue project Didaktik and/or Curriculum.

CONCLUDING REMARKS

Taking into consideration a variety of studies in curriculum research in Norway, it is possible to discern a line of development in terms of the relationship of research interest to research object. There is a development from an interest in why, and especially how, a school subject was introduced, in terms of general educational history, to an interest in elucidating the role and content of a school subject in terms of macrosocietal perspectives. This development implies use of an all-embracing theoretical perspective, which can illuminate a variety of determining factors. This line of development also indicates a move in interest from the structure of the school subject to its place and role as part of the overall school system, and, during the last decade, to some level of concern with the evolution of educational policy within a historical perspective. However, where the content of subjects is concerned, it seems that the main interest continues to be focused on textbooks and methods, whereas studies of the ultimate sources of this content have assumed a lesser role. The question of content understood as a selection of knowledge to be taught in school may be said to have been neglected. There are signs, however, that a renewed interest in the content of schooling, linked to projects of curriculum reform and coupled with an awareness of the primacy of the subject matter of schooling stimulated by the production of the Norwegian Core Curriculum for Primary, Upper Secondary and Adult Education (Gundem & Karseth, 1998; Royal Ministry of Education, 1994), will be translated into research efforts aimed at understanding the basic substance of subject matter.

Keeping in mind the different traditions in curriculum research outlined earlier, it makes sense to say that, in certain ways, the umbrella project "Curriculum and School Subjects" incorporated all of them (Gundem & Karseth, 1993). Possibly more important, however, is the impetus it gave to the establishment of curriculum research as a legitimate field of academic investigation in its own right, and not simply as a branch of educational research in general. The undertaking of curriculum research by doctoral students in, for instance, the Arts and Theology represents a widening of the scope of curriculum research that is of great significance for the future of the field (Kjosavik, 1998; Skrunes, 1995).

TRENDS AND CHALLENGES

In this part of the chapter, we aim to give an overview and discussion of theory and research in curriculum studies during the late 1990s toward the new century.

Currently, there seems to be a strong desire to examine the curriculum field from the point of view of both empirical and theoretical interests, embracing a wide range of contexts and theoretical and methodological perspectives. Indeed, one specific study may encompass several theoretical and methodological viewpoints and deal with more than one context. This may be understood in terms of an awareness of the complexities of curriculum issues in postmodern society (Doll, 1993; Pinar et al., 1995). A further marked characteristic of contemporary work is a tendency to view curriculum issues as embedded in complex philosophical, sociological, and cultural problems. This may cause difficulties when we attempt to classify specific curriculum studies. Therefore, a clear-cut description seems not possible or desirable. Instead, our focus is on compelling issues, leaving ample room for describing underlying theoretical and methodological frames of reference.

In the late 1990s, new research projects were initiated to continue the research traditions described in the first part of this chapter, and also to further develop theoretical and empirical understandings in the field of curriculum. Additionally, considerable research and systematic inquiry was going on in various Norwegian research milieus, which are empirically oriented toward the curriculum field, but which use theories other than curriculum theories as the starting point of their investigations. Our main concern is studies related to curriculum reform, which inquire into curriculum processes, the evaluation of curriculum reform, and the governance policies inherent in reform decisions. There is also in Norway an increasing interest in investigating the various facets of the curriculum of school subjects. Current trends in this type of research are also discussed. Empirical studies that focus on the practice of curriculum in the classroom are also playing a prominent role and, in the process, challenging the traditional emphasis on curriculum theory by highlighting the concept of classroom culture. Linked to classroom research is also the question of the relation between curriculum and learning and between curriculum and culture. In our overview, we also include research related to these issues.

RESEARCH ON CURRICULUM REFORM

As indicated in the introduction, the 1990s in Norway saw an upsurge of curriculum reform proposals and implementations beyond anything previously experienced. It is possible to describe the overall intention of the educational innovations that have been put in place as *systemic*; indeed, they represent a curriculum- driven attempt at major systemic reform, although what is meant by systemic reform may differ from country to country (e.g., teacher initiated, standards driven, or curriculum driven; Gundem, 1996b).

In a Norwegian setting, it makes sense to characterize systemic reform as a reform that is:

(1) Part of a wider reform of the educational and social system.

(2) Part of a comprehensive reform aimed at all levels of education.

(3) Reform positing coherence among school types within the school system.

(4) Reform striving for goal coherence, that is, based upon national overarching goals, which are translated into goals for all school subjects, and into curriculum programs at all levels.

(5) Reform which is implemented through the incorporation into planning strategies of all relevant factors and constraints, including teacher education and assessment. (Gundem, 1996b, pp. 56–61)

RESEARCH ON THE PROCESS OF CURRICULUM MAKING

Naturally, the fields of educational research and curriculum studies have focused on curriculum reform as a much preferred object of research and source of material for theory construction. One study, which makes an issue of the process of curriculum making as well as implementation and enactment, is the international research project "From Curriculum Development to Syllabus Planning." Norwegian researchers and students have taken part in this international cooperative study to compare Norwegian curriculum with similar processes in other countries. Findings from Germany and Switzerland have recently been published in articles and reports (Bähr, Fries, Ghisla, 1999; Künzli, 1998; Künzli, Bähr, Fries, 1999), and forthcoming articles will integrate further results from Norway, Finland, and the United States to complete the five-country study, which was initiated to develop both theoretical and practical understandings of curriculum processes.

A theoretic approach, based on earlier research in Germany, has already been suggested by this project. It addresses the administration of curriculum as a discourse connected to, but different from political activity, on the one hand, and pedagogical practice, on the other hand. This theoretical viewpoint is founded on existing curriculum history theory based on historical research on curriculum administration, and also on recent research on curriculum making in the German Federal Republic from 1970 to 1985 (Haft & Hopmann, 1989, 1990b; Hopmann, 1988, 1999). The focus of this research is on the rise of curriculum administration and the development of curriculum guidelines at a state level. A central topic within this research has been the ordering and selection of curriculum content as it is institutionalized as a result of the historical evolution of curriculum administration, resulting in restraint on future possibilities for development and implementation. A Norwegian example is Gundem's (1993) study on changing conceptions of curriculum administration in Norway.

In the ongoing project, however, the focus is not primarily on the historical construction of the multiple realities of the context and practice of curriculum, but on contemporary perspectives and cross-national comparison. These are the means by which the researchers are trying to analyze how reform processes are structured with reference to boundaries and processes of differentiation. From such a point of view, one may state that the curriculum serves several functions: a political function, legitimating the content of schooling; a programmatic function, producing appropriate content through curriculum guidelines; and a practical function, framing and supporting the planning of teaching and learning in classrooms. The levels of reform are correlated by virtue of the fact that they serve these different functions. If one level makes selections that disturb other levels, these react by creating constraints. Different programmatic institutions serve as linkages between the levels and mediate the topics that make up the curriculum and are eventually reconstructed from a practical point of view at the classroom level. *From Curriculum Development to Syllabus Planning* aims to investigate all three levels of decision making using empirical data collected through questionnaire surveys of curriculum designers and teachers, and through interviews and analysis of official documents. The present phase of the project may be described as one in which the concern is to develop new understandings about the relationships among politics, public administration, and agents representing various levels of praxis in different parts of the educational system (Sivesind, 1999; Sivesind & Gundem, 2000).

THE EVALUATION OF CURRICULUM REFORM

The educational reforms of the 1990s have all been followed up with evaluations. In 1994, the Ministry of Education, Research and Church Affairs asked the Research Council of Norway to organize an evaluation of the reform of the college sector. Three research institutions took part in the evaluation, which was finished in April 1999 (Kyvik, 1999). The main focus was on changes in the management and policymaking structures, but the survey also included questions about teaching (Karseth & Kyvik, 1999). However, research on higher education in Norway thus far has seldom used approaches focusing on curriculum and curriculum theory.

To evaluate the reform of upper secondary education, the Ministry of Education initiated a large project involving seven evaluation teams working closely under its supervision (Blichfeldt, 1996; KUF, 1999; Kvalsund, Deichman-Sørensen, & Aamodt, 1999). This evaluation was finished in spring of 1999. One topic was to analyze the effect of curriculum changes. In performing this analysis, Monsen (1998) used Goodlad's concept of *curriculum worlds* to stress the difference between curriculum as a written document and the curriculum conceived and used by teachers. One of his conclusions is that most teachers have an interpretation of the curriculum that corresponds with the political intention behind reform, but nevertheless argue that they have reasons for not implementing it. One explanation of this is a contradiction between aims in the establishment of new curricula.

Basing itself on the plans and intentions adopted for Reform 97 (Royal Ministry of Education, 1999), the Ministry stipulated an assessment exercise and then commissioned the Research Council of Norway to conduct it. In the fall of 1998, the Research Council invited research bodies to submit proposals for how they would design and implement this assessment. The main question that it addresses is the extent to which Reform 97 is being implemented in accordance with its objectives and intentions. The assessment program consists of three broad and comprehensive topics:

1. Curriculum, subjects, and practical educational activities.
2. Cooperation, supervision, child development, the learning environment and learning results.
3. The comprehensive school, equality, and cultural diversity. (Program Plan, 1999)

Curricular questions are central to the evaluation. However, it is too early to present results from the studies.

There are some important similarities among the three evaluation projects mentioned. They were all initiated by the Ministry, and the various evaluations have or will gather vast amounts of empirical data, both qualitative and quantitative. Yet there are also important differences between them. Although the evaluation of the upper secondary education reform was commissioned directly by the Ministry, the evaluations of the college sector and primary and lower secondary education were commissioned through the Research Council. We should also point out that, although most of the researchers so far taking part in the evaluation of primary and lower secondary education are scholars from the field of education, the research team that carried out the evaluation of upper secondary education consists of scholars from other disciplines.

An important challenge in doing evaluation research is to balance the emphasis between research questions raised by the political authorities and research questions posed by the researchers (Haug, 1998). In the field of curriculum research, this means that the community of researchers must create space to work in a way that is relatively autonomous in relation to political discourse. Although there are good reasons for being skeptical about the worth of evaluation research, it also brings one important advantage: the opportunity to gather large quantities of empirical data, which it is difficult to do without the support of outside resources. In the field of curriculum, the availability of these evaluation projects may lead to an increased interest in doing empirical research.

THE GOVERNANCE OF CURRICULUM REFORM

The governance of curriculum reform in Norway, as in other nations of the Western world, has seen a new operational style where management by overall objectives has been put in place. Management by objectives has become a key concept in the vocabulary of politicians and bureaucrats. The idea is that specific rules should be replaced by major political goals that set standards for the public sector while avoiding restrictions on professionals to organize their work. Moreover, system evaluation is regarded as a way of securing quality, efficiency, and implementation of political decisions. Although this change of approach was announced for the educational sector early in the 1980s, and strongly emphasized when the new curriculum reform was initiated in 1991 (Report No. 37 to the Storting, 1990–1991), it is still questionable whether this strategy has been reflected in actual changes in policymaking and in the work of schools.

To understand the wish for change and the problem of constructing a curriculum reform on the basis of management by objectives, sociological analyses are required. One such research project points to the different semantics used when reform proposals are communicated (Afsar, 1999). The principles of management by objectives correspond with a political discourse, which for a long time has legitimated an official school system for all children. Consequently, there arises a need for state-initiated reforms that highlight goals endorsing professional work and are capable of setting standards that can be systematically evaluated.

The Norwegian curriculum reform in the 1990s identified some main goals for the primary and lower secondary school, but differed from the Swedish curriculum in that it is promulgated as a set of regulations that focus mainly on content and principles of organization. Moreover, system-wide evaluation and correspondence with the ways in which schools and teachers evaluate their work is not given extensive attention. Therefore, the research project explores the difference between the original decision of a goal-oriented curriculum and the way this decision is eventually implemented. Two kinds of points are made and discussed with reference to systems theory. First of all, systems evaluation implies the possibility of corrections to the political activity—a perspective that can be seen as a disturbing element in the ongoing debate on a political level. Second, those who write the curriculum and those who eventually use it take part in another discourse that concerns the subjects of schooling and how these are presented to the individual student. From this point of view, evaluations have a quite different purpose than that of evaluation of the system. Consequently, subjects and their specification into a school subject are regarded as the most relevant part of the curriculum, and a systematic evaluation referring to political goals is eventually rejected politically as well as in terms of educational practice.

THE CURRICULUM OF THE SCHOOL SUBJECTS

Recent decades have seen in Scandinavia and Continental Europe a growing interest in what is called the *didactics of the school subject*—that is, in everything related to the history, legitimization, content, teaching, and learning of the subjects of the curriculum. This has been reflected in the establishment of chairs or professorships in school subject didactics in universities as part of teacher education in several disciplines (Gundem, 1992). This naturally stimulated and generated research that, in Norway, has been directed to subjects within the areas of mother tongue, science, and mathematics. An important research topic in the field of mother tongue education is the art of writing or proficiency in writing. The Norwegian research community has moved toward a theory of process-oriented writing that has been influenced by American models, but it also has important traditions of its own linked to an emphasis on the individuality and creative imagination of students as an active and positive force in written language development (Dysthe, 1987).

In the field of research on science and mathematics education, there has been an important epistemological shift toward a constructivist perspective, which views knowledge as being actively built up by the individual (Ringnes, 1993). Some research projects in science, both in Norway and Sweden, may be compared to French investigations into school subjects, where the underlying theoretical framework is linked to notions of the epistemological obstacle and the epistemological rupture (Bachelard, 1932). However, it still holds true that the mainstream of research in science education has concerned itself with questions of instruction methods, the development of instructional techniques, and evaluation. For instance, research in mathematics has been linked to the International School Effectiveness Research Project (ISERP). The underlying values perspectives of this research have, however, been severely questioned (Grøtterud & Nilsen 1998). It should also be noted that, since 1991, Norway has participated in the Third International Mathematics and Science Study (TIMMS) and is also taking part in the Program on Student Assessment Project (PISA).

An interesting recent development is that empirical research on school subjects is being linked to curriculum reforms and international comparative studies (Engvik, 2000; Hauge, 1999; Stenmo, 1999). That means making adaptations to rather complex theoretical and conceptual frameworks, as well as evolving new methodological approaches (Hopmann & Künzli, 1995). This constitutes a challenge for a research field that traditionally has been atheoretical.

There is also an increased interest in research on school subjects related to the classroom as a community with its own culture and values. This interest generates challenges to researchers from general didactics and from school subject didactics, which may result in the setting up of collaborative projects. The linking of interests in school subjects to interests in vocational education and curricular questions concerning the management of life-long learning also presents challenging opportunities for cooperative work.

CURRICULUM IN THE CLASSROOM

In the field of classroom research today, many researchers make use of an ethnographic framework (Fuglestad, 1993; Gudmundsdottir, 1992; Klette, 1998). A team of researchers, under the leadership of Annlaug Flem and Sigrun Gudmundsdottir at the Department of Education at the Norwegian University of Science and Technology in Trondheim, has established a tradition of educational research that employs microethnographic approaches to the study of teaching and learning processes in classrooms. The team has focused on the local meanings and documentation of classroom practice in all its diversity, in elementary as well as secondary schools. They have studied a variety of issues: pedagogical content knowledge among history teachers, inclusion of children with special needs in ordinary classroom activities, and the structure of teaching and learning processes (Gudmundsdottir, Reinertsen, & Nordtømme, 2000; Postholm, Wold-Granum, & Gudmundsdottir, 1999). Classroom research has also formed an important part of research efforts at the University of Oslo Faculty of Education, where there is an increasing interest in research into school subjects (Jorde, 1998; Klette, 1997).

CURRICULUM AND LEARNING: THE INFLUENCE OF INFORMATION AND COMMUNICATION TECHNOLOGY (ICT)

There is a trend in the field of educational research, and especially in classroom research, to put a stronger emphasis on studies of learning. This reflects tendencies in educational policymaking and is particularly noticeable in new education areas such as technology. This is an important move and represents a reaction against the strong effort at the beginning of the 1990s to define a canon of school knowledge. Young (1998) wrote that,

> The idea of the active learner who takes responsibility for her/his own learning is an attractive one and is a recognition of something which traditional content-dominated models of education have all too easily forgotten. However, in practice, there are some fundamental problems with the concept of learner centeredness, which are magnified in a political context in which the government distrusts the expertise of teachers as a professional group. (p. 86)

However, we must acknowledge that curriculum research in Norway in the 1980s and early 1990s almost entirely neglected the learning perspective. This is a criticism that we must take seriously into account. In contrast, within the field of educational research, generally, there is an increased interest in studies of learning activities and information and communication technology (Arnseth et al., 1999). The related issues of cognition, collaboration, and different kinds of ICT tools are having a marked impact on curriculum research.

CURRICULUM AND CULTURE

The School as a Cultural Institution (*Skole*-KULT), a research program funded by the Norwegian Research Council, has initiated research projects in many fields representing different aspects of culture. The projects that have examined the field of education have shared a common interest in the classical concept of *Bildung*, or formation of the human personality with an emphasis on compassion and solidarity, although extending it beyond its original 18th-century identification with higher culture and the bourgeoisie. Today's challenges are of a different order, characterized by a virtual separation between spheres of life that are at the root of contemporary cultural conflicts. These philosophical ideas and conceptualizations concerning differences between history and actuality have proved to be fruitful, not only as a substantive topic for research, but also to construe new perspectives on the conduct of historical research directed to the study of educational and curricular questions (Løvlie, 1997). Writing about the past is not dependent on a unique method that claims to be capable of uncovering and objectifying the reality of the past, but is a part of an educative discourse. Eventually, historical research turns out to be educative practice (Evenshaug, 2000). Similar perspectives on methods of research are promoted in historical research on the public debate about religious and moral education in the compulsory school.

In connection with the Norwegian curriculum reforms of the 1990s, a new common school subject for all students, Christian Knowledge and Religious and Ethical Education (Royal Ministry of Education, 1999), was introduced, replacing the former choice between Christian education and general religious and moral orientation. In this debate, one can analyze school, nation, and religion as discursive and historical constructs, which contribute to conceptualizations of collective identity and otherness in society ("we" and the "others"; Jørstad, 2000c). Demonstration of the historicity and contingency of such constructs opens up new arenas for discussion of *Bildung* and democratic participation (Jørstad, 2000b). As historical constructs, culture, identity, and society can be discussed and modified (Jørstad, 2000a).

Another Norwegian Project, not linked to the program we have been discussing, but also centered on issues of culture conflict, analyzes reform work from the perspectives of bilingual or bicultural minorities (Özerk, 1999). Its findings are based not only on experiences resulting from work with the new curriculum reform, but also refer to many studies of minorities, their functional capacities, and their roles in teaching and schooling. Are principles and problems concerning the experience of these groups of students taken into consideration in the design of the curriculum? This research is also conducted with reference to the past, sketching out the traditions and ways of understanding that have been applied to problems of this kind, which, although of contemporary concern, are certainly not novel. In doing so, it puts important questions on the agenda, not only affecting national policymaking and substantial areas of curriculum decision making, but also challenging the research field. Are problems of internationalization and globalization taken into consideration when curricula are made, and are politics as well as educational practice seen as a postmodern endeavor, sketching out new borders and boundaries? In such a perspective, culture may be seen as something different when compared with traditional ideas of cultural and national identity. Moreover, do curriculum researchers highlight these questions? These reflections are thought provoking and exciting, and serve as a challenge to our research efforts.

FINAL REMARKS

In the first part of this chapter, the aim was to give a portrayal of the traditions of curriculum research in Norway. In the second part, the focus has been on trends and challenges.

The field of curriculum clearly faces a challenge to produce comparative studies. For Norwegian curriculum studies, this challenge is complicated by a marked desire to find its own identity and, at the same time, see its role as subsumed within internationalization and the global society. A pertinent question to ask is whether Norwegian research on curriculum should, in defining its tradition, take as its starting point the imperatives of the national context and policies. As our overview shows, curriculum studies have, in a high degree, been open to international influences. This gives rise to both advantages and drawbacks.

We have noted a tendency toward empirical orientations. This may, to a certain degree, be due to the fact that curriculum studies are drawn toward evaluations that aim at producing directly useful data. This poses a challenge because, from a research point of view, one may question and discuss all manners of preconceptions underlying such research projects. This has led to an interest in the use of theories that yield descriptions of processes that depict them as not being the result of intentional, normative choices. In this connection, we also have to take into account approaches stemming from postmodern research orientations (Doll, 1993; Pinar et al., 1995). However, empirical research in Norway has not neglected underlying normative preconceptions. Here research has inherited a normative cast stemming from the *Didaktik* tradition (Gundem, 2000; Gundem & Hopmann, 1998a; Westbury, Hopmann, & Riquarts, 2000). This implies taking as a starting point particular rationales for understanding and interpreting curriculum guidelines. Yet empirical curriculum research has also aimed at illuminating the underlying decisions, choices, and values that shape curriculum work and curriculum development. Such an approach provides opportunities for further discussion of the preconceptions on which understanding of *Bildung* is based. This is an ongoing debate in Norway.

In summary, there seems to be in Norway a basis for curriculum studies to become aware of its theoretical and methodological starting points. However, embedded in recent trends of curriculum research, there are certain challenges and tensions. In an international context, some are related to the concept of curriculum. The Scandinavian and Continental European conception, which is linked to the idea of *Didaktik,* differs from Anglo-Saxon understandings (Gundem & Hopmann, 1998b).

This presents a concrete challenge, especially in international research projects and when national research is being mediated internationally. Another challenge is the relationship between macro- and microresearch approaches. Related to the tension between macro- and microapproaches is the relationship between theory and practice. It involves the understanding of theory by practitioners, as well as the use of theory in curriculum research and understanding. It also relates to the practical nature of curriculum problems and the role of theory in understanding them. Moreover, it challenges the conception that the aim of curriculum research must be either the development of theory or the solving of practical problems.

ACKNOWLEDGMENT

We are grateful to Dr. William A. Reid for his valuable comments and help with the language in preparing this manuscript.

REFERENCES

Afsar, A. (1999). Styringsproblem i det moderne samfunnet. Paper framlagt på konferanses. *Does History Matter: Stability and Change in Education, 7–9, October, NTNU: Trondheim.*

Andersson, H. (1979). Kampen om det för flutna. Studier i historieundervisningens målfrågor i Finland 1843–1917. *Studies Acta Academia Åboensis. Series A. Humaniora, 57*(1).

Arnseth, H. C., Ludvigsen, S., Wasson, B., & Mörk, A. (1999). *Collaboration and problem solving in distributed collaborative learning.* In Dillenborg, P. A. Euselings, & K. Hakkarainou, *Proceedings Euro GSGH. European perspectives on computer-suppored collaborative learning.* Maastricht: Maastricht University, pp. 75–82.

Bachelard, G. (1932). *La formation de l'esprit scientifique.* Paris: Librairie Scientifique J. Vrin.

Berner, B., Callewaert, S., & Silberbrandt, H. (Eds.). (1977). Skole, ideologi og samfund. Et kommentert udvalg av franske uddannelsessociologiske tekster: Bourdieu/Passeron, Baudelot/Establet, Poulantzas. København: Munksgaard.

Bernstein, B., & Lundgren, U. P. (1983). *Makt, kontroll och pedagogik. Studier av den kulturelle reproduktion.* Lund: Liber.

Bjørndal, B. (1969). *En studie i nyere amerikansk lareplantenkning.* Oslo: Universitetsforlaget.

Bjørndal, B. (1980). Om vekselvirkningen mellom didaktisk teori og undervisning: synspunkter, ideer og erfaringer med bakgrunn I Miljørlareprosjektet. Rapport fra miljørlareprosjektet; nr 24, Universitetet i Oslo, Pedagogisk forskningsinstitutt.

Bjørndal, B., & Lieberg, S. (1972). Miljørlareprosjektet et svar på naturvitenskapens og den økolcgiske tenknings utfordring til pedagogikken? Rapport fra miljørlareprosjektet; nr 7, Universitetet i Oslo, Pedagogisk forskningsinstitutt.

Bjørndal, B., & Lieberg, S. (1975). Innføring i økopedagogikk. Oslo: Aschehoug.

Bjørndal, B., & Lieberg, S. (1978). Nye veier i didaktikken? Oslo: H. Aschehoug and Co.

Bjørnsrud, H. (1995). Lareplanutvikling og larersamarbeid. Oslo: Universitetsforlaget.

Blichfeldt, J. F. (Ed.). (1996). Utdanning for alle?: Evaluering av Reform 94. Oslo: Tano Aschehoug.

Bähr, K., Fries, A.-V., Ghisla, G. (1999). Curriculum-Making: Structures, Expectations, Perspectives. Implemeitation Report. National Research Programe 33, Effectiveness of Our Education Systems.

Bourdieu, P., & Passeron, J.-C. (1970). La reproducion. Élements pour une thèorie du systëme d'enseignement. Paris: Les Editions de Minuit.

Dale, E. L. (1972). Pedagogikk og samfunnsforandring. Oslo: Gyldendal.

Dokka, H. (1988). En skole gjennom 250 år: den norske allmueskole, folkeskole, grunnskole 1739-1989. Oslo: NKS-Forlaget.

Doll, W. E., Jr. (1993). A post-modern perspective on curriculum. New York: Teachers College Press.

Dysthe, D. (1987). Ord på nye spor. Innføring i prosessorientert skrivepedagogikk. Oslo: Det Norske Samlaget.

Engelsen, B. U. (1988). Litteraturdidaktiske strømninger i en planrevisjonstid. Del I–III. Doktorgradsavhandling, Universitetet i Oslo, Pedagogisk forskningsinstitutt.

Englund, T. (1990). Curriculum history reconsidered. Scandinavian Journal of Educational Research, 34(2), 91–102.

Engvik, G. (2000). Lareplanarbeid i studieretning for idrettsfag—en solskinnshistorie i Reform 94? Trondheim: Norges Teknisk-Naturfaglige Universitet, Pedagogisk Institutt.

Evenshaug, T. (2000). Lese og skrive pedagogisk historie. Paper til den 9. fagkonferansen i pedagogikk, 29.11—1. 12 på det Utdanningsvitenskapelige fakultet, Universitetet i Oslo.

Franklin, B. M. (1986). Building the American community: The school curriculum and the search for social control. London: Falmer.

Fuglestad, O. L. (1993). Samspel og motspel. Kultur, kommunikasjon og relasjonar i skulen. Oslo: Samlaget.

Gjone, G. (1985). Moderne matematikk i skolen. Internasjonale reformbestrebelser og nasjonalt lareplanarbeid Oslo: Universitetsforlaget.

Goodlad, J. I., et al. (1979). Curriculum inquiry. The study of curriculum practice. New York: McGraw-Hill.

Goodson, I. F. (1983). School subjects and curriculum change. London: Croom Helm.

Goodson, I. F. (Ed.). (1988). The making of curriculum (Collected Essays). London: Falmer.

Grøtterud, M., & Nilsen, B. S. (1998). Effektive skoler—effektiv undervisning? Et spørmål om verdier. Oslo: AdNctam.

Gudmundsdottir, S. (1992). Den kvalitative forskningsprosessen. Norsk Pedagogisk Tidsskrift, 5, 266–276.

Gudmundsdottir, S., Reinertsen, A., & Nordtømme, N. P. (2000). Klafki's didaktik analysis as a conceptual framework for research on teaching. In I. Westbury, S. Hopmann, & K. Riquarts (Eds.). Teachiag as a reflective practice (pp. 319–334). Mahwah, NJ: Lawrence Erlbaum Associates.

Gundem, B. B. (1980). Tradition—critique—synthesis: Trends in German didactic theory with reference to Nordic curricular issues (Report no. 7, in Norwegian). Institute for Educational Research, University of Oslo.

Gundem, B. B. (1989). Engelskfaget i folkeskolen. Påvirkning og gjennomslag 1870–1970. Oslo: Universitetsforlaget.

Gundem, B. B. (1992). Notes on the development of nordic didactics. Journal of Curriculum Studies, 24(1), 51–70.

Gundem, B. B. (1993). Rise, development and changing conceptions of curriculum administration and curriculum guidelines in Norway: The national-local dilemma. Journal of Curriculum Studies, 25(3), 251–266.

Gundem, B. B. (1995). The role of didactics in curriculum in Scandinavia. Journal of Curriculum and Supervision, 10(4), 302–316.

Gundem, B. B. (1996a). School subjects history as part of an emerging curriculum history research tradition in Scandinavia. In L. B. Burlbaw (Ed.), Curriculum history. Society of Curriculum history (pp. 45–52). College Station: Texas A&M University.

Gundem, B. B. (1996b). Core curriculum—cultural heritage—literacy: Recent perspectives and trends in Norwegian education. In E. Marum (Ed.), *Children and books in the modern world: An international perspective on literacy* (pp. 55–71). London: Falmer.

Gundem, B. B. (2000). Understanding European didactics. In B. Moon, M. Ben-Peretz, & S. Brown (Eds.), *Routledge international companion to education* (pp. 235–262). London: Routledge.

Gundem, B. B., Engelsen, B. U., & Karseth, S. (Eds.). (1991). *Curriculum work and curriculum content. Theory and practice. Contemporary and historical perspectives* (Report no. 5). Institute for Educational Research, University of Oslo.

Gundem, B. B., & Hopmann, S. (Eds.). (1998a). *Didaktik and/or curriculum: An international dialogue.* New York: Lang.

Gundem, B. B., & Hopmann, S. (1998b). Didaktik meets curriculum. In B. B. Gundem & S. Hopmann (Eds.), *Didaktik and/or curriculum* (pp. 1–8). New York: Lang.

Gundem, B. B., & Karseth, B. (1993). *Curriculum and school subjects.* Report summary (Report no. 6). Institute for Educational Research, University of Oslo.

Gundem, B. B., & Karseth, B. (1998). *Norwegian national identity in recent curriculum documents.* Annual meeting of the American Educational Research Association, AERA, San Diego, Symposium Division B: Curriculum and National Identity: A Cross-Cultural Exploration.

Haft, H., & Hopmann, S. (1989). State-run curriculum development in the Federal Republic of Germany. *Journal of Curriculum Studies, 21*(2), 185–190.

Haft, H., & Hopmann, S. (1990a). Comparative curriculum administration history: Concepts and methods. In H. Haft & S. Hopmann (Eds.), *Case studies in curriculum administration history* (pp. 1–10). New York: Falmer.

Haft, H., & Hopmann, S. (Eds.). (1990b). *Case studies in curriculum administration history.* London: Falmer.

Handal, G., & Lauvås, P. (1983). *Påegne vilkår. En strategi for veiledning med larere.* Oslo: J. W. Cappelens.

Harbo, T. (1969). *Teori og praksis i den pedagogiske utdannelse. Studier i norsk pedagogikk 1818–1922.* Oslo: Universitetsforlaget.

Haug, P. (1998). Linking evaluation and reform strategies. *New Directions for Evaluation, 77,* 5–20.

Hauge, H. M. (1999). *Ei "inspirasjonskjelde" eller ei "tvangstrøye"—Ei undersøking av lararen sin bruk av L97.* Hovedoppgave: Pedagogisk institutt, Norges Teknisk–Naturvitenskapelige Universitet Trondheim.

Hertzberg, F. (1995). *Norsk grammatikkdebatt i historisk lys.* Oslo: Novus Forlag.

Hiim, H., & Hippe, E. (1989). *Undervisningsplanlegging for yrkeslærere.* Oslo: Universitetsforlaget.

Hoëm, A. (1978). *Sosialisering: en teoretisk og empirisk modellutvikling.* Oslo: Universitetsforlaget.

Hopmann, S. (1988). *Lehrplanarbeit als Verwaltungshandeln.* Kiel: IPN.

Hopmann, S. (1999). The curriculum as a standard of public education. In *Studies in philosophy and education* (pp. 89–105). The Netherlands: Kluwer Academic Publishers.

Hopmann, S., & Künzli, R. (1995, November). *Spielräme der Lehrplanarbeit: Grundzüge einer Theorie der Lehrplanung. Lern- und Lehr- Forschung. LLF—Berichte Nr. 11.* Interdisziplinøres Zentrum fur Lern—und Lehrforschung, Universität Potsdam.

Jarning, H. (1998). *Sociological imagination and didactical theorizing.* Unpublished paper, Institute for Educational Research, University of Oslo.

Jorde, D. (1998). Klasseromsforskning og naturfagundervisning. In K. Klette (Ed.), *Klasseromsforskning - på norsk* (pp. 135–153). Oslo: Ad Notam Gyldendal.

Jørstad, G. (2000a). *Historiens danningsoppdrag. "Tid - Rom - Tanke - Pedagogikk i nye sammenhenger."* Paper framlagt på NFPFs konferanse i Kristiansand 9–12 mars.

Jørstad, G. (2000b). *History and Bildung. The political and pedagogical relevance of history within a changing scientific discourse.* Unpublished paper, Institute for Educational Research, University of Oslo.

Jørstad, G. (2000c). *"VI" og "DE ANDRE." Identitetsbegrepers framtreden i norsk skoledebatt - som objektivt gitte eller historisk-diskursivt konstruerte. En diskusjon av relevansen av et historisk-diskursivt perspektiv på politisk debatt.* Paper til den 9. nasjonale fagkonferansen i pedagogikk: Kunnskap - verdier - kvalitet, Utdanningsvitenskapelige fakultet, Universitetet i Oslo.

Karseth, B. (1994). *Fagutvikling i høyere utdanning. Mellom kunnskapstradisjoner og kunnskapspolitikk. Dr.polit.-avhandling.* Universitetet i Oslo, Det samfunnsvitenskapelige fakultet. Pedagogisk forskningsinstitutt.

Karseth, B., & Kyvik, S. (1999). *Evaluering av høgskolereformen. Undervisningsvirksomheten ved de statlige høgskolene.* Delrapport nr. 1. Området for kultur og samfunn, Norges forskningsråd.

Kjosavik, S. (1998). *Fra ferdighetsfag til forming: utviklingen fra tegning, sløyd og håndarbeid til forming sett i et læreplanhistorisk perspektiv.* Avhandling (dr. polit.), Universitetet i Oslo.

Klette, K. (1997). Teacher individuality, teacher collaboration and repertoire-building: Some principal dilemmas. *Teachers and Teaching: Theory and Practice, 3*(2), 243–256.

Klette, K. (Ed.). (1998). *Klasseromsforskning på norsk*. Oslo: Ad notam Gyldendal.

Kliebard, H. M. (1986). *The struggle for the American curriculum 1893–1958*. London: Routlegde & Kegan Paul.

KUF. (1999). *Evaluering av reform 94: Sammendrag fra sluttrapportene*. Oslo: Kirke-, utdannings- og forskningsdepartementet.

Künzli, R. (1998). The common frame and the places of Didaktik. In B. B. Gundem & S. Hopmann (Eds.), *Didaktik and/or curriculum* (pp. 29–45). New York: Lang.

Künzli, R., Bähr, K., Fries, A.-V. (1999). *Lehrplanarbeit. über den Nutzen von Lehrplänen für die Schule und ihre Entwicklung, Nationales Forschungsprogramm 33*. Wirksamkeit unserer Bildungssysteme, Zürich. Verlag Rüegger.

Kvalsund, R., Deichman-Sørensen, T., & Aamodt, P. O. (Eds.). (1999). *Videregående opplæring - ved en skilleveg?: forskning fra den nasjonale evalueringen av Reform 94*. Oslo: Tano Aschehoug.

Kyvik, S. (1999). *Evaluering av høgskolereformen. Sluttrapport*. Området for kultur og samfunn, Norges forskningsråd.

Lillemyr, O. F., & Søbstad, F. (1993). *Didaktisk tenkning i barnehagen*. Oslo: Tano.

Lorentzen, S. (1986). *Ungdomsskolens samfunnsfag i historisk og komparativt perspektiv*. Avhandling: Universitetet i Oslo.

Lorentzen, S. (1990). Patriotism as part of citizenship education: A review of norwegian history textbooks throughout the nineteenth and twentieth centuries. *Scandinavian Journal of Educational Research, 34*(2), 103–110.

Lundgren, U. P. (1972). *Frame factors and the teaching process. A contribution to curriculum theory and theory on teaching*. Stockholm: Almqvist og Wiksell.

Lundgren, U. P. (1979). *Att organisera omvärlden. En introduktion till läroplansteori*. Stockholm: Liber.

Løvlie, L. (1997). Utdanningsreformens paradokser. *Norsk pedagogisk tidsskrift, 6*(97), 105–361.

Monsen, L. (Ed.). (1978). *Kunnskapssosiologi og skoleutvikling*. Oslo: Universitetsforlaget.

Monsen, L. (1998). Evaluering av reform 94. Sluttrapport. Innholdsreformen - fra måldokument til klasseromspraksis. *Forskningsrapport, 421*. Høgskolen i Lillehammer.

Özerk, K. Z. (1999). *Opplæringsteori og læreplanforståelse - en lærebok i pedagogikk, Opplandske bokforlag*. (For recent outline and discussion, see Gundem, 1992, 1995, 2000.)

Pinar, W. F., Reynolds, W. M., Slattery, P., & Taubman, P. M. (1995). *Understanding curriculum*. New York: Lang.

Postholm, M. B., Wold-Granum, M., & Gudmundsdottir, S. (1999). *"Dette her er vanskelig altså." En kasusstudie av prosjektarbeid., Skriftserien klasseromsforskning*. Trondheim: Tapir.

Program Plan. (1999). *Evaluating Reform 97*. Division of Culture and Society, The Research Council of Norway.

Reid, W. A. (1991). The Idea of the Practical. In B. B. Gundem, B. U. Engelsen, & B. Karseth (Eds.), *Curriculum work and curriculum content. Theory and practice. Contemporary and historical perspectives* (Report no. 5). Institute for Educational Research, University of Oslo.

Reid, W. (1994). *Curriculum planning as deliberation* (Report no. 11). Institute for Educational Research, University of Oslo.

Reid, W. A. (1999). *Curriculum as institution and practice. Essays in the deliberative tradition*. Mahwah, NJ: Lawrence Erlbaum Associates.

Report No. 37 to the Storting. (1990–1991). *Concerning organization and management in the education sector. Summary*. The Royal Norwegian Ministry of Education, Research and Church Affairs.

Ringnes, V. (1993). *Elevers kjemiforståelse og læringsvansker knyttet til kjemibegrepet*. Dr. scient.- avhandling, Universitetet i Oslo.

Royal Ministry of Education, Research and Church Affairs. (1994). *Core curriculum for primary, secondary and adult education*. Oslo: KUF.

Royal Ministry of Education, Research and Church Affairs. (1999). *The curriculum for the 10-year compulsory school in Norway*. Oslo: KUF.

Schwab, J. J. (1978). The practical: A language for curriculum. The practical: Arts of eclectic. The practical: Translation into curriculum. In I. Westbury & N. J. Wilkof (Eds.), *Science, curriculum, and liberal education: Selected essays of Joseph J. Schwab* (pp. 287–321, 322–364, 365–383). Chicago: The University of Chicago Press.

Schwab, J. J. (1983). The practical 4: Something for curriculum professors to do. *Curriculum Inquiry, 13*(3), 239-265.

Sivesind, K. (1999). *Task and themes in the communication about the curriculum. The Norwegian curriculum reform in perspective*. Paper for the International Symposium: Curriculum-Making Processes and Curriculum Research, University Zurich Irchel, December 2–4.

Sivesind, K., & Gundem, B. B. (2000). Läroplansreformer och lärarprofessionalitet—reflektioner om didaktikens relevans i arbetet med läroplaner. In U. Tebelius & S. Claesson (Eds.), *Skolan i centrum* (pp. 25–42). Lund: Studentlitteratur.

Skrunes, N. (1995). *Kristendomskunnskap for barn: En fagplanhistorisk undersøkelse av kristendomsfagets utvikling 1889–1939.* Norsk Lærerakademi: Bergen.

Solstad, K. J. (1994). *Equity at risk? Schooling and change in Norway.* National Education Office, Nordland County.

Steinfeld, T. (1986). *På skriftens vilkår.* Oslo: Cappelen.

Stenmo, L. M. (1999). *"Med læreplanen i bakhodet" -En undersøkelse om lærernes bruk av L97 i undervisningen.* Hovedoppgave, Pedagogisk institutt, Norges Teknisk-Naturvitenskapelige Universitet Trondheim.

Stensaasen, S. (1958). *Gjennomføringen av engelskundervisningen i Norge. Forskning og danning no. 4.* Oslo: Cappelen forlag.

Telhaug, A. O., & Aasen, P. (Eds.). (1999). *Både- og: 90- tallets utdanningsreformer i historisk perspektiv.* Oslo: Cappelen akademisk forlag.

Westbury, I., Hopmann, S., & Riquarts, K. (Eds.). (2000). *Teaching as a reflective practice. The German didaktik tradition.* Mahwah, NJ: Lawrence Erlbaum Associates.

Young, M. F. D. (Ed.). (1971). *Knowledge and control: New directions for the sociology of education.* London: Collier Macmillan.

Young, M. F. D. (1998). *The curriculum of the future: From the "New Sociology of Education" to a critical theory of learning.* London: Falmer.

CHAPTER 30

Back To Itacka:
Curriculum Studies in Romania

Nicolae Sacalis
National University of Theater and Film
Popular University Ioan I. Dalles, Romania

After the 1990s, an influx of Americanism flooded Romanian language and culture. *Management, curriculum, network, new look, weekend, lifestyle, event,* and *happening* are only a few words that have slipped into Romanian language from the American language. If we add to these words McDonald's, Pizza Hut, Ford cars, and American movies, then we may talk about an American *invasion*. Yet to understand this phenomenon, we should go back a little bit in time.

Although World War II ended in 1945, and Soviet troops occupied the country, many Romanians continued to believe that the Americans would come to save Romanian democracy. Many of them were so deeply convinced that this would happen that they died, some in jail and some outside, hoping that one day, sooner or later, the Americans would show up to rescue Romania. In the despair that followed World War II, this was the only political hope. Although the Americans postponed their coming, more and more, this belief became, in time, a kind of myth and a kind of a fading gleaming light.

I remember being a child, far away, in a remote village from Transylvania, how one day a huge balloon showed up in the sky floating majestically and smoothly like some extraterrestrial object. Soon the whole village was caught in a fever and everybody was whispering: "The Americans are coming!"

The poor militia, the representative of police authority in the village, was running all over the fields and hills trying to catch one of those mysterious balloons. It was a great scene: tragic and comic at the same time.

The average poor Romanian did not hear about the Iron Curtain, about Churchill's speech at Fulton University. So, he or she continued to hope. As late as the 1960s, there were still a few remaining partisans fighting against communism, in some remote area in the Southern Carpathian, always waiting for Americans to come. Nobody was talking about this, but everybody knew. Susman and his sons were some of these last heroes. Only now has something been said about those people who, for more than 15 years, managed to defy one of the best-organized police force: the communist security.

I was privileged to live, as a child, in that area, and I remember that one of our colleagues was a Susman. Her presence in the class was for us, children, a mysterious link with those people who were up in the mountains fighting the communist regime. Any time, when the teacher had to praise the regime and communism, all of us were somehow looking at Cathrina Susman, who incidentally was a beautiful sad girl, hidden in the last bench of the class, a tiny fallen angel. We gathered in our minds around her, trying to protect her against the Big Brother who was threatening her.

So from a very early age, we children learned to live in two worlds: the official world of propaganda, which was cold, artificial, and superimposed as a primitive, Freudian superego; and our hidden world, alive, warm, mysterious, and animated by a collective feeling that we were all up against something. These unseen bonds kept us together and gave us a special feeling, which cannot be put into words. So we pitied the poor teacher who was trying to indoctrinate us, and in the end let him talk. However, deep inside us, we all had our great secret—our *hidden curriculum* as it is called now— and our little angel, Cathrina, whom we had to protect.

Then I realized in a naive way that it is easy to teach knowledge, but more difficult to teach values, and that the soul is different from the mind. Against all the attempts made to rationalize it, the soul has remained a primitive archaic animal that does not obey the law of science and technology.

Maybe this is the reason that Socrates, who tried to teach virtue, did not do it in a class, but in the streets, in the markets, and to the banquettes. It would not have been appropriate. Values are wild flowers that do not grow in a green house. Moreover, they spring up from the most unusual and expected experiences.

That is why the communist education has produced engineers and great scientists, but only a few dedicated and convinced communists and almost no humanists. Almost all the great humanists were on the other side of the barricade.

THE COMMUNIST REFORM OF EDUCATION

After the communists took over power, one of their priorities was the reformation of the education system. After all, the communists did not want to change only the economy and the form of property, but also the people and, more important, their minds.

So in 1948, a radical education reform took place. As a matter of fact, it was not a true reform, but an imposition of soviet education on Romanian schools. As a result of the so-called *reform of education*, the bourgeois school was supposed to be replaced by a new school. The most affected were the humanistic studies at the university, where famous and valuable professors with doctorates taken abroad and long careers were replaced, over night, with illiterate party appointees. The party's imperatives and ideology were above academic standards and scholarship, and people who were reciting party slogans were the ones who got ahead.

The academic earthquake that took place in those days is felt even today. It is responsible for the low intellectual standards of the same chaps who, unfortunately, even today occupy high positions in society. What was worse, the party created special schools for its members, the so-called *workers' universities*, which produced people with diplomas and little education and training. The curriculum was tailored after Soviet models, and many textbooks were simply translation of Soviet textbooks.

The high school, or *lyceum* as it was called, and one of the best schools, which lasted 4 years, was reduced to 2 years and was, as a matter of fact, practically dismantled. *Homo Sovieticus* was looming at the horizon, and we began to learn in school that he was the best and the creator of the most important achievements of mankind; electricity, the radio, the airplane were all invented in Soviet Union.

Homo Sovieticus was a new Prometheus, and his cult was creeping into our innocent minds. The poor teachers were bewildered and had to accept the new light coming from the East. After all, *Ex Oriente Lux*. The ones who were resistant to this new form of intellectual persuasion were simply expelled from school and, in some worse cases, put in jail. Not only was the Romanian school supposed to become a Soviet school, but the whole country was supposed to turn into a Soviet republic. It was a time when my mother used to advise me before I was going to school to be careful what I said and to whom I spoke because "the windows have eyes and the doors have ears." So the school was not much fun for me, and for many children like me, after World War II in Romania.

Russian became a mandatory language in school beginning with the fifth grade. Despite all efforts made by our teacher to teach us this language, little progress was done. Somehow we could not learn Russian. I remember that I had a whole summer ruined because I failed Russian, and I had to learn to take the exam in the fall to get into the new grade. What a summer!

We had to read and learn the Romanian writers, as well as the great Soviet writers. So we read Gorki, Maiakovski, Fadeev, and others. We did it, although this kind of literature sounded strange to us. It was coming from another world. When I later learned that Fadeev killed himself, that Maiakovski died in disgrace, and Gorky also ended up in an uncertain condition, I pitied them, and I understood that *Homo Sovieticus* was a risky creature. Luckily, meanwhile, I found the great Russian writers, Tolstoi, Dostoevsky, Lermontov, and especially Lermontov, whose main character, Peciorin, a lovely romantic character, who ran away from the world in the Caucazian mountains, sounded more human than all those artificial Soviet heroes, who all were fighting all in time. His loneliness and isolation in nature impressed me dearly, like Robinson Crusoe.

HISTORY AND IDEOLOGY

When Marx died, his best friend and sponsor, Engels, at his friend's grave, called Marx a Darwin of sociology—an idea almost unknown in those times.

Unfortunately, almost a century later, it would affect all the kids who were learning history in Romania. Why? Because the communist reform of education meant a radical and dramatic change in the way history was written and taught.

Overnight, history became scientific, and everything became explained in terms of class struggle, the forces of production, and the relations of production. The people, heroes, ideas, and ideals vanished from this new history that was written under the supervision of the party. Everything moved in history under the imperative of materialistic law, as Darwin's world moved and evolved under the law of natural selection. Everything in history was meant to lead to the victory of the proletariat and of communism, and history was moving like a train from one station to another.

This myth and mythology was so overwhelming that the entirety of history and the teaching of history became a kind of gibberish. So, mumbling some Marxist words or sentences, someone could easily pass exams. Worse, this kind of ideology trained people to see history as something that occurred outside them—something that had nothing to do with their lives. We might even say that, due to this kind of communist history, Romanians learned even more to withdraw from history and boycott history as Lucian Blaga, one of our great minds, used to say.

BACK TO CAANAN

Now the market economy and democracy are coming back, and everybody wants the wealth and well-being of the capitalistic world. Yet like many Jews who left Egypt to escape slavery, many Romanians today still look back to the times when the *big pharaoh* was running their lives—when history did not have anything to do with their lives. So a new curriculum for the new generations of Romanians should be a new road to Caanan. It means getting rid of the Marxist spell. But how many are aware of this fact?

That is why, maybe, today in Romania the successful businessmen are those people less touched by higher education and communist ideology.

SAVONAROLA AND DANTE

Before the all-powerful god, communists worshipped in school. Education was science, or at least it was assumed to be science. As a result of this scientific conception, genetics, cybernetics, sociology, psychoanalyses, and, of course, all philosophy, besides materialistic philosophy, were only mere bourgeois unscientific trifle.

As a result, Romanian culture was divided in two: the good or allowed culture, and the bad or forbidden culture. The second category was placed under a tight control; only a few had access to it. I remember that in the university I attended there were two libraries: the one for everybody and the other one, less known, where were kept forbidden books, books you could not borrow without a special license. Needless to say, such licenses were granted only in the last years of Soviet rule, and even then only to special students.

I remember when, at last, I was permitted in that library, what a cultural shock I had suffered. I felt abused all those years when I had to learn all kinds of stupid things: the official trash that passed as scientific socialism or materialistic philosophy.

I was waking up, but I was still afraid to speak. Believing was, still, more important than thinking, even in the university at that time. Savonarola was stronger than Dante. Siva was more important than Vishnu. I found, for example, an old translation from Dewey, a book that was lying in the library for more than half a century, unknown and untouched by anybody. What a surprise it was when in a seminar I talked about this book. The professor raised his eyebrows and stared at me. It was obvious that he knew nothing about. Luckily the academia began timidly, here and there, to remind of its role in the city. I look back now and I cannot help saying like Elliot, "What a wasteland."

THE JUANJUANII AND THE INNER MAN

In his book *A Day Longer Than A Century*, Cinghiz Aitmatov narrates a very interesting story. A long time ago in the *cazah stepa* in the area called Sari-Ozeki, a new wave of conquerors arrived, called the *Juanjuanii*. Soon they became notorious for their cruelty, and especially for the methods they used to transform a human being into a perfect slave. After they conquered a new population, they chose the young ones and forced them to undergo a treatment that had, as a result, the complete erasure of their memory. After such treatment, a human being lost his or her memory; he or she no longer knew who he or she was; he or she had no personal wishes or will. In other words, this creature, which could hardly now be termed a human being, became a perfect obedient tool or a perfect slave. But what did the *Juanjuanii* do?

They shaved the heads of their subjects and wrapped them in a piece of raw skin taken from a camel killed for this purpose. Left in the sun for days and weeks in this way, after a while, the camel's skin was drying out and shrinking tightly around the heads of the victims, as a vice, and in the end the poor subjects become the perfect obedient tools—without will, without memory, without any trace of humanity, just a perfect human robot or zombie.

What the *Juanjuanii* tried to do, in this barbaric way, the communist education tried to do in more refined way, but the aim was the same: to produce a citizen or *new man* completely subjected to the state; a man, and a world perfectly organized, where discipline and order were everywhere, both outside and inside him. This man, as Cinghiz Aitmatov wrote, "will fallow the orders from above" and if it is necessary to sing "you will receive a signal and you will begin to sing and if it is necessary to work you will begin to work and you will work very hard."

In this world, of course, there will be no thieves and no breaking of the laws because human behaviors will be entirely programmed and planned in advance. That is why the Soviet communists, more than anybody else, were fascinated by the idea of turning schools into factories and the curriculum into a technology. As a matter of fact, the favorite slogan and definition of the teacher, coined by Soviet pedagogy, was that the teacher was "an engineer of soul." As an engineer builds machines, the teacher was supposed to build human beings.

This rationale was supported not only by the great achievements of technology the communists saw in the West, but especially, by Pavlov's theory of reflex-response, a theory that depicted more or less the human being, and especially the human mind and soul, as mere combinations of reflexes—as an architecture of unconditioned and conditioned reflexes.

It is strange, but if we had before the French revolution the book of *La Mettrie* (1709–1751), *L'homme machine* (*The Machine Man*), before the Bolshevik revolution we had Pavlov's man, made of reflexes. If the French had a blueprint of how man works, the Soviet had one as well. So the next step was, let us build this new man. Therefore, it is not unlikely that in both revolutions the human beings were chopped up and treated as pieces of machinery that were supposed to be retooled. This is the reason that Pavlov's theory played such an important role in communist education. It was the rationale that turned the school into a factory and the teacher into an engineer.

While being a student and a naive neophyte, for years I was learning Pavlov's theory, which was the only key explanation to the whole human behavior. In vain I was looking for human psyche, for human soul; we ran only into reflexes. The inner man was a shadow and a ghost that had no room in a planned and machine type of society.

When he tried to come out, the inner man was mercilessly silenced. Thus, 10 of my colleagues, some of them very bright students who proved to have their own ideas, were expelled from the university, and their lives turned into an ordeal. To be brandished as a *class enemy* was a terrible burden for young men in a communist regime.

As I am writing these lines, I go back to those times. What a dramatic and tragic experience How many lives were broken! I do not know where those colleagues are now and how they cope with life, but I do want these words to be a kind of tribute paid for their innocent sacrifice and for their ordeal.

Later, I had the chance to pass through a similar experience, when our Institute of Pedagogical and Psychological Sciences was dismantled and we were declared *enemies of socialism* and thrown into obscure and menial jobs from the margin of society. What times! For a whole summer, I did not know what would happen to me—without a job, without any social status, just an outcast.

What foolish times! How much suffering! But didn't Erasmus write a book entitled *The Praise of Human Foolishness?*

THE BEAR'S CAVE

In the Southern Carpathian mountains, there is a cave known as the Bear's Cave. It is a very unusual place with a very unusual story. Besides its geological beauty, the cave had witnessed a terrible tragedy thousands and thousands of years ago.

Being a place where the prehistoric bears used to hide, somehow the entrance and exit of the cave was suddenly blocked. The bears remained trapped inside. After trying to get out and without any food, the bears began to kill themselves until the last one. That is why the whole cave is strewn with bones, bears bones, and only somewhere, in an impressive hall of the cave, lies the bones of the last bear: crawled together as in a deep sleep.

Modern man, like the prehistoric bears, is trapped in a cave. He has severed his links with the metaphysical world. As a result, as Plato would say, he sees and deals only with physical objects and phenomena, and he does not grasp what lies behind them. He cannot go beyond this shadows because, as Rudolf Otto points out in his *Das Heilige* (*The Sacred*, 1917), the modern man has lost his ties with the sacred world. Gods no longer come down and talk with us, as they did in the Golden Age, and we do not feel the urge to climb the mountain to reach out for God. The hierophany sentiment, as Mircea Eliade says, has diminished in our scientific and technological world—in modern man.

MYSTERIUM FASCINANS

As a result, the Living God of Luther, Grundtvig, and Kierkgaard was replaced by God of philosophy and philosophers—a God that is a mere moral allegory or piece of dogmatic teaching.

The feeling of terror before the awe-inspiring mystery, or *numinous* experience, which makes man feel there is something different besides the physical world a *wholly other* (*ganz andere*), has dramatically diminished in the modern man.

Positivism has greatly contributed to the lessening of this numinous experience, and French existentialism left the man in an absurd position bewildered and bereft by despair. In a more balanced way, Dewey retained the religious experience along side the scientific experience. However, if in other parts of the world man has still preserved his link with the sacred, the communist rational completely severed the ties of man with the divine. God was not only dead for communist mentality, but He was also killed anytime when He showed up in man's life. Churches were destroyed and religion people doomed.

Like the bear's cave, the communist world was entirely and abruptly shut off from the divine. The *wholly other* (*ganz andere*), the *mysterium fascinans,* was simply eliminated from people's souls and minds. The whole communist world was plunged into the matter and physical world. Nothing beyond like in Plato's cave. Like in the Bear's Cave, a tragedy occurred. The so-called *class struggle* legitimated the killing of man by man, the murder of Abel by Cain, the celebration of Thanatos, the death instinct. This cave mentality is also responsible for two world wars, for many revolutions, for many *gulags,* and, perhaps, for the destruction of our mother nature. However, let us hope that, in the end, man will be more intelligent than bears and will be able to get out from the cave—that he will free himself and see and grasp that something else, the *wholly other,* that *mysterium fascinans,* that lies behind physical phenomena.

BACK TO ITACKA

Let us hope man will finally, like Iona, get out from the Leviathan's belly. Let us hope because hoping is the first step of believing, and believing is the first brick of life, once again in human life.

Like Ulysses, we should learn to turn back to Itacka. Like him, after a life of destruction and war, we should steer back home. Who knows? Maybe we are just beginning our Odyssey by exploring the cosmos. Maybe our place is there amid the stars. Our life on Earth was, perhaps, just our childhood. Isn't it said, in all the major religions, that God the Father is up in the sky? After growing with our Mother Earth, in her bosoms, is it the time, perhaps, to go to our Father up in the sky?

CHAPTER 31

Politics and Theories in the History of Curricular Reform in South Korea

Yonghwan Lee
Chonnam National University, South Korea

BEFORE THE COLONIAL PERIOD (PRE-1910)

Before Japan annexed the Korean peninsula as its colony in 1910, Korea had developed its own educational system and curricula through almost 5,000 years of written history. The Koreans traditionally prized the humanities and regarded technical subjects as vulgar. The nobility learned Confucian ethics and philosophy from the primary community schools, and the practical subjects were for the common people. All the primary schools and some secondary schools were established and managed privately, and the rest of the secondary schools were run by the central or provincial governments. The central government was responsible for higher education. Generally speaking, the curricula of the schools were for the state examination; that was the only means to becoming a government official.

Korea had been known to the Western countries as "the land of morning-calm" (Gregor, 1990) or "the hermit nation" (Griffis, 1905) until the feudal dynasty decided to open the country to foreign intercourse in the mid-19th century. Accordingly, the Western missionaries—Catholic, Presbyterian, and Methodist in turn—began to land in this apparently serene country, carrying their belief not only in God, but also in the priority of their own culture. They opened, with a small group of children, the modern Western-style (primary) schools as part of their missionary work and taught them arithmetic, reading, and writing of the Korean language as well as basic English. The dynasty too showed great interest in the new educational institutions. It invited some teachers (H. V. Allen, H. B. Gilmore, B. A. Bunker) from the United States and established some schools in the Western style. They began to teach foreign languages and practical technologies such as medicine in 1886. Those schools were recorded as the first modern schools in Korea (Underwood, 1926).

The government soon provided laws and ordinances for the new education, along with other policies to reform the whole society, and local educationists began to establish new private schools for children of their community. In these private schools, some

541

teachers who recognized the peril their country confronted tried to inculcate national-istic spirit in their students and especially to bring to them an awareness of Japan's sin-ister intrigue to colonize Korea.

Because of the geopolitical nature of the country, however, Korea became the arena of the power's competition, and the great powers such as the United States, Japan, Rus-sia, and China did not let it take voluntary steps to modernize. After winning the Russo–Japan war, Japan forced Korea to conclude a protectorate treaty in 1905, by which Japan intervened in almost all politics in Korea. The Japanese supervisor started to implant the Japanese educational system and curricula into Korea and oppressed es-pecially the nationalistic private schools.

Even before annexation, almost half of the officers of the central Ministry of Educa-tion were Japanese, and they regulated the whole curricula of the primary and second-ary schools. Japanese teachers came into the country and were placed in national and public schools. The proportion of class hours for the Japanese language education was the same as or more than those for the Korean language (Ham, 1976). If a private school did not educate according to the curriculum, the school could not be authorized as a regular school. Textbooks that had not been published or approved by the Ministry were banned in schools. Obviously this doctrine was aimed at those books used in pri-vate schools that promoted patriotism and the spirit of independence. Dissatisfied even with this treaty, in 1910, Japan replaced it with an annexation treaty making the Korean peninsula its colony. Thus, all the efforts of the Korean government and people to modernize the education of this country ended in vain.

THE COLONIAL PERIOD (1910–1945)

Korean education during this period can be summarized as *Japanization* and *mobocracy*. *Japanization*, or assimilation, was officially expressed as "educating subjects [to be] loyal to the Japanese Emperor" and *mobocracy* as "schools should educate aiming at making human workers according to the condition and standards of the people" (Ham, 1976, pp. 65–67). Despite that Japan was constituted of small islands, it called its land an *inner continent*, and "integration of inner land and Korea" was the official slogan which undergirded all the colonial policies. However, in actuality, the educational policy of colonial Japan was to differentiate and discriminate the Korean from the Japanese. Underwood (1926), who had been a missionary and educator in Korea since the late 18th century, summarized the policy as follows:

> The policy of the government … meant to all Koreans three things …; Against all three they mentally rebelled. First, separate and different education for Koreans in Korea and Japanese in Korea. Second, the frank and rather bald statement that the chief ob-ject of the education offered was the making of loyal citizens of Japan; third, that edu-cation in Chosen (Korea) was to be adapted to the backward conditions and low mentality of the people. (p. 192)

In other words, Korea was regarded as an object of exploitation, not of investment. They did not permit higher education for Koreans. Korean students were to learn Japanese as their mother tongue, and vocational training was enforced. Humanities were reduced to the minimum amount in the school curriculum. For example, history and geography were not taught in the primary schools. The Japanese tried to control and eventually close pri-vate schools, which were more in number than national and public schools. Regarding pri-vate schools, the Proconsul admonished the local governors as follows:

> Among private schools, many are established and managed by foreign missionaries though there are some established by Koreans. Each governor must watch if the

schools observe the laws and regulations, if the teachers perform their duties, if they are using textbooks published or approved by the Ministry of Education, and if they inspire useless patriotism and the spirit of independence by teaching some strange songs and others. Especially, mission schools have not been intervened by the Ministry because of diplomatic immunity. From now on, discipline them by emphasizing separation of religion and education, but be cautious not to offend their feelings. (M. Lee, 1948, pp. 180–181)

This policy of Japanization and mobocracy in education was salient during the first decade of the colonial period. To control private schools, the Japanese revised the Private School Law (1915) in addition to the general educational laws and regulations so they could put the private schools in double fetters (Ham, 1976; Underwood, 1926). The establishment of private schools became more complicated and difficult, and teaching the Bible was banned by law. When a private school wanted to replace its principal or one of its teachers, approval from the local governor was needed. A school teacher needed to have not merely a certificate, but also a great command of Japanese. He was required to wear a uniform and saber while on duty. Great was the surprise at this severe policy among the founders and teachers of the schools, and protests soon followed.

Even in the traditional informal community schools, which numbered almost 25,000 in the nation, they forced the teaching of Japanese and the use of textbooks published or approved by the Ministry (Underwood, 1926). As a result, the number of schools and enrollments had continuously decreased until 1917 after the annexation.

In 1919, a nationwide independence movement influenced by "the principle of self-determination of peoples" that proposed by the U.S. President Woodrow Wilson, broke out. Although the movement ended after 6 months with numerous deaths and arrests, the Japanese government changed its colonial policy, at least outwardly, from a military to a cultural one. The system of military police was abolished, and teachers did not have to wear sabers any more. School years for the Korean primary and secondary students were extended to the same years as those for Japanese students, and higher education was opened for Koreans.

The principle of *vocational education for the Korean* was partly abrogated, and humanities appeared in the school subjects along with foreign languages. They loosened the strict qualifications for private school teachers and tried to appease the foreign missionaries by mitigating the absolute principle of separation of education from religion. The missionaries had been playing important roles in the protest, corresponding with the leaders of the independence movement in Korea and with the Korean government in exile in Shanghai, China. They made known the miserable state of the Korean people to their own government and fellow countrymen on their return home. However, the change of policy was so cunning that only three Koreans were appointed to the committee of education organized (with 28 members) to examine educational demands of the Korean people after the movement. Although Korean language was inserted into the primary and secondary school curricula, credit hours for it were still a third or half of those of Japanese, and all textbooks were written in Japanese. Korean students still needed to learn the Japanese language, history, and geography as if those were their own (Oh, 1964).

The major premise of colonial policy—that is, Japanization and mobocracy—was not changed. Thus, the new educational laws regulated that the foremost goal of the primary and secondary schools was "cultivating educated workers loyal to the National (i.e., Japanese) spirit" (Ham, 1976, pp. 120, 125). Students' strikes continually broke out, and arrests of teachers and students followed.

In 1937, Japan opened war against China; accordingly, education became a part of war organization. The most salient change in education was that the name of the schools for

Koreans had the same name of the schools for Japanese, and the Korean language became an elective subject instead of a required one. They prohibited Korean students from speaking Korean in schools and forced all Koreans to change their names to the Japanese style. Students were even told to watch one another lest they speak Korean.

After the air raid on Pearl Harbor, school years in colleges were reduced so they could draft as many students as possible for the war. Humanities in the curriculum were replaced with science and technology, and the name *school* was literally changed to *training center*. All the students either went to the battle front or were utilized to provide their labor mobilizing war materials and foods or constructing runways and trenches.

PERIOD OF AMERICAN MILITARY GOVERNMENT (1945–1948)

On August 15, 1945, Japan announced unconditional surrender to allied forces, and Korea was liberated from the Japanese colonialism according to the Potsdam Declaration. However, the liberation was an uncompleted one. Because the allied forces did not appreciate the Korean people's struggles for independence in and out of the Korean peninsula, the Potsdam Declaration regulated that Korea, different from other Western countries such as France, would be under the trusteeship of the United States and Russia. Regardless of the Korean people's will, the destiny of Korea was determined according to the interests of the powerful countries in the same way that Japan had won the tug of war over the peninsula some decades before. After landing in the country, the U.S. military appointed, as the administrator of education, Captain E. L. Lockard, who had been an English professor in a city college in Chicago. He organized the Korean Committee on Education, composed of 10 boards whose chairs were all Koreans.

It was most urgent for the committee to replace Japanese officials, provincial superintendents, principals, and teachers with Koreans. In the primary schools, over 40% of the teachers were Japanese, and the percentage in the secondary and higher levels was more than that (Sohn, 1992; Underwood, 1951). However, because it was difficult to find qualified people for the places after 36 years of colonial mobocracy, they could not strictly screen those who collaborated with the Japanese colonial government. It was also natural that those who had studied in the United States and could speak English had great influence in selecting personnel and deciding educational policies. After a few months, the military government and the committee finished organizing the Department of Education. Apart from the Department, the Korean Committee on Education was rearranged and expanded to the Educational Council; it numbered about 100 members, a few of whom were from the American military.

Although the new Ministry adopted almost without modification the decisions made by the Council, the fact that the military government failed to punish traitors, or at least to exclude them from office, and that they mainly depended on opinions of pro-American or pro-Western intellectuals, laid the groundwork for a series of anti-American movements some decades later. The U.S. military's identification of itself as *occupation forces* (vs. the Russian Army calling itself the *liberation army*) did not help the American image. These rash behaviors and ignorance of the Korean history and culture of the occupation commander Gen. John R. Hodge and his staff have been frequently criticized not only by some Koreans (Sohn, 1992), but also by some American scholars (Cumings, 1981, 1983).

The military government reopened all schools and prepared temporary courses of study for these schools. They prohibited the use of textbooks written in Japanese and regulated that Korean should be used as the instructional language. However, education could not be normal because there were limited numbers of qualified teachers and virtually no textbooks written in Korean. Great efforts were made to teach Korean and train teachers. They were also concerned with adult education, by which they tried to teach the new social order and eradicate illiteracy. Probably at this time, the Korean people might have publicly heard the word *democracy* for the first time in their history. The illiteracy rate of those over 12 years old was then 77% (Committee on Compilation of History of Education, 1960). A 6–3–3–4 system, which was modeled after the American educational system, was adopted as the basic structure of education. Japanese language classes were replaced with Korean, and English was put into the secondary school curriculum. From September 1, 1946, the integrated subject social studies newly appeared in the primary school curriculum, which was an obvious influence of Deweyan progressivism and of the Korean Educational Commission, whose members had visited America for 4 months in March 1946.

Although textbooks of Korean language and Korean history were promptly published by a few Independent movement groups that had maneuvered underground during the colonial period, other classes mainly depended on blackboards and materials mimeographed by teachers because of the lack of the textbooks. The content of education could not far exceed that of the colonial period. In other words, despite getting their lost identity back (e.g., their own names, language, and history), they could not get rid of inertia because the Korean identity was not one they had won for themselves, but was one others had suddenly brought to them. At this moment, the American Educational Mission introduced Deweyan concepts such as *experience* and *life*. As a result, the so-called *New Education Movement* expanded throughout the nation. It seems to be the case that, taking into account the historical and cultural situation of the day, teachers and educationalists never fully or even well understood and appreciated the Deweyan educational theory based on democracy that undergirded the New Education Movement. Although some name this period as the *period of no educational contents*, paradoxically this was the only period when Korean teachers enjoyed their freedom and autonomy regarding the content of education. Teachers could teach what they wanted because there were no curricula coerced from the outside.

PERIOD OF SUBJECT-CENTERED CURRICULUM (1948–1962)

On August 15, 1948, the constitution was ratified, and South Korea started its new history as a Republic despite the vehement opposition from those who did not want a solid fixation of the partition of the country.

Despite the departure of the new Republic, the situation in education did not improve much. Shortage of teachers, facilities, equipment, and textbooks confused and bewildered Korean education. The most urgent need was to give some guidelines to teachers who had been just treading the colonial footsteps. According to the Law of Education enacted in 1949, "subjects of schools except for colleges, colleges of education, and informal schools shall be prescribed by a Presidential decree, and courses of study and class hours of those by a regulation of the Ministry" (Korean Education Law, Article 155). The Ministry of Education regulated that the government publish all textbooks of the primary schools and textbooks of a few policy subjects of the secondary schools such as Korean language and literature, Korean history, and social life, and that the rest of the textbooks be examined and approved by the government.

The Korean War broke out on June 25, 1950, when the government was trying to take more specific steps to provide textbooks to teachers and students. During the 3 years of wartime, education continued only nominally in the temporary tents wherever there were no battles. Even during the war, classes of the primary and secondary schools were mainly focusing on entrance examinations. Entrance examinations for both middle and high schools existed until the 1970s. Even today, the college entrance examination is still most powerful, virtually dominating the contents and methods of the primary and secondary school curricula.

The results of the war regarding the content of education manifested itself in the government's scrutinization of school curriculum and its strengthening of the ideological in education. Anticommunism permeated all humanities, and, as in the United States, communism became an antonym of the word *democracy*. This anticommunist ideology and the central control system exerted great influences on the contents and methods of education and, consequently, on teachers' autonomy thereafter.

As soon as the war ended—technically it was suspended, at least officially, by the armistice agreement between the U.N. and North Korea—the government announced the curricula for the primary and secondary schools in the form of a law in 1955, which was based on Curriculum Handbook for the School of Korea published by the third American Educational Mission to Korea (Sohn, 1992). This has been recorded as the first official Korean curriculum after 1945. In this law, *curriculum* meant the "organization of subjects and other educational activities of schools." The government decided what, how much, and when to teach. Even for the subjects whose textbooks were not to be published by the government, courses of study including detailed chapters, and contents were prepared.

Teachers and curricularists of the day seem to have accepted the General Transfer Theory or Mental (Formal) Discipline Theory. Except for broad-field subjects like social studies and an introduction of extracurricular activities (club activities) into the curriculum for 1 or 2 hours a week in the curriculum of 1955, no evidence could be found that the American Educational Mission that visited Korea 10 times from 1952 to 1961 and their Deweyan theory had any influence on classroom practices. Subject barriers were thought to be fixed and individual needs and differences subjected to the preorganized uniform curriculum.

PERIOD OF EXPERIENCE-CENTERED CURRICULUM (1962–1973)

In 1960, the authoritative President S. Lee, who had been in power from 1948, resigned and took refuge in Hawaii after a series of student protests against rigged elections. However, even before various democratic measures of the new government were implemented, the government was overthrown in 1961 by a military coup d'état. As a result, local superintendents and education officials who had previously been elected by the inhabitants' vote were now appointed by the central government. On the one hand, the military government announced anticommunism as its utmost policy to get political support from the U.S. government, who had at first been suspicious about the coup leader C. Park's ideological background. On the other hand, the coup leaders pledged economic development to console the Korean people.

In 1963, the curriculum was revised mainly to include contents justifying the coup in Humanities textbooks. Anticommunism appeared as a distinct subject in the primary school curriculum. At this time, the Deweyan theory of education as experience was officially adopted, and *curriculum* was defined as "all learning activities which students experience under the guide of the school" (Research Committee of Curriculum and Textbooks, 1990, p. 11). William Kilpatrick's Project Method was introduced to teachers, and peer group problem solving was encouraged to meet students' individual differences. However, curricular decisions were still made by the central government, and classes still focused on entrance examinations. Teachers were regarded as technicians who should sincerely transmit preselected and organized educational contents to students. Peer group problem solving was often misunderstood as solving the same problems in the same class by group.

Apart from the official introduction of the concept of *experience-centered curriculum,* the government's devotion to economic growth brought another impact on school curriculum. Efficiency emerged as an important virtue in Korean society and was used as a major excuse to amend the Constitution, and hence to justify the long-term authoritative rule. Variety, differences, and discussions were rejected as inefficient. They even instituted and forced students to memorize the *National Charter of Education* (1968), which stated that efficiency and practicality were "to be respected." In the political and social situation like this, education was almost indoctrination, and Deweyan theory had no place in curriculum practice.

Moreover, B. S. Bloom's (1956) *Taxonomy of Educational Objectives* (translated into Korean in 1966) and R. F. Mager's (1961) concept of *behavioral objectives* (translated into Korean in 1976), along with behavioral psychology were introduced and enjoyed general popularity among teachers and educators because of their efficiency-based nature. McClelland's Achievement Motive Theory was used to justify education for economic development, and B. Chung's (1970) definition of *education* was taught in colleges as the one and only definition: "Education is deliberate change of human behavior" (p. 15). Education was regarded as the means to an end imposed externally, and nobody seriously raised questions about this.

Thus, despite the official definition of it, actual curriculum managed by classroom teachers was not unlike traditional subject-centered curriculum. Curriculum was still regarded as the means to an end extrinsically imposed, whether it was economic growth of the country or the growth of students' mental ability. Teachers were to efficiently transmit curricular knowledge to the passive students. Continuing vestiges of Japanese imperialism and a powerful hierarchical Confucian tradition could not be excluded from the various factors influencing Korean education and curriculum management. There were other reasons that experience-centered curriculum could not go beyond the level of an empty slogan: the overall qualities of teachers, poor facilities of schools, and objections from parents who wanted their children to pass without difficulty the entrance examinations to junior high, senior high schools, and colleges. Entrance examinations to junior and senior high schools were finally abolished for the normal management of school curriculum in 1968 and 1974, respectively.

PERIOD OF DISCIPLINE-CENTERED CURRICULUM (1973–1981)

In 1972, President C. Park, who had already been in power for a decade, declared a state of emergency amid incessant student protests against his tyranny and amended the Constitution so that a provisory clause, which had regulated the presidential term limit, was eliminated. Right after this second and progovernment coup d'état, the curriculum was revised again. Contents justifying the coup were newly included in such subjects as National Ethics, Korean History, and Social Life. At this time, *curriculum* was defined as structures of the disciplines (Research Committee of Curriculum and Textbooks, 1990). J. Bruner's (1959) theory of the structure of knowledge was fully accepted, and all the school subjects were encouraged to be organized into spiral curricula. Bruner's structure of knowledge was thought to correspond to J. Piaget's psychological schema. These theories were combined so effectively with the already renowned Tyler–Bloom–Mager rationale that curriculum should be composed of certain steps.

First, aims or objectives should be predetermined. Broad and ideal aims should have already been set by the government, sometimes in the form of a law. Those specific to each subject should be decided by such specialists of the subjects as biologists for biology with the help of Bloom's taxonomy.

Second, the scope of the contents of each subject should be defined to achieve efficiently those aims and objectives. The contents should be structures, which could represent characteristics of each subject. Again, subject specialists would be able to do those jobs.

Third, the contents should be organized in a spiral form by the specialist. Bruner's and Piaget's theories, such as the three stages of representation—enactive, iconic, and symbolic (Bruner, 1959)—and the development of schema would be helpful in deciding when to teach particular concepts. Bloom's taxonomy and Mager's behavioral objectives would also help in this process. If the contents of each subject were well organized, teaching would not have great significance.

Fourth, teachers should measure, rather than evaluate, the degree of students' achievement according to the prespecified aims and objectives. Teachers and even curricularists had no place in the school curriculum. So long as they did not raise serious questions about the contents they were teaching, nor question the official methodology, teachers were safe. Good teachers were those who efficiently transmitted textbook knowledge. They did not have to research something because a textbook was the only thing they should be concerned about, and the content of it would remain unchanged at least for the decade in which the national curriculum was in effect.

To make matters worse, the government was so autocratic in this period that various control over the contents of classroom teaching as well as over the press was prominent. Military training had already been a required subject in senior high schools and colleges since the late 1960s, even in girls' high schools. The school picnic was officially named the *Military March.* Although national security against the bellicose communists of North Korea was always the excuse of oppression, that was actually a measure for staying in power by terrifying the people. The Korean curricular field in this period was obviously swayed by the theories of the discipline's structure. Among those theorists, R. S. Peters (1966) and P. H. Hirst (1965) contributed not only to justifying Bruner's theory of the structure of the discipline, but also to reconsidering what had been regarded as granted. Similarly to Dewey, Peters and Hirst showed, using ordinary language analysis, that the current concept of education, and therefore curriculum as a means to an end, was wrong. They began to denounce the theory of extrinsic values in education, which undergirded the Tyler–Bloom–Mager rationale, and to arouse sympathy mainly among some professors in colleges and departments of education for education as its own end.

At the same time, some dissident teachers began to be expelled from schools because of the content they had taught in classrooms, and they formed an important anti-government group. They started, as a plausible reaction to the expulsion, to study political (especially Marxist) theories of education, particularly those of P. Freire, M. Carnoy, L. Althusser, M. Sarup, and K. Harris. This was plausible because there seemed to be no better theory than those of Marxists to explain the political (and educational) situation in Korea and, moreover, to suggest a solution—namely, a revolution. For example, Freire's (1970) *Pedagogy of the Oppressed* had long been a banned book, but was read widely among radical teachers and scholars. His concept of *conscientization* became a common word describing "teaching something anti-governmental or anti-capitalistic, therefore communist."

PERIOD OF HUMANISTIC CURRICULUM (1981–1995)

Park's autocratic government, which had been in power for almost two decades, collapsed as the chief of the Korean C.I.A. assassinated the president on October 26, 1979. Despite the Korean people's bursting expectation and demand for a freer society, and for the civilian democracy that had been restrained so far, a group of generals who were afraid of losing their vested privilege carried out another military coup d'état, killing hundreds of innocent civilians in May 1980.

As had usually been the case, the national curriculum was revised once again in the next year after the new government started. This time the new curriculum claimed to be humanistic. One or two school hours per week were deleted, and extracurricular activities were emphasized to normalize the management of school curriculum by relieving students from the excessive burden of preparation for college entrance examinations. Integrated subjects were also introduced into the primary schools. However, students, especially high school students, were to stay at school until almost midnight under the name of *self-regulating classes* or *compensatory classes,* and the extracurricular activities were never conducted outside school. At the same time, the government strictly banned private tutoring, which had long been a social problem because of its high cost and hence its availability only for the rich. The risk increased the cost, and secret tutoring became a lucrative job in Korea. As a result, the overall expenditure of private tutoring became bigger than that of the regular schooling (Kong & Chun, 1990). From this time on, colleges were forced to reflect applicants' high school grades in their selection of the students.

The sanguinary coup in 1980 made the dissident groups, especially those composed of student activists, more violent and more biased to Marxist theories. Anti-Americanism began to appear openly in students' demonstrations after this coup, which was finally acknowledged by the U.S. government officials who had, as before, preferred autocracy to instability in the Korean peninsula. Dissidents were no longer afraid of the government's oppressive power, and antigovernment riots burst out more frequently. In the same way, comparatively young scholars and professors in academic circles did not conceal their interests in radical social theories. Thus, such jargon as *neo-colonial monopoly capitalism* has been used to define the nature of Korean society (Park & Cho, 1989).

In the field of education, a British version of the New Sociology of Education and the Conflict Theory from the United States were introduced into Korea. The New Sociology stimulated the Korean educationalists' taken-for-granted view of curriculum, whereas Jean Anyon's (1979) study into the American history textbooks was often quoted to reveal distorted ideological reflection in curriculum. Some of Michael Apple's books were translated into Korean. Some curricular theorists began to raise fundamental questions about the usefulness and validity of the Tyler–Bloom–Mager rationale (Lee, 1982). It was in this period that W. Pinar's (1981) reconceptualist curriculum theory was introduced as an alternative approach to the traditional taken-for-granted view of curriculum (Kwak, 1981; Lee, 1983). In his effort to classify curricular theories imported to Korea into some categories, Lee (1983) pointed out the looseness of the term *reconceptualist,* and he broke Pinar's reconceptualists into two separate camps: those who had Marxist or political backgrounds and those who showed a more humanistic interest, focusing on the individual. Pinar's study also made some Korean curricularists reconsider the nature of curriculum, which had been only of an administrative significance. However, Pinar's phenomenological and autobiographical emphases were so unfamiliar to the Korean curricularists that many were not illuminated as to his broader interest in reconceptualizing the curriculum field.

Inspired by an expanding atmosphere of more freedom in overall society, on the one hand, and in intellectual circles, on the other, some teachers tried to organize the Teachers' Labor Union in the mid-1980s. Their theoretical support was mainly provided by the teachers who had been expelled from their schools and fascinated by the political educational theory since the 1970s. Some of the parents showed an aversion to the word *laborer,* which seemed to identify their children's teachers with the vulgar manual laborer so that the government was able to criminalize the movement. More than 1,500 young teachers who refused to secede from the Union were fired and formed an important dissident group. Although some of the initial activists among the teachers were excessively biased toward Marxist theories of education as a reaction to the prohibition of Marxist theories of any kind, their on-the-spot experience enabled them to make many practical researches, and they began to publish a series of critiques of the content of the textbooks and classroom knowledge (Union of Association of Subject Teachers, 1989; Teachers Association for Korean Language and Literature Education, 1988, 1989a, 1989b, 1990; Teachers Association for Moral and Ethics Education, 1989; Teachers Association for History Education, 1989; English Teachers Association, 1991; Department of Subject in Teachers Union of Korea, 1990; Association of Korean Language and Literature Teachers in Chung-Nam Province, 1988).

Open education, which had been introduced into Korea with A. S. Neil's Summerhill School, was also revitalized as another possible alternative to the uniform national curriculum. Because it is too early to evaluate the result of the movement, which is still in an experimental stage in about 10 schools, it would be sufficient for the present to value the teachers' voluntariness and enthusiasm to respect students' individual differences, creativity, and autonomy despite the prevailing uniform curriculum.

In 1993, the first civilian president was elected after the long military regime, and various steps were embarked on toward a more democratic and free society. In 1994, most of the teachers who had been fired because of the Union Movement returned to their schools, giving up the Union, but not its ideals. Military training as a required class, which had been a symbol of both authoritative policy of education and the partitioned state of the country, was eliminated from the high school curriculum in 1995. The content justifying government power was removed from so-called *policy subjects*. Teachers' unions were finally legalized in 2000. However, the right to select and organize subjects, textbooks, teaching material, contents, and teaching methods remained in the hands of the central government.

SUMMARY AND REVIEW

One of the most noticeable features in the history of curricular reform in Korea is that the reforms always followed major changes in the political situation, especially after 1945. In other words, those who seized the political power always needed the reform of the national curriculum both to include the content justifying the process of taking the power and to accord the curriculum to the contemporary educational and curricular theories that had been introduced into Korea. Every national curriculum since 1945 was the result of the subtle, sometimes very odd combination of these two purposes, producing situations where it has not been easy to distinguish which one of these two purposes was the prior.

Consequently, official curriculum policy could not help being authoritarian, and control of the central government over planning and managing the curriculum was almost inevitable. There has been no room for teachers, students, parents, and even curricular theorists, whose roles were not neglected so completely even in the Tyler rationale, the most influential model for the Korean curriculum.

Thus, the Korean national curriculum has been most vulnerable to Marxist criticism, such as K. Harris' work—namely, that curriculum is used as a major means to present "a distorted view of the world" and to offer "a misrepresentation of reality." This line of political critique about education and curriculum was so flourishing in the mid-1980s that few dared to point out its weakness, afraid of being stigmatized as conservative. However, as many scholars have properly indicated, these political theories of education and curriculum have been successful in posing problems, but have failed in offering solutions to the problems. Especially in Korea, the harsh political condition has made some intellectuals biased toward radical political theories, which posed rather than eliminated many problems.

More than 20 years ago, a curricular theorist symbolized the history of Korean curricula since 1945 as a period of objectives model. He diagnosed rote learning and teaching as a major malignant symptom of the Korean education and pointed out that the symptom grew from the fact that the objectives model was widely held by teachers and educationists. He proposed a content model as an alternative; this idea was obviously inspired by Peters, Hirst, and Bruner, and was not very different from L. Stenhouse's *process model.* Although he suggested, leaving aside political or Marxist concerns, that Korean teachers and educationists alter the concept of curriculum, many problems still remain unsettled—problems inherent in the objectives and content models of curriculum.

Another distinctive feature of the Korean curriculum through its history is that it has continuously been influenced by foreign theories. The first national curriculum was altogether instituted by the U.S. occupation forces after the country was liberated from the Japanese colonialism, and ever since the Western theories especially have exerted a great impact on the theory and practice of the Korean curriculum. Thus, the lack of indigenous and idiosyncratic theories and practices of curriculum has been frequently mentioned as one of the problems in the Korean education. As a possible reaction to this, some radicalists sought a way of liberating the Korean curriculum from the Western, particularly American, influence. It was also in the mid-1980s that North Korean President Il-Sung Kim's version of nationalism, "Idea of Self-Reliance," was introduced to the young radicalist underground. This effort, however, sometimes showed a chauvinistic tendency and raised other important questions regarding curriculum: Can and should there be an indigenous or nationalistic curriculum? Can one be indigenous without being nationalistic or chauvinistic?

However, from the curriculum revised in 1987, the government accepted the concept of local curriculum to break the uniformity that has been pointed out as the major cause of the curricular problems in Korea. This concept of localization has further developed to become the most important characteristic of the new curriculum implemented in 1995. Although the new policy appears to be more democratic and timely in this postmodern era, this concept of localization provides grounds for its own questions and disputes. In 2000, a noticeable change occurred in the politics in the Korean Peninsula. The antagonism between two Koreas, which has exerted great influence on politics and education of both Koreas, was attenuated since South Korean President Dae-Joong Kim's official visit to North Korea in June. It is certain that financial and cultural interchange will break down the ideological barrier and the military tension between two Koreas. In South Korea, the content of the textbook unfavorable to North Korea is already being replaced with the content emphasizing the identities of the two countries. The political and educational situation in both Koreas should be bettered with this visit as a turning point.

REFERENCES

Anyon, J. (1979). Ideology and United States history textbooks. *Harvard Educational Review, 49*(3), 361–386.

Association of Korean Language and Literature Teachers in Chung-Nam Province. (1988). *Praxis education*. Tae-Jun: Nam-Nyuk.

Bloom, B. S. (1956). *Taxonomy of educational objectives I, Cognitive Domain* (E.-D. Lim et al., trans.). Seoul: Bae-Yung.

Bruner, J. S. (1959). *The process of education*. Cambridge, MA: Harvard University Press.

Chung, B.-M. (1970). *Education and the study of education*. Seoul: Bae-Yung.

Committee on Compilation of History of Education. (1960). *10 Years history of Korean education*. Seoul: Poong-Moon.

Cumings, B. (1981). *The origins of the Korean War: Liberation and the emergence of separate regimes, 1945–1947*. Princeton, NJ: Princeton University Press.

Cumings, B. (1983). *Child of conflict: The Korean-American relationship, 1943–1953*. Seattle: University of Washington Press.

Department of Subject Teachers Union of Korea. (1990). *White paper on textbook*. Seoul, Korea: Green Tree.

English Teachers Association. (1991). *English education for a right place*. Seoul: Green Tree.

Freire, P. (1970). *Pedagogy of the oppressed*. New York: Herder & Herder.

Gregor, A. J. (1990). *Land of the morning calm: Korea and American security*. Washington, DC: Ethics and Public Policy Center.

Griffis, W. E. (1905). *Korea: The hermit nation*. London: Harper & Brothers.

Ham, C.-K. (1976). *A study on the history of Korean curriculum I*. Seoul: Sook-Myung Women's University Press.

Hirst, P. H. (1965). Liberal education and the nature of knowledge. In R. S. Peters (Ed.), *Philosophy of education* (pp. 87–111). London: Oxford University Press.

Kong, E.-B., & Chun, S.-Y. (1990). *The level of educational expenditure in Korea* (Research Report 90-13). Korean Educational Development Institute, Seoul.

Kwak, B.-S. (1981). Concepts and trends of approaching curriculum. In J.-S. Oh (Ed.), *Summary of educational research: Curriculum* (pp. 1–34). Seoul, Korea: KEDI.

Lee, M.-K. (1948). *History of Korean education II*. Seoul: Eul-Yu Publishing.

Lee, Y. (1982), A critique to the taxonomy of educational objectives. *The Journal of Educational Research, 8*, 89–107.

Lee, Y. (1983). Four paradigms in curriculum research. *The Journal of Educational Research, 9*, 43–67.

Mager, R. F. (1961). *Preparing instructional objectives* (O.-H. Chung, trans.). Seoul: Educational Science Publishing.

Oh, C.-S. (1964). *History of modern education in Korea*. Seoul: Educational Publishing.

Park, Y.-C., & Cho, H.-Y. (Eds.). (1989). *Arguments about social construction of Korea I*. Seoul: Chook-San.

Peters, R. S. (1966). *Ethics and education*. London: Allen & Unwin.

Research Committee of Curriculum and Textbooks. (1990). *History of subjects in Korean curriculum*. Seoul: Korean Textbook Company.

Sohn, I.-S. (1992). *American military government and its educational policy*. Seoul: Min-Yung Publishing.

Teachers Association for History Education. (1989). *History education for life alive*. Seoul: Green Tree.

Teachers Association for Korean Language and Literature Education. (1988). *Subject teaching*. Seoul: Green Tree.

Teachers Association for Korean Language and Literature Education. (1989a). *A guide to the revised textbook of Korean language and literature*. Seoul: Green Tree.

Teachers Association for Korean Language and Literature Education. (1989b). *Korean language and literature education for reunification*. Seoul: Green Tree.

Teachers Association for Korean Language and Literature Education. (1990). *Progressive Korean language and literature education*. Seoul: Chin-Goo.

Teachers Association for Moral and Ethics Education. (1989). *Moral education together*. Seoul: Green Tree.

Underwood, H. H. (1926). *The modern education in Korea*. New York: International Press.

Underwood, H. H. (1951). *Tragedy and faith in Korea*. New York: Friendship Press.

Union of Association of Subject Teachers. (1989). *Textbooks read upside down*. Seoul: Green Tree.

CHAPTER 32

In Southeast Asia:[1] Philippines, Malaysia, and Thailand: Conjunctions and Collisions in the Global Cultural Economy

F. D. Rivera
San José State University

> *One deficit that seriously hobbles those critical voices who speak for the poor, the vulnerable, the dispossessed and the marginalized in the international fora in which global politics are made is their lack of any systematic grasp of the complexities of globalization. A new architecture for producing and sharing knowledge about globalization could provide the foundations of a pedagogy which closes this gap and helps to democratize the flow of knowledge about globalization itself. Such a pedagogy would create new forms of dialogue between academics, public intellectuals, activists and policy-makers in different societies and its principles would require significant innovations. This vision of global collaborative teaching and learning about globalization may not resolve the great antinomies of power that characterize this world but it might help to even the playing field. (Appadurai, 1999, p. 238)*

Many significant changes that have taken place in the curricula of most developing countries in decades past could be attributed to the twin metonymic conditions of greater internationalization of market economies and globalization of the cultural economy. Both late-capitalist realities define our current episteme—that seemingly *positive unconscious* that Michel Foucault has talked about—which enables us to order present history and form the conditions of what we come to regard as true. Particular to the more than 130 developing countries that account for at least 60% of the world population, the interpretive conditions of globalization and internationalization demand that these countries, despite their unstable resource capital (human and otherwise), deal with the challenges of postindustrialism of rich, developed nation-states. In this chapter, we prefer to use the term *developing countries* because it entrains a postcolonial critique about the problematic characterization often sessiled when the Three Worlds

---

[1] Japan, Taiwan, China, North, and South Korea comprise the Northeast side of Asia. Southeast Asia refers to the following countries: Philippines, Vietnam, Indonesia, Brunei, Laos, Burma (Myanmar), Malaysia, Cambodia, Thailand, and Singapore.

Theory is employed as a taken-for-granted label. Ahmad (1995/1987) articulated it clearly in the following sentences:

> [The] First and Second Worlds are defined in terms of their production systems (capitalism and socialism, respectively), whereas the third category—the Third World—is defined purely in terms of an "experience" of externally inserted phenomena. That which is constitutive of human history itself is present in the first two cases, absent in the third case. Ideologically, this classification divides the world between those who make history and those who are mere objects of it. (p. 78)

In the history of the present, such three-tiered typology seriously undermines the structure of complexity of participating in the international market. Most developing countries, in fact, participate in significant ways at varying degrees in the global condition of disorganized capitalism (Lash & Urry, 1987), which depend primarily on their economic status, of course. What is notable, as has been pointed out by present-day social theorists, are the emerging configurations that are, to a large extent, dictated by the logic of Appadurai's (1999/1990) *scapes* (ideoscapes, finanscapes, ethnoscapes, technoscapes), which perhaps at some point in time will characterize the new global cultural economy that is rhizomatic in character (in Deleuze and Guattari's sense[2] and whereby "'time' has ceased, [and] 'space' has vanished"; McLuhan & Fiore, 1967, p. 63). We could as well have said rather succinctly the simultaneous virtualization and realization of Marshall McLuhan's global village.

Withering current debates regarding a possible conceptual divide between global and international economy (see e.g., Hirst & Thompson, 1999), in this chapter we assume that attempts made by individual countries to internationalize their curricula are based on responses about the need to develop a global education through a globalized curricula. Results of various cross-cultural comparative studies on curricula show minimal differences in content. For instance, almost all countries deploy a *stateless* science, mathematics, and technology content regardless of variations in context (Nebres, 1995). Also, particular to the Asian context, various regional cooperations in education among Asian countries have led to the development of common curricular interests and collaborative programs in the areas of literacy, popular, science and technology, technical and vocational, environmental, and development education (Roy Singh, 1986). Some of the well-known results of these regional collaborations include the following: the Karachi Plan developed in Tokyo, Japan, in 1962, which transformed into the Asian Model of Educational Development and revised in Bangkok, Thailand, in 1965, and further expanded in Singapore in 1971; the Colombo Conference in 1978, which discussed educational policies relevant for the 1980s; and the periodic comparative studies of curriculum systems in Asia and the Pacific started in the late 1960s by the National Institute for Educational Research of Japan.

As a result of various forms of interaction at the regional and international levels, curriculum theorizing in developing countries in Asia has been rendered as always-al-

---

[2]Deleuze and Guattari's (1987) *rhizome* concept is a botanical metaphor that pertains to a multiplex network of forces, and thus enables "multiple entryways and exits and its own lines of flight" (p. 21). What used to be a singular model or structure (e.g., Western) has now been rendered untenable. Models are now characterized as rhizomatic—"always detachable, connectable, reversible, [and] modifiable" (p. 21). The rhizome best captures this order that is taking place in this period of late capitalism and technological success as it foregrounds the ironies, contradictions, and agnostic processes resulting from increased deterritorialization in various aspects of living. The rhizome highlights as well the possibility of those lines of flight that do not "flow along regulated pathways," but performing instead as "transversals to them, cutting across them and using elements from them in the process of doing something new [and] different" (May, 1991, p. 32).

ready, historically, and needfully an internationalized process. In contemporary times, where we witness the demise of colonial rule, the need for a globally competitive school curricula, better performances by students in cross-cultural based international examinations, and an inundant attention placed on global education, these factors and many more besides have all provided sufficient indicators that curriculum is emerging as an international text (Pinar, Reynolds, Slattery, & Taubman, 1995). The always-already internationalized component of curricula is drawn from at least two additional observations. First, specific to developing countries concerned with the aspect of developing a more stable and stronger local economy, and facing up to the demands of an international market economy that capitalize on information and technological knowledge, there are within sight vigorous curriculum restructuring efforts that they expect will enable their technological transformation (Ghosh, 1987). Second, the importance accorded to the recently concluded Third International Mathematics and Science Study (TIMSS) conducted in 1995 by the International Association for the Evaluation of Education Achievement, whose membership includes a significant number from developing countries, is indicative of a kind of global thinking aimed at the "international standardization of curricula" (Vedder, 1994. p. 11).

In the sections that follow, I explain, particularly with the Asian context in mind, the extent to which the logic of internationalization makes border wars an always-already ambivalent, agnostic process resulting from an emerging global culture characterized by disjunctive integration and increased deterritorialization in various social, cultural, economic, political, and historical aspects of living simultaneously in both the local and global spheres. Such a vectorial shift toward greater internationalization and globalization is, in Said's (1993) words, "[an] acknowledgment] that the map of the world has no divinely or dogmatically sanctioned spaces, essences, or privileges" (p. 311). Of course, Said added, "we may [still] speak of secular space, and of humanly constructed and interdependent histories that are fundamentally knowable, although not through grand theory or systematic totalization" (p. 311).

Thus, the internationalization of curriculum in developing countries doubly articulates the many conjunctions and collisions that coexist and are mutually presupposed when curriculum theorizing is performed in the "complex, overlapping, disjunctive order" (Appadurai, 1999/1990, p. 220) of the global cultural economy. As an international text, matters pertaining to curriculum are situated in some disseminated space (in Jacques Derrida's sense), where the stakes move beyond attempts at subverting binaries relevant to curriculum (euro/ethno, center/periphery, cosmopolitan/local, unified/splintered forms of curricula, homogenizing curriculum/diversified curriculum, Western (universal) academic model/Asian model, to name several) performed if only to surface a politics of privileged appropriation (a poststructuralist move) or evert strongly American and Eurocentric influences on the existing curriculum in developing countries (via a postcolonial critique). Rather, curriculum as an international text is theorized in the disseminated both/neither spaces of hybridity, especially in mind those developing countries with a colonial past and confronted by new situations that emerge from cultural globalization (thus, marking a new postcolonialism), and disjunctive syntheses (i.e., Deleuze and Guattari's rhizomes), the coming together of disparate ideas, in which curriculum and internationalization as social discourses are viewed as two simultaneously performing complex phenomena. In the next few paragraphs, I paint in broad strokes issues that I find significant.

In developing countries, proposed curriculum changes deal with the needs of global citizens, already more than 100 million in 1993 (Castles & Miller, 1993), whose shifting bodies (in the literal sense of movement, migration, and diaspora) in various locations and spaces provide different forms of productive labor in many multi/trans/national corporations and the global market in the wider context of things. In a sense, then, an internationalized curriculum articulates a marked fetishism toward bodies, doubly inscribing these bodies with use values (i.e., individuals as consumers and valued commodities in a functional sense) and exchange values (i.e., individuals as social commodities performing labor). Here it is useful to think of the emerging identities of global citizens as "perpetually in composition" (McLaren, 1995, p. 16), experiencing what Gergen (1991) referred to as the condition of "multiphrenia," marked by a "splitting of the individual into a multiplicity of self-investments" (pp. 73–74; cited in McLaren, 1995, p. 16).

An internationalized curriculum also aims for greater productivity and flexibility while seeking originality, inventiveness, and creativity. All the aforementioned aims contribute to the development of a globally competitive school curricula and to the possibility of productive collaboration among countries that share similar interests. Take, as a specific instance, the peculiarity of the Asian student phenomenon in the TIMSS and other international science and mathematics competitions (e.g., International Mathematics/Physics Olympiad), in which students from Singapore, Korea, and Japan usually perform well above average compared with their Western and "weaker Asian" counterparts. Attempts at understanding the phenomenon have led to volumes of international comparative studies and benchmarking efforts based mostly on the evaluation and assessment of curricular programs (including content, instruction, and the impact of the larger cultural and educational terrain on the curriculum). Also, developing countries that prioritize curricula aimed at progressing their own technology-based knowledge is both a political and economic imperative to collaborate productively with other countries in the same or an even higher position in the global order. Appadurai's (1999/1990) technoscape foregrounds the "odd distribution of technologies" and the emergence of technological configurations due to successful linkages among countries. For instance, the collaborative work among Middle European countries (Austria, Italy, Hungary, Czechoslovakia, Yugoslavia, and four others from the older Habsburg order) have, in fact, led to better trade and innovative developments in the areas of regional telecommunications network and rail-motorway-air links (Batley, 1991).

Although it has been widely theorized that the global cultural economy will lead to increased standardization and regimentation, it must be pointed out that an internationalized curriculum as a social discourse is most likely to explore issues of similarities and differences, such as global versus local knowledges, internationalized global practices versus nationalist ethnocentric practices, and many more besides. We note, too, that media and communications technologies, viewed as powerful instruments in the deployment of curriculum, are now making it possible for information to be obtained by all and, thus, widening spaces for individual interpretations and constructions of various images and narratives as they are made available by the technologies. Batley (1991) wrote, "The window on the world has been flung wide open more recently with the advent of audio-visual satellite reception, which supplements text-authenticity with fully contextualized discourse-authenticity" (p. 159). Even more radical in the present time is the openness by which people have started considering the many different ways individuals perceive and construct reality, which also implies that the divide between validated fact (real) and imagined world (fictional) may have finally reached an irreparably blurred status.

A fourth, but still related, point is the restive perception that the global cultural economy leads to an eschewal of heterogeneity and cultural pluralism in favor of homogeneity and universalism through various curriculum tactics and strategies (in Michel Foucault's sense) aimed at assimilation (social, cultural, religious, etc.) at the very least.

For instance, La Belle and White (1992) documented that in 19th-century Latin America, whose economy then was evolving from "labor-intensive to capital-intensive modes of production," schools were utilized as a state apparatus "in a direct and massive way to augment traditional forms of social control" (p. 245). Colonial language policies and uniform curricula were mainly deployed in schools not for the purpose of national unification, but for political, economic, and international interests, which necessarily required "subordinate populations [to adapt] to the norms and practices of the superordinate elites" (p. 260) in power. An internationalized curriculum, however, becomes a fertile ground in which to pursue plural centers and diversified viewpoints, and along with it the tensions, ironies, and contradictions resulting from the specificity of one's own cultural context as well as the complexity and general incoherence of universal claims. What used to be an enlightenment monopoly of ideas has now been assigned with different meanings in contexts. Thus, in an internationalized curriculum, one expects complex forms of discourses, refolded,[3] and in a sense reflective of the prevailing social, cultural, and economic conditions in which curriculum content and form are situated in both the local and more global contexts.

There is thus a general consensus that an internationalized curriculum has much to offer us. However, there are difficult issues that will always have to be dealt with. Particular to developing countries in Asia, which are internally plural and with a colonial past, issues surrounding what constitutes a national identity that already has been tainted by the "imprints of colonialism" (Altbach & Viswanathan, 1989, p. xii) or how to preserve one's own cultural heritage vis-à-vis the global cultural economy and various nuances of institutionalized neo-colonialism are usually pursued in the curriculum. That is the postcolonialist project imbricated in every process as developing countries participate more fully in the global cultural economy—that is, the foregrounding of the significant local in the global. Furthermore, even if globalization has been criticized for celebrating sameness and marginalizing difference, there are a few serious local efforts aimed at finding a middle ground that will link global practices with indigenous (ethno) epistemologies. An ethnomathematics curriculum, for instance, values and partakes in the tradition of Western, global mathematics while appreciating and using the situated context of mathematizing drawn from either the social or cultural environment (e.g., street mathematics of Brazilian children). There is this simultaneous sensing, call it *doubleness*, in which curriculum specialists are especially concerned with ways in which learners become competitive at the global level, as well as in ways to develop an internationalized curriculum that is drawn from the peculiarity of participating based on the contributions of the individual local culture. Thus, any attempt to frame identity or preserve one's own cultural heritage in the ambivalently both and neither same-other is already a difficult task. The self, Young (1997) wrote, "is the location of a struggle for authenticity and unity, and that most selves occupy a zone which lies somewhere between, on the one hand, heterogeneity and total plasticity and, on the other, the entirely homogenous, harmonized single self of the myth of character" (p. 499). If left unresolved, then globalization could, as During (1999) emphasized, "deprive individuals and communities of the capacity to control and know their own interests as they are increasingly called upon to produce and consume for markets driven from afar" (p. 24).

---

[3]The term *refolded* in characterizing the complex forms of discourses takes its inspiration from from Deleuze's (1986) notion of the fold, but here appropriated differently. In an internationalized curriculum, especially, issues being resolved are never about the end of an old discourse and the promotion of a new one. The same issues are constantly raised, tackled, and, in a crystallized sort of way, always-already changing as they are invested with newer meanings as a consequence of being repositioned differently.

The issues raised in the immediately preceding paragraph are exemplified in the ongoing work of Brady (1997), who wrote about how the culturally relevant practices of Australian Aboriginal and Torres Strait Islander people—their *indigenous knowledge*—conflicted with mainstream Western European concepts. Colonized in their own country for more than 208 years, the aboriginal/islander minority group developed feelings of exclusion and experienced differentiated access and limited participation when they were assimilated in the mainstream curricular activities and programs of nonindigenous Australians. Many also felt threatened that their own indigenous concepts were in danger of being colonized, commoditized by nonindigenous Australians who impose a property of ownership on acquired knowledge (through the program Aboriginal Studies) and "supplanted with industrial knowledge systems" (Winona LaDuke; cited in Brady, 1997, p. 418). Brady struggled to develop a "more holistic education [that] can become the norm rather than the exception" in which "Globally Indigenous people" and nonindigenous Australians benefit from a "mutual interaction" of differing, culturally based, knowledges. Brady, however, pointed out that even if there has been progress in the past 20 years from both indigenous and nonindigenous groups of educators to develop and implement an indigenous-based curriculum, recent moves in both the political and academic spheres are, sadly, "predicated upon nineteenth-century definitions of race, intellect and decision-making" (p. 417), which have been found to further strengthen the institutionalized colonialism that pervades in the developing context of Australian society and schools (see also Maratos, 1995).

In the remaining sections, I provide details on the current state of curriculum theorizing in the following developing countries in Asia: Philippines, Malaysia, and Thailand. The sections to follow do not deal with the history of curriculum theorizing in these countries because I situate the chapter already in medias res—that is, the main concern is curriculum theorizing in the nascent stage of globalization and greater internationalization. I begin with a brief overview of general curriculum concerns in Southeast Asia. Then I focus on the three countries. Readers are provided with two tales that complement each other—that is, realist and interpretive. The term *tales* is employed in John Van Maanen's sense to refer to the ethnographic disposition that we tell each other stories and the choice of which stories to tell already implicates us in the representational quality and validity of the stories we construct. The realist tales provide readers with important facts about the current state of curriculum theorizing in the countries mentioned. The interpretive tales, however, involve situating both curriculum and curriculum theorizing within a larger reconceptualist project (in William Pinar's sense) that focuses on possible effects of the global cultural economy and current attempts to globalize curricula on the emerging identities of individuals in these classrooms. In the case of the Philippines, I focus on the possible destructive relationship (in During's sense) between and among globalization, the problematic origin of the Filipino language, and the perceived global construction of the Filipino identity in current social studies textbooks. With Thailand and Malaysia, we deal with what Reynolds (1998) and Mee (1998) claimed as productive effects (in Foucault's sense) of globalization on the emerging identities of Thais and Malaysians.

A caveat is in order. *National identity* and *local* are two mutually related terms that are relevant in identity construction. Further, both words in tropological terms have been associated with membership in an imagined community. Yet in the history of the curriculum present, both words are problematic because different ways of characterizing them (e.g., in historical or political terms) often lead to differences in the manner curriculum changes are perceived and framed. When talking about the constitutive nature of the term *local* (local situations, local practices, local knowledges, etc.), it could, on the one hand, pertain to something that has evolved internally, reified as a tradition, or "an inert primitive or a given, which pre-exists whatever arrives from outside itself" (Appadurai, 1999, p. 231). On the other hand, it could also be viewed as a historical category that is both internally and culturally diverse and "has always had to be produced, maintained, and nurtured deliberately" (p. 231). In characterizing national identity, it could be framed in the classical sense—that is, as an aboriginal, ethnic, time-independent, and essential "cultural core" (Mee, 1998, pp. 228–229) that has defined an individual's or a community's identity or sense of authentic membership. However, it could also be viewed as a cultural category that is continually evolving and adapting. Thus, a narrow coding of the two terms leads to viewing an internationalized curriculum as constructing learners whose selves move further and further from themselves to othered selves in the service of the global cultural economy and determined by the image of the global landscape. An expanded coding of the two terms considers the possibility of an internationalized curriculum that appropriates new global registers and is characterized by learners whose identities both determine and are determined by always-already shifting categories endemic of the current temporal character of every nation-space.

GENERAL CURRICULUM ISSUES IN SOUTHEAST ASIA

Decades of war and various nuances and periods of colonization (of mind in the case of Thailand, and of both mind and body in the cases of Philippines and Malaysia) may arguably characterize significant parts of the history of most developing countries in Southeast Asia. Even if there is documented evidence that education took place during those difficult times, the intent of its deployment was anything but emancipation. At a conference in 1974, members of the Association of Southeast Asian Institutions of Higher Learning (ASAIHL) perceived the implemented curricula in the region as irrelevant, fundamentally incompatible, and mismatched with the existing sociocultural contexts, "influenced by the[ir] colonial histories" (Prachoom, 1974, p. 3), and based mostly on "the needs of societies other than those of South-East Asia as such" (p. ii). They also perceived the deployed curricula as outdated when compared with curricula in developed countries. Consequently, schools and universities produced graduates who were overspecialized, in possession of "irrelevant skills," and "wasted in the Southeast Asian context" (p. 4) because these graduates were not capable of dealing with problems that plagued their societies. Curriculum theorizing articulated a functional view of education that emphasized the development of manpower over manhood. It did not consider the impact of the prevailing social, cultural, and economic differences among groups of people. Curriculum in general was taught in a decontextualized manner and transmitted to the point that the "homogenized and inert knowledge alienated students from their backgrounds" and, thus, producing an "educated class" that was either confused or uncaring of its context (p. 4).

When the Association of South-East Asian Nations (ASEAN) was formed in 1967, consisting of the Philippines, Malaysia, Indonesia, Brunei, Thailand, and Singapore, it signified the start of a kind of global education, at least at the regional level. Vietnam became an ASEAN member only recently. The regional collaboration that took place among ASEAN members focused on both economic and educational development. Education was perceived by all as a crucial tool for growth and modernization. Curriculum theorizing at the regional level focused on basic education, particularly in the areas of reading, writing, and arithmetic (i.e., the 3 Rs). There was also a strong interest on both formal and nonformal education in the areas of literacy, vocational and technical, agricultural, health, and women's education (Hawkins, 1998).

In 1970, the National Institute for Educational Research (NIER) in Japan came out with a three-volume report that was a comparative analysis of curriculum development in elementary education among selected Asian countries. A second NIER-sponsored regional comparative study was conducted in the 1980s, but the scope of analysis included both elementary and secondary school curricula. The results of the third NIER study were published in 1999, and participating countries came from the Asia-Pacific, Europe, and North America.

The third NIER study shows remarkable curriculum changes in individual countries over the past 10 years. There has been much concern about the anticipated needs of an emerging global society as well as ways that could strengthen social cohesion and national identity and preserve cultural heritage. Curriculum theorizing focused on developing effective mechanisms for deploying cultural, ethical, and moral values and addressing both the "national and international changes and more local needs" (National Institute of Educational Research, 1999, p. 56) in the curriculum. Other curriculum theorizing concerns included ways in which to "raise the achievement for all students," establish "equal opportunity and equity," become internationally competitive, and safeguard a country's "future economic well-being" (p. 21). New subjects were introduced and new topics were incorporated in the existing curricula, such as information technology (considered a first priority), civics, environmental education, and additional foreign languages (also a first priority). Across country, almost all schools were given greater autonomy (increased devolution) in deciding how to implement state-recommended curriculum policies and deal with the local situation (p. 57) in the best manner possible. However, perennial administrative issues relevant to the deployment of curriculum have had to be dealt with, such as incompetent teachers, insufficient academic and institutional resources, and so on. Interestingly enough, all countries have participated in national or international projects and surveys (e.g., TIMSS), which for them has become the basis for monitoring and evaluating their respective curricula.

CURRICULUM ISSUES IN THE PHILIPPINES: A REALIST TALE

Basic elementary and secondary education in the Philippines takes 10 years to finish. A student who studies in a public school spends about 206 days in school, 6 years in grade school, and an additional 4 years to earn her or his high school diploma. At least based on the amended 1986 Constitution, Filipino is the national language, whereas the official languages of instruction in the schools are Filipino and English. Thus, a student who lives in a different province (state) and speaks a different dialect (local language) is encouraged to use it in everyday classroom discourse. However, he or she is required by law to learn English and Filipino.

Marinas (1999) reported that "there are no regulations that govern curriculum policies" (p. 354) except that schools are required by law to teach the following subjects: Philippine Constitution, sports, music, Filipino language, human rights, environment, dangerous drugs, and science and technology education. All schools learn about curriculum reform and changes based on orders, circulars, and bulletins given periodically by the Department (Ministry) of Education, Culture, and Sports (DECS). Curriculum reform is guided by the following provision from Article XIV of the amended 1986 Constitution, which states that:

> All educational institutions shall inculcate patriotism and nationalism, foster love of humanity, respect for human rights, appreciation of the role of national heroes in the historical development of the country, teach the rights and duties of citizenship, strengthen ethical and spiritual values, develop moral character and personal disci-

pline, encourage critical and creative thinking, broaden scientific and technological knowledge and promote vocational efficiency.

What is currently implemented is a national curriculum that contains desired learning competencies per grade and year level, including implementing guidelines. Public school teachers are given the sole responsibility for effecting change in the classroom context, which, consequently, makes the goals of reform difficult to achieve primarily because a significant number of these teachers do not have the necessary and sufficient training in both subject content and psychology of teaching and learning. The foci of curriculum theorizing in the last 5 years were in the following aspects: development of a curriculum that is both student centered and community based, formulation of appropriate learning competencies per grade and year levels, incorporation of critical thinking and values education in all subjects, and development of strong science and technology curricula in almost all aspects of the educational sector. In fact, more than 100 science and technology public high schools, which accounts for less than 3% of the total number of high schools in the country, already have been set up. Also, high-achieving students were provided with funding and opportunity to actively participate in international science and technology competitions, and the First Science and Technology Education Plan (STEP) was deployed in 1994. The following specific provision from Article XIV of the 1986 Constitution highlights the importance accorded to science and technology education:

> The State shall give priority to research and development, invention, innovation, and their utilization; and to science and technology education, training and services. It shall support indigenous, appropriate, and self-reliant scientific and technological capabilities, and their application to the country's productive systems and national life.

Curriculum theorizing in the next 5 years will be in the following areas: the development of a core curriculum, "more in-depth indigenization or localization" of curricula, and the integration of technology in existing science and mathematics curricula through the 2nd STEP, which is a revision of the 1st STEP and will be implemented at the beginning of the 2000 school year. Based on a draft copy of the 2nd STEP, the national program anticipates the "remarkable advances in the field of information and communication technology," which "shall be at the forefront of educational activities," the demands of a "global community of nations that knows no distance and time restrictions," the "indispensable [role of] technology in meeting the basic needs of humankind, and the reality of "an environment of uncontrolled information flows and global competition, trade, and investment," which places premium on knowledge and information (STEP II, 2000, pp. 9–10).

THE GLOBAL CONSTRUCTION OF THE "FILIPINO" IN PHILIPPINE TEXTBOOKS

In the Philippines, the Spanish and (early) American colonization in the periods 1521–1898 and 1898–1946, respectively, as well as its neo-colonial ties with Americans in later years, have left indelible effects on the nation as a whole, most especially in the areas of education, language, and identity. The fastness of the American influence in the never-ending process of restructuring of school curricula in the Philippines remains firm and secure to this day. Most curriculum specialists, educators, teacher practitioners, and policy administrators restructure curricular needs based on changes that take place in the North (mostly U.S.), and they justify the mis/appropriation as a manifestation of their commitment to global education. Even if there were attempts made to indigenize Western concepts, the existing curricula is far from an authentic indigenization of any kind. Hence, the absence of any meaningful kind of curriculum theorizing activity in the country is the main reason for the cacophonous manner in which significant aspects of education are currently deployed in practice. For instance, at least three shifts in emphasis were made in the country's science curriculum in the last 30 years—from inquiry to environment and low cost improvisation to the relationship of science, technology, and society (UP-ISMED Staff, 1998). The rationale for the shifts were motivated by changes in Western (mostly American) science reform movements. A similar argument applies in the case of the mathematics curriculum, which shifted from a compartmentalized framework (i.e., algebra-algebra-geometry-more algebra) to a spiral program that focuses on interconnections among various topics. The shift in the framework was, again, motivated by changes in the American school mathematics curriculum regardless of the differing contexts of the two societies.

All efforts toward developing a postcolonial-based Philippine curriculum have failed due to the larger sociocultural and historical context that have constructed the Filipino of today. The current state of popular culture, reflective of the ethos, attitude, and sentiments of the Philippine youth, is strongly Western. Indicators are aplenty. Bleaching and whitening lotions are popular with the young generation, as are hair colors and bonnets. Various themes explored in movies and TV soaps are Western adaptations. Popular songs revived by local performers and played in the airwaves are American inspired or famous American and British hits, old and new. Despite the many significant historical changes that have taken place in the country, such as the 1986 People Power Revolution that ended the 20-year dictatorship of Ferdinand Marcos through nonviolent means, the popular sentiment is far from an active reflection about nationalism. Like the social studies textbooks being used in the public schools today, students, teachers, the schools, as well as a significant fraction of Philippine media *promote,* in Mulder's (1990) words, "a bogus nationalism based on folklore, national costumes, and cultural uniqueness, while avoiding all discussion of political and economic nationalism" (pp. 98–99).

Textbooks reveal in printed discourse the social constructedness of the Filipino, whose identity is as complex as the country's language history. Mulder's critical analysis of recent World Bank and government-sponsored Philippine textbooks in social studies for college and public school elementary, middle, and high school students reveals an unproblematized celebration of the hybrid nature of the Filipino. For instance, after having read the elementary series, Mulder observed that on reaching Grade 7, every schoolchild knows that he has 40% Malay blood in his veins, 30% Indonesian, 10% Negrito, 10% Chinese, 5% Hindu, 2% Arab, and 3% European and American. This interesting cocktail explains his native qualities. Malay blood is particularly freedom loving. The Hindi strain is fatalistic. The Chinese are frugal, and the Spanish are proud and deeply religious. The American is democratic and efficient (Mulder, 1990).

On a positive note, Filipinos characterized in the prior manner appear to be legitimate global citizens, owing their lineage from a long line of strangers, which "dressed" them "in foreign gear" (p. 91) and "with all [the] good things" (p. 89) at that. Yet the half-truths claimed by the authors left out significant controversial details that could have explained why a Filipino identity has failed to emerge despite all the perceived positive contributions made. Although the textbooks celebrate the multiethnic Filipino that has evolved, they do little to explore the possibility of a Filipino with a self-contradictory identity that is as complex as the language that has evolved through the long years of colonization.

The existing social studies curricula and the textbooks, in fact, did not explore the local and precolonial contributions of the country's forebears prior to trade and colonization by strangers who first came as friends. Filipinos today benefit from a Western conception of *education*, benighted by the fact that there was already a system of education prior to the colonization of the imperial masters that took place not through the kind of schools that we know today (Arcilla, 1972). With globalization, the Filipino runs the risk of self-effacement and the predicament of total dependence that During (1999) pointed out earlier, with the help of a curriculum that does little than justify why her or his internally plural self is, as Mulder (1990) pointed out

a confusion of roots and a bastardization of descent, [marked by] a colonial mentality forever indebted for the material benefits, blessings, and civilization that foreigners brought, [and has] the near absence of a historical consciousness, the perversion of the ideas of [Jose Rizal, the national hero], a negative self-image eternally in the shadow of the great qualities of others, and a very vague (if any) identification with the encompassing state. (p. 97)

Up to this point, we have used *Filipino* without explaining how the term originated in the first place. Now it beckons us to explore the emergence of what is referred to as the *Filipino language* in the hope of providing a more or less complete characterization of the structure of complexity of the Filipino described in the preceding paragraphs. Both identity and language are contested sites that form the basic elements in any curriculum and, more important, from which colonized peoples construct their experiences that may have been "subtly and richly infused with myth" (Lamming, 1995/1960, p. 13). During (1995/1987) made an interesting point, indeed, when he insisted that language and identity are conjoined in tortile ways in the sense that "a choice of language is a choice of identity" (pp. 125–126). Whorf's (1956) insistence that our impressions and the way we come to know things about nature and the world of phenomena are shaped by the "linguistic system in our minds" (p. 213) highlight the subtle connections as well. In postcolonialist discourse, the link between identity and language has been explored, and a response given to the question regarding authenticity of identity of a colonized has been measured by the extent to which the colonized has appropriated the language of her or his colonizer. Even Anderson's (1983) notion of a colonized group's imagined community—that is, their collective identification—rests on the strength of association with a language that represents them.

The impact of the long colonial history in the Philippines that took place in the last six centuries had corresponding effects in the way the officially considered national language, Filipino, developed over time. Sibayan (1999/1994) identified six language shifts in the history of languaging in the country. The language of the forebears at the precolonial stage had its roots traced to either original Indonesian or Malayo-Polynesian (Llamzon, 1970). Toward the end of the 14th century, the indoctrination in certain parts of the country to Islam and the Muslim religion marked the first shift to the Arabic language. With the Spanish colonization in the mid-15th century, people, especially those that came from the elite and intellectual classes, were forced to learn Spanish. The shift to the English language took place with the American colonization toward the end of the 19th century. When the Philippines finally regained its independence after having experienced colonization for so long a time, the shift to Pilipino in 1935 (and then to Filipino in 1973) became a symbolic act in marking its full independence as a free state. The new language represented nationalist sentiments and was symbolic of the nation's concerted efforts to define a national identity. More recently, there has been a trend toward mixing English and the vernacular/regional language.

In 1974, Gonzalez pointed out the phenomenon of linguistic dissonance in describing the Philippines's language situation. There appeared to be a "lack of fit or disharmony" between the proposed national language and the existing official languages and media of instruction used in schools. That is, aside from English and Pilipino as the main official languages in schools and offices, the 1973 Constitution contained a provision that required the development of a national language called Filipino, which, unfortunately, had no prior existence and yet was expected to become the "expression of the [Philippine] identity" (Gonzalez, 1974, pp. 333–334). An amendment in the 1987 Constitution settled the perceived disharmony by making Filipino both the official and national language. In describing the nature of the Filipino language, Gonzalez (1974) emphasized that it is

> the product of a political settlement motivated by the emotions and cultural identities of a multilingual and poly-ethnic people an artificial symbol (like the flag, the national anthem, the name of the country, boundaries, laws, systems) of national unity not imposed but supposedly to be developed together, with representation from all sides. (pp. 336–337)

Yet there is a problem with the phrase "representation from all sides" because things are never equal at the baseline. Especially in developing countries, where concerns frequently revolve around issues that deal with better performance in the global economy, state power (through government legislations) is considered most powerful among all representations. Thus, what happened thereafter was the construction of the Filipino language in global terms that has become a compromised symbol, supposedly a confluence of the various indigenous and foreign (mostly American) elements, but that implicitly affirmed as well that no one local language was good enough. In fact, those that have been brought externally, English especially, have had greater substantial significance than the local contributions. Sibayan (1999/1994) wrote:

> In the development of the Filipino, the main contribution of the native Philippine languages will be in the enrichment of the vocabulary needed in everyday life, while English will be the main source of the intellectualized vocabulary portion. (pp. 558–559)

The privileged status accorded to the English language is due to the pragmatist nature of the Filipino who refuses to draw the line between "economic survival and being a nationalist" (Sibayan & Gonzalez, forthcoming). English for the Filipino, Sibayan (1999) wrote, will play the "economic imperative" with "nationalism" and "cultural emancipation" only as secondary priorities (p. 571).

CURRICULUM ISSUES IN MALAYSIA AND THAILAND: TWO REALIST TALES

Bahasa Melayu (Malay language) is Malaysia's national and first official language. There are three other official languages—namely, English (in second place), Chinese, and Tamil. There are three types of elementary/primary schools depending on a learner's ethnic membership: National (Malay) School, National Type Chinese School, and National Type Tamil School. In all three schools, students are required to learn both the English and Malay languages and encouraged to use their ethnic language in everyday classroom discourse as well. In high school, all students continue to learn the Malay and English languages, with their ethnic language as a possible elective. Students spend 193 days in school, and it takes them 7 years to finish elementary school, including preschool, and 5 years to earn a high school diploma. Incoming high school students from either the National Type Chinese or National Type Tamil schools are also provided with a 1-year transition program called "Remove Class" at the start of secondary schooling, which is aimed at helping them obtain adequate proficiency in the national language. High school students are tracked in the beginning of their third year of schooling (upper secondary) and allowed to pursue any one of the following streams: academic, technical, and vocational.

Curriculum theorizing in Malaysia is a centralized and systematic process and is usually initiated by the Curriculum Development Centre, a division of the country's Ministry of Education (MOE). Final decisions about curriculum changes and implementing guidelines are made by the Central Curriculum Committee comprising of the Director General of Education as chair, the various chairs of the MOE, and selected members of the academia (professors and deans). Curriculum theorizing in Malaysia is primarily guided by what is officially known as the National Philosophy of Education (NPE), which states that:

> Education in Malaysia is an ongoing effort towards further developing the potential of individuals in a holistic and integrated manner so as to produce individuals who are intellectually, spiritually, emotionally, and physically balanced and harmonious, based on a firm belief in and devotion to God. Such an effort is designed to produce Malaysian citizens who are knowledgeable and competent, who possess high moral standards, and who are responsible and capable of achieving a high level of personal well-being as well as being able to contribute to the betterment of the family, the society, and the nation at large. (National Institute for Educational Research, 1999, p. 289)

Sharifah (1999) claimed that the NPE has been developed to "achieve the nation's vision to prepare children to become knowledgeable, trained and skilled individuals to meet the growing needs of the millennium" (p. 291). To accomplish the NPE, a strong emphasis is placed on "science and technology, use of information technology, and inculcating good moral and work ethics suitable for the Information Age" (p. 291). In addition to the NPE, all education schools and school administrators are required to adhere to the Education Act of 1996, which provides the necessary laws related to curriculum policies and changes. More important, side by side with the NPE is Vision 2020, in which all Malaysians see themselves as a fully industrialized developed nation by the year 2020.

At present, there is a uniform system of education in both elementary/primary and secondary levels and a national curriculum in which content is situated based on the Malaysian context. The national curriculum promotes unity by requiring all students to learn both Behasa Melayu and English. It is equitable insofar as it allows all students to pursue the same set of core subjects. Cultural diversity is strongly encouraged at the school and classroom levels by allowing students from different ethnic groups to use their language in classroom discourse. However, central assessment and examinations are usually given in either the English or Bahasa Melayu language by the Malaysian Examination Syndicate. Students take them periodically at various points of their schooling.

A program evaluation of the New Primary School Curriculum (NPSC) was conducted in 1993, which has resulted in the deployment of the Integrated Curriculum for Primary School (ICPS) in 1995. Three new courses have been introduced—namely, Science, Living Skills (consisting of manipulative skills, commerce and entrepreneurship, and family living), and Local Studies. Further, the following areas have been given significant emphasis in the newly developed school curricula: science and technology, entrepreneurship, humanities, and the environment. At the secondary school level, the

Integrated Curriculum for Secondary School (ICSS) has been viewed as a second step toward the fulfillment of goals initially laid down in the ICPS. A key concept in deploying the ICSS is integration, which involves two parts. The first part involves the integration of knowledge, skills, and values within classroom discourse between teacher and student. The second part involves integration among curriculum, co-curricular activities, and school culture. In the next 10 years, all efforts are being aimed at advancing a curriculum that is reflective of Vision 2020 and the principles laid down in the NPE. There will also be an ongoing emphasis on science and technology and the effective deployment of information technology mainly to "foster the development of technologically literate workers for the Information Age" (Sharifah, 1999, pp. 316–317).

Thai is Thailand's official and national language. Based on the 1990 revised National Curriculum, Thais spend 200 days in school and start their education at age 3. Preprimary education takes 3 years, followed by 6 years of primary education, and 6 additional years of secondary education. Payungsak (1999) reported that 20th-century education in Thailand was used mainly to facilitate changes that took place in the social, religious, cultural, economic, and political spheres. For instance, curriculum theorizing prior to 1960 focused on issues surrounding the religious appropriation of Buddhism in Thai culture, literacy, and government service. Curriculum theorizing from the Sukhothai Period (1253–1350) up to the reign of King Rama III (1824–1851) was focused on applying Buddhist principles and Indian educational practices in almost aspects of Thai education. Boys especially were sent to the monasteries to learn basic literacy and (government) service in society resulting from processes that accompanied the acquisition of Buddhism. With the reign of King Rama V (1868–1910), curriculum theorizing shifted to the teaching/learning of the 3 Rs and to programs in which graduates were trained to become government servants. Curriculum theorizing during the time of King Rama VI (1910–1925) shifted from the development of curriculum programs for government service to general and specialized (e.g., law, education) programs for the general populace.

The curriculum in the 1990s more or less followed the 1978/1981 Revised Curricula for both elementary and secondary schools, which actually replaced the 1960 national curriculum. Curriculum theorizing in the 1978/1981 curricula focused on developing diverse programs that catered to the needs of not only those Thais who pursued advanced degrees, but those others who were forced to drop out of school and had to work. Also, an equal emphasis was placed on curricular programs that facilitated further advancement in scientific and technological fields and encouraged various socioeconomic changes that went with the country's transition from an agricultural to an agricultural-industrialized nation-state.

A more updated revision is currently underway as a result of the newly promulgated 1997 Thai Constitution and more recent changes that have occurred in the political and social spheres as well. It was expected to be fully implemented in 2000. Curriculum theorizing in the new millennium will most certainly address issues surrounding globalization and increased internationalization at least based on the following points raised by Payungsak: First, the necessity of students at all levels in developing "international communication skills" (p. 432); second, two principles drawn from the proposed basic education development which involve "comply[ing] with science and technological development while conserv[ing the] environment" and "develop[ing] harmonious nationality and internationality" (pp. 434–435); and third, the "strong influence" of globalization in today's education (p. 433). Payungsak (1999) wrote:

> Progression in academic knowledge and technology are very fast and dynamic. Worldwide dissemination and easy access [to them] not only have strong influences

on [students'] ways of life but [could] also change teaching and learning methodologies. (p. 433)

IDENTITIES IN MALAYSIA AND THAILAND: REINSCRIPTIONS, RETRENCHMENTS, AND RHIZOMES

A common feature that figures prominently in the curriculum theorizing in both Malaysia and Thailand deals with the pivotal roles of globalization and internationalization in both the content and form of their planned and implemented curricula. Why this is so invites us to consider the current situation of the larger societies and their governments that deem them as significant and a fundamental priority along with ways in which to preserve local heritage. Because curriculum theorizing in both countries is more or less a centralized task subsumed in their departments or ministries of education, curriculum theorists as contemporary specific intellectuals (in Foucault's sense) are expected to perform an instrumental function by prioritizing government thrusts in various curriculum revisions, decisions, and policies.

Globalization is a buzzword among Malaysians and Thais. In Reynolds's (1998) words, "global culture is being domesticated" (p. 129) in these societies. Malaysia's desire to establish itself as an industrialized developed nation-state in the year 2020 (i.e., Vision 2020) will be achieved partly, albeit significantly, with the assistance of schools that have been tasked to deploy curricula geared toward exploring the full potentials of advanced technologies. Mee (1998) pointed out the vigorous role being played by the present ruling body in acculturating Malaysians to the reality of "information economy, information society, global village, and information superhighway" (p. 233). In the following brief remark he made in 1991, Datuk Seri Dr Mahathir Mohamad, currently Malaysia's Prime Minister, articulated in punctilious terms the current government's uncompromised stance about the future of Malaysian society in the emerging Information Age:

> [I]n the information age that we are living in, Malaysian society must be information-rich. ... Increasingly, knowledge will not only be the basis of power but also prosperity ... [and] no effort must be spared in the creation of an information-rich Malaysian society. (Mohathir; cited in Mee, 1998, p. 234)

Specific intellectuals or experts have been assigned the following tasks: (a) "mediate between the local and global levels of the economy"; (b) perform as a "critical national resource in terms of future national development and economic competitiveness"; and (c) provide the link between "their mediation of the global economy and their control of knowledge, education, and science" (Mee, 1998, p. 234). The tasks expected of experts reveal the power they yield especially in reinscribing traditional notions of nationalism in contemporary terms. These experts, who undoubtedly are capable of exerting control and influence in current curriculum theorizing practices, work within an economic nationalist perspective, which sees "economic autonomy as the means to achieve political sovereignty" (Mee, 1998, p. 235). Also, they are in the best position to justify the necessity of redefining nationalism so that curriculum changes align with, say, Vision 2020.

In the case of Thailand, Reynolds' (1998) careful reading of Thais' formative emergence as a nation-state reveals their early cosmopolitan and later global character—that is, their historically oriented disposition "to engage with the other, an activity that of necessity establishes a tension between the local and the global" (p. 120). The migration and resettlement activities that took place among various ethnic tribes (Mon, Lao, Karen, Muslims, Phuan folks from northern Laos, and Chinese) led to the emergence of a polyethnic Bangkok in 1782, which grew in number in the succeeding centuries. The Chinese who were semiassimilated in Bangkok, especially, played a significant role in post-World War II because of the (mostly business) transactions they conducted with peoples, relatives, and various affinities in the other parts of Southeast Asia. Inter- and multicultural interactions were strongly encouraged along with the following Thai attitude that had a dual pragmatic function: Similarities between cultures resulting from affiliation were economically productive, whereas differences meant expanding the character of Thai-ness.

The international disposition of Thais became even more prominent during the period of the so-called *American era,* in which they openly embraced American principles and policies that affected almost every aspect of living and education, most especially. International communication and the manner in which Thais appropriated almost any kind of media and printing technology available further enhanced their cosmopolitan attitude. Also, even prior to Western influence, "Thai invulnerability" was described as "fragmented, repetitive, and unsystematic," which enabled Thais to appropriate and transform external (non-Thai) artifacts (knowledge, culture, material things, etc.) as if the artifacts were truly their own (Reynolds, 1998). Watson (1989) described Thais as "cultural borrowers par excellence." He wrote,

> Thailand retained its political independence by bending to the wind; adapting, modifying, and absorbing foreign ideas and customs only in so far as it was felt they were necessary. The same is true in education. … Ideas and experiments have been tried, wherever they may have come from, to see if they would benefit the Thai situation. (Watson, 1989, p. 64)

At this point, we explore how local knowledges and national identities, both elements being essential in curriculum theorizing, are viewed vis-à-vis the current social, cultural, and economic landscapes in Malaysia and Thailand. Mee (1998) insisted that the use of technologies in the emerging globalization of Malaysians only strengthened their sense of nationhood "even through the process of building extra-national relations" (p. 227). What is required, Mee pointed out, is a changing conception of what constitutes nation and nationalism (culture, identity, knowledges, practices, etc.) in their present history. In other words, the classic conception of nation and nationalism as a trope for some stable ethnic, cultural core needs to be reformulated as "a highly adaptive and always multicultural entity" (p. 229). In the present curriculum, in fact, students are exposed to a variety of nationalisms within Malaysia. They learn to speak several languages, attend schools based on their ethnic membership, and participate in religious practices and other cultural activities that are "extra-local in origin" (p. 229).

Because technology plays a significant role in the many aspects of the Malaysian school curricula, it is equally important to see how technology may have influenced the current identities of Malaysians in the larger society who have benefited from the curriculum shifts that have taken place at least in the last 10 years. Mee (1998) noted that there is now a significant number of Malaysians who are hooked up on the Internet and presently taking advantage of the various transnational relationships formed in the process of participating through webbed interactions. The Internet is also currently used as a site in which users "reinforce, construct, question and imagine national cultural practices in relation to both a local and global audience" (p. 245). Further, a semiotic analysis of various personal homepages and mailing lists reveals the "Malay presence" in the "personalized representations" (p. 252). Based on Malaysian studies on Internet communication, Mee reported there are "a host of sociocultural and geographic referents which reinstate the nation both as cultural identity and territory" (p.

232). In other words, contemporary Malaysians perceive themselves and their country as both self-reflexively global and particular—that is, premised on the concept of the world as a global, interrelated system, but differentiated in terms of national and cultural specificities" (Mee, 1998, pp. 232–233).

Reynolds (1998) reported that, in Thailand, globalization is viewed as having changed the contexts of social relations in different ways. As instances, Reynolds pointed to the increased industrialization and urbanization that have affected local standards and family and community life, including what constitutes local identities, the evolving perceptions about gayness as another form of identity in itself and no longer a problem on behavior, and "the commercialization of sex and the commodification of charismatic monks with globalization" (p. 119). Considering Thai history, various global cultural interactions inevitably have meant developing new identities for the Thais, and they certainly have proved themselves capable of localizing identities external in origin. Yet this poses a problem for some Thai intellectuals who see this predisposition toward assimilation and imitation as affecting the "viability of the 'us'" (p. 134). There is also a dilemma in the process of defining what is local because of the corresponding necessity to define what is not local. Bunrak wrote:

> It is not possible to explain the phenomenon of "inside" (*phai nai*) without making reference to what is produced on the "outside" (*phai nork*). This would seem the be the "crisis" in Thai studies everywhere. (cited in Reynolds, 1998, p. 137)

The more dominant position, however, belongs to those (including media) who celebrate the possibility of a transnational *ersatz Thai* culture, which mutually coexists with the authentic Thai culture drawn from "drama, music and literature handed down from the past" (Reynolds, 1998, p. 137). Viewed in this context, Reynolds and Kasian Tejapira before him insist on the "liberation of identity from nationality, a kind of fragmented subjectivity or split personality" (p. 137).

PROVISIONAL CLOSURE: CURRICULUM THEORIZING IN THE FOLD OF THE GLOBAL CULTURAL ECONOMY

Curriculum theorists in the critical/reconceptualist tradition foreground the necessity of looking at both internal and external factors that influence curriculum and curriculum theorizing. The various tales provide us with a purview in which to understand the complicit role of curriculum and curriculum theorizing in the social, economic, and cultural reproduction of developing societies based mostly on the hegemon of governments and schools (e.g., through texts used in the classrooms) acting as state apparatuses (in Louis Althusser's sense). The journey toward full autonomy and development in the image of Western developed nation-states requires curriculum theorists as specific intellectuals in developing countries use curriculum as a convenient site in which to materialize goals and efforts that will help their countries participate productively and competitively in both the international market and global cultural economy. Readers have been especially provided with the wider cultural context to understand why curriculum theorizing has been performed in particular ways. At the least, curriculum theorizing in developing countries always has to negotiate with the perennial emersion of complex negative factors (lack of qualified teachers, shortage of textbooks, failing bureaucracies, to mention a few) resulting from inadequate social, economic, and political structures.

The episteme we all share in the history of the present has been marked by the always-already hyperreal condition of globalization. It manifests itself in the social, cultural, economic, and political contours of nation-states that employ worldwide processes that are extralogical in nature. The trope of the global cultural economy is the rhizome—that is, various flows of images and ideas, technologies, finances, and migrants and global citizens, following Appadurai, affect both developed and developing countries in ways that render the binaries global/local and center/periphery as conceptually and practically untenable. Also, Odin (1997) talked about the postcolonial cultural experience as working within a "contemporary topology [that] is composed of cracks, in-between spaces, or gaps that do not fracture reality into this or that, but instead provide multiple points of articulation with a potential for incorporating contradictions and ambiguities" (pp. 599–600). These contemporary conditions of existence partly explain why curriculum theorizing in developing countries addresses too many complex issues all at once regardless of the fact that, say, the foreignness of science and technology being appropriated in the curriculum makes it extremely difficult for ethnobased science and technology to flourish or why mainstream scientific and technological methods appear incongruent with situated versions based on the specificity of their contexts.

The internationalization of curriculum in developing countries in Southeast Asia have both productive and destructive effects on the formation of identities, nationalism, and local heritage. The three countries explored in this chapter share the observation that, historically speaking, their imagined communities are internally polyethnic and plural. Further, because their histories reveal the extent to which their early forebears have been constructed by various forms of colonization, they appear as always-already conditioned toward globalization. Consequently, curriculum theorizing in these cases is more or less a projection of the historical conditions that shaped them. Changes in the Philippine and Thai curricula, for instance, have been preconditioned by changes in the U.S. curriculum. Western-trained Malaysian students, professionals, and experts influence ongoing curriculum restructuring activities in the country especially in the areas of science and technology.

The status of local heritage and nationalism or national identities is an important concern in a curriculum that is undergoing internationalization or globalization. The different tales, certainly biased and incomplete insofar as they have been narrated from particular standpoints, reveal the arbitrariness of categorization. The term *national identity* is quite problematic because one can be a nationalist and fail to have an identity drawn from within (like in the Philippines) or one can be a nationalist and have multiple identities (like in Malaysia and Thailand). The textbooks as curriculum tools depict Filipinos as pragmatic nationalists who have constructed, in an unproblematic manner, their imagined community in the global image of their colonizers. Malaysians and Thais, in contrast, are economic nationalists and have multiple identities, at least based on a careful reading of their respective formative histories. In other words, the significant changes that took place in the political and economic structures have resulted in different ways of appropriating the terms *local* and *national identities*.

The reality of globalization and the Information Age served as a requisite in the construction of new identities. Now more than ever do we all witness a direct link among curriculum, curriculum theorizing, and the demands of late capitalist enterprise. A globalized curriculum, like today's popular culture, is "often the product of urban, commercial, and state interests, [and] where [local, ethno-based curriculum] is often a response to the competitive cultural policies of today's nation-states" (Appadurai & Breckenridge, 1988, p. 8). Furthermore, the globalized curriculum limns new registers, images, and simulacra in the aftermath of the implosion of socioculturally constructed binaries resulting from new imaginings afforded by changing spaces/places in the disseminated order. Thus, curriculum theorizing has been inevitably employed to integrate and align national with global needs and standards. Just a few decades ago, it was noted that the old curricula of developing countries reflected the needs and influence of their colonizers. The emerging curricula at the dawn of the new millennium anticipate the demands of the new social, political, and cultural structures in the umbrae of international market and the global cultural economy.

I anticipate the immediate concerns facing the internationalization of curriculum in developing countries within the next decade or so will deal with, on the one hand, developing appropriate frameworks that will provide a clear conceptualization of the nonpareil and authentic national identities and local heritage and ways they can be sustained and reaffirmed in the face of globalization, which has widened spaces and opened up various flows resulting from increased deterritorialization and deessentialization, the very least among divers conditions of existence. On the other hand, when Odin (1997) talked about the contemporary postcolonial cultural experience as being imbricated in a "new space" that operates within the "aesthetic of the hypertext" (p. 599), there is a strong sense in which the emerging international curriculum in developing countries should be viewed in terms of, at the very least, "multivocality, multilinearity, open-endedness, active encounter, and traversal" (p. 599). The international curriculum, developed with the needs of culturally hybrid identities in mind, becomes a site in which to pursue new forms of postcolonial identities "based on the fundamental assumption of the incorporation of differences" (p. 612). The various forms are also framed within a version of reality that, according to Trinh Minh-Ha, is not a mere crossing from one borderline to the other or that is not merely double, but a reality that involves the crossing of an indeterminate number of borderlines, on that remains multiple in its hyphenation" (Trinh, 1991, p. 107; cited in Odin, 1997, p. 612).

If we consider the current situation of curriculum theorists in these developing countries whose governments make it an imperative for them to incorporate the needs of globalization and internationalization in ongoing curriculum restructuring activities, then in the service of the state they become elites who, according to C. Breckenridge and Appadurai, are transnational cultural producers and consumers, forming a global class with few real cultural allegiances to the nation-state, but who nevertheless need new ideologies of state and nation to control and shape the populations who live within their territories. As these populations are exposed, through media and travel, to the cultural regimes of other nation-states, such ideologies of nationalism increasingly take on a global flavor (Breckenridge & Appadurai; cited in Foster, 1991, p. 248). Apart from Karl Marx's notion of universal intellectuals, Foucault's specific intellectuals, and Giroux and McLaren's border intellectuals, what new roles await curriculum theorists as global intellectuals in changing times?

REFERENCES

Ahmad, A. (1995/1987). Jameson's rhetoric of otherness and the "national allegory." In B. Ashcroft, G. Griffiths, & H. Tiffin (Eds.), *The post-colonial studies reader* (pp. 77–84). London: Routledge.

Altbach, P., & Viswanathan, S. (Eds.). (1989). *From dependence to autonomy: The development of Asian universities.* Boston: Kluwer Academic Press.

Anderson, B. (1983). *Imagined communities: Reflections on the origin and spread of nationalism.* London: Verso.

Appadurai, A. (1999/1990). Disjuncture and difference in the global cultural economy. In S. During (Ed.), *The cultural studies reader* (2nd ed.). London: Routledge.

Appadurai, A. (1999). Globalization and the research imagination. *International Journal of Social Science,* 229–238.

Appadurai, A., & Breckenridge, C. (1988). Why public culture? *Public Culture, 1*(1), 5–9.

Arcilla, J. (1972). Phillipine education: Some observations from history. *Philippine Studies, 20,* 273–286.

Batley, E. (1991). Language learning and the technology of International communications. *International Review of Education, 37*(1), 149–162.

Brady, W. (1997). Indigenous Australian educators and globalisation. *International Review of Education, 43*(5–6), 413–422.

Castles, S., & Miller, M. (1996/1993). *The age of migration.* London: Macmillan.

Deleuze, G., & Guattari, F. (1987). A thousand plateaus: Capitalism and schizophrenia (B. Massumi, trans.). Minneapolis: University of Minnesota Press.

During, S. (1995/1997). *The cultural studies reader.* New York: Routledge.

During, S. (1999). Introduction. In S. During (Ed.), *The cultural studies reader* (2nd ed., pp. 1–30). London: Routledge.

Foster, R. (1991). Making national cultures in the global ecumene. *Annual Review of Anthropology, 20,* 235–260.

Gergen, K. (1991). *The saturated self: Dilemmas of identity in contemporary life.* New York: Basic Books.

Ghosh, R. (1987). New educational technologies: Their impact on relationships of dependence and interdependence for third world countries. *International Review of Education, 33*(1), 33–50.

Gonzalez, A. (1974). The 1973 constitution and the bilingual education policy of the department of education and culture. *Philippine Studies, 22,* 325–337.

Hawkins, J. (1998). Education. In R. Maidment & C. Macherras (Eds.), *Culture and society in the Asia-Pacific* (pp. 141–162). New York: Routledge.

Hirst, P., & Thompson, G. (1999). *Globalization in question: The international economy and the possibilities for governance.* Cambridge, MA: Polity Press.

La Belle, T., & White, P. (1992). Education and colonial language policies in Latin America and the Carribean. *International Review of Education.*

Lamming, G. (1995/1960). The occasion for speaking. In B. Ashcroft, G. Griffiths, & H. Tiffin (Eds.), *The post-colonial studies reader* (pp. 12–17). London: Routledge.

Lash, S., & Urry, J. (1987). *The end of organized capitalism.* Cambridge, MA: Polity Press.

Llamzon, T. (1970). On the medium of instruction: English or Filipino. *Philippine Studies, 18*(4), 683–694.

Maratos, J. (1995). Ideology in science education: The Australian example. *International review of education, 41*(5), 357–369.

Marinas, B. (1999). Philippines. In National Institute of Educational Research, *International cross-cultural study of curriculum* (pp. 348–374). Japan: Author.

McLaren, P. (1995). Critical pedagogy in the age of global capitalism: Some challenges for the educational left. *Australian Journal of Education, 39*(1), 5–21.

McLuhan, M., & Fiore, Q. (1967). *The medium is the message.* New York: Bantam.

Mee, W. (1998). National difference and global citizenship. In J. Kahn (Ed.), *Southeast Asian identities* (pp. 227–259). Singapore: Institute of Southeast Asian Studies.

Mulder, N. (1990). Phillipine textbooks and the national self-image. *Phillipine Studies, 38,* 84–102.

Nebres, B. (1995). *Mathematics education in an era of globalization: Linking education, society, and culture in our region.* Paper presented at the International conference on regional collaboration in mathematics education, Monash University, Australia.

National Institute of Educational Research. (1999). *International cross-cultural study of curriculum.* Japan: Author.

Odin, J. (1997). The edge of difference: Negotiations between the hypertextual and the postcolonial. *Modern Fiction Studies, 43*(3), 598–630.

Payungsak, J. (1999). Thailand. In National Institute of Educational Research, *International cross-cultural study of curriculum* (pp. 426–442). Japan: Author.

Pinar, W., Reynolds, W., Slattery, P., & Taubman, P. (1995). *Understanding curriculum: An introduction to the study of historical and contemporary curriculum discourses.* New York: Lang.

Prachoom, C. (Ed.). (1974). *Curriculum reform with reference to general education in southeast Asia.* Thailand: ASAIHL Secretariat.

Reynolds, C. (1998). Globalization and cultural nationalism in modern Thailand. In J. Kahn (Ed.), *Southeast Asian identities* (pp. 115–145). Singapore: Institute of Southeast Asian Studies.

Roy Singh, R. (1986). *Education in Asia and the Pacific: Retrospect–prospect.* Bangkok, Thailand: UNESCO.

Said, E. (1993). *Culture and imperialism.* New York: Vintage Books.

Sharifah, N. P. (1999). Malaysia. In National Institute of Educational Research, *International cross-cultural study of curriculum* (pp. 285–317). Japan: Author.

Sibayan, B. (1999). *The intellectualization of Filipino and other essays on education and sociolinguistics.* Manila, Philippines: De La Salle University Press.

Sibayan, B. (1999/1994). The role and status of English vis-à-vis Filipino and other languages in the Philippines. In B. Sibayan (Ed.), *The intellectualization of Filipino and other essays on education and sociolinguistics* (pp. 557–578). Manila, Philippines: De La Salle University Press.

Sibayan, B., & Gonzalez, A. (forthcoming). English language teaching in the Philippines: A succession of movements. In J. Britton, R. Shafer, & K. Watson (Eds.), *Teaching and learning English in the world.* Avon, England: Multilingual Matters Ltd.

Vedder, P. (1994). Global measurement of the quality of education: A help to developing countries? *International Review of Education, 40*(1), 5–17.

Watson, K. (1989). Looking west and east: Thailand's academic development. In P. Altbach & S. Viswanathan (Eds.), *From dependence to autonomy: The development of Asian universities* (pp. 63–96). Boston: Kluwer Academic Press.

Whorf, B. L. (1956). *Language, mind and reality: Selected writings of Benjamin Lee Whorf* (J. B. Carroll, Ed.). New York: MIT Press.

Young, R. (1997). Comparative methodology and postmodern relativism. *International Review of Education, 43*(5–6), 497–505.

CHAPTER 33

Frame Factors, Structures, and Meaning Making: Shifting Foci of Curriculum Research in Sweden

Ulla Johansson
Umeå University, Sweden

Curriculum is the place where the generations struggle to define themselves and the world (Pinar et al., 1995), and the national curriculum is thus a concentrate of answers to questions of moral, ethical, and pragmatic nature like these: What kind of citizens do "we" (i.e., various representatives of the grown up generation) want the young people to become? How do we want them to be and behave? What should they learn? This is true, not only for written curricula, but also for the delivered curriculum offered by teachers to the students. But what is taught is not necessarily learned: Students usually construct their own curriculum. Thus, my outline of curriculum research in Sweden deals with curriculum as policymaking and texts as well as processes in which teachers and students take part. Among others the following questions are treated:

- How have the research problems been defined, and what have the answers been?
- Which interests and which groups have the researchers served?

The focus is on research published between 1990 and 2000. But earlier research is also dealt with because old paradigms are still alive, and paradigmatic shifts must be understood in the light of earlier traditions in curriculum research. It is also necessary to relate the field of research to factors external to the field. Like in many countries, Swedish curriculum research has been closely connected to school policy and school reforms (Vislie et al., 1997). Hence, I begin by providing an outline of the main characteristics of the Swedish history of education.

AN OUTLINE OF SWEDISH SCHOOL HISTORY

From the early 20th century to the early 1960s, the struggle for education has been fought over the streaming of pupils: How early in life should young people be sorted into different educational tracks? After World War II, another discussion emphasized the importance of the transmission of democratic values over the transmission of knowledge and skills. A third controversial matter has been whether education should promote social justice or take care of the gifted and talented first.

In the 1940s, postcompulsory academic studies were still exclusive, and the recruitment was also biased with regard to social background and gender. At that time, the Social Democrats began to regard education as an important means for social equality and the overall democratization of society. As they formed the government on their own from 1945 to 1976, they also strongly influenced the school policy during this period. They regarded education as an essential part of an all-embracing welfare policy and as a means of realizing a classless society.

The process of reform that began after World War II eventually resulted in a fundamental reorganization of education at all levels. In 1962, the first curriculum of the reformed compulsory, comprehensive school was issued. It meant that an organizationally integrated and obligatory 9-year school replaced all previous types of different schools for the same age groups. The first 8 years of the 9-year school should be nonstreamed, but beginning in form seven, the students should be grouped within the class depending on their optional subjects and their choices of the advanced or general course in mathematics and English. In the ninth form, the students were divided into nine different programs, four of which were practical.

Thereby a school for all Swedish children would be created based on the principle of the individual's own free choice: It was the business of the pupils and their parents to choose optional subjects and programs regardless of the teachers' opinions about the students' scholastic aptitudes. However, in reality, almost everyone chose academic programs, and therefore the streaming in the form nine was abolished in the next curriculum, issued in 1969. This basic structure is still valid apart from the fact that, in the national curriculum of 1994, there are no longer any alternative courses in English and mathematics.

Similar organizational reforms have been carried through for postcompulsory education. The upper secondary school of today, *gymnasieskolan,* encompasses both academic and vocational study programs, and more than 90% of all students proceed to this school. The reform of 1977 brought almost all postsecondary schools, including teacher training colleges, into a uniform organization for higher education. Simultaneously, the entrance requirements were changed to broaden the social recruitment. Experiences of working life and the results of a voluntary SAT test may, for example, be counted as merits.

Equality was the guiding star for the reforms, and it should be accomplished by a high degree of standardization of schooling. Timetables and detailed syllabi were issued to enhance the uniformity of the teaching content. State subsidies were earmarked for specific ends, and all important decisions were made at the center of the state apparatus. People on different levels of the system were expected to turn in the right direction, and hence state intentions would eventually be realized in the classrooms and in the students' heads and bodies. On the whole, this rational planning philosophy was typical for the Swedish version of the modern project.

However, in the late 1970s, the rationality governing the school policy was questioned, among others also by leading Social Democrats. A devolution process started, giving the local authorities more freedom to make decisions about the allocation of resources. At the same time, a right-wing attack was leveled against the Social Democratic school policy, which was criticized for vague objectives, lack of order, and poor results. The conservatives argued that firm principles and real knowledge should replace the wishy-washy left-wing pedagogies, and special attention must be given to gifted children (Lundahl, 1989). When they came into power in 1991, they were able to carry out their ideas. Furthermore, the alleged failure of the school policy was used as an excuse to attack the public sector as a whole. The educational policy moved from a social welfare state model, emphasizing consensus and a centralized system of distributing values, toward a decentralized, particularized, and polarized reform model (Lindblad & Wallin, 1993).

Today, new relations between the center and periphery have been established as the local authorities are free to decide how to use the state subsidies. According to the national curriculum for the comprehensive school, issued in 1994, the timetables for the different subjects are adjustable, and the scope for local profiles and individual choices is broad. Governing through rules has to a large extent been replaced by governing through goals and results (Berg et al., 1999).

Neo-liberal currents emphasizing effectiveness and competition have also heavily influenced the Swedish education policy. A voucher system has been introduced, making it possible for parents to choose whatever school they want for their children. It has been easier to establish private schools, and the number of those is consequently growing. Diversity, not uniformity, is the order of the day. Previously catchwords like *nonsegregation, social justice,* and *education* as a joint responsibility for all citizens were central to the education policy discourse. Now they have been replaced by words like *individual options, parents' responsibility, effectiveness,* and *competition* (Carlgren & Kallós, 1996; Englund, 1994a; Kallós & Nilsson, 1995; Schüllerqvist, 1996). Thus, education is to a large extent regarded as a private instead of a public good (Englund, 1994b). In this regard, the fact that the Social Democrats came into office in 1994 has not made any fundamental difference.

Thus, Sweden has witnessed a system shift of education policy (Englund, 1996). It is true that Sweden is not unique in this respect, but in consideration of the high degree of centralization, uniformity, and detailed state regulation of schooling prevalent before the shift, there is good ground for claiming that the shift in Sweden involves a more profound break with traditional policy than in most other countries.

CURRICULUM RESEARCH IN THE SERVICE OF THE MODERN PROJECT

From the 1940s and circa 30 years on, researchers were engaged on a large scale to provide politicians with knowledge as a ground for political decisions about how to construct the comprehensive school. To begin with, curriculum research was carried out within the scientific paradigm (cf. Darling-Hammond & Snyder, 1992). In the spirit of positivism, sharp distinctions were drawn between, on the one hand, politicians who defined the education goals and asked the questions and, on the other, researchers who provided the answers (Dahllöf, 1996; Lundgren, 1999; Säfström, 1994). The research was based on a linear and static input–output model of correlations (Härnqvist, 1996; Popkewitz, 1997).

Within this positivistic paradigm, Dahllöf (1967, 1971) formulated the frame factor theory calling attention to the *black box,* previously so neglected by most researchers. He argued that it was necessary to take the processes that led to a certain result into consideration to explain why things turned out the way they did. These processes were governed and restricted by certain frames like, for instance, time at disposal, available text books, and composition of student group with regard to its degree of homogeneity of scholastic aptitude.

Dahllöf's results pointed toward the significance of the local context, but curriculum research was still dominated by a centralistic perspective. The researcher was like a social engineer who produced knowledge to be transformed into detailed rules for the schools. The teacher played the role of a technician who was expected to execute and follow the state directions. Thus, the central intentions were supposed to be fulfilled in a rather simplistic way in the classrooms all around Sweden.

Yet things were far from simple. In the 1980s, several studies showed that the goal to create a uniform, equivalent and democratic school for all had not been fulfilled (Arnman & Jönsson, 1983; Arfwedson, 1985; Callewaert & Nilsson, 1979, 1980). Lindensjö and Lundgren (1986) regarded the discrepancy between goals and results as a gap between *the arena of formulation* and *the arena of realization*. Research was carried out to explain this gap with the aim of eliminating it. The conclusion was that standardized solutions could not be applied to a complex and refractory reality, and thus the rational large-scale philosophy of planning, characteristic of the Swedish welfare state, was faulty (Lundgren, 1999).

Similar conclusions were also drawn by researchers who had used the frame factor theory to explain processes at the local level. To begin with, the frame concept included only quantifiable factors of concrete nature. Lundgren (1984) introduced two further dimensions as the goal system, and the rule system were also defined as frames. Later on traditions and mental structures, like teachers' ways of thinking about teaching, were included in the concept. In the 1990s, this elaborated and modified frame factor theory was still used as a model for curriculum research. One example is Sandberg's (1996) investigation of music education, and another is Garefalaki's (1994) study of home language instruction in Greek. However, Garefalaki concluded that the frame factors, which, according to Lundgren were important (i.e., juridical regulations, organizational frameworks, and the national curriculum for the comprehensive school) are of minor importance in shaping instruction in the Greek home language classes. Much more influential are the textbooks used, the Greek didactical tradition, and the Greek parents' ideas of proper methods of instruction. Thus, the concept of *frame factor* has gradually eroded, and in Ekman's (1992) study it encompasses all the local conditions for people's lives in a sparsely populated municipality.

In the 1990s, researchers were still preoccupied with explaining the gap between the arena of formulation and the local arena of realization. In his study of teachers in the upper secondary school, Linde (1993) identified a field of transformation between the two arenas—a field that was affected by economic conditions and the vocations for which different study programs were a preparation. Ahlstrand (1995) tried to find out whether teachers lived up to the demands of the curriculum of 1980 to cooperate. She concluded that teachers' traditional freedom to arrange the teaching as they thought fit, albeit within the stipulated frames, carried greater weight than the need and interest for cooperation. According to Ahlstrand, this could be explained by the different rationalities governing the two arenas. For the formulation arena, the technical rationality was valid, whereas the teachers' rationality was informal and adjusted to the complex, unstable, unpredictable, and unique conditions of the classroom situation.

Thus, the gap between goal and results was sometimes explained with reference to frame factors working as external determinants of the teaching process. According to some researchers, the reasons were rather to be found in human shortcomings, and therefore the focus shifted toward the teachers (Arfwedson, 1985; Berg, 1989). The aim was to understand and explain teachers' behaviors and ways of thinking about teaching to better govern them (Lindblad, 1994). The Swedish research on teacher thinking has one root in this complex of problems, but Swedish researchers have, in contrast to research in other countries, usually tried to understand teachers' actions as a result of both their intentions and the restrictions put on them by various social determinants (cf. Popkewitz, 1997). For example, Lindblad (1994) combined the frame factor theory with the Finnish philosopher Henric von Wright's concept *practical reasoning* (see also

Carlgren & Lindblad, 1991). As the frame factor concept has expanded to include also subjective dimensions, some researchers regard teachers' thinking as one frame factor among others (cf. K. Gustafsson, 1999).

THE SWEDISH RECONCEPTUALISTS
IN CURRICULUM RESEARCH

Although the frame factor theory was rooted in the positivistic tradition, it carried the seed for a paradigm shift because it undermined general explanations to educational phenomena. When nonquantifiable and nonobservable factors began to be defined as frames, the break with positivism was definite. Yet this theory also developed in another direction, which, like the reconceptualists in other countries, leveled a severe attack on the positivistic paradigm (cf. Lincoln, 1992). Inspired by critical sociological theories of education, Lundgren (1979) began to ask how the frames were constituted, whereby he identified different curriculum codes or rationalities that at different times governed the selection and organization of school knowledge. This curriculum theory also paid attention to the changing relations between production and reproduction (Lundgren, 1983).

Thus, the official goals and subject content were not taken for granted any longer. Neither was it the task of the researcher to find out measures to close the gap between the arena of formulation and realization, respectively. Nor was this gap explained by references to human shortcomings: It was caused instead by the structural function of education to reproduce and legitimize existing social relations of dominance and subordination as well as social inequalities (see Andersson, 1986; Lundgren, 1979). Bourdieu and Bernstein were influential for this direction of research (e.g., Callewaert & Nilsson, 1979; Kallós, 1978; Svingby, 1978). In the 1990s, Bourdieu's concepts of *symbolic capital, habitus,* and *field* and Bernstein's terms *classification* and *framing* were still used as analytical tools (Ahl, 1998; Broady & Palme, 1992; Frykholm & Nitzler, 1993; Holmlund, 1996; Olofsson, 1993).

Englund (1997) argued that the reconceptualists presumed that the content and practice of schooling in a direct and simplistic way reproduced the hegemonic ideology and existing social order. Englund is rooted in this tradition, but he viewed curriculum as the site for different groups' struggle over education, and the result is therefore a compromise. This view of curriculum making is shared by many researchers. For example, Elgström and Riis (1992) studied how the curriculum of 1980 came into being and, especially, how the new subject technology was introduced. This subject was thought of as the remedy for the crises of production caused by the lack of labor skilled in technology. It would also be the remedy for the increasing hostility toward technology. The issue at stake was whether the new subject should be connected to the group of science subjects or to the practical subjects like handicraft, and whether its essence should be theoretical or practical. The investigation illustrates the influence on the content of schooling exerted by different categories of teachers. The conclusion is that the curriculum is not only the result of political compromises, but also influenced by special interests of different groups of teachers.

The reconceptualist view of curriculum was also applied to studies of the delivered and experienced curriculum, and I return to those later.

THE POSTSTRUCTURALIST TURN IN CURRICULUM RESEARCH

Swedish curriculum research is not unaffected by poststructuralist currents. A small-scale linguistic turn can be observed, as some researchers emphasize the importance of language for the construction of the curriculum. Thus, in the 1990s, the term *discourse* was frequently used in many research reports. Englund and his colleagues are illustrative of this tendency. According to them, the curriculum is always open for different interpretations. Hence, they have focused on the different meanings inherent in the curriculum and textbooks. They have treated citizenship education (Englund, 1986), natural science subjects (Östman, 1995), domestic science (Hjälmeskog, 2000), the school and the media (Ljunggren, 1996), educational research as constitutive of meaning (Säfström, 1994), and education provided by the sport movement (Gustafsson, 1994). Text analyses are central to all these studies. They are also normative because one aim is to provide a guide to the realization of democratic ideals in education.

Selander and his colleagues represent a different strand of the linguistic turn. They have studied different functions of the textbooks used in schools. The textbooks set the norms for what counts as valid knowledge in school, they are the main sources of knowledge for the students, and, perhaps most important, they facilitate the teacher's work (Selander et al., 1992).

The aim of the prior studies is thus to *deconstruct* the meanings of texts. Carlgren (1995) provided an example of how these meanings are constructed within and by one dominant discourse. Together with politicians and administrators, she was involved in the process of writing a proposal to the new curriculum of 1994. Originally, the task was only to *translate* the content of the old curriculum into the new discourses of governing through goals and results, increased freedom of choice, and marketization of schooling. The task was neither to formulate new goals nor change the content of the curriculum. However, because the curriculum workers were under pressure, there was no time to discuss the underlying principles of the curriculum. Therefore, the result was not a compromise between different opinions; those who were not able to express their ideas within the new discourse could not be heard, and their opinions became nonissues. In polemics with Englund, Carlgren claimed that national curricula must be understood not as compromises, but as discursive politics instead. However, she also noted that the Swedish tradition of carrying out thorough state investigations, which are processed to get support of many groups, was abandoned at this moment. In my view, this may be an indication that the political processes producing national curricula have fundamentally changed from promoting compromises between different discourses to being governed by the hegemonic discourse. In a Foucaldian perspective the consequence would be that one single regime of truth, to a larger extent now than before, determines what is at all possible to say (Foucault, 1980).

CURRICULUM RESEARCH AND THE SHIFT IN EDUCATION POLICY

It could be argued that, in Sweden of today, Englund's thesis about the unstable meanings of curricular goals and content have been given the status of political truth. Everyone involved in the making of the curriculum, is expected to reflect on the meanings of the goals and find out how to reach the goal. The overall goals are decided at the center; the municipalities make their priorities, which result in local school plans. Then every school of the municipality produces its own working plan for how to reach the goals. The models of evaluation are in accordance with the same rationality. The state and National Agency of Education have the overall responsibility, the municipalities shall evaluate their school plans, and every school has to evaluate its own working plan. The idea is that the evaluations are incitements for development and change (Lundgren, 1999).

The abandonment of the governing through rules can be regarded as a collapse of the modern rational philosophy of planning: Cheered on by researchers the politicians have, so to say, surrendered to the complexity of reality. However, governing by goals is based on hypermodern rationality because it is still presumed that the goals can be attained by means of rational considerations and conscious acting. What is new is that the rational considerations not only originate from the center; instead the whole system is involved in the process. Therefore, the task of the researchers is not to provide the center with knowledge. Instead, they cooperate with teachers and local administrators. This fact is reflected in the principles of the National Agency of Education for the allocation of resources for local development, which requires a close cooperation between practitioners and researchers.

Thereby the gap between the arena of formulation and the arena of realization would be closed by making these arenas coincide in time and space. Yet the shift of focus from the central state to the local context has been governed by an awareness of the complexity of teaching, learning, and schooling, and the same problems of how to accomplish processes leading to the goals of the national curricula are still on the agenda. In this regard, politicians, administrators, and many researchers agree that the teachers are crucial for the eventful success, and *the professional teacher* is the catchword of today (Kallós & Nilsson, 1995). Therefore, it is significant that many theses in education deal with the role of the teacher and/or teachers' work (e.g., Ahl, 1998; Alexandersson, 1994; Arvidsson, 1995; Calander, 1999; Eriksson, 1999; Gannerud, 1999; Henckel, 1990; Hesslefors Arktoft, 1996; Kihlström, 1995; Magnusson, 1998; Numan, 1999; Robertsson Hörberg, 1997; Rönnerman, 1993; Rubenstein Reich, 1993; Stukát, 1998).

How, then, do the researchers regard the role of the teacher within a goal-governed school? Alexandersson (1999) raised the question of whether governance by rules has been abolished given that teachers are so well disciplined that they need not be explicitly told what to do. According to Hultqvist (1998), the decentralization requires a self-governed subject with the capability to interpret and apply universal rules with regard to shifting local conditions. The reflective practitioner is the political ideal; she or he is constantly prepared to reconsider the relation to her or himself, to the colleagues, the students, and to the world around the school. A requirement for this is that a dialogue is established among all the persons involved in education: The interpretations and evaluations of syllabi and reflections on pedagogical practices are collective activities aiming at the normalization of actions. Therefore, teachers' professionalism is developed by forcing them to put words to their competence—by making their tacit knowledge explicit (Carlgren, 1994). In other words, the discursive competence of the teacher is now very important (Alexandersson, 1999). Englund (1997) emphasized the importance of the *teacher's didactical competence* (i.e., the capacity to reflect on how to choose the content and methods of teaching in relation to the implicit intentions of the national curriculum).

DOES GOVERNANCE THROUGH GOALS AND RESULTS MAKE ANY DIFFERENCE FOR CURRICULUM IN PRACTICE COMPARED TO GOVERNANCE THROUGH RULES?

The curriculum of 1994 has only been in effect for 5 years. Consequently, only a few investigations of the implementation of the new governing system are yet available. In 1997, Dahn concluded that the shift of education policy had occurred first and foremost at the central level and in the dominant political discourse (Dahn, 1997). However, in the late 1990s, there were also studies indicating that the changes at the local level are sweeping, at least in some quarters. Francia (1999) concluded that the reform has promoted new organizational solutions. The marketization of schooling has forced schools to make use of the opportunities to create distinctive images of themselves, which has promoted discussions among the teachers about the what and how of their teaching to make the local profile attractive. As a result of the abolishment of school classes and specific levels of education of the comprehensive school, the students are to a larger extent organized in age-mixed groups with teams of teachers working together. Hence, the teachers can no longer close the door from their colleagues and treat didactical issues in splendid isolation.

Francia's findings indicate that the expected arenas for discussions of issues of goal and content have been established, at least at some quarters. However, there are also reasons to expect the old state of affair be revived, albeit in new clothes. The Tyler rationale may still be the rationality governing teachers' work. As a consequence of the governing through results, the outcomes of schooling may be measured against simple quantifiable criteria. The gap between the realization arena and the formulation arena still exists even if these arenas are closer now in time and space. In some municipalities, the local school plan is only a copy of parts of the national curriculum, and it does not affect the pedagogical practice. According to Berg et al. (1999), the gap is unavoidable unless the teachers' culture changes from the traditional restricted professionalism to the extended professionalism required by the new goal governing system.

Another problem, addressed by researchers, is that the restructuring of education is part of the dismantling of the welfare state. Hence, there is a considerable risk that governing through goals and results is replaced by budget governing instead (Romhed, 1999). Many groups of teachers fiercely oppose the changes; for example, they feel that discussions with colleagues about goals and content of the teaching are not meaningful because they seldom lead to tangible results. At some quarters, veritable wars have broken out between teachers and principals acting forcefully to carry through changes in the spirit of the political reform (Berg et al., 1999).

However, it is obvious that the vaguely written curriculum, to a larger extent now than before, provokes local discussions regarding goals and content. Thus, the chances of collective meaning-making at the local level are increasing. However, it takes its time to create consensus especially because the teachers can no longer choose to cooperate only with like-minded colleagues. Therefore, teachers are also experiencing a heavier workload. Furthermore, a new contract has been signed, regulating the teachers' working hours. It stipulates that the teachers must be at school a certain amount of hours every day, even if no lessons are going on. Therefore, the decentralized teacher tends to be more controlled as the control gets closer to her or him in the form of colleagues, principals, and local administrators. In addition, every teacher is accountable for the attainment of the national goals and also for the pupils of the comprehensive school to obtain a pass. With regard to the large budget cuts of school funding, the rhetoric of the increased power of the teachers rings false: There is not much for teachers and the local authorities to decide on, besides how to save money. Thus, like researchers in some other countries, Falkner (1997) concluded that it is more correct to talk about a proletarization than a professionalization of the teacher body.

CURRICULUM AS PEDAGOGICS AND STUDENTS' MEANING MAKING

Many Swedish researchers have entered into the classroom to study curriculum in practice (i.e., the delivered curriculum, like many of the earlier mentioned studies of teachers' work illustrates). Some of them have also focused on the experienced curriculum: What do students actually experience at school? What kind of people does schooling promote? The answers to such questions also support the thesis that the meaning of the curriculum is highly unstable.

Classroom studies compose a strong and living tradition with one of its roots in the frame factor theory, with Lundgren (1971) and Gustafsson (1977) as two early examples. However, within the reconceptualist tradition, the research questions were put differently. According to reproduction theories, education contributed to the reproduction of structural conditions, but which mechanisms were at work, and which roles did various actors play in the reproduction process?

As early as the 1970s, many critical researchers concluded that the notion of the comprehensive nonstreamed school was nothing but a myth. According to, for example, the curriculum of 1969, there were numerous optional subjects. As well, students were able to choose between more or less advanced courses in mathematics and English. Consequently, students only spent a small amount of time together with all their classmates (Callewaert & Nilsson, 1979). Arnman and Jönsson (1983) showed that segregated areas of living corresponded to a similar division of schools into high- and low-status schools. Special pedagogy has been another means of sorting students (Lahdenperä, 1997; Persson, 1998). Furthermore, it has always been possible to give unruly, underachieving students or students suffering from school fatigue an emergency exit out of school in the form of an adjusted curriculum. Such students spend a large part of the time at a workplace, whereas the instruction in traditional school subjects is considerably reduced (Bergecliff, 1999). In the goal-governed school, immigrants have a specific, less demanding syllabus in Swedish compared with students with Swedish as the mother tongue (Francia, 1999).

Curriculum as lived experience is explicitly addressed by Peréz Prieto (1992) in a study inspired by Paul Willis and the Birmingham school. Garpelin (1997) studied what happens when students from different primary schools meet at the lower secondary school to form a new school class and how they choose schoolmates and school perspectives—choices that in the long run affect their future and identities. Jonsson (1995) identified different student strategies or *life projects* that she interprets within the framework of the different stages of the modernization process. For example, the competitive student is in accordance with the stage emphasizing order and discipline. The self-identities of the artistic group, in contrast, are representative of the postmodern conditions.

Researchers conclude that there are many subtle mechanisms at work in the process of social reproduction. Drawing on Bourdieu, Callewaert and Nilsson (1980) argued that the teachers do not act consciously in this respect, but the interplay between their and the students' habitus make them misrecognize their own actions. Linde (1993) used the concept of *teacher repertoire* to explain this phenomenon: Every teacher has a set of methods and tricks from which she or he chooses those expected to work. Thereby different groups of students are offered different socializing meanings. In a study of teachers at the lower secondary level, Naeslund (1991) noted that the same teacher adjusted her or his way of teaching to the composition of the class. In low-motivated classes, various tricks were employed to maintain order, like pseudodialogues consisting of meaningless questions and meaningless answers. In classes with students from families with considerable cultural capital, the communication between teacher and students was of a higher quality. Naeslund interpreted the teachers' patterns of action as survival strategies.

Frykholm and Nitzler (1993) investigated the subject vocational and career education in vocational as well as academic programs of the upper secondary school. The same curriculum goals were valid for all programs, but the researchers concluded that the world of work was transformed into quite different instructional discourses, adjusted to the students' future position in the division of labor. As for the academic program of economics, for example, the students learned the concepts of political economy, and they were also encouraged to discuss and analyze various economic phenomena. The instruction at the vocational program for future metal workers, in contrast, mirrored a restricted labor union perspective, and the aim was to clarify the duties and rights of the workers.

Parts of the critique leveled against the comprehensive school claimed the pedagogical practice to be old fashioned. Catechism (i.e., teachers asking questions and students answering them) was for a long time said to be the dominant mode of instruction. At the best, the students were passive receivers of knowledge delivered by the teacher. State prescriptions stating that the individual student should be at the center of the learning process, and that the pedagogy should be less authoritarian and more democratic, had thus not been adhered to.

However, in the 1990s, classroom studies indicated that the pedagogy had not completely remained the same. Lindblad and Sandström (1999), for example, compared a tape recording of a lesson on the blood circulation from the 1970s with a lesson treating the same topic in the 1990s. In the 1970s the lesson was teacher directed, but 20 years later, the students worked with topics individually or in small groups. It seems as if the invisible pedagogy, to speak with Bernstein (1975), has gained ground at least on lower levels of education (Ahl, 1998; Gannerud, 1999; Hesslefors Arktoft, 1996). For example, a strong student centering is evident in interviews with teachers at the primary level of the compulsory school: "Earlier I used to love them in a lump. Now I love each of them individually." (Quoted from a teacher in Gannerud, 1999). The relations between teachers and students have become more horizontal, and the teachers make a point of not being authoritarian. Thus, from the student's point of view, the curriculum provides new meanings of socialization. According to Hultqvist (1998) and Österlind (1998), these new forms of pedagogy are means to construct the self-governed, free individual.

Several researchers have shown that pedagogies taking the individual student's needs, initiatives, and/or self-governed activities as the point of departure lead to differentiation of the students, often with social class or gender as the structuring principle (Ahl, 1998; Österlind, 1998; Pettersson & Asén, 1989). The students are active in constructing their own curriculum, knowledge, identity, and, occasionally, exclusion. For example, in some places, the instruction is organized in age-mixed groups. The intention is that every student may proceed at her or his own pace. This is no doubt a sound principle for learning, but there is also a risk that pupils who are not able to raise by themselves the "right" kind of motivation are left behind (Ahl, 1998).

According to Lindblad and Sandström (1999), the teacher-centered pedagogy has been replaced by desk work, with students working alone or together with a mate at their own paces and sometimes with different tasks. The researchers argued that students engaging in different life projects causes them to make use of the time spent at school differently: Every student thus carries through a unique lesson project. A similar conclusion was drawn by Österlind (1998) in her study of the lessons during the week which the pupils have planned themselves. The students' attitudes toward their planning calender were clearly related to the social background.

Bergqvist's (1990) study of how students perceive of and carry through group work tasks shows a similar phenomenon. She observed, for example, what happened during a laboratory lesson in physics. The teacher strongly believed in inductive learning. Therefore, the students did not get any clues about what they were supposed to find out. As a consequence, they focused on practical issues related to the equipment, the physical activity, and the drawing of figures. They were not able to understand any other meanings of the activities. Bergqvist is critical about the progressive rhetoric for regarding students' activities as such as valuable, and more important than whether the students actually learn something valuable.

However, the Swedish research tradition which has to the largest extent studied what and how students learn is phenomenography with Ference Marton as the prominent figure (Marton, 1981, 1994). Within this tradition, people's conceptions of various phenomena are examined. Several studies have shown that students (and teachers) experience scientific, social, and cultural phenomena in qualitatively different ways. The chemical mole (Strömdahl, 1996; Tullberg, 1997), the four rules of arithmetic (Neuman, 1987), and literary texts (Asplund-Carlsson, 1996) are only a few examples. These studies have didactical implications for how to teach the students scientifically recognized conceptions of the world. However, phenomenography has been criticized for taking the goals and content of the teaching for granted, and for losing sight of the socializing and sorting functions of education (Englund, 1997; Sundgren, 1995).

DISCIPLINE, NORMALITIES, AND THE CONSTRUCTION OF THE SELF-GOVERNED SUBJECT

Education as constitutive of the good citizen is addressed in several historical studies. For example, the concept of *citizenship* is central to the research carried out by Englund and his colleagues. Some researchers apply a foucauldian perspective, according to which pedagogies that transfer to the student the responsibility for learning can be regarded as disciplining techniques contributing to the construction of the self-governed subject. In my view, this is one of the cornerstones of schooling. Therefore, Foucault provided tools to understand the rationality of many aspects of the curriculum—the written, delivered, and experienced. However, Foucauldian approaches are not frequent in Swedish curriculum research. One reason may be that, from Foucault's point of view, knowledge produced by curriculum researchers is intrinsically linked to power, and *power* is to many of us an unpleasant word. However, if Foucault is right, power is an unavoidable element of all social relations, and is not necessarily bad. I referred earlier to studies taking this perspective as the point of departure, but in this section I return to some of those and also a few other studies.

Within this paradigm, questions are posed about curriculum as a means of shaping the ethical, moral, and disciplined self. Hultqvist (1998) studied the pedagogical and scientific discourses by means of which the preschool child has been constructed. In this respect, he distinguished three different discourses. Around the turn of the 19th century, the Fröbelian pedagogy was dominant, and its aim was to transplant a Christian morality into the child. The child of the Swedish welfare state was to develop in accordance with biological laws, and the child's own actions were therefore of less importance. However, the decentralized child in the goal-governed school of today, it is believed, participates actively in the construction of its own self: The child is regarded as potent and capable of learning many things on its own.

Dahlberg (2000) had a similar view on different competing discourses about the child. She also carried out an action research project within this theoretical framework, where the actions were inspired by Reggio Emilia. The aim was to deconstruct hegemonic discourses of early childhood education. As a result, the grown-up participants of the project have been able to understand how their thinking and practices are inscribed in these discourses. New spaces have opened up for counterdiscourses and different practices (Dahlberg, 1999). One aim of the action research is to make visible the power relations embedded in pedagogical practices. The same strategy is also applied in Berge's action research for gender equity in a comprehensive school (Berge & Ve, 2000).

Johansson (2000) treated the normalizing practices in the state grammar schools from 1927 to 1960. The grammar school students were supposed to belong to the most talented part of the Swedish youth, and in daily life at school they had to prove this over and over again. The normalizing techniques employed were of different kinds; the most important ones were the multitude of assessment measures, to which the students had to respond by proving themselves worthy of the privilege to attend the grammar school. But all the techniques played on the students' expectations of a successful career: Schooling might have been awful, but it might also have been worth it.

Österlind (1998) dealt with the so-called *students' own work* (i.e., lessons when the pupils work on their own). The teacher decides which tasks should be done during the week, but the pupils control the pacing and sequencing of the work. If anyone gets stuck and cannot be helped immediately, she or he is supposed to do something else in the meantime. Thus, there is no passive waiting time, and order is easily upheld because the pupils are busy all the time. Thereby the nature of time discipline is changed: A weaker external time structure is counteracted by a stronger inner awareness of time. At the end of the week, the students must evaluate their work against their own planning calendar. In my view, this is a striking example of technologies of the self, to which Foucault (1988) pointed. Österlind (1998) argued that the hidden curriculum for these lessons are rewritten because its old cornerstones *crowds, praise, and power* are dissolved (Jackson, 1968). Instead the individual spaces increase, the arena for public assessment shrinks, and the power balance changes (at least slightly) to the pupils' advantage. Passivity and subordination are no longer the hidden messages, but responsibility, efficiency, and self-discipline are the fundamental principles.

FEMINIST CURRICULUM RESEARCH

A relatively common view is that feminist curriculum research has not been strong in Sweden (Carlgren & Kallós, 1996). If this is true, one reason could be the close connection between curriculum research and the political reform work because, to begin with, equality between social classes, not the sexes, was the main issue (Nilsson, 1986). The pioneers of curriculum research were all men, and the strong triangle of researchers, politicians, and administrators, who met at learned seminars, was a completely male-dominated world. It was not until 1982 that the first woman was appointed professor in education.

Despite all this, it could be argued that feminism constitutes an important part of present curriculum research (cf. Yates, 1996). Feminist theories have been applied to studies of various groups of teachers (Elgqvist-Salzman, 1993; Florin, 1987; Florin & Johansson, 1991; Gannerud, 1999; Holmlund, 1996; Rönnerman, 1993). These studies show that a gender perspective is necessary not only as a supplement, but also as a means of correction to earlier research. For example, teacher professionalism has usually referred to the didactical competence of the teacher, whereas the teachers' work with developing personal relations with the pupils has been made invisible. Such social competencies are often regarded as inherent in the female genes and therefore also devalued (Gannerud, 1999). It seems as if women teachers' emotional capacities are exploited: Female teachers risk falling into the maternal nurturance trap (Berge & Ve, 2000).

Most feminist curriculum research treats schooling as reproductive of women's subordination in society. Studies deal with school policy and the organization of schooling as well as pedagogical practice, both historically and in present times. For example, in the 19th century, the state grammar schools were only open to boys, and the male monopoly on the valuable cultural capital institutionalized in education was thus kept intact. This was significant because education played a crucial part in the bourgeois meritocracy: The struggle for the power and the glory was therefore an entirely male enterprise (Florin & Johansson, 1993). However, in 1927, girls got access to the grammar school. According to Johansson (2000), the girls entering grammar schools from 1927 to 1960 constituted as adults the first large group of women, taking part in the male, White, and middle-class modern project. Those girls also distanced themselves from the housewife (i.e., the traditional representation of femininity), and in many respects they became more (middle) class than gendered subjects. Elgqvist-Salzman (1992) showed how the interplay between education and gender structures produced quite different trajectories of women and men in the moving in and out of the labor market.

Subjects like handicraft and domestic are closely connected to the division of labor within the family, and in the 19th century they contributed to reproduce traditional gender relations during a period when these relations in many spheres of society were changing (Johansson, 1992; Trotzig, 1997). In the comprehensive school of today, on the contrary, they are regarded as a means of increasing gender equity because the same curriculum goals are valid for boys and girls. Traditional gender patterns for both paid and unpaid work are to be challenged, and boys learn to take responsibility for unpaid care and domestic work. For example, both boys and girls shall take basic courses in textile craft as well as in wood and metal work, and domestic science is obligatory for both boys and girls (Berge, 1992). However, in the curriculum of 1994, subjects connected to family life lost ground, and in present hegemonic discourses schooling for the home is a non-issue compared with education for paid work (Berge & Ve, 2000; Hjälmeskog, 2000).

Another subject, crucial for the construction of gender, is physical education, which was gender-segregated on the secondary level until 1962. This fact reflected the idea that there were fundamental biological differences between men and women. The boy's body was to be hardened, whereas the girl's body would be modeled to express tenderness and graciousness. This was also in accordance with perceived differences between the male and female psyche. Female gracious movements reflected the woman's readiness and capacity to please other people. The hard and muscular male body corresponded to a manly firm and determined character (Johansson, 2000; Olofsson, 1989).

The natural sciences are to a large extent male constructions and also stable platforms for male dominance (Connel, 1989; Harding, 1986). However, because it is said to be a lack of technically skilled labor, the state has taken measures to increase the recruitment of girls to science studies. The results have not been impressive, and Staberg (1992) concluded that girls already in the compulsory school feel alienated during science lessons.

In the classrooms, gender is played out in communicative actions. In a gender perspective, Öhrn (1993) analyzed patterns of interactions between teachers and pupils at the lower secondary level of the comprehensive school. In five classes, these patterns were similar to those found in other studies: Boys dominated the classroom discourse and were also more frequently attended to by the teachers. In two other classes, groups of girls were dominant. They brought up issues of human relations and expressed publicly personal opinions, feelings, and experiences. There were also girls who tried to gain influence from a subordinate position by exaggerating and refining the role of the *good pupil*.

Taken together, feminist curriculum studies show that the social construction of gender in schools is a multidimensional process. Thus, even if Käller (1990) may be right on the whole when she concluded that girls in schools learn to be the second rank, gender structures are both reproduced and challenged by education.

CONCLUDING REMARKS

The history of Swedish curriculum research is illustrative not only of Foucault's thesis that knowledge and power are inseparable, but also that power is not only repressive. During the decades following World War II, curriculum research was used in the service of the central welfare state. Among other things, the knowledge produced was part of an overall biopolitical program aiming at a socially just and efficient distribution of the young generation into different educational tracks. Thus, the reorganization of the whole school system could be regarded as a remodeling of the educational technologies of power created in the late 19th and early 20th centuries. Yet the strong connection between researchers and the state was not regarded as problematic: The case was good, and knowledge was used to correct social injustices. There was also a space for critical opinions: According to some of the researchers involved, the strong triangle of politicians, administrators, and researchers prepared the ground for the critical tradition within curriculum research. The politicians listened to critical views as well.

Thus, the central state was the purchaser and receiver of research results, and the whole system was based on the governmentality defined by the Tyler rationale. The central governing of schooling was seen as both possible and desirable as it should provide for the realization of equality in education. However, for many reasons, this form of governmentality lost ground in the 1970s. First, when the organizational problems were solved, the focus shifted to the inner work of schooling, and the linear way of reasoning did not survive the confrontation with complex pedagogical processes. Second, the frame factor theory stressed the importance of the local context: General, large-scaled solutions could hardly be adjusted to shifting local conditions. Third, the strong triangle was replaced by a R and D model, and the contact between researchers and politicians was broken. The knowledge produced by research would now first and foremost be of use for practitioners at the grassroot level. Some of the researchers involved regret this development because, among other things, inconvenient results were put into the administrators' drawers (Dahllöf, 1996; Härnqvist, 1996). From another point of view, this development was only logical; The aim of curriculum reforms is ultimately to steer pedagogical practices.

Today the forces working to establish close connections between researchers and teachers have grown even stronger. As a consequence, the nature of the power walking hand in hand with knowledge production has fundamentally changed. Power and knowledge have diffused into all the corners of the system, and a new form of governmentality is now dominant. No longer shall large systems steer individuals, but instead all individuals are supposed to steer the system in the right direction. Therefore, a new type of human being must be constructed (i.e., the free and self-disciplined individual who is able to think on his or her own and think correctly). This does not mean that everyone must be thinking in the same way. On the contrary, each and everyone shall find local solutions adjusted to more or less unique circumstances. In this perspective, the researchers' focus on teachers work, teachers' thinking, and theories about the reflective practitioner constitute power techniques aiming at the accomplishment of desirable processes. The researchers are active in the construction of a new type of teacher. This is not to say that researchers necessarily work in the service of oppression. The overall goals of the curriculum about, for example, democracy and all human beings' equal value are potentially radical. According to Englund (1997), the duty of the professional teacher is to realize precisely this potential.

Education and curriculum research of today is thus inscribed within a new policy discourse, and researchers have also shown the breakthrough of a new pedagogical discourse. Within this discourse, the pupil is constructed according to the same kind of governmentality. The aim is to create the free and self-governed human being. The child is expected to take on responsibility for his or her own education, thus constructing his or her own curriculum and future. There is no longer any paternalistic state guaranteeing the welfare of all its citizens.

In my view, it is not likely that this form of governing will be more successful than the previous one. For example, every teacher will hardly think and act correctly, and neither will the students. The big drawback is that, for the disciplining techniques to be efficient, they have to play on people's hopes that they will benefit from adjusting to the norms However, as a consequence of substantial budget cuts, teachers' working conditions have become worse. Such a proletarization of teaching probably reduces the teachers' expectations that they will benefit from the new system.

As regards the disciplining of students, it seems as if the number of unruly young people in the schools is increasing. It may be that rebelling pupils make a realistic estimation of the profit for them to be gained from a well-disciplined way of life. Meritocratic criteria and societal structures of reward necessarily define a large proportion of the youth as *losers*. Therefore, the new educational discourses are adjusted to those equipped with a considerable amount of various forms of capital. The same is true for the neo-liberal discourse celebrating the marketization of schooling. The market does not promote equality. On the contrary, what the market is doing best is creating inequalities (Smyth, 1993).

I have argued that the shift of research focus toward the local context was logical, but it could as well be argued that it would have been natural for the research field to move in the opposite direction toward supranational structures. In a referendum in 1994, it was decided by a majority of less than 1% that Sweden should join the European Union (EU). This fact has also reduced the gravity force of the national central state, and Swedish researchers participate in large comparative projects financed by supranational organizations like the EU or OECD. Researchers in curriculum history have studied education as a means of constructing the Swedish national state, national identities, and the citizen of the welfare state. But what part does education play in this regard within the present global context? How is the center defined in relation to the periphery within the EU? A few researchers address questions like these (e.g., Andersson, 1999; Andersson & Nilsson, 2000), but on the whole there is a lack of critical research on how the changing global contexts affect curricular processes on different levels.

Finally, I return to the development of the frame factor theory, which to begin with only included sturdy quantifiable factors, but later on subjective dimensions and meaning-making processes. In many respects, this shift is logical: Curriculum reform work is a meaning-creating activity, and this is true at all levels of the system. However, meanings are unstable and produced by a multifold of discourses. One important task for critical curriculum research is to deconstruct the meanings produced. Because there are discourses that are not necessarily oppressive, the researcher should also make those with a democratic potential visible and audible.

REFERENCES

Ahl, A. (1998). *Läraren och läsundervisningen: en studie av åldersintegrerad pedagogisk praktik med sex- och sjuåringar.* Umeå, Sweden: Umeå Universitet.

Ahlstrand, E. (1995). *Lärares samarbete: En verksamhet på två arenor: Studier av fyra arbetslag på grundskolans högstadium.* Linköping, Sweden: Linköpings Universitet.

Alexandersson, M. (1994). *Metod och medvetande.* Göteborg, Sweden: Göteborgs Universitet.

Alexandersson, M. (1999). *Styrning pa villovägar.* Lund, Sweden: Studentlitteratur.

Andersson, I. (1986). *Läsning och skrivning: En analys av texter för den allmänna läs–och skrivundervisningen 1842–1982.* Umeå, Sweden: Umeå Universitet.

Andersson, I. (1999). Föreställningar och förhållningssätt i läslärans värld. In *Pedagogik-historisk forskning: perspektiv, betydelse och funktion i dagens samhälle 10-12 september 1998.* Stockholm: HLS.

Andersson, I., & Nilsson, I. (2000, June 2–6). What is social justice in Swedish education today? The political governing problem. Paper presented to the conference New Directions in Research: Education, Teacher Education and Social Justice, Umeå University, Sweden.

Arnman, G., & Jönsson, I. (1983). *Segregation och svensk skola: en studie av utbildning, klass och boende.* Lund, Sweden: Arkiv.

Arvidsson, M. (1995). *Lärares orsaks- och atgärds¹ankar om elever med svårigheter.* Göteborg, Sweden: Göteborgs Universitet.

Arfwedson, G. (1985). *School codes and teachers' work: Three studies on teacher work contexts.* Malmö, Sweden: CWK Gleerup/Liber Förlag.

Asplund Carlsson, M. (1996). Readers experience of textual meaning: An empirical approach. *Reader: Essays in Reader-oriented Theory, Criticism and Pedagogy, 28,* 67–79.

Berg, G. (1989). Educational reform and teacher professionalism. *Journal of Curriculum Studies, 21*(1), 53–60.

Berg, G., Groth, E., Nytell, U., & Söderberg, H. (1999). *Skolan i ett institutionsperspektiv.* Lund, Sweden: Studentlitteratur.

Berge, B.-M. (1992). *Gå i lära till lärare: En grupp kvinnors och grupp mäns inskolning i slöjdläraryrket.* Umeå, Sweden: Umeå Universitet.

Berge, B.-M., & Ve, H. (2000). *Action Research for Gender Equity.* Buckingham, England: Open University Press.

Bergecliff, A. (1999). *Trots eller tack vare?: Några elevröster om skolgångsanpassning i grundskolan.* Umeå, Sweden: Umeå Universitet.

Bergqvist, K. (1990). *Doing schoolwork: Task premises and joint activity in the comprehensive classroom.* Linköping, Sweden: Linköpings Universitet.

Bernstein, B. (1975). *Class, codes and control: Volume 3. Towards a theory of educational transmissions.* London: Routledge & Kegan Paul.

Broady, D., & Palme, M. (1992). *Högskolan som fält och studenternas livsbanor.* Stockholm: Högskolan för Lärarutbildning.

Calander, F. (1999). *Från fritidens pedagog till hjälplärare: Fritidspedagogers och lärares yrkesrelation i integrerade arbetslag.* Uppsala, Sweden: Uppsala Universitet.

Callewaert, S., & Nilsson, B.-A. (1979). *Samhället, skolan och skolans inre arbete.* Lund, Sweden: Lunds Bok–och tidskrifts AB.

Callewaert, S., & Nilsson, L. (1980). *Skolklassen som socialt system: Lektionsanalyser.* Lund, Sweden: Lunds Bok–och tidskrifts AB.

Carlgren, I. (1994). Professionalism som reflektion i lärares arbete. In *Lärarprofessionalism: Om professionella lärare.* Stockholm: Lärarförbundet.

Carlgren, I. (1995). National curriculum as social compromise or discursive politics? Some reflections on a curriculum-making process. *Journal of Curriculum Studies, 27*(4), 411–430.

Carlgren, I., & Kallós, D. (1996). The end of idealism or whatever happened to the Swedish comprehensive school? Further lessons from a comprehensive school system for curriculum theory and research. In I. Nilsson (Ed.), *European curriculum theory and research in a twenty year perspective* (pp. 5–28). Umeå, Sweden: Umeå University.

Carlgren, I., & Lindblad, S. (1991). On teachers' practical reasoning and professional knowledge: Considering conception of context in teachers' thinking. *Teaching and Teacher Education, 7*(5/6), 507–516.

Connel, R. W. (1989). Cool guys, swots and wimps: The interplay of masculinity and education. *Oxford Review of Education, 15*(3), 291–303.

Dahlberg, G. (1999). The Stockholm Project. In G. Dahlberg, P. Moss, & A. R. Pence (Eds.), *Beyond quality in early childhood education and care: Postmodern perspectives* (pp. 121–143). London: Falmer.

Dahlberg, G. (2000). From the "People's Home"—Folkhemmet—to the enterprise: Reflections on the constitution and reconstitution of the field of early childhood pedagogy in Sweden. In T. S. Popkewitz (Ed.), *Educational knowledge: Changing relationships between the state, civil society, and the educational community* (pp. 201–220). Albany: State University of New York.

Dahllöf, U. (1967). *Skoldifferentiering och undervisningsförlopp: komparativa mål- och processanalyser av skolsystem 1.* Stockholm: Almqvist & Wiksell.

Dahllöf, U. (1971). *Ability grouping, content validity and curriculum process analysis.* New York: Teachers College Press.

Dahllöf, U. (1996). Fran svenska kursplaneundersökningar till utvärderingar i Distrikts-Norge. In C. Gustafsson (Ed.), *Pedagogikforskarens roll i utbildningsplanering: Rapport från ett minisymposium vid Pedagogiska institutionen, Uppsala Universitet 3 maj 1994 med anledning av Urban Dahllöfs pensionsavgång* (pp. 26–39). Uppsala, Sweden: Uppsala Universitet.

Dahn, H. (1997). Omstrukturering av det svenska skolsystemet: gensvar pa globaliseringstendenser eller nationella krav? *Pedagogisk Forskning, 2*(3), 161–181.

Darling-Hammond, L., & Snyder, J. (1992). Curriculum studies and the traditions of inquiry: The scientific tradition. In P. Jackson (Ed.), *Handbook of research on curriculum.* New York: Macmillan.

Ekman, B. (1992). *Livsvillkor, livsformer, utbildning: en kommunstudie i ett pedagogiskt perspektiv.* Uppsala, Sweden: Uppsala Universitet.

Elgqvist-Salzman, I. (1992). Straight roads and winding tracks: Swedish educational policy from a gender equality perspective. *Gender and Education, 4*(1), 41–56.

Elgqvist-Salzman, I. (1993). *Lärarinna, kvinna, människa*. Stockholm: Carlsson.

Elgström, O., & Riis, U. (1992). Framed negotiations and negotiated frames. *Scandinavian Journal of Educational Research, 36*(2), 99–120.

Englund, T. (1986). *Curriculum as a political problem: Changing educational conceptions, with special reference to citizenship education*. Lund, Sweden: Studentlitteratur.

Englund, T. (1994a). Communities, markets and traditional values: Swedish schooling in the 1990s. *Curriculum Studies, 2*(1), 5–29.

Englund, T. (1994b). Utbildning som "public good" eller "private good": Svensk skola i omvandling? In H. Andersson, K. Jordheim, I. Nilsson, & V. Skovgaard-Petersen (Eds.), *Kampen om lärohusen: Studier kring statsmakt och föräldrarätt i nordisk skolutveckling* (pp. 123–150). Stockholm: Almqvist & Wicksell International.

Englund, T. (Ed.). (1996). *Utbildningspolitiskt systemskifte?* Stockholm: HLS.

Englund, T. (1997). Towards a dynamic analysis of the content of schooling: Narrow and broad didactics in Sweden. *Journal of Curriculum Studies, 29*(3), 267–287.

Eriksson, I. (1999). *Lärares pedagogiska handlingar: En studie av lärares uppfattningar av att vara pedagogisk i klassrumsarbetet*. Uppsala, Sweden: Uppsala Universitet.

Falkner, K. (1997). *Lärare och skolans omstrukturering: Ett möte mellan utbildningspolitiska intentioner och grundskollärares perspektiv på förändringar i den svenska skolan*. Uppsala, Sweden: Uppsala Universitet.

Florin, C. (1987). *Kampen om katedern: Feminiserings- och professionaliseringsprocessen i den svenska folkskolans lärarkår 1870–1906*. Umeå, Sweden: Almqvist & Wicksell.

Florin, C., & Johansson, U. (1991). Education as a female strategy: Women graduates and state grammar schools in Sweden 1870–1918. *Journal of Thought, 6*(1–2), 5–27.

Florin, C., & Johansson, U. (1993). Young men in old institutions: Culture, class and gender in Swedish state grammar schools 1850-1914: A comparative perspective. *Scandinavian Journal of History, 18*(3), 183–198.

Foucault, M. (1980). *Power/knowledge: Selected interviews and other writings 1972-1977*. New York: Pantheon.

Foucault, M. (1988). Technologies of the self: Volume I. In L. H. Martin (Ed.), *Technologies of the self. A seminar with Michel Foucault*. Amherst: The University of Massachusetts Press.

Francia. G. (1999). *Policy som text och som praktik: En analys av likvärdighetsbegreppet i 1990-talets utbildningsreform för det obligatoriska skolväsendet*. Stockholm: Stockholms Universitet.

Frykholm, C.-U., & Nitzler, R. (1993). Working life as pedagogical discourse: Empirical studies of vocational and career education based on theories of Bourdieu and Bernstein. *Journal of Curriculum Studies, 25*(5), 433–444.

Gannerud, E. (1999). *Genusperspektiv på lärargärning: om kvinnliga klasslärares liv och arbete*. Göteborg, Sweden: Göteborgs Universitet.

Garefalaki, J. (1994). *Läroboken som traditionsbärare: om hemspråksundervisningen i grekiska: ett läroplansteoretiskt och didaktiskt perspektiv*. Stockholm: Högskolan för lärarutbildning.

Garpelin, A. (1997). *Lektionen och livet: ett möte mellan ungdomar som tillsammans bildar en skolklass*. Uppsala, Sweden: Uppsala Universitet.

Gustafsson, C. (1977). *Classroom interaction: A study of pedagogical roles in the teaching process*. Lund, Sweden: Liber.

Gustafsson, C. (1999). Ramfaktorer och pedagogiskt utvecklingsarbete. *Pedagogisk forskning, 4*(1), 43–57.

Gustafsson, K. (1994). *Vad är idrottandets mening? en kunskapssociologisk granskning av idrottens utveckling och läromedel samt en organisationsdidaktisk kompetensanalys*. Uppsala, Sweden: Uppsala Universitet.

Harding, S. (1986). *The science question in feminism*. Milton Keynes, England: Open University Press.

Henckel, B. (1990). *Förskollärare i tanke och handling: en studie kring begreppen arbete, lek och inlärning*. Umeå, Sweden: Umeå Universitet.

Hesslefors Arktoft, E. (1996). *I ord och handling: Innebörder av att anknyta till elevers erfarenheter, uttryckta av lärare*. Göteborg, Sweden: Göteborgs Universitet.

Hjälmeskog, K. (2000). *Democracy begins at home: Utbildning om och för hemmet som medborgarfostran*. Uppsala, Sweden: Uppsala Universitet.

Holmlund, K. (1996). *Låt barnen komma till oss: Förskollärarna och kampen om småbarnsinstitutionerna 1854-1968*. Umeå, Sweden: Umeå Universitet.

Hultqvist, K. (1998). A history of the present on children's welfare in Sweden: From Fröbel to present-day decentralization projects. In T. S. Popkewitz & M. Brennan (Eds.), *Foucault's challenge: Discourse, knowledge, and power in education*. New York: Teachers College Press.

Härnqvist, K. (1996). Pedagogikforskarnas roll i utbildningsplanering kring 1960. In C. Gustafsson (Ed.), *Pedagogikforskarens roll i utbildningsplanering: Rapport från ett minisymposium vid Pedagogiska institutionen, Uppsala Universitet 3 maj 1994 med anledning av Urban Dahhlöfs pensionsavgang* (pp. 14-25). Uppsala, Sweden: Uppsala Universitet.

Jackson, P. W. (1968). *Life in classrooms*. New York: Holt, Reinhart & Winston.

Johansson, U. (1992). *Handicraft teaching and domestic science in the Swedish elementary school 1842–1919*. Umeå, Sweden: Umeå Universitet.

Johansson, U. (2000). *Normalitet, kön och klass: Liv och lärande i svenska läroverk 1927–1960*. Umeå, Sweden: Umeå Universitet.

Jonsson, B. (1995). Youth life projects in contemporary Sweden: A cross-sectional study. In B. Jonsson (Ed.), *Studies on youth and schooling in Sweden* (pp. 59–76). Stockholm: Stockholm Institute of Education Press.

Kallós, D. (1978). *Den nya pedagogiken: En analys av den s.k. dialogpedagogiken som svenskt samhällsfenomen*. Stockholm: Wahlström & Widstrand.

Kallós, D., & Nilsson, I. (1995). Defining and re-defining the teacher in the Swedish comprehensive school. *Educational Review, 47*(2), 173–188.

Kihlström, S. (1995). *Att vara förskollärare: om yrkets pedagogiska innebörder*. Göteborg, Sweden: Göteborgs Universitet.

Käller, K. L. (1990). *Fostran till andra rang: en studie av dominansprocessen vid skolstart och via vägar genom utbildningssystemet ur ett kvinnovetenskapligt perspektiv*. Uppsala, Sweden: Uppsala Universitet.

Lahdenperä, P. (1997). *Invandrarbakgrund eller skolsvårigheter?: En textanalytisk studie av åtgärdsprogram för elever med invandrarbakgrund*. Stockholm: HLS.

Lincoln, Y. S. (1992). Curriculum studies and the traditions of inquiry: The humanistic tradition. In P. Jackson (Ed.), *Handbook of research on curriculum*. New York: Macmillan.

Lindblad, S. (1994). *Lärarna: Samhället och skolans utveckling: Utforskningar och analyser av lärarledd verksamhet*. Stockholm: HLS.

Lindblad, S., & Sandström, F. (1999). Gamla mönster och nya gränser: om ramfaktorer och klassrumsinteraktion. *Pedagogisk Forskning, 4*(1), 73–92.

Lindblad, S., & Wallin, E. (1993). On transition of power, democracy and education in Sweden. *Journal of Curriculum Studies, 25*(1), 77–88.

Linde, G. (1993). *On curriculum transformation: Explaining selection of content in teaching*. Stockholm: HLS.

Lindensjö, B., & Lundgren, U. P. (1986). *Politisk styrning och utbildningsreformer*. Stockholm: Liber Utbildningsförlag.

Ljunggren, C. (1996). *Medborgarpubliken och det offentliga rummet: Om utbildning, medier och demokrati*. Uppsala, Sweden: Uppsala Universitet.

Lundahl, L. (1989). *I moralens, produktionens och det sunda förnuftets namn: Det svenska högerpartiets skolpolitik 1904–1962*. Lund, Sweden: Lunds Universitet.

Lundgren, U. P. (1971). *Frame factors and the teaching process: A contribution to curriculum theory and theory on teaching*. Stockholm: Almqvist & Wicksell.

Lundgren, U. P. (1979). *Att organisera omvärlden: en introduktion till läroplansteori*. Stockholm: Liber Förlag.

Lundgren, U. P. (1983). Utbildning och arbete: ett försök att bestämma utbildningens förhållande till den samhälleliga produktionen. In B. Bernstein et al. (Eds.), *Makt, kontroll och pedagogik: Studier av den kulturella reproduktionen* (pp. 9–21). Stockholm: Liber.

Lundgren, U. P. (1984). Ramfaktorteorins historia. *Skeptron, 1*, 69-81.

Lundgren, U. P. (1999). Ramfaktorteori och praktisk utbildningsplanering. *Pedagogisk forskning, 4*(1), 31–41.

Magnusson, A. (1998). *Lärarkunskapens uttryck: En studie av lärares självförståelse och vardagspraktik*. Linköping, Sweden: Linköpings Universitet.

Marton, F. (1981). Phenomenography: Describing conceptions of the world around us. *Instructional Science, 10*, 177–200.

Marton, F. (1994). Phenomenography. In T. Husér & T. N. Postlethwaite (Eds.), *The International Encyclopedia of Education* (2nd ed., pp. 4424–4429). Oxford, England: Pergamon.

Naeslund, L. (1991). *Lärarintentioner och skolverklighet: Explorativa studier av uppgiftsutformning och arbetsförhållanden hos lärare på grundskolans högstadium*. Uppsala, Sweden: Uppsala Universitet.

Neuman, D. (1987). *The origin of arithmetic skills: A phenomenographic approach*. Göteborg, Sweden: Göteborgs Universitet.

Nilsson, I. (1986). *En spjutspets mot framtiden: en analys av de svenska enhets- och grundskolereformerna i utländsk vetenskaplig litteratur 1950-1980*. Lund, Sweden: Lunds Universitet.

Numan, U. (1999). *En god lärare: Nagra perspektiv och empiriska bidrag*. Luleå, Sweden: Luleå Tekniska Universitet.

Olofsson, A. (1993). *Högskolebildningens fem ansikten: Studerandes föreställningar om kunskapspotentialer i teknik, medicin, ekonomi och psykologi: en kvalitativ utvärderingsstudie*. Umeå, Sweden: Umeå Universitet.

Olofsson, E. (1989). *Har kvinnorna en sportslig chans? Den svenska idrottsrörelsen och kvinnorna under 1900–talet.* Umeå, Sweden: Umeå Universitet.

Peréz Prieto, H. (1992). *Skola och erfarenhet: elevernas perspektiv: En grupp elevers skolerfarenheter i ett longitudinellt perspektiv.* Uppsala, Sweden: Uppsala Universitet,

Persson, B. (1998). *Den motsägelsefulla specialpedagogiken: Motiveringar, genomförande och konsekvenser.* Göteborg, Sweden: Göteborgs Universitet.

Pettersson, S., & Asén, G. (1989). *Bildundervisningen och det pedagogiska rummet: Traditioner, föreställningar och undervisningsprocess inom skolämnet teckning/bild i grundskolan.* Stockholm: Högskolan för Lärarutbildning.

Pinar, W. F., Reynolds, W. M., Slattery, P., & Taubman, P. M. (1995). *Understanding curriculum: An introduction to the study of historical and contemporary curriculum discourses.* New York: Peter Lang.

Popkewitz, T. S. (1997). The curriculum theory tradition: Studies in social/cultural and political contexts of pedagogical practises. In K. E. Rosengren & B. Öhngren (Eds.), *An evaluation of Swedish research in education* (pp. 42–67). Stockholm: HSFR.

Robertsson Hörberg, C. (1997). *Lärares kunskapsutnyttjande i praktiken: ett personligt och kontextuellt perspektiv på vardagskunskap och forskning.* Linköping, Sweden: Linköpings Universitet.

Romhed, R. (1999). Marknadsplats, myndighet eller mötesplats? In M. Alexandersson (Ed.), *Styrning på villovägar* (pp. 75–145). Lund, Sweden: Studentlitteratur.

Rubinstein Reich, L. (1993). *Samling i förskolan.* Stockholm: Almqvist & Wiksell International.

Rönnerman, K. (1993). *Lärarinnor utvecklar sin praktik: En studie av åtta utvecklingsarbeten på lågstadiet.* Umeå, Sweden: Umeå Universitet.

Sandberg, R. (1996). *Musikundervisningens yttre villkor och inre liv: Några variationer över ett läroplansteoretiskt tema.* Stockholm: Högskolan för Lärarutbildning.

Schüllerqvist, U. (1996). Förskjutningen av svensk skolpolitisk debatt under det senaste decenniet. In T. Englund (Ed.), *Utbildningspolitiskt systemskifte?* (pp. 44–106). Stockholm: Högskolan för Lärarutbildning.

Selander, S., Forsberg, A., Romare, E., & Åström, T. (1992). *Bilder av arbetsliv och näringsliv i skolans läroböcker.* Stockholm: Publica.

Smyth, J. (1993). *Schooling for democracy in economic rationalist time.* Adelaide, Australia: The Flinders University of South Australia, School of Education.

Staberg, E.-M. (1992). *Olika världar, skilda värderingar: Hur flickor och pojkar möter högstadiets fysik, kemi och teknik.* Umeå, Sweden: Umeå Universitet.

Strömdahl, H. (1996). *On mole and amount of substance: A study of the dynamics of concept formation and concept attainment.* Göteborg, Sweden: Göteborgs Universitet.

Stukát, S. (1998). *Lärares planering under och efter utbildningen.* Göteborg, Sweden: Göteborgs Universitet.

Sundgren, G. (1995). Om elevers tolkningsföreträde och rätt till en egen kunskapsprocess. *Utbildning och demokrati*, 4(1), 48–71.

Svingby, G. (1978). *Läroplaner som styrmedel för svensk obligatorisk skola: Teoretisk analys och ett empiriskt bidrag.* Göteborg, Sweden: Göteborgs Universitet.

Säfström, C. A. (1994). *Makt och mening: Förutsättningar för en innehållsfokuserad pedagogisk forskning.* Uppsala, Sweden: Uppsala Universitet.

Trotzig, E. (1997). *Sätta flickan i stånd att fullgöra sina husliga plikter: Fyra märkeskvinnor och flickors slöjdundervisning.* Linköping, Sweden: Linköpings Universitet.

Tullberg, A. (1997). *Teaching the mole: A phenomenographic inquiry into the didactics of chemistry.* Göteborg, Sweden: Göteborgs Universitet.

Vislie, L., Popkewitz, T., & Bjerg, J. (1997). Pedagogy and educational research in Sweden—History and politics. In K. E. Rosengren & B. Öhngren (Eds.), *An evaluation of Swedish research in education* (pp. 20–41). Stockholm: HSFR.

Yates, L. (1996). European curriculum theory and research revisited after twenty years: Is Europe still ahead? In I. Nilsson (Ed.). *European curriculum theory and research in a twenty year perspective* (pp. 91–96). Umeå, Sweden: Umeå University.

Öhrn, E. (1993). *Könsmönster i klassrumsinteraktion: En observations–och intervjustudie av högstadieelevers lärarkontakter.* Göteborg, Sweden: Göteborgs Universitet.

Österlind, E. (1998). *Disciplinering via frihet: Elevers planering av sitt eget arbete.* Uppsala, Sweden: Uppsala Universitet.

Östman, L. (1995). *Socialisation och mening: No-utbildning som politiskt och miljömoraliskt problem.* Uppsala, Sweden: Uppsala Universitet.

CHAPTER 34

Curriculum Study in Taiwan: Retrospect and Prospect

Jenq-Jye Hwang
National Tainan Teachers College, Taiwan

Chia-Yu Chang
National Taipei University of Technology, Taiwan

Curriculum study is not only the foundation of curriculum development and innovation; it could also serve as a watchdog over the quality of education. However, there lies a close connection between curriculum study and the social context of a country. On the one hand, the outcomes of curriculum study may lead to a social change and can promote human qualities; on the other hand, the issues and approaches of curriculum study are also influenced by the sociopolitical situation.

The R.O.C. (Taiwan) government, established on Formosa Island in 1949, has been Westernized in its education system in which there was never a lack of discussion or experimentation with the school curriculum. Yet not until the mid-1980s did the field of curriculum study appear in teacher education programs and in the top agenda of educational research. Indeed, as mentioned, the social change played a critical role.

SOCIAL AND EDUCATIONAL BACKGROUND

Social Background

Encompassed by an authoritarian political atmosphere, Taiwan's society has been underneath strict surveillance, regulation, and control. Education was merely considered an apparatus for implementing political policies and maintaining Taiwan as a stable state. In 1987, when Martial Law was lifted, new political parties and mass media sprang up and contributed to Taiwan society's moving forward to the new epoch of a genuine democracy. Shortly after, in 1991, the government declared the termination of the law, the Temporary Provisions Effective During the Period of National Mobilization in Suppression of Communist Rebellion. After decades of suppression, societal forces began to explode. Consequently, the debates and criticisms on political, cultural, historical, and educational issues that pushed forward the development of curriculum study flourished further and thus rendered Taiwan a perfect condition favorable for the blooming of curriculum study.

Moreover, Taiwan's well-known and rapid economic growth in the 1960s also raised the family income. The notions of *education as investment* and *education as consumption* that were widely circulating among the public were gradually forming. Under the influence of such notions, parents willing to invest in educating their children and to consume education as a means of promoting quality of life started to make appeals for more opportunities for their children to enter high schools and universities. Consequently, it caused a great expansion in capacity at the secondary and tertiary levels of schooling. Students were thereby able to climb higher up the educational ladder; following the increasing heterogeneity of the student population, curriculum adaptation was requested even more urgently. In such a case, many research institutes relative to curriculum and instruction were then quickly established to meet the desperate needs of curriculum development and innovation.

In the meantime, the Taiwanese political climate and economic situation were changing. The transition from traditional society to a new one had been proceeding furtively, and this gave rise to some social problems. Some characteristics about this new society have appeared as follows: (a) population growth was decreasing while the percentage of the aged rising; (b) family population was shrinking, and divorce rate during this time was gradually increasing; (c) consciousness of gender equality was suddenly awakened with its importance realized; (d) old values and traditions were deconstructed, and some new values began to emerge; (e) international exchanges happened frequently under the formation of globalization; and (f) science and technology was progressing rapidly, plus computers and communication tools were becoming very popular (Hwang, Yu, & Chang, 1993).

Educational Background

After the lifting of Martial Law and under the influence of social change, Taiwan's society has become more democratic and liberal. Constantly people demanded more participation in educational reforms. This accelerated the pace of reform. The 1990s became a critical age for rapid Taiwanese educational reforms. Not only was decentralization of educational policy finally put into effect, but autonomy, deregulation, and localization of education also took place.

First of all, the government enacted University Law and empowered universities with curriculum autonomy; second, the local educational authorities set about some projects (most important, school-based curriculum experiments) under local autonomy. Soon textbook writing and publishing were open to nongovernmental publishers, and the right of textbook selection was returned from the hand of the government back to that of schools and teachers. Moreover, the revised curriculum standards of elementary schools (1993), junior high schools (1994), senior high schools (1996), and vocational schools (1998) began, thereafter, to emphasize flexibility, localization, and applications to real life. Additionally, the Nine-Year Articulated Curriculum Guideline, which was enacted in 1998 and replaced the curriculum standards of elementary schools and junior high schools in 2001, was also undergoing an essential change in underlining (a) the articulation of elementary and junior high schools curriculum, (b) the spirit of school-based curriculum, and (c) curriculum integration. Obviously, the overall tendency of educational reforms, having created a widely different academic environment, is, so to speak, an important element that will determine future curriculum study in Taiwan.

THE DEVELOPMENT OF TAIWANESE CURRICULUM STUDY

According to the distinct aims and emphases of curriculum study that were influenced by the social and educational changes, Taiwan's history of curriculum study could be divided into the following three periods.

The Period of Orientation Toward National Policy and Practicality: 1949 to the Mid-1980s

Curriculum study in this period was mainly affected by external elements, especially political factors. The aims of curriculum study were focusing on the introduction of principles and theories of curriculum design, which focused on school formal curriculum (i.e., national curriculum standards and textbooks).

During this period of time, school curriculum was thoroughly constructed by the government, along with curriculum specialists. The major issues of curriculum study were how to construct better curriculum standards, how to implement them efficiently in schools, and how to deliver them seamlessly to students. In addition, the inquiries into curriculum thoughts at that time were subject to the field of educational philosophy. Moreover, in terms of research, government officials and curricular specialists were leading researchers, and the research methods frequently adopted then were mainly philosophical, historical, comparative, or survey ones. Issues related to national policies or those more pragmatically oriented were put as top priorities into curriculum study.

Generally speaking, there were two big achievements in this period: translation and introduction of foreign curriculum study (Chang, 1968; Chinese Education Association, 1974; Chu, 1959; Huang, 1981; Sun, 1958, 1959), and investigation into consequences and problems of curricular implementation (Department of Education, 1972, 1976; Liou, 1983).

The Period of Explicating and Criticizing: The Mid-1980s to the Mid-1990s

In this period, the domain of curriculum study began to expand vitally due to a relief from political control and the increase in the number of curriculum researchers (including the overseas educated ones). Neither of the inquiries about subject curriculum knowledge nor the techniques in curriculum development were regarded as the hottest study topics. The main objectives of study were to react against the long-term political, cultural, and social suppression.

Then the concerns of curriculum study moved toward the relationship between curriculum and social environment, especially the ideology in textbook content across the Strait, the operation of extra activities, and hidden curriculum in Taiwan. The methods of curriculum study were emphasizing theoretical analysis, document analysis, and in-depth interview and observation.

The critical thoughts of curriculum from Western scholars, such as Franklin Bobbitt, Ralph Tyler, Michael Apple, William Pinar, Herbert Kliebard, Elliot Eisner, John Goodlad, Henry Giroux, Michael Young, Basil Bernstein, Peter Freire, Paul Hirst, and so on, also became an important part of curriculum study. This period was characterized as the *explicating and criticizing* period.

As seen in the research papers, the major accomplishments of this period were primarily reached by novice researchers who just graduated from graduate school of universities (e.g., Chen, 1993; Chien, 1992; Chou, 1994, 1999; Chung, 1994; Huang, 1988; Kau, 1992; Lee, 1989; Lee, 1991; Tsai, 1992; Wang, 1992).

The Period of Localization: The Mid-1990s to the Present

The most important issues of curriculum study in this period were chiefly concerned with the local needs of curriculum study, the education for disadvantaged students, the initiation of school- based curriculum development, and curriculum integration. Namely, these issues were all concerned with localization.

The methodology of curriculum study consisted of widely adopted ethnography research, qualitative research, and action research. In addition, teachers' roles were gradually considered to be curriculum makers or even researchers. The specific emphases in this stage on curriculum study were: (a) curriculum decision making of teachers, (b) integration and differentiation of curriculum, (c) division of labor in curriculum development at each decision-making level, and (d) curriculum implementation and evaluation requested by curriculum reform. The following text explores them in great detail.

CURRICULUM STUDY IN TAIWAN

All social and educational changes since the late 1980s led Taiwan's curriculum study to a more diverse state. In the first place, the analysis of hidden curriculum, already recognized to be existing in schools, sparked off the contestation against the Han-centered and monocultural education environment; then it shifted the concern of curriculum study onto the approach of curriculum study. Accordingly, this resulted in the founding of new organizations related to curriculum study.

The Analysis of Political Ideology in Curriculum

The reviewing of ideologies in curriculum was a key issue of curriculum study in Taiwan after the lifting of Martial Law. As shown in a good deal of extensive analyses, the status and contents of subjects—including the Scout Education, Military Training, Three Principles of the People, and Thought of Dr. Sun Yat-Sen—have never been critically challenged before. It is claimed that this kind of politically related teaching subject was designed to imbue students with the KMT-led (the dominant political party, 1949–2000) governmental ideology, with a view to maintaining its vested interest and privilege and to dominantly control its ruled people. Incidentally, the less politically related subjects, like Chinese, social studies, geography, music, and so on, have also been under investigation.

In addition, the former ways, through curriculum and instruction, to implement the kinds of education such as Japanese decolonization, patriotism, and anticommunism—namely, those that intended to strengthen the political control of government—were likewise being reexamined during this period (Ou, 1990; Tseng, 1994).

Multicultural Curriculum

Aroused by the awakening of local consciousness, as well as by the controversy of mainstream cultures and values during social transformation, multicultural curriculum has undoubtedly become one of several emerging issues in Taiwan's curriculum study. The treatises and studies on multicultural curriculum are blooming. Curriculum study, particularly dealing with the multicultural issues, has come to the forefront.

At present, how to design the models for multicultural curriculum from kindergarten to university, how to select and organize multicultural curriculum contents or activities, and what the criteria of multicultural curriculum evaluation might be are put into the agenda of curriculum study (see Chen, 1999; Chuang, 1998; Hwang, 1995c; Wu, 2000).

In 1989, the Democratic Progressive Party (DPP) won a partial victory over the election of county magistrates and city mayors. By taking this opportunity, some DPP magistrates and mayors started to challenge the long-term monolanguage policy, which had been brought into force by KMT, and to undertake the new language policy of resurrecting mother tongue by means of issuing executive order to all their subordinate schools in request for compiling supplementary textbooks and to mandate native language to be taught in schools. Hereby, the previous Mandarin Policy to which the public opinions have long opposed abruptly changed its course. This was regarded as an action of educational localization and has received a favorable opinion from all circles of society. As a result, the central government also shifted its exclusive language policy and adopted native language learning into the revised curriculum standard of elementary schools of 1994 and the revised curriculum standard of junior high schools of 1996.

Meanwhile, this movement also pushed forward the issues of curriculum study regarding *local studies* content, including the analyses of its teaching materials and curriculum decision making and implementation (such as Huang, 1994; Lin, 1998; Lin & Hwang, 2000). Obviously, in Taiwan, the issue of local studies education is always subject to political struggles; educational issues related to this local studies content are commonly complicated, politicized, and at times even perverted, especially while taking the influence of localism into account. Owing to this, the evolvement, causes of problems, and improvement of local studies education, including mother tongue language teaching, have proved to be the important issues in contemporary curriculum study.

Second, the curriculum for the aboriginal is another issue and tendency of curriculum study for three reasons: (a) removal of political pressure, (b) introduction of multicultural education thought, and (c) aboriginal people's petition for school curriculum's being more responsive to the multiethnic demography of society. As the multicultural curriculum was put into implementation, the controversies in regard with this issue were (a) what counts as the worthy knowledge, (b) how to organize pertinent subject matters into textbooks, and (c) to whom it should be taught (there are at least nine tribes identified in Taiwanese aborigines besides the majority Han people). All those questions are currently listed in the agenda of curriculum study in Taiwan.

Third, curriculum research on foreign language teaching has also become another urgent issue. In response to internationalization and globalization, the foreign language teaching is, on the one hand, expanding its scope in English teaching from high school level down to the elementary school level, and, on the other hand, adding the second foreign language learning as an elective into the junior high school curriculum. However, arguably, the question of what grade foreign language should be placed needs to be researched further.

Fourth, gender equity in education is also getting more attention as shown in the works of Awakening Foundation (1988) and Hsieh (1990). The issues dealt with gender rights by researchers now aim to eliminate sexual stereotypes and prejudices in school textbooks. Arguably, how to reconstruct the whole school curriculum about the education of gender equity is no doubt another important topic in the present curriculum study (Hwang, 1995b; Lee, 1993).

Emerging Social Issues

The rapidity of Taiwanese social change has caused many social problems that need to be addressed and that surely can be resolved by means of education. Such social problems can be categorized into issues of environment protection, sex education, parents' education, human rights education, drug education, computer literacy, moral education, and career planning. Of course, all those kinds of issues are considered in Taiwan's curriculum research (Hwang, 1993).

Curriculum Thoughts

The issues of debates on the nature of curriculum as well as on the study of rationale and Western thoughts receive no less attention than the issues derived from the aforementioned social context. Especially study of curriculum thoughts were employed to castigate the domestic curriculum problems and have even shown a new direction for Taiwan's curriculum study and research.

Curriculum Control and the Politics of Curriculum Reform

Amid the deregulation of curriculum policy in Taiwan, how to share the responsibilities of curriculum control among the central government, local authorities, schools, and teachers, and what is the most appropriate model of curriculum development for each level of schooling are the problems on which curriculum researchers often contemplate (such as Cheng, 2000; Kau, 1998, 1999).

Furthermore, the politics of curriculum reform have also been incorporated into the field of curriculum study as a weighted issue in Taiwan. As time passes, the process of curriculum decision making (see the analyses of Chang, 1994; Hung, 2000; Lu, 1993; Yo, 1992) and the politics of the curriculum reform (Hwang, 1995a) have been widely discussed.

The Effects of Curriculum Implementation and Reform

There have been several vital changes in curriculum since the 1980s in Taiwan. Basically, the results of curriculum implementation, the effects of curriculum reform, and the attitudes of educators toward curriculum reforms are the ongoing issues. A number of research projects focus on studying these issues (see Wang, 2000).

Textbook Censorship and Selection

Before, due to centralization policy and practice, the highest authority of education—namely, the Ministry of Education (MOE)—was in charge of all affairs of curriculum decision making. Usually MOE, joining with specialists, took charge of developing the curriculum standards on all phases of education. Then based on the standards, the related official organizations that engaged in textbook compilation later helped with the compilation, publication, and issuing of official textbooks with the titles of *National Edition* or *Unified Edition.* What schools need to be able to do is only use these specific editions. Therefore, the school curriculum knowledge has been monopolized by the government.

Several questions arise from this situation: (a) How do the official textbooks interplay with a society full of ideologies and values? (b) In what way do these one-minded textbooks control teachers' teaching, define school curriculum, and restrict students' learning experiences? (c) What will be the relationship between examinations and textbooks? All of these are important topics in the field of curriculum study.

However, beginning in 1989, the government allowed private publishing companies to participate in textbook compiling. School teachers, therefore, gained access to textbook writing and selection. Motivated by this new policy's potential profit, publishers soon started to invite school teachers in joining their concerted efforts to restructure the previous, unified textbook content. Nonetheless, there has been investigation of how to set up a feasible textbook assessment system, what should be the reviewing standards, how the diverse content effects teaching and learning, and what is the proper or real situation of textbook selection (Chang, 1994; Chuang, 1991; Hwang et al., 1994; Ou, 1997).

Curriculum Experimentation

Encouraged by the trend of curriculum autonomy and curriculum reform, the local education authorities have given an impetus to various curriculum experiments, which were characterized as school-based curriculum, open education, and curriculum integration.

Among the three, curriculum integration aims to improve school curriculum and overcome the problems of overdivided subjects and disconnected contents condition. Based on the school-based plans, the urge for schools to invoke more autonomy in reforming and developing programs by themselves asks for schools' reflection on their own conditions and catering for each student's specific needs. The directions of reform request reestablishing national key competency standards and implementing curriculum deregulation deviating from the traditionally centralized education in Taiwan. However, in dealing with national key competency standards, not only is the pilot test necessary, but also further study is essential. Nowadays, how to operate the School-Based Curriculum Development (SBCD) and curriculum integration are two significant issues (Lin, 1998; Ye, 2000).

Approaches to Curriculum Study

Qualitative and action research have been gaining weight with curriculum study and educational researchers in Taiwan since the 1980s. To make thorough inquiries into operating curriculum, especially while dealing with the microcosmic phenomenon of school curriculum, these approaches, having been extensively used, have made a great contribution to curriculum study. These approaches are also broadly employed in discussions of various topics, ranging from the contents of textbooks to the implementation of curriculum and the use of textbooks in the classroom (Cheng, 2000; Ku, Lin, & Chu, 1999; Wang, 1996).

The Establishment of Numerous Institutes for Curriculum Study

Curriculum study could provide a sound foundation for action and evaluation when implementing curriculum reforms. During these years, following constant curriculum reforms, considerable quantities of forums, research institutes, and professional associations related to curriculum study in Taiwan have been created.

Now there are several institutes or centers of curriculum and instruction grounded in universities. They not only conduct curriculum research, but also train researchers who later devote themselves to the field of Taiwanese curriculum study. In 1996, the Association for Curriculum and Instruction (ACI, Taiwan, R.O.C), a national and nongovernmental academic organization, was founded by a group of scholars and educators concerned with the development of Taiwan's curriculum field. ACI not only publishes *The Curriculum and Instruction Quarterly*, first published in 1998, but also is the only learned and most momentous journal that focuses on curricular issues in Taiwan. There are other dedicated agencies such as the Institute of Multicultural Education, the Institute of Ethnic Relationship, the Center for Educational Research, the Center for Research in Curriculum and Instruction, the Center for Local Studies Education, and the Center for the Aboriginal Education. Moreover, various committees concerning gender equity education, aboriginal education, and so forth have also been established at schools and universities and in government offices.

PENDING ISSUES FOR RESEARCH

In making a comprehensive survey of Taiwanese curriculum study for the past half century, there are patently manifold attainments. First of all, the field of curriculum has taken root in pedagogy and has proved to be an important part of it. Second, the research population has been increased. Third, the accumulative outcomes of studies including monographs, research reports, theses, papers of periodicals, and so forth, are fruitful. This indeed shows that curriculum study is a powerful and significant field of educational research. Fourth, the different kinds of organizations that advance the curriculum study and train researchers have been built up island-wide. Fifth, the curriculum study and curriculum reform have been coupled together and dealt with as a whole. Furthermore, researchers are no longer ivory-towered; they become more and more influential over practice. However, there are still some pending issues in need of exploration when we review the development of Taiwanese curriculum study.

The Range of Curriculum Reform

There have been several periods of curriculum reform in Taiwan since 1949, and each time the range of reform was controversial. As we know, the range of reform involves debatable philosophical thinking. Some argue that only large-scale curriculum reform could bring on a thorough and fundamental success, whereas the disinclination of doing so only safeguards the status quo against advantageous change. What is more, educators, as we know, used to resist the large-scale reforms due to their conservative attitudes and were often inclined to scale down a reform's ideal. So reformers often tend to address proposals in a more radical way to ably hold the bottom line while bargaining with educators.

Yet the others who stand for the small-scale reform believe it is evolution, but not revolution, that could avoid the incoherent reform and could afford the time to take deliberate action. The small-range change is more acceptable by those people involved.

In essence, both of these approaches of reform are reasonable, and how to choose the most appropriate one depends on the social situation and claims of the curriculum reform. Definitely, how to make the right decisions is not by the intuition of decision makers, but by that information provided by curriculum research.

The Deregulation of Curriculum and the Teacher's Role in Curriculum Development

Since 1949, there has been a nationally unified curriculum standard used as a regulatory for implementing entrance examinations. However, after the lifting of Martial Law, deregulation in education has become an imperative.

As the curriculum elasticity is magnifying, things like teachers' competencies of designing curriculum, curriculum evaluation system, and other supplement measures have been installed. Whether the curriculum autonomy is implemented with responsibility and with teachers actively involved is the interests of curriculum study (see Chang, 1994; Chen, 2000; Chou, 1996; Lin, 1997; Pung, 1999).

School-Based Curriculum Development

The curriculum autonomy of schools has now become a priority in curriculum reform, and its implementation mainly emphasizes school-based curriculum development (SBCD) that can be termed *grassroots reform*.

Yet the advance to the SBCD, regardless of its advantage, also brings about some misunderstandings and panic among teachers sand parents. Some of them misconceive that the SBCD means teachers have to construct by themselves all teaching materials (e.g., textbooks) and even have to develop their schools' courses totally different from another school. For the time being, how to fulfill the SBCD idea, how to maintain educational quality, and how to justify educational equity are the follow-up issues of curriculum study (Chang, 1999; Lin, 1999).

Emerging Curricula

With regard to social transition, there are some emerging issues like environmental protection, human rights, career planning, and so on, to which our school system needs to respond urgently because they contain important knowledge for cultivating good citizens.

As these emerging issues are coming up, there are some questions that require further research. They include the limited capacity of school curriculum and the know-how for attending to these emerging curricula.

Curriculum Differentiation

Teach what to whom? is the key question in curriculum design. In our view, curriculum designers should honor two principles (i.e., education equity and adaptive development). The former, focusing on the common curriculum, aims at providing students with common experiences; the latter, stressing the differentiated curricula, points to providing opportunities for each individual student to develop his or her potential.

We should understand that carrying out the principles is quite difficult and bringing them into practice can even be painful. For example, we argue that special students should return back to the mainstream while hoping that the curriculum differentiation could serve as a mechanism in providing adaptive teaching. But when, what, and how in terms of differentiation are the tough questions that need to be resolved.

Curriculum Integration

Curriculum integration on the phase of compulsory education has been an important trend in Taiwan. Nevertheless, it is not only a complicated concept, but also a difficult task. Problems of implementation, exacerbated by resistant educators who often have only vague concepts about curriculum integration, are the main foci of current curriculum research.

Curriculum for Aboriginal Education

Originally, the curriculum for the aboriginal education was a fused approach, which aimed to melt the aborigines into the mainstream culture. But it was argued that this curricular pattern would generate a cultural lag and an identity crisis among aboriginal people due to the lack of opportunities for them and other people to recognize their cultural value and contribution to the whole society.

While stressing the importance of curricular design for the aboriginal people, the aboriginal children also need to equip themselves with social competitiveness before entering the majority society. Nevertheless, this would be lessened if they spend too much time studying their own aboriginal culture. How to strike a balance between these two curricula and better organize them into the overall school curriculum needs to be studied more.

Localization and Internationalization

Since the lifting of Martial Law in 1987, the notion of whether the indigenous people in Taiwan hold supremacy has been critically challenged. This contributed to Taiwanese indigenous' striving to return to their native culture a legitimate status in school curricula. As we can see, there are several new teaching subjects related to the local studies and the mother tongue language teaching being added into school curricula.

However, there are a few issues. First, although the addition of new subjects is a meaningful move, the source of qualified teachers is another question. Second, because the content of local culture is so multifarious, including many detached courses (e.g., history, geography, art, science, social studies, and language, etc.), the already heavy learning load becomes even heavier, making these courses hard to integrate with other former courses and giving doubt to this new policy. Third, at the age of globalization, how to make the school curriculum be responsive to both localization and globalization is also a difficult challenge to curriculum researchers.

CONCLUSION

Curriculum study is taking shape and has accumulated some outcomes after many endeavors to study, emulate, follow, and join the developed countries' curriculum studies, on the one hand, and localize them for ages, on the other hand. While envisaging the future, however, the curriculum study in Taiwan still needs to (a) establish more responsible research organizations in charge of assorted duties respectively at each national, local, and school level; (b) link up the efforts of existing institutes, schools, and nongovernmental agencies; (c) invite many more experts for more international and interdisciplinary collaboration; and (d) form systemic and integrated research by ways of concerted teamwork. The task of curriculum study belongs not only to scholars in the library, but also to teachers in schools. The aim of curriculum study is not only to establish theory, but also to improve practice.

REFERENCES

Awakening Foundation. (1988). We grow up this way: Sexual discrimination in textbooks. *Woman Awakening, 71.*

Chang, C. F. (1994). *The institutions of textbook selection in junior high schools.* Unpublished master's thesis, National Taiwan Normal University.

Chang, C. S. (1994). *An analysis of teachers' participation in educational research.* Unpublished master's thesis, National Taiwan Normal University.

Chang, C. Y. (1999). *School-based curriculum development.* Taipei, Taiwan: Shida Shuyuan.

Chang, S. C. (1968). *New theory of curriculum design and teaching method.* Taipei, Taiwan: Society of Chinese Public Relations.

Chang, S. F. (1994). *A study of the decision-making process for the elementary schools curriculum standard revising in Taiwan.* Unpublished master's thesis, National Taiwan Normal University.

Chen, M. H. (1993). *A study on the transmission of political ideology in citizenship curriculum of junior-high schools.* Unpublished master's thesis, National Taiwan Normal University.

Chen, M. Z. (1999). *A study on the idea and praxis of multicultural curriculum.* Unpublished master's thesis, National Taiwan Normal University.

Chen, S. Y. (2000). *An analysis of teachers' curriculum interpretation and curriculum operation experience in elementary schools.* Unpublished master's thesis, National Cheng Chi University.

Cheng, S. Z. (2000). *A study on curriculum development at regional level.* Unpublished master's thesis, National Hualian Teachers College.

Cheng, Z. S. (2000). *An action research on curriculum design of science stories.* Unpublished master's thesis, National Hualian Teachers College.

Chien, L. P. (1992). *A study of Paul Hirst's curriculum theory.* Unpublished master's thesis, National Taiwan Normal University.

Chinese Education Association. (Ed.). (1974). *Curriculum research.* Taipei, Taiwan: Taiwan Commercial Affairs.

Chou, P. Y. (1994). *A study of E. W. Eisner's curriculum theory.* Unpublished master's thesis, National Taiwan Normal University.

Chou, P. Y. (1999). *A study of H. Giroux's curriculum theory.* Unpublished doctoral dissertation, National Taiwan Normal University.

Chou, S. C. (1996). *The policy trend of curriculum deregulation for compulsory education in Taiwan.* Unpublished doctoral dissertation, National Taiwan Normal University.

Chu, I. Z. (1959). *Principles of curriculum making*. Taipei, Taiwan: The National Institute of Educational Materials.

Chuang, M. C. (1991). *A survey research on the utilization of textbooks for life and ethics in elementary schools*. Kauhsiung, Taiwan: Fuwen.

Chuang, T. K. (1998). *The implementation of multicultural curriculum program: A study on students' experiential curriculum*. Unpublished master's thesis, National Hualian Teachers College.

Chung, H. M. (1994). *A study of W. Pinar's methodology of curriculum research*. Unpublished master's thesis, National Taiwan Normal University.

Department of Education, Taiwan Province. (1972). *The investigation and improvement in the temporary curriculum standard and teaching materials for junior high schools*. Taichung, Taiwan: Author.

Department of Education, Taiwan Province. (1976). *An evaluation report of curriculum experiment in junior high schools: Life- centered curriculum experiment*. Taichung, Taiwan: Author.

Hsieh, S. C. (1990). The gender consciousness in education. *Newsletter For Women's Research, 18*.

Huang, F. H. (Trans.). (1981). (Written by R. W. Tyler). *Basic principles of curriculum and instruction*. Taipei, Taiwan: Kweikwan.

Huang, C. S. (1988). *The implication of Basil Bernstein's classifications and framework in curriculum study*. Unpublished master's thesis, National Taiwan Normal University.

Huang, C. S. (1994). *A theoretical framing of curriculum and transformation of social structure*. Unpublished doctoral dissertation, National Taiwan Normal University.

Huang, Y. G. (1994). *An analytical study on the development of local studies teaching materials: An example of Ilan county*. Unpublished master's thesis, National Taiwan Normal University.

Hung, Y. S. (2000). *A study on policy decision making process of articulated curriculum guidelines for compulsory education*. Unpublished master's thesis, National Taipei Teachers College.

Hwang, I. J. (1993). Social change and the curriculum design. In J. J. Huang (Ed.), *The transformation of curriculum and instruction* (pp. 1–22). Taipei, Taiwan: Shida Shuyuan.

Hwang, J. J. (1995a). The political arena of curriculum reform. In J. J. Hwang (Ed.), *Curriculum for the diverse society* (pp. 1–42). Taipei, Taiwan: Shida Shuyuan.

Hwang, J. J. (1995b). Gender education and curriculum design. In J. J. Hwang (Ed.), *Curriculum for the diverse society* (pp. 81–96). Taipei, Taiwan: Shida Shuyuan.

Hwang, J. J. (1995c). Approaches to multicultural curriculum. In J. J. Hwang (Ed.), *Curriculum for the diverse society* (pp. 97–128). Taipei, Taiwan: Shida Shuyuan.

Hwang, J. J., Lee, L. S., Yang, L. L., Chang, C. F., & Chang, C. Y. (1994). *A study on textbook censorship and textbook evaluation criteria for elementary schools*. Taipei, Taiwan: Center for Educational Research. National Taiwan Normal University.

Hwang, J. J., Yu, C. J., & Chang, C. Y. (1993). *An analysis of the issues and trends of social conditions, 2000: The education*. Research Report to Research, Development and Evaluation Council, Executive Yuan.

Kau, C. M. (1992). *A study on compulsory education curriculum in China*. Unpublished master's thesis, National Taiwan Normal University.

Kau, S. C. (1998). The strategy and mechanism of curriculum governance. *Bulletin of Taipei Municipal Teachers College, 29*, 55–72.

Kau, S. C. (1999). An analytical framework of curriculum governance. *Bulletin of Education Research, 42*, 131–154.

Ku, Y. C., Lin, S. P., & Chu, H. C. (1999). *The reform of instruction and curriculum*. Presented in a seminar on theory and practice of innovations in teacher education.

Lee, C. M. (1991). *Analysis of moral content in citizen and moral textbooks for junior high schools*. Unpublished master's thesis, National Taiwan Normal University.

Lee, L. C. (1989). *Analysis of the connotation of politics and socialization in the junior high school textbooks of Chinese*. Unpublished master's thesis, National Taiwan Normal University.

Lee, Y. C. (1993). *Examining the elementary schools textbooks*. Taipei, Taiwan: Taiwanese Professors Association.

Lin, I. S. (1998). *A study of curriculum integration models in elementary schools in Taiwan*. Unpublished master's dissertation, National Hua-Lien Teachers College.

Lin, P. S. (1999). *A case study of school-based curriculum development: Taipei county's local culture initiative*. Unpublished doctoral dissertation, National Taiwan Normal University.

Lin, S. C. (1997). *A study of teachers' participation in curriculum development of elementary schools*. Unpublished master's thesis, National Taiwan Normal University.

Lin, Z. Z. (1998). *The theory and praxis of local studies education in elementary schools*. Taipei, Taiwan: Shida Shuyuan.

Lin, Z. Z., & Hwang, K. S. (2000). *A study on the evaluation and design of local studies teaching materials for elementary schools*. Research Report to National Science Council.

Liou, D. S. (1983). *A study on the structure and content of social studies curriculum in elementary schools.* Unpublished master's thesis, National Taiwan Normal University.

Lu, Z. Y. (1993). *The curriculum development of social study in elementary schools.* Unpublished master's thesis, National Taiwan Normal University.

Ou, Y. S. (1990). *An analysis of hidden curriculum in social studies of elementary schools in Taiwan.* Unpublished doctoral dissertation, National Taiwan Normal University.

Ou, Y. S., & Hwang, J. J. (Eds.). (1997). *An evaluation report on elementary school textbooks.* Taipei, Taiwan: Association for Curriculum and Instruction, Taiwan, ROC.

Pung, Y. Z. (1999). *A study on elementary school teachers' professional ability in curriculum design.* Unpublished master's thesis, National Hualian Teachers College.

Sun, B. C. (Trans.). (1958). (Written by H. Alberty). *Principles for reconstruction of secondary school curriculum.* Taipei, Taiwan: The National Institute of Educational Materials.

Sun, B. C. (Trans.). (1959). (Written by E. F. Huggard). *Curriculum development in elementary schools.* Taipei, Taiwan: The National Institute of Educational Materials.

Tasi, C. T. (1992). *A study of Ralph Tyler's curriculum thoughts.* Unpublished master's thesis, National Taiwan Normal University.

Tseng, C. Y. (1994). *Schooling for anti-communists in Taiwan.* Unpublished master's thesis, National Taiwan Normal University.

Wang, C. H. (2000). *Concerns of elementary school teachers on innovations and influential factors of nine-year articulated curriculum for elementary and junior high schools.* Unpublished master's thesis, National Cheng-Chi University.

Wang, C. M. (1996). *The curriculum reform process of a public: Elementary school in Taiwan: A case study.* Unpublished master's thesis, National Hsin-Chu Teachers College.

Wang, L. Y. (1992). *A study of Michael Apple's curriculum thought.* Unpublished master's thesis, National Taiwan Normal University.

Wu, S. H. (2000). *Case study of teachers' multicultural instruction belief and operational curriculum.* Unpublished master's thesis, National Hua-Lien Teachers College.

Ye, S. H. (2000). *Research on implementation of curriculum integration in Taiwan's elementary schools.* Unpublished master's thesis, National Taiwan Normal University.

Yo, S. Y. (1992). *A study of teachers' curriculum decision making orientation and their inclination of participation.* Unpublished doctoral dissertation, National Cheng Chi University.

CHAPTER 35

Curriculum Development in Turkey

F. Dilek Gözütok
University of Ankara, Turkey

Rapid scientific and technological changes and developments are effective in education as in many other fields. The educational system, which has an important role both in social, political, cultural and economic development of the society and in the self development of the individuals, has got three main elements consisting of a student, a teacher and a program.

The innovations in the educational system are effective when they are used in the programs. The programs contain the targets, the contents having certain principles that are planned to reach those targets, the methods to be used, and the supporting auxiliary tools for education. They also include the evaluation measurements reflecting how much it is possible to reach the aims.

When we examine the studies of the program development in Turkey, we see the beginning of them by the announcement of the Republic. The studies of program development activities has improved systematically since the 1950s.

In Seljukians and the other Islamic countries, the primary schools, called *Mektep*, were under the names of *Darüttalim, Mektep, Mektephane, Muallimhane,* and *Darülilm* in the Ottoman period. These institutions were named *Mahalle Mektebi* or *Sibyan Mektebi* among the public. In all the Islamic societies, *Sibyan Mekteps* (primary schools) have one main lesson: The Koran. This lesson was aimed to teach how to read the Koran without explaining its meaning (Gürkan & Gökçe, 1999).

Because the students in Sibyan Schools in the First Innovation Movements Period (1773–1839) did not know how to read and write in Turkish, and because it was difficult to make innovations in those schools, new ones were opened under the name *Rüsdiye*, which formed the base of the primary schools of today. The programs of the first *Rüsdiyes* were as follows: Arabic, Grammar and Syntax, *Nubhe-i Vehbi*, Persian and *Thufe-i Vehbi*, Turkish, Calligraphy, Vocabulary (*Lugat*), and Moral lessons.

After the foundation of *Mekatib-i Umumiye Nezareti* on November 8, 1846, the primary school instructions were prepared under the name *talimat* on April 8, 1847, in the Tanzimat Period in the Ottoman Empire. These instructions included 20 articles. They consisted of the aims, rules, education period, and lessons that aimed to be taught (Büyükkaragöz, 1997).

The first secondary education institution was established under the name *Darülmaarif* in 1850 in the Ottoman Empire. The aim of this institution was to prepare students for *Darülfünun* and to train personnel for the official departments. The program of Darülfünun included Ulumu Diniye, Arabic, Persian, Hikmeti (Philosophy), Tabiye, Heyet (Astronomy), Geography, and Hendese (Geometry), (Varis, 1996). All of the lessons in these schools depended on memorization.

On June 5, 1876, the general primary school curriculum, which was prepared for 4 years of education, included lesson programs showing the method of teaching a specific number of lessons for each class in limited hours (Varis, 1996).

According to Unat (1964), the first detailed curriculum was prepared for the primary schools, known as *mekteb-i iptidai,* and the National Education System was reorganized with these regulations:

1. The duration for education in the city and the town primary schools were reduced to 3 years, and the village primary schools remained at 4 years.
2. Lessons such as the Ottoman History and Geography were extracted first from the curriculum of village schools and then from other programs, whereas the hours of Religion and Moral lessons increased.
3. A general curriculum and instruction was prepared for each of the Iptidai schools, for Istanbul Iptidai schools, and for the village primary schools.
4. To appoint a teacher for these schools, it was necessary to be graduated from *Darül Muallimin-i Iptidai* or to take a proficiency exam and be decent enough to be a teacher.

In this period, the main innovation and development were in the primary schools known as *usul-i cedide* or *iptidai mektepler,* dependent on *Maarif Nezareti* (Ministry of Education). However, in the schools known as *sibyan mektebi,* which were dependent on *Efkaf Nezareti* (Ministry of Foundations) and keep the old forms, there was no innovation about education and instruction. Moreover, the teachers of these schools tried to prevent the developments (Tazebay et al., 2000).

Before June 23, 1908, private kindergartens were established in some provinces. After this date, some private kindergartens were founded in Istanbul. In 1913, *Tedrisat-i Iptidadiye Kanununun Muvakkati* brought rules for preprimary school education, and *Ana Mektepleri Nizamnamesi* (Kindergarten Regulation) was published in 1915. After these regulations, kindergartens began to multiply in number especially in the large cities.

The programs of the primary schools were again regulated when instruction period was increased to 6 years with *Tedrisat-i Iptidaiye Kanunu Muvakkati* in 1913. Lessons in painting, music, physical education, agriculture, housekeeping, and sewing were added to the primary schools' program. Both 5 years and 6 years of primary education existed in the same system, and this created a disharmony in the education system (Varis, 1996).

After the establishment of the Turkish Great National Assembly on April 23, 1920, the government founded the central organization of *Maarif Vekaleti* (National Education Ministry). The following subjects were on the agenda of the Maarif Congress on June 16, 1921: regulation of primary schools' program, reevaluation of the education period of the primary schools, opening of village teachers' training colleges to train village teachers, and lessons and programs of the secondary schools (Cicioglu, 1985).

The Ministry prepared a program for the primary and secondary schools in 1922 and sent them to the related schools for feedback about the programs. The results showed that the lessons taught to children had to be related to the environment and to their needs. They also showed that there was a consensus for public education (collective education; Binbasioglu, 1995).

By the announcement of the Republic, there was a swift innovation movement in the educational system. When *Tevhid-i Tedrisat Kanunu* (The Law of Common Education) was put into effect in 1924, all the educational institutions were collected under the National Education Ministry, and the details of the curricula implemented in the schools were regulated. The first studies about the curriculum development in Turkey began in primary education in 1924, and these studies guided the secondary education in later phases.

The curriculum of 1924 was prepared under the name *The Primary School Curriculum* by considering the needs and conditions of the educational system of the newly established Turkish Republic. The program, which had a project quality, was in application for 2 years. The Primary School Curriculum of 1926 was prepared by considering the needs of the country at that time, the characteristics of children, and current educational and instructional concepts. The curriculum of 1926 included six main principles of the present curriculum. Tekisik (1947) explained these principles as follows:

(1) Public Educational System,

(2) The aims of the primary schools,

(3) The private aims of the lessons,

(4) The methods to be followed in education,

(5) The analytical method used in the first "reading and writing" education,

(6) To separate a five years' primary school into first and second halves. (pp. 18–19)

The 1926 curriculum was in application for 10 years. However, to train village students according to the conditions and needs of a village, a Village Schools Curriculum was prepared by focusing on the fundamental principles of the city school programs. The essence of this change in the educational programs depended on secularization, Westernization, and science.

In 1936, the previous curriculum was developed by evaluating the needs of the time. In this curriculum, the first part, "The Aims of the Primary School," included the principles of national education. Later, the subject was the "Principles of the Primary School Education and Instruction." This curriculum was in effect until 1948.

The main philosophy of the programs in this period was to train the students according to the principles of the Republican Regime. It was obvious that the programs had a national quality (MEB, 1990).

The economical, political, and social structures of the Turkish society, the developments in science and technology, the ideas of foreign experts, and the educational concept of *Atatürk* developed the educational structure in the Republican Period (Sönmez, 1994).

The first National Education Council was constituted in 1939 to increase the 3 years of village primary school curriculum to 5 years and to apply The Village Primary School Curriculum Project by the beginning of the 1939–1940 educational year. This project aimed to arrange some changes in the village schools' programs, such as the lessons related to the village life. The lessons, which can be applied, were Life Information, Nature Information, Working, and Agriculture. The program also included some lessons similar to the city primary schools, such as Turkish, Arithmetic, Geometry, History, Geography, National Information, and Painting (Tazebay et al., 2000, p. 59). To train teachers who would apply this program, Village Institutes were founded on April 17, 1940 with Act 3803.

The first formal educational program of the Institutes began in 1943. The Village Institutes had 5 years of education after the primary schools. In this period, there were 114 weeks for common cultural lessons, 58 weeks for the lessons of agricultural studies, and 58 weeks for technical works and lessons. The distribution of the lessons in a week was as follows:

Common cultural lessons: 22 hours in each class

Agricultural lessons and studies: 11 hours in each class

Technical lessons and studies: 11 hours in each class (MEB, 1953, p. 8)

There were a few changes in The Curriculum of the Village Institutes in 1947. The name of the general cultural lessons was *general information lessons,* and these lessons were given more hours than the others. Technical lessons were named *art lessons* and *workshop studies.* The instruction of these lessons was every year, but it was limited to one third of the instruction time (Akyüz, 1999).

The main resolutions that The Second National Educational Council took in 1943 were the development of morality in the schools, improvement of the efficiency of the native language studies in all the educational institutes, and analysis of history education from a methods point of view. The Council also added Art History lessons to the high schools' curriculum (Özalp, 1999).

The studies that began in 1945 aimed to remove the deficiency in the curriculum of 1936 and to prepare a program according to the needs of the 5 years of village primary schools. In this study, there were items that benefited from the inquiry results given to the teachers about the combination of village and city schools, consulting primary school inspectors and the directors of National Education, and investigating the schools by a council formed of these people. All these items show that the curriculum studies tried to establish scientific data basis.

The resolutions taken in the Third National Education Council were basically about organizations of Occupational and Technical Education and precautions to facilitate the studies of school–family organizations. Furthermore, this Council was first in which the members discussed the fundamental education and wanted to initiate the studies related to education (Özalp, 1999).

The aims of the National Education in the 1948 curriculum were collected under four items: (a) social, (b) individual, (c) human relations, and (d) economics. The Principles of Primary School Education and Instruction were rearranged. There were explanations of how to perform these principles in that arrangement. These principles and explanations also existed in the Secondary School Curriculum published in 1949 (Binbasioglu, 1995).

The aims of the courses were abridged and renewed in the secondary schools. The auxiliary tools for educational purposes were added to the curriculum of primary schools (Binbasioglu, 1995).

The Fourth National Educational Council gathered in 1949. It made several important decisions, among them to decrease the instruction period to 4 years in the high schools, regulate the curriculum of the teacher training educational institutions, combine the village institutes and teacher training educational institutions, bring closer the content and application of the lessons in the secondary schools to that of primary schools, and institute parallels between the two institutions (Özalp, 1999). After all these studies, the name *Müfredat Programi* (Curriculum) was changed to Education Program.

K. V. Wafford, who came to Turkey in 1952, investigated the conditions of the village schools and wrote a report to regulate our curriculum development studies systematically. Related to the report, 25 teachers were sent to America to get information about the applications in 1952.

The Fifth National Educational Council gathered in 1949 to review the 1948 curriculum to respond to the needs of the time. The resolution was to apply the new program first in the pilot schools and then in the other schools (MEB, 1997).

The 25 teachers in America returned to Turkey in 1954 and prepared the "Bolu Village Testing Schools Model" at the end of the observations in several regions of the country. The Committee of Instruction and Education approved this program and started its testing in Bolu and Istanbul in the 1953–1954 school year. The Testing Program Committee also prepared another model curriculum and applied it during the 1954–1955 year. These studies were accepted as the founding curriculum development studies in Turkey (Demirel, 1999; Varis, 1996).

These studies could not continue, although the elementary school curriculum development allowed students to work in a freer atmosphere and enjoy social activities, and it allowed teachers to be flexible in the arrangement of the subjects in the lessons. Moreover, the results taken from the testing studies did not affect the general education system. In addition to the aims of the National Education, the most important study was to formulate the aims of the elementary school.

The Sixth National Educational Council gathered in 1952 and discussed the Public Education and Professional and Technical Instruction. The Council made some changes on the period of school programs (Ataünal, 1994).

In the Report of the Charged Commission for the Preparation of National Educational Curriculum, which gathered in Ankara and Istanbul in 1960, the regulation of 1948 Educational Programs was discussed (Tazebay et al., 2000). In this report, the decision to evaluate students' psychological needs in the studies of program development brought a new dimension to curriculum development.

In 1961, The Ministry of National Education published a circular letter requesting the comments of the Ministry, educational institutes, and teachers regarding the 1948 curriculum. The Committee of Instruction and Education evaluated the results in cooperation with 16 experts and those who worked with the curriculum. At the end of the observations, "the changes related to the Elementary School Curriculum" were collected in a report.

A commission was formed and consisted of 108 individuals, among them experts, representatives of the school–family union, teachers of teacher training schools and secondary schools, supervisors of the primary school, and the Director of National Education. It prepared a Preliminary Curriculum Model in February 1962. This model took its last form after a commission comprised of 35 experts and teachers examined it (Gözütok, 1994).

On September, 12, 1962, the Committee of Instruction and Education examined The Curriculum Model of 1962 and put it into practice on the condition of testing and developing it in some schools by the Article of 215 for 5 years (MEB, 1997).

The Curriculum Model of 1962 collected 14 different lessons of the 1948 Curriculum under five groups and regulated the subjects of lessons according to their study fields. Especially in the second phase, it was possible to collect the other lessons around "the observations of society and country" and "the information of science and nature" items. There was a connection among different lessons and subjects of the lessons. It was important for every lesson and subject to complement each other. At the same time, the 1962 Curriculum Model was a flexible frame program allowing those necessary changes needed in local committees to be made according to the characteristics and needs of each region of Turkey (Karagöz, 1965). This model gave importance to training the students to be productive and effective members of society by giving them a chance to learn necessary information, behavior, skill, and habits (Karagöz, 1965).

Knowledge instruction is the basis of 1948 curriculum. However, increasing the number of subjects and units in each lesson created an overburdened program. It was impossible to remove all the difficulties created by this situation in practice. After teaching necessary information to students in the Life Knowledge Lesson in the first, second, and third classes, every student was face to face with 13 books in the fourth class. This was a big problem due to overburdened programs of the lessons (Karagöz, 1965).

The aim of the model curriculum was to make the student effective rather than the teacher, who should only be a leader of the student. Like the principles of locality, planning, and student activities, the model aspired to provide opportunities for students to conduct research, solve problems, criticize themselves and their studies, cooperate with others, satisfy their own needs, take on responsibilities, help others, and study systematically (Karagöz, 1965).

Education and instruction were independent from the textbook. It was possible for both the teacher and learners to apply the other sources for their research and observations.

Evaluation was a continuous activity of the model curriculum. This program did not evaluate the pupils in the middle and end of the year. At the end of each activity, it was compulsory to go over the daily, weekly, and monthly studies of units performed in a year to consider how possible it was to reach the aims (Karagöz, 1965, p. 16).

The application began in the city, town, and village schools, which had one or two teachers. Those schools were selected from 14 cities, which represented the country in some aspects. Then it was decided by the Article of 260 on November 18, 1966, to continue the curriculum until the 1968–1969 instruction period. The program was extended to include 1,881 schools, 10,099 teachers and 470,250 students (MEB, 1997).

The application of The Model Curriculum of 1962 continued during six instruction periods and was investigated and evaluated by the Education Ministry. Then a Developed Elementary School Curriculum Model was prepared by the applicators, leaders, instructors, and experts in the Ministry (Gözütok, 1994). The curriculum model was also examined by the applicators, instructors, expert, and director in the Seminar of Elementary Curriculum Evaluation. After some changes, the model was presented to the Committee of Instruction and Education for the approval and was accepted as the 1968 Elementary School Curriculum by Article 171 on July 1, 1968 (Varis, 1996).

The curriculum of 1968 gave importance to the previous study before the preparation of units and subjects, to the planning, to the group and unit studies, to research, to instruction by self-activity, to discussion and evaluation. However, it was unsuccessful due to the lack of evaluating the reorganization of the results of application. At the same time, the studies performed in Istanbul Atatürk Girls' High School and Ankara Bahcelievler Deneme High School to develop the secondary school program were also unsuccessful (MEB, 1997).

The pilot application of BAYG-E-14 Project started in 1968. Its aim was to teach science and mathematics in 3 rather than 2 years in the nine high schools and the Scientific Educational High School. The project was completed in 1970. The Scientific Educational High School was responsible for preparing the textbooks and auxiliary tools for education, organizing the conditions, and training the teachers during the testing application.

The National Education Council in 1970 discussed establishing the secondary school system and regulating the transition to higher education. The council had some resolutions on these subjects: motivation of the pupils to begin literature, science, professional fields, technical high schools, and teacher training high schools after the secondary school; and in the secondary school, based on the primary school, students between ages 12 and 17 should have general, occupational, and technical education (Özalp, 1999).

The Eighth National Educational Council gathered from September 28 through October 3, 1970, passing resolutions to modernize science and mathematics to support the secondary school model and the BAYG-E-14 project. The council instituted another project. To test the program of modern science and mathematics in the Scientific Educational High School and to improve it in all the high schools, a project called BAYG-E-23 was started in 189 schools, including 100 high schools and 89 teacher training high schools. The study of this project continued until the 1975–1976 school year. The project of BAYG-E-33 was launched in September 1976. It was designed to test and develop modern science and mathematics in the Educational Institutes, training teachers for the secondary schools and high schools and continuing for 3 years of education. However, The Commission of Scientific Development of Science Instruction dissolved due to the end of an agreement between the National Educational Ministry and Turkish Scientific and Technical Research Institution (TÜBITAK) in 1980, which aimed to improve the instruction of science and mathematics. This commission could not give enough importance to the development of science instruction. Because the Committee of Instruction and Education did not care for the extensive studies about the development of scientific education launched in 1966, these efforts failed in Turkey in 1980. The BAYG-E-14, BAYG-E-23, and BAYG-E-33 projects, which were executed by TÜBITAK, National Educational Ministry, and Scientific Educational High School, were laboratories for the secondary schools and developed their programs in the instruction of science and mathematics. In fact, this was the aim of Scientific Educational High Schools. However, these projects were not effective to develop the program of Scientific and Mathematical Instruction in Scientific Educational High School (Selvi, 1996).

With the legislation of Principal National Educational Article in 1973, the Turkish National Educational System was reorganized. This Article divided the Turkish National Educational System into intensive and extensive instruction. Basic Instruction of 8 years was put into application and included 5 years of primary education and 3 years of secondary education. Therefore, the elementary education became 8 years. According to the Article 1739, basic instruction included education of the students between ages 7 and 14. The first and second classes of the elementary school education could be established as independent schools and, if possible, could be together. Yet the improvement of compulsory education to 8 years could not be confirmed.

The Legislation of Principal National Education defined the secondary school education as "all the professional and technical institutions based on elementary school education that are teaching for at least three years" (Gürkan & Gökçe, 1999, p. 20).

The Ninth National Educational Council gathered in 1974 to decide on these subjects: initiation of orientation, which was the main principle of Turkish National Education; essentials of regulating the programs of the 9th class; aims of the selective lessons; testing of Course Passing and Credit System; and rules of regulating the testing results (Özalp, 1999). Many studies of curriculum development were reconsidered in the 1980s. There were some studies toward the consistency and standardization in program development.

The Tenth National Educational Council (1981) made some important decisions about the national educational system consisting of educational programs and students. They studied giving equal opportunities for everybody, prepared programs, and removed the differentiation between intensive and extensive education and between general and professional technical education (Özalp, 1999).

The Ministry of National Education prepared a new program model in 1982 in cooperation with the scholars in the universities to create a curriculum development model as an example to the other programs in the future. Teacher training was also the subject of the Eleventh National Educational Council (1982). There were studies on the acceptance of Course Passing and Credit System, education process, the organization of the contents, and forming a unity in the teacher training institutes (Küçükahmet, 1987).

The model developed for National Education was accepted in the 86th Article of the Committee on May 26, 1983, and was legislated in the 2142nd *Official Bulletin*. The preparation and development of programs, including working principles for the program development, were elaborated. The latter also determined the aims of the basic subjects and units in every program. Curricula should be developed after their evaluation. The model consisted of two parts. The first part included *Atatürk's* opinions on the importance of education and educational preparation appropriate to reality, the main aims of National Education, the pattern and level of the school, the principles of education and instruction, the techniques, and the methods of application. The second part included the targets of the lesson proper to the level of the school and for the target class, the sub-aims of the subjects and units, the methods of applying and evaluating the lesson, and the behaviors aimed to be gained in every unit and lesson (Yildirim, 1994). This model was reviewed on February 14, 1984, by the decision of the 16th Committee of Education and Instruction. According to this model, the curricula of the lessons should be prepared by considering the dimensions of *aim, behavior, evaluation*, and *application* of the lessons. However, several programs were prepared in different models because of not having a certain resolution. As a result, there was variation instead of standardization in the program development.

Apprenticeship and Professional Educational Law legislated by the 3308th Article in 1986 initiated the Center of Professional and Technical Educational Research and Development (Metargem), which was responsible for six items:

(1) The Program Development aimed to develop, apply and evaluate the recent developments in technology. It was also important to develop the in-service programs for teachers.

(2) The research and planning aimed to evaluate the statistical information in order to decide the needs of the qualified working power for the industry and to recommend the Organization of Governmental Planning the main titles that will appear in development programs.

(3) Project Development aimed to prepare projects including the cost analysis and the material for the educational and technical school students and the specifications of auxiliary instruments for education and laboratory.

(4) The Measurement and Evaluation aimed to develop, to apply and to evaluate the ability, success and professional proficiency tests. Another aim was to organize training courses for the management and the development of these tests, and to establish the system of mastery certification in cooperation with the industry.

(5) Technical Publications aimed to obtain the publication of approved technical periodicals and to have the translations of the books and the materials necessary for the instruction and to have the printing and the distribution in all the country.

(6) Education Technology aimed to prepare the necessary material for the application of the modern technology in the courses, to evaluate the methods and to arrange seminars and training courses about the education of technology. (MEB, 1998, pp. 65–67)

The 12th National Educational Council (1988) had these resolutions: developing the instruction of the programs with scientific methods; preparing the instruction programs in every step; considering the interest, skill, and capacity of the child; evaluating the primary school programs as a whole; and reviewing the instruction programs of the vocational high schools. It was decided that the Program Development and Research Center under the control of the Ministry, would do the activities of program development (Özalp, 1999).

To remove the variation in the program, the Measurement, Evaluation and Curriculum Development Specialist Commission formed 12 program development subcommissions. However, these subcommissions used new models to improve the curriculum instead of the one advised by National Educational Department (Demirel, 1999; MEB, 1996). Besides, the Course Passing and Credit System was decided on. Efforts toward standardization and consistency in the program development failed in this period.

The 13th Educational Council (1990) discussed the subject, "The Tendencies, Content, and Meaning of Informal Education." There were decisions to have lessons between the informal educational system and formal education, to have horizontal and vertical transfers, and to give importance to the public education subjects in teacher training institutions (Özalp, 1999).

The National Educational Ministry started the longest educational system starting at the 1991–1992 instruction period by putting Course Passing and Credit System into application in the secondary schools dependent on national education. Published in the *Official Bulletin* numbered as 20,979 on August 2, 1991, the system was accepted to support the success of the student, but not the failure, and to train the student in specific fields by considering his or her own interest, desire, and ability. In addition to 20 common lessons, students could choose from 57 selective lessons. Students of the Professional and Technical Secondary Schools and the Private Schools had to take the common lessons in this program in addition to the common compulsory lessons in the first semester.

Students were forced to drop the lesson on the condition of failing twice. However, it was compulsory to be successful in the lessons of Turkish language and literature. Students who failed in a selective lesson had the chance to select it once again (Izgar, 1994). The National Educational Ministry decided that the programs should always develop in parallel to the needs of the society and the individual, and their principles should be comprehensive and clear (Özalp, 1992).

Studies of curriculum development received important improvements by the National Educational Development Project (1990), which was supported by the World Bank. This project aimed to develop and improve the programs, elevate the quality of textbooks and instructional materials, and use them effectively. In 1993, a new curriculum was prepared by the Department of National Educational Research and Development of Education (EARGED) in accordance with the National Educational Development Project.

According to EARGED, Atatürk's directions about instruction, the laws related to education, development planning, governmental programs, and the results of research were a guide to the general aims that were fixed according to the level and type of school, as well as the type of instructional programs. The Committee of Education and Instruction decided that the main targets should be according to the changes and development in education; the needs of the individual and the society; the international, national, regional, and local dimensions; and the social, cultural, technological, political, and economic factors. The procedure of program development proper for this model was started by the Committee of Education and Instruction. The aims of the program development, members of the commission, timetable, and methods and principles were determined in this procedure. The commission consisted of teachers, scholars, program development experts, school administrators, education psychologists, sociologists, economists, and representatives of Educational Ministry (Yildirim, 1994).

The commission required needs analysis through written, oral, and literary research to determine the needs of the individual and society. The title of the subjects are decided by reviewing the literature and considering the program guide applied in the other countries, textbooks, and present program guide. Then the commission determines the aims and behaviors proper to the general aims and titles of the main subjects according to the level of the lesson and class. The relation between the aims of the lessons and class level and the titles of the subjects is put forward on a demonstrative table. The strategies, activities, materials, and evaluation of the instruction are determined according to these aims to realize the behaviors. At the same time, the lessons' unit planning is developed. The prepared programs and related instruction materials are tested on a specific number of students and teachers in the schools. The necessary corrections are made in the curriculum according to the results of the testing application. The new step is to apply it in the schools in which the teachers and executors are informed by the means of inservice education. The last step is to evaluate the whole program (Yildirim, 1994).

The 14th National Educational Council gathered in 1993 to improve the professional standards and to start family–school cooperation by considering the education–employment relation (Özalp, 1999). The General Directorate of Girls' Technical Instruction started the Project of Professional and Technical Education Development (METGE) in April 1993 to modernize the occupational and technical educational institutions and to train qualified human working power in industry and employment. The most important aim of this project was to prepare women for the working life, in public. This project was used in target schools in seven cities. At present, it is used in 57 schools in 33 cities (MEB, 1998).

The project aimed to decide which programs should be applied in which occupational field in that district and which level of education instruction should be taught at the end of the studies of standardization. This project included the studies of program development in cooperation with the universities, different foundations, and institutions. It also aimed to elaborate the activities of instruction material development through the individual instruction method (Metge, 1998).

The aims of the Metge (1998) Project was as follows:

(1) To prepare an educational system and a school structure suitable to the local needs.

(2) To obtain the cooperation and the participation of the environment (school and occupational information office and common activities of the different foundations and institutions).

(3) To prepare modular instruction programs proper to the certain needs.

(4) To be able to apply the modern technology (computer, etc.) in the educational system.

(5) To carry the vocational oriented standards of instruction.

(6) To prepare helping tools (*modules,* computer, writing for instruction).

(7) To inform the students about the working life and employment opportunities.

((8) To create sources through the sale of production, education and utility.

(9) To improve the capacity and equipment of the schools. (p. 5)

The National Educational Ministry started Curriculum Testing Schools (MLS) in 1994 to realize the aims of the National Educational Development Project. The Curriculum Testing Schools are the target schools that supported education and instruction and tested the instructional programs. For this project, 208 schools (kindergarten, elementary school, secondary school, high school, Anatolian High School Anatolian Teacher Training High School) were selected in 23 cities from seven districts (MEB, 1998).

The most important innovation with the Curriculum Testing Schools was the testing of the developed programs in these schools as pilot applications. In previous years, some programs were implemented without testing nationwide. In this case, the problems, which were not to be solved before the implementation of the programs, affected many around the country. The source of many problems was discovered by conducting this project. After discovering the solution of problems, it was possible to implement the programs throughout the country. The program development model prepared by EARGED—to be tested and corrected in the Curriculum Testing Schools—was accepted by the presidency of the Committee of Education and Instruction (MEB, 1998). This period of the program development was focused on the details of this model.

The National Educational Ministry gave importance to the program development from the center in recent years. The Ministry pointed out that the programs were not fulfilling the needs of the learners, schools, and districts. The National Educational Directorates were given the right to execute the program development studies in 1995. "Curriculum Preparation and Development Commissions' Study Instruction of the National Educational Directorate" was published in the 2428th *Official Bulletin* and put into legislation. In this regulation, six provinces of Ankara (Altindag, Çankaya, Gölbasi, Keçiören, Mamak, and Yenimahalle) were selected for pilot application. The program development commissions consisting of experts of program development, measurement, evaluation, and guide teachers. Later the pilot application was abolished, and all the National Educational Directorates were responsible for was this application. However, the commissions charged for the program development studies could not be established except Ankara. At present, the program development commissions are only organized in 11 cities (Antalya, Ankara, Adana, Aydin, Bursa, Eskisehir, Içel, Istanbul, Izmir, Konya, and Samsun) due to the wish and directions of the General Directorate Secondary School Education. It is thought that the programs will be in appropriation with the local conditions in the commission in the whole country.

The 15th National Educational Council took the most important resolution in Turkey's educational history in 1996. "The Application of 8 Years' Education" was accepted in this council. Although it existed in 1974 law, there were problems in its application.

The 16th National Educational Council gathered in 1999 to work on the Professional and Technical Educational System. The items to be discussed in the meeting were reconstruction of secondary instruction level of professional and technical education, vocational training and employment in the institutions, and training steering staff and teachers for the professional and technical educational fields and financial subjects.

The Vocational and Technical Educational Service was an important part of education legislated by the 1739th Principal National Educational Law in Turkey. The Vocational and Technical Educational Services are given in the institutions and schools of extensive and intensive vocational and technical instruction programs that are applied in secondary instruction and Apprenticeship Educational Centers.

These institutions serve in the following directorates depending on the Ministry's Central Organization in the Vocational and Technical Educational System:

(1) The General Directorate of Boys' Technical Instruction,

(2) The General Directorate of Girls' Technical Instruction,

(3) The General Directorate of Trade and Tourism Instruction,

(4) The General Directorate of Apprenticeship and Informal Instruction. (MEB, 1994, p. 33)

Foundations Dependent on the General Directorate of Boys' Technical Instruction

a.   Anatolian Technical High Schools: These schools prepare students for both life and higher education by teaching lessons based on a foreign language. After the elementary schools process, these schools follow a 5-year education, including a prepatory class that teaches at least a foreign language. These schools are science ori-

ented. They have industrial educational information together with general information courses.

b.   Anatolian Vocational High Schools: The instruction process is 4 years, including a prep year over elementary school education. The goal is to prepare students for
life and higher education by teaching a vocational foreign language, giving vocational information, and presenting some lessons in the target foreign language.

c.   Technical High Schools: These elementary instruction schools provide 4 years
of educational process. In these schools, the curriculum of the 9-year education process is common with the Industrial Occupational High Schools and Various Programmed High Schools. The students who are successful in the ninth year's
program have the right to attend the 10th-year process. Moreover, the students who
are capable of succeeding in the 9th-, 10th-, and 11th-year courses have the right to
take their diplomas before attending to 12th class.

d.   Industrial Vocational High Schools: These are schools for 3 years of educational process over elementary school. The students have their information and
technical theory lessons in the school and 3 days of the week in the institutions in the
10th and 11th classes.

e.   Turkish-German Vocational Educational Center: Vocational educational centers were established to train model adequate technical staff, foreman, and professional teachers with dual vocational educational system based on the Dual
Vocational, Educational Encouraging Project signed between Turkey and Germany.

f.   Adult Technical Educational Centers: These informal educational centers encourage the education of unemployed adults by training them in an occupation and
helping the employed adults develop themselves in their occupations. These centers, giving a year of instruction process, serve as boarding schools, too (MEB, 1994).

Foundations Dependent on the General Directorate
of Girls' Technical Instruction

a.   Girls' Professional High Schools: These are vocational schools of 3 years over
elementary school education aimed to train vocational specialists for working life
and servicing fields. The aim of these schools is to teach students common lessons of
general information in the general high schools, together with the educational instruction chosen by the students in the light of their interest, desires, and skills.

b. Anatolian Girls' Vocational High Schools: The total educational process is 4
years, including a prep class. The goal is to teach students a vocational foreign language, provide a vocational information, and present lessons in the target foreign
language.

c.   Girls' Technical High Schools: Based on the elementary school education and
having a common ninth class with Girls' Professional High Schools, Girls' Technical
High Schools have 4 years of educational process. These schools present scientific
field lessons and laboratory, workshop, and vocational field lessons.

d.   Anotolian Girls' Technical High Schools: After the elementary school, these
schools have 5 years of education process, including a prep class year. The aim is to
teach students a vocational foreign language and provide vocational lessons in the
target foreign language.

e.   Girls' Technical Educational Accomplishment Institutes: These extensive educational institutions are programmed for 2 years and have a circulating capital
structure. The students who graduated from Girls' Educational High Schools and
Girls' Practical Art Schools attend these schools to develop their skills and profes-

sional knowledge of an art field in which they are interested. These schools aim to find job opportunities to search, develop, modernize, and prosper Turkish clothing and handcraft.

f. Girls' Practical Art Schools: These are informal educational institutions teaching girls or women who never applied to education, who left formal educational institution, or who completed an intensive educational process. These schools aim to present occupational instruction by using model programs in different times and level (MEB, 1994).

Foundations Dependent on the General Directorate of Commerce and Tourism Instruction

a. Commercial Vocational High Schools: These high schools give 3 years of education process over elementary school. They aim to prepare learners as qualified participants for professions needed in private and public institutions and to prepare them for both working life and higher education.

b. Anatolian Commercial Vocational High Schools: These occupational high schools serve 4 years of education, including a prep class. They propose to train qualified participants by teaching a foreign language needed in foreign trade and in information-processing procedures, and to prepare them for vocational life and higher education.

c. Anatolian Hotel-Keeping and Tourism Vocational High Schools: Having 4 years of education process, including a prep class, these schools aim to prepare qualified participants equipped with a foreign language for hotel-keeping and tourism fields, and to train students for working life and higher education.

d Anatolian Cooking Vocational High Schools: Having qualified cooks equipped with a foreign language for nationwide and worldwide kitchens and preparing learners for employment and higher education were the aims of these schools of 4 years of instruction process, including a prep class of condensed foreign language teaching.

e Anatolian Foreign Trade Commercial High Schools: Giving 4 years of education process, including a prep class, these schools aim to prepare qualified personnel equipped with a foreign language for the foreign trade departments of the institutes, foundations, and working places and to prepare learners for working life and higher education.

f. Anatolian Secretarial Vocational High Schools: Giving 4 years of education process, including a prep class, these schools aim to prepare qualified secretaries equipped with a foreign language to be employed in institutes, foundations, and other working places and to prepare them for working life and higher education.

g. Anatolian Local Governmental Vocational High Schools: Offering 4 years of education process, including a prep class, these schools aim to train qualified personnel for the municipality and city private governing institutions and for occupational fields and higher education. Moreover, to obtain a rational study for our municipalities, these schools propose a modern urban lifestyle proper to the needs of the time.

h. Anatolian Communicational Vocational High Schools: Giving 3 years of educational process, including a prep class, these schools aim to train qualified personnel equipped with a foreign language to be employed in press, publication, and advertisement. Another aim is to prepare students for professions and higher education (MEB, 1994).

Foundations Dependent on General Directorate
of Apprenticeship and Extensive Education

a.   Public Educational Centers: These are the informal educational institutions established in the centers of cities and provinces. These centers aim to carry educational services to the people cannot attend a school, who left school or do not have a profession, who want to improve their occupation, who does not know how to read and write, who wants to develop their skills, and who want to have leisure activity or as a whole continuous service to everybody at home, work, and school.

b.   Apprenticeship Educational Centers: These institutions are aimed to train qualified personnel needed by industry in cities and professional fields included in the application of apprenticeship education by 3308th Apprenticeship and Occupational, Educational Law.

c. Professional and Technical Open Education Schools: These open schools train students who are out of formal instruction in electric installations (MEB, 1994).

The educational system of the Republican Era was based on progressive policy in education and pragmatic philosophy in general. All the government programs carried the characteristics of progressive educational movement. Although laws, constitutions, and governmental programs supported the progressive movement in theory, the application could not benefit from this. Generally, fundamentalism and perpetuity, but not progressivism, were basic elements in every school. In other words, the Turkish National Educational System was teacher and subject centered. It was not student centered.

Instead of students who were able to use scientific methods, free and flexible in their thoughts, and democratic, secular, socially just, respectable, and affectionate, our educational system had students who memorized what the teachers say and what the books write. They became shy, imitator, and dominant in their actions. They were trained as the ones having scholastic thoughts and the ones who are away from life. Moreover, the system gave importance to the interest, skill, and wishes of everybody in theory, whereas the applications did not consider these principles in general. Instead, the selective approach was used. Briefly stated, the Turkish Educational System in the Republican Era was programmed in the light of vocationalism. However, the implementation of the system based on the realist and idealist philosophies followed a fundamentalist educational trend (Sönmez, 1999).

REFERENCES

Akyüz, Y. (1999). *Türk Egitim Tarihi (History of Turkish Education)* (7th ed.). Ankara, Turkey: Alfa.

Ataünal, A. (1994). Cumhuriyet Döneminde Yüksekögretim. Jeki Gelîsneker: Ankara, Turkey.

Binbasioglu, C. (1995). Türkiye'de Egitim Bilimleri Tarihi (*History of Turkish Educational Sciences*). The Series of Research and Examination. Ankara, Turkey: MEB Publication.

Büyükkaragöz, S. S. (1997). *Program Gelistirme "Kaynak Metinler" (Source Articles in Curriculum Development)* (rev. 2nd ed.). Konya, Turkey: Kuzucular Ofset.

Cicioğlu, H. (1985). Türki ye Cumhuriyetinde ilk ue Orta Ögretim. A. Ü. Egitim Bilimleri Fakültesi Yayinlari. No: 140. Ankara, Turkey.

Demirel, Ö. (1999) *Kuramdan Uygulamaya Egitimde Program Gelistirmeye (Program Development from Theory to Application in Education).* Ankara, Turkey: Pegem.

Gözütok, F. D. (1994). *Ilkokul 1, 2. 3. Sinif Hayat Bilgisi Dersi Ihtiyaç Belirleme Arastirmasi (The Study of Defining the Needs for the Life Knowledge: Lessons of 1st, 2nd, 3rd Classes in Primary School).* Ankara, Turkey.

Gürkan, T., & Erten, G. (1999). *Türkiye'de ve Çesitli Ülkelerde Ilkögretim (Elementary School Education in Turkey and in Various Countries).* Ankara, Turkey: Siyasal.

Izgar, H (1994). *Ortaögretim Kurumlarinda Uygulanmakta Olan Ders Geçme ve Kredi Sisteminin Incelemesi (Analysis of Course Passing and Credit System Applied in Secondary Schools).* Unpublished master's thesis of the Institute of Social Sciences of Selcuk University, Konya, Turkey.

Karagöz S. (1965). *Program Gelistirmede Rehberlik (Guidance in Program Development).* Ankara, Turkey: The Publications of Teacher is at Work.

Küçükahmet, L. (1987). Ögretmen Yetistirme Düzenimizin XI. Milli Egitim Surasi Kararlari Isiginda Degelendirilmesi (The Evaluation of the Teacher Training System in the Light of Resolutions taken in the 11th National Educational Council). *Ögretmen Yetistiren Yüksek Ögretim Kurumlarinin Dünü, Bugünü, Gelecegi Sempozyumu (The Syposium of the Past, Present, and the Future of Teacher Training Higher Insutitutes).* Bulletins. Ankara, Turkey: MEB.

MEB. (1953). *Ögretmen Okullari ve Köy Ensitutüleri Programi (The Curriculum of Teacher Training Schools and the Village Institutes).* Ankara, Turkey: Author.

MEB. (1990). *Ortaögretim'de Yeniden Düzenleme ve Reform Semineri (The Seminar of the Reregulation and Reform in the Secondary School Education).* Ankara, Turkey: Author.

MEB. (1994). *Mesleki ve Teknik Egitimin Incelenmesi, Mesleki ve Teknik Egitim Raporu (The Examination of Vocational and Technical Education, The Report of Vocational and Technical Education).* Ankara, Turkey: The Center of Professional Research.

MEB. (1995). *Projeler Koordinasyon Kurulu Baskanligi (The Presidency of the Committee of Projects' Coordination).* Istanbul, Turkey: Author.

MEB. (1997). *Egitimi Arastirma ve Gelistirme Dairesi Program Çalismalari (Curriculum Studies of the Department of Educational Research and Development).* Ankara, Turkey: Author.

MEB. (1998). *Müfredat Laboratuvar Okullar Modeli Düzeltme 4. Taslak (The 4th Roughdraft of the Model of Curriculum Laboratory Schools).* Unpublished report. Ankara, Turkey: EARGED.

Özalp, O. (1999). Cumhuriyet Döneminde Egitim Politikalari ve Uygulamalari (Applications and Politics of Eduction in the Republican Era). *Cumhuriyet Döneminde Egitim II. (Education II: In the Republican Era).* Ankara, Turkey: MEB.

Selvi, K (1996). *Fen Lisesi ve Matematik Ögretim Programlarinin Deglendirilmesi, Ankara Fen Lisesi'nde Bir Inceleme (An Investigation in Ankara Scientific High School, the Evaluation of Scientific High School and Mathematics Instruction's Programs).* A Dissertation of the Institute of Social Sciences in Ankara University, Ankara, Turkey.

Sönmez, V. (1994). *Egitim Felsefesi (Philosophy of Education).* Ankara, Turkey: Adim.

Tazebay, A. (Ed.). (2000). Çelenk Süleyman; Tertemiz, Nese; Kalayci Nurdan; *Ilkögretim Programlari ve Gelismeler (Program Gelistirme Ilke ve Teknikleri Açisindan Degerlendirilmesi) (Elementary School Curriculum and Development).* Ankara, Turkey.

Tekişik, H. H. (1947). Ilkokul Programlarinin Geliştirilmesi. Ankara, Turkey.

Unat, F R. (1964). Türkiye Egitim Sisteminin Gelişmesine Tarihi Bir Bakiş. Ankara, Turkey.

Varis, F (1996). *Egitimde Program Gelistirme: Teori ve Teknikler (The Curriculum Development in Education: Theory and Technics)* (6th ed.). Ankara, Turkey: Alkim.

Yildirim, A. (1994). Program Gelistirme Modelleri ve Ülkemizdeki Program Gelistirme Çalismalarina Etkileri (The Models of Program Development and the Influences on Program Development Studies in Our Country). In *Egitim Bilimleri Kongresi.* (Congress of Educational Sciences) Vol. I. Adana, Turkey.

CHAPTER 36

Subjects, Not Subjects: Curriculum Pathways, Pedagogies, and Practices in the United Kingdom

David Hamilton
Gaby Weiner
Umeå University, Sweden

Courses of study entail notions of social order. To follow a curriculum is to be inducted into a social order. From this perspective, curriculum practice has the intention to foster social identities. The visible curriculum and the hidden curriculum are rendered as inseparable.

In this discussion of curriculum research in the United Kingdom, we adopt the framework sketched previously. We pay attention to the prefigurative relationship that exists between curriculum and social structure. We assume that courses of schooling foreshadow specific forms of social order. In turn, we recognize that curriculum change has a functional relationship to changes in the social order. However, we recognize that this functional relationship is problematic: Curricula, like schooling, may work to maintain the social order or they may operate to change the social order. Whatever form or content, courses of schooling cannot be indifferent to the social order, whether it is real, imagined, or desired.

What is the social order? How does it operate at local, regional, national, European, and global levels? How are curricula and social identities configured by these frames? To explore these questions, we focus on four areas of curriculum and practice: (a) the association of curriculum with social order; (b) the growth of curriculum federalism in the United Kingdom under the shadow of the fragile hegemony of the supernational state; (c) the advancement of new pedagogic identities (e.g., those nurtured by education feminism) as a means of injecting social justice into curriculum practice; and (d) the centralist promulgation of a school effectiveness ideology/discourse as a technology of professional and pedagogic differentiation.

CURRICULUM AND SOCIAL ORDER

The word *curriculum* first appeared in the European educational lexicon during the 16th century. The much older term, *curriculum vitae* (course of life), was reworked to denote courses of schooling. This neologism, however, was not an isolated occurrence. It was linked to other educational innovations—notably the appearance of the words class and didactics, and the transformation of earlier conceptions of method and catechism (see Gilbert, 1960; Hamilton, 1989; Martial, 1985).

This crop of educational innovations was, in turn, linked to two other historical processes. First, educational thought became reflexive as attention focused on the view that human beings could redirect their own destiny. For this reason, the European Renaissance is sometimes regarded as the expression of a humanist aspiration—in politics as much as in art. Individuals, families, communities, and nations could begin to reconcile their own desires with the dictates of earlier paradigms of social order (pagan or Judaic-Christian).

Second, educational thought began to be drawn to the idea that human powers of redirection could be applied not only reflexively, but also to other people. New additions to the European educational lexicon were the outcome of these changes in European thought. Attention turned from learning to instruction. The link among curriculum, class, method, catechism, and didactic was that, alongside the emergence of these notions, educational practice turned toward the conceptualization, organization, and accomplishment of instruction.

In its earliest form, dating from the 1570s, a curriculum denoted the pathway (or pathways) that students were expected to follow across a socially approved map of knowledge. In turn, these pathways were reproduced in the educational institutions that emerged in the Renaissance and Reformation—as, in the first instance, pathways of study and, later, as pathways of instruction. For these reasons, early curricula were associated with two conceptions of order—political and temporal. On the one hand, curricula were an expression of the social order, and, on the other hand, curricula were ordered in a sequential and, therefore, chronological sense. A curriculum, then, was an instrument that not only supported ordered instruction delivered by teachers and followed by learners, but also promoted different conceptions of social order.

A concise illustration of ordered schooling is available in the work of Johann Heinrich Alsted, a teacher of Jan Amos Comenius, whose *Didactica Magna* (Czech edition, 1632; Latin edition, 1679) is regarded as one of the most influential educational texts of the modern era. As a mapping exercise that built on earlier work, Alsted created a series of compendia in the early years of the 17th century (i.e., around the time, 1613, that the word *didactic* appeared in Germany). In 1620, Alsted published the second fruits of his synthesis of knowledge in the form of an Encyclopaedia, to be followed by a second edition in 1630, which included *didactica* as one of it subject categories.

Alsted's chapter on didactics comprises 40 pages of text. The final page, however, comprises three tables used, collectively, to represent a curriculum *universa vita scholastica* (universal school life curriculum). Taken separately, these tables illustrate a day, month, and entire course of studies for students between the ages of 7 and 25. The daily timetable, from 05.00 to 21.00 hours, indicates a pattern of private study, oral examinations, and public lectures. The monthly timetable (January is used as an example) indicates which chapters of the Bible should be studied; what arithmetic, algebra, astronomy, and *arithmetica deodaetica* (geometry?) should be taught; and what activities should be included in the students' oral examination. The entire program was divided into four stages: (a) 1 year for teaching students to read Latin; (b) 7 years of philologia (grammar) and catechesis; (c) 3 years of philosophy (i.e., further study of Latin and Greek texts in Logic, Rhetoric, Oratory and Poetry); and (d) 8 years study of higher texts (e.g., theology).

Taking our cue from these earliest conceptions of curriculum, we prioritize form over content. Further, we eschew the more recent conceptions of a curriculum as a cluster of different subjects—a view linked to discussions of the division of labor in the United States during the first two decades of the 20th century. Instead, we choose to associate curriculum with courses of schooling and, in turn, with research on courses of schooling available in the United Kingdom during the last three decades of the 20th century.

CURRICULUM FEDERALISM

When originally invited to contribute to this volume, we were asked to write about England. We chose not to follow this request because to do so would be to conceal a critical issue of social order that also envelops educational and political thought in the United Kingdom—the prospect of federalism. This federalist prospect has two dimensions: federalism within Europe and federalism within the United Kingdom. Associated curriculum discussions are similarly polarized, relating to the reconstruction and/or affirmation of national and/or European curriculum and social identities.

These federalist tensions first arose at the time of Britain's entry into the European Common Market during the 1970s. Questions were raised about the interrelations of existing educational systems. At the same time, pressure came from the smaller nations within the United Kingdom for greater control over their affairs, itself linked to the renewed assertion of national identities (Bell & Grant, 1977).

At that time, four major educational systems existed in the British Isles—one each for England, Wales, Scotland, and Northern Ireland (see Bell & Grant, 1977, for a discussion of other, smaller systems). The creation of the United Kingdom has been a process of cultural amalgamation that took over 400 years. Wales was annexed when a Welsh family (the Tudors) succeeded to the English throne in the 15th century. The parliaments and crowns of England and Scotland were merged in 1603 and 1707, respectively. Ireland, which was originally united with England in 1801, was divided into Northern Ireland (remaining in the United Kingdom) and the Irish Free State (its original name) after the Anglo-Irish Treaty of 1921.

For the remainder of the British Archipelago, sovereignty was centralized in London, but nationhood remained. A range of national-cultural institutions, including religion and education that were accepted by the English authorities, replaced economic, military, and political power. Thereafter, parliament in London could pass laws for the different systems, which in turn were administered by local interests in Edinburgh, Cardiff, and Belfast.

At times, such local interests became prominent notably around questions of national identity, language, and culture. Yet these interests have also been linked, through time, to parallel discussions of race and ethnicity. Who, for instance, are the Scots, Irish, and Welsh? Better still, who are the English? What language should they speak? More recently, migration within the United Kingdom, and the arrival of British citizens from elsewhere in the Commonwealth (the former British Empire), has fostered a complementary discourse about the *new* Scots, Welsh, and Irish, who also include the *black* British. Thus, the national independence movements that arose in the 19th century are not the same as those that came to prominence in the wake of the United Kingdom's entry to the European community. In terms of this chapter, three distinct currents flow through the course of schooling. First, there is the national question; second, there are issues relating to national history; and third, there are issues relating to cross-national identity (cf. the Europe question). These currents do not flow easily. Indeed, they flow in different directions.

The main source of this historical difference is that the constituent parts of Great Britain have changed. They are no longer univalent in their composition, politics, and religion. They have become pluralities, not least through migration and secularization. Nevertheless, the emergence of mass schooling in the latter part of the 19th century was designed to harmonize a previously dispersed schooling provision. Thus, throughout the history of schooling in the United Kingdom, curriculum practice has been tension-laden as local and national interests have not necessarily coincided (typically over religious questions).

The more recent diversity of formal educational provision in England, Wales, Scotland, and Northern Ireland can be easily mapped from the Web site created and maintained by the British Council (the United Kingdom's international organization for educational and cultural relations). Nevertheless, one notable feature of the British Council's Web pages is that they have been assembled under a common rubric. This centralist rubric, however, is not a rubric that marks stability. Rather, it notes that the pages have been assembled during a period of curriculum change. The structure of the UK educational system changed considerably during the 1990s under the impact of successive governments' aims to "improve quality, increase diversity and make institutions more accountable to students, parents, employees and taxpayers" (British Council, 2000).

This educational rubric marks, above all, a market-oriented, neo-liberal discourse in education. It accepts that formal education is a service rendered to individuals rather than to the state or a commonwealth of citizens. In effect, the British Council Web site avoids the national question because, arguably, it is a political embarrassment in England and a political project elsewhere in the United Kingdom. In the words of one influential commentator, Tom Nairn, the breakup of the United Kingdom—the cause of the political embarrassment—has been replaced by an aftermath in the 1990s—the devolution of greater political power from London to Edinburgh, Cardiff, and Belfast (Nairn, 2000).

All that remains common to educational provision in the United Kingdom is that compulsory schooling is divided into two stages: primary and secondary. Yet even this division is not uniform: Whereas statutory schooling begins at 4 years in Northern Ireland, the equivalent figure for England, Wales, and Scotland is 5 years of age.

The National curriculum in England and Wales is statutory. It accounts for approximately 80% of a pupil's time in school. The curriculum in England is divided into 9 subjects, but extends to 10 in Wales (to take account of Welsh language teaching). Further, these subjects are divided into two categories: core and foundation. The core subjects (English, mathematics, science, and, in Wales, Welsh) are followed throughout the years of compulsory schooling. A different model of distribution characterizes the foundation subjects. Technology, history, geography, music, art, and physical education are followed up to the age of 14 (plus Welsh in non Welsh-speaking schools), a modern foreign language is introduced for 11- to 14-year-olds, and 14- to 16-year-olds must study the core subjects, technology, a modern foreign language and physical education, plus either history or geography or short courses in both.

In contrast, the national curriculum in Scotland is not determined by statute or legislation. It is determined by advice from the Scottish Executive Education Department. Here the curriculum aims to provide breadth, balance, coherence, and progression through broad curricular areas, not subjects. These areas are language, mathematics, environmental studies, expressive arts, and religious, moral, and social education. In the first 2 years of secondary education, all pupils undertake a common course covering a range of subjects. Near the end of the second year, they choose courses from a menu of up to 75% of a core and 25% of optional subjects. An emphasis is placed on preparation for more specialized study and training, but all pupils are required to continue to the age of 16, with the study of English, mathematics, science, and a modern foreign language.

In Northern Ireland, the legislative basis for curriculum practice is not stated by the British Council. Pupils study a common curriculum made up of religious education, five broad areas of study, and six compulsory cross-curricular themes. The broad areas of study are English, mathematics, science and technology, creative and expressive studies, and language studies; the cross-curricular themes are education for cultural understanding, cultural heritage, health education, information technology, and, only in secondary schools, economic awareness and careers education.

There are at least three noteworthy features in the United Kingdom's curriculum pattern. First, the English and Welsh curriculum is dominated by subjects, with a concentration on knowledge or, at least, the prescribed use of old subject labels. This subject dominance can be read as a further sign of neo-liberalism. It is homage to the knowledge society where, through knowledge, pupils are equipped to meet their eventual responsibilities as workers. Their responsibilities as citizens remain secondary.

In the remaining countries, citizenship questions are paramount—the second feature of the United Kingdom's curriculum pattern. Consideration of personal and social relationships, together with their moral and political implications, suffuses school curricula. In these systems, a moral curriculum coexists with a knowledge curriculum. School pupils are inserted into a national community with identities as both workers and citizens. Such identities are linked as much to a global future as to a national past— through, for instance, the coexistence in Northern Ireland of economic awareness and cultural understanding.

Overall, the different curricula in the United Kingdom display different responses to the changing political and economic status of the United Kingdom. The federalist question is absent from the curriculum for England, but is evident in Wales by reference to the teaching of Welsh, and in Scotland and Northern Ireland by reference to the changing histories of those nations (e.g., their unionist links with England). There appears to be more space in Northern Ireland and Scotland for discussion of identity or citizenship questions (viz. who are we, how did we get here, where are we going?). There is a stronger sense, too, that these political and economic systems, self-proclaimed Celtic tigers on the Celtic fringes of Europe are actively repositioning themselves not only with respect to their former economic and cultural status, but also with respect to their future positions as small countries supported by and contributing to the European identities fostered by the European Union. Such federalist differences can help account for the dynamism of late 20th-century curriculum policy and practice in the United Kingdom.

CURRICULUM AND PEDAGOGY

The creation of statutory national curricula in England and Wales after 1988 had a number of policy repercussions. Outside England and Wales, there was a continuation of the earlier consensus—that education is a national service delivered locally. In an important sense, this meant that different policy communities have grown in the constituent nations of the United Kingdom. This important difference is revealed in the production of two texts in the 1990s. The first of these is the report of a National Commission on Education that was set up, without government support, in 1991 to consider all phases of education and training throughout the whole of the United Kingdom and to identify and examine key issues arising over the next 25 years (Learning to Succeed, 1993). The second, and much shorter, text is a comment by a distinguished English educationist on "the end of curriculum" (Reid, 1998). In effect, the first group worked despite government, whereas Reid commented that as a "nationally institutionalized form of education," curriculum is in "cultural disarray" and, therefore, "pretty well played out" (p. 499).

In contrast, the greater centralization of the curriculum policy debate in England and Wales led practitioners to look elsewhere for noncurriculum opportunities to develop their practice (e.g., as action researchers or reflective practitioners). In effect, these practitioners sought ways to maintain localism, with horizontal rather than vertical models of accountability. Teachers, parents, and pupils were held to be educational stakeholders just as much as central government.

In Scotland, the curriculum policy community reviewed the nation's education provision in a different way. A broader sweep of opinion was involved, for instance, in the creation of the 1,050 pages and 110 chapters of Scottish Education (Bryce & Humes, 1999), a volume written by teachers, professors and administrators who were asked to provide a "detailed, informed and critical account of Scottish Education at turn of the century" (p. 3). Education was still regarded as a national question.

Thus, the United Kingdom curriculum policy arena of the 1990s was suffused with a profound set of tensions surrounding the neo-liberal, free-market reconciliation of unionism and devolution, centralization and decentralization. Moreover, this influence persisted after a change in government in 1997, from Conservative to New Labor. Federalism became fragmentation, leaving cultural and institutional interstices where innovation could be considered and, in some cases, nurtured. One of these innovations—the subject of this part of the chapter—relates to discussion surrounding curriculum frameworks or codes, a discussion that has also linked curriculum codes to different pedagogies.

This new view of curriculum practice emerged, among other things, from two seminal publications: Freire's (1968) *Pedagogy of the Oppressed* and Bernstein's (1971) "On the Classification and Framing of Educational Knowledge." Freire contrasted the *banking* conception of curriculum—where "the teacher talks and the student listens—meekly" (p. 46) with a more liberatory perspective (i.e., a different pedagogy), which Freire had used to support the educational claims of oppressed social minorities. Bernstein's article on classification and framing had three features. First, it linked curriculum to "formal transmission of educational knowledge." Second, it identified "educational knowledge codes," which denoted the "underlying principles, which shape curriculum, pedagogy and evaluation." Finally, Bernstein's model proposed that:

> Formal educational knowledge can be considered to be realized through three message systems: curriculum, pedagogy and evaluation. Curriculum defines what counts as valid knowledge, pedagogy defines what counts as the valid transmission of knowledge, and evaluation defines what counts as valid realization of this knowledge on the part of the taught. (p. 47)

The historical importance of Bernstein's argument, like that of Freire's banking model, was that it injected pluralism into curriculum studies. Bernstein's parallel reference, on the one hand, to different codes or message systems, and, on the other hand, to differences in social class and control cleared the way for new curriculum analyses that focused on the interrelation and interaction of education and politics. Different forms of teaching and learning—embracing different notions of pedagogy, curriculum, didactics, and assessment—could be analyzed in terms of their historical and political modulations with respect to different social categories (e.g., gender, race, and class).

The net result of Freire's and Bernstein's efforts, particularly in the Anglo-American context, is that curriculum analysis came to be synonymous with pedagogic analysis. Curriculum analysis assumes, following Freire, that there are different pedagogies; it accepts, with Bernstein, that these different pedagogies entail different outcomes. It recognizes that a moral task for the educator—whether parent, teacher, or system administrator—is to deliberate and make choices among different curriculum codes or pedagogies.

A crucial feature of such curriculum analysis is that teaching is as much about codes as it is about methods. Put another way, a code may be understood as a framework or structure for practice, not a prescription of method. One of the best illustrations of this difference between method and code can be found in McLaren's (1998) *Life in Schools: An Introduction to Critical Pedagogy in the Foundations of Education* (3rd ed.). McLaren started with the assumption that "pedagogy must be distinguished from teaching" and continued by quoting Roger Simon who, in turn, echoed Basil Bernstein:

> "Pedagogy" [refers] to the integration in practice of particular curriculum content and design, classroom strategies and techniques, and evaluation, purpose and methods. All of these aspects of educational practice come together in the realities of what happens in classrooms. Together they organize a view of how a teacher's work within an institutional context specifies a particular version of what knowledge is of most worth, what it means to know something, and how we might construct representations of ourselves, others and our physical and social environment. (p. 165)

In the United Kingdom, such curriculum analyses were pioneered by Stenhouse (1975) and Simon (1981) and, more recently, have been explored in Murphy and Gipps (1996) and Mortimore (1999). In these later writings, a clear distinction was made between definite and indefinite conceptions of pedagogy. The definite conception is that pedagogy is the science of teaching and educational inquiry should be devoted to the search for such a science. In contrast, the indefinite conception suggests that there are many sciences of teaching that, in their turn, are dependent on specific teaching conjunctures (viz. ideological, political, and economic circumstances).

In many respects, these forms of curriculum and pedagogic analysis stem from Freire's analysis—namely, that they connect to socially excluded subpopulations of the education system (e.g., black pupils, girls, pupils with special needs). But Freire's thinking, linked to Bernstein's, has also been extended to consideration of the overall pedagogy that is appropriate to European democracies at the start of the 21st century. Again, this harks back to the neo-liberal turn in educational thought. Is schooling to be regulated by updated versions of 19th-century social Darwinism (cf. segregation and survival of the fittest), or are is it to be subject to and framed by forms of regulation that also respond to the social justice interests of oppressed and ill-represented groups?

EMERGENT PEDAGOGIC IDENTITIES:
THE CASE OF GENDER AND EDUCATION FEMINISM

Forms of curriculum regulation and pedagogical adaptation in the interests of social justice for a particular oppressed group—that of girls—has been a key focus of curriculum analysis and activism in the final few decades of the 20th century. Nowhere is there more evidence of the relationship between curriculum and social order than in the ways in which feminist pedagogical concerns have been expressed and addressed in the United Kingdom.

As already suggested and as Riddell and Salisbury (2000) recently confirmed, concepts of educational equity and inclusion have come to mean different things in different parts of the United Kingdom in the post-World War II period "depending on which aspects of social identity are seen as having greater salience" (Riddell & Salisbury, 2000, p. 8). In Wales, the importance of Welsh culture and identity has been reflected in a minority, yet widespread, concern to promote schools with Welsh as the first language of instruction. In Northern Ireland, the focus of equality has been improving the parity between Protestants and Catholics via, for instance, the creation of integrated schools. In

Scotland, social class has been the prevailing equity concern. In England, the term *equal opportunities* has been associated primarily with questions of gender, race, and ethnicity.

This has meant that those wishing to introduce equity-focused or more inclusive curricula and pedagogical forms have needed not only to address and mesh with governments and their policies, formal and hidden curricula, pedagogy, and classroom practice, but also to consider different national ethnicities, identities, and priorities. Some of the most active and, to some degree, most influential individuals and groups that have campaigned for educational equality and inclusion have been feminists. Stone (1994) coined the term *education feminism* to refer to those seeking to address the specific conditions surrounding the lives of girls and women studying and working in education. To mount a challenge to the social and educational order, education feminists have needed to understand political and ideological trends. In the United Kingdom, these have been shaped, first, by governments between 1945 and 1979, which created and developed the British welfare state according to conventional gender stereotypes and narrowly held conceptions of nation and identity.

In the case of gender, women were assumed to have greatest responsibility for the family (private sphere), whereas men were assumed to provide financially for their families through paid work (public sphere). Nationhood during this time was perceived as a unity of interests between the countries forming the United Kingdom, although England was hegemonic. After 1979, the political scene shifted as the neoliberal policies of the Thatcher, Major, and Blair administrations rejected collectivism and welfarism in favor of individualism and orientation toward the market. Paradoxically for education, such shifts were centrally administered and tightly controlled, yet they also signaled a movement away from the public/private male/female dualism that had hitherto prevailed.

Thus, in the 1990s, education feminists in the United Kingdom were confronted by three phenomenon. First, they saw collapsing boundaries between the female private sphere and male public sphere largely because of women's increased entry into the workforce while traditional male jobs in factories and industry began to disappear. Second, they came to terms with a series of attempts, starting in the 1970s, to modernize gender relations in education, regardless of which political party was in power. For instance, the requirement for gender equality in education was first enshrined in the 1975 Sex Discrimination Act by a Labor government, yet it was the Conservative administration of Margaret Thatcher that put an end to the sex-divided curriculum with the introduction, in 1988, of a national curriculum that aimed to provide entitlement to all pupils.

Third, in pursuing educational equality for girls and women from the late 1970s onward, education feminism as a politics, epistemology, and practice, and always as "a theory in the making," as Hooks (1984) termed feminism, needed to be flexible, adaptable, and alert to capitalize on the contingencies of the present. As pragmatic strategists, feminists fused their demands for equality and autonomy for girls and women working or studying within education, with individualistic "anyone can make it" ideas of neo-liberalism, and changes in culture, family life, and work patterns following deindustrialization and the growth of the service sector.

How they and others responded to the particular circumstance of the British education system in the postwar period is the main focus of this part of the chapter, particularly with regard to formal and hidden curricula and regional diversity.

Formal and Hidden Curricula

Early gender work in the 1970s and early 1980s in the United Kingdom focused on identifying evidence of female disadvantage and gender discrimination to promote the discussion of girls and women's issues in schools (e.g., Cornbleet & Libovitch, 1983). Particular emphasis was placed on educational differences between the sexes—for example, girls' lower examination results and their poorer showing in mathematical, science, and technological subjects compared with boys (e.g., Burton, 1986). The main argument made here was that the nation could not afford to lose half of its intellectual and skills potential because of outdated and discriminatory attitudes toward girls and women.

Feminists were also critical of the forms of knowledge sanctioned by the school, especially the formal school curriculum and the invisibility and/or stereotyping of girls' and women's experience, say in science or history (e.g., Kelly, 1981). They castigated prevailing psychological and sociological theories about gender because of their endorsement of female inferiority and exclusion as natural, and even functional to society (Acker, 1994). The point made was that school subjects had been distorted to portray British 19th-century and 20th-century conceptions of women as domestically oriented and confined to the sphere of the family, and that this was no longer tolerable. Feminists also focused on gender differences in classroom interaction, showing the different ways in which schools informally disadvantaged and disciplined girls and how such disadvantages could be challenged (e.g., Boaler, 1997).

Education feminism developed different orientations due to variations in the conceptual, material, and cultural perspectives of feminism, and always critically and dynamically engaged with the social forces it was attempting to transform. For example, in the United Kingdom, liberal feminists focused on girls' failure or underachievement in the schooling system to campaign for change (Byrne, 1978). Radical feminists challenged the male orientation of school subjects, the ways in which power is exercised unequally in the classroom, and girls' and women's oppression in class, on the playground, and in the staff room (e.g., Clarricoates, 1978). Marxist and socialist feminists were more interested in the degree to which education and schooling reproduce sexual inequality alongside and in relation to class inequality, and the complex relationship among the family, schooling, and labor market in maintaining dominant class and gender relationships (e.g., David, 1980). Black feminists focused on the endemic nature of racism and sexism and their interaction within schooling (e.g., Mirza, 1992). See Weiner (1994) and Mirza (1997) for a fuller discussion of the range of British education feminisms.

As a consequence of a range of political, historical, and cultural shifts and new influences, including that of education feminism, schooling in the early 1990s in the United Kingdom broke with "the traditions of the old gender order" (Arnot, David, & Weiner, 1999, p. 156). One consequence of this change is that boys and young men have begun to be seen as the losers in the examinations market. Emphasis among politicians and, to some extent, education feminists switched in the late 1990s away from girls and toward boys' and young men's responses to the new demands facing them in family life, schooling, and the labor market (e.g., Epstein, Elwood, Hey, & Maw, 1998). Indeed, such has been the so-called *moral panic* about boys' academic underachievement that recent work on gender in the United Kingdom has overwhelmingly concerned boys and masculinity.

Despite the apparent success of feminists and others in gaining visibility for gender issues in education in the post-World War II period, the normal subject of education remains the White, able-bodied male of average or above-average attainment and the working-class boy of below-average academic attainment, the latter of whom is seen as a threat to the social order. Thus, females, minorities and students with disabilities continue to be constituted as the other within schooling and education more widely (Paechter, 1998).

National Diversity

The previous section attempted to characterize the intricacies related to development of educational ideas about gender in the United Kingdom; however, these have come mainly from England and from the major conurbations such as London and its surrounding area. When we consider how gender has been treated in other parts of the United Kingdom, there are both similarities and differences to the English story. Similarities are to be found in the predominance of interest in gender differences in academic performance and examinations (rather than on gender relations in the classroom or relating to harassment or violence as in other countries) and more recently, on the better overall performance of girls compared with boys.

However, there are also striking differences. For example, conventionally, both Scotland and Wales have given a higher priority to the importance of education compared with England. In Scotland, which has a separate education system as we have seen, this has concentrated on widening access to boys from working-class families, where, in the archetype, "the sons of the laird, the minister and the ploughman, seated at the same bench, [were] taught the same lessons and disciplined with the same strip of leather" (cited in Anderson, 1985). Although there has been an idealization of the hard-working, gifted *lad o' pairts* who could rise to the highest levels in the land, there has been no similar conception of the *lass o' pairts*. One outcome has been that high-achieving girls from Scottish working-class families have tended to be funneled into the lower levels of teaching, rather than being encouraged to aspire to other intellectual and career horizons (Riddell, 2000).

In contrast, Wales, which has been more closely connected to the English educational system, has no such tradition. Yet there are proportionally more girls who leave school without any examination qualifications in Wales than anywhere else in the United Kingdom, although, according to Salisbury (2000), this has not been accepted or addressed by policymakers or educators. Northern Ireland has yet another gender profile. Due to the political conflict in recent times, antidiscriminatory legislation has been more stringent than elsewhere in the United Kingdom. Although mainly devoted to reducing religious divisions, its effects have been important to other social dimensions such as that of gender. Also, boys' relatively poor showing in examinations is not new in Northern Ireland. A long-standing feature has been that Catholic boys leave school with fewer qualifications than any other group of young people. As a consequence, gender has become a more important area of education policymaking, evoking greater expectations of success than in other parts of the United Kingdom. We would argue that the particular context created in Northern Ireland is one where the government has been obliged to take equity concerns more seriously and within which the expectations of and demands made on government are higher than is the case in Britain (Gallagher, Cormack, & Osborne, 2000, p. 81).

In summary, we can see that education feminism in the United Kingdom has played a part in challenging conventions and inequalities regarding gender, covering a range of issues in the formal and informal curriculum and emphasizing the subordination of girls. However, it is evident that in the last decade of the 20th century, the political agenda has been reinterpreted and to some extent subverted by patriarchal centralism as well as through cultural and economic priorities that are regional.

EMERGENT PEDAGOGIC DISCOURSES: THE SCHOOL EFFECTIVENESS CAUSE

A significant movement in the United Kingdom, which is the focus of this section of the chapter, has avoided attention to the pluralism of curriculum codes. The school effectiveness cause has captured not only the enthusiasm of illustrious educational researchers, but also of senior policymakers and politicians across the political spectrum. Drawing on management and systems theory, and complex statistics, school effectiveness studies have sought to establish that *school matters* and that *schools can make a difference*. This stance was partly a response to long-standing research evidence from the 1950s onward in the United Kingdom and elsewhere (e.g., U.S. research published in Coleman et al., 1966), which showed that school variables made little difference to school outcomes when matched against students' social class and ethnic background. The belief that "education cannot compensate for society" (Bernstein, 1970) sustained, for several decades, the assumption that education systems in general, and schools and teachers in particular, are hapless and helpless dupes in a capitalist project of creating winners and losers.

The view that teachers were powerless to influence their students' destiny was challenged, among others, by school effectiveness researchers. Encouraged by a study suggesting that there was a causal relationship between school process and children's progress (Rutter et al., 1979), subsequent studies sought to extend and refine this work. For many, this was a welcome departure. According to Thrupp (1999):

> After the pessimism that characterized the research of the 1970s, the popular appeal of SER [school effectiveness research] rested largely on its central message "schools can make a difference" to speak in an optimistic and "commonsense" way to the needs of educators and policy makers. SER soon became an international success story with its own "congress" membership, journal, and annual conference circuit. It rapidly took on the trappings of a movement complete with almost religious overtones. (p. 17)

In the 1990s, when educational change (both neo-conservative and neo-liberal) was on the political agenda, the SER movement's claimed ability to identify schools that were effective in achieving set targets relating to specific assessments and examinations was, not surprisingly, attractive to policymakers and politicians. School effectiveness advocates were successful in gaining public acceptance and influencing state agencies. Effectiveness discourses became predominant. As advocates joined major policymaking bodies in England and Wales (e.g., the Teacher Training Agency, the Department for Education, and the Office for Standards in Education), school effectiveness discourses began to suffuse the work of school inspections, inservice courses, and, not least, research and development funding.

Nevertheless, school effectiveness researchers were sometimes candid about their inability to realize the more ambitious claims of the SER movement and their inability to harness school effectiveness with school improvement (i.e., in transforming so-called *failing* or *bad* schools into more *effective* or *good* schools). As two senior advocates of school effectiveness practices admitted:

> Little is known about so-called "ineffective" schools in contrast to the work on effectiveness. Moreover much less is known about how to effect change in schools. More research is needed on the context specificity and generalizability of results. And of course the controversial topic on what can be learnt from international comparisons remains a little explored although increasingly important theme. (Sammons & Reynolds, 1997, p. 134)

In what ways did the school effectiveness movement order curricula? How did it help shape the social order of schooling and its pupils or clients? Its main instrument was a taxonomy of up to 11 characteristics of school effectiveness that, explicitly or implicitly, were advanced with "almost algorithmic certainty" (Morley & Rassool, 1999,

p. 122) as a basis on which to prepare for school inspections. These effectiveness characteristics that were assumed to be associated with effective schooling were: professional leadership; shared vision and goals; a learning environment (e.g., orderly and attractive); concentration on teaching and learning (e.g., academic emphasis); purposeful teaching (e.g., clear, structured); high expectations; positive reinforcement (e.g., fair discipline, feedback); monitoring of progress; identification of pupils' rights and responsibilities (e.g., raising esteem, control of work); home/ school partnership; and a learning organization (school-based staff development). Forced on an often unwilling, reform-tired, and skeptical teaching force, these characteristics were deemed as absolutely central to the development of an effective school. Critics, however, suggested that such an interpretation "bleaches context from analytic frame" (Slee & Weiner, 1998, p. 5), projecting the image of a universal subject:

> Students, teachers and head teachers are a homogenized, ungendered, non-racialized or social classed group. They are disembodied players in a larger project. The "child" has become an undifferentiated cognitive unit, and the teacher a disembodied intermediary. (Morley & Rassool, 1999, p. 122)

Few concessions were provided, for example, in lower resourced schools in the poorer urban areas, which were thus inevitably at the bottom of any effectiveness or examination league table. It was a league-table discourse that no one in education in the United Kingdom could avoid or remain outside.

Although considerable success was claimed by those advocating school effectiveness strategies, for example, regarding striking improvements in previously failing schools and in raising academic standards generally, the impact on schools and institutions in poorer areas seemed less certain. Rea and Weiner (1998), writing from the perspective of those working in such institutions, identified the way in which success and failure were measured as crucial to the ranking of schools. Staff and pupils could never be good enough. They were rendered demoralized and powerless. Teachers and schools in poorer or inner-city areas were unable to frame educational values according to the needs of their pupils and the surrounding community. Nor were they able to challenge the dominant shift in educational values, which no longer met their school and community needs. Rather they were confronted with a pathologization of themselves and all those living and teaching in poor urban areas.

It cannot be denied that many in the school effectiveness movement have been devoted to making schools a better place in which children can flourish. But the pressure to find a simple solution to schooling's many complexities and ills has led them into murky politicized territory, escape from which is difficult. A discourse of improvement and success that promises pedagogical certainty in a climate of uncertainty and instability will fail, leaving behind the kind of rejection and ignominy heaped on other so-called failing strategies and organizations.

CONCLUSION: SUBJECTS, NOT SUBJECTS

This chapter has discussed recent curriculum deliberation in the United Kingdom, largely a product of and/or reaction to the centralist, neo-liberal, free-market policies of the 1980s and beyond. It focuses more on human subjects than school subjects in its consideration of curricula as pathways through schooling, themselves also pathways through life. Thus, it regards curriculum practice and curriculum research as the reconciliation of knowledge and pathways about "what should they know?" and "what should they become?" In the process, it identifies several specific processes that have animated and will continue to animate curriculum research in the United Kingdom into the 21st century. These are first the impact on curricula and pedagogy of devolution, federalism, and globalism in the United Kingdom; second, the breakthrough texts of Freire and Bernstein in linking curriculum and pedagogy to the social and educational order, and in offering the possibility of pedagogical plurality; and third, two educational movements of late modernity—educational feminism and school effectiveness research—which have sought, in different ways, to challenge both curriculum order and social order. The extent to which the balanced is tipped toward the human subject and away from subject knowledge in forthcoming curriculum considerations (or vice versa) is important, we suggest, for the curriculum analysts and researchers of the future.

REFERENCES

Acker, S. (1994). *Gendered education.* Buckingham, England: Open University Press.

Anderson, R. (1985). In search of the "Lad o' pairts"; the mythical history of Scottish education. *History Workshop Journal, 19,* 82–104.

Arnot, M., David, M., & Weiner, G. (1999). *Closing the gender gap: Postwar education and social change.* Cambridge, England: Polity Press.

Bell, R., & Grant, N. (1977). *Patterns of education in the British Isles.* London: Allen & Unwin.

Bernstein B. (1970), Education cannot compensate for society. *New Society, 387,* 344–7.

Bernstein, B. (1971). On the classification and framing of educational knowledge. In M. F. D. Young (Ed.), *Knowledge and control: New directions for the sociology of knowledge* (pp. 47–69). London: Collier-Macmillan.

Boaler, J. (1997). *Experiencing school mathematics: Teaching styles, sex and setting.* Buckingham, England: Open University Press.

British Council. (2000). *UK Schools information.* (*www.britishcouncil.org/education/inform* consulted 2000–02–28).

Bryce, T. G. K., & Humes, W. M. (Eds.). (1999). *Scottish education.* Edinburgh, Scotland: Edinburgh University Press.

Burton L. (Ed.). (1986). *Girls into maths can go.* East Sussex, England: Holt, Rinehart & Winston.

Byrne, E. (1978). *Women and education.* London: Tavistock.

Clarricoates, K. (1978). Dinosaurs in the classroom—a re-examination of some aspects of the "hidden curriculum" in primary schools. *Women's Studies International Quarterly, 1,* 353–364.

Coleman, J. S., Campbell, E., Hobson, C., McPartland, J., Mood, A., Weinfeld, F., & York, R. (1966). *Equality of educational opportunity.* Washington, DC: U.S. Government Printing Office.

Cornbleet, A., & Libovitch, S. (1983). Anti-sexist initiatives in a mixed comprehensive school: A case study. In A. Wolpe & J. Donald (Eds.), *Is there anyone here from education?* (pp. 145–148). London: Pluto.

David, M. (1980). *The state, the family and education.* London: Routledge & Kegan Paul.

Epstein, D., Elwood, J., Hey, V., & Maw, J. (1998). *Failing boys: Issues in gender and achievement.* Buckingham, England: Open University Press.

Freire, P. (1968). *Pedagogy of the oppressed.* New York: Seabury.

Gallagher, A. M., Cormack, R. J., & Osborne, R. D. (2000). Gender, educational reform and equality in Northern Ireland. In J. Salisbury & S. Riddell (Eds.), *Gender, policy and educational change: Shifting agendas in the UK and Europe* (pp. 80–98). London: Routledge.

Gilbert, N. W. (1960). *Renaissance concepts of method.* New York: Columbia University Press.

Hamilton, D. (1989). *Towards a theory of schooling.* London: Falmer.

Hooks, B. (1984). *Feminist theory: From margin to center.* Boston: South End Press.

Kelly, A. (Ed.). (1981). *The missing half: Girls and science education.* Manchester, England: Manchester University Press.

Martial, I. K., von. (1985). *Geshichtes der Didaktik: Zur Geschiscte des Begriffs und der Didaktischen Paradigmen.* Frankfurt (Main), Germany: Fischer.

McLaren, P. (1998). *Life in schools: An introduction to critical pedagogy in the foundations of education* (3rd ed.). New York: Longman.

Mirza H. S. (1992). *Young, female and black.* London: Routledge.

Mirza H.S. (1997). Introduction: Mapping a genealogy of Black British feminism. In H. S. Mirza (Ed.), *Black British feminism: A reader* (pp. 1–30). London: Routledge.

Morley, L., & Rassool, N. (1999). *School effectiveness: Fracturing the discourse.* London: Falmer.

Mortimore, P. (Ed.). (1999). *Understanding pedagogy and its impact on learning.* London: Paul Chapman.

Murphy, P. F., & Gipps, C. V. (Eds.). (1996). *Equity in the classroom: Towards effective pedagogy for girls and boys.* London: Falmer.

Nairn, T. (2000). *After Britain: New labor and the return of Scotland.* London: Granta Books.

National Commission on Education. (1993). *Learning to succeed* (Report of the Paul Hamlyn Foundation National Commission on Education). London: Heinemann.

Paechter, C. (1998). *Educating the other: Gender, power and schooling.* London: Falmer.

Rea, J., & Weiner, G. (1998). Cultures of blame and redemption—When empowerment becomes control: Practitioners' views of the effective schools movement. In R. Slee, G. Weiner, & S. Tomlinson (Eds.), *School effectiveness for whom? Challenges to the school effectiveness and the school improvement movements* (pp. 21–32). London: Falmer.

Reid, W. A. (1998). Erasmus, Gates and the end of curriculum. *Journal of Curriculum Studies, 30,* 499–500.

Riddell S. (2000). Equal opportunities and educational reform in Scotland: The limits of liberalism. In J. Salisbury & S. Riddell (Eds.), *Gender, policy and educational change: Shifting agendas in the UK and Europe* (pp. 37–54). London: Routledge.

Riddell, S., & Salisbury, J. (2000). Introductions: Educational reforms and equal opportunities programmes. In J. Salisbury & S. Riddell (Eds.), *Gender, policy and educational change: Shifting agendas in the UK and Europe* (pp. 1–16). London: Routledge.

Rutter, M., Maugham, B., Mortimore, P., & Ouston, J. (1979). *Fifteen thousand hours.* London: Open Books.

Salisbury J. (2000). Beyond one border: Educational reforms and gender equality in Welsh schools. In J. Salisbury & S. Riddell (Eds.), *Gender, policy and educational change: Shifting agendas in the UK and Europe* (pp. 55–79). London: Routledge.

Sammons, P., & Reynolds, D. (1997). A partisan evaluation: John Elliott on school effectiveness. *Cambridge Journal of Education, 27,* 123–136.

Simon, B. (1981). Why no pedagogy in England? In B. Simon & W. Taylor (Eds.), *Education in the eighties* (pp. 124–145). London: Batsford.

Slee, R., & Weiner, G. (1998). Introduction: School effectiveness for whom? In R. Slee, G. Weiner, & S. Tomlinson (Eds.), *School effectiveness for whom? Challenges to the school effectiveness and the school improvement movements* (pp. 1–10). London: Falmer.

Stenhouse, L. (1975). *An introduction to curriculum development and research.* London: Heinemann.

Stone, L. (Ed.). (1994). *The education feminism reader.* New York: Routledge.

Thrupp, M. (1999). *Schools making a difference: Let's be realistic!* Buckingham, England: Open University Press.

Weiner, G. (1994). *Feminisms in education: An introduction.* Buckingham, England: Open University Press.

CHAPTER 37

A Random Harvest: A Multiplicity of Studies in American Curriculum History Research

Craig Kridel
University of South Carolina

Vicky Newman
University of Utah

> *Scholarship always yields a random harvest. In a developing field like curriculum history, we must expect such a harvest each year and, over years, ones varying in both yield and quality.*
> *(Davis, 1989, p. 2)*

> *If there is a direction that the history of curriculum has taken in the course of its short history, it has been mainly toward a multiplicity, if not a new complexity, in its interpretations.*
> *(Kliebard, 1992a, p. 181)*

Curriculum history as an area of scholarly study proves rather difficult to delineate. The best description seems to suggest that it is as well-defined as the field of curriculum, somewhat of a "cacophony of voices," as William Pinar characterized the field. Perhaps considered faint praise, another way to describe curriculum history's current state of the field is to suggest that this area offers many possibilities, multiplicities, and opportunities for research. Framed by criticisms of the curriculum field of the 1960s and 1970s, and by accusations of its atheoretical and ahistorical nature, curriculum historians have struggled to legitimize themselves, often seeking that legitimation from the recognized disciplinary research practices of historians of education. Yet curriculum history, most fortunately, has not fallen prey to crystalized research traditions and orthodoxies. Murray Nelson, former president of the Society for the Study of Curriculum History, while bemoaning the insular nature of the small group of scholars who engage in curriculum history, was quick to note that the area is "hardly closed to outsiders" (Nelson, 1989a, p. 27). Our review of the past 25 years of research confirms curriculum history's accessibility.

This openness, however, creates great difficulty in attempts to bring structure and delineation to this area of study. The work of Pinar et al. (1995) in *Understanding Curriculum* documented the substantive historical and "contemporary historical" dimensions of curriculum discourses. Throughout the 20th century, all contemporary curriculum discourses—political, racial, gender, phenomenological, poststructuralist, reconstructed, postmodern, autobiographical/biographical, aesthetic, theological, and institutionalized texts—include historical dimensions. Does this mean, however, that all discourses comprise different areas of study in curriculum history? Are those individuals who develop a comprehensive historical understanding of, for example, phenomenological or institutionalized text considered curriculum historians? Could any individual who draws on autobiographical narrative from the mid-20th century be considered a curriculum historian?

We think not; however, our position is not entirely stable. We celebrate "the changed status" of curriculum studies because, as Pinar et al. (1995) noted, "The pervasive sense of the field as atheoretical and ahistorical has been replaced by emphases upon theory and history, and, we might add, with a discernible sense of excitement" (p. 50). Although this excitement has opened boundaries, it has also led to divisions and conflict among the various constituencies within curriculum studies and curriculum history as well. Nevertheless, as various strands of curriculum history fuse with other areas of study—namely, educational administration, history and foundations of education, postsecondary education, teacher education, international education, and policy studies, along with the theoretical approaches of the humanities and social sciences—research distinctions continue to blur.

Clearly, the boundaries of curriculum history are obscured by transgressions across disciplines, fields, areas, texts, and discourses: testimony, archives, memoirs, analyses, theories, textbooks—bits and pieces that together comprise a story with multiple perspectives; one that renders us as readers, writers, and practitioners vulnerable to the endless oscillations that time, experience, culture, economy, imagination, and desire bring. These cross-currents represent a widespread incursion of interdisciplinary scholarship, particularly cultural studies scholarship, into research, writing, and classroom practice.

As we present *a state of the field* of American curriculum history, we must first distinguish curriculum history research from curriculum history documents. Many reviews of curriculum history begin with a discussion of Bobbitt's (1918) *The Curriculum,* which is typically described as the first publication in the then-emerging field of curriculum. However, these overviews constitute descriptions of the history of curriculum and not a state of the field portrayal of curriculum history research. For example, although Collings' (1923) *An Experiment with a Project Curriculum* now represents a historical curriculum case study, the work was written within a contemporary context and, from our perspective, does not represent an example of curriculum history scholarship. The recent examination of this account, however, brilliantly researched by Michael Knoll, clearly displays a curriculum historian at work with Collings' book as an archival source. Knoll's (1996) research, "Faking a Dissertation," represents curriculum history research in contrast to Collings' scholarship that, through time, takes on historical dimensions.

Although our view of curriculum history research is expansive and, as noted within curriculum studies, the "boundaries are porous" (Pinar et al., 1995, p. 51), our state of the field overview, for the sake of delineation, ultimately focuses on the work of two overlapping groups of curriculum historians, members of the Society for the Study of Curriculum History (a group founded in 1977 that meets prior to the AERA Annual Conference), and those participants within Division B of AERA, Section 4, Curriculum History. Years of publications and conference presentations[1] offer sufficient material to begin formulat-

---

[1]Specifically, we examined books, chapters, and articles published from circa 1976, and we reviewed and classified all presentations of SSCH conferences, consisting of 327 sessions and those 175 AERA annual meeting presentations that were (self) designated in the program index as *curriculum history* or that were noted in the SSCH program as either cosponsored or *of special interest.* We admit that many other AERA conference sessions could be classified as examples of curriculum history.

ing structure and commonality—components of a state of the field. Ultimately, we seek to be illustrative, not encyclopedic, as we portray the multiplicity, if not a new complexity, of research in the area of curriculum history. However, reliance on these documents presents its own set of problems; that is, our focus may reinscribe conflict and division rather than expand and reinterpret the scholarship of curriculum history. Nevertheless, these collections enable us to offer at least a partial representation of the field.

Our view of the state of the field does not, of course, stand alone. We wish to recognize four previously published state of the field essays, each being different than our intent. Tanner's (1981) "Curriculum History" entry in the *Encyclopedia of Educational Research* provides a comprehensive and capsulized history of curriculum with attention to burgeoning research efforts. Kliebard's (1992a) "Constructing a History of the American Curriculum" chapter for the *Handbook of Curriculum Research* describes this emerging area of scholarship and notes the historical research of curriculum doctrines, historical case studies, and histories of school subjects as well as their political and ideological assumptions and agendas. In essence, the encyclopedia chapter constitutes a history of curriculum as well as an overview of curriculum history research. A more succinct overview of curriculum history was prepared by Kliebard (1992b) as an entry in the *Encyclopedia of Educational Research*. Most recently, Franklin (1999) published "The State of Curriculum History" in *History of Education*. Although more focused than Kliebard's and Tanner's earlier overviews, Franklin described in detail certain research efforts, with emphasis on American and United Kingdom scholarship pertaining to case studies, school subjects, and social history scholarship. All four reviews describe research from the traditional areas of curriculum history and do not need to be summarized here. Researchers who seek a comprehensive understanding of curriculum history research as well as a general overview of curriculum history are encouraged to examine these essays. We wish to discuss other emerging research contexts as well as to suggest certain distinctions and definitions of curriculum history.

THE UNFOLDING OF AN AREA OF STUDY

"The History of Curriculum Thought and Practice" by Bellack (1969) in the *Review of Educational Research* is now generally viewed as "the earliest explicit recognition of history of curriculum as a demarcated area of scholarship" (Kliebard, 1992a, p. 161). This designation, however, reveals the difficulty in delineating an area of study since many notable histories of curricula were extant by 1969. Cremin's (1961) *Transformation of the School* and Krug's (1964) *The Shaping of the American High School*, not to mention the NSSE 26th Yearbook, *The Foundations and Technique of Curriculum Construction* (Rugg, 1926/1930), a legendary work that not only included a curriculum history section but also is recognized to have brought together the fields of educational administration and educational foundations "to form the field of curriculum" (Tanner & Tanner, 1990, p. 197); all of these works could be viewed as a beginning for the emerging field of curriculum history. Yet, although other forms of curriculum history research could be proposed, Bellack's essay becomes a convenient beginning for our discussion, in part, because as Bellack was demarcating the research in the history of curriculum, Schwab (1970) was declaring the curriculum field as moribund. By the early to mid-1970s, many curriculum state of the field perspectives had been published with great concern toward the relationship between theory and practice and the extensiveness of theory and history. Goodlad (1969) stated, "Curricular theory with exploratory and predictive power is virtually non-existent" (p. 374), and Huebner (1976), considering curriculum to be dead, acknowledged the atheoretical and ahistorical aspects of the field.

Readers of this collection may be more familiar with the response to this atheoretical critique of curriculum studies. By the mid-1970s, the field of curriculum saw an infusion of theoretical exploration taking many forms with the emergence of journals, conferences, and a dynamic configuration of curriculum theorists who ultimately became known as Bergamo curriculum theorists. Their work was exploratory and adventurous, and sought to make new connections among curriculum studies, the humanities, and social sciences. The Bergamo curriculum theorists brought a new element of theorizing to the field, welcomed by some, criticized by others. Although these curriculum theorists were exploring the farthest reaches of possibilities for curriculum design, they may be best understood when viewed in juxtaposition with those practice-oriented curriculum developers who were working within the organizational structure of the Association for Supervision and Curriculum Development (ASCD).

However, by the mid- to late 1970s, the field of curriculum saw the emergence of conferences, sections within journals, and a dynamic configuration of curriculum historians who formed what ultimately became known as the Society for the Study of Curriculum History. This group, too, may be better understood when viewed in juxtaposition with those activities of curricularists, curriculum designers, and developers from ASCD and AERA, and with the scholarship of educational historians from the History of Education Society.

Two events occurred in 1976 that directly influenced the developments of curriculum history research. First, ASCD released its Bicentennial yearbook, *Perspectives on Curriculum Development* (Davis, 1976), a synoptic overview of the development of the American curriculum, coupled with vignettes of curriculum leaders and summaries of curriculum documents. Through the massive membership of ASCD, this publication presented curriculum history scholarship to curriculum designers and developers as well as elementary and secondary school administrators and teachers. The intent of the collection was clear: "A particular hope is that it [the yearbook] strengthens a community of professional people and commitment through recognition of its shared past and present" (Davis, 1976, p. 15). The stage had been set. Curriculum historians would follow Bellack's caveat: Curriculum history would "help make us aware of the possibility and complexity of curriculum change and conscious of the carryover of past doctrines and practices into the present situation" (Bellack, 1969, p. 291). Research in curriculum history would offer guidance for design and development while also eliminating an ahistorical criticism of the field of curriculum.

Also in 1976, Laurel Tanner met with Hollis Caswell to discuss further a question he had posed to her earlier that year: "How do we build on past experience for a better educational program in the future?" This informal conversation led to the scheduling of an organizational meeting by Lawrence Cremin at Teachers College in 1977. Arno Bellack, Laurel Tanner, and O. L. Davis brought together 30 individuals, some of whom were suggested by Cremin, to discuss the ahistorical aspect of the field of curriculum—what was called *the problem*. Formal presentations were made by Tanner, Davis, Maxine Greene, Steven Selden, and, in absentia, Arthur W. Foshay. The 1977 Invitational Meeting on Curriculum History[2] and the extensive administrative efforts of Laurel Tanner led to the formation of the Society for the Study of Curriculum History, an organization that has met annually in conjunction with AERA since 1978.

These two events in 1976 constitute the emergence of curriculum history as not only an area of study but as a place for discourse. Both ASCD and AERA served as original settings and venues for the burgeoning interest in curriculum history scholarship, and, certainly, both organizations continue to offer an arena for discourse. Edmund Short

---

[2]Conference participants were identified by Bellack and Laurel Tanner. Interestingly, both Dwayne Huebner and William Pinar were invited guests, individuals not commonly viewed to have been part of the early days of curriculum history.

and O. L. Davis, past presidents of SSCH and editors of ASCD's *Journal for Curriculum and Supervision,* carved out substantive space for historical research in that journal. In addition, since the first volume of the *Journal of Curriculum Theorizing* was published in 1979, Pinar and Janet Miller have published curriculum history research and have accepted history-oriented conference presentations at their JCT-sponsored conference, Bergamo Curriculum Theory Conference. We concur with Pinar's (Pinar et al., 1995) more recent assessment that "the study of curriculum history ... has emerged in the 1980s as one of the most important sectors of contemporary curriculum scholarship. This has been a rapid and recent development" (p. 42).

With this rapid rise of interest in curriculum history, we must also note the apparent divergence between curriculum history and history of education. In 1976, the field of educational history was reconciling the work of the new historians of education with their close alliances to the social sciences, the significance of the "social-reconstructionist school of educational historians," and the relationship of educational history to the historical profession. Cohen (1976), in his lead article in the "Education and History" section of the *Harvard Educational Review,* suggested the degree of disarray by closing with allusions to Freud, neurosis, and repression. Much discussion centered on history of education's relationship not to education but, instead, to the discipline of history. The direction was far different from the curriculum history activities of that same year. With so many issues aloft among historians of education, it is not surprising to see so few educational historians among the invited participants at the SSCH organizational meeting (only Cremin and Douglas Sloan). One point, however, is clear in terms of Cremin's hopes for curriculum history: "Lawrence Cremin said at the time, 'I agree with Hollis Caswell and Wells Foshay that good historical studies of curriculum development are much needed to give perspective to present-day thinking in the field'" (L. Tanner, 1989, p. 17). Seemingly from the outset, curriculum historians, by Cremin's encouragement as well as their own professional, nonhistorical work, seemed devoted to "curriculum history as social action"—that is, that the insights and perspectives gained from the study of curriculum history would inform practice in the field. This proved not to hold the same importance for many educational historians. This separation continues. When comparing the invited participants at the 1977 and 1978 meetings of SSCH with those invited guests to the recent Spencer Foundation gathering of American educational historians, only one individual—Wayne Urban—appears on both lists. This split is noteworthy in terms of its political implications in scholarship. Scott (1996) noted that "most historians are [trained] to be more comfortable with description than theory" (pp. 154–155), and theorizing about historical practice itself and about implications for social change is not part of traditional historical frameworks. This separation between curriculum and educational historians proves noteworthy as we later attempt to conceive the area of curriculum history.

CURRICULUM HISTORY RESEARCH ACTIVITIES AND CONTEXTS

Although Bellack, Kliebard, Franklin, and Tanner have specified certain realms of curriculum history research, we wish to broaden somewhat the activities and contexts. Our configuration is quite porous as is evidenced by the overlappings and mergings among specified contexts that become evident as we develop our discussion. However, we designate eight contexts for curriculum history research: curriculum history as social/educational history, subject areas, case studies, synoptic introductions, memoirs and oral histories, archival documents, biography, and unsilencing voices. These contexts of curriculum history scholarship permeate and cut across one another as well as across recognized forms of curriculum discourse: political, racial, gender, phenomenological, autobio/biographical, aesthetic, theological, institutional, and international texts. Pinar et al. (1995), acknowledging the same difficulties with blurred sectors of contemporary curriculum scholarship, conceded for sake of convenience that one can distinguish work that seems to take certain "dimensions as the most important, with secondary interests in other areas acknowledged" (p. 51). We are the first to admit, for example, that Cruikshank's (1999) curriculum history scholarship on Julia Bulkley and the University of Chicago Department of Pedagogy crosses over into social history, case study, archival work, biography, and postmodern critique. Yet, for the sake of convenience, we would place these activities in a biographical context.

Ultimately, however, we see our designations merely as a way to highlight, as opposed to summarize and label, the scholarship. Our conception of curriculum history, although quite broad, cannot be encyclopedic in this abridged state of the field overview. For this reason, we present a brief account of current curriculum history research and encourage readers of this volume to explore further this work. More important, because we realize that "to list is to exclude," we underscore studies that are illustrative and apologize for those important research accounts that we have omitted. Finally, we wish to reiterate how these areas of emphasis—these primary dimensions—are often interwoven with other dimensions we subsequently designate and describe.

Curriculum History as an Area in Cultural, Social, and Educational History

> The history of curriculum thought and practice cannot be separated from the general history of American education, which, in turn, cannot be divorced from the broader stream of culture and intellectual history. (Bellack, 1969, p. 291)

This area is certainly the broadest and, for that reason, the least well-defined context of curriculum history research. Perhaps we could view this domain to constitute all research activities in curriculum history. In many respects, most examples of curriculum history research fall within the area of social and educational history. Easily, Cremin's (1961) *Transformation of the School,* Krug's (1964, 1972) *The Shaping of the American High School,* Cuban's (1984, 1993) *How Teachers Taught,* Reese's (1995) *The Origins of the American High School,* Tyack and Cuban's (1995) *Tinkering Toward Utopia,* Rousmaniere's (1997) *City Teachers: Teaching and School Reform in Historical Perspective,* Angus and Mirel's (1999) *The Failed Promise of the American High School, 1890–1995,* and Ravitch's (2000) *Left Back* would constitute such examples of curriculum history scholarship.

Curriculum History as a Subject Area Research

Among the various curriculum history contexts, subject area research constitutes the highest percentage (20%) of conference presentations at SSCH and AERA. Numerous examples of published scholarship exist—most notably, Popkewitz's (1987) *The Formation of School Subjects,* Franklin's (1994) *From "Backwardness" to "At-Risk," and Kliebard's (1999) Schooled to Work.* Although our charge has been to focus on American scholarship, Goodson's research efforts, depicting subject area research in the United Kingdom, have helped define and extend this context through the publications *School Subjects and Curriculum Change* (1983, 1987), *Social Histories of the Secondary Curriculum* (1985), and *Studying Curriculum* (1994). Curriculum history as subject area research is represented in many SSCH conference sessions. A few examples suggest the diversity of this scholarship: "The Rise and Fall of World History (Singleton & Robinson, 1985); "Science and Math Curriculum during WWII" (Nelson & Mehaffy, 1985); "Historical

Influences of Curriculum Models on the Teaching of Writing" (Kantor, 1987); "Integrated Curriculum and the Academic Disciplines" (Cruikshank, 2000); "The Social Contexts of the Committee on Social Studies Report of 1916" (Nelson, 1989b); "Examples of Elementary Social Studies School Practice during World War II" (Field, 1993); "A Social Studies Curriculum: Mississippi Freedom Schools" (Chilcoat & Ligon, 1993); and "The Facelift of a School Subject: Vocational Agriculture's Evolution into Agricultural Science" (M. Davis & Reid, 1996). In addition, book-length projects of curriculum history scholarship have been undertaken—for example, Crocco and Davis' (1999) collection in social studies education, *Bending the Future to Their Will,* and Stanic and Kilpatrick's (in press) work in mathematics education.

Curriculum History as Case Study Research

Similarly, curriculum history scholarship is well represented in this area with numerous published works and conference presentations. Perhaps this context is best represented by L. Tanner's (1997) *Dewey's Laboratory School: Lessons for Today* as well as mainstays from the history of education, such as H. Kantor's (1988) *Learning to Earn,* Labaree's (1988) *The Making of an American High School,* and the many studies of urban schools (e.g., Mirel, 1993; Urban, 1980, 1981). Semel and Sadovnik's (1999) *Schools of Tomorrow, Schools of Today* and Butchart's (1986) legendary research treatise, *Local Schools,* represent the rich work underway as curriculum historians turn to examining the lived experiences of learners in specific educational settings.

Curriculum History as a Component of Synoptic Curriculum Textbooks

This is perhaps the most common and earliest form of curriculum history research. Beginning with what is considered the first curriculum textbook, Caswell and Campbell's (1935) *Curriculum Development,* historical sections have been included in those many textbooks that have sought to provide an introduction to the field. Many examples exist, from Caswell to Alberty's (1947/1953/1962) *Reorganizing the High-School Curriculum,* Gwynn's (1943/1950/1960) *Curriculum Principles and Social Trends,* to the more recent examples of Tanner and Tanner's (1975/1980/1995) *Curriculum Development,* Schubert's (1986) *Curriculum,* Marsh and Willis' (1995/1999) *Curriculum,* and the Pinar et al. (1995) book, *Understanding Curriculum.* Even those curriculum books often perceived as more ideological statements, notably Eisner's (1979/1985) *Educational Imagination* and Hlebowitsh's (1993) *Radical Curriculum Theory Reconsidered,* include a historical synoptic component. Also, sections from synoptic texts have taken on a life of their own. Tanner and Tanner's (1990) *History of the School Curriculum* was an outgrowth of their extensive historical scholarship in their well-known text, *Curriculum Development.*

Curriculum history as cultural, social, and educational history; as subject area research; as case study research; and as synoptic textbook research has important implications for the way we document the state of the field. Given that these areas constitute the most activity and production over time, they have been given preeminence in historical analysis—that is, they have framed the way we assess the field. However, much research is currently being completed in contexts not typically discussed in state of the field overviews of curriculum history. We now turn to these contexts.

Curriculum History as Memoir and Oral History

This has been well cultivated through the efforts of O. L. Davis, Jr. and over 20 years of planned acquisitions at the Oral History in Education Project at the University of Texas,

Austin. Perhaps equally noteworthy, for curriculum historians as well as social studies educators, is Davis and Mehaffy's (1977) treatise for oral history research, *Oral History in Education.* The most innovative outgrowth of curriculum history as memoir has recently been published by a former student of Davis', J. Dan Marshall and colleagues, J. T. Sears and W. H. Schubert. The coauthors, in *Turning Points in Curriculum: A Contemporary American Memoir* (2000), weave a tapestry of memoirs, oral history interviews, and imaginary conversations as they identify recognizable turning points in contemporary curriculum history. The Society for the Study of Curriculum History conferences have provided a venue for curriculum leaders to reminisce about their work; memorable sessions included accounts by Caswell (1979), Butts (1979), Miel (1984), Tyler (1989), Taylor (1989), and Rice and Ried (1989). In addition, SSCH occasions permitted distinguished curriculum historians to reflect on others' careers—for example, Short (2000), Westbury (2000), Henderson (2000), and Reid (2000) examined the historical significance of Joseph Schwab's work in the field of curriculum. At another meeting, Jackson (1991), Passow (1991), and others reminisced about the career of Lawrence Cremin.

Curriculum History as Archival and Documentary Editing

Editing constitutes a small, yet emerging new arena in curriculum studies. One of the first documentary histories of the field, *The American Curriculum* (1994), was published by George Willis et al. The project was conceived in 1978 as a direct outgrowth of the Society for the Study of Curriculum History (for which three of five editors were past presidents). According to the authors, "during the years in which the book has taken form, historical scholarship on curriculum has burgeoned, and we hope this documentary history is a worthy addition to the resources now available to scholars and other students of curriculum history." (p. xi). Other publications, exhibits, and projects display the long-standing dimension of this research context. Schubert and Posner's (1979, 1980) genealogy of curriculum leaders and Schubert's (2002) bibliographic annotating of curriculum books represent important dimensions of this area and, in one sense, set the standard and the direction for much future research. Photographic presentations and audio recordings of curriculum leaders (Kridel, 1983), as well as the annotative bibliographic research of the books of the century museum exhibitions (Kridel, 2000), all represent the many dimensions of work with artifacts and documents. Some of the more unique scholarship with archival documents include Nelson and Singleton's (1978) review of Dewey's and Counts' FBI files, Gerald Jorgenson's (1994) graded textbook analysis, and Norrell's (1988) biblical analysis of William H. Kilpatrick's sermon book.

One innovative aspect of this curriculum history research is the acquisition and preservation of documents and materials. Various curriculum history acquisition programs are underway—most notably through the efforts of Davis, who has initiated a national acquisition project in conjunction with Kappa Delta Pi, international honor society in education, where contemporary written accounts, photographs, and oral histories of classroom activities of American elementary and secondary schools will be preserved. The collection will be archived at the Center for American History at University of Texas, Austin. Similarly, Mary S. Black, along with Davis, has initiated the Pioneer Mexican-American Educators Project, an acquisition program of documents, artifacts, and oral histories of Mexican-American teachers and administrators, also housed at University of Texas, Austin.

Curriculum History as Biographical Research

This constitutes a surprisingly large percentage of research activity in curriculum history. Numerous curriculum historians have championed biographical vignettes, beginning with Seguel's (1966) use of biography in *The Curriculum Field*. Numerous SSCH conference presentations have portrayed curriculum leaders: Romanish's (1981) depiction of the ideology of Counts, Jorgenson's (1995) examination of Franklin Bobbitt, Burlbaw's (1990) presentation of Hollis Caswell, Rudnitski's (1993) portrayal of Patty Smith Hill and Leta Hollingworth (1994), Yeager's (9195) biography of Alice Miel, Wraga's (1998) intellectual biography of Inglis, and Null's (1999, 2001) research on William Bagley and Bobbitt. The Kridel et. al (1996) work, *Teachers and Mentors*, an outgrowth of SSCH research, is composed of biographies, called *pedagogical vignettes*, of curriculum leaders. Thus far, most forms of biographical research in curriculum history have taken their guidance from the field of educational history and have resulted in a specific type of biography viewed as scholarly chronicles (Kridel, 1998). Other forms of biographical research are now being explored—notably curriculum history as narrative biography that seeks, through a research narrative form, to elicit the "warmth of a life being lived" (Newman, 1999).

Curriculum History as Unsilencing Voices

This constitutes an evolving area and our final curriculum history research context. Many curriculum historians have championed voices of the disenfranchised. Although they would not necessarily define themselves as working within postmodern discourse, their research represents a distinctive intent that does not necessarily accord with other areas. The field of educational history has provided a solid foundation through the scholarship of Anderson's (1988) *The Education of Blacks in the South*, Walker's (1996) *Their Highest Potential: An African American School Community in the Segregated South*, and Perkins' (1987) *Fanny Jackson Coppin and the Institute for Colored Youth*, as well as many other works, including *Pedagogies of Resistance: Women Educator Activists, 1880-1960* by Crocco, Munro, and Weiler (1999) and *Country Schoolwomen* by Weiler (1998). SSCH presentations have included "Curriculum Wars at Black Colleges" (Watkins, 1990); "J. L. M. Curry: Schools for Each Race" (Watkins, 1998); "Islands of Hope: A History of American Indians and Higher Education" (Bohan, 1996); "The Panopticism of Tracking: Desegregation and Curriculum Change in a Southern School 1968-1972" (Deever, 1991), and "A Study of Midway Elementary: A Historically Black Community in Central Florida" (Kysilka & Cook, 2000). Munro's (1998) "Engendering Curriculum History" provided the best example of an approach drawing from feminist and postmodern theories. Munro recognized the epistemic violence of a unified method to writing curriculum history, and she positioned curriculum history as a master narrative that progresses and evolves through the struggle between conventional narrative and liberation narrative. Such a perspective on the dominant forms of historical research and the potential for marginalizing accounts in the history of curriculum should prompt us to examine the possibilities for new directions that emerge from the contradictions and paradoxes of the field.

TOWARD A CONCEPTION OF CURRICULUM HISTORY:
A STATE DEVOUTLY WISHED

> Social scientists place a high value on research design; educational historians often wonder what that means. (Donato & Lazerson, 2000, p. 4)

Defining *curriculum* is more an act of entertainment than an enterprise that leads to any commonly accepted meaning. To a certain degree, this may be the same for any definition of curriculum history. Kliebard (1986) captured the spirit when he stated: "I was bothered by the imbalance in historical studies in education. A great deal of attention has been lavished on the question of who went to school but relatively little on the question of what happened once all those children and youth walked inside the schoolhouse doors" (p. x). This concern characterizes one generally accepted dimension of curriculum history: Curriculum historians most often seek to understand the lived life of students who "walk inside the schoolhouse doors." Other definitions of curriculum history abound, all offering differing views, beliefs, and critiques. Does curriculum history focus exclusively on the course of study, curriculum policy, the life of a school, or a recognized curriculum leader (Davis, 1977; Franklin, 1977; Hazlett, 1979)? How is curriculum history conceived in the field of higher education (Kimball, 1989; Thelin, 1989)? The questions are numerous, the responses are endless, the definitions rarely become definitive, and a careful examination is quite warranted for those who wish to enter in this research area.

Ultimately, we see curriculum history scholarship as embracing two commonalities. First, curriculum history is grounded in educational action. SSCH was first situated within the organizational context of curriculum practitioners (ASCD) and curriculum academics (AERA) where contemporary research and action was commonplace. Furthermore, the leaders in American curriculum history arise from a tradition of curriculum design and development immersed in contemporary educational practice. Curriculum historians come from the fields of curriculum, instruction, evaluation, and elementary and secondary education, where the profession assumes a degree of school involvement. In addition, they teach courses in social studies education, secondary methods, teacher education, and design and development of curriculum and instruction. Bellack's direction prevails: Curriculum history research "makes us aware of the possibility and complexity of curriculum change."

A second commonality of curriculum history research pertains to embraced understandings toward both curriculum knowledge and interpretive perspectives. Although we do not endorse any sense of cultural and curricular literacy, we accept that certain knowledge does seem to permeate most if not all curriculum history scholarship. Curriculum historians may engage in documentary editing, oral history research, or biographical scholarship, but certain social science research perspectives, or the sociology of knowledge as noted by Kliebard, are never overlooked. The work of Thomas Kuhn is never forgotten, nor are the writings of Joseph Schwab, John Dewey, or Maxine Greene out of conscious recognition. Moreover, the work of Ralph Tyler is an endnote, either explicitly or implicitly, to all curriculum history scholarship. The Tyler rationale and its critique provoked exploration in curriculum theory in the late 1970s and 1980s. We view the Tyler rationale as having an equally profound influence on all curriculum history research. We note that the critique of the rationale—what proved a litmus test in the field of curriculum for many years—was written by one of the leaders of curriculum history, Herbert Kliebard (1971). This historical analysis as well as Tyler himself, representing certain ideas, specific traditions, and particular ideologies, constitutes the backdrop for all work in curriculum history.

New directions in curriculum history should raise the question of *how* these embraced understandings are remembered and, perhaps more important, how traditional methods of analysis become means for consolidation and perpetuation of the oppositions among approaches in the field. Our review suggests that, among curriculum workers, curriculum historians, and educational historians, rifts in purpose and scholarship have diluted the strength of the field of curriculum history. We wish to assert, however, that the nonlinear bricolage of practice and interdisciplinary approaches to scholarship, and not the narrow notion of historical research, provides great richness and possibilities. Theoretical approaches that emerged from and have become mainstream in literary, historical, and sociological research have been woven from the strands of feminist studies, ethnic studies, labor studies, and cultural studies, among others. These theoretical approaches offer curriculum historians the opportunity to incorporate a range of theoretical frameworks and cultural materials into historical analyses and applications of curriculum. For example, cultural studies approaches consider the interplay among the lived reality of lives and the ideologies and policies, including the historical dimensions, that inform and are informed by material culture and practice. In addition, an "underlying motivation of the cultural studies movement [is] its attempt not just to analyze culture and its transformations," historically and theoretically, "but to actively intervene and help stimulate those transformations" (Newman, 1998, p. 1). This frees curriculum historians from the task of justifying their work through the concepts and practices of historians of education to create research and scholarship that investigates and analyzes more fully the intersections of history, theory, and practice.

These seeds for the future of the field—seeds wild and crossbred, nurtured through careful consideration, deliberation, and debate—can yield a rich and differentiated harvest, one that can nourish diversity and justice through infusing school practice with the creativity that comes from historical curiosity and intellectual adventure.

REFERENCES

Alberty H. (1947/1953/1962, with E. Alberty). *Reorganizing the high-school curriculum.* New York: Macmillan.

Anderson, J. D. (1988). *The education of Blacks in the south, 1860–1935.* Chapel Hill: University of North Carolina Press.

Angus, D. L., & Mirel, J. (1999). *The failed promise of the American high school, 1890–1995.* New York: Teachers College Press.

Bellack A. (1969). History of curriculum thought and practice. *Review of Educational Research, 39,* 283–292.

Bobbitt, J. F. (1918). *The curriculum.* Boston: Houghton-Mifflin.

Bohan, C. (1996, April). *Islands of hope: A history of American Indians and higher education.* Paper presented at the SSCH annual meeting, New York.

Burlbaw, L. (1990, April). *More than 10,000 teachers: Hollis Caswell and the Virginia Curriculum Revision Program.* Paper presented at the SSCH annual meeting, Boston.

Butchart, R. (1986). *Local school.* Nashville, TN: American Association for State and Local History.

Butts, R. F. (1979, April). *The experience of the experimental college at the University of Wisconsin.* Paper presented at the SSCH annual meeting, San Francisco.

Caswell, H. (1979, April). *General education.* Paper presented at the SSCH annual meeting, San Francisco.

Caswell, H. L., & Campbell, D. S. (1935). *Curriculum development.* New York: American Book.

Chilcoat, G., & Ligon, J. (1993, April). *A social studies curriculum: Mississippi Freedom Schools.* Paper presented at the SSCH annual meeting, Atlanta, GA.

Cohen S. (1976). The history of the history of American education, 1900–1976. *Harvard Educational Review, 46*(3), 298–330.

Collings, E. (1923). *An experiment with a project curriculum.* New York: Macmillan.

Cremin, L. A. (1961). *Transformation of the school.* New York: Alfred A. Knopf.

Crocco, M. S., & Davis, Jr., O. L. (Eds.). (1999). *Bending the future to their will: Civic women, social education, and democracy.* Lanham, MD: Rowman & Littlefield.

Crocco, M., Munro, P., & Weiler, K. (1999). *Pedagogies of resistance: Women educator activists, 1880–1960.* New York: Teachers College Press.

Cruikshank, K. (1999). In Dewey's shadow: Julia Bulkley and the University of Chicago Department of Pedagogy, 1895–1900. *History of Education Quarterly, 38*(4), pp. 373–406.

Cruikshank, K. (2000). Integrated curriculum and the academic disciplines: The NCTE Correlated Curriculum of 1936. In B. M. Franklin (Ed.), *Curriculum and consequence* (pp. 178–196). New York: Teachers College Press.

Cubar, L. (1984, 1993). *How teachers taught.* New York: Longman.

Davis, M., & Reid, J. (1996, April). *The facelift of a school subject: Vocational agriculture's evolution into agricultural science.* Paper presented at the SSCH annual meeting, New York.

Davis, Jr., O. L. (Ed.). (1976). *Perspectives on curriculum development 1776–1976.* Washington, DC: Association for Supervision and Curriculum Development.

Davis, Jr., O. L. (1977). The nature and boundaries of curriculum history. *Curriculum Inquiry, 7*(2), 157–168.

Davis, Jr., O. L., & Mehaffy, G. L. (1977). *Oral history in education.* Austin: Center for the History of Education, The University of Texas at Austin.

Davis, Jr., O. L. (1989). Opening the door to surprise. In C. Kridel (Ed.), *Curriculum history* (pp. 2–13). Lanham, MD: University Press of America.

Deever, B. (1991, April). *The panopticism of tracking: Desegregation and curriculum change in a southern school 1968–1972.* Paper presented at the SSCH annual meeting, Chicago.

Donato, R., & Lazerson, M. (2000). New direction in American educational history: Problems and prospects. *Educational Researcher, 29*(8), 4–15.

Eisner, E. (1979/1985). *The educational imagination.* New York: Macmillan.

Field, S. (1993, April). *Examples of elementary social studies school practice during World War II.* Paper presented at the SSCH annual meeting, Atlanta.

Franklin, B. M. (1977). Curriculum history: Its nature and boundaries. *Curriculum Inquiry, 7*(1), 67–69.

Franklin, B. M. (1994). *From "backwardness" to "at-risk."* Albany: State University of New York Press.

Franklin, B. M. (1999). The state of curriculum history. *History of Education, 28*(4), 459–476.

Goodlad, J. (1969). Curriculum: State of the field. *Review of Educational Research, 39,* 367–375.

Goodson, I. (1983/1987). *School subjects and curriculum change.* London: Croom Helm.

Goodson, I. (Ed.). (1985). *Social histories of the secondary curriculum: Subjects for study.* London: Falmer.

Goodson, I. (1994). *Study curriculum.* New York: Teachers College Press.

Gwynn, J. M. (1943/1950/1960). *Curriculum principles and social trends.* New York: Macmillan.

Hazlett, J. S. (1979). Conceptions of curriculum history. *Curriculum Inquiry, 9*(2), 129–131.

Henderson, J. (2000, April). *What is the historic place of Schwab's work in the curriculum field?* Paper presented at the SSCH annual meeting, New Orleans, LA.

Hlebowitsh, P. S. (1993). *Radical curriculum theory reconsidered.* New York: Teachers College Press.

Huebner, D. (1976). The moribund curriculum field: Its wake and our work. *Curriculum Inquiry, 6*(2), 153–167.

Jackson, P. (1991, April). *Lawrence Cremin remembered.* Paper presented at the SSCH annual meeting, Chicago.

Jorgenson, G. (1994, April). *Graded schools and graded textbooks.* Paper presented at the SSCH annual meeting, New Orleans, LA.

Jorgenson, G. (1995, April). *Curriculum development in 1915: Franklin Bobbitt and the Cleveland Course of Study.* Paper presented at the SSCH annual meeting, San Francisco.

Kantor, H. (1988). *Learning to earn: School, work, and vocational reform in California, 1880–1930.* Madison: University of Wisconsin Press.

Kantor, K. (1987, April). *Historical influences of curriculum models on the teaching of writing.* Paper presented at the SSCH annual meeting, Washington, DC.

Kimball, B. A. (1989). The problems in writing about higher education. In C. Kridel (Ed.), *Curriculum history* (pp. 48–65). Lanham, MD: University Press of America.

Kliebard, H. (1971). Reappraisal: The Tyler rationale. *School Review, 78,* 259–272.

Kliebard, H. (1986/1995). *The struggle for the American curriculum 1893–1958.* Boston: Routledge & Kegan Paul.

Kliebard, H. (1992a). Constructing a history of the American curriculum. In P. Jackson (Ed.), *Handbook of curriculum research* (pp. 157–184). New York: Macmillan.

Kliebard, H. (1992b). Curriculum history. In M. C. Alkin (Ed.), *Encyclopedia of Educational Research* (pp. 264–267). New York: Macmillan.

Kliebard, H. L. (1999). *Schooled to work: Vocationalism and the American curriculum, 1876–1946.* New York: Teachers College Press.

Knoll, M. (1996). Faking a dissertation: Ellsworth Collings, William H. Kilpatrick, and the "Project Curriculum." *Journal of Curriculum Studies, 28*(2), 193–222.

Kridel, C. (1983, April). *Curriculum theorist of the 19th and 20th centuries: A slide presentation.* Paper presented at the SSCH annual meeting, Montreal, Canada.

Kridel, C. (Ed.). (1998). *Writing educational biography.* New York: Garland.

Kridel, C. (Ed.). (2000). *Books of the century catalog.* Columbia: University of South Carolina Museum of Education.

Kridel, C., Bullough, R. V., & Shaker, P. (Eds.). (1996). *Teachers and mentors.* New York: Garland.

Krug, E. (1964, 1972). *The shaping of the American high school*. New York: Harper & Row; Madison: University of Wisconsin Press.

Kysilka, M, & Cook, R. (2000, April). *A study of Midway Elementary: A historically black community in central Florida*. Paper presented at the SSCH annual meeting, New Orleans, LA.

Labaree, D. F. (1988). *The making of an American high school: The credentials market and the Central High School of Philadelphia, 1838–1939*. New Haven, CT: Yale University Press.

Marsh, C. J., & Willis, G. (1995/1999). *Curriculum*. Columbus, OH: Merrill.

Marshall J. D., Sears, J. T., & Schubert, W. H. (2000). *Turning points in curriculum*. Columbus, OH: Merrill.

Miel, A. (1984, April). *Conversation with leaders in curriculum development*. Paper presented at the SSCH annual meeting, New Orleans, LA.

Mirel, J. (1993). *The rise and fall of an urban school system: Detroit, 1907–81*. Ann Arbor: University of Michigan Press.

Munro, P. (1998). Engendering curriculum history. In W. Pinar (Ed.), *Curriculum* (pp. 263–294). New York: Garland.

Nelson, M. (1989a). Does anyone out there remember it? In C. Kridel (Ed.), *Curriculum history* (pp. 27–29). Lanham, MD: University Press of America.

Nelson, M. R. (1989b, April). *The social contexts of the Committee on Social Studies Report of 1916*. Paper presented at the SSCH annual meeting, Washington, DC.

Nelson, M., & Mehaffy, G. (1985, March). *Science and math curriculum during WWII*. Paper presented at the SSCH annual meeting, Chicago.

Nelson, M., & Singleton, H. W. (1978, March). *FBI surveillance of three progressive educators: Curriculum aspects*. Paper presented at the SSCH annual meeting, Toronto, Canada.

Newman, R. (1998). Introduction. *Studies in the Literary Imagination, 31*(1), 1–4.

Newman, V. (1999). Portraits: Arresting time and infusing the imagination. *The Journal of Curriculum Theorizing, 15*(1), 63–67.

Norrell, T. H. (1988, April). *The book of sermons of Reverend William H. Kilpatrick*. Paper presented at the SSCH annual meeting, New Orleans, LA.

Null, J. W. (1999, April). *John Franklin Bobbitt: A second curriculum position*. Paper presented at the SSCH annual meeting, Montreal, Canada.

Null, J. W. (2001). *A disciplined progressive educator: The life and career of William Chandler Bagley, 1874–1946*. PhD dissertation, University of Texas at Austin.

Passow H. (1991, April). *Lawrence Cremin remembered*. Paper presented at the SSCH annual meeting, Chicago.

Pinar, W. F., Reynolds, W., Slattery, P., & Taubman, P. (1995). *Understanding curriculum*. New York: Peter Lang.

Perkins, L. (1987). *Fanny Jackson Coppin and the Institute for Colored Youth, 1837–1902*. New York: Garland.

Popkewitz, T. S. (Ed.). (1987). *The formation of school subjects*. London: Falmer.

Ravitch, D. (2000). *Left back*. New York: Simon & Schuster.

Reese, W. (1995). *The origins of the American high school*. New Haven, CT: Yale University Press.

Reid, W. (2000, April). *What is the historic place of Schwab's work in the curriculum field?* Paper presented at the SSCH annual meeting, New Orleans, LA.

Rice, T. & Ried, C. (1989). The eight-year study at East High School. In C. Kridel (Ed.), *Curriculum history* (pp. 204–212). Lanham, MD: University Press of America.

Romanish, B. (1981). *George S. Counts and the ideology of curriculum*. Paper presented at the SSCH annual meeting, Los Angeles.

Rousmaniere, K. (1997). *City teachers: Teaching and school reform in historical perspective*. New York: Teachers College Press.

Rudnitski, R. (1993, April). *Patty Smith Hill and democracy in the kindergarten curriculum*. Paper presented at the SSCH annual meeting, Atlanta, GA.

Rudnitski, R. (1994, April). *Leta Stetter Hollingworth and the curriculum at the Speyer School, 1936–1939*. Paper presented at the SSCH annual meeting, New Orleans, LA.

Rugg, H. (Ed.). (1926/1930). *The foundations and technique of curriculum construction*. Bloomington, IL: Public School Publishing.

Schubert, W. H. (2002). *Curriculum books: The first hundred years*. New York: Peter Lang.

Schubert, W. H. (1986). *Curriculum*. New York: Macmillan.

Schubert, W., & Posner, G. (1979). *Toward a genealogy of curriculum scholars*. Paper presented at the SSCH annual meeting, San Francisco.

Schubert, W., & Posner, G. (1980). Origins of the curriculum field based on a study of mentor-student relationships. *The Journal of Curriculum Theorizing, 2*(2), 37–67.

Schwab, J. (1970). *The practical: A language for curriculum.* Washington, DC: National Education Association.

Scott, J. W. (1996). *Feminism and history.* New York: Oxford University Press.

Seguel, M. L. (1966). *The curriculum field.* New York: Teachers College Press.

Semel, S. F., & Sadovnik, A. R. (Eds.). (1999). *Schools of tomorrow, schools of today.* New York: Peter Lang.

Short, E. (2000, April). *What is the historic place of Schwab's work in the curriculum field?* Paper presented at the SSCH annual meeting, New Orleans, LA.

Singleton, H. W., & Robinson, P. (1985, March). *The rise and fall of world history.* Paper presented at the SSCH annual meeting, Chicago.

Stanic, G., & Kilpatrick, J. (Eds.). (in press). *A history of school mathematics education* (Vol. 1 & 2). Reston, VA: National Council of Teachers of Mathematics.

Tanner, D. (1981). Curriculum history. In H. E. Mitzel (Ed.), *The Encyclopedia of Educational Research* (Vol. 1., pp. 412–420). New York: The Free Press.

Tanner, D., & Tanner, L. (1975/1980/1995). *Curriculum development.* New York: Macmillan.

Tanner, D., & Tanner, L. (1990). *History of the school curriculum.* New York: Macmillan.

Tanner, L. N. (1989). The 10th anniversary. In C. Kridel (Ed.), *Curriculum history* (pp. 14–18). Lanham, MD: University Press of America.

Tanner, L. N. (1997). *Dewey's laboratory school.* New York: Teachers College Press.

Taylor, H. (1989). Meiklejohn and Dewey in the 1950's. In C. Kridel (Ed.), *Curriculum history* (pp. 178–192). Lanham, MD: University Press of America.

Thelin, J. (1989). Search for the unwritten curriculum. In C. Kridel (Ed.), *Curriculum history* (pp. 66–70). Lanham, MD: University Press of America.

Tyack, D., & Cuban, L. (1995). *Tinkering toward utopia.* Cambridge, MA: Harvard University Press.

Tyler, R. (1989). Recollections of fifty years of work in curriculum. In C. Kridel (Ed.), *Curriculum history* (pp. 193–203). Lanham, MD: University Press of America.

Urban, W. (1980, April). *Curriculum change, southern style, Atlanta, 1895–1925.* Paper presented at the SSCH annual meeting, Boston.

Urban, W. (1981). Educational reform in a new south city. In *Education and the rise of the new south,* edited by R. Goodenow & A. White. Boston: G. K. Hall, pp. 114–128.

Walker, V. S. (1996). *Their highest potential: An African American school community in the segregated south.* Chapel Hill: University of North Carolina Press.

Watkins, W. H. (1990, April). *Curriculum wars at black colleges.* Paper presented at the SSCH annual meeting, Boston.

Watkins, W. H. (1998, April). *J. L. M. Curry: Schools for each race.* Paper presented at the SSCH annual meeting, San Diego, CA.

Weiler, K. (1998). *Country schoolwomen: Teaching in rural California, 1850–1950.* Stanford, CA: Stanford University Press.

Westbury, I. (2000, April). *What is the historic place of Schwab's work in the curriculum field?* Paper presented at the SSCH annual meeting, New Orleans, LA.

Willis, G., Schubert, W. H., Bullough, R. V., Kridel, C., & Holton, J. (Eds.). (1994). *The American curriculum.* Westport, CT: Greenwood.

Wraga, W. (1998, April). *Alexander James Inglis, 1879–1924: An intellectual biography.* Paper presented at the SSCH annual meeting, San Diego, CA.

Yeager, E. (1995). *Alice Miel: The career and contributions of a leader in the "second generation" of curriculum scholars.* Paper presented at the SSCH annual meeting, San Francisco.

CHAPTER 38

Hermeneutics, Subjectivity, and Aesthetics: Internationalizing the Interpretive Process in U.S. Curriculum Research

Patrick Slattery
Texas A&M University

An investigation of the interrelationship of hermeneutics, subjectivity, and aesthetics in the educational context could advance the discussion of the internationalization of curriculum research and move national educational practices beyond methodological and structuralist concerns toward a reconceptualized understanding committed to *experience* as proposed by Dewey (1938) in *Experience and Education,* by Hegel (1977) in his *Phenomenology,* and *hermeneutic conversation* as proposed by Rorty (1979). This perspective or hermeneutics resembles the process of organizing the events of our daily lives; the details are utterly unknown in advance as the process of living unfolds in a unique and unrepeatable sequence. This also describes the concept of experience that guides Hegel's (1977) *Phenomenology,* philosophies of *Bildung,* and the understanding of reading and interpretation in Gadamer (1975, 1976). Here the process of interpretation follows from Schleiermacher's 19th-century tradition of the hermeneutic circle and subsequent attention to the intersubjective nature of the hermeneutic endeavor. The intersubjective nature of hermeneutics serves as a model for contemporary efforts to internationalize curriculum research.

Schleiermacher critiqued the exegetical practice of interpreting individual passages of the Protestant Christian Bible outside of the context of the entire text and without an exegesis within the religious wider Christian community. Schleiermacher was concerned with the interrelationship between the entire text and individual passages. This understanding of hermeneutics advanced notions of interpretation as distinct from empirical accounts of lived world experience because it allowed for self-consciousness and self-formation, not in a structuralist sense of invariant constructs of human consciousness, but in a poststructural sense of emergent, ambiguous, tentative, eclectic, and sometimes contradictory identities. By the 20th century, access to poststructural notions of subjectivity through aesthetic experience began to engender a language of possibility rather than a language of certitude for hermeneutic inquiry in curriculum studies (Haggerson & Bowman, 1992). The emergence of this language of possibility offers a reconceptualized vision of the interpretive process for the internationalization of curriculum research.

A reconceptualized understanding of hermeneutics that foregrounds subjectivity and aesthetics clarifies and ameliorates the tension among the various strands of contemporary hermeneutics. Although schools, museums, and libraries are most often at the forefront of legal battles over various understandings of curricular interpretation, all educational, religious, cultural, and social phenomenon are immersed in the hermeneutic debates internationally. As the global human community enters a new millennium, the contentious and litigious sociopolitical/military milieu demands engagement with the hermeneutic question, if for no other reason than to minimize the threat of global annihilation.

The denial of the subjectivity of human persons in the hermeneutic process erases the possibility of mutually collaborative projects for global justice and ethics. Ignoring aesthetics as an integral dimension of the hermeneutic project stifles imagination, agency, and creativity—essential elements for envisioning alternative possibilities to the international modern pathos of political hegemony, fundamentalist religious intolerance, economic caste systems, worker displacement, cultural annihilation, environmental degradation, and racial, gender, sexual, socioeconomic, and ethnic oppression. A mutually interdependent understanding of hermeneutics, subjectivity, and aesthetics is a corrective not only to the current stalemate in the hermeneutic debates, but also as a language of possibility for international justice and cooperation in the postmodern era.

Postmodern hermeneutic interpretation—an apparent oxymoron—is possible if grounded in aesthetic experience and poststructural subjectivity, and if attentive to the Aristotelian sense of *application.* An educational experience that incorporates *Bildung*—without separating learning from its application to oneself as happens in technical, managerial, and behavioral models—encourages interpretation within lived world experiences and intersubjective contexts. It is here that forms of self-encounter emerge where various human communities are imaginatively engaged in individual and social transformation; where administrators and educators—management and labor—all recognize and act on their mutual needs as well as the broader interests of the environment and marginalized global societies; where teachers and students are aesthetically present to subject matter rather than assuming they possess it and can manipulate it in decontextualized projects. Possessing subject matter reduces learning to the accumulation of inert data—a notion that Whitehead (1929) vigorously critiqued. Schooling practices that foreground the inculcation of inert ideas will continue unabated until the emergence of a hermeneutic conversation based on experience—*Bildung*, application—*application*, postmodern aesthetics, and poststructural identity.

Modern political, economic, and educational projects that attempt to make sense of the tragedies and uncertainties of contemporary societies often paralyze human persons in fear, despair, and malaise. Smith (1991) located hermeneutics in such social struggles, linking social upheaval and the need for interpretation. The hermeneutical task is not a technical one solved by logic; rather, it is born in the midst of human struggle for justice, solidarity, compassion, and ecological sustainability. It enables us to ask "what makes it possible for us to speak, think, and act in the ways we do" (Smith, 1991, p. 188). Smith saw the aim of interpretation not in an infinite regression or relativization, but in "human freedom, which finds its light, identity, and dignity in those few brief moments when one's lived burdens can be shown to have their source in too limited view of things" (p. 189). The significance of the hermeneutic imagination may be to problemitize the hegemony of dominant and colonizing cultures in the international community to engage them transformatively. Thus, hermeneutics is both phenomenological and political. Hermeneutics is also a search for subjectivity. Reynolds (1989) contended that a growth of self-understanding emerges from the fusion of horizons with texts. It is here that we begin the quest to find a critical voice and sense of identity that may be transformative for the global community.

Schooling practices have the responsibility to participate in the quest for critical voice, social justice, and individual transformation. McLaren (1983) warned that education is a contested terrain that challenges singular hermeneutic interpretations or methodologies. In such a complex and conflictual milieu, some argue that schools must opt out of the social, political, and religious debates (Aarons, 1983). However, I argue that educators must enter the cultural and political debates with a commitment to justice, solidarity, compassion, liberation, and ecological sustainability—issues that are integral to international stability. As we investigate next, such a posture necessitates a commitment to the ethical and aesthetic dimensions of the hermeneutic process.

Unlike Aarons, who saw contemporary political, cultural, and religious debates as unresolvable parochial conflicts—and public schools as obsolete in such a climate—a hermeneutic conversation is an alternative mode of inquiry that affirms subjectivity and aesthetics and transforms apparently irresolvable conflicts. The hermeneutic conversation challenges deeply entrenched parochialism, intolerance, violence, hopelessness, and antiaesthetic worldviews that Langer (1957) critiqued as contributing to "a society of formless emotion." Through subjectivity, a penetrating and vibrant aesthetic sensibility is possible. Emerging poststructural theories explore this sensibility. It is here that a democratic dialogue about curriculum studies might transcend entrenched parochialism and national ideologies and move toward a vision of the role of curriculum studies in the postmodern era. I propose a hermeneutics of subjectivity and aesthetics to move toward a language of possibility for reconceptualizing the interpretative process in curriculum studies in each educational context internationally.

FROM MODERN TO POSTMODERN SUBJECTIVITY

Usher and Edwards (1994) wrote extensively about hermeneutics in postmodern education They succinctly summarized modernity as the search for an underlying and unifying truth and certainty that can render the self, cosmos, subjective experiences, and global historical events as coherent and meaningful. They wrote, "In contrast, postmodernity is marked by a view of the human and the cosmos that is irreducible and irrevocably pluralistic, existing in a multitude of sovereign units and sites of authority, with no horizontal or vertical order either in actuality or in potency" (p. 12). In this environment, knowledge is contested, constructed, and emerging. The self is also decentered and multifaceted. Subjectivity is not self-certainty, romantic individualism, or material isolationism, but rather the process of deconstructing and understanding the multifaceted layers of our postmodern identities.

At the root of modern scientific attitudes is a desire to know the world through a language that represents reality transparently and truly—where meaning is present to thought undistorted by language's fictions and where the world can reveal itself with absolute certainty. This modern certitude is extended to self-presence in the sense that knowing the self becomes the goal of consciousness. This quest has thoroughly infected the contemporary educational milieu—from the self-actualization workshops of the 1960s to the often misused personality inventories of the 1990s. It may have even been a part of the pathology of 18th-century European colonizers and their 20th-century industrial counterparts.

Traditional hermeneutics seeks the authority and certitude that encourages this modern quest for certainty through physical and psychological colonization. In the tradition of Descartes' "Cogito," the rational subject becomes immune to deception and capable of unspeakable horrors. Subjectivity is only revealed in the rational thinking being. Hence, a traditional approach to hermeneutics seeks certitude of interpretation through a voyeuristic historicity and anthropology stripped of subjectivity. This proposal for an investigation of hermeneutics, subjectivity, and aesthetics problemitizes such a positionality.

Usher and Edwards (1994) explained this problematic:

> Postmodernism shatters Cartesian certainty. Freud's introduction of the notion of the unconscious, and his disciple Lacan's (1977) reformulation of Descartes's Cogito as "I think where I am not, therefore I am where I do not think" introduced the possibility of the decentered subject where the subject of consciousness—the reasoning and thinking transparent self—is displaced by the opaque subject of the unconscious." (p. 57)

Jung (1962) expanded on Freud's unconscious to the realm of archetypes and dreams, thus introducing a new hermeneutic of understanding the self.

In summary, what we see is a multiplicity of conscious and unconscious interactions revealing the self as complex, emerging, and changing rather than fixed and rational. Mastery learning, rational accountability, canonical certitude, and metanarrative interpretations are undermined by a hermeneutic of subjectivity. The implications of a postmodern hermeneutics of subjectivity is most clearly articulated by Lacan, who agreed with Freud that subjectivity is not constituted by consciousness. Lacan emphasized the importance of unconsciousness and of desire as the locus of human actions without a Freudian biological determinism. Desire is always social and intersubjective—a hermeneutic circle rather than a hermeneutic certainty (Usher & Edwards, 1994). Lacan provided a way out of determinism through desire and intersubjectivity. It is here that a postmodern hermeneutic engages the self, enlarging our understanding of hope and despair even in the midst of malaise and fear. One reading of Lacan allows psychology to move radically beyond both scientific and humanistic positions. The self is neither an organismic subject nor a subject of rationality. It is neither pregiven nor transparent, neither self-transparent nor unitary. Lacan wrote that "the self is no longer a unified collection of thoughts and feelings, but is decentered, marked by an essential split" (cited in Benvenuto & Kennedy, 1986, p. 18). This is reminiscent of the essential tension between the *already* and the *not yet* in Bloch's (1986) eschatology. A postmodern hermeneutic of subjectivity forms the basis for this new understanding of both the human person and society as a contested terrain of ironic and conflicting positions. Truth, Usher and Edwards (1994) wrote, is not simply a matter of the intention conveyed in the speaker's meaning that acts as a guarantee of truth. "[Rather,] the meaning of the speaker's utterance and hence its veracity depends on the total intersubjective transaction—the speakers utterance, the response of the other and the dialectical relationship between utterance and response" (p. 70).

We find ourselves in this contested terrain in contemporary curriculum studies. A dogmatic and rational understanding of subjectivity and hermeneutics, rooted in theological doctrines attributed to Origin, Augustine, and Aquinas and the philosophical arguments of Kant, lingers in the modern political and religious hierarchy internationally, which in turn influences curriculum projects and curriculum theorizing. There are pockets of resistance where alternatives are being explored that offer fresh yet contested terrains of hermeneutic interpretation, which foreground subjectivity and aesthetics.

PERSPECTIVES ON HERMENEUTICS

Hermeneutics has a history of serious scholarship in Biblical interpretation and 19th-century philosophical attempts to deal with the problem of how we understand the complex actions of human beings. Contemporary hermeneutics, as derived from Heidegger and Husserl, acknowledges that discourse is an essential constituent element of textual understanding. Understanding sets free what is hidden from view by layers of tradition, prejudice, and even conscious evasion. Although these prejudices must be acknowledged as a starting point for hermeneutic inquiry for Gadamer, hermeneutic interpretation, for Heidegger, was moving toward understanding as emancipation from tradition, prejudice, and evasion.

Like Hermes—messenger and trickster—many contemporary educators revel in the irony that the official interpreter can also be a cunning deceiver. This reminds us that layers of meaning, prejudice, and intention surround all artifacts, thus necessitating a hermeneutical study to expose not only the irony of deception, but also the implications of historical analysis. Contemporary historical, textual, aesthetic, and autobiographical interpretation all acknowledge this double-edged dimension of clarity and ambiguity. However, unlike modern empiricists, who demand unbiased certainty and rational scientific proof, the ironic is celebrated by postmodern scholars who recognize that ambiguity is integral to the human condition and the natural world. Contemporary hermeneutics affirms the primacy of contested subjective understanding over inert objective information and conceives of understanding as an ontological problem rather than an epistemological problem. Therefore, Hermes the messenger and deceiver becomes a metaphor for interpretation in postmodern theory.

In schooling, hermeneutics concerns itself with the ambiguous and ironic dimensions of classroom experiences: An unexpected question triggers an exciting or provocative tangent; the changing moods and emotions of individuals create a unique and often perplexing life world in the classroom; the same methodology is not always successful with every group of students; climate changes alter the atmosphere of the school. Teachers cannot predict the ambiguous and ironic nature of life, especially in the classroom. Thus, all educational discourses reflect interpretive and hermeneutic endeavors (Gadamer & Derrida, 1989).

In this milieu, the focus of hermeneutics shifts from inert and objective data to the community of interpreters working together in mutually corrective and collaborative efforts to understand texts and contexts—an excellent model for the international community of curriculum scholars. The entire educational experience is open to reflection because everything requires recursive interpretation. Without this perspective, Hermes the trickster constantly deceives and global conflagrations escalate.

HERMENEUTICS: A PHENOMENOLOGICAL AESTHETIC INVESTIGATION

Educational philosopher Maxine Greene (1978) has been passionate in her call for *wide-awakenness* in education. She wrote that "lacking wide-awakenness ... individuals are likely to drift, to act on impulses of expediency" (p. 43). With Greene, I observe too much expediency at the expense of wide-awakenness in the schooling process. I advocate encountering *the arts*—in the broadest sense of the term—to create aesthetic moments capable of elevating the mundane to generative experiences of solidarity, agency, and liberation. Greene (1995) wrote, "Consciousness always has an imaginative phase, and imagination, more than any other capacity, breaks through the inertia of habit. When nothing intervenes to overcome such inertia, it joins with the sense of repetitiveness and uniformity to discourage active learning" (p. 21). Dewey (1934a) contended that all possibilities reach us through the imagination. "The aims and ideals that move us are generated though imagination. But they are not made out of imaginary stuff … they are made out of the world of physical and social experience" (p. x). Is it possible to release the imagination, reconceptualize the art of interpretation, and generate experiences in education that will expose sedimented perceptors and suspend final judgments?

Contemporary approaches to hermeneutics are not sufficiently committed to aesthetics, subjectivity, and imagination. Thus, they are ineffective in overcoming Greene's *inertia of habit.* Contemporary hermeneutics in both its conservative and critical application—as well as its deconstructive philosophical orientation—is not attentive to the essential role that aesthetics plays in transformative educational experience. Although Gadamer has successfully moved the understanding of hermeneutics in the direction of the aesthetic, I am impatient with his *fusion of horizons.* I seek a more dramatic break with traditional hermeneutics without the rupture created by radical deconstructionism. Contemporary scholars have attempted to mediate this contentious terrain in various ways: the mythopoetic and cosmological proposal by Haggerson and Bowman (1992), the moderate hermeneutics in the spirit of Gadamer by Gallagher (1992), the social critique by Smith (1991), the indeterminacy of interpretation in lived time by Hudak (1995), the productive process of contextualizing interpretation through hermeneutic listening proposed by Kimball and Garrison (n.d.) and Ellsworth (1989), the conversing dialogue of *Bildung* proposed by Blacker (1993), and the integration of the various strands of hermeneutics using Ricoeur's phenomenology by Bleicher (1980). Although I am indebted to these scholars for their insights, I propose an even greater emphasis on poststructural subjectivity and aesthetic experience.

A shift toward the subjective and aesthetic is accomplished by reconnecting hermeneutics to autobiographical inquiry, narrative research, lived experience, critical theory, participatory ethnographic study, arts-based autoethnographic research, and other forms of qualitative curriculum research. Nietzsche (1968) contended that "we have our highest dignity in our significance as works of art—for it is only as aesthetic phenomenon that existence and the world are eternally justified" (p. 52). My enthusiasm for Nietzsche's position does not negate, as critics often contend, a concern for ethics—for aesthetics and social justice are inseparable from my proposal (Slattery & Morris, 1999).

In the process of understanding hermeneutics from the perspective of aesthetics and subjectivity, while remaining committed to ethical issues of justice, solidarity, compassion, agency, and ecological sustainability, a vexing question remains: How does aesthetics and arts-based approaches to qualitative research promote these values, and what does interpretation mean for curriculum studies and educational research? Eisner (1994) proposed that we must shift our focus from statistical reliability and validity to what he termed *referential adequacy*—experiencing an object or situation in a new or more adequate way—and structural corroboration—linking the parts to cohesive whole. Following from the recent scholarship of Usher and Edwards, Gallagher, Haggerson, Bowman, and Bleicher, I review six current understandings of hermeneutics that inform my proposal for reconceptualizing hermeneutics by foregrounding subjectivity and aesthetics.

SIX APPROACHES TO HERMENEUTICS

First, contemporary scholars contend that *traditional theological hermeneutics* is the empirical science of interpretation of canonical religious texts within their historical context by a magesterium intent on defining the meaning of the text. Exegetes, with a concern for linguistic and grammatical accuracy, are considered experts who establish the criteria for authoritative textual interpretation.

Hermeneutic inquiry was almost exclusively empirical prior to the 19th century. As a science of interpretation, traditional theological hermeneutics was originally concerned with understanding religious texts, canonical scriptures, and noncanonical writings within their own historical, cultural, and social milieus. The difficulty of such interpretive tasks is immense—postmodernists would contend impossible—because the worldview of contemporary societies cannot objectively or completely replicate ancient cosmologies and subjectivities in which the text was aesthetically produced. Additionally, as Gadamer warned, attempting to conduct a hermeneutic study, assuming that subjectivities and prejudices of the hermeneut can be eradicated, is impossible.

Early Greek and Jewish thinkers were concerned with appropriate interpretation of the Torah, the prophets, and the wisdom literature of the Hebrew scriptures. The allegorical method was employed to understand linguistic and grammatical components of scriptural texts to appropriate this meaning within the wider spiritual framework of the time. Jeanrond (1998) explained: "Philo of Alexandria united the Jewish and Greek hermeneutical traditions and developed the thesis that an interpretation should disclose the text's spiritual sense on the basis of an explanation of the text's literal sense" (p. 462). This concept of hermeneutics expanded with the influence of Christian interpreters who sought to confirm their belief in salvation in Jesus Christ. Hebrew scriptures were interpreted in the light of the Christian faith in Jesus, arguing that the promises to Israel were fulfilled. Origen, an early Christian hermeneut, emphasized the need for text interpretation in both the historical-grammatical (literal) sense and the spiritual sense so as to provide access and understanding for every interpreter of sacred writings. Following Origen, Augustine developed his philosophy of language where the *sign* points to the *thing*.

In this sense, semiotics, like hermeneutics, is concerned with interpretation of texts, contexts, or artifacts. It provides the possibility of analysis of contemporary social problems and the possibility of explaining the processes and structures through which meaning is constituted. This emerging understanding of critical semiotics challenges Augustine's literal meaning of *signs*. In poststructural semiotics, the sign may point to nothing or to many things simultaneously, and in every case the culture–language–thought interrelationship must be interpreted. Additionally, the meaning of power and the processes through which meaning is constructed are becoming the focus of semiotic as well as hermeneutic analysis. Like Augustine, Thomas Aquinas emphasized the literal sense of language. Aquinas became the definitive authority on textual interpretation. Since the 13th century, Aquinas was presumed to support the literal interpretation as the accurate bearer of truth.[1]

Second, scholars argue that *Conservative Philosophical Hermeneutics* is grounded in the tradition of Protestant theologian Frederich Schleirmacher and philosopher Wilhelm Dilthey. It has inspired educational reformers such as E. D. Hirsch. Gallagher (1992) wrote, "These theorists would maintain that through correct methodology and hard work, the interpreter should be able (a) to break out of her historical epoch in order to understand the author as the author intended, and/or (b) to transcend historical limitations altogether in order to reach universal, or at least objective, truth" (p. 9). The

---

[1]Matthew Fox is a notable exception to this trend. A Roman Catholic Dominican priest (as was Aquinas) at the time, Fox wrote a text entitled *Sheer Joy,* in which he challenged traditional interpretations of Aquinas. Fox was silenced by the Roman Magisterium. He is not an Episcopalian priest.

intention of hermeneutics is to reproduce the meaning or intention of the text. Well-defined methodologies guide the anthropological and historical search for objectivity.

Although the literalistic practice of Biblical interpretation in the Thomistic scholastic tradition continued to dominate through the Protestant Reformation, the emphasis on the scriptures during the Reformation promoted reading and understanding biblical texts by individual believers rather than papal officials. Thus, the Protestant Reformation deemphasized the interpretation of scripture by the Roman Magisterium. Following the Enlightenment, hermeneutics was reevaluated by Schleiermacher (1768–1834), who rejected all formal, extratextual authorities as illegitimate imposition on individual acts of understanding. Schleiermacher's work discredited special theological or legal hermeneutics. Schleiermacher explained that every written text must be understood both in terms of its individual sense (psychological understanding) and the linguistic procedures through which this sense is achieved (grammatical understanding). "Hermeneutics is now understood as the art of understanding the sense of the text. Allegorical interpretation is ruled out, the text must be allowed to speak for itself" (cited in Jeanrond, 1998, p. 463).

Ricoeur (1981) contended that a movement of deregionalization began with the attempt to extract a general problem from the activity of interpretation that is each time engaged in different texts, and "the discernment of this central and unitary problematic is the achievement of Schleiermacher" (p. 45). Before Schleiermacher, a philology—historical linguistic study—of classical texts and a literalistic exegesis—critical analysis—of sacred texts predominated. After Schleiermacher, it became clear that the hermeneutical process required that the individual interpreter must discern the operations that are common to these two traditional branches of hermeneutics—philology and exegesis. However, the goal of universal truth remained intact in conservative philosophical hermeneutics even though the possibility of the value of the individual interpreter began to gain ascendancy.

Third, *contextual hermeneutics* recognizes historical and subjective conditions as essential to the interpretive process. Interpreters are now understood to move within a hermeneutical circle that requires the specification of historical conditions in textual interpretation. Gadamer (1960/1975) called attention to preunderstandings that underpin interpretation. He termed the condition and the perspectives of interpreters their "horizons" and the act of understanding the sense of a text "the fusion of horizons." Through this fusion of horizons, the interpreter enters the tradition of the text, and thus shares in the text's particular representation of truth. Gadamer (1976) wrote about relationships in the hermeneutic circle that transcend the technical sign systems of the modern age:

> Each [person] is at first a kind of linguistic circle, and these linguistic circles come in contact with each other, merging more and more. Language occurs once again, in vocabulary and grammar as always, and never without the inner infinity of the dialogue that is in process between every speaker and his [or her] partner. That is the fundamental dimension of hermeneutics. (p. 17)

Gadamer concluded by stating that genuine speaking, which has something to say and therefore is not based on prearranged signals but rather seeks words that reach the other human person, is the universal human task. This is the hermeneutic circle that educators must enter according to some postmodern theories.

Although Gadamer's hermeneutics has been criticized by some for his refusal to allow for methodological controls of the act of interpretation, many contemporary education scholars in the 1990s rely on Gadamer to support their critique of narrow instrumental views of schooling. Truth, they contend, cannot be collapsed into methods, the mainstay of the traditional approach to modern hermeneutics.[2]

For Gadamer, we must approach texts with our preunderstandings, suspend our prejudices, and engage in dialogue. For example, Blacker (1993) argued that Gadamer's effort involves a reconstruction of the humanist sense of education as *Bildung*, which emphasizes what is done *to* individuals rather than what individual persons actually *do*:

> To make the notion of *Bildung* more concrete, then, Gadamer recasts it as a dialogue between interpreter and tradition in which the latter is experienced as a Thou. This point must be stressed: he is not saying that individuals like teachers and students in every case ought to engage in an intersubjective give-and-take. ... Accordingly, sharing in this historically-constituted conversation does not mean that I experience tradition as the opinion of some person or other, but that I am able to enter into it as into a game made up of myself and other persons but not reducible to any one of us. In this edifying tradition-forming, revising and conversing dialogue taking place in language—Hegelian Spirit conversing with itself—arises *Bildung*, which I see as the normative dimension of philosophical hermeneutics. (p. 7)

Traditional theological hermeneutics and conservative philosophical hermeneutics both insist on a normative methodology. However, this normative methodology is not Blacker's conversing dialogue. The traditional normative methodology is determined by an external authority. In contrast, contextual hermeneutics validates text interpretation that arises from the dialogue of individuals working within the context of a community circle where the other, whether human person, tradition, or artifact, is experienced as a *thou* and not an *it* (Buber, 1965). For Gadamer, the hermeneutic circle is used to facilitate understanding and open up possibilities, whereas the traditional technical approach to hermeneutics is seen as dehumanizing.

Fourth, *reflective hermeneutics* is seen in Ricoeur (1981), who took a different approach when he argued that the first understanding of the sense of the text must be validated through some explanatory procedures to ensure the sense of the text. Ricoeur contended that the movement from a structuralist science to a structuralist philosophy is bound to fail. John Thompson, translator of Ricoeur, explained that structuralism insofar as it precludes the possibility of self-reflection can never establish itself as a philosophy:

> An order posited as unconscious can never, to my mind, be more than a stage abstractly separated from an understanding of the self by itself; order in itself is thought located outside itself. A genuinely reflective philosophy must nevertheless be receptive to the structuralist method, specifying its validity as an abstract and objective moment in the understanding of self and being. This imperative forms one of the principal guidelines for Ricoeur's recent work on the theory of language and interpretation. (cited in Ricoeur, 1981, p. 10)

Ricoeur's interest evolved, in part, from his initial efforts to formulate a concrete ontology infused with the themes of freedom, finitude, and hope at the Sorbonne as a graduate student with Gabriel Marcel in the 1930s. However, Ricoeur became intent on discovering a more rigorous and systematic method than he found in Marcel. The phenomenology of Husserl provided this method, and in turn led to the development of a

---

[2]It is interesting to note that Gadamer's (1960/1975) major work, *Truth and Method*, is interpreted in various ways. Gadamer delighted in the confusion of his title: "Ambiguity is the secret to a good title and promptly some reviewers would comment correspondingly. Some would say that the book discussed the method for finding the truth, others said that I claimed that there was no method for finding truth" (cited in Misgeld & Graeme, 1992, p. 64).

reflective philosophy disclosing authentic subjectivity for understanding human existence. At the same time, Ricoeur was convinced that necessity and freedom were integral aspects of that existence. Finally, he turned to the problem of language, and here he engaged hermeneutics. Ricoeur (1981) explained:

> I propose to organize this problematic [the historicity] of human experience and communication in and through distance around five themes: (1) the realization of language as a discourse; (2) the realization of discourse as a structured work; (3) the relation of speaking to writing in discourse and in the works of discourse; (4) the work of discourse as the projection of a world; (5) discourse and the work of discourse as the mediation of self-understanding. Taken together, these features constitute the criteria of textuality. (p. 132)

Ricoeur thus moved the hermeneutical process beyond traditional theological and conservative philosophical understandings to a more general level of human understanding.

Ricoeur's theory of hermeneutical understanding was judged as politically naive by Habermas. Habermas insisted that "only a critical and self-critical attitude toward interpretation could reveal possible systematic distortions in human communication and their impact on our interpretive activity" (cited in Jeanrond, 1988, p. 463; see also Habermas, 1970). Thus, in its reflective form, hermeneutics is faced with three interrelated concerns: understanding, explanation, and critical assessment. The latter implies that a community of interpreters must work to unmask ideological distortions, limited objective interpretations, and analysis of the meaning of the text. This community of interpreters opens hermeneutics to the discussion that includes a relational dimension that is mutually critical.

Gallagher (1992) used Gadamer and Ricoeur to demonstrate that no method can guarantee an absolutely objective interpretation of an author's work because readers are conditioned by the prejudices of their historical existence—prejudices embedded in language. Although language enables some access to textual meaning, it prevents absolute access to textual meaning. Interpreters never achieve complete or objective understanding because they are limited by historical circumstance, ideology, and language.

This is a clear contradiction of traditional theological and conservative philosophical hermeneutics, which seek the promise of objectivity and worry about the contamination of subjectivity in the interpretive process. Reflective hermeneutics would respond that, because interpretation has a dialogical character, it is not purely subjective. Gallagher (1992) wrote, "Interpretation involves creativity and not just reproduction; the reader participates, just as much as the author does, in putting together the meaning, or in the case of poetry or literature, in creating the aesthetic experience" (p. 10). Here Gallagher reflected the view that creativity and aesthetics provide a context for understanding interpretation. This is an important theoretical step in the reconceptualization of hermeneutics.

Fifth, *poststructural hermeneutics* is inspired by Nietzsche and Heidegger and practiced by deconstructionists like Kristeva, Baudrillard, Derrida, and Foucault. Here interpreting, like reading, is more a case of playing, dancing, or ruminating—in the etymological sense of the Latin *ruminere*—rather than application of methods. Gallagher (1992) contended that poststructural interpretation requires playing with words of the text rather than using them to find truth in or beyond the text. Additionally, poststructural hermeneutics play an interpretation of a text against itself. This becomes an endless process of critique and deconstruction—a *language game* some say—to demonstrate that all interpretations are contingent, emerging, and relative.

Haggerson, Bowman, Bleicher, and Gallagher, among others, point out that, in contrast to contextual or reflective hermeneutics, the poststructural hermeneut is skeptical about creative interpretations that establish communication with original meaning. Rather, it is believed that original meaning is unattainable, and that the best we can do is stretch the limits of language to break on fresh insights and new understandings (Gallagher, 1992). For Derrida, for example, there is no original truth of being beyond language. Thus, poststructural hermeneutics aims to deconstruct the meaning of a text—not to analyze it or reconstruct a different interpretation, but to displace traditional and conservative concepts like identity, meaning, authorship, unity, or purpose. The aim is not to establish a correct vision of the world or society, but to demonstrate that all interpretations are contingent, emergent, and incomplete.

Sixth, *critical hermeneutics* developed in the tradition of critical theorists and finds inspiration in Marx, Freud, Habermas, Marcuse, Gramsci, and the Frankfort school of social criticism. On the one hand, it is similar to poststructural hermeneutics to the extent that its social and political objectives are to deconstruct hegemonic power arrangements and create individual liberation from oppressive class structures. Critical hermeneutics deconstructs economic systems and social metanarratives by challenging false consciousness to uncover the ideological nature of beliefs and values. The goal is to promote distortion-free communication and a liberating consensus. Gallagher (1992) contended that critical hermeneutics is like conservative philosophical hermeneutics to the extent that it promises objectivity in the eradication of false consciousness (Gallagher, 1992). Critical hermeneutics expects to accomplish—in politics, religion, aesthetics, education, and psychology—a consensus beyond ideology. Thus, an absolutely objective perspective can be attained if the right methods can be employed to escape our historical constraints. Deconstructionists would contend that critical hermeneutics shares the naive optimism of theological and conservative hermeneutics that language, through ideal communication, will deliver truth and engender significant nonlinguistic emancipation and liberation.

This brief review of the scholarship surrounding six approaches to hermeneutics reveals the complexity and historical evolution of the notion of the art and process of interpretation. I now present a proposal to move hermeneutics beyond traditional theological, conservative philosophical, contextual, reflective, poststructural, and critical positions. I propose a postmodern hermeneutics that foregrounds subjectivity and aesthetics for emancipation and understanding in the interpretive process while remaining totally committed to human rights, justice, global solidarity, compassion, agency, and ecological sustainability. On the one hand, this proposal is an eclectic synthesis of the six approaches to hermeneutics reviewed before. On the other hand, this proposal is an attempt to jettison all of these approaches in favor of a hermeneutics of subjectivity and aesthetics. Such a position is problematic. How might subjective-aesthetic interpretations be possible and viable in the postmodern era?

HERMENEUTICS AND SUBJECTIVITY

Dewey (1934b) wrote, "In the end, works of art are the only media of complete and unhindered communication between man and man [sic] that can occur in a world full of gulfs and walls that limit community of experience" (p. 105). This is a phenomenology based on the assumption that we cannot speculate about what beings are in themselves. Rather, the emphasis should be placed on *possibility* and *becoming* as a goal of education because human consciousness can never be static. Sartre argued that human consciousness (being for itself) can never become a substance or an objective thing (being in itself), and this is why possibility rather than a static ontology must be the focus of educational inquiry. Hence, each new experience adds to the accumulated meaning of experience for each individual and sets the stage for present and future possibilities.

Although the present is conditioned by the past, every moment is also full of future possibilities for change and new directions. The aesthetic experience inspires these new realizations, as Dewey (1934b) explained:

> A work of art, no matter how old or classic is actually not just potentially, a work of art only when it lives in some individual experience. A piece of parchment, of marble, of canvas, it remains self-identical throughout the ages. But as a work of art it is re-created every time it is aesthetically experienced. ... The Parthenon, or whatever, is universal because it can continue to inspire new personal realizations in experience. (pp. 108–109)

Pablo Picasso (1971) also described artistic creation in a similar way:

> A picture is not thought out and settled beforehand. While it is being done it changes as one's thoughts change. And when it is finished it still goes on changing according to the state of mind of whoever is looking at it. A picture lives a life like a living creature, undergoing the changes imposed on us by our life from day, to day. This is natural enough, as the picture lives only through the man who is looking at it. (p. 268)

Picasso and Dewey reflected one of the important dimensions of this proposal: Events find their meaning in subjective encounters where knowledge is constructed and reconstructed in every unique situation. In this sense, a work of art truly exists only in the encounter. If locked in a darkened vault, a painting is simply an aggregate of materials. Aesthetics, like education, is the process of becoming and re-creating in each new context. Hermeneutics, then, must foreground the interpretive process and subjective interrelationship of text and hermeneut.

The complexity of understanding aesthetic experiences is difficult for those committed to a modern mechanistic understanding, where such experiences do not conform to the logic of positivism, behaviorism, rationalism, and structural analysis. I propose that multiplicity of understandings must replace binary hierarchies, and subjectivity replaces pastiche. Here synthetical experiences can give meaning and sustenance to Gadamer's *fusion of horizons*, where the individual is not subsumed nor imitated, but integrated within the context of the lived world experiences all around waiting to be discovered, uncovered, created, and shared in the hermeneutic circle.

The self-formation that emerges from these experiences is seen in the concept of *Bildung* presented at the beginning of this chapter. Gallagher (1992) expanded on this notion and wrote,

> This transformation is the result of recognizing "one's own in the alien," which is "the basic movement of spirit, whose being consists only in returning to itself from what is other." In this sense every individual is always engaged in *Bildung*. ... The re-emergence of the self, however, is neither a Hegelian synthesis of the old self with the new nor simply a repetition of the old, inauthentic self. The self that is reappropriated is the self that has undergone transformation. (pp. 50–51)

Such transformative pedagogy challenges curriculum scholars and the entire educational community to reevaluate the traditional understanding of the learning environment. The postmodern world demands awareness of the environment and openness to the deep ecology of leaning:

> The forests speak out, the oceans beckon, the sky calls us forth, the plants want to share their story, the mind of the universe is open to all of us, the planet wants to in-

struct. Educators, through their methods and their content, can either open wide the doors to this wonder or narrow the doorways to offer only a partial view which they can then control. (LePage, 1987, p. 162)

LePage argued that participation in the environment is far more educational than passive observation. Participation in new environments and expanded horizons provides students and teachers with insights into alternative strategies for living, and therefore expanded possibilities for the transformation. These possibilities, in turn, offer a vision of hope to people who otherwise would be unaware of alternatives because hermeneutic interpretation has been limited to either theological, conservative, reflective, or poststructural options. In this sense, aesthetic theories also inform social and political theories of education that challenge dominant paradigms.

Attention to the alternatives that provide hope was called *wide-awakenness* by Greene (1978). Greene argued for a strong emphasis on arts and humanities in education to promote this wide-awakenness and self-understanding that emerges from synthetical moments. Greene turned to the poet Henry David Thoreau for inspiration: "Thoreau writes passionately about throwing off sleep. He talks about how few people are awake enough for a poetic or divine life. He asserts that to be awake is to be alive" (p. 162). Eisner (1994) wrote:

> Knowledge is considered by most in our culture as something that one discovers, not something that one makes. Knowledge is out there waiting to be found, and the most useful tool for finding it is science. If there were greater appreciation for the extent to which knowledge is constructed—something made—there might be a greater likelihood that its aesthetic dimension would be appreciated. (p. 32)

Phenomenological and aesthetic understanding replaces the modern obsession with standardized interpretation, predetermined investigative methodologies, and universal master narratives that can be applied to knowledge acquisition.

Although hermeneutics involves critical reflection, it is also a kind of knowing called *praxis* by Freire, Greene, and others—a knowing that becomes an opening to possibilities, agency, and empowerment. Greene (1978) called it "a poem about one human being's self-formation, recaptured through a return (in inner time) to an original landscape, the place where it all began" (p. 15). This experience of returning is not only necessary for wide-awakenness, but also for hermeneutics. The emphasis shifts from the external to the internal, interconnectedness, and solidarity. Without that awareness, teachers and scholars find it unimaginably difficult to cope with the demands of modern schools and society, and they "neither have the time nor energy, nor inclination to urge their students to critical reflection: they themselves have suppressed the questions, and avoided backward looks" (Sizer, 1984, p. 38).

This, then, is a reconceptualized vision of hermeneutic subjectivity and aesthetics in curriculum studies: Transformation and learning are stimulated by a sense of connectedness, solidarity, becoming, and future possibilities of what might be. Once engaged in the journey, the traveler no longer remains isolated and separated from the dreams and visions that give sustenance for exploration and praxis. A transformative pedagogy is most clearly seen as the engagement of this process of interpretation by students and teachers who are confident that the consummation of education is liberation and synthesis without knowing the precise destination in advance. A hermeneutics of subjectivity and aesthetics empowers educators to resist methodological approaches that seek to certify inert information for canonical accountability. Resistence to limited interpretive practices mandated by accountability models of teaching and learning find theoretical and philosophical support for reconceptualizing the interpretive process. Hermeneutics now becomes a critical political project for reconceptualizing the nature of curriculum—not in an attempt to overcome false consciousness, but to promote agency and liberation through the freedom of the subjective aesthetic experience. Foregrounding the subjective and aesthetic in the interpretive process offers hope for transformative experiences in the current international paralysis of the social, religious, economic, educational, and political structures of the modern era. Maybe *postmodern hermeneutics* is not an oxymoron after all?

REFERENCES

Aarons, S. (1983). *Compelling belief: The culture of American schooling.* New York: McGraw-Hill.

Blacker, D. (1993, March). *Education as the normative dimension of philosophical hermeneutics.* Paper presented at the annual meeting of the Philosophy of Education Society in New Orleans, LA.

Bleicher, J. (1980). *Contemporary hermeneutics: Hermeneutics as method, philosophy and critique.* New York: Routledge.

Benvenuto, B., & Kennedy, R. (1986). *The works of Jacques Lacan.* London: Free Press Association Books.

Bloch, E. (1986). *The principle of hope.* Oxford, England: Blackwell.

Buber, M. (1965). *I and thou* (R. G. Smith, Trans.). New York: Scribner.

Burke, P. (1995). *Collected poems.* Unpublished manuscript, Scottsdale, AZ.

Dewey, J. (1934a). *A common faith.* New Haven, CT: Yale University Press.

Dewey, J. (1934b). *Art as experience.* New York: Milton, Balch, & Co.

Dewey, J. (1938). *Experience and education.* New York: Macmillan.

Eisner, E. (1994). *The educational imagination: On the design and evaluation of school programs* (3rd ed.). New York: Macmillan.

Ellsworth, E. (1989). Why doesn't this feel empowering? Working through the repressive myths of critical pedagogy. *Harvard Educational Review, 59*(3), 297–324.

Gadamer, H.-G. (1960/1975). *Truth and method.* New York: Crossroads.

Gadamer, H.-G. (1976). *Philosophical hermeneutics* (D. E. Linge, Ed. and Trans.). Berkeley: University of California Press.

Gadamer, H.-G., & Derrida, J. (1989). *Dialogue and deconstructionism: The Gadamer–Derrida encounter.* Albany: State University of New York Press.

Gallagher, S. (1992). *Hermeneutics and education.* Albany: State University of New York Press.

Greene, M. (1978). *Landscapes of learning.* New York: Teachers College Press.

Greene, M. (1995). *Releasing the imagination: Essays on education, the arts, and social change.* San Francisco: Jossey- Bass.

Habermas, J. (1970). *Knowledge and human interests.* Boston: Beacon.

Haggerson, N., & Bowman, A. (1992). *Informing educational policy and practice through interpretive inquiry.* Lancaster, PA: Technomic.

Hegel, G. W. F. (1977). *Phenomenology of spirit* (T. M. Knox, Trans.). New York: Harper.

Hudak, G. M. (1995). We are all related: The formation of the "sound" identity in music making and schooling. *Discourse: Studies in the Cultural Politics of Education, 16*(3), 297–315.

Jeanrond, W. (1998). Hermeneutics. In J. Komonchak, M. Collins, & D. Lane (Eds.), *The new dictionary of theology* (pp. 462–464). Wilmington, DE: Michael Glazier.

Jung, C. G. (1962). *Memories, dreams, reflections* (A. Jaffe, Ed.; C. Winston & R. Winston, Trans.). New York: Random House.

Kimball, S., & Garrison, J. (n.d.). *Hermeneutic listening.* Unpublished abstract. VA Polytechnic Institute, Blacksburg, VA.

Lacan, J. (1977). *Ecrits: A selection.* London: Tavistock.

Langer, S. (1957). *Problems of art.* New York: Charles Scribner.

LePage, A. (1987). *Transforming education: The new 3 r's.* Oakland, CA: Oakmore House.

McLaren, P. (1999). *Revolutionary multiculturalism.* New York: Macmillan.

Misgeld, D., & Graeme, N. (1992). *Hans-Georg Gadamer on education, poetry, and history: Applied hermeneutics* (L. Schmidt & M. Reuss, Trans.). Albany: State University of New York Press.

Nietzsche, F. (1968). The birth of tragedy. In W. Kaufmann (Trans. & Ed.), *Basic writings of Nietzsche* (3rd ed., p. 52). New York: Modern Library.

Picasso, P. (1971). Conversations. In H. B. Chipps (Ed.), *Theories of modern art: A source book of artists and critics* (p. 268). Berkeley: University of California Press.

Reynolds, W. M. (1989). *Reading curriculum theory: The development of a new hermeneutic*. New York: Peter Lang.

Ricoeur, P. (1981). *Hermeneutics and the human sciences* (J. Thompson, Trans. & Ed.). Cambridge, England: Cambridge University Press.

Rorty, R. (1979). *Philosophy and the mirror of nature*. Princeton, NJ: Princeton University Press.

Sizer, T. (1984). *Horace's compromise: The dilemma of the American high school*. Boston: Houghton-Mifflin.

Slattery, P., & Morris, M. (1999). Simone de Beauvoir's ethics and postmodern ambiguity: The assertion of freedom in the face of the absurd. *Educational Theory, 49*(1), 21–36.

Smith, D. G. (1991). Hermeneutic inquiry: The hermeneutic imagination and the pedagogic text. In E. Short (Ed.), *Forms of curriculum inquiry* (pp. 187–209). Albany: State University of New York Press.

Usher, R., & Edwards, R. (1994). *Postmodernism and education*. London: Routledge.

Whitehead, A. N. (1929). *Aims of education*. New York: The Free Press.

Author Index

Subject Index